6

Hamlyn Encyclopedia of
PHOTOGRAPHY

HAMLYN
London · New York · Sydney · Toronto

Editor John Farndon
Art Editor Trevor Vertigan

Published 1985 by Hamlyn Publishing,
a Division of The Hamlyn Publishing Group Limited
London New York Sydney Toronto
Astronaut House, Feltham, Middlesex, England

Produced by Marshall Cavendish Books Limited
58 Old Compton Street
London W1V 5PA

ISBN 0 600 50077 2
Printed and bound in Hong Kong by Dai Nippon Printing Company

INTRODUCTION

In its early days, photography was an expensive, awkward, unpredictable and sometimes positively dangerous process, and to be a photographer called for considerable dedication. Photographers not only had to process their own pictures, they had to coat their own photographic plates with light-sensitive chemicals as well. Cameras were bulky and very awkward to use and exposures typically lasted many minutes, even in the brightest light. And if the photographer actually managed to record the picture successfully, he or she may well have been brought to an untimely end by an explosion in the darkroom or a lingering death from the materials handled gradually proving poisonous.

Today, fortunately, photography is not quite so hazardous, and advances in technology – in the last decade especially – have meant that taking pictures could not be simpler. Indeed, many cameras are sold, with justification, as being almost entirely foolproof – photography is almost 'as easy as winking'. Cameras for the amateur 'snapshot' market incorporate a whole host of automatic features, from auto exposure to auto film loading, and even complex professional models have some automatic features.

However, automatic systems do have limitations, and if you are to take anything but snapshots, you need to be aware of these limitations and learn to exploit them. This book is intended to guide you through all the basic techniques of photography, from handling cameras through exposure and focusing to flash photography, pointing out where auto systems can help and where they can hinder, and showing how you can achieve the degree of precision needed for quality results.

Yet none of these techniques will result in good photographs unless you combine them with a flair for seeing pictures. So there is an extensive section on subjects, such as portraits and sport, to help you develop your eye and to show you how to apply the techniques in practice.

More and more photographers nowadays are becoming aware of the possibilities of the photographic studio, and a large section of the book is devoted to studio techniques, showing you how to set up a studio in your own home, what lights to buy, how to use them, how to handle photo-sessions and much more.

The final section of the book explains the background to the techniques and explains most of the important technical aspects, for only by understanding just what is going on can you learn to exploit the potential of your films and equipment to the full.

CONTENTS

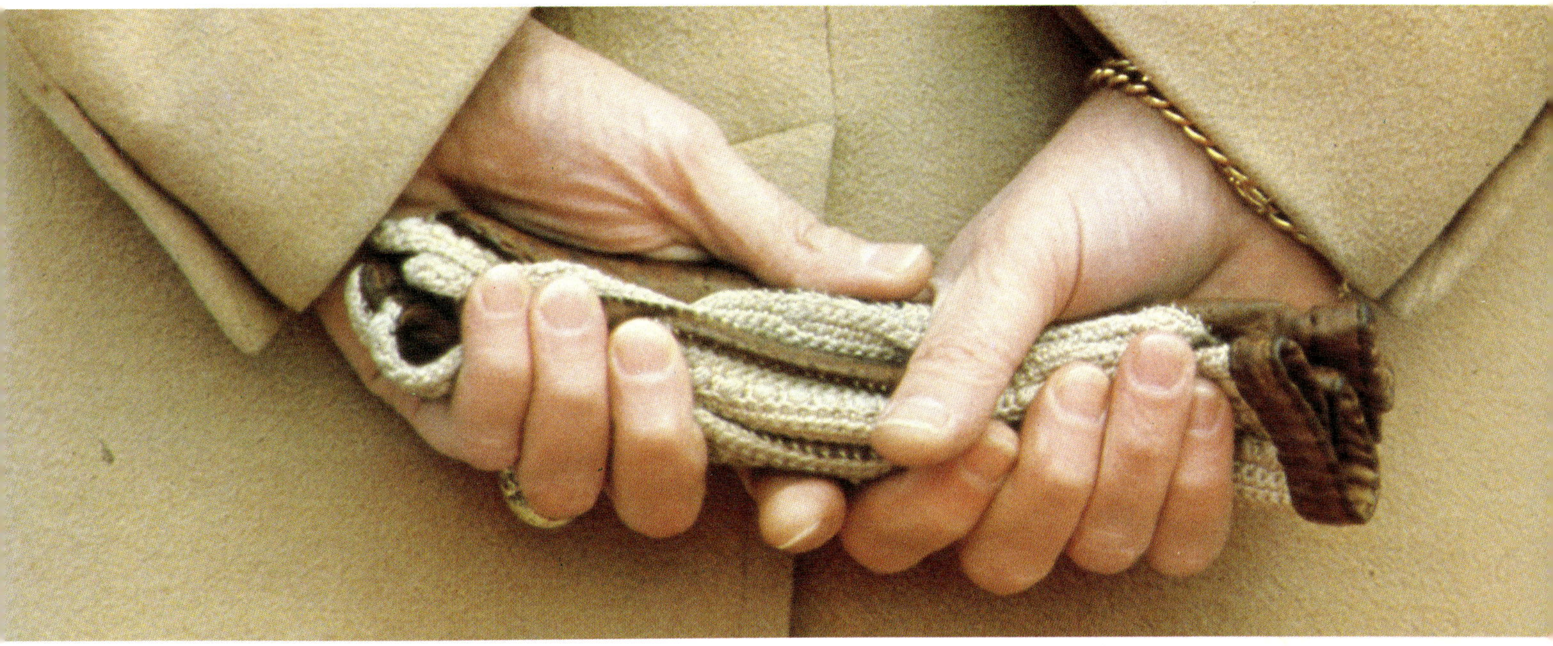

CHAPTER 1
CAMERAS
The 35mm SLR

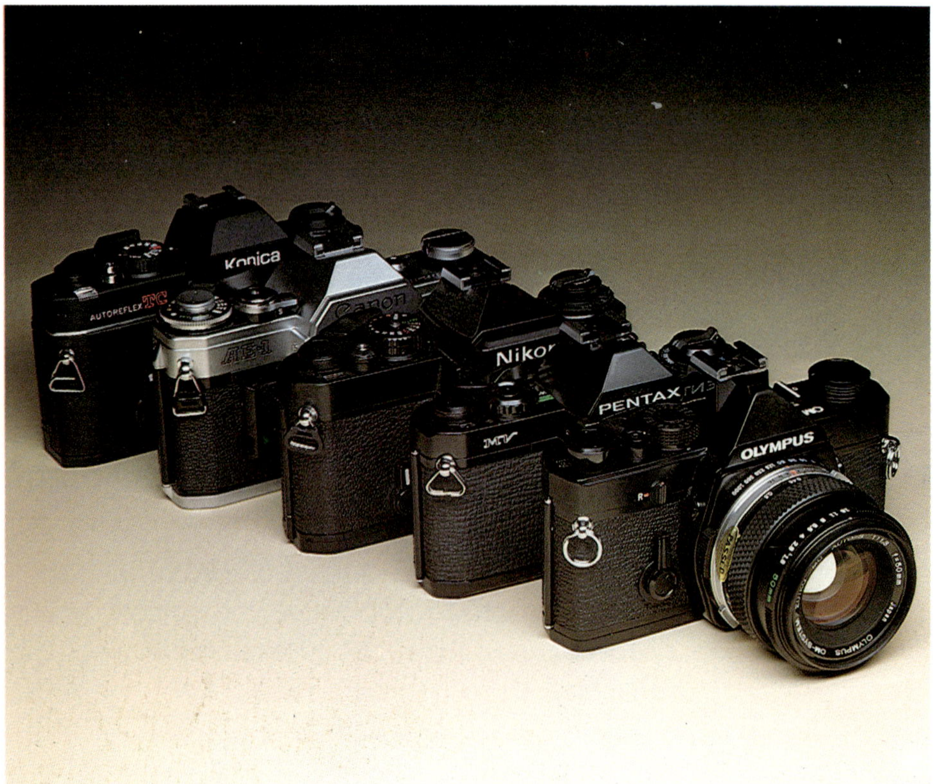

35mm SLRs *use a number of different exposure systems. From back to front: automatic; aperture priority; shutter priority; multi-mode; manual*

There are many different types of camera, but for the serious amateur photographer, the choice is usually between three basic types of camera: 35mm SLRs, 35mm 'compacts' and roll film cameras. Both 35mm SLRs and 'compacts' use cassettes of 35mm film which gives negatives or slides 36 x 24mm—the film, including sprocket holes, is 35mm wide. Roll film cameras, however, use film that comes in rolls almost twice as wide, which means that each film frame can be 60mm wide—the length varies with the camera. Because the roll film frame is much bigger, roll film cameras give better quality pictures than 35mm cameras using 35mm film and are preferred by many professionals. Unfortunately, they are generally more expensive to buy and load with film, and tend to be very bulky.

Of the three types of camera, the 35mm SLR has long been the most popular with serious amateur photographers—although the increasingly sophisticated compacts are gradually gaining ground. The 35mm SLR owes its popularity to its sheer versatility and its tradition of high quality optics. The camera gets its name from its viewing system (SLR stands for Single Lens Reflex). The viewfinder shows the scene directly through the picture taking lens—the light is reflected via a mirror (angled at 45° behind the lens) and a specially-shaped prism called a *pentaprism*. This system has two advantages.

First of all, it shows the scene exactly as it will appear on film. This means that the picture can be composed very accurately. It also ensures accurate composition even when different lenses are fitted to the camera. Consequently, there is a vast range of alternative lenses for every SLR which can be fitted in place of the standard lens to give a desired effect. This is what makes the SLR so versatile.

Secondly, it makes the camera very suitable for a through-the-lens (TTL) exposure metering system. This measures the amount of light actually coming through the picture taking lens and so helps give precise exposure.

Every modern SLR has TTL exposure metering, but there are a number of different systems for controlling exposure. In each camera, the meter reading must be translated into exposure settings (aperture and shutter speed) to give correctly exposed pictures. On some cameras, the exposure settings are set completely automatically (*auto exposure* systems). On others, the photographer sets either aperture or shutter and the camera sets the other control automatically (*aperture* or *shutter priority*). On others the photographer has to set both controls *manually*. On the fourth type, there is a choice of exposure systems (*multi-mode*). Each exposure system has something different to offer the photographer.

Aperture priority-Nikon FE

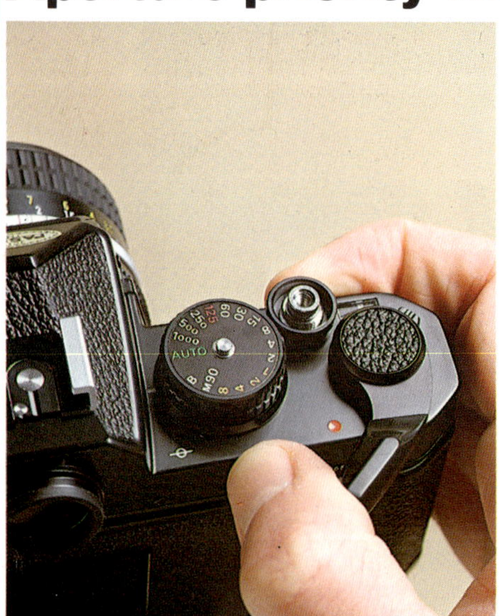

1 Meter on *The exposure meter is switched on. The switch for the meter on the Nikon FE is in the film wind lever, which is pulled out to switch it on*

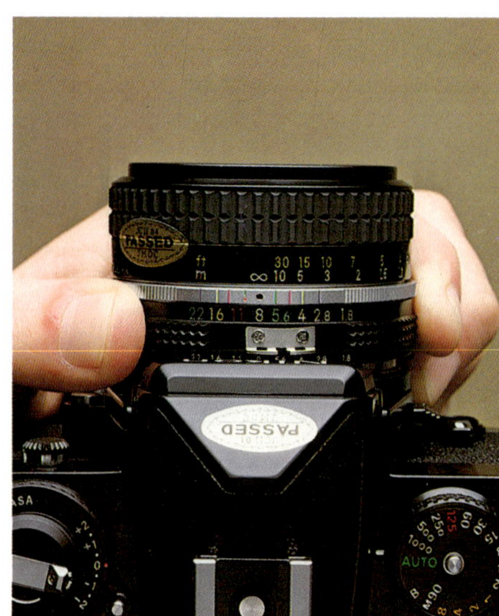

2 Set aperture *On aperture priority cameras, the aperture ring on the lens is then set to the f-number that the photographer has chosen*

Foreground grasses *Aperture priority automatics work well when depth of field is important. A small aperture was chosen here to keep everything in focus*

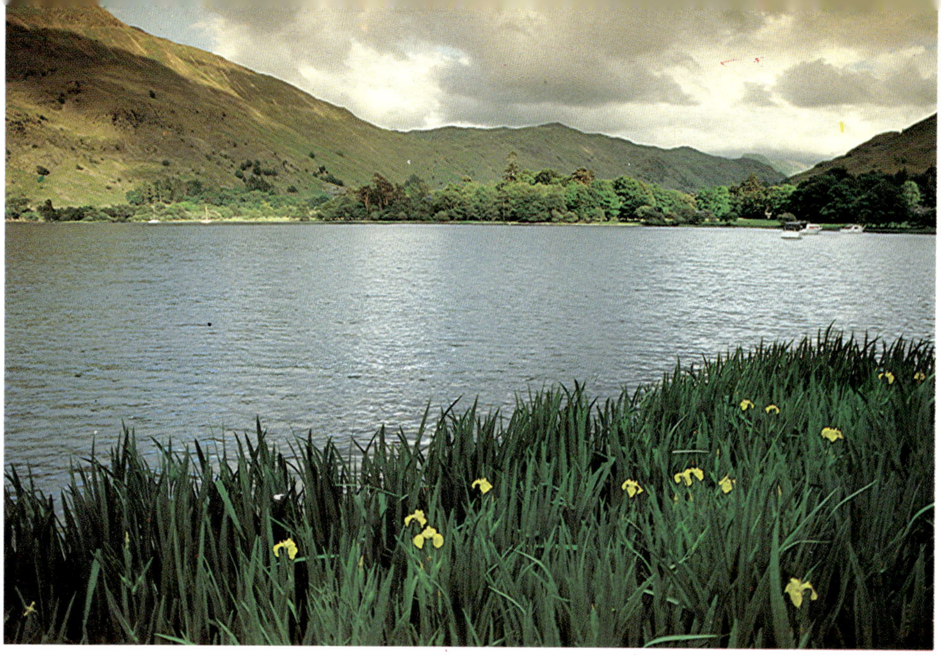

Aperture and shutter priority

On a shutter priority camera, the photographer first sets the shutter speed that is required, the camera takes a light meter reading, and adjusts the aperture to give the correct exposure to the film.

Because this type of camera allows the user to set the shutter speed that is needed, it tends to find favour with camera users for whom the shutter speed is the most important factor. Sports photographers, for example, need to know exactly what shutter speed is set on the camera at the time of exposure, because it is usually important that the subject of the picture will be 'frozen' in motion rather than blurred. The user of a shutter priority automatic gives up control of the aperture that is used, but can select the best shutter speed.

With aperture priority automatics, the situation is reversed. Instead of setting the shutter speed, the user picks the aperture, and the camera selects an appropriate shutter speed. The Nikon FE is a camera of this type. The sequence of operations for this camera begins with the user setting an aperture on the scale around the lens. The choice of aperture would usually be dictated by the depth of field required in the photograph (see page 220). Having set the aperture, the photographer looks through the viewfinder and pulls the lever wind backwards. This switches on the meter and moves a small needle in

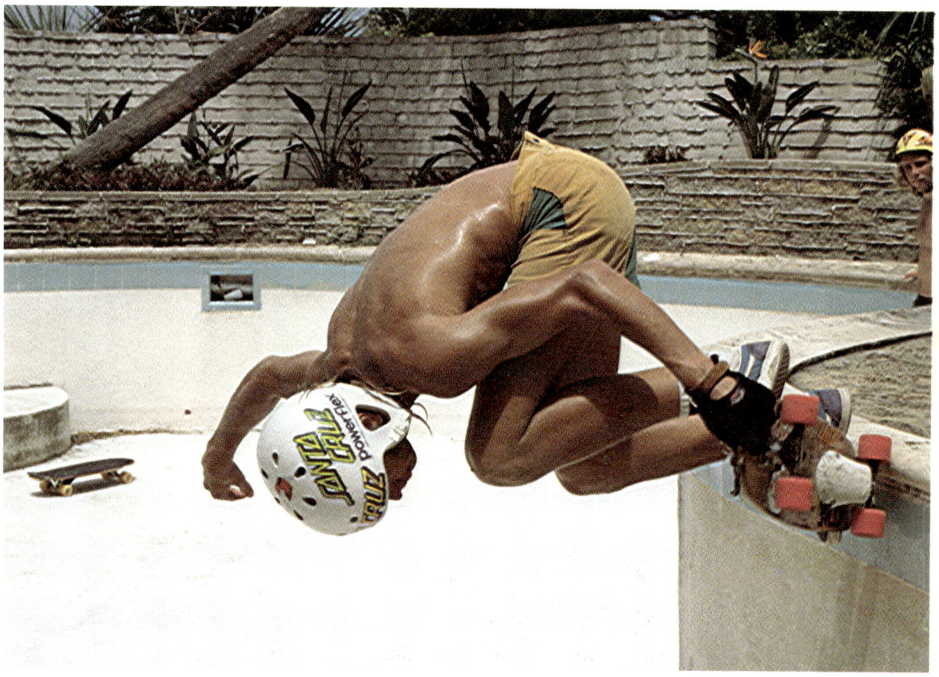

Speedy skateboard *If the subject of the picture must be frozen in motion, a shutter priority automatic will be easiest to use*

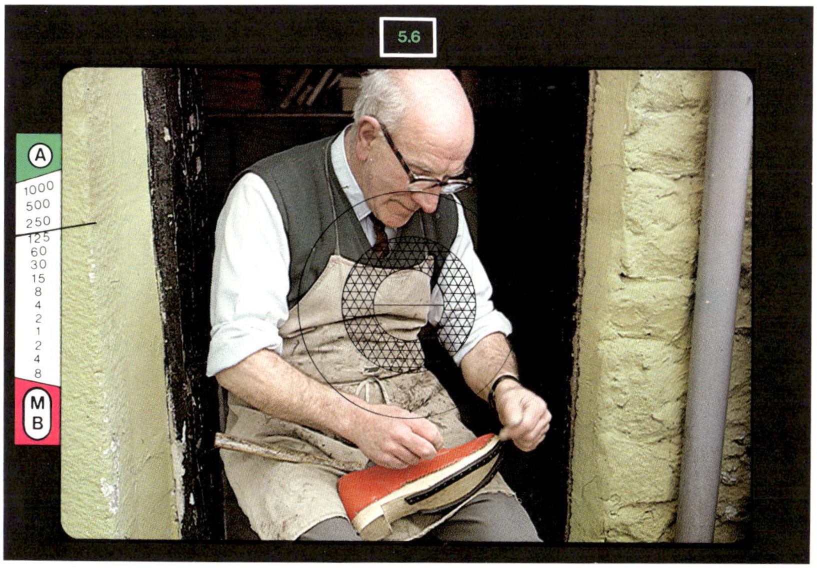

3 Viewfinder *Looking through the viewfinder, a scale is visible on the left hand side of the focusing screen, on which shutter speeds are marked. A needle swings over the scale, and comes to rest at the shutter speed that will be set by the camera's automatic meter*

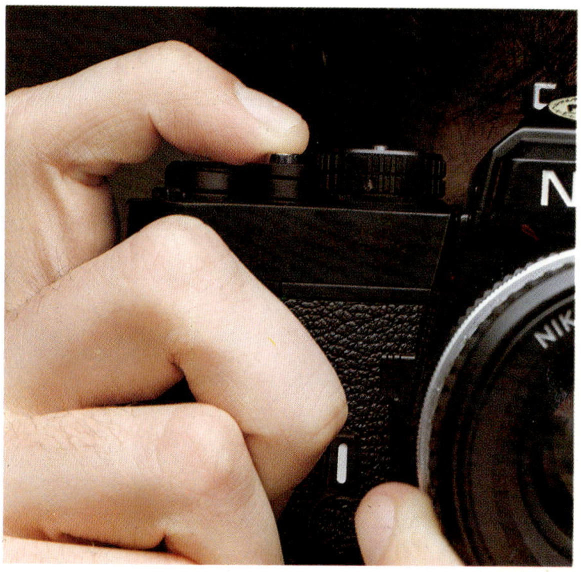

4 Releasing shutter *At the moment of exposure, the aperture closes to the f-number chosen by the photographer, and the shutter speed is set by the camera to give the correct exposure*

Manual metering-Olympus OM1

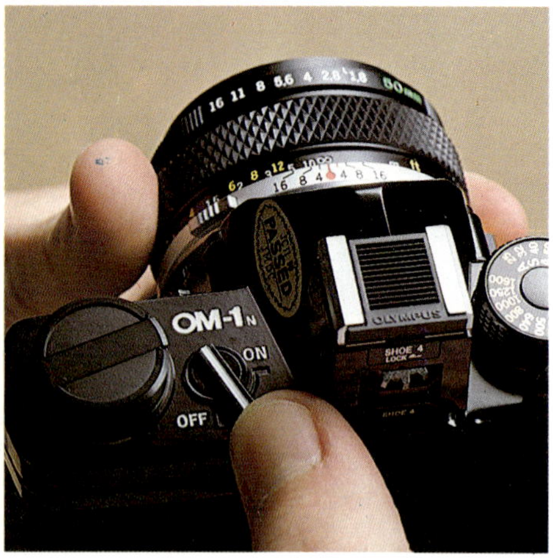

1 Meter on *The Olympus OM1 has a separate meter switch. This must be operated before a light meter reading can be taken with the camera*

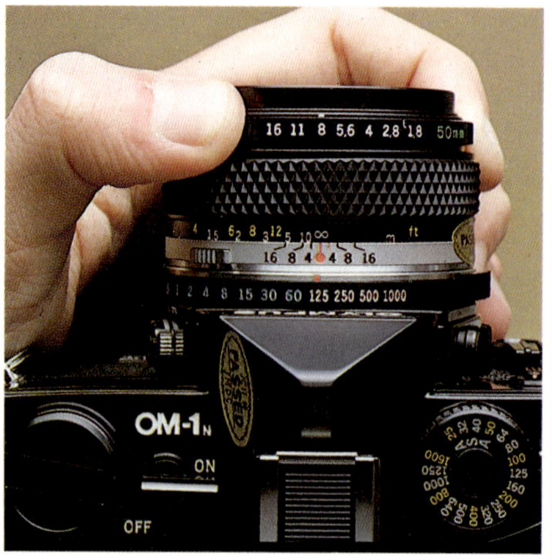

2 Set aperture *In this instance, the photographer first sets the aperture to a value that will give sufficient depth of field for the subject*

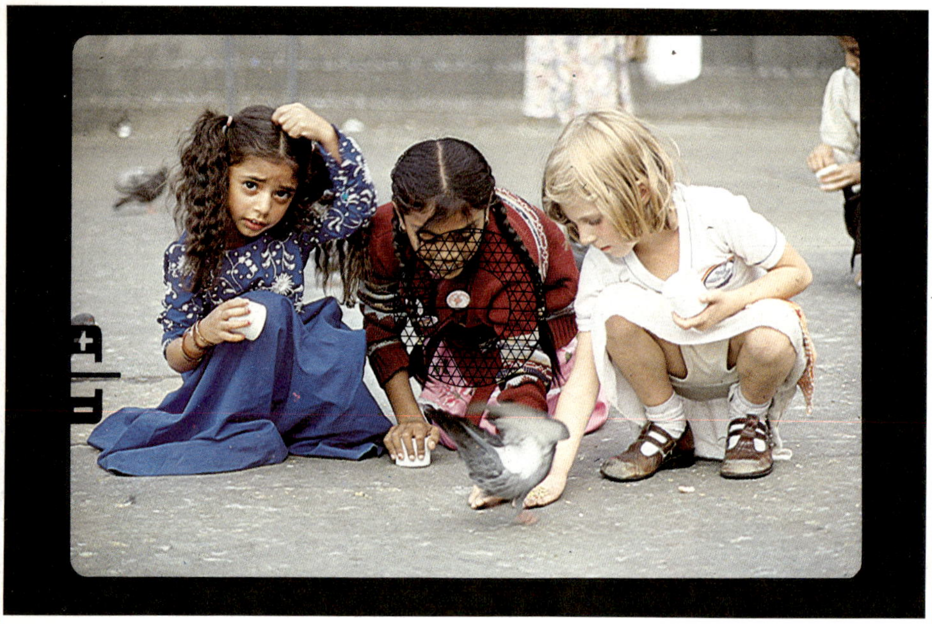

3 Viewfinder *A needle on the left hand side of the focusing screen moves over a pair of marks. Exposure is correct when it is centred*

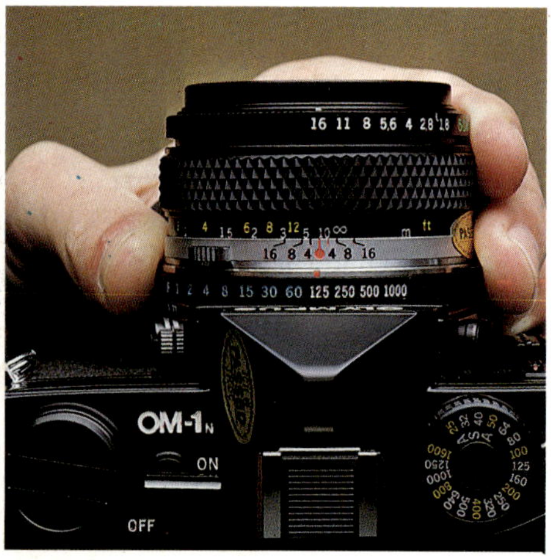

4 Shutter speed *In this case, the photographer adjusts the shutter speed to balance the meter needle. The shutter speed dial is around the lens mount*

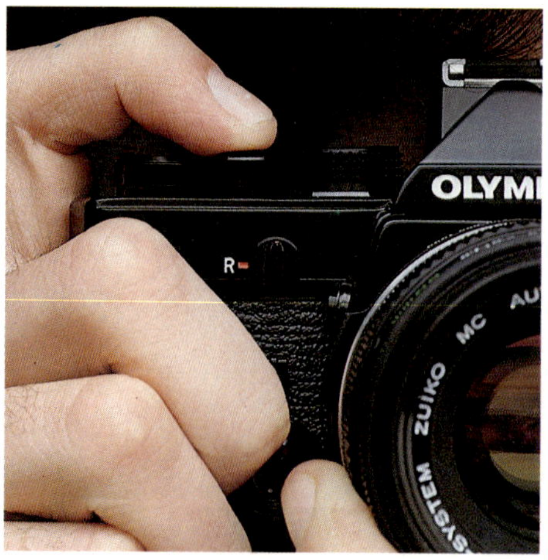

5 Release shutter *After focusing and composing the picture, the shutter release is pressed. Both aperture and shutter have been manually set*

the viewfinder to indicate the speed at which the shutter is going to operate. When pressure is applied to the shutter button the shutter will be released at the speed indicated in the viewfinder.

This system of operation is no better or worse than the shutter priority method, but is suited to a different type of photography, in which the aperture is considered by the photographer to be more important than the shutter speed. If a portrait is the subject of the picture, for example, the photographer must be sure that the whole of the model's face is in focus, so the aperture that is set is of great importance. Since the subject is unlikely to move very much, the shutter speed is less crucial.

Aperture priority automation is favoured by a lot of camera manufacturers, because the system requires fewer connections between the camera lens and body. To build a shutter priority automatic, on the other hand, some kind of mechanical linkage is needed between body and lens, to ensure that the correct aperture is set at the moment of exposure.

Manual cameras

Although shutter priority and aperture priority automatic cameras are the most common types, some other cameras fit into neither of these two categories. These are fully automatic cameras, and those which set the exposure without any intervention by the photographer—so-called 'programmed' cameras.

Manual cameras, such as the Olympus OM-1, have a meter needle visible through the viewfinder, but leave the photographer to do the work of changing the shutter speed and the aperture. To set the correct exposure on the OM-1, for example, the photographer first switches on the meter—on some manual cameras this is incorporated into the shutter release—and sets either the aperture or the shutter speed to the chosen value. Looking through the viewfinder, a meter needle is visible, and a pair of pincer-like claws. By adjusting either the aperture or the shutter speed, the photographer can bring the needle to rest between the claws—a position which indicates that the film will receive correct exposure. Over and under-exposure are indicated by the needle being too high or too low.

There are a number of variations on this method of exposure metering, which are similar in their method of operation, but which differ in the way that the meter reading is indicated. In the match-needle type of camera, there are two needles. Instead of lining up one needle between claws in the viewfinder, the photographer aligns the two needles to set the correct exposure. Over- and under-traffic light displays, where an LED of a particular colour or a certain combination of LEDs lights up when the exposure is correct. Over and under-exposure is indicated in this case by an LED of a different colour, or in a different position in the finder, lighting up.

This manual system of exposure sett-

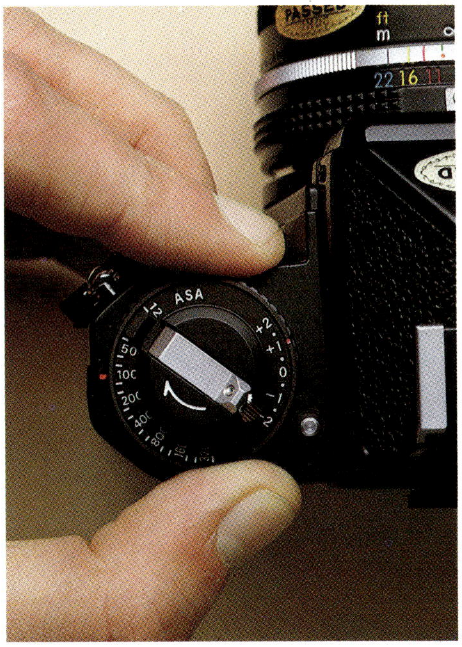

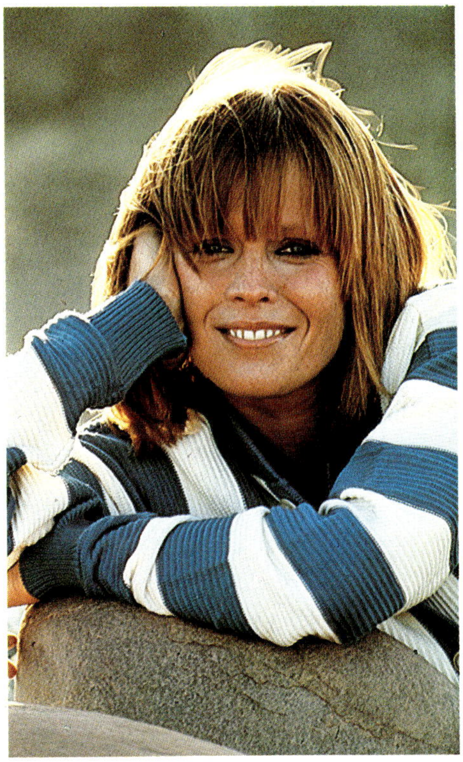

Exposure compensation *Backlit subjects require extra exposure, and some auto cameras have an exposure compensation dial to provide this facility*

ing, while more time consuming than an automatic system, does allow the photographer full control of the aperture and shutter speeds that are being set, and for this reason is often preferred by professional photographers. It is also marginally cheaper to build into a camera, so is often found on the more inexpensive models in a camera range.

'Programmed' automation

This system, used in cameras at both ends of the price range, has a pre-programmed sequence of apertures and shutter speeds which will be set according to the lighting conditions. In the brightest light, a fast

Manual metering-Olympus OM1

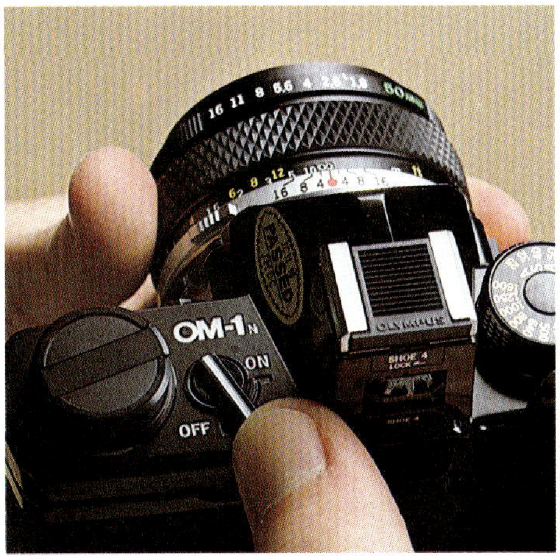

1 Meter on *Manual cameras can be used in two different ways. The procedure in this second example again begins by turning on the exposure meter*

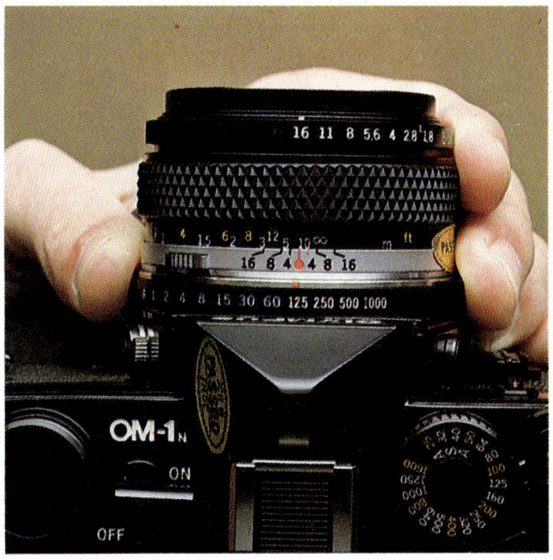

2 Set shutter *Here the photographer is especially concerned that the right shutter speed is set, so he adjusts this control first*

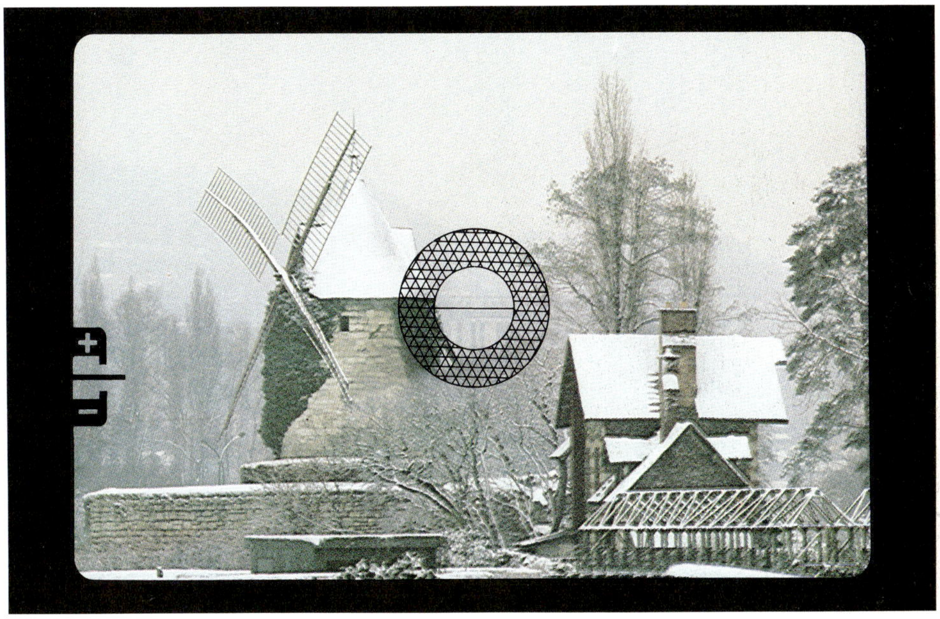

3 Viewfinder *To centre the needle this time the photographer adjusts not the shutter speed control, but the aperture ring*

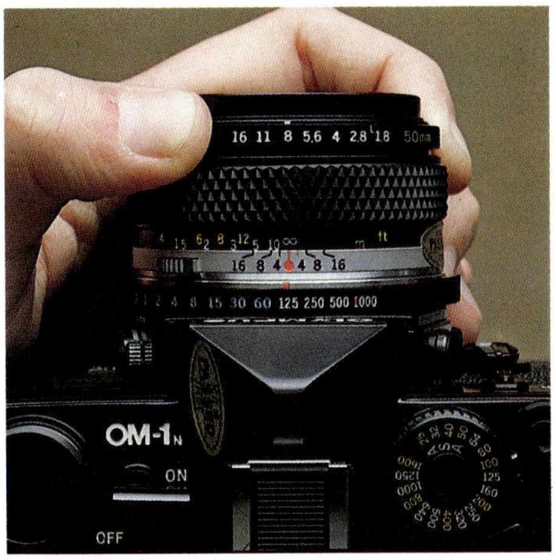

4 Adjusting aperture *Since the photographer considers the f-number to be of secondary importance, he can adjust it freely to balance the meter*

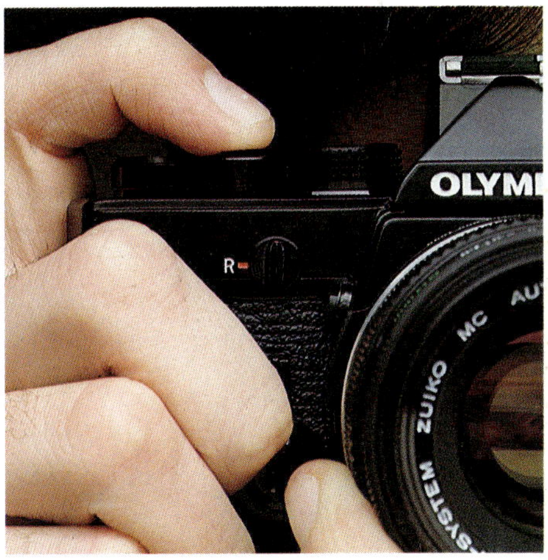

5 Release shutter *If the meter needle is between the claws, the film will receive the correct exposure when the shutter release is pressed*

Shutter priority-Canon AE1

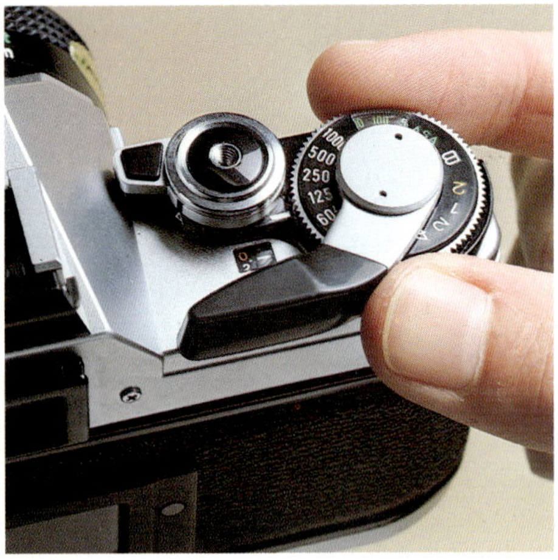

1 Set shutter *On shutter priority automatics such as this Canon AE-1, the first stage is to set the shutter speed to the chosen value*

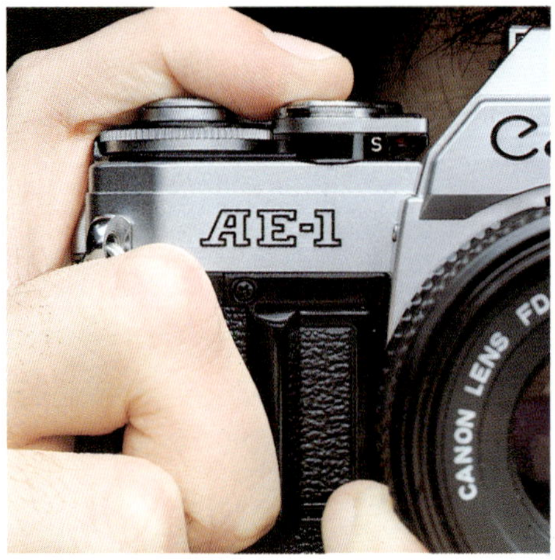

2 Half press release *Gentle pressure on the shutter release switches on the camera and activates the through the lens exposure meter*

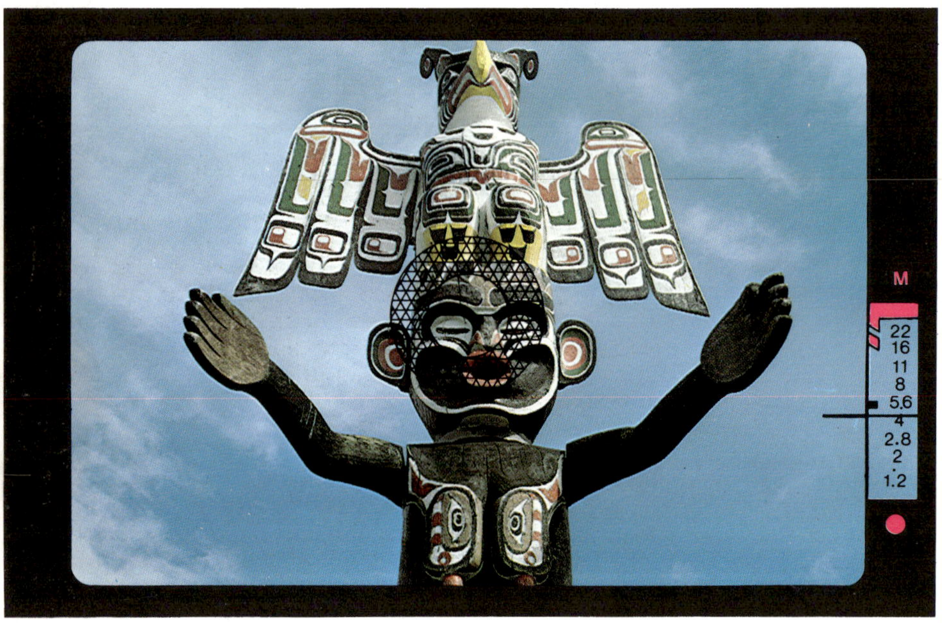

3 Viewfinder *A needle indicates the aperture which the camera has chosen. If this is off the scale, chose another shutter speed*

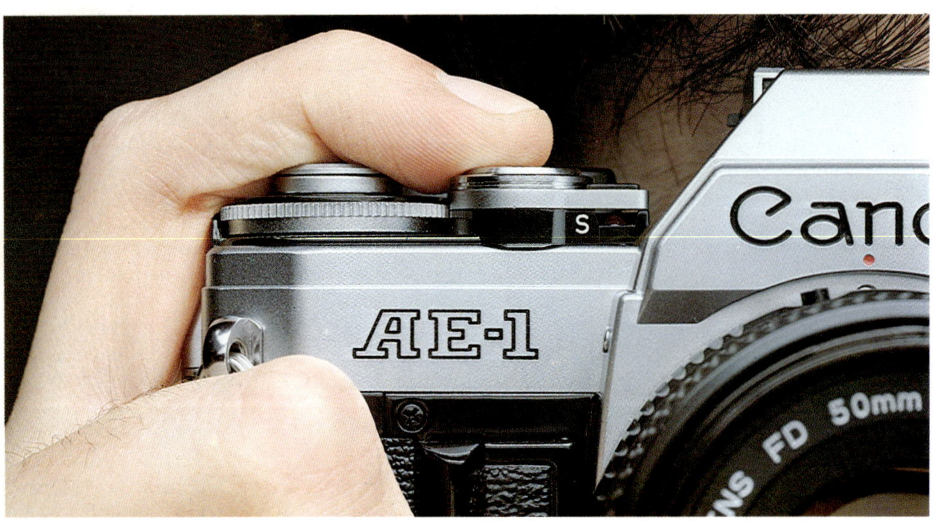

4 Release shutter *When the shutter button is pressed all the way down, the aperture is closed to the value selected by the exposure meter*

shutter speed and small aperture will be set by the camera, and as more exposure is required, the camera will automatically change the shutter speed to a progressively slower setting, and open the iris diaphragm to a wider aperture. The photographer has no control over the speeds and apertures that are used. Although this system is fine for quick snapshots, it can be restricting for serious photography.

Many automatic cameras have some sort of manual override, or compensation for unusual lighting. The most common example is the provision of a switch which allows the photographer to use the camera manually, in the same way as any non-automatic camera would be operated. Though this is a useful feature, many photographers find that automatic exposure gives perfect results for 98 per cent of their exposures, and they rarely take advantage of the switch.

The most common reason for wanting to change the exposure that the camera has set is because the subject is backlit, and so the automatic facility on the camera would produce underexposure. This is because the light meter usually averages the light reaching a certain portion of the focusing screen, and is unduly influenced by the bright light behind the subject. Early through the lens meters averaged the light from the whole frame, and produced serious underexposure in backlit conditions. Modern cameras are more selective—many of them have a meter that gives more emphasis to the centre of the screen—and so if the subject is central, backlit pictures will not be quite so heavily underexposed. Some cameras have a backlight switch which gives a one stop overexposure increase when pushed, and others have an exposure compensation dial, which allows the photographer to dial in a preset amount of exposure compensation. On cameras that lack either of these facilities, exposure compensation can still be made by changing the film speed set on the dial of the camera, halving the speed set to give an extra stop exposure.

A few cameras have what is described as a 'memory lock'. This is a switch or button, which locks the meter when pressed. If a backlit portrait is the subject of the picture, the photographer will move in close to the subject, take a meter reading from the model's face, depress the memory lock and then move back to recompose the picture before pressing the shutter release. The camera will give the correct exposure for the model's face, and ignore the backlighting. This system generally works well in practice.

The big advantage of an automatic is that you never miss a shot through fiddling with the exposure controls—even if exposure is not perfect, it will be nearly right every time. But there is no doubt that a manual gives you a better 'feel' for exposure, and this makes it the ideal camera for the beginner as well as for hardened professionals.

Choosing an SLR

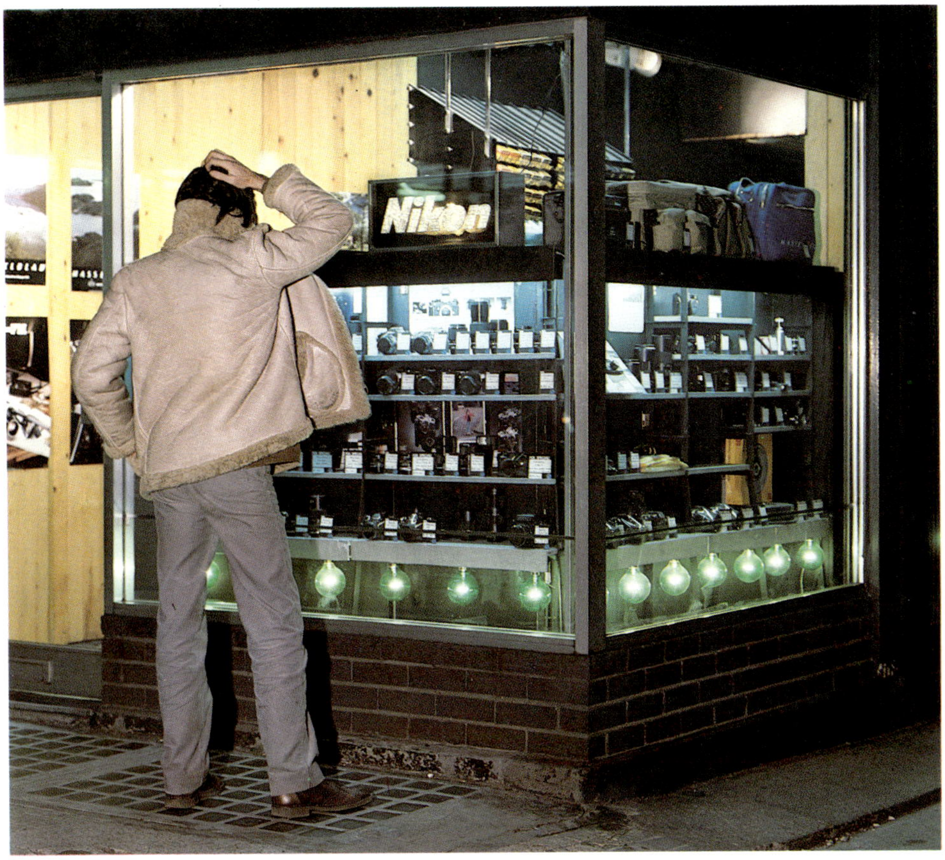

Camera choice *There are so many cameras on the market that choosing an SLR is no longer an easy matter*

Once you have decided which type of exposure system best suits your needs, you can start to look at individual SLRs. There is an enormous range on the market, some makers offering ten or more models, and it can be difficult to make a choice. Fortunately, very few modern SLRs are bad value for money – the price is nearly always a genuine reflection of the quality.

It usually makes sense to buy the best you can afford, but it is worth thinking about how you expect your interest in photography to develop. If you never buy any more equipment, then the best you can afford may indeed be the wisest choice. But if you plan to improve your outfit gradually, it may be better to pay slightly less and buy an economy model from the range of one of the big SLR systems manufacturers. That way, you can uprate piece by piece without making all your accessories redundant.

Specifications are important – a high-flash synchronization speed or off-the-film metering may prove invaluable. But do not go on specifications alone. Remember, to achieve impressive specifications at a low price, the maker may have had to skimp in other areas. This section gives an idea of the most important qualities to look for.

Weight and size

Most 35 mm SLRs have a basic body weight in the range 500 to 600 g, approximately the weight of three average size paperback novels. This does vary from model to model but most SLR cameras are now quite a lot lighter than the models of a few years ago.

Clearly a very light camera is the most suitable for a photographer who intends to use it hand-held for long periods, as in the coverage of sporting events. Photographers who pursue energetic hobbies—like walking or climbing—will also find that small cameras take a load off their shoulders. With photographic work where the stable support of a tripod is likely, such as bird photography, the weight of the camera is a much less important consideration.

Since Olympus introduced their OM-1 model, the first of a new generation of smaller SLRs, most manufacturers have tried to make cameras small as well as light. Given the fixed size of the film, lenses and reflex viewing system used by SLRs, however, a further significant miniaturization of overall size seems unlikely—which is why photographers often turn to the pocket-sized compacts.

It is an easy matter to measure the dimensions of a camera or to weigh it, but judging the robustness of a camera is a different matter. Just because a camera is heavy and looks solid does not mean that it will stand up to rough treatment. A poorly engineered bracket or hinge will fail whatever its dimensions. The only practical way of judging robustness is by reputation, and the fact that professionals who do demand a lot of their equipment have tended to buy Nikon or Canon is something of a guide.

Lightness is often achieved by the increased use of plastics and thinner castings—in most cases this reduces the strength and resilience of a camera.

Few amateurs, however, need equipment that will withstand a great deal of wear and tear. Only if you enjoy exotic locations or go in for a strenuous hobby, such as free-fall parachuting, will you really need such a rugged SLR.

The lens

Cameras are often sold complete with a standard lens. In the case of 35 mm SLRs this means one of either a 50 mm or 55 mm focal length. Such a lens gives an image that closely resembles the way the human eye views the scene.

There is usually a choice of several standard lenses, which normally have maximum apertures of f/1.4, f/1.8 or f/2. The first of these has the largest maximum aperture, and will be the most expensive. However, choosing a good standard lens purely on the basis of price will not necessarily result in the model that produces the best pictures. An f/1.4 lens may well cost twice as much as an f/2 lens, but when used at full aperture, the f/2 lens will probably produce better pictures. It may seem surprising then, that people are prepared to pay more for wide-aperture lenses.

The reasons are simple—if a lens has a wide maximum aperture, it gathers a lot of light. This means the focusing screen is brighter, and focusing more accurate. Also, in dimly lit conditions, more light will get to the film and it will be possible to use a faster shutter speed with a lens that has a wide maximum aperture. These advantages make such lenses attractive to photographers who need fast shutter speeds, and who often shoot pictures in bad light—candid photographers, for example, frequently need lenses with

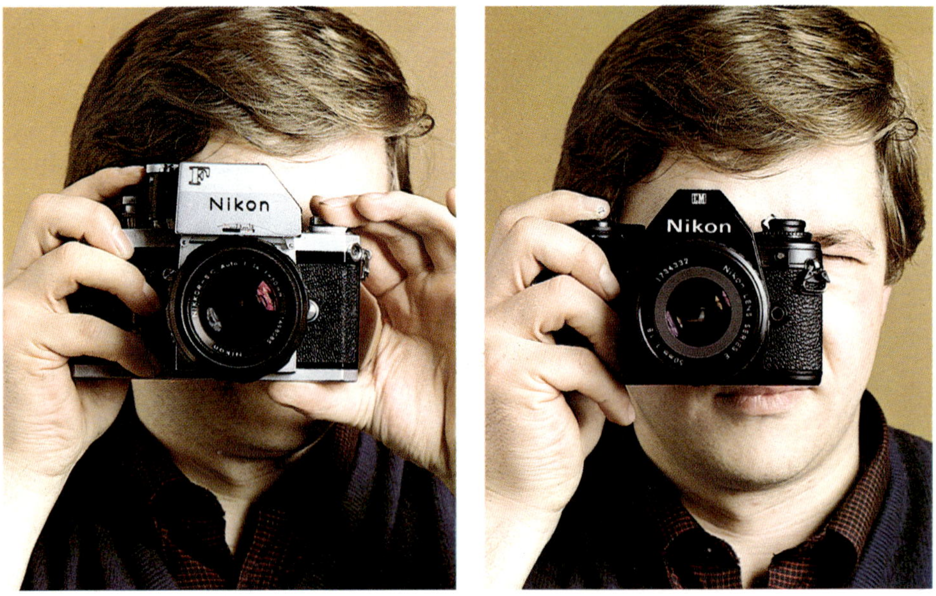

Old and new *Most modern cameras are much lighter and less bulky than their predecessors. The larger one shown here was made in 1973*

wide maximum apertures.

Unless you are convinced that you need the extra light-gathering power of a lens with a wide maximum aperture, it is a better idea to buy one with a more modest specification, and save your money to buy film.

In the quest for more compact cameras, lens design has now followed the lead of camera bodies. Fortunately, mass-production has ensured that these lighter lenses are not significantly more expensive than older, more bulky, types.

Some manufacturers offer two ranges of lenses. The smaller lenses are mechanically less rugged, and optically different from their heavier counterparts, but the results that are produced with a compact lens from a reputable manufacturer should be every bit as good as those from a bulkier lens.

The lenses for most SLR cameras are fitted with a bayonet mount—a simple twist and lock action mounts the lens on the camera body. In the past, many cameras used a screw thread to mount the lens on the camera, and this at one time was almost universal. Though there are many secondhand cameras and lenses of this type available, only one or two manufacturers now use the screw thread method of lens fitting on their current models.

The disadvantage of the bayonet system is that it is far from universal. Although a few manufacturers share the same mount, it is generally impossible to use the lenses from one maker on the body of another. Independent manufacturers make lenses with a variety of mounts, so choice is not limited to lenses made by the manufacturer of your camera (see box).

One thing that has improved enormously with the development of the modern SLR is the range of interchangeable lenses. All the major manufacturers offer a comprehensive selection ranging from 6 mm fisheyes —that gather everything in front of the camera into one circular image—to 2000 mm mirror lenses that act like telescopes, magnifying the smallest distant detail. Many of these lenses are not only expensive but of limited use, and their availability is only relevant if you have a specialist application in mind. For example, if you are interested in wildlife photography, a comprehensive range of telephoto lenses could be most useful.

The shutter

All 35 mm SLRs use focal plane shutters These shutters are in the camera body placed right in front of the film and controlled either mechanically or electronically. Mechanical systems usually have twelve speed steps from 'B' (which means that the shutter stays

Interchangeable lens mounts

The manufacturers of SLR cameras usually take a very independent approach to the development of their new models. Nowhere is this more obvious than in the design of lens mounts. Most camera manufacturers have adopted a unique way of fitting lens to camera, that is used by no other company. In recent years, though, there has been some degree of co-operation between companies, and a few cameras share the same mount.

On the other hand, some manufacturers have developed their own bayonet mount, and then found that it limited the further development of their cameras, so they introduced a second type of bayonet mount. A range of models from one manufacturer has used no less than three different systems of coupling lens to camera!

When buying an SLR, remember that independent lens makers—those who do not also make cameras—also supply lenses in a number of fittings. Make sure that the camera you want has lenses available from sources other than the camera manufacturer, or you may find that your choice is very restricted.

Pentax, Cosina, Chinon, Ricoh and Topcon all use the Pentax 'K' bayonet mount that is quickly becoming a standard fitting. A lens from any one of these manufacturers will fit the body of any other, and the camera will work perfectly. Topcon, however, also use a different unique bayonet on their Super DM model.

Contax and Yashica use the same lens mount. Lenses are freely interchangeable.

Rollei and Voigtlander also use the same mount as each other—so both brands can share the same lenses.

Zenith, Praktica and Alpa all use the 42 mm 'universal' screw thread, not a bayonet, on their cameras. Alpa use a unique bayonet on one of their models, and Praktica, similarly, employ a unique bayonet fitting. To complicate matters still further, Praktica also have another system —electrical coupling. This feeds information from lens to camera, so some of their lenses, and one of their cameras, have electrical contacts fitted to the screw thread fittings.

Mamiya use two separate, non-interchangeable bayonet lens mounts and all other manufacturers, including Canon, Nikon, Olympus and Minolta, use exclusive bayonet lens mounts.

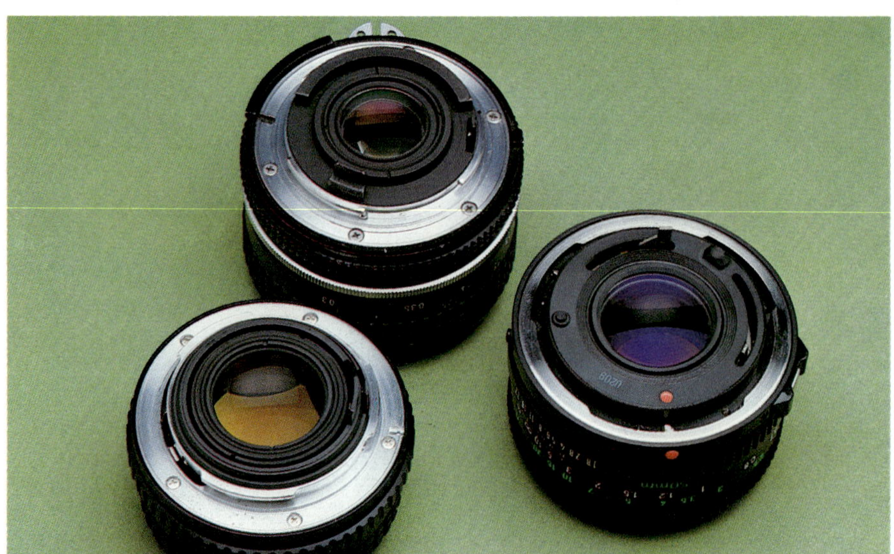

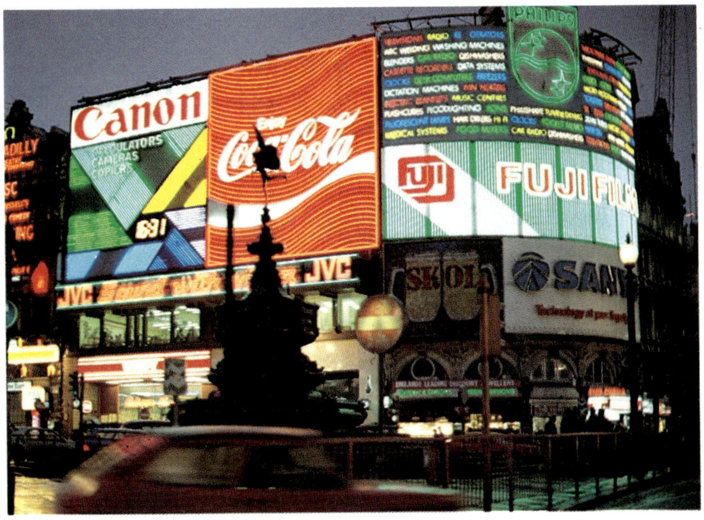

Wide aperture *Standard lenses with wide aperture are not always better. This picture was taken with an f/1.2 50 mm lens at full aperture. Definition is poor—look at the digital clock*

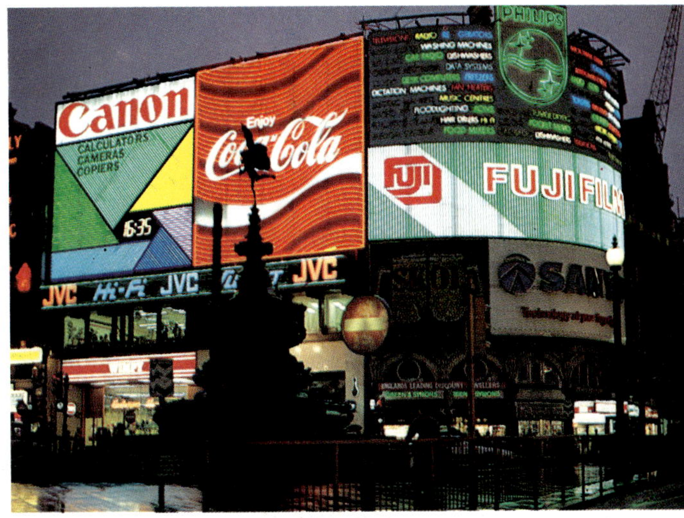

Better quality *An f/1.7 standard lens produced much better results, but a longer shutter speed was necessary. The lens was only half the weight of the f/1.2 equivalent, —see comparison below—and a third of the price*

open as long as the button is depressed) through one second, ½ second and so on up to 1/1000 second. The mechanism is controlled by either a dial on the top plate or a ring on the lens. The dial is marked not with fractions, but with numbers—½ second is marked as 2, ¼ second as 4 and so on to 1000. This series of steps is also used in those electronic exposure systems that give shutter speed priority. A few aperture-priority automatic cameras have no shutter speed dial. Since these cameras are designed to be used automatically at all times, the lack of a manual shutter speed control is not a great problem. If you require control over the shutter speed, however, it is highly unlikely that you will have much use for a camera of this type.

Viewfinder and focusing screens

The incorporation of more and more electronics into the camera and the use of the viewfinder to display information has concentrated attention on this part of the camera. Some manufacturers produce cameras that have easily interchangeable viewfinders. The normal eye level pentaprism can be exchanged for a finder that can be used at waist level, or one that gives a greatly magnified image which is useful for copying work. As such viewfinders are intended for special purposes it is easy to decide whether or not their possible applications will interest you.

Although a standard focusing screen is suitable for most applications, many cameras accept interchangeable focusing screens, even if the viewfinder itself is fixed. While this used to be a feature found only on the most expensive cameras, it is now available even on quite cheap ones. The screen fitted as standard to many cameras may have several focusing aids—usually both microprisms and a split image rangefinder—and the screens that are available as alternatives differ from one manufacturer to another.

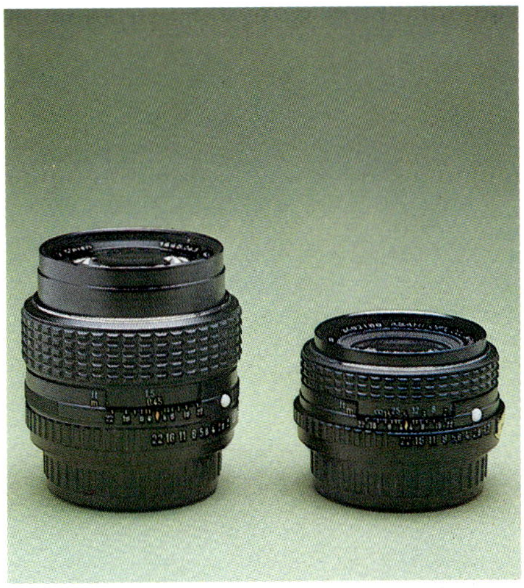

Some cameras accept screens that have no focusing aids at all, while others have microprisms all over, If you have very special interests, and want to take photographs through microscopes, for example, you may need a special screen.

Since the range of screens available varies so much from one company to another it is a good idea to check details of the more unusual screens with a camera salesman, who should be able to explain what is available to fit the camera that you are considering buying. For most applications, though, a standard screen is quite satisfactory.

Viewfinder information

Most cameras have some information in the viewfinder about the shutter speed or aperture that has been set. Some have a great deal more information, such as the number of frames of film that have been used, or whether the camera is set on manual.

This information is passed on to the photographer in a number of ways. There may be a scale of apertures down one side of the screen. A small LED lights up alongside one of these to indicate the aperture in use. An alternative is a needle which swings across a scale and comes to rest alongside the aperture or shutter speed that has been set by the photographer.

A more direct method of indicating the aperture is a device which is sometimes called a Judas' window. This looks like a tiny window at the top of the viewfinder image, through which the photographer can see the aperture setting ring. Though this works well with lenses made by the same firm that made the camera, lenses made by other companies may not have the aperture ring in the same place, and no indication of aperture will be visible.

Viewfinder information systems work well in average conditions, but when buying a camera it is a good idea to see whether the settings are visible both in very bright light (point the lens at a bright shop spotlight) and in very dim light, or when the subject is very dark in colour.

Some photographers prefer an uncluttered viewfinder, and like to have the bare minimum of information visible.

Hot shoes and flashguns

On top of the viewfinder most manufacturers provide a slide-on connection, a *hot shoe* or *accessory shoe,* for one of the small electronic flashguns currently available. The built-in contacts link the gun to the camera and fire the flash at the moment when the shutter is open. Because of the way the shutter works, you should not usually set a faster shutter speed than 1/60 or 1/125 while using a flashgun (see page 99). On the more sophisticated electronic cameras the use of the hot shoe automatically programs the shutter to fire at one of these speeds.

Some electronic cameras that have so-called dedicated flash capability can provide even more sophisticated couplings between camera and flash. For example, some cameras will operate at the correct synchronization speed for flash only when the flashgun is ready to make an exposure. If it is not, the camera will revert to the normal automatic mode of working, and will make an exposure

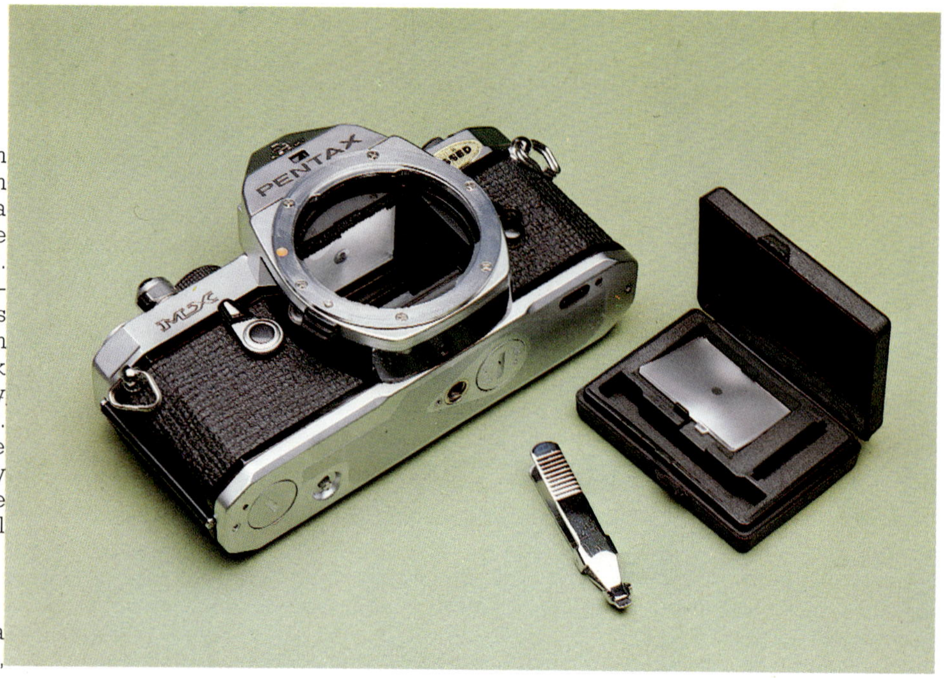

Interchangeable screens *For special uses, you can change the focusing screen of some cameras. This is often fiddly, and sometimes needs tweezers*

using available light. Such cameras often have a 'flash ready' indication visible in the viewfinder, and some also have a 'confidence light' that comes on if the subject is within the range of the flashgun.

It is probably clear from this description that a few dedicated flash systems are extremely sophisticated. When buying an SLR, it is as well to think carefully about whether you are likely to need this degree of complexity. Sophisticated dedicated flashguns are more expensive than the more ordinary types, and the extra expense may not be justified unless you have special requirements.

Motor drives and winders

The first time that you use a camera fitted with a motor winder or autowind, the feeling is very seductive. There is no need to do anything but press the shutter release—all the winding on is done for you. In fact such units can create a different approach to camera handling, because you never have to move your eye from the viewfinder. This is particularly true if the motor is coupled with fully automatic exposure control. The disadvantage is that it is easy to take frame after frame indiscriminately without concentrating hard enough on getting the 'decisive moment'.

Motor winders are easy to attach they are usually screwed into place on the camera base plate. They are powered by a set of batteries fitted into a compartment in the winder. The speed of winding on is usually about 2 frames a second. Not all cameras can be used with an autowinder, and if they can, only a unit made for a particular camera will fit. Autowinders are not interchangeable between different makes of camera.

A few cameras have two different types of motor available—a simple, inexpensive motor winder, and a more sophisticated unit called a motor drive. Since the two motors often look very similar, it is difficult to see why the drive is twice or three times the price of the winder. The reason is twofold—speed and robustness. Motor winders usually operate quite slowly in comparison to drives, some of which can run a roll of 36 exposures through a camera in three and a half seconds. Such high speed operation demands more heavily built components and more complex and sturdy mechanisms.

Since motor drives are made to professional standards, and should run many thousands of rolls of film without trouble, they are clearly going to be expensive. Unless you need really fast operation, then you are unlikely to need the sophistication offered by a motor drive, and an autowinder would be adequate.

Other features

A few cameras have a mirror lock—the mirror that reflects the image on to the focusing screen can be locked in the 'up' position. In practice, this feature is of little use for everyday photography, but some photographers like to lock up the mirror to reduce vibration. This procedure blacks out the viewfinder screen. The facility is of greatest value when using very long focus lenses or photographing through telescopes, where any vibration is undesirable.

A self timer, or delayed action, gives about a ten second delay before the shutter is released, and this allows the photographer to get into the picture. It is

Bayonet mounts *Except on a few cameras, lenses are changed by a bayonet mount. The twist and lock action is quick and positive*

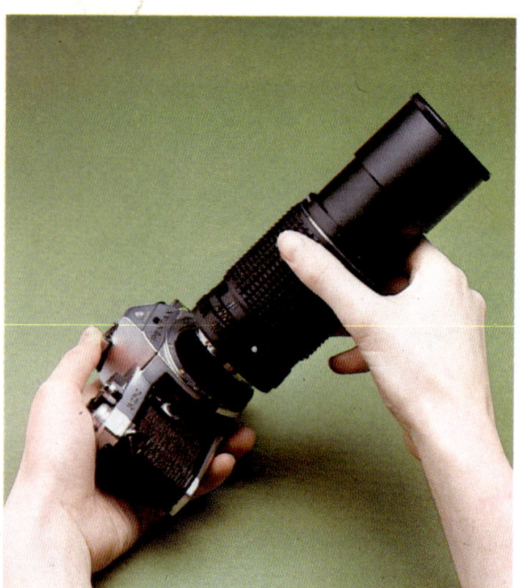

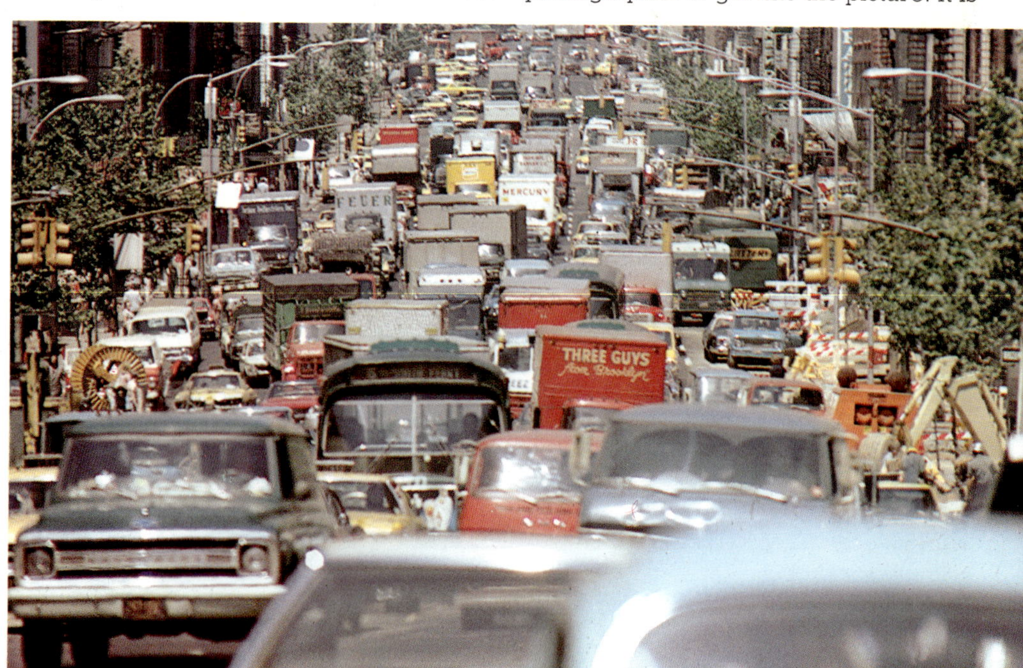

Telephoto traffic *The greatest advantage of using an SLR is the ability to use interchangeable lenses. A telephoto lens was used for this shot*

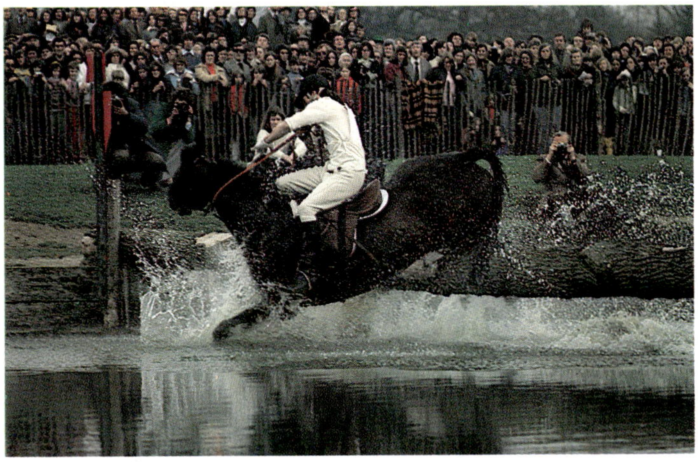

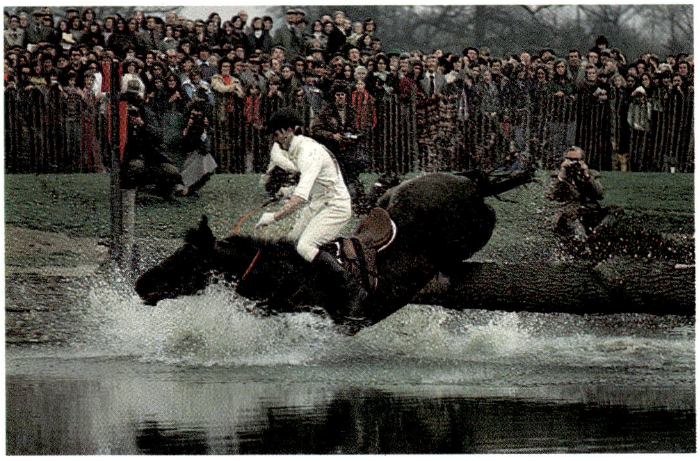

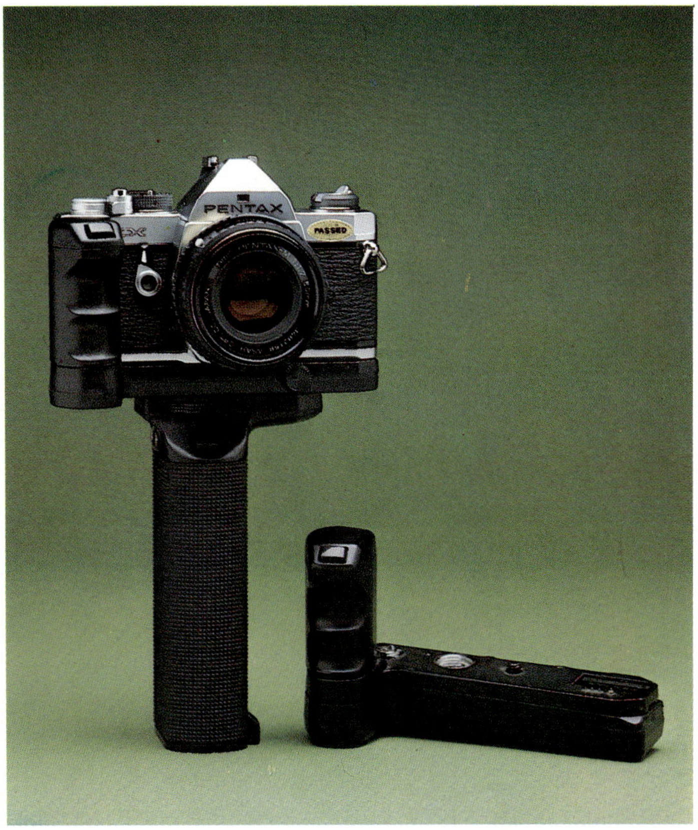

Motor drives *Professionals often use costly motor drives (attached to camera) to catch action like this, but an autowinder (alongside) is adequate for most purposes*

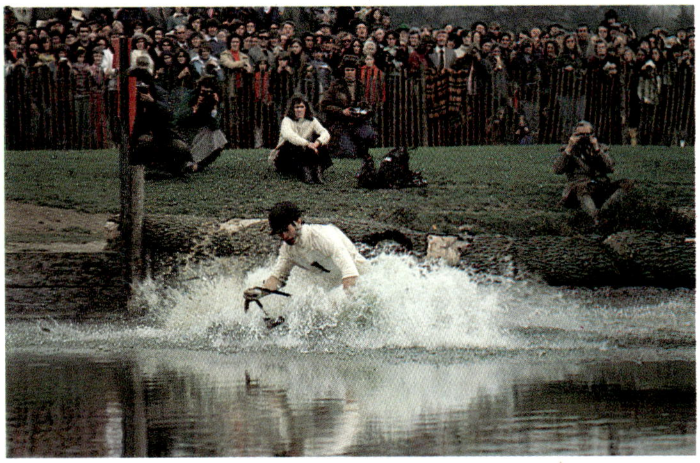

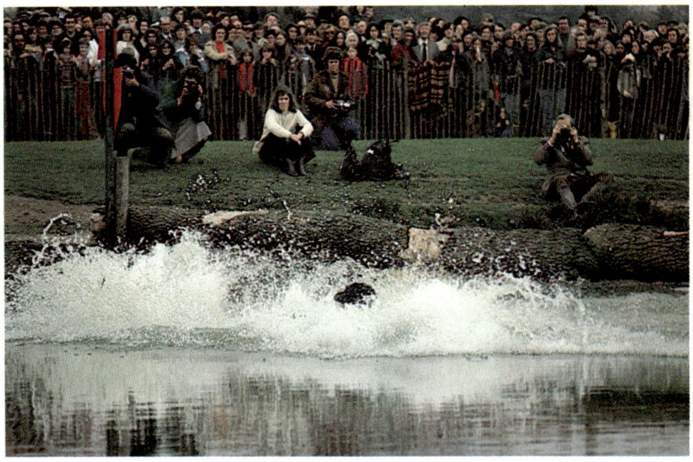

also useful for damping down vibration, as the photographer's finger is not on the shutter release at the moment of exposure. In this respect it is useful if you are using the camera on a tripod, and you do not have a cable release with you.

Exotic extras

Those cameras designed for professional use are the basic units of entire systems intended for use in special situations. Underwater housings and radio-controlled shutter releases can look very glamorous to those unacquainted with them but you should remember that they are all intended to do specific jobs. The purchase of such equipment, which is often very expensive, should only be contemplated if you are absolutely sure that you are going to use it for quite a while. If you want to try something out, then the nearest big city will usually have a company specializing in photographic equipment hire. The availability of such items, which you may rarely or never use, should never be allowed to colour your judgement as to the camera that you buy.

Making a selection

When trying to decide which camera to buy, first sort out those areas of photography that interest you most. If you are not sure, you may have to purchase equipment that is flexible enough for use in a variety of situations. But if you are only interested in taking portraits of friends, or landscapes, you will only need simple equipment.

Once you have narrowed the area of choice a little, get some brochures on the cameras in which you are interested. Try to ignore the sales talk as much as possible and concentrate on the facts. Publicity leaflets have technical data pages where the hard information is collected. If one particular aspect is emphasized by the manufacturer and seems impressive, ask yourself whether it is of any advantage to you. A shutter that works at 1/2000 of a second is of little use if your interest is architecture. However, a good motor-drive facility and a well matched range of zoom lenses may be just what a budding sports photographer is looking for.

Once you have narrowed the choice, go into a shop and try out the cameras on your short list. Do not let the shop staff try to hurry you into an inappropriate selection. Whatever your choice, you will have to use the results of that decision for quite a while. A few hours consideration may save frustration in the years to come.

Compact cameras

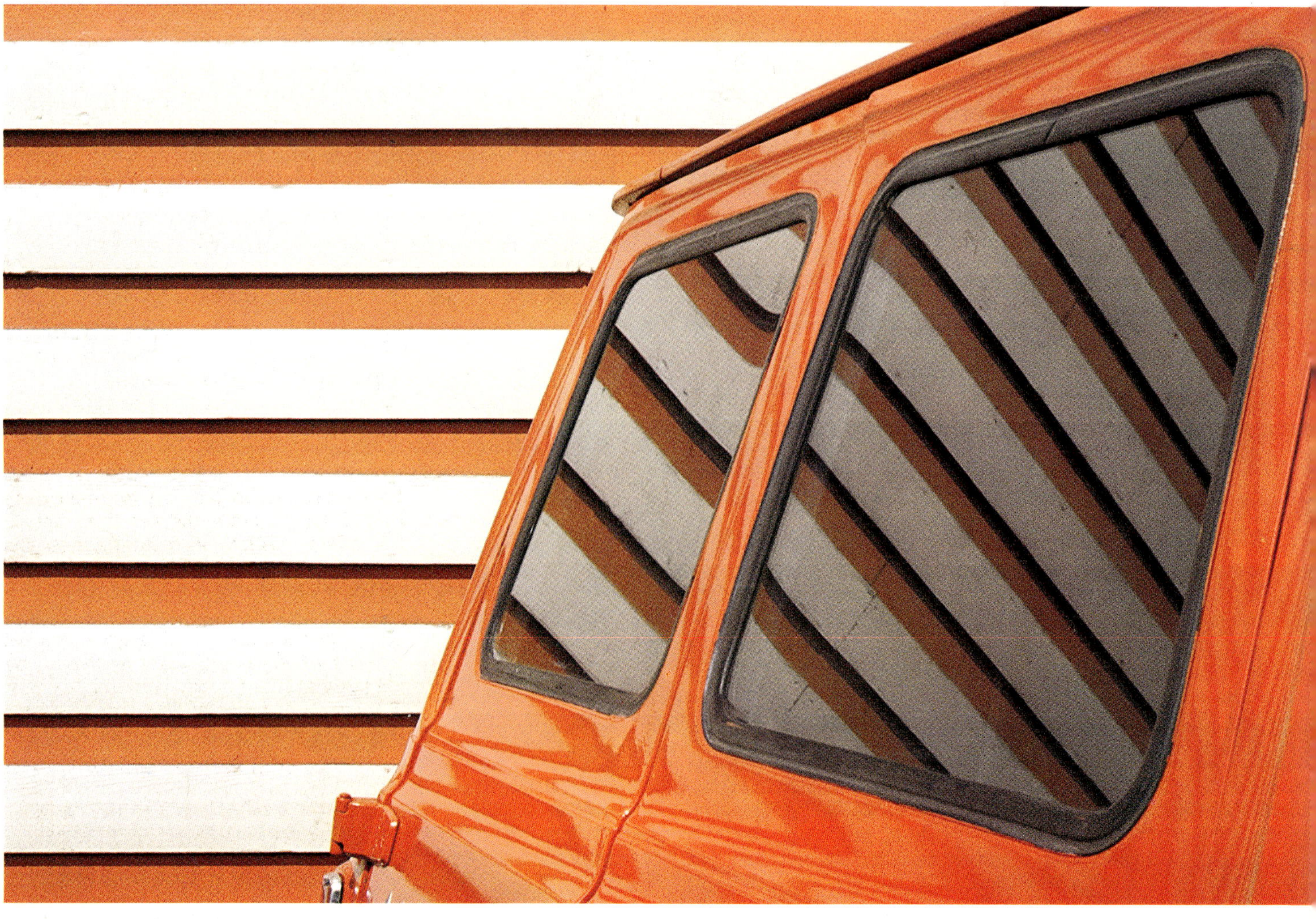

Today's simple compact cameras, if used with care, can give results which are practically indistinguishable from those taken by an expensive single lens reflex. Indeed, in some circumstances they can be more suitable than an SLR, so the results will actually be better. Many of them have excellent lenses, and if you choose the right subject, they can produce results of professional standard.

Quite a few professional photographers carry small 35 mm cameras around in their spare time, and leave their heavy SLRs at the studio. The best way to make the most of a compact camera is to recognize its limitations and its advantages, and to use it in the most appropriate circumstances. Compared with an SLR, a compact's drawbacks are its fixed lens, its often limited control over exposure, its separate viewfinder sometimes with no indication of correct focus, and its lack of versatility. Its advantages are light weight, simplicity of use, and in some cases its less complicated lens. Some of these advantages can work against the unwary photographer, however, so it is important to recognize what the problems are.

Hold the camera steady

One of the most common causes of bad pictures from small, simple cameras is camera shake. Some small cameras weigh very little, particularly if there is extensive use of plastic in their construction. Every little movement of the hand is liable to jar the camera and blur the picture.

Camera movement can be overcome by using a sufficiently fast shutter speed, but on many compact cameras there is no indication of the shutter speed in use. On the popular Olympus Trip, for example, the shutter may be set at either 1/200 sec or 1/40 sec. Camera shake is

Red van *Compact cameras give their best results when the subject is composed of large bold shapes and colourful patterns. Try to avoid images like that below, where the subject is scattered across the frame, or blends into the background*

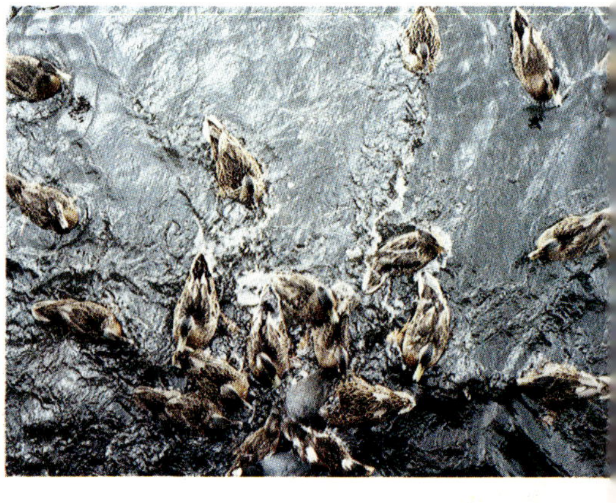

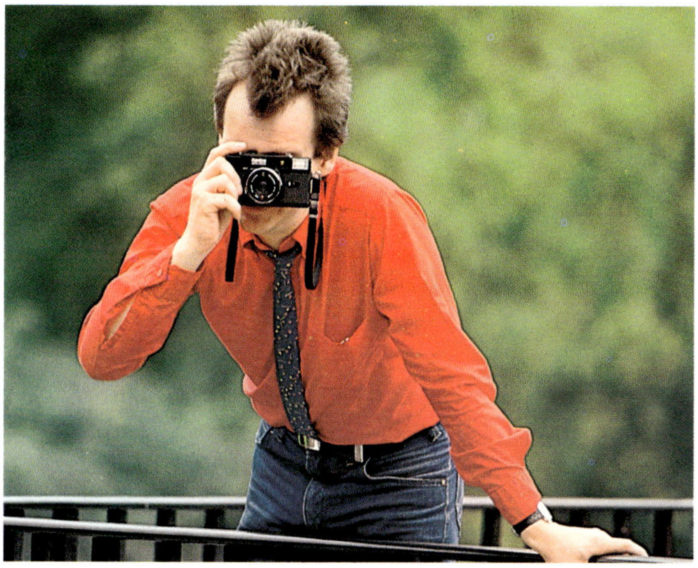

Unsteady posture *Camera shake ruins many pictures made by compact cameras, and a posture like this encourages it*

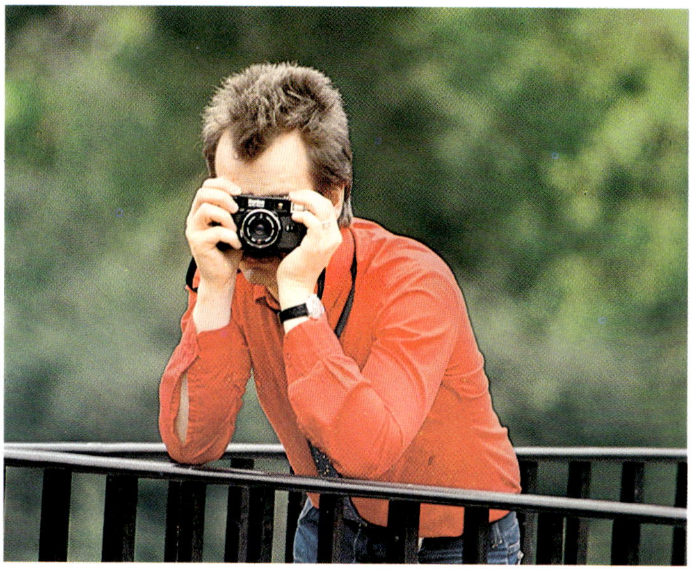

A firm grip *By bracing yourself against a railing or wall, it is easier to grip the camera and eliminate vibration*

quite likely at the slower speed so you should take extra care in holding the camera steady.

Whenever possible, therefore, brace yourself against a wall, or against a chair, or any other solid object. If you cannot do any of these things, take up a stable posture with your legs apart, and the camera pressed firmly against your face. More information on camera steadiness is given on pages 54-57.

If your camera has more than one shutter speed, try and use a speed faster than 1/30 sec if you can, as speeds slower than this increase the risk of camera shake. Fortunately, compact cameras usually have lenses with quite a wide angle of view, and this in itself helps to reduce the effect of camera movement. A few automatic cameras have a warning light in the viewfinder, which lights up when extra support is needed, and it is important to pay attention to this. Camera instructions frequently emphasize that a flash or a tripod is necessary when the light is on, but if you take great care to brace the camera solidly, you may be able to make use of available light without the need for a tripod.

Many automatic cameras leave the user to set the aperture, after which the camera decides on a shutter speed according to the *f*-stop chosen and the prevailing light. If you select a small aperture, these cameras will always set a slow shutter speed, so try and avoid stopping the lens right down, which will increase the likelihood of camera shake. Using a fast film also helps, as the shutter speed will be faster for the same exposure at any given aperture.

Keep your distance

Unlike SLRs, compacts cannot be focused visually. Indeed, some of the simplest have a fixed focus and only give sharp results if the subject is between two metres and infinity. With these cameras, then, it is important to ensure that your subject is no closer than two metres. You can only photograph subjects closer than this if your camera has a variable aperture, set either by the autoexposure system or by the photographer, using 'sunny' or 'cloudy' settings. In bright sunshine, the aperture is narrow, giving better depth of field (see page 220). Even so, subjects should not be closer than 1.75 metres.

On more expensive compact models, there is a focusing scale, with distances marked on the lens, either in feet or metres, or in symbols—a mountain representing infinity, a group of people four metres, and a head and shoulders about one metre. If your pictures are unsharp, it may well be because you are not using the focusing scale correctly. It is certainly

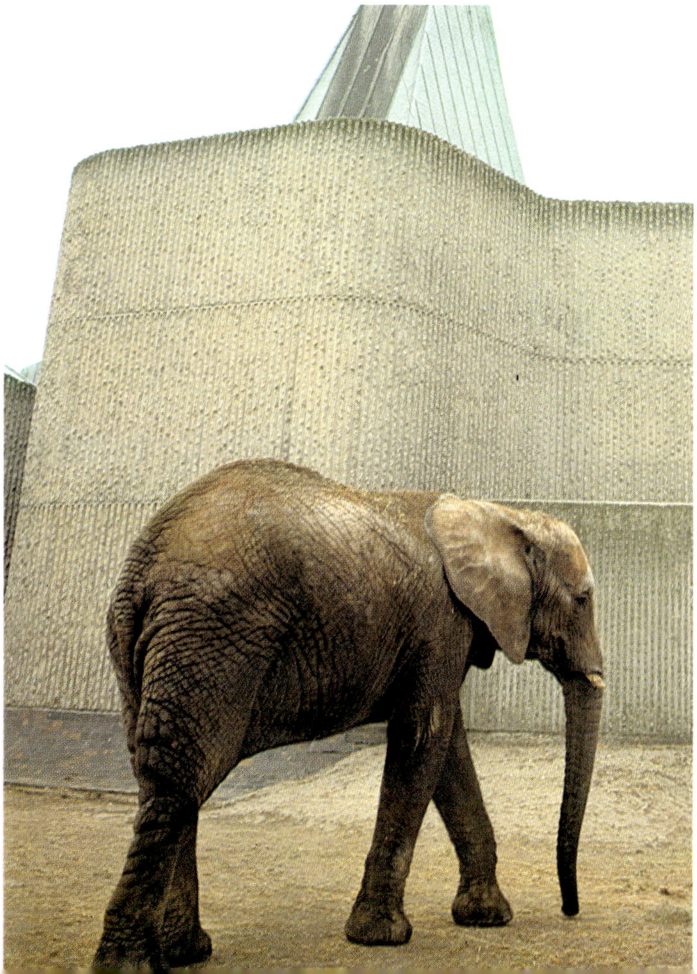

At the zoo *Small subjects usually make disappointing pictures with a compact. Stick to big animals that easily fill the frame and are not obscured by the bars of a cage*

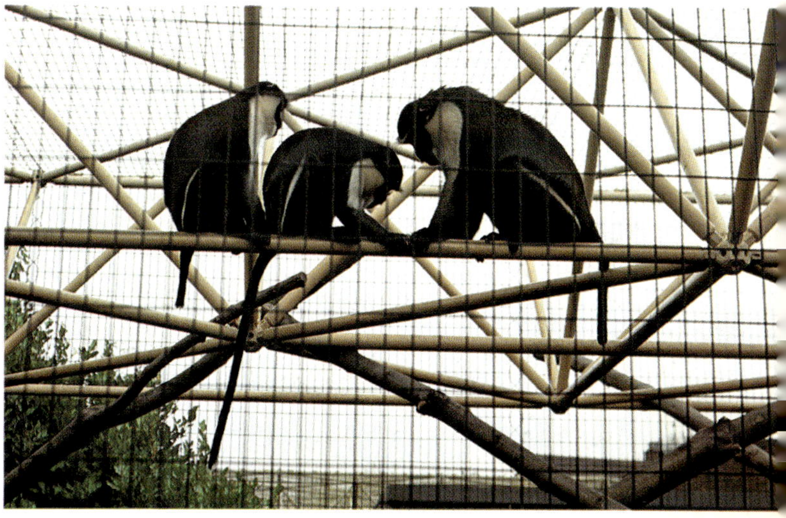

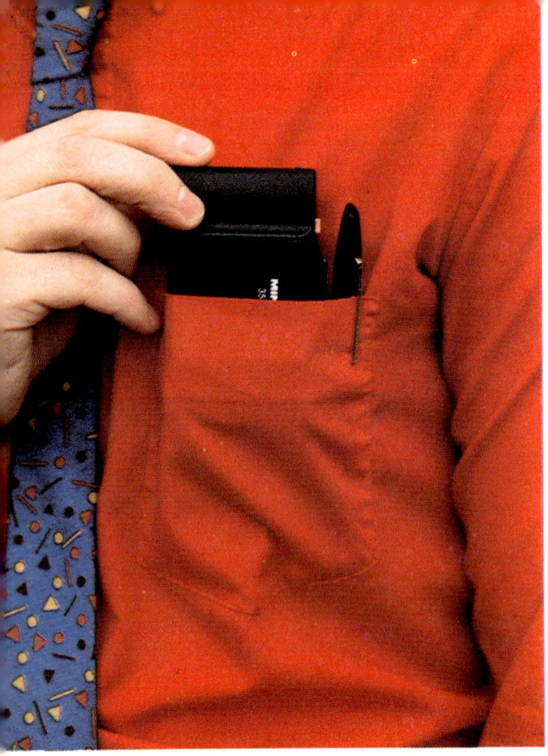

Carry a compact *Make a habit of taking your camera wherever you go—that way, you will never miss a picture*

easy to forget to focus at all if you are used to an SLR, for the viewfinder in a compact will show a sharp image whether the lens is focused or not. Using a focusing scale requires some care, for it is not always easy to estimate the distance to your subject. It is well worth spending a little time judging distances by eye and then measuring with a tape measure to test your accuracy.

In dim conditions, where a wide aperture is needed for correct exposure, focusing is especially critical, and it is important to remember that only a small distance will be in focus because of the small depth of field. In bright light, however, you can afford to be less careful about focusing. And, if you set the focusing scale to about four metres, you can virtually ignore focusing, because there will be sufficient depth of field (due to the narrow aperture) to ensure everything further than one metre from the camera is in focus.

Autofocus cameras

An increasing number of compacts at the upper end of the market now incorporate autofocus systems as well as autoexposure. These systems are either *active* or *passive*. The passive system uses two rangefinder windows to match the contrast of two images. Active systems work by sending out an infrared light or sound signal, which bounces off the subject. Most passive systems only work properly only when the light is reasonably bright. Active systems, however, function equally well in bright sunshine and pitch darkness—although infrared can be fooled by highly polished, reflective surfaces, and ultrasound autofocus systems may be thrown by glass. The Olympus XA-1 avoids these problems with a rangefinder. It does not focus automatically, but aids quick and easy manual focusing, achieved by matching two split images.

In the right conditions, all autofocus systems work well, and they are particularly useful for off-the-cuff shots, such as candids, because you can literally raise the camera, point and shoot. They are also valuable for shots of moving subjects, when you cannot be sure how far they are away at the moment you shoot. With fast moving subjects, though, it is worth remembering that the autofocus mechanism delays the firing of the shutter fractionally. This means you may have to anticipate a little to ensure the subject is correctly framed.

Autofocus systems have their limitations, however, and certain subjects can cause problems. Subjects in which the point of interest is not in the centre of the frame are particularly awkward—because the autofocus mechanism focuses on the centre of the picture. If you photograph two people side by side with a gap in between, the camera may well focus on the background through the gap, not the people themselves. There are two solutions to this problem. The simplest is to move the two people close together. The alternative is to use the *focus lock* if the camera has one. To do this, simply frame the main point of interest in the centre of the frame, operate the focus lock and then swing the camera round to achieve the desired composition.

Use the viewfinder properly

Compact cameras use direct vision viewfinders that do not look through the lens in the way that an SLR viewfinder does. At short distances, this separation of taking and viewing lenses often leads to

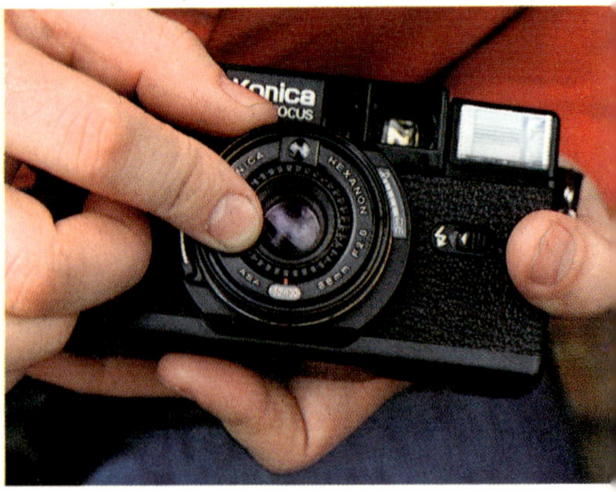

Changing ASA *You can compensate for backlighting by changing the film speed —you do not need a special switch*

errors in framing (known as *parallax error*). Almost all compact cameras have marks to show the extact area covered by the lens, and within this frame there is either a secondary line or small parallax correction marks, which indicate what the lens sees at short distances. Unless you pay attention to these markings, you may find that not all of your subject is included in the picture.

If the framing on your camera is wildly inaccurate, there may be a fault in the alignment of viewfinder and lens. To check this, set the camera on a tripod facing a brick wall. If it does not have a tripod socket, place it on a support such as a chair or ladder. With the aid of a friend, make clear chalk marks on the wall where the markings for corners of the frame appear in the viewfinder. When you have done this, photograph the wall without moving the camera. On processing the film, the chalk corner marks should be visible at the corners of the picture. If they are displaced by a small amount, you will be able to allow for this when taking pictures in future, but if the discrepancy is large, you should have the camera adjusted.

Keep your distance *Compact cameras have a limited focusing range, and it is easy to get out of focus results when you are close to your subject. Instead of trying to fill the frame with the subject on its own, move back and add another element to the picture*

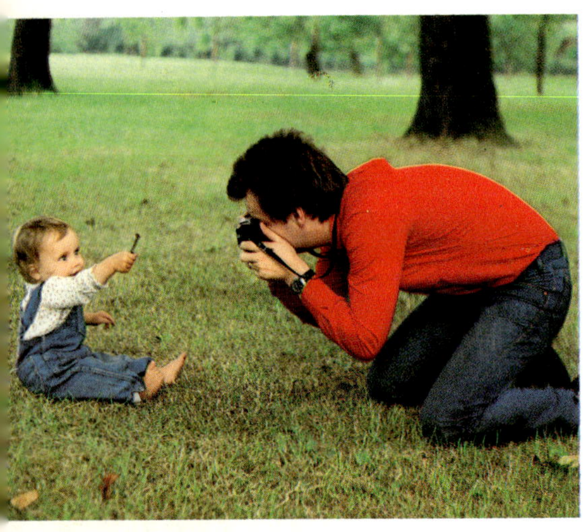

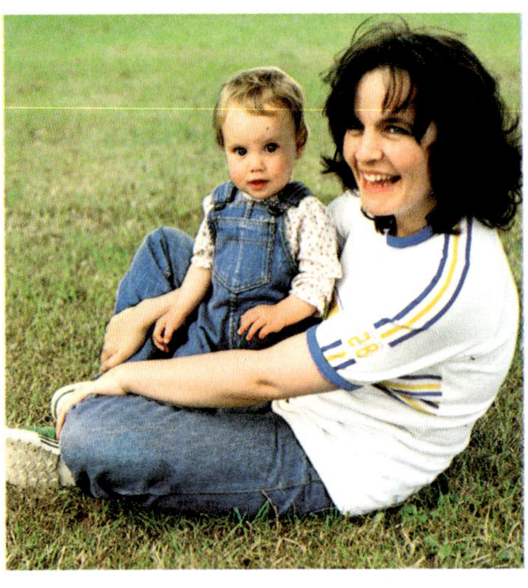

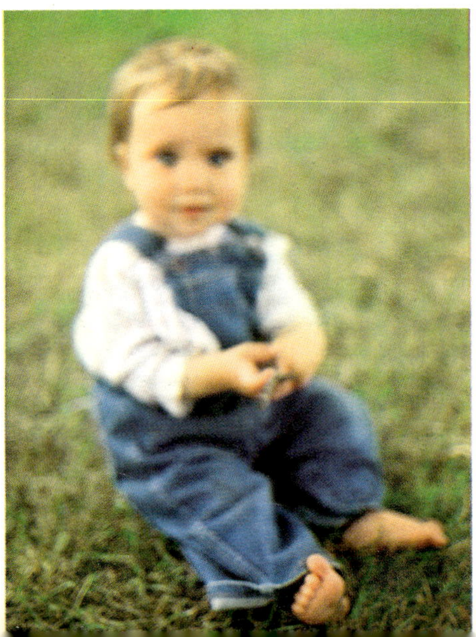

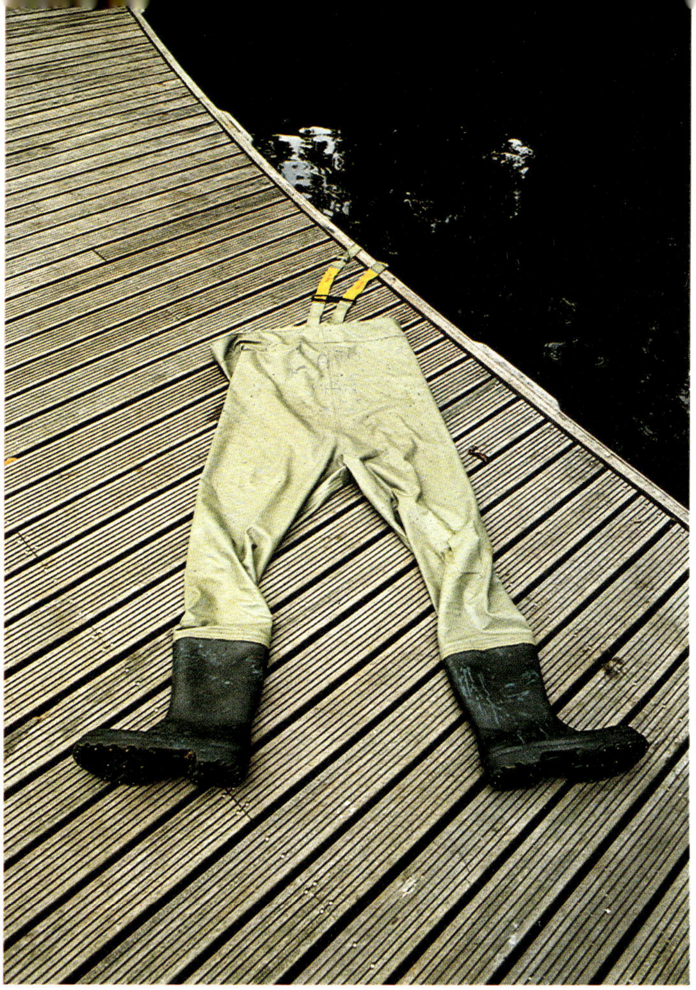

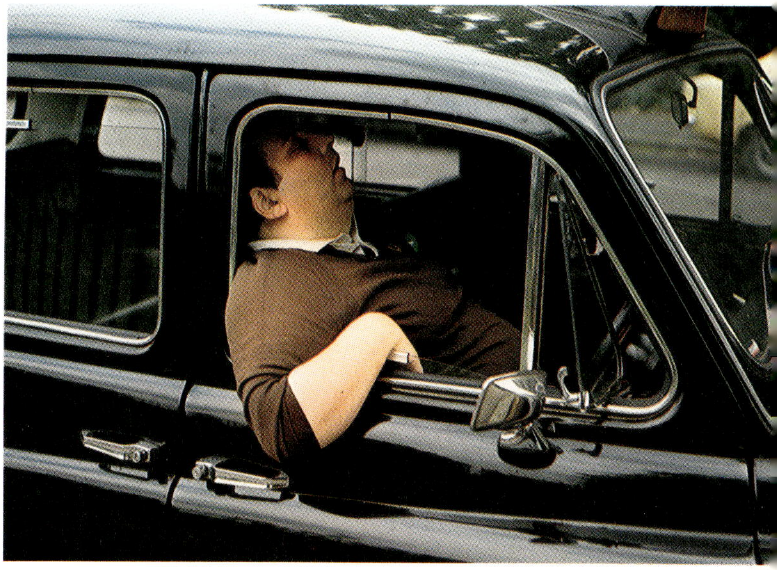

Simple subjects *Compact cameras give their best results when the subject is not too far away. Pick out uncomplicated scenes without many distracting details*

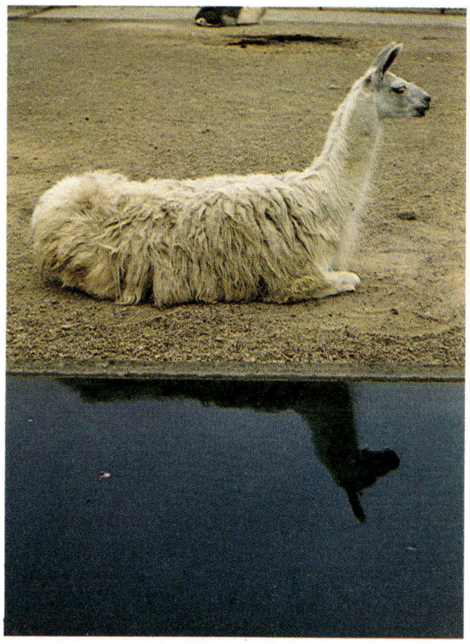

Unusual lighting needs care

Compact automatic cameras are designed to work well with low contrast lighting, or when the sun is coming from behind the photographer. Crosslighting or backlighting needs special attention.

When the light is coming from behind the subject, it is quite likely that the camera will underexpose. This is a result of the design of the meter, which, instead of reading through the lens, generally takes a reading through a small window alongside the lens or viewfinder.

If you are taking pictures in back- or sidelit conditions, always give about one stop extra exposure, and then bracket the exposures on either side of this so that you have a greater chance of success. You can do this by setting the film speed on the camera to a speed which is lower than the film that you are using. If you have 100 ASA (ISO) film in the camera, for example, make exposures with the ASA dial on 100, 50 and 25.

Better composition

When using a simple camera, particularly with print film that will give enprints, try and fill the frame with the subject—this avoids the common fault of a small area of interest in the middle of the frame, with rather boring surroundings. Move in towards the subject, and get as close as you can without cutting off important parts of the image at the edges of the frame. Unless you will be able to print the film yourself, so that you can make selective enlargements, do not bother taking a picture unless the subject appears fairly big in the finder.

When the subject is too small to fill the frame, even at the camera's closest focusing distance, try and add something to the picture in order to fill the frame. A picture of a small child on a bicycle looks much better than one of a small child standing in a wide expanse of grass.

Avoid photographing distant scenery. Unless the view is very dramatic, you will find it hard to make a good picture of a scenic view because fine distant detail that your eye picks out disappears when the pictures are printed. The only way to deal with such a subject is to include something in the foreground to provide a point of reference and a sense of scale. Alternatively, use a tree to frame the view and fill in some of the broad expanse of sky. It is often a good idea to choose an unusual viewpoint, particularly a low one, in order to make the most of the foreground.

Look out for bold, striking shapes and colours, and avoid subjects that include fine detail that is important for an understanding of the picture. Pictures taken on dull days can look very drab unless there is plenty of colour in them.

Avoid small subjects—if you take a compact camera with you to a zoo, for example, only photograph animals that fill a reasonable proportion of the frame. Small birds and animals, however attractive they may look at the time, are invariably disappointing without a telephoto lens to compress distance.

Fast film gives more scope with a compact camera, and allows you to take correctly exposed pictures in much dimmer conditions without running the risk of camera shake. Although there is a small loss of quality compared with slower film, this is often unnoticeable on small enlargements.

Above all, remember to take the camera with you as often as possible. The beauty of a compact camera is that it is no great burden to carry around, and to leave it behind is to waste much of its potential. Make a habit of slipping it into your pocket when you leave the house. This way you need never miss a picture.

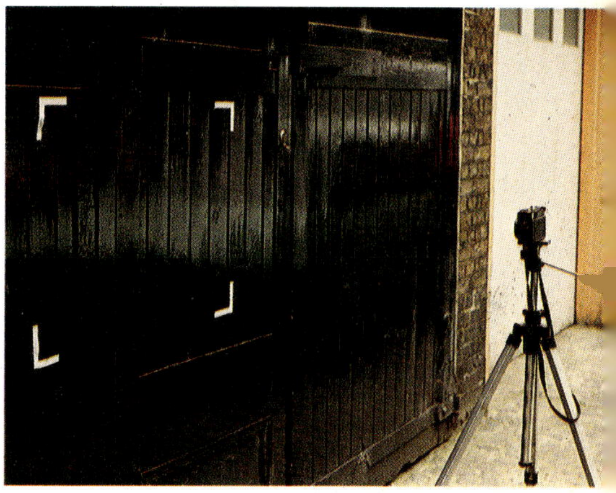

Check for parallax *If the framing of your pictures is consistently wrong, you can use this simple method to check the accuracy of the viewfinder*

Roll film cameras

The advantages of the single lens reflex camera are familiar to almost every serious photographer—it has a viewfinder which shows exactly what is recorded on film, and is compact, convenient and easy to use.

For the amateur, 'SLR' is synonymous with '35 mm', but Single Lens Reflex cameras which use the larger format rollfilm are commonplace in professional circles. These offer most of the advantages of their smaller 35 mm cousins — compactness and convenience and a viewfinder that shows exactly what is recorded on film—but they produce pictures that are four times the size of a 35 mm frame, and have other additional features which make them particularly versatile.

The habitual 35 mm user, however, may find rollfilm cameras clumsy and unfamiliar. They are quite heavy, and with the exception of one camera, none of the controls are where you would expect them to be. Nevertheless, these cameras are easy to use once you get to know them and are ideal for producing big, high quality pictures.

The first step is learning how to load the film. Loading methods vary from model to model—two examples of fairly typical loading procedures are shown on pages 22 to 23. Although loading seems complicated when compared to the simplicity of a 35 mm camera, it is a routine which is actually much easier than it looks, and after a little practice you should have no difficulty.

Film can be loaded either with the magazine separated from the camera, or attached to it. You may find it easier to leave the magazine attached to the camera body so that you have fewer pieces to cope with—an important consideration if you are standing ankle deep in mud.

Cameras that have removable magazines invariably have a film shield—a stainless steel or plastic blade that prevents the film being fogged when the magazine is separated from the camera body. Most of them also have safety interlocks which prevent the shutter from being fired when the shield is in place, and lock the magazine to the camera when it is withdrawn. This system prevents film from being inadvertently fogged, and assures that the photographer does not 'shoot' a whole roll of film with the shield in place.

A few cameras have a compartment for stowing the shield when it is not in place in the magazine. If your camera

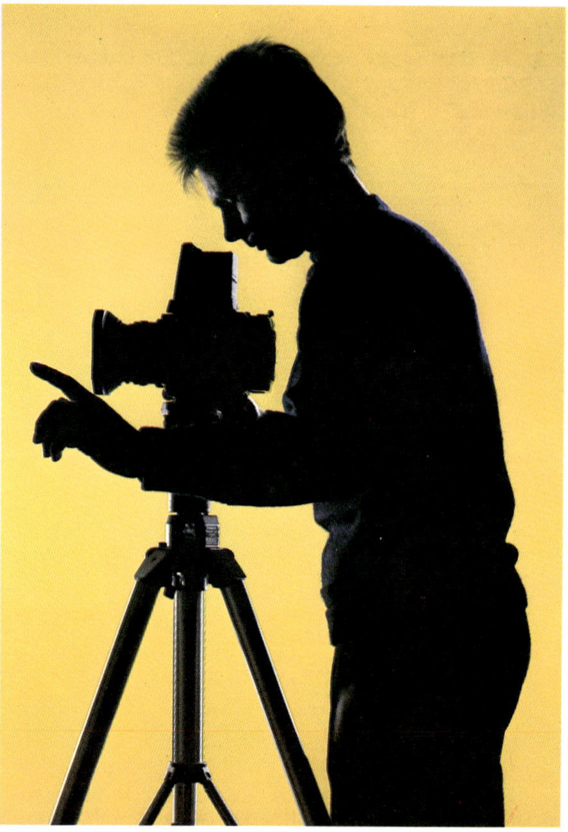

In the studio *The rollfilm SLR is possibly the ideal studio camera. It is compact and convenient, yet produces a negative four times the size of a 35 mm frame*

Traditional model *The Hasselblad 500 C/M is a traditional, mechanically operated camera, and is shown here with the waist-level finder fitted as standard. It has a leaf shutter, and most of the controls are grouped on or near the lens*

Electronic automation *The Bronica ETR is typical of the modern breed of rollfilm SLRs. It too has a leaf shutter, but this is electronically controlled, and the shutter speed dial is on the side of the camera body. This model is fitted with a speed grip, and the metering prism converts it to a fully automatic camera*

does not have this facility, you should develop the habit of always putting the shield in some safe place—in a particular compartment in your camera bag, for example or in your top pocket—rather than simply stuffed in your back trouser pocket where it will be bent if you sit down. It is very easy to lose, or at least temporarily mislay such a small object, and this can be very irritating if you are working quickly, and want to change magazines.

Changing lenses is a more straightforward process, similar in most respects to lens changing on smaller cameras. All rollfilm cameras have bayonet mount lenses, and these are usually removed by pressing a button and turning the lens. Several rollfilm SLRs have leaf shutters in their lenses, and when mounting or removing a lens on one of these cameras, you must make sure that the shutter in the lens is tensioned, and that the film has been advanced. If you neglect this, you may damage both camera and lens because the coupling is not in the correct position.

Besides advancing the film and cocking the shutter, cranking the wind knob or lever performs a further vital function; it lowers the mirror in the camera body. Unlike 35 mm cameras, few rollfilm SLRs have instant return mirrors. When the shutter release is pressed, the mirror rises, and the image disappears from the viewfinder. If you find this loss of image disconcerting, you should use one of the few cameras that have an instant return mirror.

When you take your first shots on a rollfilm SLR, the first point to consider is how to hold it. This largely depends on the viewing system you are using—the standard fitting on most cameras is the folding waist-level finder. If you are using this, you should support the camera with your left hand, so that your left index finger rests on the shutter release button. This is usually on the front of the camera at the bottom right. You can then use your right hand for focusing and winding film. The Rollei SL66 is awkward to use because the lens is focused using a knob on the left of the body, and the film is wound with crank on the right. When this camera is used hand-held, it must be switched from hand to hand as the lens is focused and film is advanced. Bronica cameras present similar problems, because the film speed control is on the left hand side of the camera body.

Traditional mechanical SLR

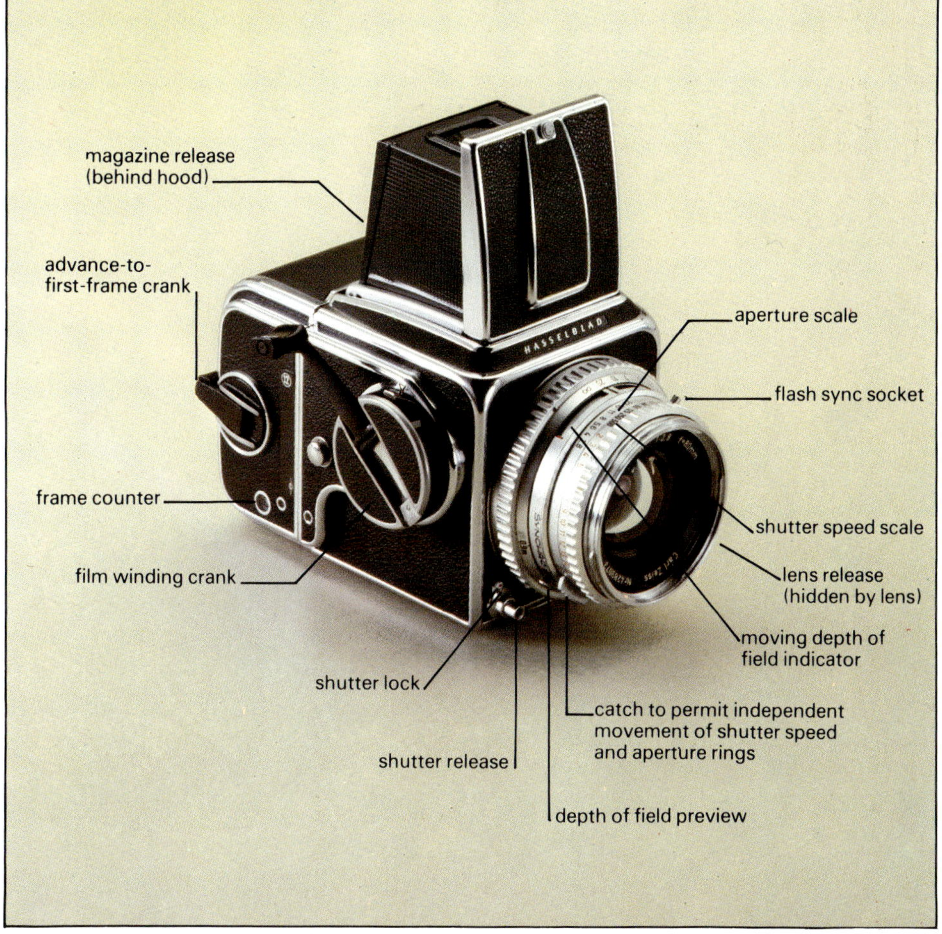

Cameras which use the 6 × 4.5 cm format are generally fitted with pentaprisms, because of the difficulties of using a waist-level finder when the camera is turned through 90° to take vertical format pictures. Holding a camera at eye level can be quite tiring, and you may find that a pistol grip takes the strain off your arms, and makes handling easier. Some of these cameras can also be fitted with a *speed grip*, which has a coupled shutter release and film wind crank, and makes operation much quicker and easier.

With a couple of exceptions, focusing is accomplished by turning a ring around the lens—just like a 35 mm camera. With a waist-level finder, however, you may find it difficult to accurately judge the point of sharp focus. It is best to do this using the flip-up magnifier fitted to the inside of the folding hood—with the screen up to half a metre from your eyes at waist level, focusing without a lens is not sufficiently accurate.

Although split-image and microprism focusing screens are available for rollfilm SLRs, these are not very easy to use (except with prism finders), and photographers generally prefer a plain matt screen.

Depth of field preview facility is available on most cameras of this type, though it is of limited use, because the focusing screen darkens considerably when the lens is stopped down. The depth of field available at any particular aperture is indicated by scales around the lens barrel, or on a panel on the camera side. In order to check on depth of field, you should take a Polaroid test shot and examine it using a magnifier.

Setting the exposure

Controls for setting the aperture and shutter speed are easy to identify by their familiar series of numbers. The shutter speed control is usually on the camera body, and the aperture ring on the lens, but on the Hasselblad, the two controls are on adjacent rings around the lens. These are linked together by a spring clip, which must be pressed if the two rings are to be moved independently of one another. This feature can be infuriating when you want to quickly bracket a series of exposures, but can be useful if you are using fill-in flash.

TTL light meters can be fitted to virtually any rollfilm SLR, but most photographers prefer to use a separate handheld meter, perhaps because these medium format cameras do not lend themselves to the kind of rapid-fire shooting that demands snap decisions about exposure.

Once you have focused the camera, and set the aperture and shutter speed, you are ready to take a picture. If nothing happens when you press the shutter release, there could be a number of things you have forgotten. Check that you have removed the darkslide, If there is one fitted, and that the film has been advanced to the first frame. Check that

Modern electronic SLR

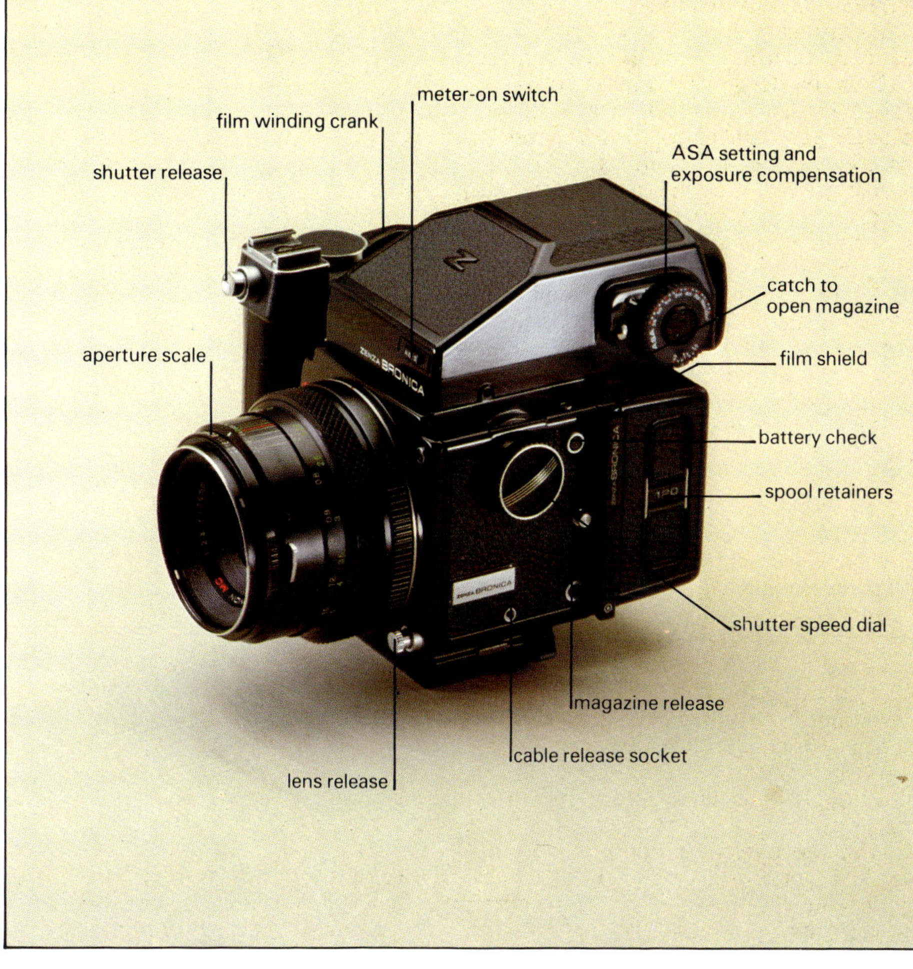

Bookform holder loading

The rollfilm holder of the Mamiya RB 67 is typical of bookform holders—the magazine at the back of the camera opens up like the cover of a book

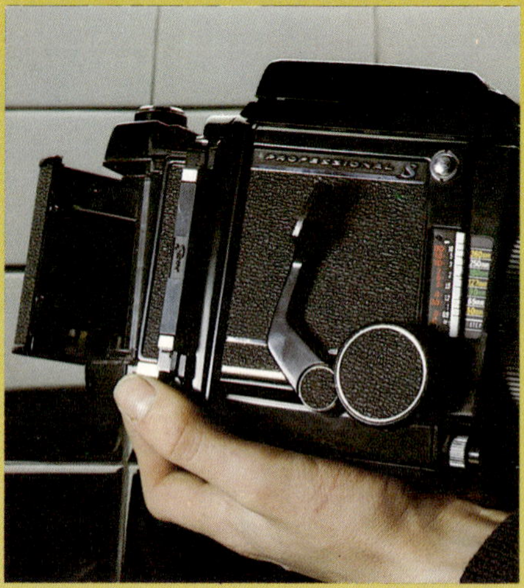

1 Open back *A catch releases the back cover, and frees the rollfilm holder. This is removed from the magazine for film loading*

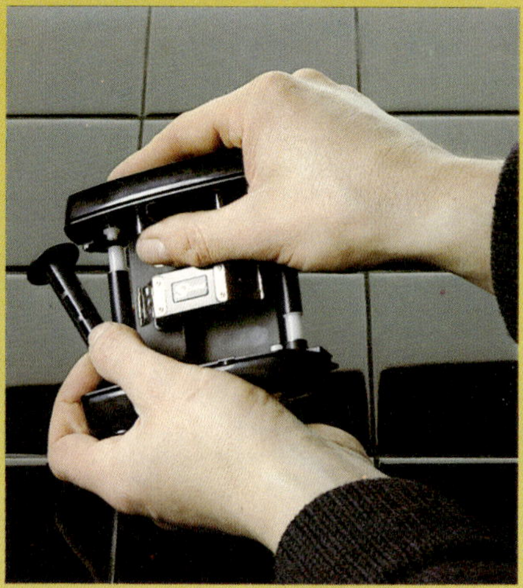

2 Lift out spool *A button inside the holder retracts a pin, releasing the film spool. Transfer the empty spool to the take-up spindle*

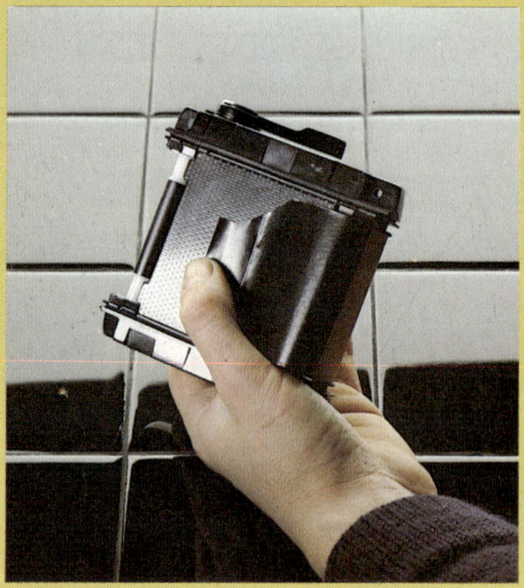

3 Pull out leader *Fit a new roll of film on the supply side of the magazine, and pull the backing paper across the pressure plate*

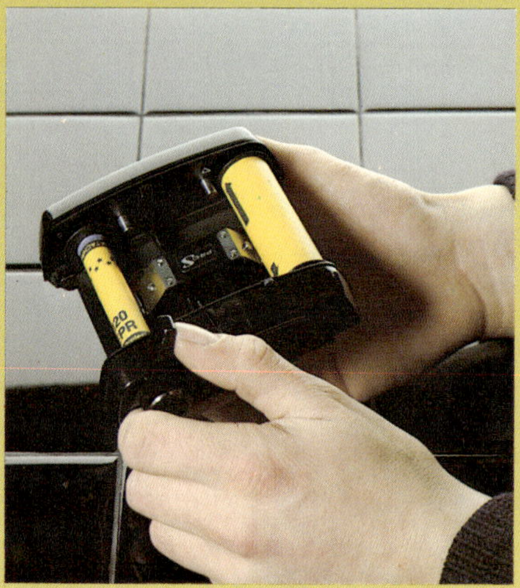

4 Line up arrows *Crank the film until the arrows on the backing paper are aligned with the white triangle engraved on the holder*

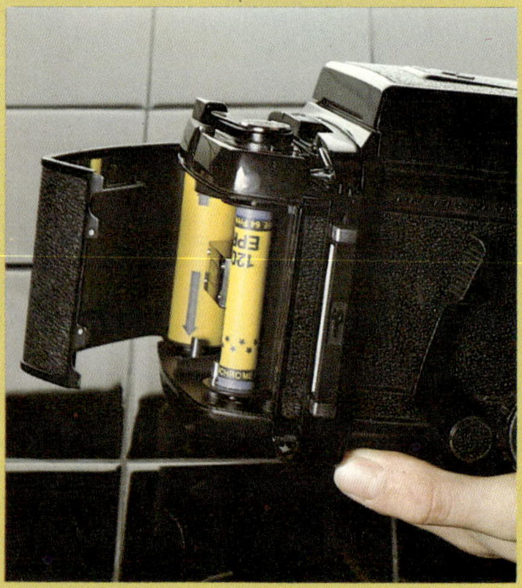

5 Replace insert *Slip the holder back into the magazine, and close the bookform cover. A latch on the magazine locks the cover closed*

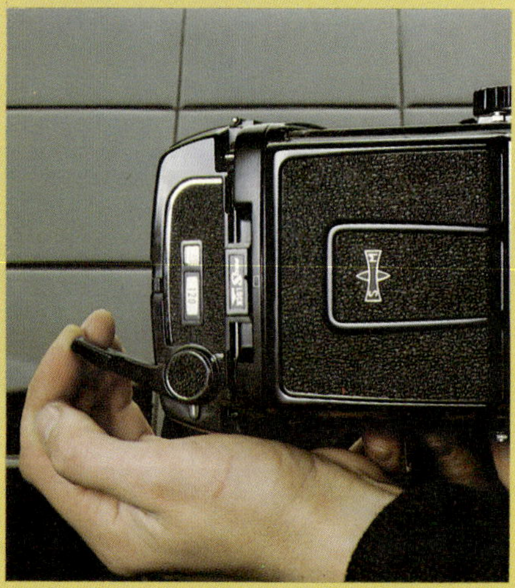

6 Advance the film *Crank the lever wind until it locks. A number 1 appears in the window, and the magazine is ready for use*

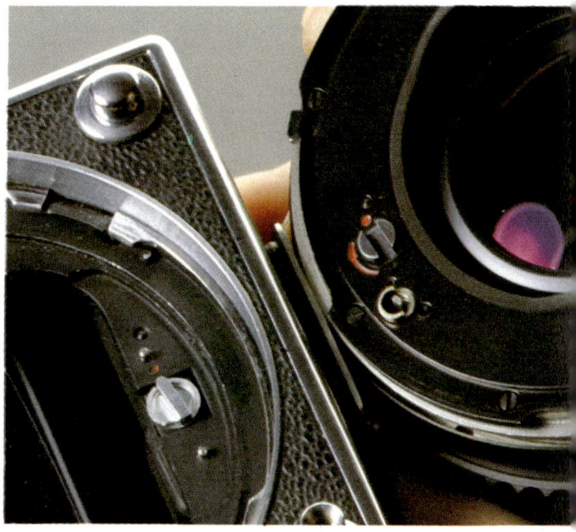

Camera couplings *These delicate couplings cock and release the shutter. When changing lenses, they can be damaged if their positions do not match*

the shutter is cocked—though in most cases, if you can see an image in the viewfinder, you can be sure that this has been done. If your camera has an electronic shutter, check that it has been switched on, and that the batteries are not flat. Finally, check that there is not a catch which locks the shutter release.

If you are making an exposure which is longer than 1/15 second, keep the release depressed until the shutter has closed. This is important, because on models of cameras which utilize a leaf shutter, there is an auxiliary capping shutter in the camera body. This shutter closes the instant that you take your finger off the release button, and it can easily close before the primary shutter in the lens, thereby curtailing the exposure prematurely.

Rollfilm SLRs which have leaf shutters offer significant advantages with electronic flash, because there is no upper limit on the synchronization speed that can be used. If the camera you are using has a focal plane shutter, you may be limited to speeds slower than 1/60 sec. This is such a severe limitation that the manufacturers of these cameras have made available accessory lenses which are fitted with quite separate leaf shutters, so that flash can be synchronized at all speeds.

Special features

Certain rollfim SLRs have controls or features which you may not immediately understand. The most common of these is the facility for changing from 120 to 220 film. In outward appearances, these two film types seem identical, but there are important differences between them. 220 film is twice the length of 120, and to accommodate the longer strip of film on the same size spools, the emulsion is coated on to a thinner base. The backing paper, too, is different. Instead of running the full length of the film, it is fixed to the film only at the beginning and end—a paper tail and leader.

Before loading a roll of 220 film, the pressure plate at the back of the camera must be moved forward to compensate for the different film thickness, and lack of backing. This forward movement is accomplished by rotating or sliding the pressure plate, or operating a catch. An adjustment must also be made to the frame counter, so that it does not stop counting halfway through the film.

Not every magazine can be used with 220 film—Hasselblad and other cameras must be fitted with a special 220 back.

A feature which you may recognize from 35 mm cameras is the *mirror lock up*. This raises the mirror to reduce vibration when the camera is used on a tripod, and reflex viewing is not required. On Hasselblads, it also closes down the lens to the working aperture, so that the only vibration at the moment of exposure stems from the shutter itself. A further advantage of using this prerelease is that it reduces the elapse between the release and the exposure.

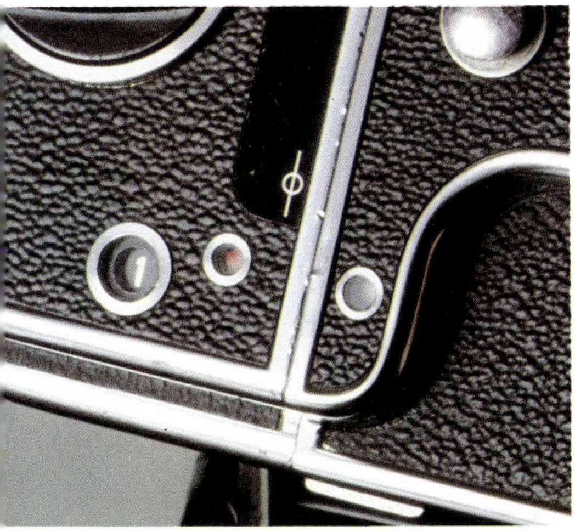

Coloured index *The red and white windows indicate whether film is wound and shutter cocked. To prevent double exposure, the colours must match*

The Rollei and Pentax

Two rollfilm SLRs are quite different from the rest, and have characteristics which make them exceptional. One is the Pentax 6 × 7, which has a layout reminiscent of a 35 mm SLR. It has a focal plane shutter, and an instant return mirror, and many of the comments about camera handling do not apply to it—it is probably the quickest and easiest to use of all rollfilm SLRs.

Another highly unusual camera is the Rollei SLX. Although very compact, it incorporates motorized film advance, and automatic TTL metering, both as standard features. It has an electronically controlled leaf shutter and, like the Pentax, it is much more convenient to use than other rollfilm cameras.

The motorized film advance fitted to the Rollei is not unique—several other models can be fitted with motordrives as accessories, and the Hasselblad EL/M has one permanently attached. In all other respects, though, this camera is identical to the Hasselblad 500 C/M and both models can be fitted with the same range of lenses and accessories.

Separate magazine loading

The backs of Hasselblads and other cameras can be removed. This means they can be preloaded with film, and changing rolls just means swapping backs

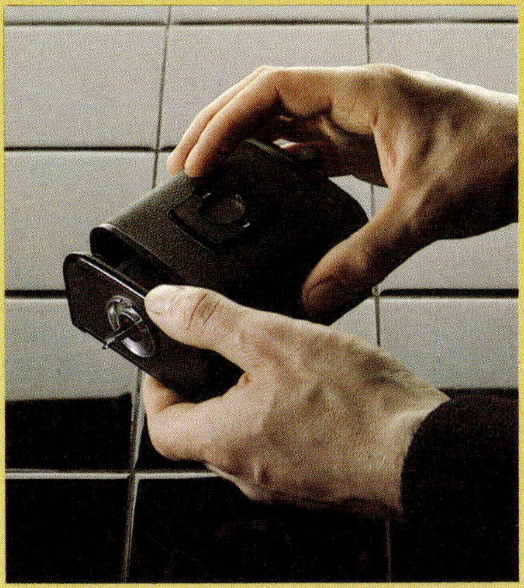

1 Remove insert *Lift and turn the catch on the magazine's side. This releases the rollfilm holder, which is withdrawn to load the film*

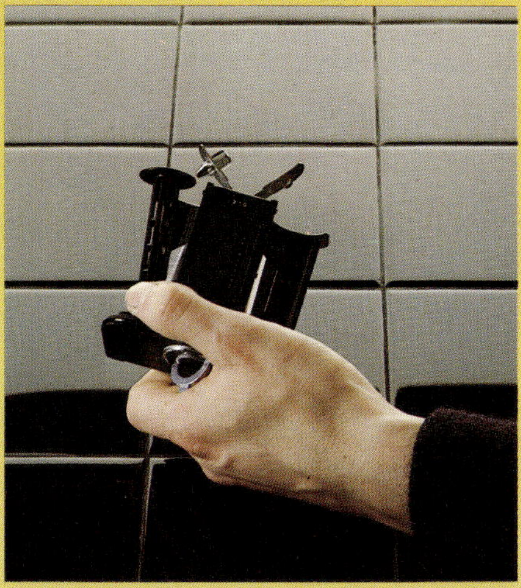

2 Lift flanges *Raise the flanges that retain the spools, move the empty spool to the take-up side, and replace it with a fresh film*

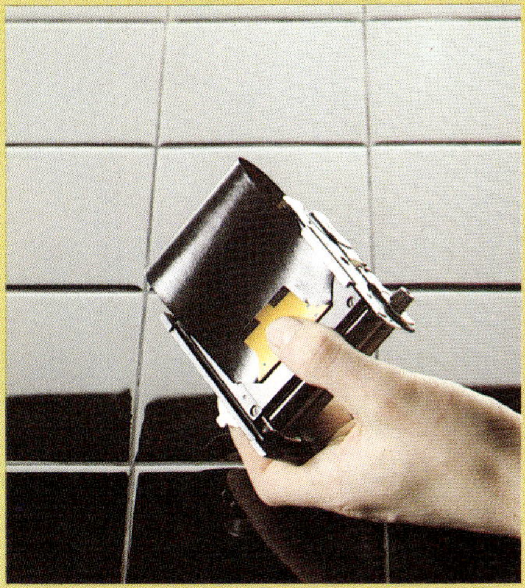

3 Extend leader *The backing paper runs under a bar at the edge of the pressure plate. This is lifted by the catch used in the first step*

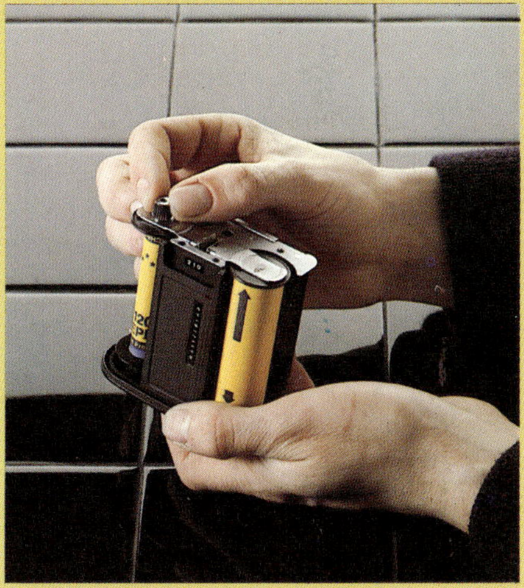

4 Line up arrows *Wind the knurled knob until the arrows on the film and holder line up. Then replace the holder in the magazine*

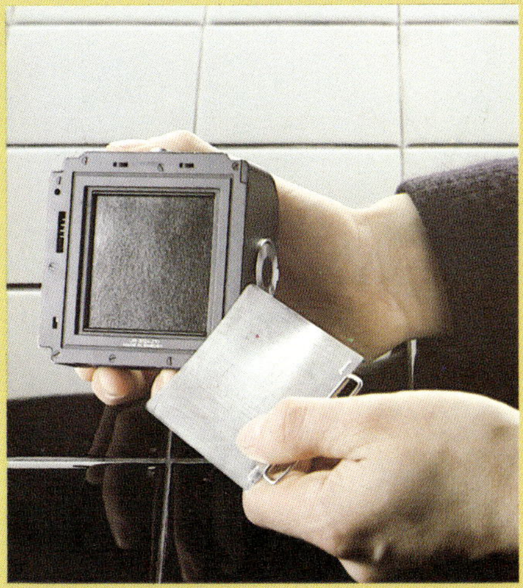

5 Check for dirt *Check the film aperture to ensure that no dirt or hairs are trapped between the film and the magazine shield*

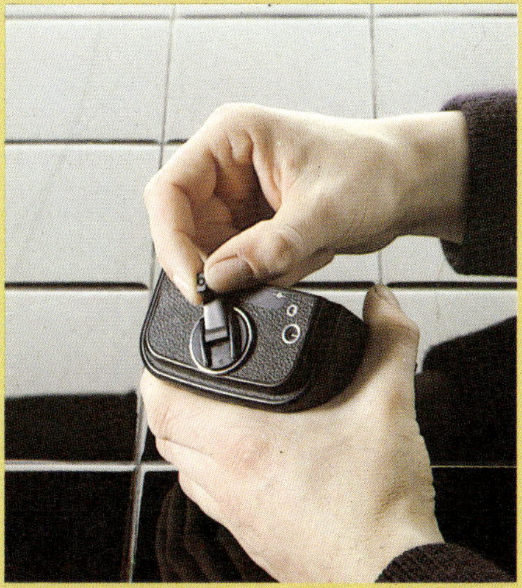

6 Wind to first frame *Crank the wind-on until a number 1 appears in the frame counter window. The magazine is then ready for use*

CHAPTER 2
FILMS
Types of film

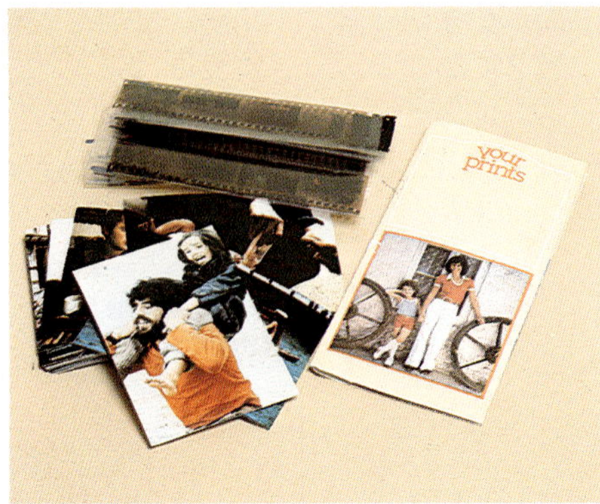

Colour negatives *If you want cheap prints, these are the best choice*

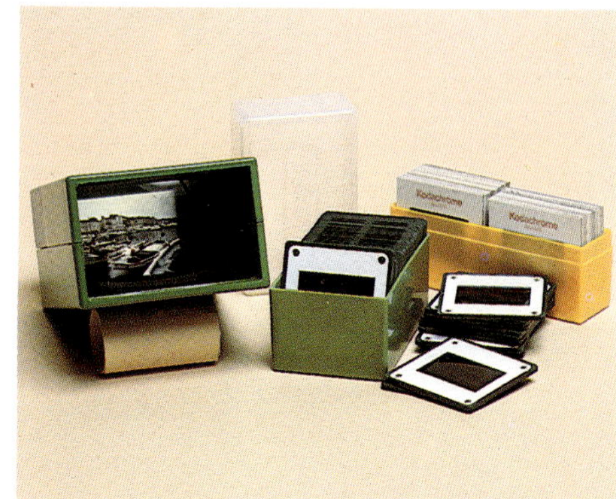

Colour transparencies *Better quality but viewing is not as easy*

The range of film types available often seems bewildering. When faced with a choice between different films, each with its own peculiarities, there is a great tendency to simply stick to one well-tried type and not experiment.

This can be a big mistake. Although it is a good idea to get used to one film type before you branch out, so that any variations in results are definitely due to yourself and not the film, after a while it is worth looking at the choice available.

The choice breaks down into three categories—colour negative, colour transparency and black and white. Everybody is familiar with the appearance of negatives—with the light parts of the image appearing dark and vice versa. While black and white negatives appear with black images on a clear background, colour negatives usually have an overall orange colour, with the images in colours different from the originals—a red object appears greenish for example. The print that is produced from negatives is sometimes called a *positive* copy.

Transparencies or slides are also positives, but are produced directly from the original material by a process of *reversal*. The film is first processed to give a negative, then immediately reversed in its tones to give a positive. The continental name for slides is *diapositives*.

Colour negative films

By far the most popular type of film in use is colour negative film. The negatives, once processed, are used to make colour prints of whatever size is required. This accounts for the popularity of negative film—the results are easy to handle. For most people, processing is simply a matter of taking the film to a shop which sends it to a laboratory to be processed. The negatives and the prints can then be collected later.

It is possible for the enthusiast to develop and print colour negatives, and the process is not particularly difficult. But unless you intend to do a great deal of printing, or enjoy the darkroom work involved, it is easier to leave the job to the developing and printing firms.

One advantage of negative film is that any number of copies can be made from the negative, all to the same quality. This means that not only can you send copies to people but, should you lose a print, you can always get another made from the negative which you can keep safely out of the way. Even if you lose the negative, it is still possible to get copies from the surviving print. This is an advantage not enjoyed by users of colour slides.

The exposure *latitude* of colour negative films is extraordinary—that is, they can tolerate under- or overexposure and still give printable negatives. With heavy overexposure, the colours may change, but there will still be an image on the print. Tolerance to underexposure is much lower, so it is a good idea to give the film too much light rather than too little. There is also considerable leeway as regards the lighting conditions in which pictures can be taken. Though the colour of daylight is much bluer than the colour of domestic light bulbs, for example, it is possible to use many of today's colour negative films in any kind of light, and still get prints that are acceptable.

This versatility is also the source of the major disadvantage of colour prints. The colours that they give are the result of the way the print is made, and a negative can be printed to appear generally too blue, or too green, or any other colour. This allows flexibility, but it also means that it is possible for the prints to give the wrong colours entirely. This can easily happen when the prints are made on the automatic machines used in d & p firms.

This kind of problem will only occur in extreme cases, and generally the quality of machine printing is quite high. Should you require really good prints from your colour negatives, many laboratories offer a de-luxe service, which can produce superb prints, at a price.

Of all the films on the market, colour negative film is by far the most easily obtained and processed. It is available in almost all countries, in all popular sizes including 35 mm and 110 and 126 cartridges. The choice of emulsions is greatest in 35 mm with films as fast as 1000 ASA (ISO) and as slow as 40 ASA (ISO) available, but ranges from 80 to 400 ASA (ISO) in most formats.

Colour transparencies

Colour slides, or transparencies as they are more correctly called, rank second in order of popularity. The film is sometimes also called *reversal film*, as the image is reversed from a negative to a positive slide during processing.

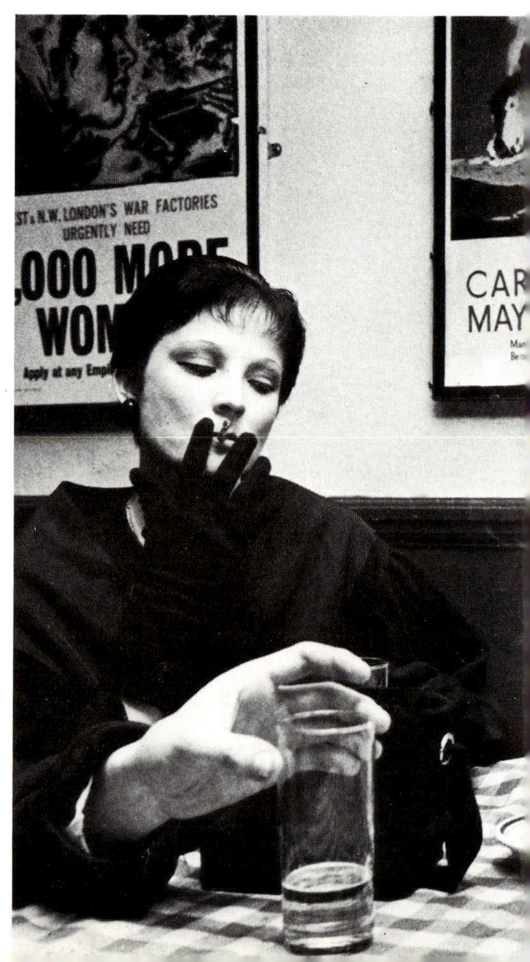

Punchy monochrome *Black and white film can sometimes give a much more striking result than anything in colour*

Though they undoubtedly give the best colour, transparencies have the drawback that they cannot be handed round and viewed as easily as prints. They must either be projected or looked at through a hand viewer. If more than one person wants to see them, using a viewer becomes a time consuming business, and there are few practical alternatives to projecting them in a darkened room.

If this is not a problem, then colour transparencies present an attractive alternative to colour prints. The choice of film types is broader, with films widely available in speeds ranging from 25 ASA up to 1600. The fast films can be processed to give speeds as high as 3200ASA. In addition, there are specialist films available, some of them sensitive to infra-red light (which would enable you to take pictures in total darkness).

The cost of processing colour transparencies is lower than the cost of colour prints, as only the film itself is involved. So if your aim is to get the cheapest possible colour photographs then colour slides are the best choice. The quality of the final images is generally higher than for colour prints, because the images have only been through one process, whereas colour prints are one step further removed from the subject of the photograph. The colour quality of a slide depends only on the film. But with prints from negatives, it depends on the film, the paper, and the way the print was made. And each time an image is copied, there is a drop in quality. Though you may not think of a colour print as a copy, that is what it really is —a reversed, negative copy of the colour negative.

All the drawbacks of colour printing are eliminated with slides, but on the other hand the advantages are lost as well. The colour balance of colour slides is critical, and to get good results, it is sometimes necessary to use filters on the lens of the camera. On a sunny day out of doors, no filter is necessary, but if the weather is heavily overcast, for example, you would need a filter. It is also necessary to use different types of slide film in daylight and artificial 'tungsten' light, or use very strong colour correcting filters.

Similarly, the exposure has to be more carefully judged if the slides are not to look washed out, or dark and muddy. Indeed, the exposure latitude of colour slide film may be less than half a stop—that is, the exposure must be accurate to within half a stop. Colour negative films, on the other hand, will take up to three stops overexposure and perhaps a stop underexposure without an undue loss of quality. In fact, you can often get some kind of picture even if the exposure error is greater than this. The image on slide film will effectively be lost if exposure is more than two or three stops out and, for optimum results exposure must be spot-on.

Colour slide films are particularly sensitive to overexposure and photographers trying slide film for the first time end up with pale, washed out slides. Unfortunately, nothing can be done to rescue overexposed slides—unlike negatives, where you can compensate during printing. So if you have to err at all when exposing slide film, underexpose a little. Indeed, some photographers like to underexpose slide film by half a stop all the time because it gives richer, more saturated—though not necessarily correct—colours. You can do this even with an automatic camera by setting the film

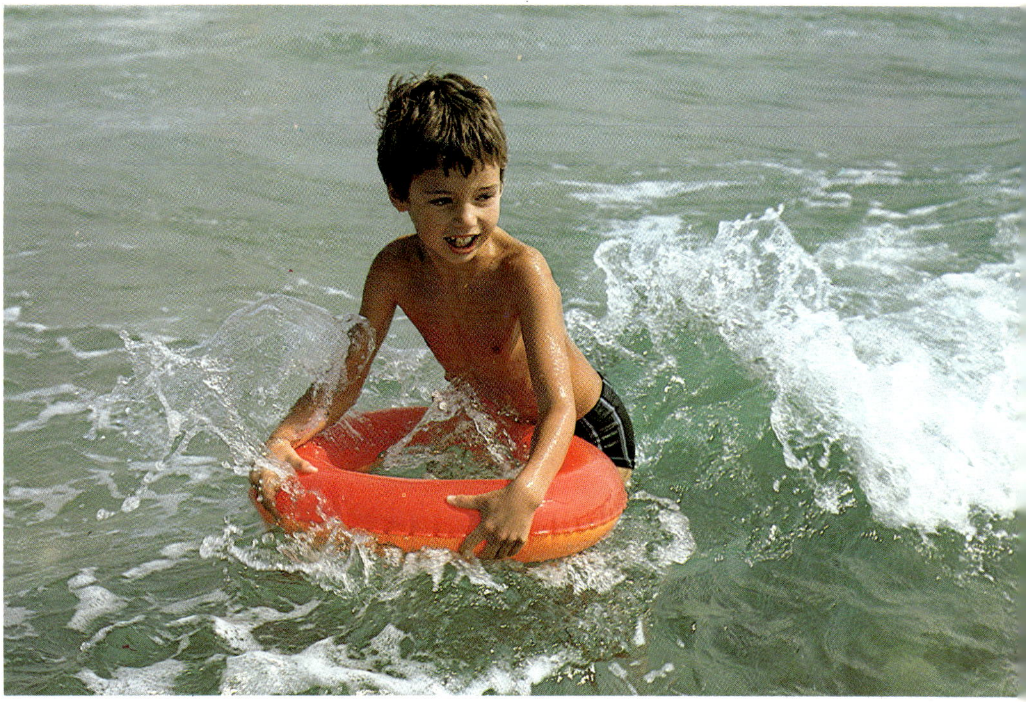

Holiday snaps *Negative film does not need careful exposure metering, and is most suitable for casual photographs taken over a long period of time*

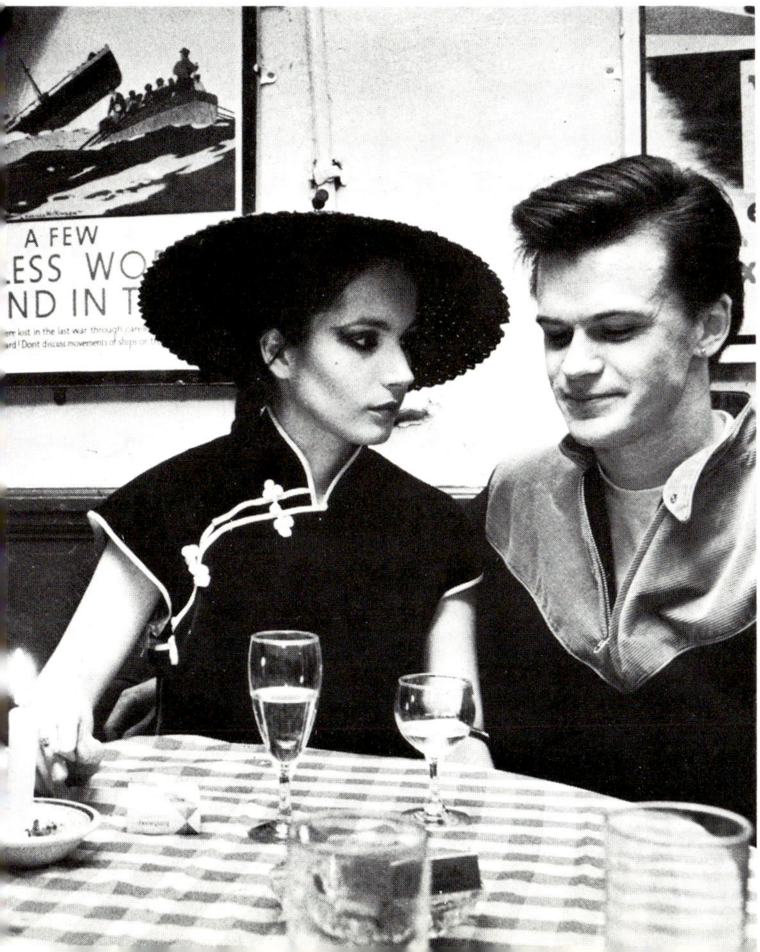

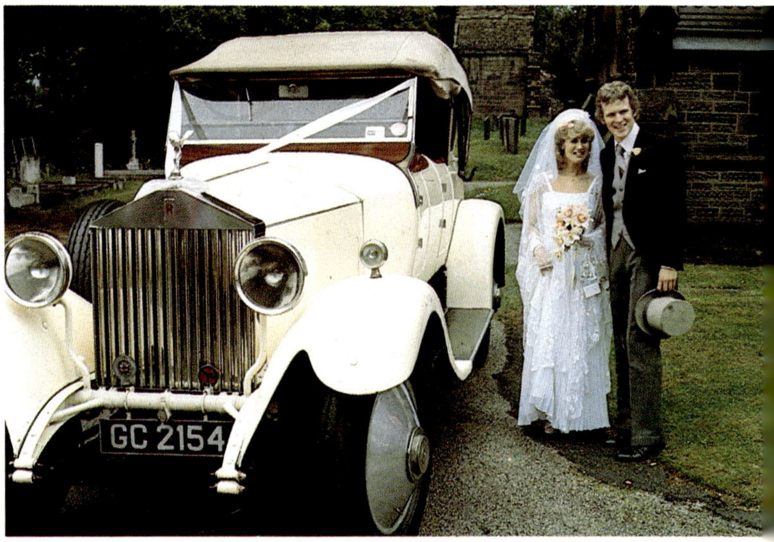

Wedding colour *Social and family occasions, such as weddings and parties, are perfectly suited to negative film. Prints are cheap and easy to get processed quickly*

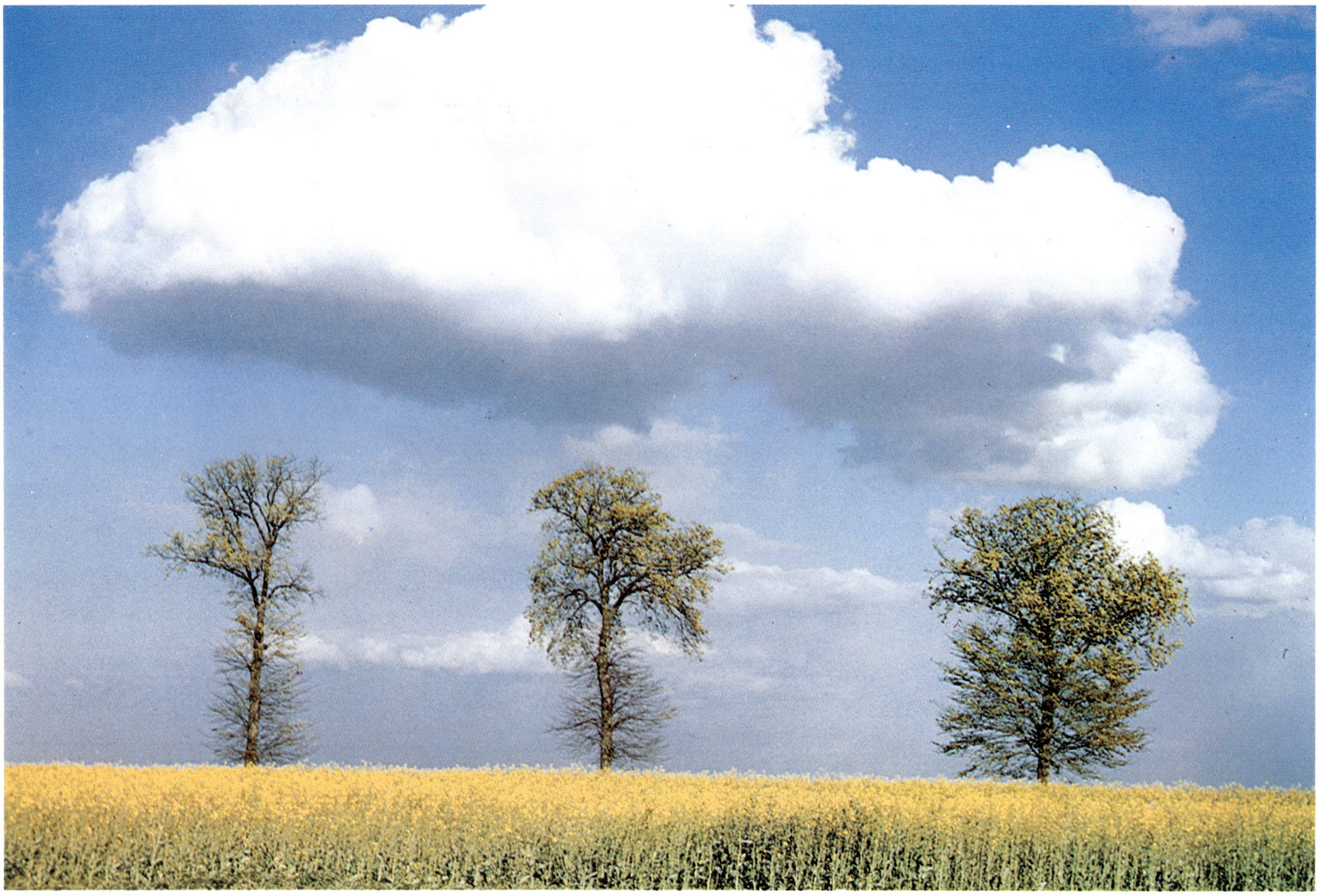

speed dial at 50% faster than the recommended ASA(ISO) rating. Kodachrome 25, for instance you could expose at 35 ASA (ISO).

Virtually every type of slide film can be bought as 35 mm film, but only a small choice is available in 126 and 110; usually one film from each manufacturer.

Black and white

Though colour films occupy most of the market, b & w film still has many enthusiasts, most of whom process it themselves. Almost all black and white films give negatives, from which prints can be made. B & w printing, like processing, is easy and can be done at home.

For some people, the reduction of all colours of the spectrum to shades of grey is too much of a sacrifice to make, but the rewards of working in b & w are considerable. It is easier to process and print your own pictures in monochrome than it is in colour, and costs are far lower than for colour prints or transparencies. On the other hand, it is far less easy to find laboratories which will process and print black and white film, if you cannot do it yourself, and the cost may be as high as for colour.

The range of b & w films is formidable, and even for films that are in day to day use, speeds range from 25 ASA to 400. Specialist b & w films abound, with the slowest of these being only a fraction of 1 ASA used for scientific photography. At the other end of the scale, b & w films are often rated at 2000 ASA or more.

Careful colour *Scenes with a wide brightness range will reproduce more accurately on transparency film*

Colour for landscape *Slides give colour that is true to life. Negatives can be more variable because of printing errors*

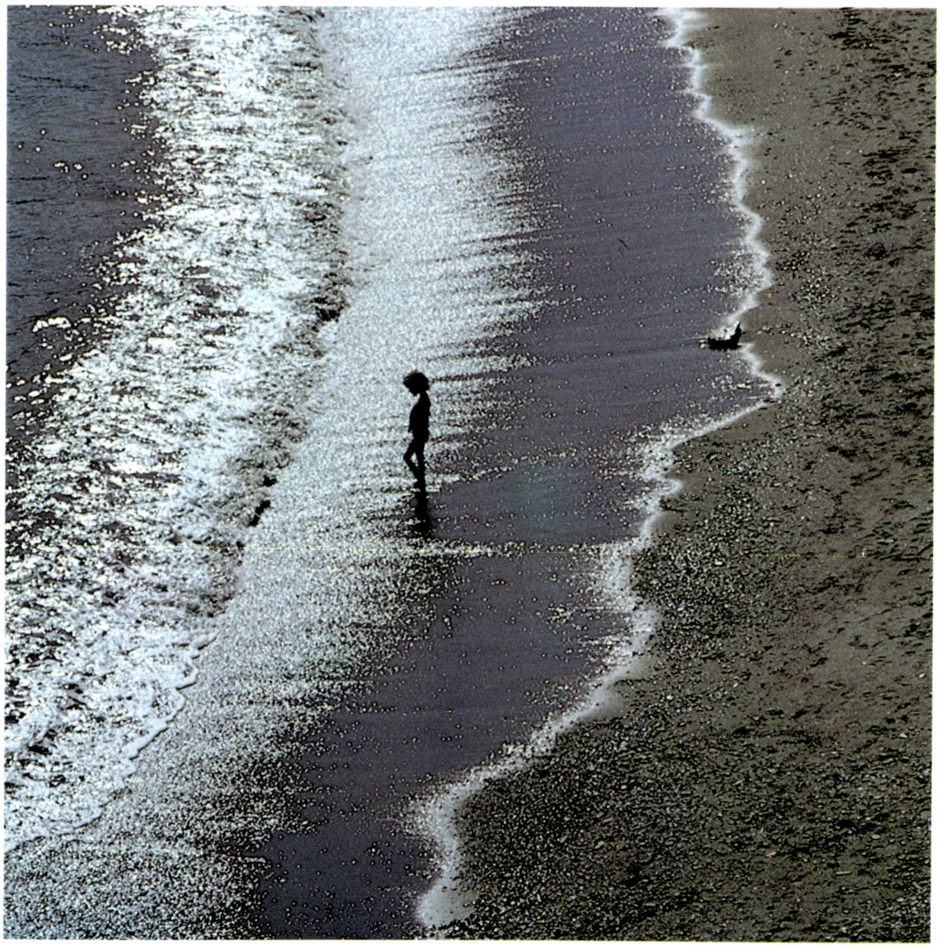

Film speeds

Every now and then, just as the light is fading, you come across a potentially beautiful picture—a group of children playing in the twilight under the boughs of an old tree or fishermen mending their nets in the shadow of the harbour wall—but when you check your meter, you find that there just is not enough light for the shot.

The moment is lost, but it need not have been; with the right *speed* of film there would have been no problem. A faster film gives you that bit of extra film sensitivity to shoot in very low light. At another extreme, in bright sunlight, a slow film can be just as valuable, giving all the control over depth of field and all the fine detail you need for a really high quality picture. Learning to use the right film speed for each situation can make a tremendous difference to the range and quality of your photographs.

Choosing the speed

With a basic cartridge-loading camera, you have little choice of film speed—there is often just one film of each type—black and white, colour negative (for prints) and colour reversal (for transparencies). This film performs well over a remarkably wide range of conditions but there is no scope for using different film speeds for different effects. Once you graduate to a 35 mm camera, however, a wide range of films of various speeds is available and many possibilities open up.

Film speed is a property of the thin

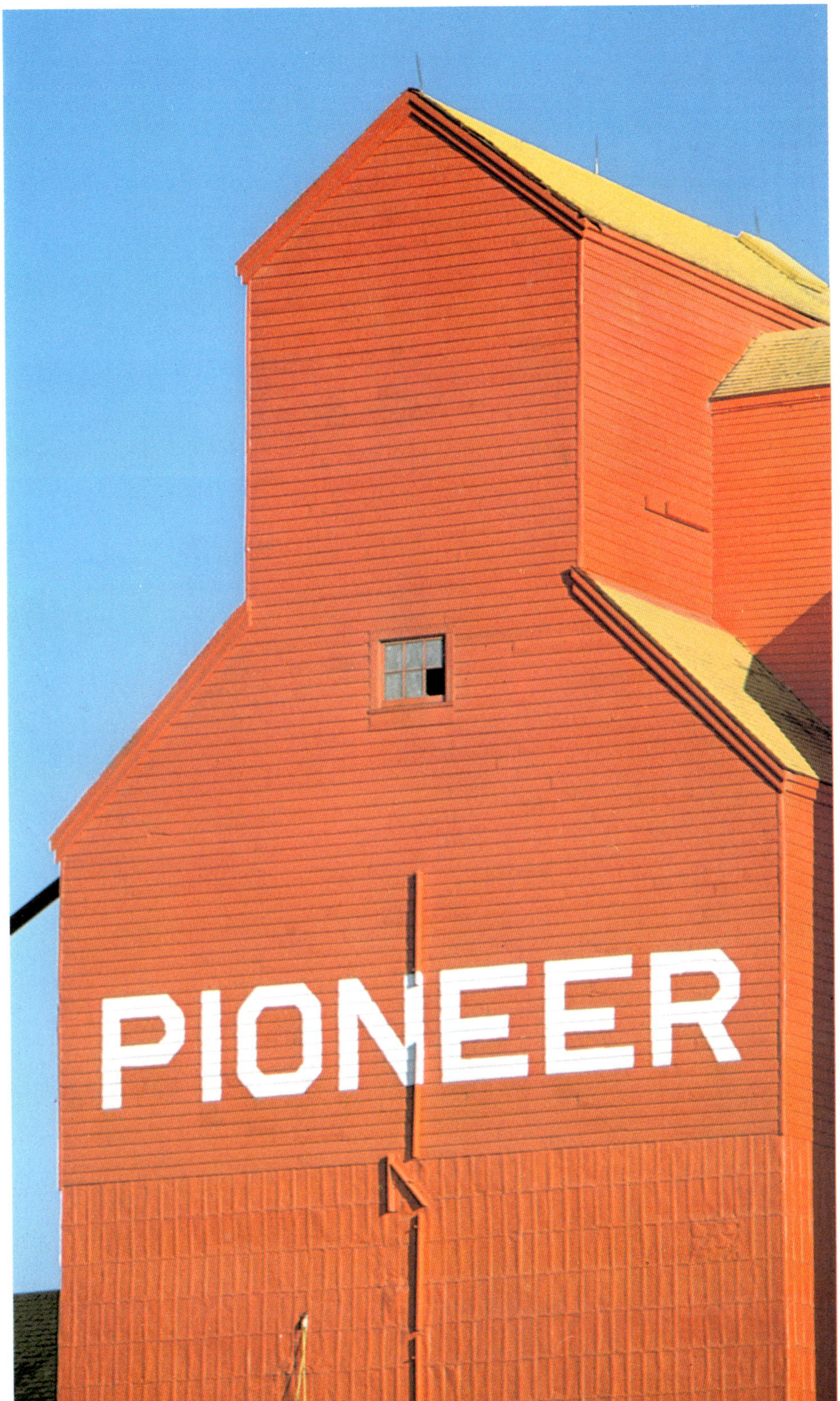

Slow film *In bright, clear weather, use a slow film to give really full colours like those in the picture*

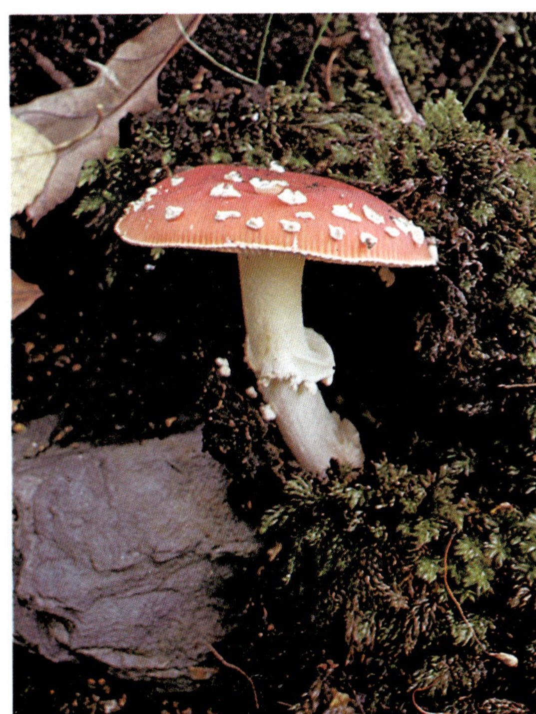

Fast film *When there is little light available shots like this could be impossible on anything but fast film*

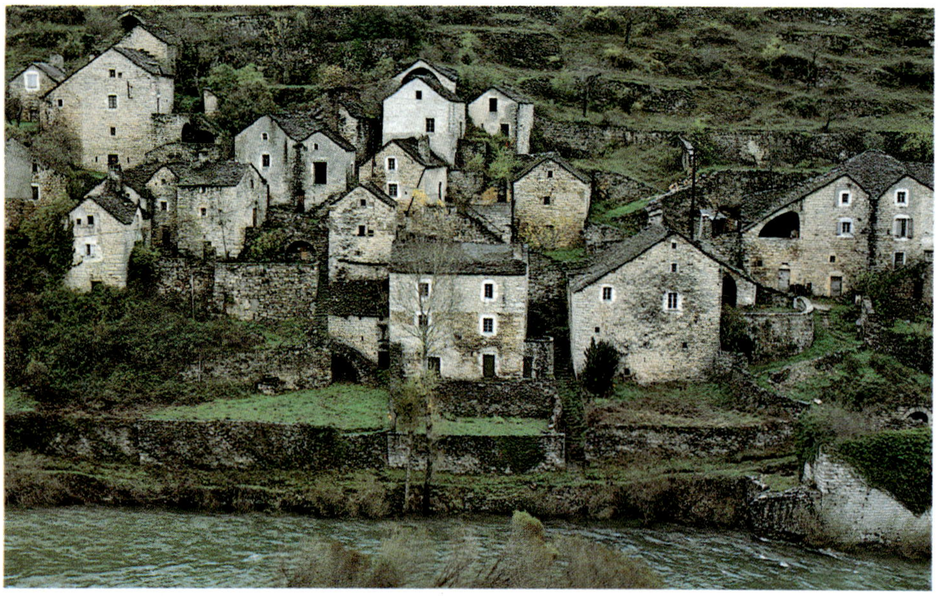

coating of light sensitive *emulsion* on the film that reacts to record the image when you open the shutter. You can see the emulsion by looking along a strip of negatives. One side of the film is glossy and smooth but the emulsion side is dull and very slightly less smooth.

With a fast film, the emulsion is very sensitive and reacts rapidly to light once the shutter is opened. A slow emulsion, on the other hand, is much less sensitive and reacts slowly to record the image. In any situation, therefore, a slow film needs much more exposure than a fast film. You get this extra exposure either by increasing the aperture or using a longer shutter speed.

Alternative ratings

The speed of a film is indicated by the film speed rating marked on the package and on the cassette. Various speed rating systems have been devised, but most films are still marked with numbers according to both the ASA (American Standards Association) and the DIN (German system) standards. These ratings are established by the amount of exposure needed which in turn depends on the film's speed or sensitivity.

There is now also an ISO (International Standards Organization) rating for every film, which is identical to the ASA and DIN speeds and simply combines the two numbers. Thus a film rated 400 ASA and 27 DIN is rated ISO 400/27°.

Most people prefer to use the ASA number because it is far simpler to convert into exposure requirements. With the ASA system, the speed number is arithmetically proportional to the film's sensitivity. That is, doubling the ASA number doubles the sensitivity. If the film is twice as sensitive, it needs half the exposure. One way of halving the exposure is to double the shutter speed. Another is to halve the aperture. Because every increase in *f*-number halves the aperture, halving the exposure simply means taking down the aperture by one stop.

Fortunately, if your camera has a light meter, you won't have to make this calculation every time you change films. You simply reset the film speed dial and use the meter in the normal way.

Tone and contrast *Scenes like this need a slow film to bring out the subtle tones and enhance the contrast*

Black-browed albatross *When using a long telephoto, fast film allows you to set a high shutter speed to avoid blur*

There is a bewildering variety of films on the market, each with its own characteristics and capabilities, but they can be divided into five broad groups according to their speed: fast, very fast, medium, slow, and very slow.

Using fast film

Fast films are rated at anything from 200 ASA upwards. A particularly popular speed with all types of film—black and white, colour reversal, and colour negative—is 400 ASA.

It is in low light conditions that a fast film really pays off. With its extra sensitivity, it can allow you to shoot normally when there is not enough light available to take your picture on a standard medium speed film without very long exposures or wide apertures.

This quality is particularly valuable on dull, rainy days or in European winters where cloud and low angle sunlight reduce the amount of available light. Often the only way to continue your photographic activities throughout the year and take advantage of the abund-

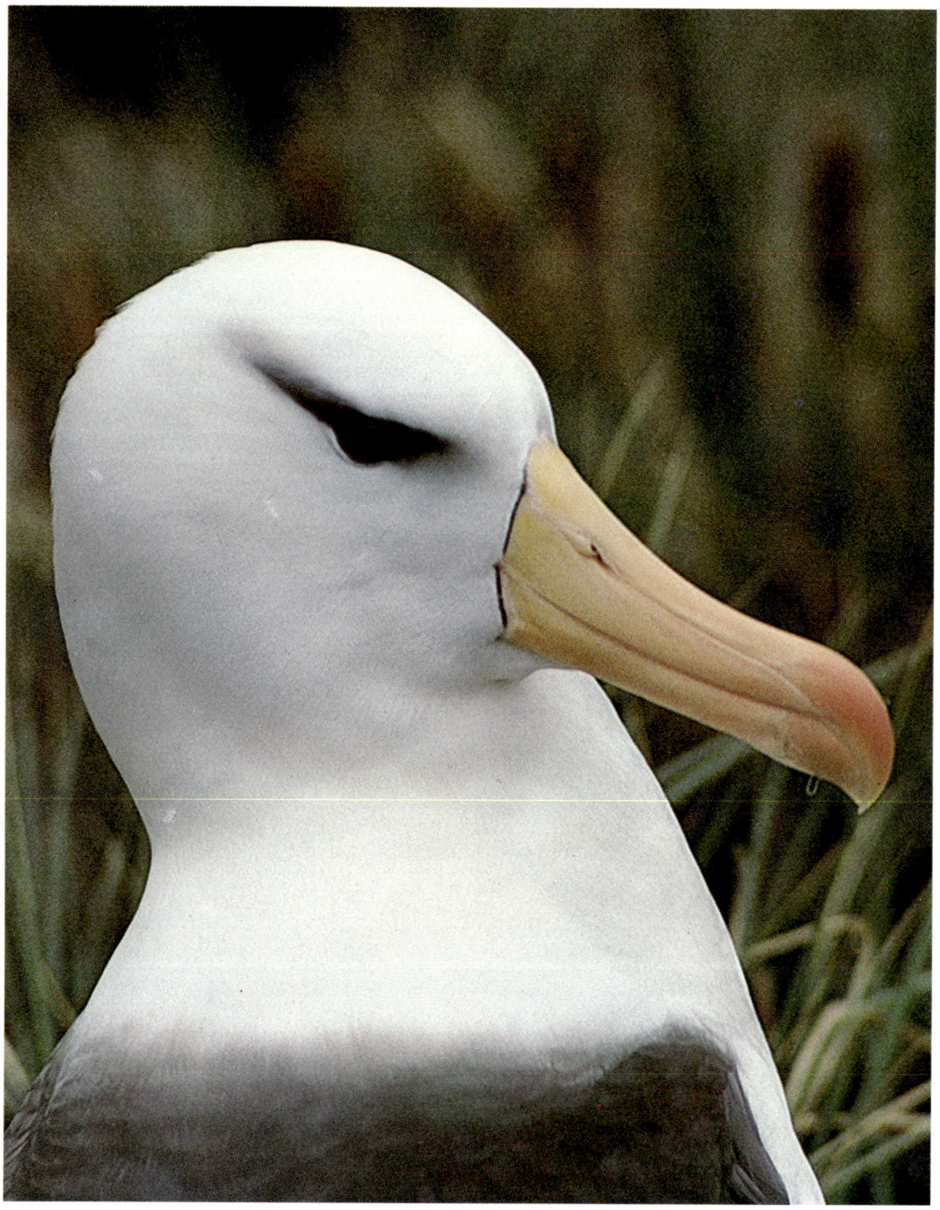

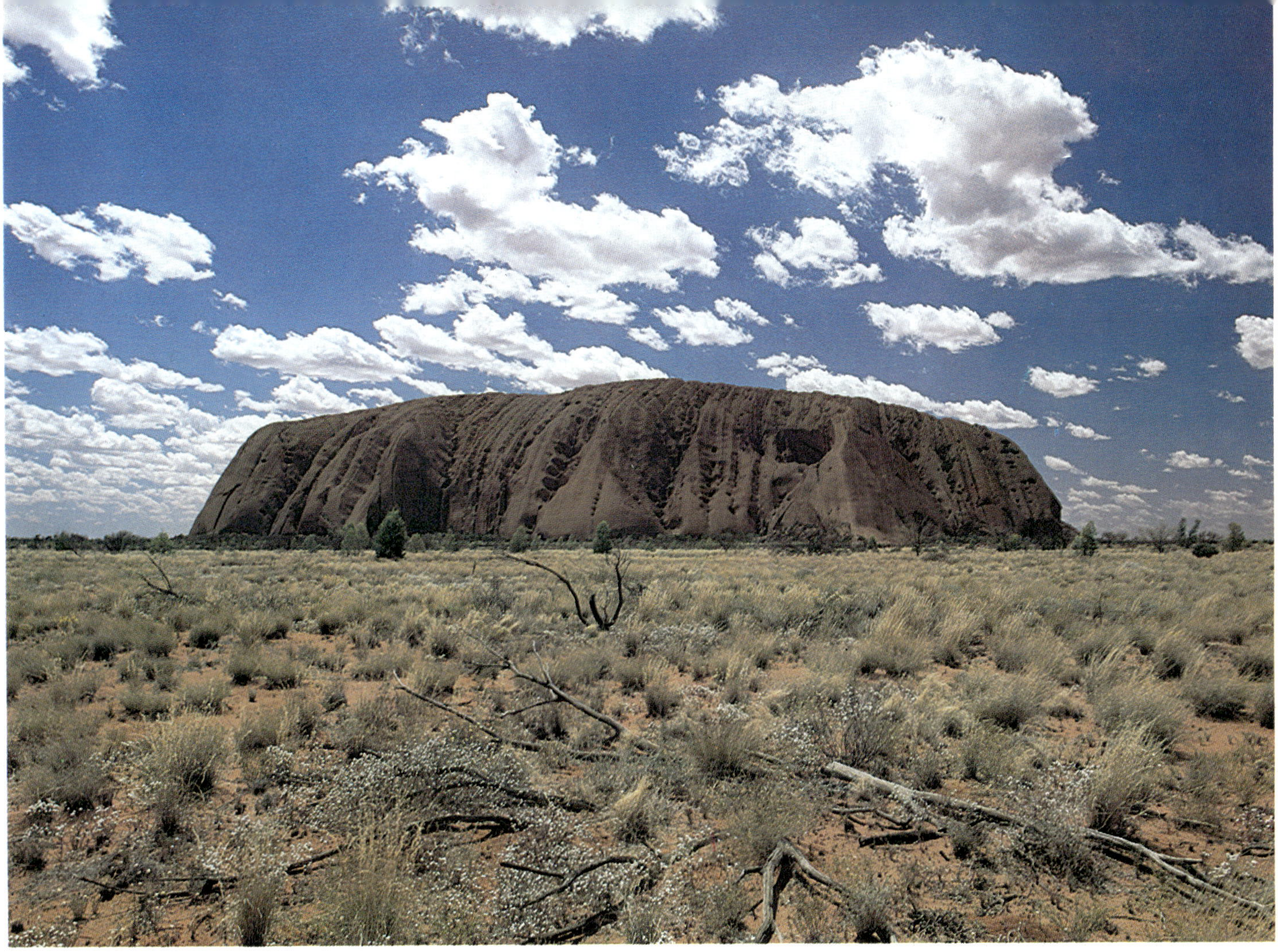

ance of highly photogenic material that occurs in winter is to use a fast film. Many of the beautiful atmospheric pictures of misty winter scenes or frosty puddles will probably have been taken on fast films. Indeed, unless you are fortunate enough to live in a climate that is sunny all the year round, it is probably a good idea to keep your camera loaded with a relatively fast film in winter.

Similarly, indoor photographs by available light are rarely possible on standard film without extreme exposures. Usually flash or photographic lights are needed, either of which can ruin the lighting effect or spontaneous event you were trying to capture—and they cost money. By using a fast film you may not only be able to shoot indoors by available natural light during the day, but also by the normal room lights at night.

If you do shoot with a fast film in artificial light, though, remember that colour slide films are balanced for either natural or artificial light. If you use a daylight film in artificial (electric) light, the final photograph will have a distinct colour cast.

Another big advantage of fast films is that they allow you to use a higher shutter speed. This can be useful even when conditions are good enough for a slower film. With a fast film, the shutter can be set at 1/500 second or even 1/1000 second for freezing fast moving action, while a sufficiently wide aperture is retained for good depth of field. If you are photographing sport on anything but the brightest day, this can be invaluable.

Alternatively, you can take advantage of the higher shutter speeds available with fast films under any conditions to reduce the chances of camera shake. When using a hand-held telephoto lens in particular, you can easily get severe camera shake, but changing to a fast film may give you the extra shutter speed to avoid this becoming too obvious. A faster film may also be valuable with a long telephoto anyway because of the tiny maximum aperture.

With so many points in their favour, you may wonder why people do not

Texture *On anything but a fairly slow film, the fine textural details on Ayers Rock, Australia, would be lost*

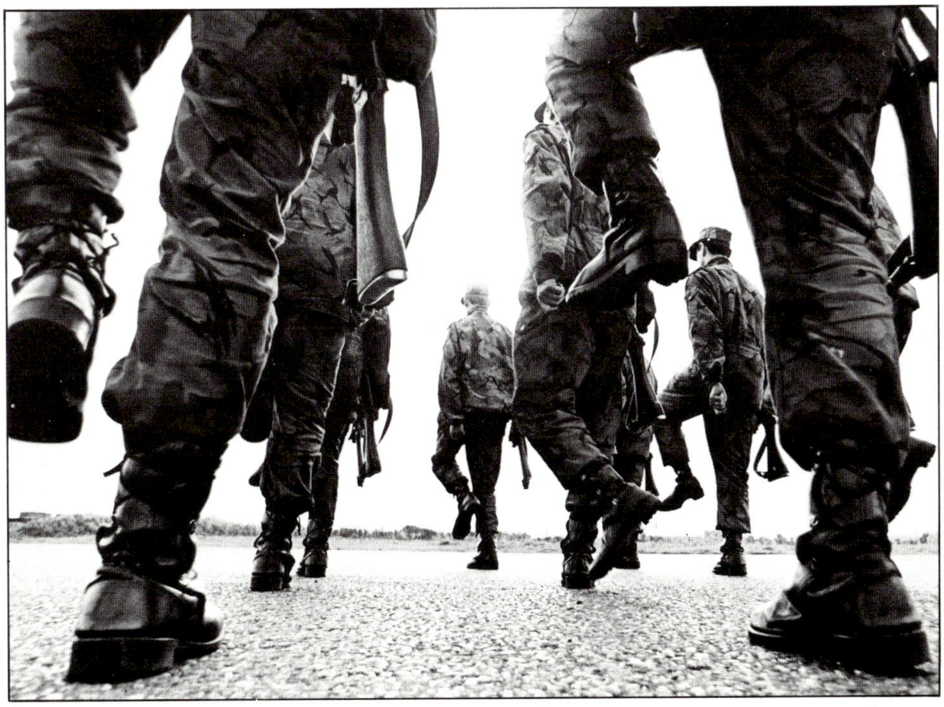

Depth of field *With a fast film, you can get good depth of field and fast shutter speeds even on a dull day*

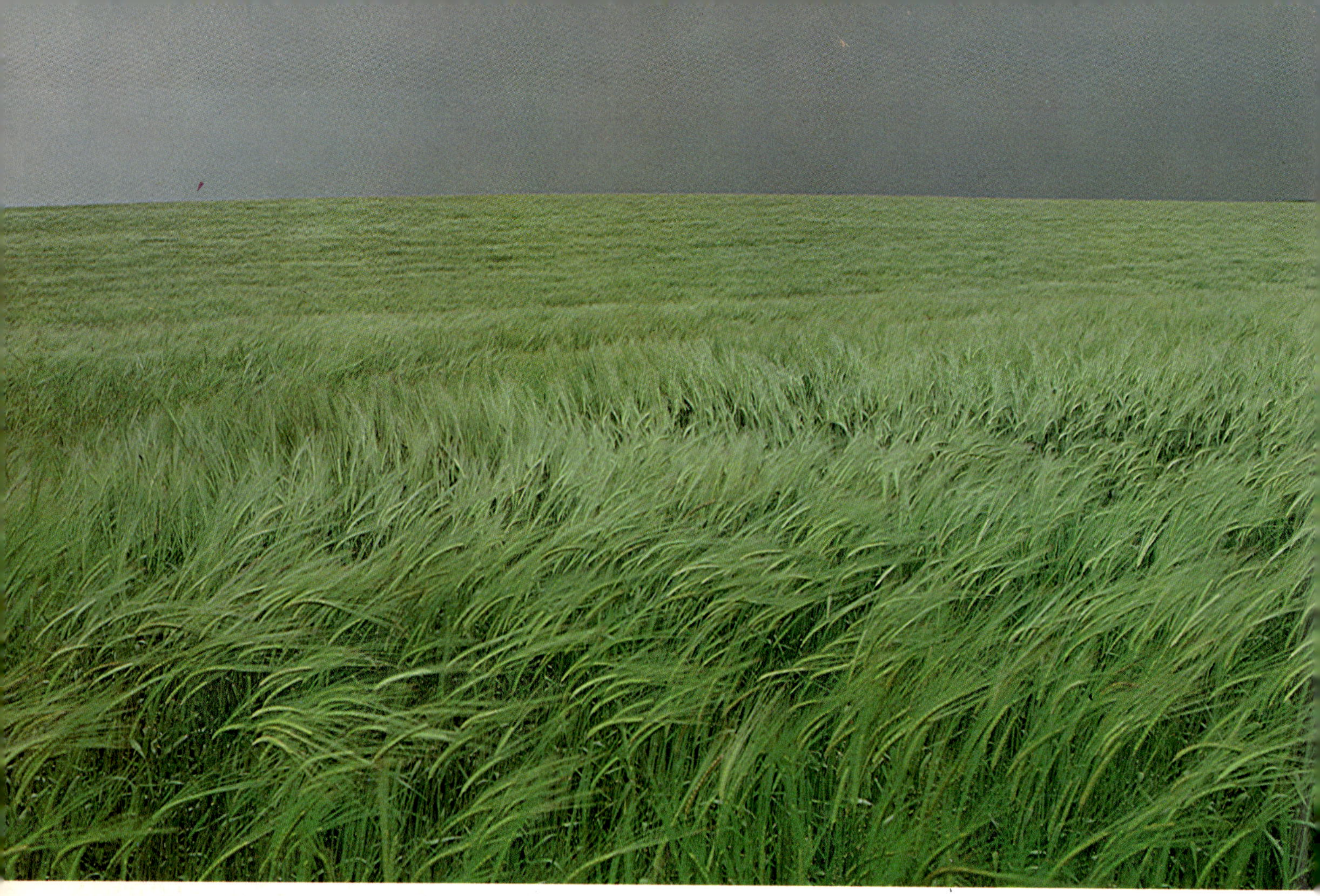

Medium speed film *In changeable weather load the camera with medium speed film to cope with all conditions*

shoot with fast films all the time. Indeed some photographers do. But, like every type of film, fast films do have their disadvantages.

One of the most significant drawbacks of fast film is reduced picture quality. Fast films not only give a *grainier* image than slow films, but they also tend to suffer from lack of contrast.

With a grainy image, sharpness is necessarily poor because outlines are coarse and less well-defined. Study an enprint made from a fast film through a magnifying glass and you can see what appears to be the individual grains—though in fact the effect is caused by the clumping of individual grains.

If you only intend to make small prints from the negative, this extra graininess does not really matter. However, as the picture is progressively enlarged, the grain pattern and poor definition become more and more obvious. So if you want really large prints, it might be better to use a slower film if at all possible. With really fast conventional film (see panel), the grains can be so big that they are easily visible to the naked eye even at fairly small enlargements. Such coarse grain can sometimes be used creatively and even heightened deliberately for special effects, but the reduced image quality is generally undesirable.

Similarly, the softness of the slightly lower contrast negative of high speed

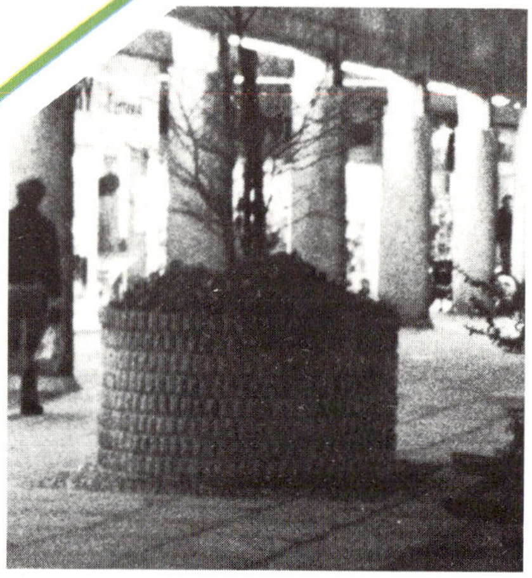

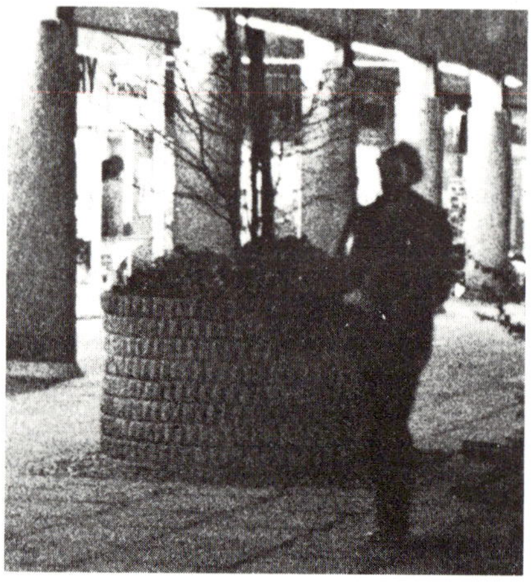

Very fast films

Sometimes, when the light is very poor, you may find that a standard fast film is inadequate. In this case you could use one of the special high speed black and white films that are available. These can be rated at 1600 ASA or above.

Although 1600 ASA sounds very fast, it is only worth two more stops than a standard fast film like HP5. A 1600 ASA film, therefore, will not enable you to take pictures in very dark conditions, such as a dimly lit road at night. But it may give you the extra latitude to shoot at the aperture or shutter speed you want, or to use a telephoto lens in gloomy conditions.

There are two basic groups of very high speed black and white film: conventional films and 'chromogenic' films. Conventional very fast films such as Kodak 2475 professional recording film give very grey and grainy results when rated at 1600 ASA. An alternative is to use a slower film such as HP5 or Tri-X and 'uprate' it by increasing the development time. This tends to give burnt out highlights with lost shadow detail. The left-hand picture was taken on HP5, which is nominally 400 ASA, developed to give 1600 ASA.

Chromogenic films such as Ilford XP1 and Agfapan Vario-XL, on the other hand, work in a different way from conventional emulsions and can be rated at anything between 400 and 1600 ASA. At their rated speed they can give excellent performance, with much finer grain than a conventional very high speed film.

Chromogenic films are, however, more expensive than conventional ones and require more complex processing.

The picture on the right was taken on Ilford XP1, also rated at 1600 ASA.

films can sometimes be attractive, but it certainly reduces their usability. Where there is little natural contrast in your subject, such as in a landscape on a wet day, you should use a slow film if possible to bring out what contrast there is. High speed colour films also tend to give slightly less than the full value to colours, and for really strong *colour saturation*, a slow film is necessary.

While fast black-and-white films suffer from lack of definition, however, there is hardly any difference in sharpness between the standard and fast emulsions of many colour negative films. Neither do they suffer from graininess to quite the same extent, even when up rated. Unfortunately, colour films are generally much less sharp than their black-and-white counterparts in the first place, since colour emulsions are made from a sandwhich of three layers. Each layer has its own grain structure and these tend to overlap and diffuse the final image reducing its sharpness.

Fine grain

For really high quality, high definition work in both black-and-white and colour, particularly if the picture is going to be much enlarged or reproduced, a slow film with fine grain and high contrast is essential. Unfortunately, because such films are less sensitive, they need either a great deal of exposure or bright light.

Most of the high quality still life pictures used for large colour advertisements are taken on slow, very fine grain film. The extra exposure is usually obtained not by opening the aperture wide, since this might reduce depth of field too drastically, but by using fairly long exposure times. For this, a tripod is absolutely essential. Any still life is probably best done in this way if you want high quality results. The process requires some time and effort, but the final picture should justify all the work.

Out of doors, stationary well-lit subjects with subtle shades of colour, minute details or interesting textural qualities benefit from the superb colour saturation and fine definition of a slow film. In fact, wherever conditions are bright enough to permit the use of slow film without excessive loss of depth of field through use of wide apertures, then a slow film is best for really high quality results. In bright Mediterranean or Alpine summers, a slow film such as a 25 ASA Kodachrome can be ideal.

Pictures of flowers for gardening catalogues, landscapes for travel brochures and architectural shots are generally taken on slow film. Sometimes a tripod may be needed if apertures are to be narrow enough to give good depth of field, but in brilliant sunshine there will usually be enough light to give both narrow apertures and high shutter speed.

In fact, in bright sunshine, anything but a very slow film may not give you the degree of flexibility you want. In bright sunshine, a fast film will always have to be exposed with high shutter speeds and narrow apertures if it is not to be overexposed. Indeed, it may not even be possible to stop down sufficiently to avoid overexposure. A narrow aperture ensures that everything is in focus whether you want it to be or not; you cannot keep the background out of focus to avoid distracting from your subject. Neither can you avoid freezing any motion if you have a high shutter speed. So in certain circumstances, the creative possibilities might be greater with a slow film than a fast.

It would be nice if there were a film which could combine all the advantages of both fast and slow films. Of course this is not possible and you have to commit yourself to either one or the other when you load the camera. Medium speed films combine some of the advantages of both slow and fast films with some of the disadvantages. They are not ideal compromises by any means and each film should only be used in the appropriate circumstances.

Medium speed films are best for a wide range of photographs in all conditions. They will not work in extremely low light, but neither will they have the graininess of a fast film. Medium speed films, particularly black-and-white are ideal for portraits. Even the most beautiful complexion has minor blemishes and a slow, fine grain film shows every single one. A medium speed film provides sufficient graininess to disguise these blemishes while retaining enough contrast and definition to record all the textural definition that is wanted.

Whatever result you want, though, you should choose your film to suit the photograph you are looking for. Whether you want the fine detail of a slow film, the value of a fast film in low light, or the versatility of a medium speed film, you should load your camera with the film that gives the best results in the conditions you are most likely to encounter during your photography.

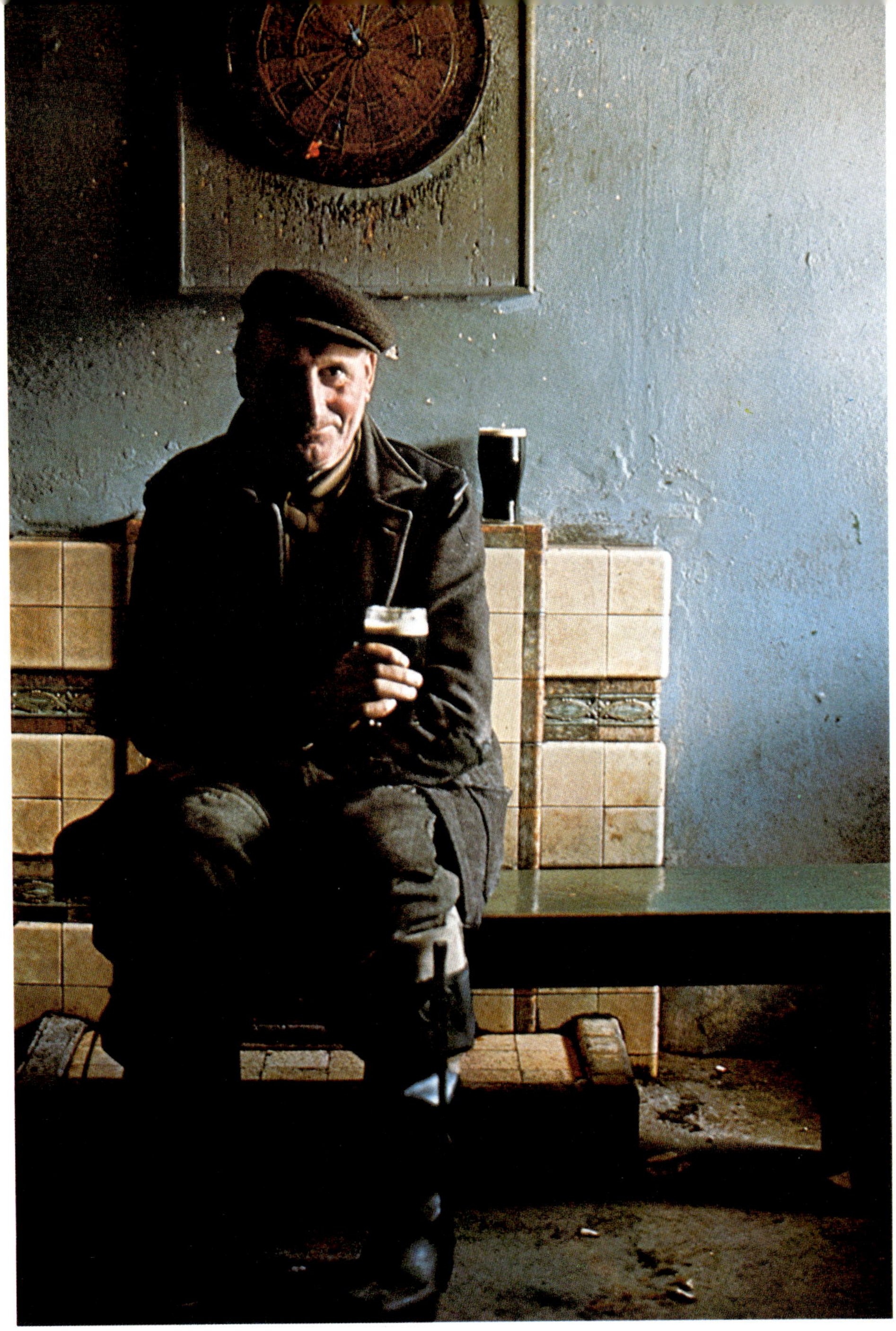

Available light indoors *Fast film may enable you to get candid shots indoors where light levels are generally low*

Specialist films

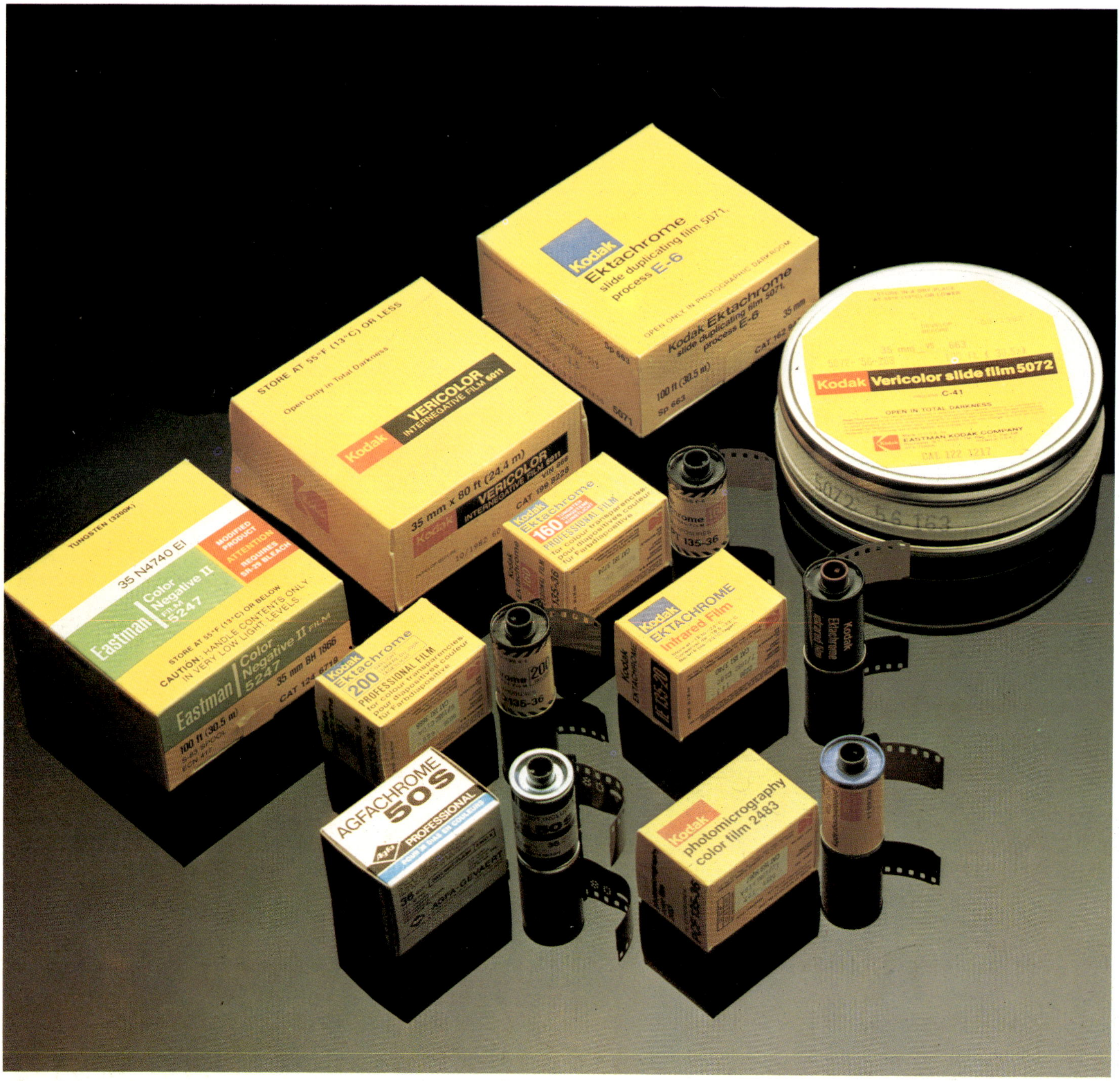

The range of colour films on the dealer's shelf is usually restricted to those which are most popular for amateur use. But there are other films available, in both colour and black and white, which you might find worth using on occasion. These are only stocked by the largest dealers, or by professional suppliers. In some cases it may be necessary to obtain them on special order. Some of the films are available in 35 mm cassette form, in the normal exposure lengths, while others may be sold only in bulk form, and must be loaded by the user into reusable cassettes.

This section deals with colour films suitable for use in the camera that are relatively easy to obtain.

'Professional' films

Many films are described by the manufacturers as 'professional', even though they are basically very similar to their amateur counterparts. Such films as the Ektachrome series are sold in a 'professional' form, for example, as either cassettes, roll films or sheet film.

The main difference between 'professional' and 'amateur' films lies in the way that they must be stored. It is expected that an amateur film will spend some time on the dealer's shelf, some

Special films *for special purposes. A wide range of such films is available, most of them produced by Kodak. Each is designed for a specific purpose and would give widely different results if used to photograph identical subjects*

time in the amateur's gadget bag, often a considerable time in the camera, and then possibly some time before it is returned for processing. At all these stages, it may be subjected to extremes of temperature. No colour film can maintain perfect colour balance over a length of time, so the films are made to give their optimum results a matter of six months or so after manufacture. They carry a 'process by' date to indicate when they will start to suffer from poor quality, if stored at average temperatures.

Professional films, on the other hand, are designed to give their best performance shortly after manufacture. They must be stored at low temperatures, in order that they maintain this optimum performance until used. Once taken from storage, they should be used within a short time, then processed very soon afterwards, to prevent fading of the latent image, or latent image regression. These are the conditions under which most professionals work, and the films therefore give highly consistent results.

In addition to the normal information, each batch of professional film is provided with specific speed data by the manufacturer. A bath of Ektachrome 200 Professional, for example, has a nominal speed of 200 ASA (ISO) but may be rated at, say, 250 ASA. Manufacturers also provide supplementary filter information with professional tungsten film. Sometimes a correction filter may be suggested for a professional tungsten film for 'long' or 'short' exposures.

Some professional films are described as 'Type S' or 'Type L'. These are designed for either 'short' or 'long' exposures respectively. Short exposures are those encountered in normal daylight conditions, in the range 1/10 to 1/100 second. Long exposures are those often used in artificial light, for such purposes as advertising shots, in the range 1/10 to 30 seconds. Such films are made by both Kodak and Agfa, and may be either colour negative or slide films.

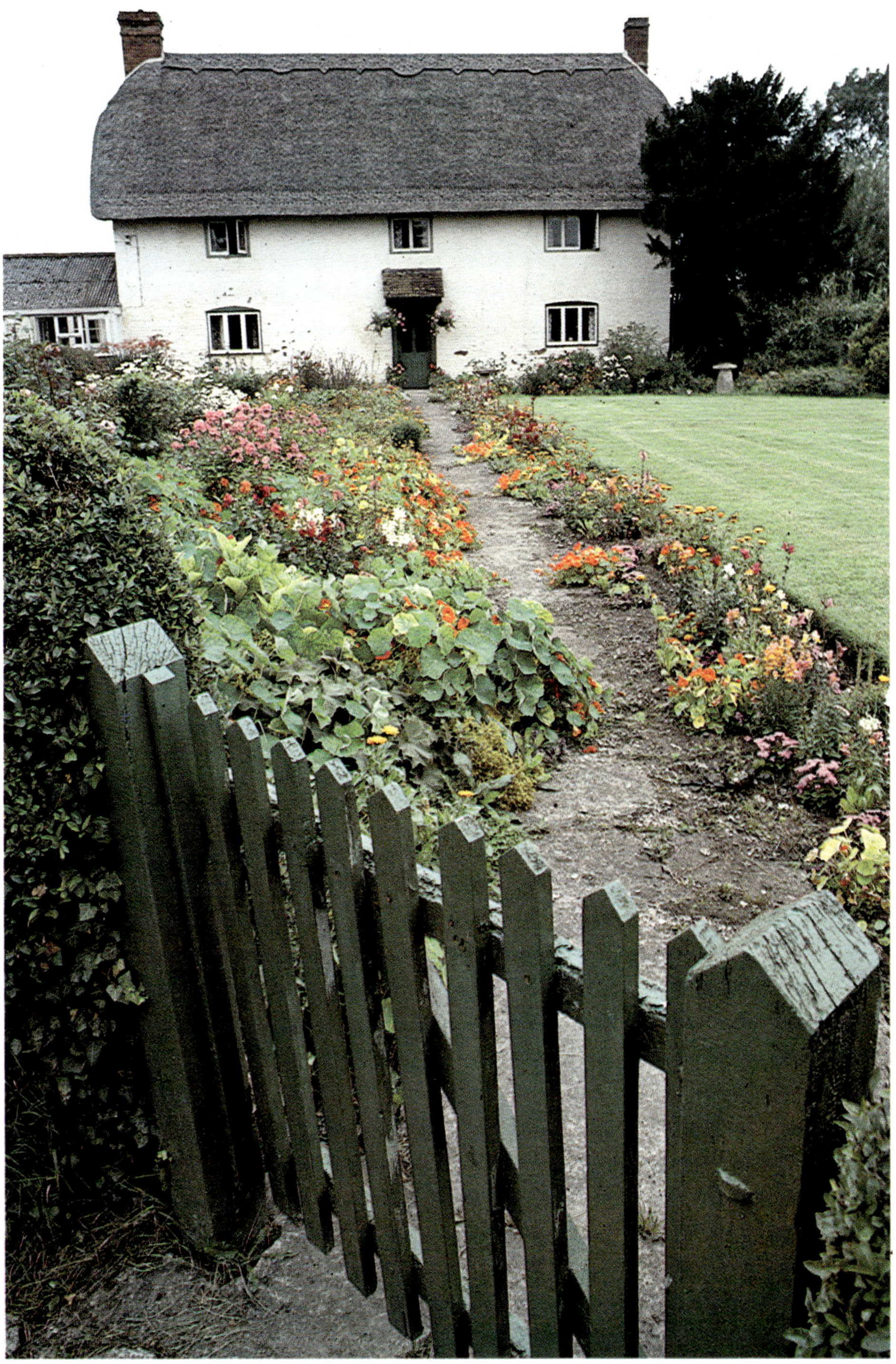

Infrared colour film

Perhaps the most popular specialist film available to the amateur is Kodak Ektachrome Infrared Film. Intended for military, land survey, medical and archaeological uses, it gives transparencies in false colours when used for everyday purposes.

Its three colour layers produce the same colour dyes as other films, but the sensitivity of each is shifted along the spectrum. Instead of being sensitive to blue, green and red light, it is sensitive to green, red and infrared. The film must be used with a Wratten 12 filter to remove blue light.

Intended to detect peaks in the amount of infrared light reflected by an object, its unusual colour response makes it popular for creating surreal effects. Techniques for infrared photography are explained in a subsequent article.

The film is available in 20 exposure 35 mm cassettes, at a cost some 20 per cent higher than conventional colour films. Its main drawback, apart from its limited availability, is that it currently requires the obsolescent Kodak E4 process, only available from a small

Infrared film *The infrared shot (below) emphasizes the high infrared reflectiveness of vegetation, which appears green on normal film (left)*

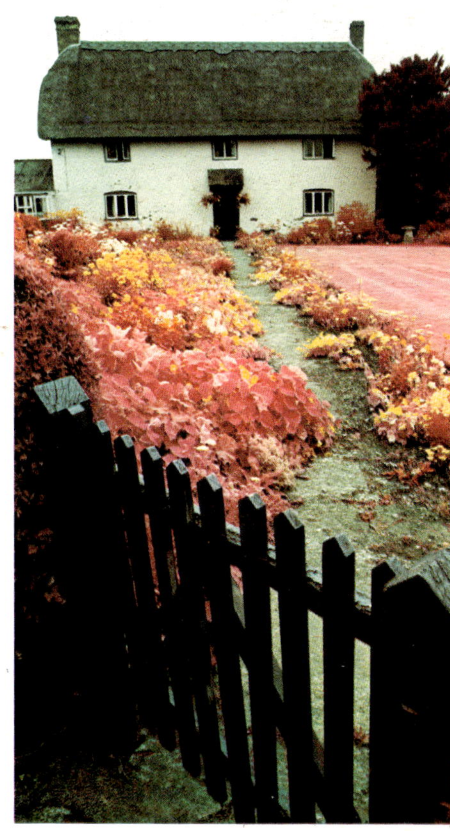

number of laboratories, and now almost unobtainable in kit form.

Infrared film was originally designed for aerial photography, so its contrast is very high. This means that its exposure latitude is very small—less than half a stop either way. With a yellow Wratten 12 filter in front of the lens the effective speed of Ektachrome Infrared film is 100 ASA.

Photomicrography film

Kodak's Photomicrography Colour Film 2483 is a very high contrast film suited to the kinds of image seen through a microscope where many stained specimens have very low contrasts of tone and colour. Its speed is 16 ASA in daylight, making it the slowest camera film available. But as photomicrography uses tungsten lamps for illumination, its speed drops to only 4 ASA when the necessary Wratten 80A colour conversion filter is used. Although balanced for use by daylight or electronic flash, it tends to suffer from colour casts, because of reciprocity failure problems at exposure times longer than 1/10 second. Outdoor shots often have a generally blue cast, and the high contrast and colour saturation make the reds reproduce particularly strongly.

Photomicrography film is available only as 35 mm 36 exposure cassettes. Like infrared film it gives colour slides after processing through the obsolete E4 process. Apart from the use of this film for its intended purpose of micrography, it can give strangely coloured, high contrast images when used in the camera, and may also be useful for copying line drawings in colour.

Like most specialist materials, micrography film should be kept in a refrigerator before and after use. If you want to use this material and your camera's film speed control does not go down to 16 ASA, set it to 32 ASA—often the slowest setting—and give 1 stop extra exposure, either manually or using a '+1' exposure compensation control. As with all high contrast material, the exposure latitude is no more than half a stop either way, so you should bracket your exposures.

Slide duplicating film

Kodak's Ektachrome slide duplicating film is a very slow speed, low contrast film of high resolving power that is used for making facsimile copies of colour slides without the usual contrast increase that is inevitable when making copies of slides on conventional film. Though it must be specially ordered through a dealer bulk lengths may work at only half the cost of ordinary camera film. It can be processed in the normal E6 chemistry used for other Ektachrome slide films, but you should let the laboratory know that your cassette has been loaded from a supply of bulk film.

Kodak market two types of slide duplicating film, one balanced to give correct colour with daylight (SE 371) and one balanced for tungsten light at 3200K (Slide Duplicating Film 5071). The tungsten balanced film is ideal for use with simple slide duplicators used with a photoflood as a light source, with some professional bench top duplicators, or if you copy slides using an enlarger or projector. Daylight-type film is needed, however, when you copy using electronic flash as the light source—as most bench top copiers do.

Although the films are balanced for light of a particular colour temperature, additional filtration is necessary when making duplicate slides, in order to correct for the different types of film being copied. Kodak recommend the use of filters with each batch.

Used in the camera for general purposes, the films give low contrast results which for most subjects will be disappointing. A sheet film version, Kodak Ektachrome Duplicating Film 6121 is available in sizes from 4 × 5 inches to 20 × 16 inches. You could use this to make large transparencies for display from 35 mm originals.

Internegative film

Kodak's Vericolor Internegative Film 6011 is a colour negative film for making negatives from slides.

Such a negative is known as an 'internegative' and can then be used to make a print in the normal way. This film is really for darkroom use and is only available as 35 mm film in 23 metre rolls and in sheet film sizes as Kodak Vericolor Internegative Film 4112 (Estar Thick Base). It would be possible to use it in a 35 mm camera in much the same way as duplicating film. In practice, its original function, that of producing a negative for prints from slides, has been largely superseded by easier reversal processes such as Ektachrome R14 or Cibachrome paper.

Internegative film is balanced for a colour temperature of 3200 K and recommended exposure times are between 1/10 second and 30 seconds, with an optimum of about 10 seconds. It is processed in normal C41 chemicals, as used for conventional colour

Photomicrography film ***(below)****, used for photographing low contrast images through a microscope, produces more contrasty pictures than normal film (left)*

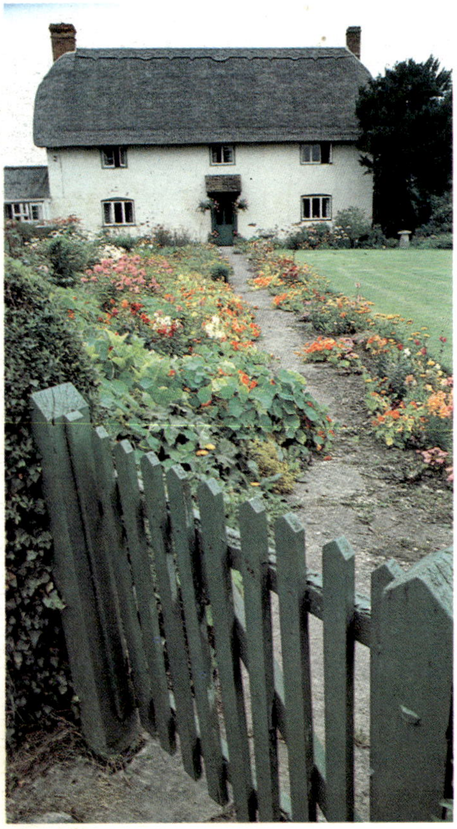

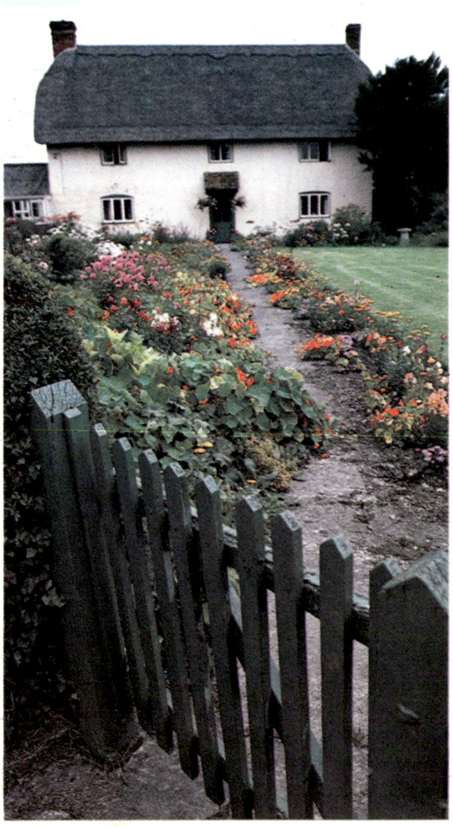

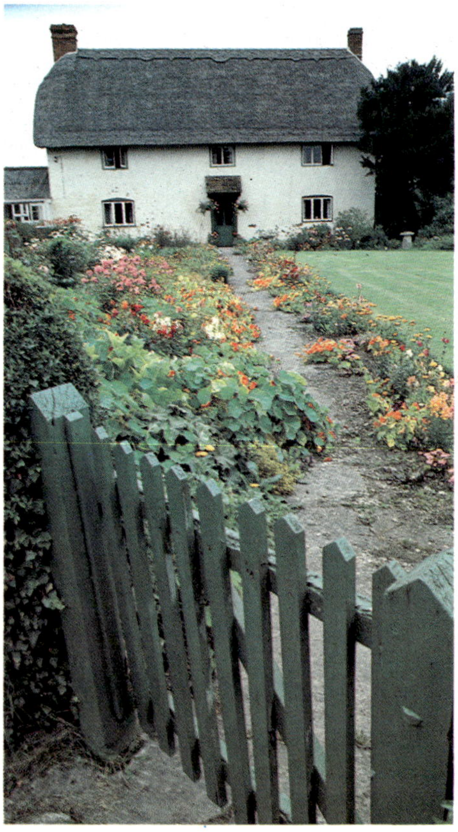

negative film processing.

One unusual property of internegative film is that each of the normal three layers of the emulsion is a mixture of a fast, low contrast emulsion and a slow, high contrast emulsion. This is intended to cope with the high contrast of the original colour slide without the need for contrast reducing masks. The fast emulsion records the mid tones of the slide at a reduced contrast, while the slow layers record only the highlights but maintain a higher contrast for better reproduction. This means that the film has the unusual property of offering a contrast increase as the exposure time increases, the slow emulsion then playing more of a part.

Because of its special properties, another application of internegative film is in copying colour line diagrams for making colour prints.

Vericolor Slide Film 5072

This film is made for producing colour slides from colour negatives and it is only available in the same lengths as slide duplicating film mentioned earlier. It is handled and treated in much the same way as colour paper, except that it may be used in a camera or slide copier rather than in the enlarger. It is a high contrast film with its colour balanced for 3200 K and an exposure time range of 1/4 second to 8 seconds. As in conventional colour printing, you must determine the appropriate filtration by means of tests for each negative. A suggested starting point for a Kodacolor II negative is 30 Y + 50 M for a dichroic head enlarger.

Vericolor slide film is processed in C41 chemicals but if the chemicals are used more than once the replenishment rate has to be adjusted and an additive used in the colour developer. Because of this film's high contrast properties, it can be used to copy black and white text to make colour line slides for titles or captions. If it is 'flashed' during development, it can give unusual Sabattier effect images.

Kodak 5247 film

Until recently, this film was of little interest to the amateur. It is a 35 mm movie negative film, used in the camera for making feature films. It is normally available only in bulk, the smallest length being 30 m.

Some laboratories in the US and Canada, however, are now loading this film in normal 35 mm cassette lengths. The negatives, once processed, are suitable for both print and slide making. The prints are made as normal, while slides, if required, are made by contact printing on release print film, the same film that is normally used for making films for release to cinemas.

The main advantage of the film is that it can offer either prints or slides, though the quality of either cannot be expected to be as high as when using the material designed for the task. In addition, the film can be rated at 100, 200 or 400 ASA, with appropriate processing. This is a common feature of the film when used in movie making.

The film is balanced for a colour temperature of 3200 K, but the laboratories who reload it claim that it can be used in daylight or fluorescent light with no further filtration. Ideally it requires a Wratten 85 filter when used in daylight, the speed being reduced from 100 ASA to 64 ASA.

The process, while similar to the standard negative C41 process, has to be modified to remove the special black 'rem-jet' anti-halation backing. If a normal C41 process is used, the backing will not be completely removed and the chemicals will be spoilt. The film must, therefore, normally be processed by a lab accustomed to dealing with it.

It is, however, possible to process the film at home using C41 chemicals if the backing is first removed by rubbing it gently, in total darkness, with a cloth soaked in a 5 per cent solution of sodium carbonate.

The release print film used for making the transparencies is processed in Ektacolor 3 print chemicals.

However, the use of 5247 film for still camera photography is not encouraged by Kodak. Certainly there are a number of problems involved. First, the exposure and colour balance are adjusted for 1/50 sec—the normal movie camera exposure. Second, it is more difficult to process than still colour negative film. Third, it does not have all the anti-scratch layers of still films intended for use in cassettes.

Generally, it is true to say that still negative films are more suitable for still camera photography since they include a family of compatible chemicals, paper and print film suited to the production of prints or slides.

Slide duplicating film *(below) is intended for photographing high contrast slides and the results are lower in contrast than normal film (left)*

Kodak 5247 film *(below) produces acceptable images but they lack the sharpness and clarity of those taken on normal film (left)*

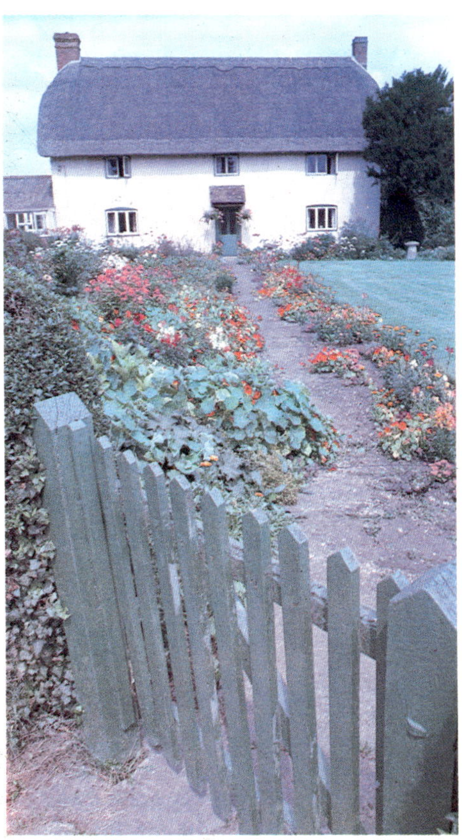

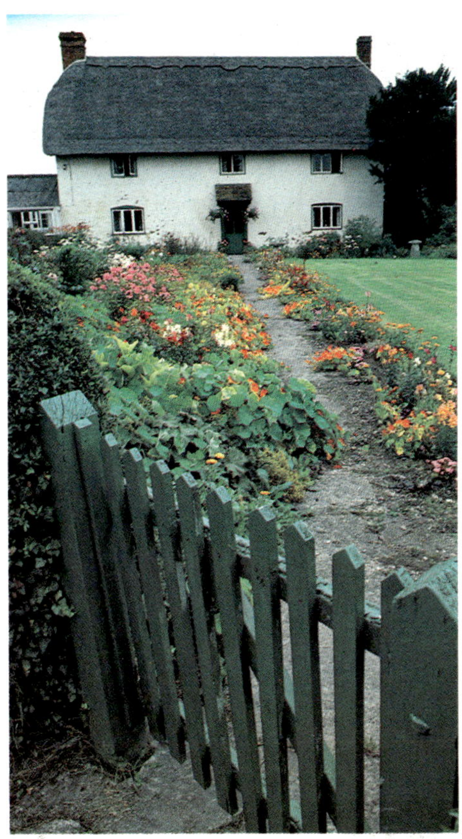

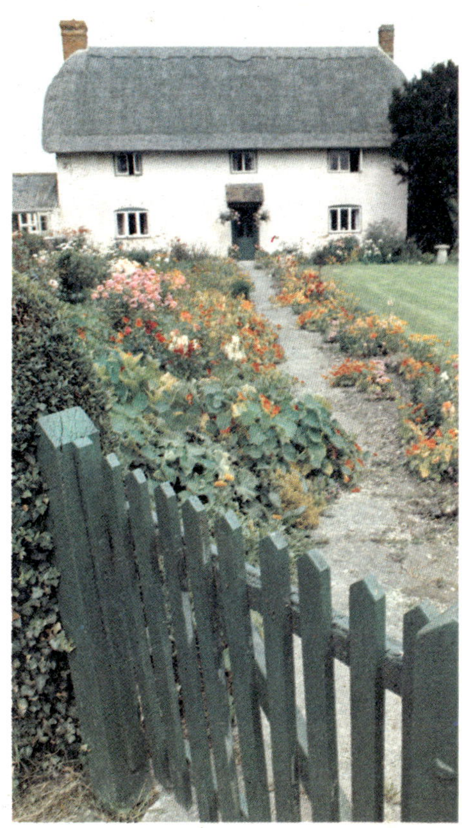

CHAPTER 3
EXPOSURE
Shutter speed and aperture

To record colour and detail properly, the film must be exposed to just the right amount of light when the shutter is fired. If it receives too much light—if it is *overexposed*—the colours and tones will be pale and washed-out and detail will be barely visible in the *highlights,* the brightest parts of the picture. However, if the film receives too little light—if it is *underexposed*—colours and tones will be very dark and shadows so dense that detail cannot be seen. Only when the film is correctly exposed will colour and tone be good and fine detail be visible in both shadows and highlights. This is why good exposure is so important.

Of course, scenes vary considerably in brightness, and so the amount of light available to expose the film (the *available light*) also varies considerably. So, to ensure the film always receives the correct exposure, the amount of light that actually reaches the film must be carefully regulated. This is done by two camera controls, shutter speed and aperture. Shutter speed controls the length of the exposure, and the aperture controls its intensity, simply by varying the size of the window in the lens called the *iris diaphragm* (see page 222).

On the simplest 110, Disc and 35 mm compact cameras, there is only one shutter speed and one aperture. This means they are simple to use, for there are no exposure controls to set. But they will only give good results in bright sunlight. Some simple cameras, though, have two shutter speeds, indicated by 'sun' and 'cloud' symbols, which must be seen according to conditions.

However, all SLRs, many 35 mm compact cameras and some Disc cameras have a full range of shutter speeds and apertures. This means that they can give correct exposure in a wide variety of conditions, but exposure is that much more complex.

Shutter speed and aperture

To set the right shutter speed and aperture combination, you must assess the brightness of the scene you want to photograph. Photographers used to rely on experience to judge the brightness of the scene. Nowadays, however, photo-electric light meters make this task very simple. Most modern SLRs incorporate this meter within the camera body and it measures light coming through the lens (TTL). On other cameras, the meter cell may be just above the lens.

With automatic cameras, the exposure controls are adjusted automatically according to the light reading, following a set programme. With semi-automatic cameras, you set either the aperture (aperture-priority) or the shutter speed (shutter-priority), and the camera does the rest. With manual cameras, you set either the shutter speed or the aperture and then adjust the other control until the signal in the viewfinder tells you the setting is right. The exact procedure for each type of camera is shown in Chapter 1.

The important thing to remember when setting the exposure controls is that there is not just one correct shutter speed and aperture combination but a whole range. This means that you can choose either the aperture or the shutter speed you want to create a particular effect. The effects you can achieve by varying the shutter speed are described in the remainder of this section. The effects you can achieve by varying the aperture are covered in the Chapter 4.

When you deliberately alter shutter speed or aperture to achieve a particular affect, always keep in mind that their effect on exposure is *reciprocal*—that is, when you increase one you must reduce the other by the same amount to give the same exposure. Fortunately, the click stops on both the aperture and shutter speed controls are stepped to avoid any complex calculations. A stop movement on either control either doubles or halves the exposure, depending on which way you turn the control. If you set the shutter speed one stop slower, for instance, this doubles the exposure time. To compensate, you halve the aperture by taking it down a stop. So if the correct aperture with a shutter speed of 1/125 second is *f*/2.8, the correct aperture at 1/60 second is *f*/4; at 1/30 it is *f*5.6, at 1/15 it is *f*/8 and so on. Choosing the combination that best suits the subject is the true art of exposure.

Choosing the shutter speed

Probably more shots are ruined by using the wrong shutter speed than by anything else. If the shutter speed is too slow, either the subject or the camera can move during the exposure and the resulting picture may be blurred.

If the blurring has been caused by camera movement (usually called camera shake), it will be noticeable all over the photograph. No part of the picture—neither subject nor background—will be sharp. If the blurring has been caused by only the subject moving, the background, or at any rate some other part of the picture, will be sharp while the subject will be blurred.

Camera shake is cured either by putting the camera on some suitable support, or by using a fast enough shutter speed. Subject movement can be cured only by using a sufficiently fast shutter speed.

To be absolutely certain of eliminating shake when you are hand-holding your camera, you should use a shutter speed not slower than 1/125 second when using the standard lens. This is the 'safe' speed: with practice, most people can successfully hand-hold a camera perfectly steady at 1/60, even 1/30 or 1/15.

You also need to take into account the

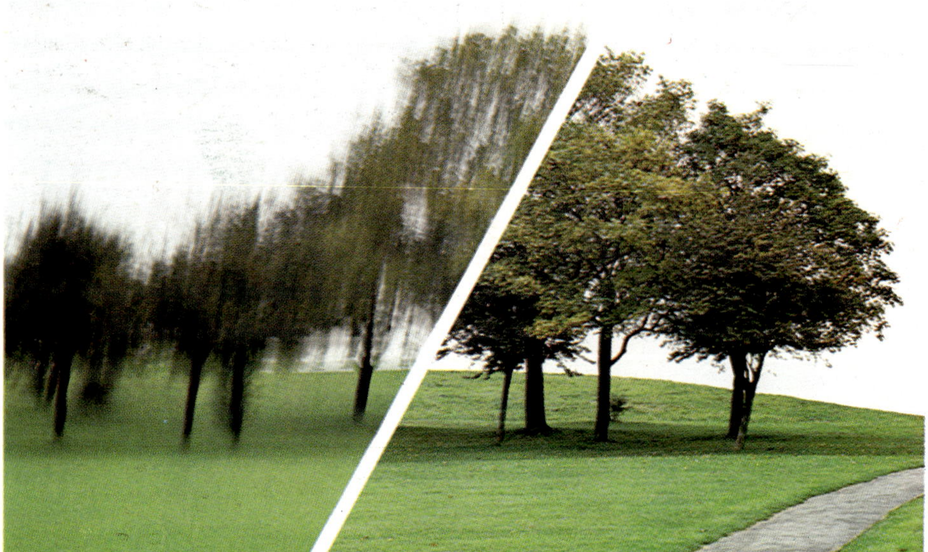

Camera shake *Two hand-held shots of the same subject. One,taken at 1/15, failed to eliminate camera shake. The other, at 1/125, is perfectly sharp*

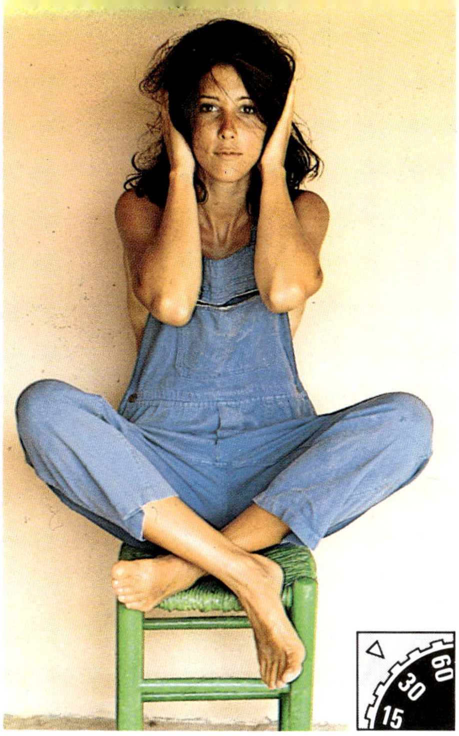

A still subject *Photography indoors without extra lighting often calls for the use of slow shutter speeds—in this case 1/30—as long as the subject is not moving*

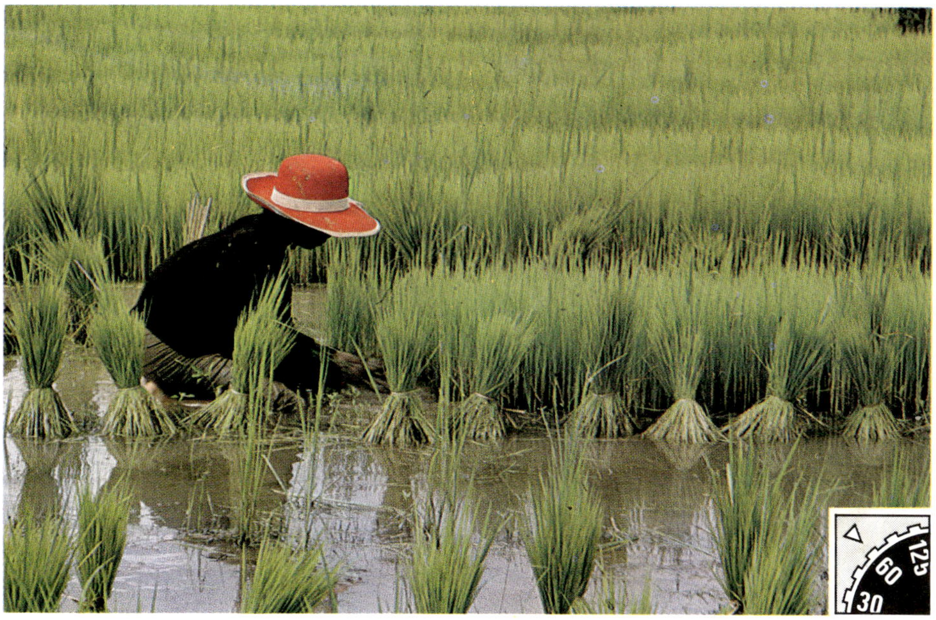

Cloudy day *With slow films and a subject with little movement, 1/60 is an acceptable shutter speed in poor lighting conditions*

Walking subjects *Unless the subject is very close, 1/125 is adequate to prevent blurring in horizontal movement, such as in a shot like this*

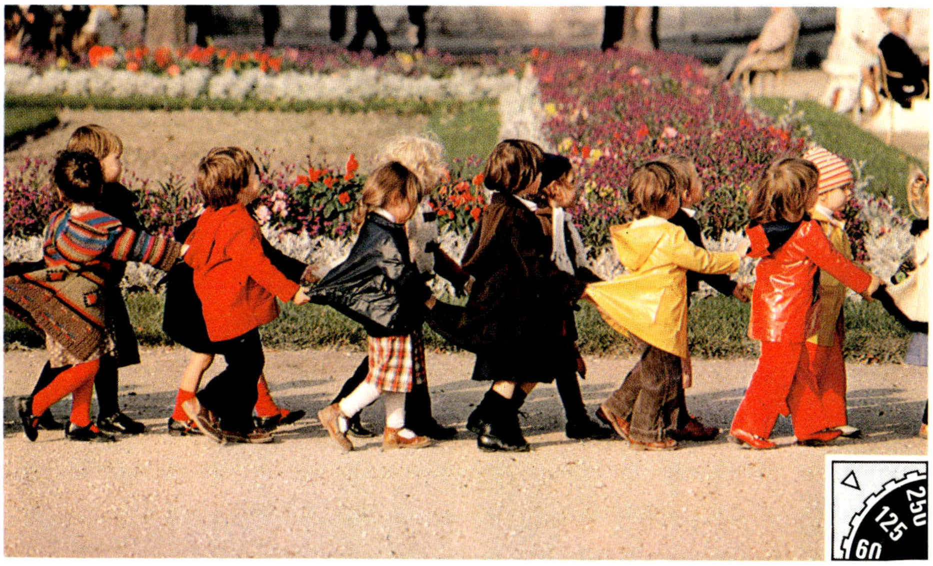

conditions in which you are taking photographs: it is surprising how much unsteadiness is caused by strong wind. Not so surprising is that being on a boat or in a car or aeroplane inevitably causes camera shake. So if you are in doubt about hand-holding the camera, use 1/125 or faster to be sure.

One catch: if you are hand-holding a long focus (telephoto) lens its magnification will exaggerate camera shake. This means using a faster-than-normal shutter speed, and for 35 mm camera users there is a useful rule of thumb for calculating this: you simply match the speed to the focal length of the lens being used. With a 1000 mm lens, you need 1/1000 second; with a 200 mm lens, 1/200 (or 1/250) will do. This rule gives about 1/60 second as the slowest speed for the camera's standard lens. Slower speeds can safely be used with wide angle lenses.

If you are at all worried that you cannot hand-hold, make use of doors, fences, walls, posts—in fact, whatever is to hand—as a support for the camera. Stand with your feet apart but do not tense yourself. Squeeze the shutter gently rather than jab at it. According to your own preference, release the shutter while holding your breath, or just after exhaling. This can make a noticeable improvement to the sharpness of your pictures.

With a reasonable range of shutter speeds—this is generally taken to mean speeds of up to 1/500 or 1/1000—freezing subject action presents few problems. But a more restricted range of speeds—or lack of light on a particular day—does not prevent you photographing moving objects, though you must be aware of problem subjects.

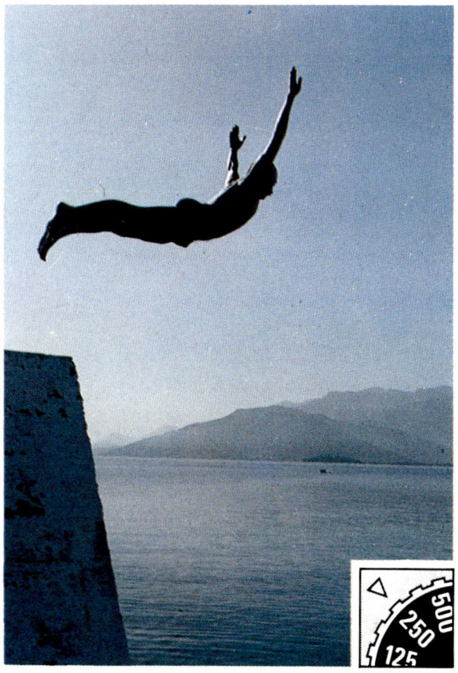

Frozen diver *If the shot is timed to coincide with the peak of action, even fast movement can be stopped using a shutter speed of 1/250*

Can you choose your shutter speed?

The very simplest and cheapest cameras have only one shutter speed—usually around 1/90 second. This is adequate for general photography, and usually prevents blur due to camera shake. Rapidly moving objects, however, will be blurred; so your photography is restricted by such a camera.

An increasing number of modern automatic cameras give you no indication of your shutter speed, but instead just warn you by means of a light in the viewfinder when the shutter speed will be less than, say, 1/30 second. You can control the shutter speed by varying the camera's aperture so that the auto-control will be forced to change the shutter speed accordingly to give a good exposure. But you will not be certain of the speed chosen, so for good results auto exposure can be a drawback.

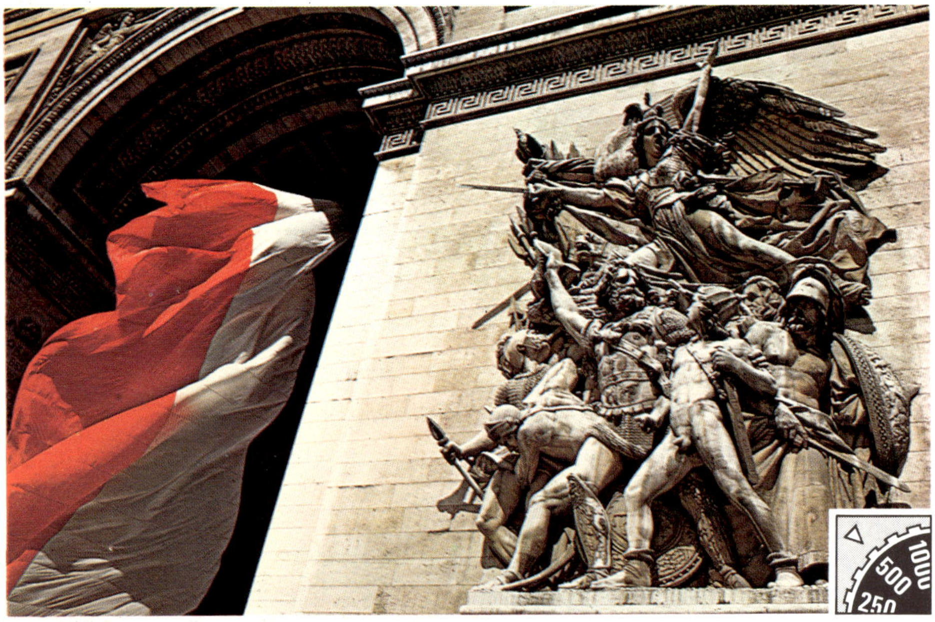

Fireworks *A time exposure on 'B' of several seconds is sufficient to record several firework bursts. The time depends on the film and lens aperture*

How to choose

When working out the right choice of shutter speed, a useful first step is to ask yourself what sort of movement you are shooting. If it is a normal movement, such as walking, you can work in the region of 1/125 provided the action does not take place too close to the camera, or directly across the field of view. With violent action—the hurdler, the child on a see-saw, the pole vaulter or the motor cycle scrambler—the slowest you can work at will be 1/250.

Many modern cameras have a range of shutter speeds that goes up to 1/1000, and sometimes 1/2000 second, but for certain types of action, such as a nearby car, or a skier hurtling across the frame, even these will not freeze it absolutely.

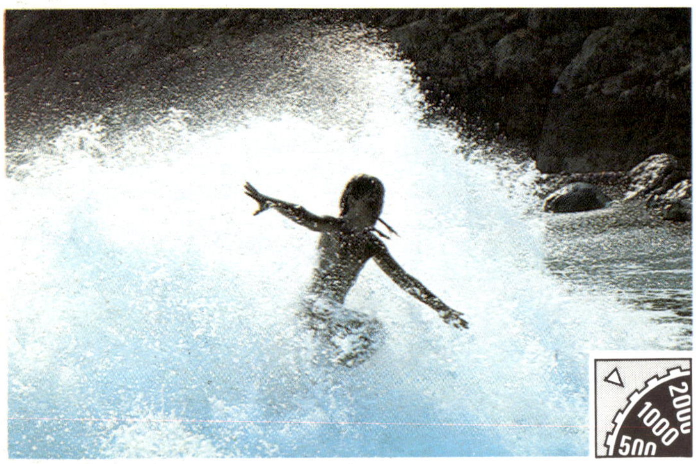

Statue and flag *Although the main part of the subject is not moving, a very rapid 1/500 is necessary to halt all movement of a thrashing flag*

Frozen spray *To 'freeze' movement such as the spray in this shot, use the fastest speed of your camera, ideally 1/2000. Any less may give blur*

There is no need, however, to put the camera away when faced with this type of situation. Much of the point of taking action photographs is, after all, to convey the feeling, the visual impression, of action—and in this, a little blurring is a positive help. The secret here is to use the technique known as *panning*: following the subject's movement within the viewfinder and releasing the shutter while continuing to swing the camera so it tracks the subject movement—even after taking the shot.

Done properly, this results in a sharp, or almost sharp, subject against a blurred background. Only those parts of the image which move smoothly will register

The first thing to bear in mind about subject movement is that it only matters when it results in movement across the film. This means that if a car is speeding straight towards you at 50 km/h, to a camera it will appear as if it is hardly moving at all, and register quite sharply on film if you only use 1/60. If, however, it is moving across the camera's field of view, then its speed will be only too apparent. To be certain of freezing it, you will need to use 1/500 or 1/1000.

But if the same car moving across your field of view were 100 metres away, rather than 5 metres away, its movement would be much less apparent, and you could safely use a slower speed.

Finally, if the same car were coming towards you diagonally, its movement would be less apparent than when moving straight across. In this case you would probably freeze the action at 1/250 even if the car was close.

As before, long focus lenses exaggerate the effects of movement, while short focus lenses reduce them. There are formulae for working out the appropriate shutter speed for all subjects with various lenses, but they are not usually to hand when you are faced with a particular problem. The only way to be sure of good results is to use common sense and experience—after a while you will be able to do this automatically.

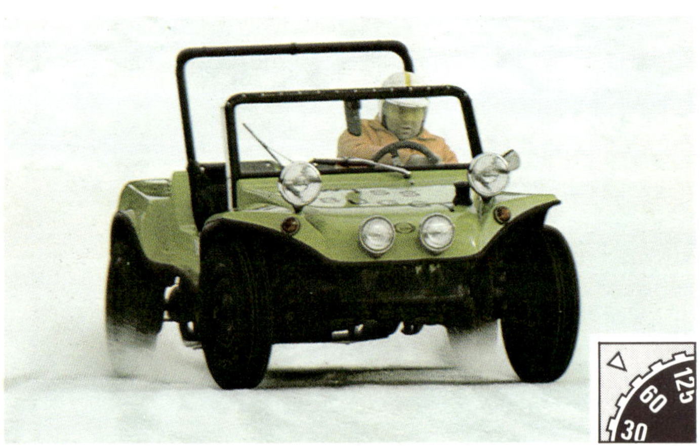

Snow buggy *You can use relatively slow speeds if a fast-moving object is coming towards the camera—1/60 was sufficient in this shot*

Racing car *By using the technique of panning, moderate speeds such as 1/125 can be used even for fast subjects*

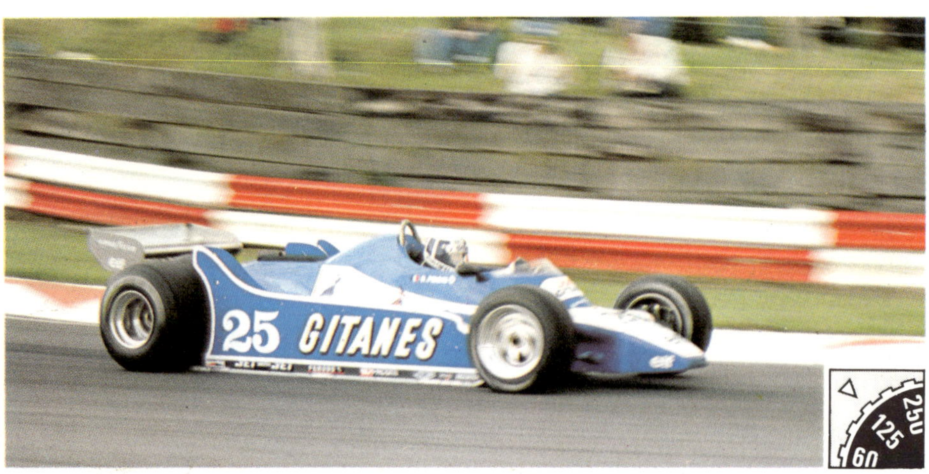

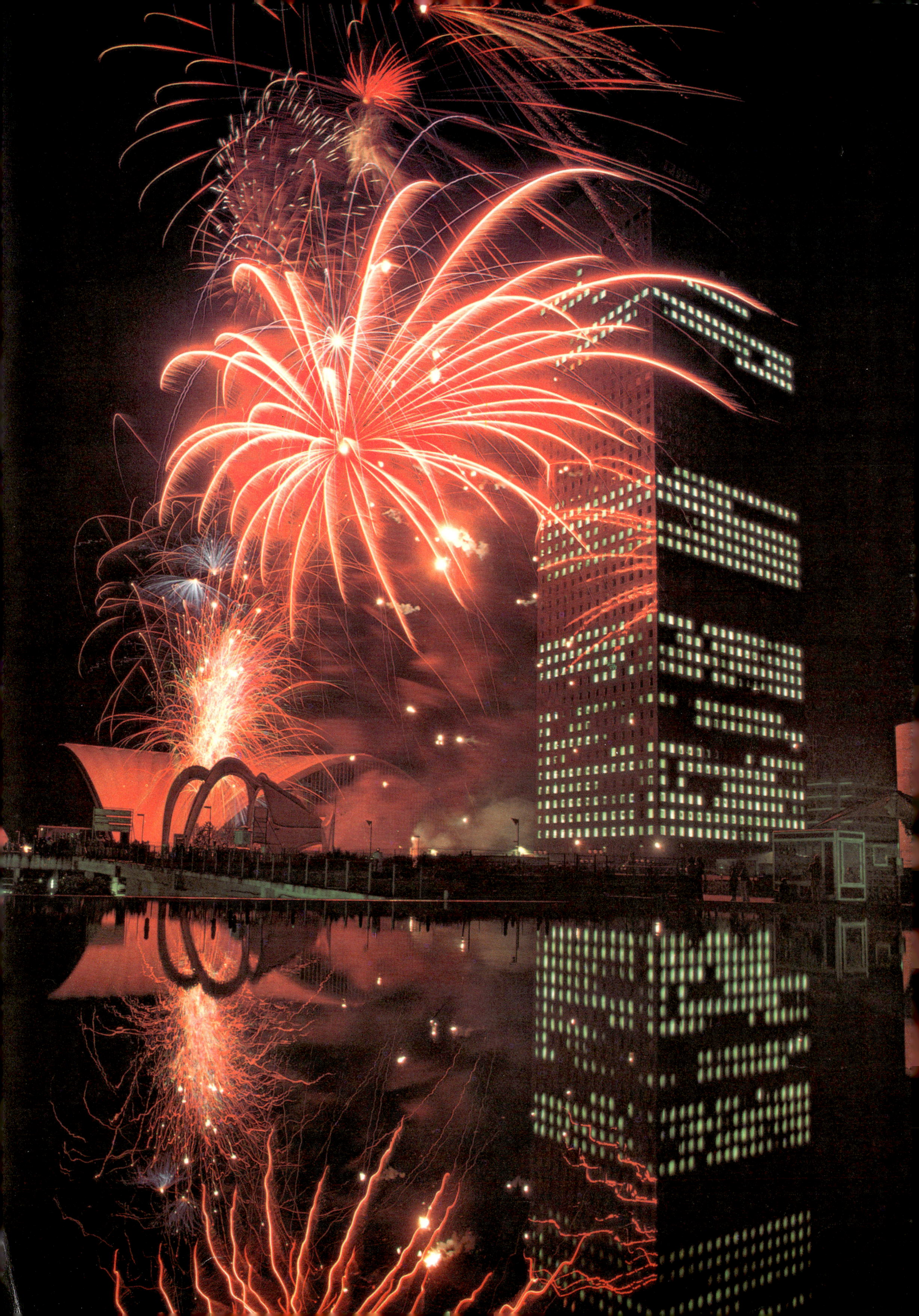

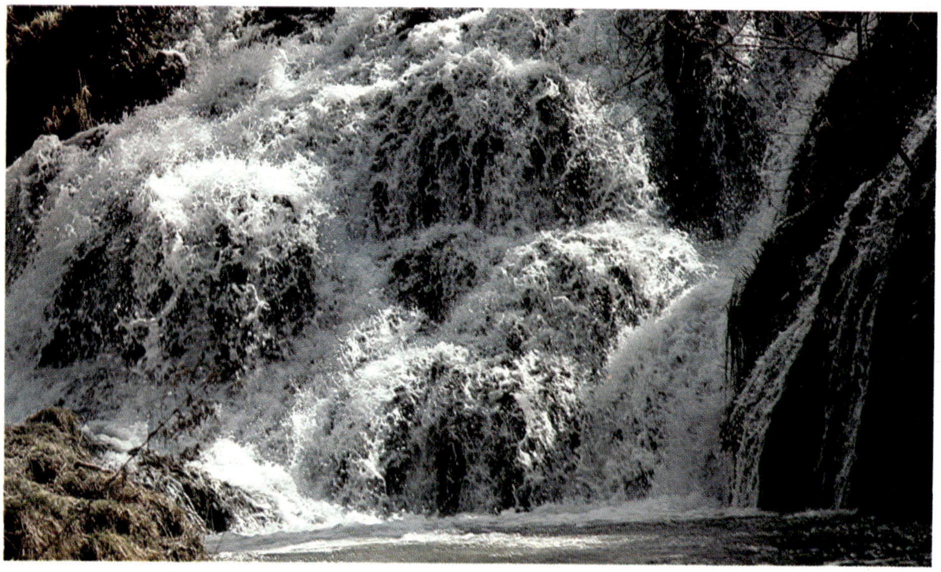

Waterfall impact *The sheer power of the water is suggested by using a brief shutter speed to freeze all movement in the subject*

Flowing waterfall *In marked contrast, but no less effective, is the result of using a slow speed (1/4 or longer) to indicate movement in the subject*

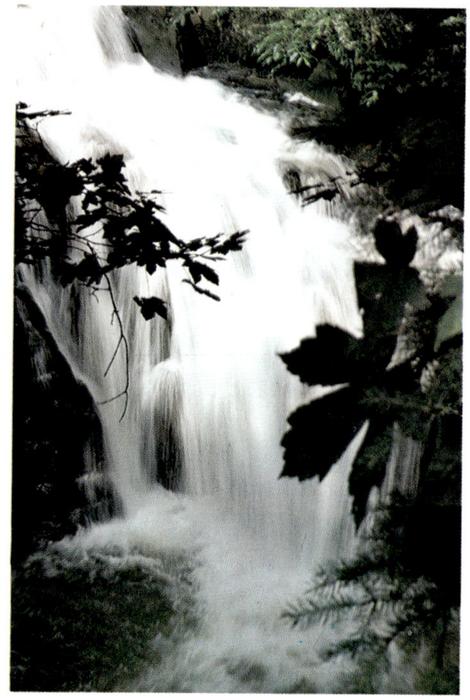

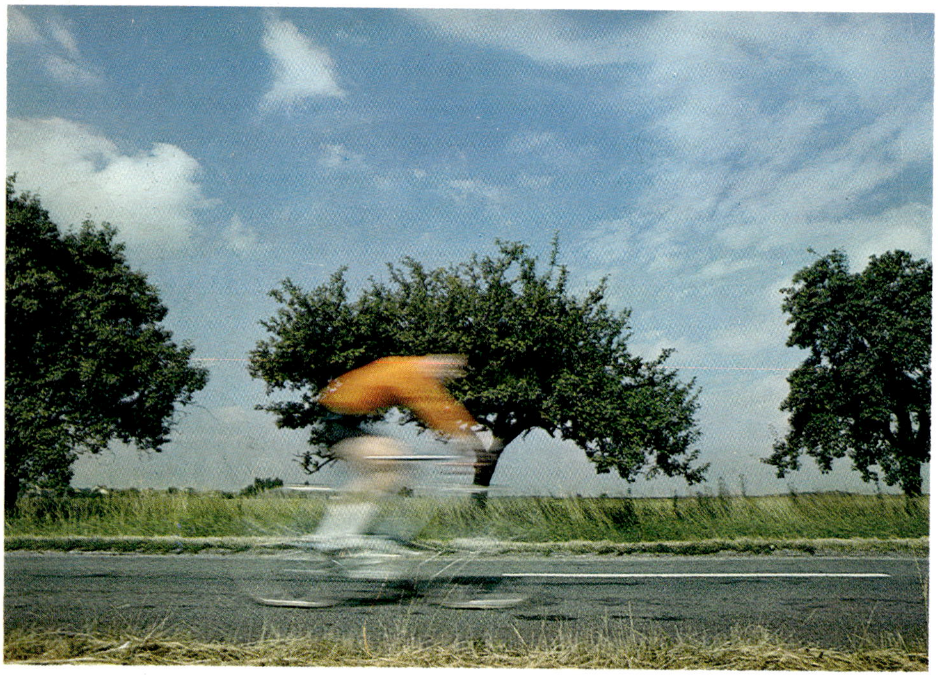

Cyclist *If you keep your camera still and use a fairly slow shutter speed, any subject movement is likely to show as blurring*

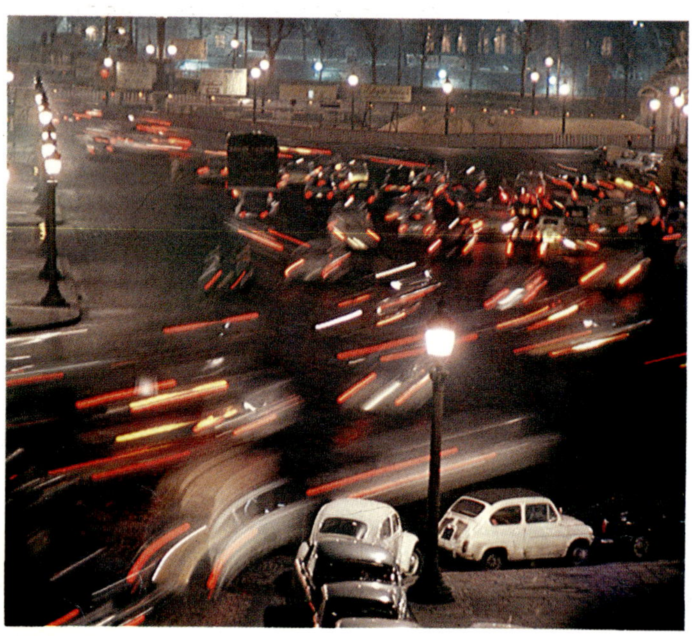

Traffic trails *You need to use slow speeds and time exposures for shots at dusk or at night. Trails formed by the lights of moving traffic can look particularly effective. A continuous trail requires use of long exposures and a really firm camera support*

sharply: a galloping horse, for example, will come out with a sharp body, but blurred legs. However, the impression of speed given by a blurred background, or smudged hooves, can be the making of a fine, atmospheric shot. The best way to pan is with the camera on a tripod with a *pan and tilt* attachment but with practice excellent results can be achieved by hand.

Sometimes it is better to hold the camera still and allow the subject to move, so that its image is just a blur. While this can be effective, it doesn't always work: it depends on the amount of detail that remains. But the principle is always worth bearing in mind: you need not necessarily 'freeze' a moving subject for the most effective shot.

Long exposure times

The shutter speed dial of your camera has many speeds on it which most photographers hardly ever use—those longer than 1/30 second. These speeds almost always require the use of a tripod, but they can give exciting results when used properly.

Times between 1/30 and 1 second are invaluable when lighting conditions are poor and there is not much movement in the subject. Additionally, they can be used to create the impression of movement in comparatively slow subjects, such as people walking.

For exposure times longer than a second you must use the 'B' setting. The 'B' stands for 'bulb'—recalling the days when all exposures were made by opening the shutter for a period of time, with an air bulb and flexible tube for vibration-free operation.

A remote release—either the air bulb variety or a cable release—is very useful for operating the shutter without jogging the camera. Exposures can range from a few seconds to several minutes, depending on the subject and the amount of light which is available.

Precision exposure

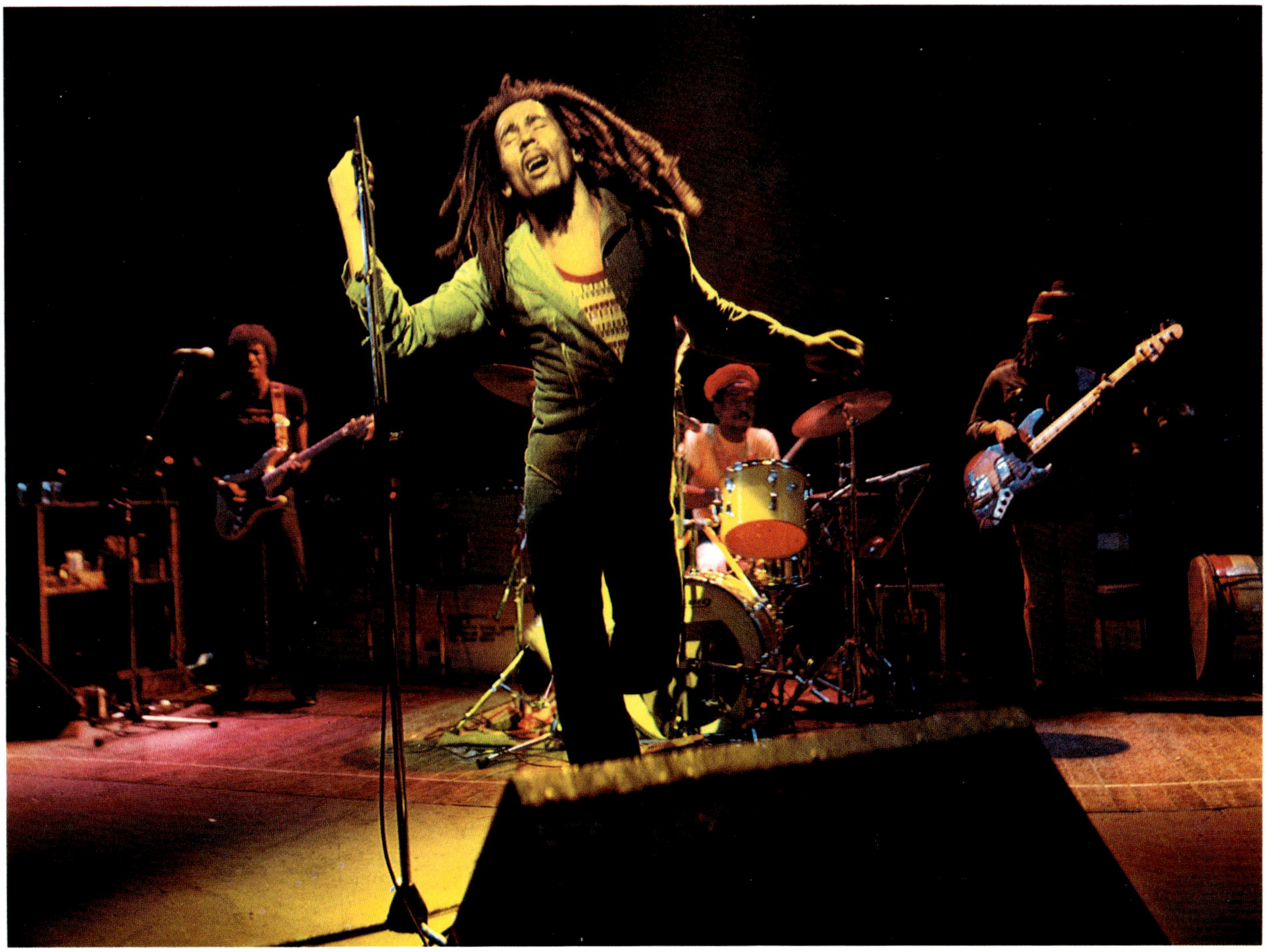

By far the best way to assess how much light there is in a scene—and what exposure is needed—is with a light meter and most new cameras now have built-in meters. Built-in meters undoubtedly help even the most inexperienced photographer to achieve good results in most situations, but there are occasions when it pays to use a separate hand-held meter or use your built-in meter in the same precise, controlled way.

Hand-held meters are intrinsically no more accurate than built-in meters and measure light in much the same way. The difference comes in the way photographers tend to use them.

With a built-in meter, the normal technique for taking a reading is simply to line up the camera on the subject as if you were going to take a picture. The meter then gives a general reading for all or part of the scene you can see through the viewfinder—depending on whether the meter is *overall, centre-weighted* or *spot*.

This system is quick and easy to use and gives good results most of the time. However, it is only reliable if there is a fairly even mixture of tones in the scene—some dark, some light, some in between—with no particular extremes. More significantly, perhaps, it also assumes that all or a large part of the scene is equally important and that there are no small areas of interest. With centre-weighted and spot meters the middle of the picture has more effect on the reading, but even with these the 'read' area is large.

A hand-held meter encourages far greater care in exposure although it takes longer to use. It encourages you to not only make the general reading that you make with the built-in meter, but also to single out areas within the scene and meter them individually. There are a number of other special metering techniques that can be used to ensure correct exposure and all of these are much easier with a hand-held meter than a built-in type.

Bob Marley *A good overall exposure reading of a brightly lit stage can be taken by briefly pointing an incident meter into the stage spotlight beam*

It is possible to adapt these special metering techniques to a built-in meter, although it is generally more awkward. It can be a nuisance, for instance, to have to unclamp your camera from a tripod to make special readings. Similarly, because you have to put your eye to the viewfinder to read a built-in meter, special readings can be physically awkward—to take a light reading for a portrait 10 cm away from someone's face, you actually have to stand that close. Indeed, some metering techniques, such as incident light metering (see below), cannot be done with a built-in meter without a little trickery.

For the special metering techniques outlined here, then, you should really use a hand-held meter.

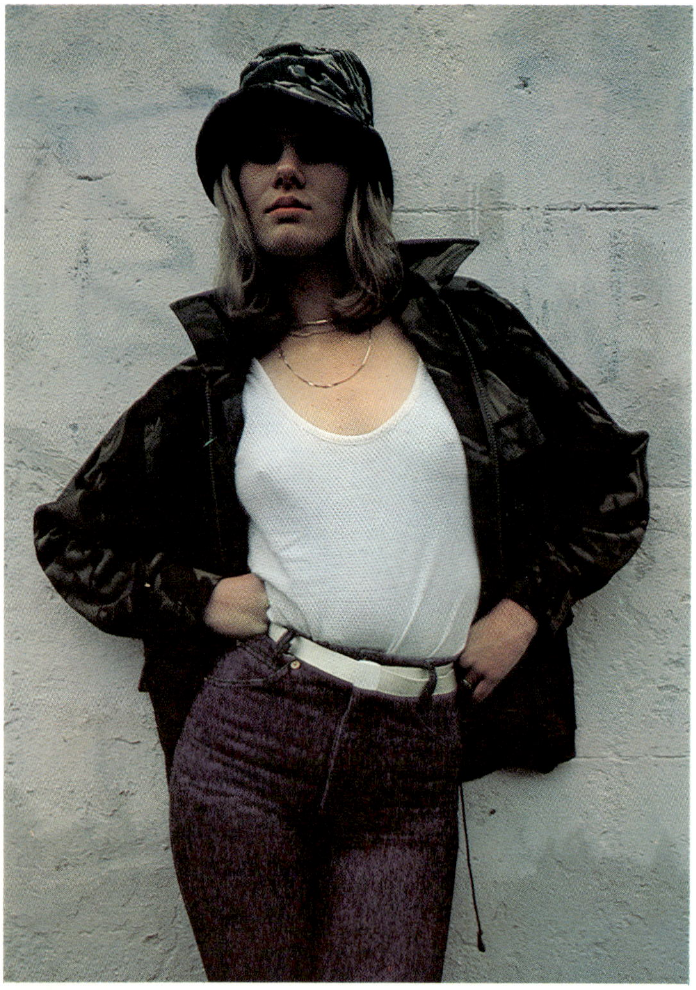

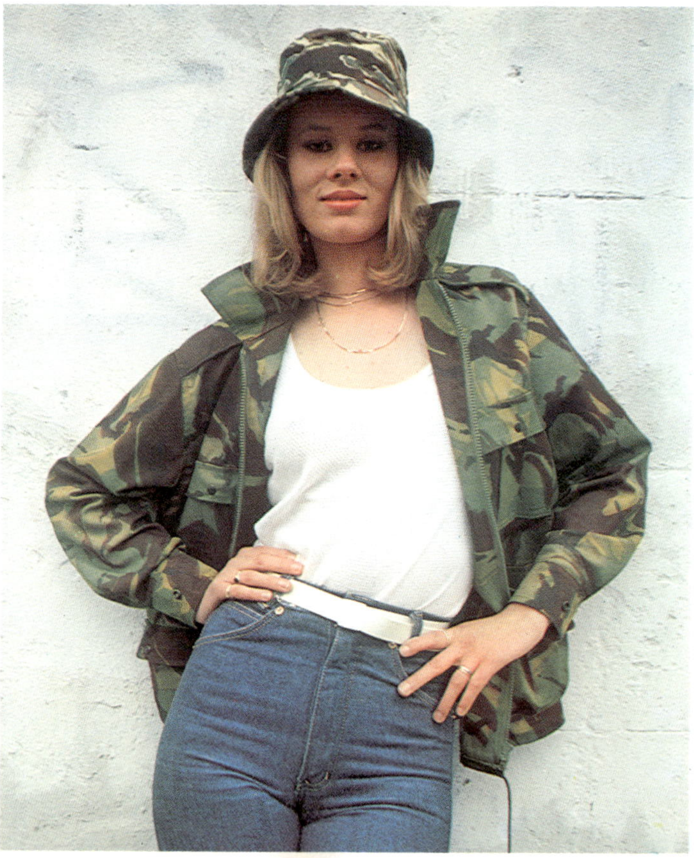

Light background *Taking an exposure reading from a light background can lead to underexposure, left. A built-in meter 'sees' the background as a brightly lit grey surface. A shot with incident metering, right, give better results*

Dark background *The opposite problem occurs with a dark background, left. Reflected light meters cannot be relied on to determine correct exposure, but incident meters are unaffected by subject reflectivity*

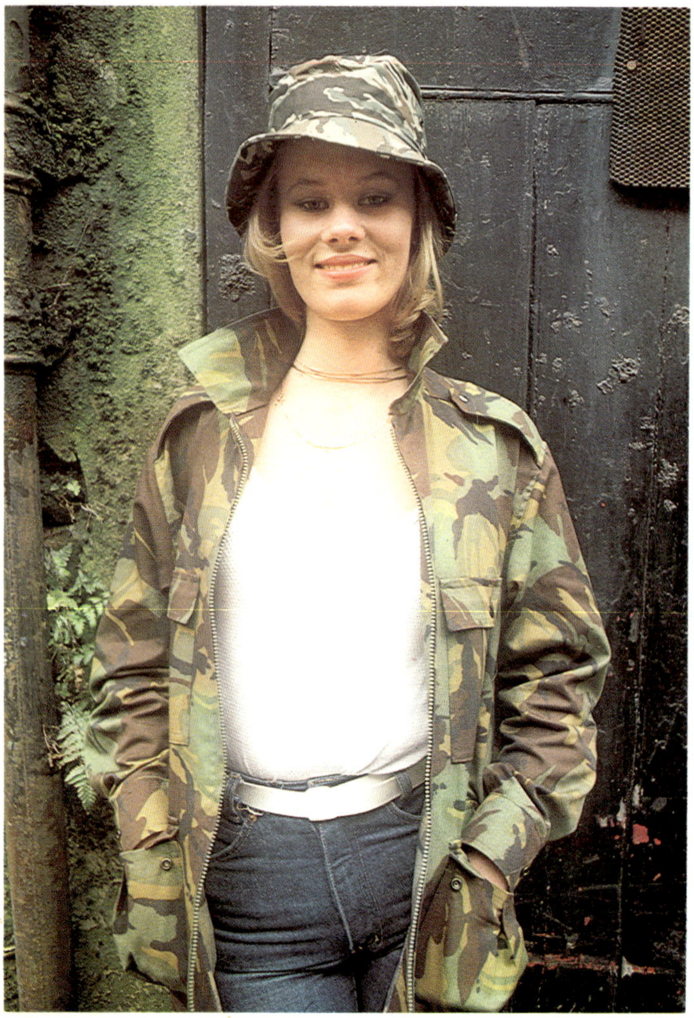

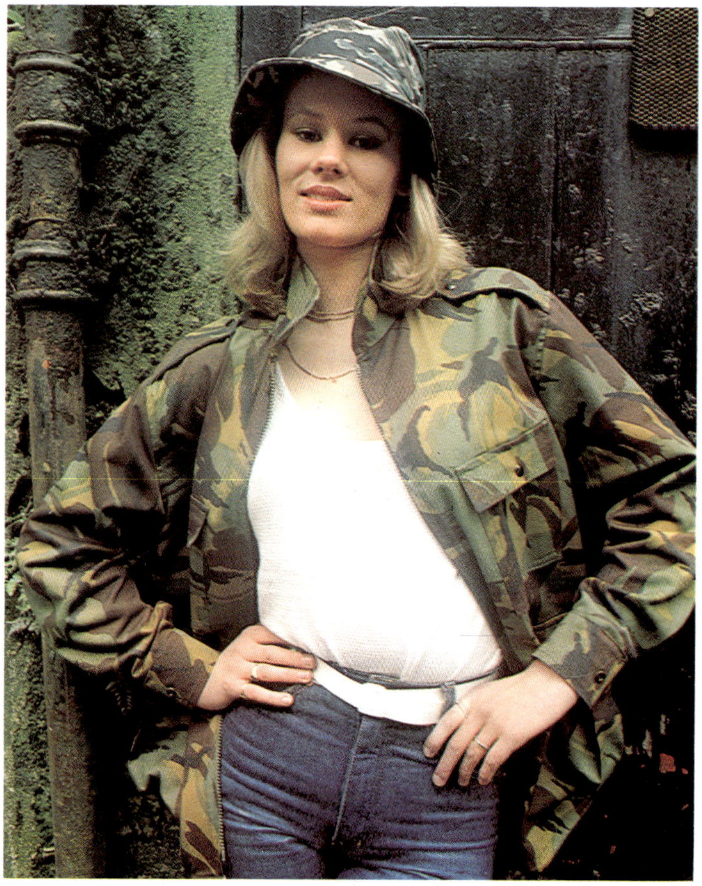

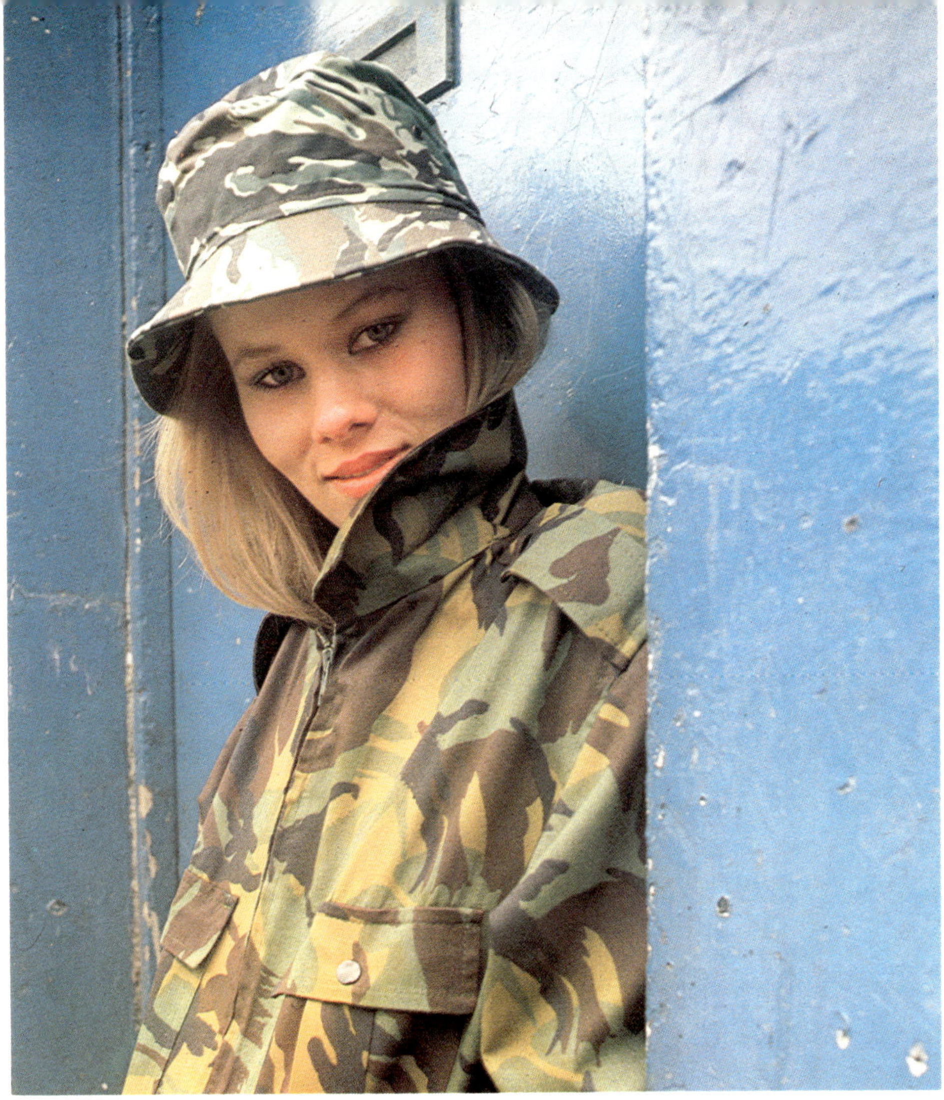

Average background *A subject with an average range of tones is interpreted similarly by both incident and reflected light meters*

Exposure

Although the precision of the light meter may lead you to believe that there is only one 'correct' exposure for every scene, exposure is often very much a compromise. Normally, the aim is to record detail in every part of the scene, both shadows and highlights, including all the tones between white and black that correspond to the tones in the original scene.

However, the human eye can cope with shadows and highlights far better than a film can. While the human eye will see detail in both shadows and highlights when the highlights are 1000 times as bright as the shadows—a brightness range of 1000 : 1—a black and white film can only cope with a range of 128 : 1.

You can use a hand-held light meter to see if the brightness range is too great for the film to cope with. Move into the scene and take a reading from the lightest part of the subject and then the darkest. If the difference between the two readings is more than seven *f*-stops, the brightness range is too great for black and white film to cope with. This does not mean that you cannot take your picture. It simply means that you must compromise and decide whether to overexpose the highlights or underexpose the shadows.

Colour print film can show detail in dark and light areas with about seven stops difference in brightness. Colour slide film can only manage a five stop range of brightness.

Inevitably, then, some of the detail the photographer sees in the original scene must be lost. Just what is lost depends upon the exposure. If you give a short exposure, shadow detail will be lost; if you give a long exposure there will be good detail in the shadows but the highlights will be 'burnt out'.

For black and white film, the traditional method is to expose for the shadows and let the highlights take care of themselves—that is, exposure is the minimum necessary to give good detail in the shadows. This does not mean that you take your meter reading from the shadows only, but simply that it is normally preferable to allow the highlights to burn out a little in order to get good detail in the darkest areas.

This policy works reasonably well for colour negative film as well, but not for colour slide film which gives unpleasant desaturated colours in the highlights when it is overexposed. Exposure for slides, therefore, is normally biased towards the highlights.

The exposure should really be chosen to give the sort of photograph you want. If you want detail in the highlights most, expose for these; if you want shadow detail picked out, expose for these. Once you have decided what you want, you can use a hand-held meter to help you establish what exposure gives you the effect you want.

Reflected light

Like built-in meters, most hand-held meters are designed to measure light reflected from the subject. These meters are referred to as *reflected light* meters. *Incident light* meters are also available and they are used to meter light incident (falling) upon the subject rather than reflected from it. Some meters can take both reflected and incident light readings. The procedure for taking a reading varies from meter to meter and you should refer to the manufacturer's instructions.

Reflected light readings can be taken in a number of ways, the most common of which is a general reading similar to the reading you take with a built-in meter. The meter is simply held next to the camera and pointed at the subject. Because the meter responds to exactly what the camera records—the light reflected from the subject—this method normally gives good results.

You should check, however, that the meter has a roughly similar angle of acceptance to the lens fitted to your camera. Typically the meter's angle of acceptance is about 45° which corres-

Pointing the meter *Unlike a built-in meter, a hand-held meter does not make allowances for bright skies. For accuracy, aim it slightly downwards*

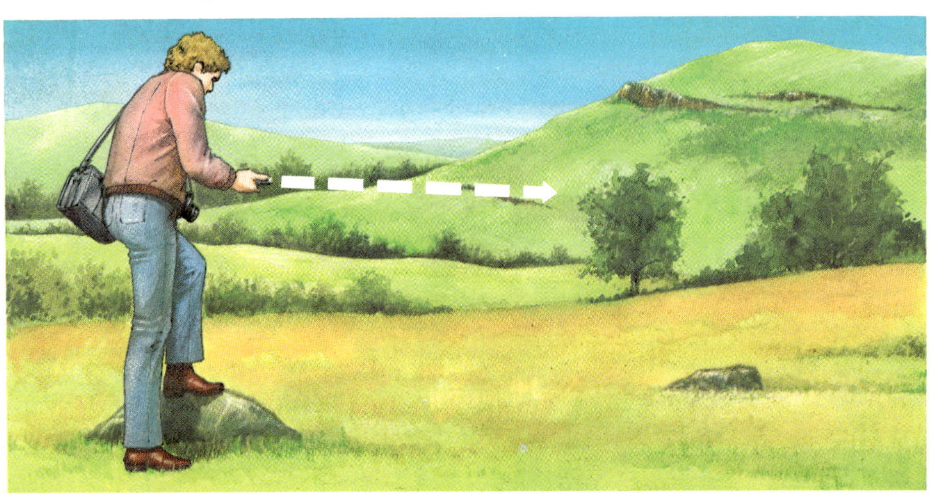

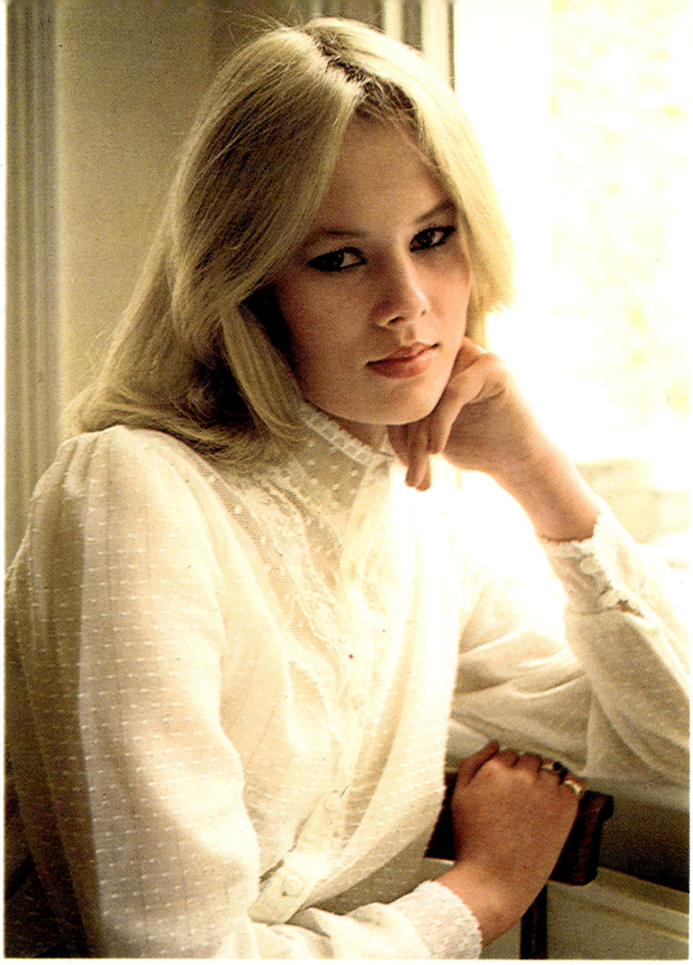

Exposing for shadows *Giving a greater than normal exposure reveals detail in the shadows, but tends to wash out the detail in the highlights—in this case, the window*

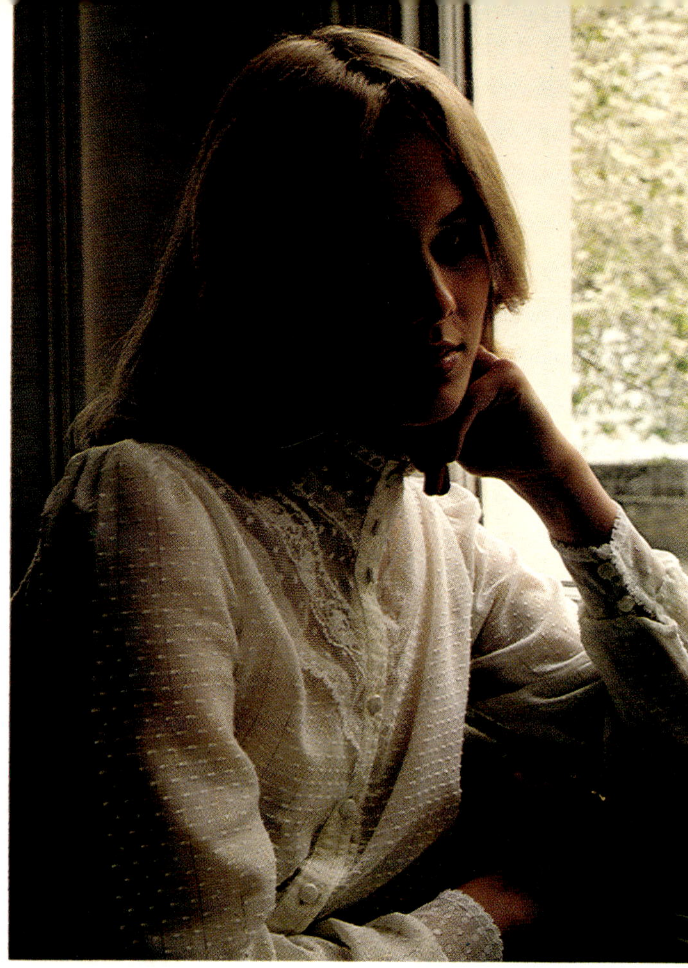

Exposing for highlights *With a shorter exposure, detail in the highlight areas is visible and colours are more saturated but shadow and midtone detail are lost*

ponds to the angle of view of a standard 50 mm lens. You should bear this in mind when changing lenses. While a TTL meter automatically adjusts for different lenses, a general scene reading with a hand-held meter may give incorrect exposure when you have anything but the standard lens on the camera.

Nevertheless, as long as direct sunlight does not catch the meter cell—shade it with your hand if necessary—a general scene reading gives acceptable exposures for most subjects. However, it is worth examining the scene to see if you might improve your results by exposing for particular areas.

Tilting the meter

Landscapes, for example, and indeed other photographs, often include a large sky area. This has a considerable influence on general scene readings, and you may get two widely different readings with two similar views, simply because you include different proportions of sky. If you include a large area of sky in the frame, shadow detail could be lost on the ground if you only take a general scene reading.

Whether it is a landscape or a building you are shooting, aim the meter down towards the ground to get your reading. Start with the meter towards the sky and slowly tilt it downwards. The reading will drop rapidly at first and then become steady once all the sky is excluded. If you use this steady reading directly for your exposure, the sky may well be a little burnt out. Unless you want a featureless sky, therefore, you should expose at one stop less than indicated.

Closing in

When the main point of interest is fairly small in the frame—a small figure against a seascape, for instance—a general scene reading may again give an unsatisfactory reading since it will be influenced mostly by the brightness of the sea. In this instance, move in close to take a reading directly from the figure.

Portraits particularly benefit from this metering technique, whether outdoors or in the studio. Your reading should be taken with the meter held at a distance of 15 cm in front of the subject's face.

Out of doors, close-up meter readings may sometimes give false results if your point of interest is some distance from the camera. Haze between the camera and the subject can result in overexposure, especially on a sunny day. So you should again expose at one stop less than the close-up reading indicates.

Key tones

Areas that are coloured very dark or very light can also fool a reflected light meter. Even under identical lighting conditions, a meter will indicate that more exposure is needed for a very dark coloured object than for a very light coloured object. This is because dark colours reflect less light than light ones. A meter simply indicates that there is less light, without showing why. If you follow the exposure indicated by

Compromise exposure *Taking an exposure reading from a middle tone gives an exposure that fully exploits the contrast range of the film*

the meter, therefore, a black curtain would be rendered grey in the final photograph. To keep the curtain black, you must use an exposure that is less than that indicated by three or four stops.

A white subject, on the other hand, may need three or more stops exposure than that shown. Learning to predict whether or not you need to adjust the recommended exposure, and by how much, only takes a little experience. For mainly dark subjects, you should normally give less exposure than the meter suggests by using a smaller aperture or a faster shutter speed or both. For mainly light subjects the opposite is true.

Tone cards

One valuable technique for ensuring that important areas of the picture are correctly exposed, whether in shadow or light, dark or light coloured, is to measure exposure against a reference tone.

This reference tone may be anything that corresponds to the subject. If shooting distant grassy hills, for instance, you can point the meter at the grass nearby. Providing the lighting is identical, the meter reading for the grass gives the right exposure for the distant hills.

Similarly, you can point the meter at your hand to get a reading for a portrait—again providing the lighting on the hand is identical to the light on the subject. This can be useful when shooting in a hurry or when you cannot move near enough to the subject to take a close-up reading. Many news photographers prepare their exposure in this way, while waiting for a celebrity to emerge from a building.

One of the most useful reference tones is a grey card and Kodak produce a neutral, 18 per cent reflector card for just this purpose. In the final picture, this card would come out medium grey if given the correct exposure. Exposing for this grey card gives a good range of tones either side of a medium grey. It may miss out on detail in the extreme highlights or dark shadows, but ensures that the negative is neither very thin nor very dense.

Some photographers also use a white card in some circumstances. This provides a highlight reading. The highlights will be properly exposed on black and white film if you give about 3 stops more exposure than indicated when you point the meter at the card. It may be particularly valuable when using colour slide film and helps to avoid over-exposing the highlights. It can also be valuable in very low light conditions when your meter is insufficiently sensitive to give a reading.

Subject brightness range

Exposure adjustment in f-stops	Brightness level	Typical subject
+3	Diffuse highlights	White clouds, snow, white paint
+2	Light tones	Very pale skin, light blue sky, dry white sand
+1	Medium light tones	Pale skin, weathered wood, foliage, red brick, deep blue sky
0	Middle grey	Kodak neutral test card
−1	Medium dark tones	Dark skin, dark foliage, tree trunks
−2	Dark tones	Very dark skin, most dark clothing
−3	Very dark tones	Textured black objects
−4	Black	Untextured black

To use this table, take a light reading from a subject of about the same tone as one of those listed in the right-hand column. The exposure adjustment that needs to be applied to correctly expose the subject is listed in the left-hand column. These figures are only approximate and may vary in individual cases.

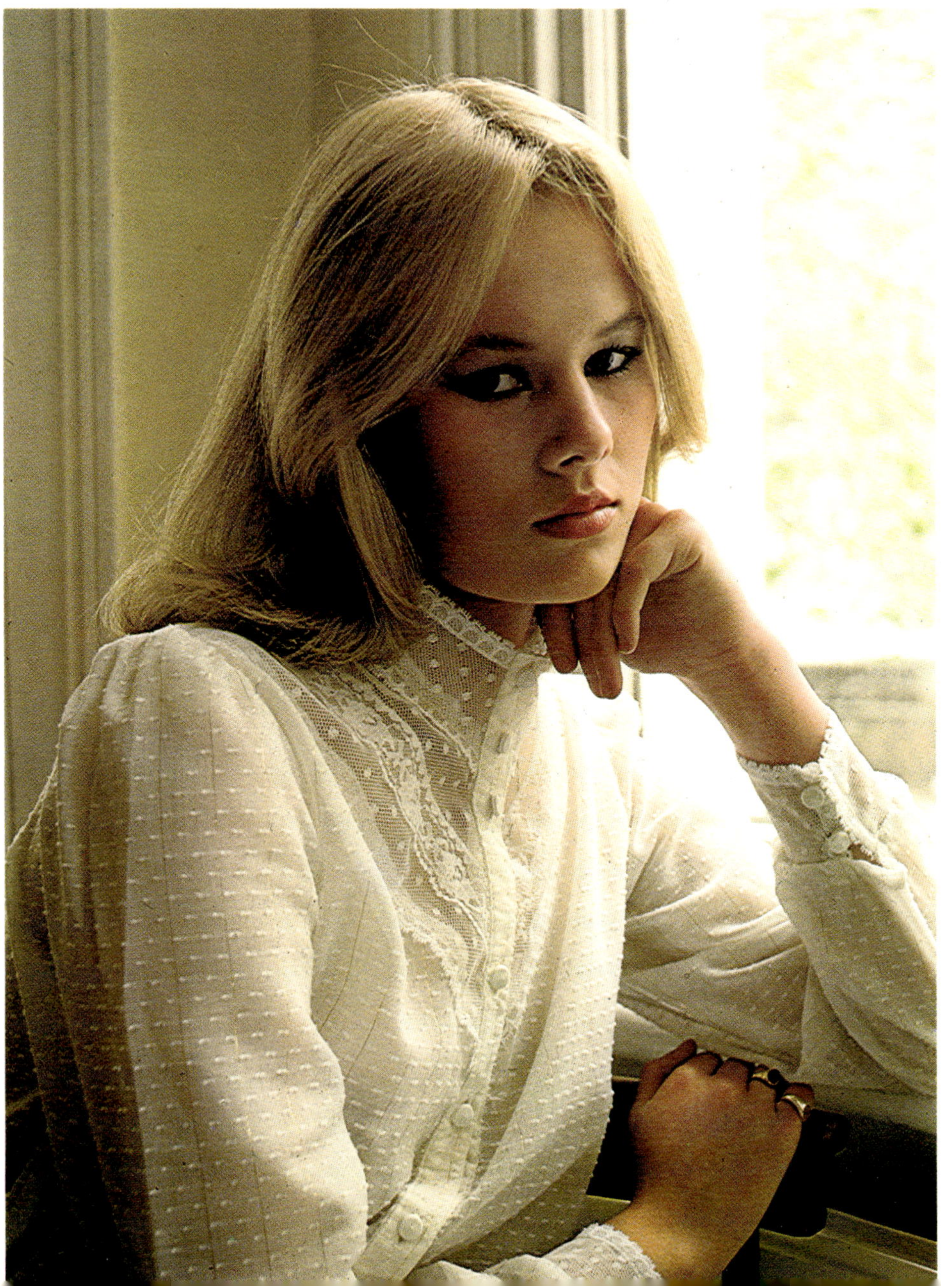

Advanced metering

Experienced photographers often use complicated systems to determine the correct exposure. Such methods as the Zone System and the YOB System are ways of working out the precise effects of exposure on the final picture. The Zone System is dealt with more fully in the next section, but such systems generally mean taking several brightness measurements from various parts of the scene, usually with a spot meter that takes exposure readings from a very small area. The different brightnesses of the scene are then related to the way they will appear in the final print or slide.

For example, if the photographer knows that pale skin tones usually look best in the print if they have been given twice as much exposure as a neutral subject, such as a Kodak grey card, then he can simply take a reading from a skin tone and set an exposure that is one stop higher than that indicated by the meter. With the exposure needed for this important tone known, the photographer can then determine which other tones will be over- or underexposed. Then, adjustments to the composition of the picture or the lighting, if some important detail of the subject needs to be brought into the brightness range of the film, can be made. More advanced applications of these methods may even involve adjustments to the development time given to the film in order to adjust the contrast of the picture. The accompanying table uses information determined by Kodak, and shows the relative brightness of several subjects lit by the sun. Use the table to work out the exposure compensation you need to apply to a meter reading from any part of your subject.

The zone system

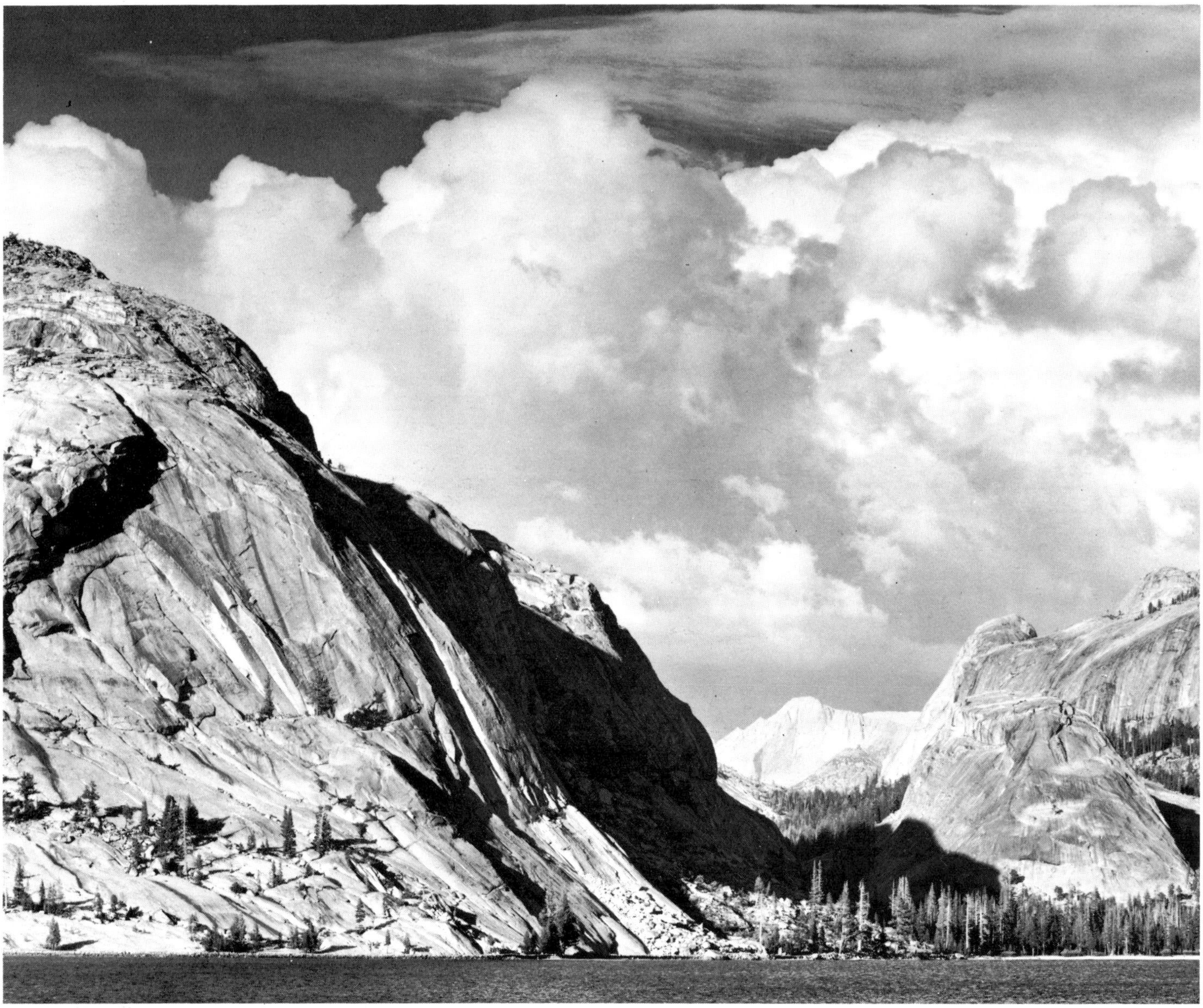

Fine print *By using the zone system with large format film, Ansel Adams achieved superb quality in his prints*

Of all the techniques for metering and exposure, the zone system is the most advanced—and the most complicated. Originally developed by Ansel Adams in the 1940s, it is intended mainly for black and white work, and involves preliminary darkroom work to set up the system. But once you have mastered the system, you will find that your understanding of exposure and your control of tones is much better.

The system is based on a scale of fixed tones—or *zones*—each of which is given a number (see box). By relating zones in the subject to tones which will appear in the final print, and relating both to an exposure meter reading, it is possible to finely control the range of tones in your pictures, and so get the most out of the materials. To enable you to do this, however, the processing and printing procedures must be standardized. And even the film speed may have to be altered to suit your own set-up and equipment.

First steps

Start in the darkroom to see what information a normally developed negative produces. Mark on the enlarger column a height for the enlarger which produces a convenient print size. Marking it allows you to repeat the test accurately, though you should also make extensive notes of everything that you do.

Having chosen a convenient aperture —say *f*/8—make a test strip using the unexposed edge of a negative or, better still, an unexposed frame. This means that the density of the negative is just base density plus fog. It is important, though, that the film stock and development are strictly standardized.

Make the test on grade two or three paper (whichever you use, you should use the same grade for all future prints). Give several exposures, increasing by two seconds each time, and develop fully. When dry, examine the result under a bright light. If the exposure is about right, at some point the tone steps become dense black and indistinguishable from each other. This is the deepest black of which your system is capable—zone 0. The exposure time for the first of these dense black tones is your standard printing or *standard negative exposure time*. Depending on the enlargement and your equipment it will be about ten seconds.

Having found the standard print time, you must now determine the correct film speed to use with your system, and this is done by producing a mid grey print. In effect, this calibrates your exposure meter and camera.

Set up a sheet of plain white or grey card under even illumination. Out of doors on an overcast day is ideal, provided the light level is constant. Take a reading with your usual meter at the film manufacturer's speed rating, making sure that the meter reads from the card only. Move in close if necessary, but try to standardize your procedure so that you can repeat it.

The meter will suggest an exposure which would make the card mid grey in the print, which is precisely what you want. Take a number of shots of the card at different exposures—about two stops either side of the metered reading, in half stop increments, should be sufficient. Try to keep the shutter speed constant—though it may be worth running the test several times with different shutter speeds as a check for any inaccuracies in the camera. Develop and fix using your standard procedure.

Now print the resulting negatives at the previously determined standard printing time. Compare the prints with an 18 per cent grey card and find the one which comes closest in tone. Providing you know which negative this print is made from and what exposure it had, you can determine your personal film speed, relevant to your equipment and processing. For example, if the nearest print came from the negative which was given double the metered exposure, then the true film speed should be one stop less than the recommended rating —say 64 ASA (ISO) in place of 125 ASA. This sort of adjustment is quite common with black and white film (though not so usual with colour).

At this point it is useful to make a *zone ruler*. This is a scale which shows you what the zones look like with your usual printing paper. Making such a scale involves shooting the grey card again. This time the first exposure should give four or five stops underexposure, to give zone 0 or 1 (in 35 mm photography zones 0 and 1 tend to merge due to the limited tonal range of most films). Make nine or ten exposures, giving one stop extra exposure each time. Once again it is best if you can keep the exposure time standard—preferably around 1/60 second, but in any case less than one second to avoid reciprocity failure.

Develop and print as for the other tests. The result is a series of prints from deepest black to pure white demonstrating the full range of tones. Trimmed neatly, these can serve as a reminder of the tones your equipment will produce. Of particular interest are the differences visible between zones 1, 2 and 3, and

Making a zone ruler

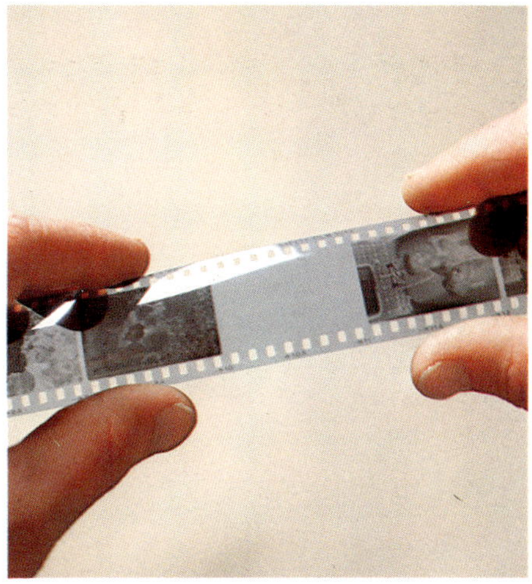

1 *Use a blank frame on a normally developed film. This gives you the minimum density (film base plus fog) which you will encounter in your negatives*

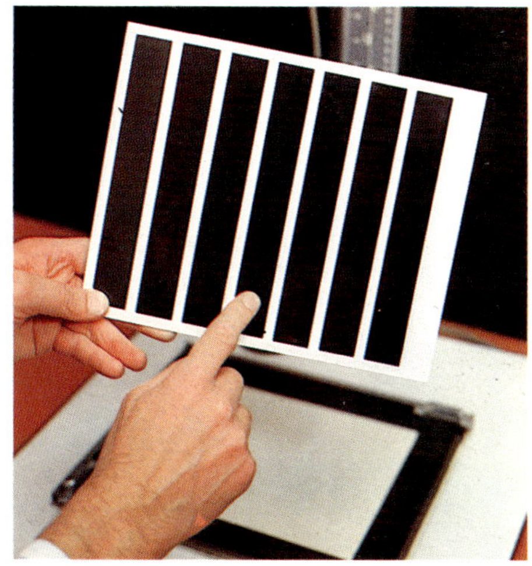

2 *Make a series of test prints, noting the exposure time for each. Your standard exposure time is that which produces the first maximum black*

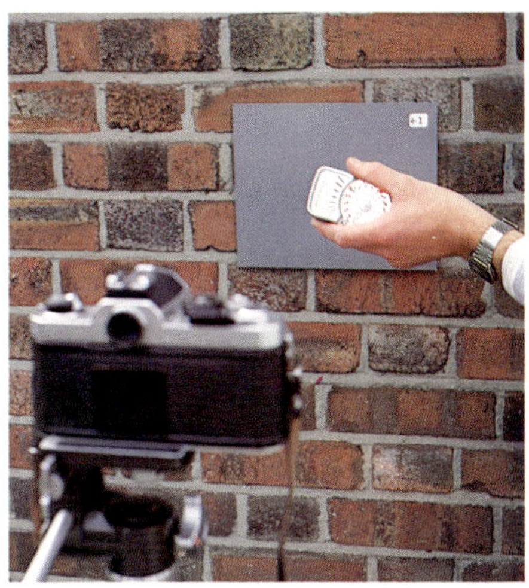

3 *Next, take pictures of a standard grey card at the exposure suggested by a meter and bracketed exposures, marking in the frame the compensation given*

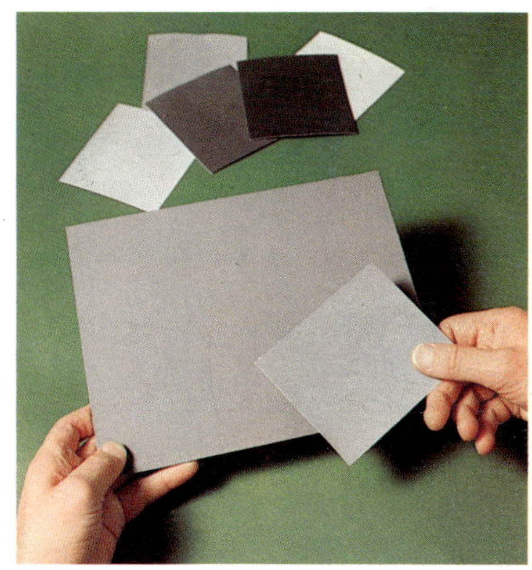

4 *Using the standard printing time, make a set of prints and find the one closest to the grey card. This shows any necessary changes to the film speed rating*

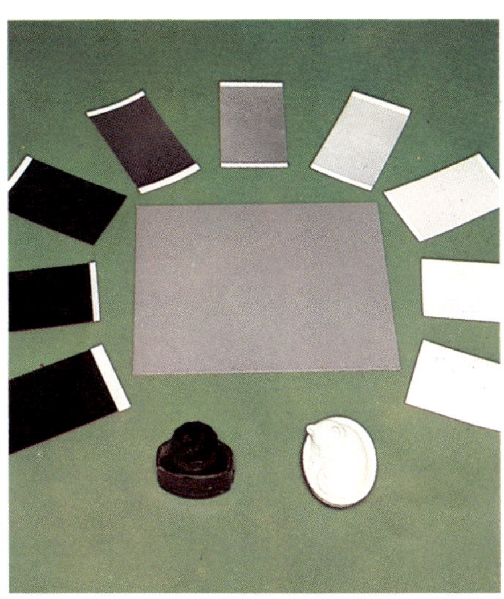

5 *Using bracketed exposures in the camera and the grey card as the subject you can make a set of prints from white to black at one stop intervals—the zone ruler*

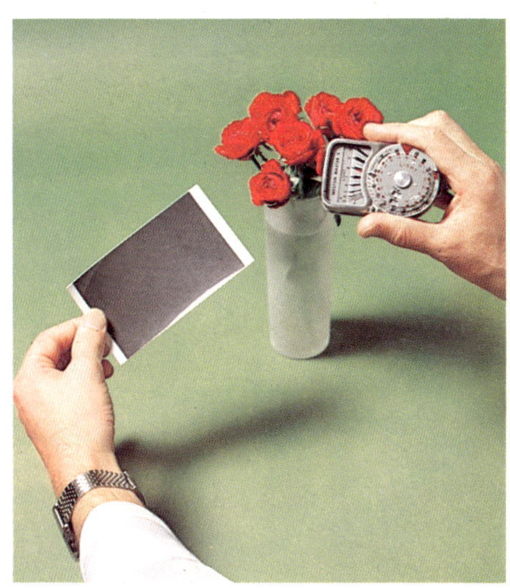

6 *Use the zone ruler to decide what tone you want an object to be. Then meter the object and use the index mark on the dial corresponding to that zone*

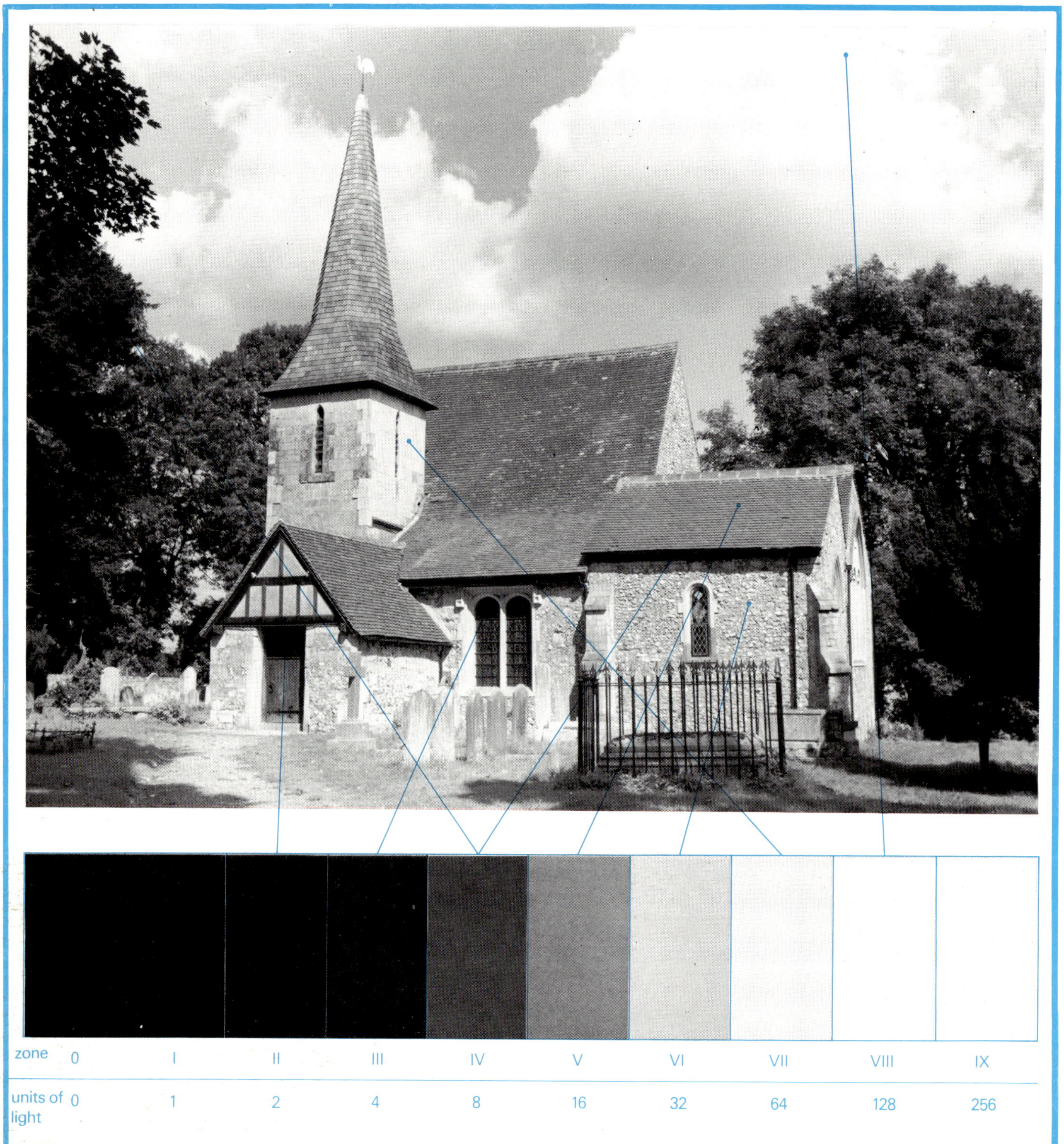

Note: rendering of sky here is between zones V and VI, achieved with a yellow filter

zones 7, 8 and 9.

All of this assumes normal development in fresh developer. Even so, it sometimes happens that the zone ruler is not quite right. You might find, for example, that although zone 5 is a reasonably good match to the grey card and zone 0 (or 1) is a good deep black, zone 9 may not be pure white. This implies that the development should be increased slightly to produce a denser negative result for the highlights. This slightly alters the density of zone 5, but hardly changes the darkest zones at all.

Whenever you have a few frames left over at the end of a roll of film, use them to experiment. Try over- and under-developing by various percentages and see what the effect is on another zone ruler series. Determine what development times enable you to keep zone 0 black, but move the higher zones up or down the brightness scale by one zone or more. Having done this, you can apply the results in the field—for example, when you need lower contrast with contrasty subjects.

Using this method to control contrast is much more accurate and predictable than any other technique—certainly much better than just guessing, which is what many photographers do. These procedures may seem complicated, but they are an important foundation, allowing you to predict what the result will be when you make the actual camera exposure.

Using the system

Compared with setting it up, using the zone system is fairly simple. You must be well acquainted with the print zones, and it is a good idea to carry the zone ruler with you, especially when you first use the system.

Zones and tones

The zone system divides the intensities of the objects in any scene into a number of bands, or *zones*, each double the brightness of the previous zone. The zones are numbered from 0 to 9 as follows:

Shadows

0 The deepest black of which the paper is capable
1 The darkest tone distinguishable from black, but without texture visible
3 Adequate texture in dark materials

Middle greys

4 Dark mid tones, such as dark leaves or shadows in portraits
5 Standard middle grey—18 per cent reflectance. Clear blue north sky
6 Light mid tone. Average white skin in sunlight or shadows in snow

Highlights

7 Very light areas, but with texture clearly visible
8 Almost white, with very little or no texture. Brightest reflections in face
9 Pure paper base white with no detail. Snow in sunlight and bright reflections in, for example, chrome

This scale represents a tonal range of 512:1 for the negative, which is reduced to about 50:1 in the print. It is possible to adapt the zone system for use with colour transparency film, but you will find it necessary to use a different set of zones. Transparency film records a tonal range of only five stops, so the zones above should be grouped in pairs (0 combined with 1, 2 with 3, and so on). You should also use a more limited range of index marks on the exposure meter itself.

The best approach is to use a meter which has a range of exposure index marks, such as the famous Weston Master. These marks represent zones 1 to 8. The absence of marks for zones 0 and 9 is not a problem as these zones are simply pure black and pure white, and will rarely need to be metered for. In any case, with 35 mm photography, zones 0 and 1 often merge, as do zones 8 and 9.

The basic metering method is to first decide what zone you want a particular object tone to appear in. Say, for example, you want a flower to reproduce as zone 3. You should meter from the flower going very close if necessary to avoid metering other objects as well. Then use the mark corresponding to zone 3 as your exposure index.

The other object tones will arrange themselves according to their brightnesses relative to the flower. But you may find that the range of brightnesses is too great, or that you lose detail in another important object.

It is worth, therefore, taking readings from the brightest and darkest objects in which you want detail to appear. If both of these fall outside the normal range of zones you should either reduce development to compress the tonal range, or be prepared to sacrifice detail.

Alternatively, you may find that the range of zones is not very great. The brightness range might only be from 2 to 6, for example. In this case you could increase development slightly. But whenever you alter development, it should always be done according to previously made tests.

Another problem is that the zones might go off the scale at just one end. Putting the flower on zone three may only give you a range of zones from 0 to 5. In this case it may be wise to change the flower to zone 4 or 4½. On the other hand, such a limited tonal range is not always a problem, particularly if you actually want a low key picture (high key shots are obtained in a similar way). Although it may seem tempting to compensate for contrast problems by using different paper grades, the point of the zone system is to get the best possible negative, so that such compromises do not have to be made. Only this way can you get perfect exposures.

Using the zone system with flash

The zone system can help predict how fill-in flash will operate. Consider trying to photograph a person while the light is harsh. The meter indicates a difference of three stops between the highlight and shadow details. If the brighter parts of the face are placed on zone VI as they should be, the shadows will fall on zone III—almost featureless. If a flash gun is used to add light to the shadows a simple diagram can be drawn to show what will happen. A flash gun at normal power will give 16 units of light contribution to the scene—in other words a zone V amount.

zone No.	I	II	III	IV	V	VI	VII
equivalent units of light	1	2	4	8	16	32	64
metered subject			shadow			highlight	
add flash, 16 units			16			16	
Total resulting			20			48	

The facial highlights are now at 48 units, about zone VI½ whereas the shadows have moved proportionally more, from 4 to 20 units, ending up on zone V½. The overall exposure could be cut ½ stop to place highlights in zone VI.

Just over a stop difference between highlight and shadows may be thought too little (too much fill in) so draw another diagram to find out what will happen if a half power flash is applied. Half power equals 8 units of light.

zone No.	I	II	III	IV	V	VI	
units of light	1	2	4	8	16	32	64
metered subject			shadow			highlight	
add flash, 8 units			8			8	
Total resulting			12			40	

The difference between the two is just under two zones, about correct, and the added light would not require a decrease in exposure as between 32 and 40 units is only a quarter stop

Ansel Adams

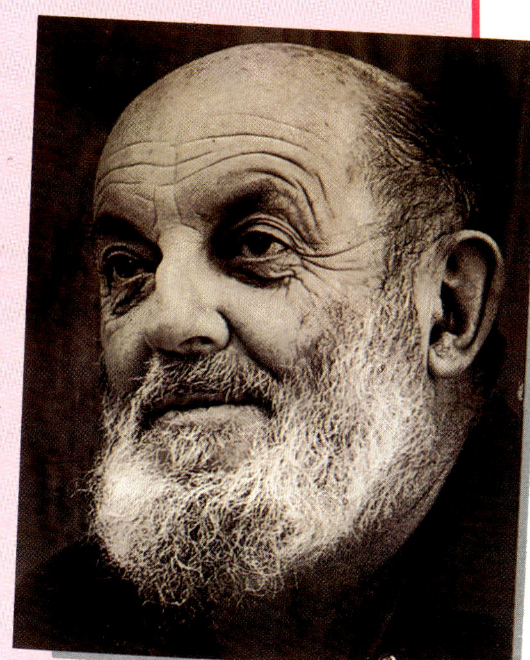

Ansel Adams (right) was the father of the zone system. Using this system enabled him to produce pictures with stunning tonal ranges which, when combined with his undoubted creative talents, resulted in prints with great intensity and power. Original Adams prints are among the most expensive on the market, some fetching as much as a luxury car.

To get the utmost quality from his b & w film he used large format cameras, usually 5 × 4 and 10 × 8 inch. But his introduction to photography was much less auspicious.

It was in 1916, at the age of 14, that he first took up photography. His imagination was fired by the great vistas of the Yosemite Valley in California, and he attempted to record these using a box Brownie. He studied photography assiduously and quickly mastered the basic techniques. By the mid 1930s he had made his mark as a leading American photographer, highlighted by a one man exhibition at Alfred Stieglitz's gallery, *An American Place*.

The main influence on Adams was Paul Strand, and he collaborated with people like Edward Weston, who all shared a love of the 'fine print'. Two of his most important photographs—*Banner Peak* (1923) and *The Half Dome* (1926)—were steps on the way to realizing that the photographic medium is a craft which needs to be carefully controlled and understood. To this end he developed the zone system—a method which demands that the photographer be aware of the precise effects of exposure and development.

The zone system has been known to inspire almost fanatical devotion in some of its most ardent followers, who tend to rate technical quality above aspects such as interesting subject matter, or good composition. Nevertheless the Zone system remains, forty years on, the standard technique for ultimate print quality.

CHAPTER 4
FOCUSING
Where to focus

When you first start taking pictures, your only thoughts about focusing are probably along the lines of 'Is it in focus, or is it out of focus?' But it does not take very long before you begin to realize that focusing a camera is not quite that simple. Unless the subject is distant scenery with nothing in the foreground of the picture, there will always be some objects which are closer to the camera than others. Under most circumstances, you must decide which part of the scene is to appear most sharp on the film.

In simple cases, such as a figure standing against a nondescript background, the decision of what to focus on will be simple — you can just focus on the figure. But in a more complex situation, where no one part of the subject seems more important than any other, and there is not enough depth of field to include everything it can be difficult to decide what to focus on.

The way you focus the camera will depend on what the picture is for, and which part of the picture is most important. For example, the kind of photograph that an archaeologist requires of Pompeii will be altogether different from the picture that a holidaymaker may take of the same subject. The archaeologist will need a picture that gives the maximum amount of information about the buildings and the setting, whereas someone who is seeing the sights is more interested in

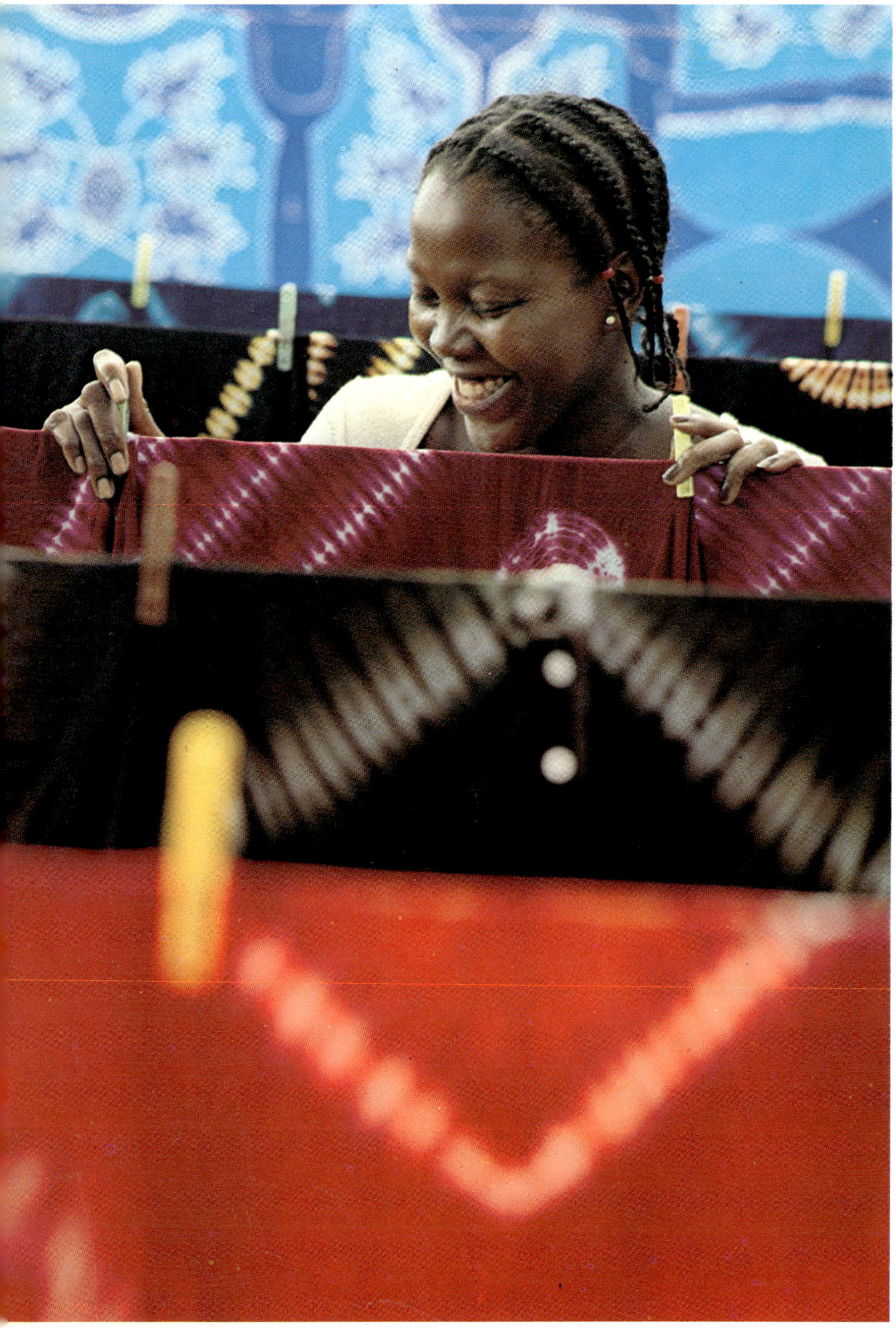

Washing *By deliberately restricting depth of field with a narrow aperture, you can focus on a single part of the subject*

Chairs *Careful use of the depth of field and focus point allows comprehensive focus of near and far objects*

Crowd *Isolating a figure. By focusing on a single figure, it is possible to pull one face out of a large crowd*

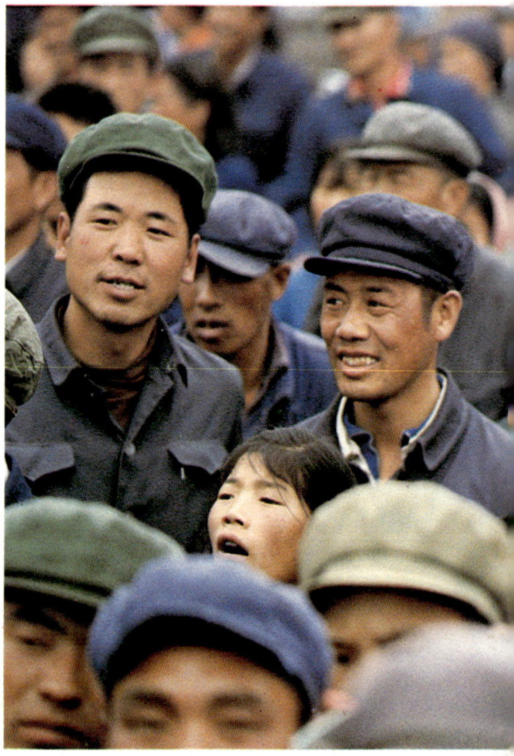

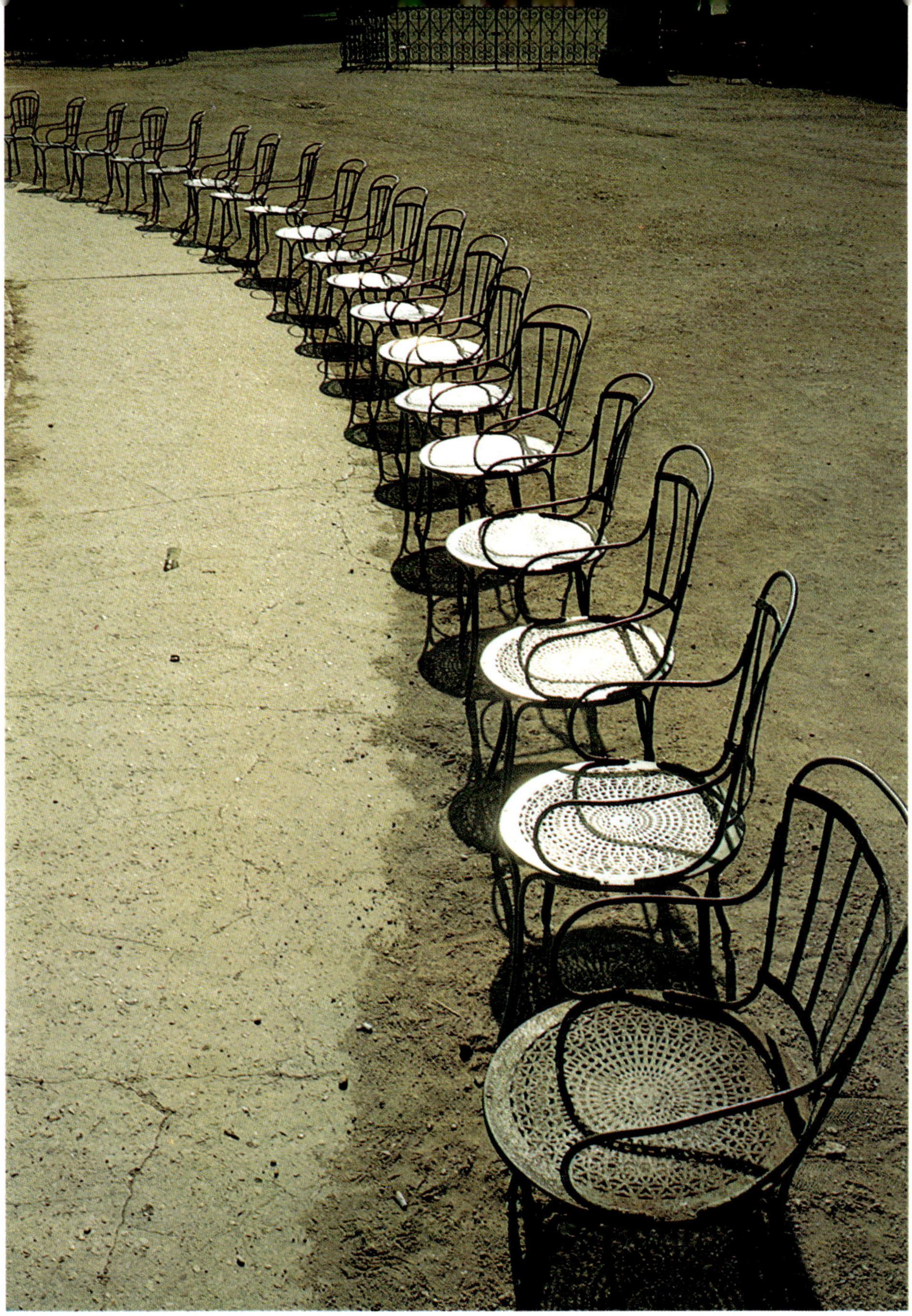

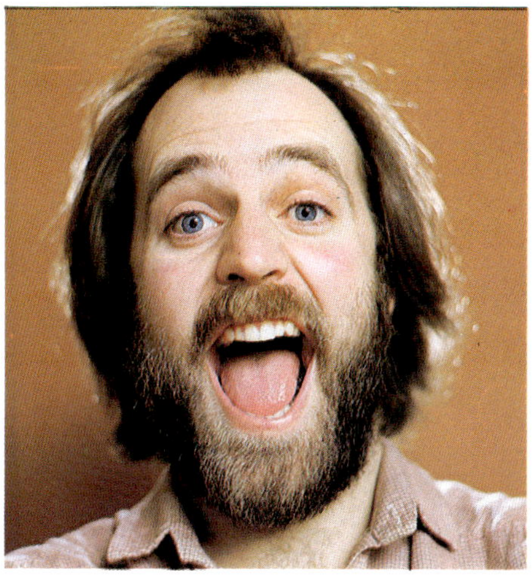

Eyes in focus *Where there is not enough depth of field to keep the whole face in focus, focusing on the eyes alone does usually produce an acceptable portrait*

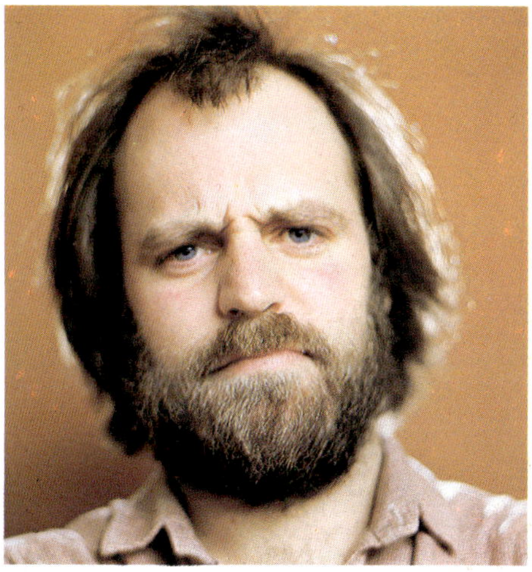

Unsharp eyes *On the other hand, a portrait in which some other part of a sitter's face is in focus, and the eyes are not, tends to look distinctly odd*

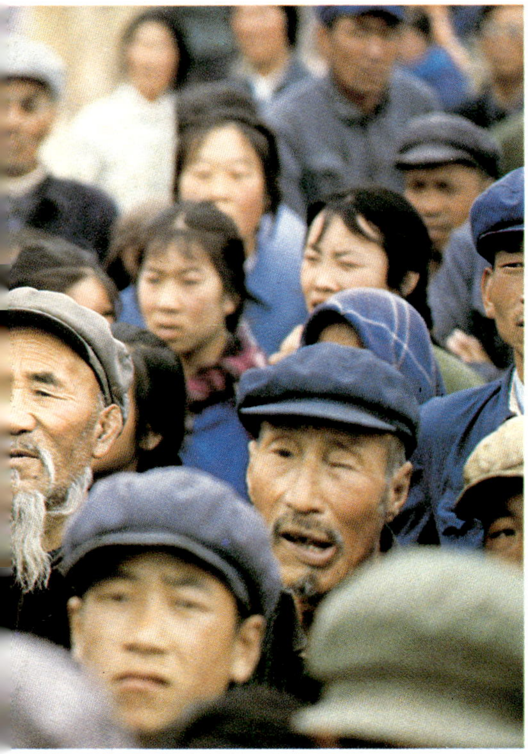

taking a picture which will bring back the atmosphere of the place, than in creating a strictly literal interpretation.

These requirements will dictate what the two photographers choose to focus on. The archaeologist will try to make sure that absolutely everything in the picture appears pin-sharp on the film. He might do this by estimating the distance to the nearest point of the picture, and to the most distant part of the scene, and then consult the depth of field scale on the camera lens to focus on a point between these two distances. When the lens is stopped down to a small aperture, both near and far points will be in focus.

The kind of picture that is suitable as an accurate, scientific record will, however, often look out of place in a picture album. Such pictures are often sterile and lifeless, despite their technical perfection. In photographing the same scene, a tourist may well spot a particularly interesting feature of a building and decide to emphasize this, rather than concentrating on getting everything perfectly sharp. In this case, it would be best to focus carefully on the feature that is to be the centre of attention, and use a wide aperture to restrict depth of field.

What you focus on will depend on which part of the picture is most important, and what you wish to include or eliminate. Do not forget that those parts of the picture which are unsharp are not necessarily wasted. You can use out of focus portions of the image to frame a part of the subject that you wish to emphasize, or to provide an impression of depth in the picture.

The way you focus the camera, and how much of the picture is in focus, can be broadly divided into *selective focusing*, where you use shallow depth of field to isolate the subject, and *comprehensive focusing* where maximum use is made of the available depth of field.

Selective focusing

It is always necessary to be selective in focusing, so this term is misleading, but it is generally taken to mean the use of shallow depth of field to isolate or emphasize the subject. This may be a decision that is taken for a specific reason—such as a distracting background to the picture. It may be forced upon the photographer, for example by poor light where it is not possible to close down the aperture of the lens to produce greater depth of field. The subject may be moving quickly, so a fast shutter speed is needed. In order to give adequate exposure, it would be necessary in this case to use a wide aperture.

All modern SLR cameras focus at full aperture, so the image in the viewfinder when you are taking the picture will be more selective than the final picture. Unless you are taking photographs at full aperture, there will be more depth of field when the lens is closed down to the working aperture. If you want to produce a blurred foreground or background, then it will be necessary to close the lens down in order to preview the depth of field. Most manual and semi-automatic SLR cameras allow you to do this, usually in the form of a catch or switch on the camera body. When pressed, this closes down the lens to the working aperture. If you are using a viewfinder camera, there is no alternative to using the depth of field scale.

When shooting portraits, it is very useful to be able to eliminate a background, particularly if the pictures are taken in a city setting where it is often difficult to find an attractive backdrop against which to take the pictures. A telephoto lens (which has very shallow depth of field) will do this more effectively than a standard lens, and the opposite applies to wide angle lenses. These have more depth of field, and consequently are not as useful when using selective focus techniques.

In most cases, the rule of thumb 'focus on the most important part of the picture' will apply, but there are one or two instances where this will not give you enough guidance about what part of the subject to focus on. If, for example, you are shooting portraits at a wide aperture, depth of field is often so shallow that only part of the subject's face will be in focus. In this case always focus on your sitter's eyes, unless you have a particular reason for wanting the eyes out of focus. Surprisingly, a portrait in which only the eyes are in focus will often be acceptable, whereas one in which only the tip of the subject's nose is sharp will look ridiculous.

There are cases of portraits in which this rule could be broken successfully. One such case would be a picture of a potter or other craftworker. Here you might choose to focus on the hands, and let the whole face fall outside the depth of field of the lens. This would draw attention to the hands at the expense of the subject's face.

If you are photographing a landscape which seems to lack a focal point, you might consider focusing on an isolated tree or wall in the foreground, and using a wide aperture. This would confine attention to one part of the picture by the use of selective focusing. It would also prevent the viewer's eye from wandering all over the picture, as it might if you were to adopt the more obvious solution of focusing on the scene behind.

A background or foreground does not have to be in perfect focus in order to set the scene of a picture, and by isolating the main subject using selective focusing, the surroundings can give an impression of the setting without being so clear on the picture as to intrude. Images of cars and buildings in a city street do not have to be absolutely sharp in order to be recognizable, and will still add atmosphere to a picture in which the principal subject is isolated by selective focusing.

Similarly, photographs in a garden do

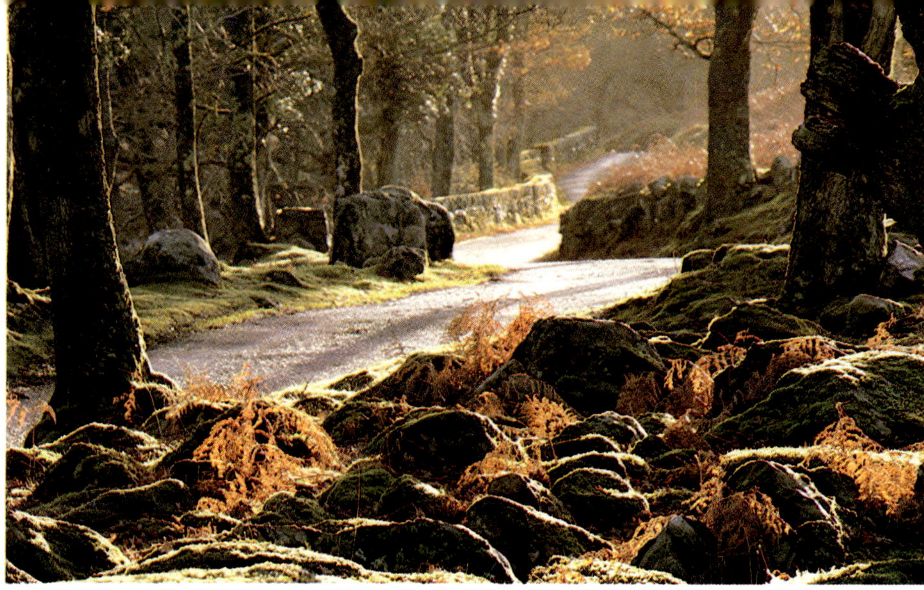

Centre of interest *With no obvious subject matter, choose a feature which will most attract the attention in a scene*

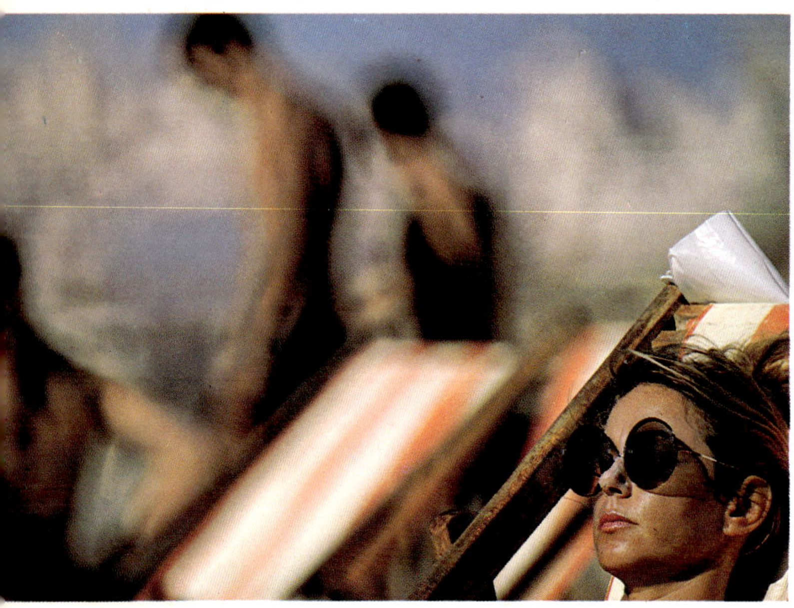

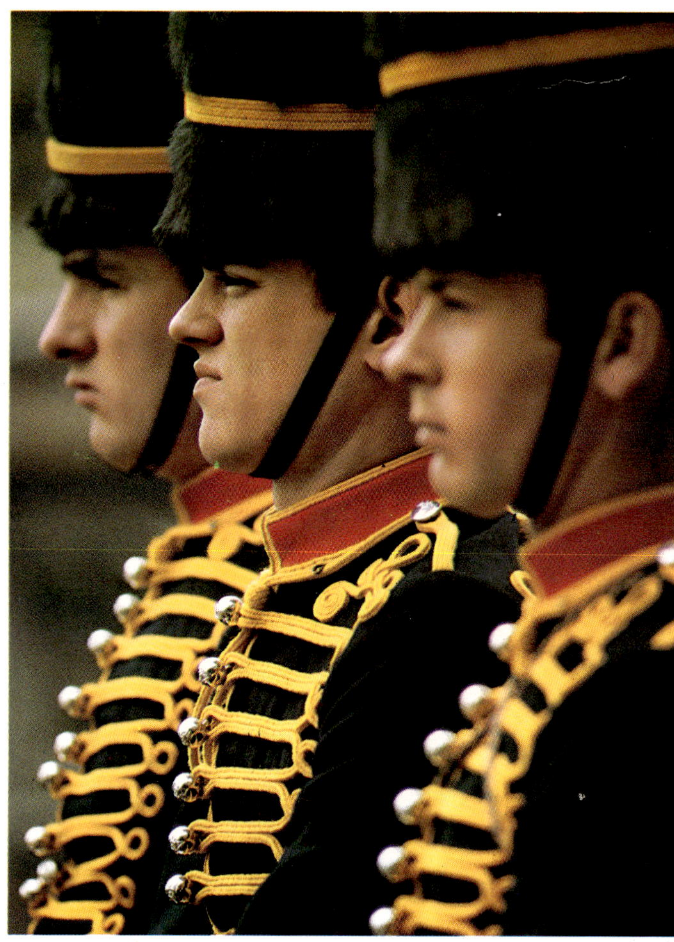

Groups of people *When there are large numbers of people in a picture, it can often look cluttered. By focusing on one figure, the beach scene becomes a backdrop, and the soldier ceases to be so anonymous*

not have to show every flower head sharply drawn in order to get across the idea of flower beds. Out of focus flowers will appear as blobs of bright colour which do not draw attention away from the gardener in the middle of them.

Comprehensive focusing

Once you know a little about depth of field, obtaining sharp focus throughout the picture seems an easy matter, but it depends as much on where in the picture you focus as it does on the aperture that you use. Ironically, when photographing a distant scene the best point on which to focus is not infinity.

If you are taking pictures at a medium aperture such as *f*/8, and you focus the lens on infinity, depth of field will extend from a point closer than infinity, around nine metres on a standard lens, to some point beyond infinity. Any depth of field that extends beyond infinity serves no useful purpose. Instead of wasting it it is possible to focus on a point closer than infinity. This brings the near point of sharp focus closer to the camera, while still keeping the far distance sharp. If the point of distant focus is at infinity, the lens is focused on what is called the *hyperfocal distance*. This is different for each aperture on a lens. Though it is never marked on the lens barrel, it is easy to locate—just align the infinity marking for the lens with the depth of field mark for the aperture in use, and the lens will be focused on the hyperfocal distance. For a scene that includes infinity, this will give maximum possible depth of field.

To get the maximum amount of depth of field in a picture that does not include infinity, do not simply focus on a point, because there is always more depth of field—usually about twice as much—on the far side of the point of sharpest focus than there is on the near side. Consequently, the best place to focus the lens is about one third of the way between the nearest point that has to be sharp, and the most distant point.

Wide angle lenses have much more depth of field than standard lenses. A 28 mm lens, for example, when stopped down to *f*/22, will give sharp focus from infinity to 0.6 m when focused on a point about 1.3 m from the camera. This extra depth of field can be useful in situations where it is difficult or impossible to focus, such as in a dark room when using flash.

Focusing problems

There are situations where it is impossible to focus through the lens. Sometimes the subject of the picture is reluctant to be photographed, or is camera-shy, and freezes when a camera is pointed at him. There are a number of ways of getting round the problem, besides using a wide angle lens at a small aperture. The most obvious solution is just to estimate the distance and set it on the focusing scale of the camera. If your estimates are not accurate, you could try focusing on another subject the same distance away then turn to your original subject and release the shutter.

SLR cameras are particularly difficult to focus when used in low-light conditions, or with wide angle lenses, and these are situations where rangefinder cameras excel. If you are using an SLR much of the light that enters the camera lens is absorbed by the viewing system—the mirror, prism and viewing screen. In bright light, this does not matter, but when the light gets dim it becomes increasingly difficult to focus this kind of camera. If a wide angle lens is fitted, the point of sharpest focus is often hard to locate precisely, particularly if the lens does not have a wide maximum aperture.

Rangefinder cameras such as the Leica use a viewfinder that is separate from the taking lens, and are easier to use in low light situations, since very little light is lost in the viewing system.

How to focus

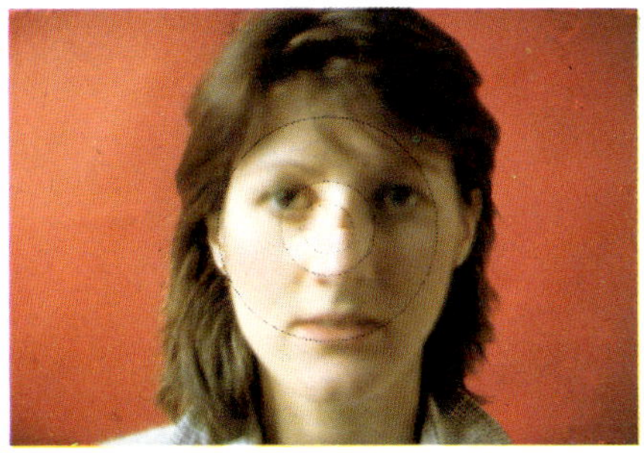

Split screen focusing 1 *Tiny prisms break up the out of focus image*

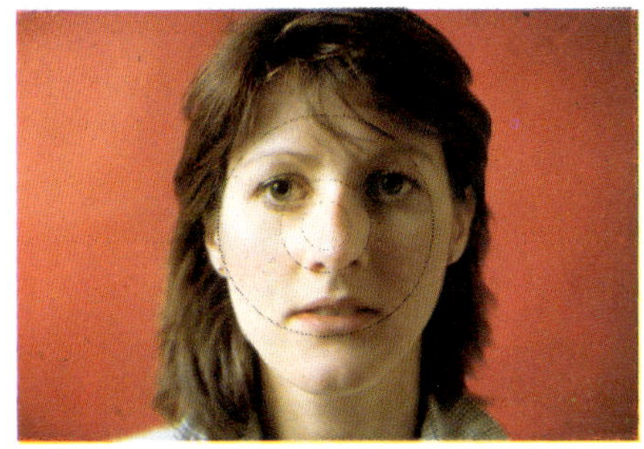

2 *The broken up image becomes smooth when the subject is in focus*

With non reflex cameras, the lens is focused by estimating or measuring the distance to the subject and then setting this on the focusing ring. With an SLR, however, you can see the scene through the lens itself. This means you can set the focus visually, adjusting the focusing ring until the subject is sharp in the viewfinder.

To focus the lens, look through the viewfinder at some clearly visible detail in the chosen subject. Then slowly turn the focusing ring one way or the other until the detail is pin sharp. The lens is now focused.

This may seem laborious at first, but you will soon find that, with practice, you can focus almost instantaneously. And providing your eyesight is good, or you use the proper corrective eyepiece, your pictures should be perfectly sharp every time.

Nevertheless, it can be difficult to focus a wide angle or standard lens in this way and most SLRs now include some type of focusing aid in the viewfinder. These are of two main types: split image screens and microprisms.

Split image focusers

The split image focuser is simply a way of showing you more clearly when the rays of light from the subject converge precisely on the focusing screen—that is, when the image is in focus. It consists of two tiny wedge-shaped prisms set into the focusing screen and relies on the way prisms bend light for its focusing effect. The two wedges slope in opposite directions, but cross in the middle at exactly the same height as the focusing screen.

When the image is in focus, the light rays converge at the same place as the prisms cross over. So the light is bent equally by each prism and the image seen on the two halves of the focuser match. When the image is out of focus, the light converges either behind or before the crossover. Either way, the images in each prism are displaced in opposite directions.

Focusing with a split image

Split image focusers are very easy to use and make focusing considerably more accurate. Simply look through the viewfinder at the small circle on the focusing screen and turn the focusing screen and turn the focusing ring in the way described above for unaided focusing. With the subject out of focus, the images in each half of the circle are offset. To focus, keep turning the focusing ring until the two images mate perfectly.

A point to remember with split image focusers is that they need a lot of light to work properly. If there is insufficient light coming through the lens, either one or both halves of the circle will black out. Generally speaking, they will not work at apertures of less than about *f*/4, even in fairly bright conditions. So this renders them inoperative with many telephoto and zoom lenses which have a maximum aperture of less. And even with a large aperture, they will not work in very low light conditions or with a dark subject— often just the times when you need them most. If you find that half of the screen *does* black out, you may be able to make it reappear by moving your eye around. But in many situations, even this will not work.

Consequently, the focusing screens of many modern SLRs include a microprism focusing aid as well. This is the shimmering ring around the outside of the split image circle. Some cameras have microprisms alone.

Microprisms

Microprisms work on much the same principle as split image focusers, but instead of using two prisms, they use many hundreds. They are so small that they cannot be resolved by the eye, but when the image is out of focus they appear to shimmer. This is due to multiple splitting of the image. When the image is focused, the microprism clears, giving an undistorted view.

Advanced focusing

Inaccurate focusing probably spoils more photographs than any other technical fault. Most modern cameras automatically set the correct exposure, but usually leave the user to set the focus. Under most conditions focusing is relatively simple—you decide what to focus on (see pages 50 to 53) and then set the appropriate distance on your lens, using whatever focusing aids may be built into your camera. However, there are occasions when the conditions or the subject make focusing difficult.

There may be times when you do not wish to make your presence obvious, such as in candid street photography. For such occasions you need a focusing method which enables you to produce a sharp image without drawing attention to the camera by holding it up to your eye and focusing it in the normal way. You may also have to deal with a rapidly moving subject, in which case you will not have time to set the focus. In low light, you may not be able even to see the subject clearly enough to focus properly. At other times, the subject itself may be the problem—its surface texture may defeat the camera's focusing aids, or it may extend beyond the depth of field of the lens you are using. While focusing in such situations is more difficult than usual, there are several techniques you can use to make it easier.

Girl on swing *With moving subjects, preset the point of sharp focus, and shoot when your subject reaches it*

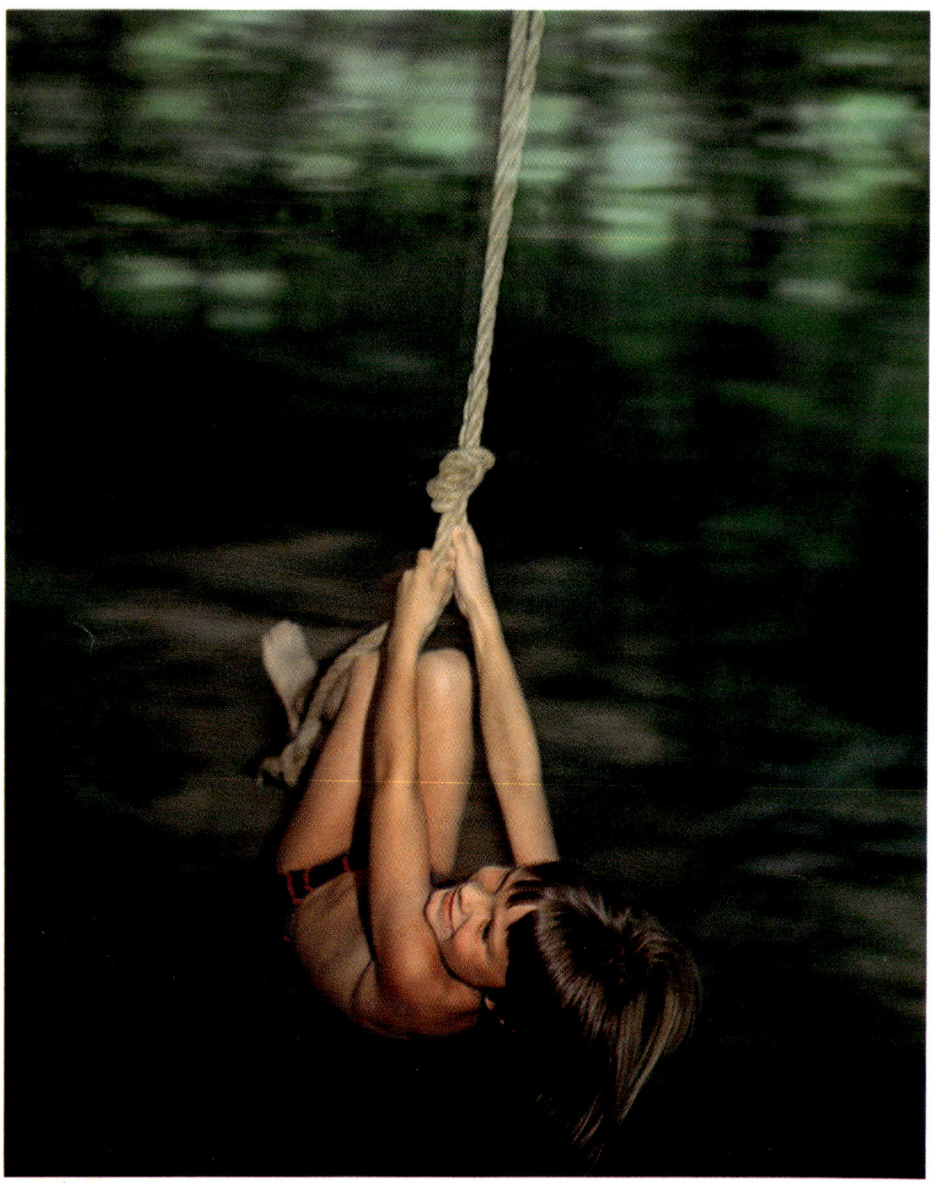

Fast focusing

Parties and street scenes are typical situations where the rapid and irregular movement of the subject can make focusing a hit-or-miss business. Indoors, low light aggravates this, and asking people to stop for the camera destroys the spontaneity of the situation.

If you are using a camera with interchangeable lenses, you can make fast focusing easier by fitting a wide angle lens. This gives you greater depth of field, so that more will be in focus, and also has the advantage that the focusing ring usually rotates through a relatively small arc, making focusing quicker. If you use high speed film with such a lens you can choose a small aperture, thus increasing your depth of field so that almost everything will be in focus.

At parties or similar gatherings, a portable flashgun fitted to your camera can allow you to set a small aperture on your normal or wide angle lens so that you need not worry about focusing at all—you just have to make sure that your subject is within the depth of field of the lens and within the range of the flash gun. If you have an automatic electronic flash, set the lens aperture to match the aperture indicated on the flash calculator dial. Usually the dial indicates a maximum distance at which the flash can be used. If your lens has a depth of field scale, set this distance on the focusing ring opposite the mark on the scale for the aperture you have set. This technique will give you maximum depth of field, allowing you to take photographs at a range of distances knowing that as much as possible will appear sharp.

Take care when using a wide angle lens and a flashgun together—you may need to fit a diffuser panel to the flash head to increase the illumination coverage and light the edges of the subject (see pages 102 to 105).

Zone focusing

For candid photography and for other occasions when you do not want to use flash, there are other ways of ensuring that the subject is kept in focus. When there is insufficient time to focus through the viewfinder in the regular way you can try adopting the method used by some manufacturers of rangefinder cameras, known as zone focusing. Instead of precise distances in feet and metres, symbols are marked on the focusing ring—a head for the close-up setting, a group of figures for the middle distance and a mountain for the infinity setting. When the lens is set for a given zone,

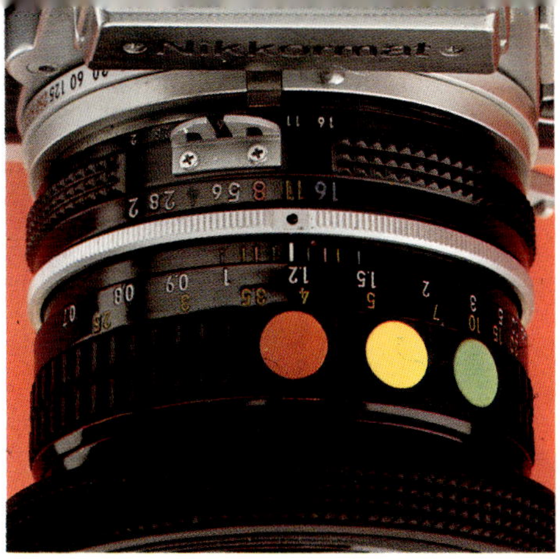

Zone 1 *Focused on 1.1 metres*

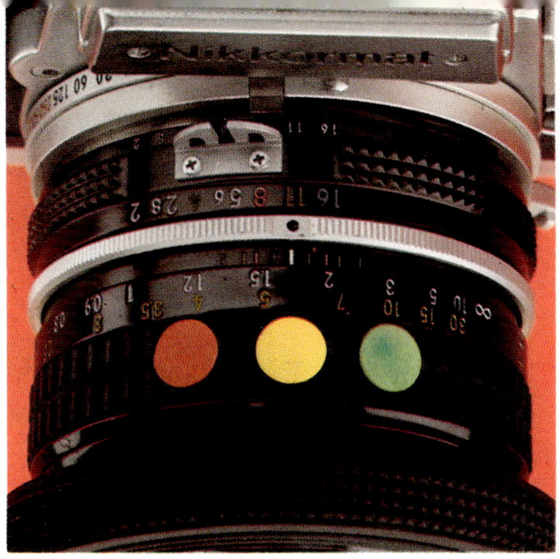

Zone 2 *Focused on 1.75 metres*

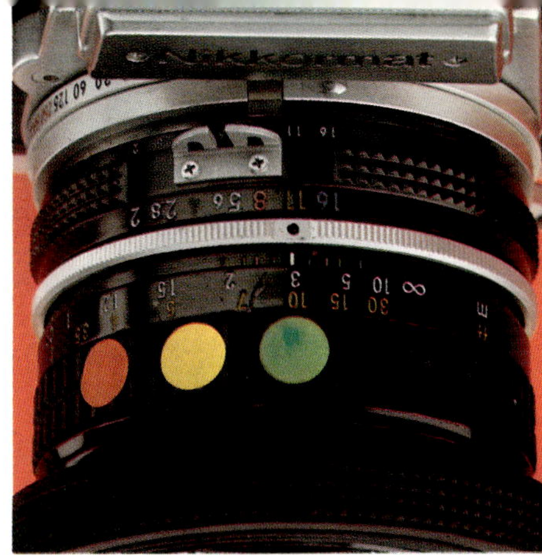

Zone 3 *Focused on 3 metres*

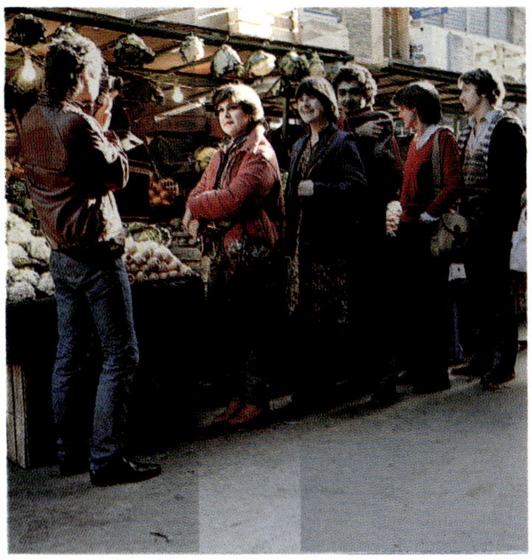

Front of queue *With the lens focused on 1.1 m, only the stallholder and the first customer are in focus*

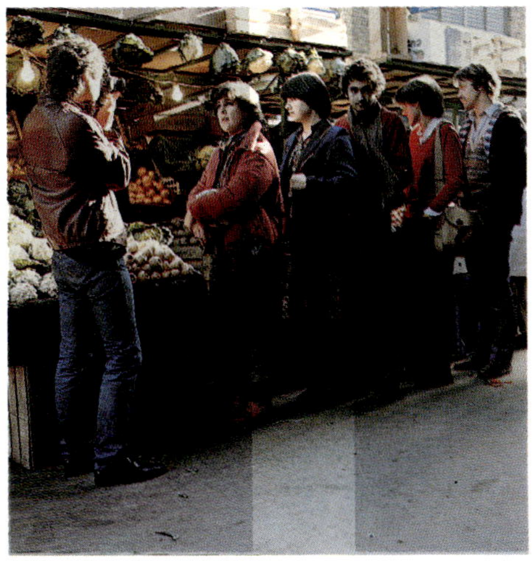

Middle of queue *The second zone of sharp focus includes only the next of the figures in the queue*

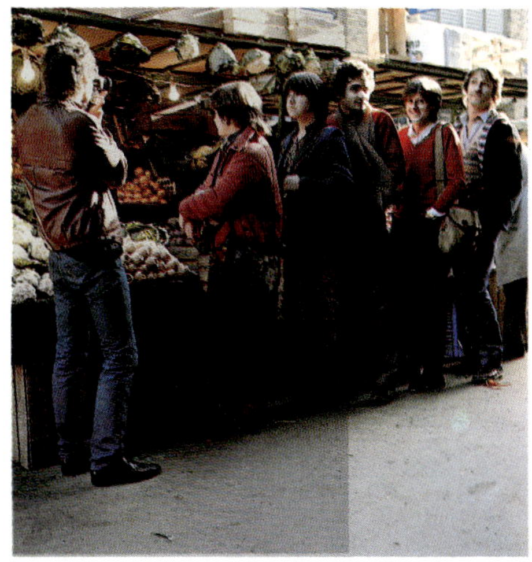

Back of queue *With the lens set to the green mark, the first two figures are unsharp, and the rest are in focus*

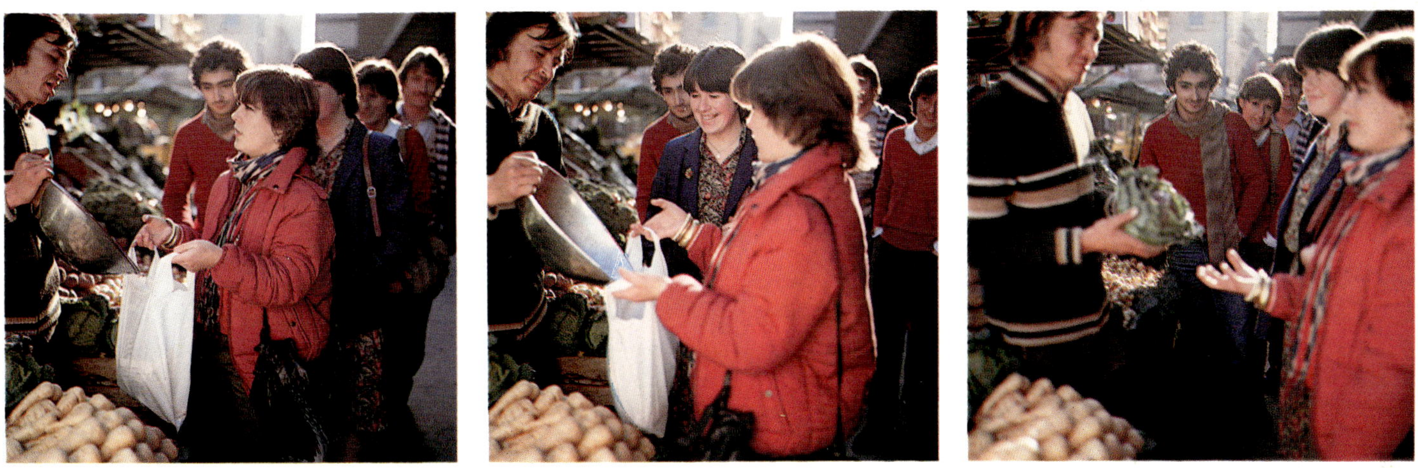

Zone focusing ***By using preset zones it is possible to make snap judgements about where to set the focusing ring without having to lift the camera conspicuously up to your eye***

all objects within the zone are sharp. Of course this system works better if you are able to benefit from the broad depth of field of a wide angle lens or a small aperture. Focusing becomes very much more difficult to accomplish with this method if a lens longer than 50 or 55 mm is used or if a normal lens is used at full aperture.

If you have a rough idea of how far away your subjects are likely to be, you can identify these distances on the focusing ring so that you can rapidly preset the focus before you raise the camera to your eye. To accomplish this, some photographers use the night photography technique described on page 95. Tape small pieces of matchstick to specific focus positions—in this case, for example, one match might indicate what is likely to be the closest distance to be used on your lens's focusing scale. This is followed by two pieces side by side at a middle distance, and three pieces at a farther distance. Rotating the focusing ring until the appropriate zone is at the 12 o'clock position and aligning the matchsticks with the index mark on the focusing scale by touch, you can set an estimated distance without even looking at your focusing scale.

All this presupposes that you are reasonably familiar with the controls of your camera so that you can handle it literally with your eyes closed. It also assumes that you can make a reasonably good estimate of the distance to your subject. This sort of ability is the result of practice. An hour or so of guessing distances and then checking them against the distances given by the focusing aids in your camera is usually enough to improve your ability considerably.

For candid shots outdoors, there are other methods often practised by photographers who specialize in catching people unawares. One method is to focus on another subject a similar distance away, then turn the camera on to the subject you are really interested in and quickly press the shutter. With a wide angle lens, you can even include people in the frame without them knowing it. They will think you are shooting past them and are unlikely to realize how much your camera is taking in. Another method involves anticipating where your subject is likely to walk into view. By prefocusing on a point on the ground and waiting for the subject to walk past that particular spot, you can take a photograph very quickly by just raising the camera to your eye at the last possible moment.

Fast moving subjects

Cars, trains, aircraft and other fast moving subjects present special focusing problems. Sometimes the subject may be moving across your field of view at an angle or at a considerable distance, and you have to successfully adjust the focus continuously to keep the subject sharp. This technique is known as follow focusing but can only be employed effectively if the subject is at a reasonable distance away. To make follow focusing easier, Novoflex manufacture a range of telephoto lenses with pistol grips to control the focus. Squeezing the control focuses the lens progressively closer, and relaxing it allows the focus to return towards infinity.

However, if the subject is close or moving more or less directly towards or away from you, you may have to preset the focus, just as for walking subjects. Find a point on the ground that the subject can be expected to pass over and focus on this. When the subject reaches this point it will be in focus.

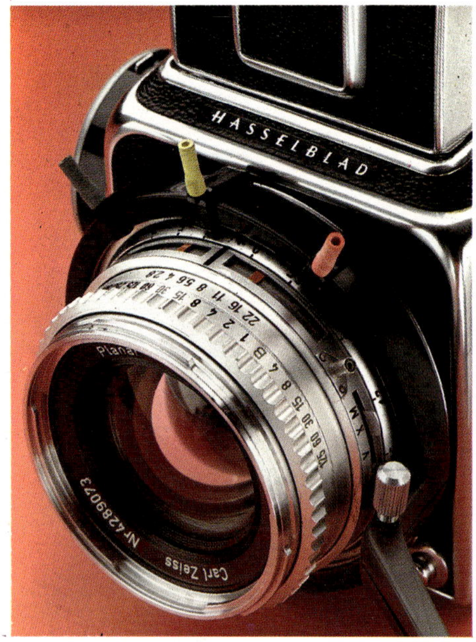

Focusing markers *Certain cameras have quick focus rings fitted with movable markers to indicate focus zones*

There is a slight complication, though—if you wait until the subject is in focus before you release the shutter, the brief time delay between pressing the shutter release button and the operation of the shutter mechanism may be enough to let the subject pass out of focus, especically if it is moving quickly. This delay is known as time parallax, and it varies in duration from camera to camera. In general SLRs have greater time parallax than rangefinder cameras since their viewing mirrors have to be raised before the shutter can operate.

The solution to the problem is to release the shutter slightly before the subject reaches the focused point. If, for instance, the subject is a racing car, you may well decide that the driver's cockpit is the most desirable position to have in focus. But if the car is coming towards you at speed, you will need to press the shutter at the moment when the nose of the car crosses the point of prefocus. This will allow for the time parallax so that the cockpit will be crossing the focusing point at the time the actual exposure is made. Consistent success can only be achieved if you practise this technique and learn from your mistakes.

Parallax focusing

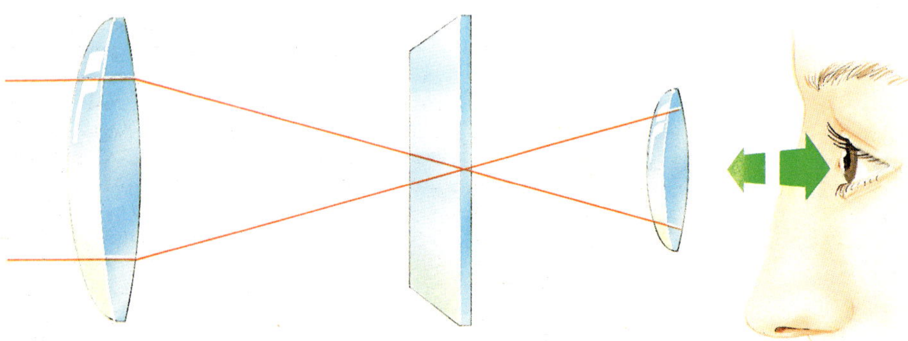

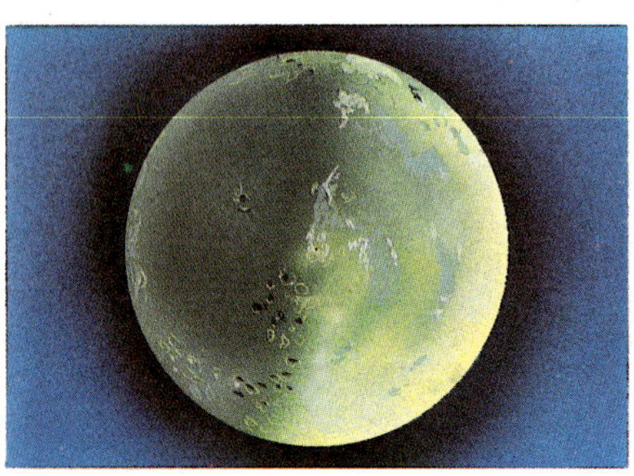

Using clear screens *In certain conditions, it may be impossible to use a matt glass screen, and instead a clear screen with cross hairs is used*

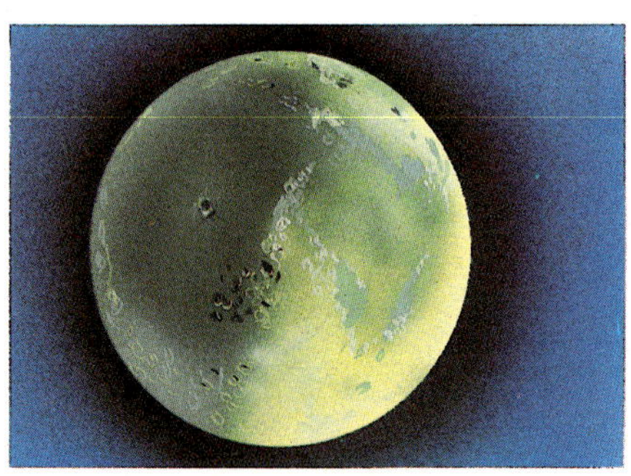

When the image of the subject is in focus, it does not move in relation to the screen if the photographer's head is rocked gently to and fro

Split image screens

The focusing aids built in to SLRs can cope with most situations. However, there are some subjects that are difficult to deal with even with the combined help of split image rangefinders, microprisms and glass focusing screens.

Cats and rabbits, for example, are often physically uncooperative—they tend not to sit still when you want them to—and their fur is difficult to focus on yet must be really sharp to be effective in a photograph. Fur is impossible to focus with split image rangefinder prisms unless it has a strong pattern. Microprisms are somewhat more effective but can be misleading when you are dealing with long-furred animals at close ranges. Try to focus on the centre of the animal rather than its outline. If you are shooting a portrait of your pet, try to focus on the eyes, just as when you photograph a person.

Some subjects can mislead your focusing system. Split image rangefinders are usually effective with subjects having strong horizontal or vertical lines on their surface, but not when the lines form a regular pattern as with striped wallpaper. In such cases you may find that you have matched the wrong lines of the pattern, giving an image that looks satisfactory in the split image prisms yet is out of focus. With such subjects you should always check your focusing on the matt glass area of your focusing screen.

One difficulty widely experienced with focusing is that one half of a split image screen may black out. This only happens with lenses of a relatively small maximum aperture. But this itself is particularly irritating since lenses with smaller apertures tend to be of longer focal lengths and require more critical focusing techniques. In some cases you will find that this difficulty can be overcome by placing your eye closer to the viewfinder or by using a rubber eyecup. However, often there is no way of improving matters and one of the other focusing aids has to be used. Usually a camera which offers a split image screen also allows focusing to be accomplished by microprisms or by the plain matt glass area of the screen. Cameras with

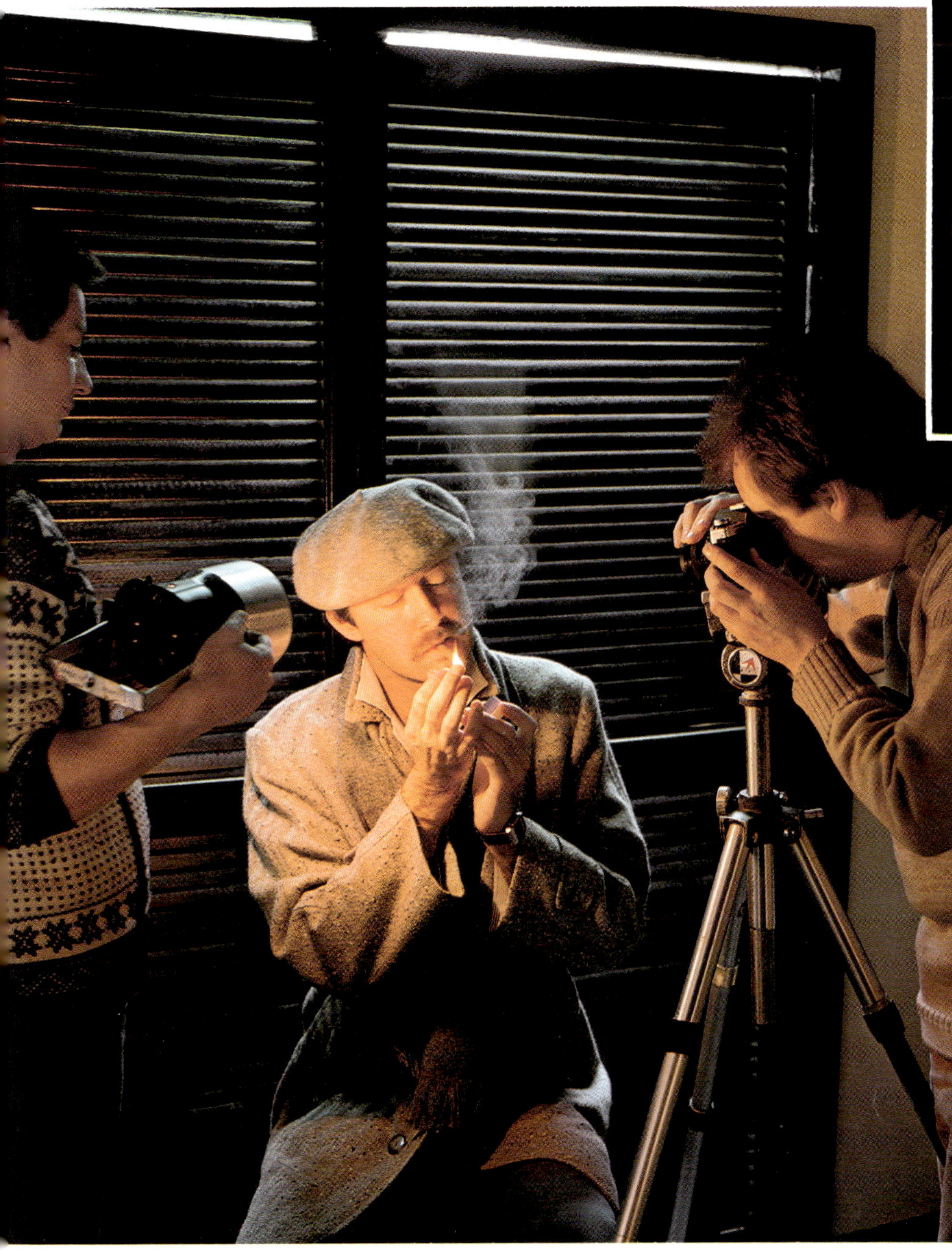

interchangeable screens can be fitted with the appropriate screen which will make focusing much easier (see page 13) for certain subjects.

Using a tape measure

There are occasions when the easiest way to overcome focusing problems is to measure the distance from the camera to the subject with a tape measure. Dark subjects, for instance, can be particularly tricky to deal with. However, in such cases you can try to bracket the focusing by taking several exposures with the focusing ring moved slightly between shots.

If your subject is close and stationary you may find it easier to measure the distance and to set this distance on your focusing ring.

To make certain that this is done accurately, the distance should be measured from the most important part of your subject to the film plane. The location of the film plane is indicated by a mark which is usually scribed on the top plate of the camera.

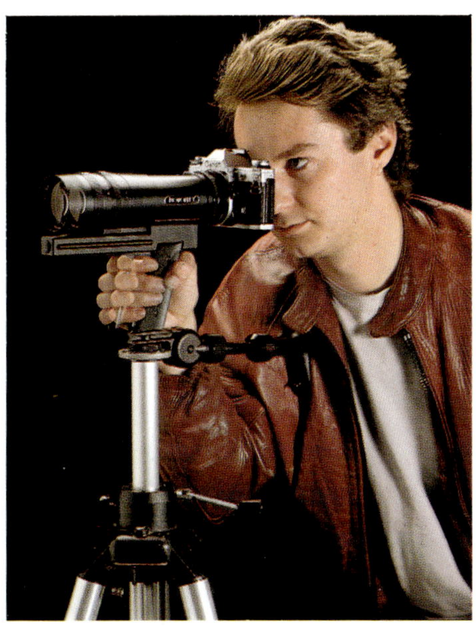

Fast focusing *Novoflex lenses have an ingenious squeeze-to-focus action that makes follow focus techniques easier*

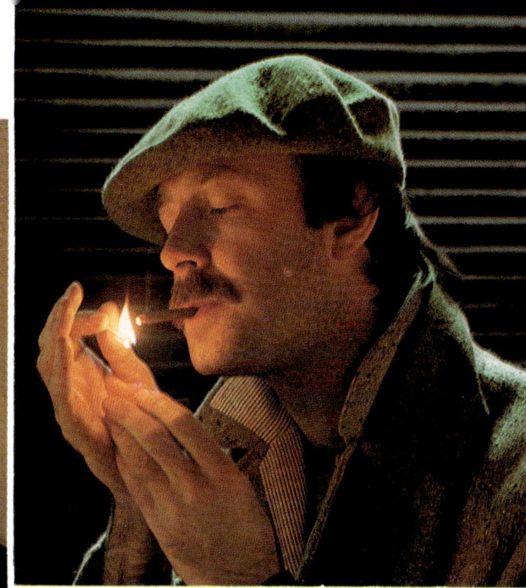

Adding light *Sometimes, you may need a light to focus by. Remove it to take the actual photograph*

Where possible, a simple solution to focusing on dark subjects is to shine more light on to the subject while you focus. After focusing, the extra light can be removed or extinguished while the exposure is made. Additional light can be supplied by a mirror, domestic lights or a torch.

Autofocus problems

There are two main types of autofocus systems—active and passive (see page 18). Both are likely to make mistakes under some circumstances. Active systems work by emitting a pulse of light or sound and computing the distance to the subject either by measuring the angle at which the pulse is reflected, or in the case of the Polaroid Sonar system, the length of time taken for the pulse to return to the camera.

In either case, if the subject does not act as a suitable reflecting surface for the pulse from the camera, results may be unsatisfactory. With the Sonar system, some hard surfaces at an angle to the line of sight can reflect the sound pulses away from the camera altogether, leading the camera to set focus at infinity. The only practical way to avoid these problems is to make sure that there are no steeply angled surfaces within your field of view, and that you do not exceed the close focusing limit of your camera.

Passive autofocus systems are just as prone to error. Most work by detecting subject contrast, although mechanical details may vary. All need light to operate, and some may not be able to focus in light levels that are still bright enough for ordinary photography. Flat, even surfaces without much subject detail usually defeat contrast measuring systems. Some systems are sensitive to the angle of lines on the subject, and may work better when held vertically rather than horizontally.

Both active and passive systems are often fooled by intervening objects such as foliage, bars or panes of glass. Fortunately, most autofocus systems can be manually overridden.

CHAPTER 5
CAMERA SUPPORT
Steadying techniques

Keeping the camera completely steady during exposure is much more important than is generally realized. While few serious amateur photographers get really blurred pictures through 'camera shake', many pictures are less than critically sharp because the camera is not held firmly enough.

In normal circumstances it is unwise to attempt hand-holding your camera at shutter speeds of less than 1/30 second. Longer lenses need even faster shutter speeds. As a rough guide, use a support when shooting with a 500 mm lens at less than 1/500 second or with a 200 mm lens at less than 1/200 second.

There are various methods that can be used to keep your camera steady. The best is a tripod but if you do not have one on the spot it is possible to improvise with varying degrees of success.

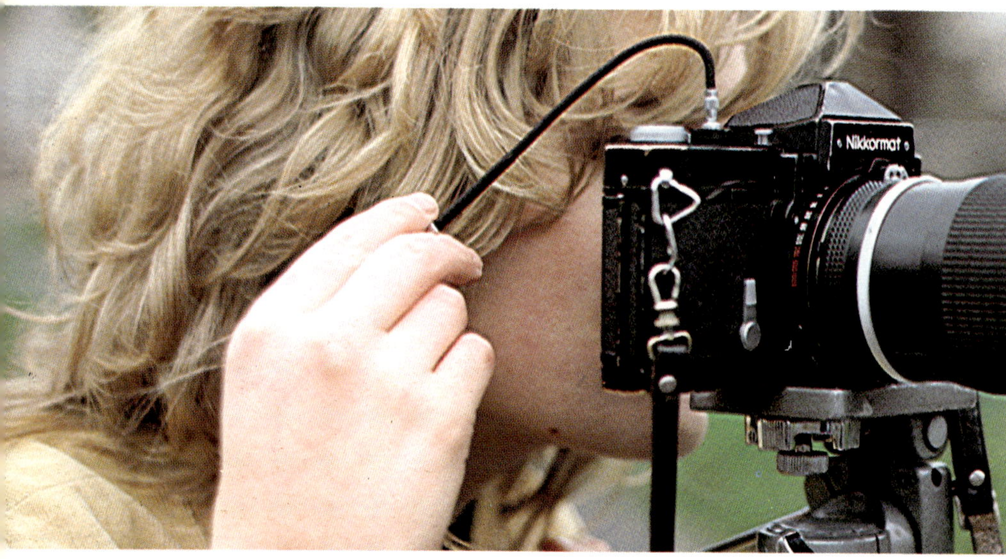

Camera support *The best method to use is a sturdy tripod and a cable release. This is essential for telephoto shots or in low light*

Adding support

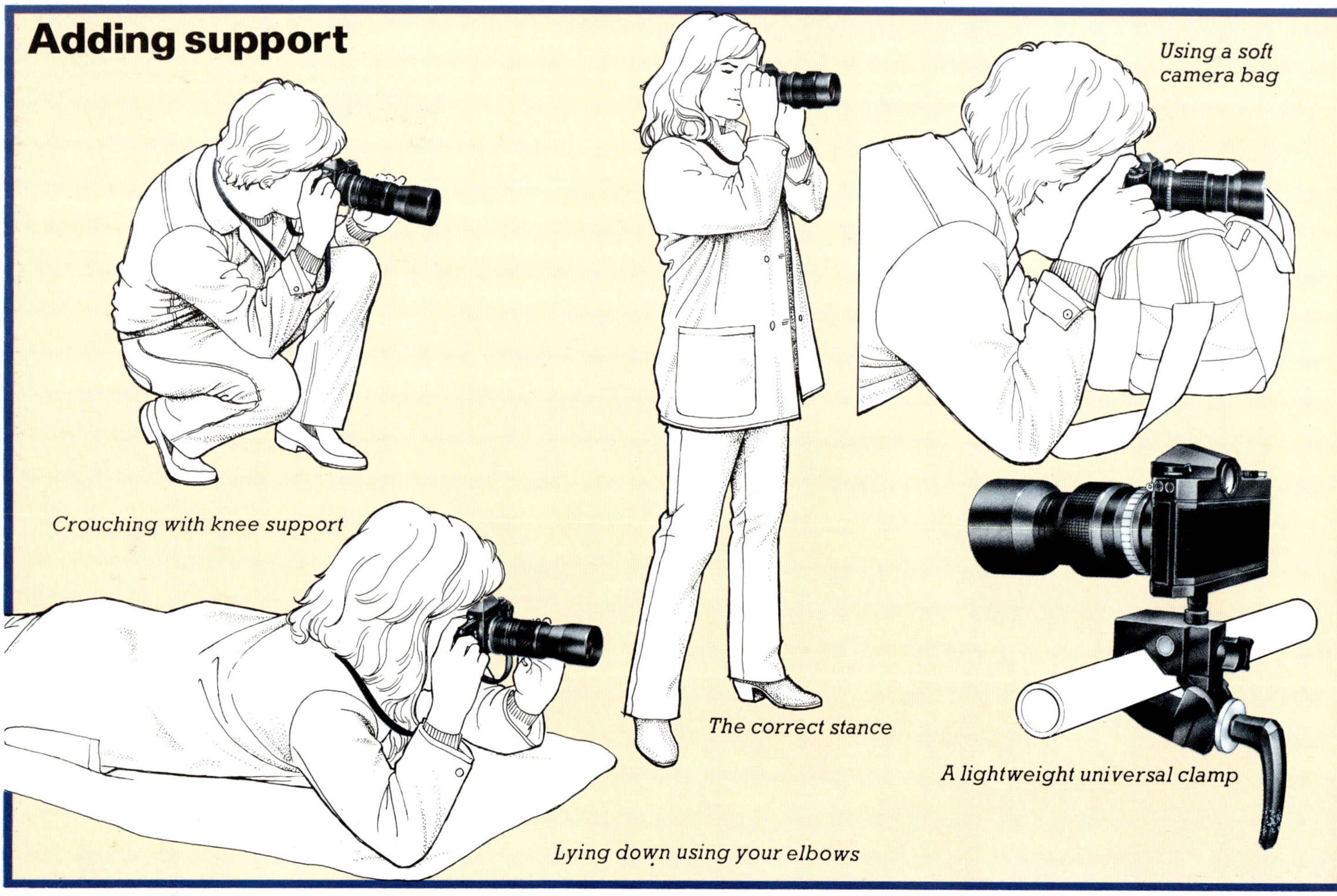

If you have nothing else to support your camera but yourself, you could try sitting down or squatting and firmly resting your elbows on your knees, keeping perfectly still during the exposure. Even if you simply dig your elbows firmly into your rib cage this can be better than simply using the normal hand-held position.

Since in this situation your body is acting as a sort of bipod, you could try steadying yourself—and thus the camera—somewhat more by leaning against something solid, such as a tree, and becoming more like a tripod. Even better results can be obtained if you instead place the camera on a solid object, such as a wall or rock.

Lying on the ground with the camera in front of you is a further simple, but obviously restrictive way to keep your

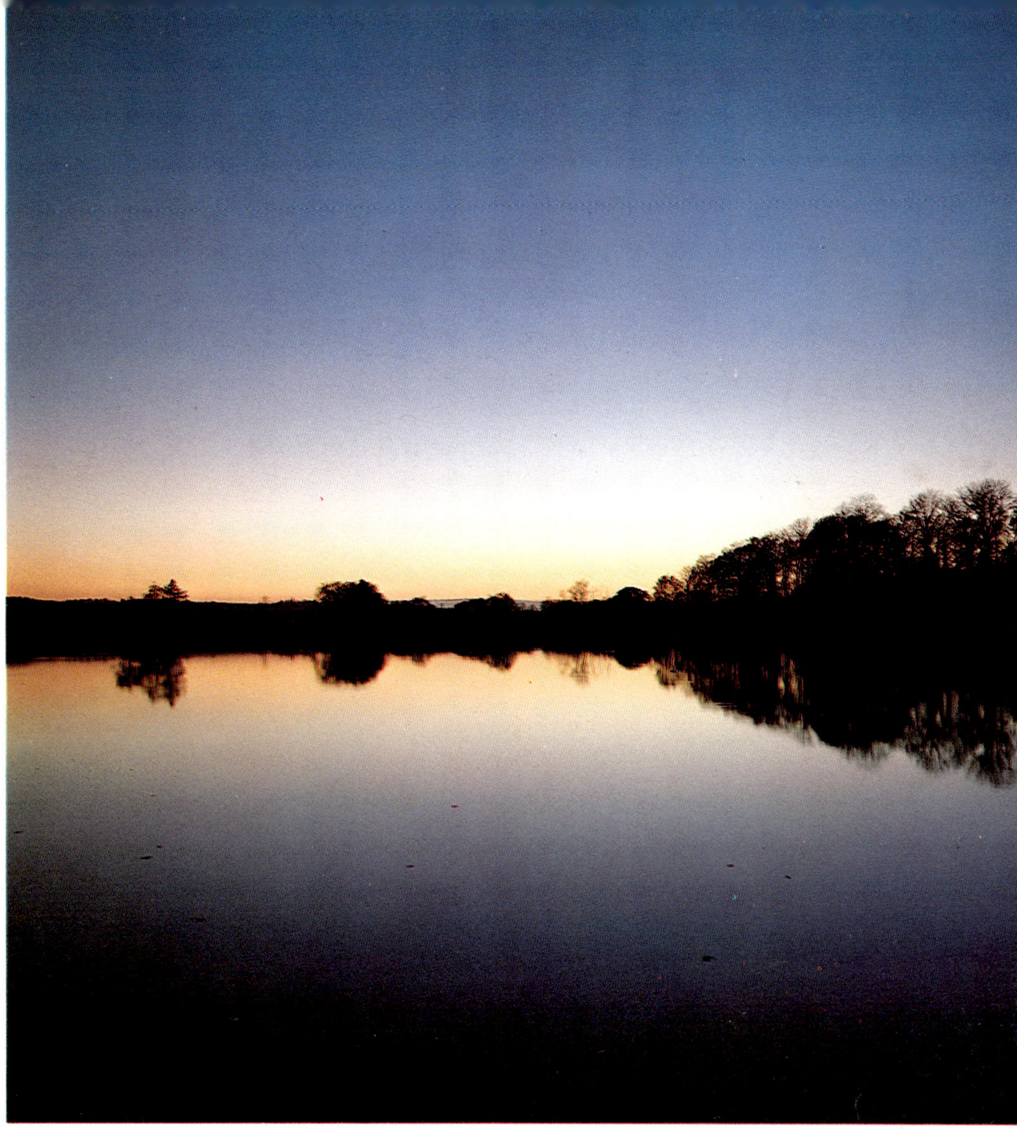

Low light shots *Unless your camera is firmly supported, it is impossible to take shots like this without camera shake spoiling your picture*

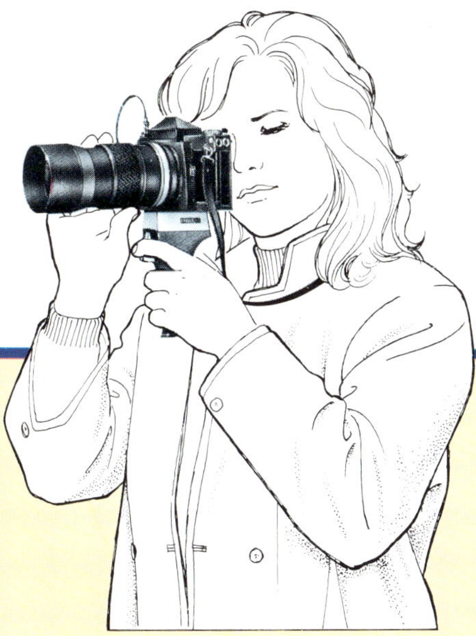

A pistol grip with cable release

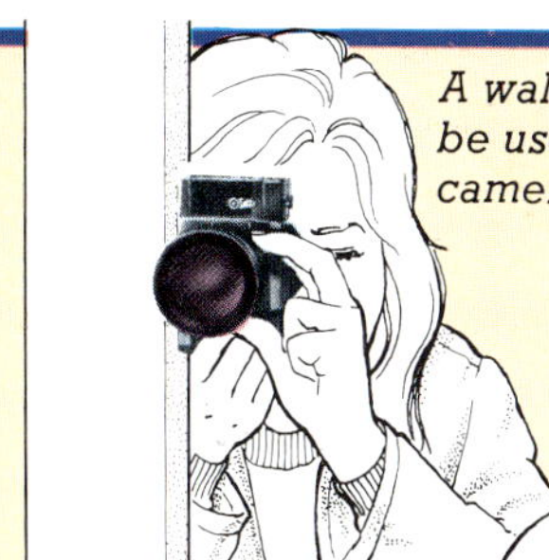

A wall or a nearby post can be used to stabilize the camera or the lens

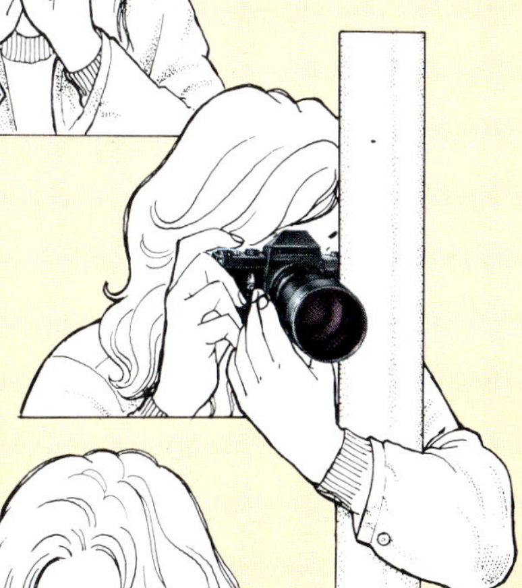

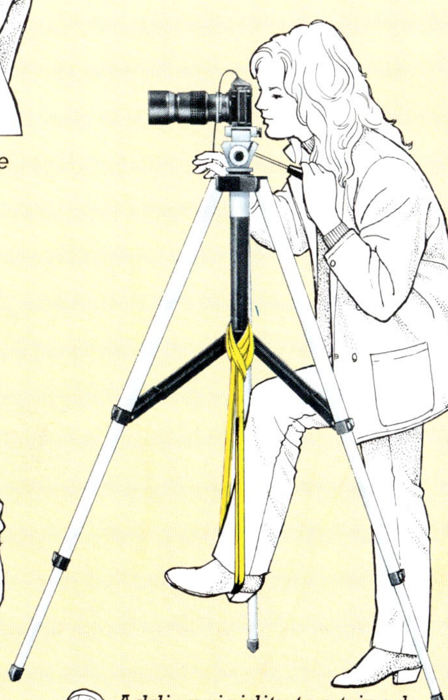

Adding rigidity to a tripod

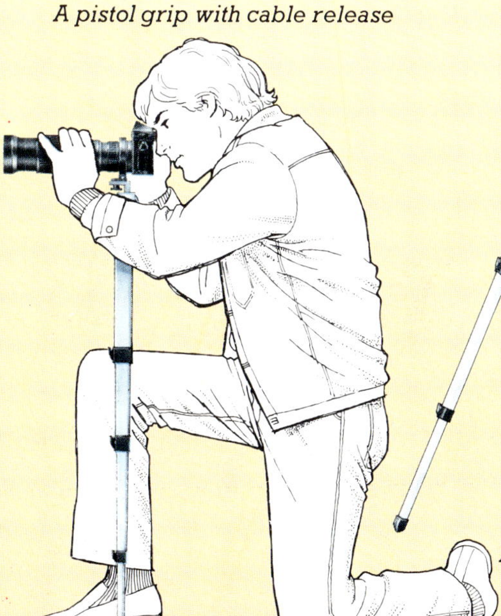

Monopods need extra support

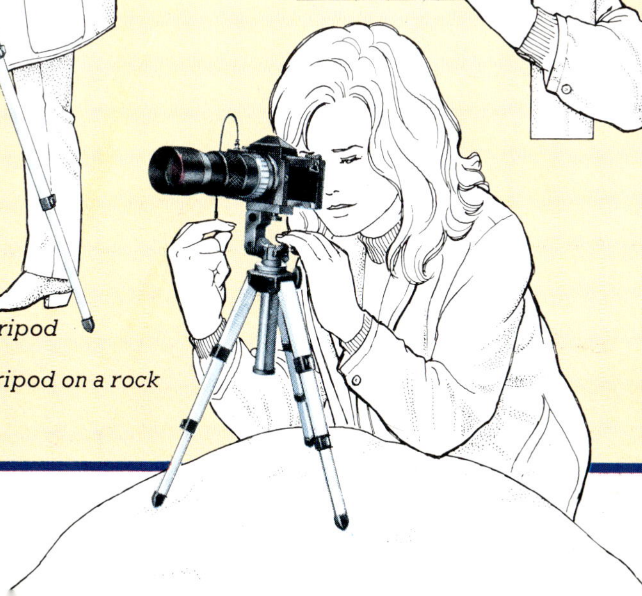

A mini tripod on a rock

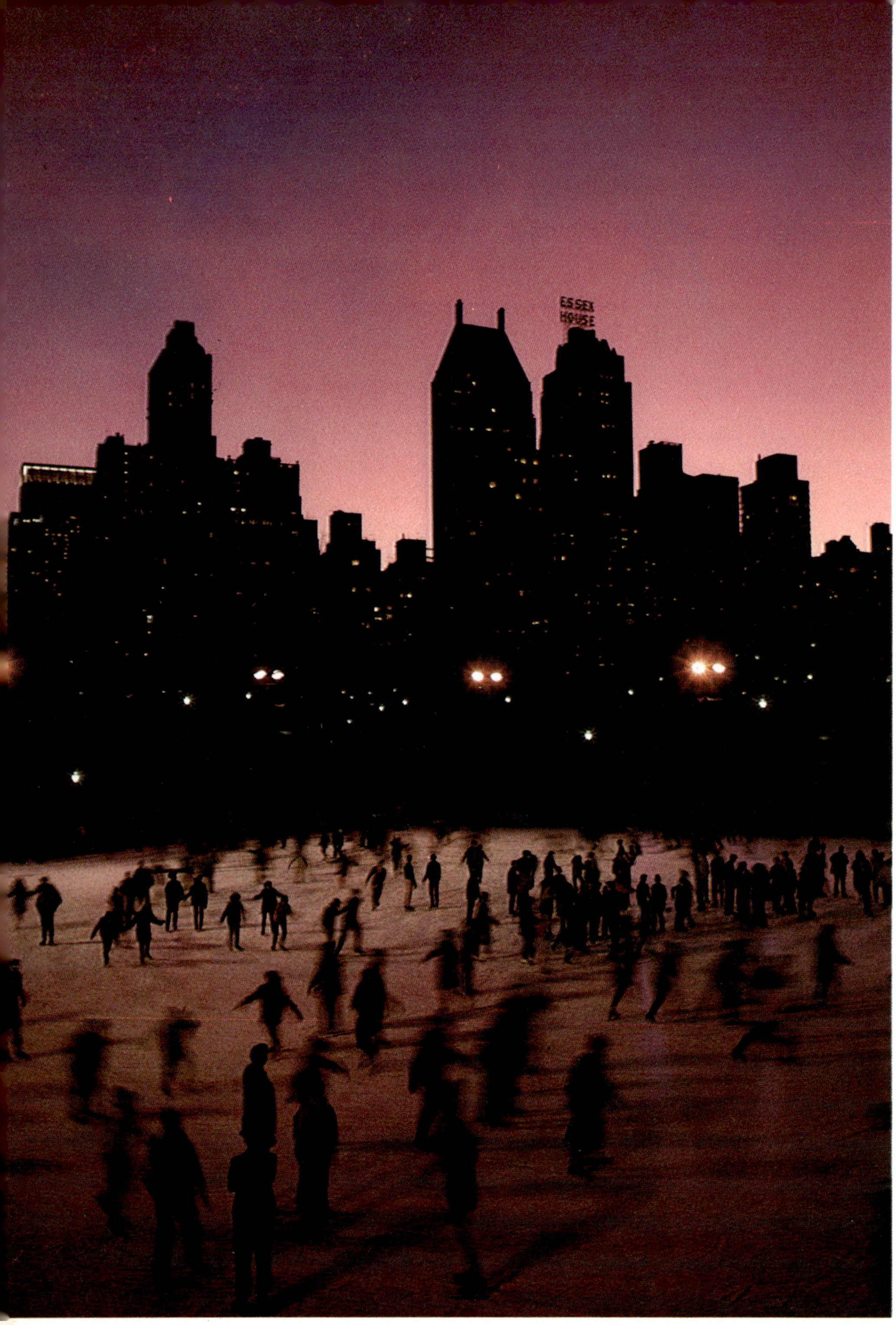

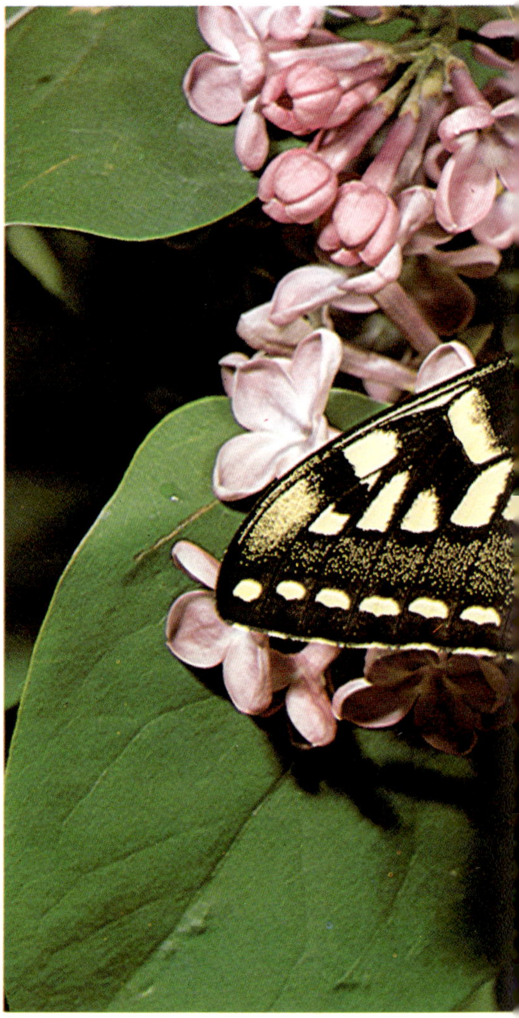

Skaters *To shoot in low light you will need slow shutter speeds, and moving subjects will blur. If the rest is sharp this is an effective technique*

Butterfly *For close-up work extra support is essential. The light level is low and absolute steadiness is needed for focusing*

Lion *Wildlife shots are nearly always taken with long focus lenses, which exaggerate the slightest movement of the camera*

camera reasonably steady. Another useful technique is to use your camera strap, stretching it out tightly in front of you, either from your neck or, say, a branch or railing.

With a twin lens camera you could hold your camera steady upside down against a roof or other object within easy distance above your head, such as under a low bridge, archway or firm branch.

A useful and simple support which is easy to carry around is a bean or sand bag, or better still a piece of 10 mm thick foam, which is even lighter and more compact. This type of support can provide a solid base, especially for low level shooting or when a ledge such as a car window is being used as a rest. Sometimes a soft camera bag can be used for the same effect.

An efficient way of supporting the camera is to use one of the wide range of clamps that are available for this purpose. A typical clamp has a mount which screws into the camera's tripod bush, and has a pair of jaws which allows it to be attached to any convenient object. Attachments are available for fixing clamps to fences, posts, furniture or any other firm anchor points. There is even a clamp which can be fitted to windows by means of suction pads.

If you intend to use such a device, choose one which is easily portable as well as one which has more than one use. You should also try and find a clamp which is strong enough to support your camera with a long lens fitted.

Another type of portable and compact support is the pistol or rifle grip. These are particularly useful when covering fast events, such as Grand Prix racing, when a tripod would be too cumbersome to operate. These types of supports are

Reducing vibration

Some cameras have facilities which help reduce camera shake. With the single lens reflex camera, the mirror jumps up when the shutter is clicked, and this can cause quite a lot of vibration. On some SLRs you can lock the mirror up before taking the shot to avoid this, although there is the disadvantage that nothing can then be seen through the viewfinder.

The pressure of one's finger on the shutter can also cause some camera shake, and this can be avoided on models which have delayed shutter releases, allowing the shutter to be fired automatically. Similarly, a cable release can enable you to click the shutter without handling the camera.

In addition, there are some cameras which have a specially built soft shutter release.

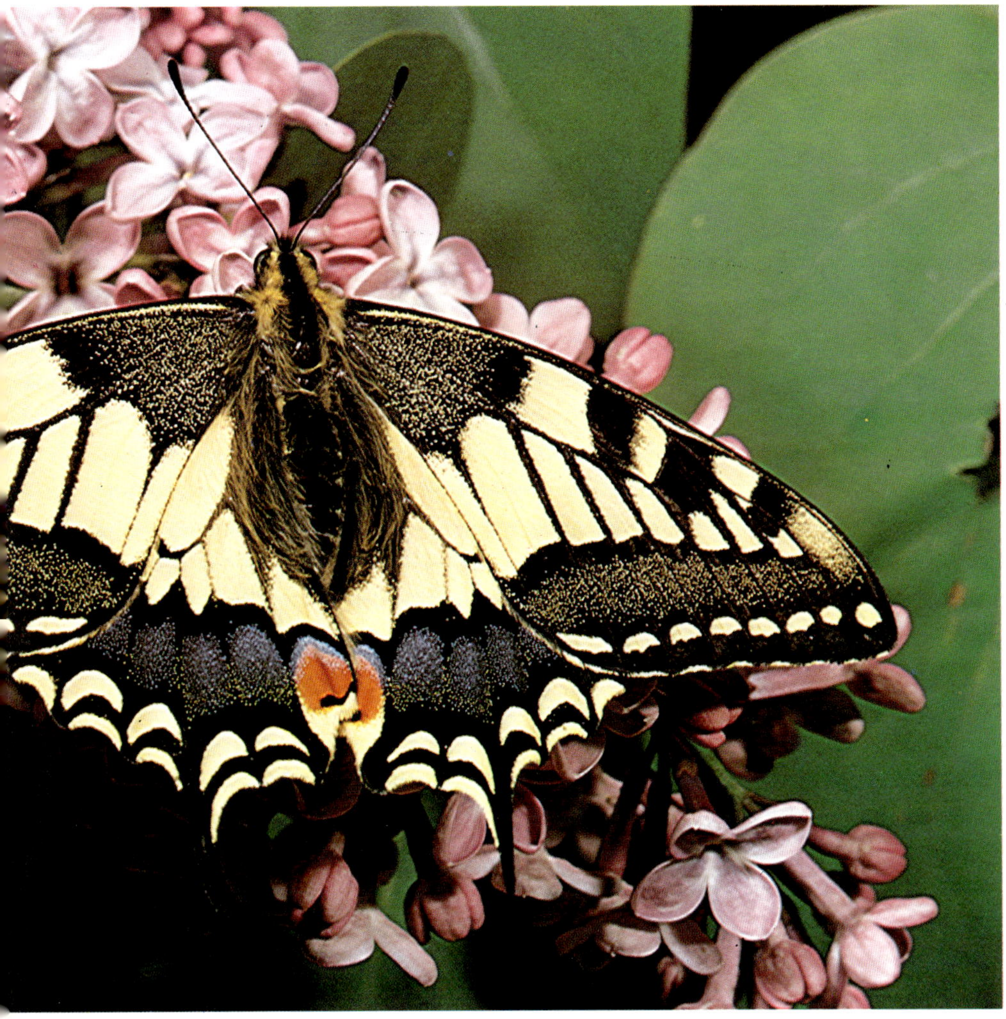

Rigidity, however, can be markedly improved by hanging a bag of stones or some other weight from the tripod head. This can be especially useful in high winds or blustery weather.

Another method is to join together two or more straps and hang them from the tripod head. This can then be used as a foothold on which to exert downward pressure. This can be useful for adding rigidity to the tripod when either the camera and lens are a heavy unit or when there is a strong wind.

Miniature table-top tripods are also available and are small enough to be used almost anywhere where a flat surface is available, such as a table or even a wall. Some makes are extremely solid, sometimes more so than a heavier stand. In addition, a table-top stand can be braced against the photographer's chest. These tripods can easily be slipped into a camera bag and are very useful things to take along if you are travelling or if you take your camera with you on walks or other occasions when a large tripod is too heavy. The versatility of the table top tripod makes it a valuable accessory.

There are many situations where holding the camera by hand is simply not sturdy enough to secure a shake-free exposure. In such circumstances, a rigid tripod is obviously the best thing to use, but there are many other alternatives. It is really a question of using your head —or more likely, some other part of your body!

often fitted with a cable release for the shutter and are braced on the shoulder.

A monopod—a single pole with the camera fixed to the top and the bottom firmly pushed to the ground—is very useful for keeping the camera steady for location work, when a tripod would prove too bulky or difficult to use.

They are light to carry and inexpensive, but not advisable for cameras with a larger format than 35 mm or for shutter speeds below 1/15 second.

By standing or kneeling with the monopod braced firmly against one's body, it is possible to turn it into an effective tripod. The effectiveness of a monopod is largely determined by the way you use it. It will not do all the work for you, so it needs careful use.

The best way to support one's camera, however, is with a firm rigid tripod, although this is also the most expensive method. Tripods come in a variety of designs, sizes and weights. The heaviest —and therefore the firmest—are best of all, but if the tripod is too heavy it will not be portable. As a general rule, the heavier your camera, the heavier and stronger your tripod needs to be.

The heavy duty tripods are mostly used with cameras larger than the 35 mm format and are therefore often limited to studio or location work, when an extra-sharp photo can be critical.

Portable tripods should be rigid if they are to be any use, but some of the lightest full size tripods are far too flimsy.

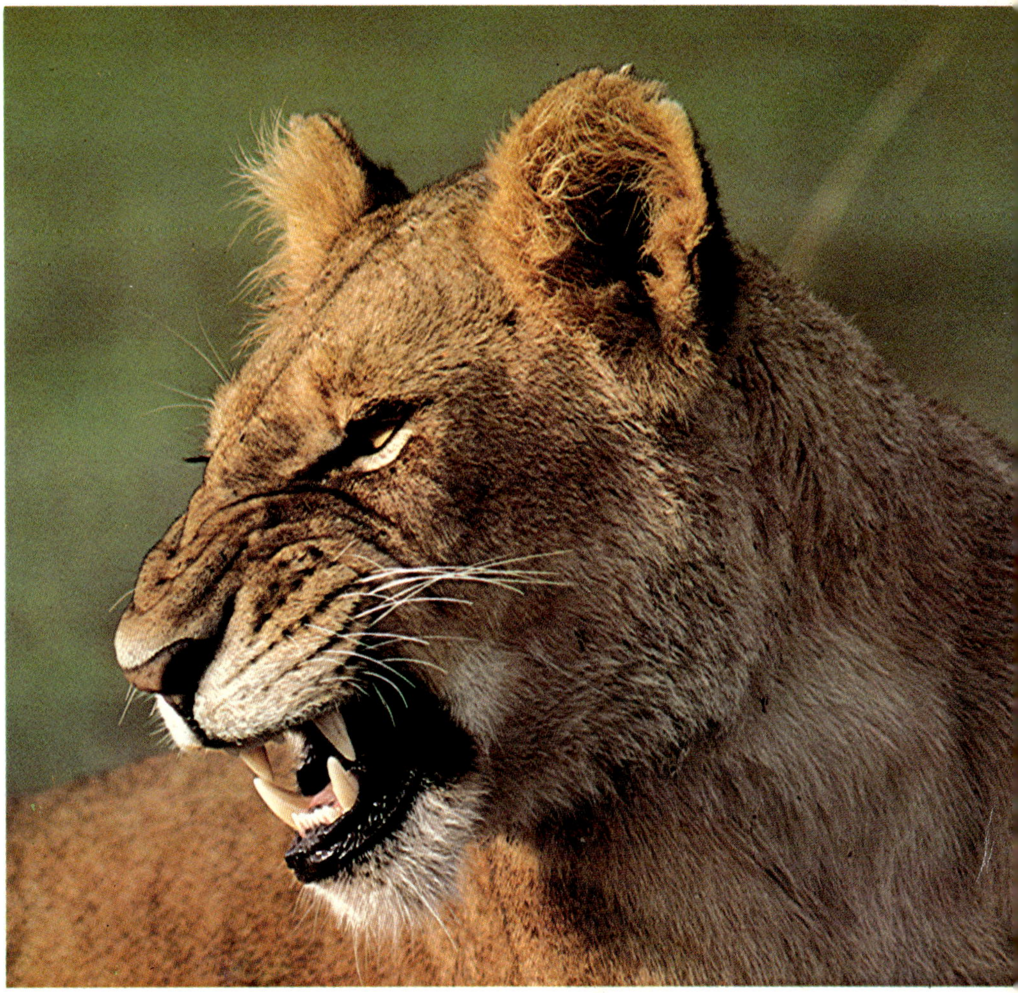

Tripods

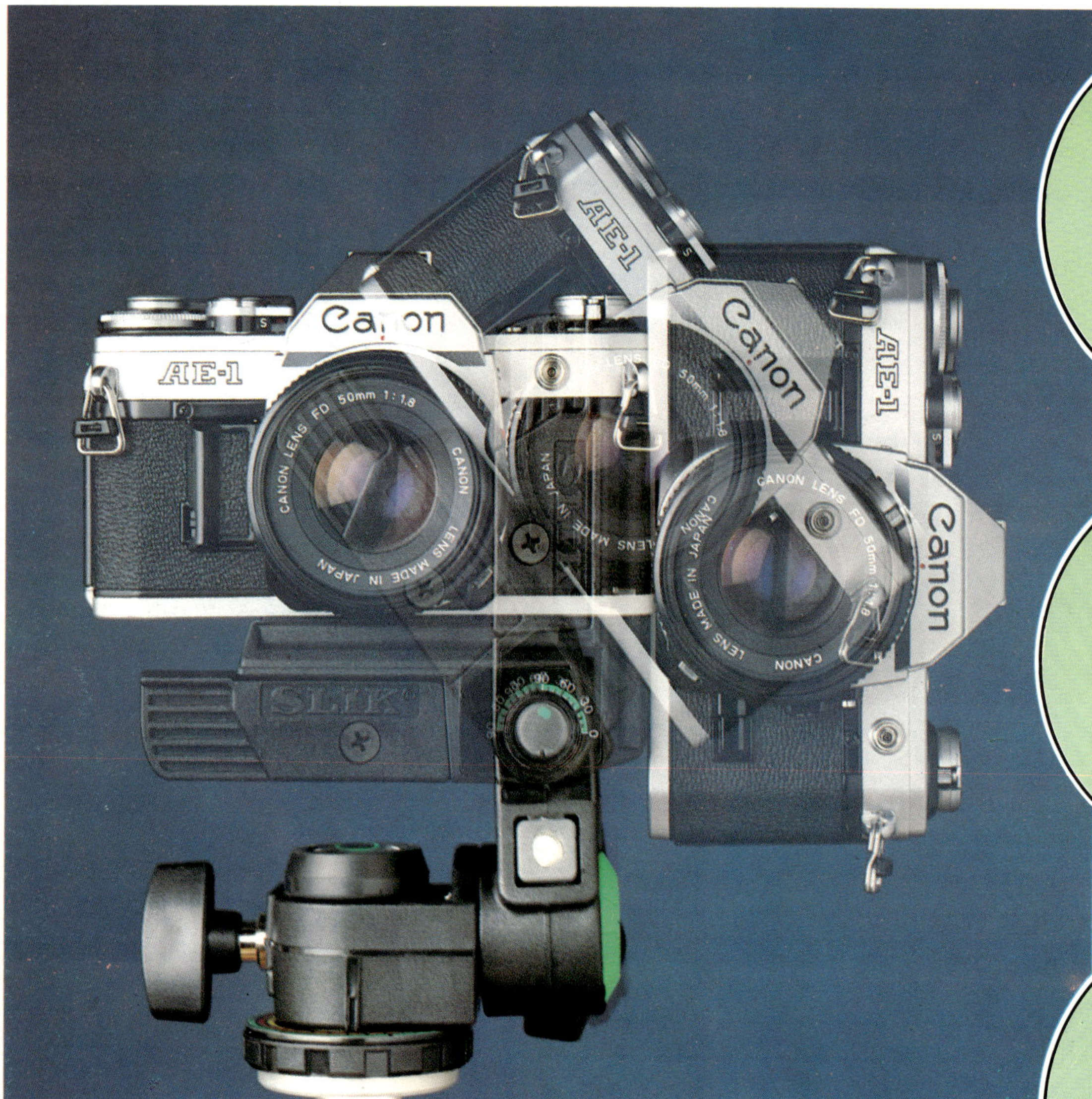

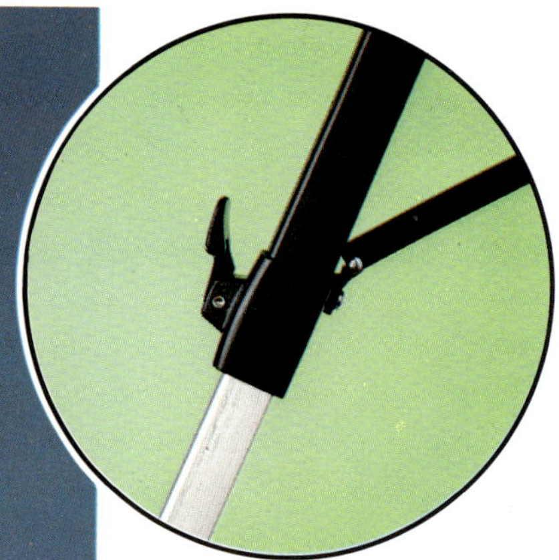

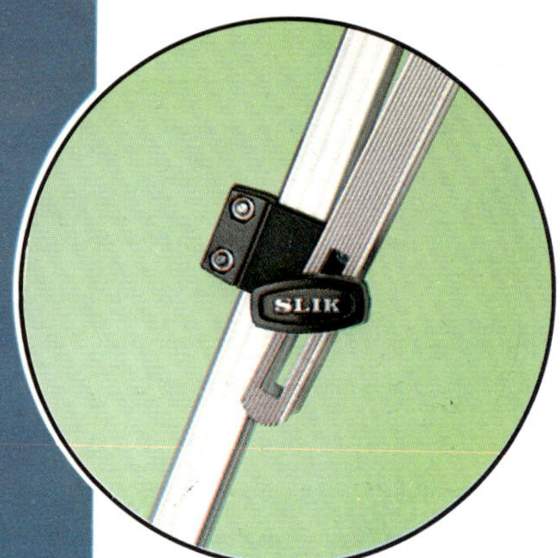

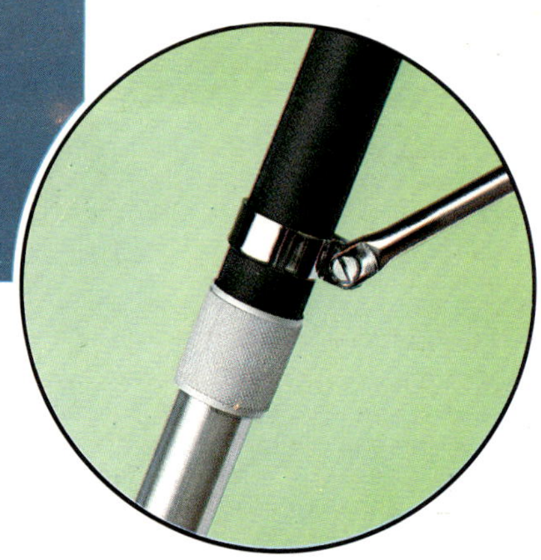

For many people, a tripod seems low on the list of necessary accessories for, unlike lenses, filters and flashguns, it does not obviously extend your range. However, a tripod makes more difference to the *quality* of your photography than virtually any other additional piece of equipment, and it should perhaps be the first piece of new equipment you buy after your camera. Used properly in conjunction with a cable release, a tripod guarantees the minimum possible movement of the camera during exposure and so helps ensure pin sharp pictures. In fact, a tripod will extend your range as well, opening up a variety of effects and techniques impossible without one, such as low light photography, multiple exposures, panoramas and stereo pictures, all covered elsewhere in this book. This section shows what to look for when selecting a tripod.

Travelling light

Tripods must be light enough to carry easily and sturdy enough to withstand light breezes or vibrations, so almost all modern tripods are built from aluminium alloys. The legs are made as tubes or as a U-chanelled, box-like construction. The circular tube style is generally more rigid than other types but is usually a feature of heavier and more expensive models.

For the photographer, the shiny, natural finish of aluminium tripods can sometimes be a disadvantage. In close-up photography, for example, or in copying work where you are focusing down on the subject through a sheet of glass, it is sometimes hard to avoid a reflection of the tripod appearing in the picture. And when photographing birds or other timid animals, a bright silvery

Leg locks *Channel section legs have either flip locks (top) or a threaded handle (centre). Tubular legs are locked by a threaded ring (bottom) which provides a very secure joint that is not prone to wear*

Tilt top *Many tripods have a pivoting camera platform. This is a valuable feature—it allows you to take both vertical and horizontal shots and the changeover can be made in a single action. Tripods without this feature are much less versatile*

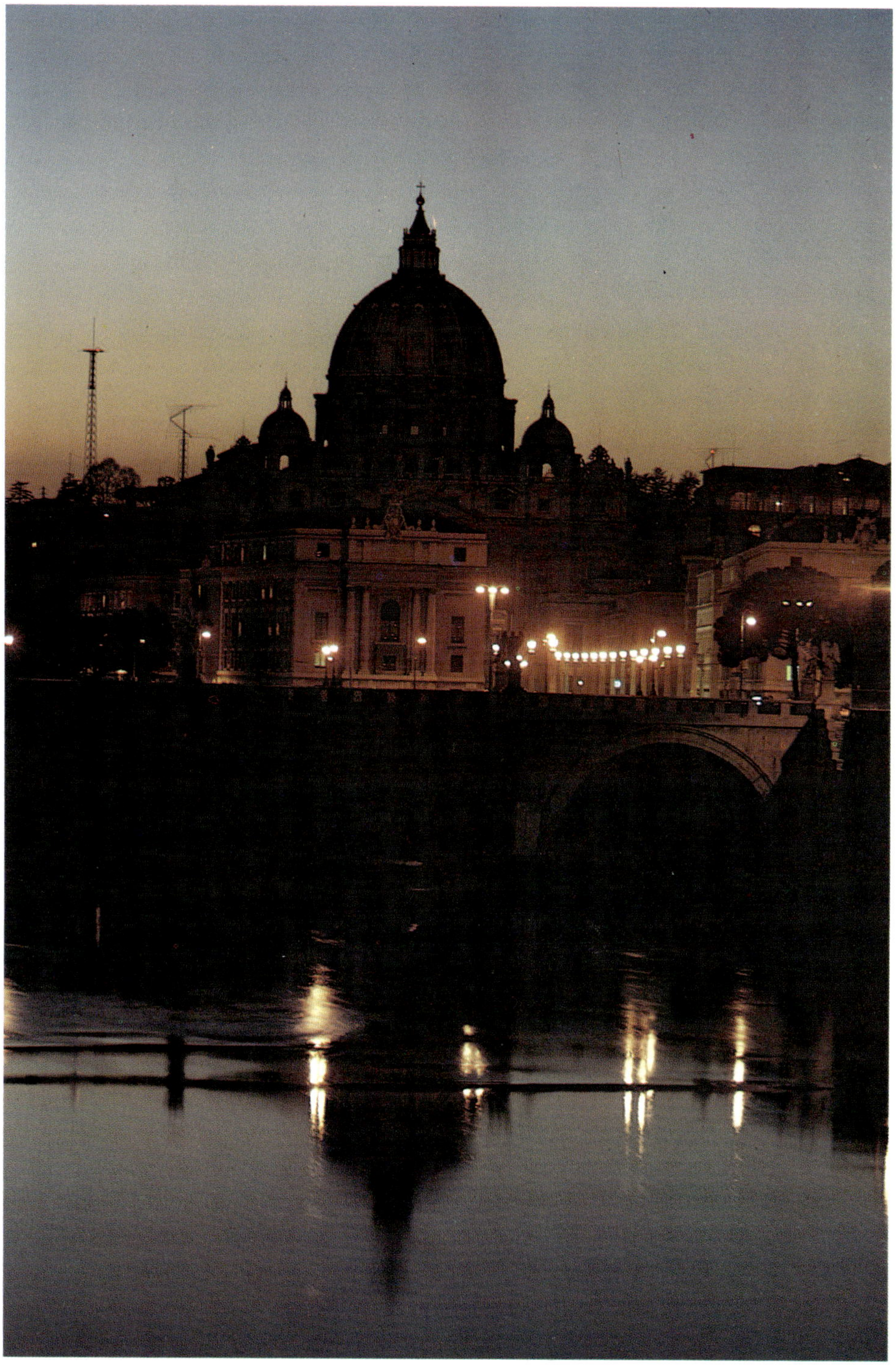

Leg locks

There are two common methods of locking tripod leg joints into their extended position: screw threads and flip levers. The sections on tubular legs are normally locked by a screw thread mechanism—each section is pulled out to its full extent and locked into place by tightening the screw. U-chanelled leg sections are normally fixed by the flip lever type of locks.

Both locking systems have points for and against them. Legs fitted with flip lever locks, for instance, can be set up much faster than screw thread leg sections. But though this may seem a great advantage, in practice speed of assembly is of limited value, because tripods are rarely used in situations where time is pressing. Inner leg sections, on some tripods with flip lever locks, can wear loose and may drop violently to the floor when the lever is flipped open. The jolt can damage or knock off the base plate of the bottom leg section.

Screw locking, on the other hand, provides a very rigid joint. In fact the screw locks on some professional tripods are so sturdy that they can be used as footholds when a photographer climbs up the tripod to reach the viewfinder—but this kind of treatment is not to be recommended for most ordinary tripods!

Whichever kind of leg locks you have on a tripod, it is important to make sure they are securely fastened before fitting the camera to the top. If one leg collapses suddenly your camera could be ruined. To prevent such accidents, some of the more expensive tripods have air cushion devices, built into the legs, that make it impossible for the legs to retract suddenly. And should the leg locks come loose, the legs telescope together only very slowly—giving you plenty of time to catch the camera.

To stop the tripod slipping, the feet must suit the surface. Most tripods are equipped with both rubber feet for hard shiny surfaces and spikes for soft ground. On a few tripods the feet are reversible, but on most the spike is fixed and the rubber feet are screwed down when they are needed.

On the waterfront *For night-time pictures, a tripod is essential, as it allows you to use long exposures without running the risk of camera shake. Even at dusk, exposure times may still be too long for hand-held shots*

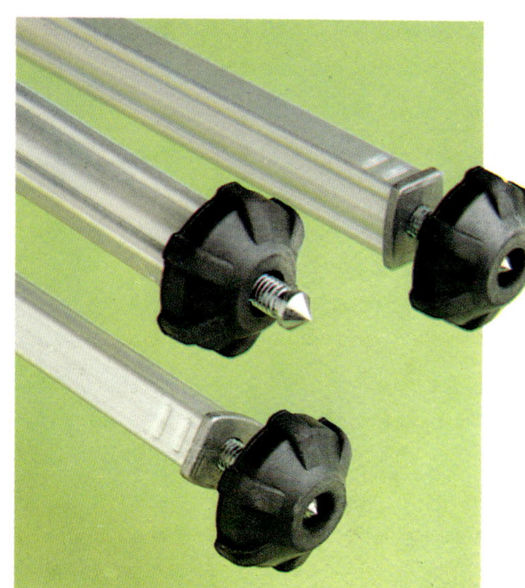

Rubber feet *In order to get a firm grip on soft ground, almost all tripods have spikes at the end of their legs. But make sure that the spikes have rubber covers, or, better still, are retractable, or they may slip on flat, hard surfaces*

tripod might attract unwanted attention. In these circumstances it is better to use a tripod with matt-black legs. An anodised finish is preferable to black paint because paint can easily become chipped or scratched, revealing the shiny metal.

Leg length

Tripods vary enormously in size from small table-top models only 10 cm high to professional giants that can take a camera up to 3 metres off the ground. For portability and easy storage tripods need to fold up into a small space.

The legs on modern tripods are usually telescopic with anything between two and eight sections, though most have three or four. The more sections a leg has, the smaller it is when folded up. Unfortunately, each joint in a tripod's legs is a possible source of unsteadiness and for maximum rigidity it is best to buy a tripod with as few sections as possible—even though this type may not pack down to as small a size as some others. It is better to have a bulky tripod that performs well than a compact type that may prove to be unstable.

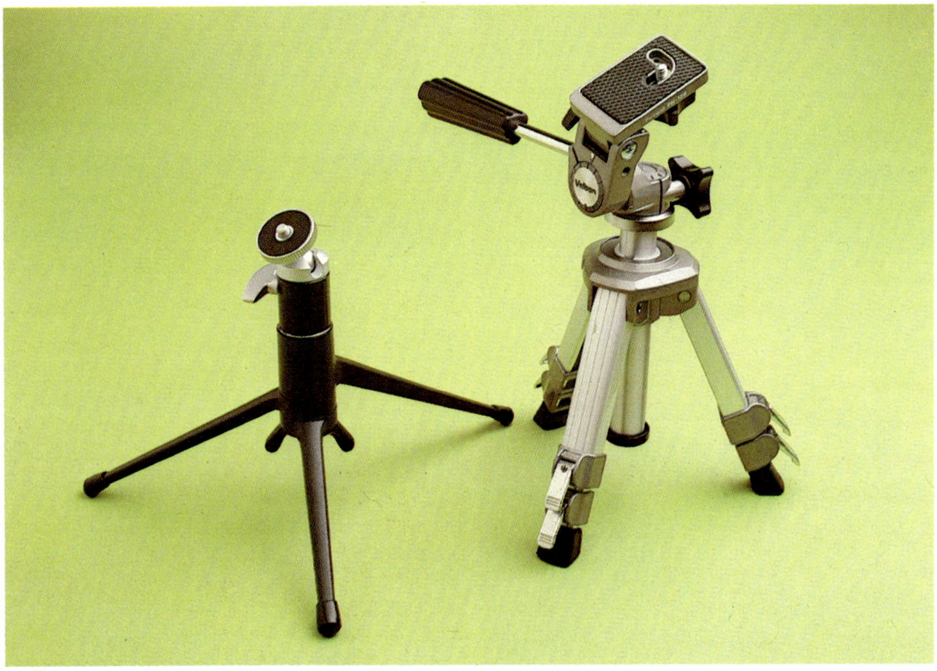

Table-top tripods *If space and bulk are at a premium, choose a table-top tripod. Some of these are very simple, but others are like miniature replicas of their full size counterparts*

Centre column *A rising centre column is an invaluable feature. This one is geared, and winding a handle on the body of the tripod moves the head steadily up or down*

Holding the camera

One of the most important decisions to make when you buy a tripod is which of the two types of head to choose.

The ball and socket head uses a metal ball with a tripod-screw attached. The ball joint allows you to move the camera round through a full circle in the horizontal plane, and to tilt it up and down through about 40°. A narrow channel cut in one side of the cup allows the ball and camera to point straight down at one place only. The disadvantage of this system is that the camera must be locked in each position. This means that to move the camera around you have to undo the screw, choose a new position, and then tighten it up again. The operation is therefore awkward and not very positive.

Camera movement is made much easier and much more definite on a tripod fitted with a pan and tilt head. Not surprisingly, this type of head is the more popular. The direction of the camera is controlled by a long slim handle. With this the camera can be panned horizontally through 360°—and tilted back wards or forwards. Twisting the handle locks either the tilt or the pan, or sometimes both. In addition to the pan and tilt, some tripods allow the camera base to be turned up through 90° for taking photographs in vertical format.

Some of the more expensive tripods have one or more bubble levels fitted to the head. These work in the same way as a spiritlevel—when the bubble is in the centre of the tube or dish of fluid, the tripod head is horizontal.

If you are taking only a single picture, levels are not important because the camera can be levelled with the pan and tilt or ball and socket head. Levels are more useful if you decide to take a series of pictures to show a wide panorama by panning the camera on the tripod between pictures. Unless the tripod is completely level, the camera moves up or down as you pan. You can judge whether the tripod is level by eye, but a bubble level makes it much easier.

On every tripod, the camera is locked on to the rubber-surfaced platform by a screw thread. This locking screw can often be very difficult to undo and a few tripods have a quick-release system consisting of a circular or wedge-shaped metal block. The block is screwed on to the camera base using the tripod socket,

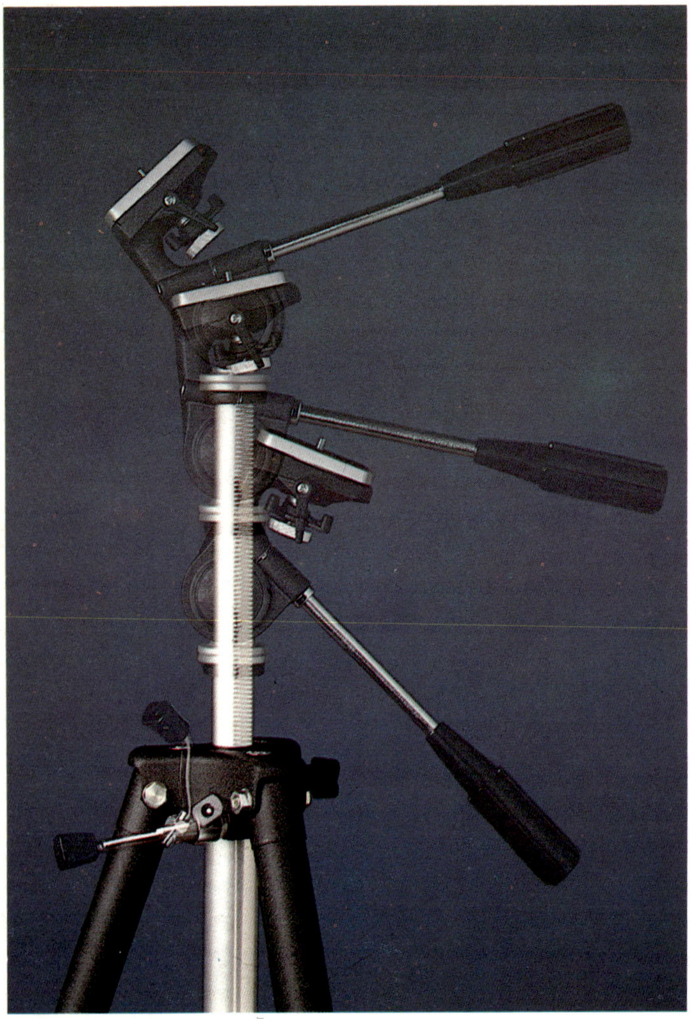

Two heads *A pan and tilt head (left) has individual locks for each action. Ball and socket heads, on the other hand, are smaller and use just one knob to lock all movements of the camera*

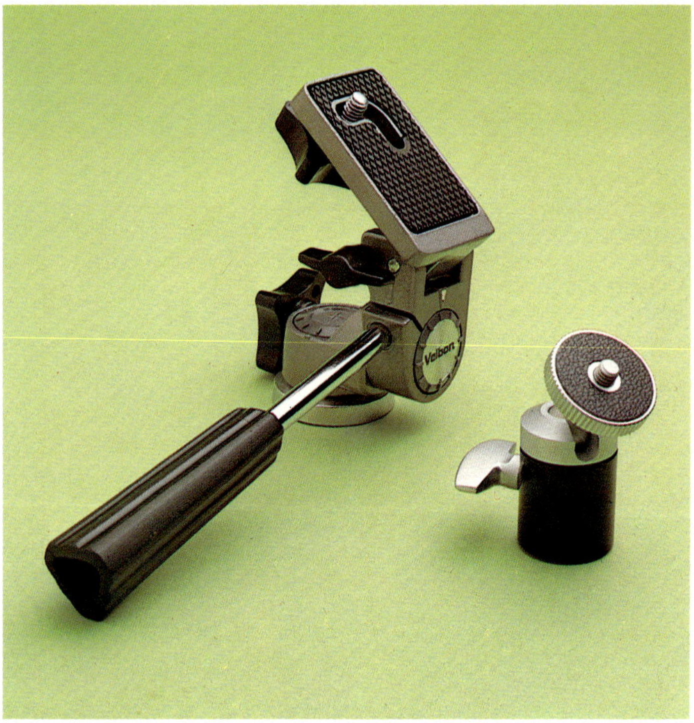

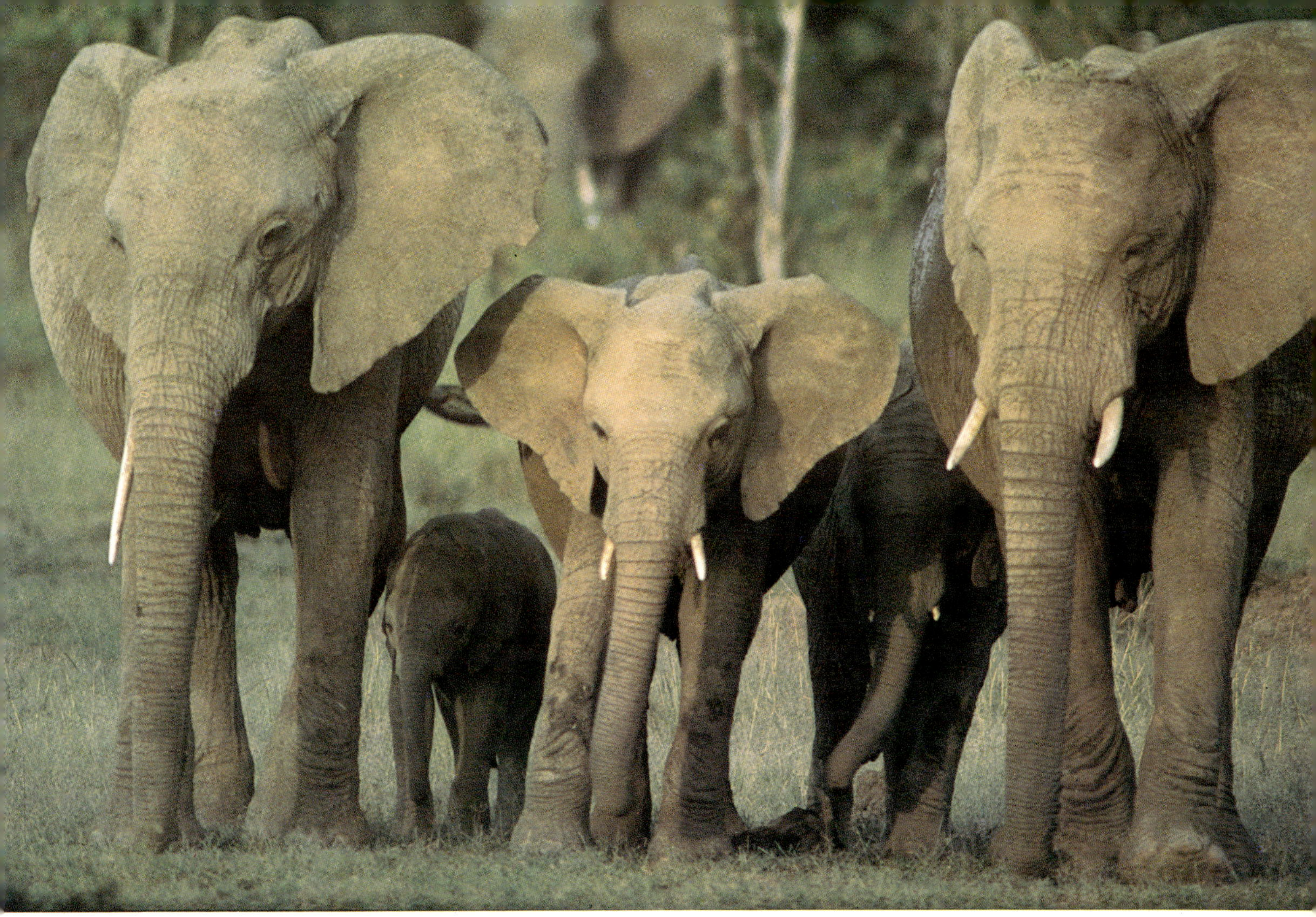

and the whole apparatus is then fixed into a recess on the tripod and locked into place by a lever or knob. A good quick release mechanism can make life much easier but a poor quality or worn device may fail to hold the camera rigidly. Since the main purpose of the tripods is to hold the camera rigidly, it may, therefore, be better to avoid cheaper tripods incorporating quick release heads.

Tripod heads are usually attached to a centre column which can be moved up or down through a boss at the top of the legs. On some tripods this column has teeth cut into one side and is raised or lowered by a small, geared crank handle. A non-geared centre column is moved simply by lifting or lowering the column to the appropriate height and securing it with the column lock. Crank handles, though convenient, usually prevent you inverting the centre column for copying, and low level photography.

Special tripods

If you cannot afford a full scale tripod it may be worth buying a miniature table-top version that holds the camera 20 cm or so above a surface. These are basic and can be very cheap and this is their main feature, along with ease of handling and portability, when viewed against full scale tripods.

One common type of miniature tripod has a hollow metal tube not much longer than a hand, with a ball and socket head at one end. When you unscrew the base of the tube out come three legs, each pivoted to the base (often rather loosely). The legs unfold outwards and the base is screwed back into the main column to secure the legs. The height of these tripods is not adjustable.

Because of their size—when packed away the column is only about 10 cms high—table-top tripods can be carried anywhere. They can be placed on top of any convenient object such as a brick wall, a table-top or a car roof. The only limitation is that you must find something of the appropriate height on which to set the tripod.

Unfortunately, though relatively steady when set on a firm base, table-top tripods are not generally very stable. Any adjustment to the ball and socket must be made very carefully because they are very top heavy with the camera in place. A camera can easily topple over, especially if there is a long lens to help it over-balance. Nevertheless, the low cost and lightweight make these small tripods attractive alternatives.

A simple variation on the tripod is the monopod, sometimes called a unipod. This is really just a single tripod leg. Sometimes a tiny three-legged base is fitted in the base of the column and can be screwed into place when needed. More usually, it is stuck into the ground on a spike.

Monopods cannot give the steadiness of a tripod but they can often be used in situations where a tripod cannot. With a single leg, they are much lighter to carry and do not need a large, relatively flat area to stand on. If, for example, you were going for a walk over hilly ground where a tripod might be awkward to set up and cumbersome to carry, then a monopod could be a useful accessory. Some sports photographers prefer monopods because they can move the camera much faster to follow the action than they could even on the smoothest pan and tilt head tripod.

Safari family *Long telephoto lenses are always difficult to use hand-held, and should be supported with a solid tripod whenever possible*

A firm base

Though a light tripod is easy to carry, it can sway with the slightest breeze or vibration, so it may be worth spending the extra effort and money on a heavier model which will provide a firmer base. Remember, though, that some tripods are heavy because they have many leg joints and their weight advantage may be offset by the greater chance of eventual unsteadiness and trouble following wear and tear on joints. So, your final choice will probably be based on a compromise between weight, size and ease of use.

Finally, whatever tripod you choose, you should use a cable release or other remote control device for shutter control to gain the full benefit from the extra steadiness. Used properly, a tripod can make a substantial difference to the quality and range of your photographs.

CHAPTER 6
LONG LENSES
Telephoto lenses

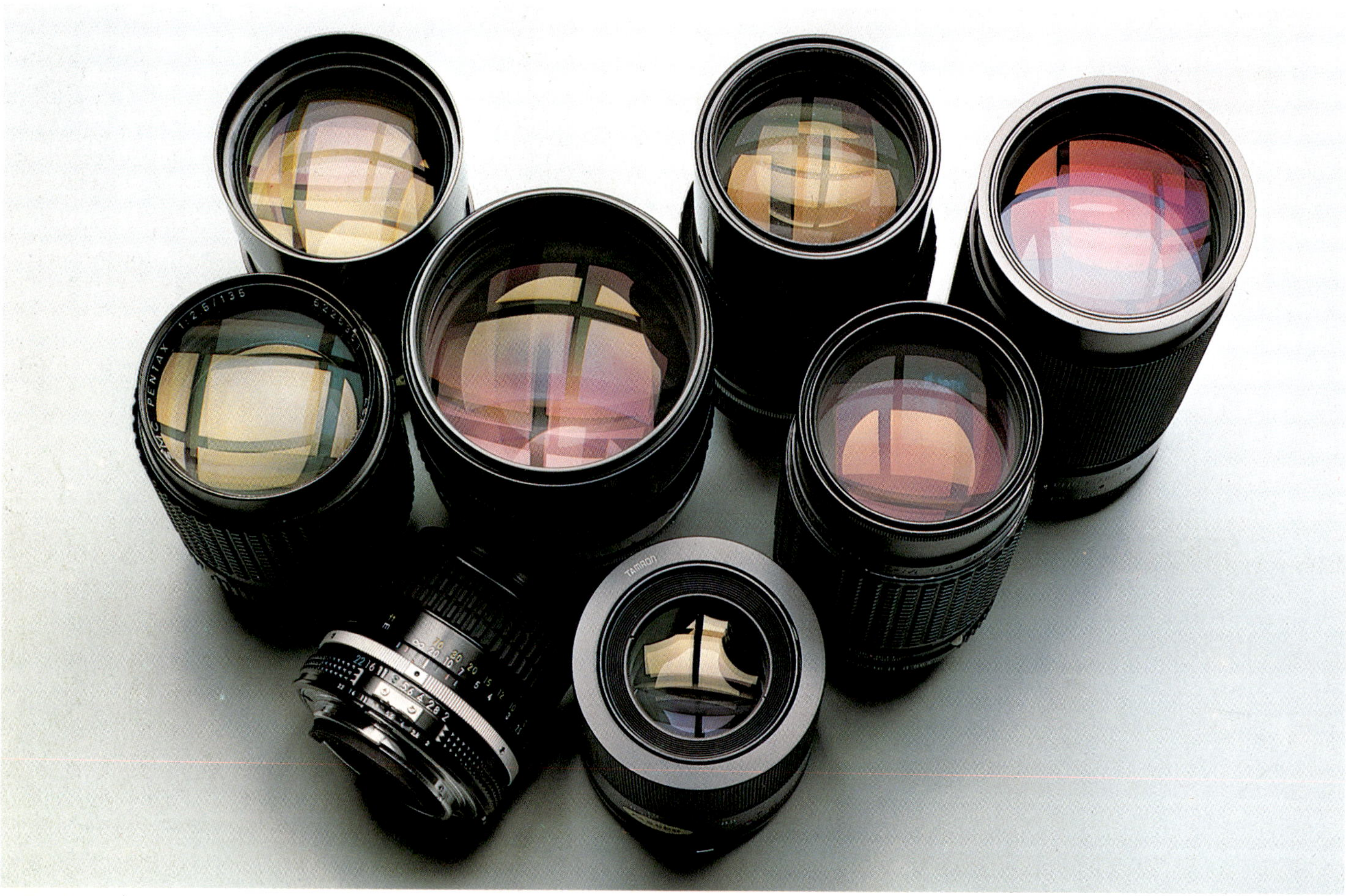

Long lens choice *All these lenses give an enlarged image on film. The smallest is little bigger than a standard lens*

There is nothing more disappointing than developing a roll of film and then finding that the main subject occupies a tiny area in the middle of each picture. It is not therefore surprising to find that after buying an SLR and standard lens, many photographers buy a telephoto lens or a zoom, because a focal length longer than the standard 50 mm produces an enlarged image. This seems to bring the subject closer to the camera, and gives pictures of distant subjects more interest and impact.

Looking through a camera fitted with a telephoto lens is like looking through a telescope, and telephotos have many uses in the same kind of circumstances that demand a telescope or binoculars. For photographing sport or wildlife, or picking out faces in a crowd, telephoto lenses are essential.

There is, however, another use for a telephoto lens which is less obvious than the enlargement which it produces on the film. On some occasions, getting close enough to the subject is not really a problem—portraiture is an example—but there are advantages to be gained from moving back, and putting some space between the camera and subject.

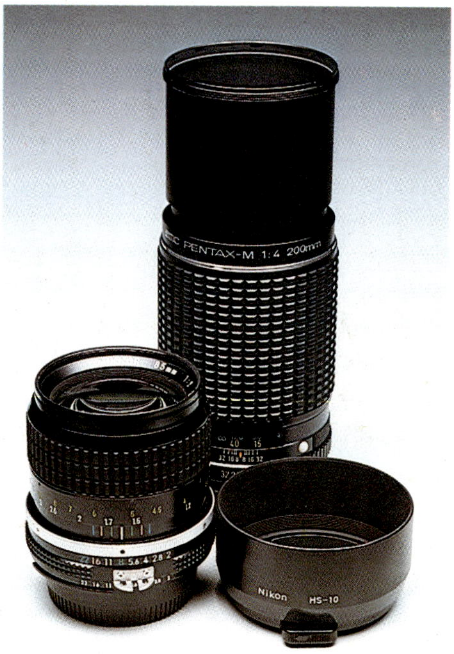

Lens hoods *The contrast of many pictures can be improved by the use of a lens hood, but this is often not included in the basic price of a lens*

In order to fill the frame with a head and shoulders portrait, it is necessary to stand within about 60 cm of your subject when using a standard lens. Fitting a 105 mm lens enables you to move back to double this distance, and still get an image that is just as big. With a 200 mm lens, there will be nearly two and a half metres between you and your subject for the same image size.

Moving back from a portrait sitter can improve your pictures in two ways. First, by changing the perspective of the portrait, the nose of your sitter does not look so large in comparison to the rest of the head. Secondly, the sitter will be more relaxed; it is not easy to wear a serene expression when there is a camera a short distance from your face.

For both these reasons, most tightly cropped portraits look a lot better when shot on a long focus lens, and if you expect to be doing a lot of portrait work, it is worth considering buying one, even if you will have little use for it in other types of photography.

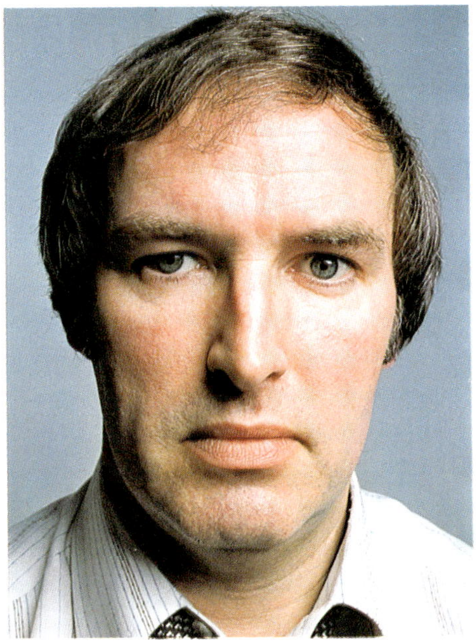

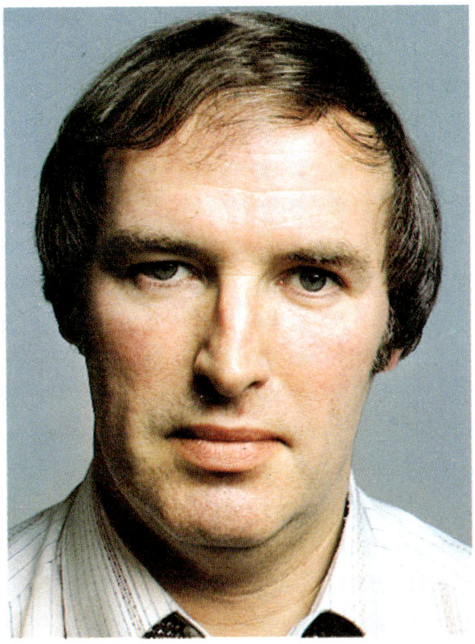

Portraits and telephotos *The picture on the left was taken with a standard lens, and looks distorted because the photographer was so close to his subject. Using a 85 mm lens enabled him to move back, so the perspective is more pleasant*

Few 80 to 200 mm zooms have maximum apertures wider than f/3.5, but an f/2 135 mm lens is not unheard of. This means that photographs can be taken in dimmer light with the telephoto, or a faster shutter speed can be used.

Medium telephotos

The most popular focal lengths for telephotos range from about 85 mm to 200 mm. Anything shorter than 85 mm would not offer any significant advantage over a standard lens, and above 200 mm the weight and bulk of the lenses increases rapidly, and their maximum apertures are smaller. This means that, because of their bulk and weight, such lenses are hard to hold steady, and because their maximum aperture is smaller, a slower shutter speed is necessary. Consequently, lenses longer than 200 mm often need to be used on a tripod for best results. Such lenses are dealt with on pages 75-79.

The most popular focal length in this range is the 135 mm lens. This is a useful all purpose telephoto which is usually

Telephoto or zoom?

At first glance, it may seem that zoom lenses are more useful than fixed focal length telephotos. Zooms have a range of different focal lengths: some of them range from wide angle, through standard 50 mm, to telephoto. But fixed focal length telephotos have retained their popularity for a number of reasons. The most important of these is performance. For a photographer who demands top quality, zoom lenses are often inadequate. Few, if any, zooms are as good as the best lenses of fixed focal length.

Fixed focal length lenses are cheaper than zooms, too, because the optical construction of a fixed telephoto is much less complex and costly to assemble. This is especially noticeable at the cheaper end of the lens range—cheap telephoto lenses often produce acceptable results, whereas cheap zooms are frequently very poor indeed. If you do not have a lot of money to spend on a lens, a fixed telephoto will usually produce better results than a zoom lens of the same price.

Zoom lenses tend to be much heavier, and more bulky than fixed focal length telephotos and although a zoom might cover the range of several telephotos, many photographers find that they habitually use only part of the range of a zoom lens. If, for example, you own a 80-200 mm zoom lens and only use the lens at its 200 mm lens setting, it would be much less cumbersome to carry only a 200 mm fixed lens.

The final reason why many photographers prefer fixed telephoto lenses is the maximum aperture available—some telephoto lenses have one or two stops more than their zoom equivalent.

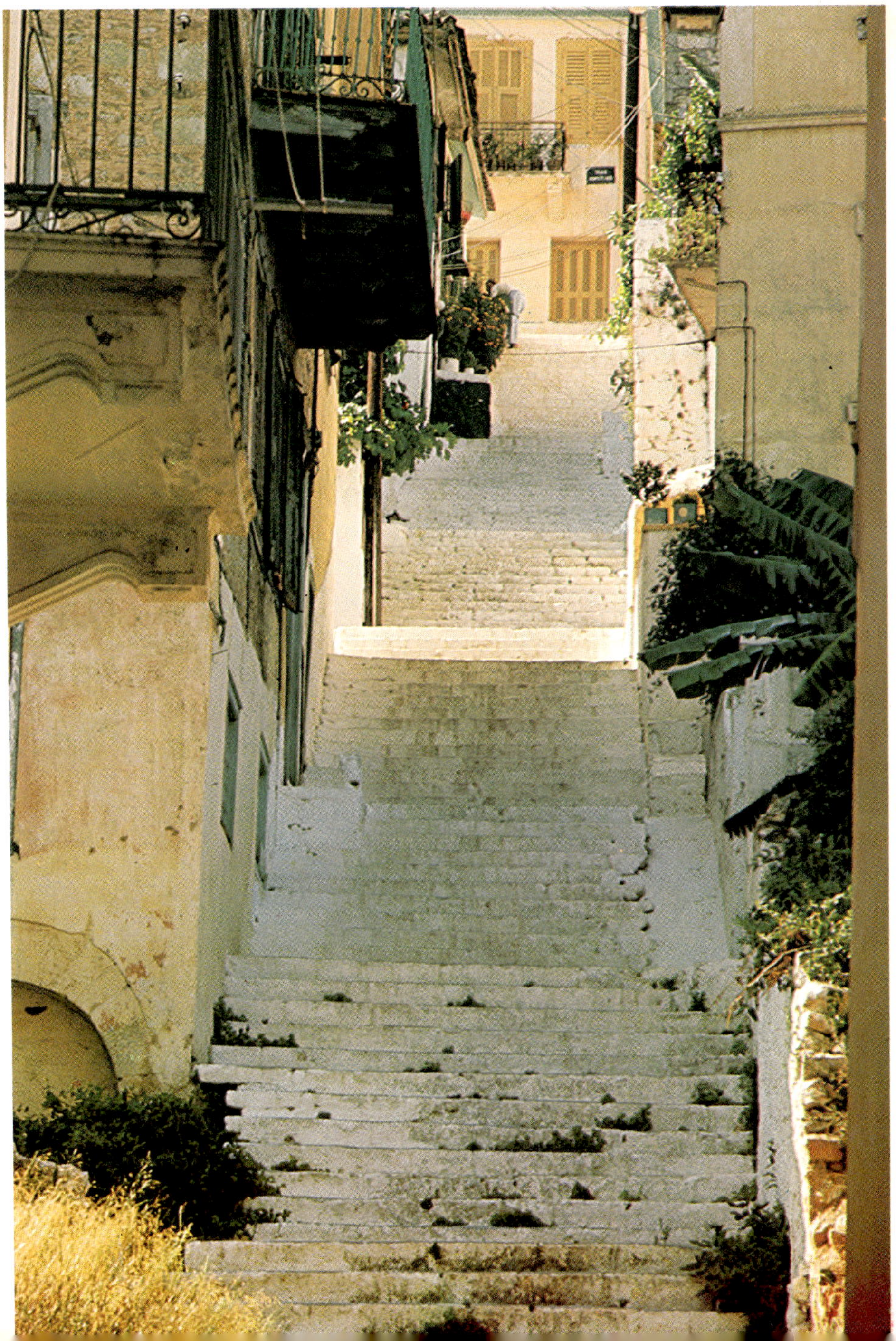

Steep steps *Telephoto lenses allow the photographer to move back, and this appears to compress depth and flatten out the subject*

quite light and easy to hold, yet provides a convenient enlargement of about two and a half times compared to the image formed by a standard lens. It is perfectly suitable for portraits, and is not so long that you find yourself shouting instructions to your model, if you are taking portraits out of doors. For sport photography, or any picture where a larger image than normal is necessary, the 135 mm lens is a good compromise between lightness, compactness and high magnification.

Since there is so much demand for 135 mm lenses, economies of scale have brought prices down, and they are usually the cheapest telephoto in a manufacturer's range. The cheapest ones available cost no more than four rolls of process paid colour slide film.

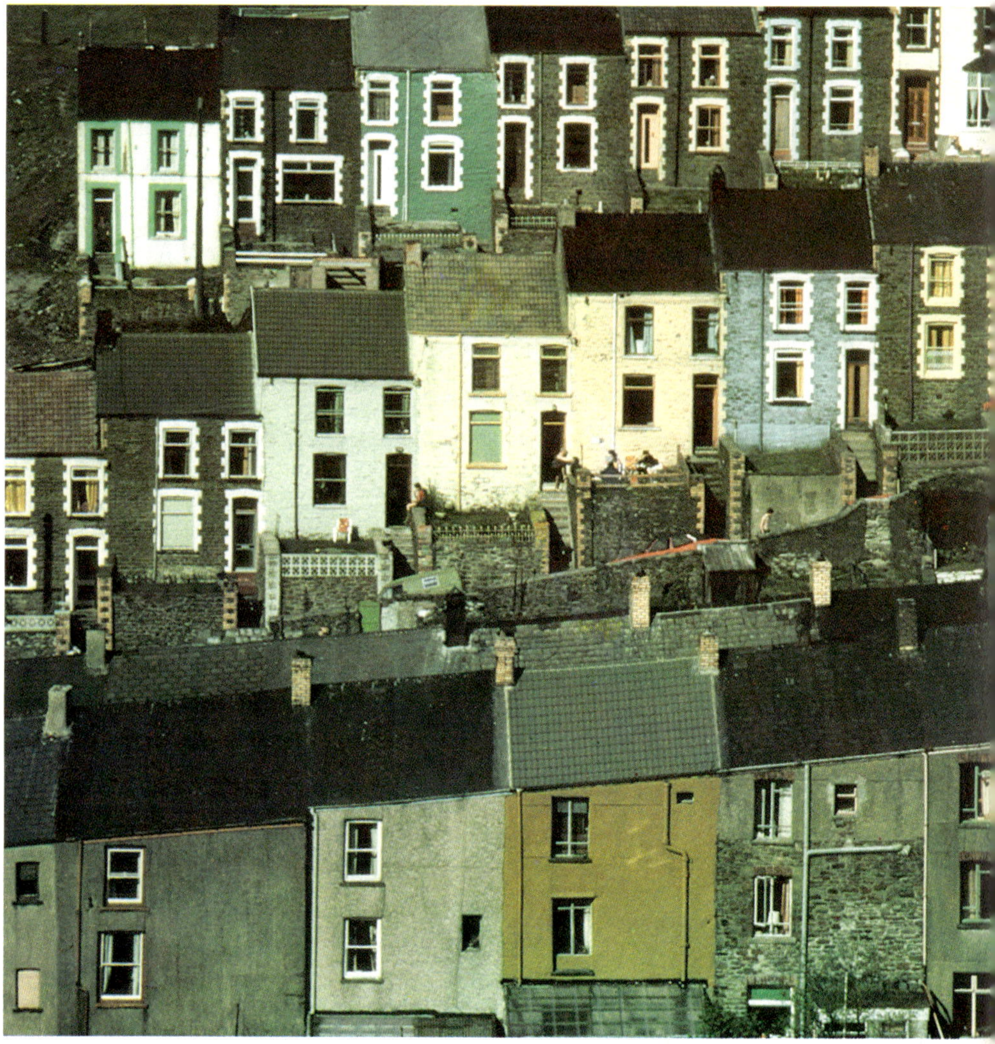

Small telephotos

With the increasing popularity of compact 35 mm SLR cameras, there has been a swing towards smaller telephoto lenses, and this has frequently been achieved by simpler construction and so reduced size and weight. It has also meant that photographers have started buying shorter telephotos, such as the 85 mm and 105 mm focal lengths. These have long been popular among professional photographers, particularly photojournalists. They eliminate the unflattering perspective that close working with a standard lens can produce when taking portraits, and are often available in wide apertures—typical examples include an *f*/2 85 mm and an *f*/2.5 105 mm.

Some photographers consider these focal lengths too short to be useful, but they are compact, and produce an image which is double the size of that formed by a standard lens—quite ample under many circumstances.

200 mm lenses are at the upper end of the medium telephoto category. They produce a magnification of about four times compared to a standard lens, and are very popular for sporting events where the crowd is quite close to the competitors. They would be useful for tennis, but not so useful for soccer if the football players were at the other end of the pitch. Here, a much more powerful lens, such as a 400 or 600 mm, would be better for covering the distances involved.

A 200 mm lens forces the photographer to stand quite a way back from the subject compared to the camera-to-subject distance for a standard lens. This has the effect of compressing apparent perspective. A line of cars, for instance, appears packed tightly together when photographed with a 200 mm lens.

This 'compression effect' is what a lot of photographers look for in a telephoto, but it can have drawbacks. It also compresses dust and haze in the atmosphere, and photographs of distant scenes with a 200 mm lens are often spoilt because of this. The atmosphere is only clear enough to get really crisp results over long distances on a few clear, frosty winter mornings. Over shorter distances, haze in the atmosphere is less of a problem, and will only intrude in very hot, dusty weather. A 200 mm lens should be useable over distances of up to 200 metres on most days of the year, without atmospheric mistiness becoming objectionable.

Camera shake

Just as a 200 mm lens magnifies the image four times compared to a standard lens, so also it emphasizes any camera shake by a factor of four. This means that faster shutter speeds are necessary if all camera movement is to be eliminated. A rough guide to the slowest shutter speed that can be used hand-held is that it is equal to the reciprocal of the focal length—a 50 mm lens can be hand-held at a 1/50 sec, (nearest common equivalent 1/60) a 135 mm at 1/135 sec (approximately 1/125) and a 200 mm lens at 1/200 (1/250). This can be very limiting, and may force the photographer to use a fairly wide aperture if a tripod is not available.

This may in turn lead to problems of depth of field—when a 200 mm lens is focused on a point ten metres away,

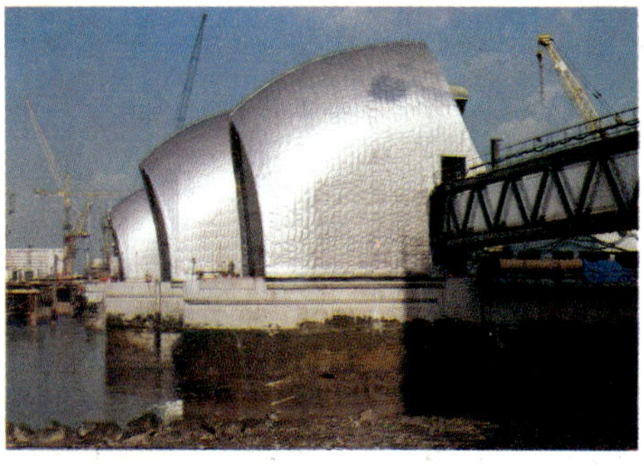

Standard 50 mm lens

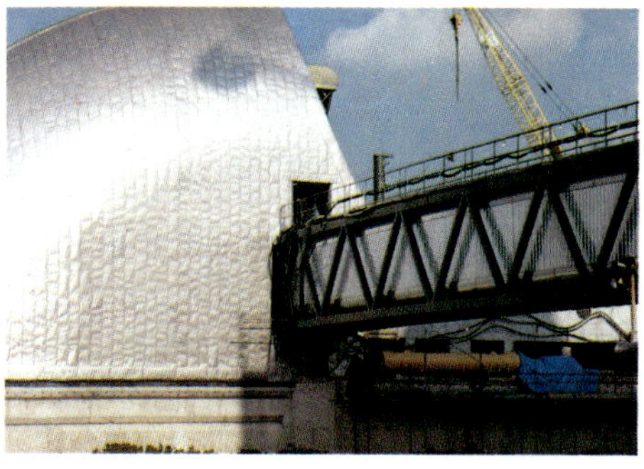

85 mm telephoto lens

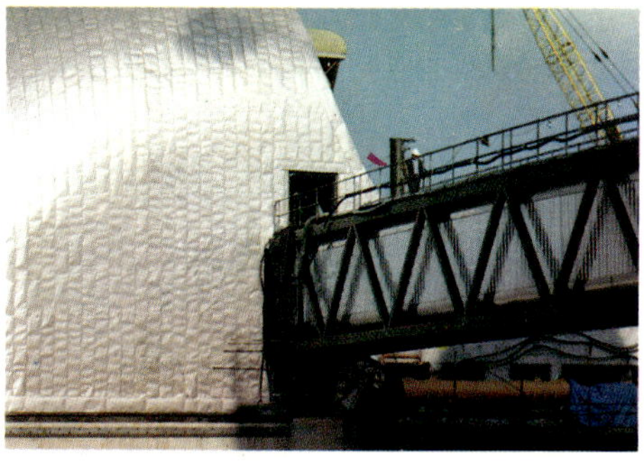

105 mm telephoto lens

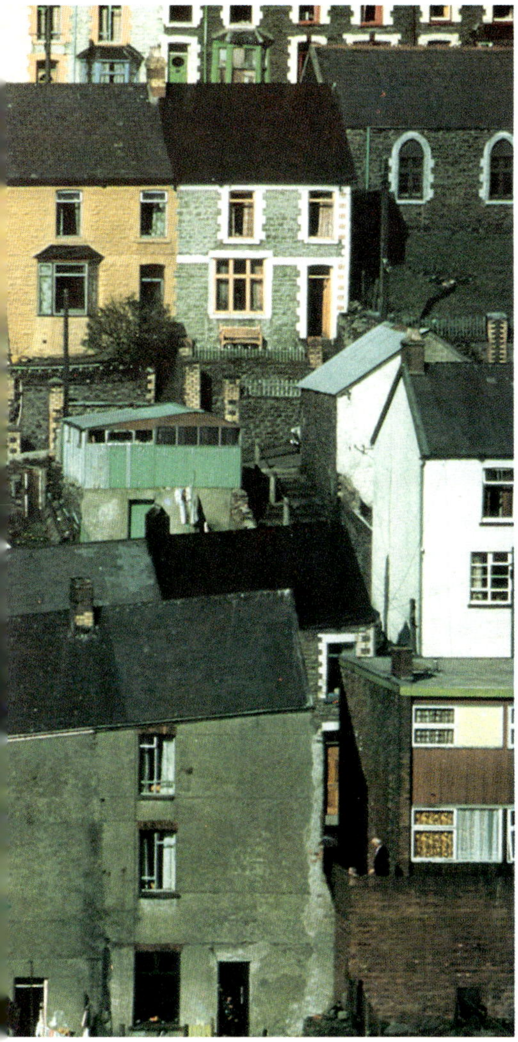

Roofs and houses *Because a long focus lens includes less of the subject, it is possible to crop really tightly for striking, dramatic compositions*

the depth of field is only 60 cm at an aperture of *f*/4.

This vicious circle—fast shutter speed needed to eliminate camera shake, so wider aperture selected, which in turn means inadequate depth of field—is shared by all telephoto lenses, not just the 200 mm. But the problems become more pronounced as focal length increases. The only real solution is to use either a tripod or a faster film.

The focal length of lens that will be most suitable for each individual photographer will largely be dictated by the type of photography for which he or she anticipates the lens will be used. For most people, the actual view through the lens is the deciding factor. By looking through a range of telephotos, and pointing them at people in the shop or in the street outside, it should be easy to judge which lens is best fitted to your requirements. This is a subjective decision in the end, and as often as not, people will reject a lens because the viewfinder image is not 'right'.

Choosing a lens

The choice of focal length is usually fairly easy, but the problems arise when it becomes necessary to choose between many similar brands. If you get the chance, it is worth testing a lens before you buy by taking photographs with it. Look for sharpness and contrast at various apertures, both at the edges and in the centre of the picture, and for signs of vignetting—darkening at the edges.

All long focus lenses should be used with a lens hood to give best results. The size of hood required will vary according to the focal length of the lens—a hood for a 200 mm lens will be unsuitable for a 105 mm lens. The better lenses of 135 mm and longer have built-in hoods, and those that do not often have hoods included in the price. A lens hood is an essential accessory and it may add a significant amount to the cost of a lens if purchased separately.

Similar comments apply to lens cases. Some people never use them, but other people consider them vital for keeping equipment clean. If you want one, make sure it will not add to the price, or at least take this into account when comparing prices of lenses.

Filters

If you use filters frequently, it is a good idea to take a close look at the size of filter needed for the lens you are buying. A number of manufacturers have standardized the filter size of their lenses as far as is practically possible, and all of the commonly used focal lengths from any one of these manufacturers take the same size.

Although adapter rings are available if filter sizes are not compatible, it is much simpler to buy a lens that will takes the same size filters as your standard lens.

A point which is often overlooked when buying a lens is the direction of movement of the focusing ring. Some lenses have a ring that must be turned clockwise to focus to infinity, others anticlockwise. It can be very disconcerting to have to switch between the two systems, so check this, too, when you are looking at lenses.

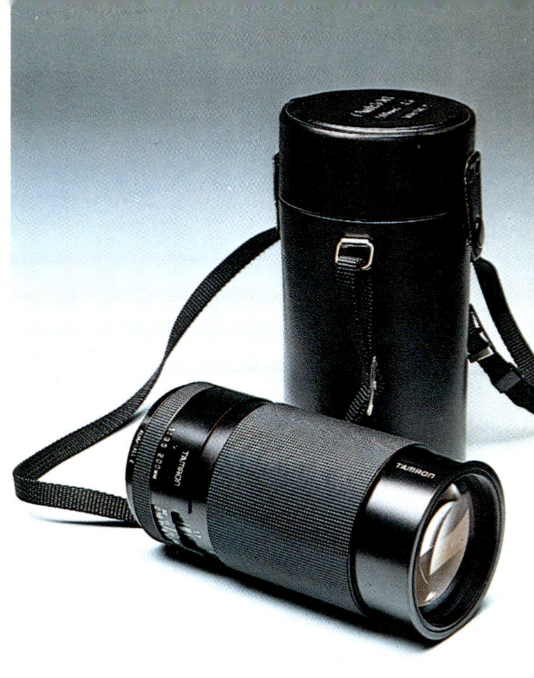

A good case *If you do not have a camera bag, check that the lens price includes a case. This lens has a case and strap*

Very cheap lenses often use a mechanism called a preset diaphragm to close the aperture from fully open to the working aperture. This eliminates all mechanical couplings between camera body and lens. Just before exposure, the photographer turns a ring, which looks identical to an automatic aperture setting ring. This closes the diaphragm, and comes to a halt at a point preset by the photographer. Although this system works perfectly well, it is very cumbersome and slow to use. Unless it is essential to buy the cheapest possible lens, it is worth spending the extra money and buying a lens with an automatic diaphragm.

The best lenses on the market are almost always expensive, and for most photographers it is necessary to strike a balance between cost and quality. Even if money is no object, compromise is sometimes necessary—the extra light gathering power of an *f*/2 lens may seem desirable, but has to be considered in the context of the extra weight of the lens when compared with an *f*/3.5 of the same focal length.

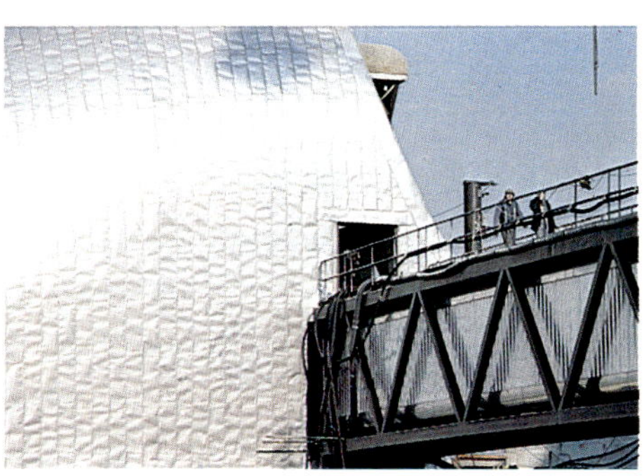

135 mm telephoto lens

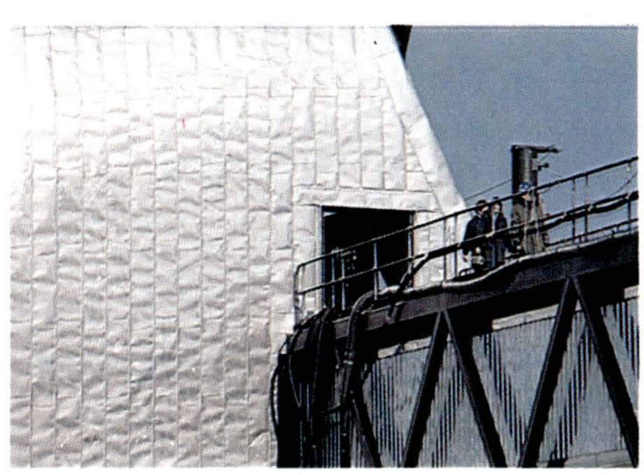

200 mm telephoto lens

Silver cowls *This series of pictures shows the field of view through the most popular telephoto lenses. All the pictures are printed from the whole of the 35 mm frame, so that it is possible to make a size comparison between them. Perhaps surprisingly, the 85 mm lens, which many photographers dismiss as being too short for most purposes, actually produces a very useful degree of magnification. The longest lens, the 200 mm, allowed the photographer to emphasize a small area of the subject*

Mirror lenses

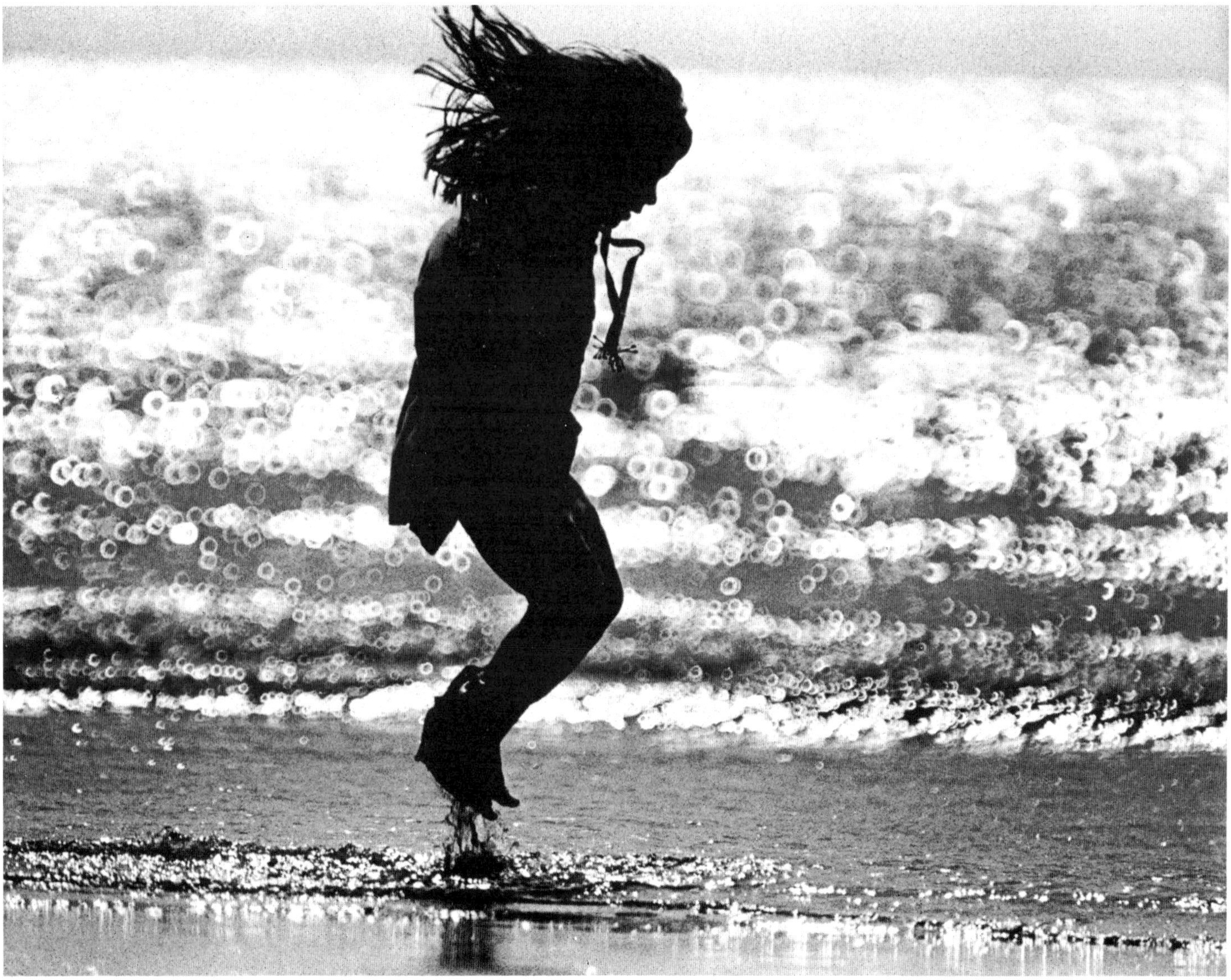

Pictures taken with super telephoto lenses always look impressive—perspective is flattened, and distant scenery is dramatically enlarged. But most people are put off by the size and weight of the lenses—the longer ones are virtually impossible to hand hold, and few lenses longer than 300 mm will fit into the average camera bag.

Mirror lenses have overcome these problems of size and weight. By folding the optical path of the light entering the lens, so that it travels three times along the barrel, it is possible to cut down bulk and mass to a small fraction of that of a conventional lens.

Mirror, or *catadioptric*, lenses are not new—they have been around since the earliest days of photography, and the first portrait was taken using a lens that reflected light, instead of refracting it. For a long time, though, problems of design and construction made the commercial use of mirror lenses impractical and until recently they were a costly novelty. This has changed, and mass production has brought the cost of mirror lenses down to a level comparable with ordinary telephoto lenses.

Mirror lenses are no longer confined to the upper reaches of the focal length range, either. Focal lengths as short as 250 mm and 300 mm are available, though 500 mm 'cat' lenses are more common. At the other end of the scale, there are 2000 mm mirror lenses in routine production, and longer focal lengths can be made up to order—though these are really astronomical telescopes adapted for use as a camera lens.

Jump for joy *Mirror lenses form ring-shaped highlights on out of focus parts of the subject*

Reflector or refractor?

There are a number of important differences between mirror lenses and conventional refracting lenses, and these differences affect the way that mirror lenses are used.

In a conventional lens, an iris diaphragm is fitted to control the width of the beam of light which enters the lens. It is impractical to fit an iris diaphragm to a mirror lens, however, because of the large diameter and optical construction, with a central obstruction. Reducing the aperture would seriously degrade performance. All the mirror lenses which are commonly available therefore have a fixed aperture. This makes exposure control more difficult, and the light falling on the film has to be controlled by the shutter in the camera, or by inserting neutral density (grey-black) filters into the light path.

A second, equally important, consequence of the lack of diaphragm is that the photographer has no control over depth of field—the lens must be used at full aperture, and depth of field is always very limited.

The image formed by a mirror lens is reflected twice—once by the main mirror, and then again by a smaller mirror attached to the inside of the glass corrector plate at the front of the lens. This smaller mirror obscures the central portion of the lens, so the beam of light that reaches the film is not circular in cross section, but doughnut shaped. Though this does not affect the image when it is in focus, it causes out of focus spots of light to form circles instead of discs. This can make out of focus subjects look peculiar, particularly if they have very bright highlights. A few photographers avoid mirror lenses for this reason but most people find these doughnut shaped circles attractive, and use them for creative effect.

Against these drawbacks must be considered the enormous savings in weight and size that stem from the use of a reflecting lens design. Typically, a mirror lens is half the weight and a third of the length of a comparable refracting lens. 300 mm mirror lenses are often no longer than a standard 50 mm lens.

Mirror lenses in use

Because they have a long focal length and narrow angle of view, mirror lenses have similar limitations to conventional long telephotos (see page 75). They are prone to vibration and camera shake, so it is best to use some kind of camera support such as a tripod or monopod. The shorter focal length mirror lenses have no tripod socket of their own, since they are quite small and light, but those over 500 mm generally have a standard $\frac{1}{4}$ inch threaded tripod bush.

An ordinary medium weight tripod is quite adequate for 500 mm and shorter models. For a 1000 mm lens, a heavy duty tripod is needed to eliminate vibration, and the monstrous 2000 mm mirror lens that is sometimes used by professional photographers needs a special cast alloy mounting cradle, similar to a telescope mounting. This is used on a special plinth—an ordinary tripod is more or less useless.

Mirror lenses offer less wind resistance, and are better balanced than conventional telephotos. If you do not

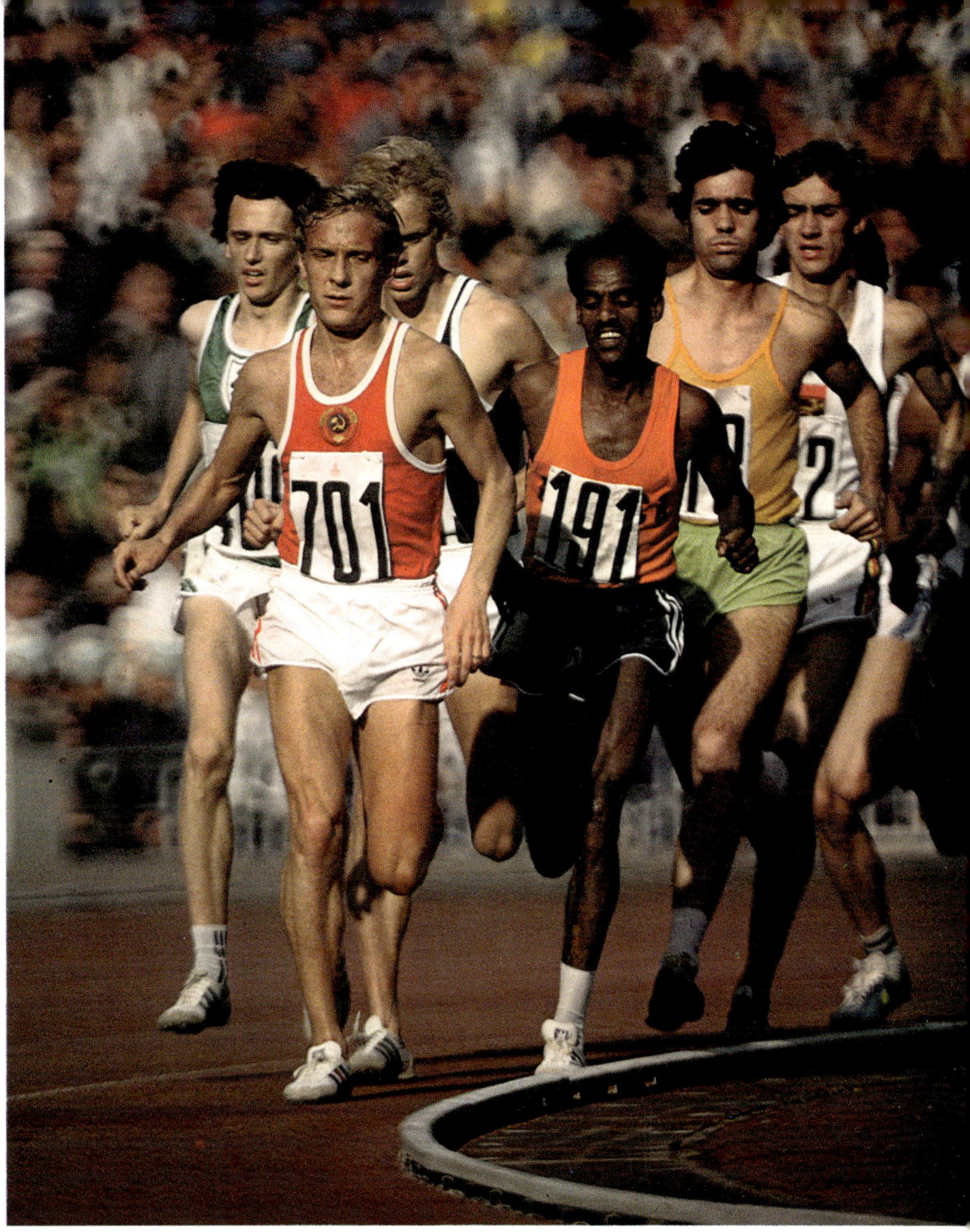

In the lead *Because they can only be used at full aperture, mirror lenses have very little depth of field*

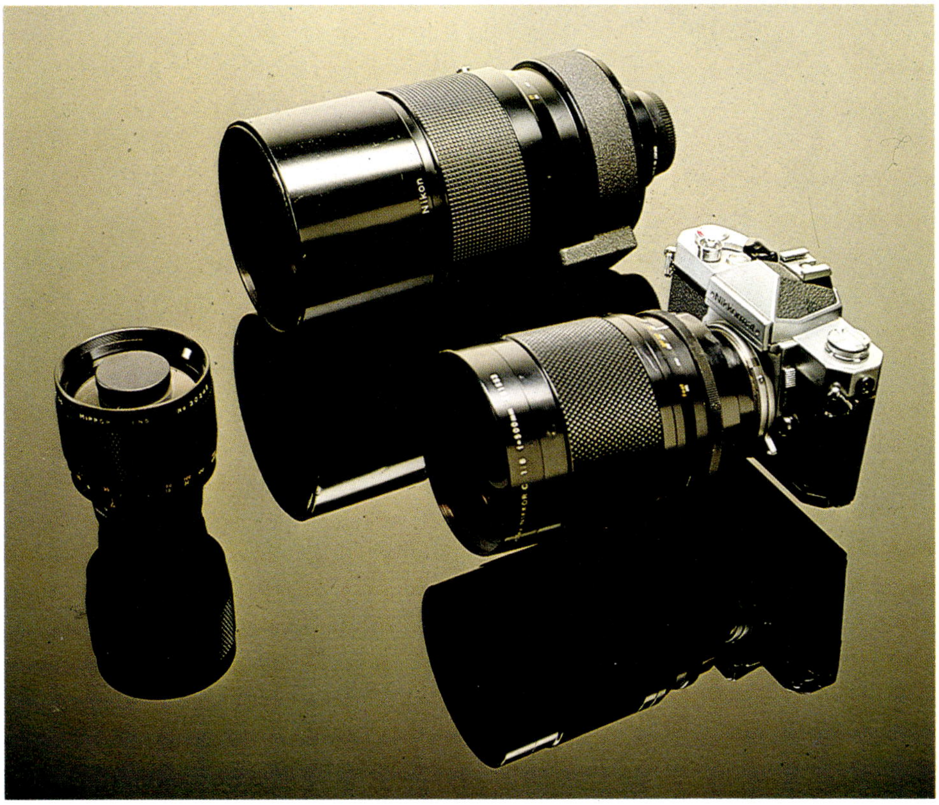

Small wonders *These lenses—300 mm, 500 mm and 1000 mm—are only a third the length of their refracting counterparts*

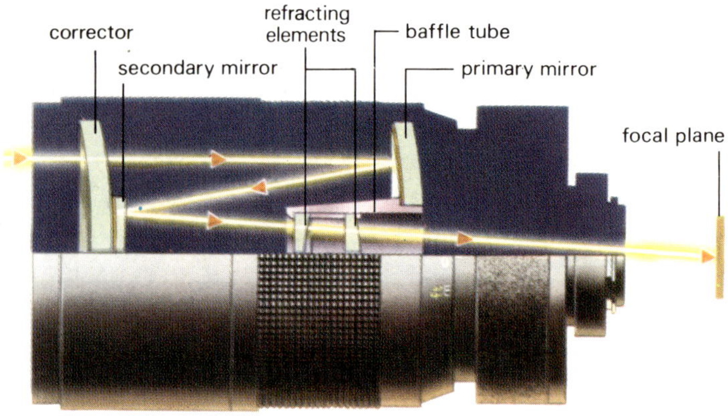

Curved mirrors *Two reflections of the image take place in the barrel of a mirror lens*

want to be encumbered by a tripod, you may find that it is possible to hand-hold a mirror lens at the higher shutter speeds. 250 mm, 300 mm and 500 mm lenses give acceptable results at 1/500 second or faster, but as a general rule, it is best to use the fastest speed possible. Remember that the pictures from any long lens will seem sharper if you use a tripod.

Focusing a mirror lens is not as easy as focusing a standard or short telephoto lens. The small aperture—usually *f*/8 or smaller—causes the microprisms and rangefinder wedges on standard focusing screens to black out. The solution is to use the plain ground glass portion of the focusing screen, or if your camera accepts interchangeable screens, to fit a different one. Screens are available which have plain matt glass all over, or which have focusing aids with prism angles more suitable for slow lenses (see page 12).

Mirror lenses have two unique features that affect focusing. First, there must always be a filter in the path of the light if the lens uses rear mounted filters. Although some mirror lenses accept filters on the front, many of them have a huge front element, and filters would be very costly. If it is fitted behind the lens, the filter becomes an integral part of the camera's optical system, and if it is removed, the resulting pictures will not be as sharp. Even if you do not need a neutral density filter for exposure control, you should use the UV filter supplied with the lens.

The second feature that you will notice is that mirror lenses have a focusing scale that carries on turning when you get to the infinity marking. This is because they are particularly susceptible to temperature changes, and the exact position of infinity focus varies according to the ambient temperature. When focusing on distant subjects, therefore, it is not sufficient to turn the lens until it stops, as this could lead to incorrect focus, particularly in cold weather. The focusing scale is a guide only, and should not be relied

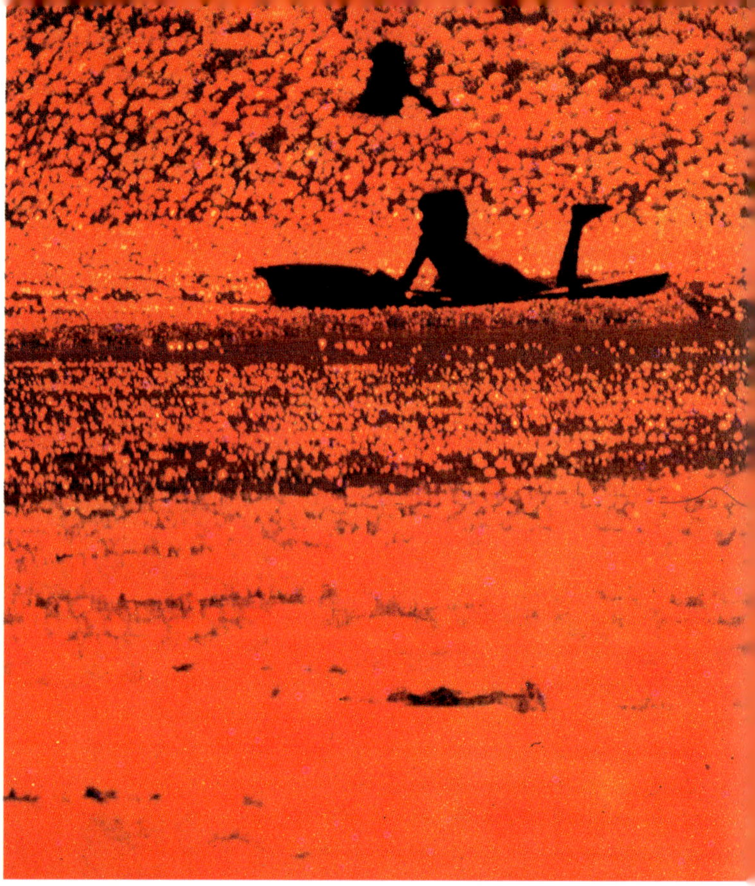

Red raft *The red filter that is built into some mirror lenses may give striking results with colour film*

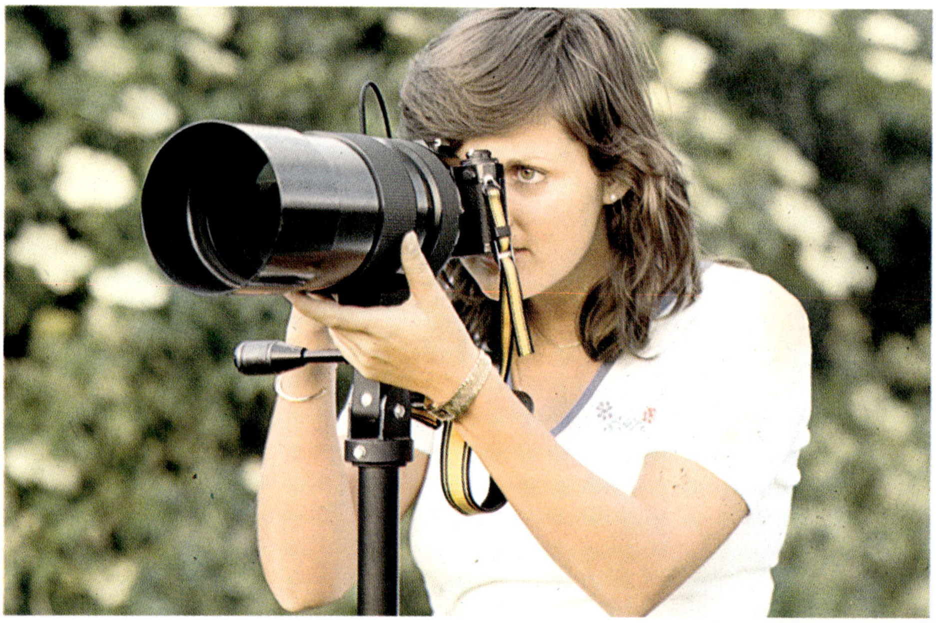

On a tripod *For the longer mirror lenses—such as this 1000 mm—a tripod is absolutely essential*

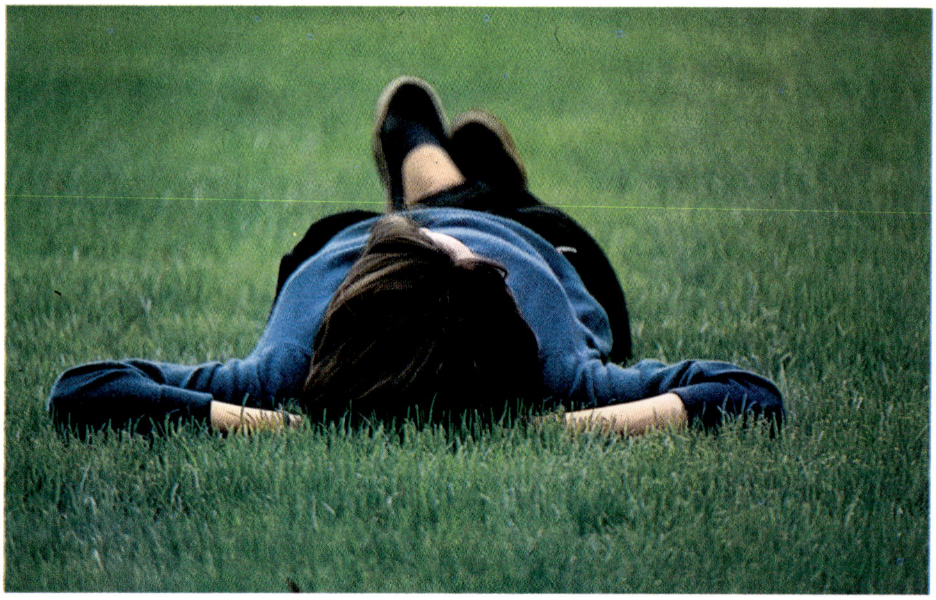

Dark corners *All mirror lenses give slightly uneven illumination—this shows up as a central 'hot spot'*

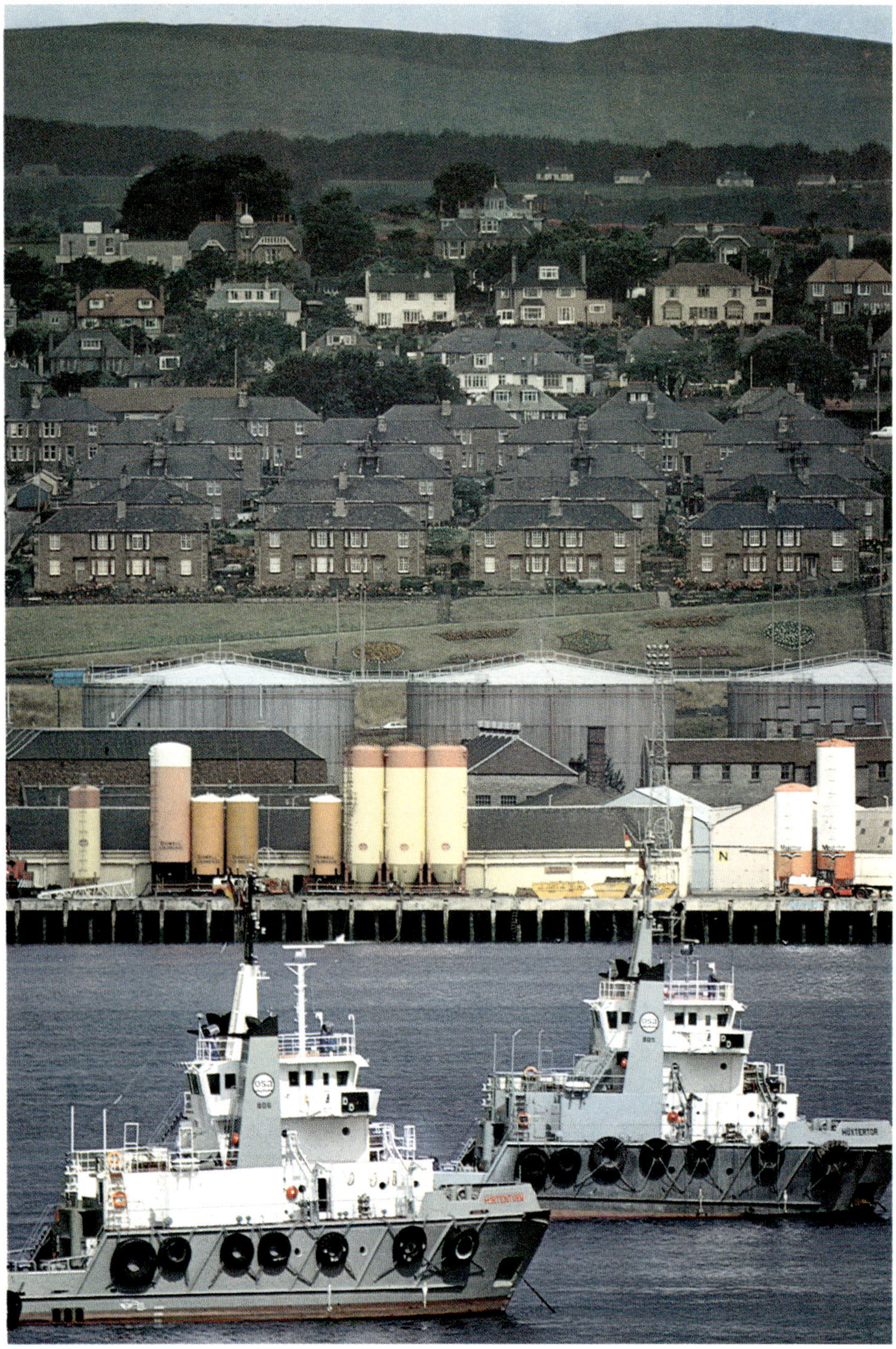

upon for accurate results.

Some of the newer mirror lenses have a close focusing facility which enables the frame to be filled by a small subject, and with a 2× teleconverter, macro pictures are possible at a distance of a couple of metres. While this is a handy feature for occasional close up photographs of flat subjects, the shallow depth of field of mirror lenses limits their usefulness at close range. Another consideration is that they give their best results when focused on infinity, and performance is not as good at short subject distances.

You might notice a slight darkening at the top of the focusing screen when you have a catadioptric lens fitted to the camera. This is caused by the reflex mirror in the camera body not being quite big enough to reflect the whole of the image. This is not a great problem, and does not show up on the film, though it may affect the exposure meter in your camera.

Exposure control

Metering systems in SLR cameras are designed with an average lens in mind, and they work well with lenses in the 20 to 200 mm range. Outside these limits, the indicated exposure may not be quite correct, though this will depend on the exact position of the light sensitive cells in the camera body.

The lack of iris diaphragm does not help, because shutter speed priority cameras rely on this to set the exposure. Before you take any important pictures using a mirror lens, it is a good idea to check that your built-in meter works correctly with it.

First, find out whether it can be used on the automatic setting. If the camera has aperture priority metering, this should be possible, but if it is a shutter priority model, you must use it in the manual mode. In this case, the meter is balanced using the shutter speed control and neutral density filters, though these are only necessary with very fast film or in bright sunlight.

Cameras with manual metering are operated in the same way, but if your camera does not have a TTL meter, you may have problems. The angle of view of a mirror lens is much narrower than that of a hand held or non-TTL meter, so a separate spotmeter is necessary to make sure that the exposure is correct.

Even if the camera's meter appears to function normally, it still may not be giving the correct exposure to the film. It is best to make a series of test exposures on slow colour transparency film before using the lens for serious photography. This film has little exposure latitude, so metering errors show up clearly. Make the exposures at the setting indicated by the camera, and then at ½, 1, 1½ and 2 stops over- and underexposure. Keep a careful record of the exposures, and from the series of nine pictures, pick the best, and work out whether your exposure meter needs to be set to a different ASA value to compensate for over- or underexposure.

River estuary *Like any long telephoto, a mirror lens can produce very dramatic pictures by flattening out perspective*

Getting the best results

Mirror lenses are no better or worse than conventional long telephotos. The two types of lens have different characteristics, and are subject to different applications.

Bright sunlight and contrasty lighting suit mirror lenses, because in overcast

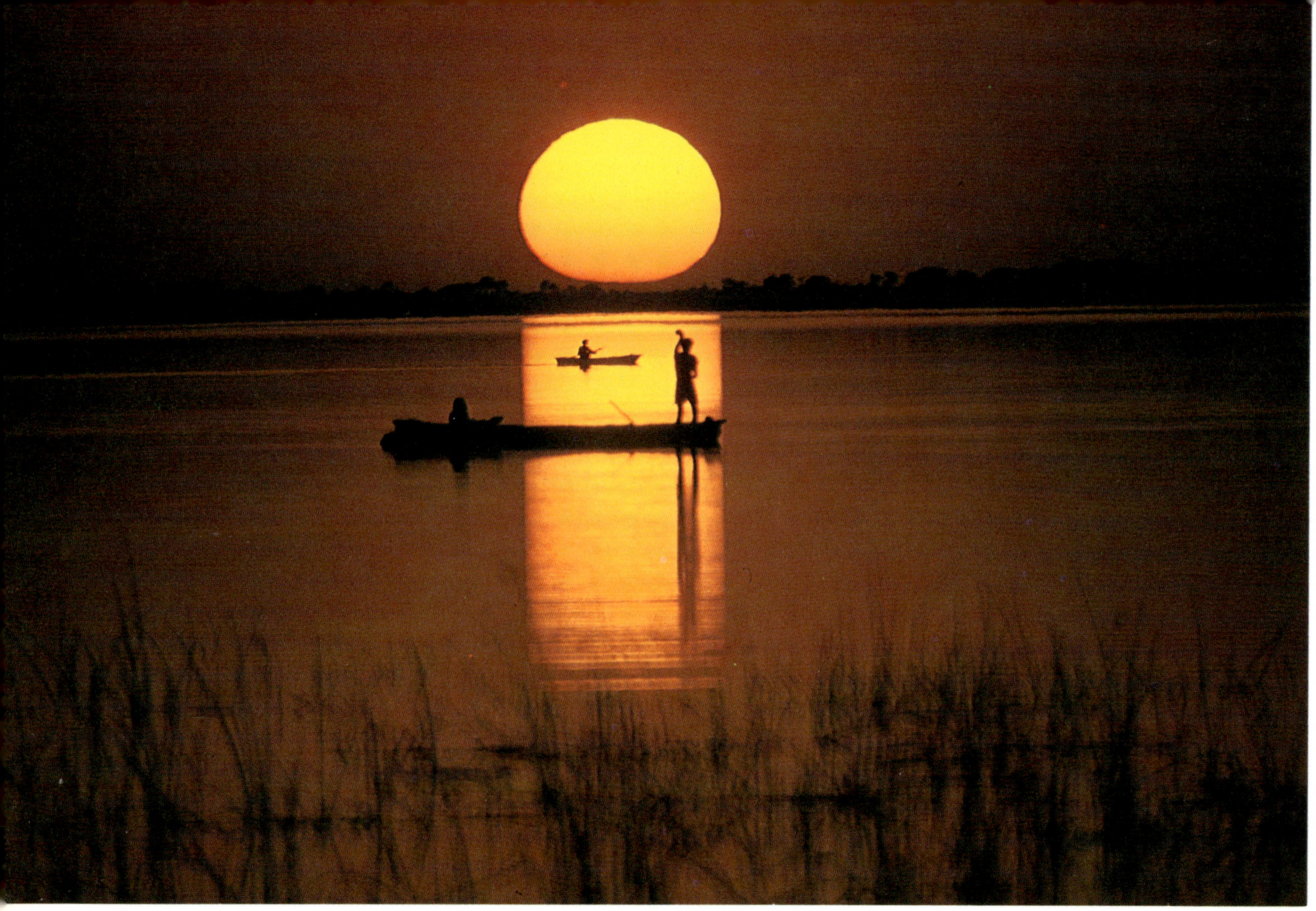

Setting sun *The moon and sun can make exciting subjects if you use a long catadioptric lens*

conditions and with very flat subject matter, they tend to give a hot spot in the middle of the frame. This slight unevenness of exposure is a characteristic of all mirror lenses, but is minimized on the newer designs. In contrasty light, it is unnoticeable and even in dull light the darker corners may not be noticed.

The central obstruction of a mirror lens reduces the contrast of the image, so when photographing through haze a conventional refracting lens will give more contrasty results.

If you need to be very mobile, a mirror lens is a good choice—its light weight and small size make it the first choice for travelling photographers, or in situations where there is a lot of action going on which would make the use of a tripod difficult or dangerous. If you need to move quickly, or to pack a lot of equipment, a conventional long lens is a tremendous handicap.

Whenever there are bright highlights in a picture, the out of focus circles produced by a catadioptric lens can make a very attractive picture. Backlit portraits take on a sparkling, unreal quality. Pictures at night, or over expanses of sunlit water, offer a lot of potential for a mirror lens user.

The shallow depth of field produced by a mirror lens can be used to isolate subjects—a figure can be picked out in a crowd, or the subject of a portrait isolated from a background. The dough-nut shaped circles of confusion shatter background detail to an even greater extent than with normal lenses, so objects at close distances seem even more isolated.

This shallow depth of field can cause problems—when a 500 mm mirror lens is focused at 20 metres, depth of field extends only 20 cm on either side of the plane of sharp focus. When you need a lot of depth of field, stick to a conventional lens and stop down.

Just like any long lens, a catadioptric will appear to compress perspective when focused on distant objects. Buildings and hills appear to be stacked up on top of each other, and this can be used to produces very striking pictures. Over long distances, atmospheric haze gives a veiled appearance to a picture, and cuts down contrast. This can cause problems, because of the inherent low contrast of mirror lenses. The solution with black and white film is to increase development, but there is little you can do if you are shooting pictures in colour.

Because they have quite a small aperture, mirror lenses must be used with fast film, and to hand hold them, you must use film faster than 125 ASA. In overcast weather, you may find yourself using 400 ASA(ISO) film, pushing it by one stop if you do not wish to use a tripod. Fortunately, this procedure will give a boost to film contrast, which is very welcome in dull conditions.

Military man *At its closest focusing distance, a mirror lens can take an unusual view of a familiar subject*

The unique characteristics of mirror lenses make it crucial that you use them with care, and pick the right subjects. They are not the answer to every photographer's prayer, and there are some circumstances where a conventional lens does a better job. On the other hand, if you stick to the general principles outlined here, there is no reason why you should not get some striking pictures which make good use of these compact, lightweight lenses.

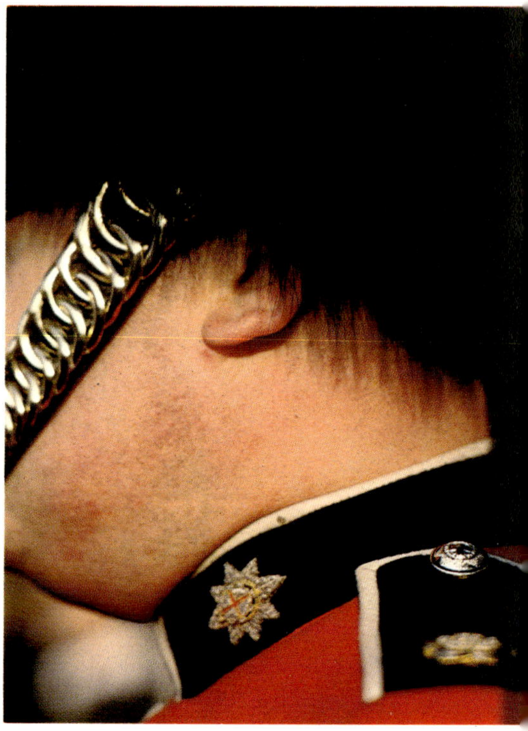

Long telephotos

Although many photographers think of a long telephoto simply as a lens for magnifying distant objects, lenses in the range 200 to 600 mm have a number of other equally valuable properties. You can use these lenses to pick out fascinating details close by. Or you can exploit the shallow depth of field to throw a distracting background out of focus. For the best results, however, a long lens requires special handling.

There are lenses much longer than 600 mm available. Indeed, a lens with a focal length of 5200 mm was made as recently as 1980 by Canon. But such giant super-telephotos are expensive specialist items that cost a small fortune even to hire.

Supporting the lens

With any long lens, the camera must be kept completely steady during exposure, and even a good tripod fitted in the camera baseplate is not always adequate. The unsupported weight and length of a long telephoto can exert considerable leverage and may unsteady the camera. The leverage may even put enough strain on the lens mount or the tripod socket to damage them.

It is essential, therefore, to support the lens as well as the camera and to make lens support easier, most long telephoto lenses have their own built-in tripod socket.

Ideally, the camera and lens should be supported by a pair of tripods, one under the lens and another under the camera. Unfortunately, this sort of arrangement is extremely unwieldy and impractical. Not only does it mean carrying two tripods around but finding a suitable site to place two tripods firmly on level ground. A satisfactory compromise is to use a single tripod and to mount both camera and lens by the lens socket, which is usually close to the point of balance of the camera and lens.

If you find even a single tripod too unwieldy, a monopod screwed into the

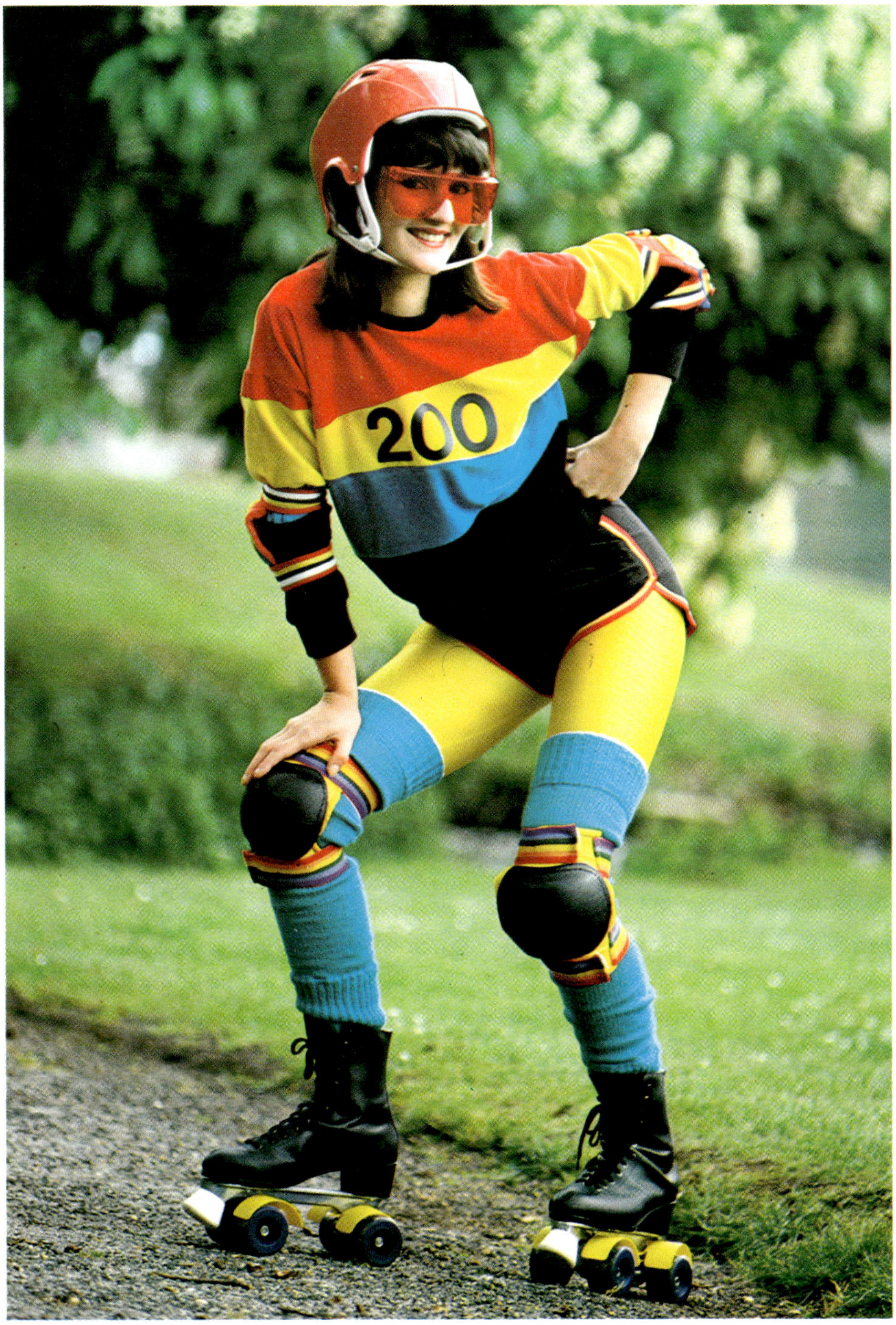

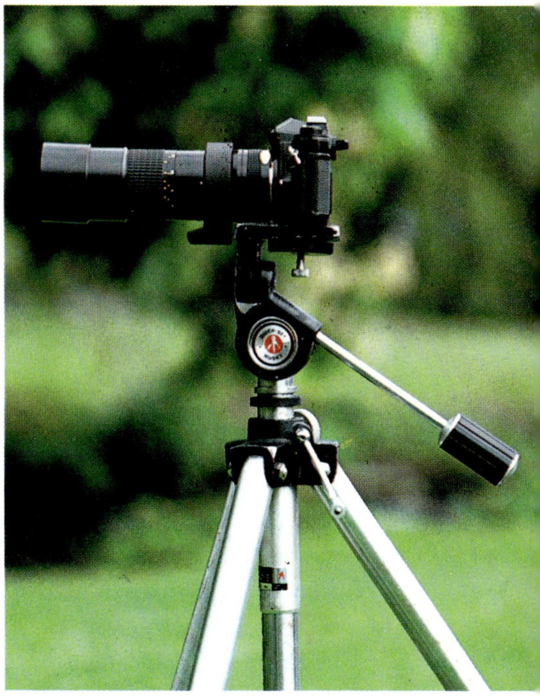

200 mm *Taken from about 10 metres with a 200 mm telephoto. Following shots show the increase in image size with larger lenses*

Camera mounting *Smaller long telephotos can be supported normally, but longer lenses may need their own tripod or support*

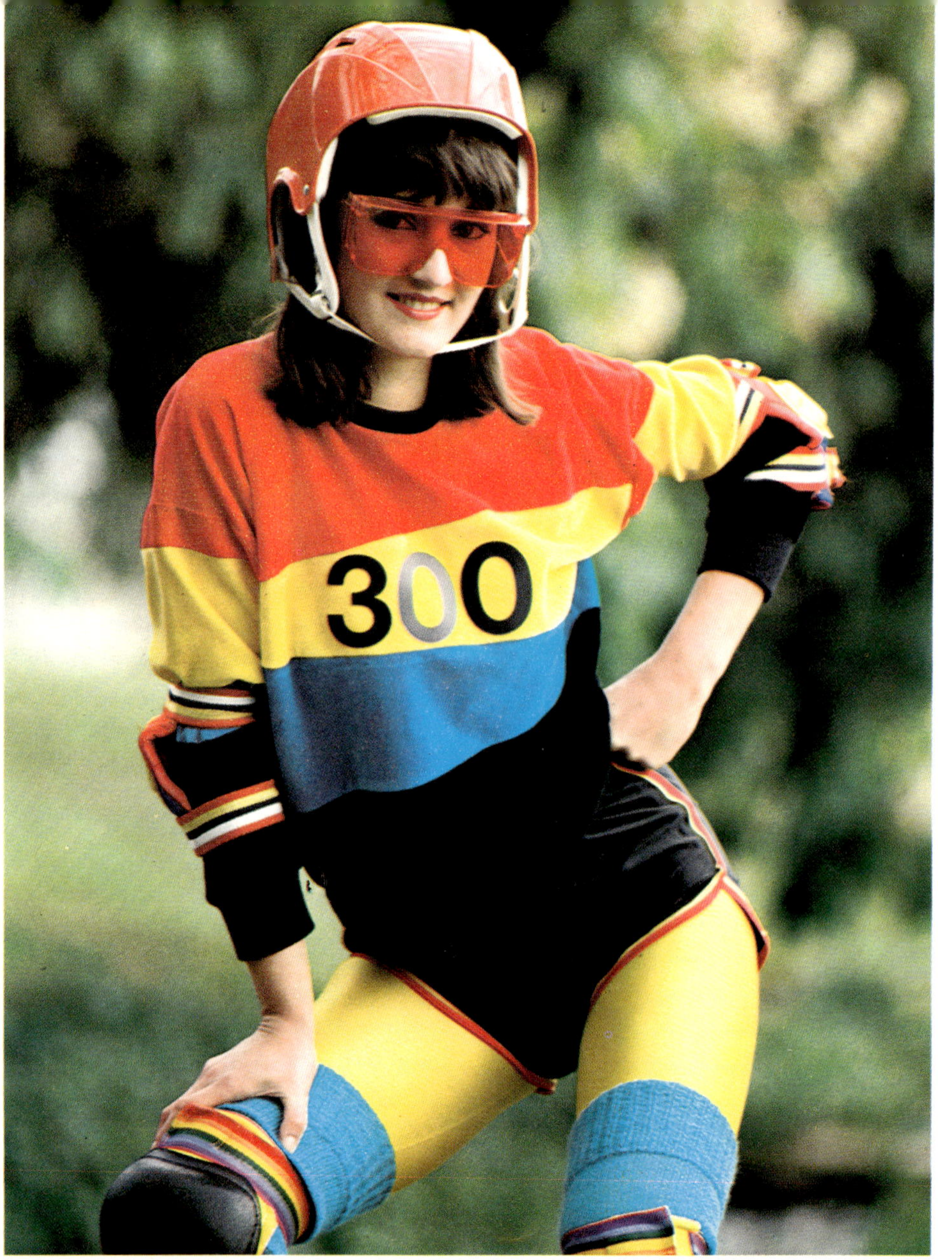

Monopod *To avoid the need for a bulky tripod, a 300 mm can be mounted on a monopod by its built-in tripod socket, but careful operation is necessary*

300 mm *From the same distance, a 300 mm lens brings the subject significantly closer than a 200 mm. The lens is just small enough to be portable*

lens tripod socket may be adequate. The monopod supports the lens, and your body supports the camera. Pistol grips and rifle stocks (see page 58) can also help to hold the camera firmly. In this instance, a cable release should be used to avoid the tendency for the camera to tilt slightly when the shutter release on top of the camera is pressed.

Monopods, grips and stocks are not only easier to carry, but also make it easier to move the camera around to adjust the framing. A tripod head must be unlocked and relocked to make every small change in aim. All too often, simply relocking an inexpensive tripod head will move it slightly out of position, losing the accuracy of framing which is so essential with long telephotos.

Fitting an autowinder or motor drive adds weight underneath the camera, and this may improve the balance, as well as allowing a firmer grip.

Viewing and focusing

Long telephotos have a very limited depth of field and, although this can be a great disadvantage at first, with practice it can be used to remove distracting backgrounds and foregrounds in a controlled way. While you can easily throw backgrounds out of focus, it can require great skill to keep all the subject in sharp focus or to reach the best focus point quickly and positively, especially with moving subjects.

To ensure sharp pictures, you must focus very carefully, and it is important to keep a few points in mind. Most microprism focusing spots do not work with long telephotos, and you must focus by eye in the ground glass surrounding the microprism centre instead. Similarly, split-image rangefinders usually black out at small apertures and with a long telephoto you may not be able to open up enough for the split-image to be visible. Again, you must

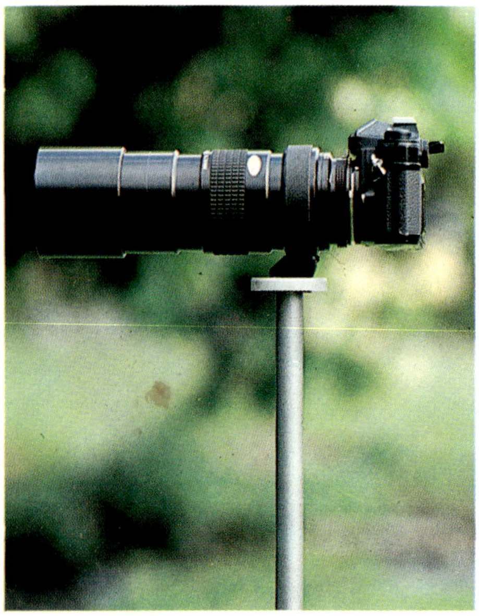

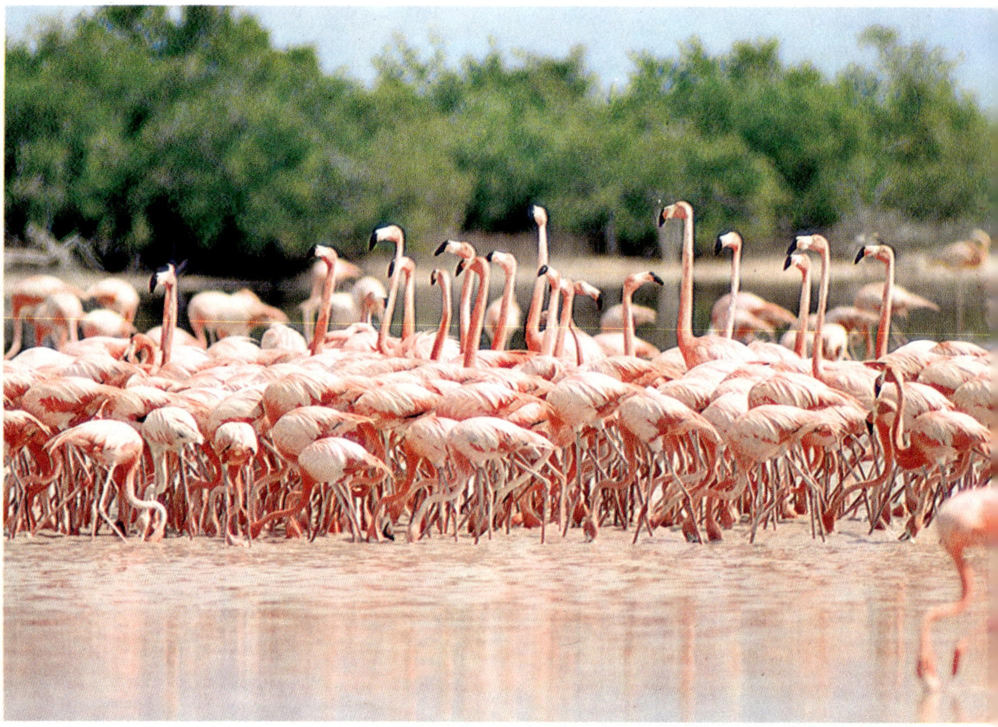

Pink flamingos *Long telephoto lenses are often used to photograph wildlife. They allow greater flexibility in choice of viewpoint and framing*

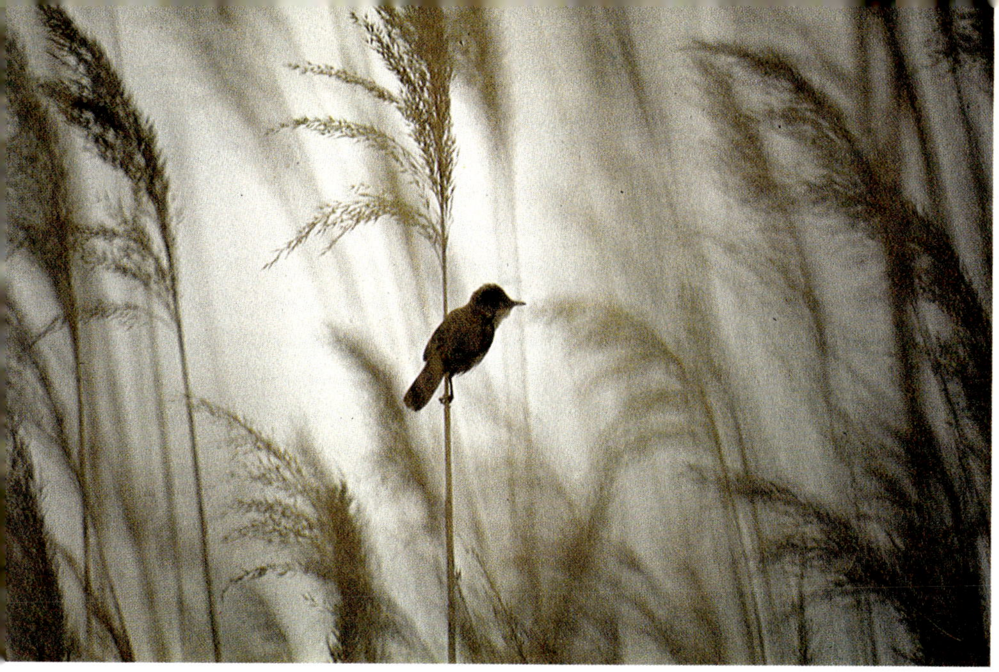

Bird in foliage *The limited depth of field of long telephoto lenses can be used to creative advantage. Here it has given a moody background blur*

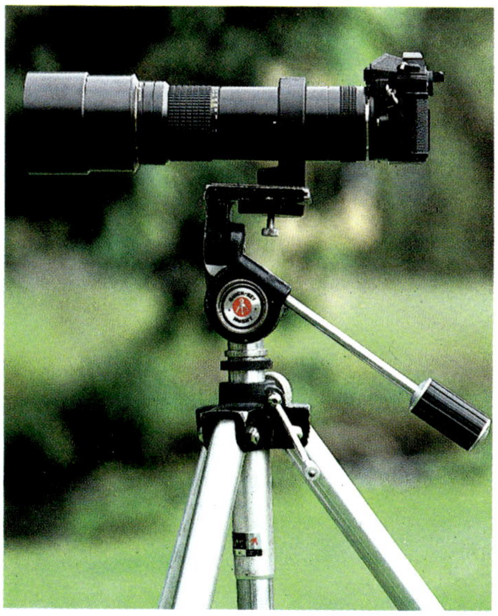

Lens mount *A 400 mm lens needs very firm support and should be mounted on a solid tripod by the lens. This also balances the unit well*

focus by eye in the ground glass area when using small maximum aperture telephoto lenses.

If your camera has interchangeable focusing screens, it is worth using a plain ground glass screen instead—this makes focusing by eye easier. Some camera makers produce special split-image and microprism focusing screens that can be used with lenses with limited maximum apertures, but these are usually better suited to wide angle lenses than telephotos.

When using a long telephoto on a static subject, focus with great care. If your camera has a depth of field preview control, use it to make sure that all important parts of the subject are sharp. If not, use the depth of field scale on the lens. Judge the distances by focusing first on the most distant part of the subject that you want to keep sharp, and note the setting on the lens distance scale, perhaps marking it with a soft china pencil directly on the focusing ring of the lens. Then focus on the closest part and mark this distance. You can then check these markings against the depth of field scale.

If there is insufficient depth of field even at a very small aperture, part of the subject will have to remain out of focus (see page 50-53).

Presetting the focus

When shooting fast moving subjects with a long telephoto, presetting the focus is a useful way of avoiding the problems brought about by the narrow angle of view and the shallow depth of field. When covering motor sports, athletics and wildlife, for example, the rapid movement of the subject across the field of view and perhaps towards the camera can combine to make it very difficult to change the focus manually as you try to follow the subject in the viewfinder.

Instead you should pick a noticeable

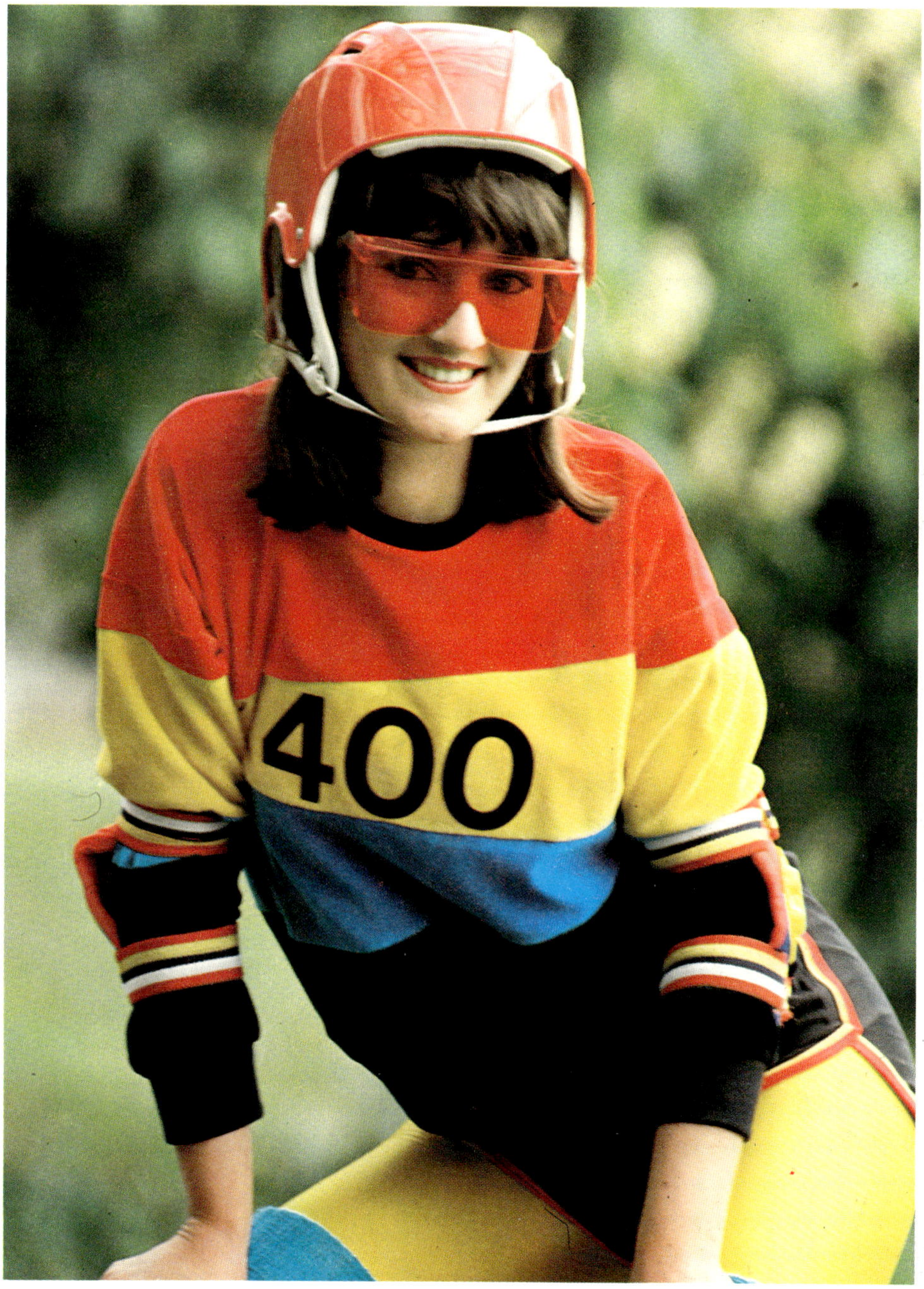

400 mm *Long enough to bring distant subjects in close, but too bulky for casual use, a 400 mm demands careful subject framing for good results*

feature that you know the subject is likely to pass—a feeding table for wild birds or a mark on the road for racing cars, for example. Focus on this point and do not shift the focus even if you move the camera to view the approaching subject. You may find it disconcerting to view the subject as a total blur, but providing you press the shutter as the subject passes the preset focusing point, the picture should be sharp.

With very fast moving subjects you should also allow for the brief period that elapses between pressing the shutter release and its actual opening. Camera mechanisms take time to operate—the lens aperture has to stop down and the viewing mirror has to flip up before the shutter actually fires. In this brief instant, a fast moving subject can move past your preset focus point. It may even pass out of the frame. The shutter must therefore be fired an instant before the subject passes the preset focus point, but perfect framing needs considerable practice.

Follow focus

If you can find no preset focus point, you may have to try changing the focus as you follow the subject in the viewfinder. With a long telephoto, this can be very difficult and again the only way to perfect the technique is to practise. Football matches and other team sports give good opportunities for testing your skills on fast moving, unpredictable subjects. Shooting a few rolls of film for practice purposes will help you take better pictures later.

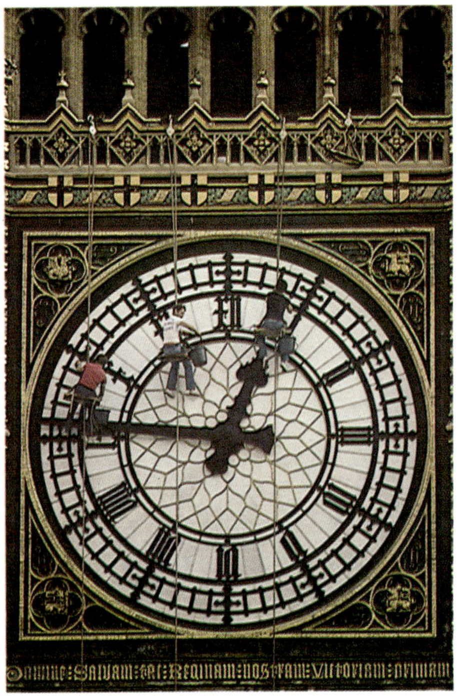

Clock face *To bring architectural detail in really close, a 600 mm lens is ideal. Clarity is good even from a distance of more than 200 metres*

Racing car *To produce sharp pictures of rapidly moving subjects with a long lens it is necessary to pre-focus. The lens was focused on the crest of the hill*

Choosing shutter speed

With any long focus lens, particularly those above 200 mm, camera shake can be a problem and, for hand-held shots, you should use the fastest shutter speed you can. A wide aperture may sacrifice depth of field, however. In this case, use a fast film and push process if necessary (by up-rating the film speed and increasing the development time to compensate) in order to achieve an additional one or two exposure stops.

When using a lens longer than 200 mm, hand-held shots will not normally be sharp at shutter speeds of less than 1/250 second. With a 500 mm lens, at least 1/500 is necessary and it is better to use a 1/1000 or 1/2000 if possible.

Slower shutter speeds can only be used with a firm support—such as a tripod—or with the panning technique. Given a firm support, such as a monopod or a tripod with a pan and tilt head, you can use speeds as slow as 1/15 second as long as you pan smoothly and evenly.

Light and metering

For long distance shots in particular, long telephotos can result in reduced contrast, and it is worth setting the exposure and choosing the lighting

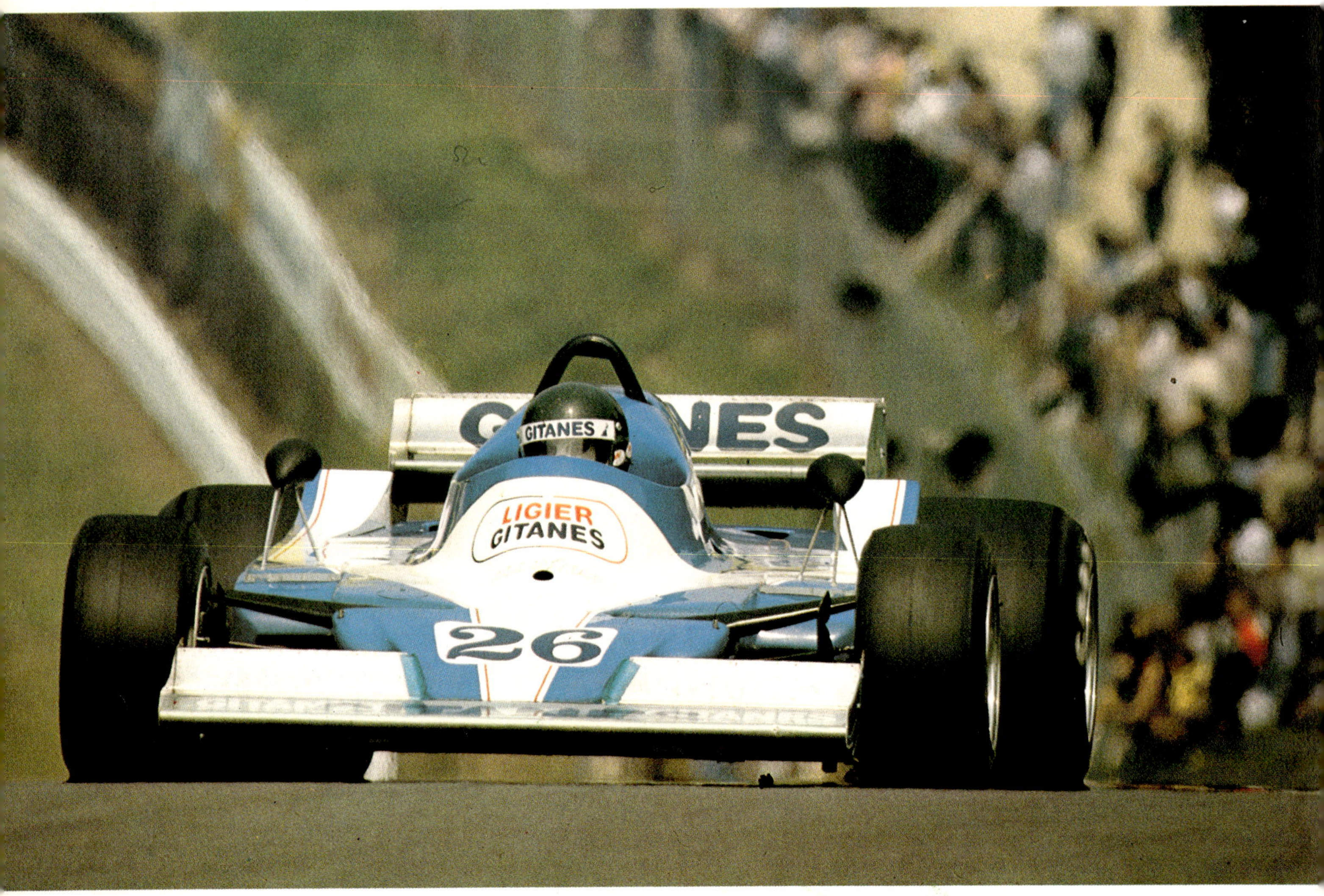

conditions that bring out the maximum contrast in your subject.

When using slide film with a long telephoto, it is usually best to give the minimum acceptable exposure. A slide that is slightly denser than normal may appear to have improved contrast and definition. Similarly, slight under-exposure combined with overdevelopment can improve the contrast of black and white telephoto pictures.

Even in low light you should still aim for minimum exposure. At concerts and shows, for instance, try to base your exposure readings on the performers rather than on the stage as a whole. An average reading will make the picture look grey and the performers washed out. It is better to have good contrast and a pure black for all the shadows than to try for an exposure that gives good shadow detail. Fortunately, the narrow angle of view of long telephotos combined with through the lens metering makes it easier to take selective readings from small areas of the subject. Simply move in close enough to fill the frame with your subject and use the reading taken at this distance as the basis for exposure of the whole view. If, however, you are forced to take a distant viewpoint—say at the back of a large concert hall—exposure setting may be more difficult. If you have to record the whole of a dimly lit stage rather than a single spotlit performer, the indicated meter exposure will have to be corrected by stopping down slightly.

Choose subject lighting carefully. Side or backlight will appear to increase sharpness. Flat frontal lighting or dull light will reduce it. Subjects picked out in full light against dark backgrounds will look sharper as well. In these circumstances be especially careful to avoid lens flare. Long telephotos can be fitted with very deep lens hoods, often deeper than those supplied with the particular model. You may be able to improvise an effective lens hood from cardboard tubes painted black inside.

Finally, sunsets or moonrises are ideal subjects for long telephoto lenses, particularly if they are the main points of interest—a long lens helps to ensure that they are not tiny spots in a vast frame. You should always be extremely careful when viewing and photographing the sun, however. Even when the sun is low on the horizon and dim enough to look at without discomfort it may still produce enough heat to damage your eyesight permanently. It may also damage your camera's viewing system. So, when photographing the sun, point the camera at the sun for the briefest time necessary for framing and metering. A straightforward through the lens meter reading will usually be correct, but bracket exposures a stop on either side of the 'correct' reading in any case. Each exposure setting will change the mood and colour of the final result, and give you a wide choice of effects in the final pictures.

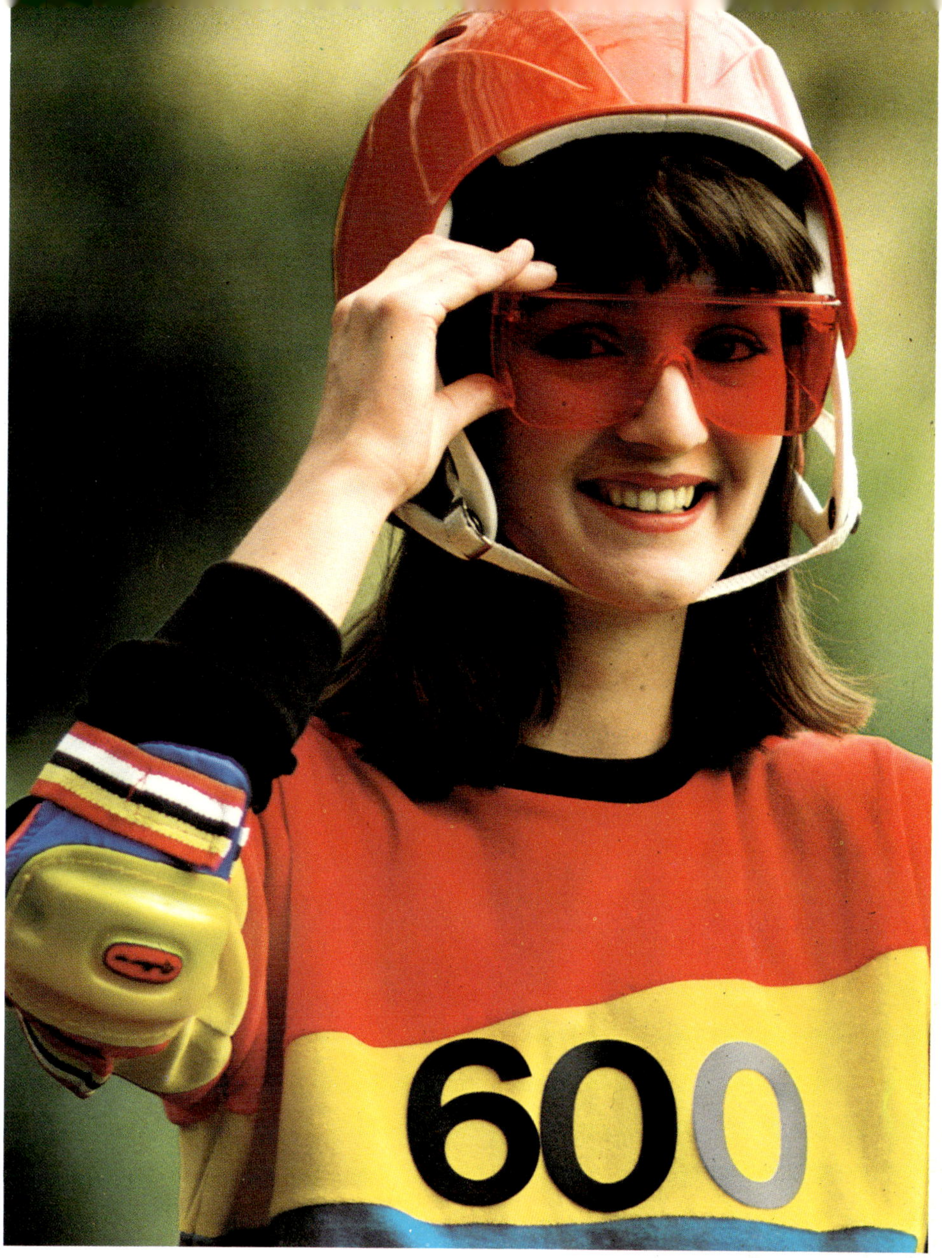

600 mm *For a tight close-up from a distance, a 600 mm is hard to beat. Powerful lenses are usually mirror designs to reduce overall length*

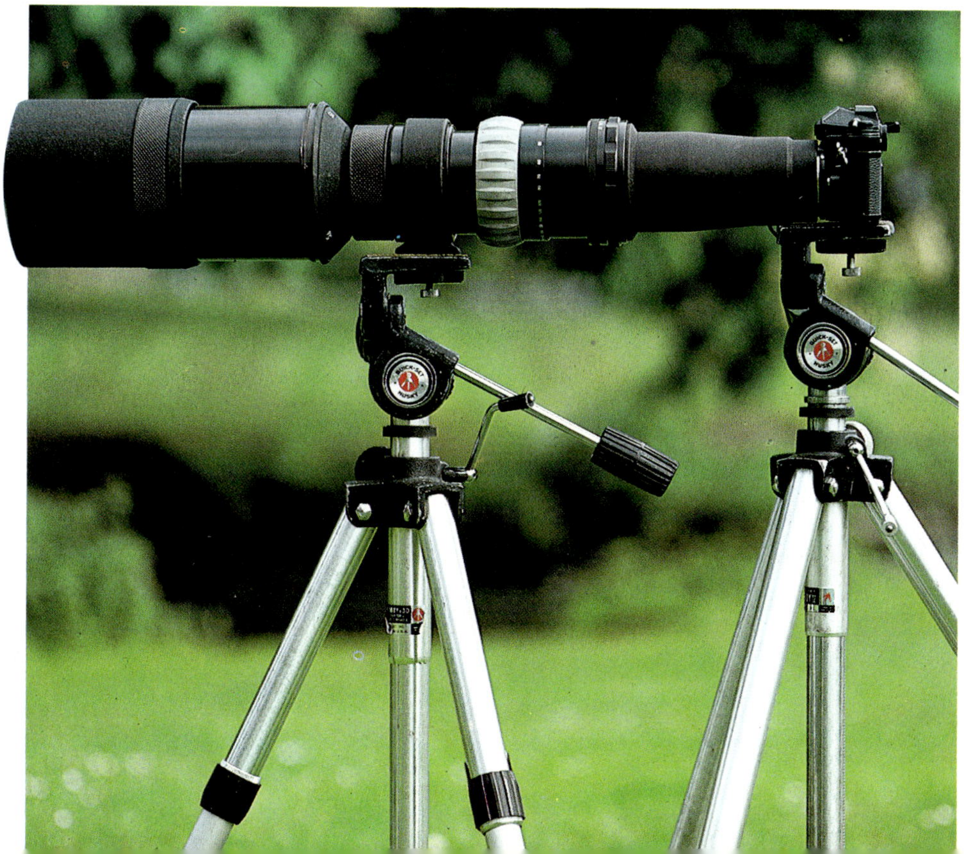

Two tripods *With very long lenses, extra precautions are needed to ensure stability. Tripods under lens and camera eliminate shake*

CHAPTER 7
WIDE ANGLE LENSES
Medium wide lenses

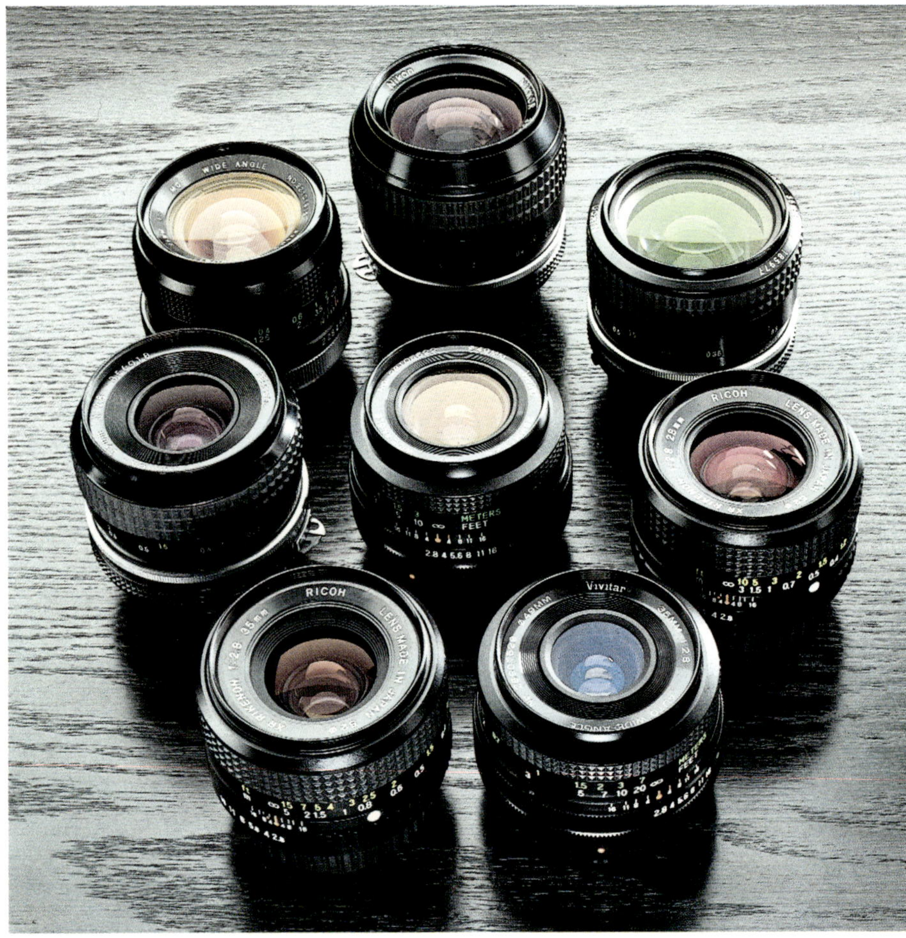

Wide angle choice *Picking a wide angle lens is not easy. There are 150 different lenses which have focal lengths in the 24 to 35 mm range, and price is not always a guide to quality*

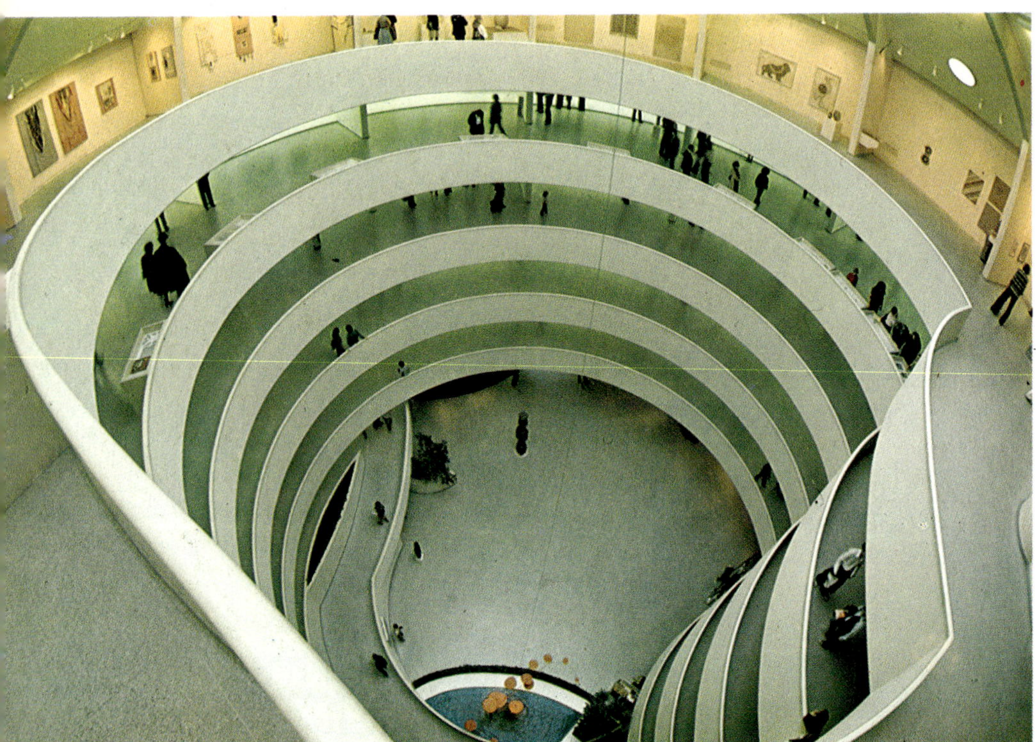

Looking down *The classic use for a wide angle lens is in a confined space. Here a 24 mm lens has been used to emphasize the curving spiral lines of the Guggenheim Art Gallery in New York*

Of all the additional lenses you can buy for your camera, perhaps few are more useful than a wide angle, and, increasingly nowadays, people are using a wide angle, not just as an accessory lens but as their main lens, in preference to the traditional 50 or 55 mm.

Giving that extra coverage to include all the subject and greater depth of field to ensure that it is all in focus, wide angles can be invaluable in many situations. An additional attraction is that you can shoot to include more than the main subject area and then crop at your leisure to achieve the desired framing. For close-ups, wide angle lenses can also give dramatic perspective effects.

Surprisingly, perhaps, the traditional 50 or 55 mm lens is actually a little too long to give completely 'normal' looking results on a 35 mm format: a focal length of about 43 mm is actually correct—this distance corresponds to the diagonal of the 24 × 36 mm frame. Some camera manufacturers already offer 38 mm, 40 mm or 45 mm lenses as options for standard lenses. If one of these focal lengths is not available for your camera, but you want to use a short focal length lens as standard, you could buy a 35 mm wide angle.

Wide angles of 35 mm are usually the cheapest wide angle in a manufacturer's range, and are often as small and light as a 50 mm. They usually take the same filtration attachment size, focus quite close, and even the cheapest usually give reasonably good results. Another point in the favour of 35 mm lenses is that they are easy for an inexperienced photographer to use—some of the more disturbing effects of wide angle lenses are not produced at this focal length. In fact, the 35 mm is one of the easiest of all lenses to use, giving plenty of margin for error in framing and focusing and reducing the chances of camera shake.

The angle of view of a 35 mm lens just matches that of most flashguns at around 60°, so flash pictures will be

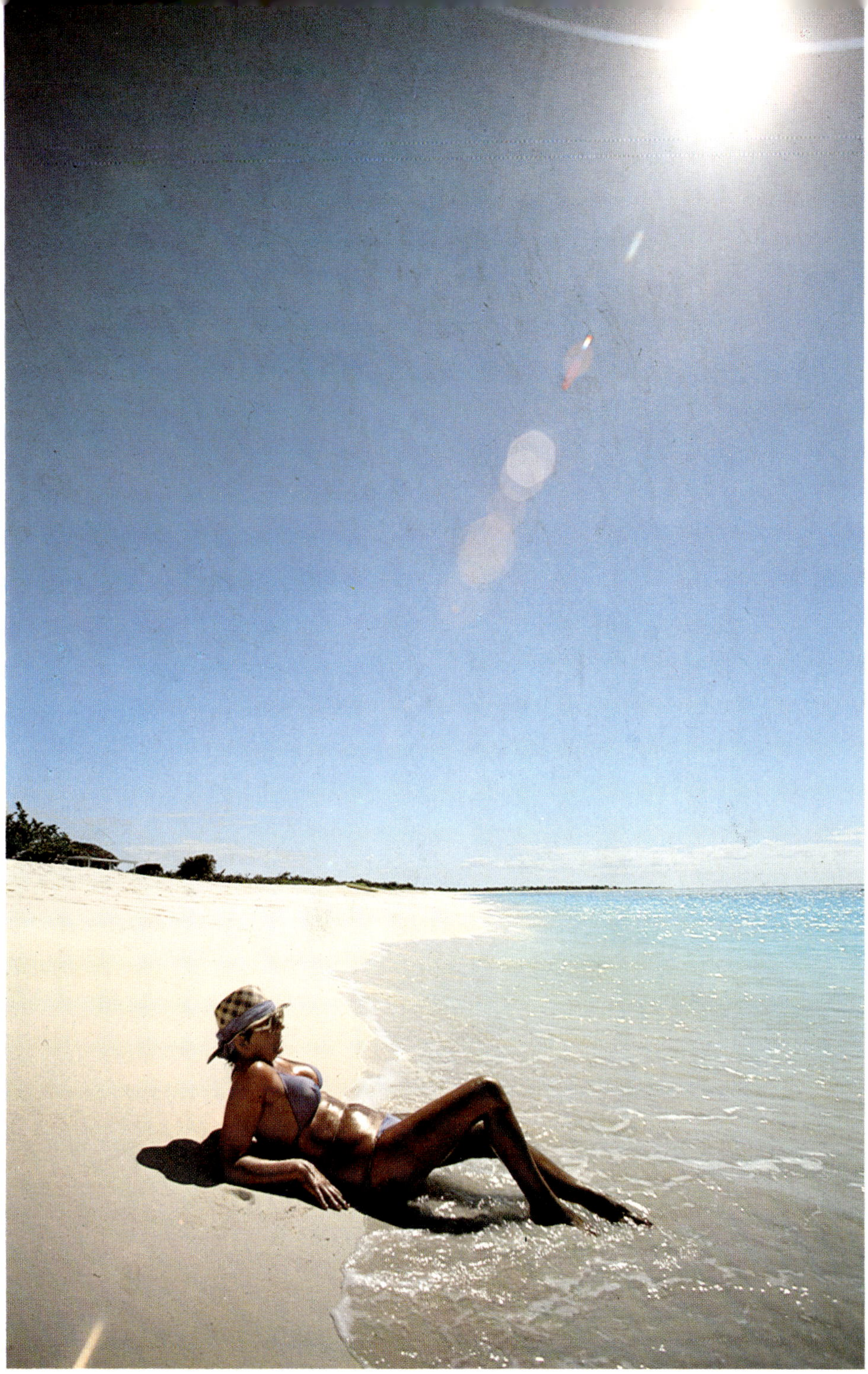

frame, perspective is very pronounced. Depth of field is also great enough to keep both foreground and background sharp, when properly focused.

This can be invaluable for news photographers who have to take pictures in fast moving, crowded situations where there is little time to focus the camera.

28 mm lenses are usually a little larger and heavier than standard 50 mm lenses, but are generally quite reasonably priced. This is because it is a popular focal length, and the lenses can be made in comparitively large numbers. Image quality is usually fairly good, but the optical performance of a cheap 28 mm lens is unlikely to be up to the standard of a similarly priced 35 mm.

24 mm lenses may seem only a little shorter in focal length than 28 mm, but the difference in angle of view is considerable. Pictures on a 24 mm lens seem to 'spread out' obviously at the edges and corners of the frame. Perspective also tends to be much more pronounced than with a 28 mm lens, because the photographer must move in closer to fill the frame with the subject.

The corners of the picture taken with a 24 mm lens are inevitably darker than the centre. This is not a sign of bad manufacture, but an inherent problem with wide angle lenses. All lenses suffer this loss of brightness towards the edge of the frame: it simply becomes more obvious at short focal lengths.

This combination of factors makes it easy to spot picture taken with a 24 mm lens—the photographs have a characteristic 24 mm 'look'. This 'look' can often

Sun, sea and sand *Taken with a standard lens, this would have been just another beach snapshot. A wide angle lens takes in more of the sky, and a dramatic trail of flare spots lead to the sun*

Fast or small *Wide angle lenses that have a large maximum aperture tend to be big and heavy. These three lenses have a focal length of 35 mm, but range from f/1.4 to f/2.8*

completely illuminated. With any wider angle of view, the edges of the picture may not be properly lit unless you use a diffuser to spread the light.

Because the angle of view is close to that of the standard lens, pictures taken on a 35 mm lens do not look like typical wide angle pictures—it is often hard to tell them from those taken with a standard lens. If you want to use the 35 mm as your standard lens, this is obviously an advantage. But if you wish your wide angle to supplement a 50 mm lens, the difference should be more marked and you may prefer a lens with a shorter focal length.

A 28 mm makes a useful combination when paired with a 50 mm standard lens, or one of the newer 40 or 45 mm standards. It covers almost twice the area of the 50 mm lens and gives the typical wide angle 'look'. Whenever any strong foreground objects are included in the

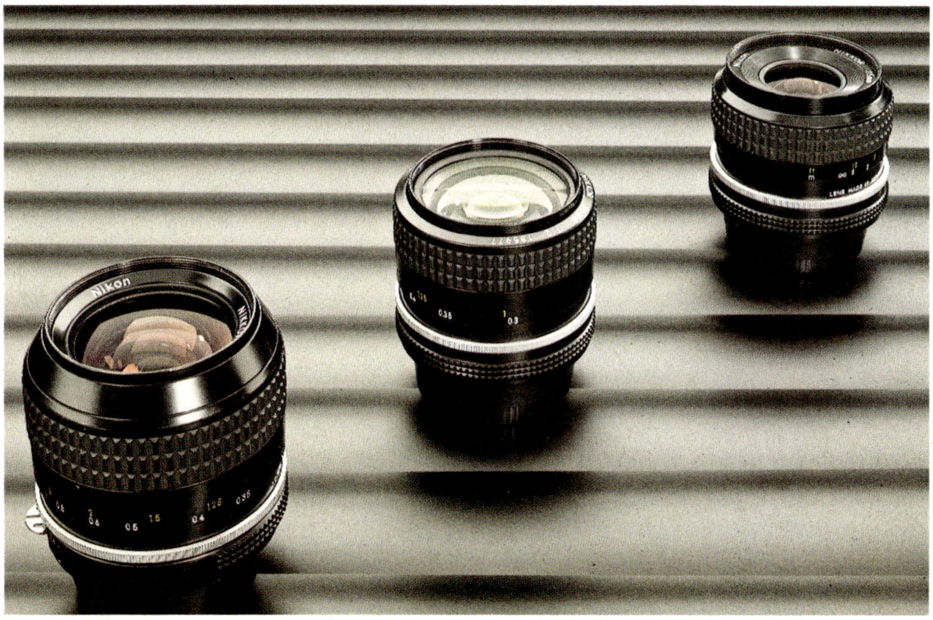

be difficult to use effectively and it is probably best to avoid 24 mm lenses as your first wide angle, unless you are confident of your ability to exploit its characteristics. If you own a 24 mm and a 50 mm, you may find the gap between them uncomfortably large, and that you need a more moderate wide angle—like a 35 mm—to fill it.

Maximum apertures

All three wide angle focal lengths are widely available, with a choice of different maximum apertures from most manufacturers. Although very fast 50 mm lenses—lenses with a wide maximum aperture—are available, it is much more difficult to make a wide angle lens that has a really large maximum aperture. There are some mass produced fast wide angles which are very good value for money, but they cannot match the slow lenses for quality. Unless you can afford the best, avoid fast wide angles.

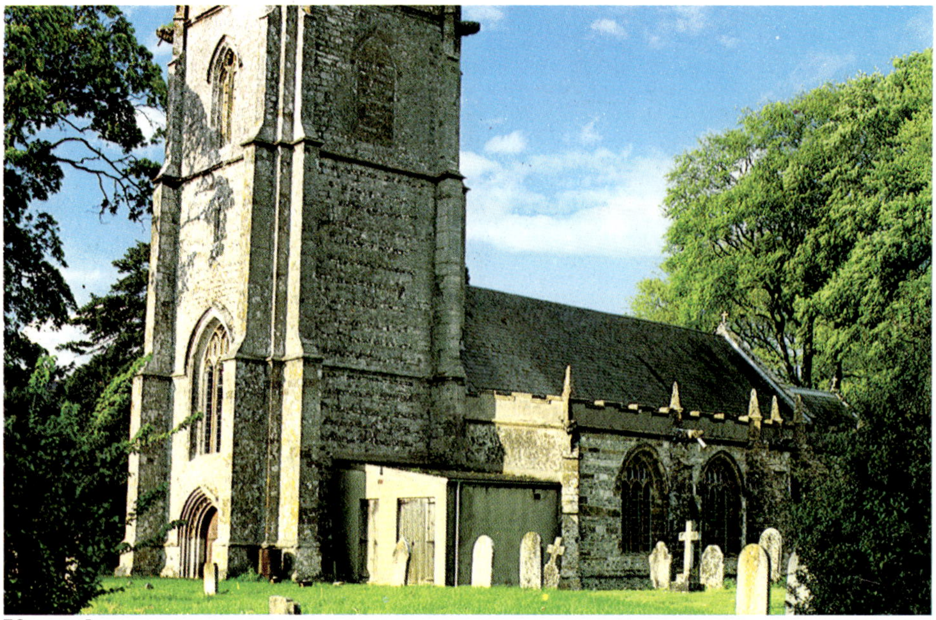

50 mm lens

Church in the trees *A high wall in the churchyard prevented the photographer from backing away from the subject and, with a standard 50 mm lens, the tower top is lopped off. Using a 35 mm lens (right) cured this, and some photographers use this lens as standard. 28 mm and 24 mm lenses include even more of the surroundings*

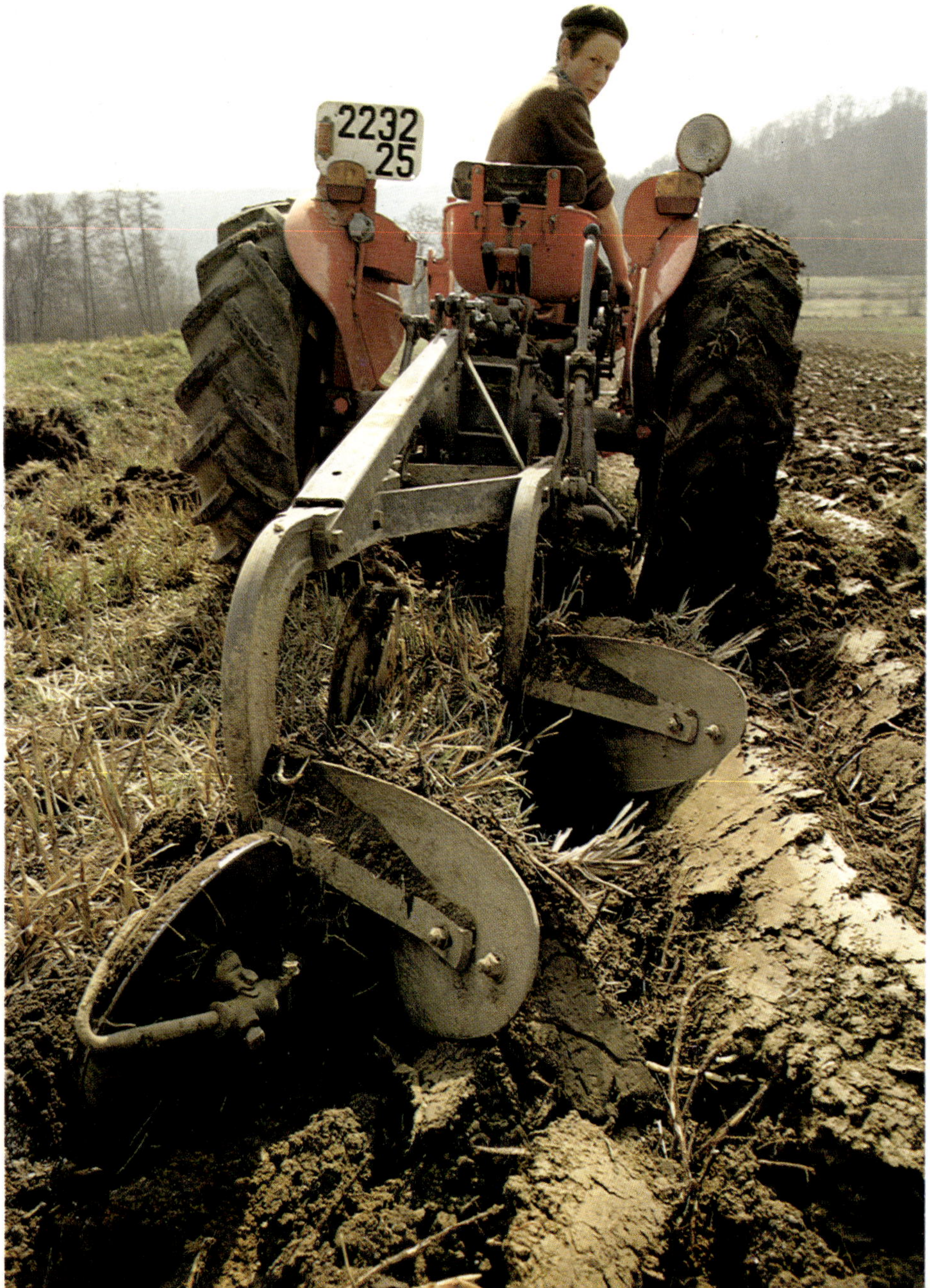

Down on the farm *By showing both the horizon and the ground at the feet of the photographer, a wide angle lens lends itself to dramatic images*

The most common maximum aperture for a 35 mm lens is *f*/2.8, though there are many *f*/2 lenses. Like the *f*/2.8s, the *f*/2 lenses generally give good quality results, but they are physically much larger. There are a few lenses as fast as *f*/1.4 and even *f*/1.2 and this extra speed may be invaluable in low light conditions, but they do not give as good definition. At the other end of the range, there are a few *f*/3.5 lenses available at 35 mm but these are usually at the cheaper end of the market, and have a rather conservative specification by today's standards.

The typical 28 mm lenses are, like 35 mms, usually *f*/2.8s, and there are many good quality *f*/2.8 lenses available at a reasonable price. There are several *f*/2 lenses in this focal length, but unless you pay extra for a good lens, performance may be disappointing. 28 mm lenses with a maximum aperture of *f*/2.8 also tend to be considerably more bulky and heavy.

Again, most 24 mm lenses have maximum apertures of *f*/2.8, though there are a few *f*/2 versions available. One manufacturer even makes an *f*/1.4, but this is both large and expensive.

As a general rule, then, any wide angle lens with a maximum aperture larger than *f*/2.8 tends to be more expensive, heavier, bulkier, and does not produce such good pictures as a lens with a more moderate specification. However, performance varies not only with the speed of a lens but also from manufacturer to manufacturer.

Lens faults

Although most wide angle lenses made by camera manufacturers are generally very good, some of the cheaper lenses made by independent manufacturers may have noticeable design faults. These

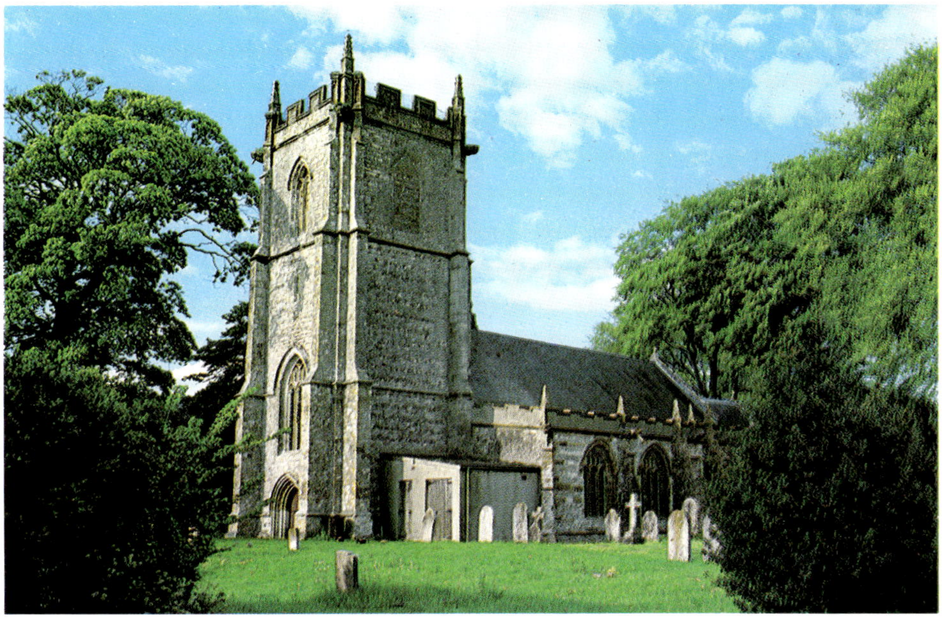

35 mm lens

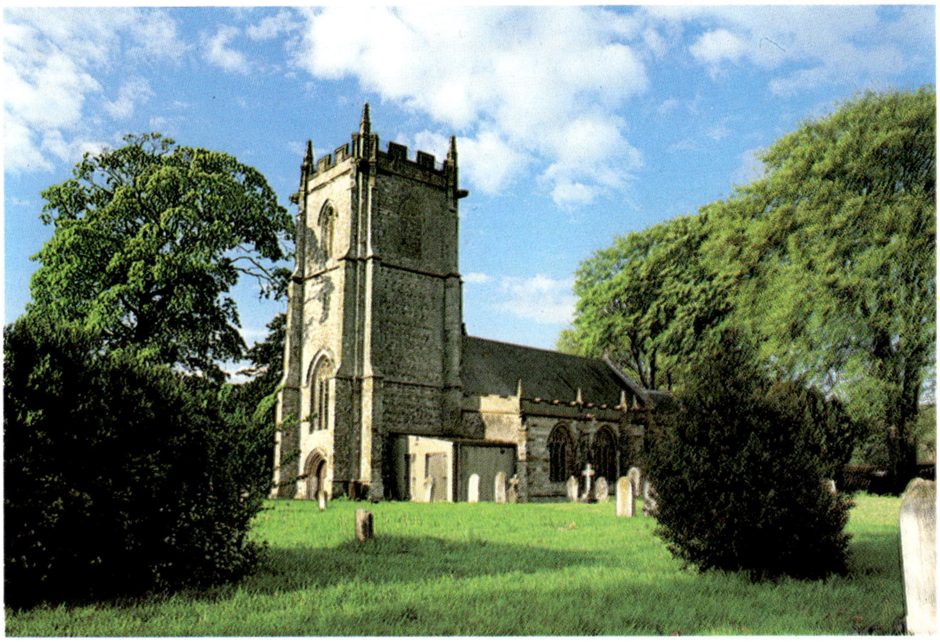

28 mm lens

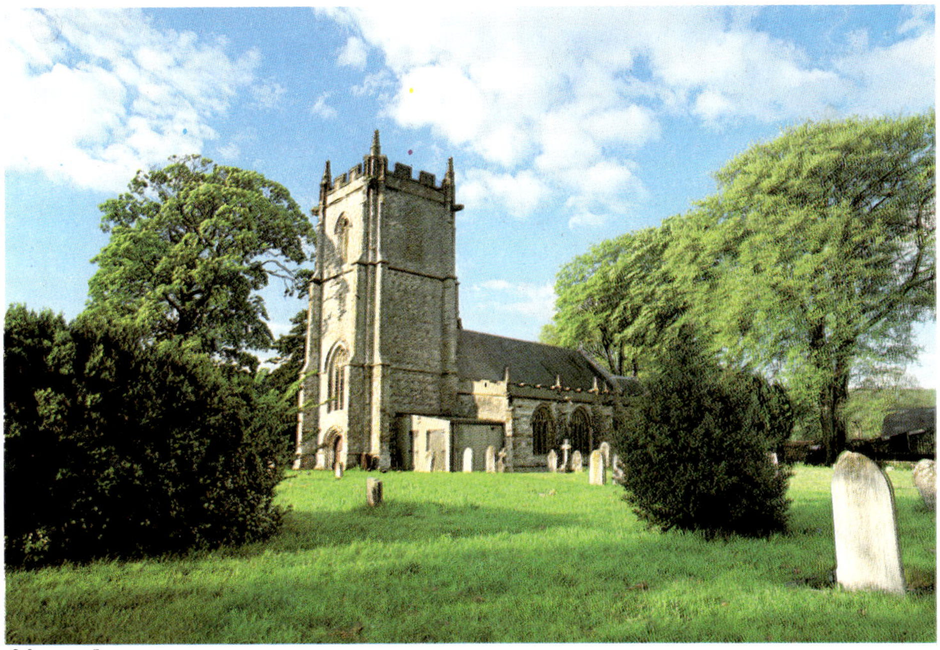

24 mm lens

faults fall into three main categories: 'barrel' distortion: uneven illumination: and focus fall-off.

Most wide angle lenses suffer some 'barrel' distortion (bowing out at the edges) particularly with close-ups. With a few lenses, however, this can reach a level that you may not accept. Be careful not to mistake distortion produced by the lens with distortion that you see on some viewfinder systems, notably the Zenith E—viewfinder distortion will not appear on film. When checking for barrel distortion check the viewfinder first with a standard lens by focusing on a distant horizon. Then repeat the check with the wide angle in place. If the horizon bows up in the centre much more with the wide angle in place, it has barrel distortion.

Uneven illumination often occurs at full aperture and is partly cured by stopping down, but it cannot be totally eliminated. The poorer quality wide angles may suffer badly from this fault, but costly lenses are usually better.

Focus fall-off to the edges is another very frequent fault, as a wide-angle may tend to have curvature of field, an aberration which can mean a lens focused at one metre in the centre of the picture is focused at two metres at the corners. The best wide-angles have floating elements to correct this fault, which is normally worse at close focus distances and is absent, even in the cheapest lenses, at infinity. Floating elements make a lens very costly, and most lens-makers produce their lenses to give best results at around 3 metres. You cannot trust wide angle lenses to give a flat focus field for close-ups unless specially designed or corrected to do so—which most wide angles are not.

Making your choice

There are over 150 different lenses between 24 and 35 mm available, and it can be difficult to decide which to buy.

If you are buying a wide angle to use as a standard lens, then a 35 mm is most useful, but if you already have a 55 mm lens, a 28 mm is probably more suitable. A lens as short as 24 mm is only really necessary for very specific uses, or if you already have a more moderate wide angle, such as a 35 mm.

If you use colour negative film, and only produce enprints, then there is little to choose between different lenses. But if you enlarge or project your pictures, quality is an important factor. Remember that the lenses that have less ambitious specifications are likely to give better results than those that sound good to be true. For example, an *f*/1.2 compact 24 mm lens that weighs next to nothing should make you immediately suspicious. If you can afford to buy from a reputable manufacturer, then do so, because wide angle lenses are particularly difficult to design and manufacture. If you have a limited budget, avoid 24 mm lenses altogether and those with large maximum apertures—stick to an *f*/2.8 35 mm or 28 mm.

Ultra wide lenses

Ultra-wide angle lenses produce pictures which look different from those taken with standard, telephoto or moderate wide angle lenses. The images from such lenses, with focal lengths between 13 and 21 mm, are instantly recognizable from the outward sweep of detail near the corners.

On looking closer, however, one notices that the centres of the pictures are virtually the same as those produced by less extreme focal lengths, with little distortion of straight lines. In contrast, still shorter focal length lenses, which come into the fish-eye category, have fields of view wider than 120°, and suffer from barrel distortion (see page 83) so that straight lines appear curved.

Ultra-wides have a variety of uses. They are valuable in confined spaces, or for including more of the surroundings than a more conventional wide angle lens. For such purposes they are simply a more extreme version of a straightforward wide angle. But the edges of the field of view do tend to show more extreme distortions than those of, say, a 24 mm lens. These distortions are sometimes useful for creating a bizarre effect, but usually they are undesirable and the photographer must take a number of precuations to avoid them.

In this case, if a less extreme wide angle lens is not available, keep your main subject within the central area of the frame so that a normal enprint or masked-down slide mount will cut off the extremes of the picture. The very wide angle of view covered means you must hold the camera precisely parallel to any subject you want to record accurately. If there is any tilt on the camera, parallel lines in the subject immediately appear to converge or diverge. This is a result of the greater perspective effect caused by having to move closer to the subject.

If you want to use an ultra-wide for accurate architectural shots, it is a good idea to have a spirit level on the camera's flash-shoe. To avoid converging vertical lines, align the camera parallel to the ground with the spirit level, then check by comparing verticals in the picture with the upright ends of the viewfinder frame, unless this has a slightly curved appearance. On a tripod, adjust the camera as accurately as possible by this method and check by panning so that a vertical wall end or pillar lines up, first with one end of the frame then the other. When it matches both frame ends exactly, your camera is perfectly aligned for architectural shots.

Once positioned in this way, the camera height may have to be adjusted by racking the tripod up or down, or by choosing a different viewpoint, in order to get the whole building in the frame. This may also result in the desired composition occupying only part of the frame. If you enlarge your own pictures, this is not a problem as you can just use that part of the negative containing the building.

For colour slides, however, it may be inconvenient to use this method. In this case the secret is to look for a suitable foreground area which completes the full frame of the picture, instead of cropping the unwanted parts of the image away. Then you have a full frame with a balanced composition and perfect vertical perspective.

Coping with distortion

Many photographers use the edge distortion of ultra-wide angle lenses to create unusual effects. To gain a vivid impression of this distortion, try positioning identical objects in a row or pattern across the whole frame—circular dinner plates work very well. The change in shape will be very noticeable.

For very dramatic shape changes, use only the corner of the frame. By employing as little as one quarter of the negative or slide, and enlarging or slide copying later on, you will produce a shot which is distorted on one side, and which looks unbalanced and often grotesque.

You should not be afraid to use an ultra-wide in situations where longer lenses are more usual. For example, an ultra-wide is capable of taking a head-and-shoulders self portrait from arm's length. Held above your head, you can photograph yourself full-length. Try high or low viewpoints even if they are no more than a metre higher or lower. This sort of approach will often produce unusual distortions, but these can be used creatively. Furthermore, a camera with an ultra-wide lens can often be inserted into a gap or hole, such as in a fence, and reveal far more than you could see by eye alone.

The use of unusual viewpoints needs a lot of care and thought. A common fault in ultra-wide technique is the use of too low a viewpoint, so that a small part of the nearby ground takes on far too much significance. Dirty carpets, patchy concrete floors and so on, which might not show with a normal lens, suddenly become very prominent. When possible, avoid too much foreground, perhaps by choosing a higher viewpoint.

Ultra-wides are unique in the way they reproduce the various planes of the subject. They create impact by showing these planes from different angles, from a viewpoint between them. For example, only the use of a wide angle allows you to increase the amount of sky you include, as you cannot change it by moving closer!

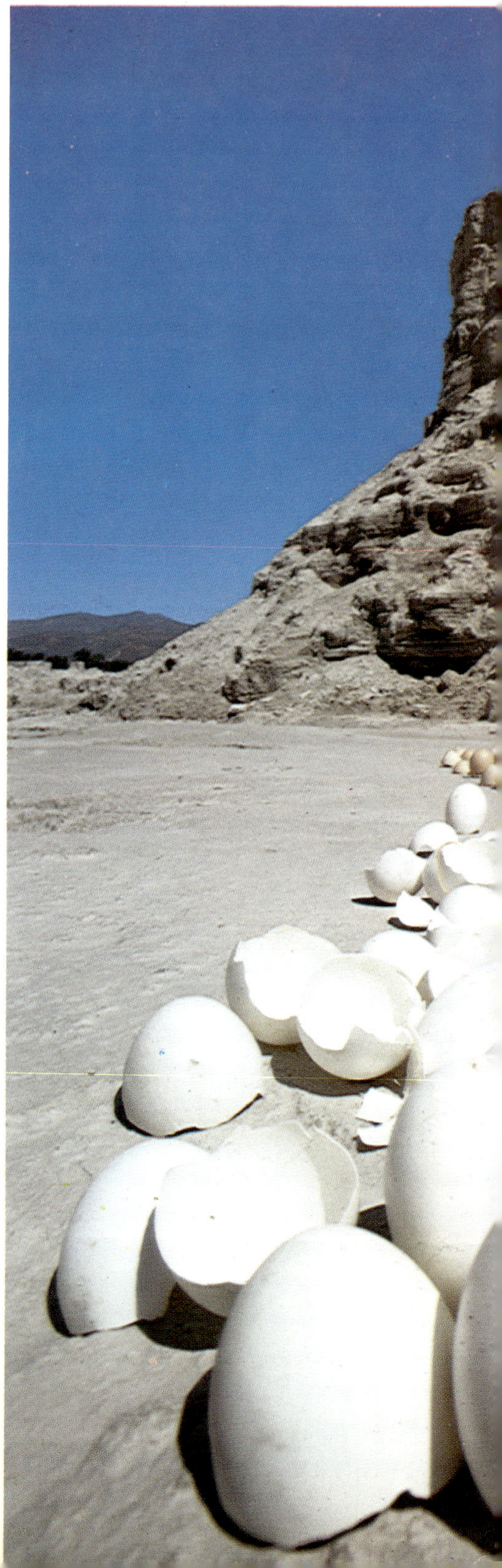

One of the most dramatic features of the ultra-wide lens is its effect on parallel lines. The normal convergence of such lines to a vanishing point is exaggerated by the extremely wide field of view. This effect is not unique to ultra-wides, but is more noticeable when using them. It is important when taking pictures with converging verticals to balance the angle at which the subject apparently leans. The amount of convergence must balance on each side of the subject, so that the whole picture does not appear to be about to fall over sideways. This does not always mean ensuring that a line running through the centre of the frame is perfectly vertical or horizontal. It means looking carefully through the finder, and deciding when the overall feel of the picture seems balanced. You can usually tell mistakes straight away. Often the horizon is tilted, or the subject seems about to drop out of the frame altogether.

Changing scale

For dramatic images, use the steep perspective of the ultra-wide to juxtapose small, nearby foreground details, such as a face, against wide background vistas. There will be a great scale difference between the close subject and the general view, because of their widely different distances from the lens. By concealing middle distance detail, such as empty ground, the foreground subject, a picture is produced which is all foreground and background with little visual connection. This is useful for making visual points or messages in a picture, or for introducing humour.

Because of its special features, the ultra-wide is often used for trick pictures. A small subject, placed very close to the camera, will have its scale changed or made unrecognizable. Try this effect with accurate scale models, model railways and similar subjects. You may have to crop the edges off the picture to get rid of unwanted details and distortions.

With ultra-wides, an object will often appear larger at the edge of the frame than it would at the centre, due to the lens design. This difference of image scale creates strange effects when you pan the camera during a long exposure. The blurred effect looks stronger at the

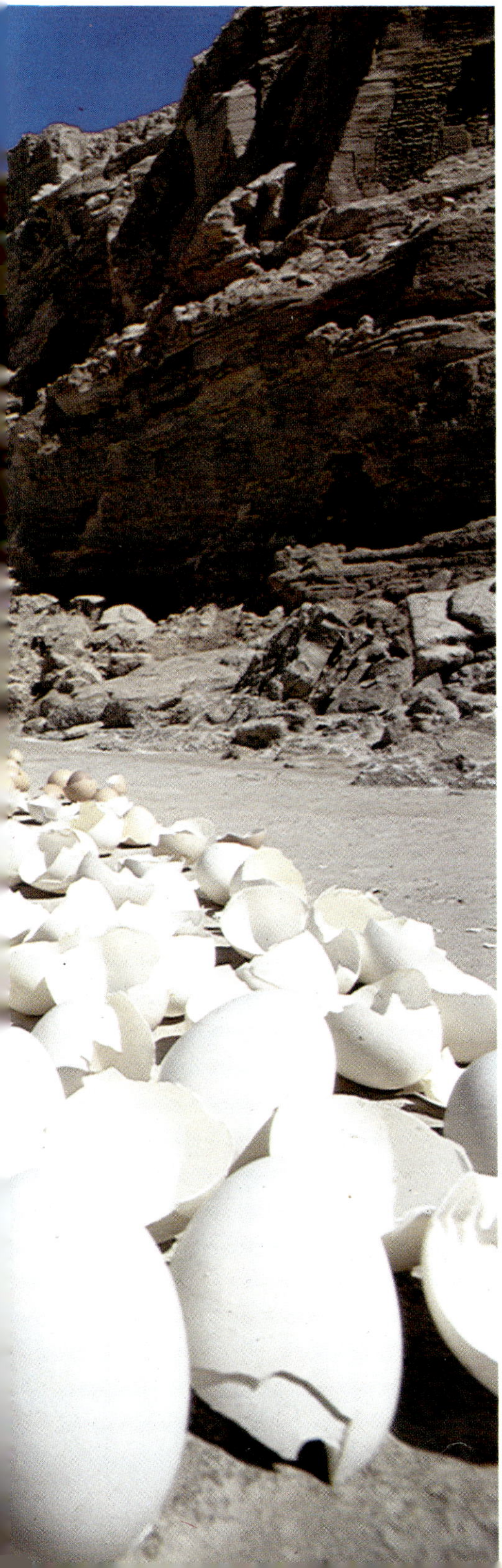

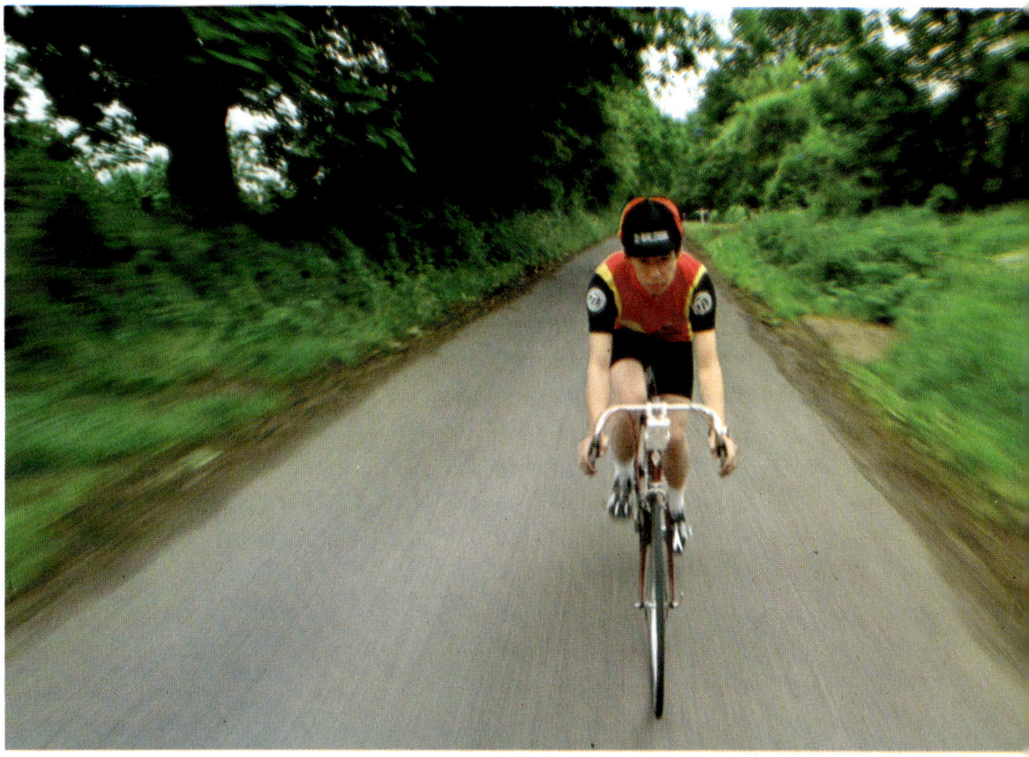

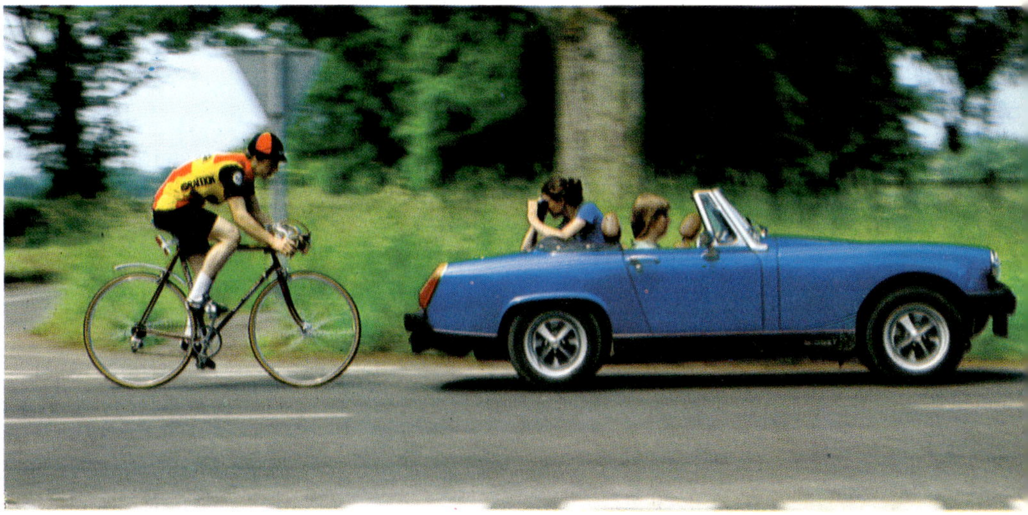

Seaside shells *An ultra-wide lens has enormous depth of field, and if it is stopped down, everything from a few centimetres to infinity is in focus the dramatic perspective that this can give may be used to make small foreground objects seem unnaturally large*

Cycling shot *With a long exposure shot of a moving cyclist taken from a car, the 'edge rush' effect of an ultra-wide gives a tremendous impression of speed—but this kind of shot needs a straight, empty road and extreme caution. The effect can be achieved at fairly low speeds*

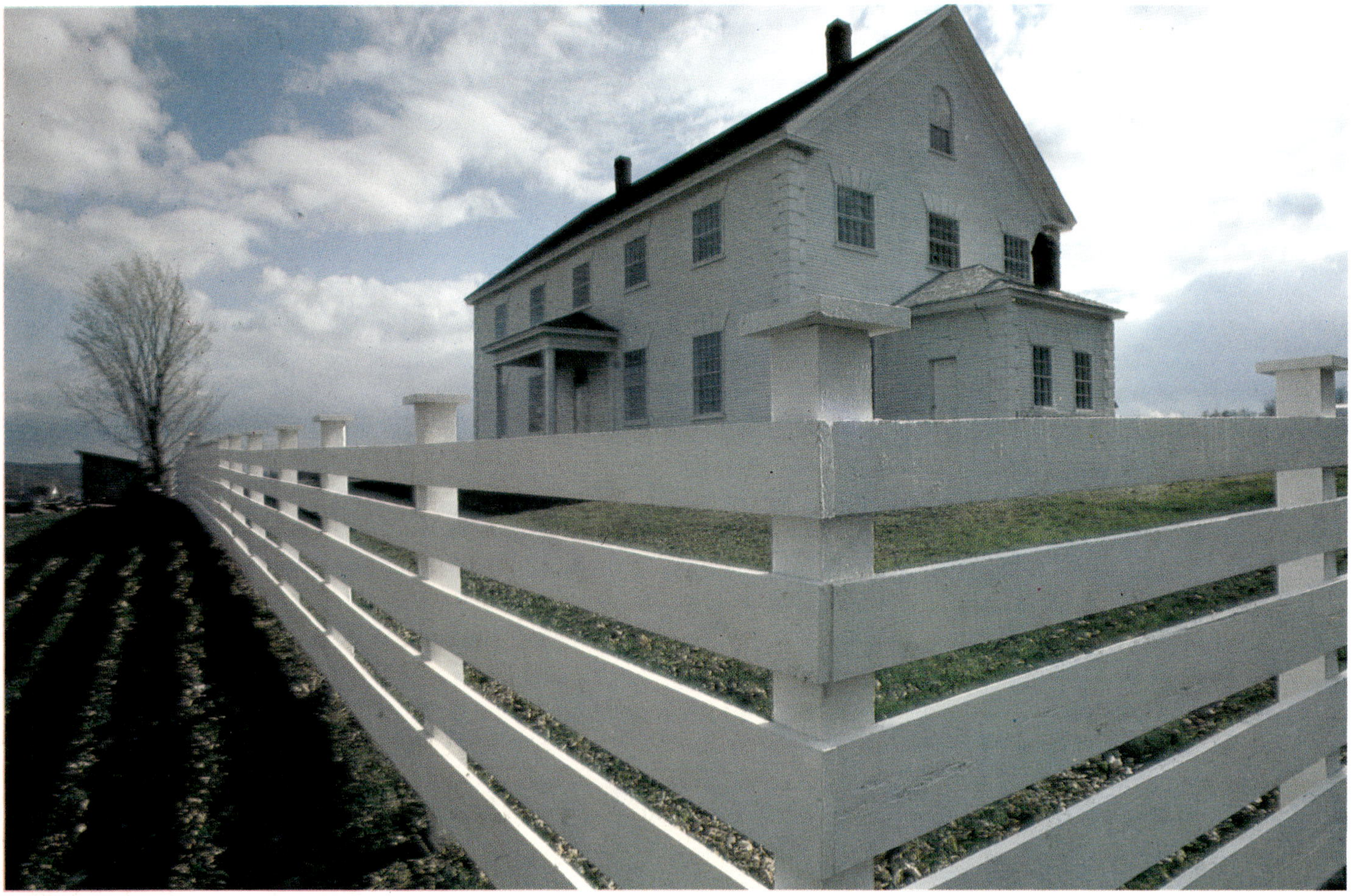

edges than in the middle. If you shoot from a moving vehicle, you get the same effect, with the addition of nearby ground detail that appears to rush by much faster than distant detail.

These 'edge-rush' effects, the increase of blurring towards the limits of the frame, convey a strong impression of speed, whether across the frame or forwards into the picture. Keep part of the centre sharp for the greatest effect. You will need to experiment to find the best way of doing this.

Ultra-wides have an enormous depth of field. But this can be a problem when you do not want it. You should not hesitate to work at full aperture if you need to pick out a close object against an out of focus background. You may need to focus slightly closer than the subject to keep the background blurred. However, using the scale difference produced by moving in close can often create a better effect than shallow depth of field and increases the impact of the subject.

The great depth of field of ultra-wides can also be a problem when focusing. It is not always obvious when a subject is not sharply in focus, especially in low light conditions. When using a medium or small aperture, this is rarely a problem as the depth of field will make up for slight mistakes. But if full aperture is used, poor focusing may become apparent when the picture is enlarged or projected. Split image focusing screens are very useful aids and help to ensure that every shot is perfectly sharp.

One possible drawback with ultra-wides is that they have complex groups of elements which, because of their design, cannot be totally free from flare and ghosted patches of light. Lens hoods are rarely effective as they have to be very short to prevent cut off at the edges of the frame. By aiming towards the sun, you may throw off a whole string of hexagonal coloured flare patches across the frame. Put these to good use when you cannot avoid them, by making them part of the picture.

Another feature of the ultra-wide is that the far edges of the frame may only receive one quarter of the exposure of the central area—the effect known as vignetting. As the lens is stopped down, this 'fault' is reduced. But pictures often gain from controlled gradual darkening towards the edges. Try working at full aperture, or only a single *f*/stop down, and use the fall-off to contain the frame visually.

With flash, very few guns, even when fitted with wide angle attachments, will cover the field of view of a lens less than 21 mm. This also results in fall-off, with only the centre of the image properly lit. If even lighting is needed, you can use two flashguns, each aimed at half of the subject—two flashguns can be connected to the camera flash socket using a Y-shaped adaptor, readily available from most dealers. Another way of achieving overall even illumination is to use bounce flash (see pages 106 to 109).

Most ultra-wides will focus as close as about 15 cm with no trouble, but extremely strong visual effects can be obtained by fitting a close-up lens. Extension tubes

are invariably too long and may cause the lens to focus on a point inside its own front elements. Split field close-up lenses do not work well with ultra-wides as the division between the lenses clearly shows as a line across the picture, due to the great depth of field.

In the same way, graduated filters with a hard division between the tones are not suitable for ultra-wides. Those with a soft edge to the colour are better, and the amount of sky included in an ultra-wide shot is ideal for this kind of effect. Because the division between the coloured and clear halves will be crisp even when using a soft-edged filter, the sliding type of filter holder is better than the rim mounted type, as it lets you adjust the position of the division, to hide it or make use of it.

Special effects filters and prisms do not work well with ultra-wides. Starburst and cross screen filters, diffraction gratings and prisms all give effects linked directly to the focal length of the lens used. With an ultra-wide you must use a much stronger star or cross screen to get a good light burst effect. Prisms meant for 50 to 35 mm lenses may fail to work altogether with ultra-wides, as well as cutting off the edges of the picture and, unfortunately, there are no special effects prisms for ultra-wide work.

Interesting cloud shots can be taken by day or night with an ultra-wide because of the extra sky area it covers. At dusk, put the horizon at the bottom of the frame and use a long exposure so that moving clouds record as a sweeping pattern.

Indoors, use the ultra-wide for photographing small items, but be careful with large subjects because simple backgrounds are difficult to arrange—most backgrounds that are suitable for normal lenses, such as rolls of paper, will not be large enough to cover the full frame. If you are using paper as the background, one way to fill the whole frame is to set the roll on end in the form of a deep curved bay, suitably supported.

The combination of unusual image geometry and critical handling make ultra-wides difficult to master. Often it is better to start with a less extreme wide angle and learn the technique in stages. An ultra-wide will offer you new possibilities. You will have to get closer, and rethink your approach to the subject. But, for all this effort, you may be rewarded with an unusual photograph.

Sun and clouds *Flare can be a problem with cheap ultra-wides, but if you cannot prevent it, use it creatively*

House and fence *With an ultra-wide lens, move in close to the subject for dramatic perspective effects*

Towering brick *A mundane object given a touch of drama with an ultra-wide and double exposure. The brick was shot first with an ultra-wide and the moon added during a second exposure using a much longer lens*

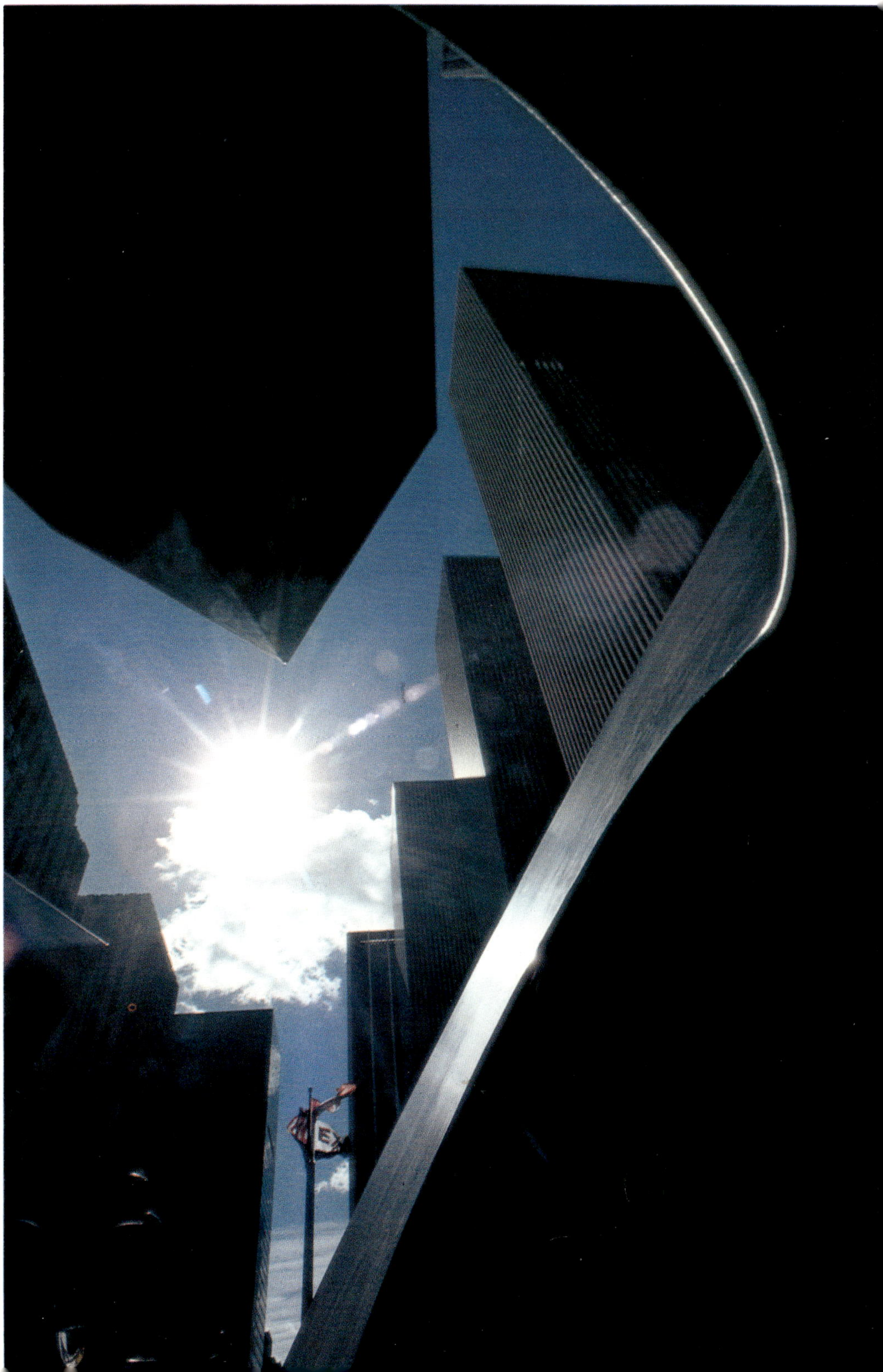

CHAPTER 8
DAY AND NIGHT
Light through the day

Light is the raw material of photography. If you want to make the best use of outdoor light in your pictures, you should know how it changes in character at different times of the day throughout the year.

Natural light

Natural light comes from only one source—the sun. But the sun's light can be diffused and reflected in different ways so that it behaves much more subtly than any single light source in the studio.

As well as the direct light of the sun, natural light can be made up of scattered blue light from the sky, light reflected from clouds, light diffused through clouds, light reflected from the ground and from buildings and objects, and light filtered through such things as trees and bushes.

The sun's light changes in colour, depending on its position in the sky and on atmospheric conditions. It changes in intensity through the day and during the year. When the sun is highest in the sky, at midday in summer, its light is much stronger than at dusk or dawn in winter. And the direction of the sun's light changes constantly; a building or landscape that is lit by flat direct light on a summer's morning will be lit completely differently on a winter's afternoon.

Geography is important. The quality of the light—its strength, intensity, colour, and the contrast ratio between those parts of the subject lit by the direct light of the sun and those in shadow—is affected by both natural and man-made factors. In areas like the Mediterranean, California and Australia, the light is generally much clearer and brighter than in more heavily industrialized areas at higher latitudes, such as north-east United States and Britain.

Despite all these influences on the character of natural light, you can think of light outdoors as having two main parts: direct sunlight and reflected sunlight. How these components interact determines what the light is like.

The sun

At an average distance of about 150,000,000 km, the sun is the nearest star to the Earth. Terrestrial distances are insignificant by comparison, so the sun's light is one light source that does not vary in intensity according to the distance from the subject for practical purposes. As seen from the Earth, the angular diameter of the sun is a tiny half a degree. Sunlight is therefore close to being a point light source, and would give sharp edged

Stonehenge at dawn *The strong contrasts between the brightening sky and the deep shadows of dawn provide excellent opportunities for silhouettes*

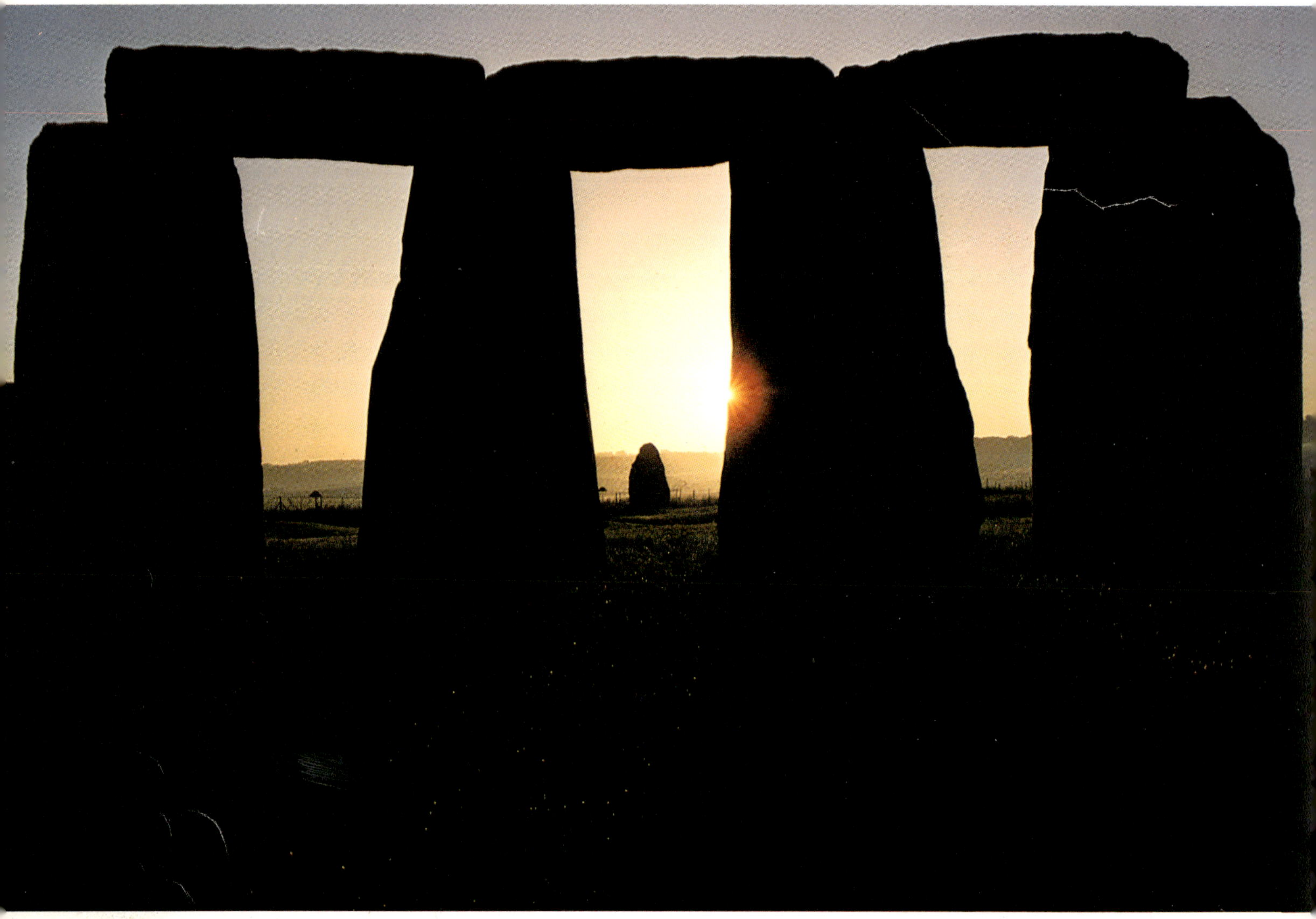

shadows and very high contrast between lit and unlit areas of the subject if it were not for the softening effects of the many sources of reflected light on Earth.

The sun's light has a colour temperature of about 5,500 K, a slightly yellowish-white (see Understanding Colour Temperature, pages 238-239). But the Earth's atmosphere can effect the colour of sunlight considerably.

The sky

As seen from the ground, the daytime sky is a dome across which the sun and clouds appear to move. The blue colour of a clear sky is a result of scattering and selective absorbtion of sunlight by the atmosphere.

When objects are in shadow under a clear sky, they will be lit mainly by skylight and will have a blue cast when photographed on colour film. The colour temperature of a clear blue sky is about 10,000 K. The saturation of the sky's blue tint is influenced by the amount of airborne dust and water vapour in the atmosphere. Over industrial cities, skies are rarely as deep a blue as they are over the countryside, where there are usually fewer airborne particles.

When the sky is a paler blue, shadows are less deep and pictures have less contrast because relatively more light comes from the sky. Pictures taken under such skies often have better shadow detail than those taken under bluer skies, while still retaining a sunny look. Yet because proportionally more skylight is falling on the subject you may need to use a yellowish 81 series filter to obtain natural looking colour photographs, even when your subject is not in shade.

The light from the sky is quite different when the weather is cloudy. At midday, the light falling on a subject from an overcast sky has a colour temperature of about 7,000 K, which is distinctly blueish. Without the direct rays of the sun the lighting is soft and shadowless, but may need an 81C filter for neutral colour balance. You should be careful not to over-correct colour temperatures, though. If your pictures combine completely neutral colour balance with grey, overcast skies they may not look natural. You expect to see slightly colder colours on dull days—they help to capture the mood of the scene.

A sunny day: dawn

Because the position of the sun has such a great influence on the quality of natural light, it is useful to follow the effects of the sun's position in the sky

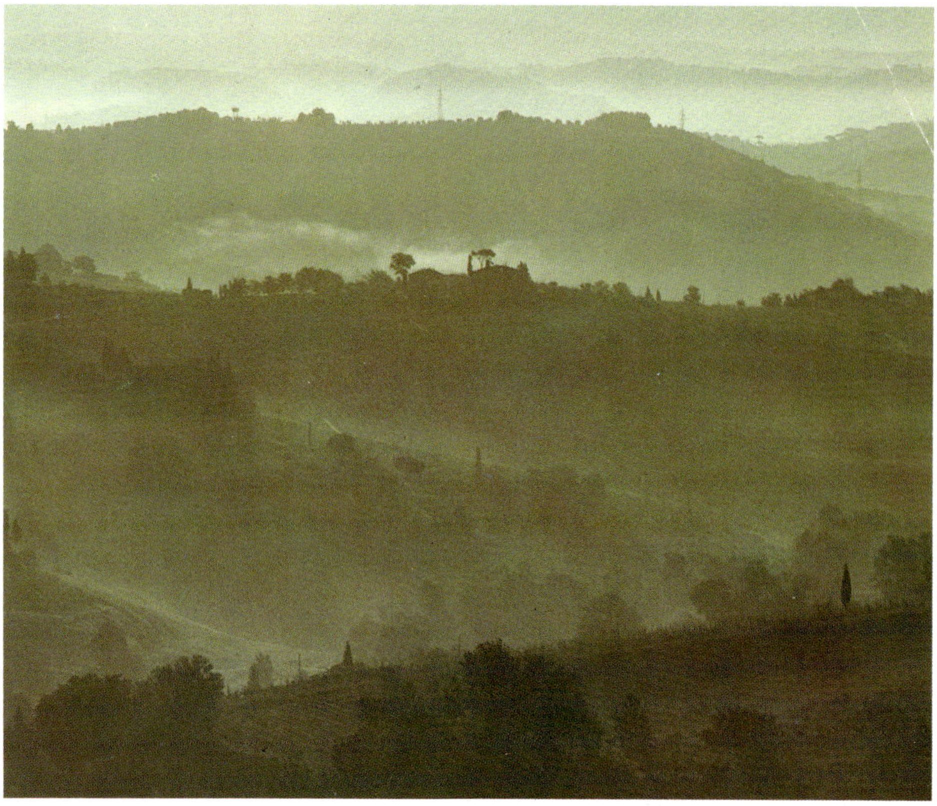

Morning landscape *Early morning mist in Tuscany shows an extreme example of the effect of aerial perspective—the loss of detail over distance*

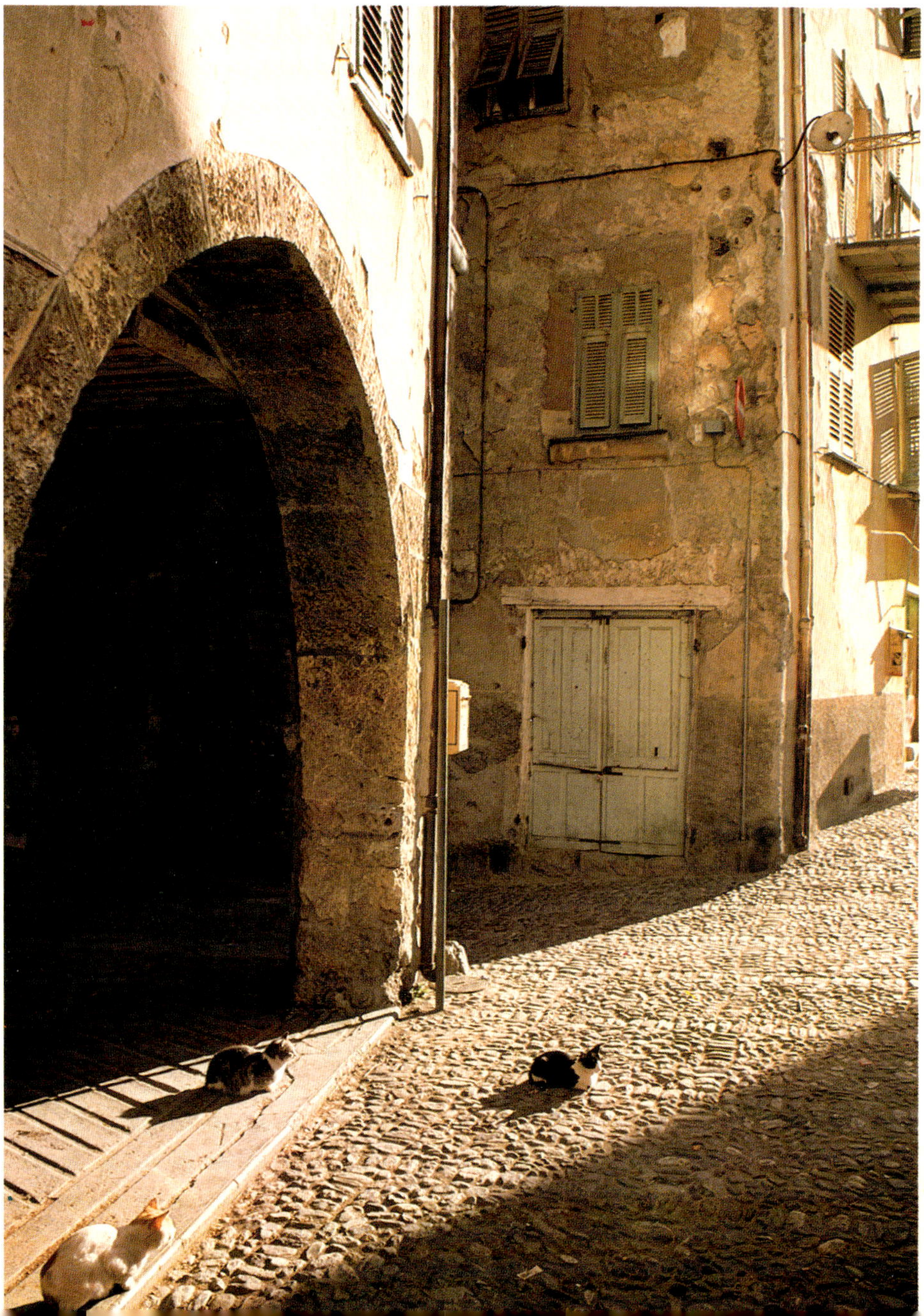

Cats on cobbles *Later in the morning, the slanting light helps to emphasize textures on walls and streets, which disappear when the sun is higher*

through an idealized sunny day.

Shortly before sunrise the sky begins to glow softly. How long it will glow depends on latitude and atmospheric conditions. At higher latitudes, the sun moves more obliquely towards the horizon, and both sunrise and sunset take longer than in regions near the tropics. If the atmosphere contains many particles of fine dust and other contaminants, more light will be diffused up into the sky before sunrise and the dawn will be more protracted. Nevertheless, although the light reaching the landscape is essentially blue skylight, it is more directional than the skylight later in the day. Shadows are long but soft, because the light is coming from a low angle.

Photographically, early dawn twilight presents some problems. Even with high speed film, exposures are long. A tripod is usually necessary, and static subjects such as landscapes and buildings are more suitable than living subjects. Yet the cool blue tones of early morning can be very attractive, and you should not overlook the possibilities that an early start provides for photography. Large cities are usually almost deserted at this time of day and have a special mood not found at any other time. Interesting effects can be achieved in landscape photography, particularly of mountains: the reddish direct light of the sun will strike the peaks of the mountains while the rest of the landscape is still lit by the cool blueish light from the sky, creating interesting contrasts of brightness and colour.

As the sun rises above the horizon, the long shadows become hard-edged. If the night has been clear, the air is clean and distant views have great clarity. Early sunlight has a lower colour temperature than later in the day. Contrasts between areas that are lit by sun and those in shadow are high, a difference accentuated by the coolness of shadows and the warm tone of the sunlight. Landscapes with long shadows and golden highlights look particularly effective. The strong contrasts give a greater appearance of sharpness.

Portraits taken at this time of day have strong modelling, and the colour of the sunlight is flattering to skin tones. If the contrast between shadow and sunlit parts of your subject is too strong for your taste, a reflector can be used to bounce some extra light into the shadows. Use a sheet of white card or a piece of aluminium foil stuck to a board.

Morning

As the sun rises higher in the sky, the balance between sunlight and skylight moves closer towards the norm for which the film is designed. The sun no longer has to shine obliquely through so much of the Earth's atmosphere, and its colour temperature increases. The sky brightens, and contrasts between shadows and sunlit areas lessen. Shadows shorten, but are still long enough to give interesting modelling to subjects. How high the sun will rise depends on the time of the year and the latitude, but in general, mid morning on clear days gives a good all purpose light with excellent modelling and colour balance that is close enough to neutral not to need any corrective reddish or blueish filtration.

Noon

The sun is at its highest at noon. In the tropics the sun will rise to be directly overhead at certain times of the year. At such times, shadows are extremely short and the sun's light is very strong. Even at higher latitudes the light will have relatively high contrast with deep shadows, but the overall colour balance will be neutral.

If you are using colour slide film in high contrast conditions, it is usually best to give slightly too little exposure rather than too much. Pale, washed out highlights are less desirable than full shadow tones with richly coloured light areas. The bright light of noon gives good colours if you do not overexpose your film.

Nevertheless, it is often worth using a little filtration to increase the depth of colours. A polarizing filter, for instance, can be used very effectively to deepen the blue of the sky. In tropical areas, in particular, the effect of filtering out polarized light is maximized because the sun, almost overhead, is at right angles to the camera. A polarizing filter can also cut down heat haze and give stronger, more saturated colours in landscapes, though this effect may be more pronounced later in the day.

If you are photographing on the beach, it is often worth underexposing slide film a little, because the strong overhead sun tends to bleach all the colour from the sand and sea. Skin tones can also suffer, and it sometimes helps to use an 81 series warming filter to give a slight sun-tanned look. This has to be subtle, though, or all other colours in the picture may tend to appear muddy.

If the sun is very high in the sky, portraits can be unsatisfactory—deep shadows under the eyes and nose can obscure facial features. Once again, this is a time to use fill-in reflectors, either artificial or natural. A sandy beach can work well as a reflector, or you can move your subject under some trees to exploit the natural diffusing qualities of foliage. Colour balance in the shade of trees can be a problem—the blueish light of shade is mixed with green light filtered through leaves and may call for the use of a magenta colour compensating filter. A CC 10M is usually sufficient correction.

Afternoon

When the sun starts to drop in the sky, the modelling quality comes back into the light, as in the morning. Shadows lengthen again, but in the opposite direction to those cast in the morning. Subjects that were not lit the way you wanted in the morning may now be

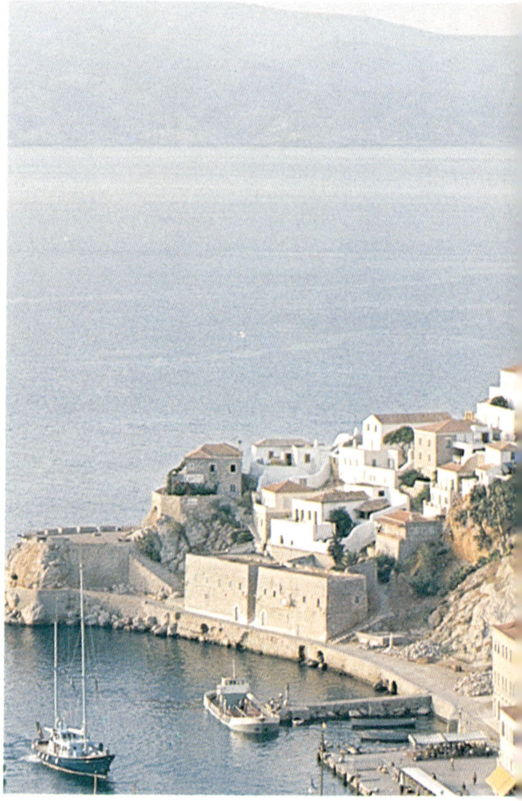

ready for you to photograph. When you photograph static subjects such as buildings and landscapes you should always pause to think how the changing direction of the sun's light will affect their appearance.

The skylight is usually paler in the afternoon, especially over cities where the day's activities stir dust and other particles into the atmosphere. Afternoon light is therefore generally warmer than at other times of day. Haze softens colours over distance, and this *aerial perspective* can give emphasis to the scale of city views and landscapes.

Sunset

At the end of the day, the sunlight again turns a golden yellow, as it was at dawn. Because of aerial haze, however, the colour is likely to be even redder than at dawn, and will be spread over a larger area of the sky.

As light levels drop, so the colour response of the human eye varies. In particular, its sensitivity to red light diminishes progressively as the sunsets and night falls until, in twilight, we can see little besides blue. (In near darkness, our colour vision disappears altogether and we see the world in shades of grey alone.) The colour response of films, on the other hand, remains constant regardless of the light level—unless exposures have to be so long that reciprocity failure (see page 236) occurs. This means that sunsets are often recorded redder on film than they looked to the human eye. This does not usually matter, because fiery red sunsets look attractive. But sometimes it is worth trying to achieve a cooler, more natural look by using a bluish 82A filter over the lens.

Light readings for sunsets should be

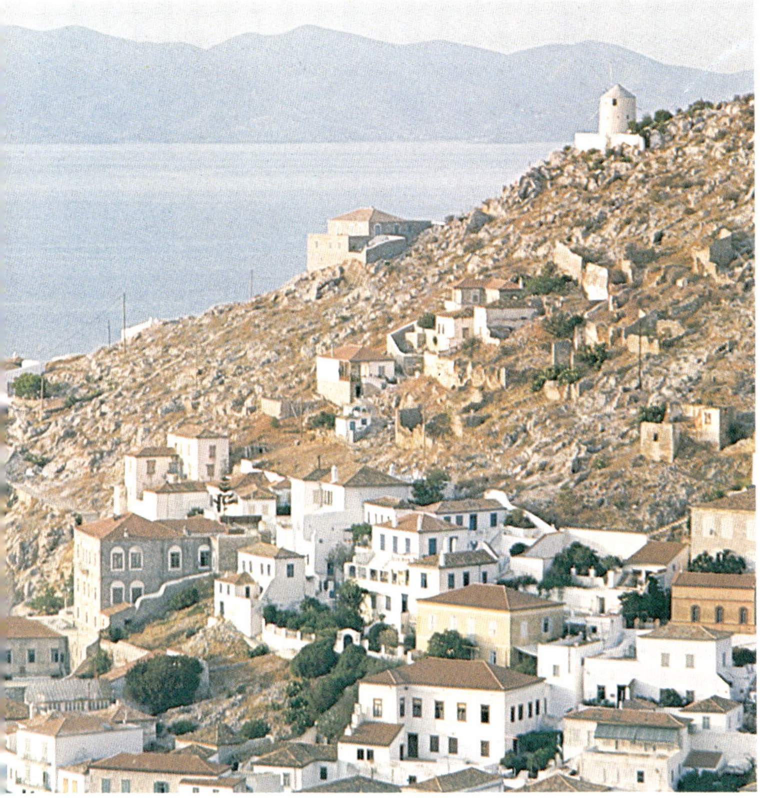

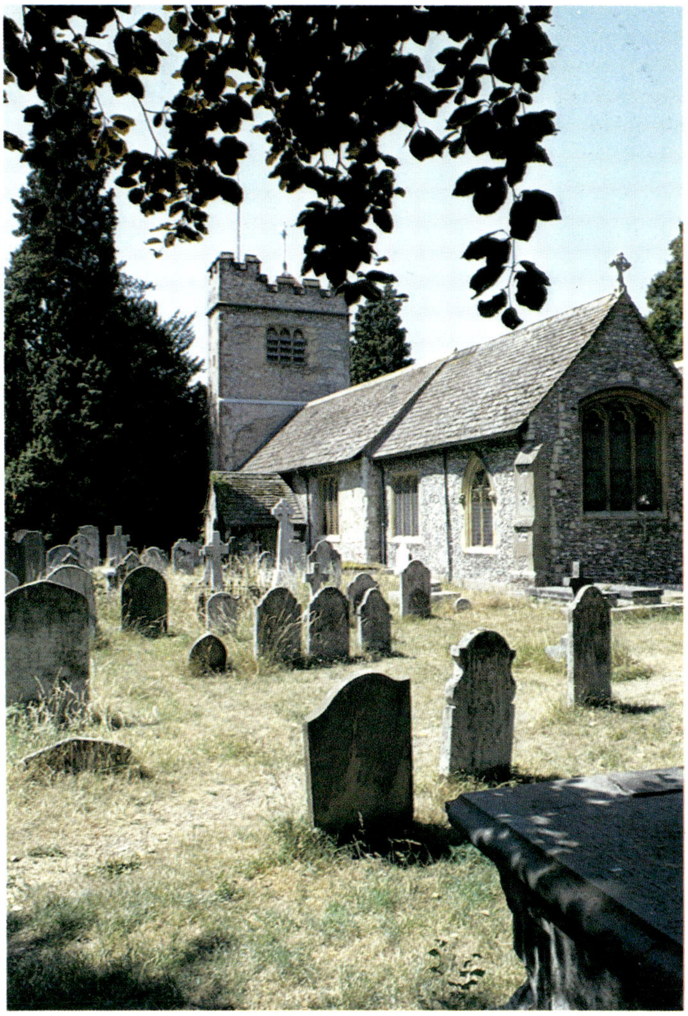

Harbour village *Light depends on atmospheric conditions. A slight haze lowers the contrast of the light, giving a timeless, dreamy quality*

Churchyard at noon *In the countryside during summer, midday light can produce deep shadows and high contrast. The effect is reduced in towns by air pollution*

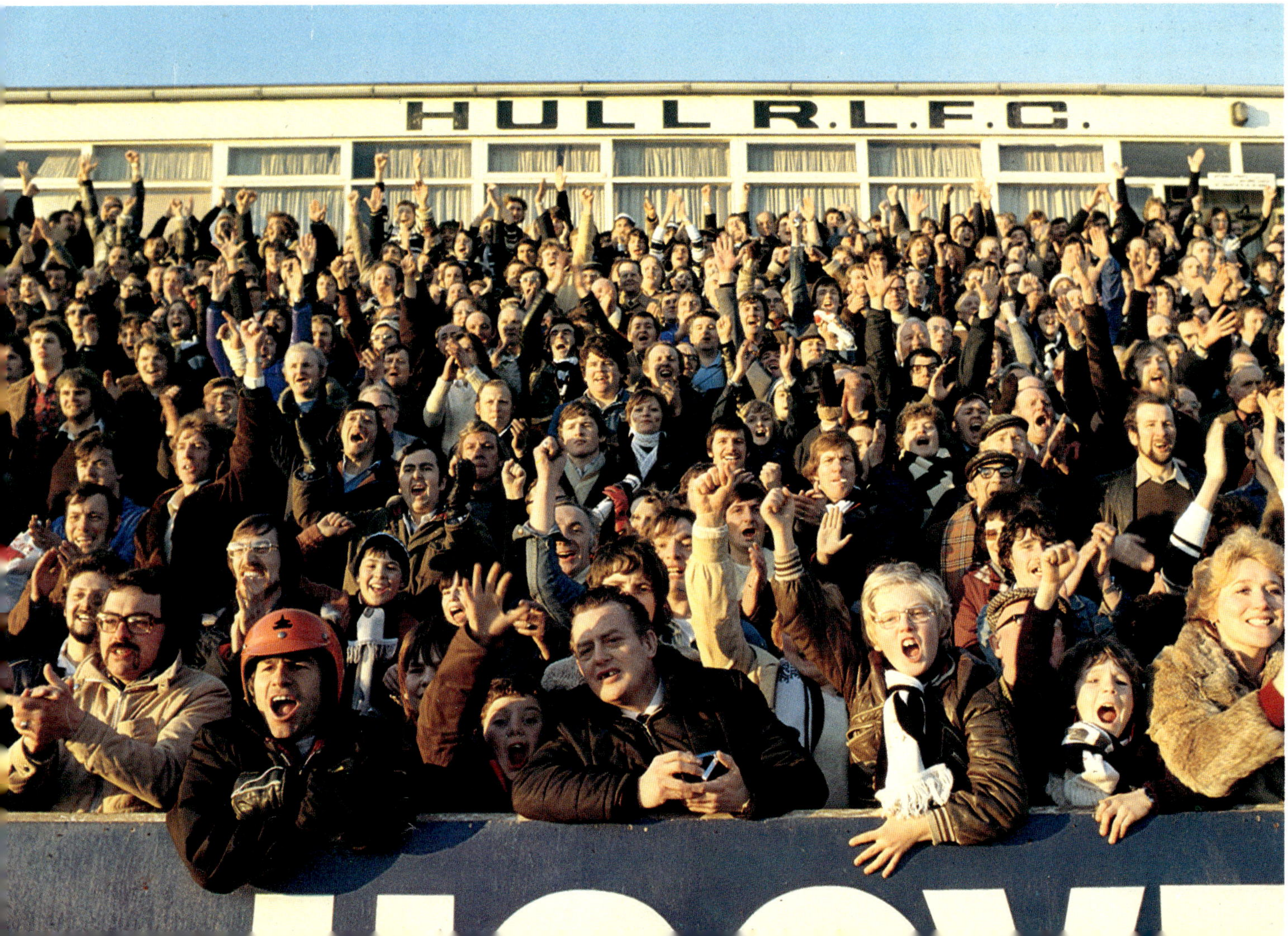

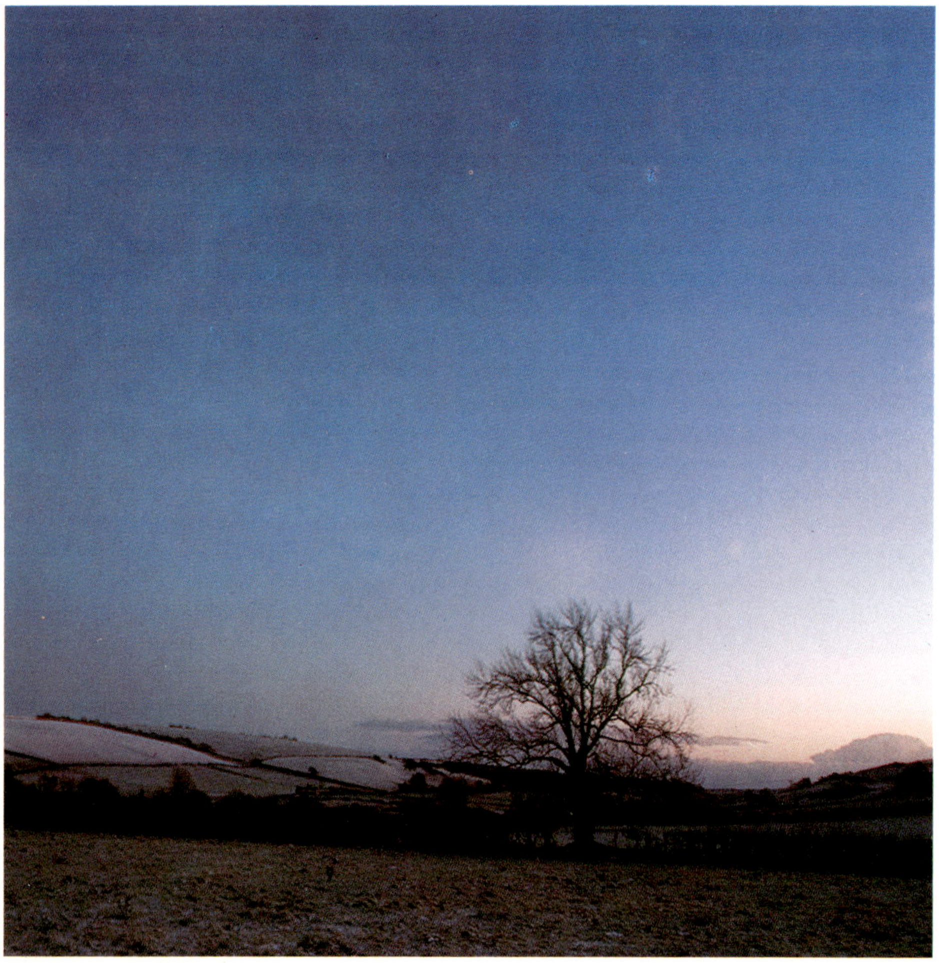

Landscape *As dusk settles, the colour of the light sinks towards the deep blue of night. Keep exposures short to avoid trailing of the Moon's image*

taken from the brighter clouds rather than from the sun itself, but small changes in exposure can cause considerable differences in the final effect. It is difficult to photograph a sunset badly—if you see a particularly spectacular sunset, take several shots at different exposures. Most of them will be satisfactory in their own way.

If morning light is flattering for portraits, that in the late afternoon and at sunset even more so. Golden skin tones, rich colours and contrasting deep blue skies in the background are easy to obtain. Your subject is often able to face the sun directly for flat but revealing lighting. The sunlight is weakened by atmospheric haze and does not make your subject screw up his or her eyes as much as in the morning.

Dusk

After the sun has dropped below the horizon, the remaining light from the sky has a very high colour temperature. Towards the sunset horizon there are usually some fast disappearing traces of pink and red in the sky, but the predominant colours are violets and blues. You need not attempt to correct colour temperature with filters at this time of day. The light changes so quickly in colour and intensity that even if you use an expensive colour temperature meter you are unlikely to be able to convert its readings into a corrective filter pack before the light changes.

If you have a tripod, colour film, and can work quickly, you can make photographs of cities and buildings at this time of day that capture the impression of night particularly effectively. There is still enough light in the sky to reveal the forms of buildings, but the interior lights glowing through the windows give pictures a night-time feel. The period in which the light from the sky and the light from windows is balanced is short. Set up your camera beforehand, use tungsten film to accentuate the blue of the sky, and make as many exposures as quickly as you can before the last of the day's light vanishes. Night photography is dealt with in the next section.

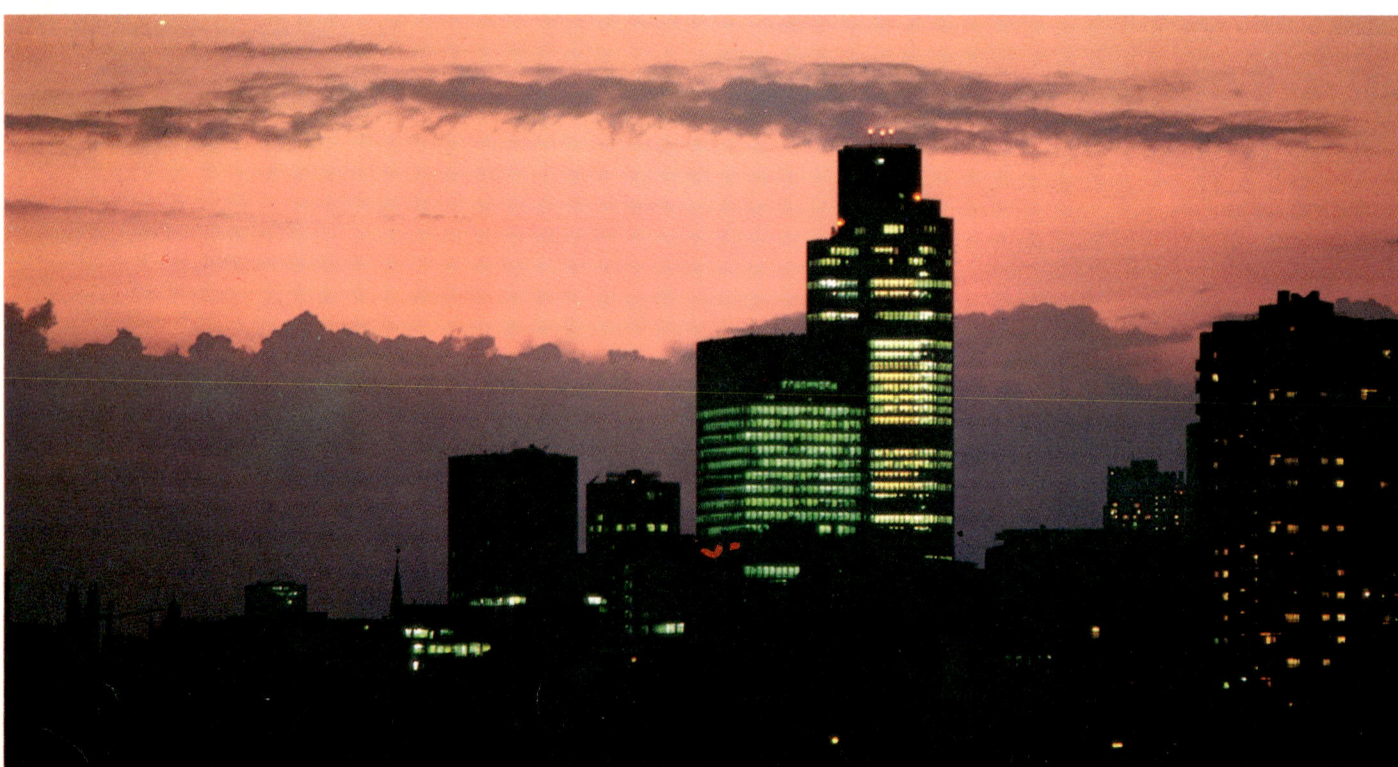

City sunset *Even when it is too dark for normal photography, light in the sky and windows can give good pictures of silhouetted buildings*

Photography at night

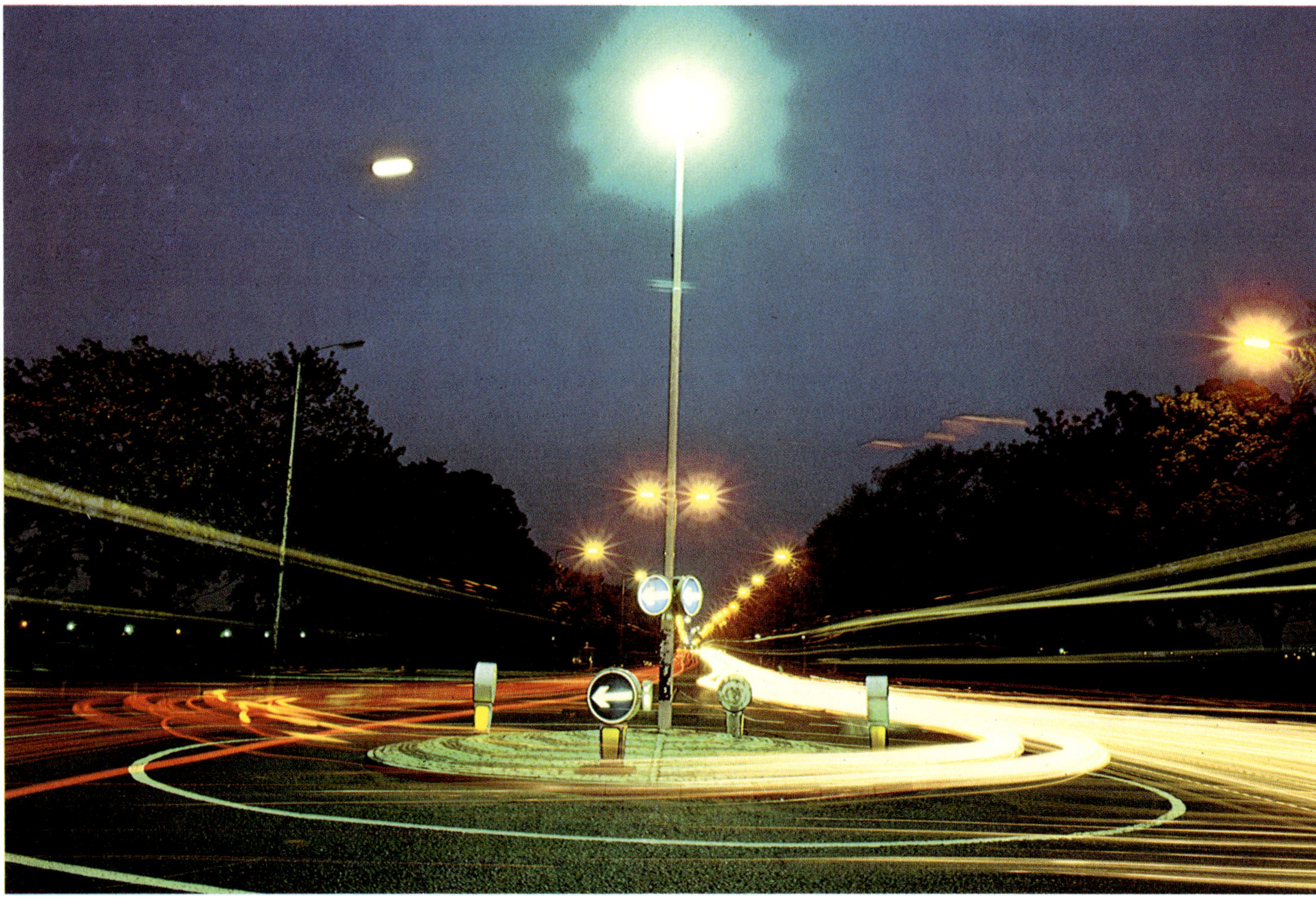

Night scene *Using a long exposure, with the camera on a tripod, produces bright streaks from the head and tail lights of all the passing vehicles*

Taking pictures in the dark seems a contradiction in terms—and indeed it is, for every photograph needs light. But it is very rare to find yourself in total darkness—other than in your darkroom—so there is generally some chance of a picture even in very low light.

It often happens that pictures present themselves at night, but remain unphotographed either because there was no camera to hand or because there was hardly any available light. Even modern emulsions are not as sensitive to light as the eye, so inevitably it is not possible to photograph some scenes, particularly those involving some action, just as you saw them. But it is often possible to take some sort of shot by using the right technique.

The range of low-light photographs that you might want to take includes street scenes at night, candid photography in dark locations, views of floodlit buildings, illuminations, and dimly lit interiors. And there are special effects which make use of the fact that the only light appearing in the picture is what you put there.

In general, night photography subjects divide into those where convential daytime camera techniques with a handheld camera are adequate, and those where extra help is needed. The first category includes street scenes in brightly lit areas, some illuminations and interiors. Subjects where there is not enough light for conventional photography include such subjects as moonlit landscapes, streets where there is little light, and occasions where you are not prepared for low light photography and have to use whatever means are to hand.

Hand-held camera

Many low light scenes can be photographed normally using a hand-held camera. It is often necessary to do this: you may be trying to take candid photographs in the street, or there may be some action which you have to keep up with. The limitations are the amount of light available, the speed of your film, the maximum aperture of your lens and its focal length.

With slow films, it gets too dark for normal picture taking shortly after sunset, unless you photograph the night sky. Fast films (see page 27), however, allow you to continue somewhat longer in to the twilight, using a shutter speed of 1/60 second and the camera's maximum aperture of, say, *f*/2. One normally tries to avoid taking pictures at shutter speeds slower than 1/60 second, but as the light gets dimmer this becomes necessary. It is usually possible for most people to hand-hold exposures of 1/30 and even 1/15 second using a standard lens, with care (see page 58).

Once you have reached 1/15 second, your first option is to change to a wide angle lens, if you have one. Any blur caused by camera shake will be less noticeable with a wide angle lens. But even this will only allow you to use 1/8 second exposure with extreme care.

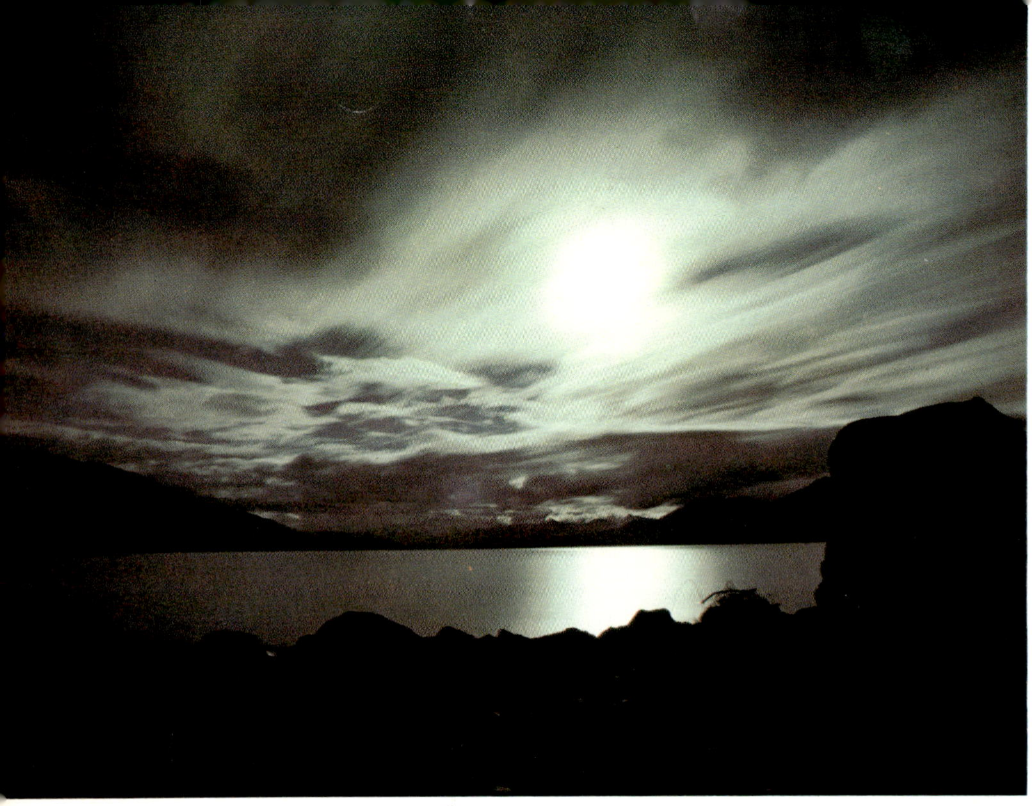

that you can use slower films for better definition. The limitation, however, is that moving objects will record as streaks, or may not even register on the film at all—though this can be used to advantage.

When using a tripod or camera support, it is advisable to operate the shutter using a cable or air bulb release. These usually screw into the shutter release button and allow you to fire the camera off without touching it. As well as making it unnecessary to touch the camera, a cable release tensions itself against the top of the camera body into which it is screwed, rather than pushing down on to the tripod itself. This also helps to prevent vibration.

A cable release at least 30 cm long is desirable. Air bulb releases are generally at least 2 metres long, so the photographer can be some way from the camera operating it.

Most cameras these days, other than the simplest, have facilities for long exposure times. Most often there is a 'B' setting, either on the shutter speed dial, or as an alternative to the automatic exposure setting. With the camera on 'B', the shutter stays open for as long as the shutter release is pressed. If you want to give exposures longer than a few seconds, it is a good idea to use a cable release with a screw lock on the end. The procedure is to press the cable release to open the shutter, screw the

Your next option is to rate the film at a faster speed, tolerating the loss of picture quality which this involves. This can only be done with certain films—it is impossible with Kodachrome, and while colour negative films will tolerate some underexposure they cannot be processed specially for higher speeds. Ektachrome and other E6 process films can, however, be push processed by one or two stops, as can most black and white films. You can do this by extending the development time (see page 235). Alternatively, many processing laboratories will push the film speed for an extra charge.

Using film at 800 ASA(ISO) in a camera fitted with a wide angle lens, with a maximum aperture of *f*/1.7 and a shutter speed of 1/15 second, will allow you to take pictures in quite poor street lighting, or in dimly lit interiors. You are limited, however, to slow moving subjects. Any subject movement will require a shutter speed of at least 1/60 second for sharp results. Depth of field will also be very restricted under these conditions.

One further option available if you need to take low light level pictures is to use a larger camera format. This will not result in extra light on the film, but it will be possible to use fast film without the graininess becoming excessive, since your negatives or transparencies will be bigger compared to the grain size. Roll film or larger format cameras do not usually have lenses as fast as those on 35 mm cameras, however, so there may be no overall gain. And the extra bulk of the camera may make it more difficult to use in those situations where a hand-held camera is needed.

Using a camera support

If you hold the camera steady by using a tripod or some other support (see pages 58 to 65), many more things become possible. Exposure times can be as long as desired, which means

Passing clouds *At night in a moonlit landscape, time exposures can transform a picture. Here the movement of the clouds has spread them across the frame*

Spaghetti junction *A high viewpoint sometimes produces a picture which is totally different to one taken at ground level—these roads look map-like*

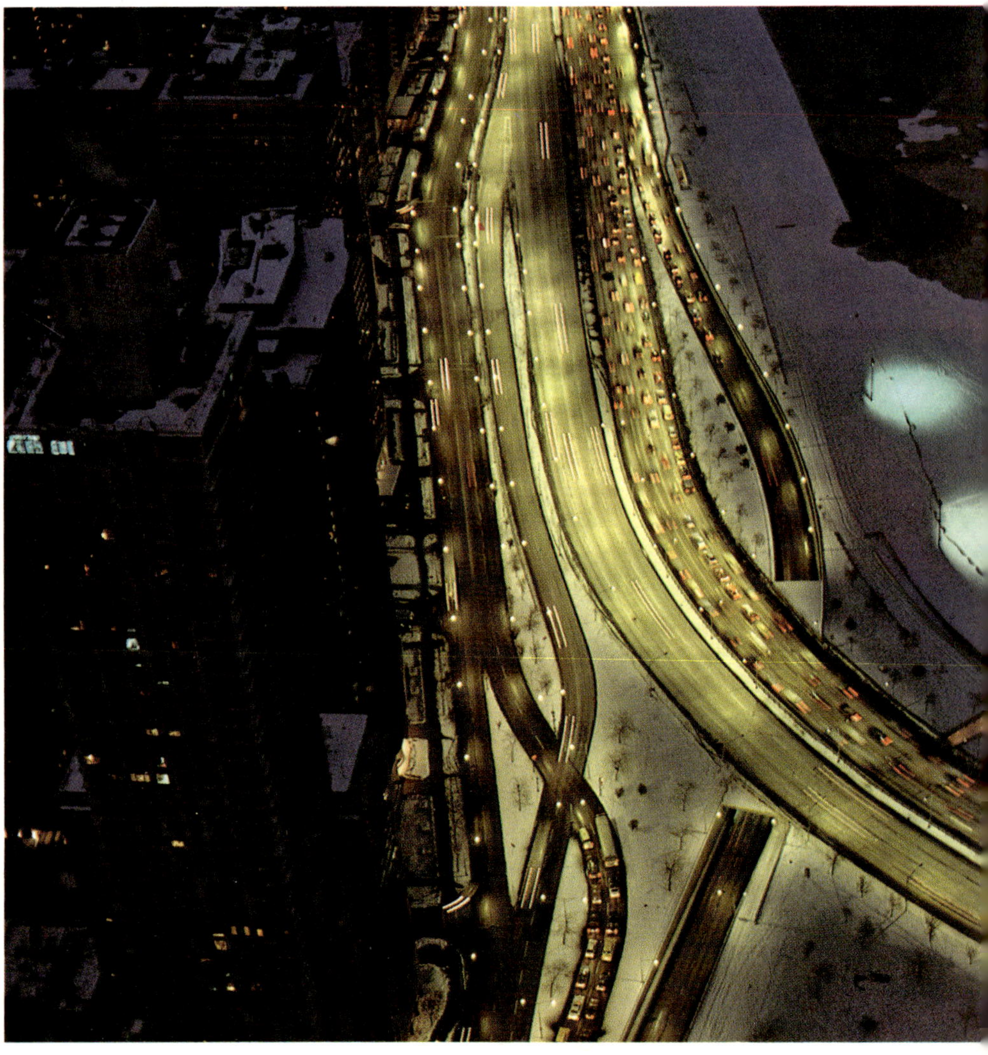

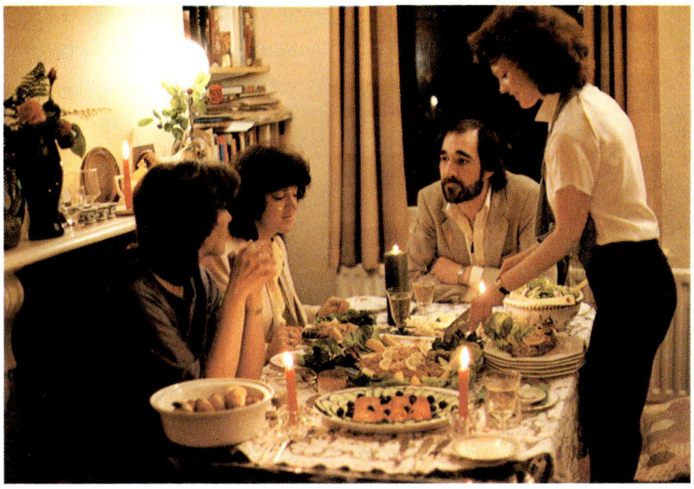

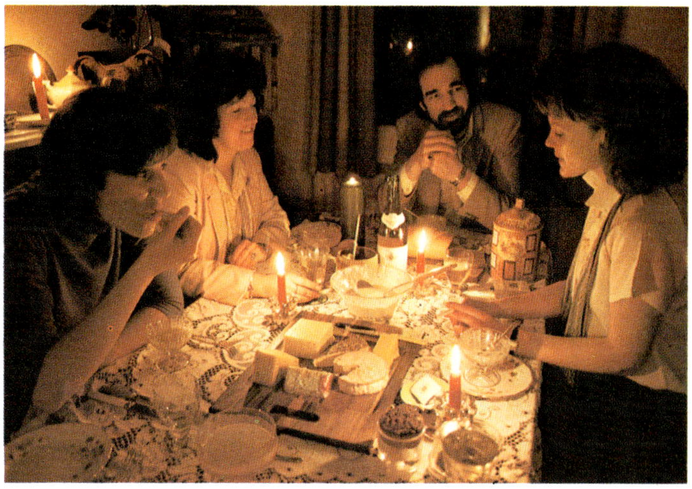

Dinner party *With fast film, it is possible to take pictures even in dim lighting. The exposure here was 1/30 sec at full aperture—f/2—using a standard 50 mm lens*

Candlelight *Wide angle lenses can be used without danger of camera shake at even slower shutter speeds. Switching to a 28 mm f/2 lens made this shot possible at 1/15 sec*

locking knob tight, and leave the camera for as long as desired. When the time comes to close the shutter, hold a finger against the cable release end, undo the screw lock and close the shutter by relaxing the spring tension of the cable release. This prevents the violent jerk which may happen if you simply undo the screw lock.

If an unwanted object seems about to enter the field of view during the exposure, you need not end the exposure prematurely. If the surroundings are dark enough you can interrupt the exposure by holding a dark card, cloth or even a hat over the lens. As long as you do not disturb the camera, you can remove it when the object has gone.

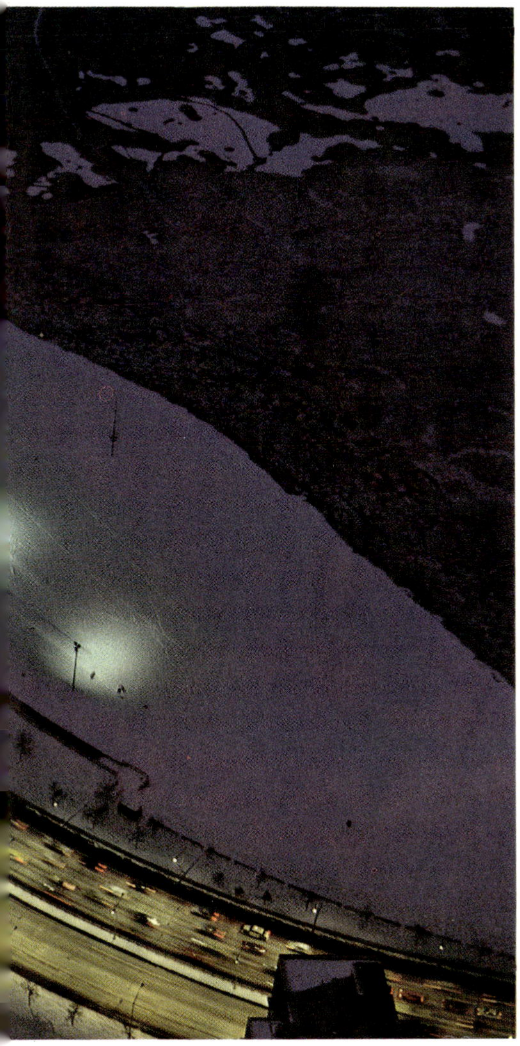

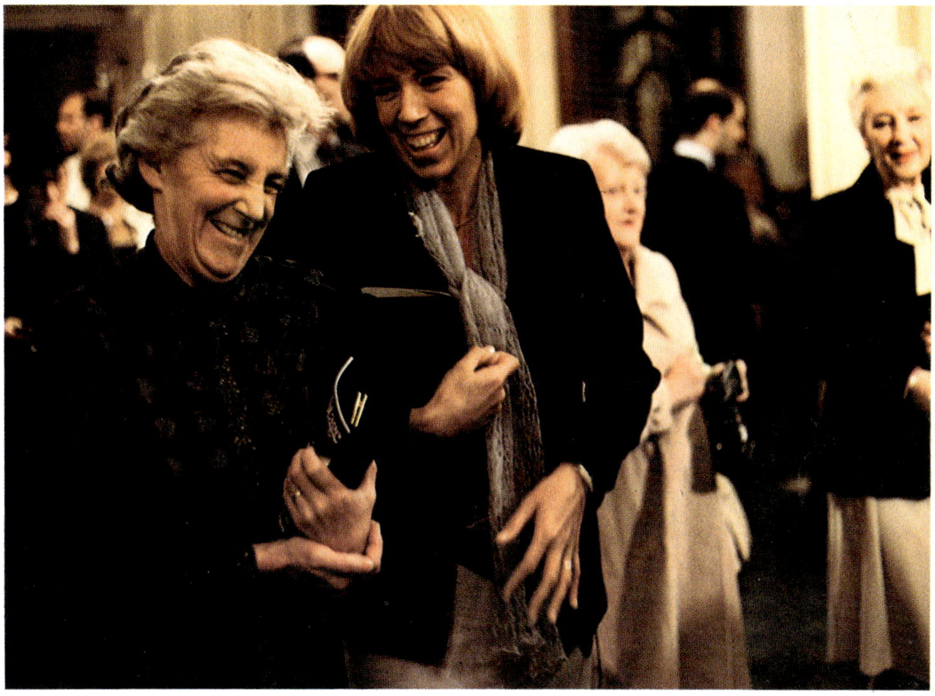

Party snaps *When your subjects are moving, flash is not the only answer. Here the 400 ASA film was pushed by one stop to allow a speed of 1/60 at f/2*

Time exposures of this sort can be used in a wide variety of situations. As well as allowing you to take pictures in places where there is very little light, or where you want to use slow film or a small aperture, they enable you to create special effects. The classic example is the trailed lights of moving cars: it may be necessary to stop down the camera in order to get a sufficient number of trails for an interesting shot. Alternatively you can experiment with a wide range of similar effects by walking along with a torch pointing towards the camera during the exposure.

People in a street will blur in an exposure no longer than 1/4 second, while retaining enough characteristics to show who they are. Dark moving objects may disappear altogether if they have a light background, as the brightness overpowers any trace of them. Time exposures can be used to make a busy street appear completely deserted or at least populated only by ghostly figures.

By operating a flashgun at some point during the exposure, a sharp but faint image of a person may register within the blur. The exposure which the film receives depends on the aperture it is working at rather than on the total exposure time. If you calculate the flash exposure as you would normally, then you may get overexposed results if the subject in the flash appears against a light background. On the other hand, if it is possible to operate the flash when the subject is against a black part of the picture, the exposure will be normal.

There are, however, additional problems to be borne in mind when using

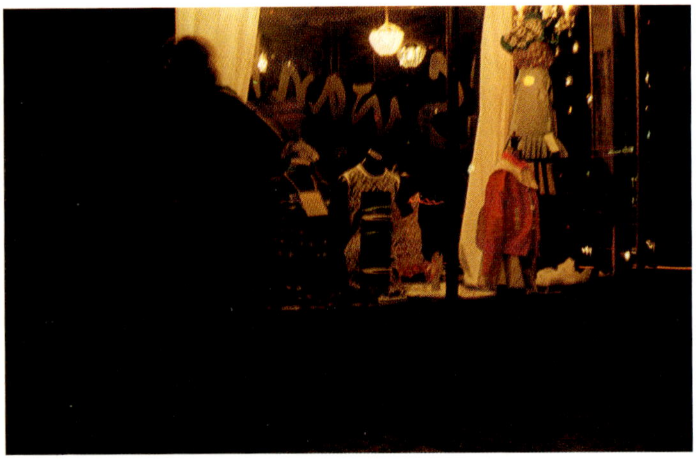

Dark street *Shop windows at night make an interesting subject, but without additional light the shadows are black and empty, and the glare of the window is all that appears*

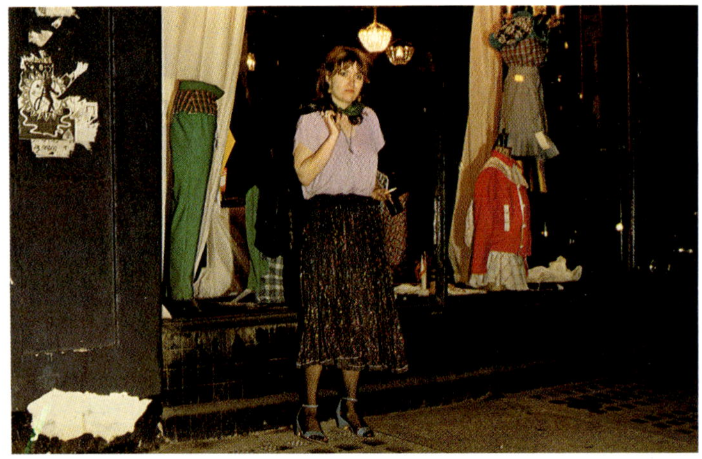

Add a flash *Using a flash in addition to a time exposure produces a much better picture. Detail appears outside the window, which still retains a cheery glow*

flash at night. The guide numbers on flash units usually assume that there will be some reflections from walls, so in the open the flash apparently has less power. And anybody with dark hair, complexion or clothes may tend to disappear against a black background. For these reasons, it is not possible to give rules about how to tackle such situations, as the results depend entirely on the conditions at the time.

This technique of using flash can be extended to 'painting with light'. This involves moving around an otherwise dark subject with a portable flashgun, setting it off to illuminate parts of the subject at a time. The operator has to make sure that he or she does not appear silhouetted against the surface being illuminated unless this is specifically required.

Using this technique, you can either use a single flash on each part of the area to be covered, or you can add flashes from the same location to produce more illumination. As for exposure, you can use the guide number system to calculate the aperture needed on the camera for a given flash distance. Then as long as you do not overlap the flashes, you can use the camera as far away from the subject as desired providing the distance from the flash to the subject remains the same as your calculated flash distance. The size of the well illuminated area in the picture, however, decreases as the camera is moved farther from the subject.

This system only works if the flash is pointing more or less away from the camera. Side illumination requires much more exposure, and also runs the risk of allowing the flash to shine directly into the camera.

It is possible to use tungsten lighting, or even a bright torch, to paint a surface with light in the same way, but unless you use the appropriate film or filters (see page 119) the results may have a warm colour when using colour film.

When giving time exposures in this way at night, watch out not only for cars and people entering the field of view, but also for the flashing lights of aircraft in the sky beyond.

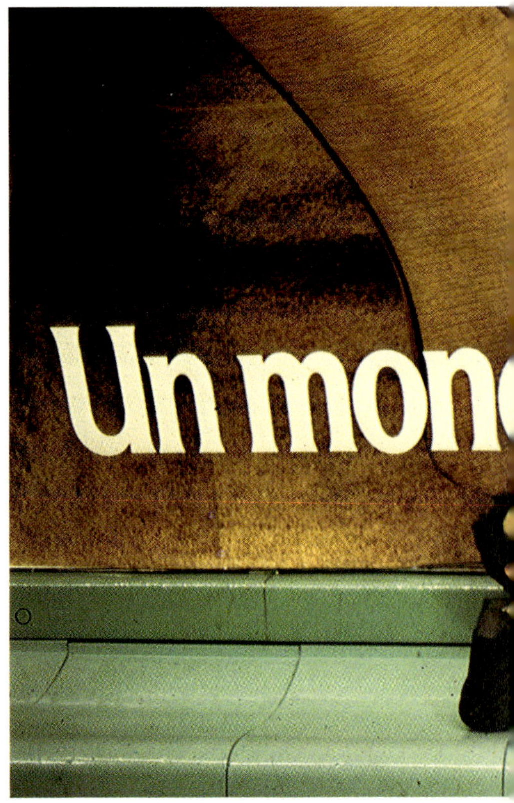

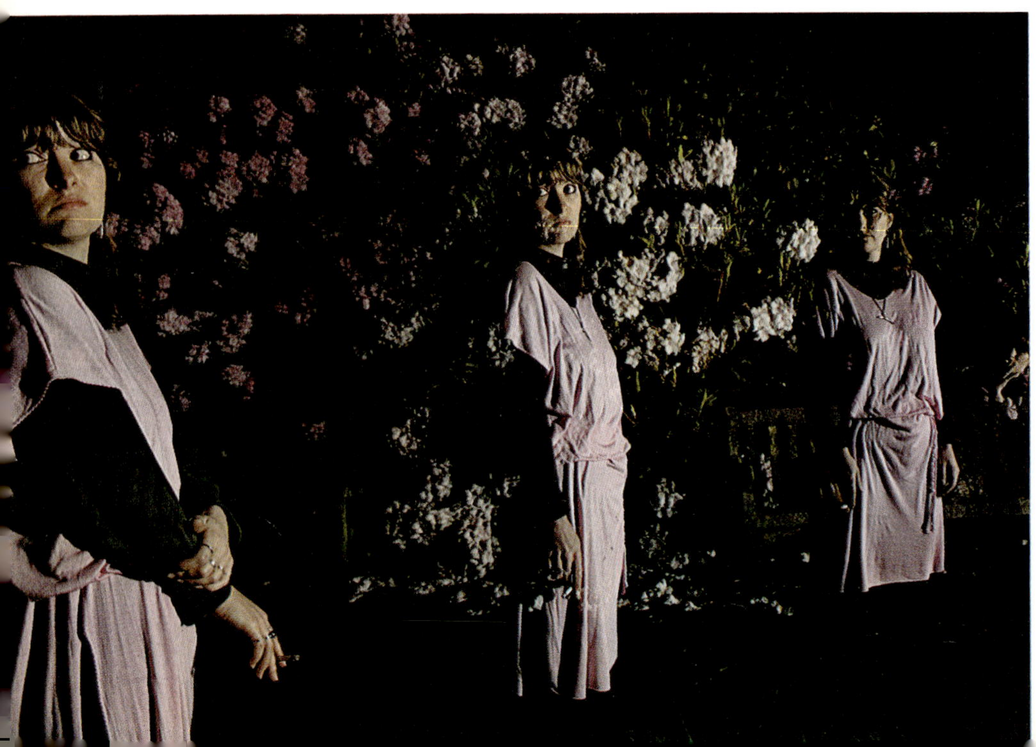

In the garden *By leaving the shutter open and 'collecting' a series of images on the film, you can produce a wide range of imaginative pictures*

Exposure and metering

One major problem when photographing at night is that the camera's own meter may not be sensitive enough to give a reading. Alternatively, it may be misled by bright lights in the field of view into giving less exposure than is really needed. In many viewfinders the reading may not even be visible as the numbers can only be seen against the brightness of the subject.

If you are using slow film and want to give a time exposure, many meters will not give an indication as their scales stop at one second. In such cases put the meter on a higher film speed until you do get a reading. Then work out how many stops extra exposure you must give. For example, if your meter does not respond at 64ASA and full aperture, but gives a reading of one second at 500 ASA, then you must give three stops extra exposure (doubling the film speed

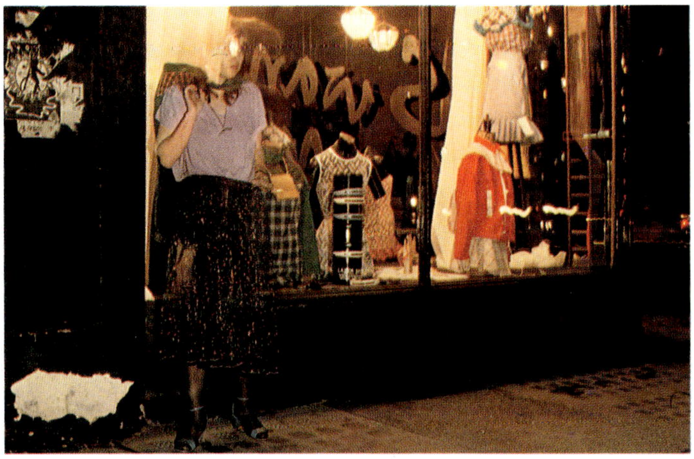

Moving subjects *For pictures like this, it is essential that parts of the subject lit by the flash keep still. If they move about, the lights behind can burn out their image*

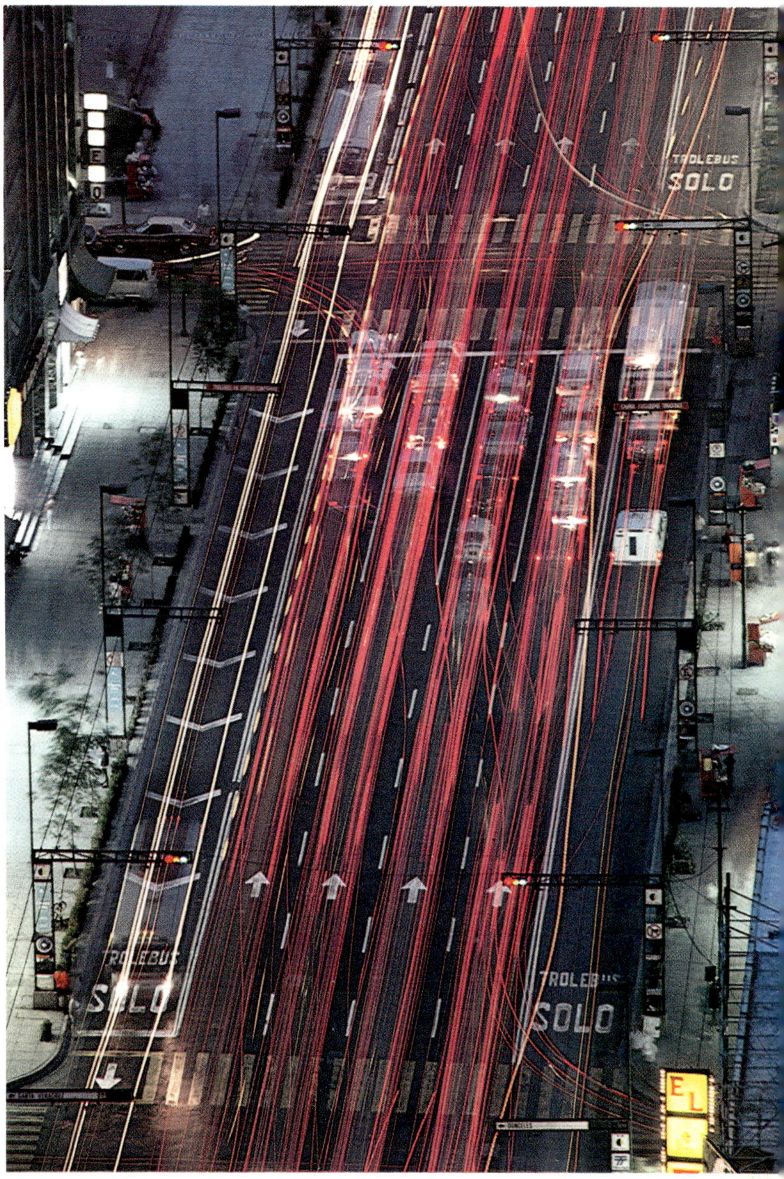

Freeway in focus *Night scenes are sometimes surprisingly bright, and to allow really long exposures you may find that you have to stop the lens down to a small aperture*

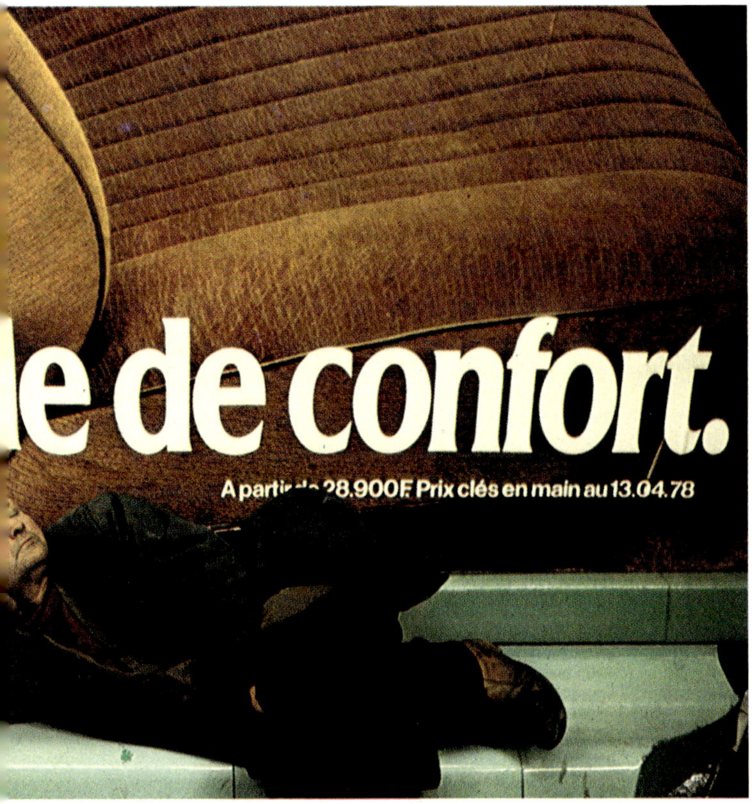

Subway scene *Lighting in many public places is bright enough to permit hand-held candid shots with fast film. Fluorescent lighting gives a characteristic green tint*

gives one stop: the sequence is 125 – 250 – 500). So you must give 8 seconds' exposure on 64ASA film.

To this must be added the complication of reciprocity failure (see page 236). This may result in an 8 second exposure being extended to 30 seconds.

Faced with such problems, many photographers take the easy way out and *bracket* their exposures—that is, they give several different exposures in the hope that one will come out. This is often the best procedure, but it is also good technique to be fairly certain of your starting point.

To prevent the meter being fooled by bright lights, aim to avoid them when metering, and give the indicated exposure even if the lights are to be part of the picture. With fully automatic cameras this may involve guesswork or resetting the film speed dial.

If you cannot read the camera's internal meter, you may have to turn it so as to be able to see the needle or figures against the brightest part of the view. If this is not possible, then guesswork again has to take over.

Working in the dark

As well as there being too little light to take pictures, photography in the dark also means that you may have trouble in operating your camera.

A most useful accessory is a small torch. As well as allowing you to see the camera settings, it can also be used either to throw some light on the subject, or to place on the subject to give you a reference point to focus on. It also comes in handy should you have the misfortune to have to search for some small item of equipment on the ground.

When taking candid shots at night, it is not possible to use a torch for focusing. One solution to this problem is to glue or tape small pieces of matchstick to the focusing ring index mark of your lens. Suitable points might be at the two and four metre marks, for example. Then you can either line up the pieces of matchstick or guess some midway position. With the two focusing extremes, this method gives you four reference points for focusing.

To operate the aperture ring in the dark, get used to how many click stops there are between maximum and minimum apertures. The wider apertures usually have half click stops, so memorize how many there are.

Strips of tape, such as masking tape, can help you distinguish between lenses of similar size in the dark. Stick different numbers of strips round the barrels.

Practice loading and unloading in the dark. To prevent loading a film already exposed, be sure to wind each film fully back into its cassette.

CHAPTER 9
FLASH PHOTOGRAPHY
Flash on the camera

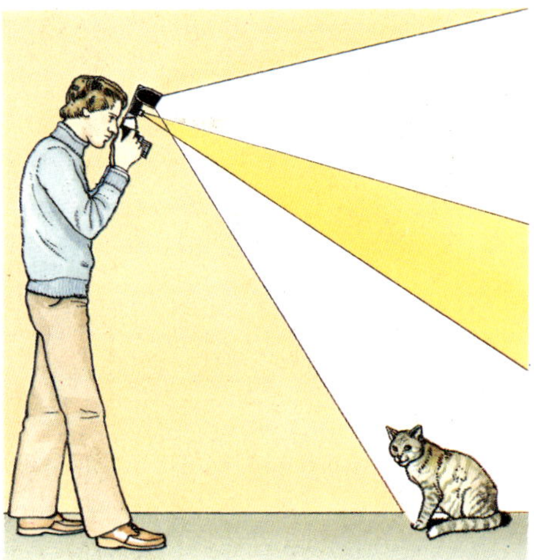

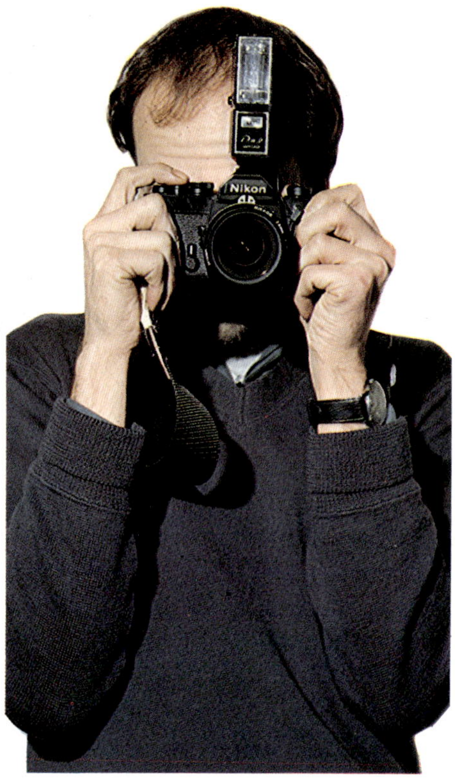

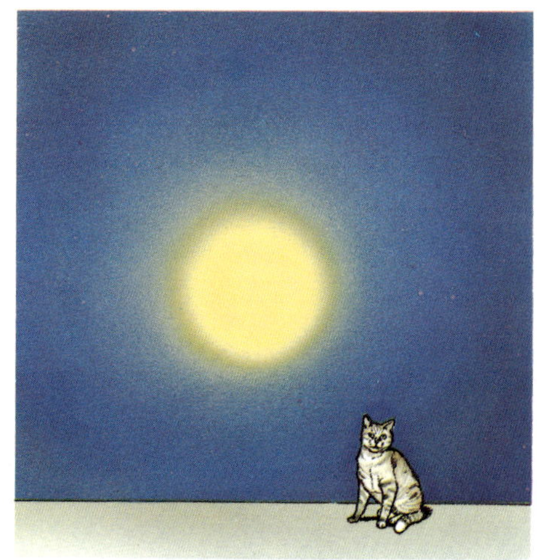

Fooling the sensor *An automatic gun has a sensor to control the light output. Since its beam is smaller than that of the flash, you can have problems if the subject is not framed centrally*

Modern flashguns are the answer to the prayers of a good many photographers. Shooting indoors always used to be a problem. You either had to work in the artificial atmosphere of a studio or carry a lot of bulky and often fragile equipment round if you wanted to work on location, or trust the available light. The modern convenient, sophisticated small electronic flashgun overcomes those problems for all but the largest subjects. In addition, the light given out is very similar in colour to daylight so you do not need to use special film or filters to ensure correct colour.

Most people tend to use flashguns indoors to light portraits, often in a rather indiscriminate fashion, working on the basis that any record is better than none at all. However, it only takes a little experimentation and effort to improve these results, perhaps extending your technique into other, more adventurous, areas. And it is also worth using flash to make interesting records of subjects such as wedding presents, before and after shots of redecorating schemes, or your baby's first steps—just as likely to take place in a dimly lit living room as outside on the lawn.

How they work

Unlike flashbulbs and cubes, electronic flash guns are completely reusable. The flash is produced by passing an electric current through a tube filled with an inert gas. For those smaller models that fit easily on to the camera, the electrical power is supplied by a set of small dry batteries fitted into a compartment in the unit. Larger models use separate re-

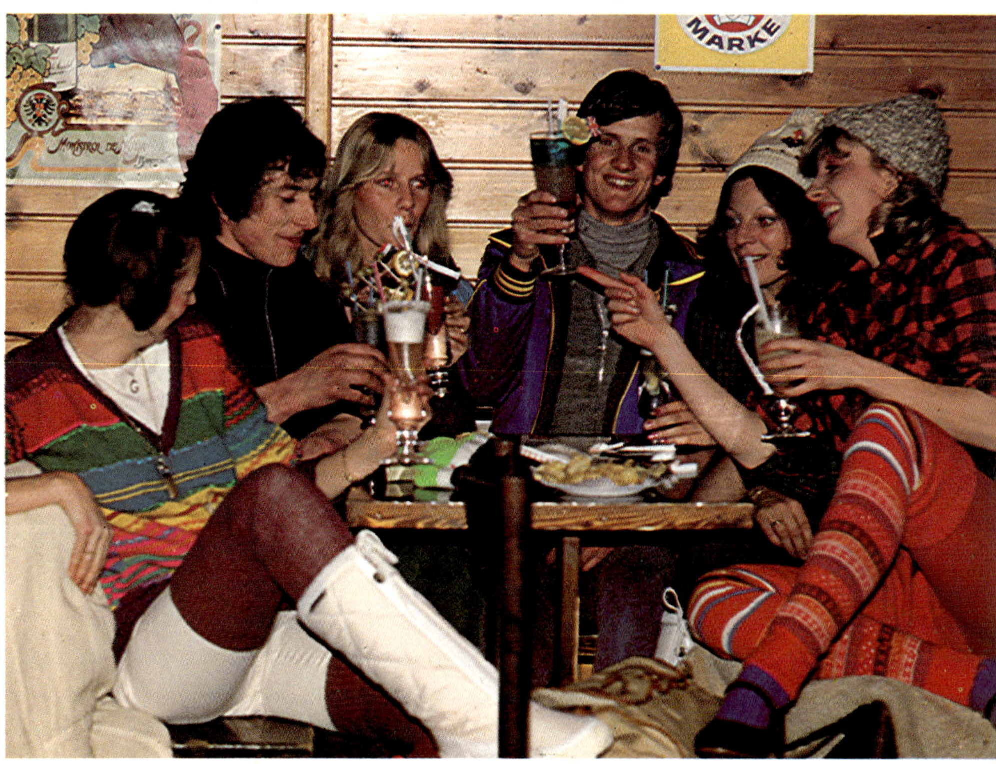

A group of people *A flashgun mounted directly on the camera is useful for taking off the cuff shots like this*

chargeable nickel–cadmium batteries. These are more expensive but much more economical.

Synchronization
No matter how powerful the gun, however, the subject will not be properly illuminated unless the flash is discharged exactly at the moment when the shutter is open. Such synchronization is ensured in two ways. Some cameras are fitted with *hot shoes*, usually on top of the camera. These are slide-in brackets into which a foot on the base of the gun is pushed. When this is done an electrical connection is established between the two that fires the flash as the shutter reaches its open position.

Not all cameras have hot shoes but all 35 mm models have connection points for synchronization leads. These sockets are usually located on the camera body close to the lens mount but this is not invariable. The lead is plugged into both gun and camera, and the gun then fires whenever the shutter is pressed.

Older cameras may still have an M and X setting. The M setting was for synchronizing bulbs, which have a slightly different firing time. If you have such a facility on your camera always keep it set at X, which is the setting for electronic flash. At the M setting using electronic flash, you will get no pictures.

Automatic guns
Modern designs can be divided into two types, manual and automatic. The latter guns all have a manual option which you can use when necessary.

Automatic guns have a photoelectric sensor—a 'magic eye'—on the front of the unit. Its job is to measure the amount of light reflected back from the subject when the flash goes off. As soon as the programmed amount of light has been received back, it cuts off the flash, giving the correct exposure.

It sounds as if this system should guarantee perfect results every time, but unfortunately this is not always true, and there are occasions when a light or dark background can fool the sensor.

The sensor will also be misled if you are taking a shot of a highly reflective subject or one which has a mirror or a piece of glass behind it. The light is then bounced straight back at the sensor causing extreme underexposure.

In addition, the sensor measures an angle of only about 12° to 20° of the total subject area so if your subject is out of its path, the sensor will read off the background. In this case the gun will have to be used manually.

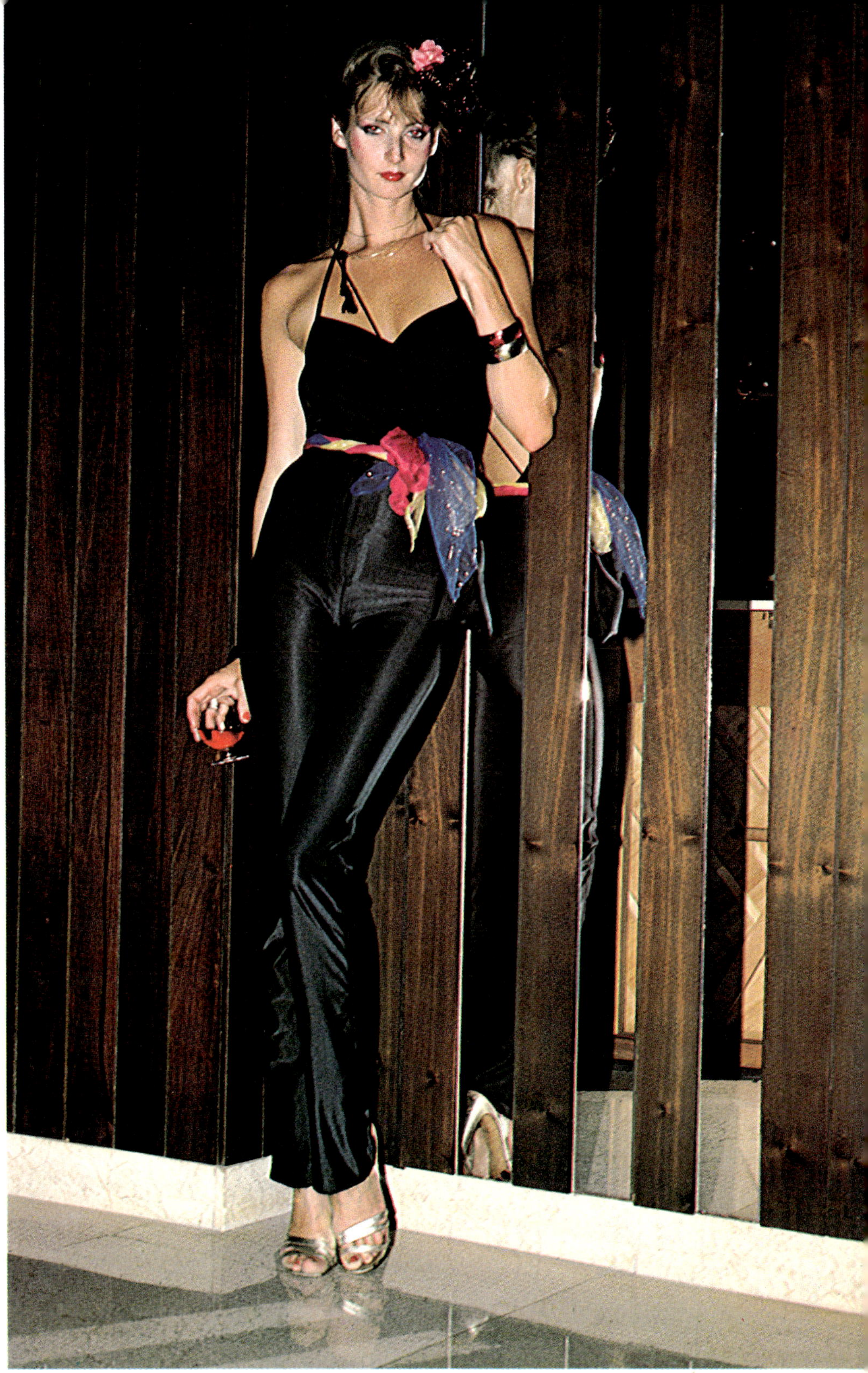

A touch of glamour *If you are careful when using the flash mounted on the camera, you can use it for a range of subjects. A diffuser was used here*

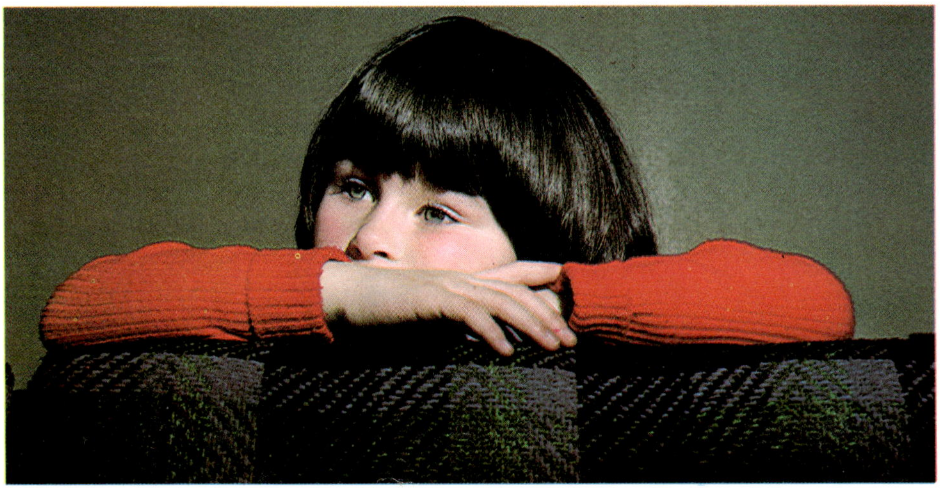

Small children *With young children you have to be ready for spontaneous shots. Using the flashgun fitted to the camera can help you to act quickly*

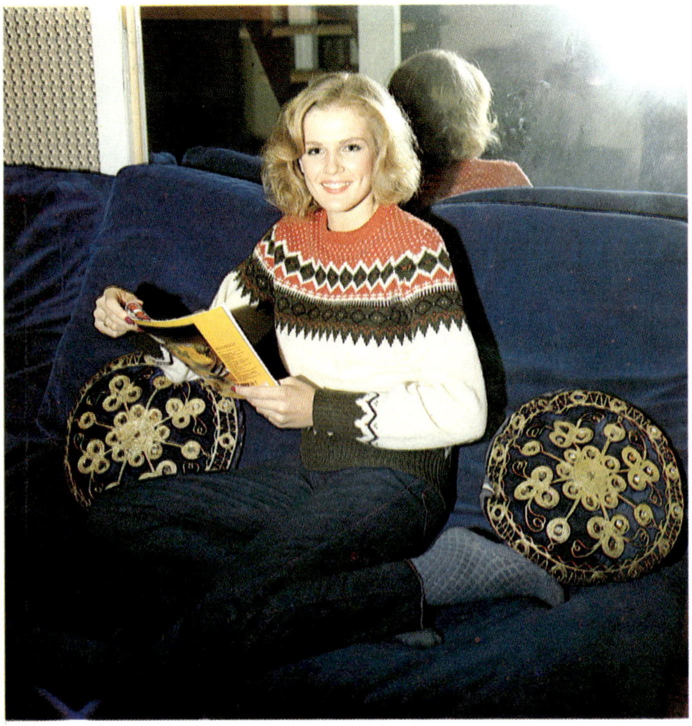

Reflections *One of the things you must watch out for is a reflective surface, such as a mirror or even a framed picture, in the background. This may cause a distracting reflection*

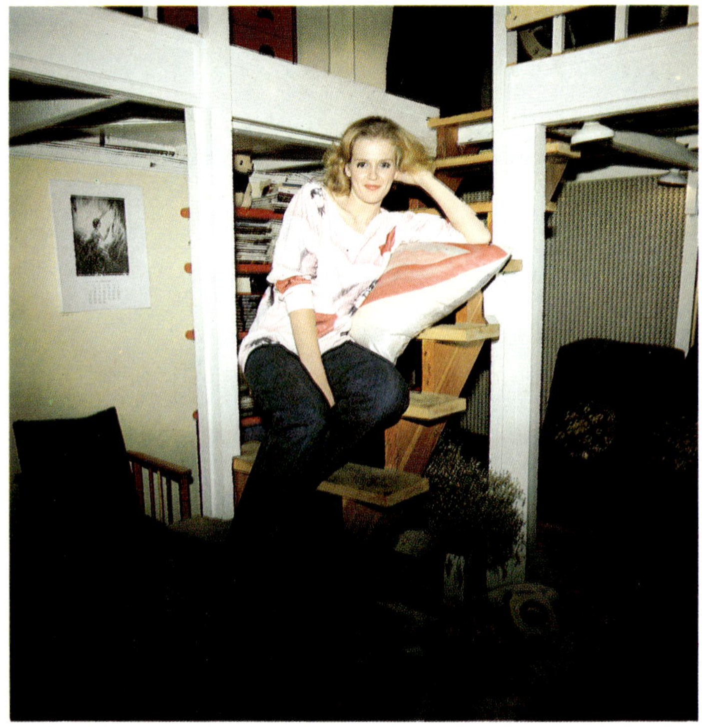

Insufficient coverage *Another problem is that of not getting enough illumination for a wide angle lens, as here. Diffuser panels will increase the coverage*

Auto guns have a further drawback in that there is a limited range of distances over which the auto sensor will work. But within this range, which is normally adequate for indoor work, they allow you freedom of movement without constantly having to worry about the exposure setting.

The simplest automatic flashguns allow you just one aperture for each film speed. The camera must be set to the aperture appropriate to the speed of film you are using, and all shots taken at that aperture will then be well exposed. More expensive guns have a choice of output powers, so you have more control over the aperture you work at.

Manual flashguns

When using a purely manual gun or an automatic gun set to the manual mode, you will need to make a simple calculation to get the correct exposure. Although it requires more effort, it avoids incorrect flash exposure caused by deceptively reflective surfaces.

Every flashgun has a guide number—the higher the number the more powerful the flash. To get the correct exposure, divide this number by the camera-to-subject distance and you will have the appropriate aperture. For example, a typical guide number for a gun in the medium power range is 23 when using a film rated at 100 ASA (ISO). The subject is 2 m away. This gives an aperture of approximately *f*/11.

If you have an SLR or a rangefinder camera it is a simple matter to measure the distance. Just focus the camera and read the information you want off the focusing ring. If you do not have such a camera, you have to estimate the distance.

Guide numbers are now in metres but feet guide numbers may be encountered so be careful not to confuse the two otherwise you will get some odd results. They are also given in relation to a specific film speed, usually 100 ASA. With the gun you should get a chart giving you the guide numbers for other film speeds. If there is no chart the new number can be calculated fairly easily. If the speed of the film in your camera is double the given one, that is 200 ASA instead of 100 ASA, you multiply the number by 1.4. If it is 400 ASA, that is 4 times the original given speed, you multiply by 2. If it is only half, that is 50 ASA, you multiply by 0.7. The reason for these odd numbers is that the scale is based on a square law.

Fortunately, most manual guns have a calculator dial or sliding scale set into the side of the unit on which you can work out apertures for given distances.

Outdoor flash *There are numerous shots which you can take outside using a flash to provide the light. This photograph was taken when it was almost dark*

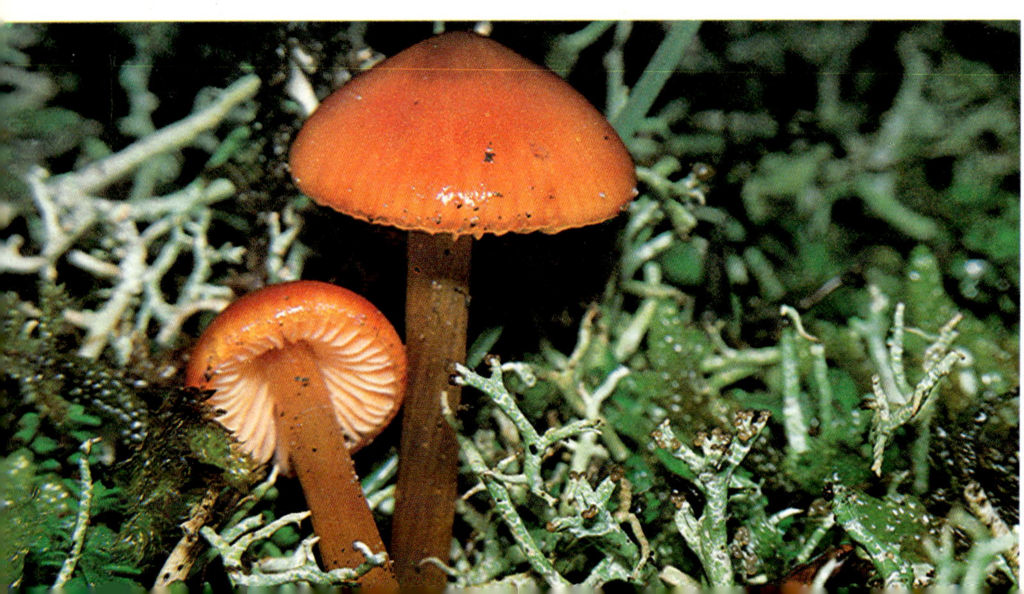

Shutter speeds

So far shutter speeds have not been mentioned. This is because the duration of the flash is only 1/1000 sec or less. Close-ups with an automatic gun can reduce the time to as little as 1/40,000 sec. This can create a problem with those cameras fitted with focal plane shutters, which include all modern 35 mm SLRs. Because the blind moves across the frame, the gap exposing the film in a continuous action, such very short flashes of light will only reach the film during part of the shutter movement, unless a relatively long exposure time is chosen where the gap in the blind is as wide as the film. In practice this means that shutter speeds faster than 1/60 or 1/125 cannot be used with most SLRs.

Testing the flash

Before you begin shooting it is a good

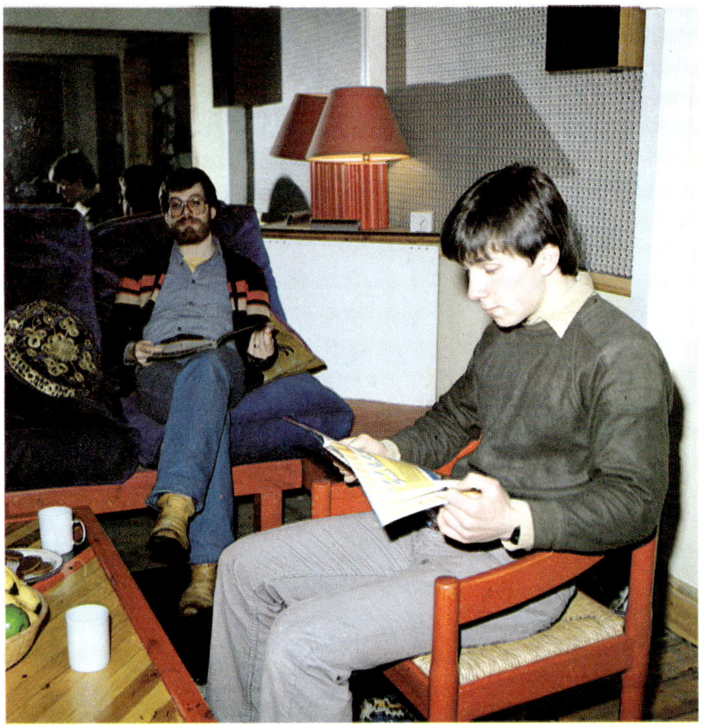

Foreground and background *Another problem arises if subjects are at different distances. The sensor reads off the foreground so the rest is underexposed*

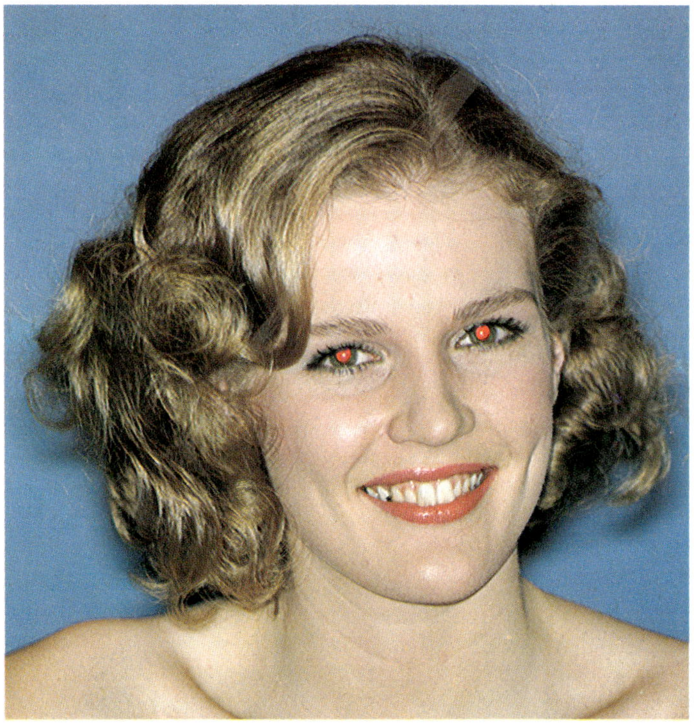

Red eye *If the flashgun is positioned close to the camera lens it is likely that the pupil of the model's eyes will turn bright red because of light reflected off the retina*

idea to test the battery, particularly if you have not used the gun for some time. Many units have a test circuit that lights a bulb if everything is all right.

If you get an underexposed set of pictures but the batteries are good, make a series of careful tests before you return the gun to the shop or take it to a photographic mechanic. It is quite possible that you set the controls incorrectly or miscalculated without realizing it.

Recycling time

Each time that the gun is fired all or part of the electrical charge, which is stored in the capacitor, is discharged through the flash tube. Before you can fire again, the capacitor must recharge. In a modern gun with fully charged batteries this can happen in a fraction of a second, particularly if it is an automatic with a thyristor circuit that channels excess power back into the capacitor. However, as the power of the batteries diminishes the recycling time will increase. If you try firing before the capacitor is ready the flash will lack full power and you will get an underexposed picture.

On-camera flash

The simplest way to use a flashgun is by attaching it to the camera, particularly if the latter has a hot shoe. Since the lens will be pointing at the subject you can be sure that the flash will be as well. As long as the gun has enough power to bridge the intervening distance, you can expect at least some sort of picture.

Unfortunately, with such direct illumination, the result is rather harsh with sharply defined shadows. If you are taking a portrait you will, in addition, get a reflection from the skin that makes it look unpleasantly shiny. Colours can also look rather garish.

Another unpleasant result of on-the-camera flash is an effect called *red eye*. This occurs in a portrait when the light source is very near to the lens. The light enters the eye and is reflected off the retina, which contains many blood vessels, straight back to the lens. So the centre of the eye appears red, which is very disturbing. The only cure is to move the gun away from the camera.

Diffused flash

A diffuser that scatters the light emitted by the flashgun is one way of avoiding some of the problems without taking the unit off the camera.

The simplest diffusers are tissue paper, muslin or even a clean handkerchief taped over the tube and reflector. If you have an automatic gun be careful to avoid obscuring the photoelectric sensor. Some manufacturers make plastic diffusing screens as accessories.

However you diffuse the light one thing is certain: some of it will be absorbed and this has to be allowed for when judging the exposure. If you have an automatic gun the sensor takes care of this. If you do not, the aperture should be opened up by at least one stop, although you will need to experiment a little before you can be sure of the precise effect on exposure.

Whatever the means you choose to create the diffusion, the effects are roughly the same. Shadows are lighter, containing more detail and the edges are less distinct. However, the effect will still be a little flat. As the flash is close to the lens, most of the shadows created are on those parts of the face hidden from the lens. If you want a more rounded effect to capture subjects modelled by shadow, then you have to move the flash off the camera away from the lens.

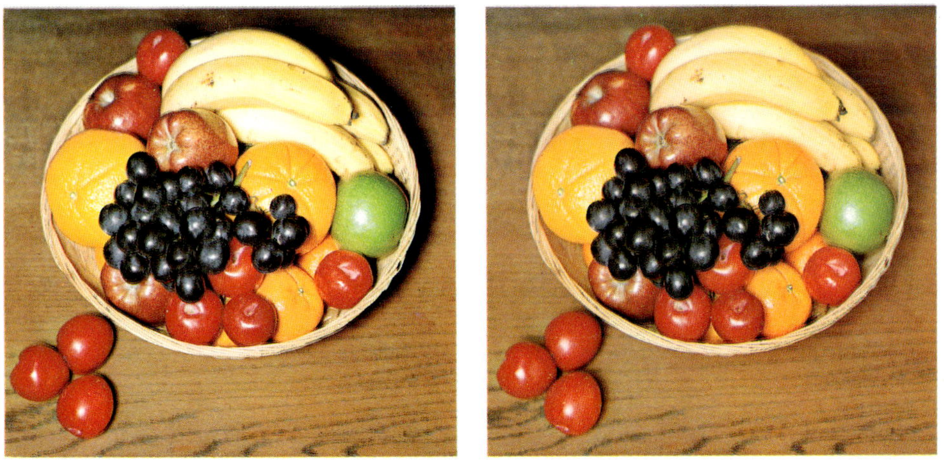

Diffused flash *Without a diffuser (left) the light is harsh. The diffused shot (right) has softer shadows and reflections*

Flash off the camera

Keeping the flashgun attached to the camera is a very straightforward way of lighting a subject. The light is automatically aimed at the same subject as the camera and there are no trailing cables to impede movement. It is a flexible system and simple to operate, but the results are rather limited for effects. If you want a broader, more subtle range of lighting effects with flash, you will have to detach the gun from the camera.

Flashbars

The simplest and most convenient way of moving the flashgun away from the camera, if only for a short distance, is to mount it on a flashbar. These take various forms but basically consist of a bracket which fastens the flashgun to the camera. The camera is attached to the bracket by the tripod bush in the base plate, while the gun is attached by the foot on its base or by a similar bush. A short lead connects the two and synchronizes them.

If there is some distance between the gun and the camera, the light will strike the subject at an angle that is slightly different from the lens to subject line. This means that both highlight and shadow areas will be apparent to the lens. If the gun is still relatively close to the lens, the shadows will not overwhelm the highlights, but some shadowing or modelling will be introduced. The flexibility and mobility of a self-contained hand-held unit are very useful advantages for parties or similar situations where you wish to move around freely. You have fewer problems with awkward or ugly shadows, and you avoid trailing synchronization leads that can easily be damaged or disconnected.

Mounting the flashgun on a flashbar instead of on the camera itself makes little difference to lighting the subject except at quite close viewpoints. If the subject is more than about a metre away, the difference in lighting is negligible.

Hand-held flash

An even broader range of lighting effects can be achieved by completely separating the camera and the flashgun. With a

Miss World 1970 *Many photographers here are using flash bars or separate hand-held units to give better lighting quality*

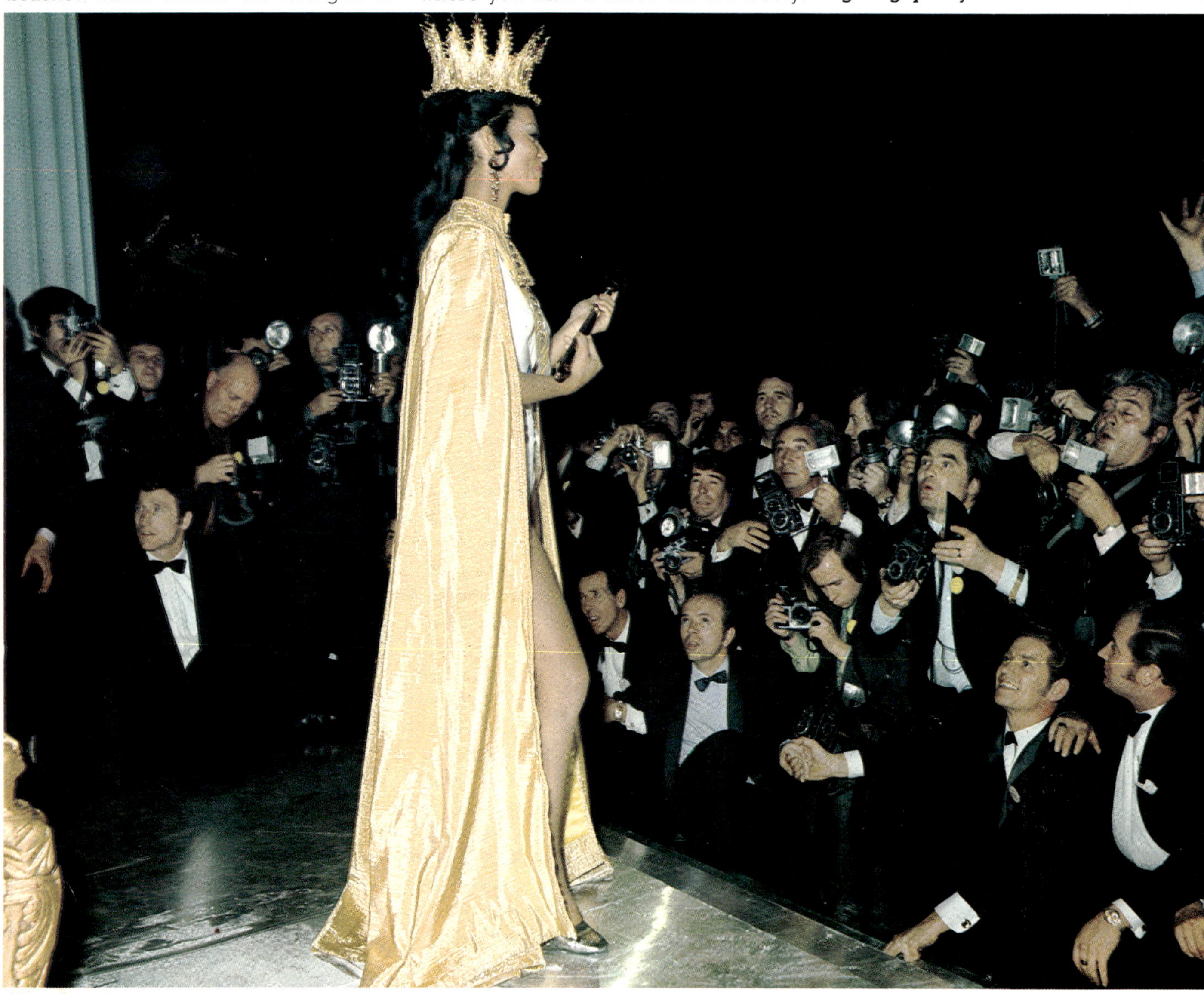

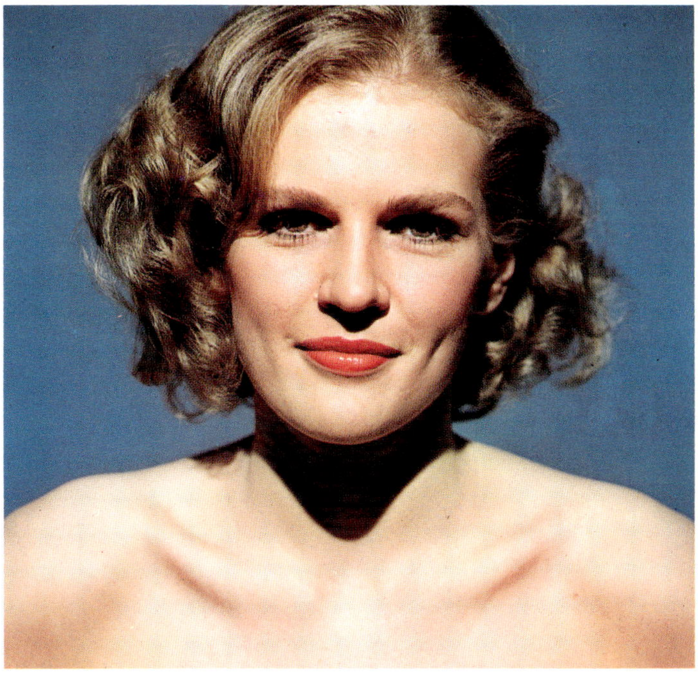

Girl with shadows *Lit from above—eye sockets blacken, the nose casts a triangular blob, and the neck disappears*

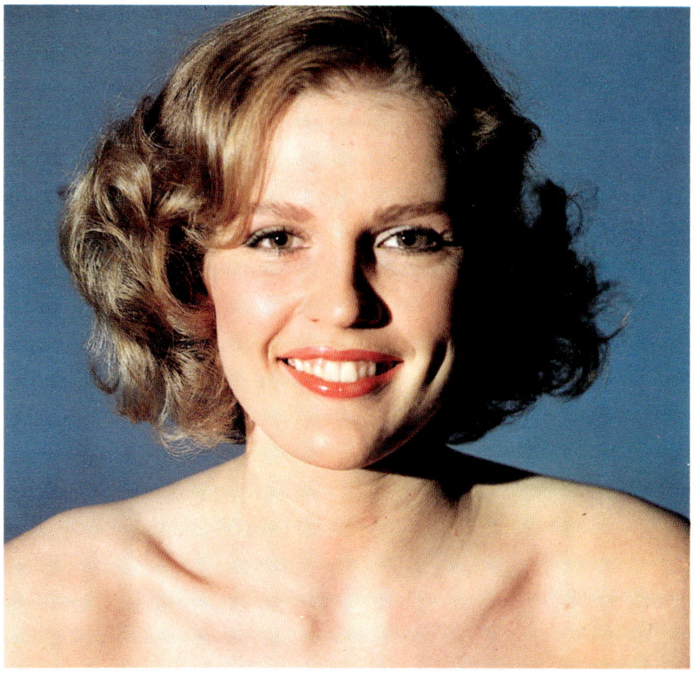

Girl with modelling *Lit from side with hand-held flash, features are defined by soft shadows to one side*

small gun and a lightweight camera, the juggling of the two is not much of a problem once you develop your technique. The most important thing is to keep the camera straight and the gun pointing in the right direction.

As you cannot know the exact effect of holding the gun in any particular position, it is a good idea to experiment a little at first. As a guide, the higher you hold the gun, the more the shadows will resemble those created by sunlight or the ceiling lights in the room. The further to the left or right you hold the gun, the more shadow will be formed on the opposite side of the subject.

The distance from the gun to the subject will also affect the shadows produced. Subject to the length of your arm, the maximum height of the gun will be approximately 2 to 2.5 m. If the subject is only 2 m away the lighting angle can be varied from camera height —with the light parallel to the lens to subject line—to an acute angle, with the light held at arm's length. At a distance of 10 m, the difference in the lighting angle between these two points is considerably less.

This technique is ideal for an informal portrait. The location of shadows on the face is the key to a good picture. If in doubt and you want to be certain of a usable shot, try holding the gun a little above your head and to one side. If you avoid getting so close to your subject that you have an acute lighting angle, you will create some shadows that give form to the face without making them too obvious. With both a flashbar and a hand-held camera, the auto exposure of a flashgun will still operate.

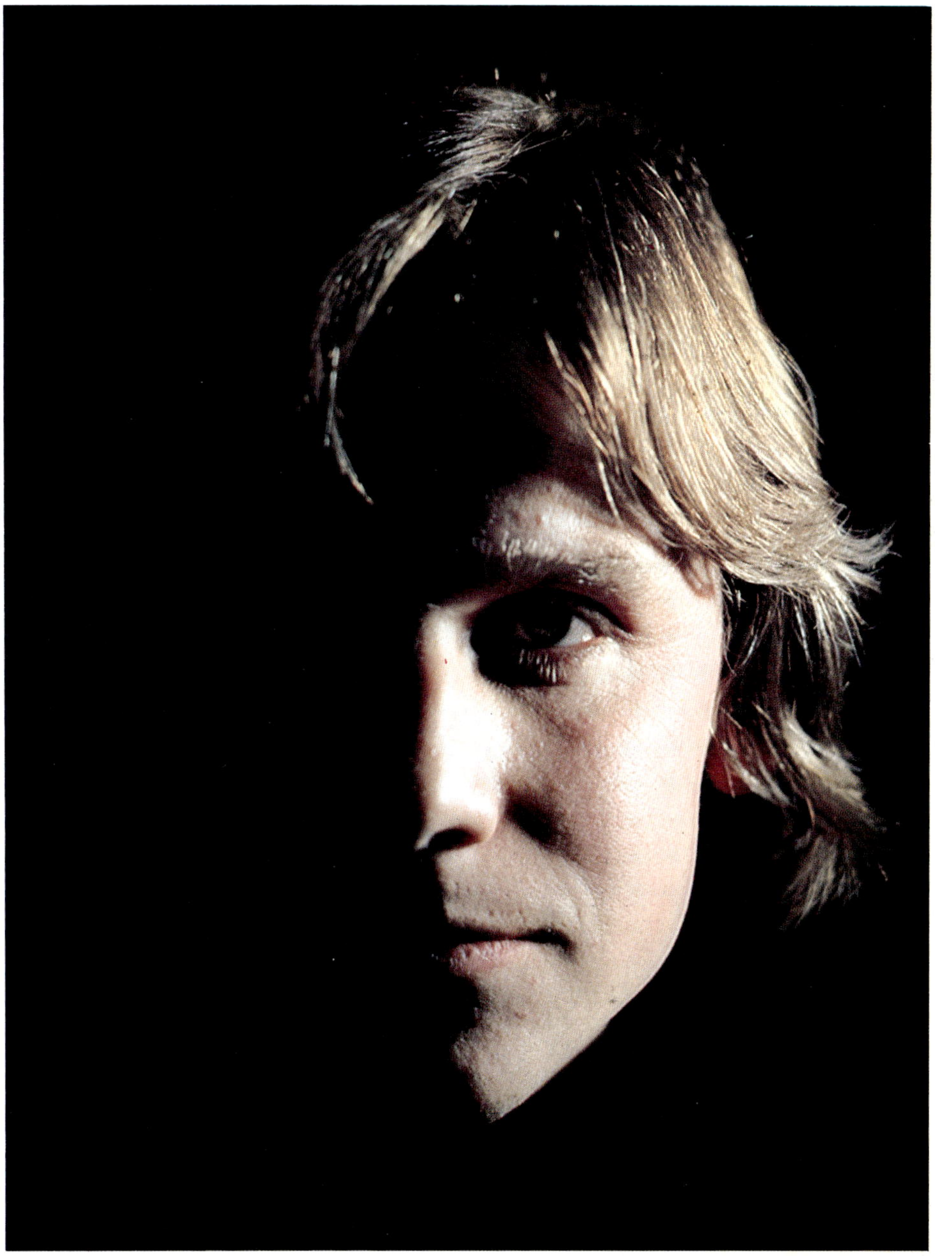

Side lit *With the flash to one side and black velvet draped to 'lose' his neck, the subject is dramatized—a good technique to show character*

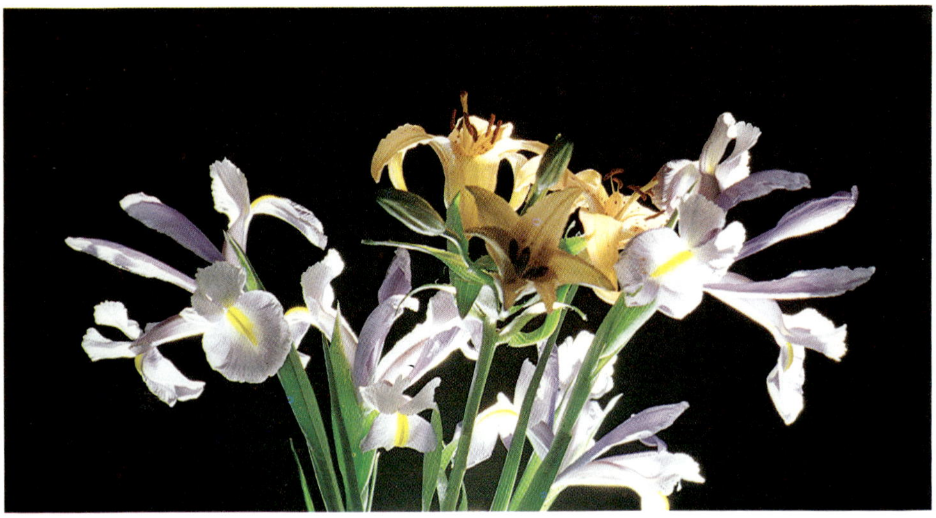

Backlit flowers *With the flash behind and below the flowers, petals become translucent and seem to glow against the black background*

Lighting for shape *Shadows can accentuate a shape lit from the side or back. Forward-falling shadows can be very effective too.*

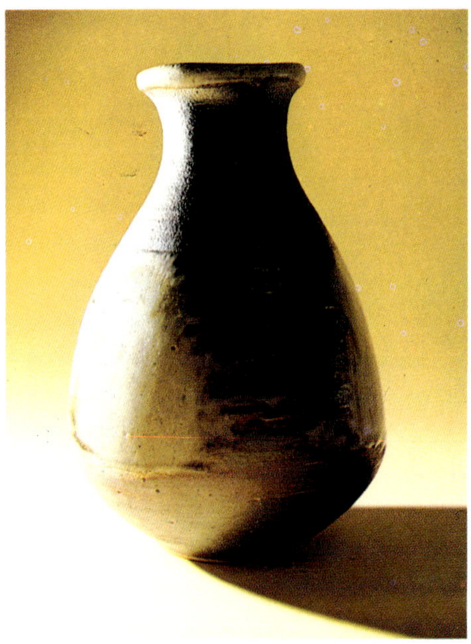

A separate stand

Fixing either the camera or the flash, or both, to a tripod or stand overcomes the handling problems sometimes encountered when trying to hand-hold your equipment. If you have a long synchronization lead, you can get a range of lighting positions impossible with flashbars or hand-held flash. The disadvantage is that stands are static and you often have a long trailing lead that can become a nuisance.

Removing the flashgun from the camera confuses its automatic function. With the flash and camera at different distances from the subject, the automatic sensor is misled. Some manufacturers solve the problem by supplying a removable sensor which can be attached to the camera's accessory base and connected by cable to the flash unit. This way the sensor still measures the reflected light from the camera position regardless of the position of the flash and fires it for the correct time.

Use of stands is best restricted to stationary or formal situations. A stand is ideal if you want to take still life subject such as vases of flowers or other table-top subjects. It is also suitable for formal portraits or shots where a person is limited to a particular spot by what they are doing, such as making some piece of pottery or carrying out some other work.

As well as allowing you to vary the flash angle, a separate stand will also let you move the flash unit closer to the subject, or to one side of it. This gives greater flexibility and offers greater creative opportunities. But at the same time you may give yourself problems of exposure.

If the gun is only slightly closer to the subject, you can still use its auto exposure system. But for more extreme variations, it is best to switch it to manual use, and work out the camera aperture using the table on the unit. In this case, the distance involved is that from the flash to the subject, rather than camera to subject.

Flash guide numbers are computed from the basis of flash on the camera giving front lighting. When the flashgun is removed from the camera, the guide number has to be reduced. For example, under average conditions the guide number for 45° lighting is the guide number for flash on the camera multiplied by 0.7; thus, a guide number of 33 becomes 23.

The alternative to this is to leave the flash on automatic, but to calculate the alteration in camera aperture that will be needed. If you would normally use the camera at *f*/8, but the flashgun is now at halfway between you and the subject, you will need to reduce the aperture by one stop to *f*/11.

You have more choice in the lighting angle with a stand than when the gun is hand-held. You also have the freedom to move round a static subject checking on angles and considering the effects of placing your equipment in different arrangements.

The basic principle for positioning the gun is simple: the further it is from the lens to subject line, the greater the shadow area will be. When taking a portrait, be aware of the shadow cast by the nose. It can form a dark triangular blotch on the face if the gun is placed in the wrong position.

Lighting effects

The amount of shadow should relate to the character and appearance of the subject. In a portrait, smooth, soft skin should be matched by light, inconspicuous shadows, while more rugged

Flashbar *A bracket fastens the flashgun to the camera. This distancing introduces some modelling*

Hand-held flash *For stronger modelling, especially of a close subject, hold the flash at arm's length*

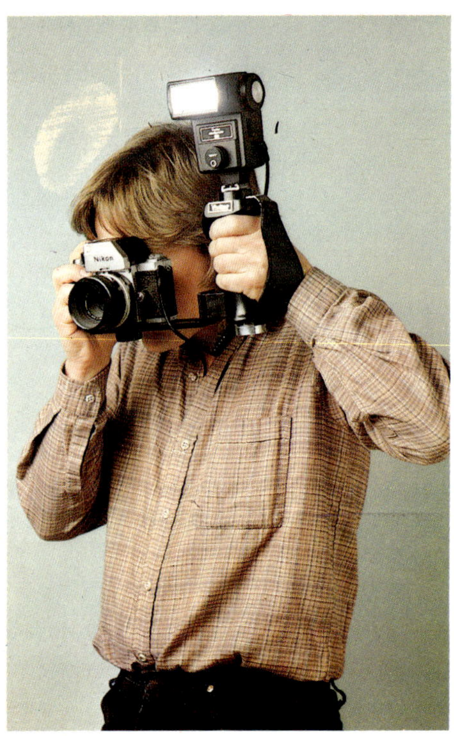

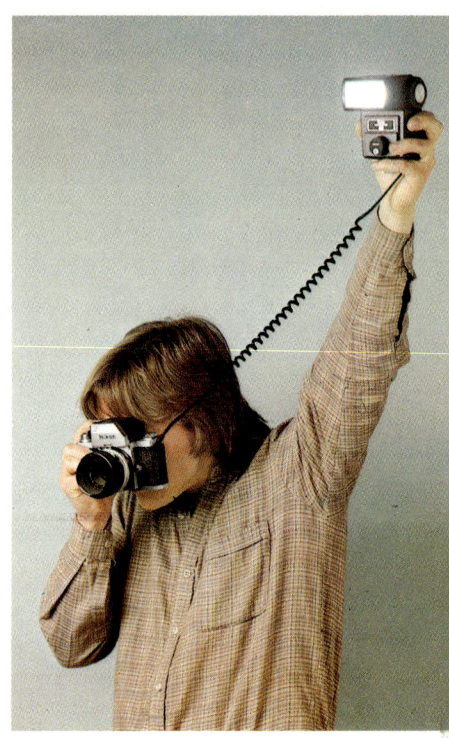

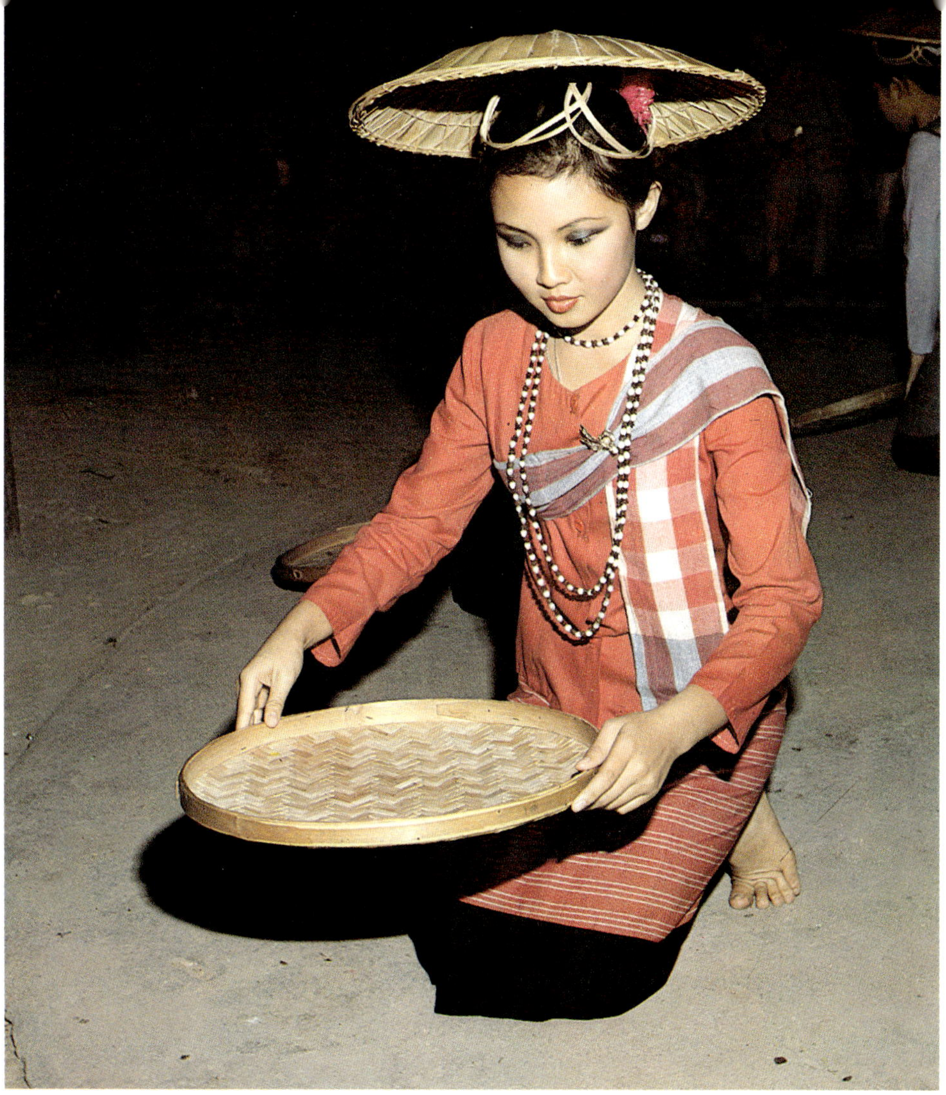

features can be depicted more dramatically. This simple approach can be varied once you have gained experience.

Still life subjects will often allow you great freedom over lighting effects, as long as there are not too many surface projections creating ugly shadows. The first thing to consider is whether you wish to emphasize the colour, shape or texture of the object. If you decide on colour, then you will probably find that placing the gun near the camera will provide the virtually shadowless lighting that gives colour prominence. Emphasizing the shape of the object often means separating it from the background by means of lighting. With a single flash gun this can be achieved either by shading the background by means of a board placed between it and the gun, or by lighting the object from behind. Back lighting is best confined to translucent objects such as glass. The texture of a surface is usually brought out by using side lighting.

All these effects are limited by having only one light to work with. Using flash for more subtle effects is described in the sections on studio flash.

Oriental woman *The flash was placed to one side and slightly above to give a pleasing result*

Soft shadows *A diffuser over the flash unit softens the shadows and gives a more glamorous picture*

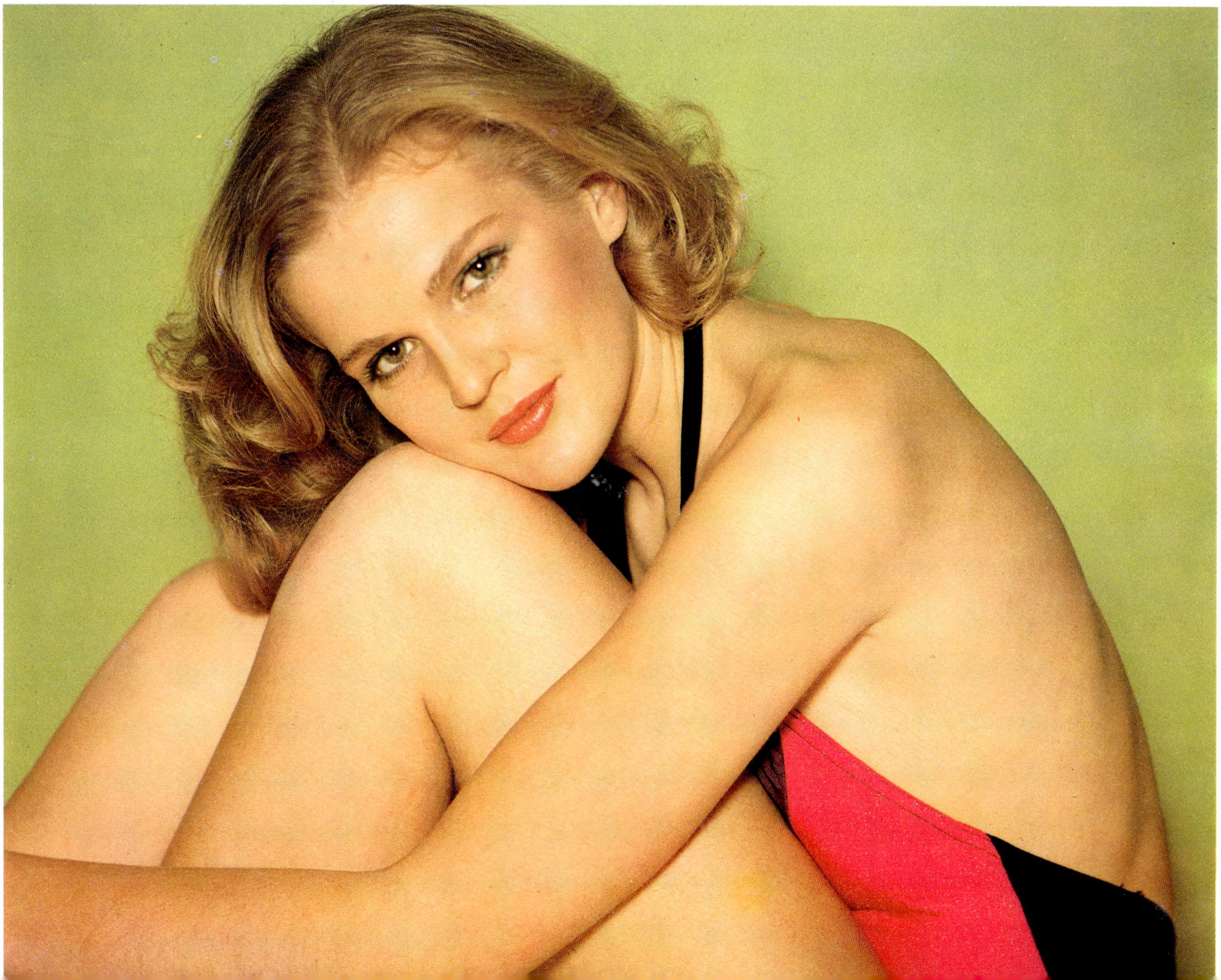

Bounce flash

Pictures taken with small flashguns mounted on the camera and aimed straight at the subject are rarely very pleasing. If the light in your pictures always comes from the same direction and has the same character—flat, but with deep, hard edged shadows and pronounced fall-off over distance—then you need a different approach. Taking the flashgun off the camera's flash shoe is one answer (see page 102), but perhaps the most effective technique is to point the flash unit at some reflecting surface, using the reflected light to illuminate the subject.

This technique, known as *bounce flash* because the light from the flash is bounced off the reflecting surface, produces a light that is softer and more enveloping. This suits many subjects better than simple, direct flash on the camera.

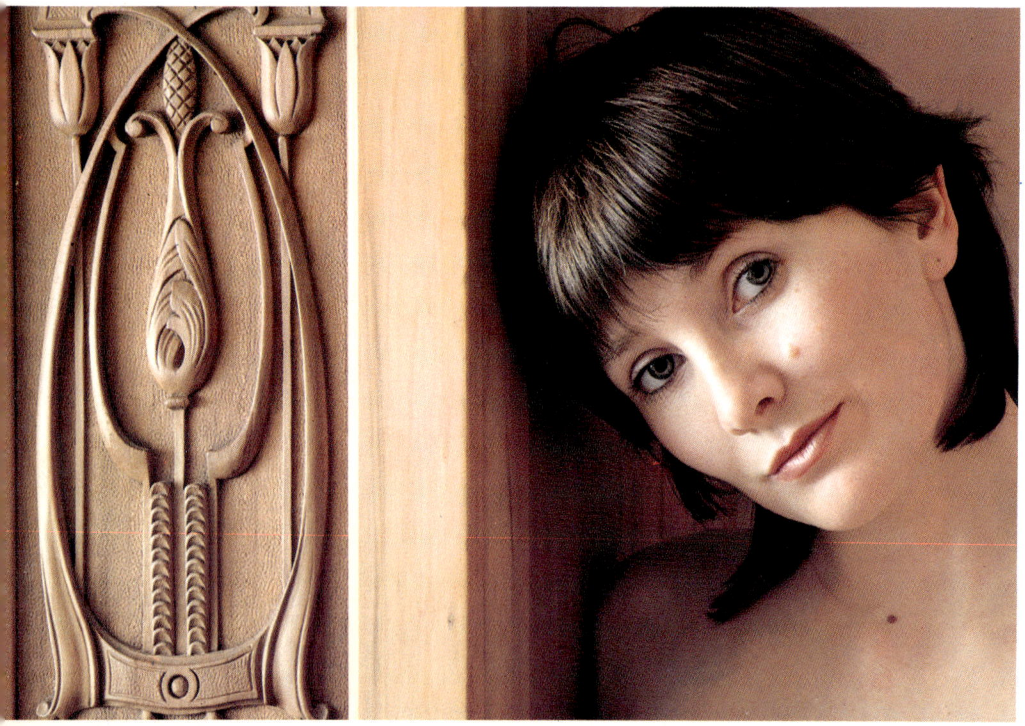

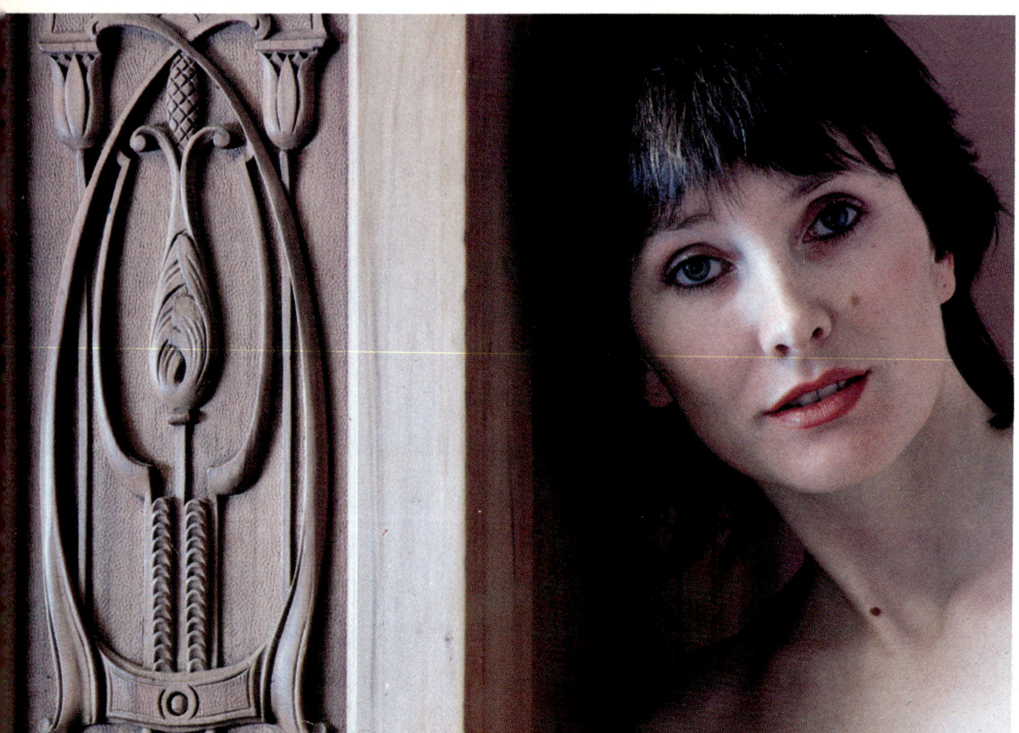

Using walls and ceilings

Bounce flash from a white surface is as close to natural lighting as you can get with a portable flashgun. Obviously, any white surface reflects light, but a ceiling is usually the most convenient reflector. The illumination then comes from above and shadows fall in the same way as by natural light. The light is scattered over a wide area and diffused by the matt texture of most ceilings, giving a soft, even illumination that still clearly comes from a single source.

The main disadvantage of bounce flash is that you are totally dependent on the location. Ceilings vary widely in height and colour. A ceiling that is dark toned or discoloured by tobacco smoke can absorb a great deal of light. With a high ceiling, the light from the gun has to travel further and may be too weak to properly illuminate the subject.

Many small flashguns are not powerful enough for most bounce work, even though they may be fitted with tilting flash heads. Relying exclusively on bounce flash for lighting interiors other than normal domestic rooms can lead to problems with exposure, though the flash can be used as a fill-in to supplement the existing lighting.

Some automatic flashguns have an exposure confirmation light that blinks if enough light has reached the subject for correct exposure. These can be a useful reassurance. If you have an automatic flashgun, this takes care of the exposure under most circumstances.

If your gun only offers a limited range of aperture settings for use on automatic and none of these is suitable for the distance you are working at or the reflectivity of the ceiling, you may need to switch to manual. Calculate the proper lens aperture yourself, and add the distance the light travels from the flashgun to the ceiling to the distance from the ceiling to the subject. Make an extra

Bounce from a wall *The even sidelight given by bouncing your flash off a wall can often resemble natural daylight from a side window*

Coloured bounce *Beware of coloured walls, especially cool blues and greens. The results will have a cast which may not be what you wanted*

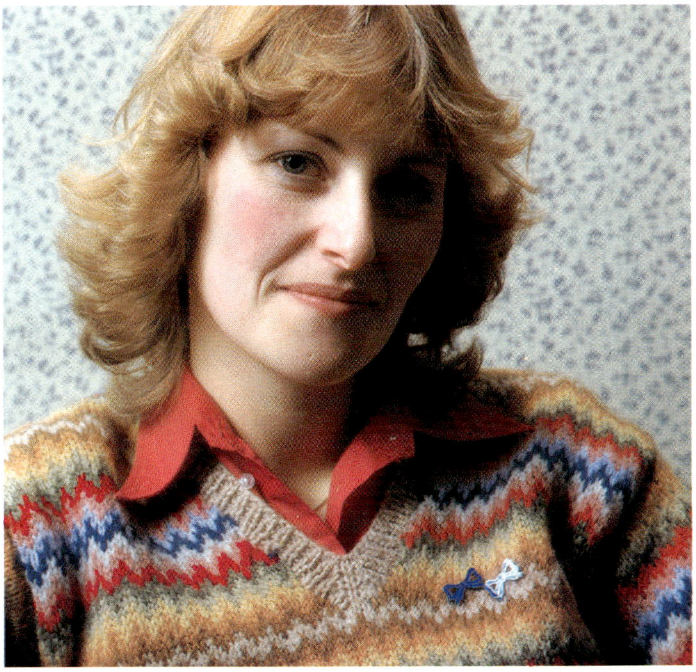

No reflector *Side bounce from a short distance can give deep shadows with insufficient detail*

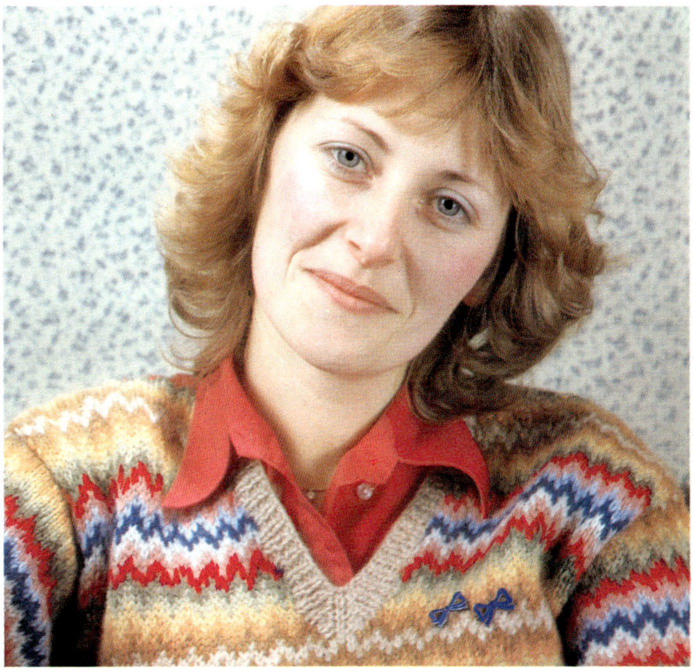

Silver reflector *A sheet of silver foil held on the shadow side of the subject improves the lighting ratio*

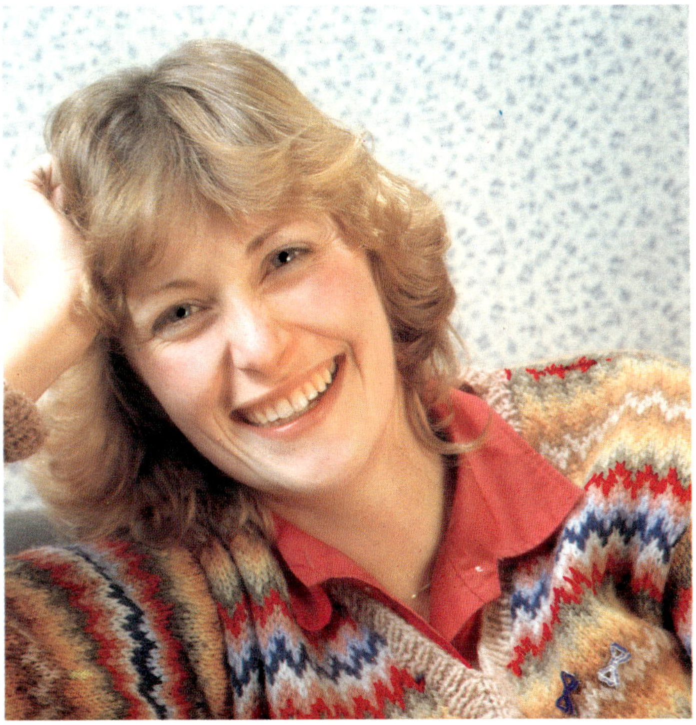

Gold reflector *A more pleasing effect is given to skin tones by using gold-coloured foil rather than silver*

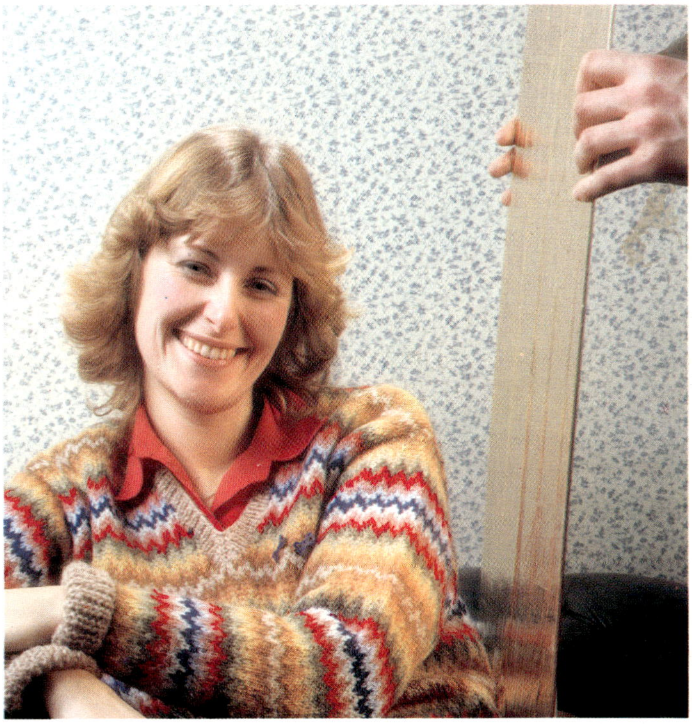

Reflector distance *The amount of shadow fill can be varied by altering the distance from reflector to subject*

allowance for the light absorbtion of the ceiling. A plain white ceiling normally requires at least an extra stop exposure, but this may vary considerably from room to room.

You can make reliable estimates of the necessary correction with experience. Until you have gained this experience, bracket your exposures: make extra shots at one stop more and one stop less than your calculated aperture setting. When working out the correct exposure for manual bounce flash, it is safer to assume that the ceiling is slightly higher and slightly less reflective than it looks.

Bounce flash can create pictorial problems too. If the angle of bounce is too acute, your subject may suffer from heavy vertical shadows. Strong shadows under the eyes and chin can spoil a portrait and are as unsightly as direct flash on camera. Shadows like this are inevitable if you attempt to bounce the flash virtually straight up and down. One answer to the problem is to use a more powerful flashgun and stand further back from your subject, but a better solution may be to bounce the light off a wall rather than a ceiling. In this case, light strikes your subject from the side, giving a similar form of illumination to that from a large window. If you are using colour film, beware of coloured walls. Any light reflected from a coloured wall gives a cast to the subject you are photographing. This is not much of a problem if the wall is pale pink or buff, but green or blue walls can give unpleasant skin tones.

Reflectors

The next logical step after bouncing light off a wall is to use a reflector to direct light into shadow areas. A white sheet pinned or taped to a wall makes a simple and reliable reflector. Sometimes you may want a brighter reflection than a white surface can give. In this

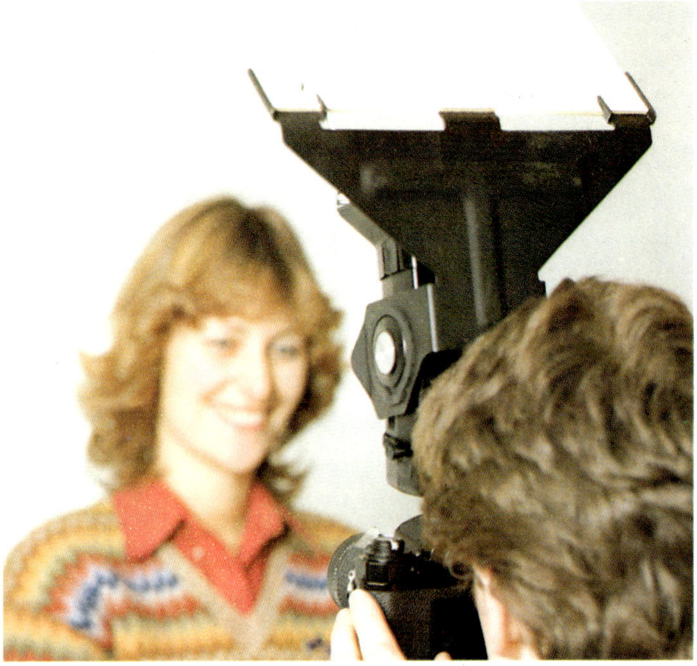

Bounce boards *These attachments can provide soft frontal light at close distances, and are easily portable*

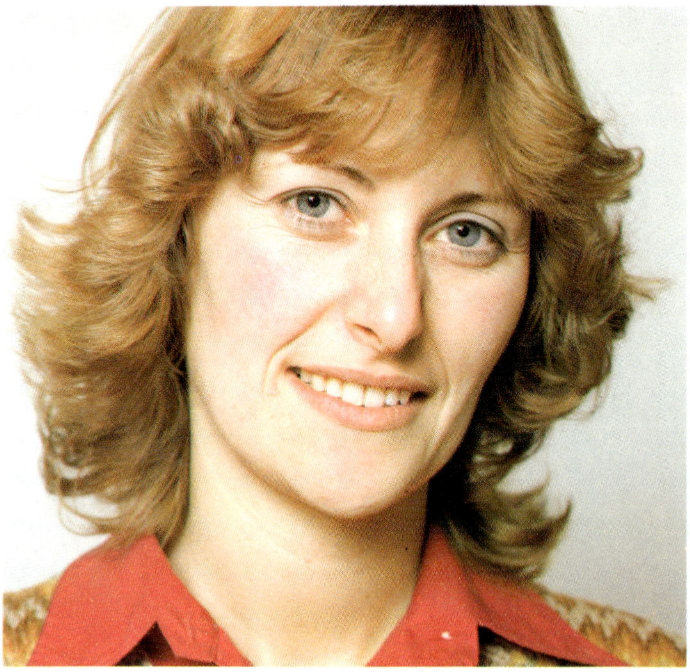

Soft lighting *The effect given by bounce board flash attachments is particularly suitable for close portraits*

case, you need a silvered surface. There are sophisticated reflector sheets, coated silver on one side and white on the other, that fold up small enough to fit into a camera bag. An inexpensive alternative is to stick aluminium foil on to a sheet of expanded polystyrene of the sort sold by builders for home insulation.

Unfortunately, there are few occasions when the subject can easily be placed by a wall, and a wall mounted reflector is not very versatile. At home you can make a mobile reflector by draping a sheet, or a large piece of paper, over a clothes-horse or any suitable piece of furniture. When setting it up, angle it so that light is reflected into the areas that you wish to illuminate. This can be difficult if the flashgun is mounted on the camera, but with an extension cord you can move the flashgun around until you achieve the best illumination.

Outside the home, providing reflectors can be a problem. There are rarely any suitable walls, and it can be awkward carrying your own reflector everywhere. Even if you do persevere and carry a reflector to the location, it can be difficult setting it up. The best solution is to ask a friend to hold your reflector, but if this is not practical you can often get by with sticky tape and spring clips. Bear in mind that reflectors have to be large and conspicuous if they are to be effective. They need to be used quite close to the subject, so it is not really possible to take unposed candid photographs with reflectors.

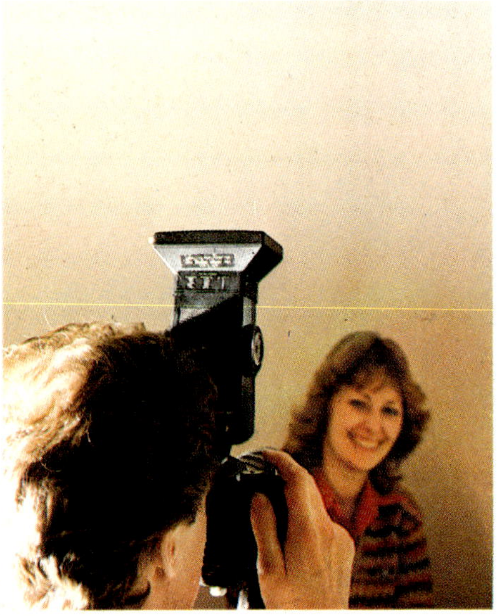

Poor aim *If your bounce angle is too steep, the result can be uneven illumination of the subject*

Manual bounce

When using bounce flash with a manual flashgun in a room or studio, you need to increase exposure to allow for the light absorbed by the ceiling or wall and the distance from flash to ceiling to subject. The table below gives the increase in exposure necessary for a range of subject distances in a typical domestic room. If the ceiling is much higher than 2.5 m, exposure must be increased accordingly.

Distance from flash to subject	Extra f/stops
1 m	3 stops
1.5	2
2	$1\frac{2}{3}$
2.5	$1\frac{1}{2}$
3	$1\frac{1}{2}$
3.5	$1\frac{1}{3}$
4	$1\frac{1}{3}$
4.5	$1\frac{1}{3}$
5 and over	1

Bounce boards

Some manufacturers have sought to overcome some of the problems of using bounce flash by making brackets that clip on to their flashguns. These brackets hold a piece of white board that is angled towards the subject to provide a directional form of bounce lighting.

When used properly, these devices can be very effective. The distance from the flash to the bounce surface is constant, and so is the reflectivity of the board. This simplifies exposure calculations considerably if you decide to set your flash manually.

Problems arise when you try to use these reflectors at too great a distance from your subject. Light from the flashgun illuminates the reflector board so that the subject is in effect lit by the large board rather than by a small flash tube.

If you stand close to your subject so that the width of the board relative to the distance from the subject is large, then the light will fall on the subject evenly from many different angles. The effect will be to give a soft frontal lighting if the flash and reflector board are mounted on the camera. But if you move too far back, so that the ratio of board size to distance is smaller, then the effect will gradually become almost indistinguishable from ordinary direct flash.

Bounce boards also tend to be bulky and may not mount very securely on your camera. These drawbacks reduce the usefulness of bounce board attachments for photography outside the home or other more controlled situations. They are most useful for highly mobile subjects such as young children and pets, when you wish to avoid the contrast and hard shadows of direct flash. Their effect is also particularly useful for head-and-shoulder portraits.

Twin tube flashguns

Another attempt by flashgun manufacturers to solve the problems created by direct flash on camera is the twin tube design. Bounce flash from a ceiling usually requires a powerful flashgun so that you can stand sufficiently far from your subject to reduce unpleasantly hard vertical shadows. Twin tube flashguns use a small second flash tube pointing directly at the subject to fill in these shadows and allow you to work close to your subject while still keeping some of the advantages of bounce light. Since you do not need to be so far away, the flashgun itself can be smaller, cheaper, and easier to carry.

A certain amount of thought is needed to use these units effectively. Because they produce results under a wide variety of conditions, it is easy to forget that the main light is supposed to be provided by the bounce tube pointed at the ceiling. If the ceiling is too dark or too far away, the subject will be lit entirely by the direct light of the secondary flash tube and you will be back where you started—using direct flash on camera. In such cases, it is best to accept the inevitable and point the main flash tube at the subject to use the full power of the gun.

Twin tube flashguns provide more attractive lighting than ordinary direct flash units, but the effect they give can become just as routine as direct flash if used too often. Try to vary the way you use these units as much as you can. Remember also that the proportion of bounce to direct flash on which the manufacturer has preset the unit may not suit your pictures. If this is the case, you can make adjustments by taping pieces of opaque card or paper over the flash tubes until the effect is just right to suit your style.

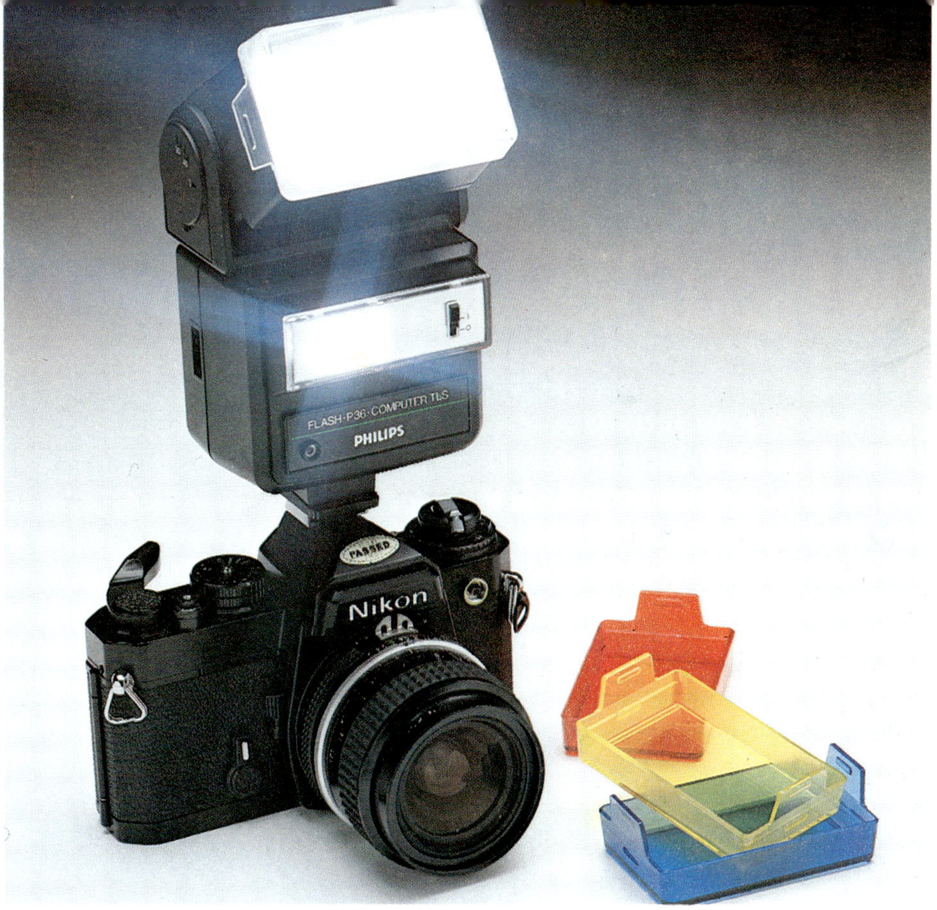

Twin tube flash *A compact compromise between direct and bounce flash, above. The results, below, show agreeably soft, indirect light combined with the greater liveliness of direct flash on the camera. The direct flash helps to fill in the shadows*

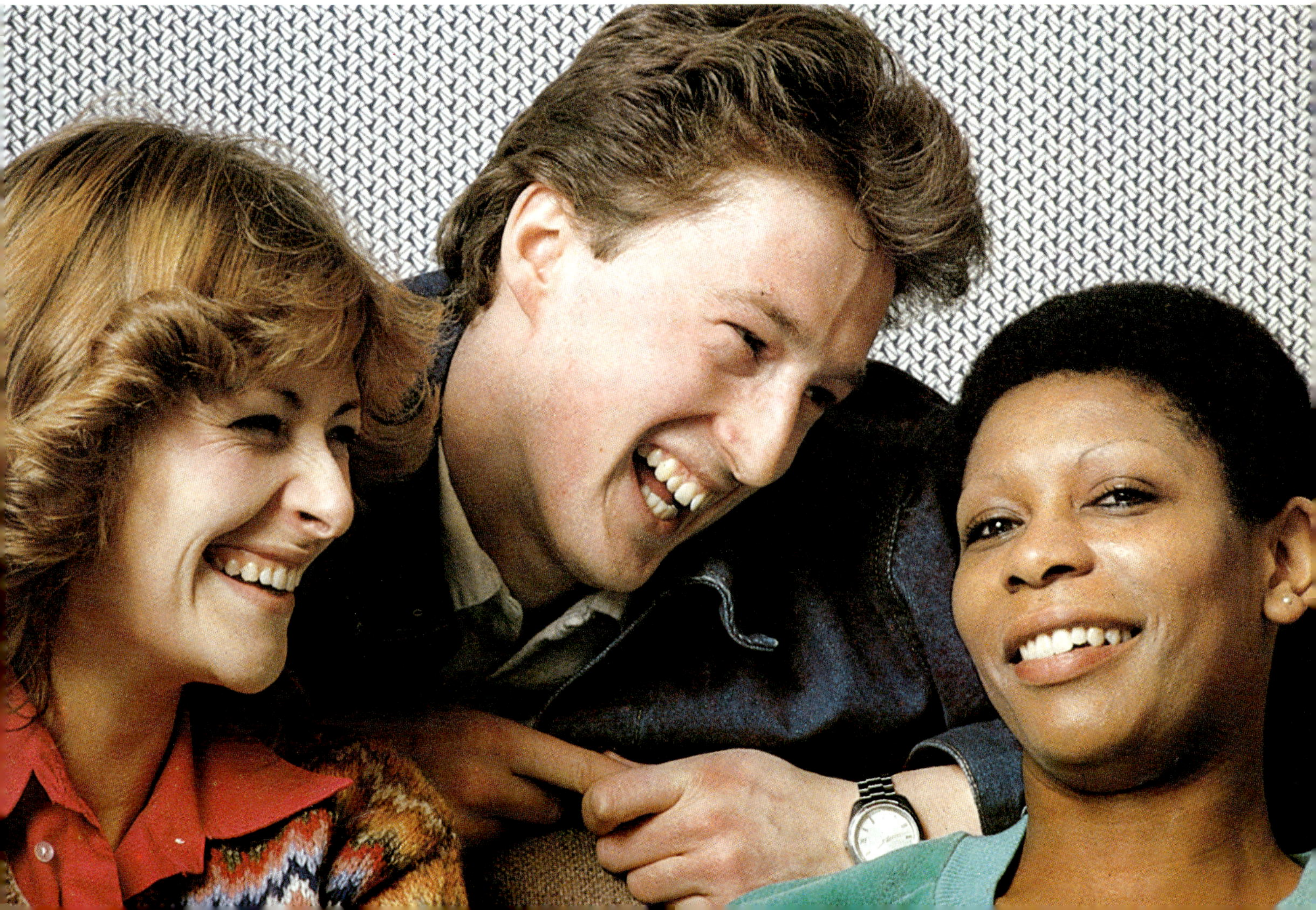

Natural flash

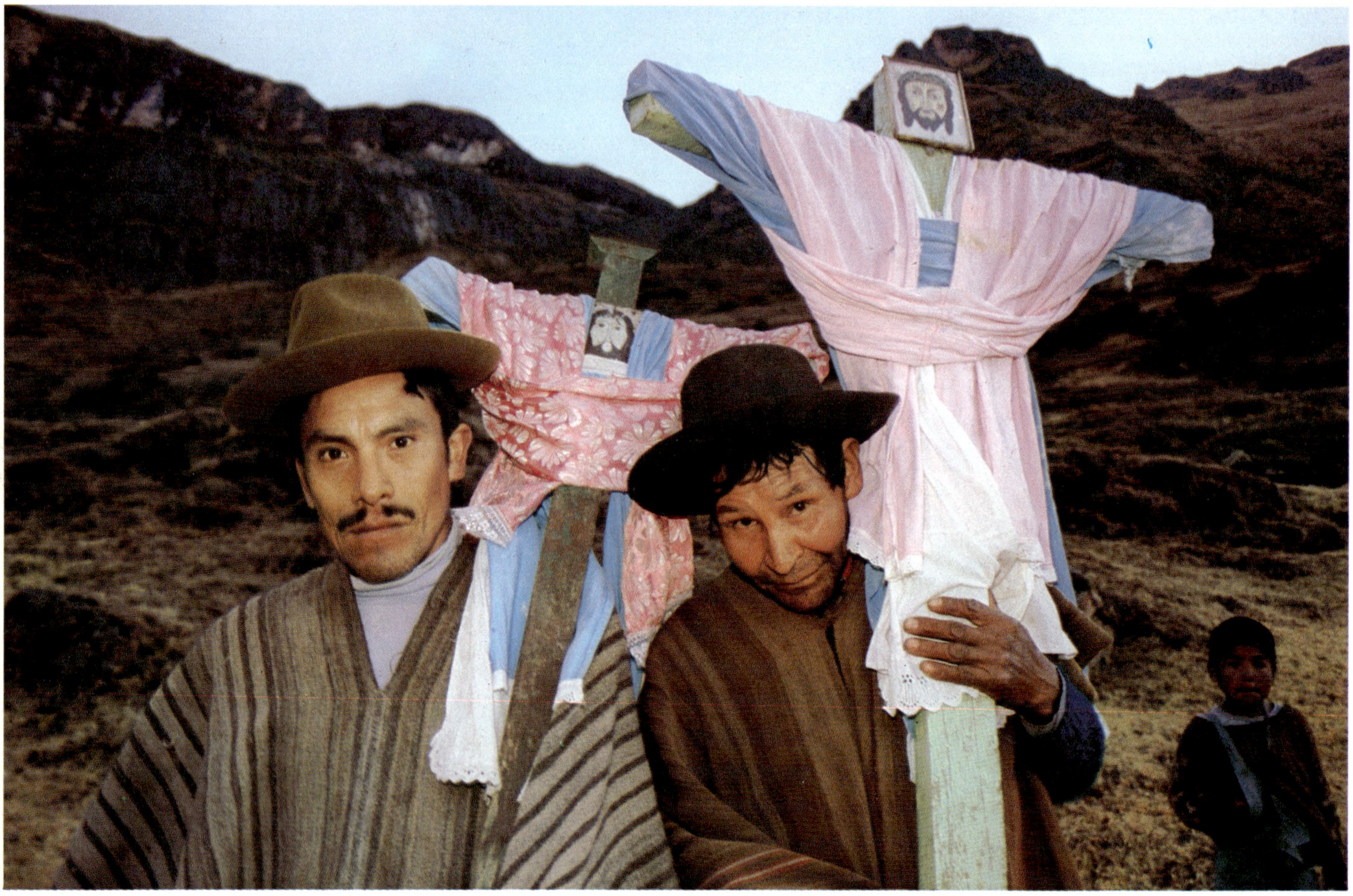

Flash is undoubtedly a valuable weapon in the photographer's armoury and in many circumstances it is the only way of achieving a picture. But many photographers will not use it because they feel it destroys the atmosphere of the available light, particularly natural daylight. However, used in the right way, flash can not only be used without upsetting the quality of the available light, it can positively enhance it, by controlling contrast, adding detail and improving colour and sharpness.

If you wish to retain the feeling of natural light but wish to use flash to fill in shadows in indoor shots, it is important that the use of flash should not be obvious in the picture. There are a number of ways of achieving this, but it is undoubtedly simplest to keep the flash light weaker than the available light.

Weak flash

With an automatic flashgun the flash can be weakened quite simply by altering the settings. First set the aperture on the camera to give the correct exposure for

Sharp crosses *Adding flash to the picture not only lightens the shadows, so giving a more reasonable contrast range, but also helps to make the image look sharper. This is because the flash 'freezes' any movement*

the light available. Then set an aperture one stop larger on the flashgun dial. If the exposure for the available light is 1/30 second at *f*/4, then you could set the flashgun at *f*/2.8. This means that the flash will be too short to give a full exposure but is sufficient to lighten shadows.

Use a warm coloured filter such as an 81A to reduce the blue highlights produced by direct flash, and try to avoid the tell-tale shadows running back from the subject, either by having no close background, or else one which is so close that the shadows are too small to be noticed. You can either come in very close, so that the light source is effectively larger, or keep back a little, so that all the clues are smaller and so less noticeable.

When you wish to achieve a really subtle effect, you can increase the

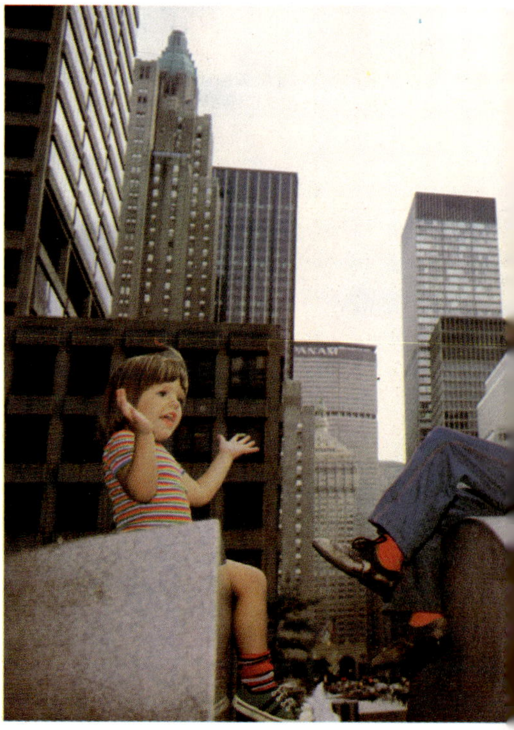

aperture setting on the flashgun by two or even three stops. Used like this, the flash will be almost imperceptible but it helps to introduce a little colour, shape and texture into shadow areas and lift the picture generally.

Subtle fill-in flash may also help to make your pictures look sharp because the flash is so brief. The flash exposure does not, therefore, suffer from even a trace of camera shake and this ultra sharp flash image helps to give the whole picture an extra crisp look, especially in hand-held shots.

Another application of weak fill-in flash is to reduce colour balance problems when using daylight film in fluorescent or tungsten lighting. Aim the flash at the important features of the subject so that even if the rest of the picture suffers from a slight colour cast, it may not be noticeable because the focal point is rendered in the true colours. With the flashgun set one stop larger than the camera, the use of flash may be undetectable.

If, for any photographs you wish the flash and available light to be equally balanced, beware of simply setting the flash for the same aperture setting as the available light exposure. This merely results in an overexposed picture. Where the flash duration is brief, it has little effect on the overall exposure. But once the flash exposure is one to one with the available light, it increases the amount of light in the picture considerably. The solution to this problem is simply to reduce the aperture on the camera by one stop.

Using the flash on a one to one basis will of course change the overall effect of the lighting quite considerably, but the existing light may well hold its own remarkably well. One reason for this is that backlighting is more obtrusive than front lighting, but the light from the flash, even when bounced, is usually more frontal than the existing light. Indeed it is the lack of backlighting that often makes flash (on its own) such a limited form of lighting. If you mix flash with available light you can often make use of a window, a table lamp or any other bright source to provide some backlighting. Backlighting not only separates each part of the subject from the background, but puts highlights on to every flat surface, bringing out shape and texture and subtly increasing the tonal range.

Quality control

While the simplest way of keeping pictures taken with flash natural is to use a weak flash you can also control its *quality* so that it looks like available light. To do this, you have to imagine the natural lighting for your subject, and then use the flash to reproduce it. You need to estimate not only the size and power of the light source correctly, but also its distance and angle.

The size is important because the type of shadows, the size of the highlights and the graduation of tone between the two are controlled by the size of the light-source. If you want to make light which, for instance, looks as if it comes from a window, then you need a light source the size of a window. This can usually be done quite simply by bouncing flash from a white wall. The patch of flash on the wall will tend to be the same size as a window. If there is no white wall in the right place, you can bounce the flash off a reflector. This can be either a proper studio reflector, a large white umbrella, or even a white bedsheet, a sheet of white paper or polystyrene, or just a couple of pages of newspaper taped together.

Remember that for bounced flash the autocell on the flashgun has to be pointing at the subject. With some flashguns this is awkward, especially when they are mounted on the camera. An ex-

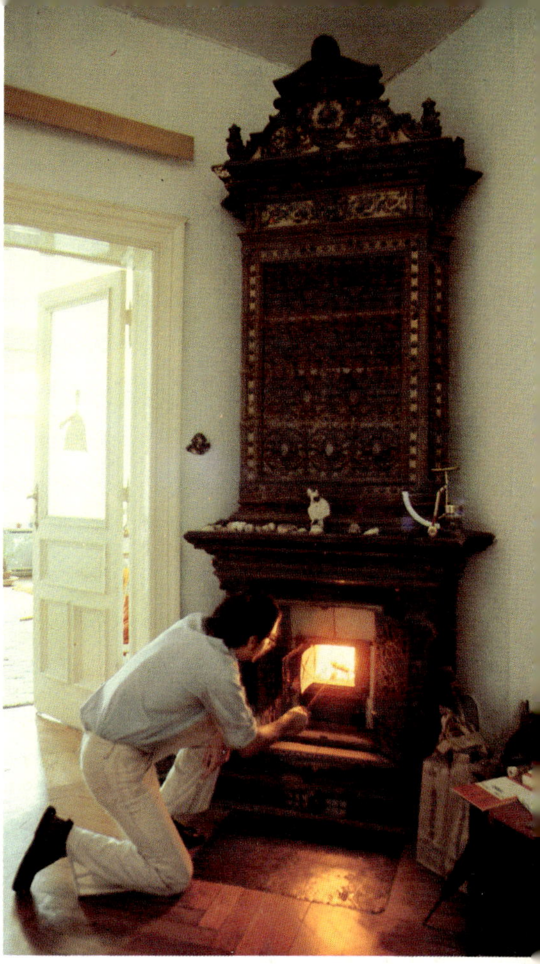

Backlighting *In the shot above, the flash has played an important part in showing detail in the room. But the available light is still crucial—the light from the fire picks up detail in the face, and the light from the doorway helps to outline the figure and pick up texture in the floor. For the pictures below, it was important to keep the detail in the background, by careful choice of exposure time, to provide a setting for the children, who were in shadow (right) and so were lit almost entirely by flash in the final shot. There is very little mixing of flash and available light as each lights a different area of the subject*

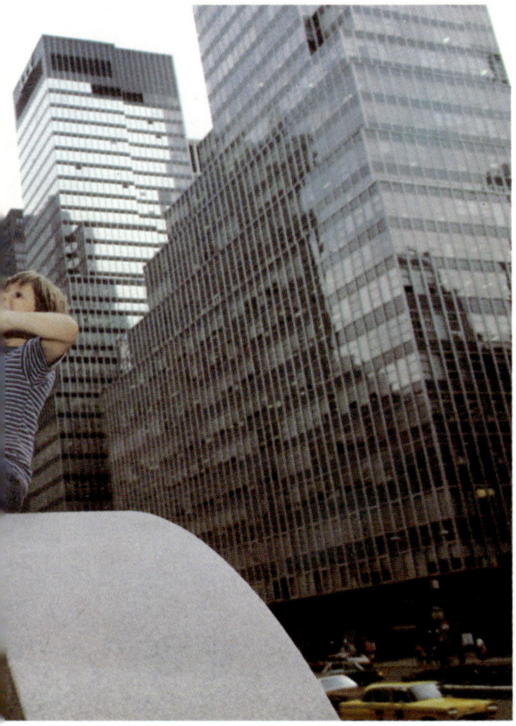

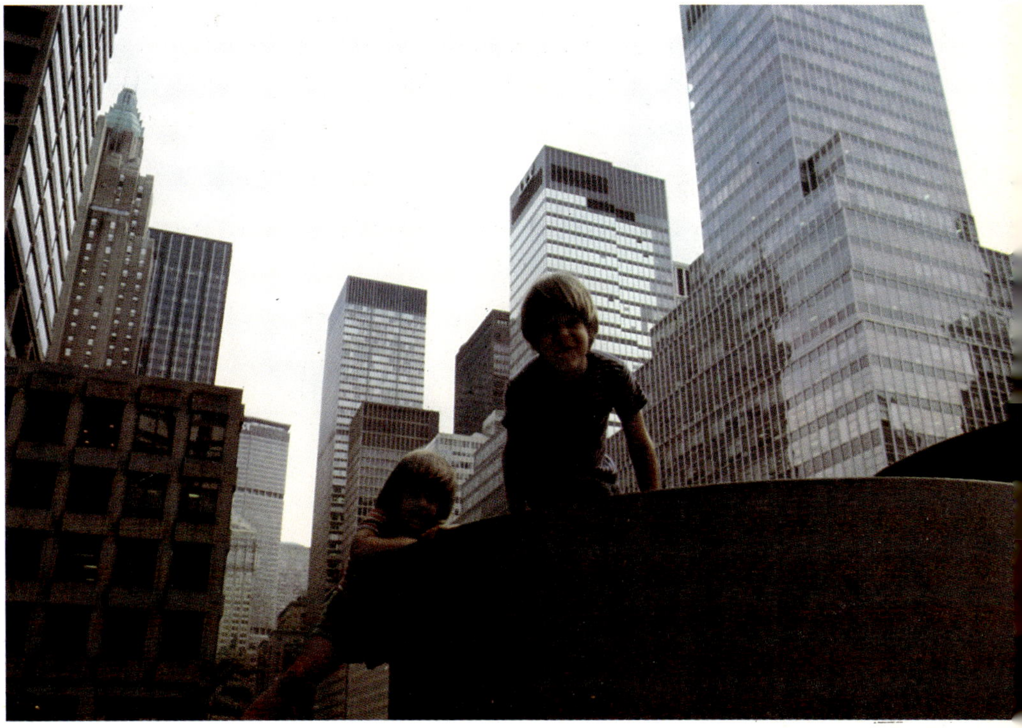

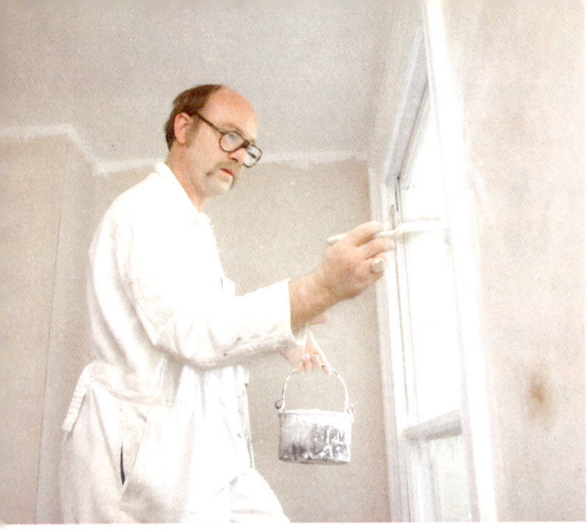

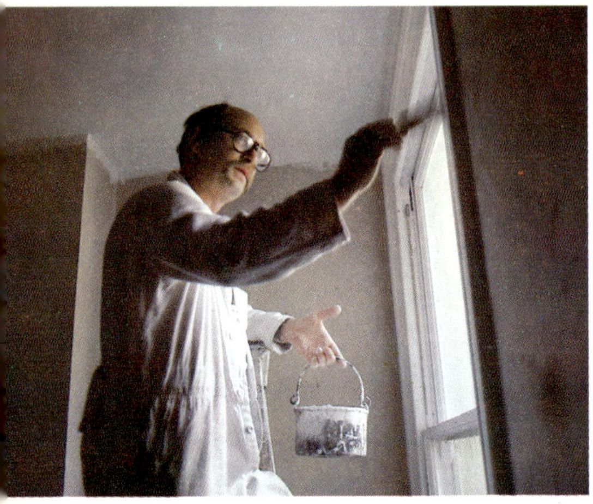

Flash proportions *It is very easy for the flash to dominate the picture, as can be seen from the pictures above. In the top shot most of the light is from the flash, although the daylight from the window (shown in the lower shot without flash) helps to illuminate the face and overalls. In the three shots below progressively greater amounts of flash were used, in ratios of 1:4, 1:2 and 1:1 to the available light. It can be seen how the flash has gradually become more noticeable until it finally destroys the natural quality of the light. The frontal lighting of the flash is artificial and so looks wrong when allowed to dominate*

cellent solution is to have the autocell mounted on the hot-shoe and the rest of the flashgun on the end of a lead, so that it can be held as you wish. Some flash units have autocells which can be unplugged and used in this way, others offer the autocells, or 'remote sensors' as they are also called, separately.

In the same way, when you bounce flash from the ceiling you are, in effect, mimicking strip lighting because the overall effect of many fluorescent tubes is to turn the whole ceiling into one large light source—bounce-flash from the ceiling does exactly the same.

If you use direct flash it looks artificial unless you can position it to imitate some naturally occurring light source. If you want to imitate direct sunlight with a flashgun, take it off the camera and position it above and to the side of the subject, pointing down at the same angle as the sun might be expected to—say around 30°.

Because the sun is very distant, the flash must also be as far away as possible. You can even use a mirror to extend the effective distance if necessary. Obviously this means using a fairly powerful flashgun or else a fast film and a wide aperture, though if the subject is static and you can darken the room, you can fire the flash several times.

If the subject is small it is easier to fool the eye that the light source is infinitely far away. Distant light sources cast virtually parallel shadows. Shadows from nearby lights tend to narrow rapidly. So a nearby source is immediately obvious from the shape of the shadows—particularly with large subjects. As a rule of thumb, if the light source is further than about ten times the width of the area being photographed, the light looks reasonably natural. A light orange filter helps add to the impression especially if the 'sun' is at a low angle. Try a blue reflector in the shadows for a hint of blue sky, but be careful not to overdo it!

Another common light source you can imitate is a table or reading light. In this case the position must be *close,* just as the lamp would be. You may need to place a neutral density filter over the flash head when you are using the auto function, if the flash is less than about a metre from the subject. You can use the flash direct in imitation of a naked bulb, or bounce/diffuse it to look like a shaded lamp. For this purpose a small umbrella is ideal. If you have a remote sensor the flash head can be attached to the handle of the umbrella so that it points into it, and you can position the whole thing close to your subject, right up to the edge of the picture, so that it imitates the quality of a table or standard lamp. With some white umbrellas you can either shine the flash through the fabric of the umbrella which then acts as a diffuser, or else use it to bounce the flash as a reflector. The remote sensor overcomes the problems of working out how much light is transmitted or reflected. Alternatively, you can use a flashmeter.

You can also bounce flash off the television screen to look like the light from a television or bounce it off a sheet of yellow paper placed low down to look like the light from a fire—the possibilities are endless.

As long as you can think of a particular light source which could be in the position you need, you just have to set the flash to that angle, distance and size of source (by bouncing or diffusing) and it will look perfectly natural.

In many situations, there may not be an obvious surface for bouncing the flash from. But it is surprising how many things can be used as reflectors. Virtually any nearby surface can be used. Though strongly coloured objects may give unpleasant casts in colour shots, almost anything can be used in black and white.

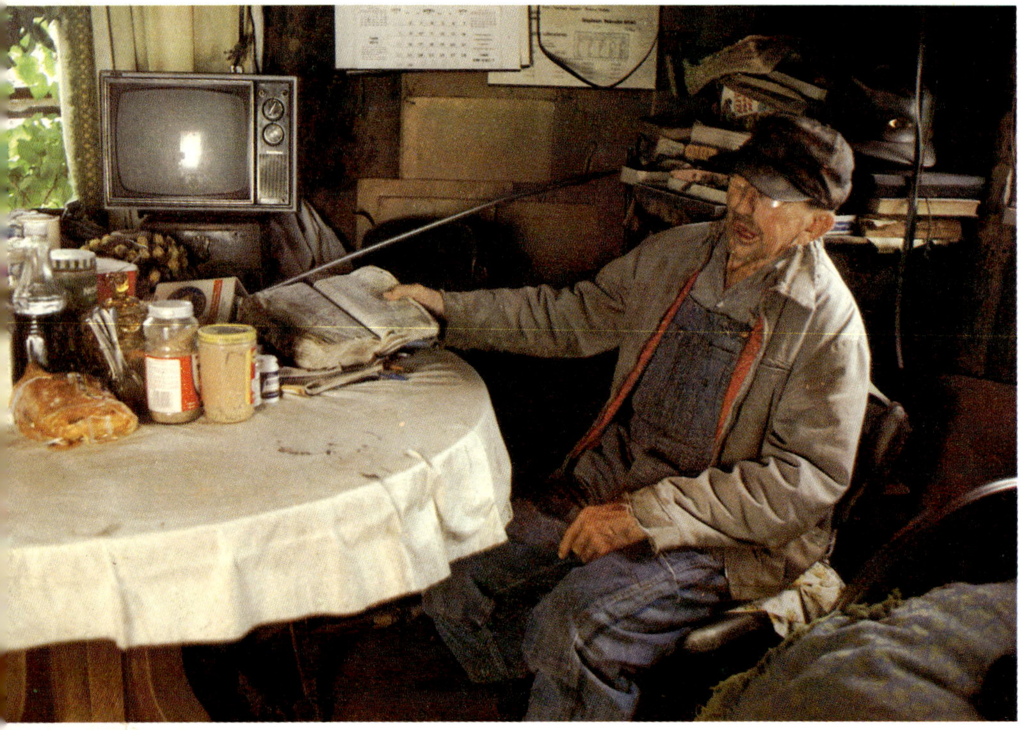

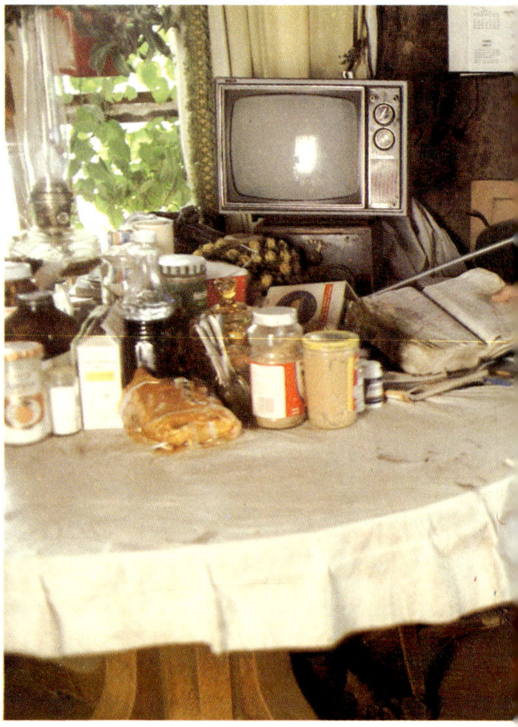

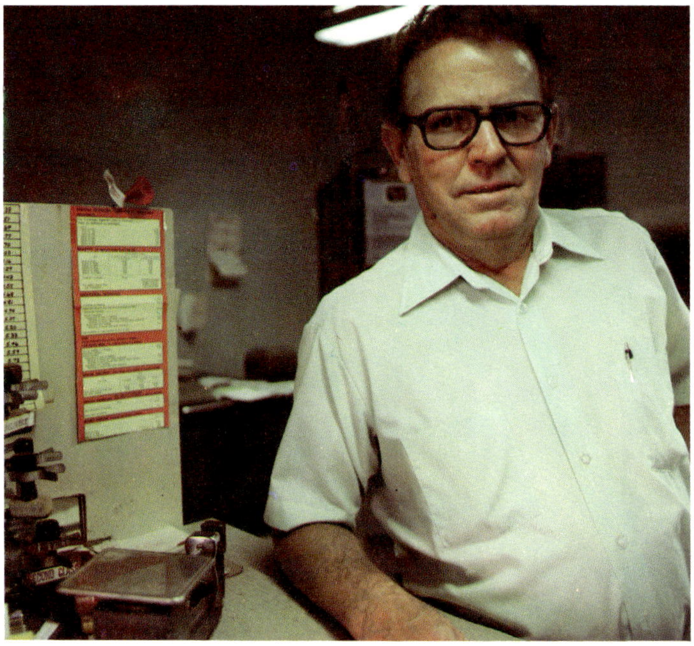

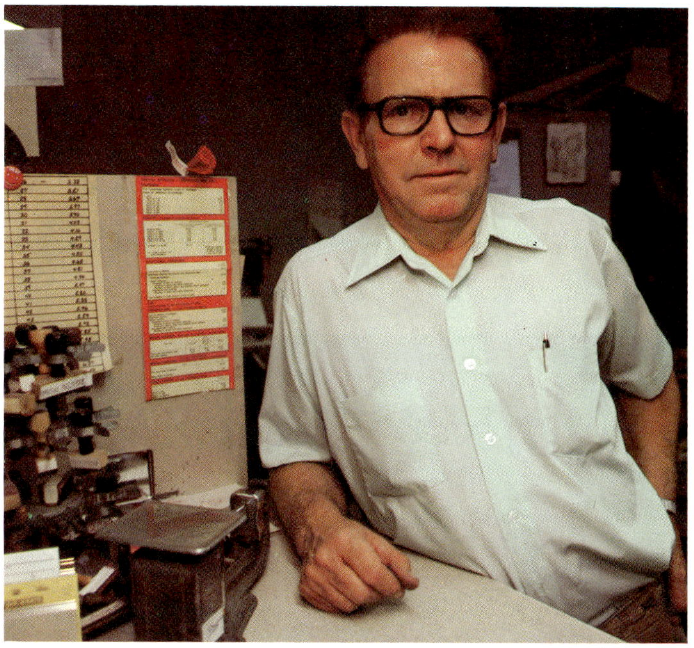

Colour change *Even quite small amounts of flash can be used to clean up colour. Here a small unit was used (right) to remove the unattractive green cast caused by fluorescent lights (left) without changing the atmosphere of the light*

Daylight and flash

When you wish to mix daylight with flash, perhaps to light a portrait against a window, there are different methods of doing it. To obtain a natural result, you could either bounce the flash to one side, to look like the light coming from another window, or bounce from the floor, perhaps from a white sheet if the floor is dark-toned: or from a large reflector behind the camera, to provide the large-source front lighting which might come from a white room. Since the flash is to provide the main light on the subject's face, it is easier to set this first. This is done in the normal way, setting the camera to the same *f*/stop as the flashgun's calculator dial—unless of course, you want it a little darker or lighter than normal.

The daylight is 'controlled' by the shutter speed, and you can make it weaker or stronger just by turning the shutter speed dial. As a starting point take a reading on the general scene outside. This will probably indicate quite a fast shutter speed. If you were to shoot at this setting the light would appear to be the same inside and out and this gives a dull look to the shot.

To brighten the picture, slow down the shutter speed by one or two settings. This will not affect the flash in any way; only the daylight changes. At some point, depending on the exact configuration of the window, and your composition, you will notice that the needle indicates 'correct exposure'. At this point it might be a good idea to check that the subject's face, not lit by the daylight, is still registering 'underexposed' on the camera's meter. Move in close and check: *some* light from the window is sure to reach it. As long as it is still reading 'underexposed', you can go on increasing the shutter speed for a few more stops.

There is no 'correct' setting for the shutter speed in this situation, it just depends what sort of picture you want. In any case the tolerance is enormous. A stop of two either way is not going to do much damage. You may find that the shutter speed is too short to synchronize (see page 98) in which case you could either select a smaller aperture and work from that, or accept a brighter scene outdoors by lengthening the shutter speed. If the shutter speed is too *long*, either use a tripod, accept a darker outdoor exposure, or, if the flash provides for it, set a wider aperture.

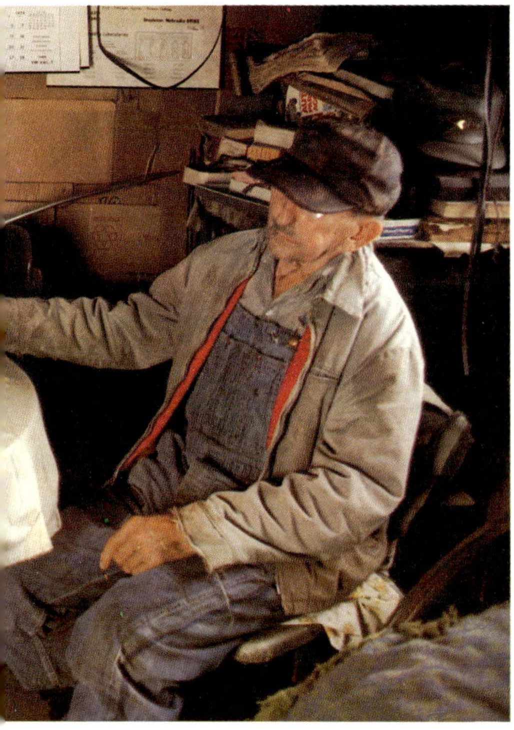

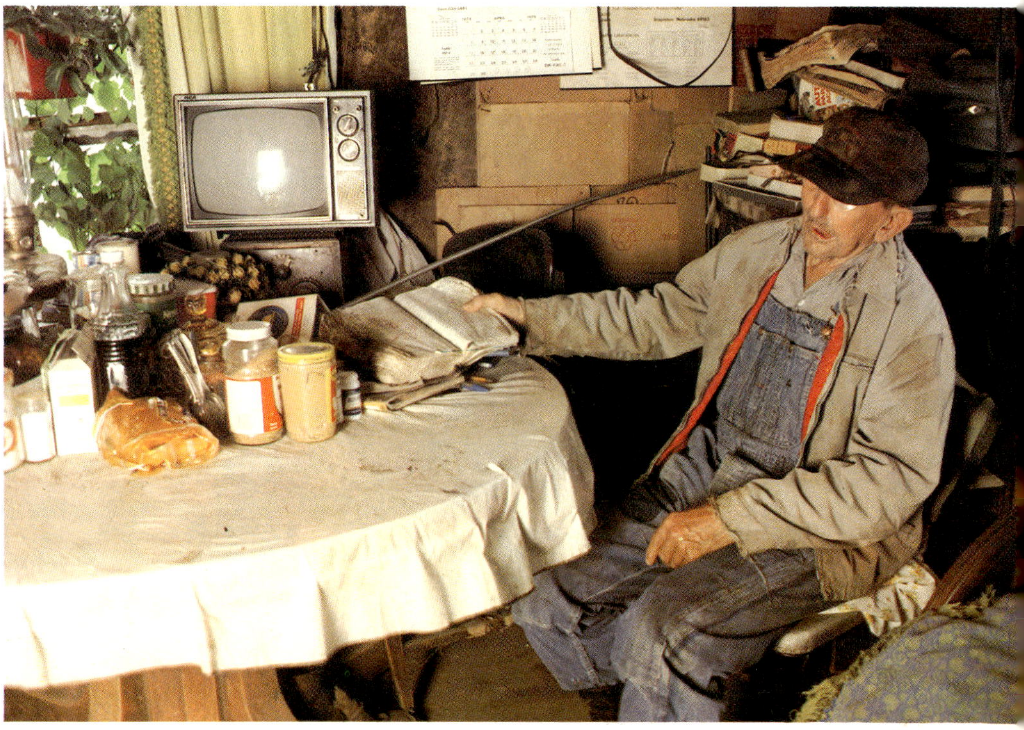

CHAPTER 10
PHOTOGRAPHY INDOORS
Available light

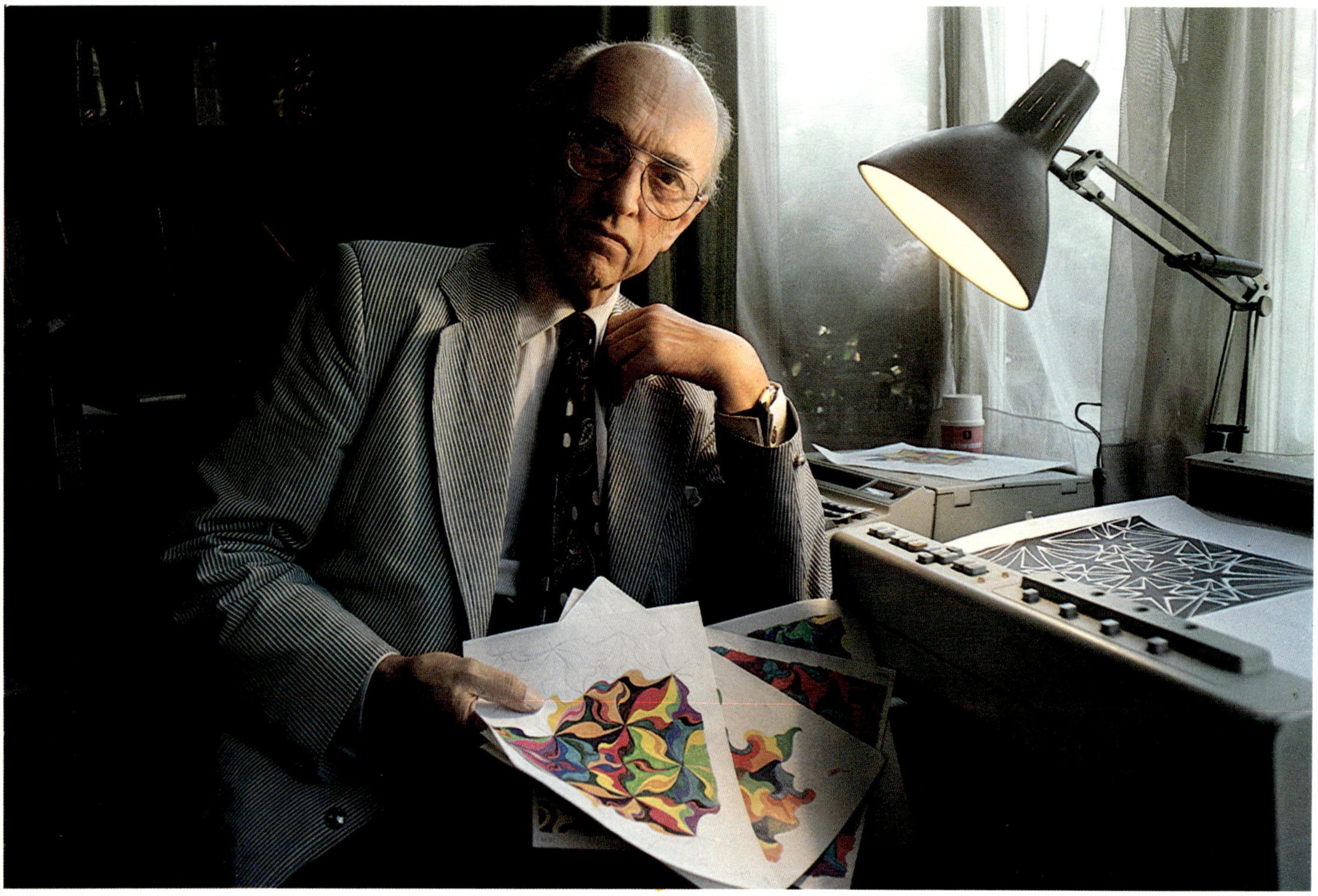

Mixed lighting *Deliberately adding a tungsten light to the window light has produced a more atmospheric portrait*

The available light you find indoors cannot be controlled in the way that flashguns and other lighting equipment can and calls for the use of different techniques. Without being able to alter the strength, direction or nature of the light being used, the photographer has to learn to make best use of what is already there.

Available light, sometimes called existing light, refers to the normal lighting which you find in a room. In daylight, this would mean the natural light coming through the windows and perhaps supplemented with some artificial lighting. It may also mean a small amount of daylight with artificial light as the main illumination. At night, the available light will consist solely of artificial lighting although this itself may consist of a mixture of tungsten bulbs and fluorescent tubes.

Many people think that taking photographs indoors without special lighting equipment inevitably leads to poor results. This should not be the case and, although there are problems coping with the variations of available light, the results are usually more natural than the harsh effects often created by a flashgun.

Contrast problems

One of the difficulties associated with using available light indoors is the inherent contrast of the light source itself. This is usually daylight coming through a window which produces hard side light, but it can also be domestic lamps.

Exposures indoors will normally be rather long with slow or medium speed films so that, on the whole, it makes more sense to use fast films such as Tri-X or HP5 (400 ASA/ISO) for black and white. For colour transparencies use films such as Ektachrome ET 160 for tungsten light, and Ektachrome ED 400 if either daylight or flash is the main light source. These higher speed films will allow you to use shorter exposures to freeze movement or increase depth of field. Fast films are inherently less contrasty than slower ones and this has the advantage of helping to counter the problem of increased contrast indoors.

One further advantage of using fast films is that they can be *uprated*. Most black and white and colour transparency film with speeds of 400 ASA can be uprated to 1600 ASA quite safely where it would have been either impossible or inconvenient to use the film at its recommended speed. Suppose, for instance, your exposure meter gave a reading of 1/8 second at *f*/2 for a shot indoors at 400 ASA. By uprating the film to 1600 ASA you could use 1/30 second at *f*/2 which would allow you to hand hold the camera whereas with the former setting you would have to use a tripod to eliminate camera shake. Do not forget that if you uprate films an adjustment in the processing will have to be made.

An alternative worth considering, even if you normally shoot on colour slide film, is to use fast colour negative film now avail-

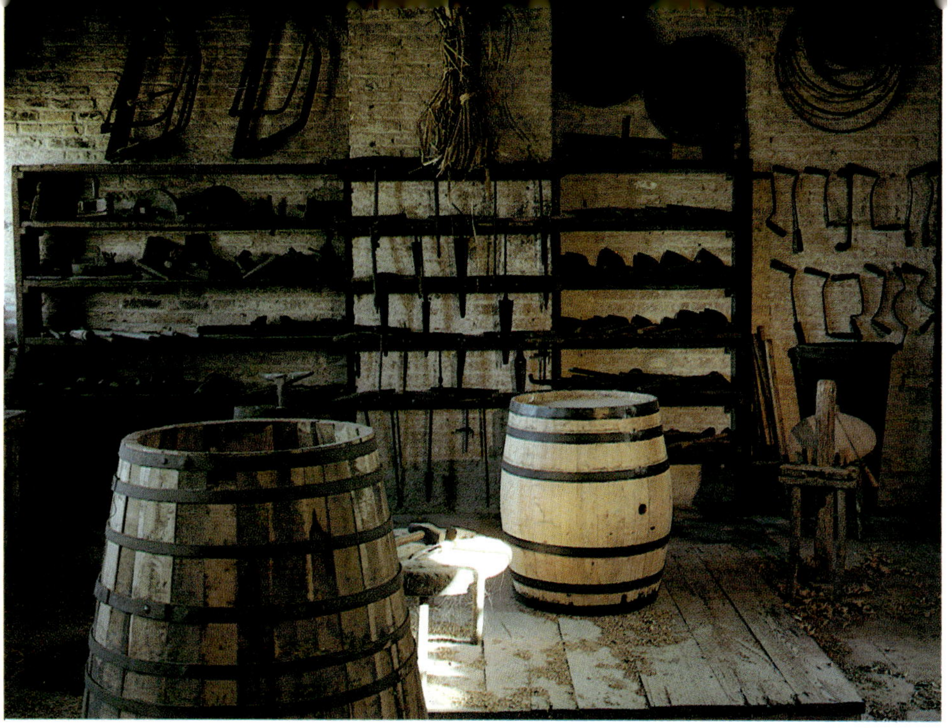

Natural light *The mood created by natural light can influence the whole shot. A tripod is needed in low light*

able, such as Fujicolor's HR 1600 which is normally rated at 1600 ASA and can be uprated to twice this rate without severe loss of quality.

However, if the light is so low that not even the fastest film will give you shutter speeds shorter than half a second, or if you want the grain-free quality of a slower film, it is better to use tungsten balanced slide film rather than daylight slide film—even when the available light is natural daylight. Tungsten films are designed for studio use and so are more suitable for long exposures. Daylight films tend to suffer from reciprocity failure earlier. While daylight film is designed to work best at shutter speeds of around 1/125 second, tungsten film works well at half a second. But if you use tungsten balanced film in daylight, you must remember to put an 85B or other appropriate filter over the lens to give correct colour.

Unless the room in which you are shooting is white or lightly coloured, the lighting contrast is likely to be very great. For this reason it is important to position the subject carefully in relation to the light source. There will probably be several stops difference between the highlight areas adjacent to the light source and the shadow areas in the background. This calls for very accurate and intelligent use of the exposure meter. It is usually better to take light readings off the relevant portion of the main subject. If necessary you can use a reflector, which need be nothing more elaborate than a piece of white card, paper or sheet to fill in shadow detail. Obviously large areas to be filled in will need either a large reflector or an additional light source.

It is very important to realize that low levels of illumination, such as from a 80 watt bulb, do not necessarily mean soft light. On the contrary, most domestic lighting is very contrasty because its position high up on the wall or ceiling throws big, harsh shadows.

Assessing lighting contrast and deciding whether what you see through the viewfinder of your camera will actually be recorded by the film is perhaps the single most important aspect of photography. Modern film, whether colour or black and white, is unable to cope with the same brightness or contrast range as the human eye. This means that what your eye sees in a particular scene will not necessarily be recorded in its entirety on the final negative or transparency. There is a very simple trick which artists have traditionally used to evaluate the shape and contrast of their subjects. This is to squint at your subject—to close your eyes so that you can just see a dim outline of the scene in front of you. Note that the shadow and highlight areas which contain detail with your eyes fully open now no longer register. The film will react in a very similar fashion.

Once you get used to using this discipline every time you view a difficult shot you will avoid disappointing results where what you saw in the first place does not appear in the photograph.

There are occasions, particularly with architectural interiors, when you want not only to record detail in the deep shadow areas but also to highlight detail such as bright daylight streaming through a window. With normal average exposure readings and film development, only the mid tone areas will record any significant detail. The highlights will be burned out while the shadow areas will go black. There is not much to be done in this kind of situation with colour materials, short of using supplementary fill-in lighting. But with black and white film over which you have development control you can 'compress' the tonal range of the film. The secret is to expose for the shadows and develop for the highlights. Normally this technique is used with large format cameras where single sheets of film can be exposed and developed individually to give the exact effect required but there is no reason why the same technique cannot be applied to 35 mm format, as long as you treat the rest of the film this way.

Using window light

To get used to available light, begin by taking portraits or simple still life arrangements just using the daylight coming through a window. A variety of

Railway coach *Although these tungsten lamps have made the colours artificially warm, this shot is still attractive*

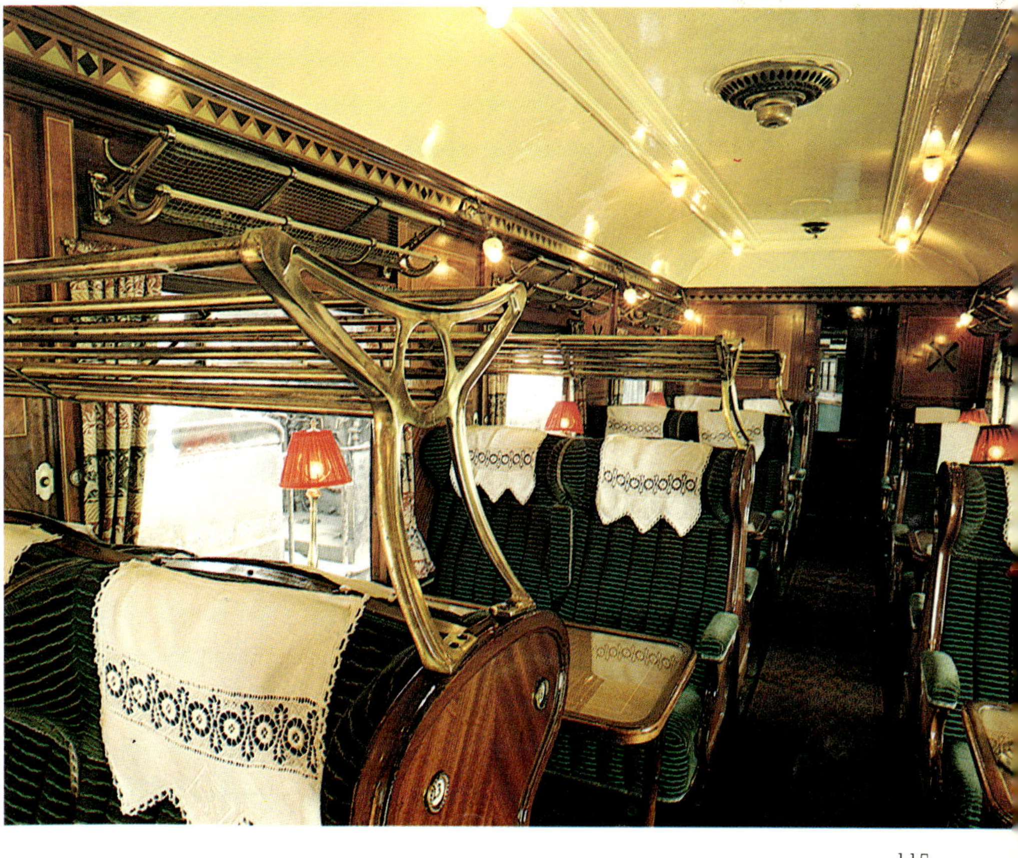

effects can be treated in this way by moving your subject experimentally in relation to the window light. You can light from the front by positioning your subject face-on to the window and taking the photograph from outside facing in. Alternatively, use sidelighting so that half the face is brightly lit while the other side is in deep shadow. A silhouette can be achieved by shooting directly into the window with your subject facing you. The variations are endless, especially if you use a white reflector to fill in the shadow detail.

Watch very carefully for background detail such as bookshelves and standard lamps interfering with your subject; because of the great difference in contrast between the foreground and background you may not be aware of obtrusive detail. Exposure readings also have to be very carefully evaluated in view of the enormous range of brightness levels.

Even with fast film, when you are using available daylight indoors, you will usually have to use fairly slow shutter speeds—1/60 or slower—if your aperture is to be anything but wide open. To avoid camera shake, especially with longer focal length lenses, you will need to support the camera in some way. A sturdy tripod is ideal but a table top with a pile of books for final height adjustment will suffice with care. A tripod is also a very useful disciplining element in that it makes you much more decisive about the framing and positioning of your final shot. Full details on keeping the camera steady are covered on pages 58 to 65.

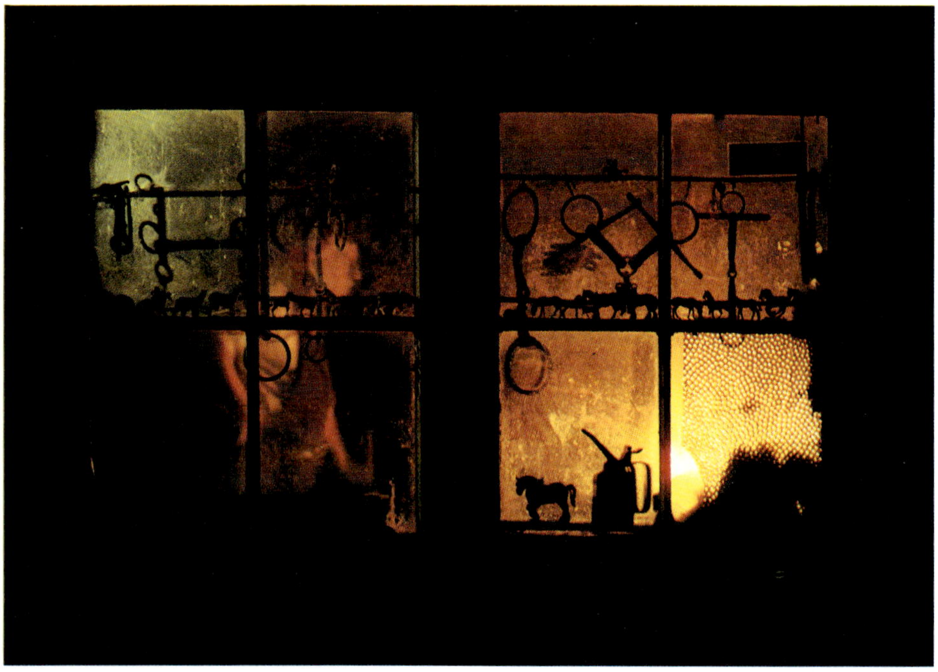

Blacksmith *In pictures like this the light itself is the strongest point. A flashgun would have spoilt the mood*

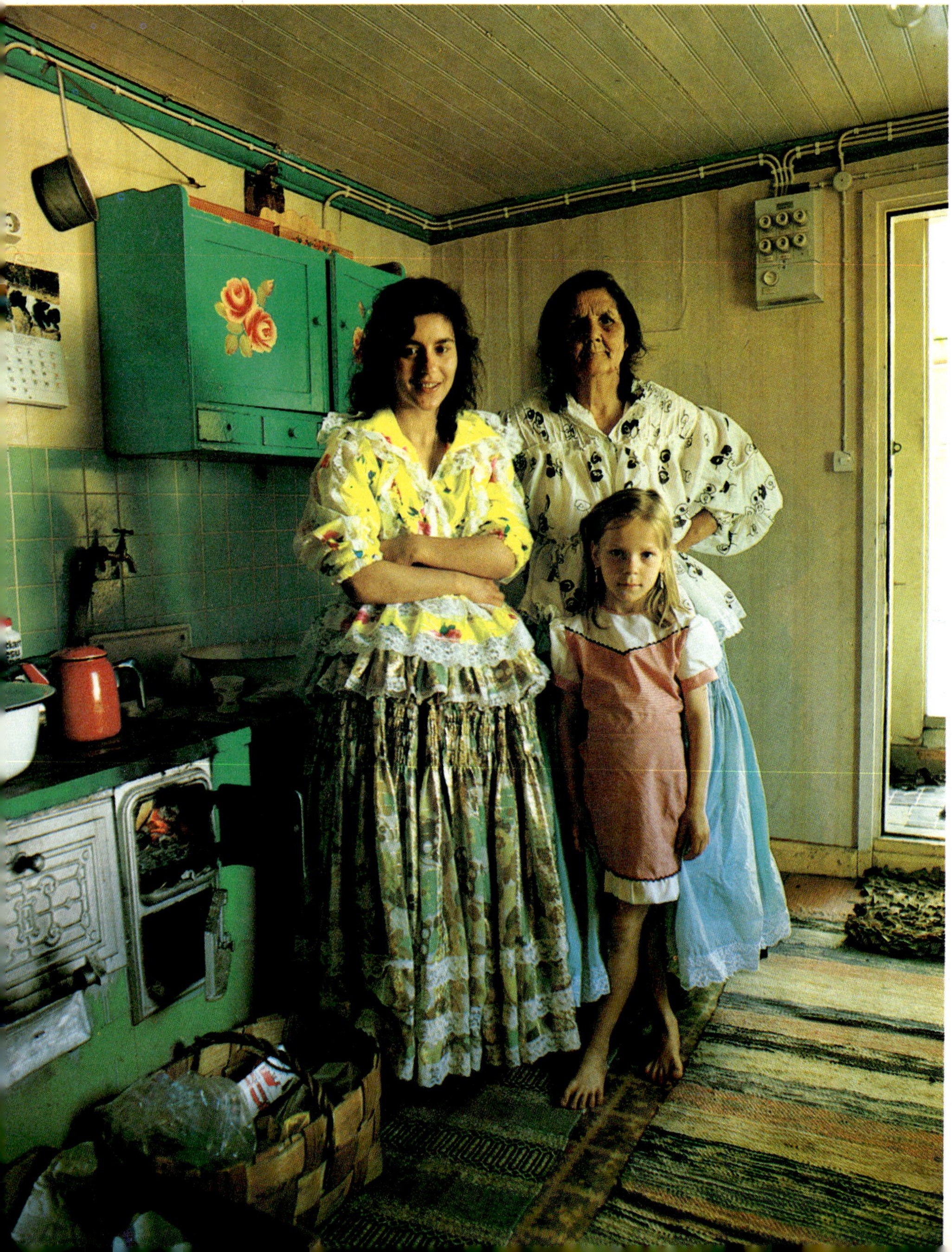

Finnish gypsies *The warm tones in this shot are caused by an overhead tungsten bulb which supplemented the daylight*

Colour temperature

The quality of daylight varies considerably according to the time of day and the season of the year. Winter sunlight, where the sun is low and casts long shadows, is entirely different from summer sunlight, where the sun is high in the sky and casts short shadows.

This clearly makes a considerable difference to the amount of light available. While the winter sun is generally weaker, it may actually illuminate a south facing room more because more direct light comes through the window.

The colour temperature (page 238) also varies according to the time of day and prevailing weather conditions. An obvious instance is red sunset light compared to the bluishness of a cloudy, rainy day. Although it is fairly easy to assess the quality and colour temperature of daylight outdoors, it becomes more difficult indoors since there are other factors which influence it. The colour of walls, floors, carpets and curtains can influence the final colour of the film. Windows themselves can diffuse light or concentrate it depending on the angle of light and the optical quality of the glass.

Shooting with black and white material obviously eliminates many of these problems since there is no colour to worry about—the main factor, apart

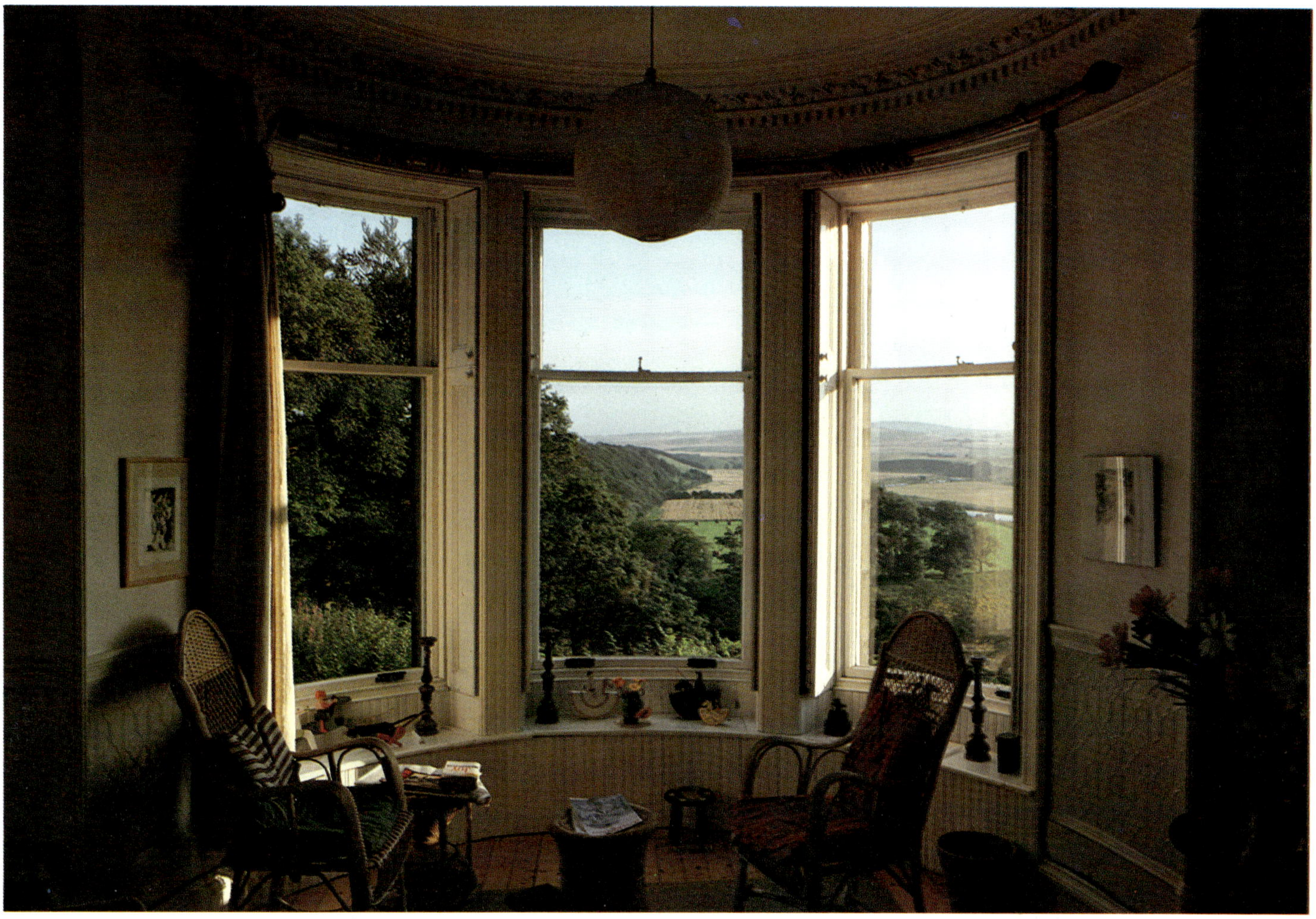

Inside looking out *The interior need not be correctly exposed as long as there is enough detail shown to hold the interest*

from composition and lighting, is being able to cope with contrast.

Apart from daylight, which is the commonest photographic light source there are other manmade light sources which are used indoors when there is little or no daylight to make short enough exposures.

Daylight is a general term describing mean noon sunlight plus skylight. But as mentioned, it can vary in its colour temperature. Mean noon sunlight contains equal quantities of blue, green and red light—the primary colours which, mixed together, produce what we see as white light. Electronic flash and blue flashbulbs also have the same colour temperature as daylight. This is a great advantage when shooting in colour since flash can be used with daylight type colour slide film.

The tungsten lights used indoors are deficient in blue so that photographs taken using daylight type colour film will have a warm reddish colour cast. To combat this problem colour reversal films are made in two types—one for daylight and one specially for tungsten lighting. Tungsten balanced colour transparency films, because of their chemical make up which compensates for the lack of blue in artificial light, will produce a blue colour cast if they are used with daylight or flash.

Fluorescent light is something of an unknown quantity as a photographic light source since the colour temperature emitted by a fluorescent tube depends entirely on the type of tube being used. There are at least seven types in general domestic and industrial use—all of which emit different colour compositions. This light is very difficult to cope with and since it is so varied, there is no film made to match it. It usually gives colour transparencies a greenish cast but it can also cause blue or red casts. The colour bias depends entirely on the type of tubes used.

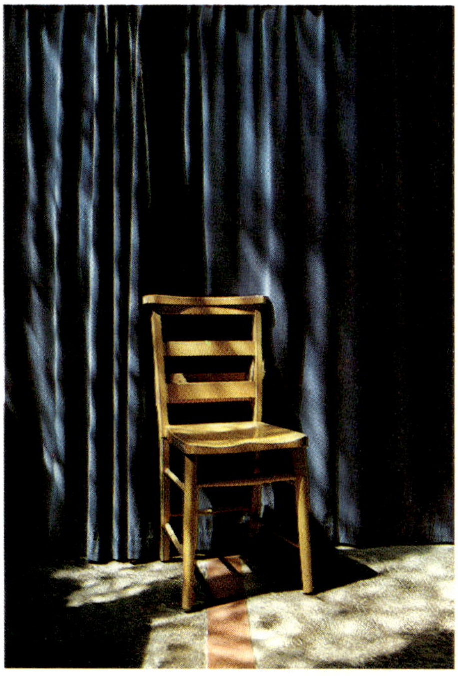

Chair *Shafts of sunlight can be a useful light source indoors even if they do not fill the whole room*

Mixed lighting

Since different light sources emit various colour temperatures, it is highly probable that if you take pictures by available light you will encounter one of the photographer's nightmares—mixed lighting. When taking a simple shot of a living room and kitchen interior, for example, you are likely to have a mixture of daylight, tungsten and fluorescent lighting, all of which would produce different colour casts.

What you have to establish before all else is the dominant light source. This can be done by roughly assessing the lighting ratio by eye. Turn the artificial lights off and stand back to see what difference this makes to the shadow detail if there is a lot of daylight streaming through the doors or windows. Alternatively, use an exposure meter to measure the relative brightness. Do this by taking a reading from the areas lit by daylight and another from the tungsten lit areas. Use the appropriate colour film for the light source which is strongest.

If the room in which you are photographing has a fairly equal mix of daylight and tungsten light the decision is

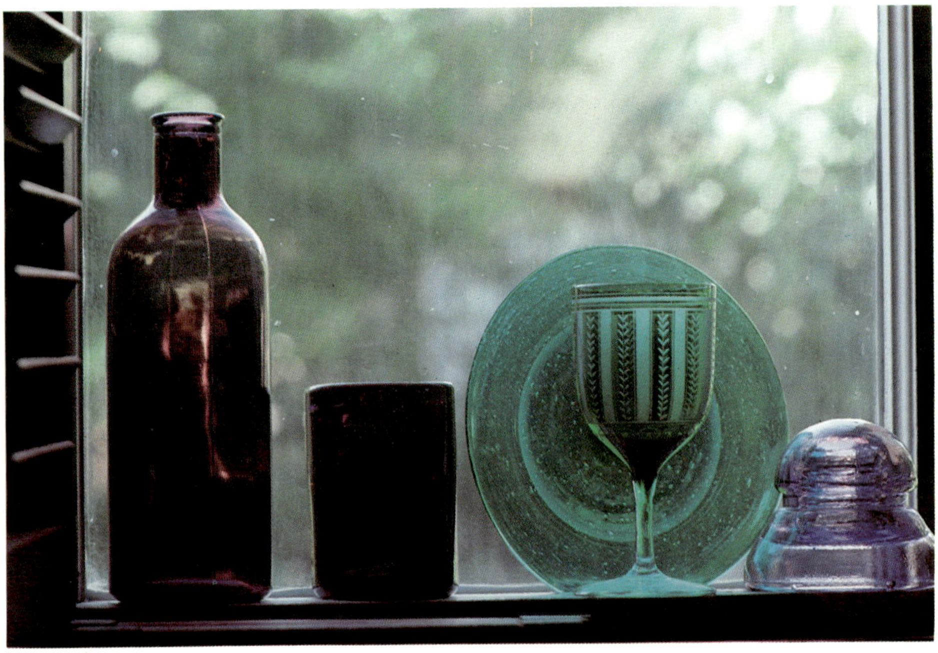

Still life *Backlighting from a window can be used effectively for a wide range of still life shots*

more difficult. If you use daylight type colour film to record the daylight parts of the picture accurately, the tungsten lit portions will have a warm reddish cast over them. If on the other hand you decide to use tungsten type film then the daylight portions of the pictures will go cold and bluish. Pictures with a warmish cast are generally far more acceptable than ones with a cold bluish cast so that it is usual, if in any real doubt as to what film to use, to shoot with daylight type colour film.

When you run into problems with mixed lighting, try and increase one single source of lighting to produce a more dominant type of light. This will help you to decide which film to use and you may find that all you have to do is open the curtains more fully or add an extra reading lamp or reflector.

Conversion filters

Another method of balancing colour film to different light sources is to use various colour conversion filters over the camera lens.

Two of the most useful filters are those numbered 80A and 85B. The 80A is a blue filter for exposing daylight colour film in tungsten illumination. The 85B is an amber filter which is used for exposing tungsten balanced film in daylight. Both of these filters cut down the amount of light reaching the film and you need to increase the exposure by 2 stops for the 80A and about 2/3 stops for the 85B.

Compensating for fluorescent lighting is slightly harder. If the fluorescent light is fairly weak you may find that the warmth of the tungsten lighting will eliminate its influence. With stronger fluorescent lighting, however, the colour cast is so obvious that more careful correction is needed.

Some manufacturers now produce filters which are designed to adapt ordinary daylight film for use with fluorescent lighting. *FL-D* filters are designed to cope with daylight-type fluorescent tubes while *FL-W* filters are for use with white or warm tubes. These filters can produce good results, but to get the best correction possible you have to choose a specific filter, or pair of filters, to compensate for a particular type of tube. But, because tubes are replaced occasionally, a single room may have more than one type of tube. This problem is difficult to solve and is the subject of a separate article.

Once you become aware of the effects different types of lights have on your subject you can juggle around with them to produce very creative shots. The most striking pictures are almost always those taken with very simple lighting—wonders can be done with nothing more elaborate than an Anglepoise lamp and a piece of white card. Look carefully at your subject. Squint at it to evaluate the broad tonal areas. And, above all, experiment with different film, lighting and positioning.

Cat and rabbit *A window gives a diffuse and natural illumination which can be ideal lighting for portraits*

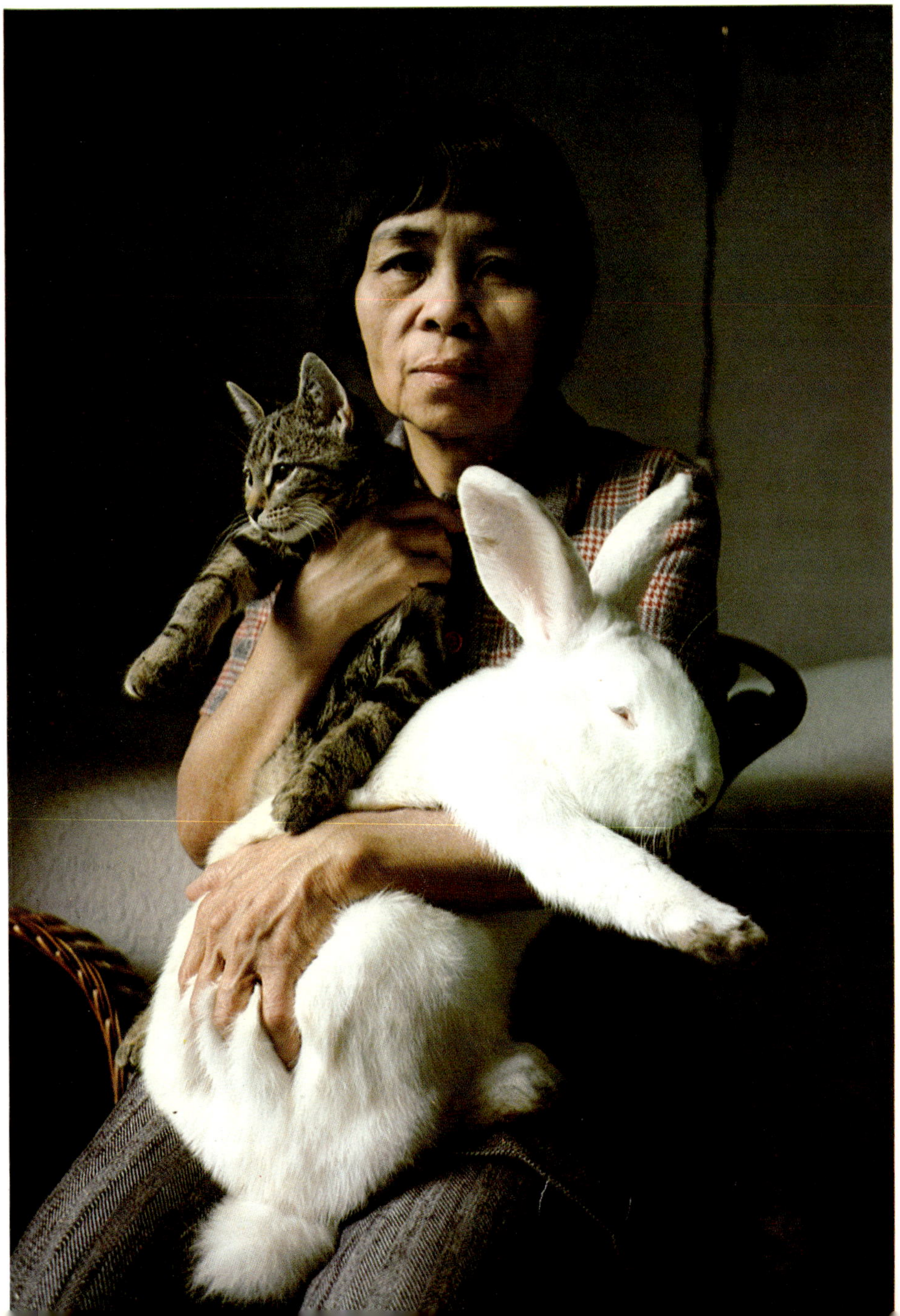

Artificial light

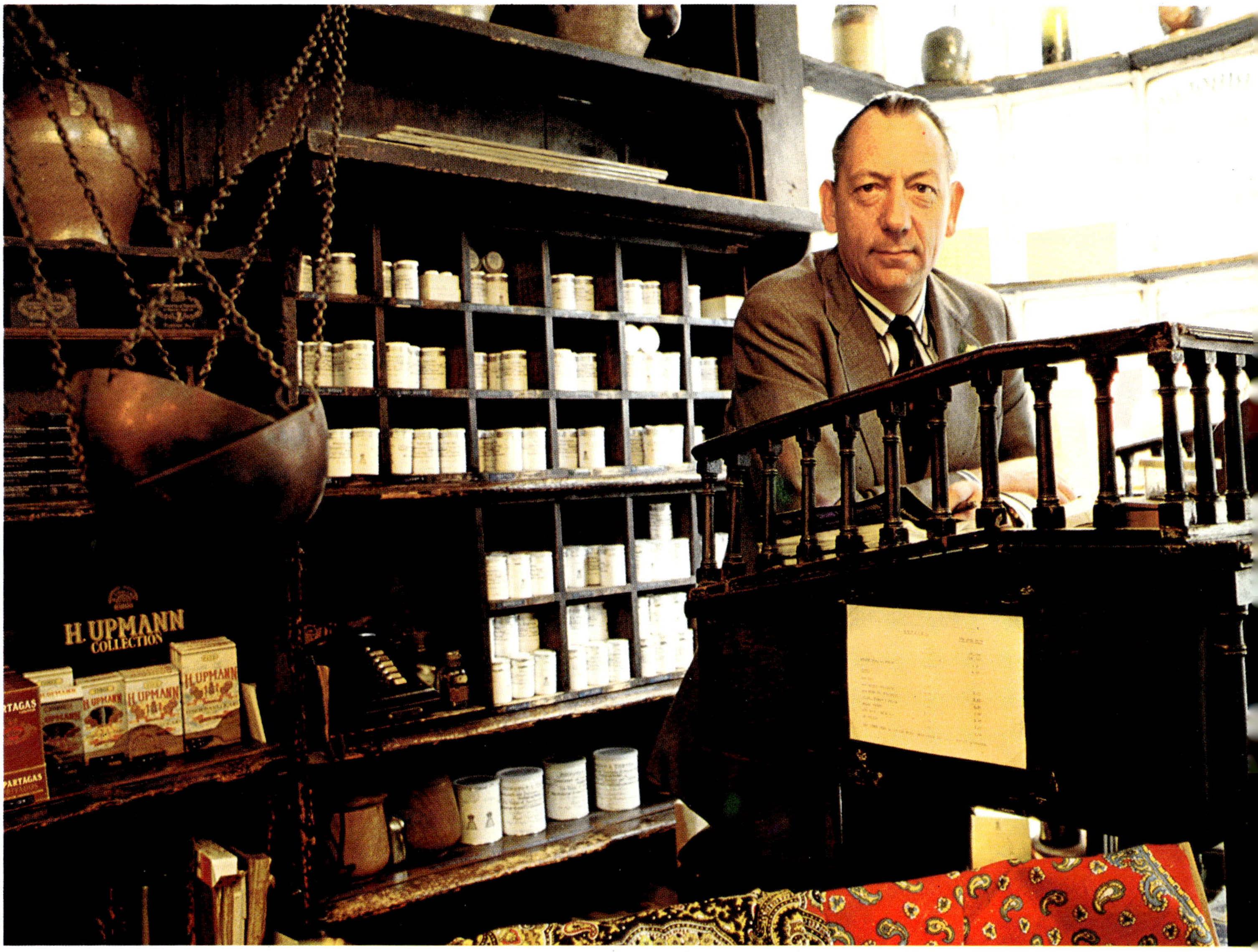

Shop interior *Film colour balance need not always match the light. Daylight film was used here to good effect with the warm predominantly tungsten lighting*

To the human eye, colours tend to look much the same in every light—a red pen is red and a blue pen is blue in both daylight and electric light. But there are significant differences in the colour of every type of light source, and an object that appears one colour in fluorescent light is a slightly different colour by candlelight. While the eye quickly adapts to changing light and may not see these colour variations, they may be only too obvious on film unless you make appropriate adjustments.

Earlier articles show how to correct for variations in the colour of daylight (see pages 88 to 92), but it is just as important to correct for the differences between various types of artificial light otherwise your pictures may turn out with an unpleasant colour cast.

Good colour balance is particularly crucial if you are using colour slide film because it is virtually impossible to adjust the colour during processing. But even with negative film, it is worth trying to get the colour correct when you are taking the picture—if the colour is nearly correct, filtration for printing will be that much easier and if the colour is too far out, it may be impossible to correct even with the strongest filters.

Techniques for colour correction of artificial light sources are, like those for daylight, relatively straightforward, consisting largely of matching the film to the light source as closely as possible and making further adjustments with filters placed over the lens. With artificial light photography, however, you have additional scope for correction because you can often adjust the light source. You may be able to change the light source completely, or adjust its colour with the aid of filters placed over the bulb or reflector.

The problems with colour correction of artificial light come in deciding what correction needs to be made. It is essential, therefore, to identify your light source or light sources. Beware of mixed light sources, though. If you are shooting indoors, for instance, daylight may be coming through the window and mixing with the electric light. Mixed lighting should be avoided if possible.

For indoor work, there are four major types of light—tungsten studio lighting, domestic light bulbs, fluorescent light, and flash—though there are many others such as candles or gaslamps. Artificial light outdoors, however, is much more varied and often hard to identify. Street lamps differ and may use, for instance, sodium, mercury vapour, tungsten, gas, or oil. Only once you are sure of the type of light source can you begin to make corrections for the type of cast they give.

Tungsten studio lighting

Like many forms of artificial light, tungsten studio lights—such as photofloods and 'photographic' lamps—produce a light that looks almost as white as daylight but in fact has a much lower colour temperature (see page 238); that is, it has a much lower proportion of blue. Pictures taken in tungsten light on daylight balanced slide film, therefore, have a rather orange cast.

The orange cast from tungsten lighting can be attractive, giving a warm cosy look to the scene and adding colour to skin tones, and you may not always want to correct for it. However, in most circumstances the cast is much too strong and must at least be partially corrected.

Perhaps the simplest correction to make is to buy film balanced for certain kinds of studio lighting. Both colour slides and colour negative films can be bought in versions that are balanced for tungsten studio lights. Colour slide films for studio lighting are normally referred to as Tungsten or Type B films; the colour negative films are usually referred to as Type L. Both these films are designed to give the correct colour balance with photographic lamps at 3200K. These films give fairly good balance with most tungsten studio light and you will rarely need to make any other corrections.

If for any reason you wish to use daylight balanced film, you must use filters. You can place filters over the lights, but if all your studio lights are similar it is far easier to use a filter over the lens. Unfiltered, daylight slide film gives a very orange cast, and to correct you must use a deep blue filter, such as the Kodak Wratten 80A.

Unless you have TTL metering, you must remember to make the necessary exposure adjustments whenever you add a filter.

For nearly all your studio shots, either tungsten balanced film or daylight film with an 80A filter give good results, but there are times when you want the colour balance absolutely perfect. On these occasions you may have to make further adjustments.

First, you must discover what colour temperature your lights run at. Photographic lamps are normally rated at 3200K and may need no special treatment, but photofloods are slightly bluer and are rated at 3400K. So, when using photofloods, many photographers would recommend a pale amber 81A filter to remove the blueness with tungsten film, or 80B filter with daylight film.

Unfortunately, even this extra care does not ensure perfect colour because the lights cannot be relied upon to stay at their rated colour temperature. Manufacturers of photofloods, for instance, only guarantee that their lamps are within 100K of 3400K, but no closer. Even if you could buy a perfectly rated bulb it would have to be run constantly at the correct voltage. Unfortunately, most domestic electricity supplies vary noticeably in voltage from time to time. You can buy special voltage stabilizers, but these tend to be very expensive.

The colour temperature of studio lamps also varies with their age—photographic lamps, in particular, tend to redden as they get older. Again, you can buy special intensifiers that increase the voltage to maintain the colour as the bulb gets older, but these are an unnecessary expense for the amateur. A final point to remember is that colour temperature also varies with how long the light has been on.

There is little you can do to overcome these variations unless you have an expensive colour temperature meter, but you can keep them to a minimum by taking certain precautions. First, avoid plugging any other electrical appliance into the socket that supplies your lights. Second, whenever you buy new photographic lamps, let them burn for 15 to 20 minutes before you take any pictures because when new they are slightly bluer than the rated 3200K. If you can afford to, it is also a good idea to replace bulbs after five sessions. But there is no need to discard the old lamps altogether: they can be used for black and white work with good results.

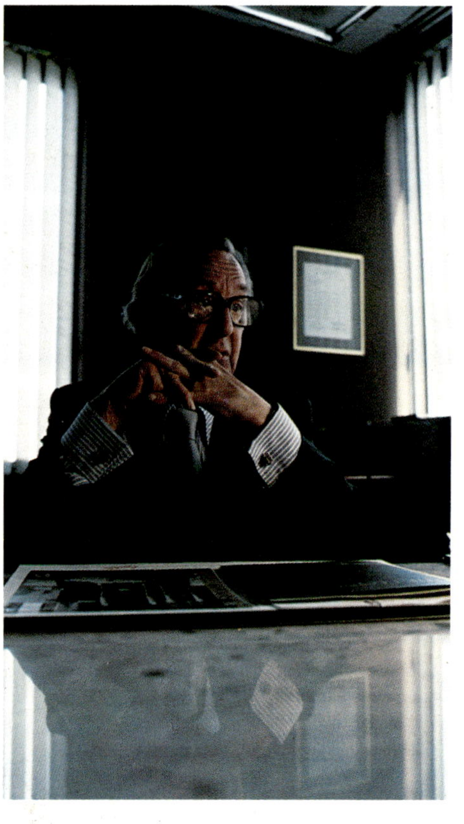

Boardroom *Tungsten balanced film was used in daylight to give a cold blue cast. But a desk lamp directed on the face improved skin tones*

If you take these basic precautions, and make the adjustments recommended above, there is no reason why you should not achieve good if not perfect colour balance on every shot. Problems only arise when you get reflections from strongly coloured surfaces. Keep your subject well away from such strong colours unless they contribute positively to the image.

Normal domestic lighting, however, may be slightly harder to deal with.

Domestic lighting

The problem with average domestic lighting is that it can take so many different forms. Although it is normally in the form of tungsten bulbs, these can be anything from 15 watts to 200 watts and upwards. Each wattage gives a different colour temperature—a 25W bulb, for instance, gives out a light of about 2600K while a 200W bulb may work at about 3000K. Colour temperature varies between individual bulbs of the same wattage even more than it does with photofloods.

If you are working at home, colour temperature may also be affected by the colours of the furnishings and decoration, and the colour of the lamp shade.

With all these complications, it is clearly impossible to achieve perfect correction. Fortunately it is rarely needed. People are used to wide variations in the colour and appearance of domestic rooms and so will not usually be upset by minor colour casts. In fact, an orange colour cast may actually give an attractive warmth to the picture.

Nevertheless, if you want your pictures to look fairly natural, you must make some sort of correction. Domestic tungsten lighting is very yellow, so when correcting you should aim to reduce the yellow content. Using tungsten film or daylight film with an 80A filter will eliminate most of the yellow and in many instances this will be adequate.

If results are still too yellow, however, you may have to use an 82A filter with the tungsten film. You could use the 82A in combination with 80A and daylight film but two filters restrict the amount of light reaching the film considerably and you may need inordinately long exposures to compensate. If you do decide to use to use a combination of filters, it is best to use gelatin filters because they are much thinner and will have less optical effect on the film.

Fluorescent lights

If you often take pictures in any public building, such as a shop or office, you will almost certainly come across fluorescent lighting. Yet fluorescent lighting is one of the hardest of all light sources to correct for. Unlike tungsten light, fluorescent light does not work by heating a thin piece of metal with an electric current, and colour temperature does not apply (see page 238). So you cannot simply look at the colour temperature and make an appropriate correction.

More importantly, although fluorescent light looks as white as daylight, the basic light emitted by a fluorescent tube is *discontinuous*. Instead of emitting all the colours in varying proportions, it only gives out bands of light of certain wavelengths: some wavelengths are not emitted at all.

If certain colours are missing it may be virtually impossible to put them back, even if you can identify which colours to replace. The fact that pictures taken by fluorescent light have a green cast does not mean that you simply filter out the green, because you might be left with little else. Fortunately, most fluorescent tubes are designed with a continuous spectrum of colours overlaying the discontinuous spectrum. This means that you can make some attempt at correction.

Lighting technicians use a colour temperature meter as a starting point, and correct fluorescent light using colour correction (CC) filters by trial and error, but a simpler alternative if you do not have such a meter is to use a filter specifically designed for correcting daylight colour film in fluorescent lighting. This filter is referred to as FL-D and is available from most filter manufacturers.

Street lamps

Many types of street lamps, like fluorescent light, give a discontinuous spectrum and are therefore very difficult to correct. In fact, there is no correction you can apply to give correct colour rendition in sodium lighting because if you put a filter over the camera lens, you filter out all the illumination in the scene. If you want to take colour pictures in sodium lighting, therefore, all you can do is illuminate the scene with a flash. There are a number of different types of streetlight in general use, recognized by their colour and appearance.

The most common streetlights are mercury (blue-green) and sodium (orange-yellow). Sodium lights are produced in two varieties—low pressure and high pressure.

Mercury streetlights have a spectrum which consists of several bright lines (several colours) of varying strength, with virtually no red content at all. It is therefore impossible to filter the light to produce a white result, since there can never be enough red. The exact colour which mercury streetlights appear on film depends on the lamps themselves and the type of film used.

While they will always show a blue-green cast, they do give a certain amount of colour rendering to their surroundings.

Low pressure sodium lamps, however, are almost completely one pure colour, yellow-orange. As a result, different colours are indistinguishable in their light. Examine the spectrum on page 199 under sodium lighting and you will see it solely in different tones of yellow.

Again, it is impossible to filter the colour of low pressure sodium lamps, and any photograph taken solely by their light will appear the same colour as the lamps.

High pressure sodium lighting has a much mellower pink colour. While it has a strong yellow content, there are enough other colours to give a reasonable colour rendering, and for this reason these lamps are often used in city centres—where it is felt desirable to provide lighting that shows colours.

High pressure sodium light is fairly close to tungsten lighting in its characteristics, so for most purposes either artificial light film or daylight film with an 80B filter will be adequate. For perfect results, 'fine tuning' using colour correction filters is needed. Streetlights of this sort tend to vary widely in colour, so the correction which you establish for one particular lamp may be quite wrong for another lamp of the same type some way down the street. For most purposes, however, it is not important to fine tune the colour in this way as viewers will not expect pink street lighting to give white results.

Filters

When deciding on the filtration you need to achieve the right colour balance, it is important to remember that there are three different types of filter used for altering colour balance. *Colour conversion* filters are used to convert daylight for tungsten film (amber 85 series) or tungsten light for daylight film (blue 80 series). *Light balancing* filters are paler versions of the conversion filters, designed to make small adjustments to the colour temperature—the 81 series is pale amber and the 82 series pale blue. *Colour Compensating* filters, which must be slid into square filter holders, are designed to give you complete control over the colour of the light. They are usually written in the form CC 05 M, for example—this is a pale (5%) Magenta filter.

Stock Exchange ***The green cast caused by fluorescent lights can be extremely difficult to filter out. An FL-D filter gives some improvement, but the result is still far from perfect.***

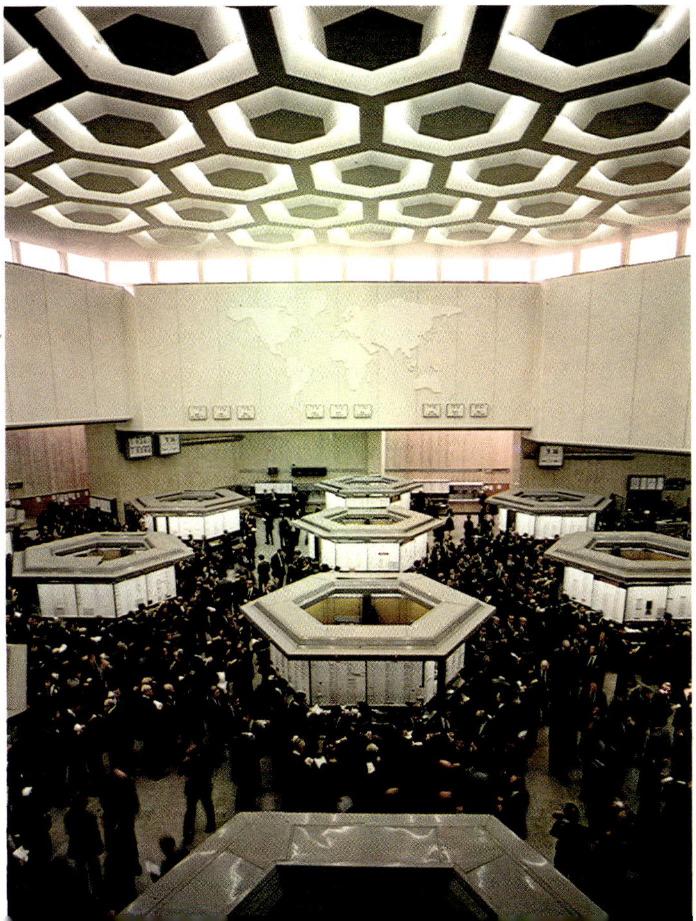

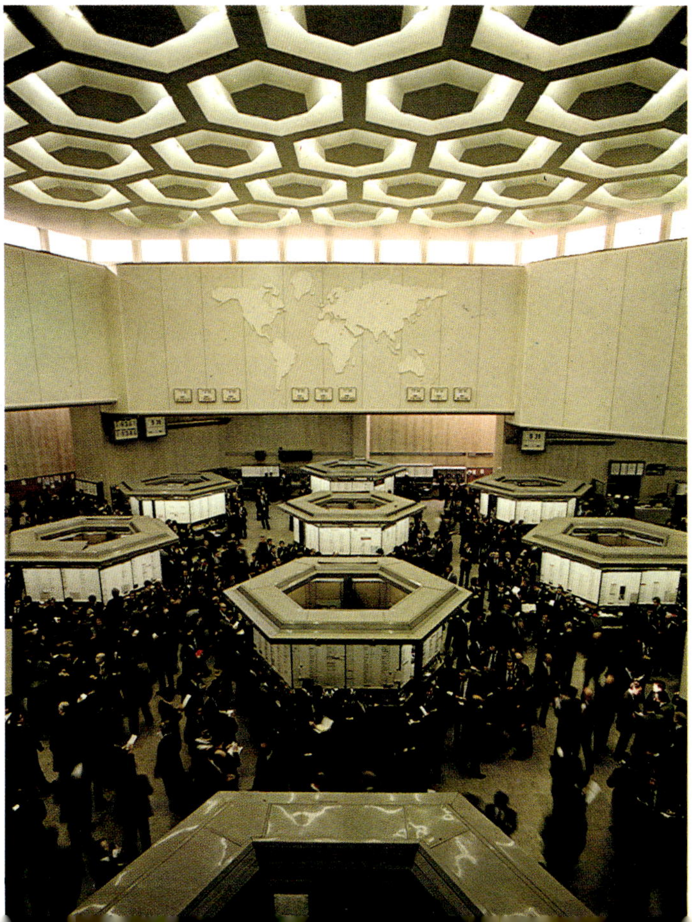

CHAPTER 11
PEOPLE
Portraits

The very idea of taking formal portraits fills many photographers with horror. The word 'formal' itself suggests something straightlaced and rigid, out of the Victorian era, and possibly even with clamps to hold the subject in place. Or one thinks of the portrait taken at school, where the photographer set up a standard plain background and lighting arrangement, and every child had to sit in a standard way.

Yet even in Victorian times some photographers were beginning to let their subjects 'breathe', and the portraits of well-known people taken by such photographers as Julia Margaret Cameron are far from the stylized mould. Today, there is a wider range than ever, and it is hard to tell where the formal photograph ends and the candid shot takes over.

Most formal portraits, however, are better termed 'posed' photographs. Here, the session is set up with the aim of

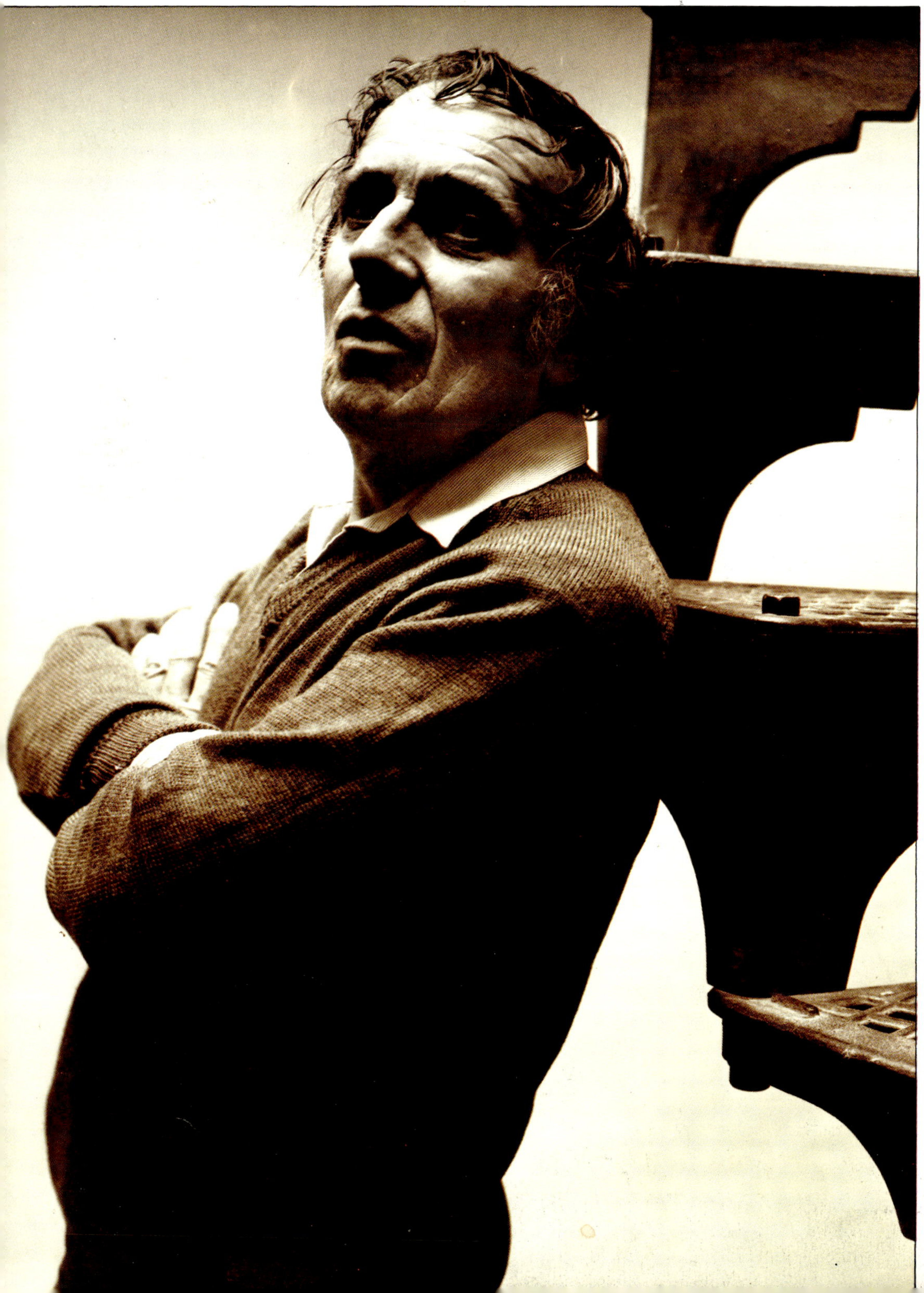

Folded arms *The position of the arms can add an extra means of expression. Note the way in which the staircase has been used in the composition*

Smoker *By positioning the subject's head high up in the frame, the photographer has been able to feature the hand as part of the shot*

Lady at home *The subject's own surroundings often prompt a more relaxed pose. However, be careful to avoid distracting backgrounds*

Frame within frame *To make a statement about the man and his work—he is an architect—the photographer created an organized, graphic shot*

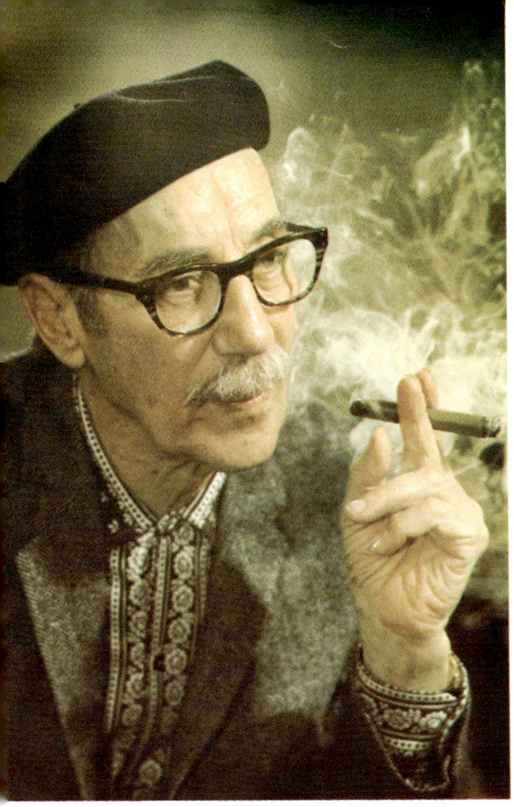

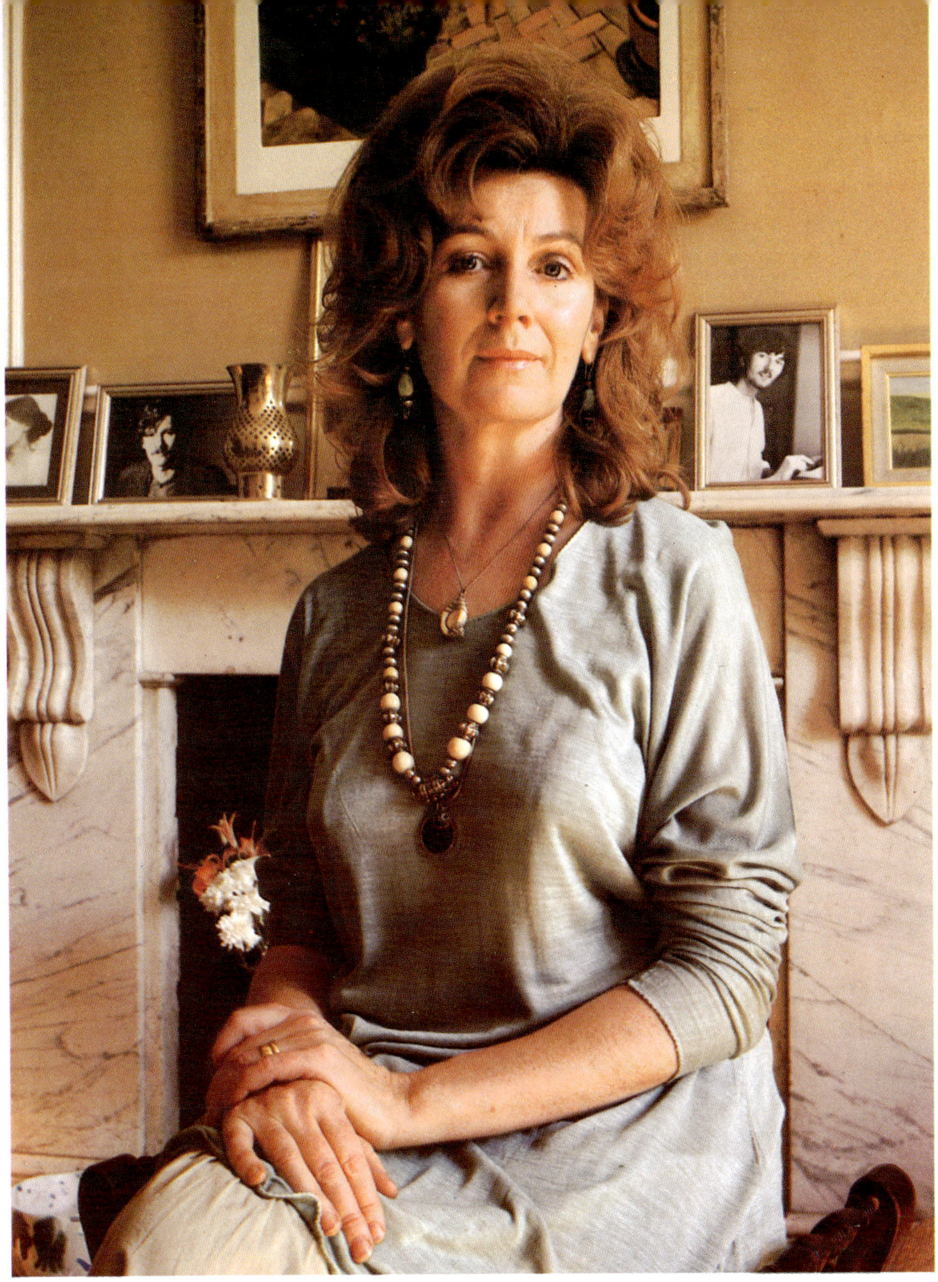

taking the subject's picture, and the subject expects to cooperate with you in order to achieve this. The traditional portrait is taken in the studio, or at least a temporary studio, but it is quite possible to take the same carefully posed, studied portraits either outdoors or in an ordinary room.

Studio photography is in many ways the hardest of all types of portrait photography—paradoxically because so much is under your control. You must attend to every part of the picture, instead of letting the background worry about itself or putting up with whatever light happens to be around at the time. For both you and the subject it is a novel experience, which means that you must pay great attention to detail.

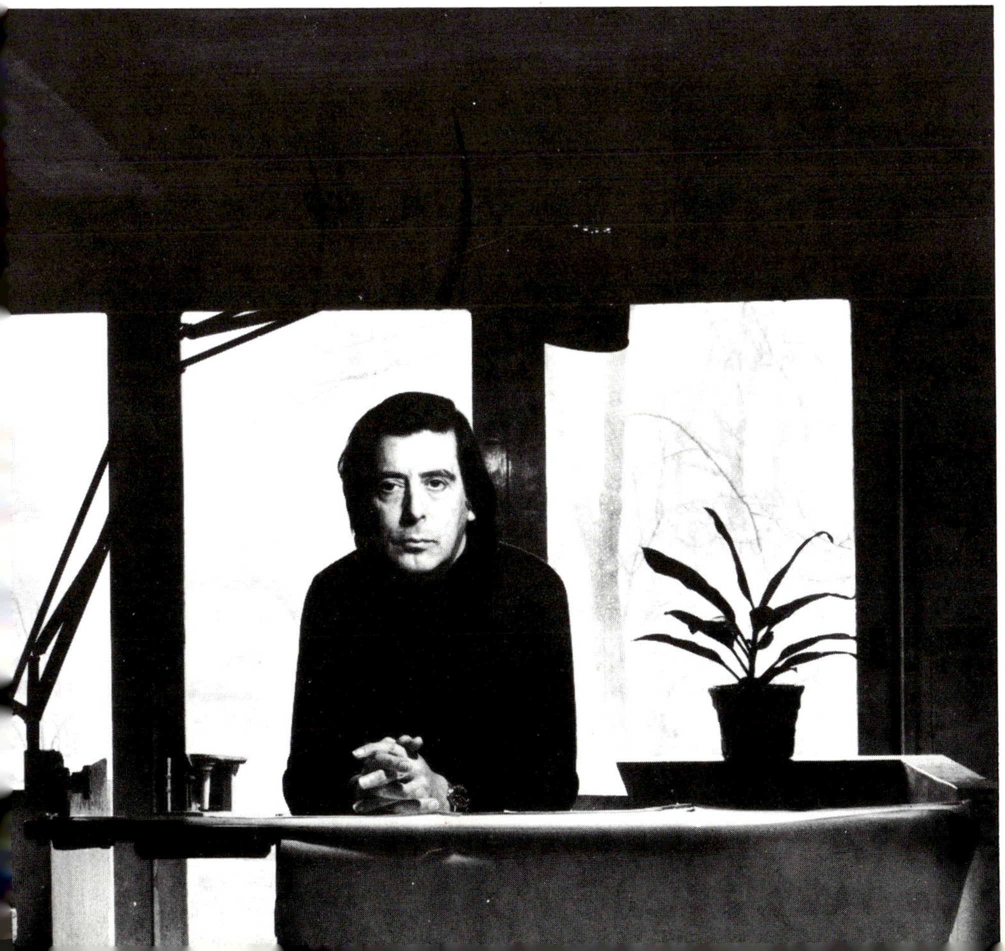

A professional portraitist, for example, will even wear clothes which are appropriate to the session, in cases where a stranger is to be photographed. A judge or mayor, for example, may well respond better to a photographer wearing a suit than one casually dressed, while the owner of a trendy wine bar might be the opposite.

You should also take a professional approach to the session, even when photographing a friend, in the way you set things up. It is vital to prepare the set thoroughly beforehand, so that your subject does not quickly get bored with the whole thing. You ought to have some sort of idea what kind of pictures you want before you start. This is easier in the case of friends than of strangers whose personality you have no idea of until you meet them. A true character study, rather than a simple likeness, means much more than putting your subject on the ready-lit set, however. It is important to be able to make rapid changes to the set-up during the session as the subject's personality emerges, and again this means having things ready beforehand. To start with, it is best to

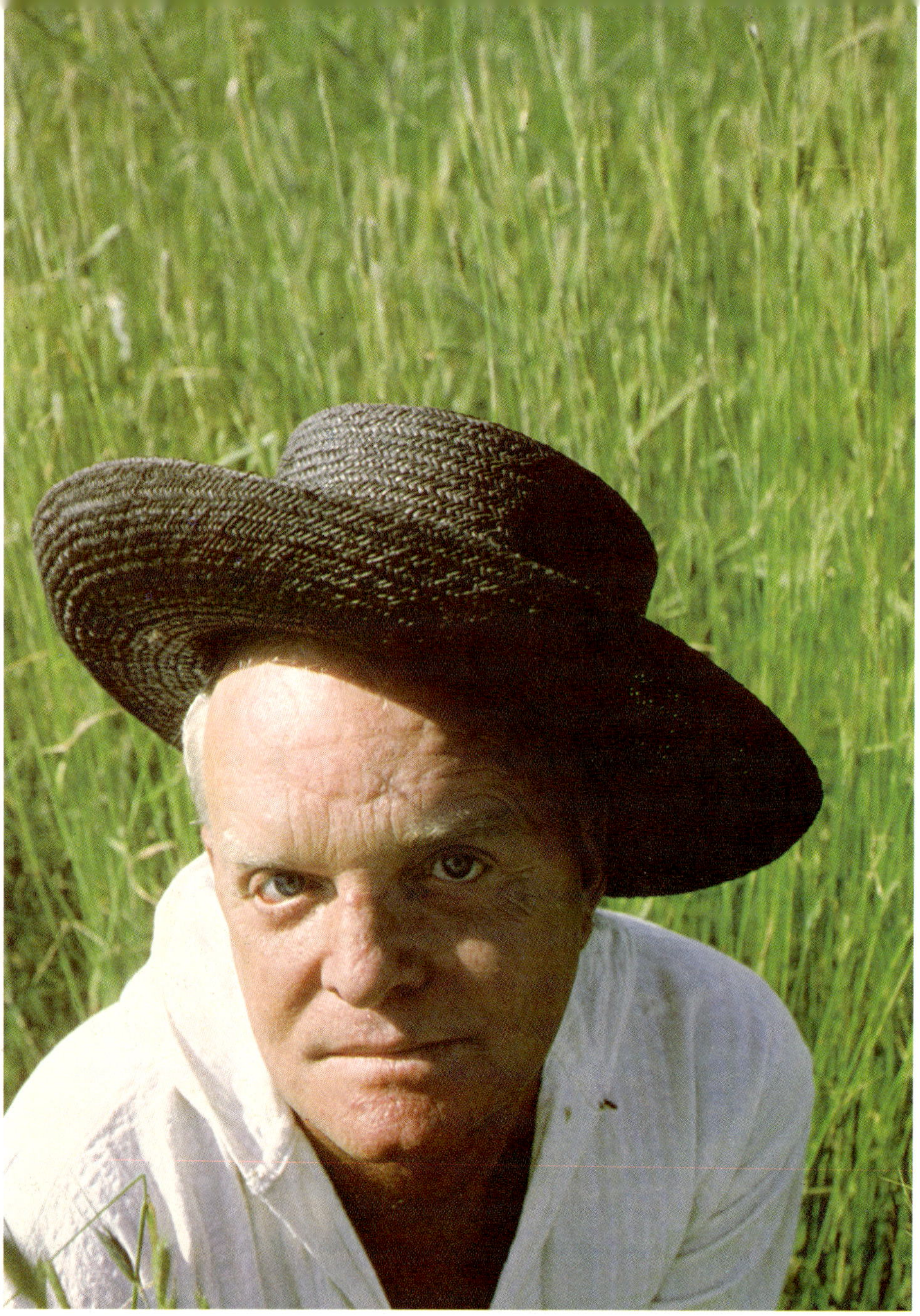

Truman Capote *The shape of the hat and the positioning of the subject low in the frame created this striking composition*

photograph a range of friends, experimenting with showing their characters in different ways, before tackling portraits of strangers.

The problem of assessing your subject's character is central to the success of the portrait. Different photographers have different ways of doing this. Inevitably you form snap judgements, in which case you are likely to portray the personality that the person is trying to project rather than their true inner self. Your ability to judge people and to get on with them is not the sort of thing that can be developed in any way other than by experience, however. It is safe to assume, though, that if someone dresses and behaves in either an aggressive or timid way, that they will be quite happy with portraits which reinforce those characteristics.

There are also different ways of handling the session itself. It is usually preferable to talk directly to the subject, and to get them to respond to you, rather than to the impersonal lens of the camera. This means using a tripod, so that you are not hidden behind the camera as you speak. Having focused, take your eye away from the viewfinder and talk normally to the person. Once you have the pose looking good, you can ask them to look at the lens for a picture which you take using a cable release, without even looking through the viewfinder.

On the other hand some portraitists will virtually ignore the camera, and will bustle around attending to various details so that the subject is caught virtually off guard and does not assume a fixed pose when the cable release is pressed. This method tends to produce a rather serious portrait, since the subject has made no effort to look pleasant or interested, but it may reveal more personality than a posed shot, since the subject is less self-conscious.

When faced with your subject, often the hardest thing is actually getting the session under way. Even professional portrait photographers can have this problem, and one solution is to have a stock of poses which you know work well. The beginner does not have such a stock available from experience, so a useful alternative would be to collect a library of poses that you like and show them to your subject. If the pictures are good they will probably be quite keen to be photographed in such a way, and will instantly get an idea of what you want. Having established common ground, you can then explore various possibilities, developing an idea from a basic theme.

The subject's personality can be revealed in a wide variety of ways by the pose itself. There is no secret to discovering such poses—they are mostly fairly obvious. A subject who leans forward will appear aggressive, while one who leans back will appear either relaxed or submissive.

The graphic appearance of the body and clothes also have considerable effect on the viewer. Rounded shapes are soft and are often thought of as feminine, while sharp or angular patterns, with cutting eges, are aggressive or masculine. These shapes can be produced by the subject's arms or legs, often subtly. Arms, for example, may be folded across the chest to produce an angular, aggressive effect; or hands can be cupped around the face to give a pensive, possibly shy look. Including a subject's hands in a close-up shot introduces another element to what might otherwise be a rather bland picture of a face. The angle from which you take the shot can also affect appearances. Cecil Beaton, the English society photographer, often photographed women from above eye level because he said it made their faces appear heart-shaped. You can experiment with your subject by trying the same pose from above eye level, moving down as far as waist level. Given the

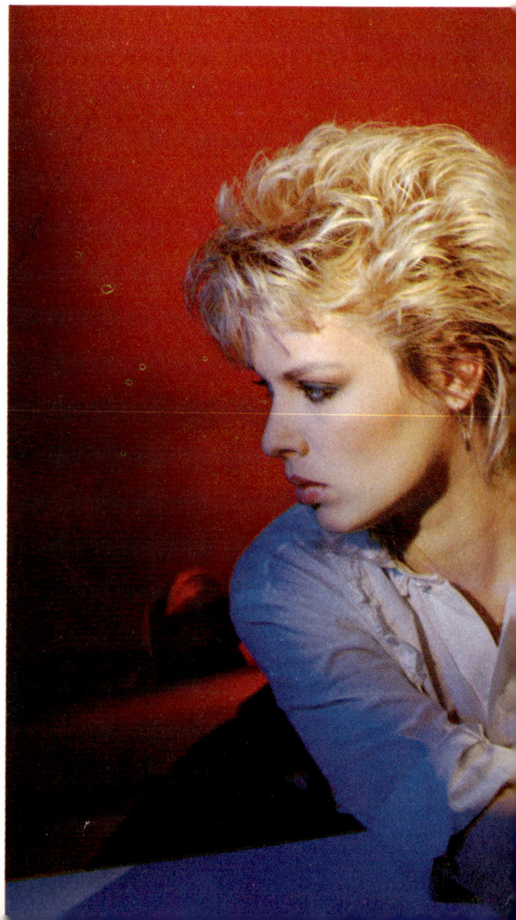

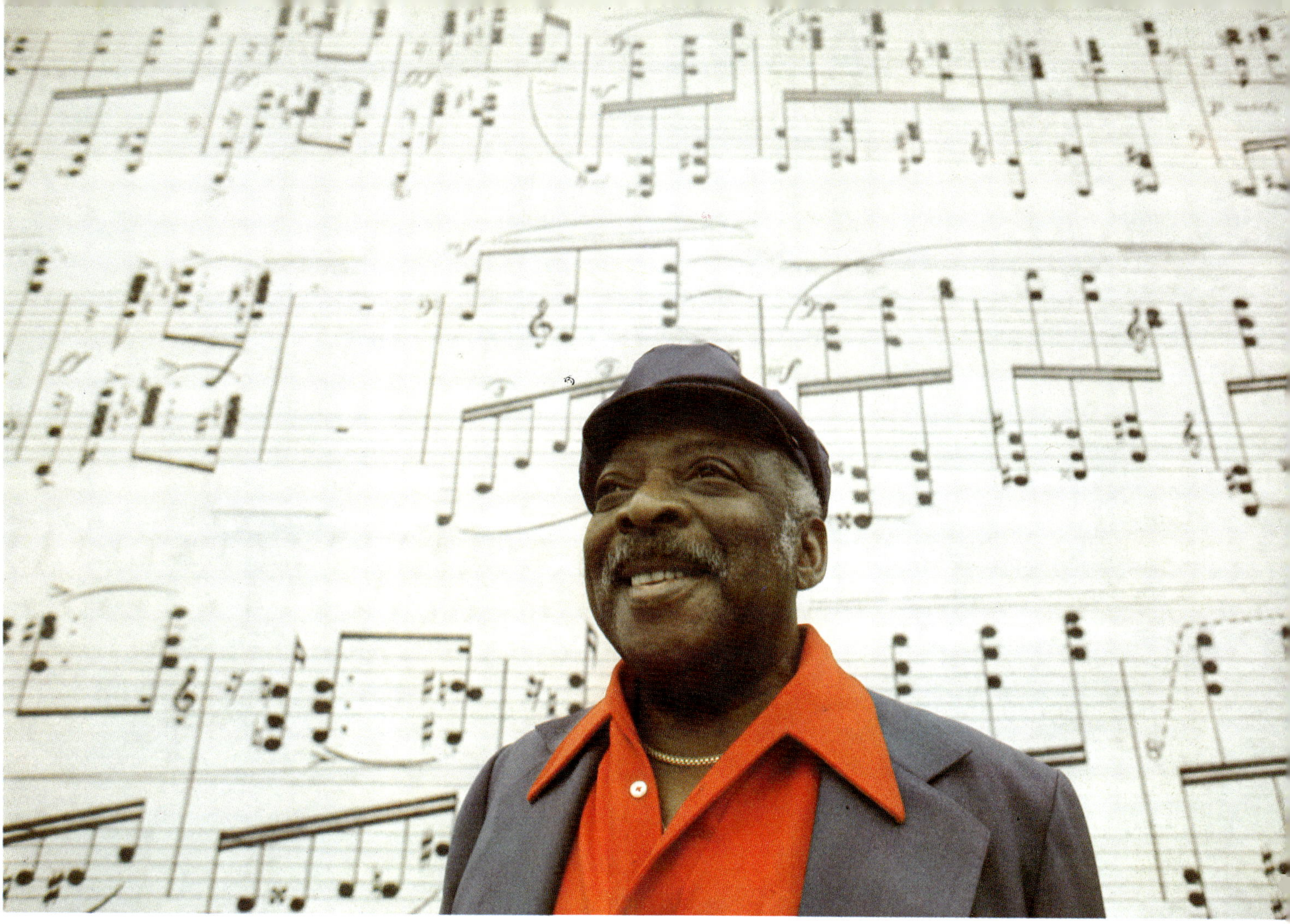

Man and his music *While backgrounds should usually be kept simple, there are always cases for breaking the rules*

Fashion designer *For portraits where the subject is positioned centrally, try using the surroundings as a frame*

Singer's profile *The sweeping lines formed by the arms balance the composition and give it strong, graphic qualities*

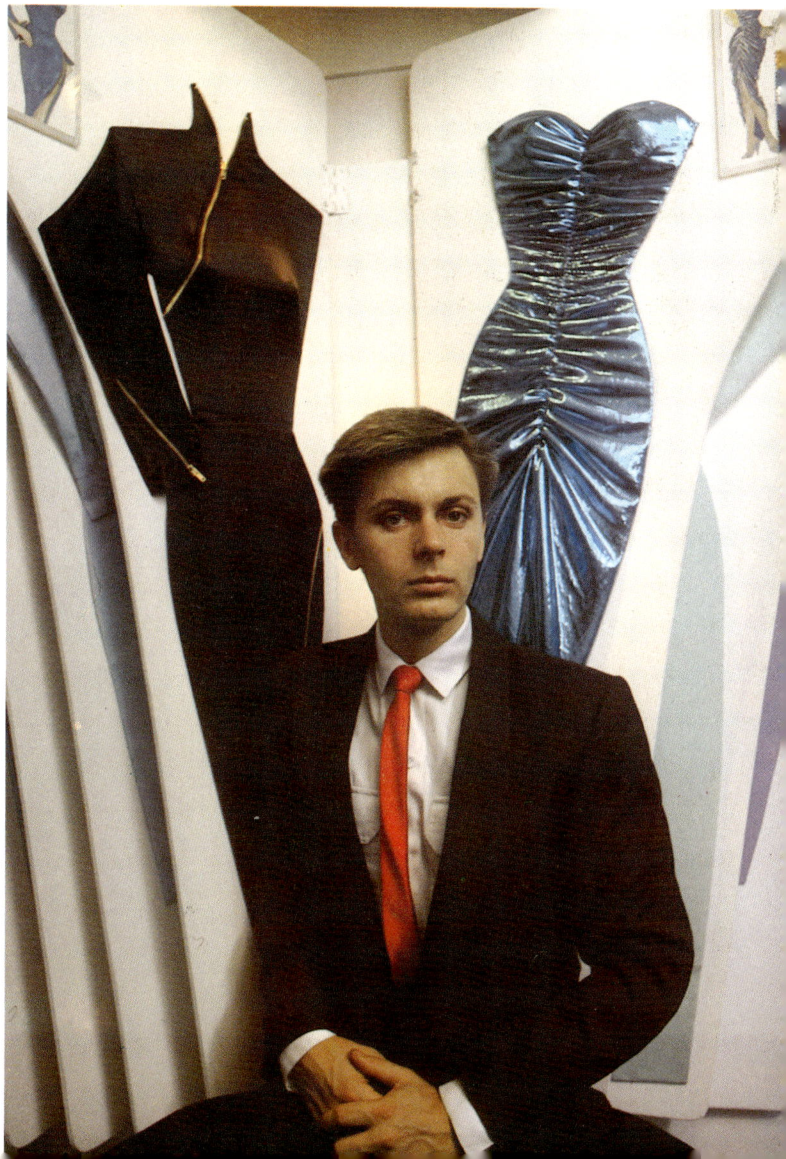

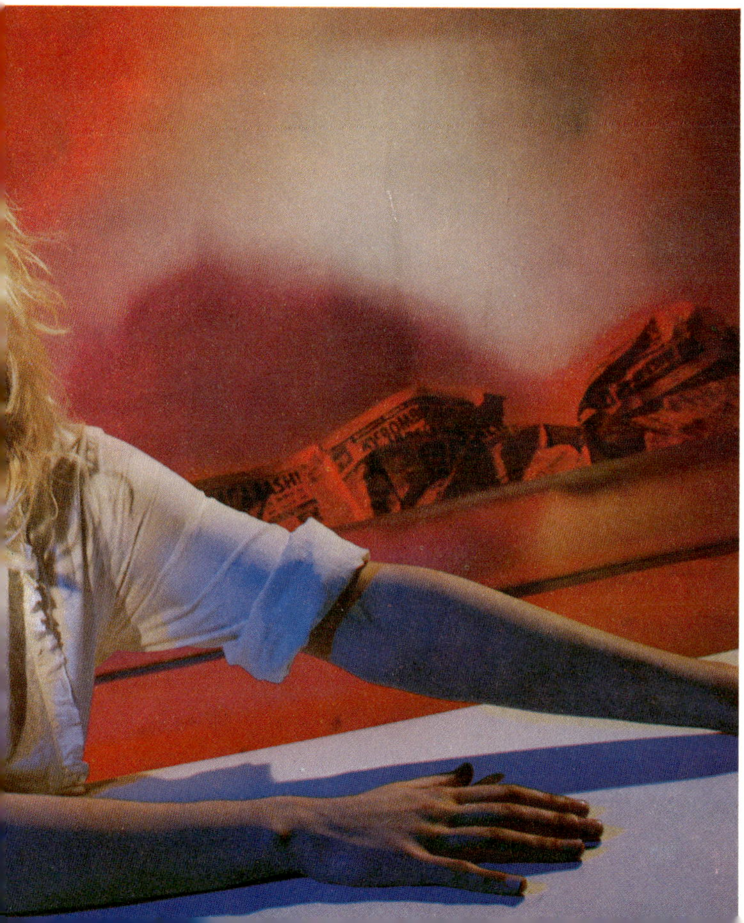

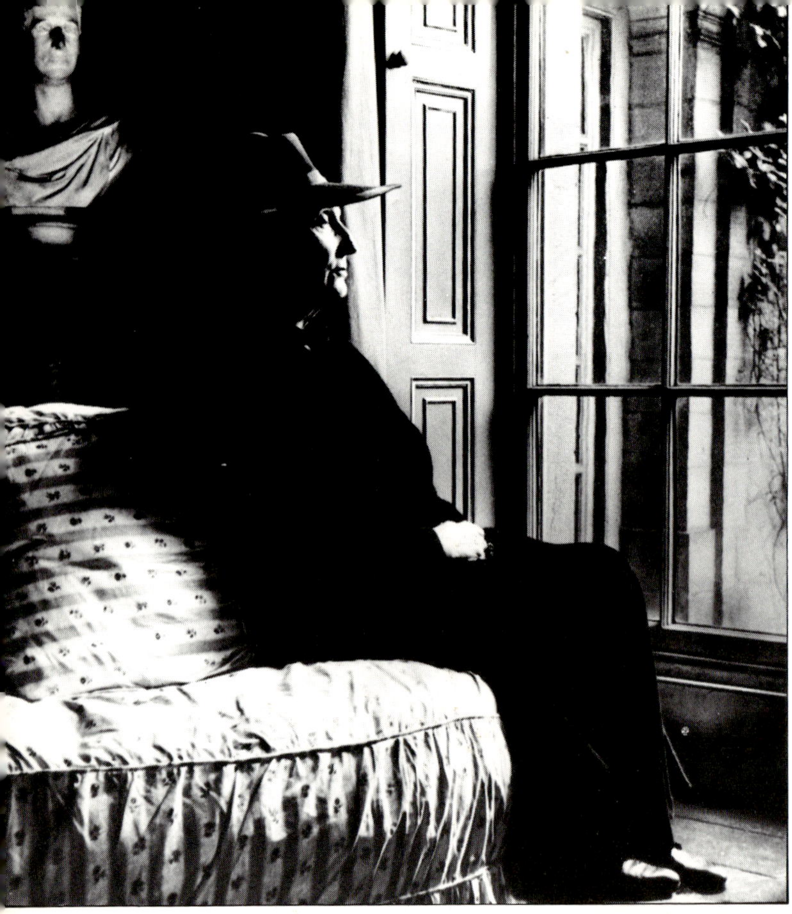

Window light *Daylight can be a very effective light source for portraiture and can also allow you to use the window itself as part of the shot*

Young girl *Flash can also be used in a way that simulates daylight. Here the directional illumination has been used to bring out the texture in the wall and to cast unusual, striking shadows*

Lana Turner *This has all the elements of a classic portrait—careful lighting, composition according to the rule of thirds and the bold shapes described by the subject's limbs*

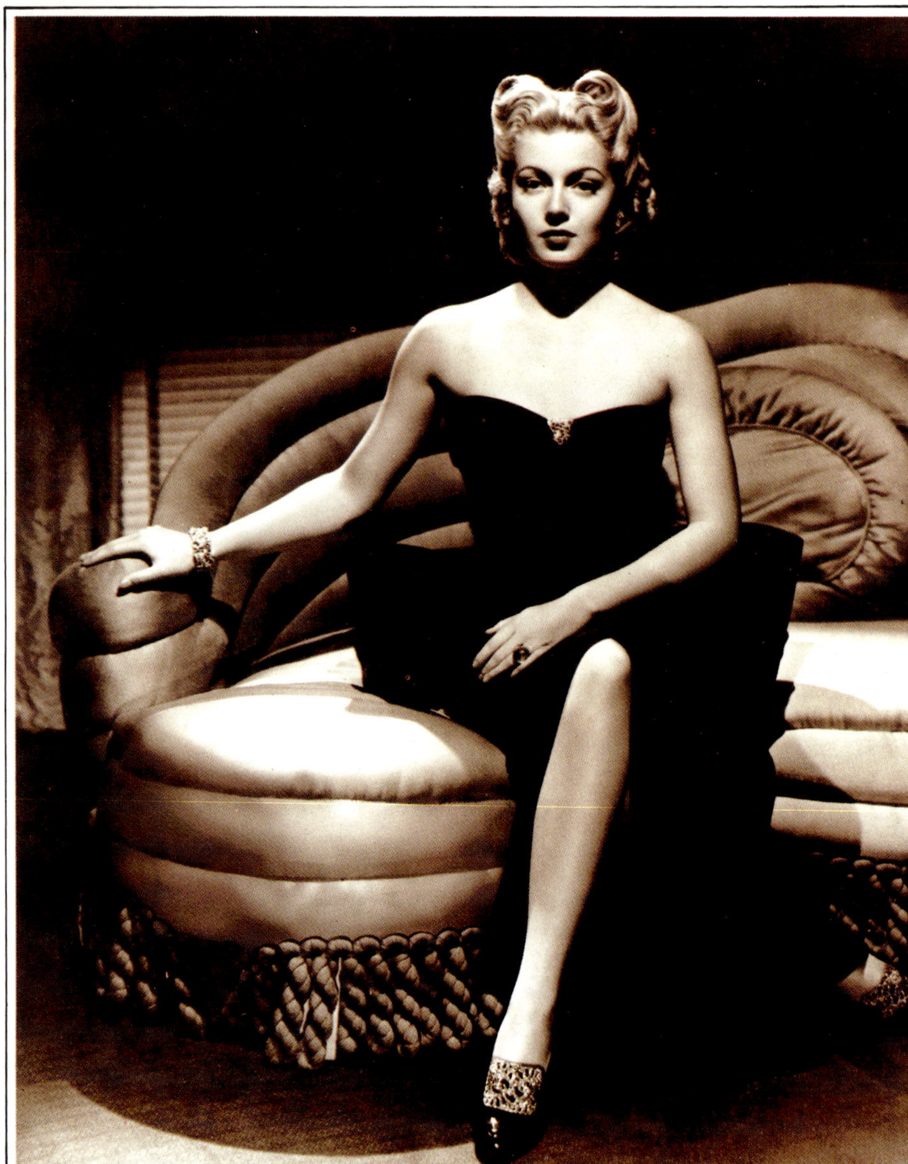

fairly long focal lengths common in portrait work, this is not as extreme as it sounds.

Other techniques used to reveal character are often aimed at helping the subject to lose self-consciousness. A profile, for example, enables them to look away from the camera, though they might find the result unflattering, as most people rarely see their profiles. Any imperfections of the profile, such as poorly shaped chins or noses, will become very obvious. To avoid this, yet still achieve a different pose, you can ask your subject to look away then look back at you. Using a rapid shutter speed or flash, take the picture when they are not quite facing you, though their eyes are looking at the camera.

For head and shoulders shots where the subject dominates the frame, there is just as much need for careful composition as with full length shots. One consideration is whether or not to frame the shot so that there is space around the edges or so the portrait fits exactly into the confines of the viewfinder. There is justification for both, depending on the effect you want to achieve. There is also a strong case for framing just a selected area—perhaps cropping out the top of the head, for instance.

There is also a need to think about whether or not the main subject should be framed centrally or to one side of the centre. General principles of composition apply just as much to portraiture as to landscape or any other type of photography, so that framing the main subject in accordance with the 'rule of thirds' is often a safe choice. Of course, though this does not have to be observed rigidly and it is a mistake to adhere strongly to a fixed set of rules.

Some portraits aim to flatter the individual, rather than reveal aspects of character. In this case, extremes are undesirable. A standard rule among portrait photographers is that you should never allow the subject to look down on you. Double chins become pronounced, wrinkles sag and you find yourself confronted with distended notrils. If in doubt, therefore, you should keep your viewpoint at or above eye level, foreshortening the face. Other techniques for flattering subjects are to use diffuse, fairly frontal, lighting to soften wrinkles, and to keep the main lighting above eye level, but not so high as to produce shadowed eye sockets. Bear in mind, too, that dark skinned people often prefer to appear lighter, while a fair skinned person will usually like to appear to have a tan. Ask your subject whether they have a good side, and ignore this information at your peril!

In formal portraits, backgrounds should be kept as simple as possible—unless you have a particular interest in trying to relate the subject to his or her surroundings or interests. Generally, the best background is either a plain wall or background paper—or even an expanse of sky. Watch out for distracting

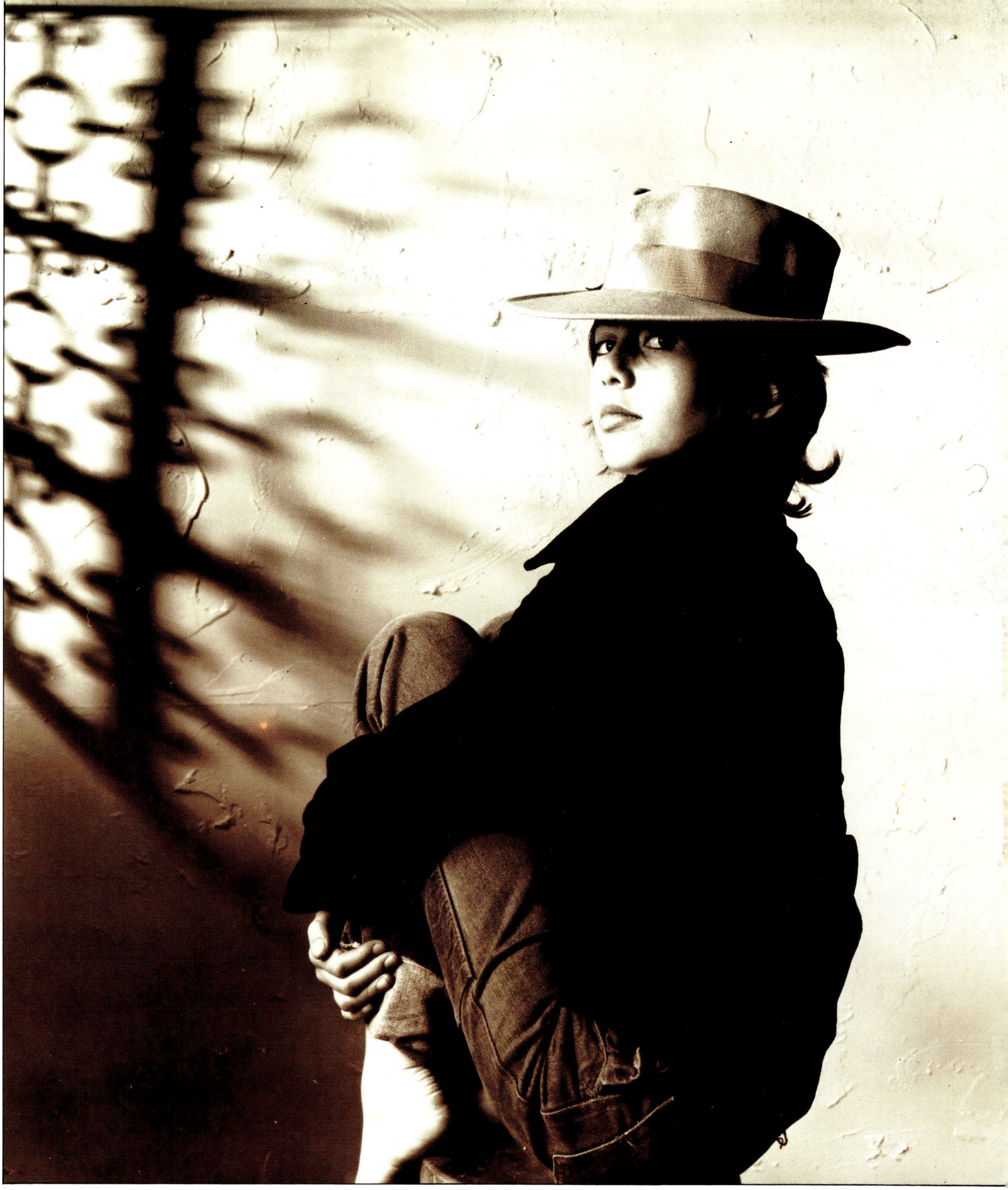

shadows, although, of course, it can be very effective to deliberately make a strong shadow part of the portrait.

In your search for an interesting and revealing portrait, it is a good idea to look at those taken by famous portraitists. There is often a clear style associated with each one, and with specific eras. Pictures taken in the first half of the century, for example, tended to be rather stylized and relied on strange or dramatic lighting for their originality. In the 60s, people became keen on lighting each shot with several lights—main light, fill-in, highlight (or kicklight) and maybe one or two others. This showed that the picture had been taken in a studio with plenty of facilities around. The trend since then has been towards more naturalistic photographs, often completely forsaking the studio in favour of everyday surroundings.

Photographers have tried a wide range of techniques to reveal character. Grain, blurring, contrast, multiple exposure, double exposure, montaging and practically every other technique can be added to the armoury of lighting and poses to reveal facets of character. It is inevitable that you may repeat ideas used by others, either knowingly or unwittingly, but the vast range of human characteristics makes it possible to treat every subject differently, so that each portrait is as individual as the person it represents.

Candid photography

Posed deliberately in front of the camera, nearly everyone becomes a little self-conscious. For this reason, many people feel that the only way to get natural and totally candid portraits is to catch people by surprise or, better still, without them knowing at all.

By exploiting the ability of the modern camera to freeze an instant, men and women can be pictured going about their lives in their normal environment, and fleeting expressions or moments of human drama can be transformed into striking permanent images. Taking pictures of people without their knowledge may seem a little unfair, but it certainly produces some fascinating results.

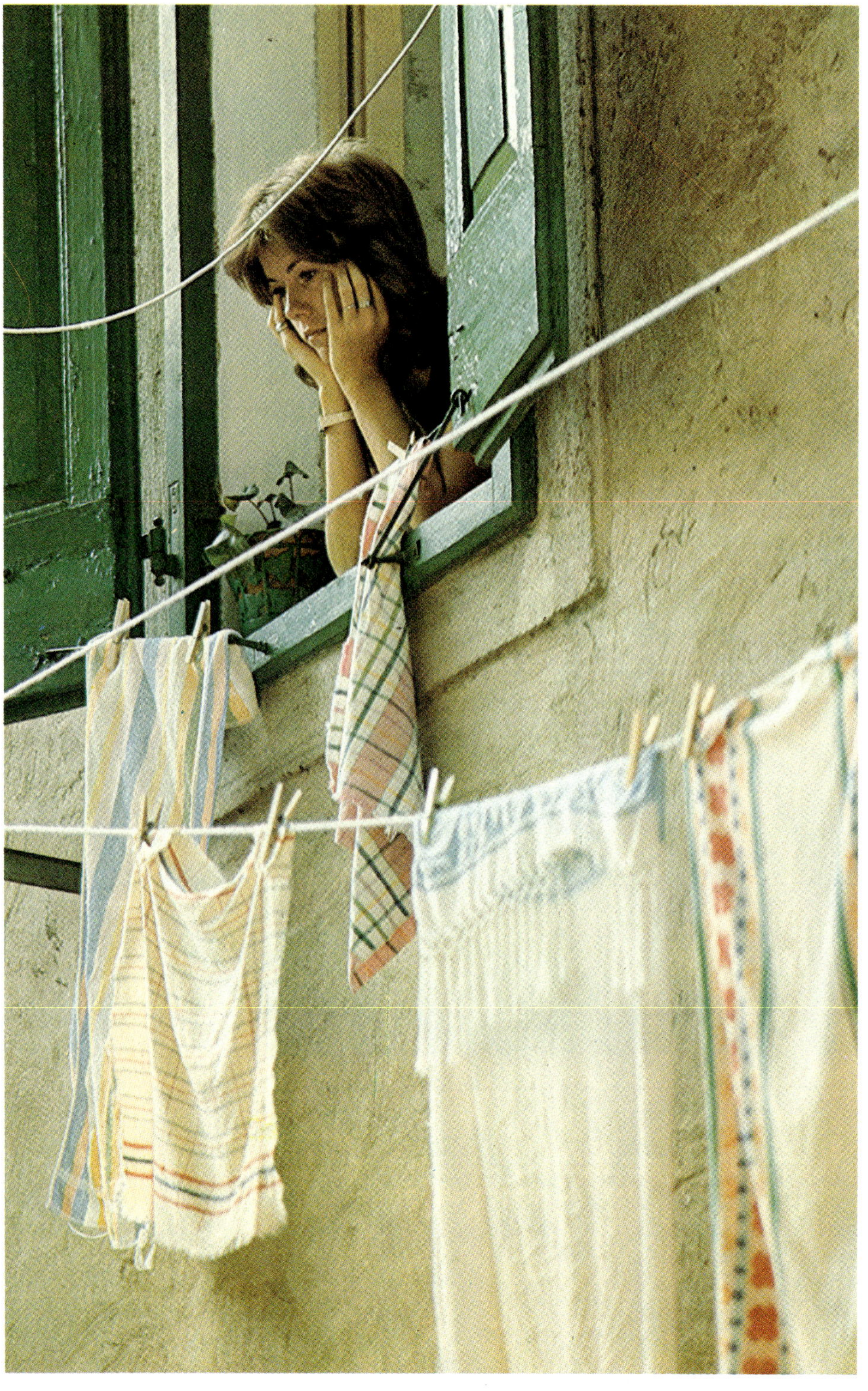

The word 'candid' means, literally, 'frankly truthful'. Related to photography, however, it has come to mean 'unposed', and candid photography can be approached in one of two ways. You can either go out deliberately to provoke a reaction and attract your subject's attention. Or you can try to avoid being noticed and try to capture life as it happens.

The fascination of the first approach is capturing people's snap response to the camera, whether it be surprise, hostility or laughter. It is an ideal way of taking informal portraits of friends and family, and many shots of this type are taken by framing up the subject unobtrusively, attracting their attention and then shooting. But it can also produce dramatic results in less familiar situations.

Surprise photographs of strangers, for example, can produce a whole variety of interesting responses. Strangers will react to the camera in different ways. Some will enjoy the attention and play up to the camera. Others may be resentful and sullen or even aggressive. Some may simply be surprised. Whatever the response, though, the results can be very revealing.

Reaction shots

Because most people react positively to the camera—if only to positively ignore it—press photographers and photojournalists often use this technique to portray people in their own environment. If, for instance, they want to illustrate life in a really depressed urban area, this sort of reaction shot often gives the impact that the photographer wants. It might be that the surprised or aggressive look on the subject's face is simply a response to the suddenness of the camera's intrusion, but the result conveys the tough environment far more strongly than any posed photo would.

In its extreme form, this sort of photojournalism becomes posed rather than candid and many colour supplement pictures are taken by placing the subject deliberately in his or her natural environment. A shepherd, therefore, would be photographed against a back-

Girl in a window *Washing-lines across the subject are usually distracting, but here they add to the natural look and to the moodiness of the picture*

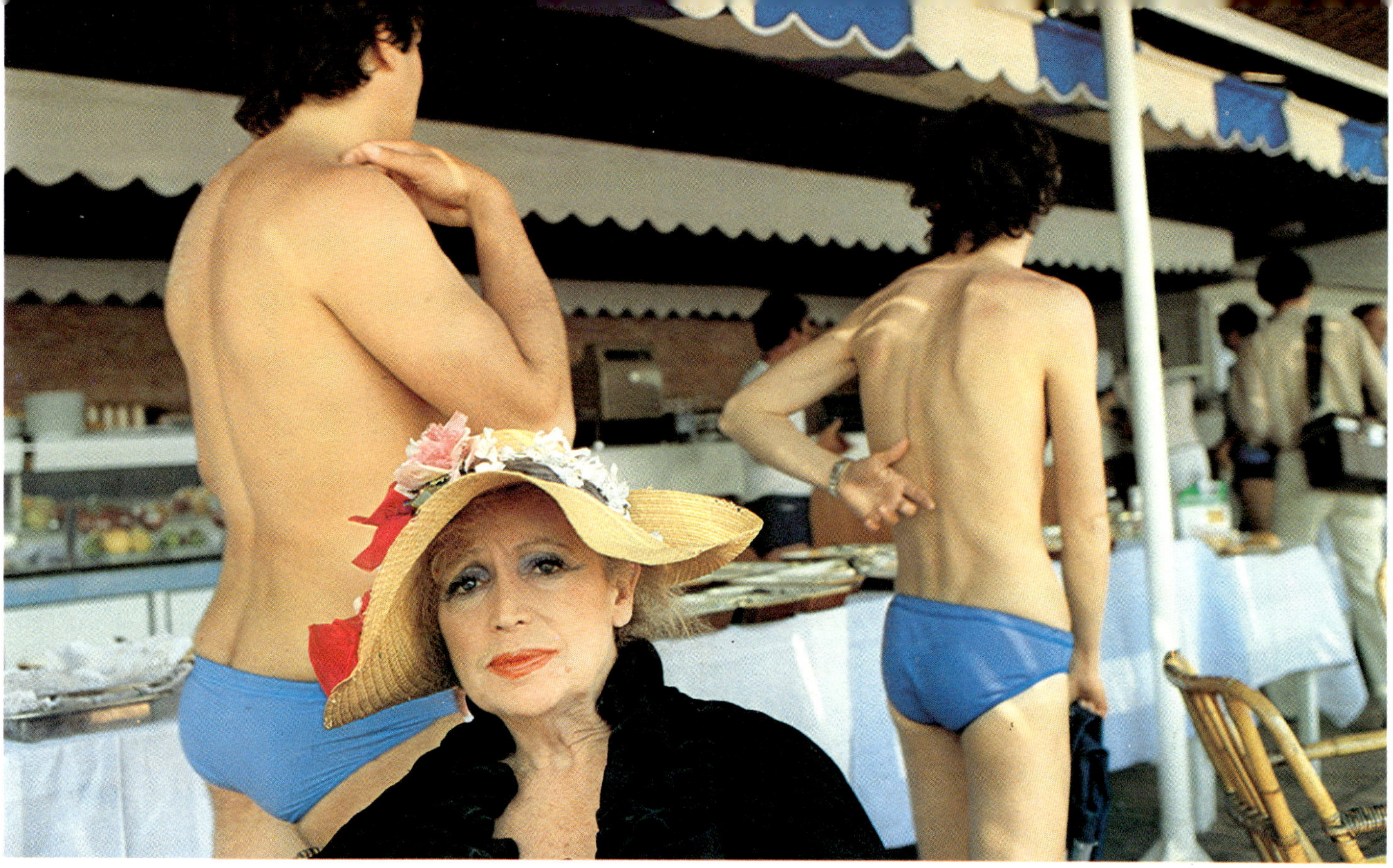

ground of sheep and green hills, a docker against ships and cranes and an architect against his own buildings.

The kind of response depends to a considerable extent on the photographer. An aggressive, impatient photographer will generally get a similar response and may be lucky if the hostility is only recorded on film. Unless that is the sort of photo you want, then you should behave with consideration towards your subject and remember that you are indeed intruding.

Whatever the response, though, these reaction shots are, to many photographers, rarely candid—truly candid shots are only taken when the subject is totally unaware that there is someone around with a camera. People are pictured doing normal things—sleeping, waiting for a bus, talking in the streets, buying the groceries—in their natural environment. The idea is to show people as they really are or to capture a fleeting moment of humour or pathos, anger or kindness. The camera must be a detached and totally unnoticed observer. The photographer's job is never to arrange the subject; but simply to spot the situation 'frame up' and decide on the moment to capture the situation with the maximum impact.

Shooting unobserved

This sort of picture can be taken anywhere—the only essential ingredient is people. As long as there are people around, there is potential for a candid shot. Crowded places naturally provide plenty of scope, but an isolated figure can often provide a poignant subject. But it is important that the photographer remains largely unobserved, and it helps if people are absorbed in their own activities rather than ready to look round at the first click.

Taking candid pictures unobserved on a crowded rush hour station, for instance, is generally fairly easy because everyone is concentrating on getting home. Unfortunately it can be difficult spotting potential subjects and getting them in focus in the fast moving crowd.

On a crowded beach, on the other hand, there is much less movement, but people are less absorbed in what they are doing. Not surprisingly, many candid beach pictures just show people asleep in deck chairs or reading newspapers. Places where movement is slow or predicatable but where everyone is sufficiently absorbed to leave the photographer unobserved make the best locations for candid photography. Markets have plenty of potential. So too have crowds at outdoor events.

Candid pictures often tend to be of older people or are set in working class urban districts. This is not necessarily because such subjects are more photogenic, but often because they are easier to photograph. In areas of densely populated terraced housing, there are usually plenty of people walking around; in affluent and spacious suburbs, the few people around tend to be in cars. Old people are similarly easier to photograph because they are generally slower moving and have more time to stop and pass the time of day with friends in the street. And while young people tend to be much the same the world over, older people often retain local dress and traditions.

Again, while candid shots are to be found anywhere at any time, there are occasions when it is easier to shoot unobtrusively. In summer, plenty of people are on the streets and there are many potential subjects. In winter, on the other hand, there are fewer people around, but you tend to be less obtrusive, particularly if you wear a heavy coat to conceal your camera. It is possible to stand shooting for hours on a street corner on a gloomy winter's day without anyone noticing, but you will be spotted instantly in your shirt sleeves in the summer sunshine.

Lady *Candid photographs can be direct and revealing portraits, but shots like this require an eye for an arresting face, a gentle approach and a sure technique*

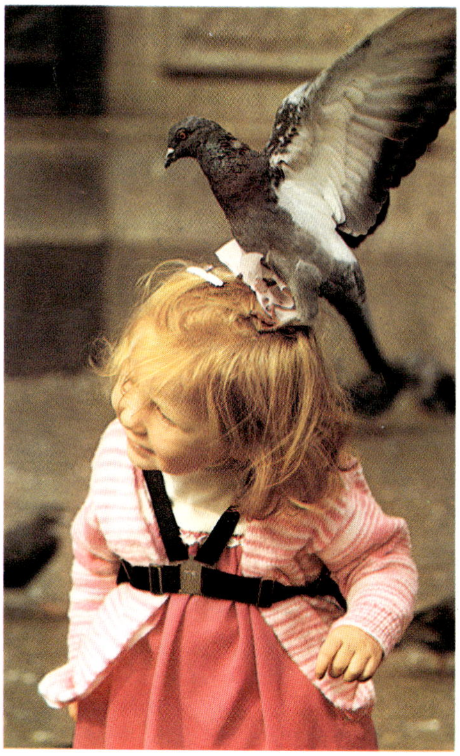

A bird on the head *Children make ideal subjects for candid work, so when out with children keep your camera prepared for amusing moments*

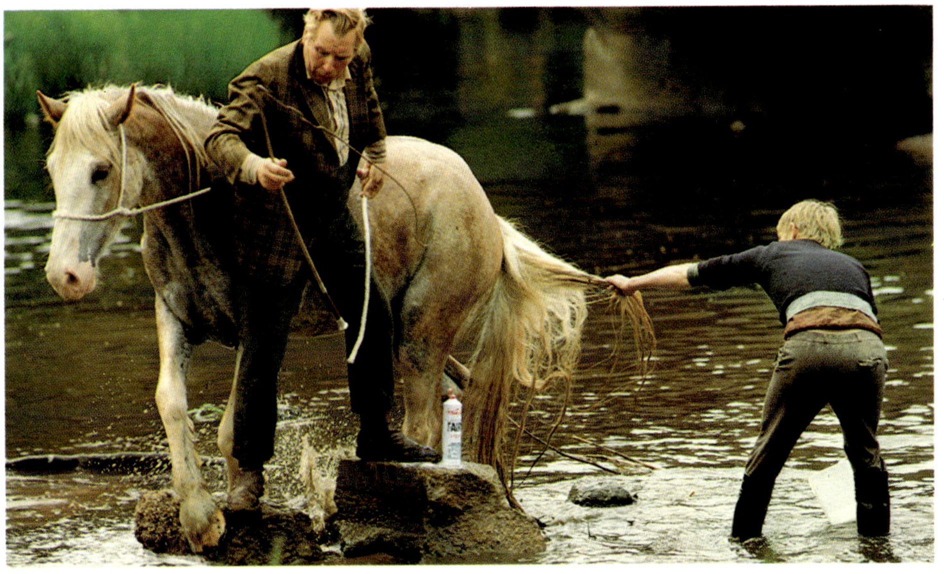

Washing the pony *People absorbed in some task are again ideal for candid shots and you often have time to compose your picture leisurely and properly*

But wherever and whenever you go out to take candid pictures, it is important to attract the minimum attention. Bright, flashy clothes are clearly out, but so too is a flashy, aggressive manner. The best candid shots are taken not by a cartoon-image loud, khaki-clad press photographer bristling with lenses and equipment, but by the quiet observer.

If you cannot help being noticed when you arrive at your location, wait for a while and let people get used to you and your camera before you start shooting in earnest. Unfortunately, you will rarely remain unobserved for long and even if your subject does not react, other people, may interrupt your activities. If this happens, you must be patient and polite—any sort of argument will ruin the situation—and carry on shooting if possible.

Many photographers avoid candid photography because they find it embarassing, particularly if they are noticed. There are no easy answers to this problem and it is up to the individual photographer to overcome it. However, many of the most experienced candid photographers suffered from self-consciousness when they started and gaining confidence is largely a matter of practice. Nevertheless, it may be worth going along to the local amateur dramatic society to take pictures during rehearsals. Obviously you must get permission first, but most actors and actresses will be only too pleased to have their performances on film. This should help you become accustomed to the idea of taking impromptu shots of people before you try your technique on total strangers.

It is often thought that the best way to take candid pictures without being noticed is to use all sorts of elaborate equipment—concealed cameras, subminiatures, telephotos—but these are usually unnecessary. Indeed, people are understandably suspicious and resentful of these 'sneaky' techniques and in some countries the surreptitious use of a miniature camera can be positively dangerous. Some people suggest that a twin-lens reflex camera, of the sort traditionally used by wedding photographers, held at waist level is the ideal for candid work because it is much less obvious when you shoot. But you can generally take pictures much faster with an SLR, and an eye-level viewpoint is generally more pleasing, although it may be worth bending down or shooting from above to create a bit of variety.

There is one drawback to using an SLR, however, and that is its noisiness. While it is very useful to be able to focus quickly and accurately, the system that allows you to do this, with a mirror that must flip out of the way before the

Crowd shots *Spectators at a sports event make good subjects—they are usually too absorbed to notice cameras. Try to concentrate on a few faces*

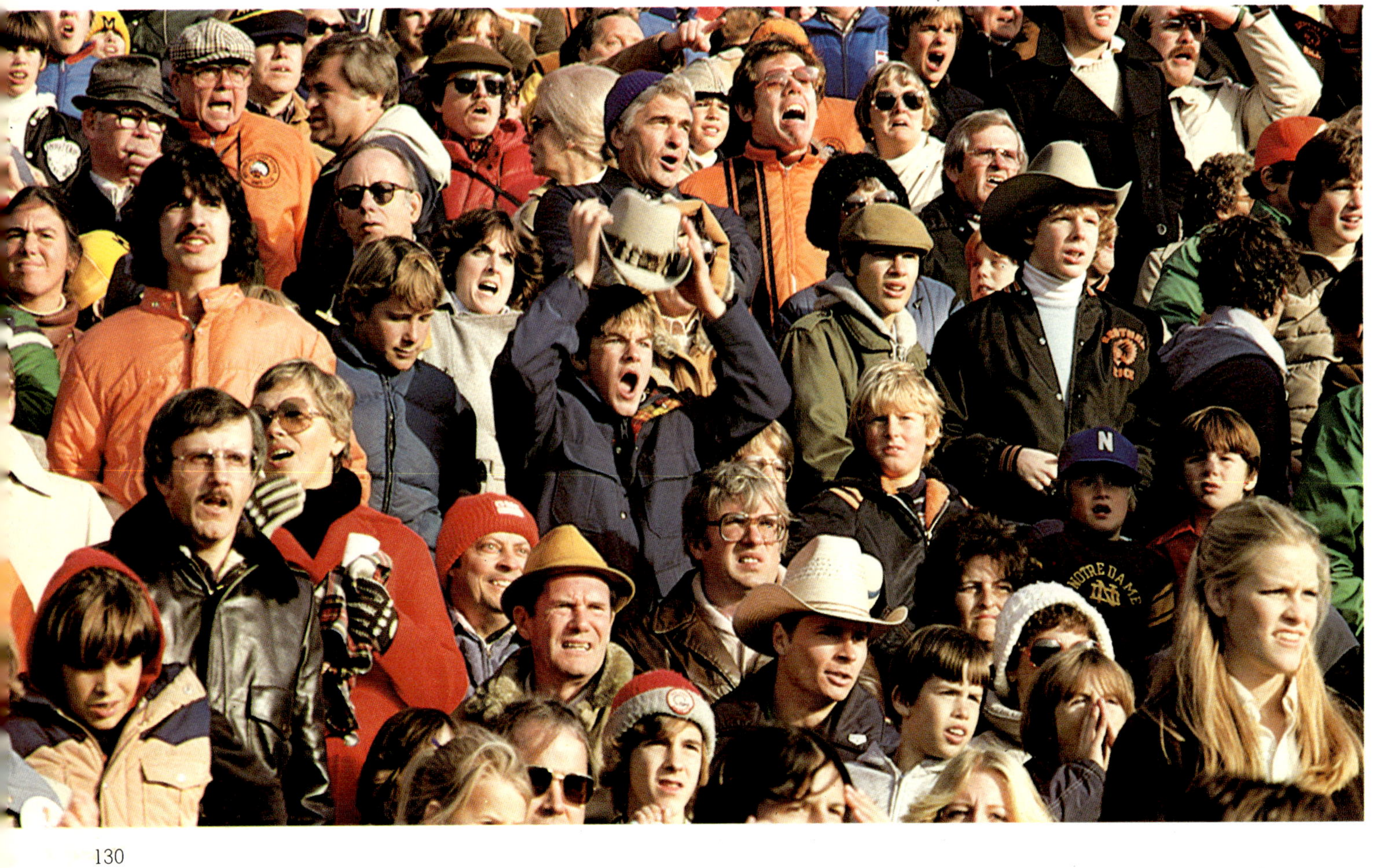

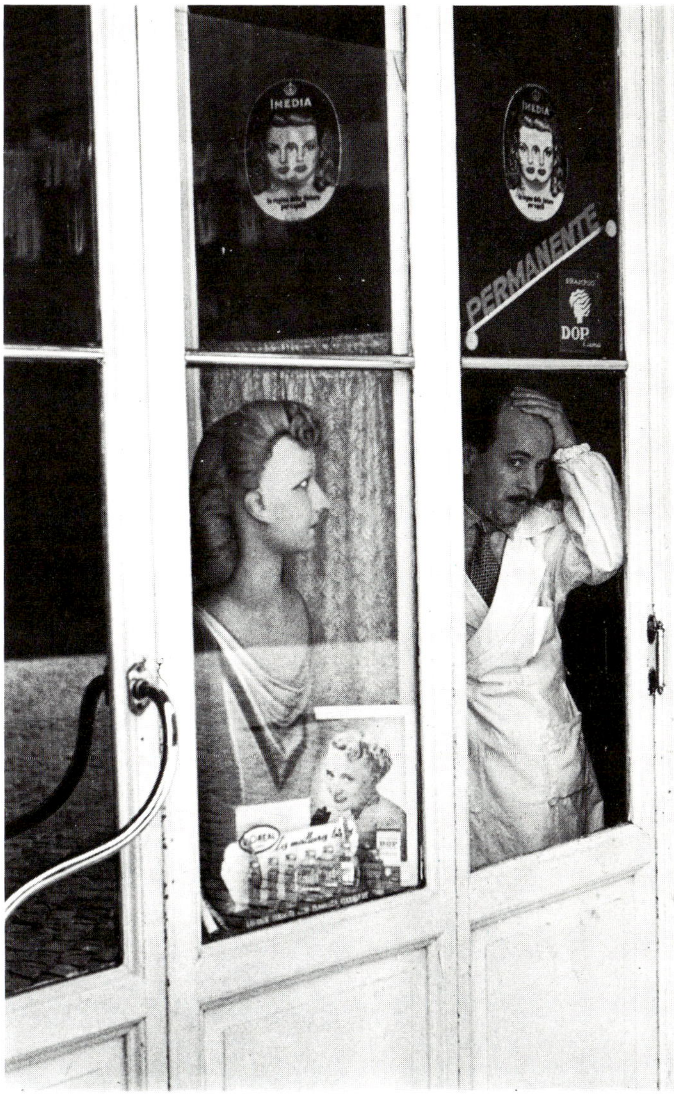

Hair today? *Photographs like this need a keen eye for humour and an ever ready camera—this belongs to the master of the candid shot, Henri Cartier-Bresson*

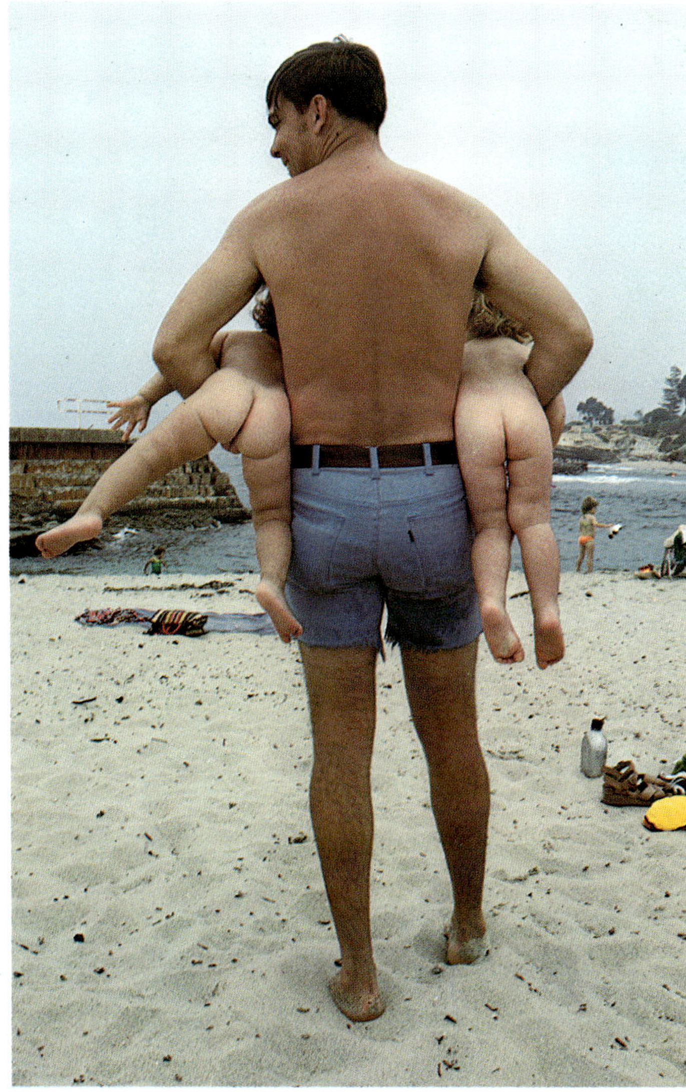

On the beach *With people at play and plenty of light, crowded holiday beaches provide plenty of scope for catching revealing moments on film*

picture can be taken, gives a noticeable click as you press the shutter.

Some SLRs are less noisy than others, but quietest of all are non-SLRs which do not have mirrors or focal plane shutters. This is where compact cameras come into their own, since they generally have comparatively silent leaf shutters. Twin-lens reflex cameras, of the sort mentioned above, also have leaf shutters and offer the additional advantages of accurate focusing and interchangeable lenses.

Speed is perhaps the most important factor in candid photography—not so much the shutter speed or the speed of the film, but the speed with which you can decide on the framing, focusing and exposure, and take the shot. Any time lost here may lose you the picture or may give your subject time to see you. Automatic exposure and focusing certainly help in this respect, but neither of these will make much difference if you are not alert or, more significantly, unfamiliar, with your equipment. It is essential to be completely at home with your camera if you are to operate quickly and unobtrusively. Seconds spent fumbling with the focusing and aperture can only help draw attention and may prove embarrassing. The famous candid photographer, Henri Cartier-Bresson, once claimed to be able to adjust the focus, aperture and shutter speed while the camera was still in his pocket!

In fact, it is rarely necessary to readjust all the settings for each individual shot. When you go out for a day of candid photography in a particular location, the same settings will probably be adequate for most of the day, unless you go into dark shadows or shoot from extremely close quarters. On a bright, cloudy day outdoors, for instance, a setting of *f*/8 at 1/125 of a second will give the correct exposure in most candid situations. It will also give you reasonable depth of field and you can be sure that if you set the focus to around 3 metres, or whatever the average shooting distance is, your picture will probably be sharp.

Candid lenses

There is something to be said for all focal lengths and lens types. A telephoto will allow you to fill the frame without getting too close and may get you pictures of inaccessible subjects, but the result will look as distant and detached as indeed you are. Pictures taken with a standard or wide angle lens are far more immediate and involved, but have to be taken at a much closer range. Nevertheless, you may be able to photograph someone with a wide angle lens even if he sees the camera if you only include him or her at the edge of the frame—people rarely believe they are being photographed unless the camera is pointing straight at them. Furthermore, such a lens will include some background—often invaluable to help place subjects in their normal environments. Most professionals are happiest with a standard lens, or a 28-50 mm zoom, and only use a long lens when absolutely necessary.

However you tackle candid photography, you must remember that not everyone appreciates having their picture taken, particularly if the result could be embarrassing. Indeed, it is well known that some people, such as the African Masai tribe, find it highly worrying. The Masai believe that if you take their picture you take away their souls—though they may accept financial compensation. Either way, you must consider the feelings of the people you photograph. It might be a nice gesture to offer them a copy of your final shot.

CHAPTER 12
SPORT
Outdoor events

Few subjects provide a greater range of photogenic material than sport. Action and drama, atmosphere and colour—sport has it all. Whatever type of picture you want to take, a sporting event seems to offer a wealth of possibilities.

Action is there in abundance—the athlete sprinting for the ribbon, the burly forward powering his way out of a ruck—but there are many other photographic opportunities. If you want pictures of human drama, for instance, what better place to look than on the sports field?

If you are simply looking for attractive pictures, there is endless potential in the grace of the gymnast or the sparkle and colour of windsurfing. And when there is little happening on the field of play there are usually plenty of fascinating shots to be found in the crowd.

So where do you go to take good sports photos? Good pictures can be taken anywhere, at any sporting event, and it requires the skill of the photographer to seek them out. Nevertheless, some sports are much easier to photograph than others.

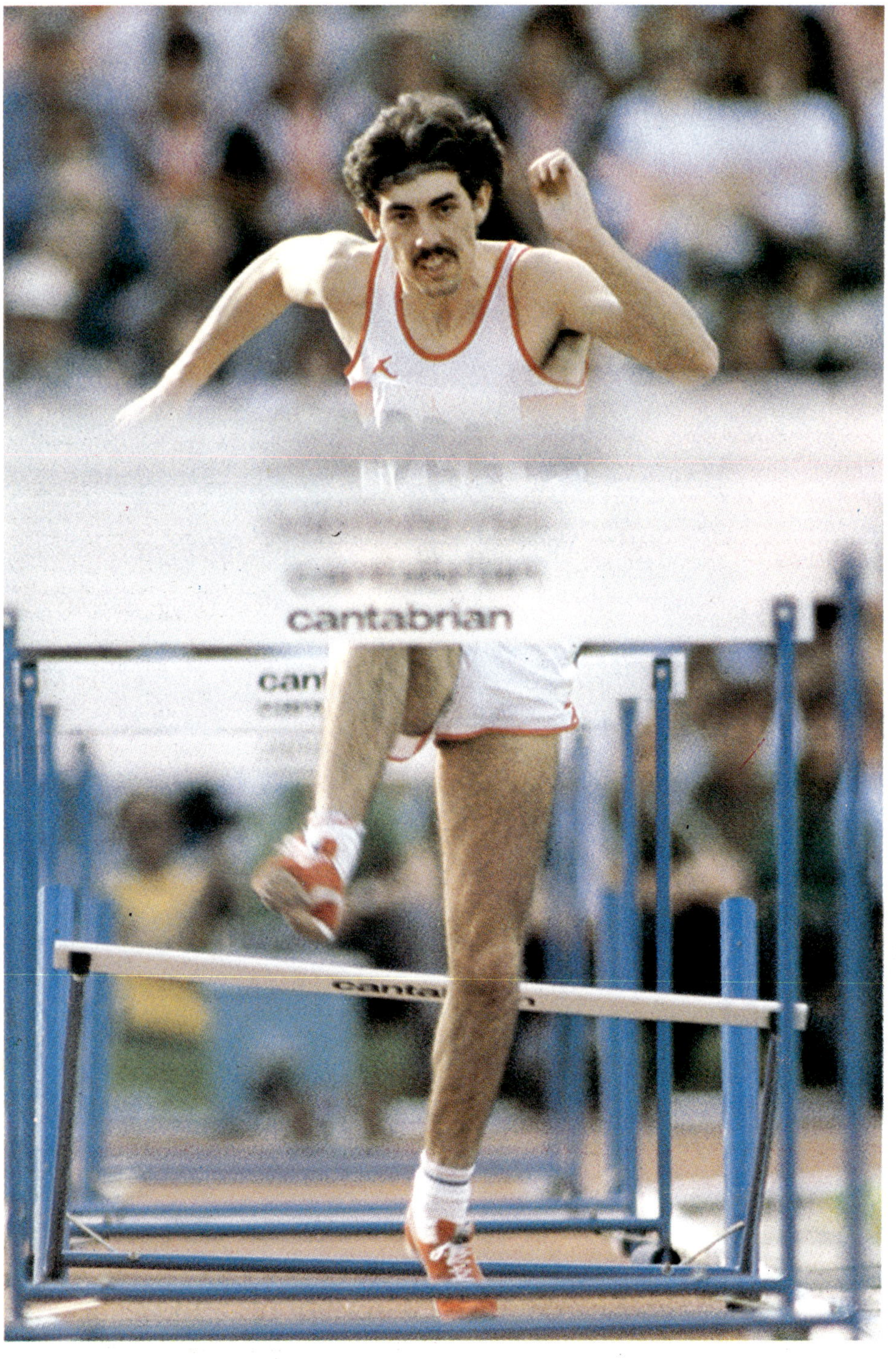

Pulling for focus *For shots like this, with crowd and hurdles nicely blurred, you must 'pull' the focus carefully to keep the moving athlete sharp*

Looking for action

Any sport where there is plenty of natural action makes an excellent starting point for the budding sports photographer. Rugby's heaving scrums, crushing tackles and flying touch-downs provide plenty of scope for action shots. Tennis and football provide similarly good opportunities. And if you are able to get there, you can hardly go wrong with an Alpine skiing event for subject matter, with its high speed twists and turns, dramatic take-offs and spectacular falls. Although the vast expanse of snow presents a number of technical problems with exposure, these are easily overcome by careful positioning and judicious use of a light meter. Basically, though, any sport with plenty of large scale moments makes a good subject.

Where action is slow or small scale, however, exciting pictures can be difficult to find. Cricket might seem to be the obvious example, and certainly it is not an easy sport to cover, but there are many shots to be had in the bowler's run-up and delivery, and, because much of the action takes place in the same position every time, the camera can always be ready to fire at the right moment. While cricket may be slow moving for television, the photographer with the still camera can isolate the sporadic moment of high drama to create surprisingly lively pictures.

Getting exciting pictures from golf or swimming, on the other hand, is a real challenge. If you watch golf regularly you may have noticed that photographers never press the shutter until after the golfer hits the ball—otherwise the sound of a hundred shutters clicking simultaneously might put him off his stroke. In the normal course of events, then, there are little more than three basic golfing action shots—the follow-through on the tee shot, down on the fairway and in the bunker. It is possible to get good golfing shots, but it is far from easy.

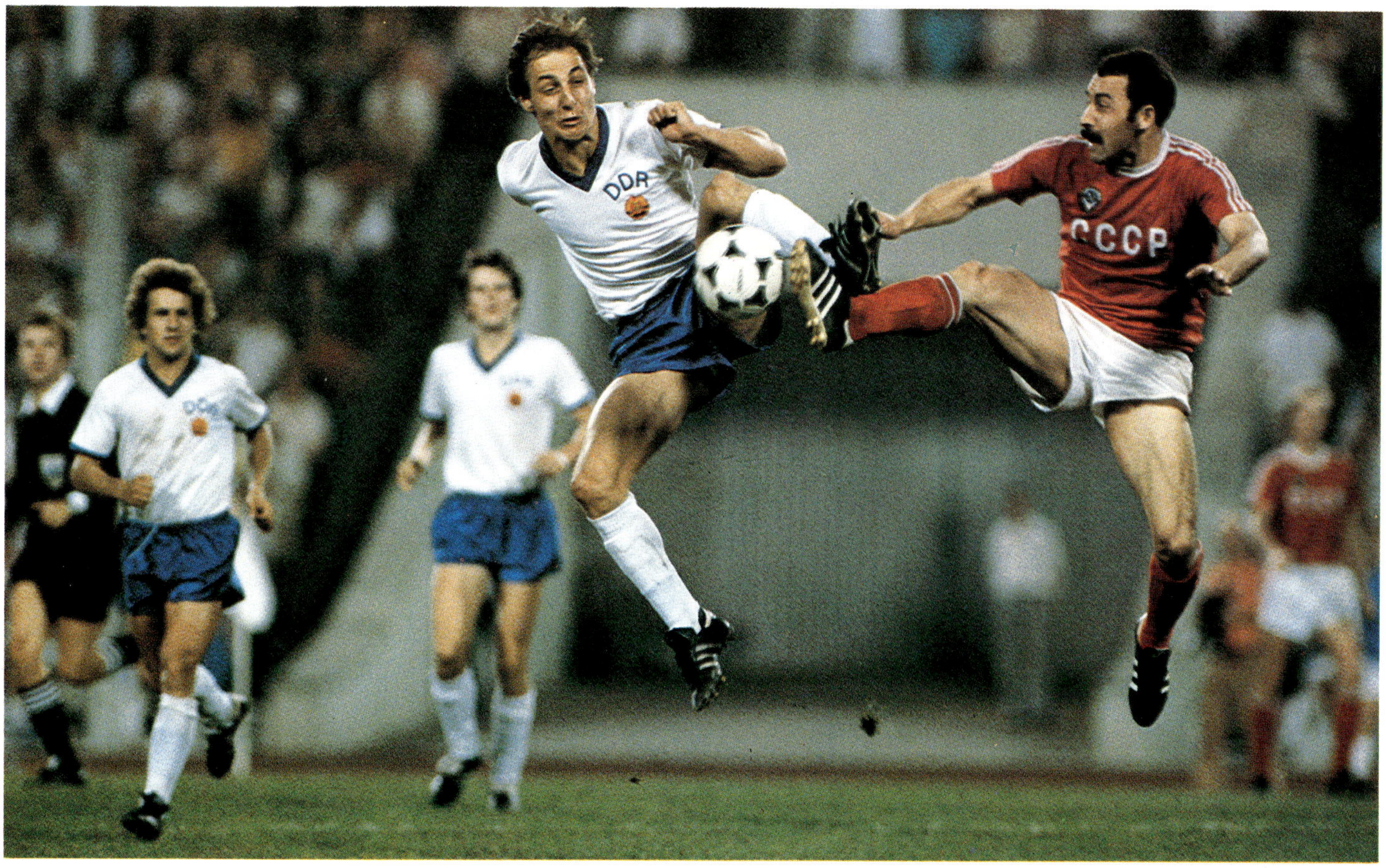

Good swimming pictures are possibly even harder to come by since much of the action takes place below water—often all you can see is a slow moving head hidden beneath a black bathing cap. Certainly a row of swimmers plunging into the water at the start of a race can be spectacular, but everyone else shoots at the same moment!

Choose a sport with plenty of movement at first, and move on to the more awkward subjects when you have some experience behind you, unless you have a particular interest in an event.

Personal interest is certainly a big advantage because, if you know the game well, you will have a good idea where to stand to capture the heart of the action and you will know when to expect dramatic moments. If you know little about the sport you intend shooting, read up about it before the day. No more than a basic working knowledge is necessary.

Shooting football *With the grandstand out of focus, this superbly caught peak-of-the-action shot comes across strongly*

Pro v. amateur

The glamour of professional sport acts like a magnet to photographers, and at any major event dozens of hopeful cameramen, both professional and amateur, are to be seen waiting around for the big moment. With so much competition, the chances of getting a good position to shoot from are not very high—even the professionals have problems. Most big venues have limits on the numbers of photographers they allow on the field and the chances of an amateur being given permission to sit on the pitch during a major football match or on the Centre Court at Wimbledon are extremely small.

Yet while the big names of sport make the headlines, they do not necessarily make good photographs. A tiny figure in the corner of the frame against a distracting background does not make a very exciting picture, even if the figure is a superstar—there are already thousands of bad pictures of any major personality. It is far better to get a good position at an amateur event than a bad position at a big professional game.

Many of the great sports pictures of history have been shot by amateurs at obscure events. There is always scope for pictures wherever you are. Because it is live action, there is always a chance of something unexpected happening whether you are at a Saturday kick-around or the Cup Final, and it is the element of surprise that makes sports photography exciting.

When it comes to the ideal range of equipment for sports photography no two people agree, because different situations require different treatment. At a tennis match, for instance, professionals shooting from the courtside tend to use a 135 mm lens for whole body shots up to the net and anything between 180 mm and 300 mm for baseline

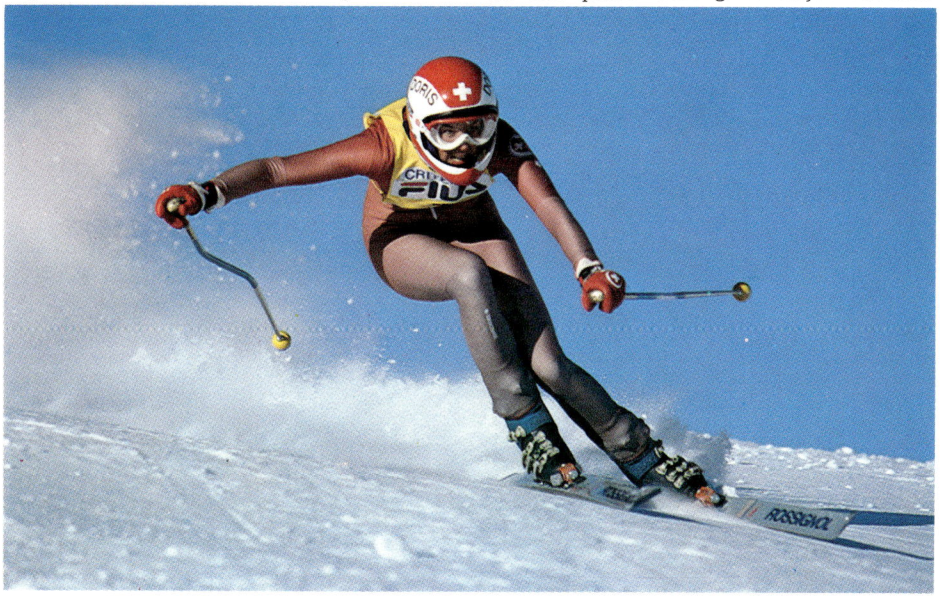

Winter sports *With plenty of light, bright colours and an abundance of dramatic action, ski events offer tremendous scope for the photographer*

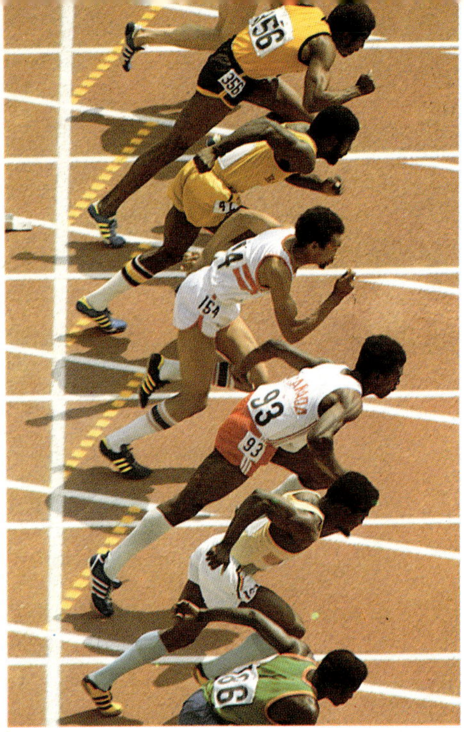

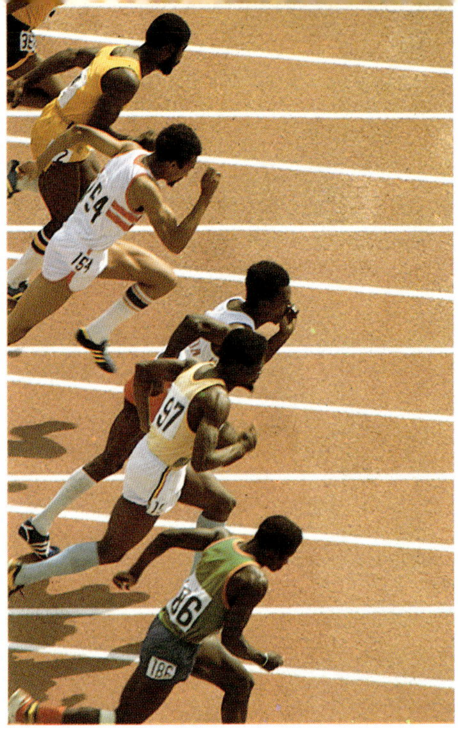

Creating drama *Without thoughtful composition, the intense drama of the sports field can often be lost. While both of these pictures are pleasing, that on the left has more tension because the front runners, closer to the leading edge of the frame, seem to be straining to get out of the picture*

rallies. At a football match their choice would be completely different. Then, unfortunately, most amateurs do not have such freedom of choice.

You can get good results with virtually any camera and standard lens, given the right conditions, but probably the best combination is a basic 35 mm SLR with a 200 mm telephoto. The advantages of the telephoto over the standard lens are quite significant. A telephoto allows you to single out the interesting areas and blur out background distractions by differential focusing. But above all it moves you right into the heart of the action so that you fill the frame with your subject. Anything bigger than 200 mm, though, would be unwieldy and difficult to use.

A zoom lens might seem an obvious choice for a sports photographer, providing a whole range of focal lengths and allowing him to switch his attention from one part of the field to another and still fill the frame. But most professionals use a zoom only for special effects or when conditions restrict them to carrying a single lens. In normal conditions, a fixed focal length telephoto offers equivalent or superior performance and a wider maximum aperture for a given weight.

If you are using a telephoto, you will almost certainly need some sort of support for the camera. Hand held 200 mm shots can be taken, but the results are rarely completely sharp. A monopod—a one-legged version of a tripod—is probably the best solution. It is light, easy to carry, needs the minimum of space to erect and allows you complete freedom of movement with the camera, far more than a tripod with even the best pan-and-tilt head. Professionals find a monopod indispensable.

One other piece of equipment that may be useful though by no means essential, if you are keen on sports photography, is a motor drive for winding on the film automatically. Because in many sports the action happens so quickly, you have to keep your eye to the viewfinder all the time. Look away even for a second to wind on and you may miss a terrific picture. A motor drive solves this problem, though it can only be fitted to a camera designed to take one.

As for film, this depends on the weather conditions more than anything. The speed of the action tends to suggest a fast film for maintaining fast shutter speeds, but except in really gloomy conditions a fast film can be more of a nuisance than a help. Fast films tend to produce grainy results, and on a bright day they prevent you from opening the aperture to blur the background. In most conditions a fairly slow or medium speed

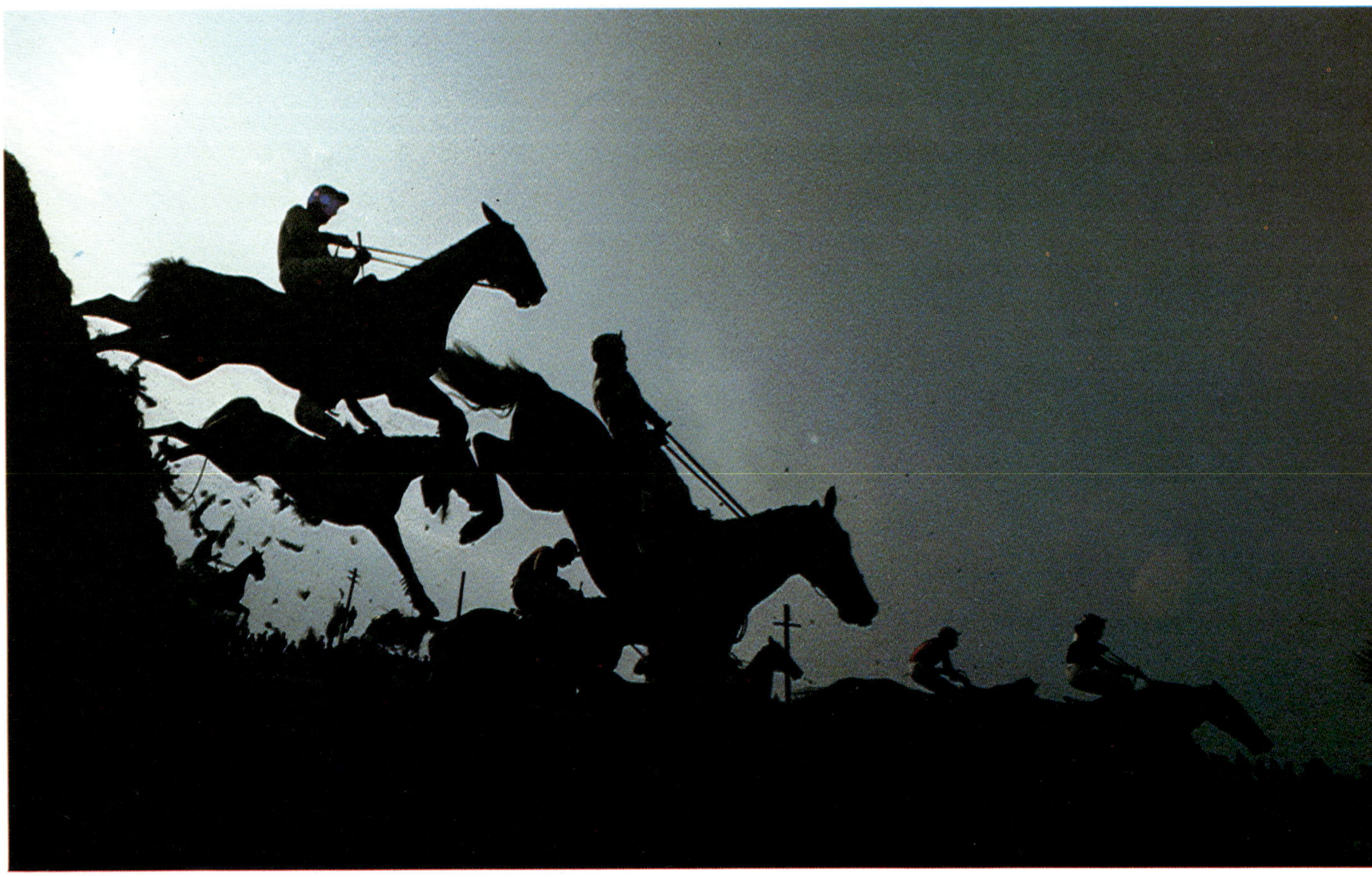

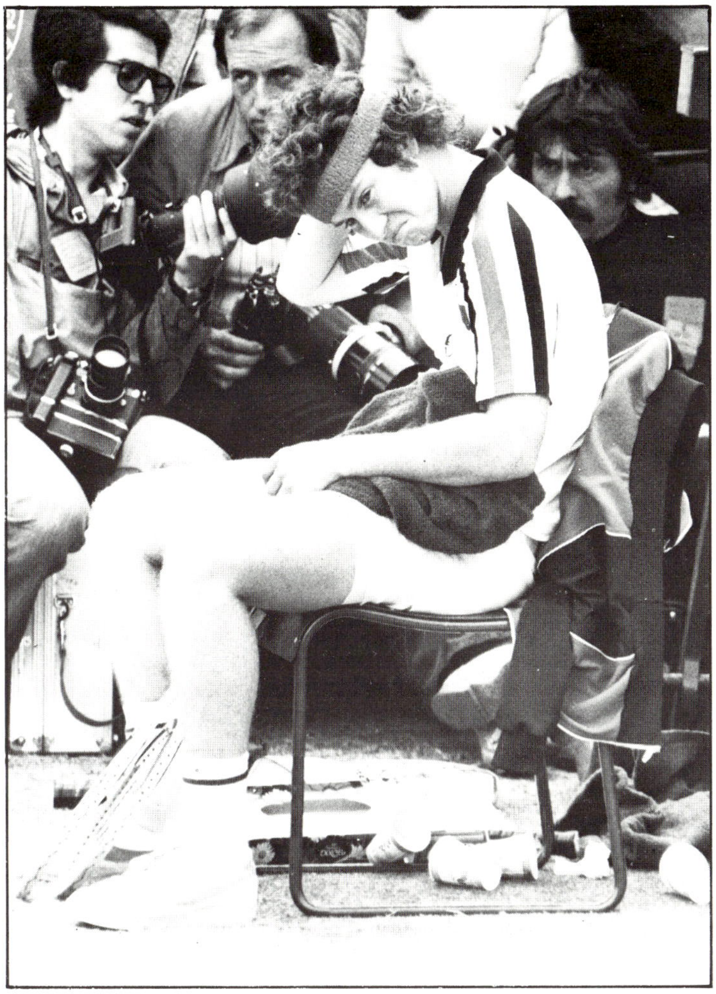

Exhaustion *It is the human element that often makes sports photographs—look out for the reactions of players in between the action*

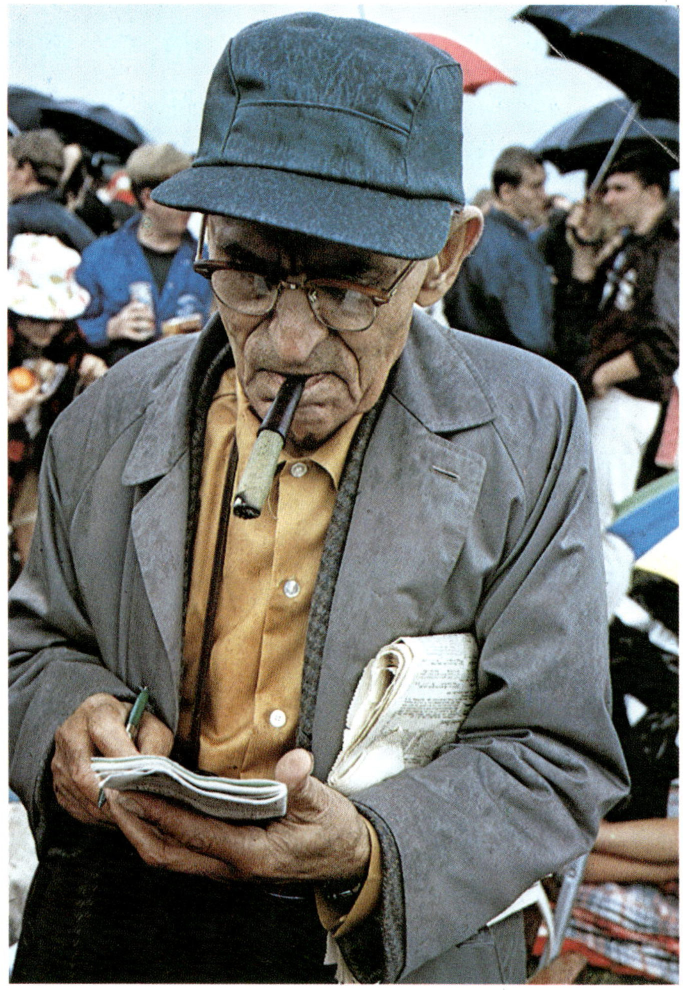

Candid shots *If there is nothing happening on the field, there is often tremendous potential for candid shots among the crowd of spectators*

film—in the range 64 to 100 ASA (ISO)—is fine, but in a fickle climate it is probably a good idea to take along a faster film—a 200 or even a 400 ASA in case the light closes in.

With continuous action on the field, there is a great temptation to shoot with a high shutter speed all the time. Although you can't go far wrong by doing this, it does not necessarily produce the most interesting pictures. It is true that high shutter speeds freeze the action and also allow you to use a wide aperture to isolate the subject against a blurred background. Indeed professionals tend to use high shutter speeds all the time because their pictures must be clear and 'artistic' effects are out of place—there is no such restriction on the amateur. Dramatic pictures with a tremendous amount of movement can be made by panning—following the subject in the viewfinder while taking the picture—with a slow shutter speed of 1/60 or even 1/30 second. This keeps the subject's body sharp, the limbs slightly blurred and the background an indistinct streak.

Too many panned shots, however, could become boring, and a good compromise shutter speed is 1/250 or 1/500 second which freezes most of the action while allowing just enough movement to give the picture a little life.

Choosing the viewpoint *It is always worth looking for the unusual angle. Here a low viewpoint makes the horses loom over the camera dramatically*

Blurring the background

While in most situations you can move your subject around, or move around your subject, to find a good background, in sports photography you are usually stuck with whatever happens to be behind the players. Invariably this is totally unsatisfactory—a crowd of spectators or an unsightly scoreboard, detracting from the main picture. The only way to overcome this is by using a wide aperture to keep the background out of focus.

But when the subject is moving about at high speed—and at worst is running towards you—it requires a lot of practice to get the hand-eye co-ordination just right so that you can 'pull' the focus as the subject bears down on you. Until you are absolutely sure of your ability to do this perfectly, it is probably better to shoot at $f/3.5$ or even $f/4$ rather than opening up all the way to $f/2.8$, if your lens allows it.

Deciding when to make the final commitment and press the shutter is largely a matter of experience. Once you have been to a football match or an athletics meeting a few times you learn to anticipate moments of high drama. There are numerous highlights in tennis, for example, but an experienced sports photographer will be particularly wide awake when there are close-to-the-net volleys being played. There may be dynamic shots of players lunging for difficult returns or falling as they miss. But tennis is a very reactive sport and it is worth keeping your eyes open for emotional expressions between shots. One of the features to look for in all sports is signs of effort, not just in the face but in the whole body movement. The final result will look far more lively if the player seems to be really working. In tennis, this means that the best shots tend to come immediately after a player has made a stroke rather than before.

Every sport has its own set of standard 'peak of the action' pictures. They can be moves from set positions—the line-out in rugby or the service in tennis. Or they could be classic action shots of stars—Borg's backhand or Pele kicking the ball. Any number of shots of these situations have been taken. Professionals' files should be full of them, because they have to provide such basic shots for newspapers on demand. These pictures are visual clichés and it is a good idea to look for new situations for potential pictures. Look around for less obvious points of interest—a footballer does not need to have the ball at his feet to make an exciting picture.

Indoor events

Put off by the technical problems of shooting in difficult lighting conditions, many photographers steer clear of indoor sporting events. Yet for the tremendous range of action subjects—the glamour and gore of the boxing ring, the grace of the gymnast, the breathtaking speed of an ice hockey match and much more—it is well worth overcoming any apprehension about technicalities and accepting the challenge of capturing the drama and excitement on film.

As with outdoor sports, it is useful to know a little beforehand about the rules and the way the play flows in the event you wish to shoot. It is especially important with indoor events to work out exactly where all the action will take place and choose your viewpoint accordingly. Space can be limited indoors and there is usually little chance to move around after the event has started. In basketball, for instance, all the drama takes place around the baskets—a seat in the centre of the pitch might give a good view of the game but is a poor position for photographs. If you are able to, go to the hall or arena a few days earlier and spend a little time trying out various viewpoints with alternative lenses.

Some indoor sports are almost impossible to photograph successfully. Squash is a case in point because the players are nearly always playing away from you and your viewpoint is inevitably from above. Squash courts also use fluorescent lights which give a green cast to colour pictures.

At outdoor events, the professional sports photographer normally has an advantage over the amateur because he has greater access to the action. This is less true with indoor events. Even at a world championship boxing match there are very few seats at the ringside for photographers. This area is taken up by sports writers and television commentators. However, you can use this to advantage in your shots by including the crowd in the composition to provide more atmosphere. The boxing ring is brilliantly lit and you can use the first few rows of people in silhouette as a natural frame for your shot. However, the professional photographer can set up shots with the athletes before the event or during training. Unless you have very good contacts you will not be allowed near a world class athlete during training. Nevertheless, there is no reason why you should concentrate on professional events. There can be just as much drama and excitement at

Ice hockey *Keep your eyes open for an incident or argument during any sport, and frame tightly, using a telephoto lens to isolate the main action*

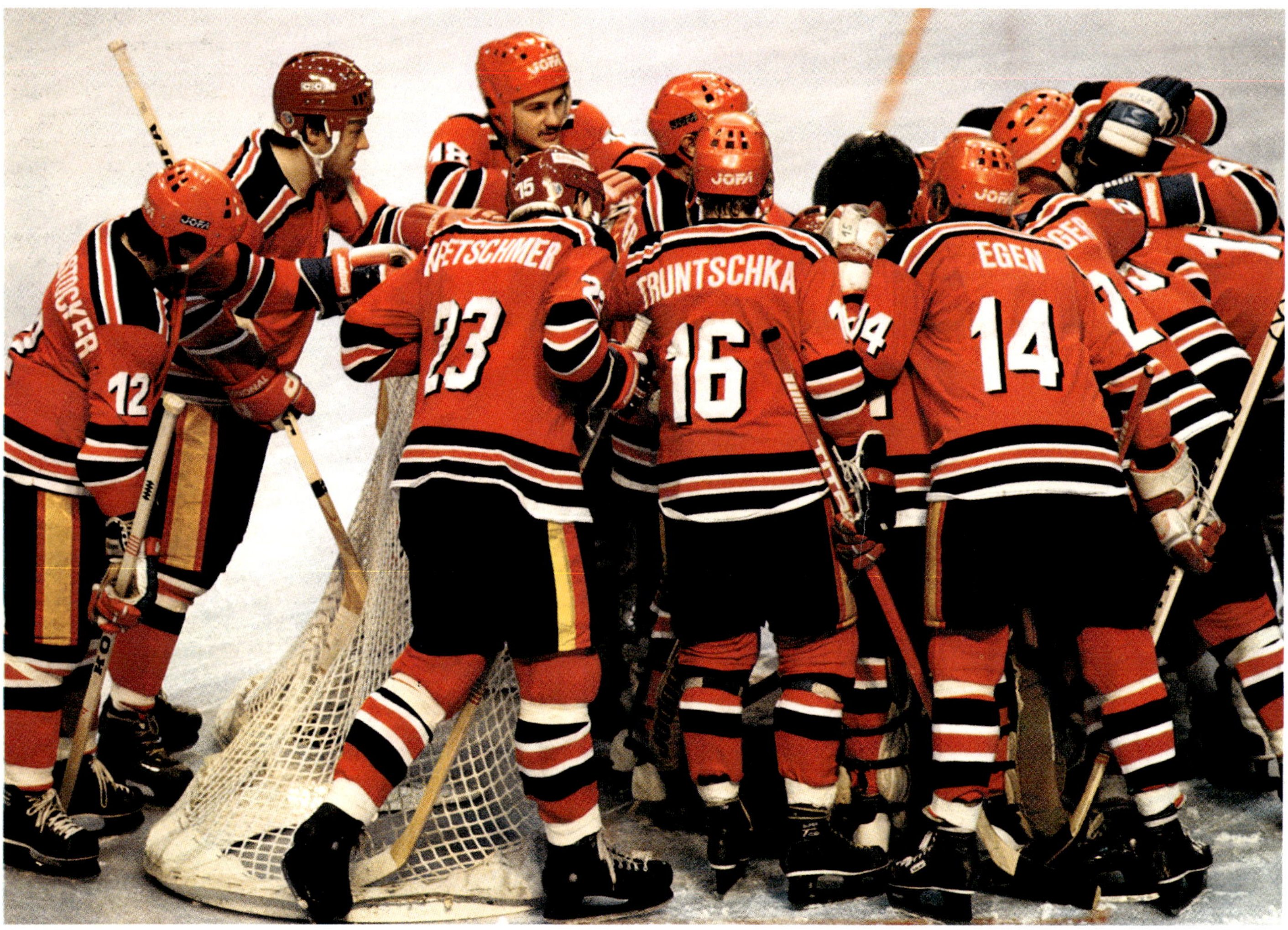

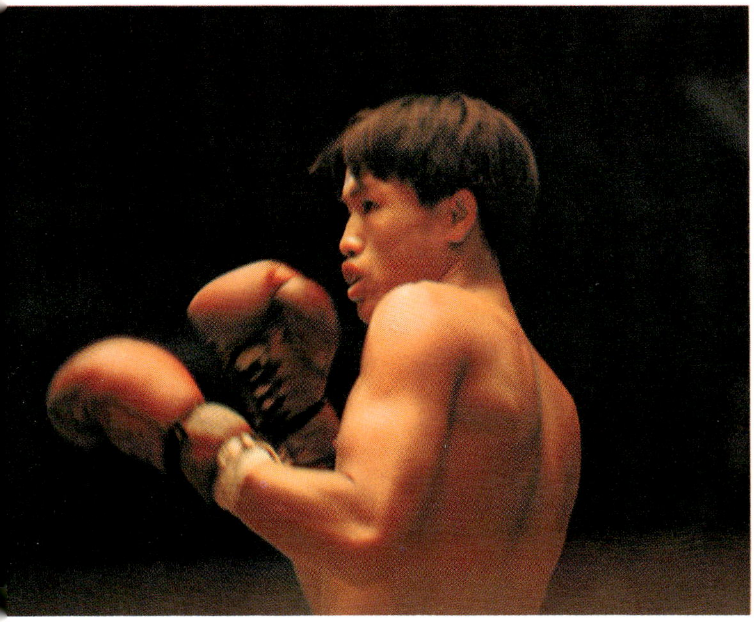

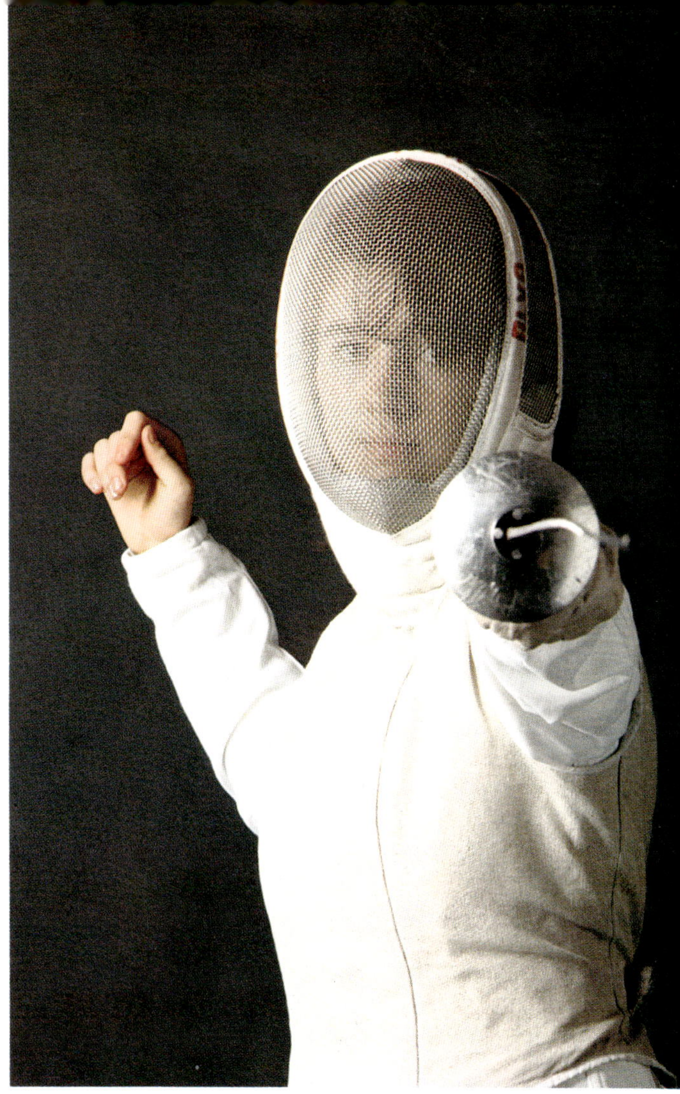

amateur events and you should be able to get a far better viewpoint at the local indoor sports centre. It may even be possible to arrange a meeting with the club secretary to outline the sort of pictures you would like to take. In fact, the secretary may be very receptive to the idea of a set of pictures which can be used for publicity.

During an amateur practice session you often have the chance to get the participants to repeat certain activities for your camera. You will also be able to work in locations which would be out of the question during an actual event. It is far better to have a great picture of a relatively unknown athlete than a shot of a champion who may be too far away to be recognized.

Another advantage of shooting at amateur sessions is that you may be allowed to use flash, something that is normally absolutely prohibited at major events. If you are able to arrange a session with a gymnast, try to pick viewpoints that not only illustrate the tremendous effort that they put into their exercises, but also show them in a way that they are never normally seen. If you are using flash, keep it as a fill-in and allow the main area lights to create a rim around the subject so that they stand away from the background. Even so, it is worth moving around until you have a dark and uncluttered background.

In particular, pre-arranged shots give better results than action shots with the martial arts. In both judo and fencing, the action is very jerky and it may not be easy to take anything but straightforward shots of the action. But if you can organize a session with the fencers you could, for instance, put yourself and your camera in the place of the opponent. In this way, the fencer and sword appear to be coming straight at you, and you can convey something of the real feeling of taking part in that event. A session at a martial arts club will also allow you to take pictures from floor level. From this position, you could use a wide angle lens with the camera pointing upwards at the judo expert who appears to be towering over you.

Boxer *Normally unacceptable, the deep shadows and orange cast of poor tungsten light can convey the drama of the event*

Fencer *In practice sessions, you can arrange a striking, opponent's eye view of the fencer in action*

In most sports there are similar picture opportunities before and after the event. A carefully set up portrait can be very rewarding. Boxers and the people connected with boxing are often colourful and flamboyant figures, making good subjects for portraits. Straightforward shots against a plain background can be very effective. With the boxers themselves, try to arrange the pictures after they have finished a bout so that their skin glistens with perspiration—or cheat with baby oil to achieve the same effect. Remember though, that with some portraits, the nature of the sport may not be immediately evident and the shot loses some of its impact. Try to include the 'tools of the trade' to set the shot in context. With a cyclist, make sure the bicycle is in the frame: shoot an ice-hockey goalkeeper in full body armour, holding or wearing his face mask.

Of course, during events light is a problem. The light level is seldom sufficient to allow you to use your camera's full capacity for freezing the action. Most professional photographers take a full range of films with them on an assignment, but the most popular films are probably the 200 and 400 ASA (ISO) transparency types which can be pushed by two stops, giving speeds of 800 and 1600 ASA respectively.

Colour balance, however, can be more difficult to achieve—particularly where there is a mixture of daylight and artificial light. It is essential to identify the nature of the light source. If you are in doubt, ask the organizers what type of lighting the hall uses. When the event is being televised or is coming from a venue that is often used for television, artificial light may give correct colour balance for daylight film since television cameras need daylight balanced light. Even with this kind of lighting, you may well need to apply some corrective filtration to give good colour balance—any deficiencies in the colour will show up particularly badly in skin tones. The only way to be absolutely sure of the colour balance of the available light is to use a colour temperature meter. If you cannot obtain one, carry out a number of tests, shooting frames with different filtration, at your local venues. And if at all possible, use a powerful flashgun to provide your own illumination. This avoids all problems with colour.

Whatever the lighting, though, be sure you have your camera at the ready all the time, particularly at the moments when the action has just finished, because often the best shots are momentary, unexpected incidents. The look of elation or dejection on the face of a weightlifter who has either succeeded or failed with a difficult weight may say much more than pictures during the activity.

There is a tendency to assume that sports shots must freeze the action and many people shoot at high shutter speeds all the time. But sports with graceful movement provide the oppor-

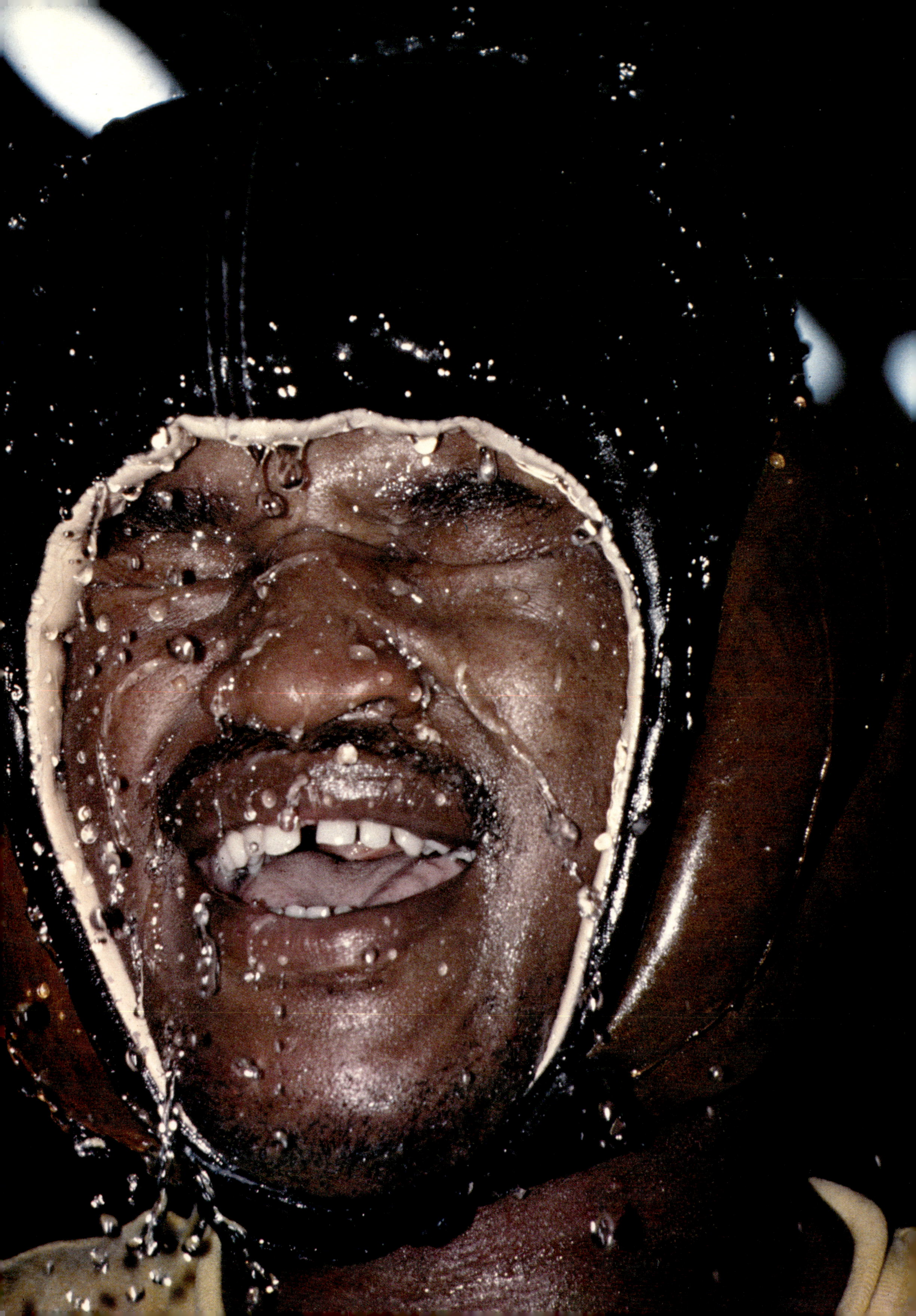

tunity to use slow and even very slow shutter speeds to capture the flow of the action and the balletic movements of the competitors. Both skating and gymnastics particularly benefit from this approach.

With the camera mounted on a tripod, you can use exposures of up to a second and the free flowing movements can give very graceful abstract shots. Some care is needed with ice skating since the skaters move very quickly around the ice. It is best to pick a moment when the subject is moving on the spot. Slow shutter speeds can also be very effective with the martial arts on certain occasions. If you anticipate the action carefully, you should be able to start your exposure as one of the participants begins to make a throw. The long shutter time records the whole of the subsequent movement.

At a cycling race you can mix flash with a long exposure, freezing the cyclist with the flash and showing the speed of the event by the blur created by the long exposure.

Multiple exposures with the camera on a tripod are similarly effective with indoor sports—providing you can ensure a dark background. A simple shot of a gymnast performing on the parallel bars or on the beam can show the whole exercise in a single frame.

For every kind of shot, though, look carefully at the background. Since a large aperture is often needed in the poor light, the background can normally be thrown out of focus. Nevertheless, look out for distractions and try to exclude them from the frame. Move higher for instance, so that the floor becomes your background—this is particularly useful with a sport such as skating where the crowd can be visually very distracting.

Think of the subject in the context of the background—certain backgrounds complement the subject better than others. A fencer in his white outfit stands out well against a dark background, whereas a coloured boxer does not. With some events the background can be a great help, particularly if it has a strong graphic element. At major weightlifting events, for example, the weightlifter performs in front of the scoreboard with all the competitors' names on it and the various weights they have achieved. With this in the background you have a picture that tells the whole story.

If possible, allow the various competitors space to move into in your composition. You may find that this will only come with experience, since composing a picture carefully while following a moving sport is not easy at first try.

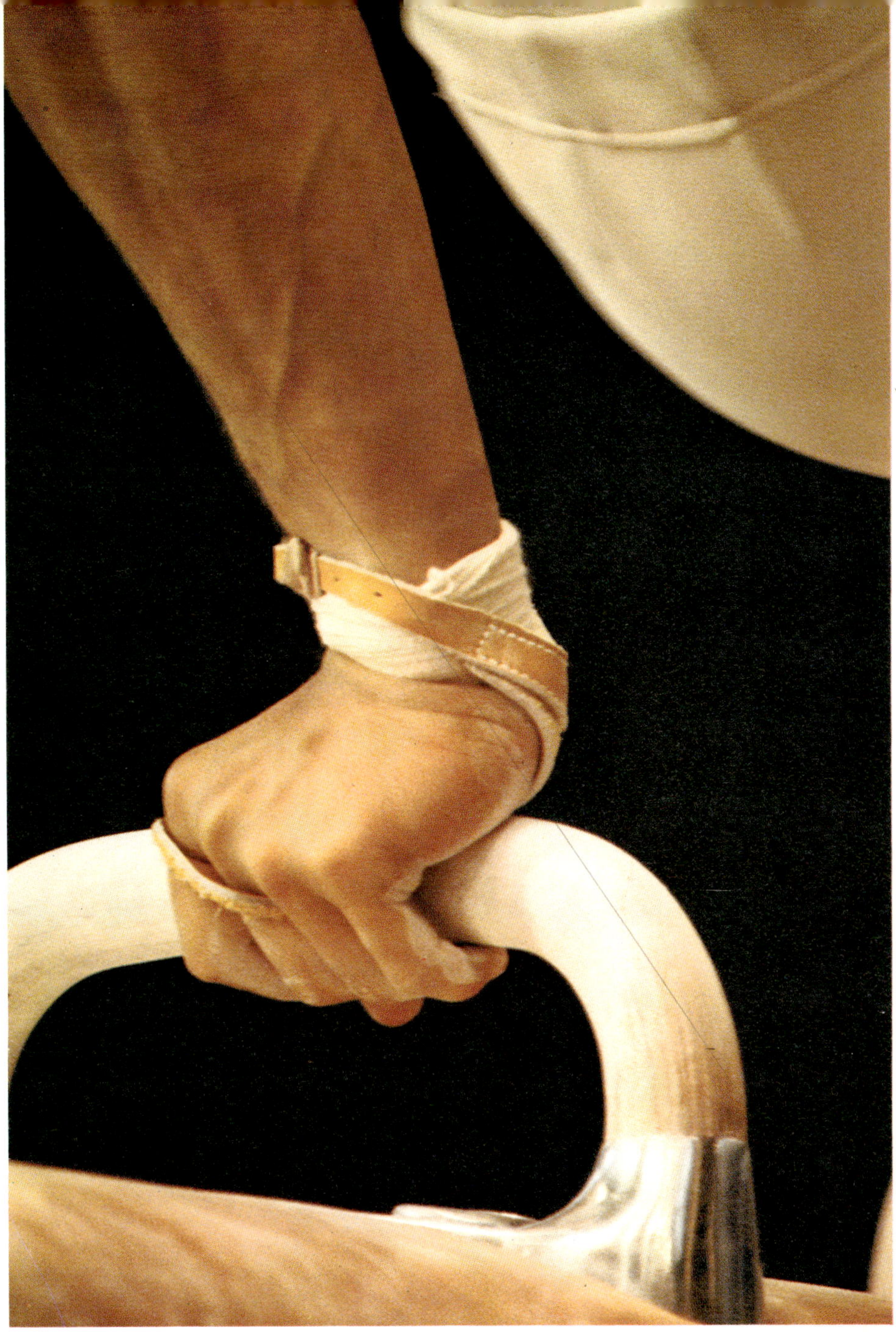

Gymnastics *A small detail can sometimes capture the flavour of a sport much more effectively than a general shot*

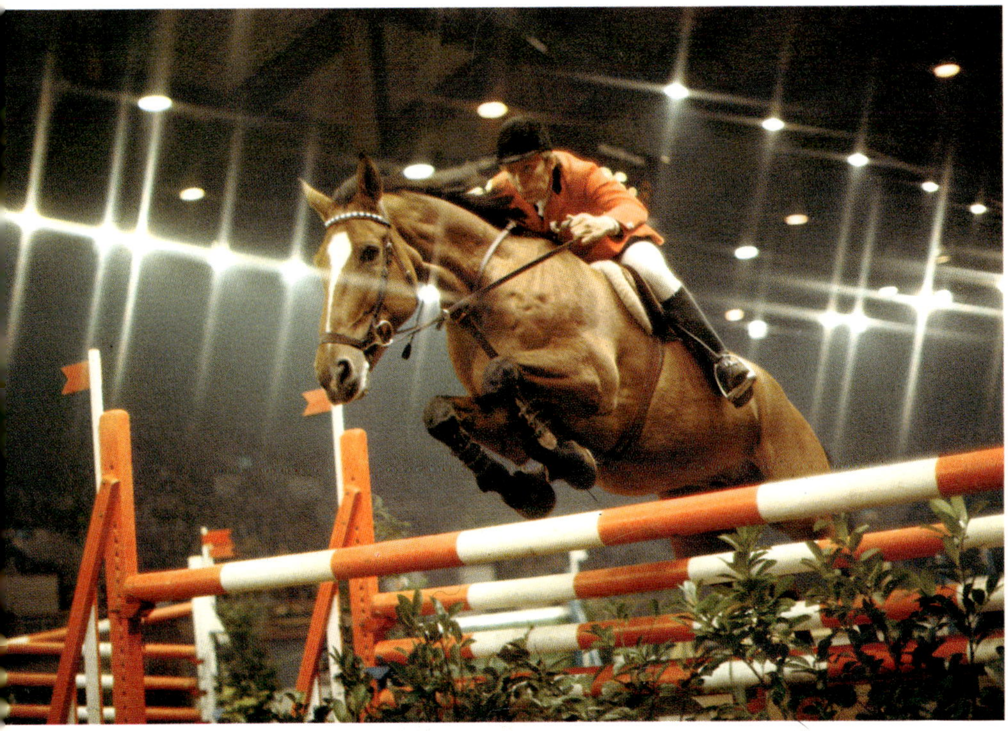

The jump *Lighting in an arena can intrude on the composition, but you can make a feature of this by using a starburst filter*

CHAPTER 13

WILDLIFE

Photographing birds

Birds are the only form of wildlife that most of us notice regularly—even for a city dweller, hardly a day goes by without seeing a bird or hearing its song. It is hardly surprising, then, that so many people choose birds as subjects for their first attempt at wildlife photography. Getting a picture is often only a matter of leaving food out in the garden and waiting for the subject to swoop down, but if you are prepared to look farther afield, it is easy to photograph many of the less common species in their natural, rural habitat.

The single most important factor affecting the quality of your pictures of birds has little to do with photography—it is your knowledge of the birds themselves and the techniques of getting close enough to them. If you know where you are most likely to find a particular species, your chances of coming back with a good picture are that much greater than if you are totally ignorant of birds' habits.

Learning about birds has another purpose. As cities grow, and woodland is uprooted for farmland, there are fewer available habitats for many species of birds. If you have learnt something about the creatures you want to photograph, you will soon learn how best to go about it without disturbing them or their young. Some birds are relatively tame, and will tolerate attention from a photographer, but other species must be approached with much more care to avoid disturbing them. In many parts of the world, birds of all species are protected, and you can be heavily fined for intimidating them. Even if this is not the case, the bird should come first, not the photograph.

Equipment and materials

The photographic equipment that you need to get effective pictures of birds varies according to the species that you are photographing, and how close you can get to it. For stalking birds, for example, you ideally need a lens with a focal length of 200 mm or longer, but if you lay bait, and sit in a hide, even a 135 mm lens may prove more than long enough. In general, you should use the shortest possible focal length that allows the bird to occupy a reasonable portion of the frame. You can then minimize such problems as camera shake and shallow depth of field. There is no point in using a 400 mm lens if you can move in closer and use a 135. However, probably the most useful focal length for expeditions in the field is the 300 mm—this is neither too long to be unmanageable, nor too short to pull in images of more distant birds. Even a lens of this focal length, however, will be inadequate for anything but the largest birds unless you can move in quite close. You can use a ×2 teleconverter, though, to double

Gulls in flight *Not all birds are naturally timid—many will come quite close to the photographer*

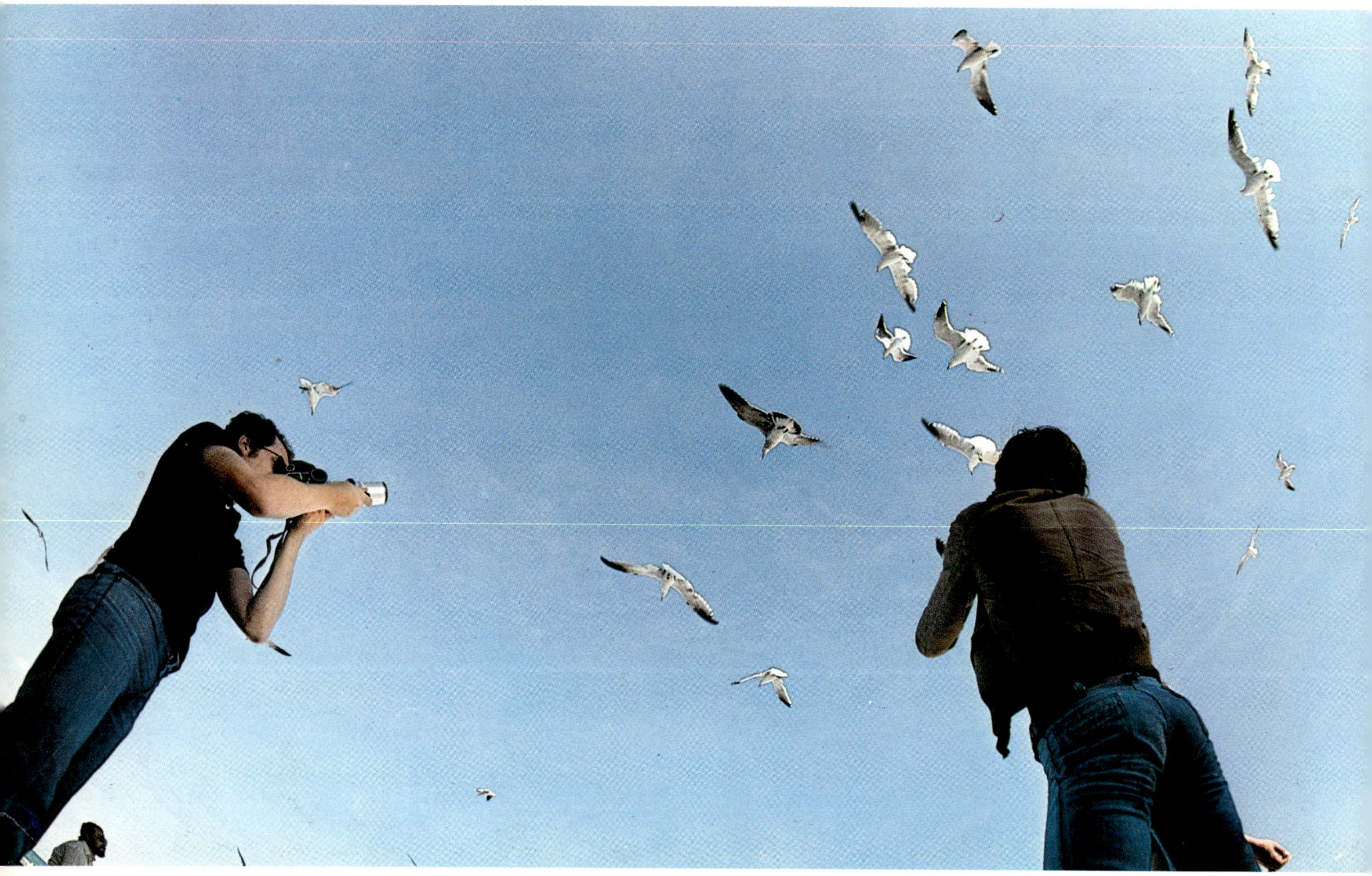

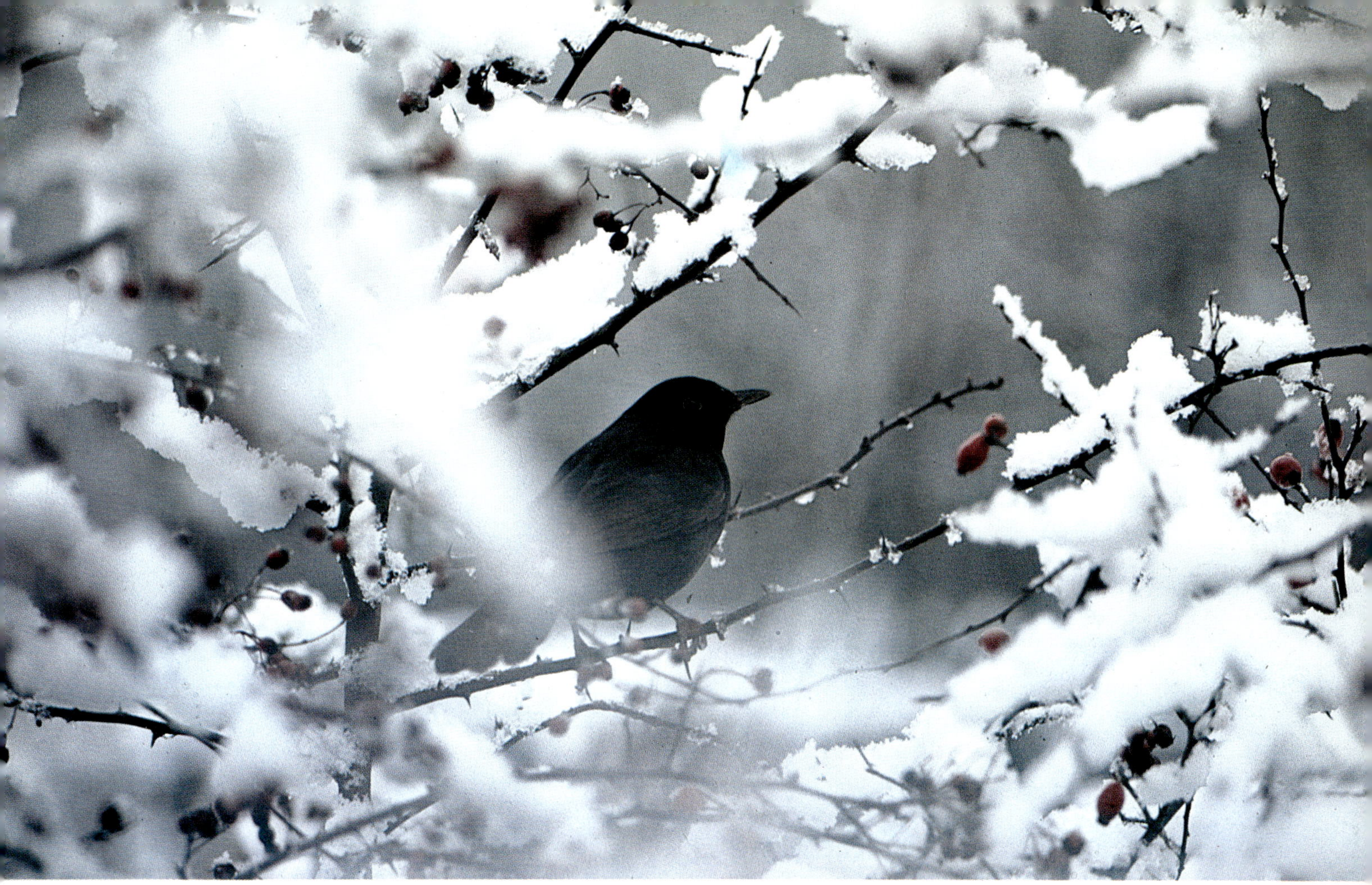

Blackbird *A fall of snow makes birds that are normally well hidden stand out against a clean white background*

Thinly disguised hide *Camouflaging a hide is unnecessary—it is the shape of the human figure that scares birds*

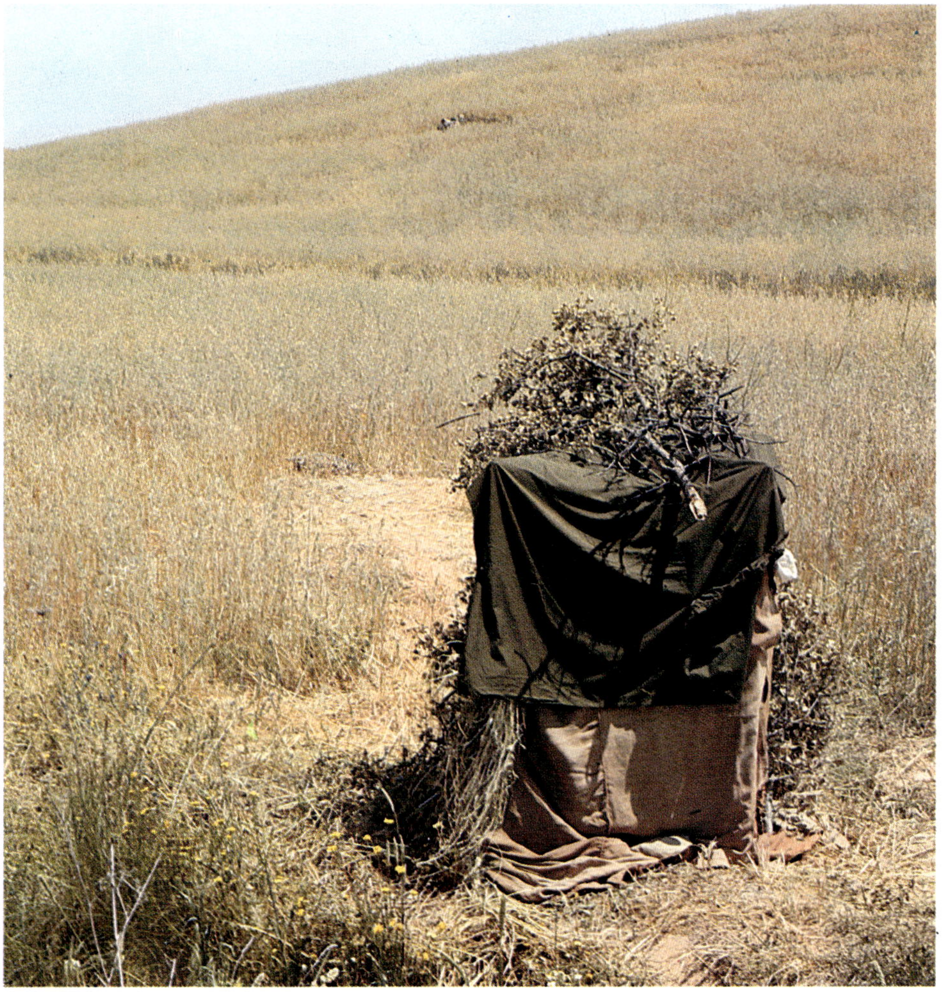

magnification of a long lens.

Zoom lenses can be very useful because they make it possible to photograph a whole group of birds together and then to close-frame one individual specimen quickly, without moving the camera or lens. Only the longer zooms are suitable, though, and a wide to tele zoom is not sufficiently powerful.

A camera support is vital, and some photographers never take a single picture without one. Use the sturdiest tripod you can comfortably carry, particularly if you are using a long telephoto lens. Four or five section lightweight tripods may be less of a burden on your shoulder when you are walking, but they cannot hold the camera steady, particularly in a fresh breeze. If a tripod is out of the question, then use a monopod, shoulder brace or car window clamp instead. The more rigidly supported the camera is, the better—more wildlife pictures are spoilt by camera shake than by any other fault.

Choice of film is dictated by conditions. As a general rule, use the slowest film that you can. Fashions in bird photography do not change, and the graininess that is apparent on fast films is never an asset. If the lighting is very bad, or you need to stop action, you may need to use a 400 ASA film, but if there is plenty of light, try to use a slow film such as Kodachrome 64. Not only does this give fine grain and better definition, but it also fades more slowly than other emulsions.

The exact choice of the film and equipment that is most appropriate for a particular photographic trip depends on how you approach the problem of getting pictures of a bird in its natural surroundings. Broadly speaking, there are three quite distinct ways of getting pictures: stalking the bird; wait and see —where the photographer lies in wait in a hide until the bird appears; and finally, nest photography.

Stalking birds

For stalking birds, you should use the longest lens possible because the farther you are from a bird, the less likely it is to see you and fly off. Always wear inconspicuous clothing, so that you blend in with the surrounding scenery. If you are going to be walking on the mud flats of a river estuary, then a grey outfit offers good cover, but inland, the brown and green of army camouflage battledress is less likely to be noticed.

Once you reach the general area where you plan to take pictures, first use binoculars to establish exactly

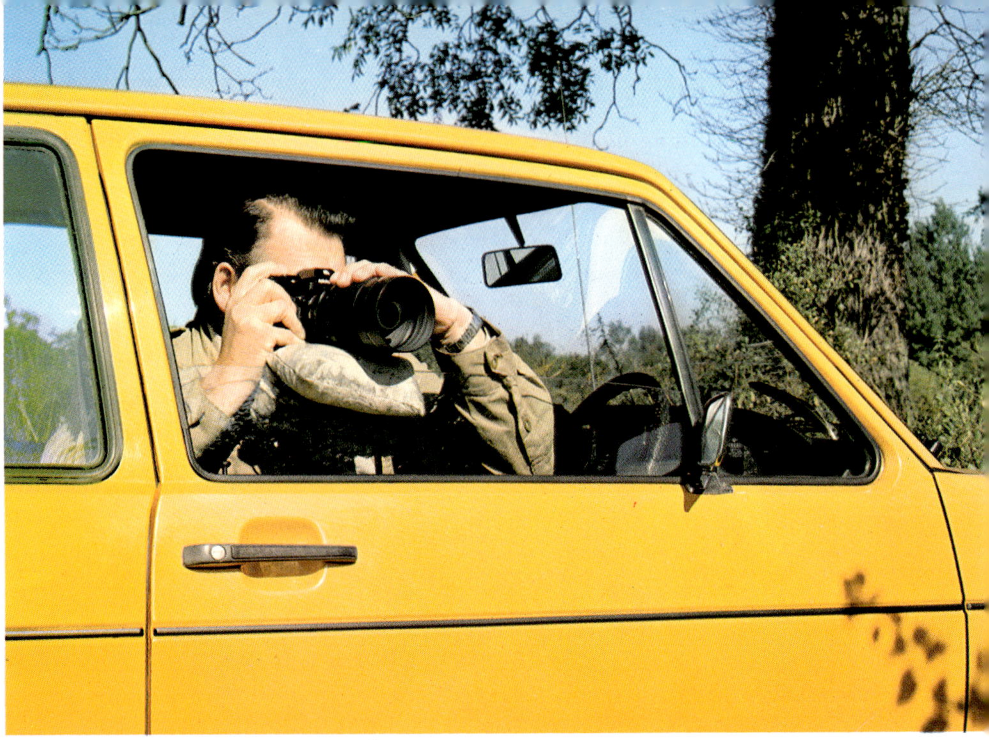

Car and beanbag *Even a car can be used as a hide, with the camera rested on a beanbag over an open window*

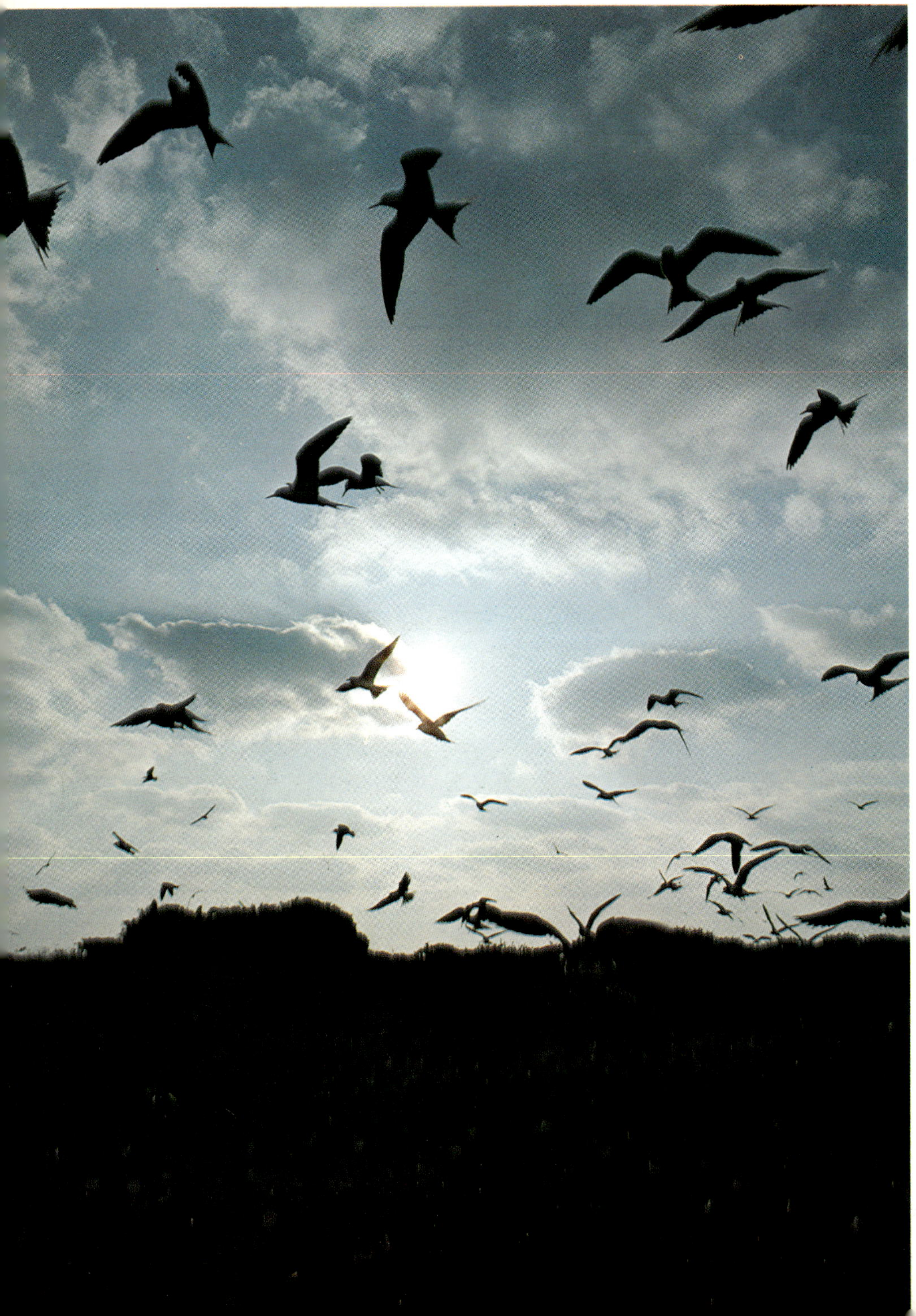

where the birds gather. Then approach as slowly as possible, moving forward when the bird is looking away or feeding. Birds only feed when they are relaxed, so this is the best moment to move forward, or to release the shutter. If the bird stops feeding and looks up, freeze immediately, as the slightest movement may cause it to take flight. As soon as it starts to feed once more, you can safely continue your advance.

Birds are much more sensitive to movement than they are to noise, and the sound that a camera makes is often drowned by the wind, or by the noise that a flock of birds themselves make. But even a slight movement is enough to scare a bird, and it is worth bearing this in mind when you spot a new arrival landing at the edge of your field of view. Resist the temptation to suddenly swing your head, or your camera lens, round to look at the bird. Wait until the other birds in the area settle down again, and then slowly turn your camera round to photograph the new bird. If you fail to do this, every bird in sight may fly off.

Wait and see

Putting out bait to attract a bird is the opposite approach to stalking it—instead of going to the bird, you wait for it to come to you. Although this may seem easier than stalking, it actually requires more organization on the part of the photographer. If birds are to land and take the bait, the photographer must not be conspicuous, and this generally means using some sort of hide and keeping out of sight.

A simple one person hide usually consists of a small upright frame, about

Sooty terns *You do not need to fill the frame with a bird to make a good picture. Look out for atmospheric scene-setting shots like this*

one metre square, and 1.5 to 2 metres high. It should be as light as possible, and easy to put up quickly. Guy lines will be necessary if the wind is very strong, and there should be no loose pieces of canvas to flap around and frighten the birds. A tiny window at the front of the hide provides space for the photographer to poke a lens out.

Perhaps surprisingly, birds are not frightened by a hide that does not blend in with its surroundings, so camouflage is not necessary. It is necessary, though, to conceal the hide from curious onlookers, who might otherwise come and frighten off the birds. Try and place your hide in a position where it is not visible from nearby footpaths or roads.

Even a vehicle can be used as a hide, as birds seem quite oblivious to human figures inside. It is even possible to drive a car slowly forward without being too much of a distraction. As soon as the windows are wound down, though, the birds may become aware of being watched and will be much more sensitive to your movements.

Laying bait outside a hide is not just a matter of sprinkling seed and waiting for some action. Although this may attract some attention by chance, regular feeding at the same spot is needed to establish a routine and the birds' confidence. Once birds know that there is food to be had at a particular spot, they will keep on coming in increasing numbers, and you will be able to get the pictures that you want.

Bait can be bird seed, pieces of raw meat, or just household food waste, depending on the natural diet of the bird you are trying to attract. Do not just throw the bait on the ground though—hang it up from branches, or scatter it on the top of rocks. This approach may give your shots a better background. You may even be able to photograph the bird against the light of the sky if the bait is well above ground level. If you erect your hide near an area where there is already an abundant supply of food, you may need no bait at all. Suitable locations for hides are river estuaries, where waders constantly feed at low water, and sewage plants, where birds gather to feed on insects.

Even in your own garden, it is possible to attract a large variety of birds if you put food out regularly. Set up a feeding table near the house, where you have a good view from a window. Build a perch alongside the table, and change this regularly, using natural materials such as rocks, or twigs and old tree stumps. Before feeding, birds invariably alight near the food, and look around for predators. Your perch provides an ideal viewpoint for this purpose, and if you change it regularly, you can introduce variety to pictures that are all taken at the same place.

On the nest

The third, and most difficult, approach to photographing birds is to catch them at the nest. The earliest bird pictures were

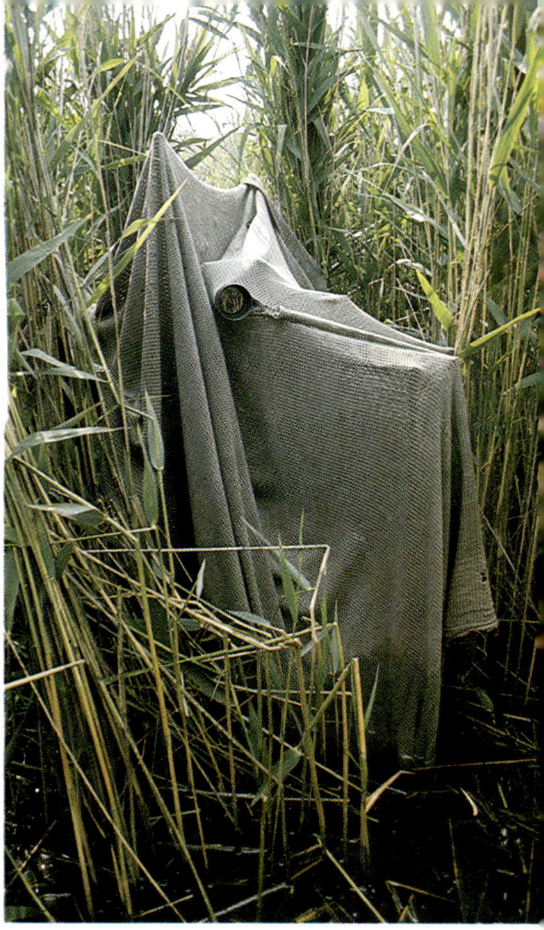

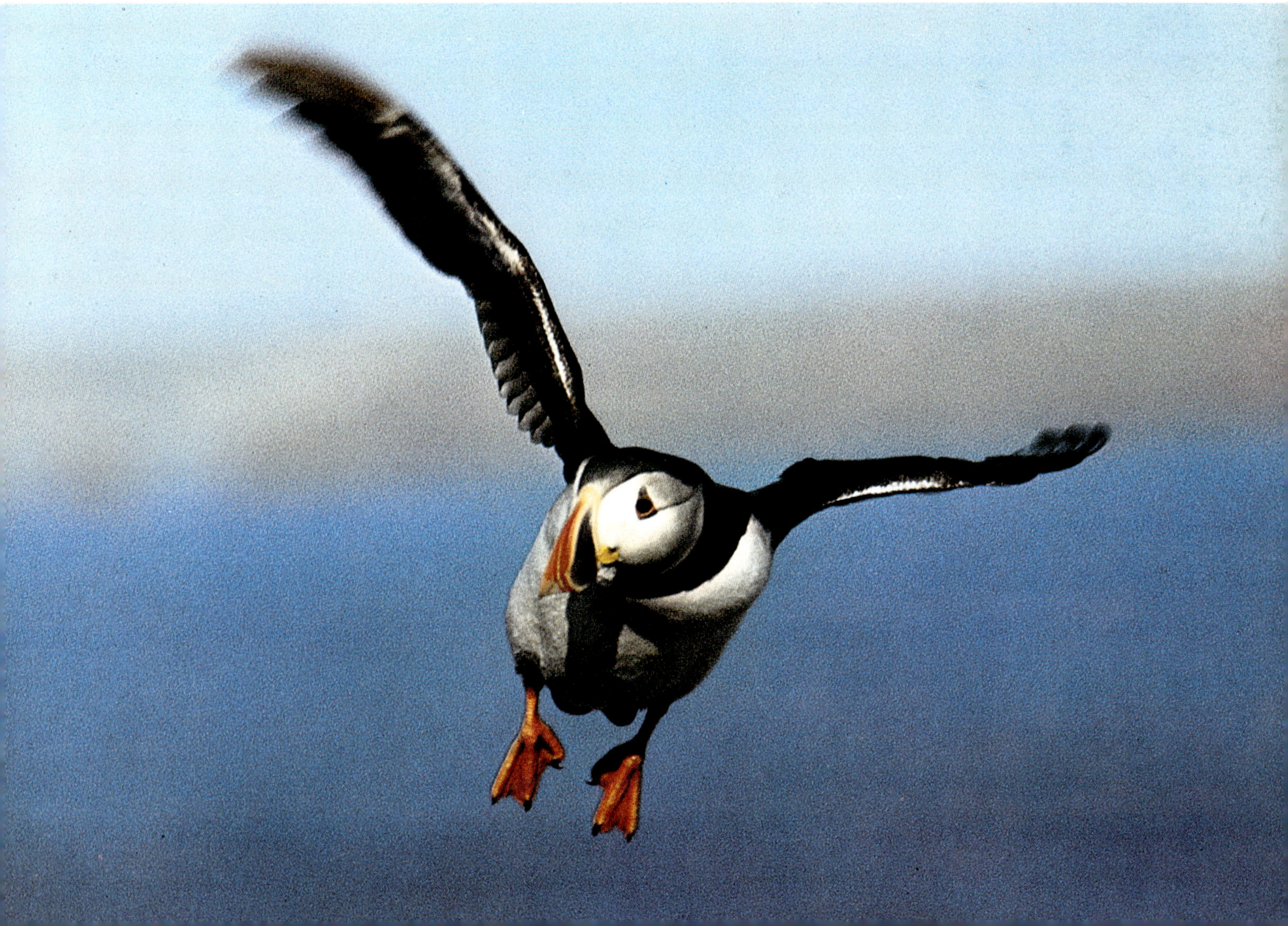

Home-made hide *As long as the photographer is concealed, almost anything will do as a hide*
Soaring puffin *A cliff top can provide a useful vantage point from which to photograph all kinds of sea birds*

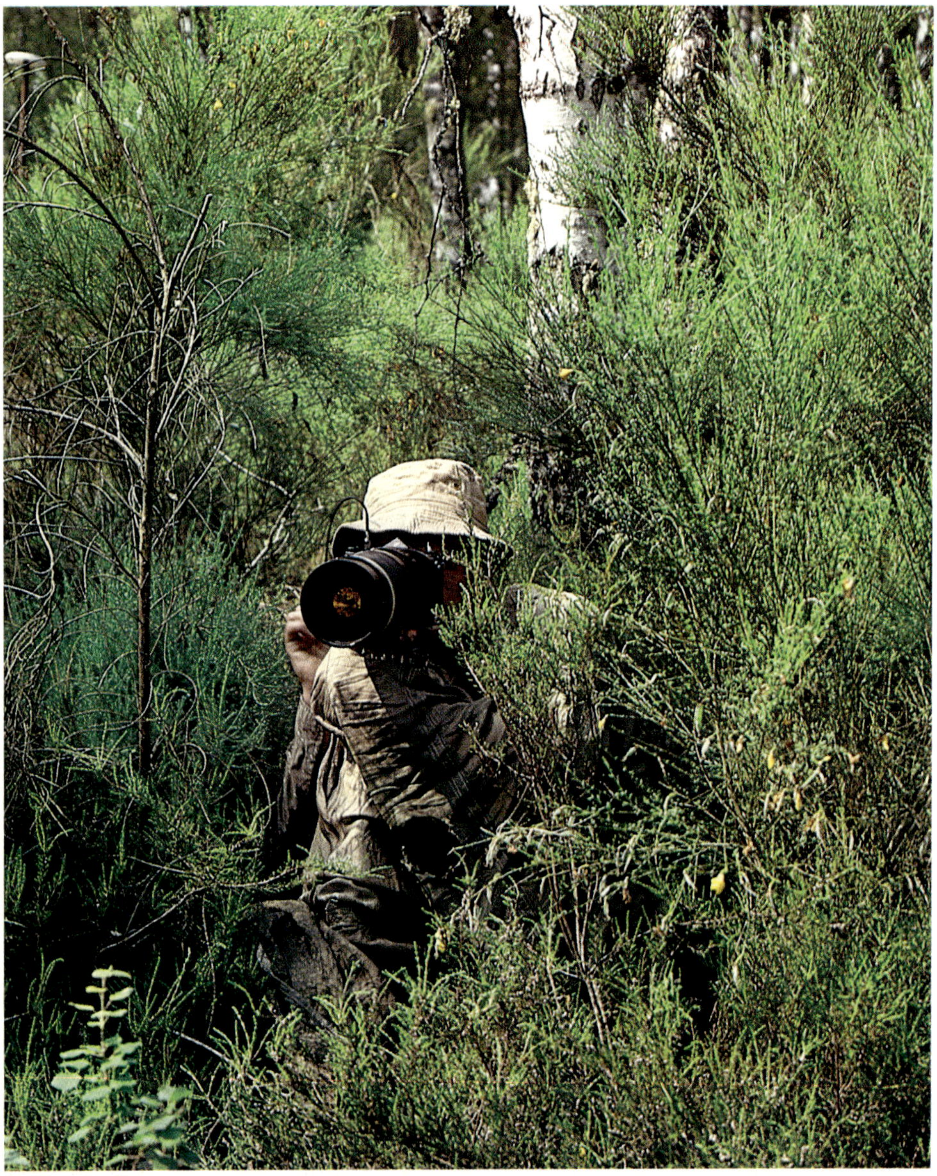

all taken in this way, because the necessary equipment was so cumbersome, and exposure so long, that a nesting bird was the only one that kept still long enough to be caught by the camera.

This is no longer the case, and ornithologists try to avoid photographing a bird at the nest unless it is strictly necessary for scientific reasons. Usually, it is possible to get a picture of a bird by baiting or stalking it, and neither of these two approaches are as much of a threat to the survival of a species. A brooding bird is very sensitive to interference, and will often desert the nest and eggs at the slightest disturbance.

If you are an experienced ornithologist, and you want to photograph nesting birds, then you should get in touch with your local ornithological society. They will give you a list of protected species, and give you advice on how best to get the pictures you want without causing distress to the bird or its young—precautions vary from species to species.

If you are inexperienced, it is probably better to stick to stalking birds or putting out bait—neither of these methods constitutes a great threat to the survival of the bird, and they both make it possible to take quite beautiful pictures, sometimes without leaving your garden.

Creeping close *For stalking birds, you need a long lens and great patience. Here, the photographer has concealed his tripod and himself with a blanket*

Blue heron *Large species of bird are often easier to photograph, because you do not need to get close or use a long lens to fill the frame*

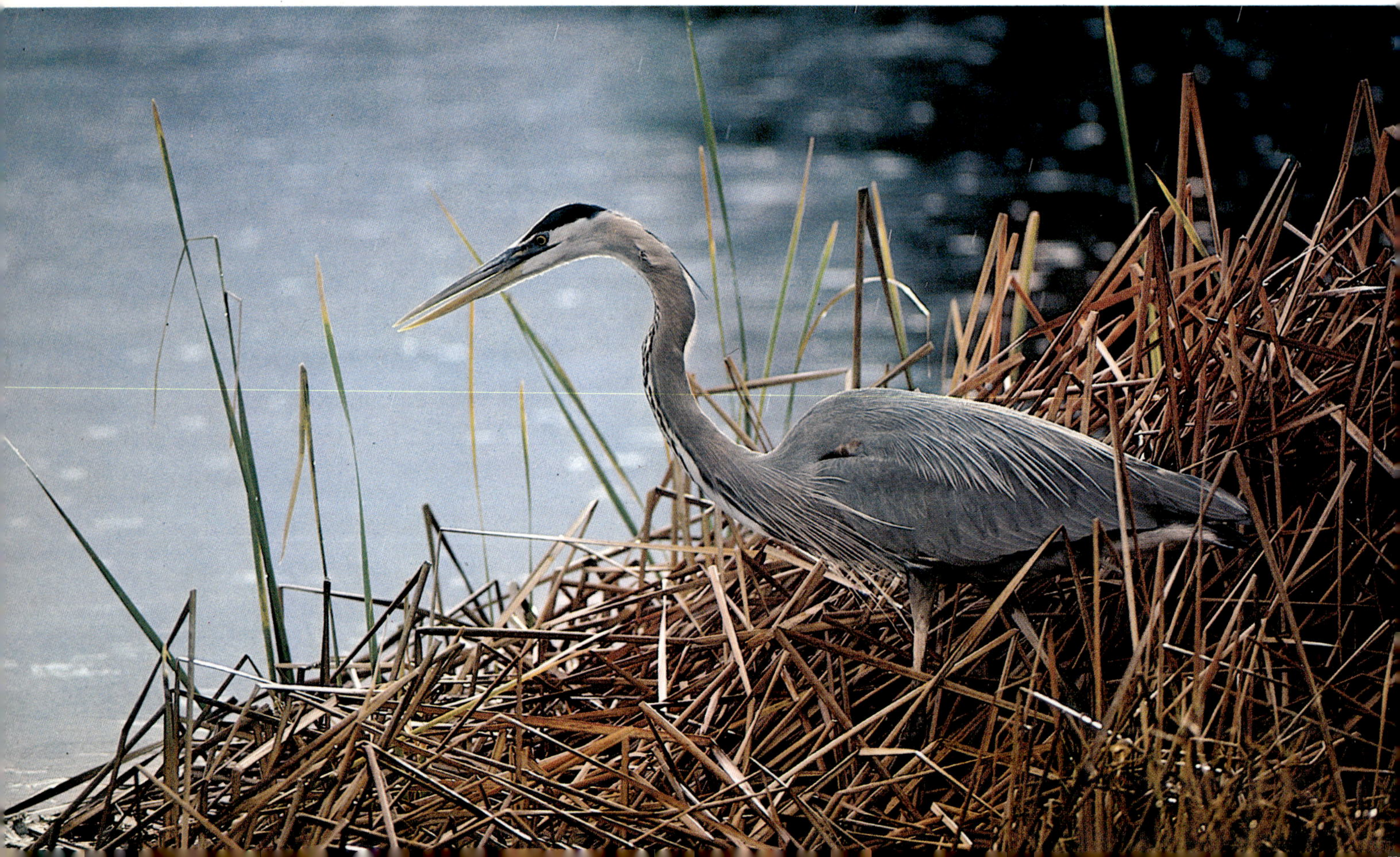

Wildlife at night

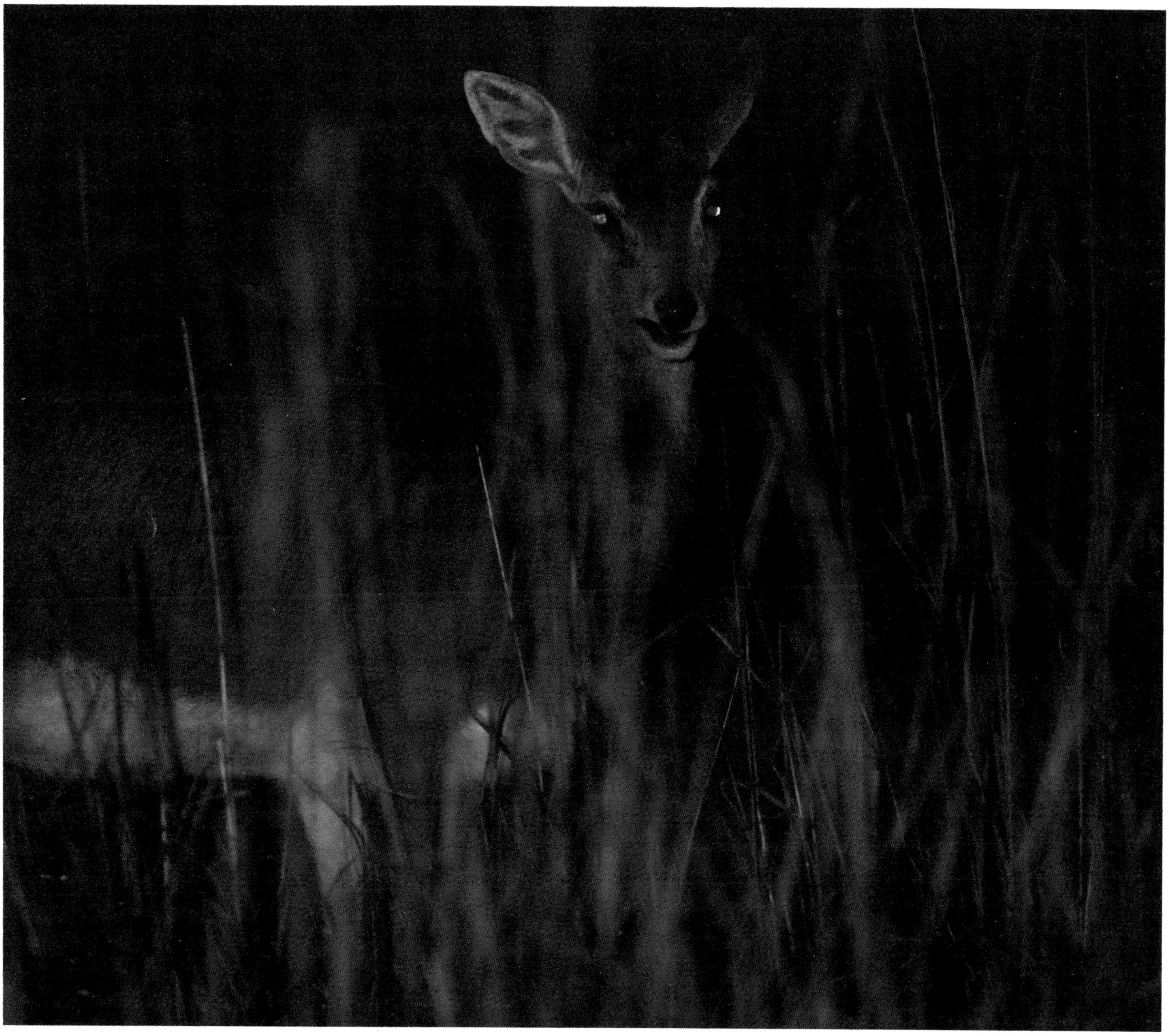

Nocturnal birds and animals make a particularly challenging subject for the photographer. Not only are they active during the hours when most of us are asleep, but they are also hidden from our eyes by darkness. The very fact that this section of the animal kingdom is normally invisible makes it that much more interesting when we see it in photographs.

The challenge lies in securing these pictures against what might seem to be formidable odds. Most wild creatures try to avoid human contact if possible and, to take photographs, you must take them by surprise. This can be particularly difficult at night—many animals see better at night than we do, and have highly developed senses of smell and hearing. Furthermore, such simple photographic tasks as focusing the camera can prove almost impossible in the dark, and camera controls must be operated by feel rather than by sight.

None of these difficulties is insurmountable, however, particularly if you have a knowledge and understanding of the creatures you plan to photograph, and the patience to wait silently and motionless until they appear.

Blinking oribi *The direct flash on the photographer's camera picked out a dramatic glint in the animal's eyes*

Equipment and materials

Surprisingly little extra equipment is needed for night shots of animals and you can use most cameras, providing they are quiet in operation, and easy to use in the dark. It is often possible to set up and focus the camera during the day, so complex viewing systems are not necessary and a 35 mm rangefinder or a 6 × 6 cm TLR is ideal. If you use an SLR, it may need to be muffled, or used

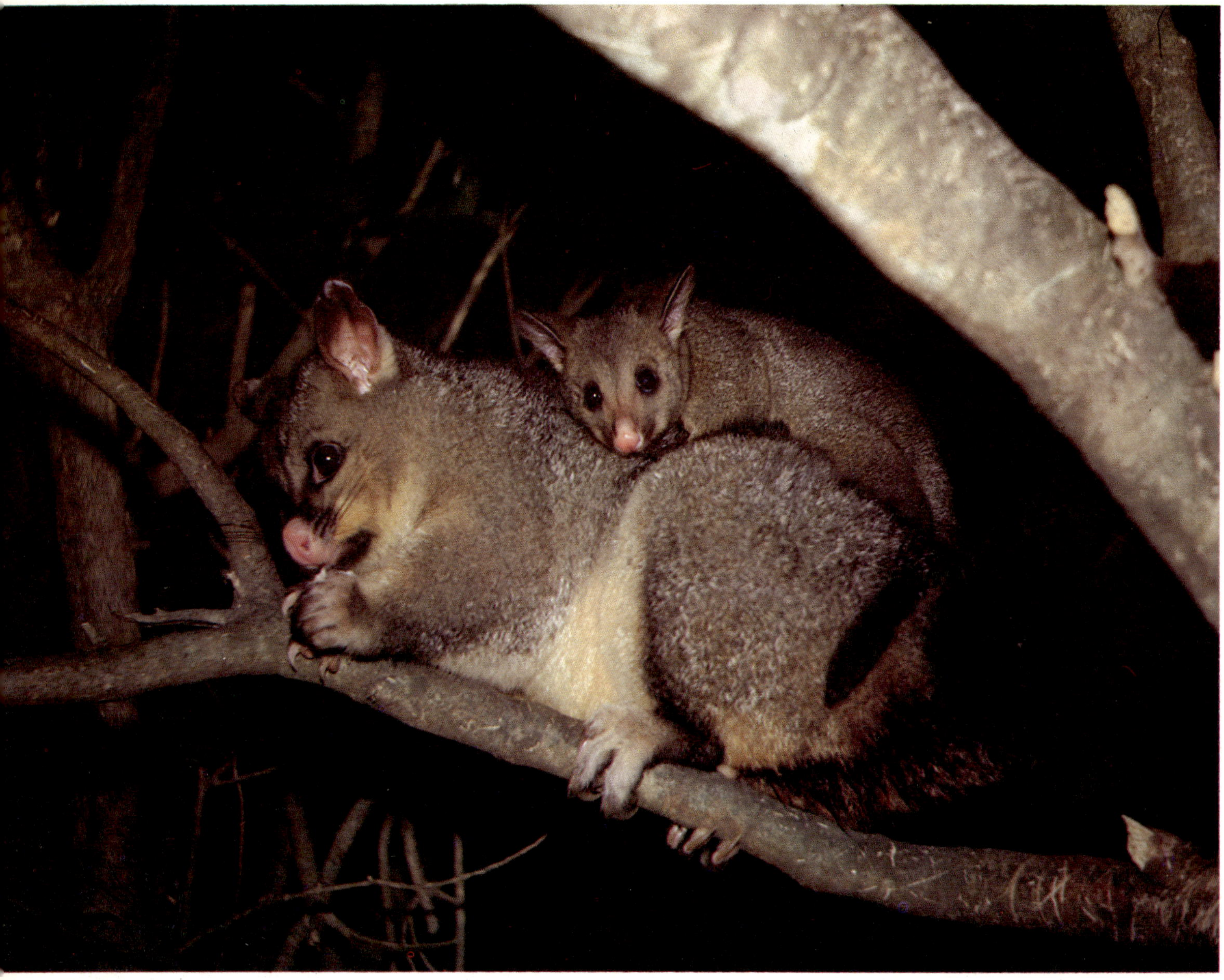

Possum and young *At night, focusing is a problem, and for this picture, the photographer was aided by a torch*

with the mirror locked up, so that the noise of the mirror is eliminated and the only sound comes from the shutter.

For many pictures, a standard focal length lens is sufficient, and will enable some of the animal's habitat to be included in the picture. For more tightly framed shots, a medium telephoto is more useful. Long lenses are usually impractical—on an SLR they are difficult to focus, and on a rangefinder camera they do not couple with the focusing mechanism. Furthermore, their relatively small apertures can present exposure problems.

Flash is essential for working at night, and if a large area of ground is to be lit, you will need a powerful gun. Flash guide numbers are usually calculated for average indoor conditions, and in an open space you may have to use a wider aperture than usual. If you are using a telephoto lens, you may be able to overcome this problem by using a special condenser lens attachment over the reflector of the flash. This concentrates the beam on a smaller area, and effectively increases the power and reach of the gun.

A single flashgun produces very harsh lighting, so wherever possible use two instead. Use a powerful gun to provide the main or key light, and another, smaller, unit to fill in the shadows. To avoid trailing wires it is best to use a slave cell to fire one of the guns. You will have to experiment to achieve the right lighting balance between the two units, but a good starting point is to have the main light twice as powerful as the camera-mounted fill-in flash. To estimate the correct exposure using this twin flash method, follow the guide lines on the larger flash, then close the lens aperture by half a stop to take account of the extra light from the smaller gun. Try and shoot a few test exposures before going out to photograph a live subject.

Even with flash, some sort of camera support is essential. This frees your hands, and allows you to carefully compose the picture around the spot where you expect the subject to appear. Choice of film depends very much on the power of your flash, and its distance from the subject, but you should use the finest grain film that is practical.

The final choice of equipment and materials depends partly upon what you already own or can borrow, but there are three basic techniques for shooting wildlife at night, and each calls for a number of minor variations in equipment.

Baiting

The simplest way to attract animals for the camera is to put down food regularly in the same place, and be prepared to photograph the animals that come to eat. Use seed and grain for the smaller mammals, or pieces of meat to attract carnivores and owls. Even in a suburban garden, a surprisingly wide range of wildlife can be attracted by this method.

Try and avoid unnatural looking bait such as white bread—this never looks good on photographs. Some kinds of bait, particularly meat, can be mixed with earth, or staked to the ground, so that your subject cannot just pick it up and run off with it. If you are using grain, on the other hand, lay it in a line parallel to the camera back, so that as the feeding animal works its way along the line, it stays in focus.

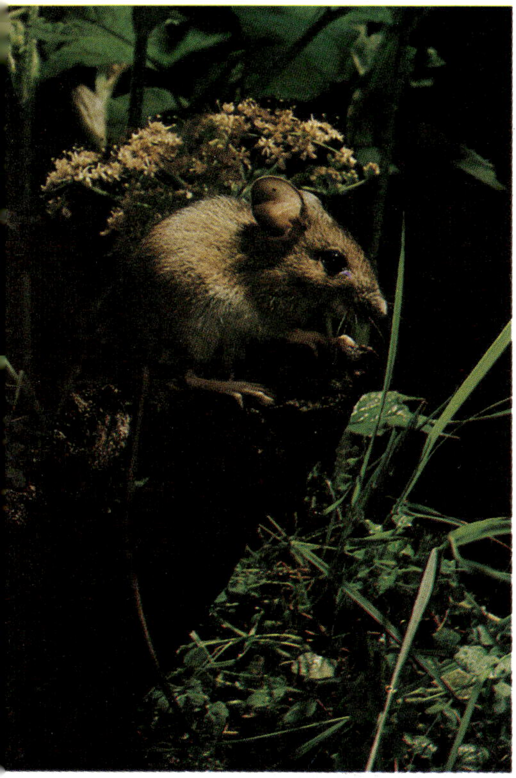

Mouse and frog *Small animals abound in woodland and long grass, but they tend to be nervous and elusive. For these difficult subjects, you may have to use a special remote trigger, so that the animal itself releases the shutter by breaking a beam of light*

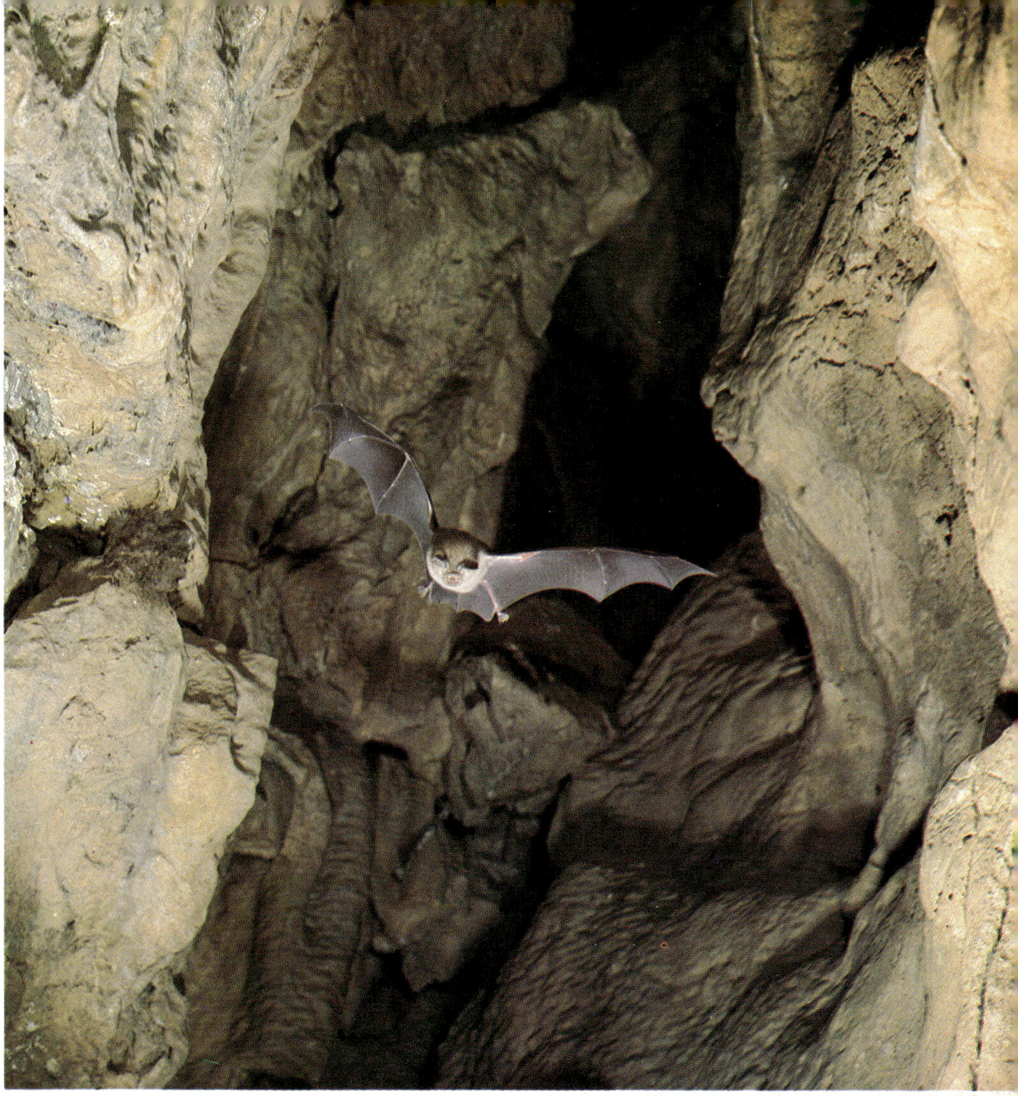

Bat in flight *Fast-moving subjects leave no time for focusing, so the camera must be preset on a fixed point*

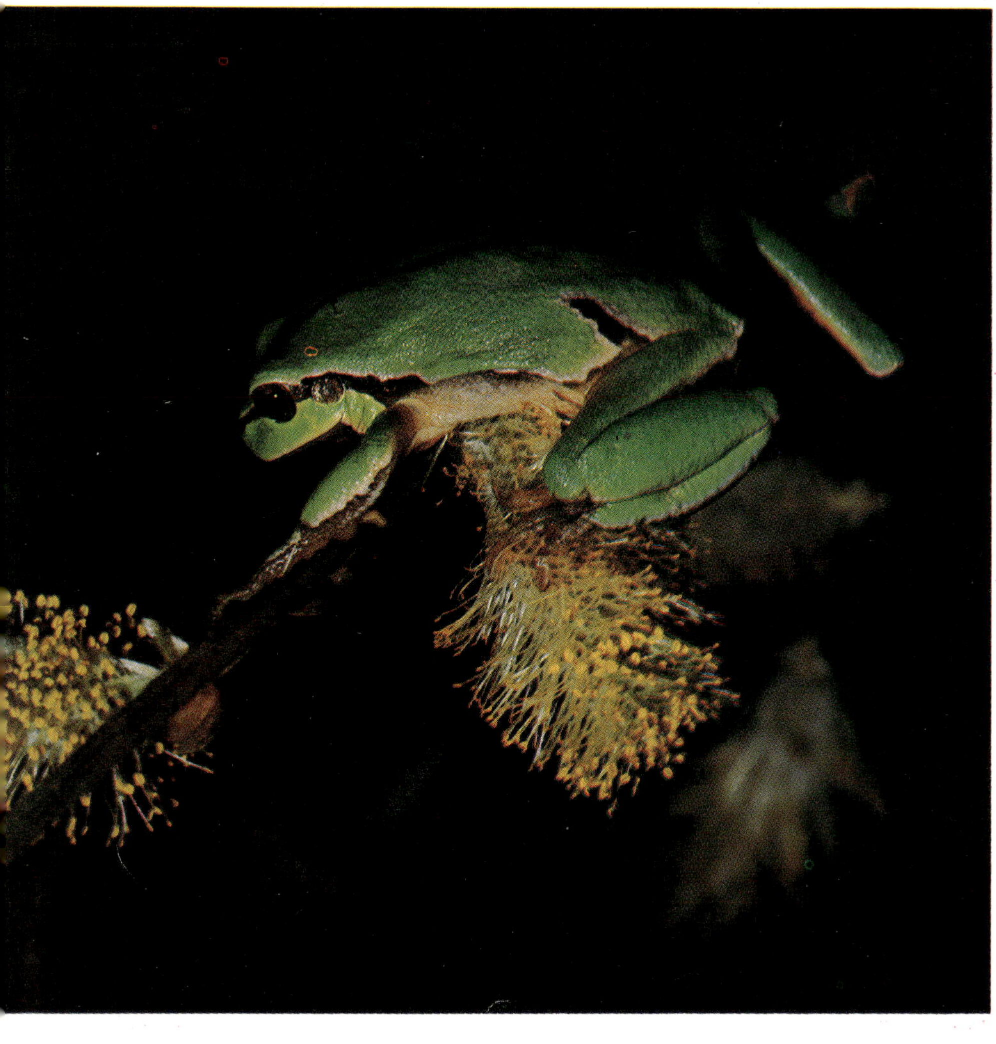

The most important thing to bear in mind when laying bait is that most nocturnal animals are timid and wary. It is no good sprinkling crumbs on the ground and expecting immediate results. It may take days or even weeks before the animals get used to a new source of food.

Once you have established that the bait is being taken regularly, you can start to make preparations for photography. First, remove any unsightly rocks, twigs or rubbish, at least a day or two before you take the pictures.

Before it gets dark on the evening of the shoot, set up the camera, making sure that it is downwind from the bait. Make yourself as comfortable as possible, as you may have to stay in the same position for several hours. Try and wear warm clothes that do not rustle when you move, and wear plenty of them—it can get cold at night, even in summer. A car makes a very good place to sit if you can get one close enough to the site.

When the time comes to take pictures, release the shutter using a cable release. A useful type is the pneumatic release, which works at distances of up to ten metres from the camera. Other methods of remote control appear on page 161.

Unless you are using some sort of automatic trip device, you will need to be able to see the subject. In total

Nonchalant badger *Some species will ignore electronic flash, once they have had time to get accustomed to it*

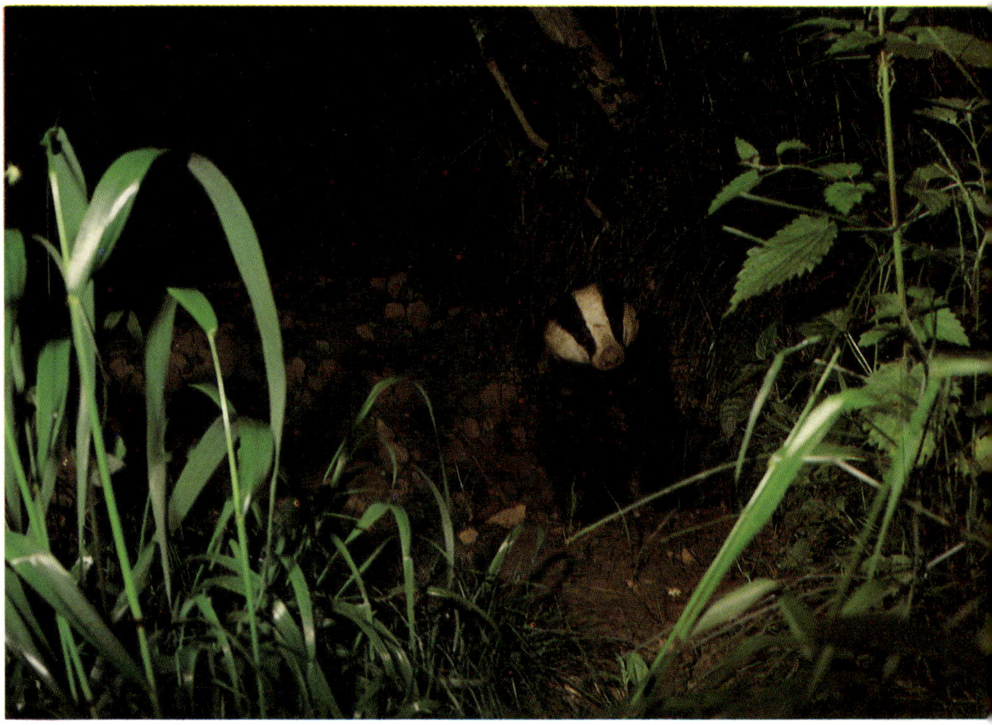

darkness, you can use a torch covered with a simple red filter—cellophane will do—to illuminate the subject. Most animals do not notice a dim red light as long as it is kept reasonably still.

When you are about to take pictures, wait until the creature is relaxed and feeding before pressing the shutter. After this, wait a few seconds before winding on the film, or taking another picture. The noise of the shutter may initially startle the creature, in which case you must muffle the camera, but very soon most will get used to the sound of the camera, and do not react to it.

Prefocusing the camera

If you can find a spot that is regularly frequented by the animal that you wish to photograph, you can dispense with the bait, and set up the camera nearby. This location might be the entrance to its den, a stream where it drinks, or even a favourite tree where it sharpens its claws. When photographing near to an animal's den, you must keep disturbance to an absolute minimum. As with nest photography of birds, the slightest disruption may cause animals to desert their young, or at least move them to a safer place. When setting up your equipment, always avoid treading near the entrance hole, and try to approach silently and downwind. A hide is generally unnecessary, but try and sit against a tree or bush so that your silhouette does not show on the skyline.

Some animals follow very regular hours, emerging at the same time every evening, but others are not so predictable. If an animal has very regular habits, you can photograph it at a number of different places, and soon build a collection of shots illustrating various aspects of its behaviour. In spring and early summer, you may be lucky enough to see the young emerging for the first time. Young animals are more inquisitive than adults, and may come quite close to you, providing a good opportunity for close-up pictures. Do not be tempted, however, to touch or stroke the animals, because not only will you leave your scent on them, thus running the risk of their parents deserting them, but you may also be bitten.

When trying to photograph this sort of activity, you will probably need to move and refocus the camera quickly and quietly. This may at first seem difficult, but with experience and practice, it becomes surprisingly easy. Get to know your camera well—remember which way to turn the focusing ring if the subject moves closer, or use the focusing techniques described on page 653. Also make a note of the direction in which the aperture ring must be turned to stop the lens down. Only by becoming thoroughly familiar with your equipment can you hope to respond quickly when animals move around.

Stalking for pictures

Of all the methods of photographing wildlife at night, stalking is by far the most difficult, and least likely to yield an acceptable result. Any animal in its own environment is able to see and hear far better than you can, and knows the terrain much better. On the other hand, you may gain the occasional shot of animals which cannot be photographed by the other methods.

You will need to carry a camera, a flash and a torch. It is possible to mount the torch on the camera or strap it to the barrel of the lens to make it less cumbersome, but a more convenient solution is to use a caver's helmet with a lamp fixed to it. This leaves your hands free to operate the camera. Use a long lens, and a tele attachment on the flash.

It is sometimes possible to follow an animal along a path once it has become

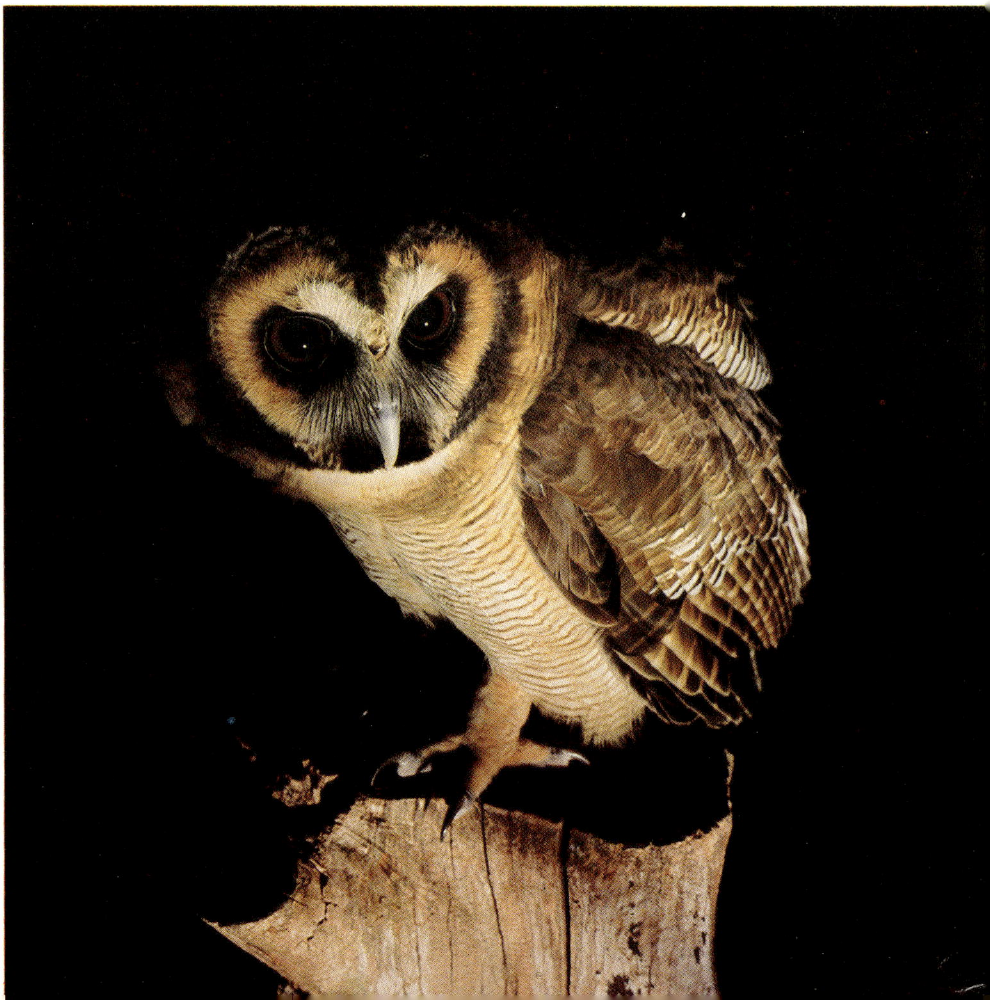

Lone owl *Night pictures often need powerful flash units to prevent dark subjects merging with the background*

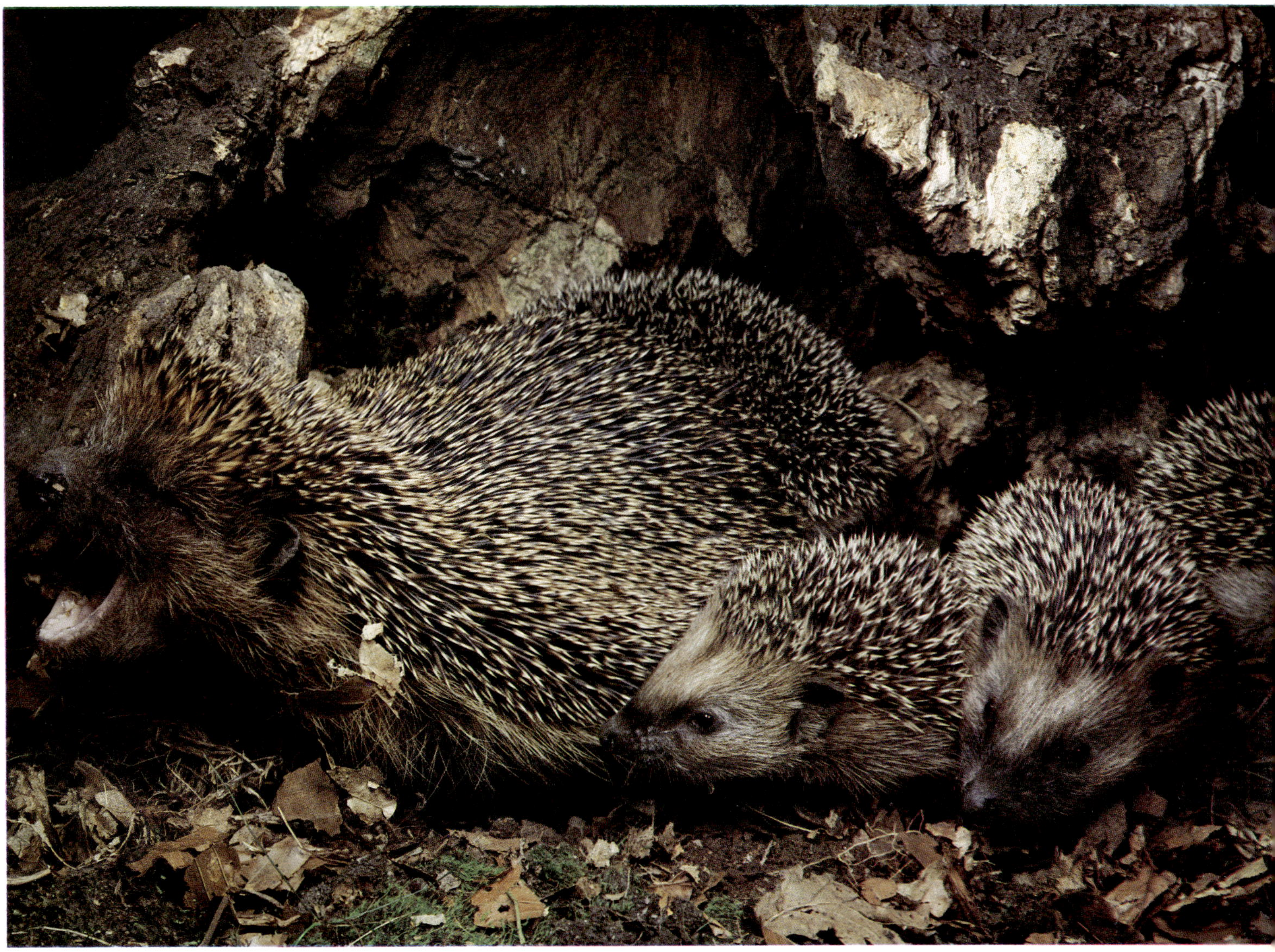

preoccupied in its search for food. Animals may scratch the ground looking for roots and grubs, and often become oblivious to observers, and it is then that you can take a picture. The animal will probably run off when it sees the flash, so you may only get one picture.

Never relentlessly pursue an animal just to get a picture. At certain times of the year food supplies may be limited, and by continually following the animal, you may cause it to go hungry.

Whenever walking through the countryside at night, either stalking or returning home, be very careful where you tread. Woodland paths are often slippery and fraught with obstacles such as tree roots which can easily be over-looked at night. Before you set out, tell someone where you are going, and what time they should expect you back. Walk the route in daylight first, and get to know any potential obstacles.

If you have never tried photographing animals and birds at night, then make a start by laying bait, and use this method to get to know more about wildlife and the photographic techniques involved. Local natural history societies should be able to offer you help and encourage-ment, and with patience, skill and good luck, you should be able to produce interesting and informative images.

Hedgehog family *Even in your back garden, regular baiting can attract good subjects—these hedgehogs were lured by a saucer of milk.* **Coyote** *In wilder areas, a regular supply of meat soon brings larger mammals*

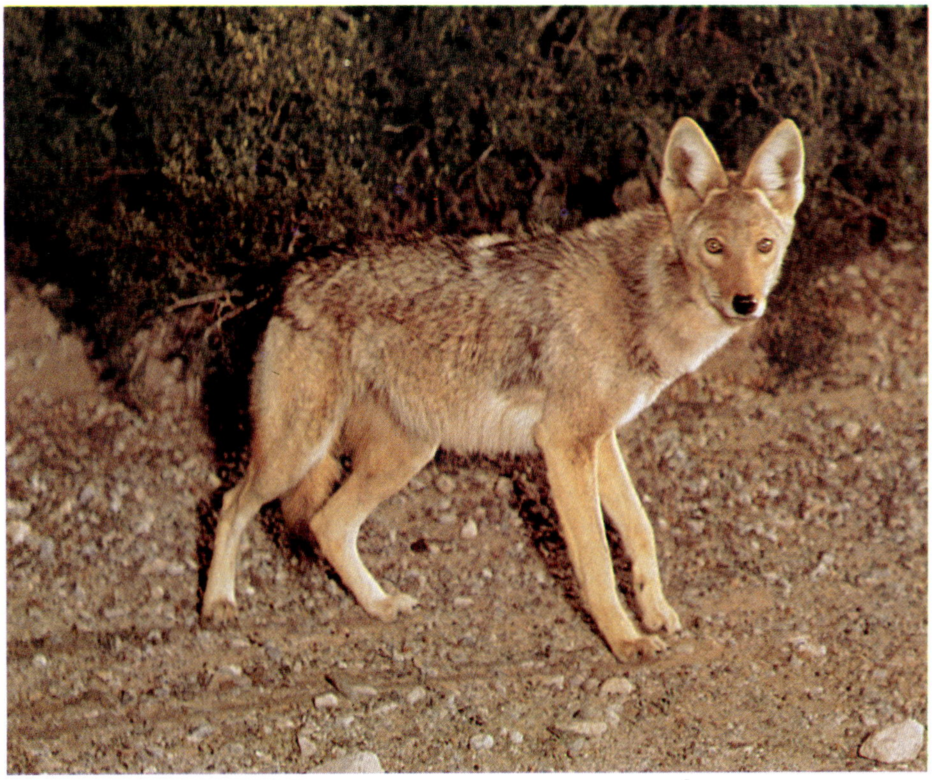

CHAPTER 14

MACRO PHOTOGRAPHY

Simple close-ups

Any photograph looks better when the frame is filled by the subject, but when you are photographing objects only a short distance away, it is sometimes impossible to focus the camera close enough to do this. Most 35 mm SLRs focus down to about half a metre—close enough to fill the frame with this page. It is not difficult to make lenses that focus closer—macro lenses do just this—but as you get nearer to the subject special problems begin to crop up. Half a metre is about as close as you can get without using special close-up techniques, so it is a sensible point to fix as the minimum focusing distance for standard lenses.

Close-up equipment

If you already own a zoom lens, you may not need any special equipment to take close-up pictures. Many zooms have a macro focusing facility, which makes it possible to focus on much closer objects than standard lenses can cope with. Some of these lenses focus as close as 15 cm, but are used at a long focal length. In this way, they are able to form images as big as 1:3—that is, where the image on the film is a third of the size of the original object. The quality of the pictures is usually poor, however, and for serious close-up work, macro zoom lenses are not really adequate.

True macro lenses are quite different from macro zooms. They are specially constructed for close-up work and usually focus from infinity right down to 1:2 (half life size) with a single turn of the focusing ring. Another feature that distinguishes them from other lenses is the design of their optical components. The aberrations of macro lenses are balanced so that they give their best results at short distances. Most other lenses work better when the subject is three metres or more from the camera. Unfortunately, macro lenses are bulkier than ordinary lenses, have small maximum apertures, and are expensive.

A much cheaper way to take close-up pictures is to use extension tubes, or supplementary close-up lenses. Supplementary lenses screw into the front of the camera lens, just as a filter does. They change the effective focal length of the lens, which enables you to focus on objects nearer the camera.

Extension tubes are simply short metal rings which fit between the camera body and the lens. Because they move the camera lens out from the body, nearby objects are brought into sharp focus. Both extension tubes and close-up lenses are sold either individually or in sets.

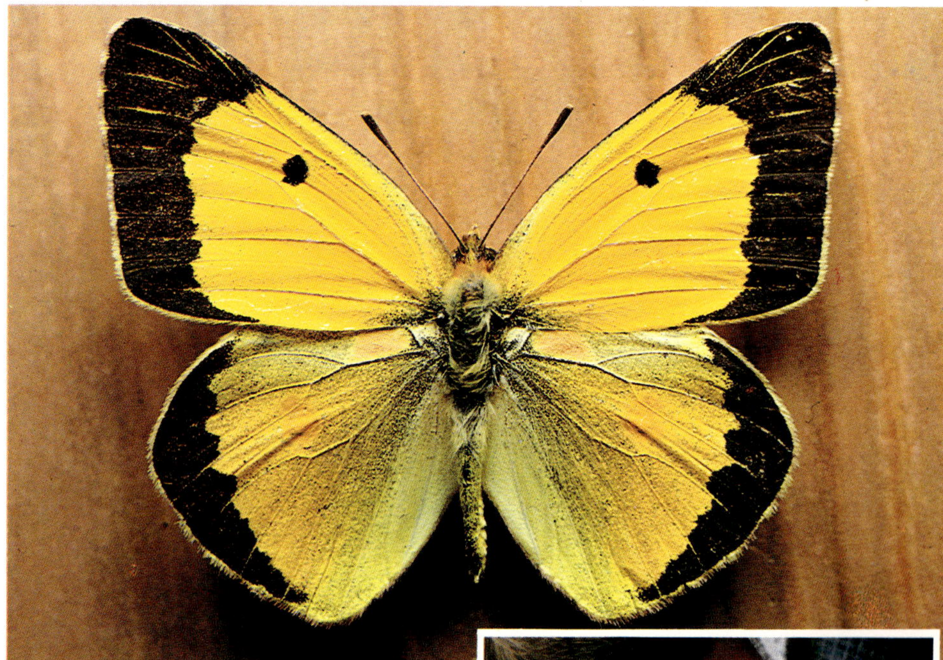

Butterfly *To fill the frame with a small subject, you will need to move in very close. A set of extension tubes moves the lens far enough out to bring a tiny subject like this into focus*

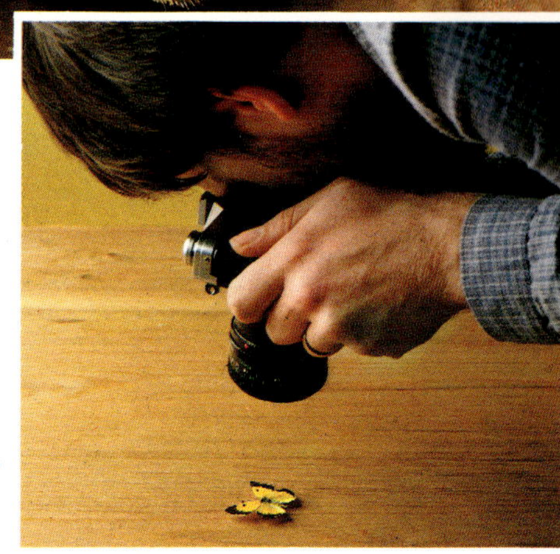

Best of all for close-up work, however, are expanding bellows. They act like extension tubes but give a continuous and much greater range. Some bellows will give up to 20 × magnification with a standard 50 mm lens. But all this comes at a high price—they are really items for the professional.

Whatever equipment you use, close-up photography needs more care than that of distant subjects. Because the images on film are bigger, camera shake becomes more obvious, and it is essential to keep the camera very steady. Focusing is critical, because depth of field is greatly reduced—often to a matter of millimetres—and there is no margin for error. Exposure measurement is sometimes complicated by the fact that certain close-up methods require extra exposure according to the magnification of the image. The secret with close-ups is to plan each shot meticulously.

Supplementary lenses

Close-up supplementary lenses minimize these problems. This is partly because only moderately close subjects can be handled by this method, and pictures in extreme close-up—where the problems are greatest—are better left to other types of equipment. Because they are simple to use, however, a set of close-up lenses is a good introduction to close-up photography.

Close-up supplementary lenses look rather like clear glass filters, but with a slight curve. Their power—simply, the degree of effect they have in focusing the lens closer—is measured in dioptres. The dioptre power is equal to the reciprocal of the focal length of the close-up lens. A one dioptre lens has a focal length of one metre, a two dioptre 0.5 metre, a three dioptre 0.3 metre, and so on. The higher the power a lens has, the more effect it will have when it is attached to the camera lens. When lenses are used in combination, the powers are added together to get the new power.

If you focus your camera lens on infinity, and then fit a close-up supplementary lens, the new point of sharp focus is equal to the focal length of the

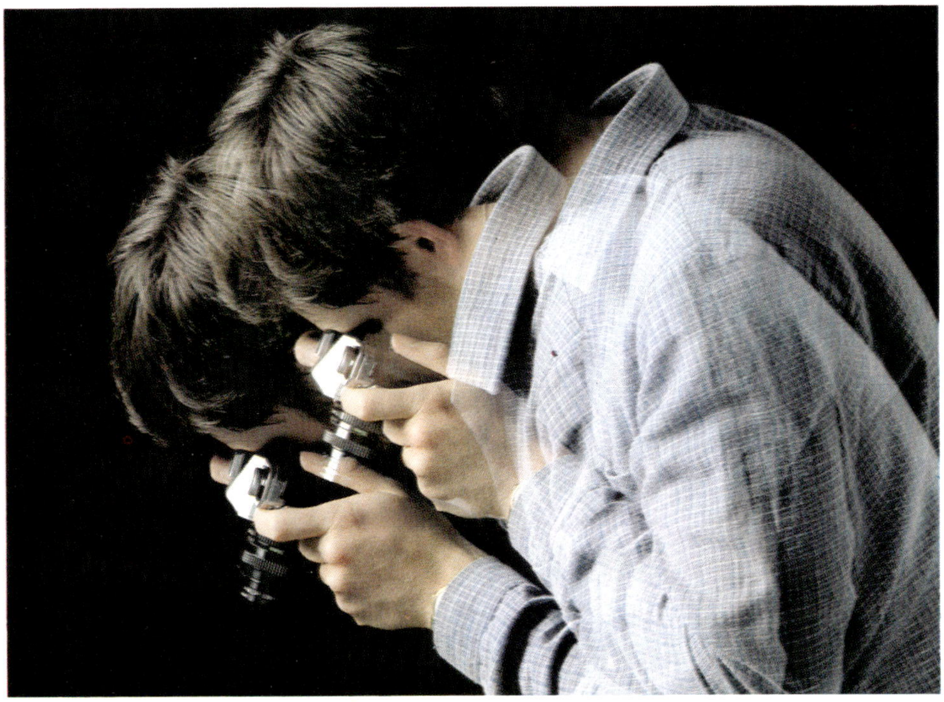

Focusing for close-up *At short range it is easiest to focus by moving back and forth until the subject appears sharp in the viewfinder*

supplementary. If you are using a two dioptre lens, for example, the new focus point will lie half a metre from the camera. With the lower power lenses, turning the focusing ring brings the point of sharp focus closer to the camera, but high power supplementaries have such a strong effect that the focusing ring becomes virtually useless. In this case, the simplest way to focus is to move back and forth, nearer and farther away from the subject, until the image snaps into focus in the viewfinder. This technique is useful for all kinds of close-up work, since at short distances a small change in camera position produces a dramatic change in the plane of the subject that is in focus.

Because a close-up lens provides only a limited focusing range, it is most convenient to buy two or more of them to use either in combination or individually. The most useful powers are +3 and +2 dioptre—lower powers have too little effect when used with a standard lens, and higher powers, too much.

Although there are formulae which can be used to calculate the new point of sharp focus when a close-up lens is fitted to a prime lens, these are unnecessary when using an SLR camera, because the image can be viewed directly through the lens. Once you get used to using close-up lenses, you should not find it difficult to pick out the one that you need.

Close-up lenses have less effect on wide angle lenses, and more effect on telephotos, so if you have a range of lenses, it might be worthwhile trying out a close-up lens with several of them, as this will make a wider range of magnifications possible. This is only possible if all the lenses take the same diameter of filters, or if you have step-up or step-down rings to suit all your lenses.

The greatest advantage of using close-up supplementary lenses is that, unlike other close-up methods, no exposure compensation is necessary, and the viewfinder does not darken. This means that focusing and composing the picture is easy, and can be done in the usual way. A further advantage is that even if your camera does not have a TTL exposure meter, exposure readings from a hand-held meter will still be accurate—this is not the case with other close-up systems.

A few non-SLR cameras accept close-up lenses, but these are usually of quite low powers, and focusing must be done by guesswork or calculation. Higher powers make the camera viewfinder useless, because parallax becomes a serious problem, and with twin lens reflex cameras focusing becomes a tedious routine involving swapping the close-up lens from the viewing to the taking lens and back again. Rangefinder cameras can sometimes be fitted with a close-up lens and a special adapter, which simultaneously corrects parallax and alters the rangefinder to work at short distances.

The major drawback to close-up lenses is that the image quality they produce is not very good. This is particularly true with high power close-up lenses, but whichever one you are using, you should stop the camera lens down to the smallest practical aperture, as this will improve the performance of the combination. Use the weakest close-up lens possible, and never use two supplementary lenses if you can get away with one. If you have to use two, fit the stronger one nearer the camera.

Using extension tubes

Extension tubes are much more expensive than close-up lenses, but they are capable of much better results. They can, however, only be used with SLR cameras. They are generally sold in sets of three tubes, each with a different length.

In use, one end of the tube is fitted to the camera body with the lens fitted into the other end. With the more expensive tubes, your camera's meter remains coupled to the lens by a series of rods and levers, but the cheapest tubes do not have this facility, and the meter can only be used in the manual mode.

The focusing distance—and also how much the image appears enlarged—depends partly on how far the lens is from the film. The larger the lens exten-

Fitting a ring *Attaching an extension ring is no more difficult than changing a lens. Bayonet mounts couple the ring to the camera body and lens and take just a few seconds to fit*

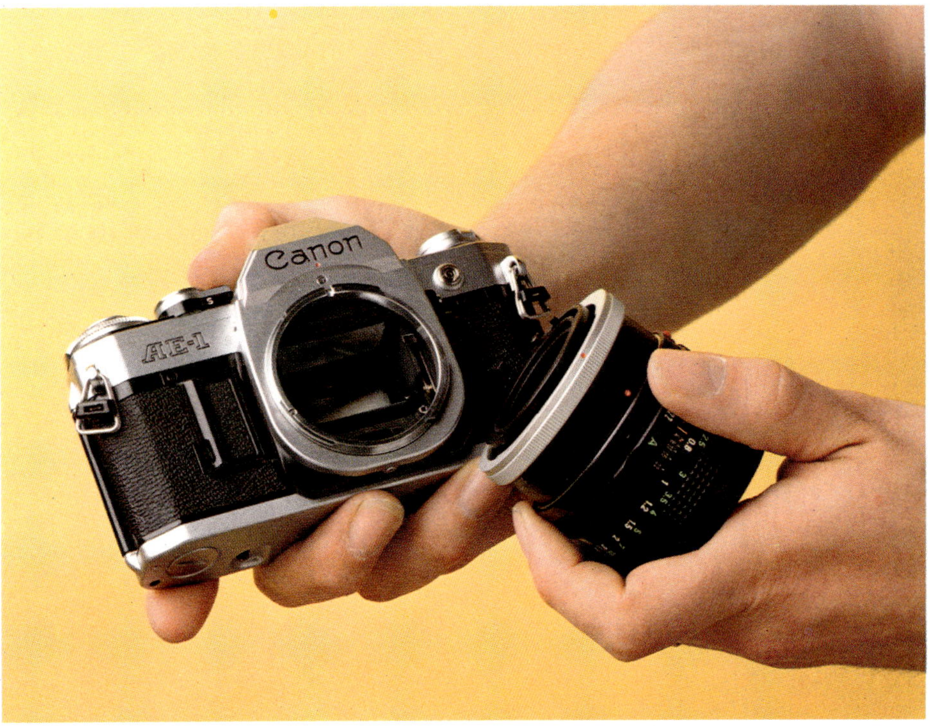

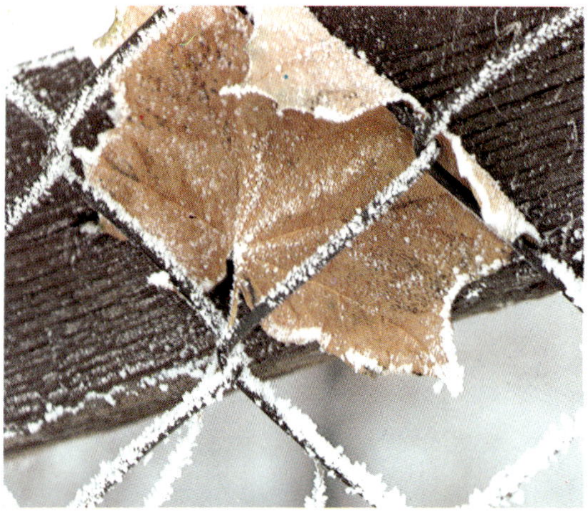

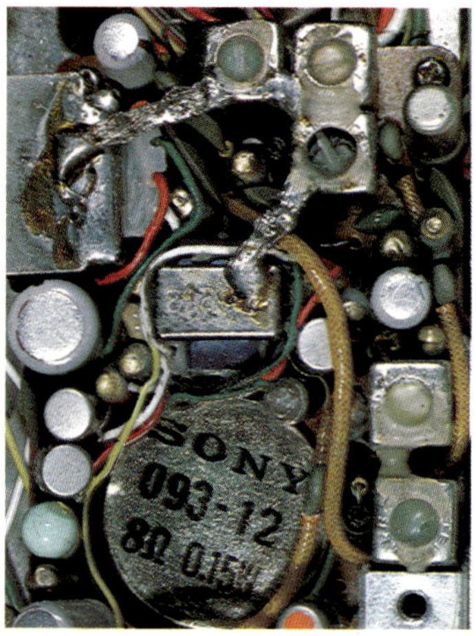

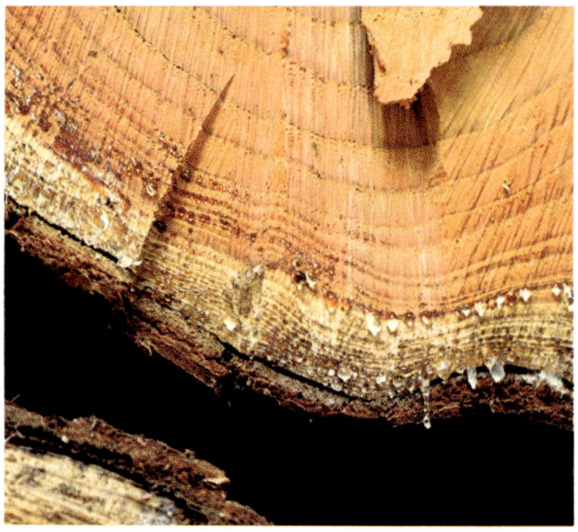

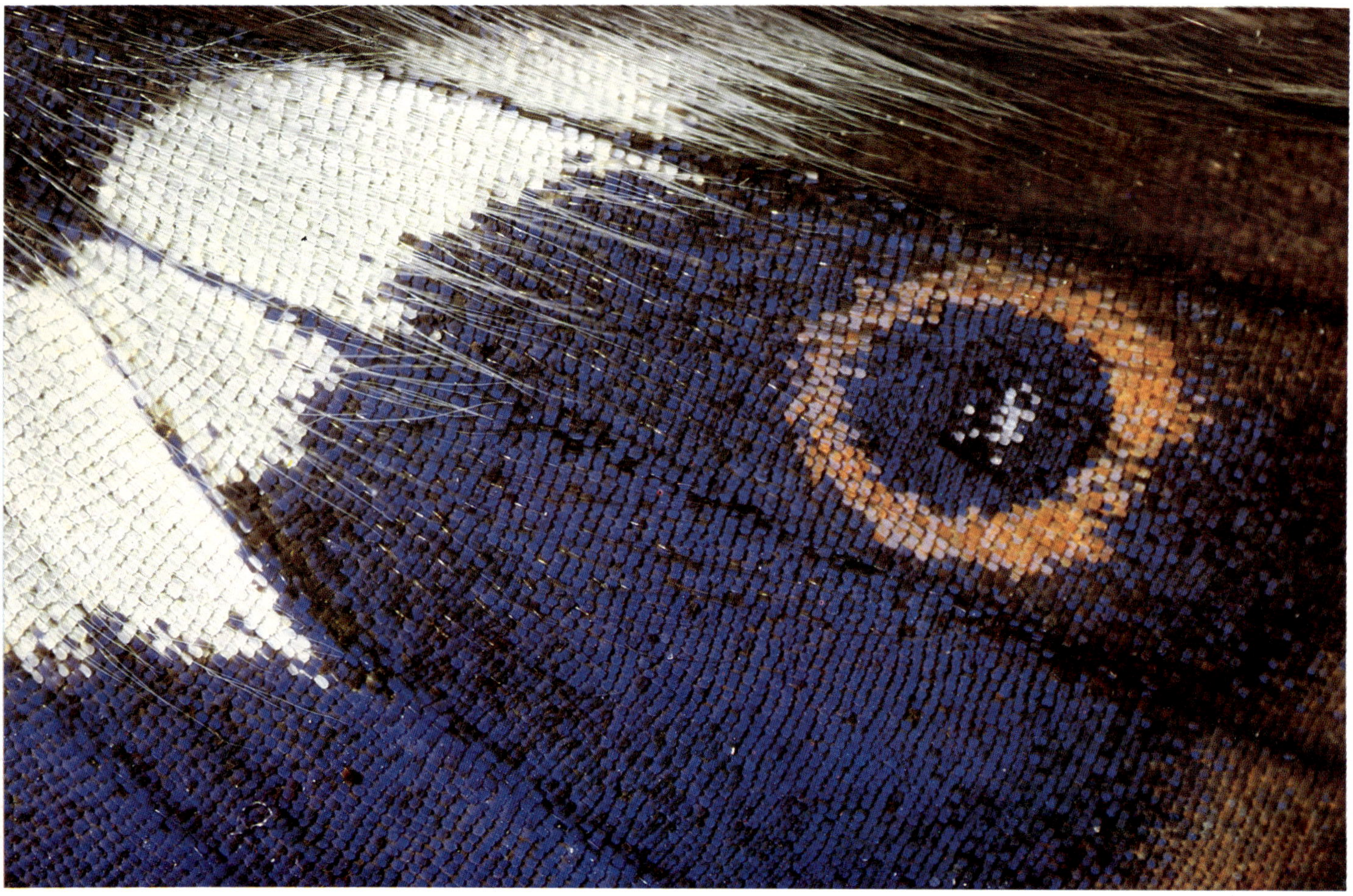

sion, the greater is the degree of enlargement, so stacking up three extension tubes behind a lens allows you to focus much closer than if you just use one. The focal length of the lens in use also has an effect. The longer its focal length, the greater extension is needed to reach a particular magnification.

If a lens is moved from the film until it is twice its focal length away, the image on the film will be exactly the same size as the subject. This means that to form a life size image, a 200 mm lens needs a four times as much extension as a 50 mm.

The exact size of each extension ring varies between manufacturers so the precise degree of magnification also varies. The ideal set of rings would enable the photographer to focus on any point from the minimum focusing distance of the lens alone, right down to life size or closer. In reality, this would need more than three rings, and most sets either leave gaps in the focusing range, or cover a more limited range of magnifications. However, most close-up pictures can be cropped at the printing stage if the subject does not fill the frame perfectly, so this is not a really serious drawback.

Focusing with close-up lenses is partly a matter of knowing which tube to fit in order to get the subject in focus at a certain distance, though this is easy to learn with practice. Once you have fitted a tube, moving back and forth brings the subject into the plane of sharp focus. As with close-up lenses, the focusing action of the lens itself is only of limited use, though it can make quite a difference with the shorter tubes.

Focusing is hindered by the fact that at high magnifications, the light from the image is spread out over a larger area

Common or garden close-up *The beauty of macro photography is that it enables you to see ordinary objects in a new light. Photographed from a few centimetres away, even the most mundane objects become almost unrecognizable and can take on an interesting abstract quality. Look especially for subjects like these where all the important detail lies in a flat plane—depth of field is very limited at high magnifications*

than normal. This means that the focusing screen becomes dark, and the microprisms and rangefinder wedges may black out. Focusing must then be carried out using the matt glass part of the screen.

This darkening also affects the image on film, so when you are using extension tubes, you must allow some extra exposure to take this into account. A TTL meter will automatically make the adjustment. When using a separate non-TTL meter, the extra exposure must be carefully worked out. The procedure for doing this is explained in the panel.

Automatic extension tubes retain all the normal functions of the camera with which they are used, but manual tubes may present some difficulties, particularly if the camera is fully automatic with no manual override. Since each type of camera has different characteristics, you should carefully read the instruction booklet before buying a set of extension tubes—particularly if they are not made by the camera manufacturer.

Movement and depth of field

Regardless of which method you use to take close-up pictures, depth of field is always a problem. As you get closer to your subject, it shrinks dramatically. At high magnifications, it is effectively zero, and the part of the subject that is sharp forms a flat plane—the *plane of sharp focus*. This means that there is no margin for focusing error, and objects only a couple of millimetres in front of or behind the plane of sharp focus will be recorded on the film as a shapeless blur. Focusing must be done with great care and precision, and the lens should be stopped down as much as possible to maximize depth of field.

Subject and camera movement take on increased significance in close-up work, for this very reason. Not only does camera movement cause blur if it takes place while the shutter is open, but it can also throw the whole image out of focus. Moving the camera by a centimetre has little effect when a lens is focused on infinity, but it can render a close-up of a bumble bee totally out of focus. This makes a tripod essential for all but moderate close-ups.

A tripod can eliminate camera shake, but it can do nothing to stop subject movement. A slight breeze can blow a flower right out of the picture, and unless your subject is static, you should use the fastest possible shutter speed. This in itself brings problems, because a fast shutter speed usually means using a wide aperture.

Since a small aperture is needed to give good depth of field, close-up pictures can present enormous exposure difficulties. The only simple solution is to load the camera with fast film, which allows both a high shutter speed and a small aperture. Electronic flash can help considerably, since it provides extra light and freezes motion, but the use of flash at short distances is in itself a fairly specialized technique, and a subsequent article deals with this.

Most of the problems with close-up work only crop up at high magnifications, or when a separate light meter is being used. If you have an SLR camera with through the lens metering, it is easy to take successful close-up pictures with the relatively simple equipment described here. All the pictures on the opposite page were taken with close-up lenses or extension tubes, and you can easily take equally effective pictures without even leaving your home.

Exposure compensation

All exposure meters which do not read through the lens are calibrated on the basis that the camera lens is focused on infinity. At closer subject distances, the lens is moved farther away from the film, and the light passing through the lens is spread over a wider area, so it is dimmer. This fall-off in illumination obeys the inverse square law so doubling the lens extension cuts the brightness to only a quarter.

Whenever the film-to-lens distance is increased to take a close-up picture, you must allow extra exposure to take this into account. Since close-up lenses focus closer without moving the lens farther out from the film, they need no compensation, but all other close-up systems do.

The necessary correction is affected not only by the lens extension, but the also by the focal length. To work out the correction, divide the total lens extension by the focal length, and square the result.

If you are not mathematical and use a 35 mm camera, you may find the chart below helpful. Set up your close-up picture, then place the chart in the subject position. Line up the right hand side of the panel with the right hand short side of the viewfinder frame, and you can then read off the compensation on the left hand side, either in the form of the number of *f*-stops by which the lens aperture should be opened, or an exposure factor, by which the exposure time should be multiplied.

You can also calculate the exposure compensation by measuring the total lens extension. Note, though, that this will not work with telephoto or retrofocus lenses.

Example

A 50 mm lens is fitted to a 30 mm extension tube to take a close-up picture, and the focusing mount of the lens provides some extra lens extension.

Since you cannot measure the lens-to-film distance directly, it must be worked out indirectly. When the lens is focused on infinity, its extension from the film position is exactly the same as its focal length. The extra extension for closer subjects can be found by seeing how much the overall physical length of the lens increases over its length when focused on infinity. When focused on infinity, the lens extension must be the same as its focal length.

In this case:

Lens length for close up = 48 mm (A)
Length at infinity = 43 mm (B)
Subtract B from A = 5 mm (C)
Extension at infinity = 50 mm (D)
Extension tube length = 30 mm (E)
Add C, D, and E = 5 + 50 + 30 = 85 mm
The total extension, then, is 85 mm.
Divide this by the focal length $= \frac{85}{50} = 1.7$
Square the result to get the compensation $1.7^2 = 2.89$
The estimated exposure time should be nearly tripled.

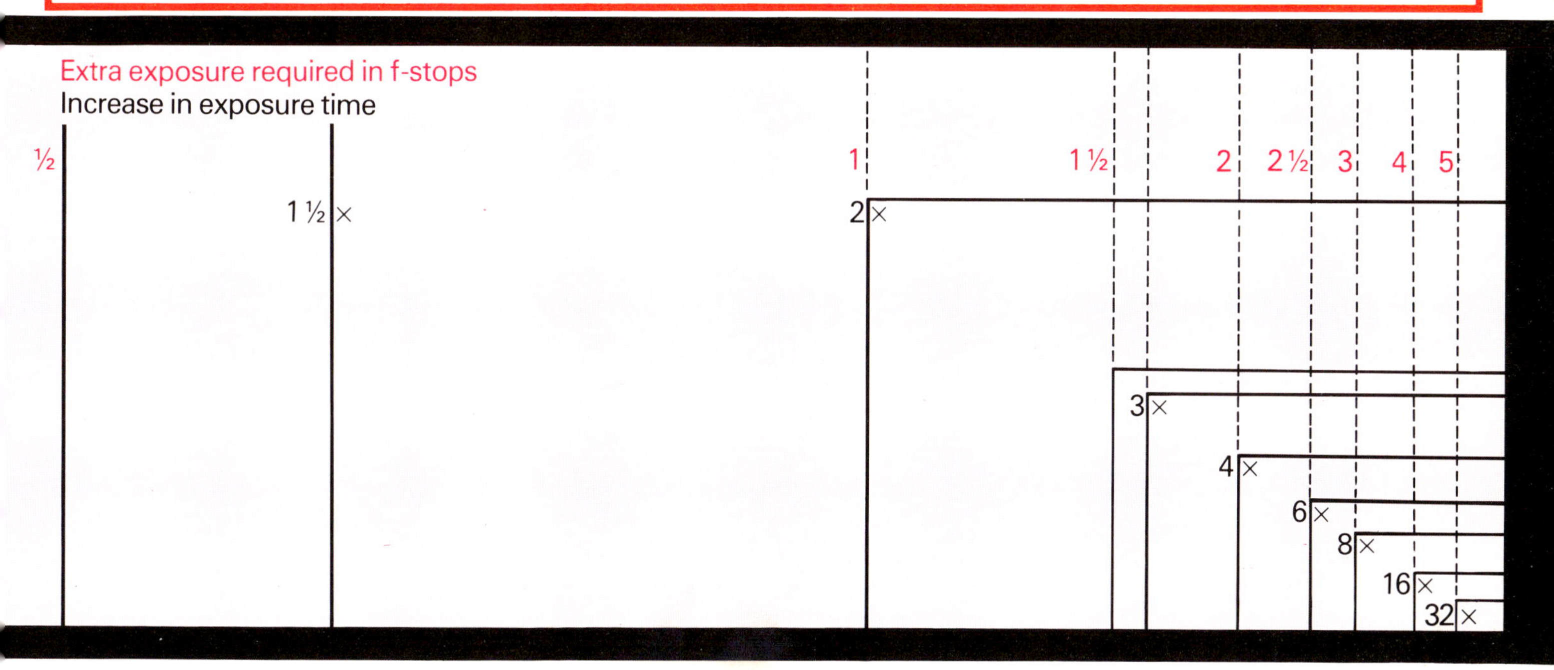

Lighting for close-ups

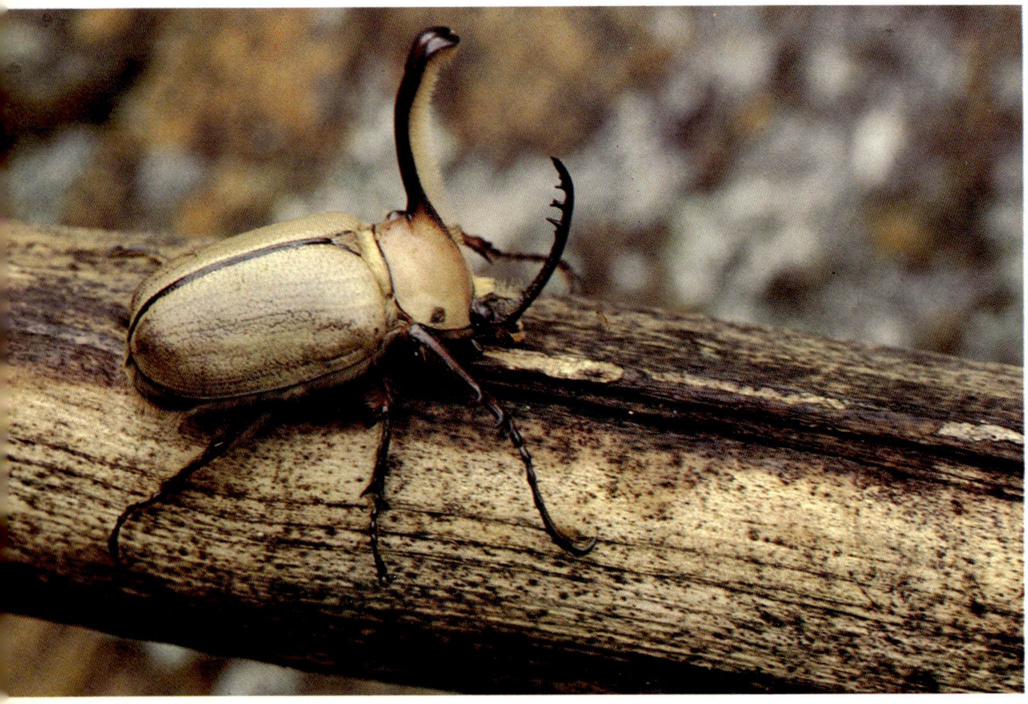

Rhinoceros beetle *In overcast weather, when shadows are gentle and soft, natural daylight may be all you need to light close-up pictures*

Fungus in focus *In most cases, however, some extra light is necessary. This mushroom was lit using a single flash unit on the right, with a reflector card opposite to fill in the shadows*

Small subjects present the photographer with special lighting problems, because when camera and subject are very close together, seemingly tiny patches of shadow are often enlarged until they fill half the picture. To combat the high contrasts and loss of detail that can spoil close-up pictures, you need to light your subject even more carefully than usual. Careful illumination is also needed to ensure that the subject is properly lit for, with such a small subject area, the total amount of light available is very small. The table in the previous chapter showed how to compensate for this by increasing exposure. But sometimes it is better to provide your own light.

Outdoor close-ups

Natural daylight is one of the most convenient light sources—it is usually quite bright and, unlike electronic flash, it provides continuous illumination, so it is easy to see how the subject is lit. For these and other reasons, many photographers take their first close-up pictures out of doors, often of a natural history subject such as a flower.

Despite its advantages, however, daylight has some drawbacks as a means of illuminating small objects. For one thing, it is difficult to control, and if you are working out a trip in advance it is impossible to predict whether you will be working in sunny or overcast conditions. In brilliant sunlight the strong shadows may help you to bring out a sense of depth in a subject, but in close-up work you must make sure that important detail is not obscured by heavy shadow. If this seems to be a problem, there are two possible solutions—either you can wait until the sun is covered by a cloud, so there is a much softer light, or you can control the sunlight by the careful use of reflectors and diffusers.

For this purpose, it is worth carrying several pieces of white and grey card, each about 20 × 25 cm, if you frequently take close-up pictures outdoors. A diffuser can be made from a sheet of tracing paper or acrylic lighting gel, which is more durable. Or you can buy a portable, foldaway diffusing ring, such as the Lastolite (see page 208).

Both reflector cards and diffusers are used outside the picture area to direct light into the shadows of the subject and reduce the overall contrast of a picture. Diffusers are used between the light source—in this case the sun—and the subject to provide an even, less directional source of illumination than direct sunlight. A reflector card can have an even more dramatic effect, and can lighten shadows considerably. White card is useful for this purpose, but a card covered with crumpled kitchen foil is

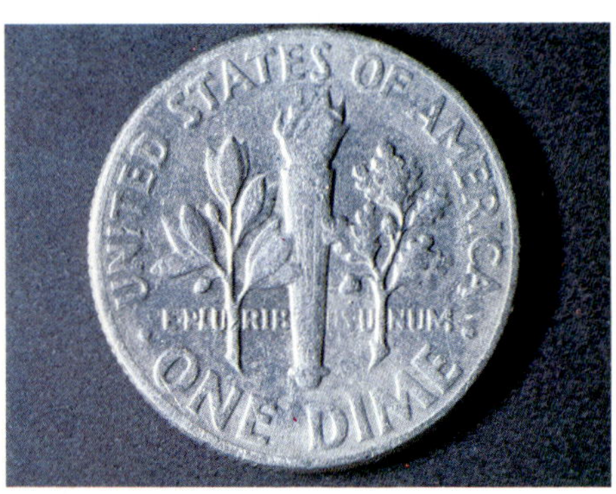

Single flash *The simplest form of lighting is a single flash directed straight at the subject. This produces heavy, well defined shadows and relatively harsh modelling*

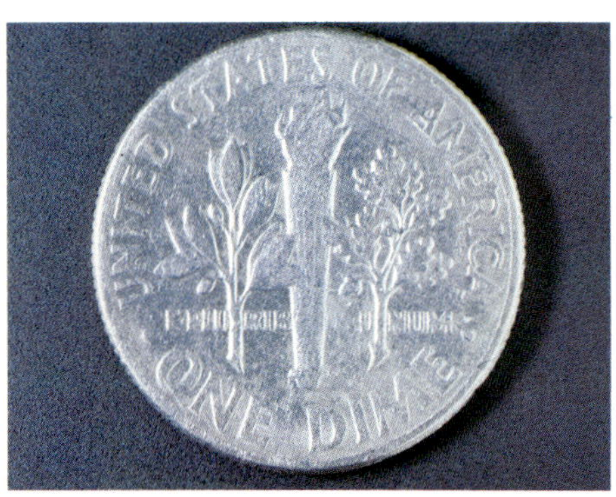

Diffused flash *A cylinder of tracing paper around the subject, lit by a single flash, improves the lighting. But it can sometimes eliminate the highlights, producing a dull result*

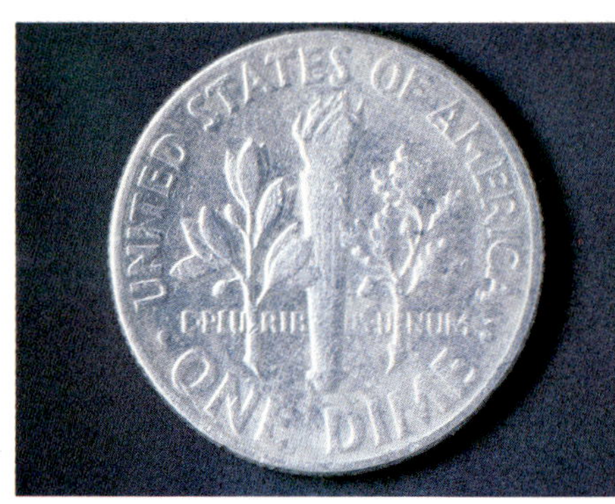

Twin flash *Flat objects such as stamps can be lit by two undiffused flashguns. Three-dimensional objects, however, cast harsh shadows, and this method of lighting may not be suitable*

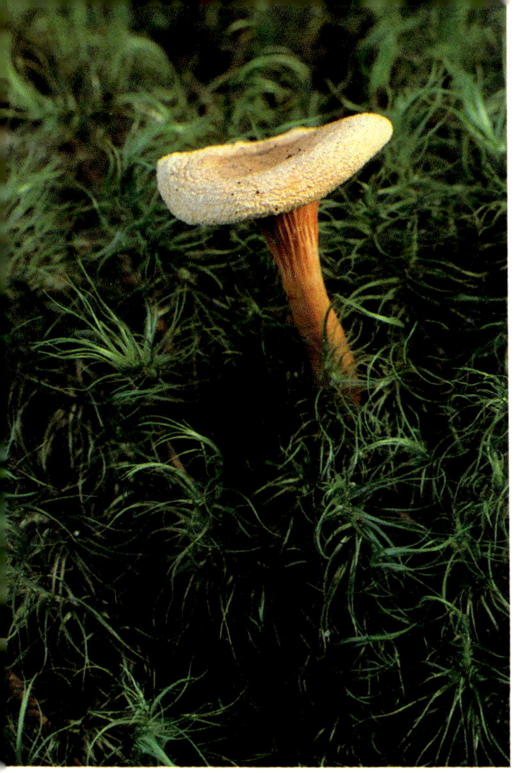

often more efficient. Its many faceted surface reflects light in a similar manner to a sunlit pool of water. Flat silver card tends to have a very directional effect if used in bright sunlight, producing a very unnatural appearance, and it is unwise to use this or coloured reflectors unless you have a very clear idea of the effect you are trying to achieve.

Reflector cards can also be used as neutral backgrounds, but if you use white card as a background when photographing a small subject such as a plant, remember that the reflective surface of the card also affects the overall lighting. It introduces an element of diffuse backlighting, and the apparent transparency of the flowers or leaves is changed. The effect is less noticeable with a grey or coloured card.

Although direct sunlight presents the photographer with problems of harsh shadows and burnt-out highlights, not all outdoor subjects are found on exposed ground which is reached by the direct rays of the sun. Fungi, for example, often grow in dark, dank woods where even on the sunniest day the light is dim and diffuse. This means that the outline of the plant can easily disappear into a leaf covered background unless some additional lighting is used. There are exposure problems, too, simply because the light is so dim, and because depth of field considerations require the use of a small aperture. Even with a tripod and fast film, available light photography may not be feasible. In such cases, the most satisfactory solution is to use an electronic flash unit, and to control it so that the flash is used as the main light with daylight as fill-in.

The commonly available computer type unit is best avoided for close-up work, and the smallest, cheapest manual gun is almost certainly adequate for most requirements. A very powerful flash may actually prove difficult to use, and a weaker flash makes it easier to strike a balance between flash and natural daylight.

Whatever flashgun you use, it is essential that you are completely familiar with its power output and method of operation, so that you can predict the precise effect and determine the exposure accurately.

Using flash and daylight in combination takes some practice, and although there are some circumstances where direct flash on camera is acceptable, it is more likely that you will need an extension lead to allow you to use the flash unit well away from the camera. For example, when photographing a toadstool deep in a wood, flash on camera would give very flat illumination over a limited range, with a totally black background. More natural lighting is produced if you try to simulate the quality of light that would fall on the toadstool if it was growing in an open spot in sunlight. In the open, sunlight would fall on it from above and to the side so you should place the flashgun in a position which reproduces this kind of lighting.

In this case, you should direct the flash so that it is at about 45° to the camera axis in both vertical and hori-

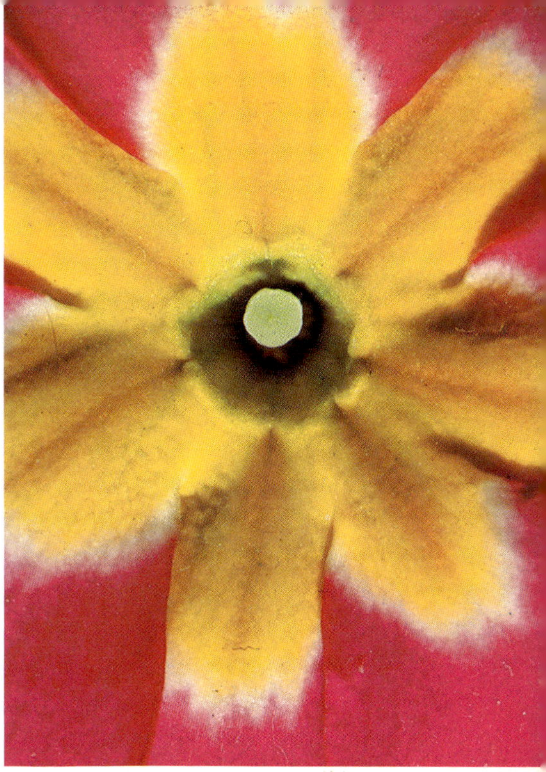

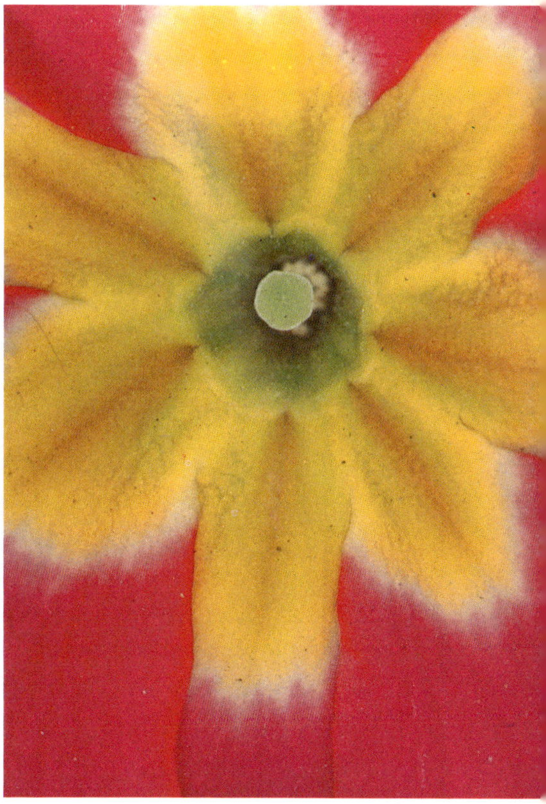

Bright flower *All types of lighting must be used with discretion. Axial illumination (bottom) eliminates shadows but colours are richer when a single direct flash is used (top)*

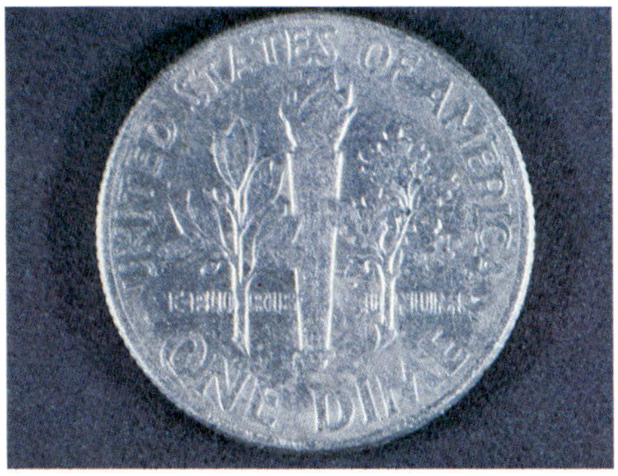

A hole for highlights *By cutting a hole in the cylinder of tracing paper that surrounds the subject, some of the flash falls directly on it, to give a more sparkling result*

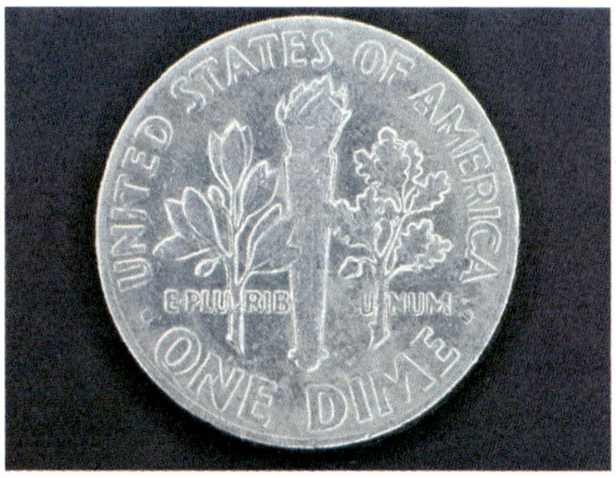

Ring flash *The shadowless illumination that makes ring flash so suitable for heavily textured subjects can actually be a disadvantage in some circumstances, flattening out important detail*

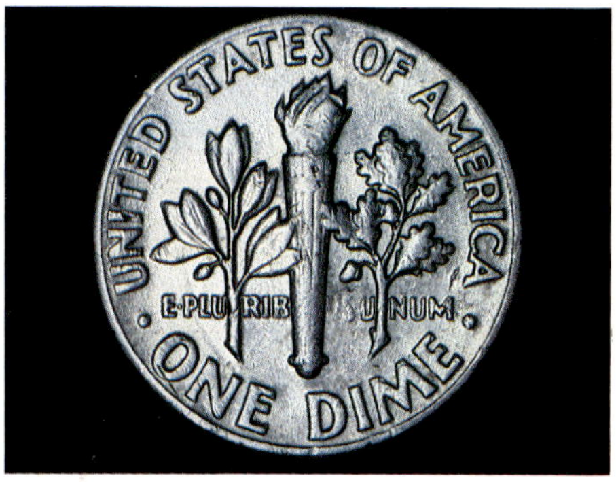

Axial lighting *can sometimes be useful for illuminating particularly difficult subjects, and is ideal for objects that have reflective surfaces at odd angles*

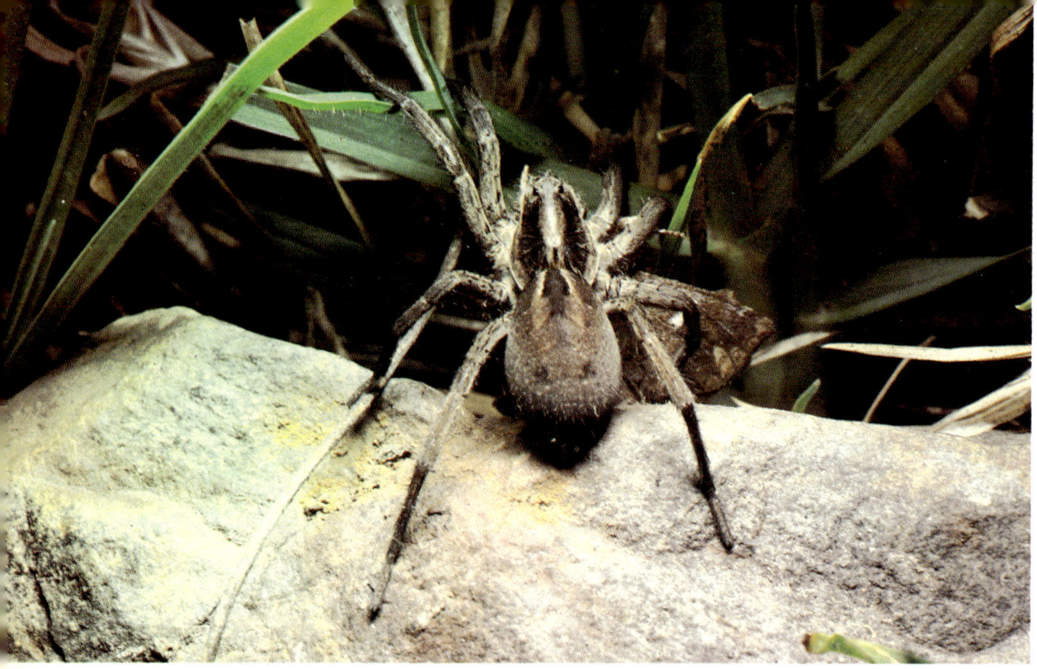

Spider and moth *For this picture, flash was diffused by bouncing it off a piece of white card, which was held directly above the spider and its prey*

Diffuse lighting *A simple and effective way to light a small subject is to surround it with a cylinder of tracing paper, and light this from the side*

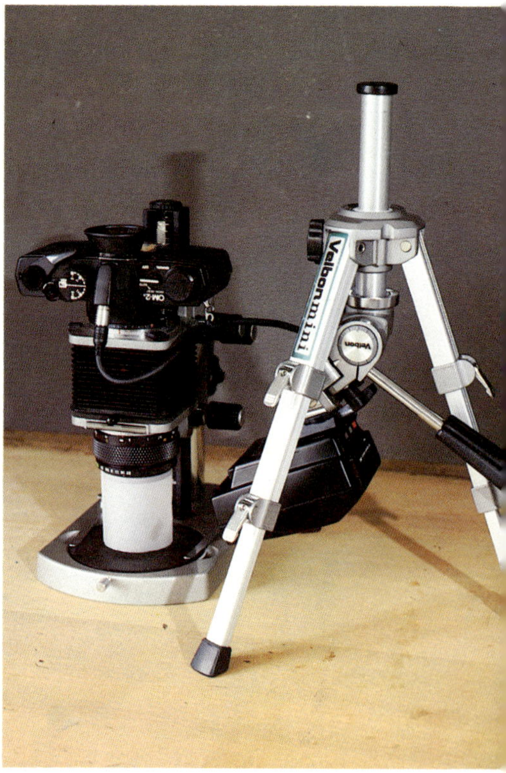

zontal planes—similar to conventional portrait lighting. This reproduces natural sunlight, but unfortunately it also brings with it the same problems of deep shadows that you encounter when using sunlight as a light source. One solution to this is to use reflectors and diffusers to fill in the shadows formed by the flash, but by using a long exposure, you may be able to use the daylight itself to brighten the dark shadows and reduce the contrast of the subject.

This is done by carefully balancing the exposure for flash with that from the daylight. The aim is to give a normal flash exposure combined with a daylight exposure one stop less than normal. This will give twice as much flash as daylight, so the daylight will fill in the shadows.

The first step is to work out the aperture required for the flash exposure. If you have an automatic unit which will work at close distances you can use the aperture it recommends on the table on the side or back of the unit, but remember that if your flash unit is at a angle to the line of sight you will inevitably lose some of the effect of the flash. With a manual gun you will probably need to know the guide number, since the tables on the units rarely cover very close distances. If you do not know the guide number, work it

Special techniques

Axial illumination

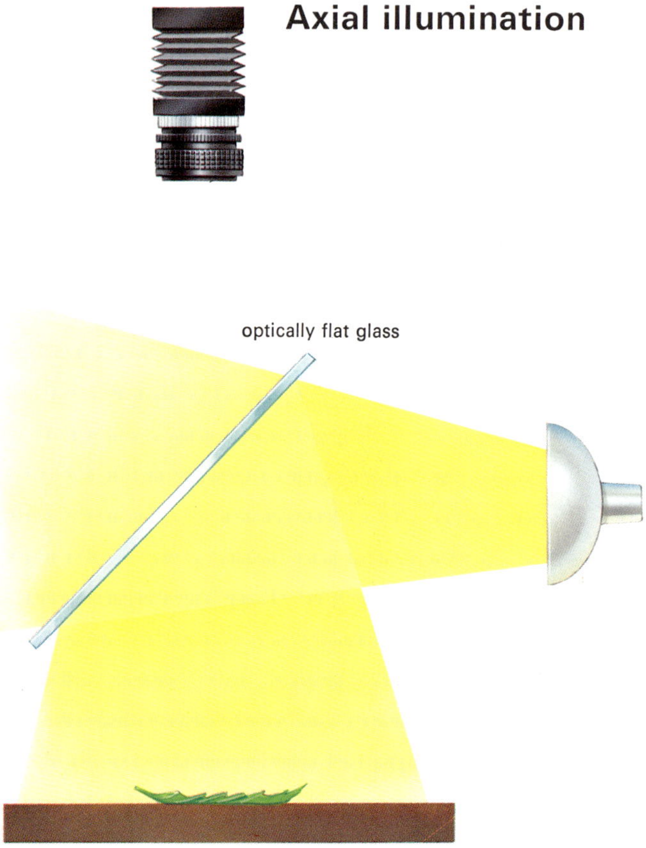

Darkfield illumination

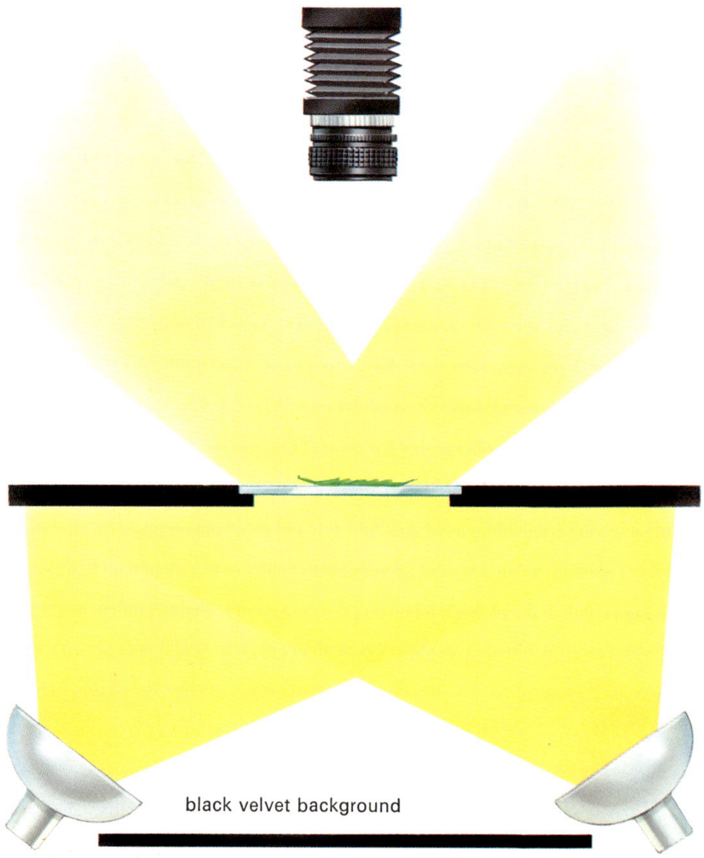

out from the table by multiplying any flash-to-subject distance by the aperture it recommends. Use this GN to find the aperture for the actual subject distance. This will be your working aperture for the shot.

Next, find the shutter speed required for the daylight exposure by opening up by one stop from the working aperture and taking a reading. Remember to stop down again to the working aperture before taking the shot.

This procedure results in a flash to daylight ratio of 2:1, and though this is fine for colour materials, a ratio of 4:1 or 8:1 is better for black and white materials whose contrast can be controlled in printing. Greater contrast between the flash and fill-in is achieved by taking the daylight exposure reading at a proportionately wider aperture, before stopping down as before to the working aperture. Do not forget that if you are using extension tubes or bellows, a reduced amount of light reaches the film, and you must compensate for this as shown on page 153.

Close-ups indoors

Certain types of subject require close-up photography outdoors, but most small objects can be brought indoors and shot in the studio. This eliminates the inconvenience of carrying bulky camera gear out on location.

Elaborate equipment is not necessary for close-up lighting indoors. Because such a small area is being photographed, low power flash or tungsten lighting is all that is needed. A simple lighting set-up might consist of one lamp, a couple of white reflector boards to fill in the shadows, and a few small mirrors to add sparkling highlights.

The first decision to be made is whether to use flash or tungsten light. Tungsten is easier to control, but heats up small subjects rapidly, and requires either tungsten balanced colour film or heavy filtration. Electronic flash, on the other hand, can be used with the more widely available daylight balanced film, but makes it more difficult to see what the final result will look like.

To get round this problem, professional studio flash units incorporate modelling lights, and you can simulate the effect of these on a simple level by setting up the shot using a small reading lamp as a light source, then replacing it with a flash unit immediately before exposure. The effect of the flash is likely to be slightly different, but this technique can still provide a useful guide if you are using only one light source. With more than one, it may be difficult to match the output of the flashguns and tungsten lamps.

General lighting techniques indoors are very similar to those outdoors when it comes to the placement of lights and reflectors, but a studio allows even greater versatility. This is important when extremely soft lighting is required—when the subject is very shiny, for example, or when it has a deeply convoluted surface which casts heavy featureless shadows.

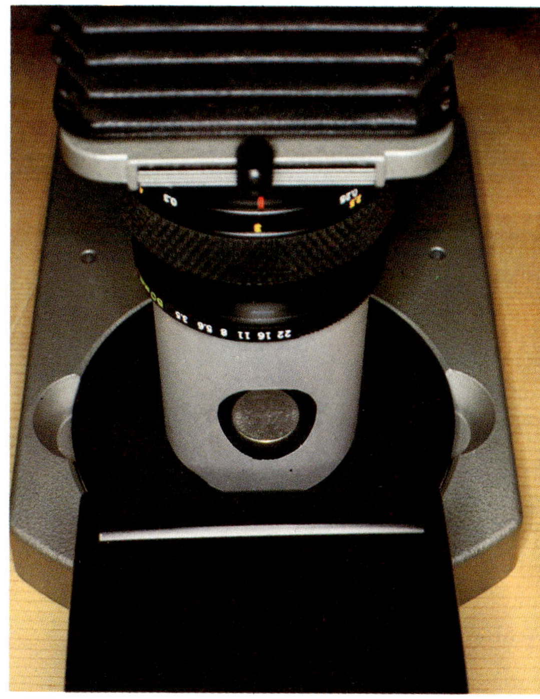

More sparkle *With reflective subjects, diffuse lighting may be too dull. Holes cut in the diffuser add highlights, and black card inside puts in shadows*

A cheap and simple way of providing this flat lighting is to surround the subject with a cylinder of tracing paper, then shoot from one end. You can create soft but directional lighting by using only one light source, at one side of the cylinder, but by using two lamps—one on either side—you can make the lighting completely even. For really tiny objects, use a clean white eggshell instead of a tracing paper cylinder, and for larger ones, construct a tent out of thin white fabric and light this in the same way as before.

Sometimes, these techniques provide light that is too flat, particularly if you are photographing a small reflective subject. To add bright highlights, make a hole in the diffuser which surrounds the subject. Light from the lamp can then be shone on to the subject, either directly or by using mirrors. 'Shadows' can be created by putting strips of black paper or card inside the diffusing enclosure.

When very flat lighting is required for a non-reflective subject, a useful if expensive option is ring flash. This provides completely shadow free lighting by effectively bending the flashtube—in a suitable reflector—around the front of the camera lens. The quality of light produced by a ring flash is ideal for an objective, precise record of a small subject. This has led to it being widely used by medical photographers and for other scientific purposes, but for many subjects the effects it produces are too flat and lacking in depth .Unless you have very specific reasons for using ring flash, it is better to stick to more conventional methods, and deal with each and every close-up lighting problem on its own merits.

Some subjects demand special treatment, maybe to emphasize their texture or their transparency. To bring out detail in shiny, textured objects without creating burnt-out highlights, you can use an effect called *axial illumination*. This completely shadowless form of lighting is produced by arranging the axis of the lamp and that of the camera lens so that they lie at right angles to each other. A sheet of flat picture glass is set at 45° and reflects the light down on to the subject.

The reflection of the light is only partial, because most passes straight through the glass sheet, and you should take this into account when calculating the exposure.

For translucent objects, *darkfield illumination* is particularly useful. The subject is placed on a sheet of glass at a distance from a black background, and backlit in such a way that the lamps do not shine into the camera lens. The subject then appears to be floating in space, and glows brightly against a solid black background.

If you decide to try this technique, you will undoubtedly find it easier to master if you use tungsten lighting rather than flash. You must also take great care to prevent dust from falling on the glass plate, as every speck will be picked up by the bright backlighting.

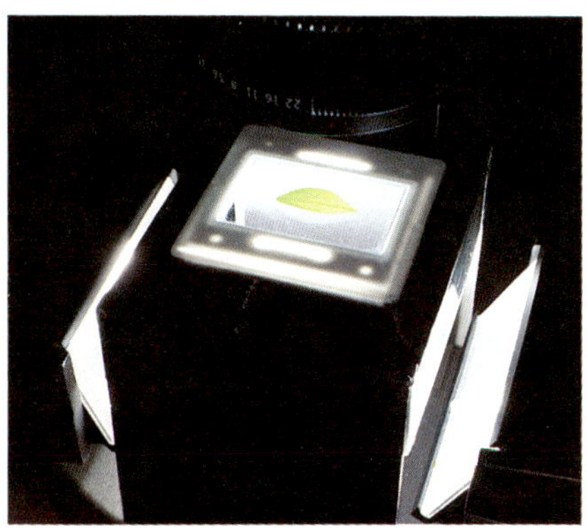

Darkfield illumination *A method for bringing out detail in translucent and semitransparent objects. The specimen is supported by a sheet of glass, with a sheet of black paper or fabric behind. The glass is lit from below by flash or tungsten light*

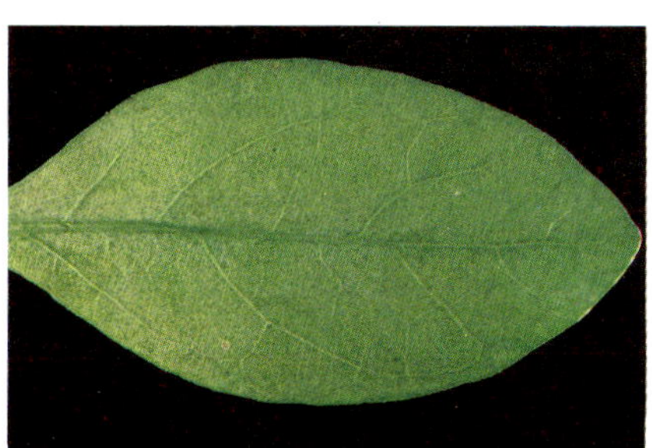

CHAPTER 15
SPECIALIST TECHNIQUES
Photography underwater

Most of us think of the sea as a backdrop for photographs of harbours, boats and beaches. But the surface of the sea is like a curtain that conceals another world—a world where the photographer is weightless, and can move easily in all directions.

Snorkel and scuba diving provide the key to this hidden world, and if you are learning to skindive, you may want to take pictures of what you see underwater. Readily available nowadays is a wide range of special cameras and waterproof housings that make this a practical proposition, but underwater photography is not just a matter of picking up a suitable camera, and diving head-first into the water. There is a lot more to it than that.

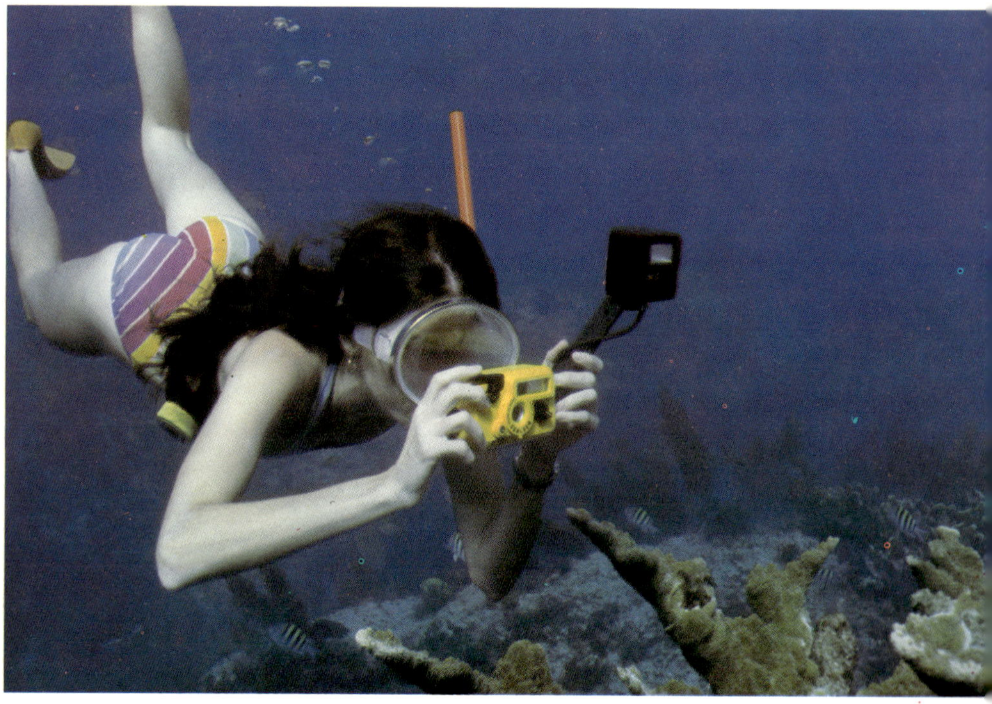

The basic approach *You can get very interesting pictures with nothing more than a snorkel and a simple underwater camera and flashgun*

Safety first *Diving equipment should always be checked before use. It is dangerous to cut corners for the sake of a few extra minutes*

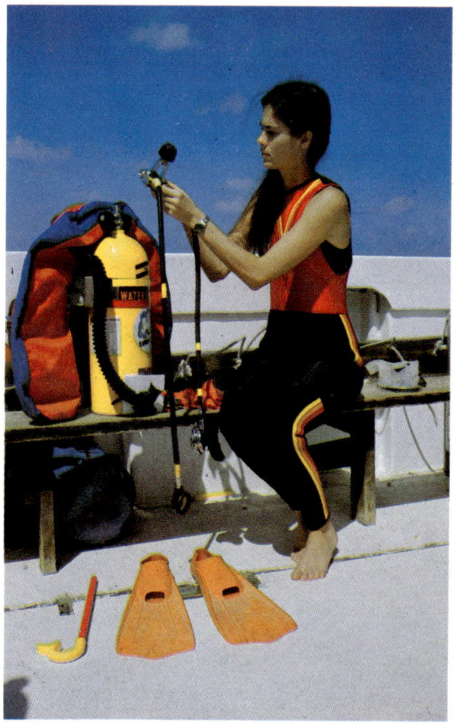

Diving and the photographer

The most important point to remember when taking photographs underwater is that you are a diver first, and a photographer second—safety must have priority over picture taking.

Before you plunge into the water, make sure that you know what you are doing. Despite the apparent simplicity of the apparatus, even snorkel diving can be highly dangerous if you do not know how to control your breathing. If you plan to go diving while on holiday, you may find it useful to take a short course at a local swimming pool before you leave home. This can save you valuable time when you arrive at the holiday resort.

For the diver—and the photographer—the sea can be thought of as three distinct layers. The first extends about five metres down from the surface, and in this region you can dive using only a face mask and snorkel. In this layer too, photography is comparatively simple, because daylight penetrates the water, providing sufficient natural illumination for taking pictures, and pressure is not great, so that even simple underwater cameras can be used. The inexpensive plastic 'EWA' bag underwater housing is quite adequate at these depths.

The next layer extends from five metres down to about 50 metres. Scuba gear—Self Contained Underwater Breathing Apparatus—is essential. And because much less sunlight penetrates this far, artificial light is also needed for photography. The water pressure increases at greater depths, and you must take great care to ensure that water does not seep into your camera. Very sophisticated housings are needed when you dive to the limits of scuba apparatus.

The remainder of the oceans—deeper than 50 m—are strictly out of bounds for the amateur diver. Very elaborate equipment is needed both for photography, and for survival. The water above filters out almost all light, and generates enormous pressures that can force moisture through even the tiniest opening.

These restrictions on depth may seem discouraging, but the most interesting and attractive region of the sea, as far as the photographer is concerned, is within about ten metres of the surface. Here the ample daylight nourishes a great variety of fish and plant life, and in fact, you do not even need to dive to take pictures near the surface—in shallow seas, it may be enough to just splash along the surface with face-mask and camera. This is particularly true in warm waters where coral reefs lie only a metre or two down.

Taking the plunge

Besides the obvious problems of keeping the water out of your camera, there are other difficulties involved in taking photographs underwater. The most important of these is refraction.

Because light travels more slowly in water than it does in air, all objects underwater look closer through the flat glass of the face mask than they really are. This is important because it increases the effective focal length of the camera lens by 25 per cent. This means that the angle of view of the lens is reduced when it is used underwater, and the depth of field is reduced.

Surprisingly, this does not create focusing problems. With an SLR in an underwater housing, the camera can be focused visually using the focusing screen (though this is usually possible only if a speedfinder or action-finder is fitted). You simply focus the camera on the subject as you would on land, even though everything seems nearer.

With non-reflex cameras, however, you must focus largely by guesswork. If you are using a conventional viewfinder camera in an underwater housing, you can use the focusing scale just as you would on land, but you must estimate how far away the subject appears to be and set the *apparent* distance, not the *actual* distance as it would be measured with a tape or a rule. The same is true of underwater, or amphibious cameras. In all cases, the focusing scale on such cameras is marked with the apparent distance from camera to subject, rather than the actual distance.

The narrower angle of view and reduced depth of field present more difficult problems. Seawater is often very murky, and you cannot usually see farther than 10–20 m. The majority of underwater photographs are taken at distances of less than three metres, so the angle of view becomes of crucial importance.

A lens for a 35 mm camera which has a focal length of 35 mm in air becomes the equivalent of a 47 mm when used underwater, and if you use it to take a full length picture of another diver, you must be about four metres from your subject. At this distance, the dirt suspended in the water between you and the other diver is often sufficient to reduce definition and contrast considerably, and there is no alternative but to move in closer to get a sharper result.

Naturally, this means that less of the subject appears in the picture, unless you use a wide angle lens. With a simple fixed lens amphibious camera, this is impossible, and such cameras are of limited use for this very reason. With a Nikonos camera, or an SLR in an underwater housing, you can fit a lens which has a shorter focal length, and takes in more of the subject.

An alternative to changing the lens is to use a dome port over the front of an underwater housing. This is a large, deeply curved front glass, and it corrects for the refraction caused by the water. It has to be used with a supplementary close-up lens fitted to the principal camera lens within the housing, —without this, there is a considerable focus shift. Even with a correction lens, there is usually some change in the point of sharp focus, and the focusing scale on the camera must be recalibrated by experiment.

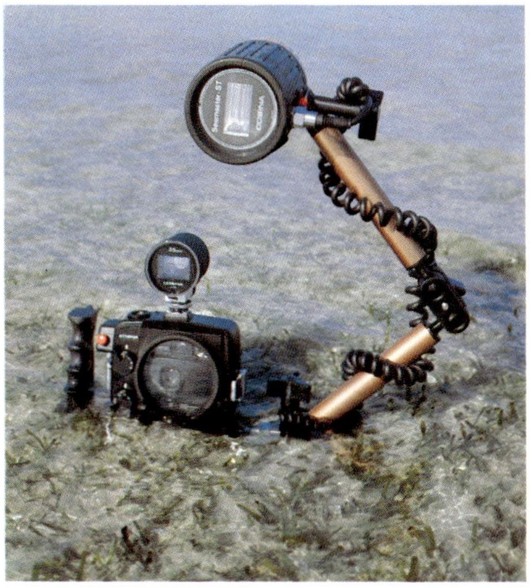

Subaqua flash *An underwater flashgun, like the one above, is an extremely useful item. Water absorbs much of the daylight so that the naturally lit scene is often dim and lacking in colour (below right). Using flash gives a better level of illumination and greatly improves the colour rendition of the scene (below left)*

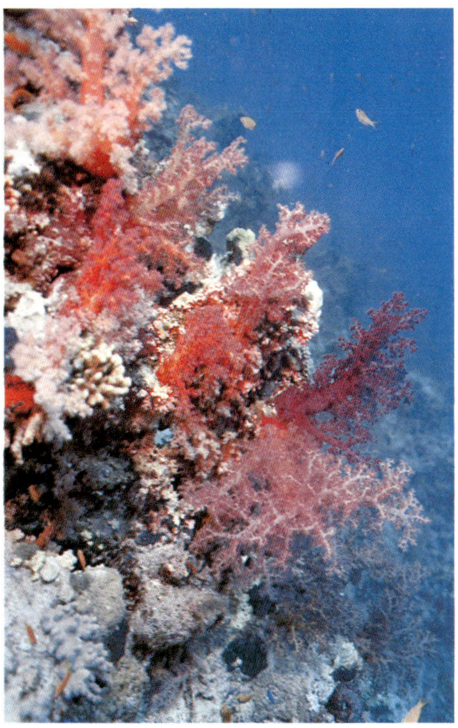

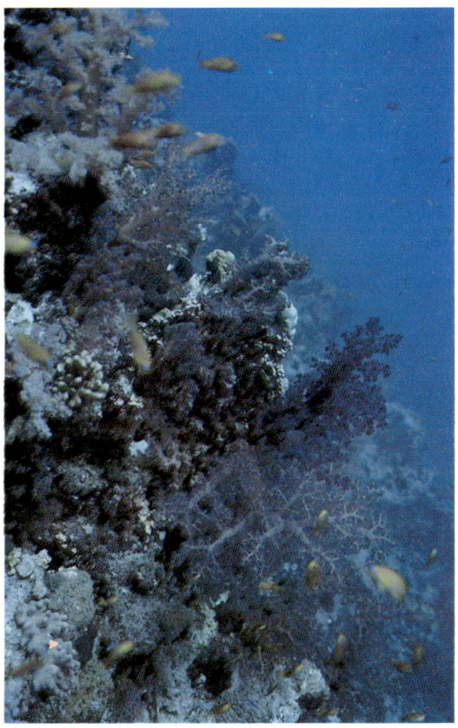

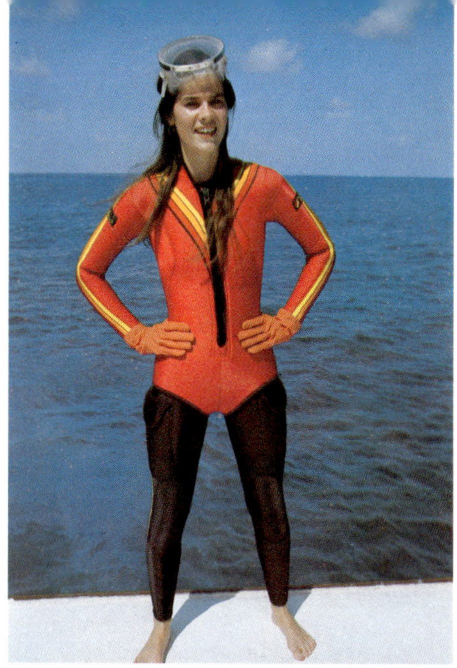

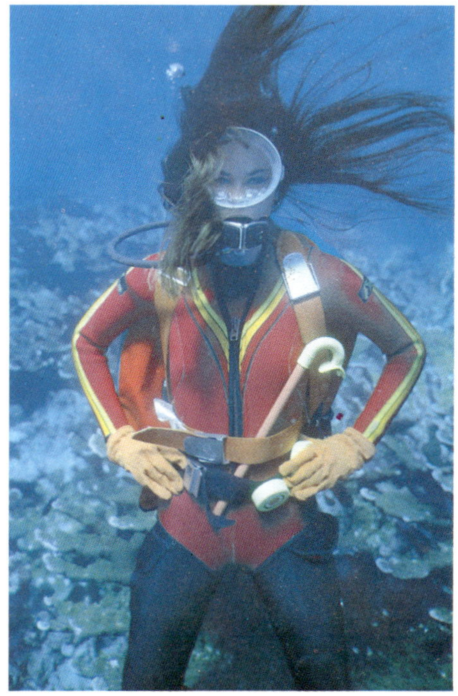

Altered size *The two pictures (right) were taken with the same lens at the same distance, but in air and water. The subject appears larger in the lower shot because of the refracting effect of the water*

Colour and exposure

Not only does water refract light to a greater extent than air, but it also absorbs it. Some of the daylight that falls on the surface of the sea is reflected, and never penetrates the water, and the light that does penetrate becomes dimmer at increasing depths. Even in quite clear, shallow water—five to ten metres down —you must give one or two stops more exposure than you would normally give on the surface.

If your camera has a built-in meter,

exposure measurement is unlikely to be a problem, but for other cameras, you must use either a separate hand-held meter in an underwater housing, or rely on guesswork. Since the cost of a meter and housing is quite high, guesswork is frequently the only practical alternative.

If you are used to relying on a light meter, this may seem a haphazard technique, but it is usually sufficiently accurate for negative films. Transparency film has very limited exposure latitude, and you should bracket exposures heavily if you are guessing the settings for colour slides.

You can quickly increase the accuracy of your exposure estimates if you arrange to have film processed soon after exposure. This way you can shoot a test roll underwater, and judge from the results whether your estimates were sufficiently precise. This procedure also serves to check whether your equipment is operating correctly. If you are away from home, you may be able to find a local processing laboratory, or simply develop the film yourself within the film cassette by using special monobath chemicals (only with b & w films).

Light absorbtion by water is not even across the spectrum, but is differential—red light, for example, is absorbed more strongly than blue. Despite the fact that a glass of seawater looks clear, it actually has a pale blue tinge. While this is unnoticeable in normal conditions, it is of increasing importance as light travels through greater and greater depths of water. Its effect is to gradually and progressively filter out all colours of light except blue as the diver swims down from the surface of the sea.

This means that as you go deeper, there is a progressively stronger blue cast, and yellows and reds become weak. Even in clear water, red light is missing from the spectrum by the time the diver has descended to a depth of five metres, and red objects appear dark grey or black at these depth and below. At 20 m only blue light remains, and photographs taken at this depth by available light appear monochromatic—just blue and black.

The blue-black tones of a colour picture taken underwater cannot be improved by filtration, because a filter can only remove colours, not replace them. The only way to photograph submarine objects in their true colours is to use flash—either electronic or bulb.

Bulb flash has a number of advantages underwater—it is compact, cheap to buy, and relatively powerful, but electronic flash is undoubtedly more convenient. You can buy special underwater units, or put your own land-flash into a waterproof housing. Whichever system you opt for, the principles are the same. The most important point is that the axis of the flashgun must be as far from the camera as possible, to avoid *backscatter*. This is the reflection of light back to the camera from suspended particles in the water, and it shows up on film as tiny white dots across the whole frame. Good quality underwater flashes have large connecting bars to move them far out from the camera to avoid this effect, and the tiny built-in flashes found on compact amphibious cameras are all but useless, as they are too close to the lens.

Treat with caution the guide number of any flash unit that you use underwater. Just as the water soaks up sunlight, so it reduces the power of a flash. Even the most powerful flash unit is useless at distances over four or five metres because the light from the flash has to travel twice this far—once to the subject, then back to the camera.

If you are using flash, exposure testing is especially important, because your initial estimate of the power of the flash

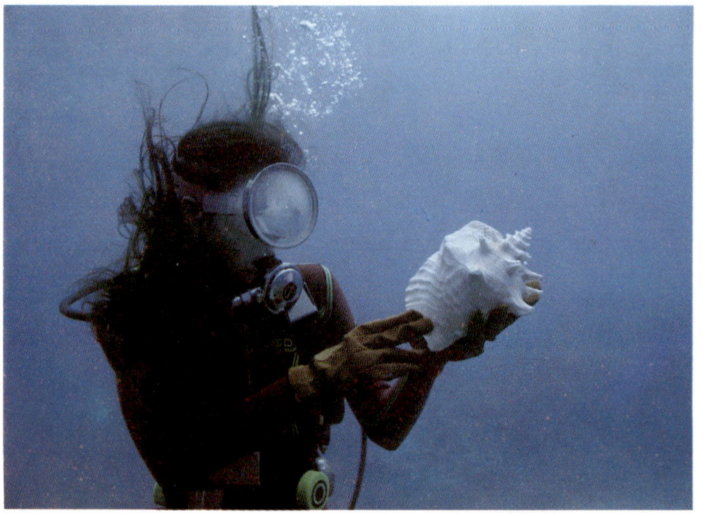

Distance density *The further you are from the subject the lower the contrast becomes, as can be seen from these shots taken at distances of 1, 2 and 7 metres. Many sub aqua photographers use wide angle lenses as these allow them to get close to the subject and still show all of it*

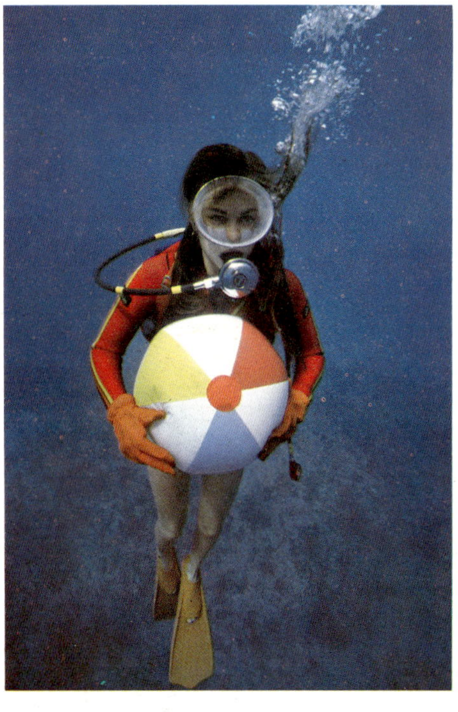

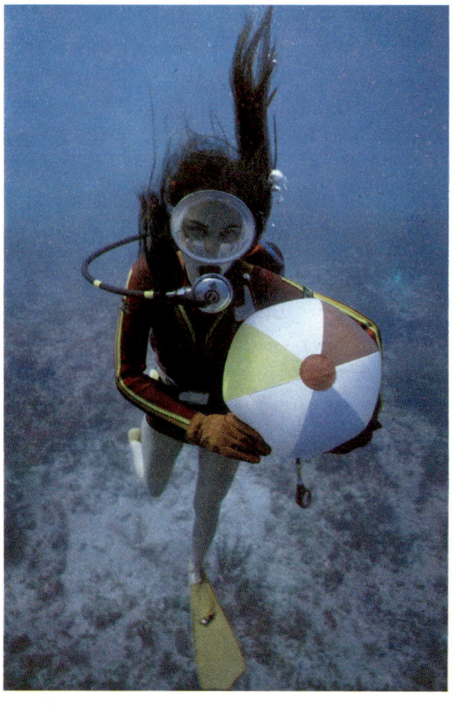

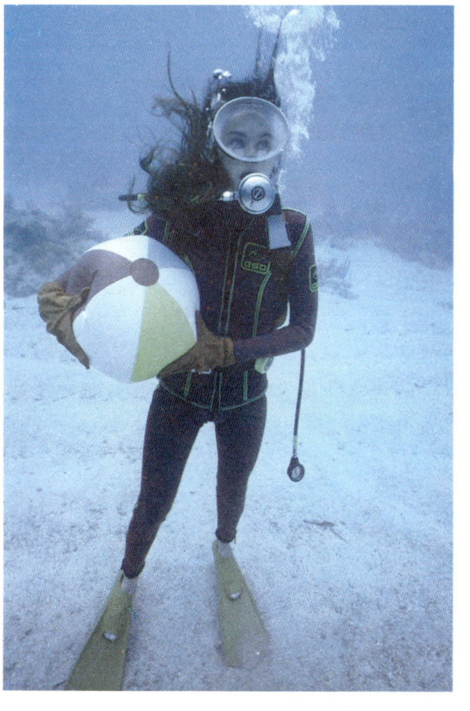

Colour and depth *The deeper you go the more blue the light becomes, due to absorption by the water. At a depth of three metres (left) colour saturation is still reasonable. But at six metres (middle) the yellows and reds are very weak, and at 12 metres the blue cast is so pronounced that the picture is almost monochromatic (right)*

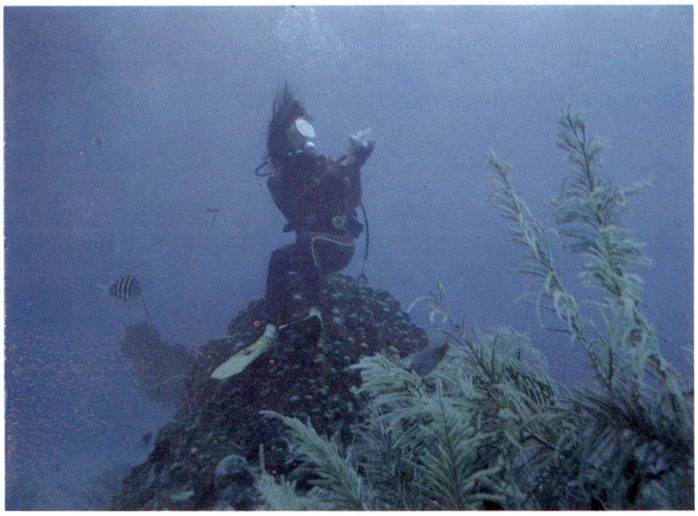

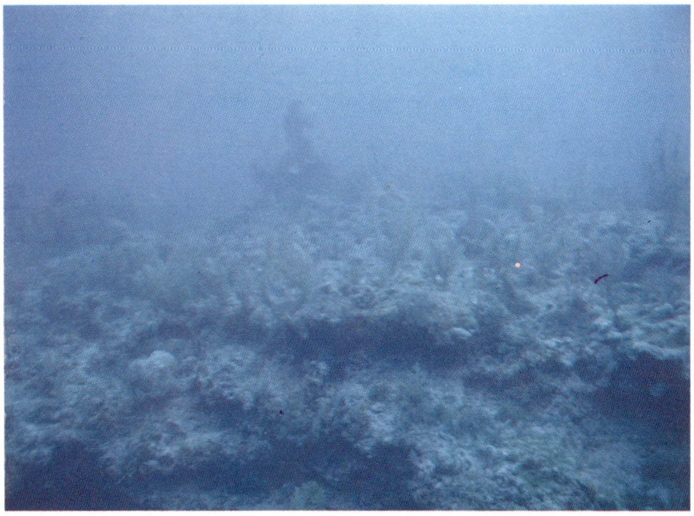

unit will probably be too optimistic. Once again, the only answer is to process films on the spot, and compare the negatives with the exposure settings that you used underwater—bracket generously to include the correct exposure.

Underwater technique

Photography underwater is so different from photography on land, that even things that you normally take for granted have to be thought out carefully. The only way of becoming really skilled is to actually practice the techniques described here, until they become second nature. There are, however, a few general points that may help to safeguard your equipment, and improve your pictures.

Check the O-rings Almost all sub-aqua equipment is sealed with rubber rings, which rest in a shallow groove. These rings, and the grooves, must be kept perfectly clean and well greased. A small grain of sand is enough to break the seal, and flood the camera.

Condensation If you are diving in cold water, the inside of a housing can quickly mist up. A bag of silica gel packed inside with the camera can cure this.

Move in close Distant scenes are usually disappointing. Use a wide angle lens if you can, or else just avoid subjects which are more than three metres away.

Think about backgrounds In shallow water, the surface of the sea makes a splendid background, and the sun shining through the water can be used to backlight other divers—this works particularly well with fill-in flash.

Take your time It is easy to run through a roll of film in a matter of minutes, particularly with 126, or 110, both of which have a maximum of 20 frames. It is impossible to load film underwater, so when you run out, you will not be able to take any more pictures without surfacing, rinsing the camera in fresh water, and reloading—a time-consuming routine.

Do not trust the viewfinder The simple frame finders used on underwater cameras are frequently innaccurate. A test roll of film helps you find out how much of the subject is really appearing on film.

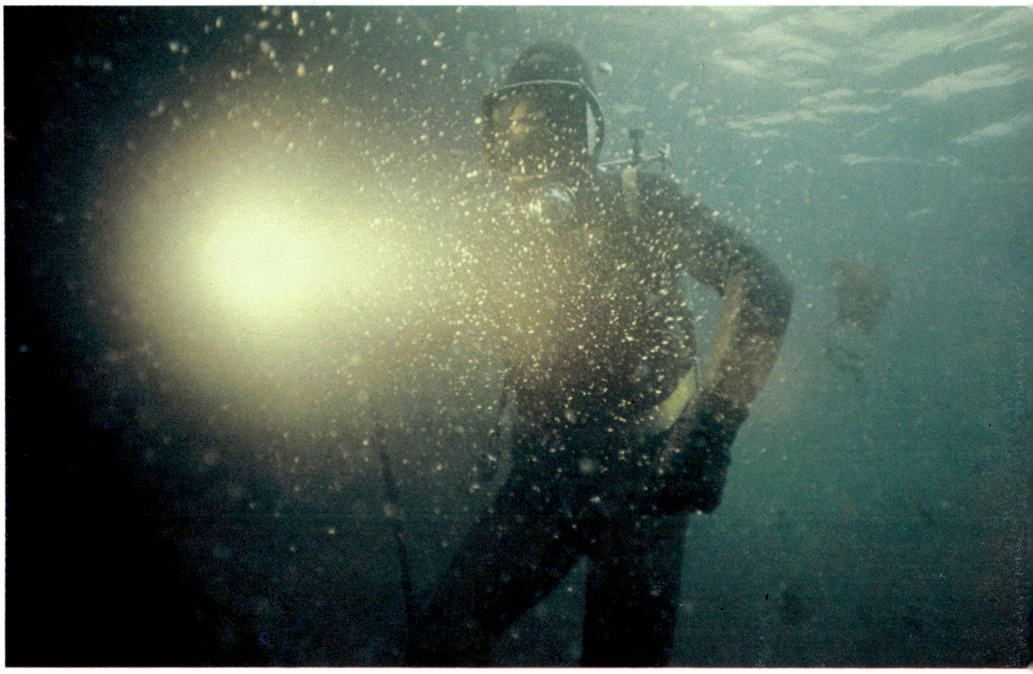

Flash backscatter *Using flash in water is very different from using it in air. The light is picked up and reflected by particles suspended in the water (above). This is an effect known as backscatter, and the result is low contrast (below). One way to overcome this problem is to move the flash well away from the camera*

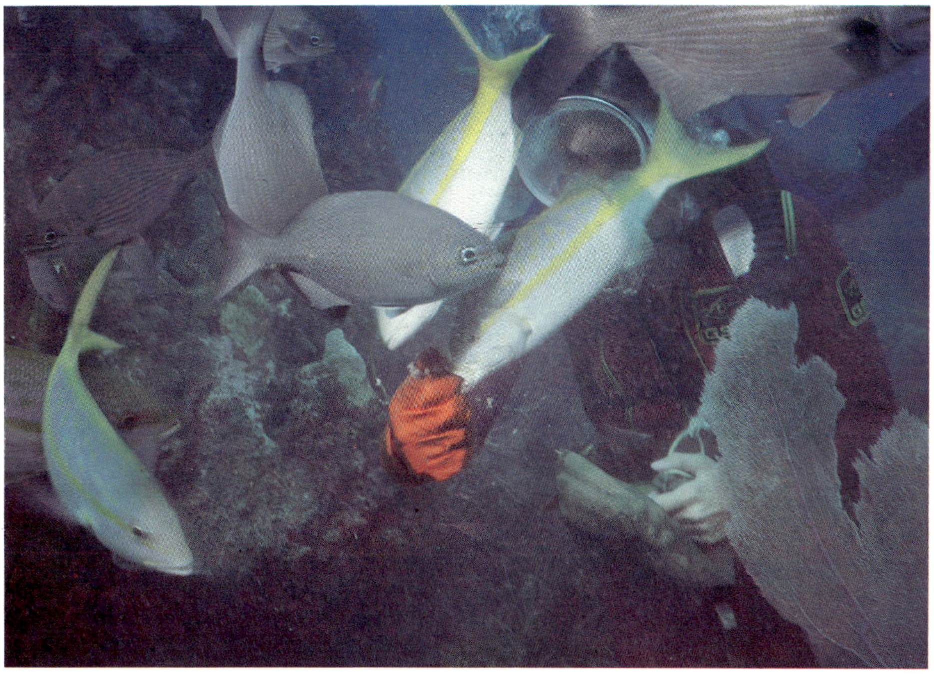

Adapting binoculars

Super-telephoto lenses produce dramatic images which seem to cut across long distances, flattening far off objects into a bold pattern of shapes. But for most people, the cost of the really long telephotos puts them out of reach, and their weight and bulk make them unwieldy to use. The largest ones are not even designed to be particularly portable—they work best from a fixed plinth.

Many photographers, though, own a telescope or a pair of binoculars, and these can easily be pressed into service to take the kind of photographs that are usually associated with much more expensive super-telephotos. Furthermore, they are more portable than conventional long lenses, and produce the maximum image magnification at the minimum cost.

Clearly, though, neither a telescope nor a pair of binoculars can give you quite the same quality as a super-telephoto lens, but the best makes can give more than acceptable results with the right subject.

Telescopes generally give greater magnification than binoculars. So since only one eyepiece is needed, not two, when used in combination with a camera, a telescope is better for high magnification. However, it is undoubtedly easier to mount a pair of binoculars firmly. If you have the choice, then, a pair of binoculars will probably give best results.

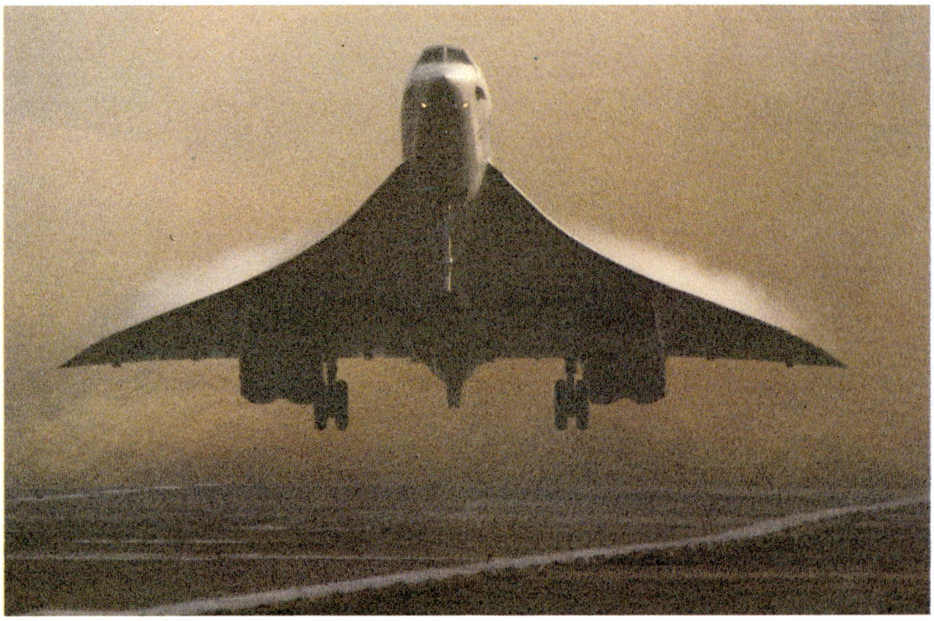

Concorde *Extremely long focal lengths—such as the 1200 mm lens used for this shot—allow you to photograph otherwise inaccessible subjects with dramatic effects though shots of very distant subjects encounter problems with interference by haze*

Quick and simple

The easiest way to link a camera to binoculars or a telescope is simply to put the camera, with its standard lens, against the eyepiece, where you would normally have your eye. This technique is known as *afocal photography*, and in this case the optical system works in the same way as front-of-lens tele converters.

There are several advantages to this method: no modifications are needed to any of the components of the system, it costs very little to set up, and a rigid support for the camera is not necessary—it is even possible to hand hold it if need be. A mount for the telescope or binoculars is needed, but this can be made at home from plywood, and bolted on to a tripod. Some telescopes have their own tripod mount, making this unnecessary, and special clamps can be purchased to hold binoculars to a tripod.

In use, the telescope or binoculars are first lined up on the object to be photographed, and focused in the usual way. The camera is then brought into position behind the eyepiece, and the camera

Adapting for binoculars

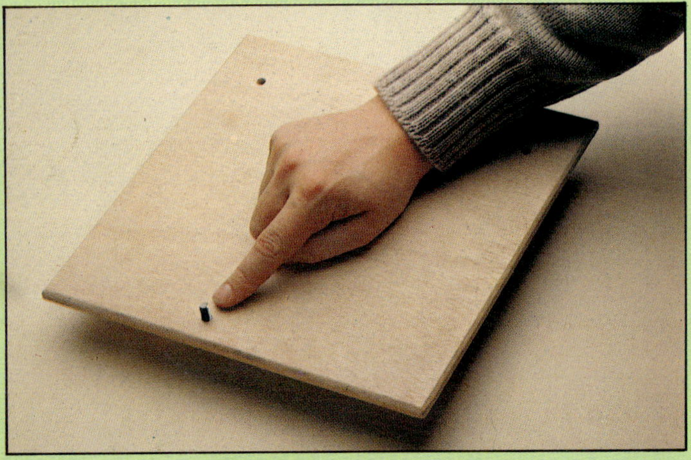

1. *The first step is to cut a baseboard and to drill a hole for the bolt which will hold the camera in place*

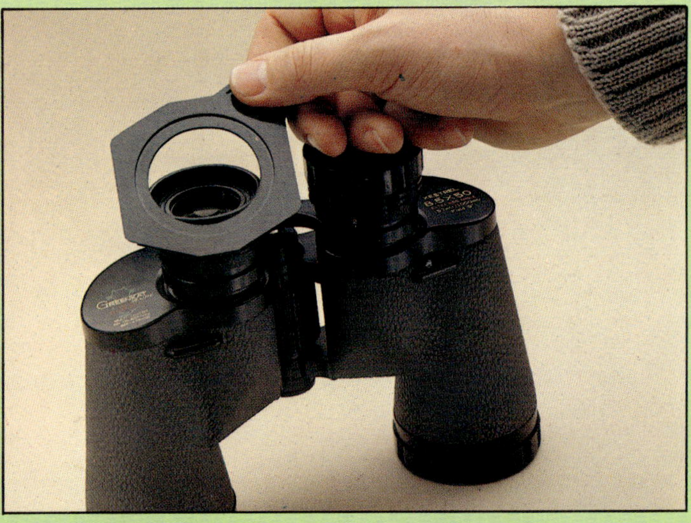

2. *Cut a hole in the blank plastic sheet from a filter system. It should be a snug fit over the eyepiece*

lens focused on infinity—binoculars and telescopes are designed to be used with the eye at rest, and when correctly adjusted they always form an image which appears to be at infinity, regardless of how far away the subject is.

Not all users focus optical instruments correctly, but there is a simple way of making sure that a telescope or binoculars are focused on infinity. In the case of a telescope, look through the eyepiece with one eye, but keep the other eye open. Focus the telescope until you can see both the real and the telescope image sharply. If you normally wear spectacles, keep them on for this test. It does not matter if you can only see a small part of the image.

For binoculars, focus the half of the instrument that you plan to use in this way, before going any further.

If you follow this procedure, you do not even need to use an SLR camera, because focusing and framing are done before the camera is moved into position. A simple camera may in fact produce better pictures, because the uncomplicated design of the lens on a cheaper camera is often more compatible with the optics of a telescope or binoculars than the five or six element designs found on most SLRs.

In fact, the ideal camera to use is a rangefinder or twin lens reflex type. Such cameras usually have comparatively straightforward lenses of small maximum aperture and have no moving mirror to cause vibration. The large maximum aperture that is essential for focusing with an SLR becomes a liability in afocal photography, because to provide a distortion-free image, the manufacturers use five or six glass elements, well spaced out. This arrangement, when applied to the eyepiece, causes vignetting—your pictures look as if they are taken down a cardboard tube. If your only available lens is of this type, the best solution is to confine the subject to the centre of the frame, and crop off the dark edges of the picture at the printing stage if this is possible.

In practice

While it is possible to hold the camera up to the eyepiece and line it up by eye, it is preferable to have the camera and optical system firmly fixed together. It is unlikely that the telescope or binocular manufacturers will supply a ready-made adapter which allows you to fit your camera directly to the eyepiece of a telescope or binoculars, so usually you will need to make an adapter yourself. The simplest way to do this is to buy one of the popular 'creative' filter systems, and adapt the rigid black plastic sheet—supplied for use as a lens cap—to hold the camera lens close to the eyepiece.

Make a large hole in the centre of this plastic sheet, and use a round file to ream it out until it fits neatly over the eyepiece. Slide the plastic sheet into the holder, and check for fit. When the eyepiece is inserted into the round hole, and the filter holder attached to the lens, the front element of the lens should be as close as possible to the rear element of the eyepiece, without actually touching it. The whole assembly must be centred as carefully as possible—the centre of the eyepiece should be perfectly aligned with the centre of the camera lens.

When you have arranged the fit as well as you can, dismantle the adapter, and glue the black sheet into the holder, using a 'superglue' or epoxy adhesive. Ideally the eyepiece should also be glued into place, but this is not essential, and you can probably get away with a push-fit.

Whether you use a purpose-built adapter, or a home made one, you will need to hold the entire set-up steady. The best way of doing this is to mount everything on to a baseboard. A suitable material for making a baseboard is plywood, about 1 cm thick. This is rigid and easy to work with. Start by drilling a hole at one end so that you can mount the camera on the board with a tripod screw—a $\frac{1}{4}$ inch Whitworth bolt. Take care that this bolt does not protrude more than 5 mm from the board, or there is a danger that you will damage the camera's tripod bush by overtightening. Lay the binoculars or telescope down on the board, and align the various parts of the system using packing material such as pieces of card or thin wood. When you have established the amount of packing material needed, and where it should be placed, glue it into position.

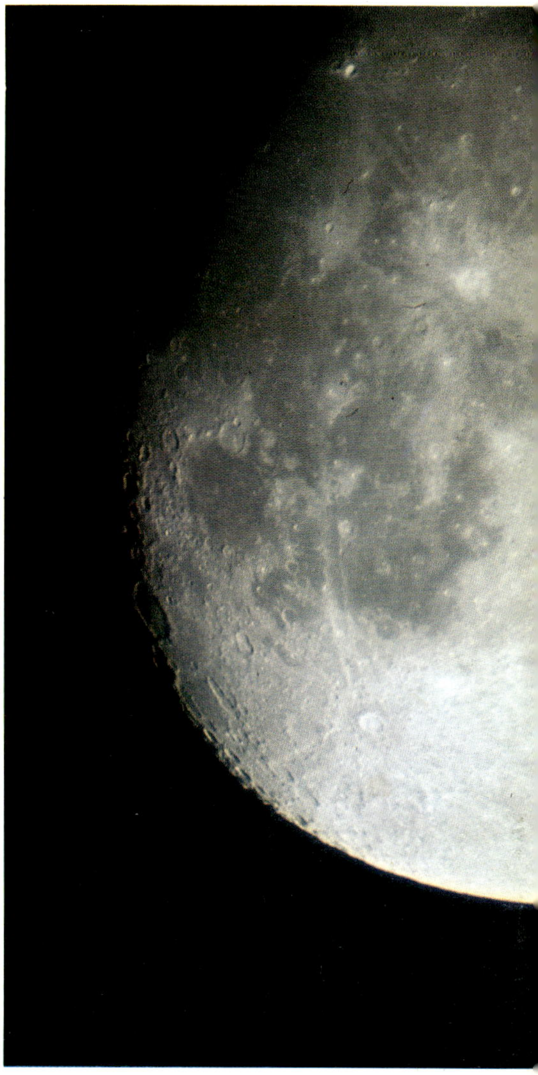

Full moon *photographed through a 16 × 50 binocular set-up*

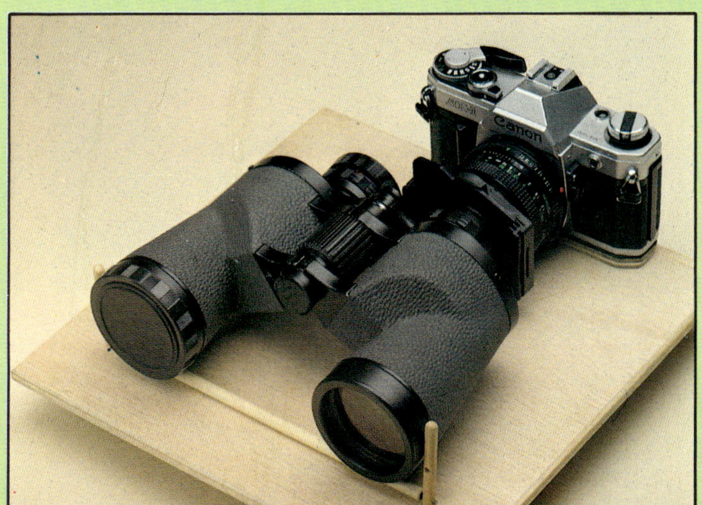

3. *Use shims of card or wood to align the camera and binoculars and then glue the shims in place*

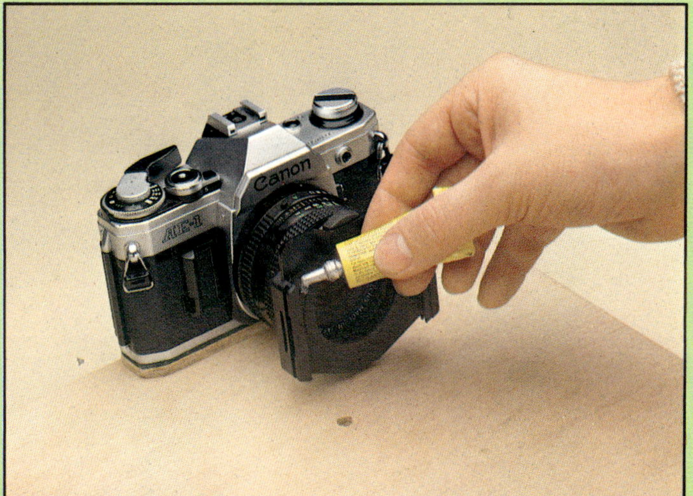

4. *You can now glue the black sheet into its holder to preserve the correct alignment*

continued

To prevent the binoculars or telescope from sliding around, hold them down with heavy gauge rubber bands.

Finally, find the point of balance and drill a hole in the baseboard at that point. Tap or glue a ¼ inch Whitworth nut into the hole so that the unit can be fixed to a tripod.

Although somewhat ungainly, this set up works well, provided that there is enough play in the system to allow the units to be focused, and that no light can enter between the eyepiece and lens. Light leaks can be eliminated by draping a large piece of black cloth over the whole apparatus.

Other methods

Afocal photography is not the only way to use a camera with a telescope or binoculars. By removing the camera lens and the eyepiece of the other unit, you can project images directly into the camera body. This system, known as direct projection, is really only useful for photography with astronomical telescopes, though, and is dealt with in a subsequent article.

Eyepiece projection is a third method, and is identical to direct projection except that the eyepiece on the binocular or telescope is retained. High magnifications are possible by increasing the separation between the two components, but the system is of limited practical use—stray light is a problem, the aperture is very small, and all the units must be rigidly clamped together.

Making exposures

The restrictions that apply to ordinary super-telephoto lenses also make photography through binoculars or a telescope difficult. Atmospheric haze and turbulence can reduce definition and hinder focusing when the subject is very distant, and it is best to concentrate on photographing things which are quite close—less than a kilometre away. At the other extreme, you may be interested in photographing the moon or stars, though this calls for special techniques

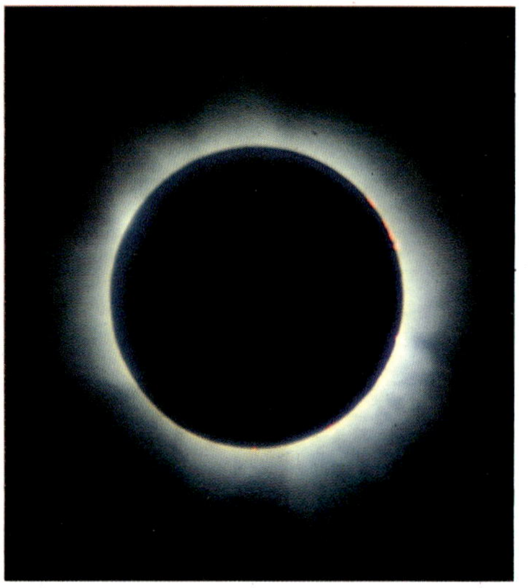

Eclipse *The total solar eclipse of February 1980, photographed from Kenya using apparatus similar to that shown below*

because of the Earth's rotation, and is discussed subsequently.

Try to avoid using the focusing system of the camera if you can. The split image rangefinder and microprisms black out when used at high magnifications, and although the procedure of focusing by eye and then moving the camera into place is tedious, it is the surest way of getting sharp pictures. Because the working aperture of the combination of lenses is quite small, the focusing screen of an SLR goes very dark, and it is difficult to detect when a subject is in focus.

If you must use the camera's focusing screen—for example, when the subject is moving—a simple method of increasing screen brightness is to dab a small quantity of distilled water on it through the lens mount, with the lens removed. Light transmission increases dramatically—sometimes the screen image becomes eight times as bright. The water quickly evaporates, and if it is confined to the centre of the screen, it should do no damage. A more permanent solution is to use a drop of oil, though this can be very difficult to remove.

The amount of exposure that you will need to give for any particular subject depends not only on the subject brightness, but also on the effective aperture of the set-up that you are using. If your camera has a through-the-lens exposure meter, you should have no trouble measuring the exposure—use the meter in the stopped-down mode. If it does not, then you will have to make a series of test exposures. If you are using a 50 mm camera lens at full aperture and 8 × 30 binoculars, a good starting point is about *f*/16. This is the effective aperture of the whole system and is fixed, so exposure must be controlled using the shutter speed. Closing down the aperture of the camera lens only has the effect of increasing vignetting.

Apart from these operational problems encountered with combinations of camera and binoculars or telescope, pictures can be taken in very much the same way as they are with a conventional telephoto lens. More detailed information on this subject is given on pages 75 to 80.

WARNING

Never under any circumstances whatever attempt to view or photograph the sun with any of the set-ups described in the text without the correct high density absorbing filter over the lens.

Not all the filters on sale are safe, and many are easily damaged by use. You must seek expert advice first and the best way to do this is to contact your local astronomical society.

The only safe way to view and photograph the sun is by projection on to a screen. This reduces the light to a safe level. It may also be possible to photograph it when the sun is very close to the horizon at sunrise or sunset, but only when the disc is comfortable to view with the naked eye. Do not attempt it at any other time or you run the risk of permanently damaging your cameras or your eyesight.

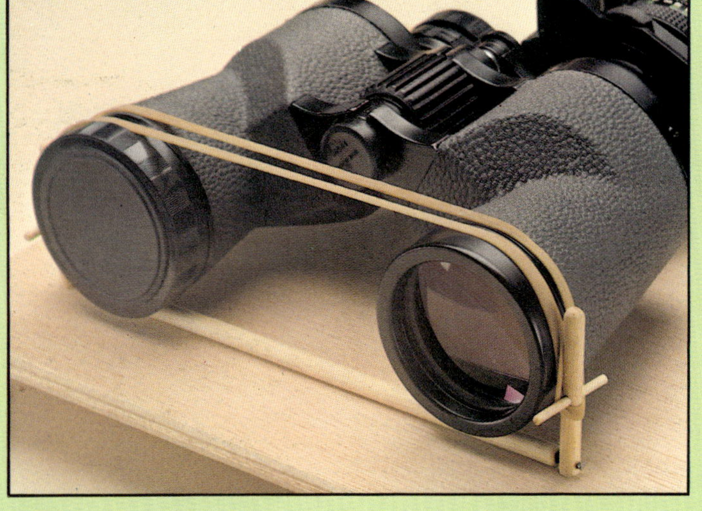

5. *The binoculars are held very simply by a rubber band. The dowelling also keeps them closely in line*

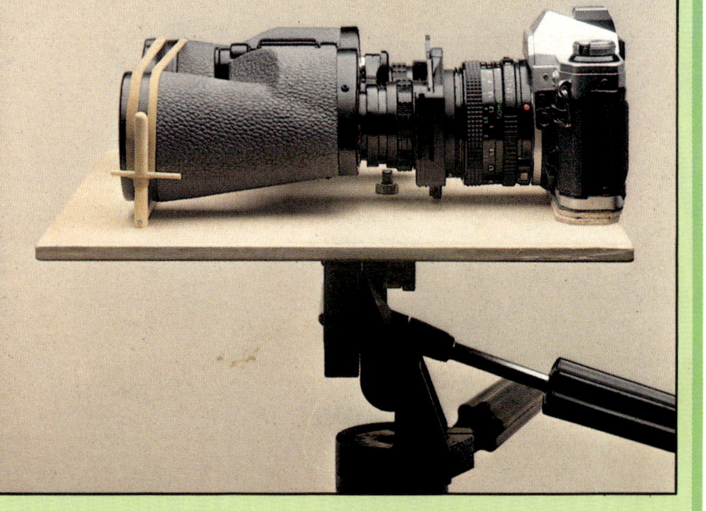

6. *The finished assembly can be mounted on a tripod—but be sure to drill the hole at the balance point*

Remote control techniques

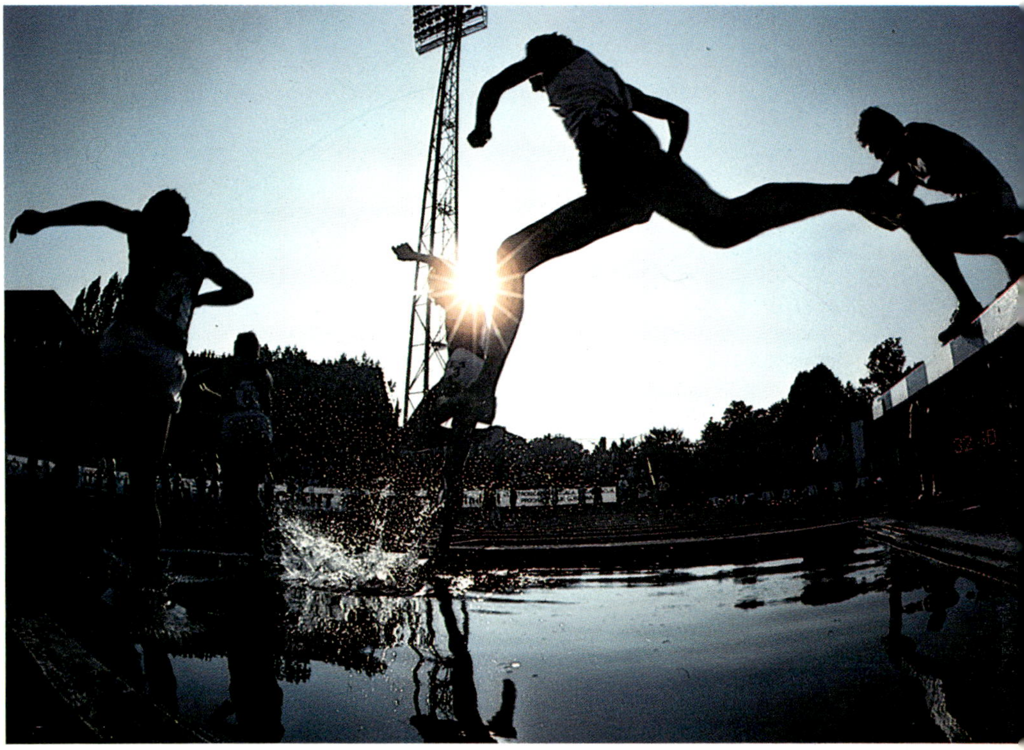

Over the water *For this dramatic effect, the camera was fitted with a fisheye lens, and fired with an infrared device*

In some situations, it is not possible for the photographer to stand by the camera ready to release the shutter at the right moment. It might be too dangerous, as in the case of a rocket launch, or the subject might be too timid, as in the case of wildlife photography.

In these and many other situations, some way of releasing the shutter from a distance is needed. Any camera which has provision for a cable release can be triggered mechanically from a short distance. Those which can be fitted with motor drives, however, can be operated by a number of remote control methods, even at considerable distances.

Mechanical methods

The easiest way of releasing the shutter at a distance is to use a long cable release. Although this is the simplest solution, the frictional resistance of the cable limits its length to about two metres. Another system is the pneumatic release, in which the shutter is released using a long rubber tube filled with air, with a plunger at one end and a bulb at the other. When the bulb is squeezed, the air pressure in the tube is increased, which forces the plunger outwards and releases the shutter. This method allows the photographer to work up to 10 metres from the camera.

Both methods are reliable because of their simplicity, but they have certain drawbacks which make them unsuitable for certain situations. Apart from the important limitations on the distance from photographer to camera, there is the problem of winding the camera. Unless you fit a motor drive or a winder to the camera, you have to wind it manually after each shot—this means moving up to the camera. Fitting a motor or a winder might seem to be the solution, but, in most circumstances, a cable cannot give fine control over the number of shots you take.

More elaborate remote control systems allow the camera to be operated from a much greater distance, but they are harder to arrange and may be less reliable than mechanical methods.

Electrical control

Using an electrical system, you can operate the camera at almost any distance, and it is cheaper and simpler than the majority of long distance remote

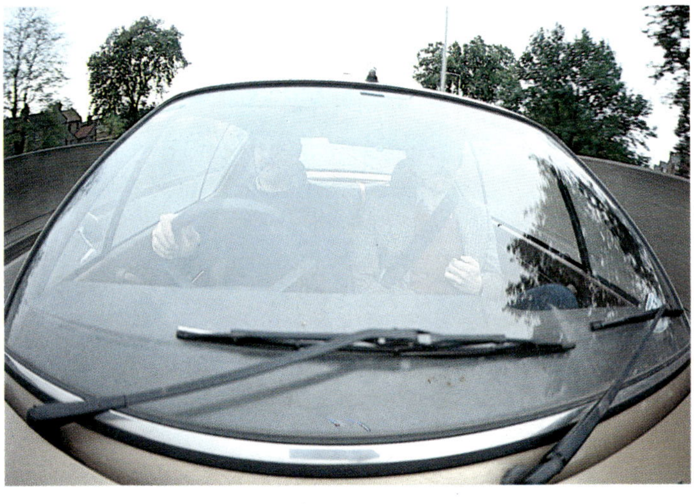

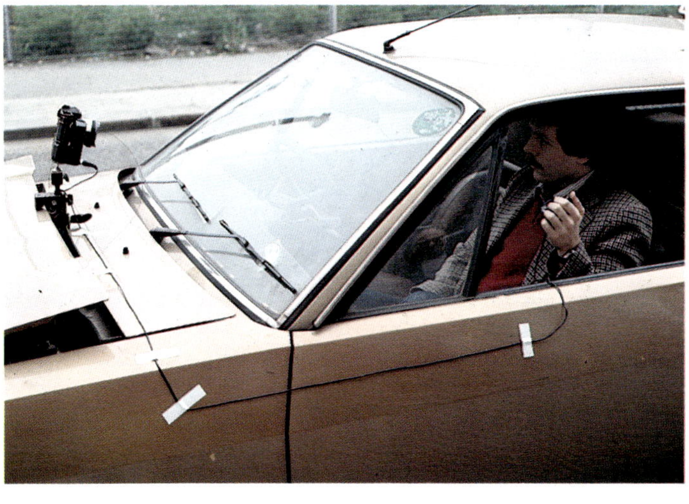

On the move *To get this unusual self-portrait, photographer Jerry Young clamped his camera to the bonnet of the car and fired the shutter on the move via an electric switch connected to the motor drive. To give an impression of speed, he set the shutter at 1/60*

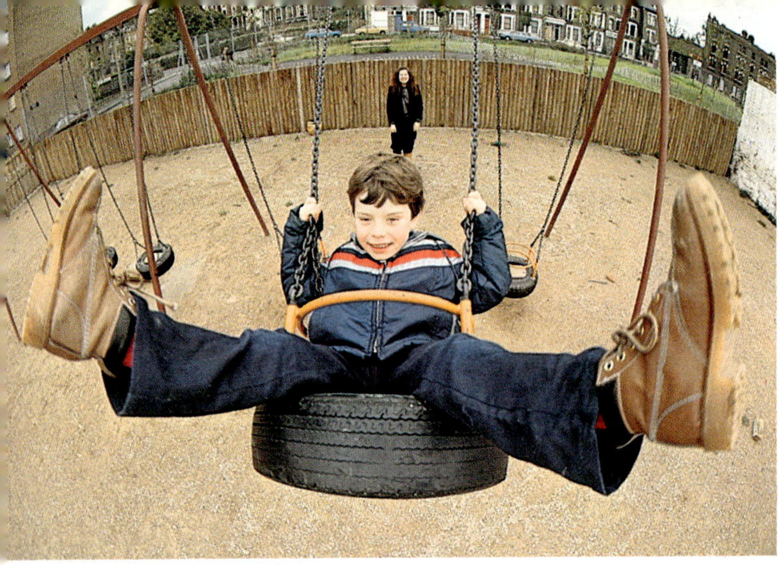

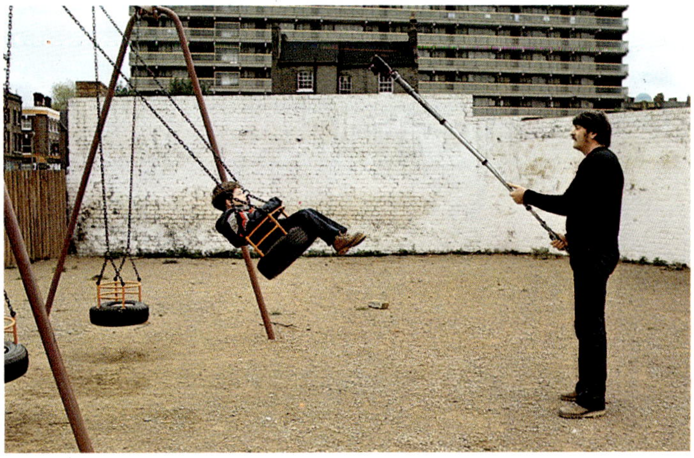

On the swing *The cable operating the camera was taped to the monopod. For a simple shot like this, either a cable or a pneumatic release would be suitable*

control systems, since all it consists of is a piece of cable connected to the motor drive or winder. Most motor drives have a facility for electrical operation, consisting of two electrical terminals. The remote control cable is simply plugged into the terminals, and when the photographer closes the circuit by means of a switch at the other end of the cable, the motor drive or winder fires for the period of time the switch is kept on.

Most manufacturers supply cables for use with their motor drives and winders, but you can easily make your own using ordinary lightweight flex soldered to a suitable plug and an ordinary switch. Lightweight flex is adequate for lengths up to about 35 m, but beyond this length resistance becomes too great and thicker cable should be used.

Electrical remote control has the advantage of economy—the cable, plug and switch can be bought for very little. It is the ideal system when the camera is fairly close to the photographer but is inaccessible, such as when it is bolted on to a canoe, a racing car or a hang glider. In these cases, the camera is operated by the pilot or driver—often, solitary sailors use this system to photograph themselves on lone ocean crossings.

Unfortunately, this method of remote control has the disadvantage that there must always be a cable between camera and photographer. This not only makes it difficult to set up in certain circumstances, but it restricts the photographer's mobility. In situations where the camera is visible but inaccessible an infrared system is better.

Infrared control

Infrared systems, which cost roughly the same as a good medium telephoto, depend on an infrared transmitter, rather like a flashgun with a deep red filter over the window, which transmits a powerful infrared pulse when the switch is pressed. The pulse is picked up by the infrared receiver which is usually mounted on the hot shoe of the camera. This operates a solenoid, closing the circuit and switching on the motor drive or winder. It is best to direct the transmitter towards the camera as far as possible, though precise alignment is not always necessary.

Some powerful sources of infrared, such as the sun, might fire the remote control system accidentally. For this reason, many infrared releases emit more than one wavelength, or quality of light, not all of them infrared. The receiver is 'tuned' to these light frequencies, and does not respond to any other combination. Some types of release have two or more frequencies or 'channels', allowing the photographer to operate more than one camera independently, using the same set.

Different systems work in slightly different ways, but the popular Nikon Modulite can operate in two modes. In the first, one press on the release button starts the camera and a second press stops it. This is ideal for sequences such as a 100 m sprint, which lasts little more than ten seconds. The camera can be started at the beginning of the race and left running to shoot the entire event. You can then select the best shot, or sequence of shots, from the film. For a wildlife photograph, however, when the action takes place over a long time, you do not want the camera running continually and the second mode is more useful. In the second mode, you shoot a single frame each time you press the button on the infrared transmitter.

Infrared releases are efficient up to

Camera on the wing *Remote control is essential for this type of shot. The camera and motor drive were securely clamped to the wing of the biplane, and fired electrically by the pilot. A 16 mm fisheye lens was used to obtain maximum depth of field and give the characteristic distorted effect*

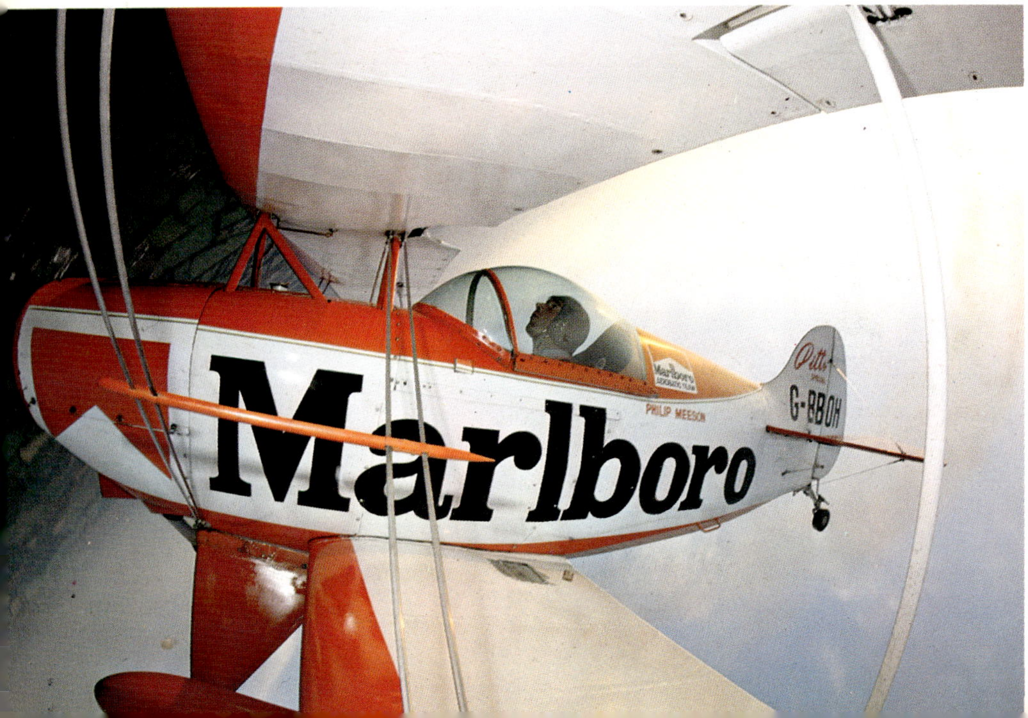

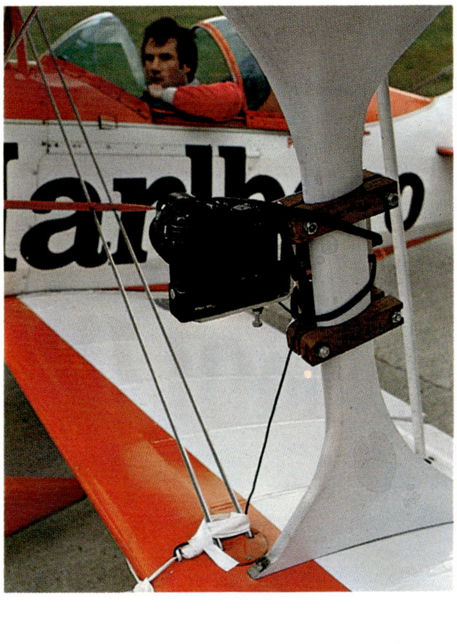

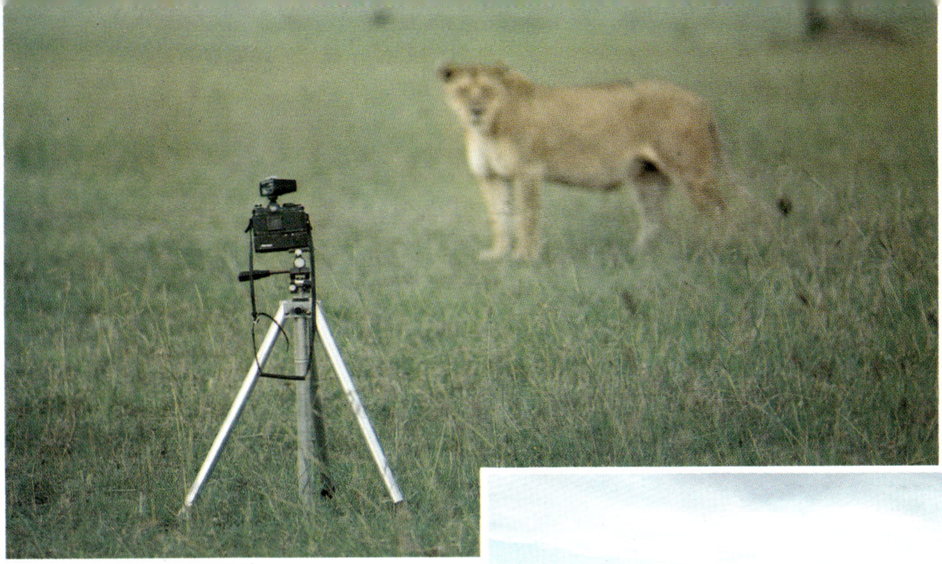

about 60 m in most built-up areas, though this is reduced in open country. Mist, rain and snow all absorb infrared, reducing the range of the system. However, you can increase the range of your transmitter by fitting an improvised lens system to it. A cardboard snoot with a converging lens on the end, fitted to the window of the transmitter, can increase the range to as much as 90 m. Initially, a little trial and error may be required to achieve the right arrangement. With luck, though, you can operate the camera away across the far side of a fairly wide river.

Infrared release systems do have a number of drawbacks, however. The first is that if two units of the same type are used at the same event by different photographers, the signal from one unit can start the other running. Though the choice of frequencies does get round this to a certain extent, it does not rule out accidents, and there have even been cases of photographers deliberately winding off the film of rivals using a compatible release. The only solution to this problem, which at some sporting events can be a real obstacle, is to have your unit specially modified to operate on a unique frequency. Manufacturers cannot do this, however, and it should only be attempted by a technician.

The other problem is that, over a long distance, infrared releases are limited to line-of-sight operation. This means that the transmitter and receiver must be exactly aligned, with no obstacle in between. If this is not done, the camera will not fire at a long distance. At shorter range, however, some infrared releases, notably the Nikon, can be operated by bouncing the beam off suitable reflecting surfaces.

Radio control

The problem of line-of-sight operation is solved by using a radio-controlled release. These function in the same way as a walkie-talkie radio. A transmitter sends out a signal at a given frequency, which is picked up by a receiver mounted on the camera, firing the motor drive or the winder. Such systems can work efficiently at much greater distances than either electrical or infrared releases, and are ideal for use when the camera is fixed to a moving object but the photographer is stationary.

Unfortunately, though, there are other problems associated with radio remote control. First, radio frequencies are strictly controlled by governments, and private devices of this type are illegal in some countries. In Britain, for example, ready-made radio controlled units for operating cameras are illegal, though custom built units can be licensed, and operated legally in certain areas.

Second, radio waves abound in built-up areas, and the camera can be easily

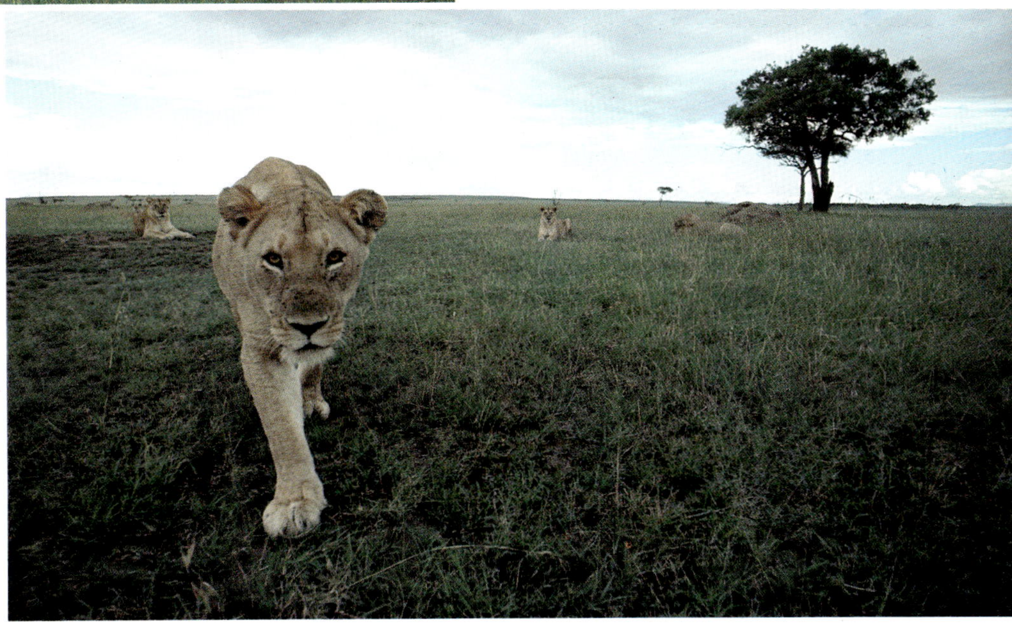

Lions *A Nikon Modulite was used for this wide angle shot—the receiver is clearly visible, mounted on the hot shoe of the camera. The lion, attracted by the whirring of the motor drive, knocked the tripod over and chewed the camera which, fortunately, was almost undamaged*

Bike *Shots like this are simple to set up. Tape the monopod to the bicycle frame and pre-focus the lens—here, an 18 mm —on the child. As the bike goes past, the infrared transmitter (inset) fires the motor drive. To obtain an impression of speed, use a 1/60 second shutter speed to give a blurred image*

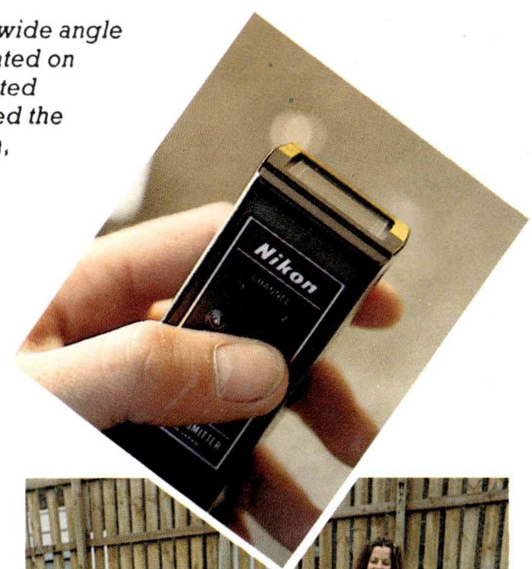

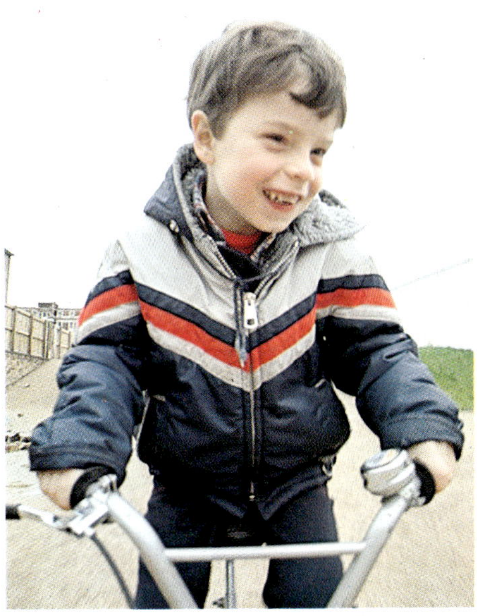

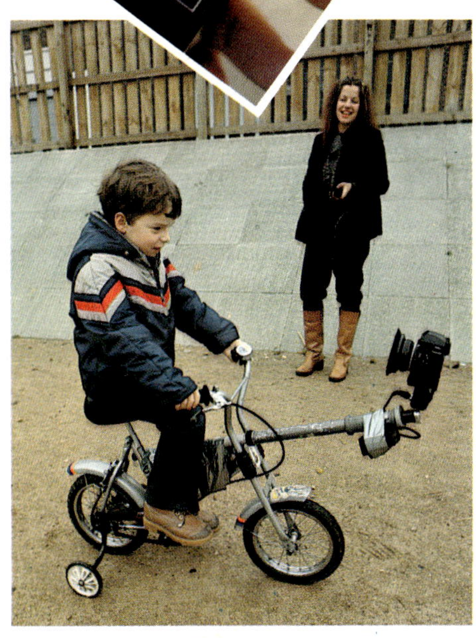

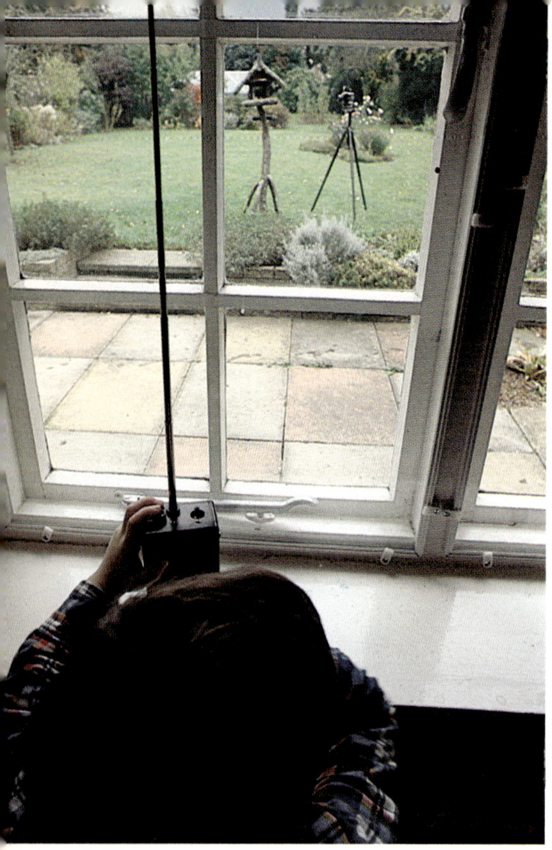

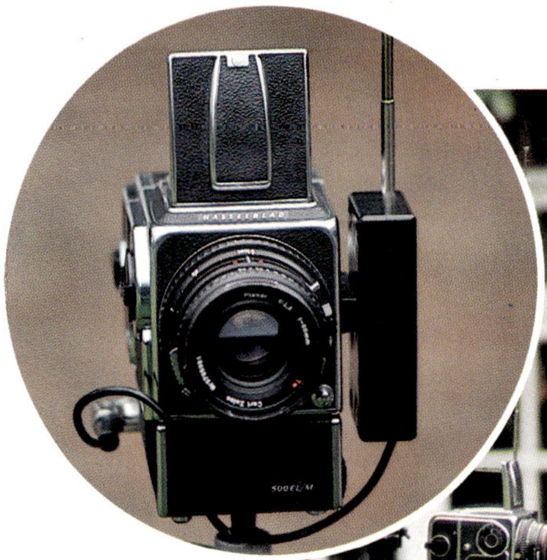

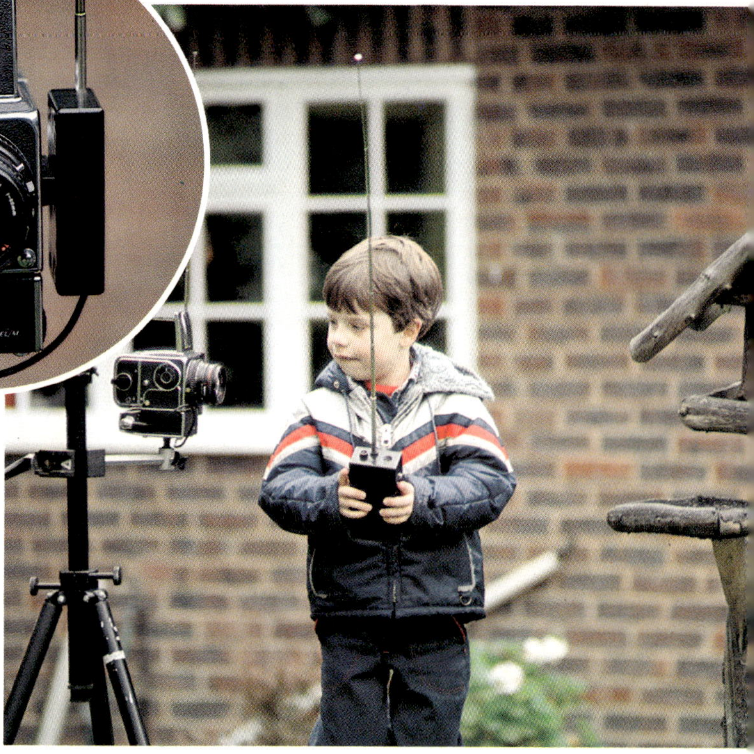

Bird table *When the camera is invisible, infrared cannot be used, and radio control is the answer. The receiver (inset) is mounted on the camera and can be triggered from several kilometres*

fired by outside interference. Even vehicles can generate radio waves, so this can be a real problem if you want to operate your camera near a road or in a busy city centre.

If for some reason you need to use a radio release in a country where, for legal reasons, they are not available, you might be able to adapt a device manufactured for use with model aircraft. These are usually very compact, and can be bought for little more than the price of a camera body or a mid-range medium telephoto lens.

Automatic detection

Sometimes, the photographer cannot even observe the subject or release the shutter at the right time. A typical example is wildlife photography. To photograph a bird at night, the camera must be positioned according to the bird's habitual flight paths, but the photographer cannot see the subject.

This is where systems designed for surveillance and security are the only solution, since no purpose built photographic equipment of this type is available. A common device is a transmitter which gives out a continuous infrared beam, and a receiver. When the

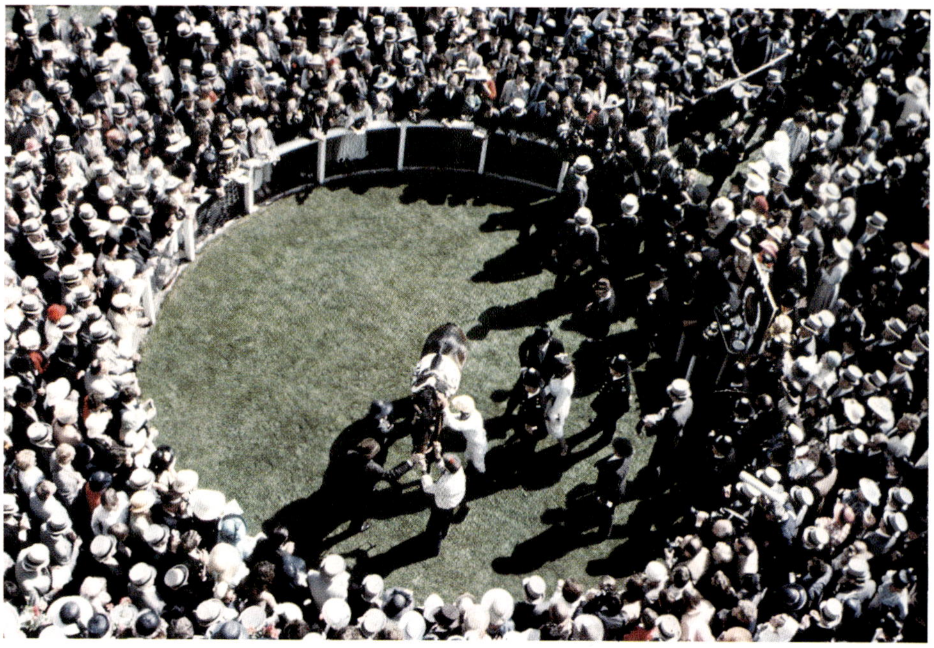

White water *A specially constructed waterproof box attached to the canoe held the camera and motordrive, while a special switch, placed between the canoeist's legs, fired the camera when he squeezed his knees together*

Derby winner *Remote control allows some unusual viewpoints—here the camera was at the top of a pole, and operated by infrared. Careful framing and prefocus are required—a moderate wide angle lens also helps framing*

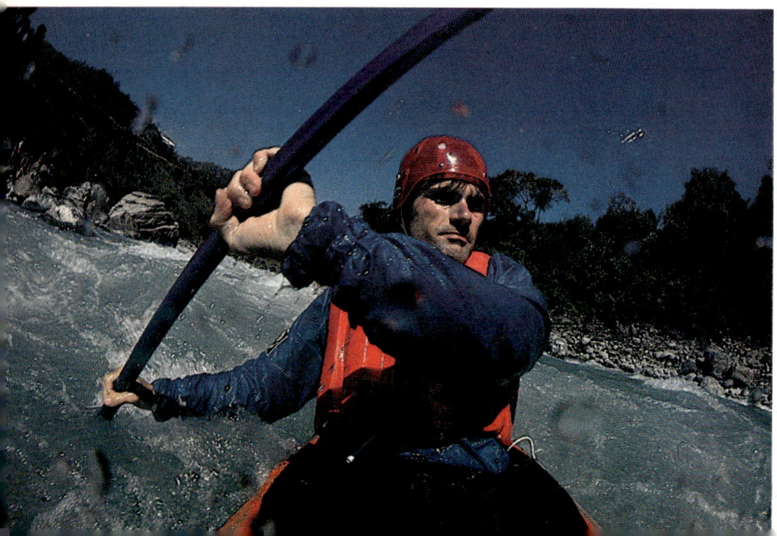

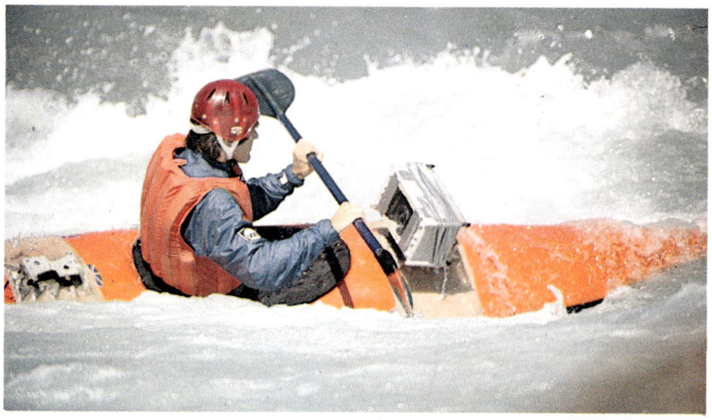

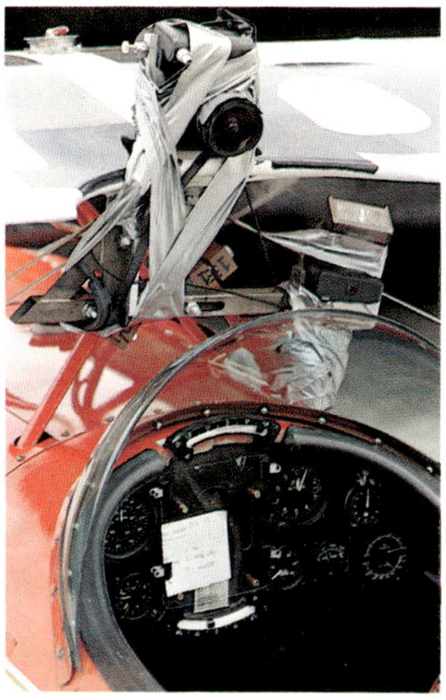

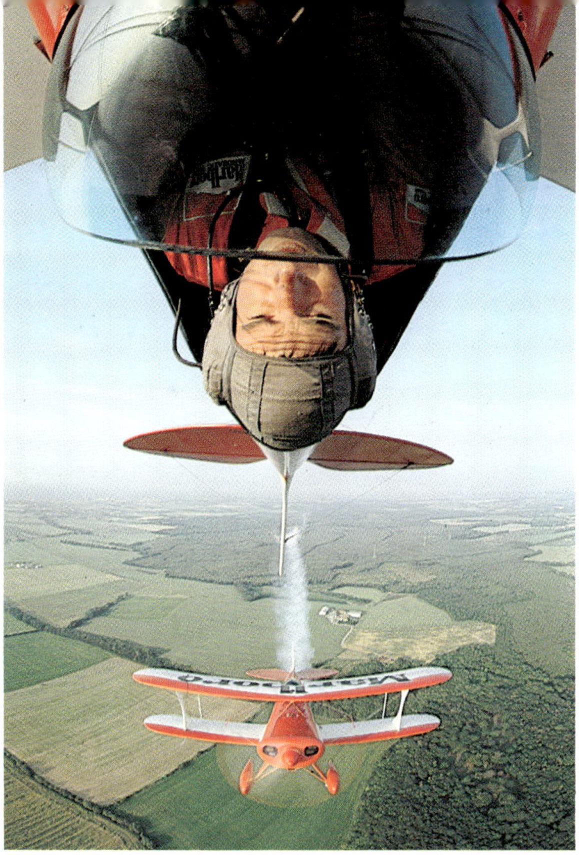

Pilot *The close viewpoint and a wide angle lens gave this shot added impact. In situations like this, the photographer cannot control the camera. Here the pilot operated the unit with a hand switch*

beam is broken, an electrical circuit is completed and this triggers off the camera. The two units, transmitter and receiver, can be mounted side by side, and the beam bounced off a reflector. Some devices incorporate a rotating fan, as on a strobe light, which breaks the beam up into a fixed rate of pulses. If the beam is broken or the frequency changed, the camera is fired.

This system is ideal for use in daylight if the weather and lighting conditions are constant and the subject slow moving. However, if the light is changing rapidly or the subject needs to be frozen in motion, you must use some form of flash. Not only is lighting then consistent, but the flash is sufficiently short to freeze the action.

There is a short time lag between the breaking of the beam and the release of the shutter, so you must frame your picture to allow for this. On most 35 mm cameras, the delay can be as much as 1/10 of a second, but on some cameras with leaf shutters it can be as little as 1/400 of a second. A leaf shutter can also be synchronized at high speeds, allowing you to use flash to freeze action even in daylight using a wide aperture.

Another factor is the sensitivity of the unit. Most units have a screw which adjusts their sensitivity to a given size of subject. If you want to photograph a small bird, you must set the sensitivity so that insects do not fire the shutter. Similarly, if your intended subject is much larger, set the sensitivity lower, or the camera will take many pictures of smaller creatures.

When working outdoors, make sure all your equipment is well wrapped in polythene to keep it dry. Conventional power supplies will probably be inadequate, especially if you are using flash—a very small area of undergrowth may need several guns to light it properly, so even a large source of power can be quickly exhausted. The best solution is to use lead acid batteries. Motor cycle cells give the right voltage, and several of these set up in series can power a remote release device for the best part of a night.

Exposure

The 'break the beam' system used with flash at night allows complete exposure control, but most other remote control situations are more complex. Often, the camera has to be set up a long time before the event to be photographed.

Automatic exposure is not necessarily the best solution. If your camera has aperture priority automation, you might set it to obtain an acceptable shutter speed for a given light. If, however, that light diminishes, your pictures will be blurred, because your camera will have compensated by setting a slower shutter speed.

Whether you use your camera on automatic or on manual, the only solution to the problem of exposure is to compensate at the processing stage.

Bear in mind that, however efficient your remote control system is, it is always a good idea to use it, whenever possible, only as a back-up to a camera operated manually.

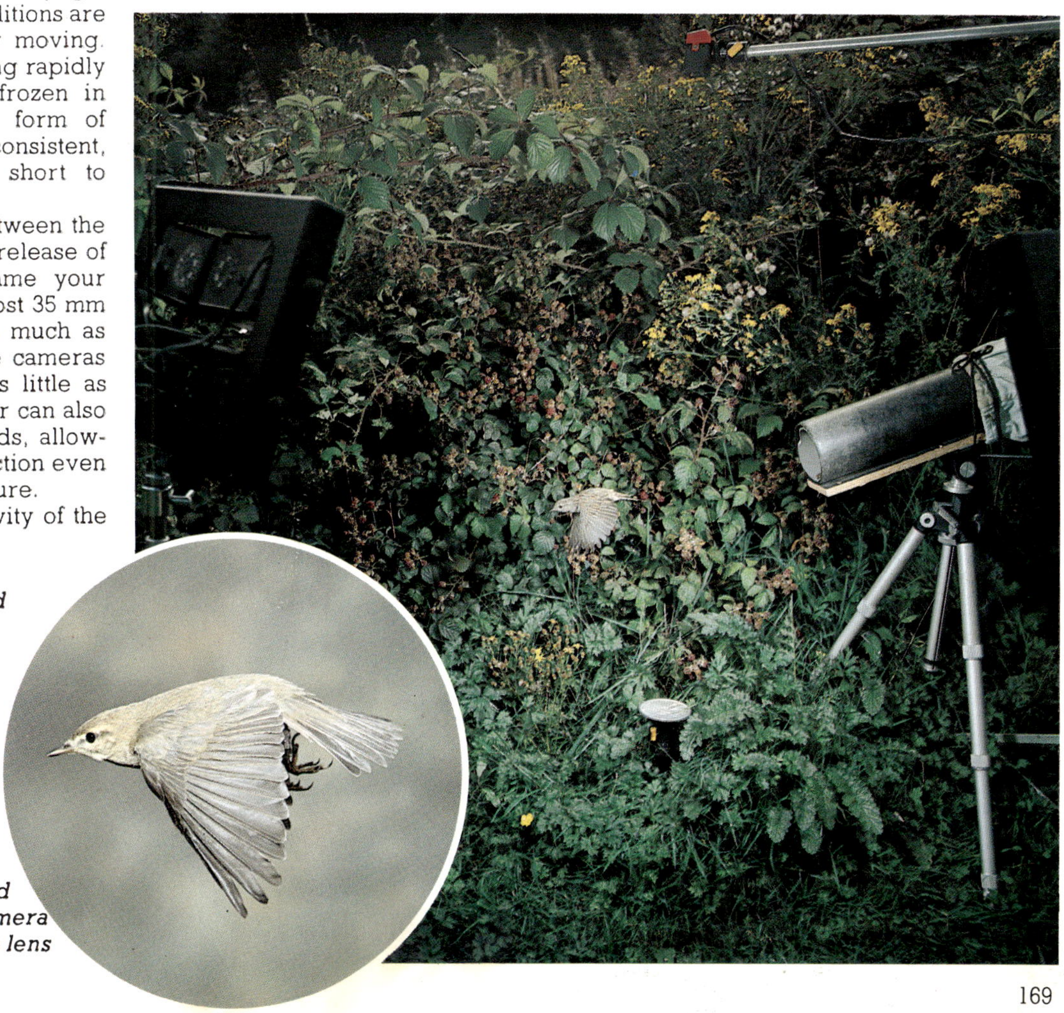

Frozen in flight *A flash of 1/10,000 second freezes rapid movement. Eight flashguns, of which four are visible on the left, were used to light this small area of undergrowth. A transmitter, at the top of the picture, directed an infrared beam at the receiver on the ground. The bird, released through the tube on the right, flew through the beam, activating camera and flash in 25 milliseconds. The camera was a Hasselblad with a 150 mm lens*

CHAPTER 16
SETTING UP A STUDIO
Home studio

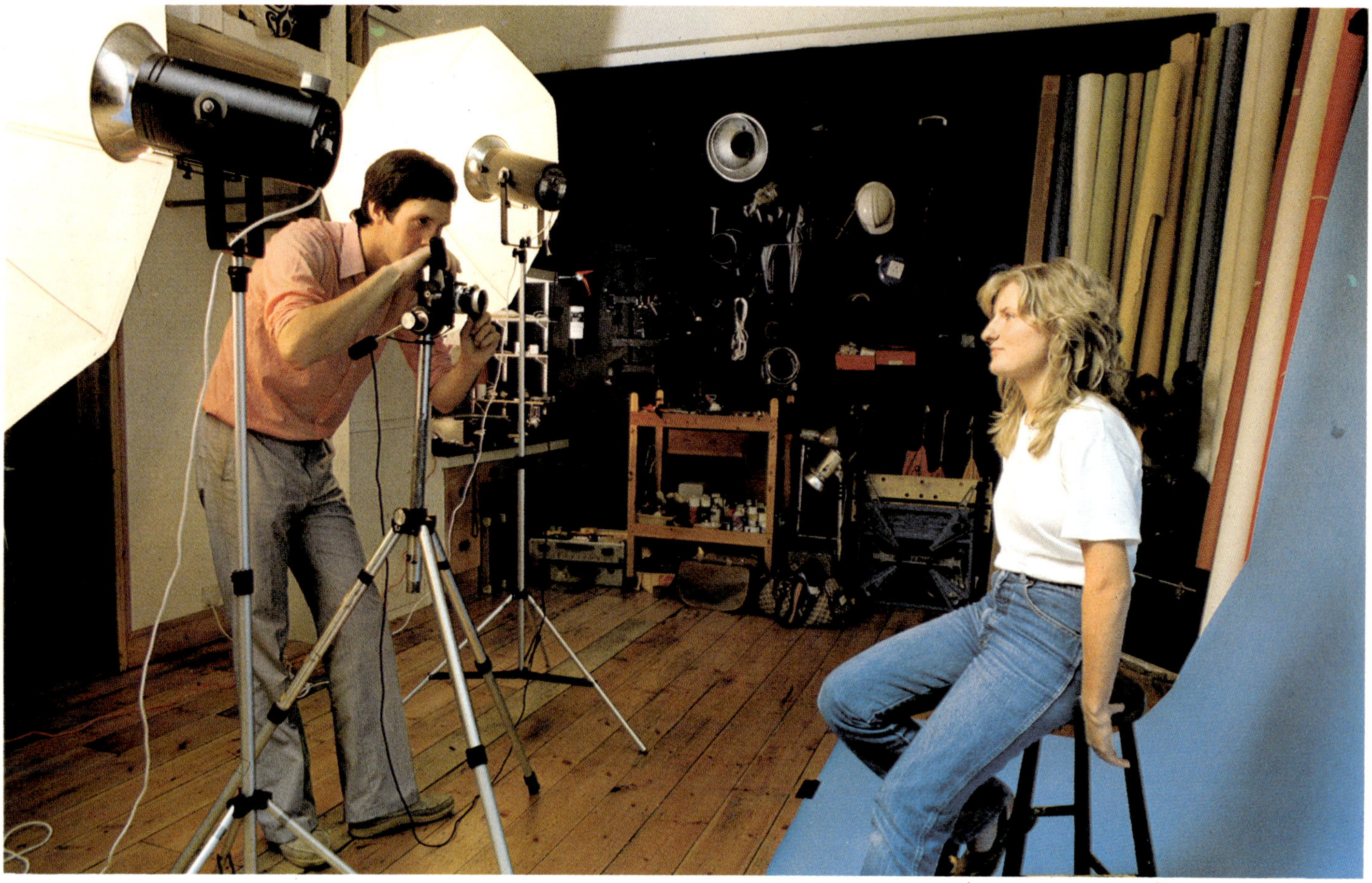

Full time studio *If you have a big house, you may be able to convert one room into a permanent studio.*
Tungsten or flash? *Quartz lamps are cheaper to buy, but get very hot and cost more to run than flash*

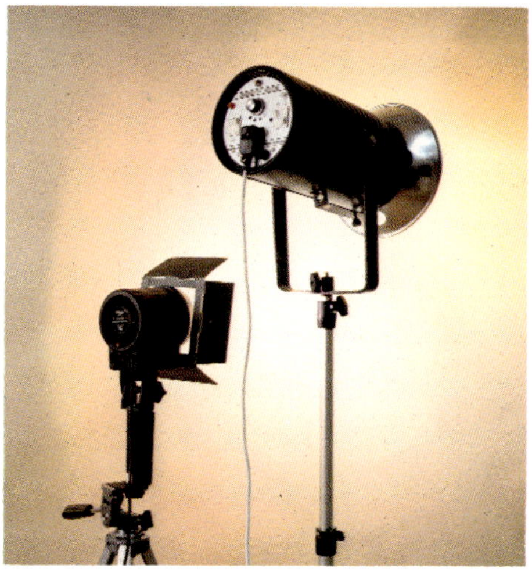

Photographic studios take many forms. Some are as vast as aircraft hangars—big enough to hold several buses with room to spare, others are small enough and light enough to be carried around on photographic expeditions—the American portrait photographer Irving Penn once built a tiny, tentlike canvas studio, which he took with him when photographing primitive tribal people.

Whether grand or humble, though, a studio has only one purpose—to give the photographer more control over the way a picture is made. This is achieved by protecting subjects from the elements, providing a support for backgrounds, and permitting controlled lighting of the subject.

A studio at home
Very few amateur photographers can afford the luxury of a purpose-built studio, and most people have to make do with a room that is less than perfect for photography. If all the rooms in your house seem too cramped, or unsuitable, do not despair—take advantage of what you have got. Your studio may double as a living room, or even a garage. Despite this there is much you can do to create a successful working studio in almost any room. So, what should you look for?

Choosing a room
Although you can take photographs in a room of almost any dimensions, your photography will be much easier if the scale of the studio matches the scale of the work you do regularly. There is no sense in having a huge studio if you only ever photograph small still lifes. On the other hand, if your main interest is portraiture, you may need quite a large room, where you can move back from the model for full-length portraits. If you want to use rolls of coloured background paper, your room must be wide enough to fit these in. There must also be space at either side, so that you have room to roll up the paper and fit lights in. Background paper—also called seamless background and Colorama—is made in standard-sized rolls 2.74 metres wide, and you need at least one metre of free space either side. Your studio should be at least five metres wide if you plan to use background paper rolls. These can, of course, be sawn down to a smaller

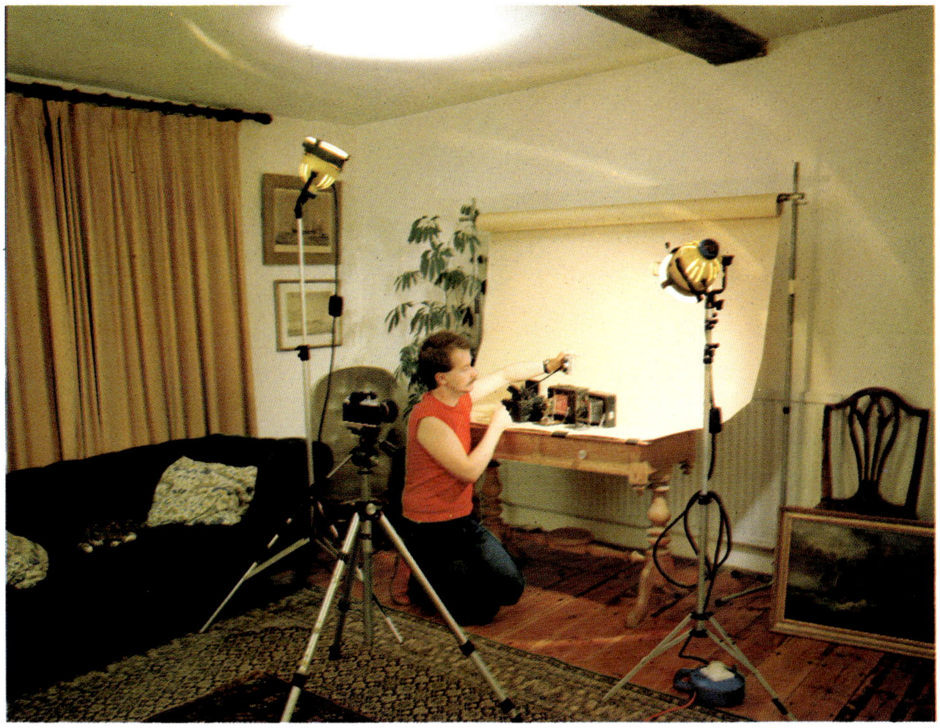

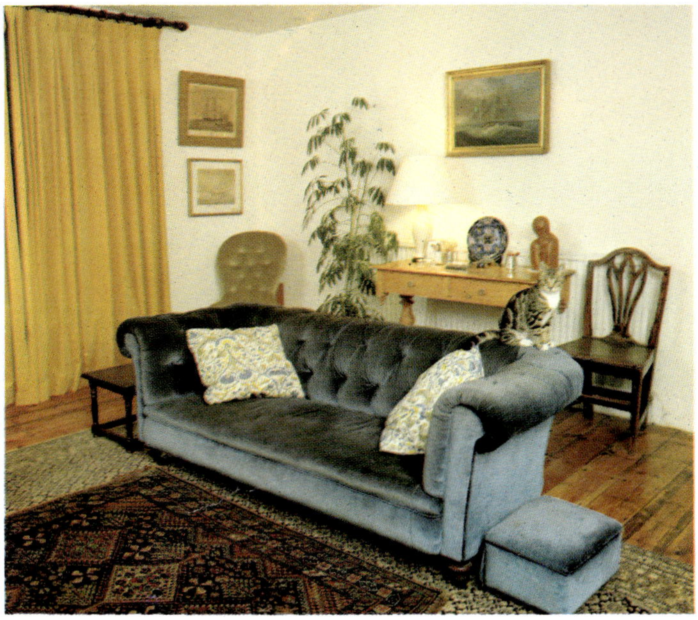

Studio at home
You can set up a studio with a minimum of equipment and space. Often it is just a question of pushing the furniture aside and setting up a couple of lights. The room can be quickly restored to its normal role when the session is finished.
The ideal size
A bigger studio gives you scope to shoot with longer lenses

size so that they will fit smaller rooms, but this is rather expensive and wasteful.

The length of your studio will dictate the largest subject you can photograph, but it will also influence the focal length of the lens you can use. To get an idea of space, think of how far back you need to stand to take a full length portrait. With a 35 mm camera turned in vertical format and fitted with a standard lens, the head and feet of an average standing figure will be tightly framed when the camera is 2.5 metres away. With the same subject and a 105 mm lens, the camera must be positioned 5.3 metres away and with a 135 mm lens, 6.8 metres. These distances are not true room lengths, because they allow no space for the photographer to get behind the camera. There must be sufficient space behind the model, too, so that shadows do not fall on the background, which often has to be lit separately. Allow an extra metre behind the camera, and at least 1.5 metres behind the model. Further, to avoid very tight framing, the studio needs to be even longer by a metre or two.

There is no real alternative to a long, wide studio if you want to use longer focal length lenses. It is no solution to choose a short lens such as a wide angle because this simply introduces perspective distortion of the subject. Compare the two portraits on page 67, and you will see that the photograph taken with a telephoto lens is by far the better shot. Had the other portrait been taken with a wide angle instead of the standard lens it would look even odder. A further reason for not using a wide angle lens is that such a lens sees more background—which you would have to accommodate. A long lens though, gives you more room for manoeuvre, and prevents the edges of the background creeping in at each side of the picture.

If you do not have a long enough room available, remember that you can shoot through an open doorway for the occasional full length picture. This has the added advantage that the doorway

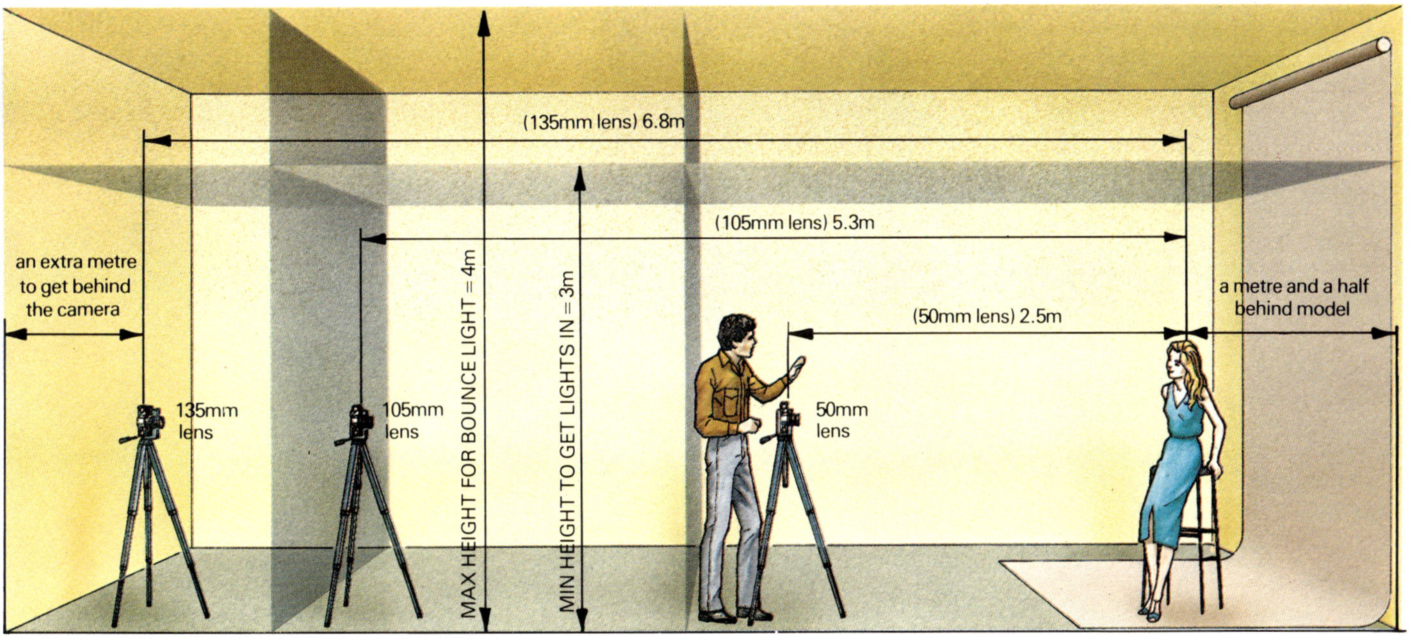

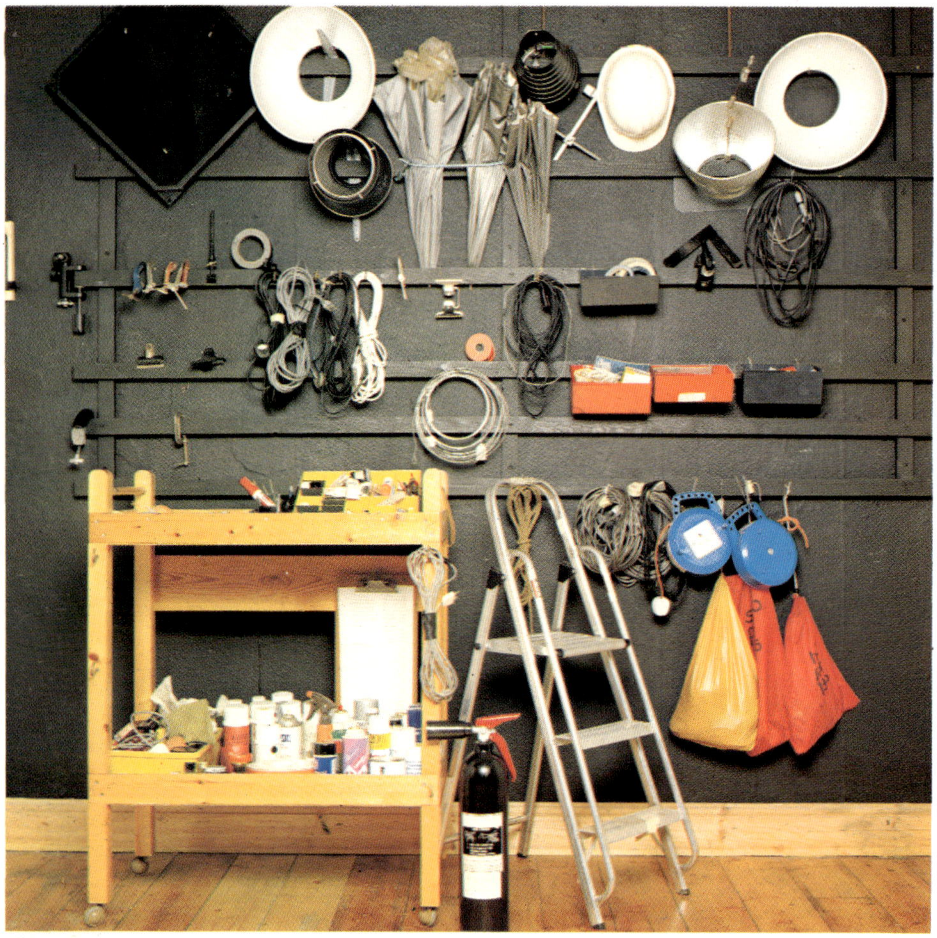

Equipment storage *Even in a home studio, it is important to have all the essential acessories close at hand*

acts as a very deep lens hood, cutting out any stray light.

A studio that is too long or wide is rarely a handicap, but a ceiling that is too high can cause problems. It is useful to have a fairly low, white painted ceiling, so that you can bounce light off it. Light bounced from a ceiling, like bounced flash, gives very pleasant, soft illumination but if the ceiling is higher than about four metres, bounced lighting effects become more or less impractical.

On the other hand, a very low ceiling may be restrictive—sometimes you may need to put a light above a model.

The ideal room to use as a studio, then, is at least five metres wide, nine metres long, and three to four metres high. A balcony is a useful feature, because it makes topshots—pictures from above—much easier to achieve. Natural light from two sides is an advantage, but not essential, and it is quite feasible to rely entirely on electric light.

Flash or tungsten?

One of the most important decisions facing a photographer setting up a studio is whether to use tungsten lights, or electronic flash. Both have their advantages: tungsten lights are cheaper to buy than studio flash units, but consume more electric power. Electronic flash freezes all action in the picture, but without Polaroid tests, it is difficult to see whether the lighting and exposure are correct. Tungsten lights give off more heat than electronic flash units, but are more reliable.

Perhaps the biggest factor is cost—studio flash units are too expensive to justify the outlay unless you use them very regularly. If you are working on a low budget, or have a lot to learn about lighting, it is probably better to buy tungsten units.

Tungsten lights are available in many forms. The cheapest are the type shown on pages 174 to 177, but these can only be used with quite low power photoflood bulbs. Although they are suitable for lighting at close quarters, the level of illumination from them drops considerably when they are moved back from the subject. This means that, unless you use a lot of lights, long exposures at quite large apertures are sometimes needed.

Professional photographers rarely use photoflood bulbs for tungsten lighting, instead, many prefer quartz-halogen lighting units. These take small glass tubes instead of bulbs, and usually have a power output of 1000 watts. Professional quartz lighting units are fairly expensive, but movie lights, which take the same lamps, are just as powerful and much cheaper. Check before you buy that the lights can be used for continuous running, and not just intermittently.

Quartz lights do not accept interchangeable reflectors, though some of them have a variable beam angle. Lighting effects must be controlled by using umbrellas, diffusers, or reflective sheets. Although this may seem more complicated than swapping from one

Useful equipment

Besides the basic fixtures and fittings for a studio, there is a whole range of small items that can be useful around the studio. Many are ordinary domestic tools or utensils, others are quite specialized. The list is not comprehensive and no single item is essential. However, all of the following items should help you get the best out of your studio and are all quite cheap.

Supporting, sticking and fixing: a general purpose tool kit comes in very handy for holding bits of a set or background together. Six house bricks can be used as supports or weights. A theatrical stage weight, or any heavy lump of metal is useful for similar purposes. A beer crate is good for standing on or to give a bit of extra height to a prop, and a laboratory retort stand can be used to support an object at any height or angle. Double-sided tape is invaluable for adjusting or fixing the position of props as is a plasticene type adhesive. Conventional tape, such as black PVC, or heavy carpet tape, has a thousand uses in the studio.

Lighting aids: reflectors of various sorts are essential. Large sheets of expanded polystyrene need very little support, and make excellent reflectors. Foil covered card, either high gloss or dull matt can be cut up and concealed in a still life to lighten shadows. Diffusers made of acrylic or tracing paper stretched on a frame, allow careful control of light. (Some diffusing material comes in a deep blue colour equivalent to an 80A filter, and converts tungsten light to daylight colour.) Black velvet stretched on a frame can be used to take light out of a portrait. Double-sided spring clips can be used instead of barn doors to 'flag' a light and prevent it shining into the lens. A *French flag* has a similar function but is attached to a tripod with a clamp.

Electrical leads and a long extension cable are essential, but tend to get snarled up. Store them in small fabric bags so that they are out of the way, but easily accessible. A peg board or a plastic rack such as those used for storing vegetables is useful for storing odd bits, but a wheeled trolley is better. Cover the shelves in ribbed rubber mat, so that lenses and other items do not roll around—a raised lip stops them falling off altogether.

For still life work, a dulling spray is very useful. This puts a fine matt lacquer on to shiny objects, so that they do not flare into the lens. A sheet of plate glass is a necessity if you photograph glassware, as it allows you to light from below.

Finally, do not neglect safety, particularly with hot tungsten lamps. Buy a fire extinguisher of the foam type—water is dangerous where there is electrical equipment in the room. A small step ladder is much safer to stand on than a wobbly chair or stool, and can double as a projector stand—but make sure all four legs are firmly on the ground.

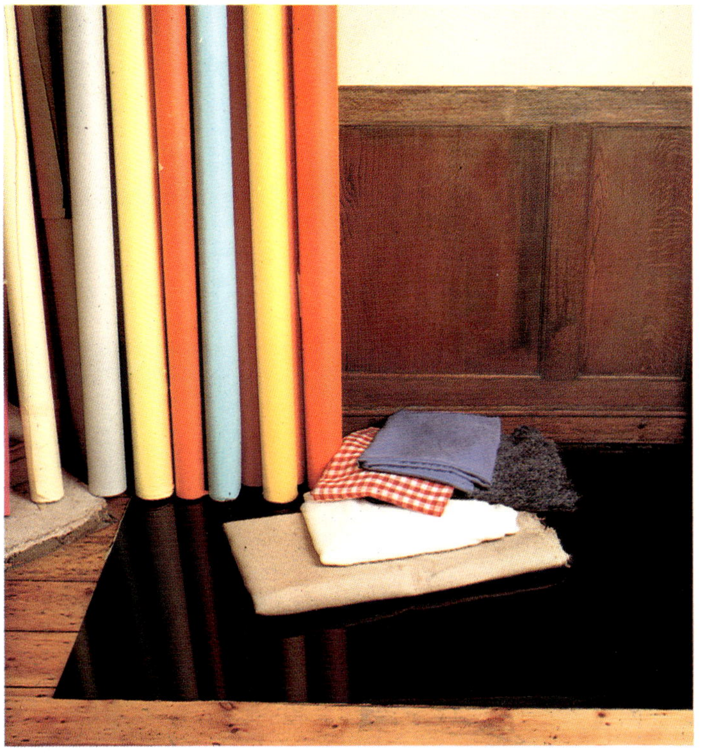

Bold backgrounds
Seamless paper rolls come in many colours, but scraps of fabric are just as useful, and have more texture

Lighting aids
A French flag (fixed to the tripod) stops light shining into the lens, and black, silver and diffusion sheets help to control lighting

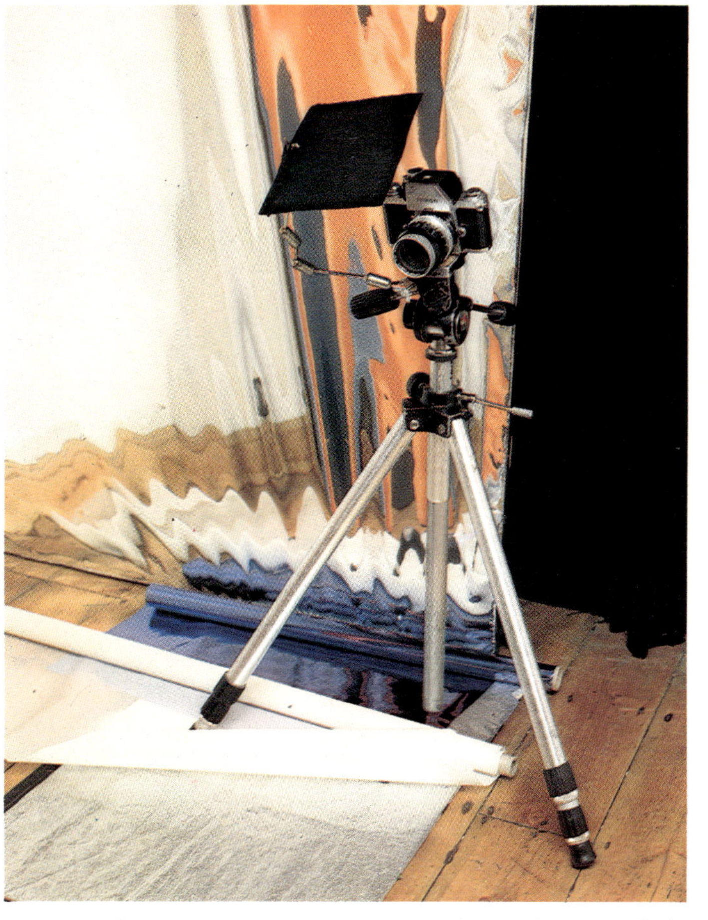

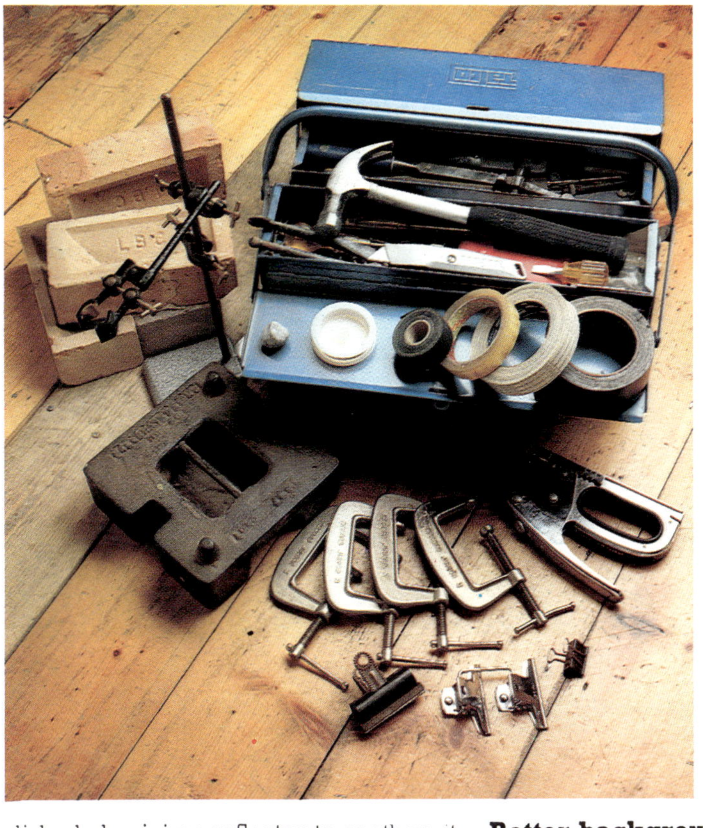

Useful tools
All sorts of non-photographic items have a use in the studio

dished aluminium reflector to another, it can provide a more versatile method of lighting the subject. It also cuts down on cost—diffusers can be made cheaply and easily at home.

If you decide to use electronic flash, it is worth considering the purchase of a small monobloc studio flash unit. Unlike portable flashguns, these studio units have a modelling bulb close to the flash tube, and this gives you some indication of how the light changes when the model or the flash is moved. Portable flash guns are difficult to use in the studio, because you cannot see how light is falling on the subject—you are 'working in the dark'.

Better backgrounds

Rolls of seamless background paper are ideal for portraits and many other types of photography. By concealing distracting details, they draw attention to the main subject and, with careful lighting, can make the join between the floor and wall of the studio invisible. Background rolls come in a wide range of colours, but if you buy a roll of white paper, you can use coloured gels over the lights to provide variations of hue. The paper is rolled in lengths of 11 or 25 metres and has a tubular cardboard core, by which it can be supported. Though special stands are available for this purpose, you can easily use a bamboo pole, a couple of pulleys and a length of rope to raise and lower the paper.

For some purposes, paper rolls are unsuitable—some photographers feel they are featureless, bland, and lacking in character. If you want a background with some texture in it, lengths of fabric make a useful studio accessory. With a 135 mm lens, you only need a piece of fabric one metre square for a background to a head and shoulders portrait, and this sort of length can easily be bought as an 'end of roll remnant' at very low cost.

Wood, and plastic laminate panels make very good backgrounds, too, if you have enough room to store them. Plastic laminate wipes clean, and is waterproof and flexible. It is a good substitute for seamless background paper, and though the initial cost is higher, it can work out cheaper in the long run.

Whatever sort of background you use, it is convenient to be able to fix it to the floor, so that it does not move about in draughts or when someone walks past. If you have a wooden floor, this is a simple matter—you can staple it down, or put pins or nails through it. If your studio floor is solid concrete, however, it is well worth laying a plywood floor over at least part of the area of the studio. If you are using background paper in a studio which has fitted carpets, a temporary plywood floor cover becomes a necessity, because it prevents the paper being creased each time someone walks on it, or puts something down.

Budget lighting

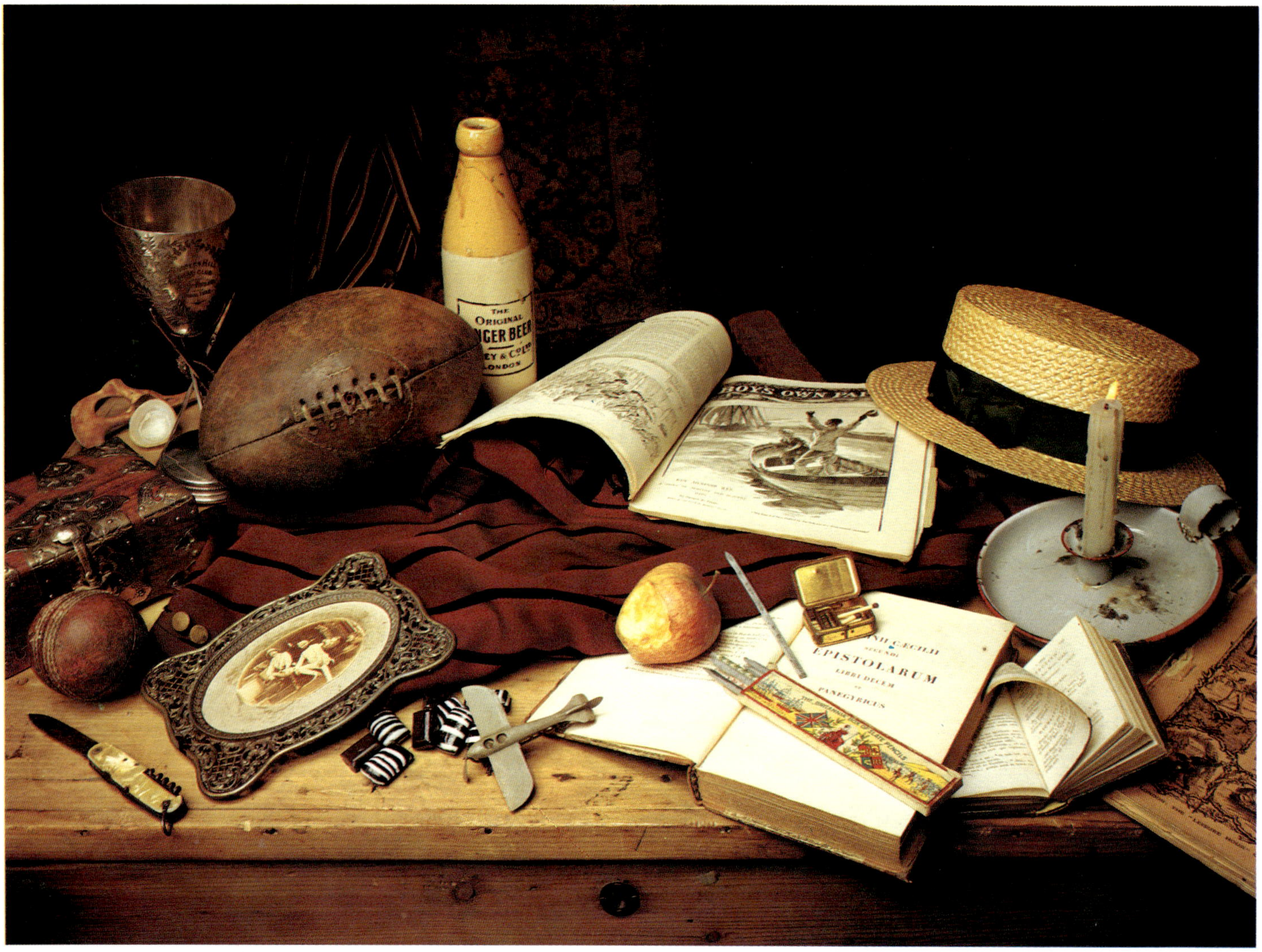

Light is essential to photography. Without it, you would be unable to take pictures. But whereas the use of available light will normally give satisfactory results out of doors, you will often require artificial light if you wish to take good photographs indoors.

Full studio lighting can cost a lot of money, but if you choose carefully from the range of budget equipment available, you will be able to create excellent and easily controllable sources of artificial light for a relatively modest outlay.

There are basically two methods of providing light for an indoor subject—flash and tungsten lighting.

Bulbs

The term *tungsten lighting* is generally used to describe sources of light that are illuminated continuously, rather than lighting up for a very brief instant in the way that a flashgun does. Because it is a general term, tungsten light is used to refer to all sorts of light sources, ranging from ordinary household bulbs to football stadium floodlights. For photographic purposes, the type of tungsten lamps that are most commonly used range from 275 watts to 1000 watts, though for the home studio anything brighter than 500 watts is rather unmanageable. Lamps dimmer than 275 watts emit light that is too yellow in colour, and are therefore not really suitable for colour photography.

There are many different types of lamp which are made specifically for photography, but the most useful of these, as far as the non-professional user is concerned, is the photoflood bulb.

Photofloods are made in a variety of sizes and power outputs, the outputs of the most popular sizes being rated at

Schoolboy still life *For this sort of still life, a cheap, simple lighting set up is perfectly adequate to achieve well lit pictures*

275 watts and 500 watts. Although photofloods look very similar to domestic light bulbs, they are made with a different electrical element within the glass globe. But photofloods get much hotter, shine brighter and last for less time than conventional light bulbs. Their most important advantage, however, is that they burn with a bluer light.

Photofloods have a colour temperature of around 3400 kelvins, (see pages 238 to 239) which makes them much more suitable for use with tungsten balanced colour slide film than conventional light bulbs. Some filtration must still be used, though, because tungsten film is balanced for light with a colour temperature of

3200K (see films and filters, below).

The cap fittings of photofloods are the same as those of ordinary domestic light bulbs, so they could be used in place of ordinary bulbs. Although this is feasible with the smaller bulbs for short periods, it can be dangerous to use large photoflood bulbs in fittings that have not been specifically designed for this purpose. The bulbs heat up very rapidly, and could damage light fittings in a few minutes. A burnt out lampholder may just mean a blown fuse, but there is a serious risk of fire if the bulb touches flammable material. Photoflood bulbs, particularly the larger ones, should be used in ceramic lampholders with metal fittings.

There are other types of tungsten lamp available, some of which offer significant advantages over photofloods. Photopearl lamps, also called Argaphoto bulbs, are in many ways similar to photofloods —they consume either 500 or 1000 watts and have a colour temperature of 3200 kelvins, which means that they can be used with tungsten film without the need for filters. The major difference between photofloods and photopearl lamps is in burning time: photopearl bulbs burn for 100 hours or so, while photofloods will burn out after only 3 to 6 hours. Although the cost of the longer lasting bulbs is as much as five times greater than the cheaper photofloods, they cost less in the long run.

Photoflood lamps are now commonly called 'photolamps' and photopearl lamps are generally known as 'tungsten (3200K) lamps'. Without the colour temperature in brackets the term tungsten is virtually meaningless because all filament lamps have tungsten filaments.

Lampholders and stands

On its own, a bulb is useless—it needs to be supported and its light directed. There are a variety of lighting systems on the market which provide a good selection of stands and lamp-holders, and can be fitted with a number of different reflectors.

There are three common types of lamp fitting available for photographic purposes—one is a bayonet cap (BC) fitting, and the other two are Edison screw (ES) fittings. Some photographic lamps are available in a choice of fittings, but all photoflood and photopearl lamps that are likely to be used at home are available in the smaller of the two Edison screw fittings. It makes sense, therefore, to base any home studio around this one standard size, which is also the size most commonly used in domestic screw-thread light fittings in Europe and the USA.

Most domestic light fittings are made of plastic, and while this is a perfectly suitable material for bulbs up to 200W, it will probably char or melt if used with powerful photographic lamps. If you plan to use one of the more powerful bulbs for extended periods, make sure that the lampholder you buy is made of metal, and that the insulators inside are made of a ceramic material—you should be able to see these insulators by looking into the lampholder with the bulb removed.

Lighting stands for the lampholders are available in a wide variety of shapes and sizes. They are usually collapsible, and fold up quite small for ease of transportation. The more portable stands are made of aluminium alloy—this makes

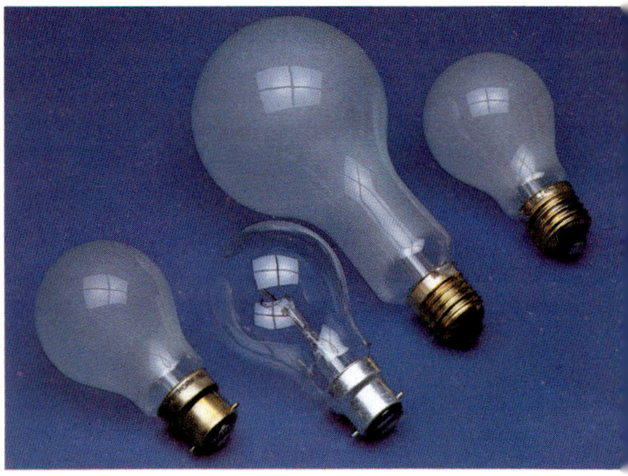

Photographic lamps *The opal bulbs are photofloods—two are 375W, one 500W. The clear bulb is an ordinary 60W lamp*

Budget lighting *Even unexpensive lighting systems offer a choice of stands and reflectors. Some allow you to use your electronic flashguns as a light source*

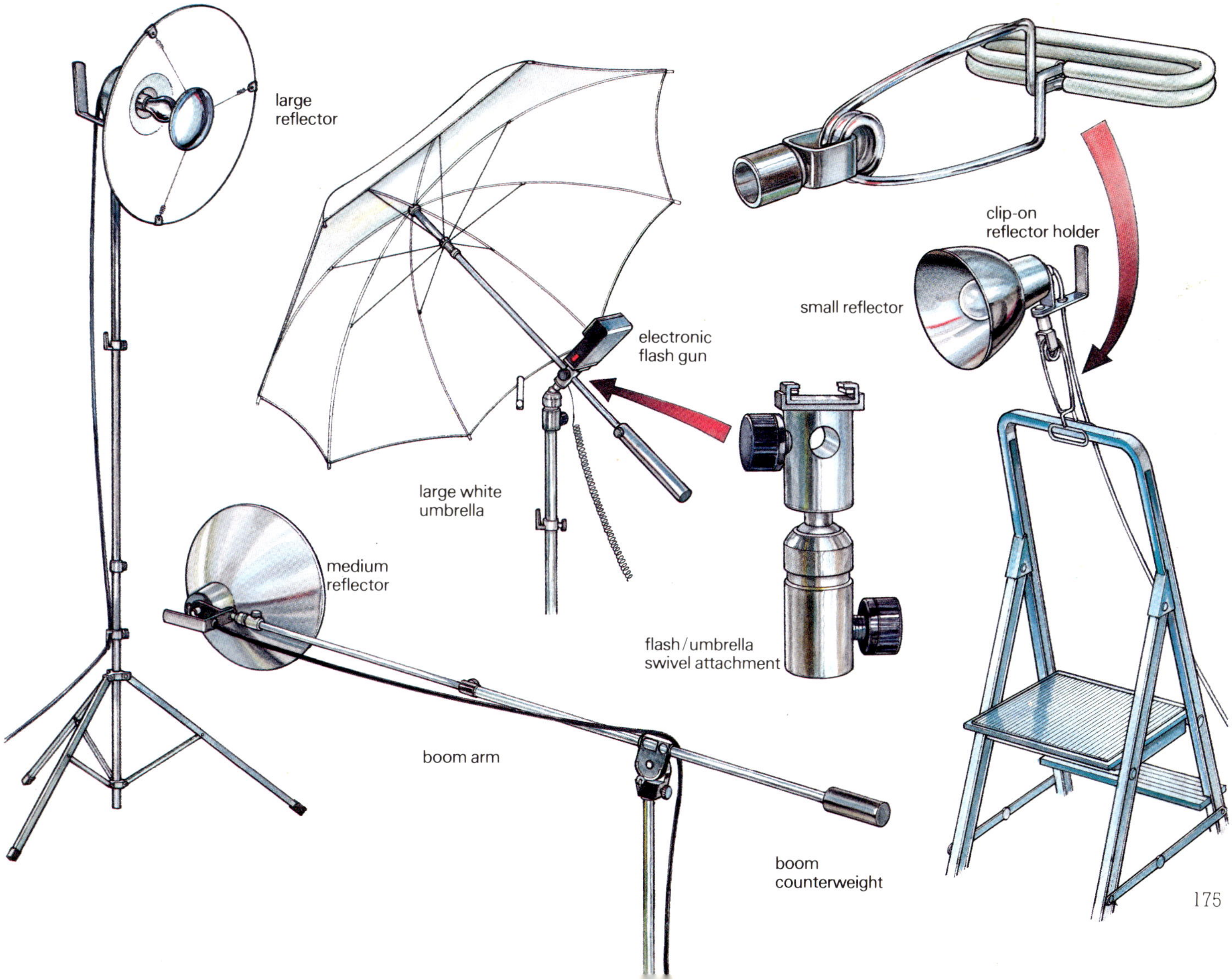

them a lot lighter to carry around. Unfortunately, aluminium is both expensive and rather soft, so the better makes of aluminium stand are quite substantially built, and therefore tend to be quite costly. If you intend to use your lighting frequently, or if you will have to carry it around a lot, it is probably a good idea to spend your money on heavy duty types.

On the other hand, most amateur lighting set-ups are used infrequently, being stored in a cupboard when not in use, and in such a case a strong aluminium stand would be a waste of money.

The most rigid types of stand are those made of aluminium tubing. Although the stands constructed from aluminium extrusions are adequate for most purposes, they can be more difficult to assemble, and are not usually quite as steady as the tubular type.

Cheaper stands are often made from pressed steel—they have telescopic steel tubes in the centre, and flat metal strip legs. These stands only extend to about 2 m, but this is usually adequate for portraits and still life photography in the home. When these are not being used they can be stored in boxes which take up very little space.

It is very useful to be able to get a light down low, almost at floor level. This is sometimes necessary when lighting a portrait, because a low light can be used for backlighting—it will come from behind the subject, but will not be visible in the picture. In such cases you can buy a small tripod attachment which will take the lampholder. Some manufacturers produce a clamp that can be fitted to one leg of a lighting stand serving the same purpose.

Lighting stands are not the only means of fixing lamps into position. Strong spring clips are available that have a lampholder and reflector attached. These can be fixed to the back of a chair or onto a shelf, and usually have a ball and socket joint which allows the lamp to be pointed in a number of different directions. These devices work well for improvised lighting set ups, and can be usefully pressed into service as extra reading lights when not in use for photography.

Another useful accessory that comes in handy for occasional photo sessions is a small steel bracket that hooks over the top of a door. Most internal doors have a small amount of clearance at the top, so the door can often be closed with the bracket in place. The light is then fixed onto the bracket, which again has a ball and socket joint so that it can be pointed in the required direction.

Getting a lamp above a subject is often a problem, particularly for portraiture where a dark haired sitter will need extra light on the hair for good results. A long horizontal bar is usually used for this purpose, with the lamp fixed to one end. A counterweight is attached to the other and the whole arm, called a *boom,* is clamped to the upright of a lighting stand. The lamp hangs above the sitter's head, but does not appear in the picture.

Reflectors

Even the most inexpensive lights can be used with a range of different reflectors. As a general rule, the smaller the reflector, the sharper and harder the light source will appear to be. A bare light bulb is the most extreme example, forming very hard, abrupt shadows. It also wastes a lot of light.

A small shiny reflector directs more light from the bulb onto the subject, but still forms fairly hard shadows. A larger reflector is less efficient in concentrating the light from the bulb, but produces less harsh shadows. Very large reflectors give extremely soft illumination, with very gentle shadows, but the light is spread out so that it is much dimmer.

These three types of reflector can be fitted to most types of economical lighting units. They are generally made from spun aluminium, which makes them light, reflective, and easy to move around. The smallest reflectors are usually about 17 to 18 cm across, and are highly polished inside. They are best used for backlighting, where a small source of light is required, or for a dramatic main source of light. They produce narrow beams with little spread.

General purpose reflectors are not so highly polished, measure about 24 cm across, and produce a softer, wider beam of light. This is the type of reflector that is supplied as standard with many lighting units.

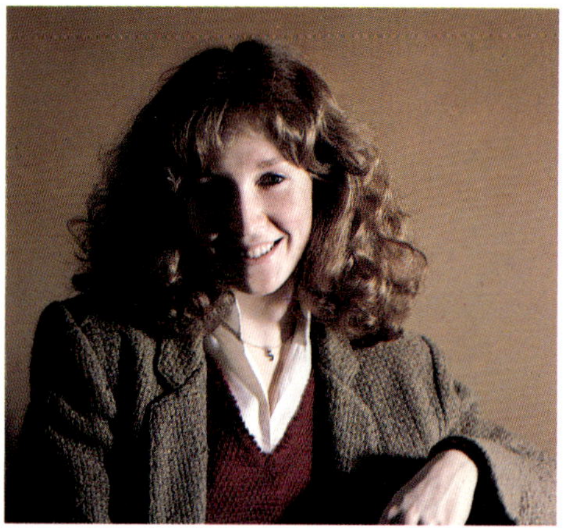

Hard light *The smallest reflectors produce a concentrated, harsh beam*

Fill in reflectors are much larger—40 cm or bigger, and are painted matt white on the inside. They often have a cover which prevents light from reaching the subject directly from the bulb. These reflectors are used to fill in harsh shadows in a picture, without forming disturbing secondary shadows themselves. They are also useful as a soft, flattering main light for portraiture.

Some photographic lamps also have a reflector built into the bulb. Since the reflector is fixed in place these bulbs are of limited use. They produce fairly narrow beams of light, and can be pressed into service as a last resort.

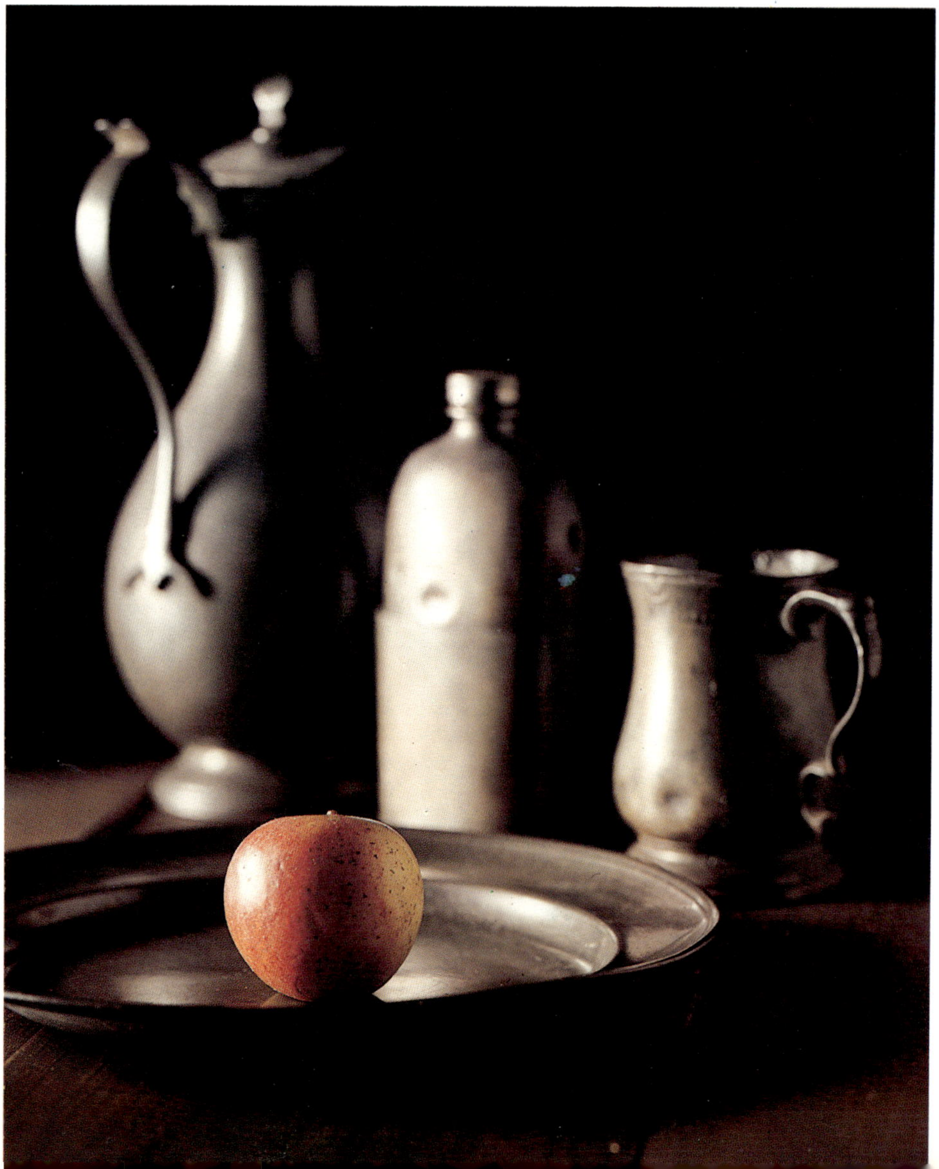

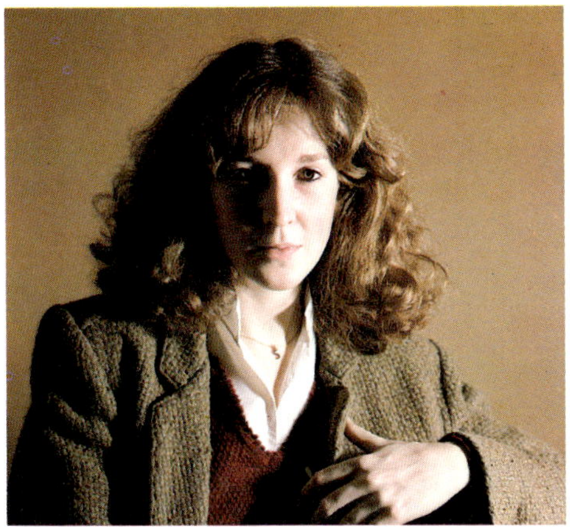

Slightly softer *Medium size reflectors form a beam that is marginally softer*

Lighting accessories

The most expensive lighting systems have custom built systems of accessories available, such as *barn doors* and *snoots*. Barn doors are black metal flaps that control the area of the subject that is lit by the lamp, and can also be used to prevent light falling directly on the camera lens.

Although these are rarely made for the cheaper lighting systems, a substitute can be improvised using pieces of black card and a pair of spring clips.

A snoot is a long cone-shaped cover that is fixed to a lamp to produce a small spot of light on the subject. Some of the cheaper lighting systems have snoots available, but you can easily make snoots for lights without them from black card and adhesive tape.

Dimmers and cost-cutting

Tungsten lights are expensive to run—the bulbs are costly and use a lot of power. The lives of photoflood bulbs are very short, and towards the end of their working life the colour of the light they emit becomes redder. For this reason, many photographers use a dimmer in the lighting circuit. This is set to a low level for focusing and composing the picture, and is turned up to full power for the exposure itself. Since the power to the lamps is reduced, they consume less electricity. The life of the bulbs is prolonged considerably—an eight per cent cut in voltage to a photoflood doubles the life of the bulb. It is easy to see that the use of a dimmer can halve the number of bulbs used.

Cutting the voltage to a bulb also lowers the colour temperature of the light, so it is important to remember to turn up the power before pressing the shutter release on your camera.

The same effect can be achieved by using a series/parallel circuit. This has a two-position switch with one position for exposure, and one for focusing. Unfortunately, it can only be used with even numbers of bulbs, and will not work if one, three or five lamps are in use. Some manufacturers produce ready made units of this type, and even if they are unobtainable, any competent local electrician should be able to make one up to order for minimal cost.

Solitary apple *The lighting for this picture was very straightforward—just one lamp in a large white reflector on the left of the subject, and a reflecting sheet on the right to put some light into the shadows*

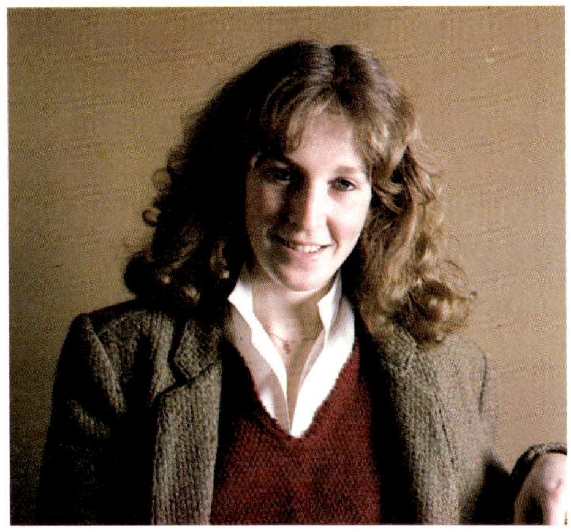

Big and soft *Large white reflectors are much more suitable for portraits*

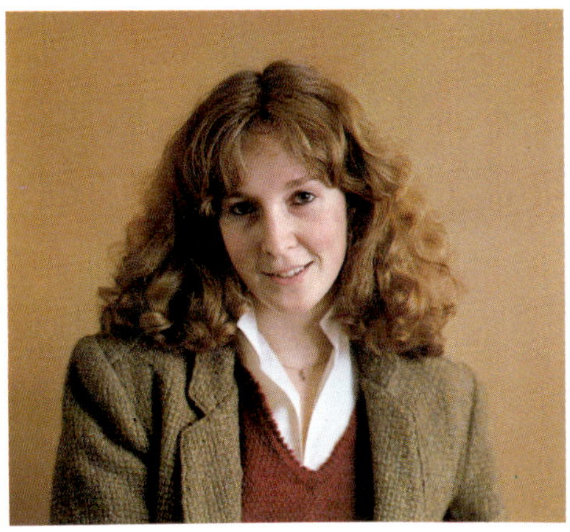

Flattering flash *Best results are produced by flash and an umbrella*

Portable flashguns

A lot of professional photographers prefer to use electronic flash for studio work, and it is easy to see why. Electronic flash does not heat up in the same way that tungsten light does—and it freezes all movement in the subject. Daylight balanced colour slide film can be used with electronic flash, which is an advantage, because there is less choice of film balanced for tungsten than there is of film balanced for daylight.

Professional studio flash units are often very powerful, and most of them are fairly expensive—the cheaper units are discussed in the following section. The advantages of using flash are so great, however, that many people use small portable flashguns as light sources for portraiture and still life indoors. The biggest drawback to this is that you cannot see the effect that the flashes will have until you develop the film, and you cannot use a conventional meter to measure the light. Professionals get round these problems by using *modelling lights*—small halogen bulbs placed close to the flash tube to simulate the effect of the light—and by using flash meters. Polaroid test shots are also used as lighting checks.

Clearly, then, a photographer using a portable flashgun rather than a custom built studio unit is at a considerable disadvantage. However, the versatility of a small flashgun can be increased by using accessories designed to direct and control the light. The most useful of these is a bracket that enables a portable flash gun to be directed into a reflective white or silver umbrella or *brolly*. This produces a much more diffuse source of illumination than direct flash, though much of the flash's power will be lost.

The advantages of a brolly are that it is the correct shape for a directional reflector, with the flashgun at its focus pointing into the umbrella, and that it can be folded up for convenient storage.

Umbrella brackets are usually quite cheap, and are made to fit either onto a tripod, or onto a conventional lighting stand. Since the area of the umbrella reflector is quite large, the light produced by such a unit is soft and gives gentle shadows. Quite acceptable portraits can be produced by using just one umbrella and a fill-in reflector.

Films and filters

Most colour films are carefully balanced to give perfect results in sunshine—light with a colour temperature of 5500 kelvins. Electronic flash emits light with this colour temperature, so daylight film will give good results with flash without any filtration on the camera lens being necessary.

If daylight balanced colour slide film is used in tungsten light, the pictures will have an orange cast. This can be prevented by the use of an 80B blue filter over the lens, although even this precaution may not result in perfect colour reproduction.

The best solution when using tungsten lighting is to use film that is specifically balanced for this kind of light. Tungsten balanced film, such as Ektachrome 160 Tungsten, will give accurate colour when used in light with a colour temperature of 3200 kelvins. Photopearl lamps have this colour temperature, so they can be used without filtration when the camera is loaded with tungsten film. Photoflood lamps are slightly bluer in colour. They have a colour temperature of 3400 kelvins, and if they are used without filtration, they will give a pale blue cast to pictures on slide films. The solution is to use an 81A or an 81B filter. Either of these filters will eliminate the blue cast from the picture, but the 81B has a more pronounced effect.

Colour print film is only available in a daylight balanced version and, though correction can be made at the printing stage if the film is exposed in tungsten light, it is better to use an 80B blue filter over the lens for photofloods or an 80A for photopearl lamps. This will give better colour reproduction, and make printing the negative that much easier.

Studio flash

While budget lighting systems work reasonably well for a limited range of studio shots, you may eventually find them rather restrictive. To exploit the potential of the photographic studio to the full and to achieve professional results like the picture on the right, you really need proper studio flash units.

The cost of these units varies considerably, according to power and specifications, but the cheapest costs more than a basic SLR and the most expensive more than a top-of-the-range car. Clearly, to justify such a massive outlay, you must be sure that you will use the lights regularly and frequently—and preferably recoup some of the investment by selling pictures. Otherwise, it is probably better to hire the equipment as and when you need it. This, after all, is what many professionals do.

There are hire firms in most big cities, and you should be able to find these by looking in the telephone directory or one of the professional photographic journals. Unfortunately, you may find many large rental companies are unwilling to hire equipment to amateurs because their lack of experience can put the equipment—and possibly themselves—at risk. However, if you can convince staff that you know what you are doing, most will usually accept you as a client. Before you try to hire equipment, read up all the relevant information and ask photographers who have already used the equipment for their advice. Hiring is not cheap, and you have to leave a large deposit, but before you decide to buy studio flash instead, think carefully just how many times you would actually use it.

Unlike portable flashguns, studio flash units are mains powered and have very short recycling times—between one and four seconds—with a ready light to show when the flash is ready to fire again.

One of the great advantages of studio flash units is that they always have built-in modelling lamps. These are mounted next to the flash head, and shine continuously, giving off a light whose directional properties are very similar to that of the actual flash unit. In this way you can see the effect of a given light combination.

Many modelling lamps are switched to suit the power output of the flash. The higher the flash setting, the brighter the modelling light. This is an invaluable feature, especially if you are using two units, because by switching off all other

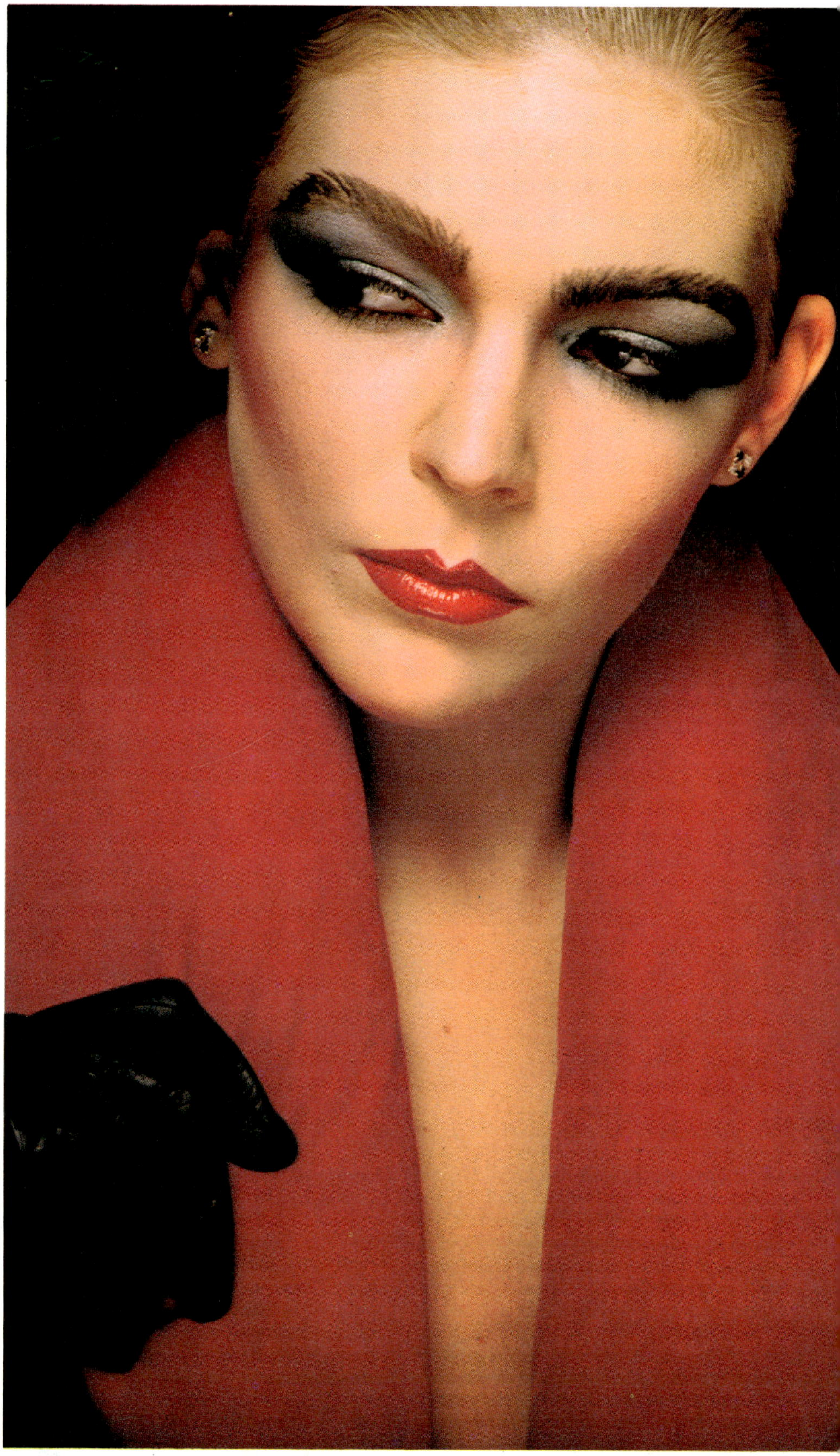

Girl in red *Sophisticated, professional looking lighting arrangements are possible even with the most basic electronic studio flash units*

light sources you can adjust the light balance visually with the modelling lamps. The flash units then give out the light in the same proportion, giving the modelling you want.

Some units have a special device which switches off the modelling light just before the flash fires, and turns it on again afterwards. They also have a socket for a synchronization lead, allowing you to use them at any distance from the camera. Others include built in photocells or 'slave' units, which are connected to the circuit of the flash unit and trigger it off as soon as another unit is fired. In this way you can synchronize any number of flash units. Slave units can be bought separately and plugged into flash units which do not already have them built in.

Most flash units are built on the *monobloc* system, with the power pack and the flash head together in one unit. At one end there is the flash head with the modelling lamp, while the power socket, sync socket and the controls are at the other end. Most studio flash units can be combined with all kinds of accessories, so you can build up your own flash 'system', with facilities for controlling the light in many ways.

All manufacturers offer a range of accessories, designed to direct the light as required. Umbrellas are used for bouncing flash, and snoots have a similar effect to a spotlight, while honeycombs provide large areas of concentrated light. Barn doors are flaps which prevent light from going into unwanted areas.

Flash power and exposure

The power output of studio flash units varies from model to model, and in addition each one can generally be used at half power or quarter power. For a single unit, the exposure may be calculated using the guide number supplied by the manufacturer. However, when using umbrellas, diffusers or more than one flash head, these numbers become useless, because so many factors are involved.

Some manufacturers only give a power rating for their units in joules or watt-seconds, and with these units you should follow the manufacturer's instructions for calculating exposure. (A joule is a unit of energy equivalent to one watt of power flowing for one second—the higher the joules or watt-seconds rating, the brighter the flash.)

The smaller units have a maximum output of 100 joules, while the more powerful ones go up to 500 joules, though this is far from the most powerful flash available as some professional units go up to 20,000 joules. All units have variable power output, an essential feature when you are using them for fill in or for close-ups, where full power would be too bright.

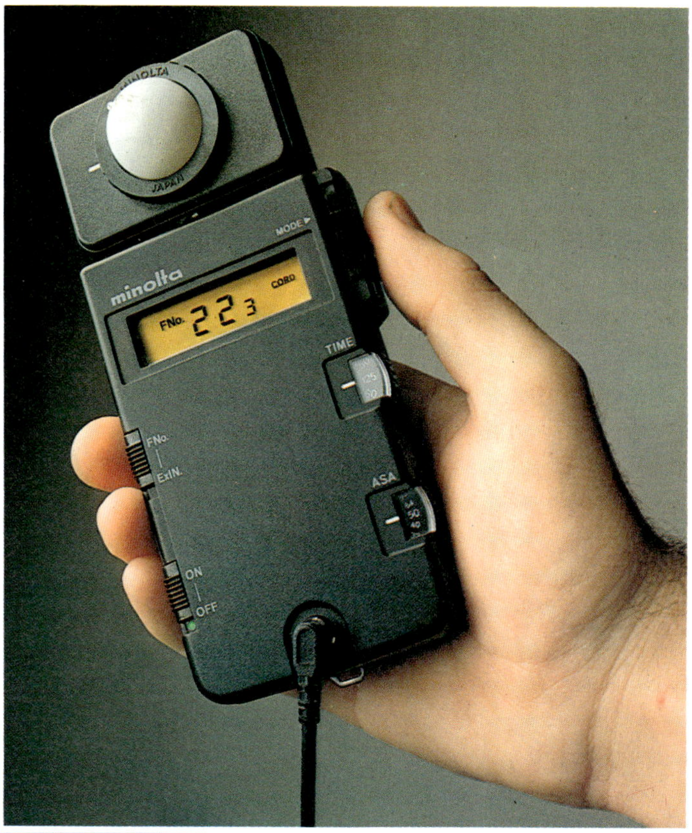

Flashmeter
Manufacturers' recommendations cannot always give the accuracy needed for exposure and a proper flashmeter can be an invaluable extra. Unlike some, this Minolta meter gives a reading directly in f-stops.

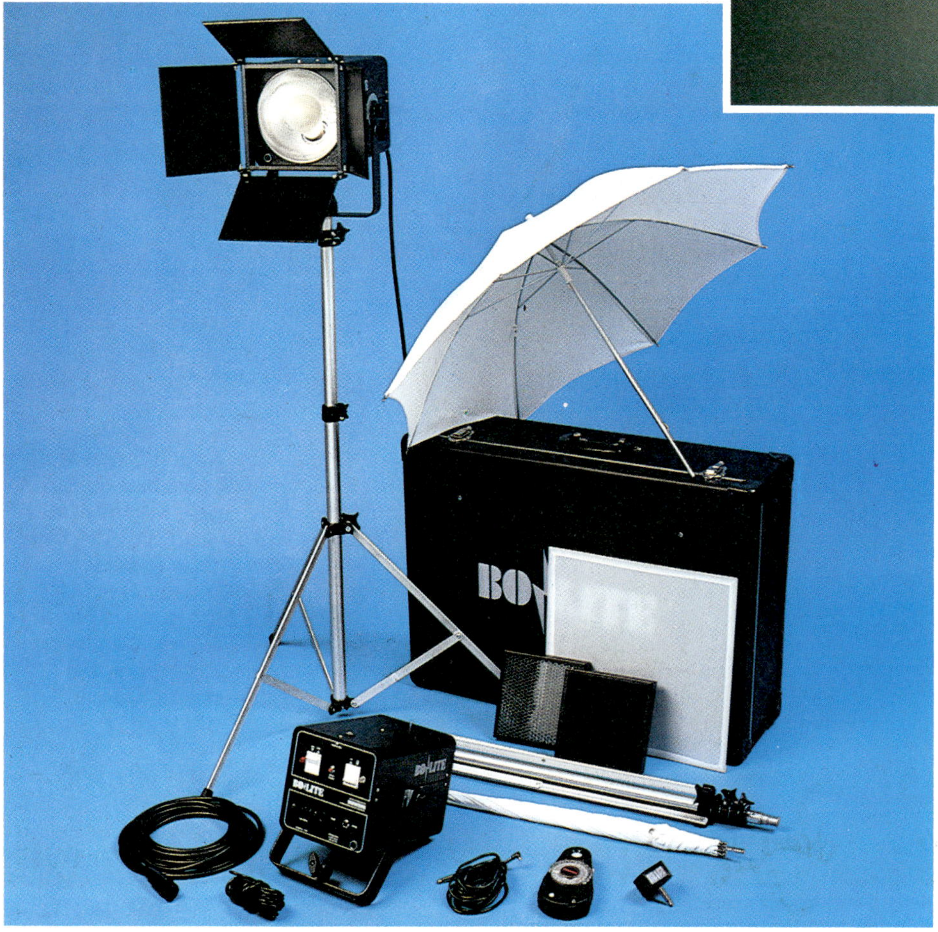

Studio flash
The Bowens Bo-lite 200 is an inexpensive unit that comes with reflector and modelling lamp. A wide range of accessories is also available

There is no simple conversion between joules and guide numbers. While the joule rating gives an indication of the overall power of the unit, it is of no use in calculating the exposure, as the light output depends on other factors. These include the type of reflector behind the flash tube, and the degree of spreading of the flash. In fact, a 127 joule unit from one manufacturer has a similar guide number to a 100 joule unit from another.

The only way to ensure completely reliable exposure calculation is to use a flashmeter. This device measures the brightness of the flash, and either gives you an index number which you then convert to an *f*-stop, or it gives you a direct *f*-stop readout. This is an essential piece of equipment to accompany studio flash, and well worth the extra expense.

Flash systems

There is a wide range of flash systems available, and your choice depends on the type of work they are intended for as well as on how much you can afford.

At the inexpensive end of the scale, a unit such as the Bowens Bo-lite costs about three times as much as the average on-camera electronic flash, or about the same as a budget SLR. The Bo-lite has a built in reflector and modelling lamp at one end, with clearly laid out controls at the other. Its power output is 100 joules, giving a flash factor of 33 (metres with 100 ASA (ISO) film).

The accessory kit consists of a four panel barn door, a silver and black honeycomb, and a 'softlite', which is a 36 cm square diffuser panel. All these attachments are easily fitted to the flash head, and the unit can also be used with an umbrella. All studio flash outfits require a sturdy lighting stand, and the Bo-lite can be bought as a complete kit which contains all you need for basic studio flash. This consists of a carrying case, two Bo-lites with stands, two umbrellas and other accessories, a slave cell and all the necessary leads.

Another low priced system is the Courtenay Colorflash 2 and 4 series. The Colorflash 2 has a similar power output to the Bo-lite, giving a guide number of 27 to 34 with 100 ASA film. The Colorflash 4 is more powerful, with a guide number of 38 to 46 with 100 ASA film. Courtenay also supply a full range of accessories, all of which can be fitted in their specially built carrying case.

More expensive are units such as the Multiblitz Mini Studio 202, which has an output of 200 joules and a recycling time of 2 seconds at full power and only 1½ seconds at half power. The accessories are fundamentally the same as those for the other makes mentioned, namely a soft box or diffuser, honeycomb, reflectors and umbrellas. The 202 system can be bought as a complete kit, with three heads, lighting stands and accessories, all in a compact carrying case. The flash heads have built in slave cells.

Another system, the Multiblitz Profilite system, combines the advantages of both portable and studio flash, constituting a multi-role system suitable for both studio and location work. The unit consists of a power pack, flash head and power source adaptor. The essential feature of this system is that it can be used as a portable flash when fitted with a battery pack and a flash head without a modelling light. Alternatively, it can be used as a studio lighting system when the flash head is changed for one with a modelling lamp, and a mains adaptor attached. There is even an adaptor available which allows the unit to be

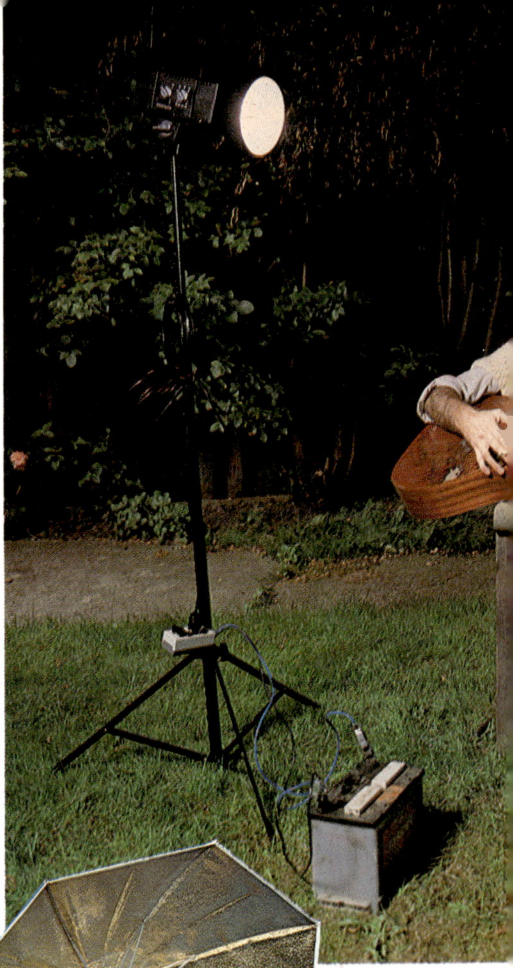

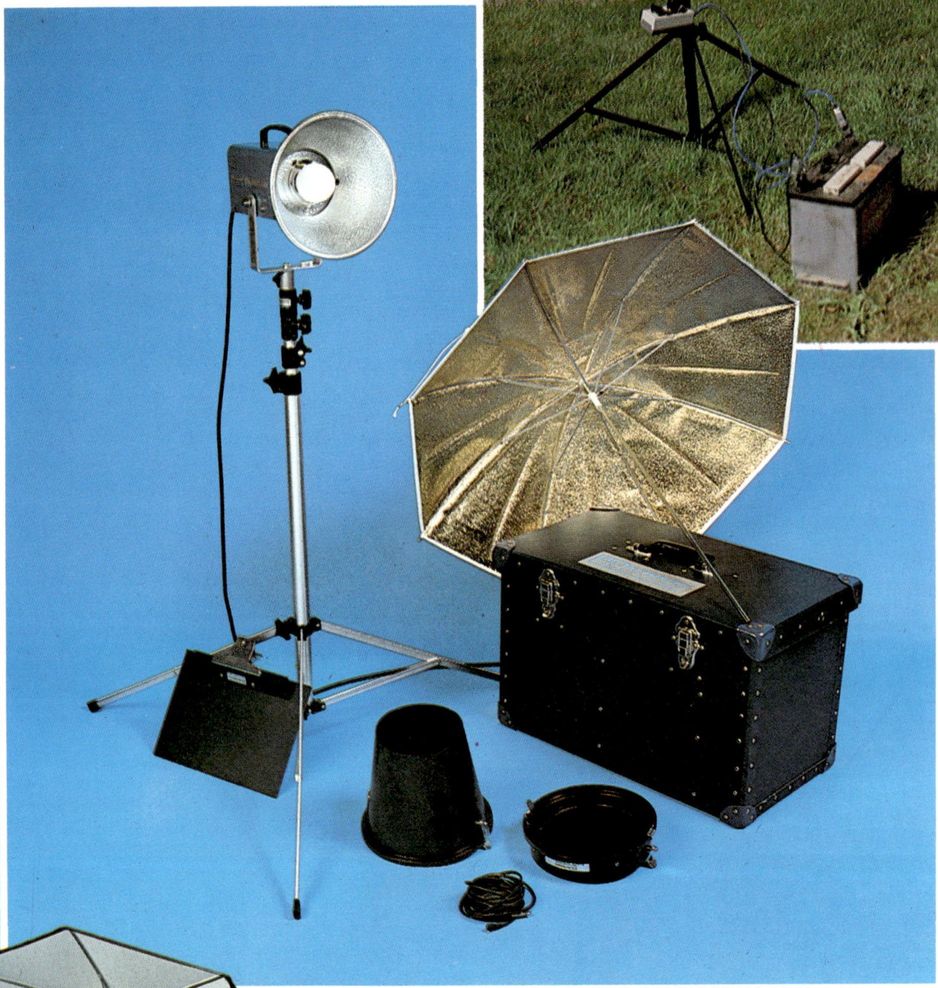

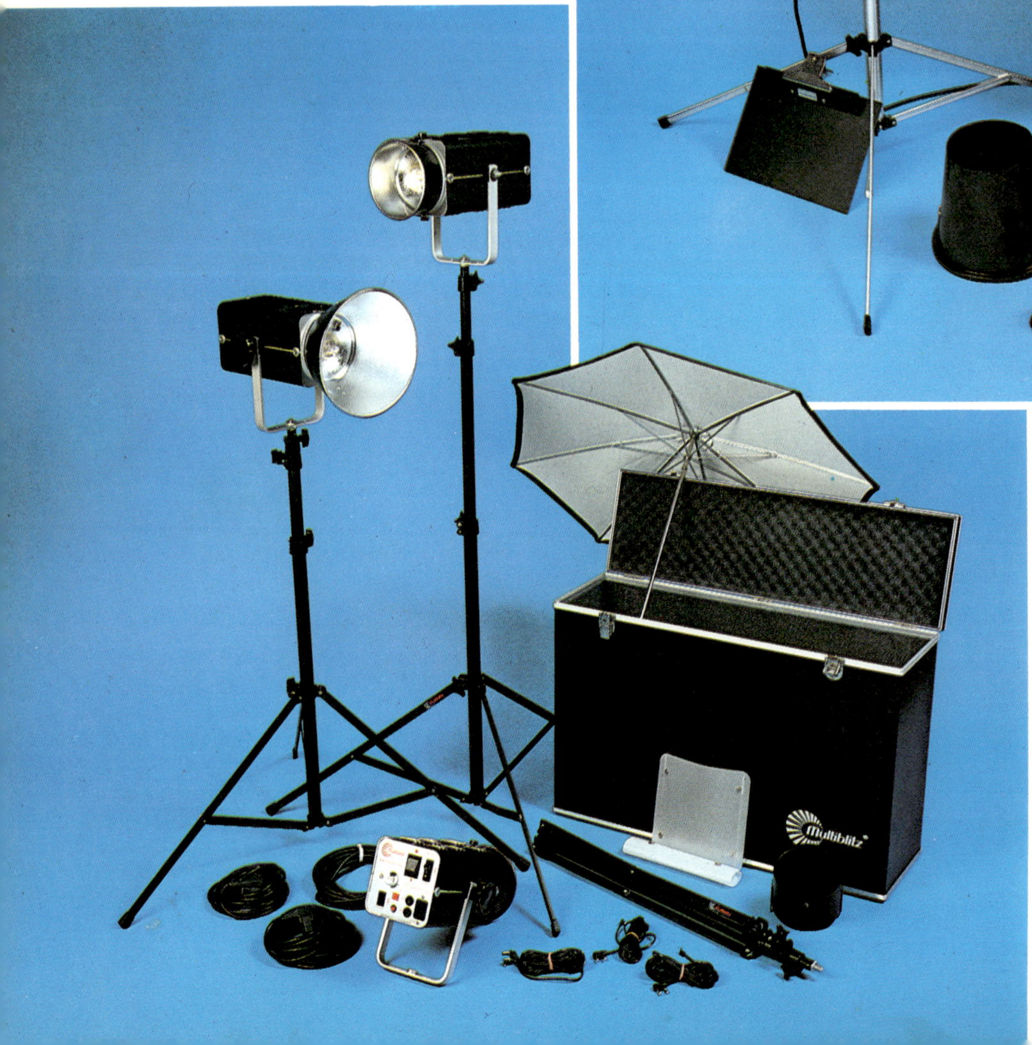

Studio flash systems *Like the Bo-lite the Courtenay Colorflash (above) is an inexpensive unit with a power output of 100 joules giving a guide number (in metres) of around 30 with 100 ASA film. The Multiblitz Mini Studio 202 (left) gives twice the power and recycles rapidly, but costs a little more. The sophisticated Bowens Monolite system (right) is even more expensive, but it can be built up gradually rather than purchased outright*

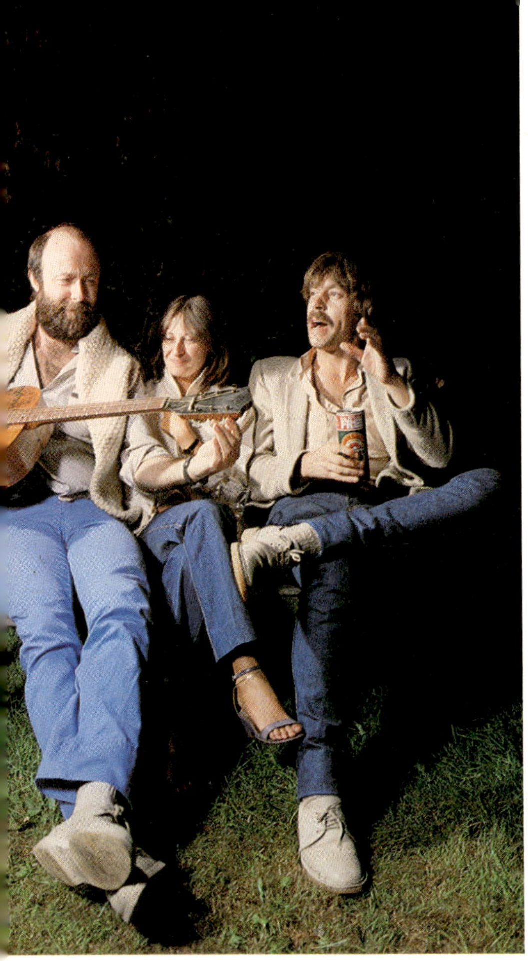

powered by a car battery, and the full range of accessories is available, including a carrying case.

Among the more sophisticated units is the Bowens Monolite series. The Monolites are cylindrical monobloc units with built in modelling lights. These are switched on in proportion to the flash power output. There is also a control for switching the modelling lamp to full brightness, which is very useful when focusing, and a device which extinguishes the modelling light as the flash fires, switching it on afterwards. The Monolite 200 E has a rating of 127 joules and a guide number of 34 with 100 ASA film.

A more powerful version, the Monolite 400 E, gives a maximum power of 254 joules, and a guide number of 50 m with 100 ASA film. Top of the range is the Monolite 800 E, with a power output of 508 joules, and a guide number of 67 m with 100 ASA film. This model also has a recycling time of $1\frac{1}{2}$ seconds and a four power output selector.

The Monolites have sockets for flash slave cells, and an overheat cutout device. The accessories available form a very comprehensive range, and there are a variety of reflectors and devices for controlling light. The stands available run from lightweight to heavyweight, with a boom type stand also available.

On the bench *Some systems can be used outdoors as well as in the studio—the Profilite runs off a normal 12 volt car battery*

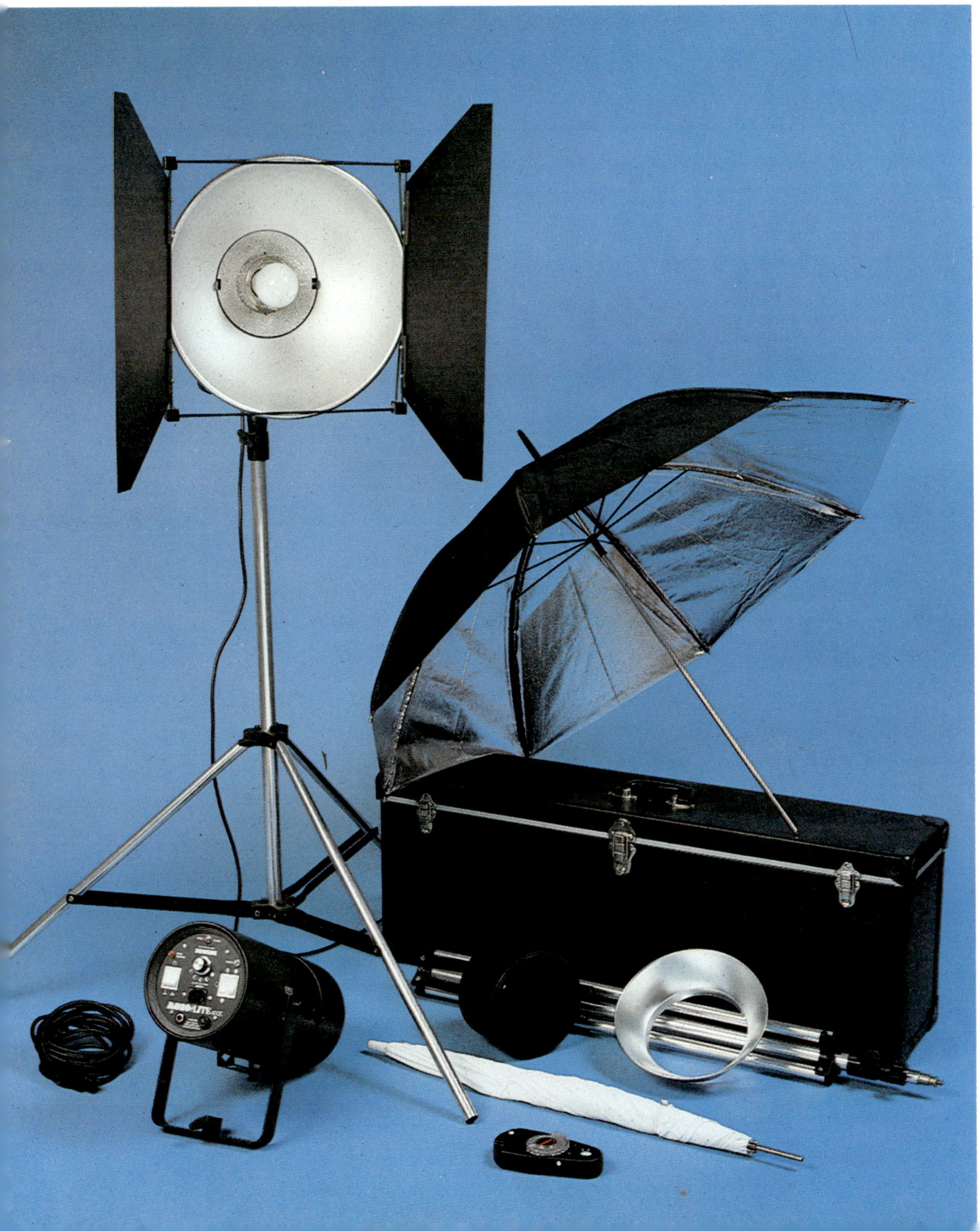

Similar to the Monolites is the Courtenay Sola studio flash. There are three models in this range—the Sola 2, the Sola 4 and the Sola 8, giving guide numbers identical to the Monolite units.

Choosing a system

The first thing you must consider if you decide to buy studio flash is the power output you will need. If, for example, you only intend to shoot close-ups or head and shoulder portraits on fast or medium speed film, then an ordinary amateur flash or one of the less powerful studio units, say one with 100 joules output, should be quite adequate for your needs. On the other hand, if you want to photograph groups, then you need a much more powerful unit. It is better to buy more power than you need than to buy less, because you can always turn a unit down if necessary, but you cannot increase its maximum power output.

The number of accessories you buy depends on the amount of work you intend to do, as well as on the type. The range of accessories is vast, and not all of them are essential, at least at first, while others can be improvised. An umbrella is probably the most useful item, but diffusing screens can be made with tracing paper, while you could make snoots from heavy black paper or card.

Bear in mind that the more accessories you buy, the heavier the equipment will be, and it can become very troublesome to carry around. If you do not intend to move about too much, this is not too important, but you should still avoid buying items you do not really need. The best method is probably to build your system up slowly, starting with essentials and adding things you need one at a time.

You might also try looking at what is available on the secondhand market, as a system in good condition might be much cheaper than a new system, and is certainly an alternative worth considering if you are working on a budget.

Although not all the units described are as powerful as some of the more expensive hand held guns, and they are also much more cumbersome to use, the advantages far outweigh the disadvantages if you intend to do studio work at all seriously. The control you can achieve over the direction and quality of the light gives you a far wider range of possible modelling effects.

For a photographer who plans to do studio work regularly, a studio flash system is essential equipment. If you decide that studio work is for you, then you must decide what power output you require, and base your choice on this consideration. If you choose the right studio flash system, it should prove to be a very worthwhile investment.

CHAPTER 17
STUDIO LIGHTING TECHNIQUES
Using studio flash

Electronic flash has clear advantages as a light source, both on location and in the studio. Its colour is balanced for use with transparency film, and the duration of the flash is brief enough to freeze all but the fastest action.

Studio flash units, however, are not quite as simple to operate as the small, hot shoe mounted guns that are frequently used with 35 mm cameras. They are much more powerful, and are always manually operated, so the direction, quality and intensity of the light they produce is completely under the control of the photographer.

For the occasional user of studio electronic flash, however, learning how to get the best results is the second problem—actually finding out how to use the units at all is the first.

Studio flash is actually easy to use though the controls and operation may seem rather daunting initially. First, plug the flash in and switch on at the mains supply and at the unit itself. Once the capacitors are fully charged, the modelling light should come on. The synchronization lead plugs into the camera in the same way as the flashgun, but at the other end there is a large jack-plug which must be plugged into a socket on the flashpack.

Once you have connected the camera and flash with the sync cable, you can proceed in much the same way as you would with a hand-held unit.

If you are familiar with a low power hand flashgun, the fast recycling may come as a pleasant change—often, the flash recycles as quickly as you can wind on. The high power of studio flash is a great asset, too—with 100 ASA film, you are likely to be working at an aperture of *f*/8 or smaller, though this also depends on the size of reflector you use.

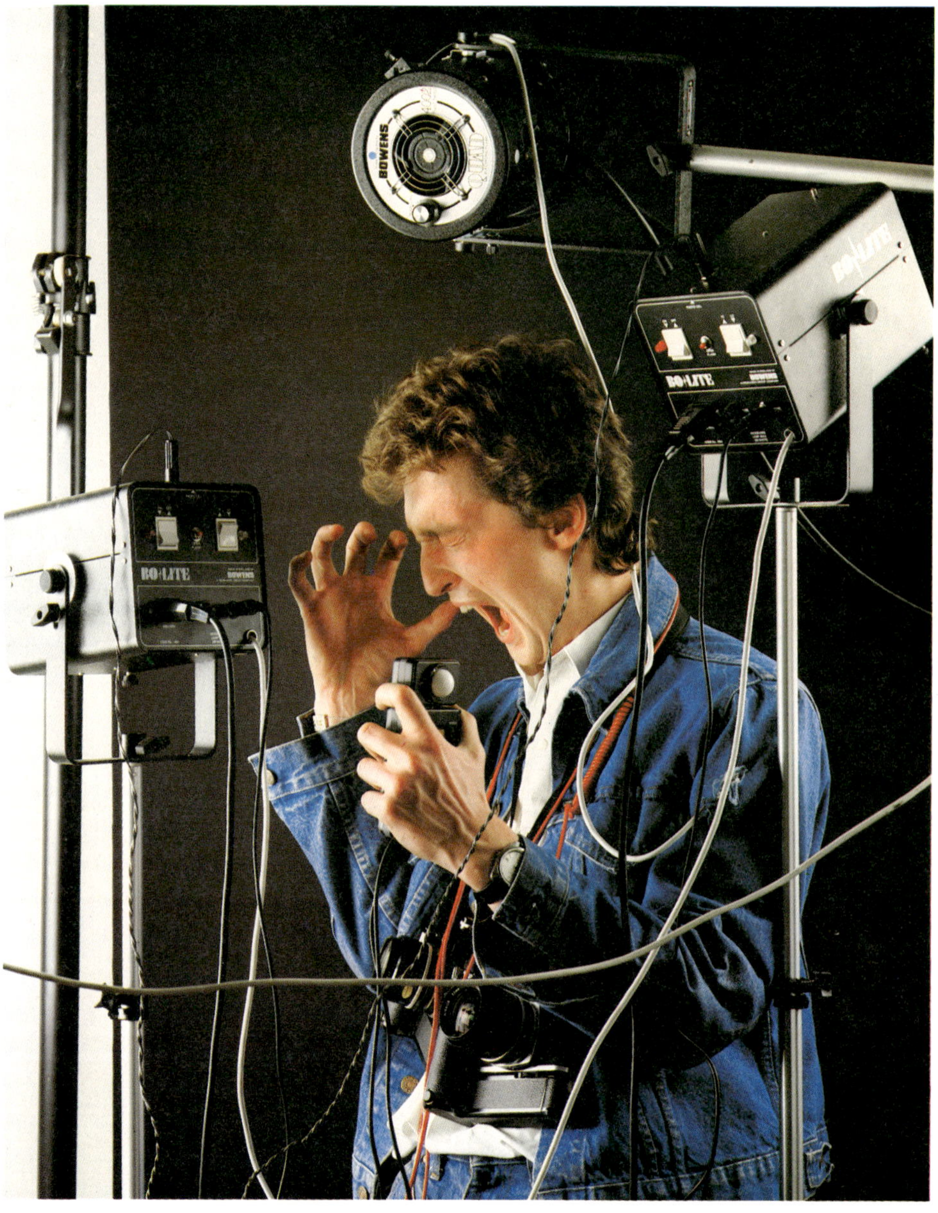

In a tangle *Although studio flash may initially seem complex, a systematic approach can soon sort things out*

Controlling the light

One of the major advantages of studio flash units is that they can be used with a wide range of reflectors and accessories. You can change the reflector to give the right type of light for every subject. The simplest reflectors are just shiny metal dishes, and these come in a range of sizes. Generally, the smaller they are the harsher and more contrasty is the light they produce.

For a softer effect, use a larger reflector, with a white surface on the inside. Some of these white dishes have a cap to prevent light from the flash tube reaching the subject directly. This softens the light even further but still retains quite definite modelling.

A very popular way of using flash is to bounch it off the interior of a silver or white fabric umbrella. These behave as giant size reflectors, but they are light in weight and can be folded up like an umbrella for transport.

The large reflective surface of an umbrella gives a very soft light which is ideal for portraiture. Silver umbrellas give a slightly harsher, more contrasty light that looks good on black and white film, while white umbrellas produce softer, more gentle results. But the softest results of all are produced by white nylon umbrellas. With this type of umbrella, the flash is fired through the material instead of being bounced off it and so it acts like a giant diffuser.

Professional studios go in for even bigger diffused light sources, which are often referred to as *fish friers* or, the larger sizes, *swimming pools*. These produce extremely soft lighting, and for lighting shiny objects, for example, which reflect the shape of the light source clearly, they are ideal. Here, the rectangular shape of the fish frier scores over the octagonal reflections created by umbrella.

Changing the reflector is not the only way of controlling the light from the

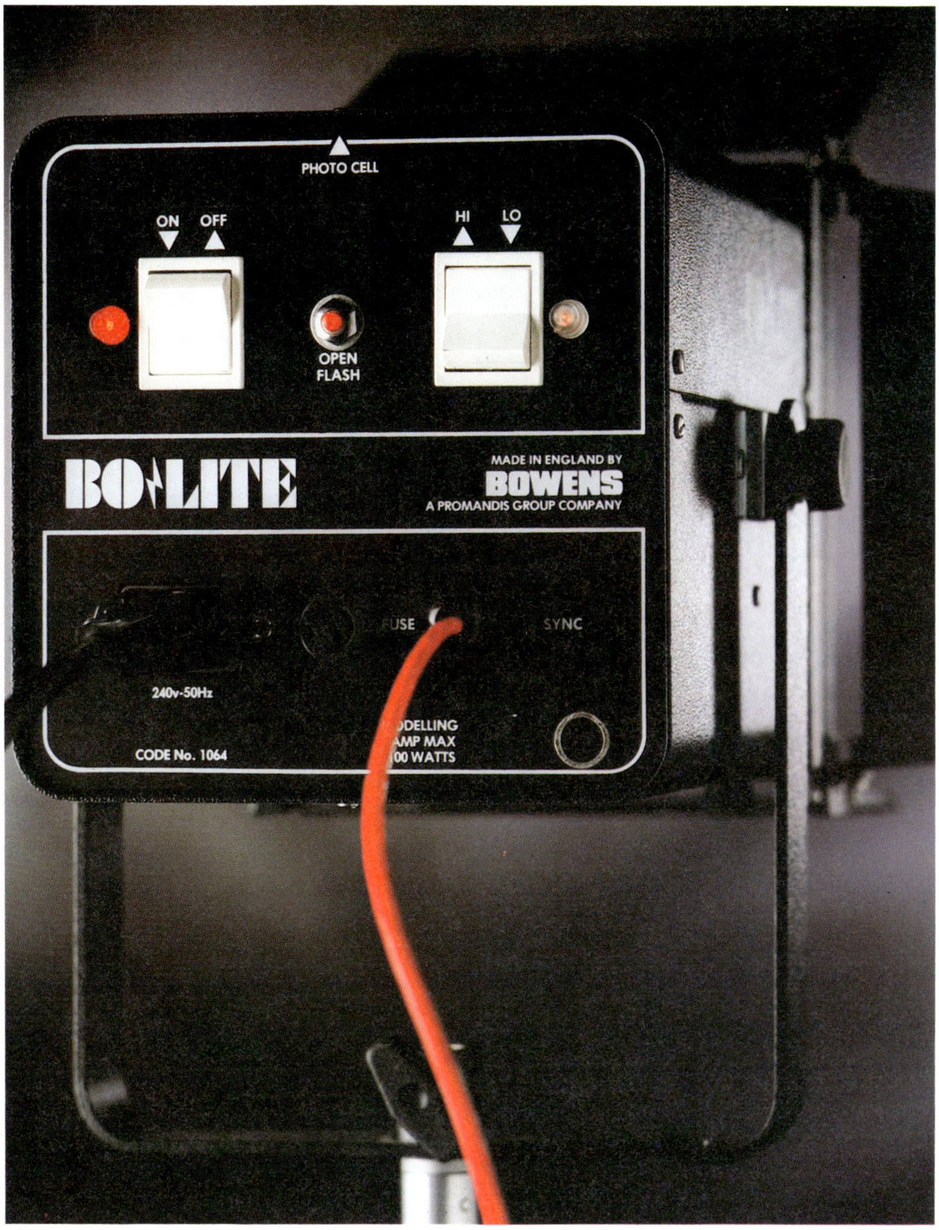

flash. By bouncing the light off the ceiling, or by sending it through sheets of diffusing material, you can further modify how it falls on the subject. You can control its colour with acrylic lighting gels, which can be placed in front of the reflector—double ended spring clips are useful for this—and you can shade parts of the subject using barn doors.

One of the big advantages of studio flash, in comparison to tungsten or quartz-halogen lighting, is that flash rarely gives any problems with colour balance. Providing you use daylight film, colour should always be reasonably good, though skin tones sometimes benefit from using a pale warming filter over the lens, or gold rather than silver reflectors. This means that the effect of any gel over the lights will be much the same on film as it appears in the studio. The only thing to remember is that the modelling lights are not the same colour as the flash, so a colour meter will only read correctly if you fire the flash.

Obviously, the effect of the light varies considerably with its position and you should experiment using the modelling light to find the best position.

Light control *A Hi/Lo switch controls power output, and reflectors can be changed for softer or harsher lighting. Below, fitting a white umbrella*

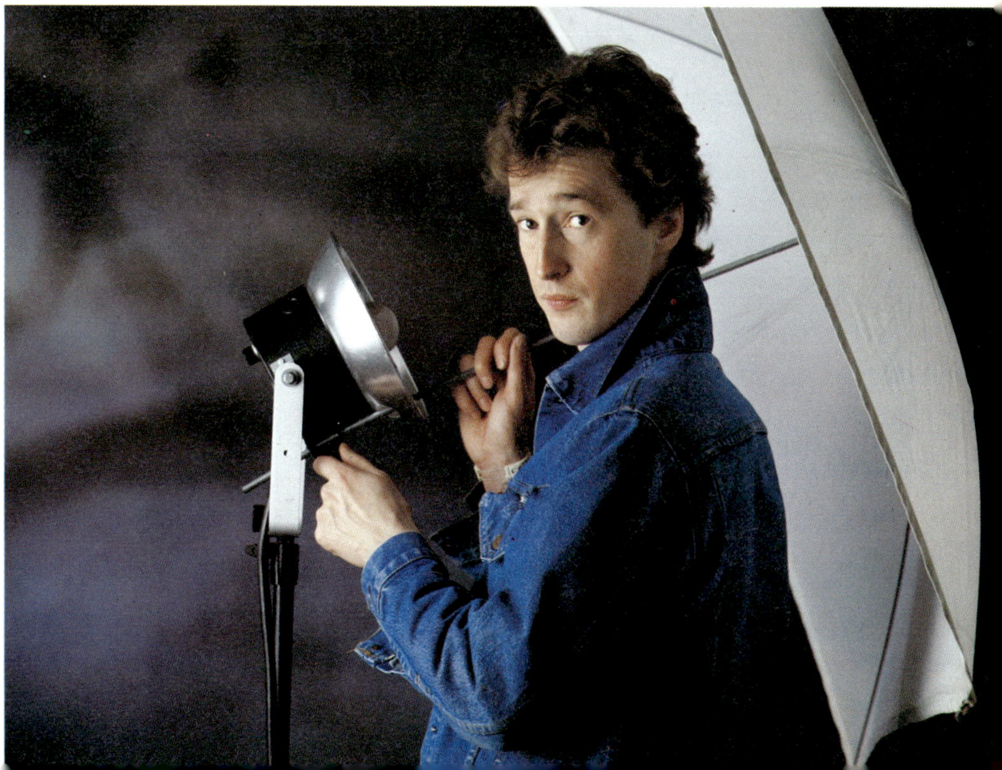

Controlling the power

The size and shape of the reflector that you use has a direct effect on how efficiently the power of the flash is used. Small, silver reflectors concentrate the light and make the fullest use of it. Large white ones dissipate power, forcing you to use a wider aperture. Umbrellas, particularly white ones, soak up light, reducing the output of the unit by up to three stops.

This is the reason why professional flash units are so high powered and have considerable power in reserve. Smaller units which are less powerful may present problems when used with umbrellas, and you may find yourself working at an unacceptably wide aperture.

A solution to this problem is to move the lights in towards the subject—large reflectors and umbrellas can be moved in much closer than small ones—or to use faster film. Another solution, which is popular with still life photographers, is to completely black out the studio, and fire the flash several times with the camera's shutter locked open. Obviously this only works with a static subject.

At the other end of the scale, you may find yourself with too much power. All but the smallest units have a power reduction switch, for this very reason. They can be turned down to $\frac{1}{2}$, $\frac{1}{4}$, or even $\frac{1}{8}$ power, and if you are working at very close range, you may need to take advantage of this facility to enable you to work at a reasonable aperture. For example, when the flash head is only a metre from the subject, and set to full power, you may need to use an aperture of *f*/32 or *f*/45 on 100 ASA film. With small format cameras, this is out of the question, and reducing the power is the only practical alternative.

If the power of the flash is not switchable, it is a simple matter to use grey neutral density lighting gels to cut down on the output, and these are also useful with switchable units should the $\frac{1}{2}$ or $\frac{1}{4}$ power setting still prove too bright.

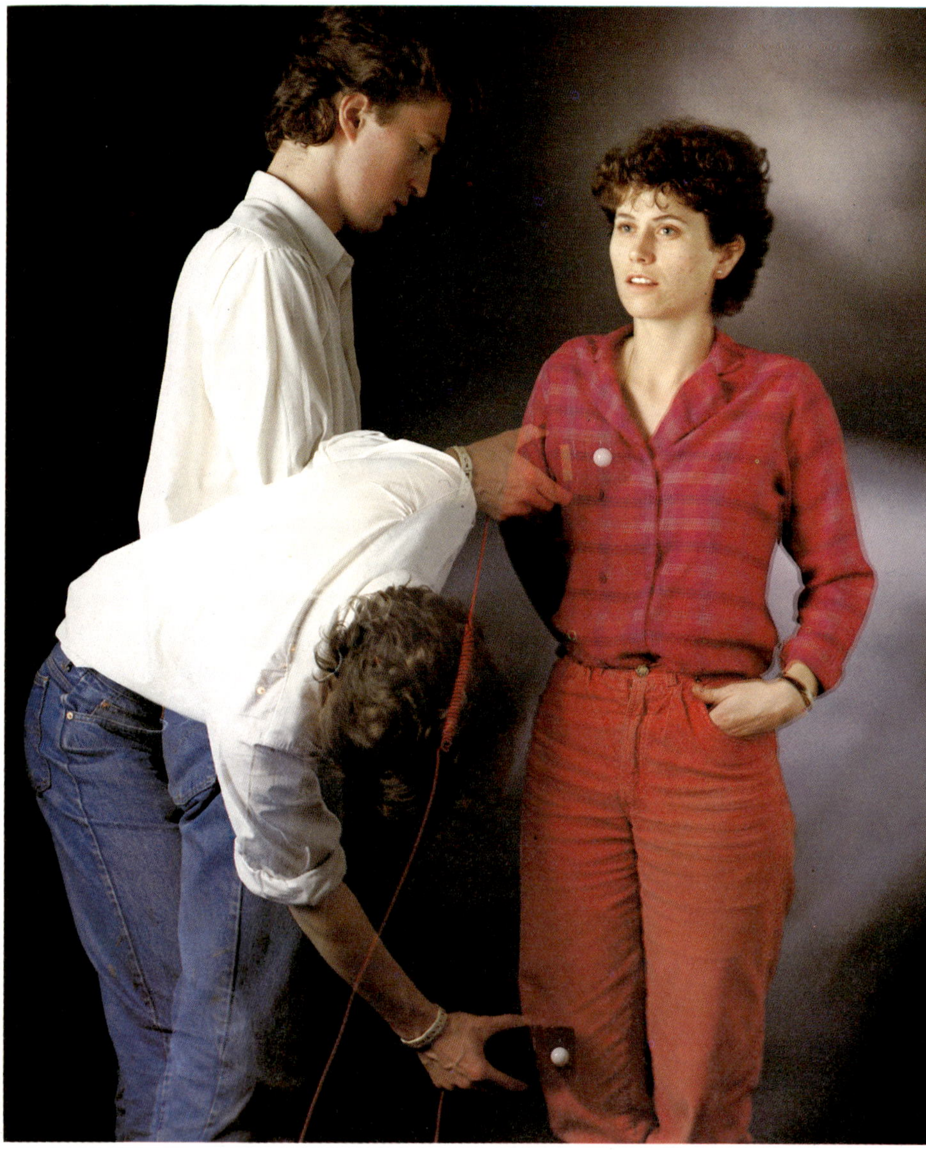

Checking exposure *When using flash, it is often difficult to judge whether the subject is evenly illuminated, so it is important to take flashmeter readings both at the centre, and at the edges of the picture area*

Switching to a lower power setting usually alters the modelling lights too. These are dimmed in proportion to the flash tube so that you can get some idea of the balance of light between two or more flash heads. To get a true picture of the relationship between the power of several lights, all other sources of light must be blacked out, particularly if any of the units are operating on low power settings.

Modelling lights, even proportionally dimmed ones, cannot give any indication of the brightness of the flash in relation to ambient lighting. Only an actual exposure on either conventional or Polaroid film can do this.

Controlling exposure

With a small hot shoe flash, determining exposure is a simple matter, but with large studio units, the situation is more complicated. The only satisfactory way of setting the right aperture on the camera is to use a flash exposure meter. This looks similar to a conventional incident light exposure meter, but has no scale of shutter speeds—only film speeds and apertures. Its internal workings, however, are quite different, and it is only sensitive to the sudden surge of illumination produced by the electronic flash unit. Ambient light has no effect on the flashmeter reading.

To take a flash exposure reading, the meter is placed as close as possible to the subject, with its white domed diffuser pointing at the camera. The flash is then fired, either using a cable linking the meter and the flashpack, or—with meters that can be used in the cordless mode—by pressing the open flash button on the flashpack. A display on the meter then indicates the aperture to be used, either directly with a digital readout, or indirectly, using a needle and a calculator dial. Some models of meter can be used to accumulate readings, so that repeated firings of the flash either move the needle up the scale or light different LEDs.

When using a flashmeter, remember that it can be used to check the ratio between shadows and highlights of the picture, so that you can make sure that the film is capable of accommodating the full tonal range of the subject. You can also use it to check the fall-off of illumination, and this is particularly important if you are lighting a large set, or if you have placed most of your flash heads high up above the subject. With a full-length portrait, for example, you should take readings at both face and floor level; there may be a fall-off of one or two stops which you can remedy either by moving lights or adding reflectors.

In addition to a flashmeter reading, many professionals like to take a picture on instant film to check the lighting. All large format cameras can accommodate instant film backs, and most roll film

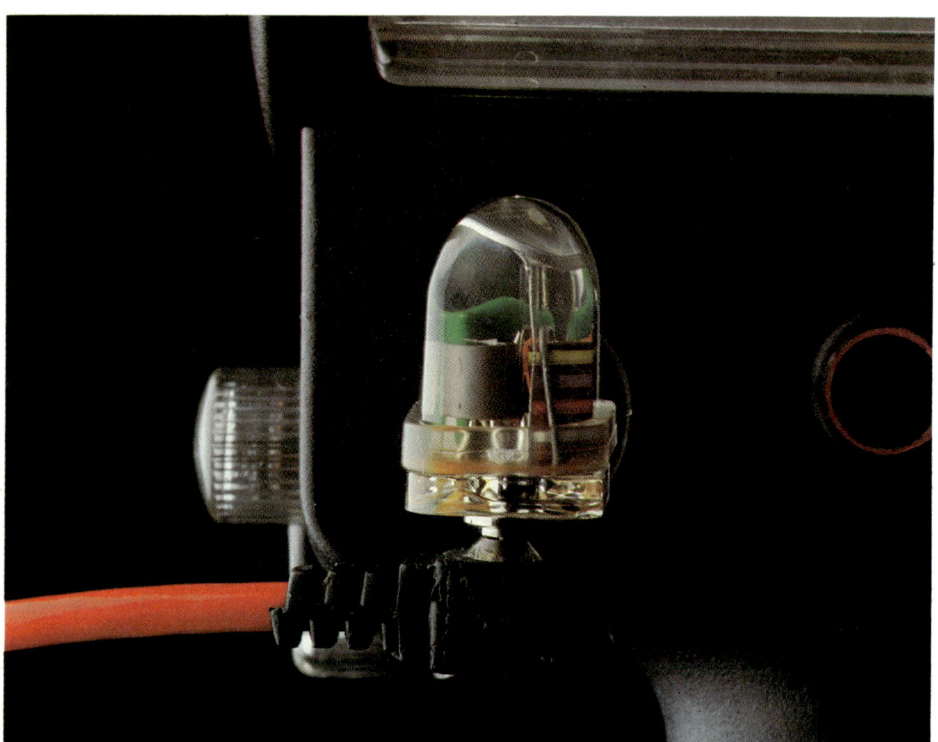

Slave sync *Cordless flash triggering is possible using a plug-in slave cell on a general purpose unit such as this*

cameras can be fitted with a special Polaroid back. A New York company even adapts 35 mm camera backs for use with Polaroid film.

An instant picture allows you to assess the degree of contrast that will appear on film, and lets you balance flash and daylight. But neither Polaroid test shots nor flashmeter readings guarantee that exposure will be exactly right. To be absolutely sure of getting the pictures you want, you must bracket a series of exposures—at half stop intervals for transparency film, and full stops for negatives—or else run a *clip test*. This is a facility offered by professional labs, and consists of snipping off the first few frames of a film, processing them and asessing them for exposure, and pushing or pulling the rest of the film so that the density is exactly right. The asessment can be done either by the photographer or the lab.

The advantages of this system are that it avoids the frustration of finding that the best picture from your portrait session is one stop underexposed. On the other hand, there is an extra charge for a clip-test, not all labs run them, and you have to wait longer for your film.

Check everything

Working with studio flash can seem difficult if you are not used to it, but after a while you will find it is as simple as working with tungsten light. Photographers who are constantly in the studio often develop an ability to estimate flash exposure very accurately, just by glancing at the power output of each flash head, though such skill comes only with years of practice. There are, however, a few of the professionals' habits worth adopting.

First of all, check everything—twice. It is very easy to do a session without noticing that there is something fundamentally wrong. Do not forget that cameras with focal plane shutters must be used at slow speeds if they are to synchronize with the flash. It is easy to inadvertently move the shutter dial.

Think of safety first. Do not leave a camera on a table with the sync cable trailing across the floor, because someone is bound to walk past, catch the cable with their foot, and send the camera crashing to the ground. The same is true of the flash heads, particularly the monobloc units which are top-heavy. If there are a number of cables snaking round the studio floor, tape them down so that they do not pose such a safety risk.

Remember that electronic flash generates very high voltages, so never touch anything with wet hands, and do not try to repair faulty units yourself. Take special care with older units. Some of them must be unplugged from the mains before changing the flash head configuration. Failure to do this can result in a fatal electric shock!

Check all the synchronization cables. If you are using more than one flash head, use a cable to synchronize the first, with slave cells to fire the others. Slaves plug into the jack socket that usually takes the sync cable. Some photographers use slave cells on every head, and fire them with a low power flash on the camera.

Check the readylights. With multiple flash set-ups, these should all go out after the exposure has been made. If they do not, check the sync cables again, or turn the slave triggers to point at the main flash. If your system can be switched so that the modelling lights go out after each exposure, use this facility to check that every head is firing. The modelling lights come back on after the pack has recycled, and this is a reliable indication that it is safe to make another exposure. With other units, keep your eye on the readylight—it is easy to get carried away and try to work too fast.

Finally, a tip about bracketing. If you can, bracket the pictures using the power output of the flash, and not the lens aperture. This way, depth of field will be the same in all pictures.

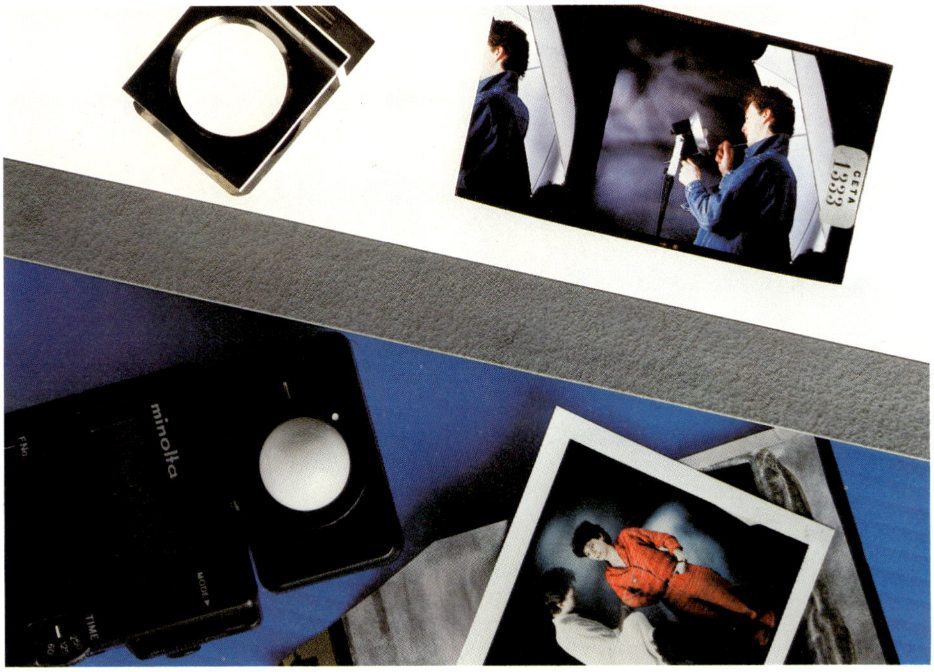

Exposure control *A flashmeter and Polaroid film help gauge exposure, and a clip test makes fine tuning possible*

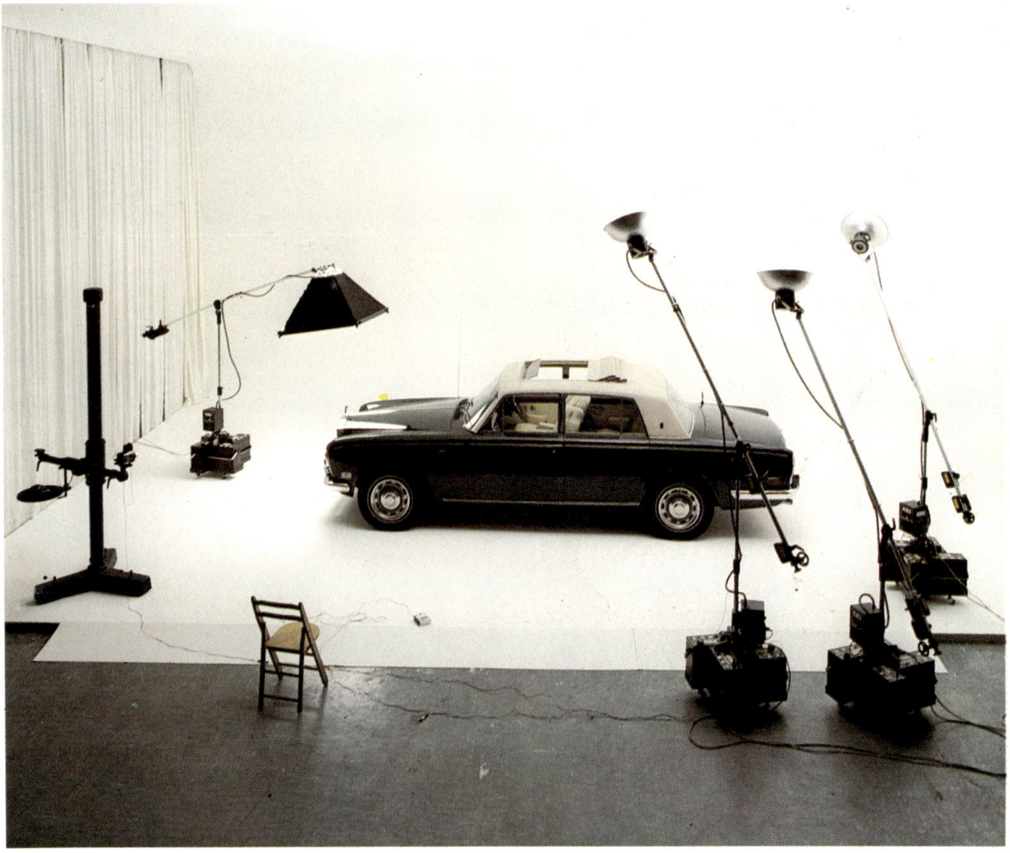

High power flash *A large studio needs lots of light. This one is equipped with a system 1000 times more powerful than the average hot shoe flashgun*

Simple lighting set-ups

Some people believe that to take successful photographs by studio light, you need massive banks of lamps and an expensive array of complex equipment. But with careful positioning of your subject, camera and light source, you can produce effective and often dramatic results using just a single light.

Indeed, one of the best ways of learning to exploit studio lighting to the full is to begin with a single light source and observe how different angles mould the subject in different ways and create different effects. Portraits, still lifes and many other subjects are well within the scope of the most basic lighting set-up.

Many professionals prefer to use electronic flash. Such lights illuminate only when the shutter is pressed, except on the very expensive models. This means you can only see the effect of the lighting set-up in the resulting photograph. Once you are experienced with studio lights, this will not matter, but when you first begin it is essential to have a continuous light source, such as a simple tungsten light. With the light on all the time, you can try out different positions and experiment with various effects without wasting valuable film.

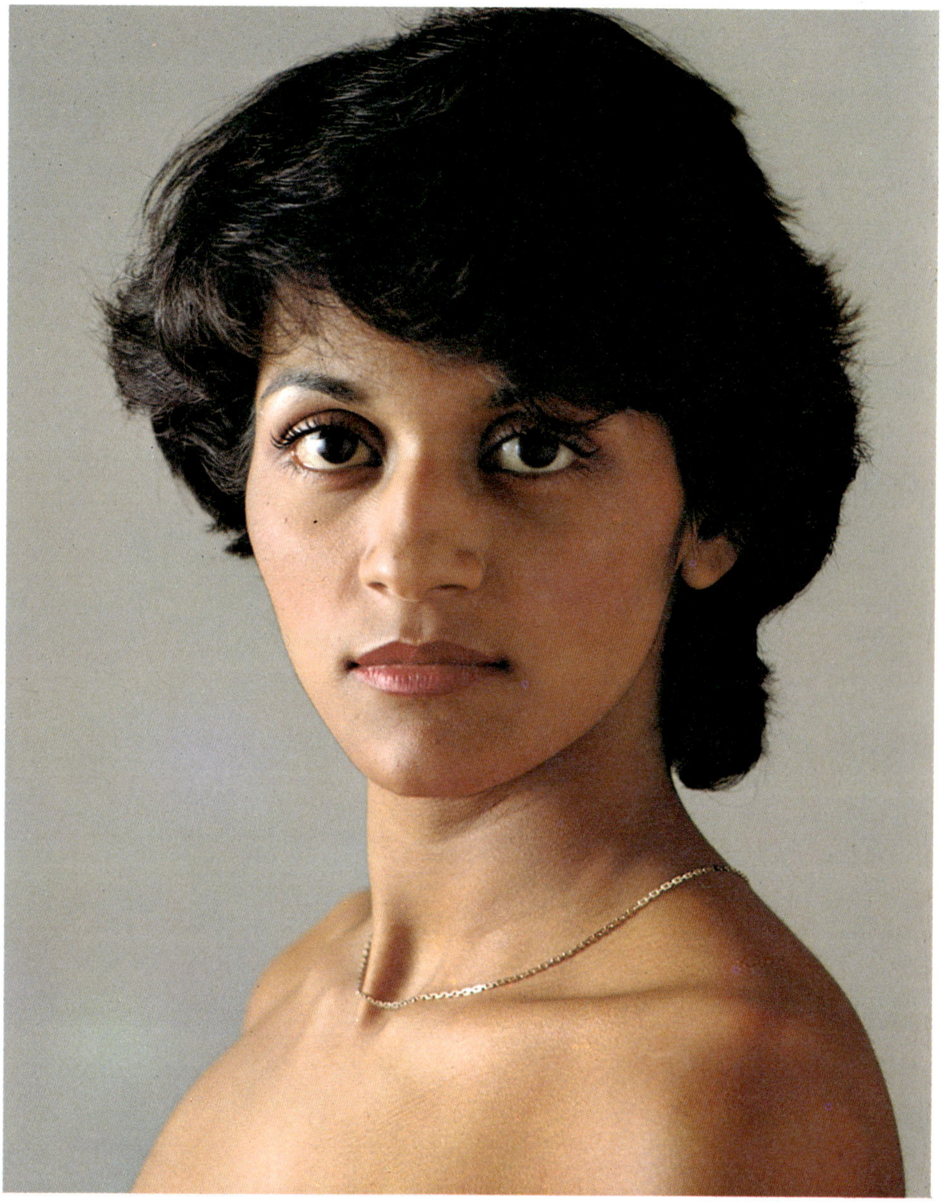

Head and shoulders *The effect of just one light, bounced off a large oblong reflector. To lighten shadows, a square reflector was also used and a small silver reflector threw light on to the model's neck*

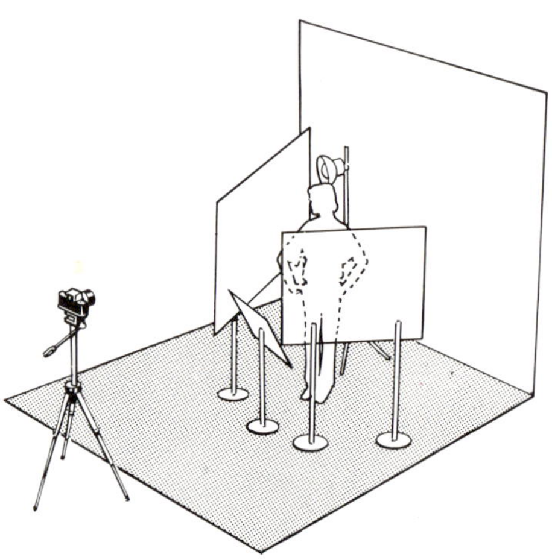

Lighting for portraits

Before you move into your 'studio' to try out lighting for portraits with a live subject, it is useful to conduct a few experiments with a model head and a desk lamp. An ordinary metal-shaded desk lamp and a polystyrene model head, like those used in hat shops, will do. Set the head on a table in a darkened room so that the lamp is the only form of lighting. Move the lamp all round the head and note how different angles cast different shadows and accentuate different features. Move the lamp in and out as well and observe how the distance of the light source affects the modelling. And try lighting the head obliquely rather than shining the lamp directly at it. These experiments should give you a basic idea of the way different lighting angles and positions can change the look of your subject. When you move into the studio you will have a basic frame of reference to work from when trying out various effects.

In the studio

Your choice of lighting set-up depends very much on the type of picture you want. Portraits can be high key or low key, in profile or head on, dramatically stylized creations or plain likenesses—all of these require a different position for your single light.

For a straightforward frontal shot, one of the best places for the lamp is in front of the subject and pointing down from an angle of about 45°. This position gives a relatively natural look because shadows fall in much the same way as they would in normal daylight.

With the light at a much steeper angle,

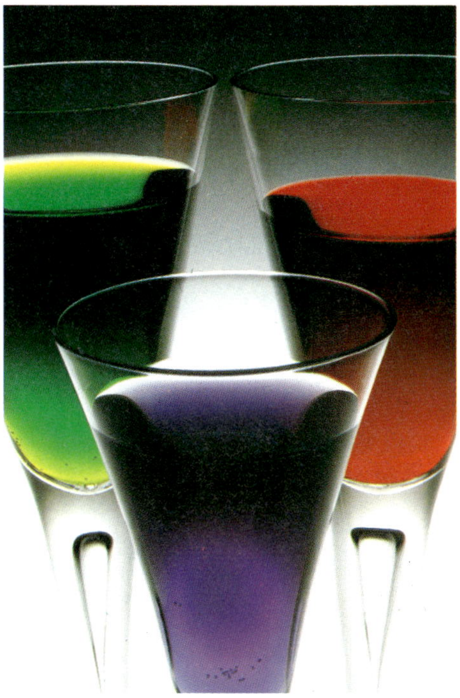

Glasses *One lamp, pointed upwards through a sheet of curved Perspex backed with tracing paper, was used to light these glasses of coloured liquid*

some parts of the face are thrown into deep shadow. If the sitter has shallow features, this can sometimes help to give them more strength, but the eyes should usually have some light unless you are striving for an unusual effect. However, a high lighting angle invariably produces a long shadow under the nose and this can look very odd indeed.

Lowering the light much beyond 45°, on the other hand, tends to have a flattening effect. A shallow lighting angle may give complete illumination, but the result is usually dull and rarely flattering to the subject. And once the light is taken down to the same level or below the sitter's head, the face begins to take on a very unnatural look. Old 'horror' films often used a light shining directly upwards from beneath the chin to produce a sinister mask appearance.

When you choose the height for your light, you must also choose whether to place it directly in front, to one side or even behind your sitter. Again, for a straightforward portrait, the best lighting is probably achieved with the lamp offset to one side by about 45° or perhaps slightly less. A direct frontal setting produces a very flat image while side-lighting tends to look rather unnatural and throws awkward shadows. In the 45° position there are clear shadows to reveal the contours of the face but these are not so large as to obscure much facial detail.

Naturally, because the 45° position is so suitable for simple portraits, it is commonly used. But there are alternatives, and if you want to produce a picture with an unconventional approach, it may be worth experimenting with alternative settings. You must be sure of your subject's cooperation, though, because these unusual lighting positions may give a portrait that is far from flattering.

Sidelighting throws one half of the face into deep shadow and on a strongly featured face this can be very dramatic. Lighting from unusual angles often produces striking effects on the right face and it is worth experimenting. If one half of the face is virtually invisible, the lighting helps to create an air of mystery. Actors playing the lead role in a tragedy may often be photographed in this sort of lighting. But for maximum effect the background must be completely dark.

Sidelight also helps to reveal texture and by moving the light slightly forward so that it skims across the face from a very low angle, you may get some fascinating shots of skin texture. Remember again, though, that many subjects will not want any skin blemishes shown.

With the light right behind the subject, the subject's face is in darkness and all you see is a silhouette. The outline of the sitter, however, will be softened by bright highlights and this lighting is known as *rim* lighting. The highlights are particularly obvious on people with thick curly hair catches the light to create a bright halo.

Because of the bright, dreamy quality this halo produces—looking soft and innocent in some cases, glamorous in others—such lighting is a very popular way of photographing girls. But you need an additional form of lighting on the face. Even though *you* may be able to see the face clearly, the camera cannot unless you increase exposure to the point where the rim becomes an indistinct white blur and washed out highlights spill on to the face. While the eye can cope with the contrast range, the camera cannot.

Although contrast is extreme with backlighting, even with frontal lighting the contrast between the shadow areas and the highlights produced by a single light source may be too great for the film. While the illumination from a single

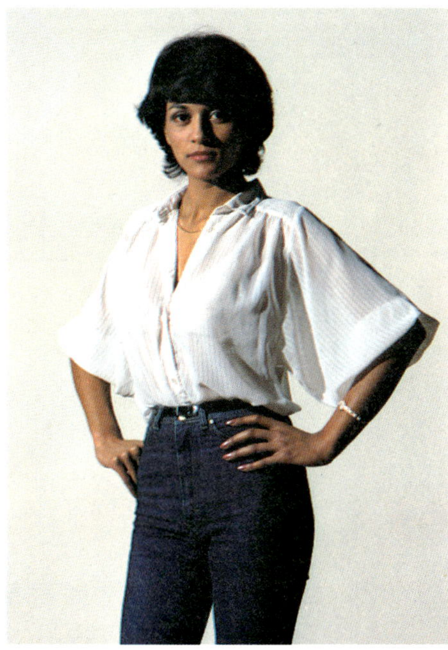

Direct light *The simplest lighting arrangement of all—one light on a stand, shining down on the model at an angle of 45°. Without a reflector, shadows tend to be harsh and black, but the effect suits some subjects*

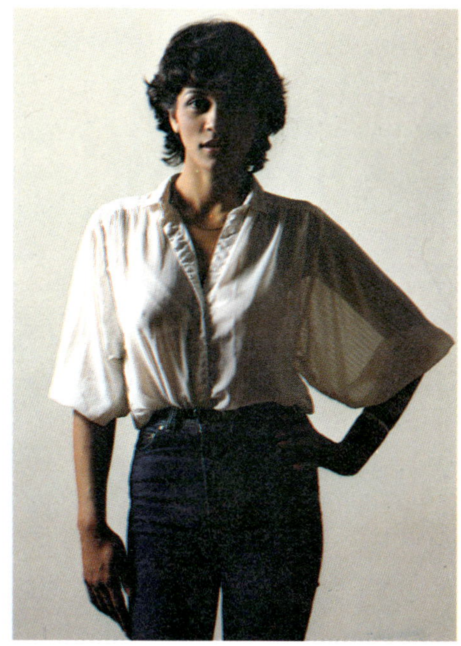

Side light *Placing a lamp directly to one side of the model produces high contrast even when the light is bounced off a large reflector to give it a broader spread. But this can be used to dramatic effect*

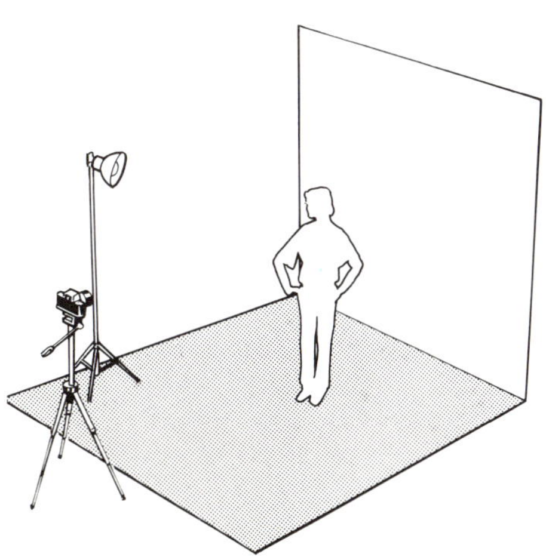

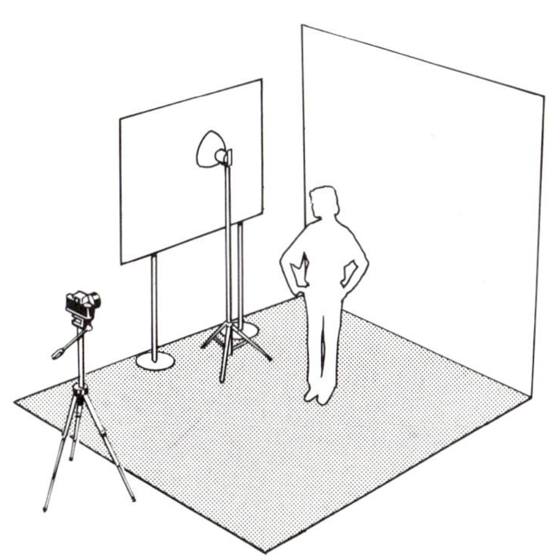

light placed at a 45° angle above and to one side looks good through the viewfinder, some parts of the face will be in deep shadow in the final photograph. Deep shadow and bright highlights are ideal for the more dramatic approaches, but they are quite unsuitable for straightforward portraits.

Reducing contrast

It is relatively easy to tell whether the contrast range in the subject is to great for your camera by measuring the *lighting ratio*, the ratio between the darkest and lightest parts of the subject. You can measure the lighting ratio simply by moving in close to the subject with a meter—either a separate meter or that in your camera. Take a reading from both the lit and unlit areas of the subject and compare them.

If you are using colour film, there should not be more than about two *f*/stops difference between the readings from each area. Black and white film is more tolerant and can cope with a three stop difference, and possibly even more with careful development. But even with black and white film the lighting ratio is likely to be too great with a single light source, so you must find some way of increasing or *filling in* light in the shadow areas.

The most obvious fill-in method is an extra light and this is dealt with in the following section. If you have only one light, however, a simple and very effective method is to use a reflective surface.

Almost any smooth, light coloured surface can be used as a reflector—a piece of white card, a sheet, a white wall or even a mirror. The main problem with a reflector is often finding a way to support it in the appropriate position. Rigid surfaces such as card are therefore better than sheets, although a white sheet provides a large surface.

Finding the right position for the reflector is not always easy and it is worth experimenting with different reflector positions and angles until you achieve the effect you want. To catch light from your studio lamp, the reflector must be on the opposite side of the subject. It cannot be directly opposite, or the subject will block off the light from the reflector. It must also direct light towards the part of the subject you want illuminated. For a 45° light, the reflector should be to the side and slightly in front of the subject.

There is no reason why you should restrict yourself to a single reflector. Combinations of large and small reflectors may be useful. A large reflector can brighten large shadow areas while a small reflector could be used to highlight important areas of the subject.

Still life

Although this section has concentrated on portraits, there is certainly no reason why you cannot successfully use a single light and reflectors for still life. But when lighting still lifes you must decide what aspect of the subject you want to bring out, as different lighting positions bring

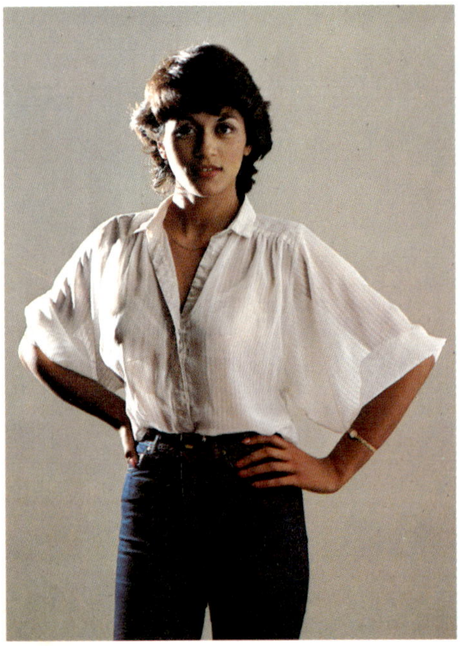

Rear light plus reflector *With the lamp positioned behind the model and a large white reflector in front, shadows are less dense. When photographing towards the light, a long lens hood should be used to reduce distracting flare*

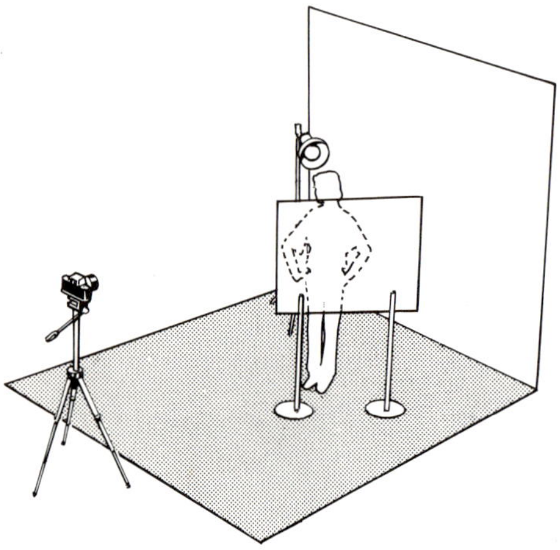

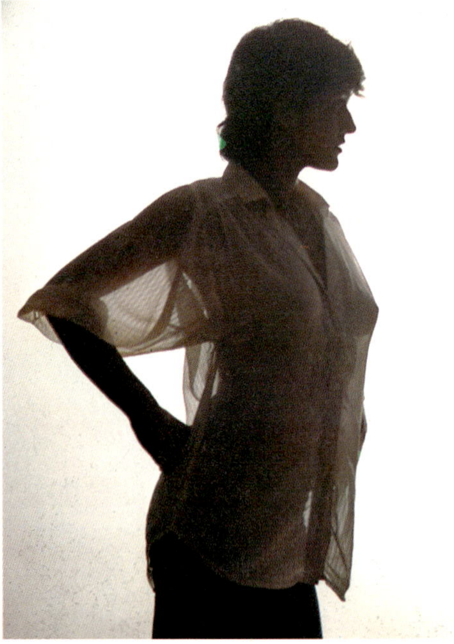

Back lighting *Bouncing the light off the background directly behind the model throws her into silhouette. This gives strong emphasis to her outline, and is particularly effective with portraits taken in profile*

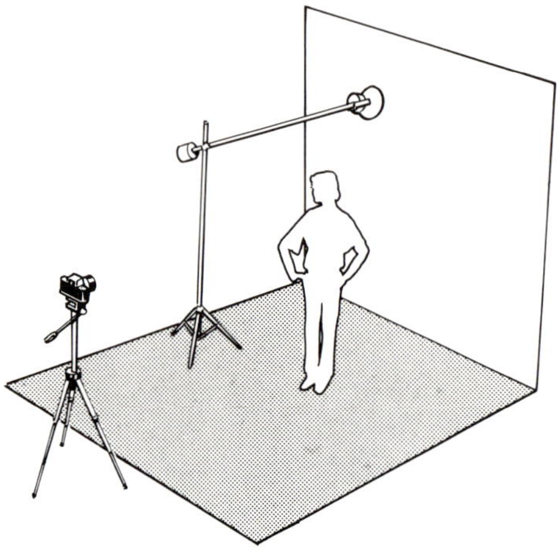

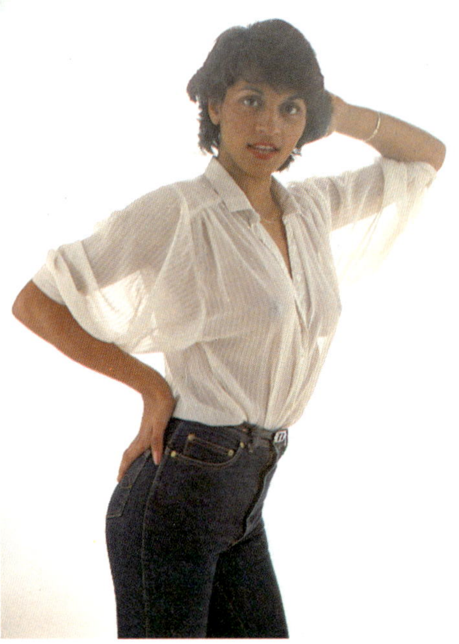

Back light plus reflectors *The same light as for the silhouette picture, but with two large white reflectors in front of the model. The gauzy translucence of the blouse is emphasized, and shadow detail is retained*

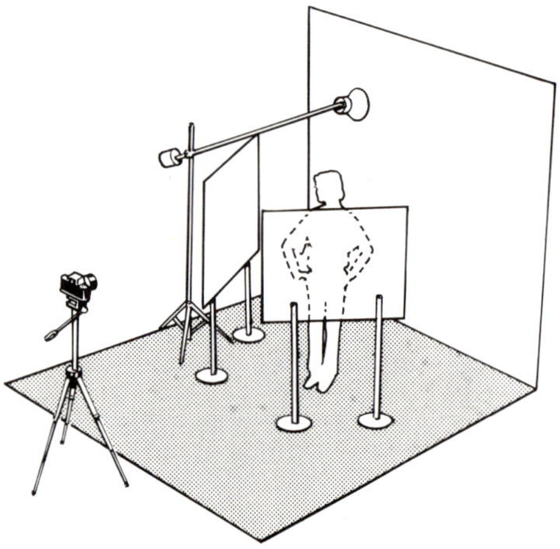

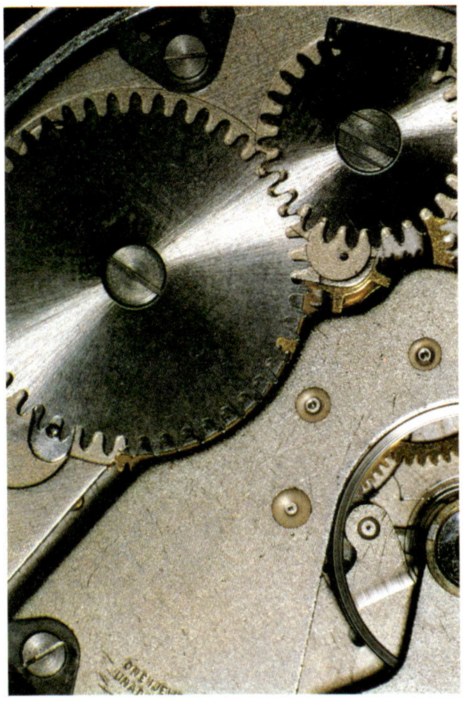

Watchworks *A single lamp, without a reflector, placed above the subject is enough to light this close-up of a brightly reflective mechanism*

out different qualities—detail, form and tone, for example.

For maximum detail, you usually need the light in front of the subject and ample use of reflectors to fill in shadows. Textures, on the other hand, are often best revealed by strong lighting from a shallow angle—almost sidelighting. An effect often used by advertising photographers to create a sense of luxury and opulence is to light their subject from above and slightly behind, with only a little fill-in.

Colour balance

If you are using colour film, particularly colour slide film, with tungsten light, you must place an appropriate filter over either the light or the camera lens to give the correct colour balance. The long-lasting 500 watt photographic lamps give correct colour with film balanced for artificial light, but the popular short life photoflood bulbs burn hotter and need an 81A filter. Ordinary domestic 100 watt bulbs are redder and need a bluish 82B filter for correct colour.

Filters for the lens are cheap and quite easy to use but many professionals prefer large filter sheets placed over the lights. These sheets are available from shops that sell professional film equipment. Although widely known as 'gels', these filter sheets are usually made of dyed acetate or tough polyester.

The main advantage of this filter method is that it allows you to mix various light sources such as tungsten and daylight. If you use this method, do not attach the filter too close to the light because they can be damaged by the heat. Remember too that gelatin sheets cannot be used over the camera lens because their optical quality is not sufficiently good. For further details of colour balance for tungsten lights, see pages 174-177.

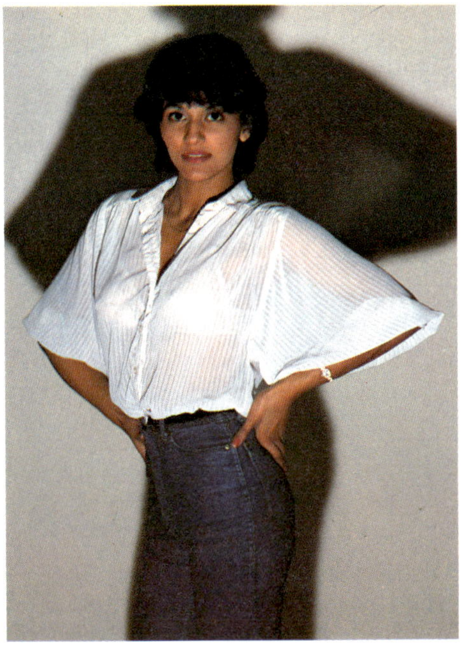

Light from below *Positioning a lamp below your model gives a disconcerting effect. Even more bizarre results can be produced by moving the lamp in closer to the model, so that it shines upwards from foot-level*

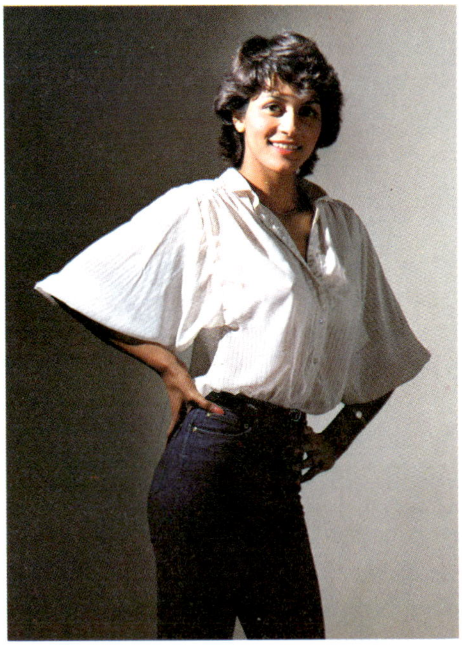

Silver and black *A small silver board, to lighten shadows, combined with a large black board. The black board reduces the light on the background and changes the nature of the reflections on the model*

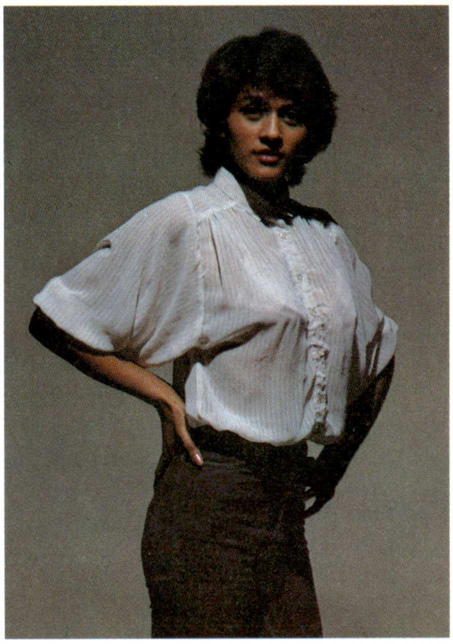

Two black boards *Frontal lighting from above combined with black boards on either side. All boards used for these pictures were made of lightweight sheets of expanded polystyrene, available from builders merchants*

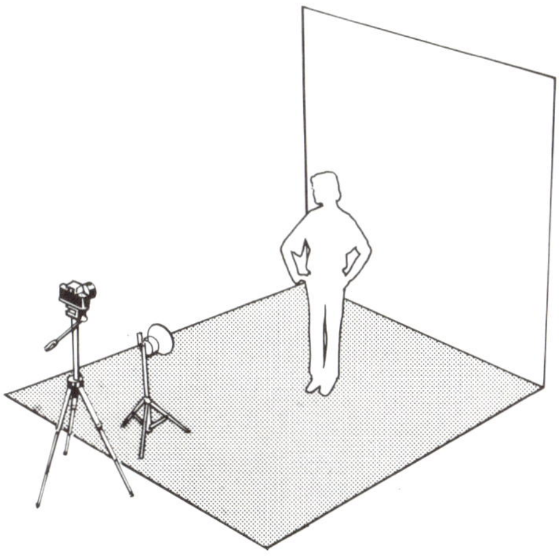

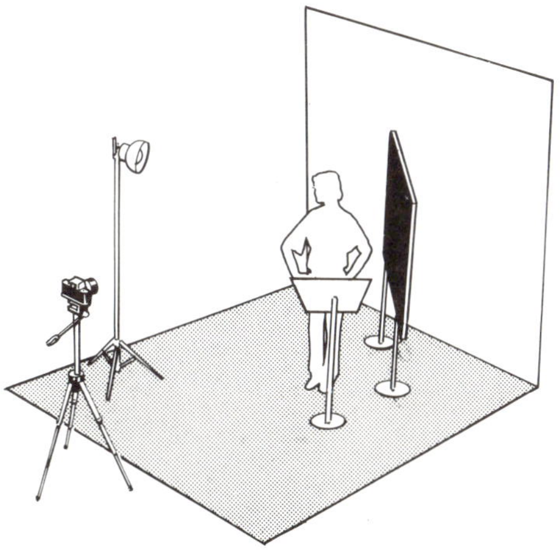

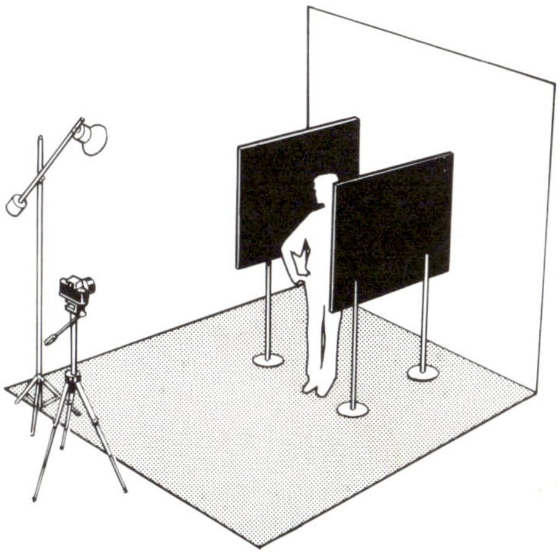

Multiple lighting set-ups

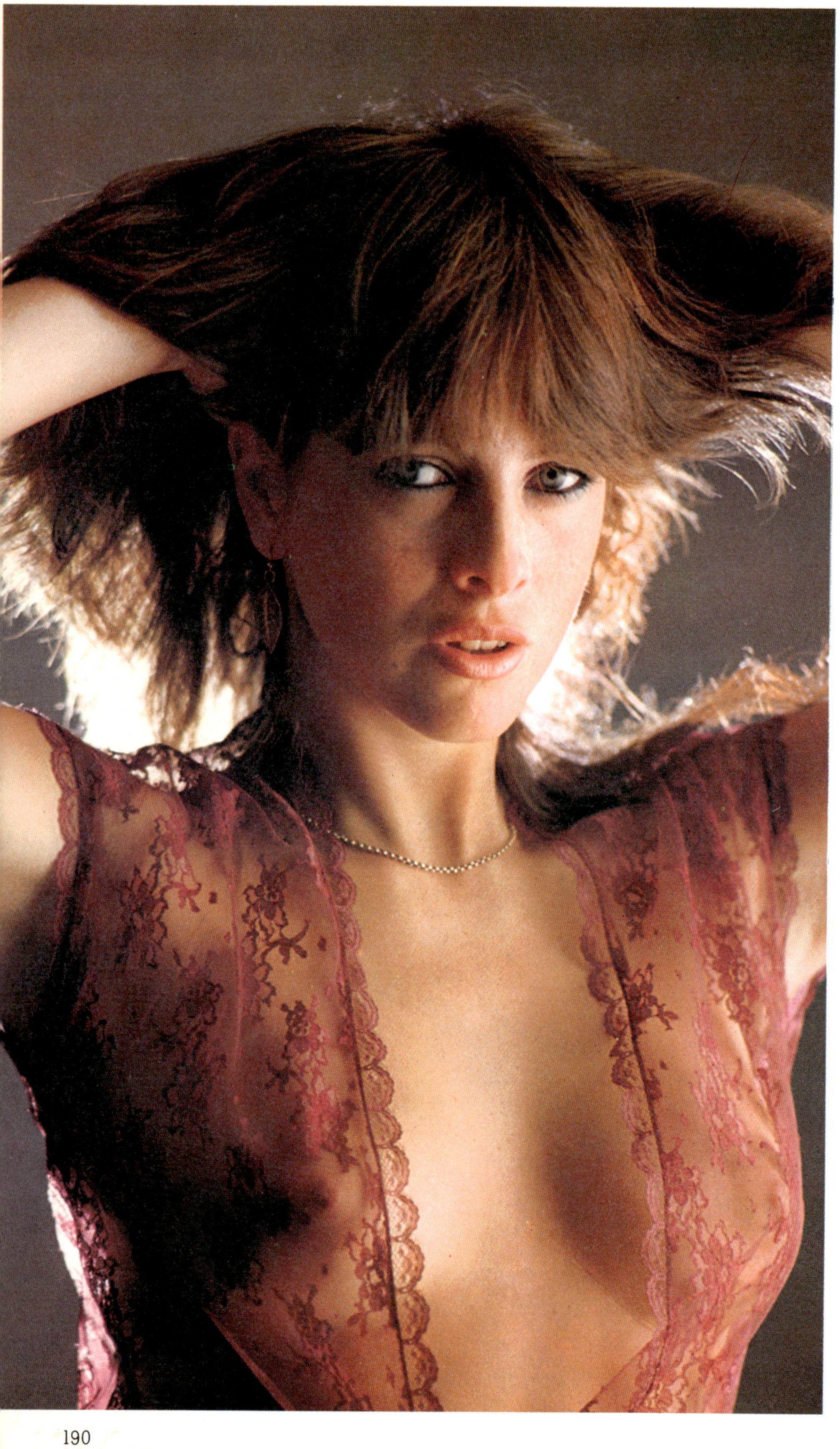

Although you can achieve impressive results with just a single light source, your control over the appearance of the subject is broad rather than subtle. By adding extra lights, you can fine-tune the illumination to give a wide range of highly-controlled effects.

The secret to handling multiple light set-ups is actually to use as few lights as possible. Natural lighting usually comes from one main source such as the sun or a window, although there are many minor sources of reflected light. So for a portrait to look natural, studio light must also appear to come from a single principal source. You need just one main light, usually diffused with a broad floodlight reflector, to set the key for the picture. Other lights must never be allowed to compete with the main light if you want a natural look to the photograph.

Setting up the main light follows largely the same process as that outlined for single source lighting, although with extra lights available to fill in deep shadows, slightly more extreme positions can still give natural looking results.

Nevertheless, one particular lighting set up has become widely accepted for conventional portraits, and provides suitable illumination for a wide range of sitters. The main light is positioned in front of the sitter and to one side and pointing down towards the face at an angle of 45°. With the right additional light, the effect is natural and revealing.

Unfortunately, although this lighting arrangement shows up the subject well, it tends to give rather flat results if the sitter faces the camera directly. Most

Lighting control *Diffused light from two lamps in a reflector placed behind tracing paper on the right, and a back light to shine through the hair and frame the face, give a flattering picture. Lively posing helps the total effect*

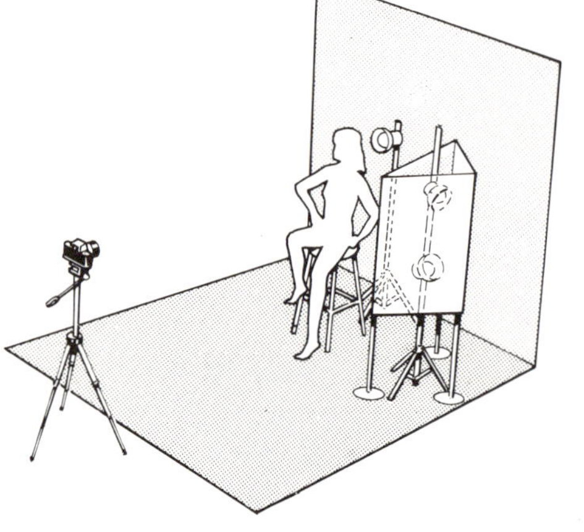

photographers prefer to move the camera round to shoot obliquely at the subject. If you decide to do this, it is probably better not to move the camera but to ask the sitter to turn his or her head slightly and then move the lights accordingly.

As the subject turns away from the camera, however, the effect of 45° lighting changes. If the light is to the left of the subject and the subject turns to the left, the light is then on the far side of the face from the camera. It shines across the face and, for the camera shooting the shadowed side of the face, much less of the face is illuminated. Only the more prominent features—forehead, cheeks, nose, chin and so on—are brightly lit and the effect is to make the face look narrower than usual. So if you have a subject with a broad face, you may be able to make it look narrower by using this form of lighting.

If, however, the light shines on the side of the face nearest to the camera, much more seems to be illuminated and the effect is to make the face look broader and flatter. Very little textural detail is revealed and this type of lighting is better when you want the appearance of a smooth complexion. But unless the subject has sharp, narrow features, fill-in lighting should be kept to a minimum to stop the face appearing too broad and flat. You can play down or emphasize either of these techniques—broadening and smoothing with the light on the near side of the face, narrowing and accentuating texture with the light on the far side—by moving the light through different angles.

Fill-in light

Once the main light is positioned, you must set another to fill in the shadows to prevent them becoming too deep. The best place for this light is usually fairly close to the line between the camera and subject, on the opposite side of the camera to the main light. Move it around from this position until the unpleasantly deep shadows are softened.

Normally, even if the main light is a sharp spotlight, the fill-in should be a diffused flood light. If the main and fill-in are equally bright, the fill-in should be placed one third further away from the sitter than the main light. If the fill-in is only half as bright as the main light, it should be set at approximately two thirds the distance.

You can decide when the amount of fill-in is correct by making measurements in the way shown in the article on single source lighting. However, with a fill-in light, you can measure the effect of each light separately and this is usually easier. Simply switch on the main light, take a light meter reading and switch off. Repeat the process for the fill-in light. The difference in exposure in *f*-stops gives an idea of the contrast in the subject after the fill-in has been added. The range of contrast needed depends on the subject: for those which require a soft effect, such as babies and girls, the difference in exposure settings should not normally be more than 1 to 1½ *f*-stops. With older men, and shots where you want to emphasize masculine character, you can afford to give 2½ to 3 stops. Only for really unusual, dramatic effects should the difference be four stops or more.

Remember to allow for the skin tone of your subject when estimating exposure, however. If your subject is very dark skinned, the exposure meter tends to over-compensate. This does not matter with black and white film, but with colour slide film, you should aim to underexpose by one *f*-stop.

Additional lights

In addition to the main and fill-in lights, many photographers add a number of other lights to produce special effects and enhance the picture in small but important ways.

One of the most popular extra lights is a hair light. With only two lights, even the healthiest hair can look dull and uninteresting. The hair light is added to introduce highlights into the hair and make it glisten brightly. It is usually set in one of three places—either above the head, above and to one side, or to one side and level with the head.

Exact positioning is important, particularly with an overhead light. If it is forward of the crown, light can spill onto the face and upset the shadow pattern. Arranged directly above the crown, it produces a pancake of light on top of the head that is rarely flattering. Ideally, it should be set a little behind the crown so that light is reflected brightly through the strands of the hair.

Hair light is most effective on brunettes and people with thick hair. Very light blondes need little hair emphasis, and if you use a hair light with people who are slightly balding, it may show up the very feature they want to hide.

A well shaded domestic lamp will often provide a good hair light, but if

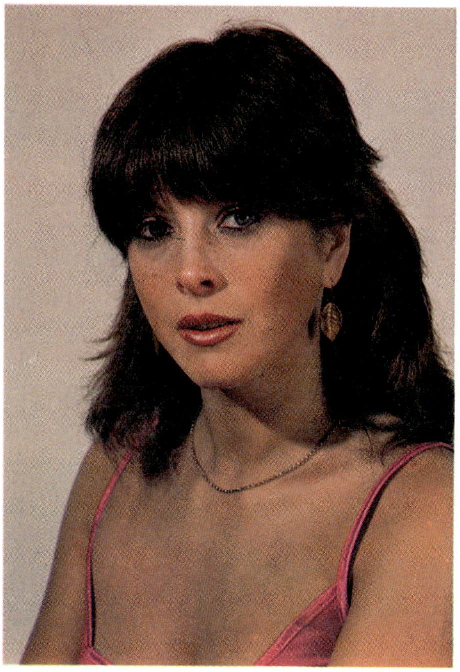

Directional light *Strong light from the front gives direct main lighting on the subject. A weaker lamp, with a reflector board to the side of the model, gives a similar effect to a broad floodlight fill-in*

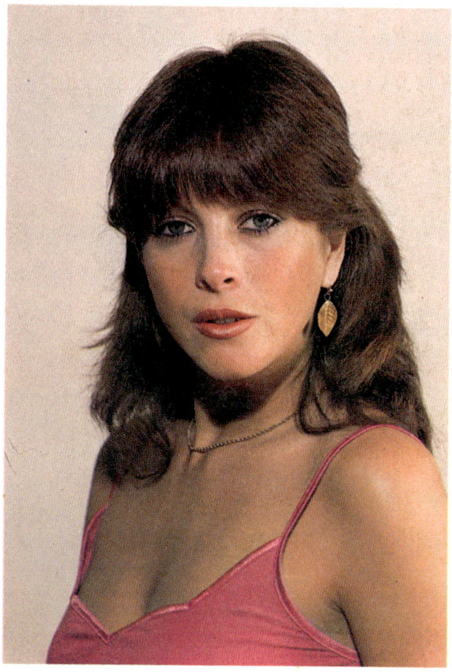

Broad light *Moving the directional lamp further back and around towards the camera axis changes the effect. The reflector board has also been moved, so that most of the light comes from the right of the picture*

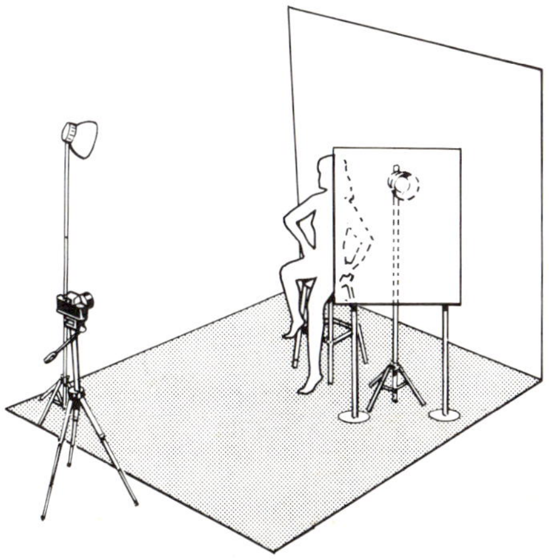

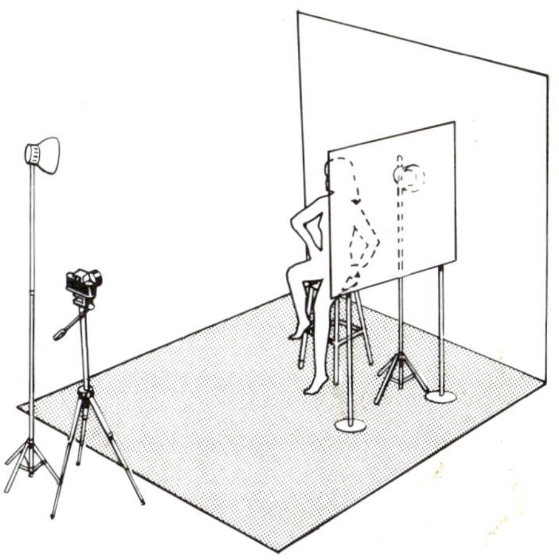

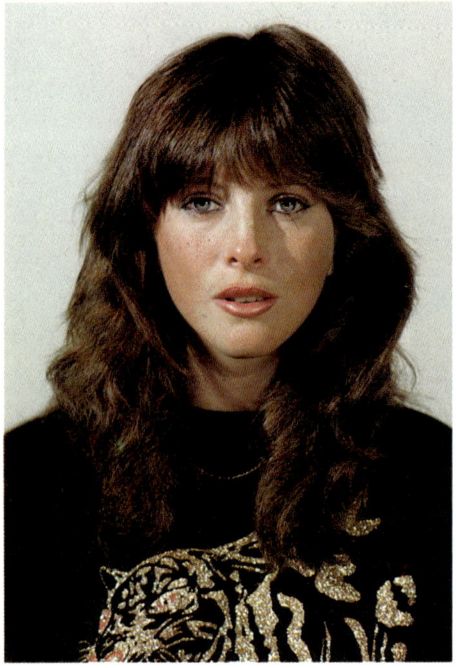

Rear light *Placing a light directly behind the model hides it from the view of the camera and gives a glamorous halo effect. The main light is placed high up and almost directly behind the camera for frontal illumination*

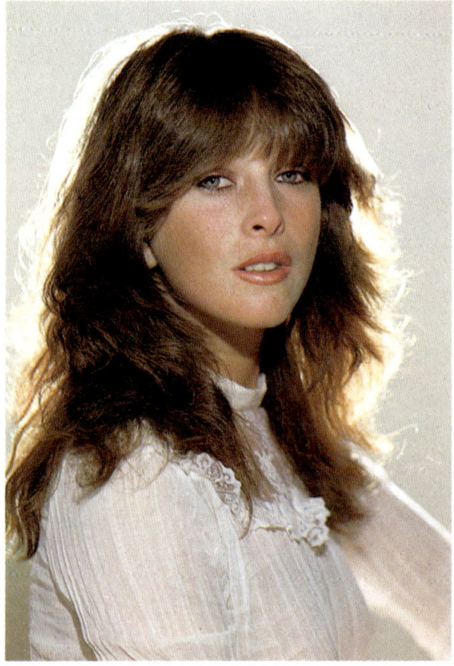

Lighting angle *A minor adjustment to the position of the main light and to the pose of the model gives a major change in mood. Both direct and reflected lights are now at similar angles to the subject*

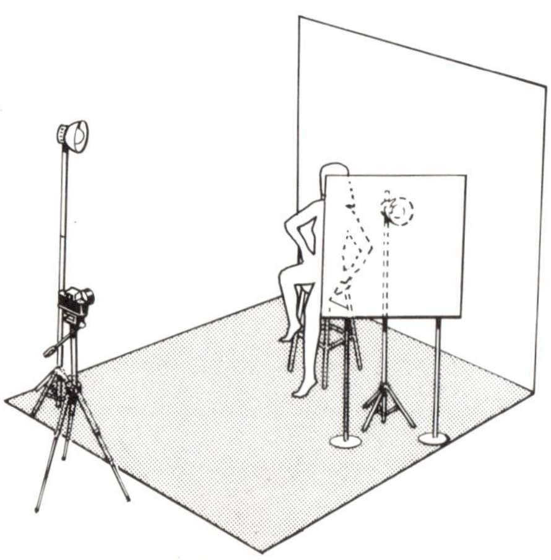

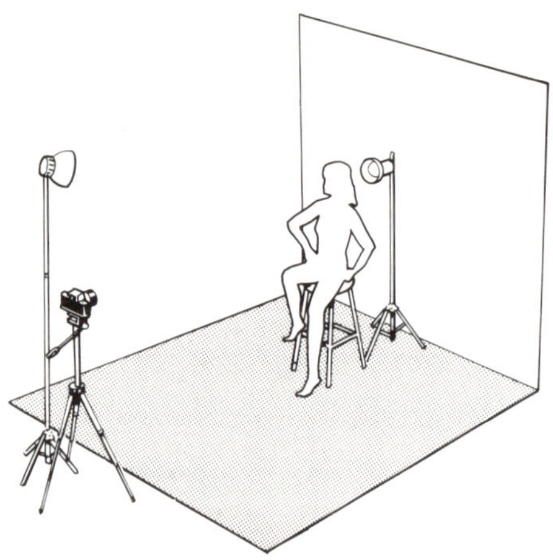

this is suspended from the ceiling it should hang low. Move your subject around until he or she is correctly placed in relation to this light. A proper spotlight is better but it can be very expensive. A spotlight can direct a beam of light upon the sitter from several metres away.

Another light can be added to illuminate the background. If you have not arranged a special background this light is unnecessary. It is better to sit the subject well away from any walls and leave the background dark. Dark backgrounds do not suit all subjects, however, and you may want to use a light background. More interesting backgrounds can be used, providing they do not distract from the subject, but for straight portraits a very smooth plain surface is probably best. A plain white painted wall is ideal. If you cannot find a suitable wall, you may have to buy a roll of special background paper from a photographic supplier.

It is very easy to set up the lights to illuminate the head and forget about the background. While this does not matter with a dark and distant background, a light background will pick up various distracting shadows from the front lights, particularly if it is close behind the subject. Ideally, the subject should be placed as far in front of the background as possible.

In small studios where there is little room for manoeuvre and a shadowed background is unavoidable, the background light is often used to kill the shadows in the background. It must be a very strong light and the background will appear very bright.

Even where the background is sufficiently distant to avoid unpleasant shadows, the background light can be used to brighten the background so that it complements but does not compete with the subject—there should be at least one stop difference in the readings between the background and the subject.

A popular effect is to place the background light on the floor and point it upwards so that the background is light at the bottom but gradually darkens towards the top. This helps to 'frame' the subject, and the dark top of the background contrasts with the hair light.

You can place the background light in many positions, but prevent stray lights and trailing wires from intruding into the picture. The light can even be set behind the backdrop, shining through it. This can produce a soft, even circle of light around the head and avoids awkwardly placed lights near the sitter.

Other lights can be added both in front and behind the subject to create small bright highlights and to give the picture extra sparkle. A small spotlight aimed on the cheek to reflect straight into the camera is a good example. You find the correct position for this light by setting the spotlight right by the camera. Have your sitter hold a small mirror right on the spot to be highlighted. Then walk

Portrait lighting step-by-step

Building up an arrangement *Three lamps are enough for most types of portrait.*

1 *A main light with a broad reflector is placed to one side of the model to illuminate the important features*

2 *An accent light behind, and on the other side, adds extra highlights and brings out form more strongly.*

3 *Accent light and main light are not enough on their own, however. There are several distracting shadow areas that should also be dealt with.*

4 *The answer is to add a third light almost in line with the camera. This serves as a fill-in to lighten the shadows without overpowering the other lights*

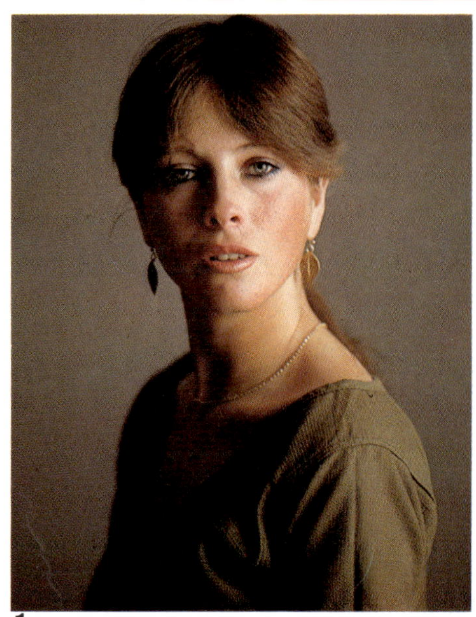

1

around the sitter until you see the image of the spotlight reflected in the mirror. The spotlight should be placed where you are standing when you see this reflection. Position the spot carefully and check through the viewfinder.

Other lighting schemes

Once you have experimented with conventional portrait lighting, you can try other techniques. Ideally the lighting should be tailored to suit your subject, and although formal portrait lighting arrangements usually work well, there are times when a different arrangement is more suitable.

'Glamour' lighting uses exactly the same sort of arrangement as 'standard' lighting, but the main light is taken further back and the fill-in light is the more dominant. First switch the angled light off to ensure even coverage of the features by the main light, then bring the fill-in light slowly forward until shadows begin to appear. The correct position can be found by very carefully moving the fill-in light back again until the shadows just disappear.

Another example is a form of lighting named after the well known portraitist Karsh. This consists of lights placed either side of the sitter equally illuminating both sides of the head. Each light is positioned individually, lighting only one side of the head, then both are turned on together. If all has gone well an extremely effective form of lighting will be achieved, flattering to the sitter but not corresponding to that usually seen in real life. Great care as to be taken in positioning the lights: they should both be of equal strength and at equal distances each side of the sitter and from the camera. With a full-face shot, if the lights are set too far back they produce a black line down the centre of the nose, but if too far forward, awkward looking shadows will spoil the result. But do get these positions worked out before your sitter arrives!

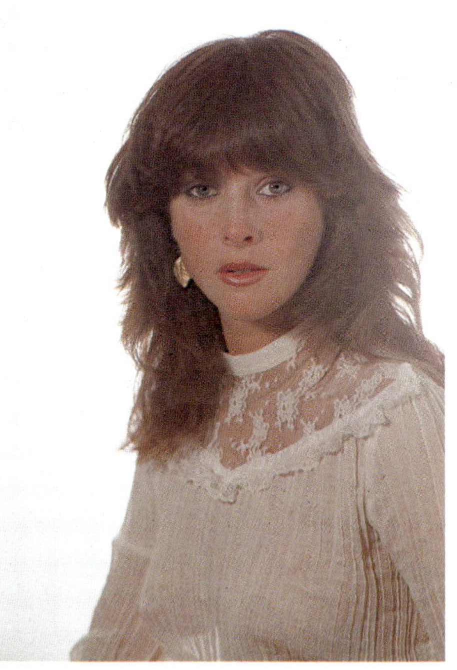

Tracing paper diffusion *A sheet of tracing paper is used as a background, and light is directed through it towards the camera. Another sheet of tracing paper over the main light gives a final result that is both soft and high key*

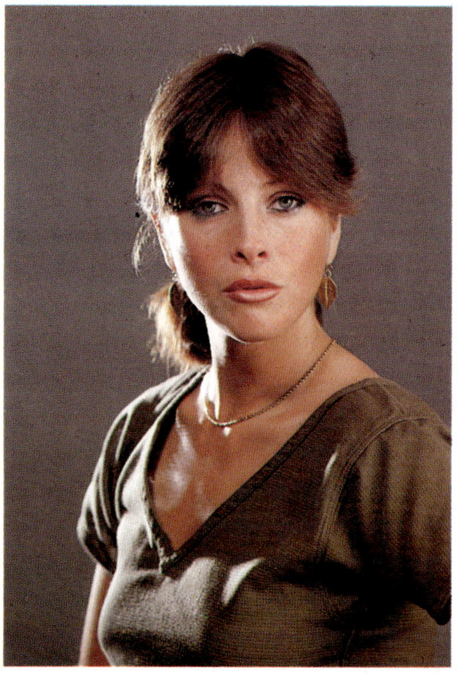

Three lights *The result of the lighting in the sequence below. The main light comes from an angled reflector, while the accent light is provided by a small spot. Tracing paper is used to diffuse the fill-light*

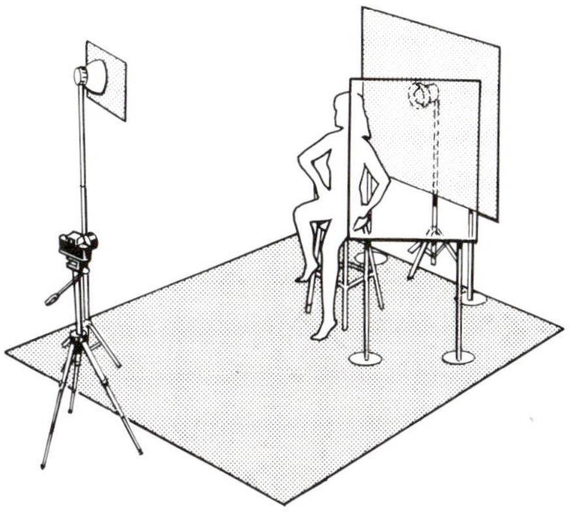

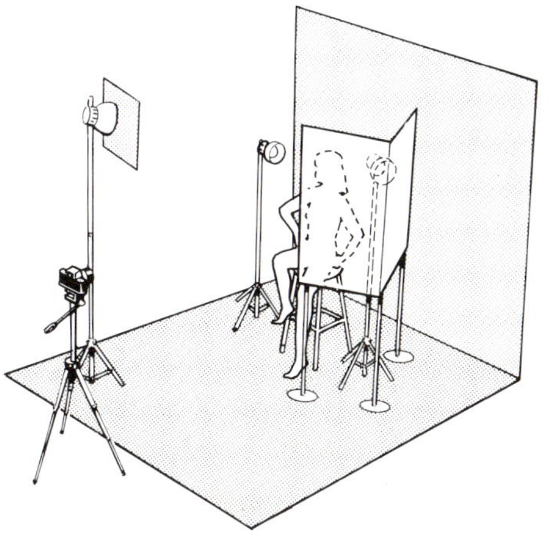

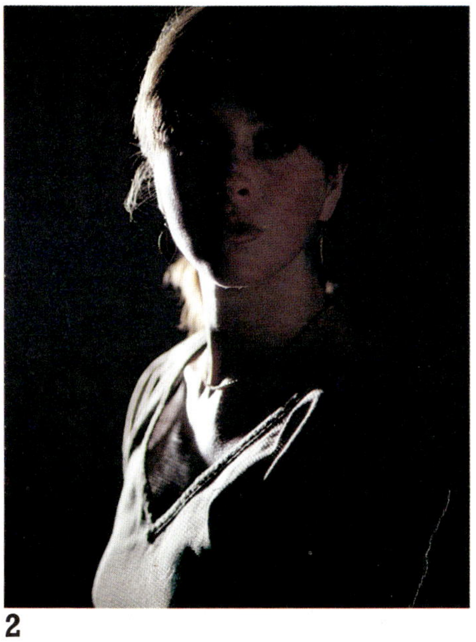

2

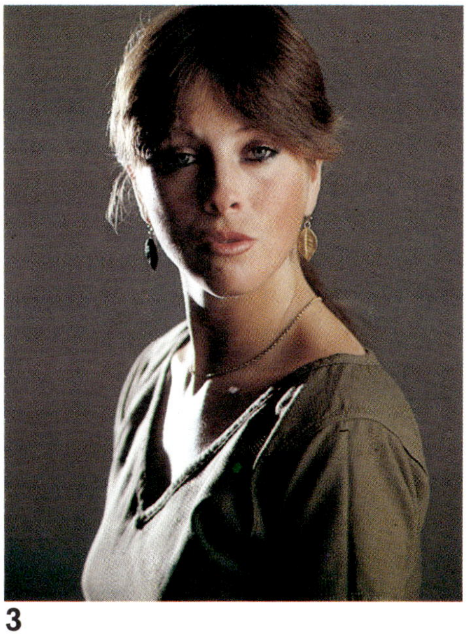

3

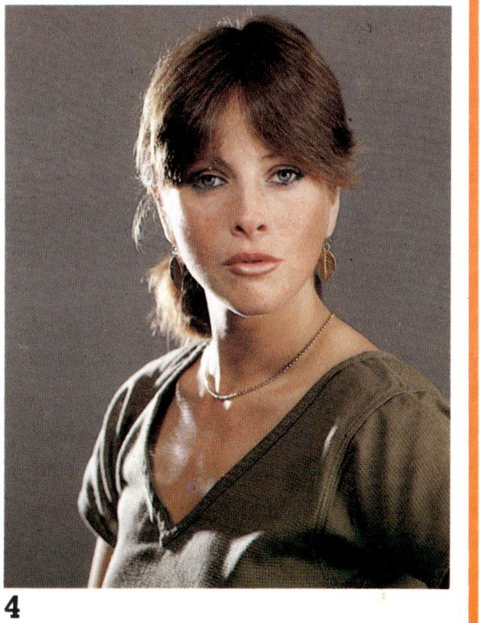

4

CHAPTER 18
THE PORTRAIT STUDIO
Directing a session

Many people have an image of the professional photographer working slickly through a session with a model, moving swiftly from pose to pose with just an occasional 'Hold it!' to break the flow. Few amateurs can work this easily with a model, though, and results from even the most informal session often look stiff and lifeless. There is no easy solution to this problem, but here are a few tricks of the trade to help improve your confidence and make it easier for the model to settle into the session.

It is usually easy to tell when a photographer has a rapport with a model, just by looking at the contact sheet or slides from the session. Poses are relaxed, and the pictures have a natural look to them. When the photographer has had difficulty with a session, this too is frequently obvious. The pictures look stilted, the model looks awkward and uncomfortable, and it is clear that there was very little communication between photographer and subject.

Perhaps the most important thing is to know before you begin the session exactly what type of pictures you want. Write down as much as you can about each photograph. Make a note of the kind of lighting you want to use, the location you have in mind, and the general atmosphere of the final image. With a clear idea of what you want, you can explain your plans to the model briefly and confidently. If you are unclear in your own mind, your directions to the model will be unclear too.

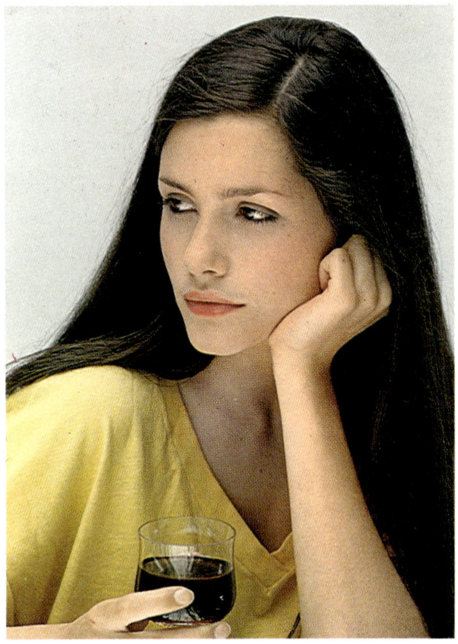

A relaxed pose *Inexperienced models are often given away by their hands. A simple prop gives them something to do*

Discuss with the model what sort of clothes are needed for the pictures—it is a good idea to have a change of clothes on hand if possible, to add variety. Think about hand props too, because these can give a nervous model confidence. Smokers particularly find it hard to know where to put their hands if they are not holding a cigarette. Holding an umbrella can give a model something to do, and take away the feeling of having 15 fingers.

Immediately before meeting your model to take the photographs, check that you have everything you need, and in the case of film, more than you need. This may sound obvious, but scrabbling in a gadget bag for a lens you left at home quickly breaks a model's concentration, and running out of film brings a session to an abrupt end.

Helping the model to relax

Professional models are expert at looking calm and comfortable in front of the camera, but for people who are unused to it, having a picture taken can be an ordeal. Do all you can to make your subject feel at ease. If you are working in a studio, whether it is purpose built or improvised, make sure it is warm and reasonably comfortable. Music is a great help, and fills any awkward silences while you are changing film or lights. If possible choose the music to suit the mood of the shots you want—it is difficult to look cool and sophisticated while assaulted by 'The Ride of the Valkyries'!

If your model seems nervous on arriving, do not be too eager to start taking pictures, and allow time to relax.

If you are working with an inexperienced model, it is sometimes a good idea to suggest that they bring a friend or relative along. This can give a much needed boost to their confidence: the friend might also help by holding reflectors, or touching up make up. Try and exclude all other people since it is difficult for anyone to look relaxed and natural if they are surrounded by a curious crowd. Professional models though, should be used to a busy studio.

Make as many preparations as you can before the session. Arrange the lighting as far as possible and take exposure meter readings from a stand-in in the model's position. Unless the lighting changes, you should be able to retain the same reading for the whole of the session. With adequate planning and preparation, you can concentrate on taking pictures without worrying about the technicalities.

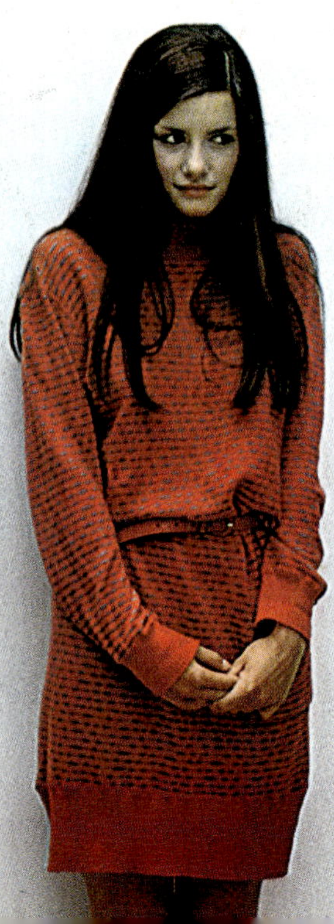

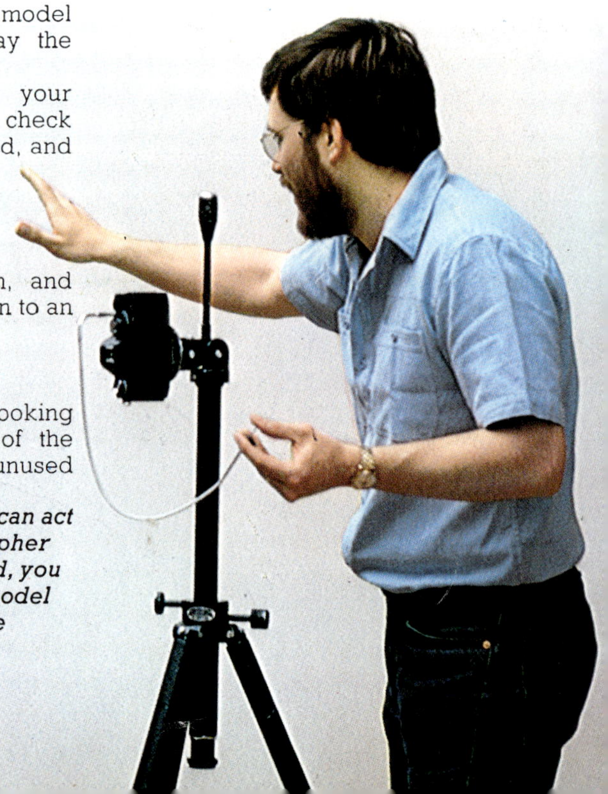

Use a tripod *A hand-held camera can act as a barrier between the photographer and model. But if it is set on a tripod, you can concentrate on directing the model without having to spend lots of time framing up*

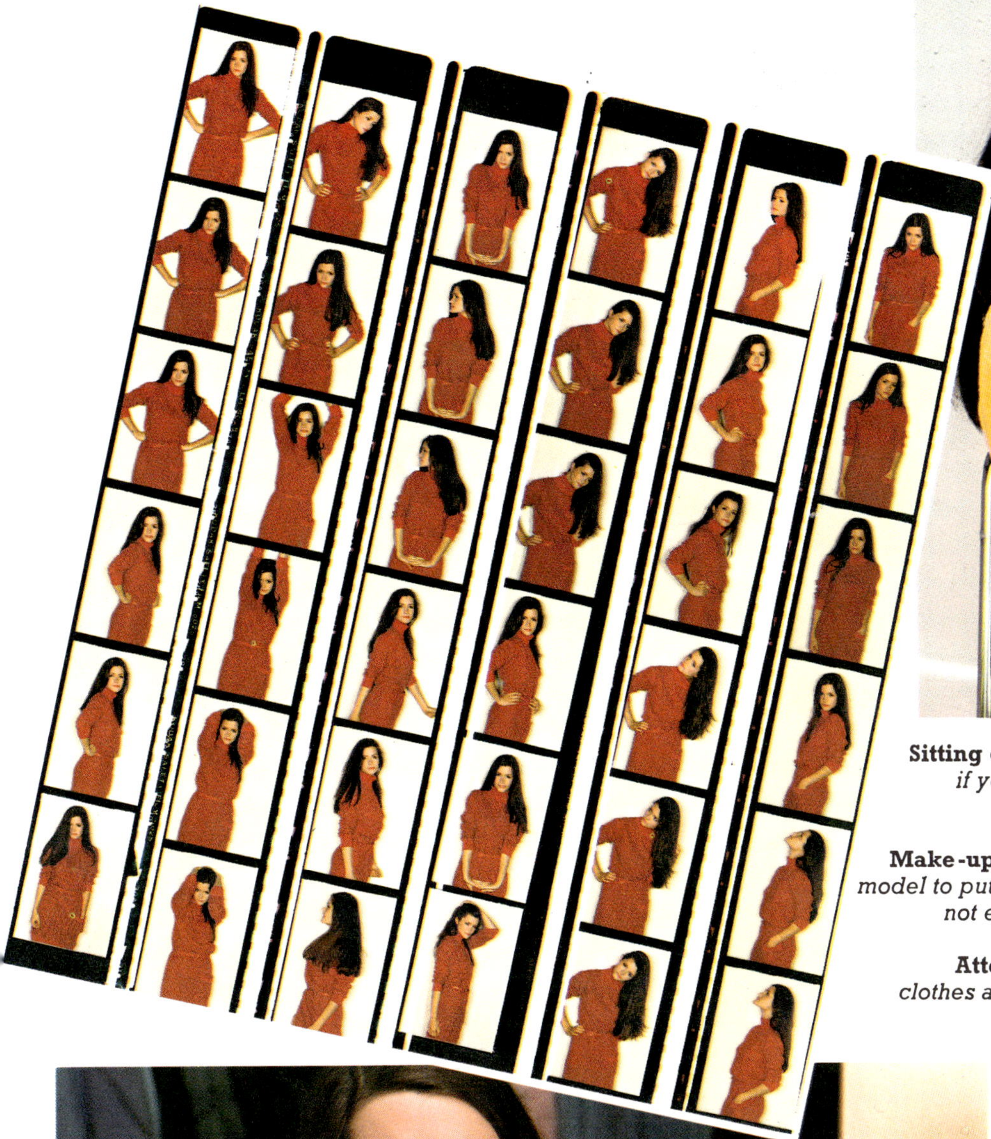

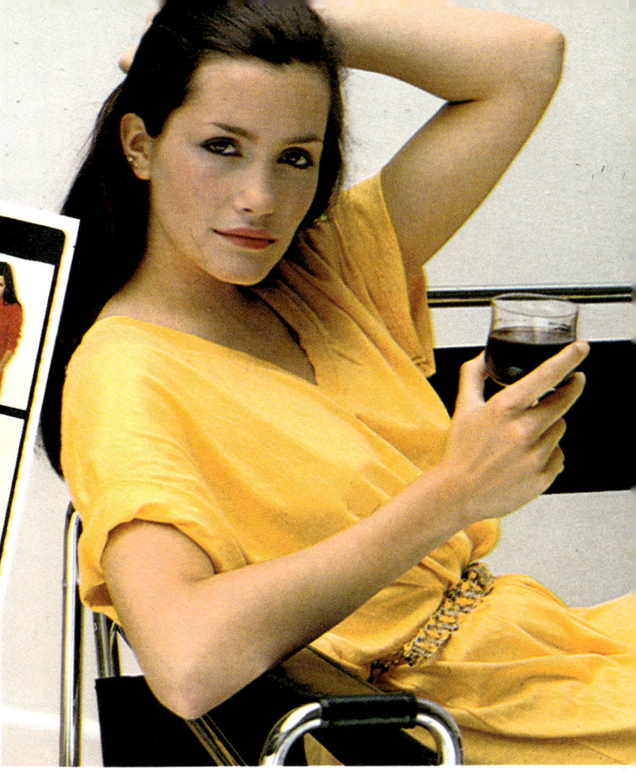

Sitting down *Pictures are more likely to be better if your model is comfortable. A seated pose is easier than standing*

Make-up *Remember to provide somewhere for the model to put on make-up. A proper theatrical mirror is not essential, but the area should be brightly lit*

Attention to detail *Take great care arranging clothes and hair. Small details that look insignificant at the time can easily spoil the picture*

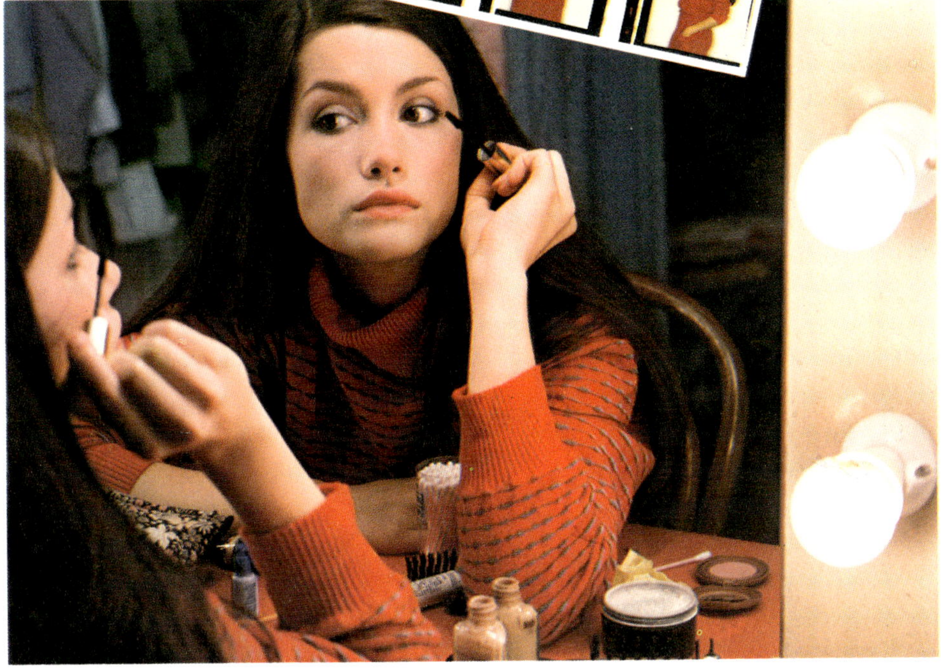

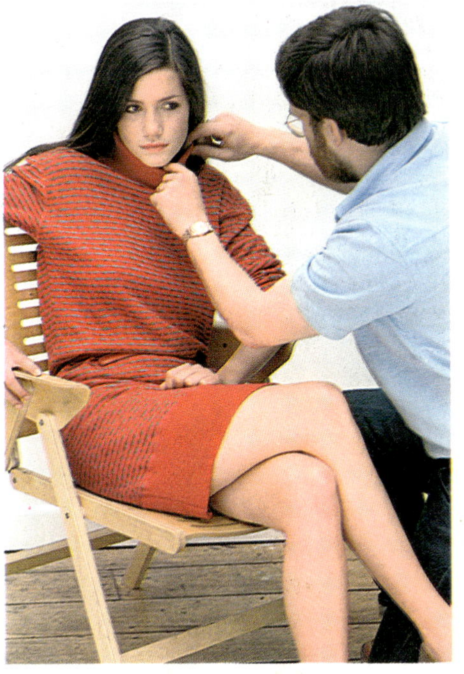

Once you begin shooting, try and keep the model occupied all the time. A regular flow of conversation and encouragement helps a lot—everybody wants to be told that they are doing well, and you should try and provide this reassurance, even if you are not convinced that the pictures are any good. Work quickly, and do not try to economize on film. People tend to tense themselves just before the shutter is released, and then relax when they hear a click. A series of exposures in rapid succession is often better than a single frame, because the model does not have time to assume a fixed expression before each picture is taken. This is one reason why so many professional photographers shoot many rolls of film and use motor drives so they can work quickly.

Most models relax as a session progresses, so if things start badly, do not worry too much—they usually pick up momentum later. Often the best pictures from a session are the last dozen or so on the final roll of film, and the earlier shots are generally poor.

On the other hand, do not allow yourself to get carried away and push the model to the point of exhaustion. As soon as attention begins to flag, take a break and have a cup of coffee, or bring the session to an end. Working as a model can be very tiring, and it is easy to forget this, particularly if the session seems to be going well.

Using a tripod

Many photographers feel that clamping a camera to a tripod produces a rather rigid, inflexible type of picture. While this may be true for certain types of photography, a tripod can be a great asset when working with a model. It allows you to set the camera up at a fixed point, and take pictures without constantly squinting through the viewfinder. You can stand beside the camera, or just behind it, instead of bending down and hiding your face behind the lens. Using a long cable release and an autowinder allows you to get closer still. This makes it much easier to build up a relationship with a model, who can watch your reactions to a change in pose or expression. If you are unsure about the framing of the picture, mark the background with tape or string so that you can see where the edge of the viewfinder frame comes without having to look through the camera.

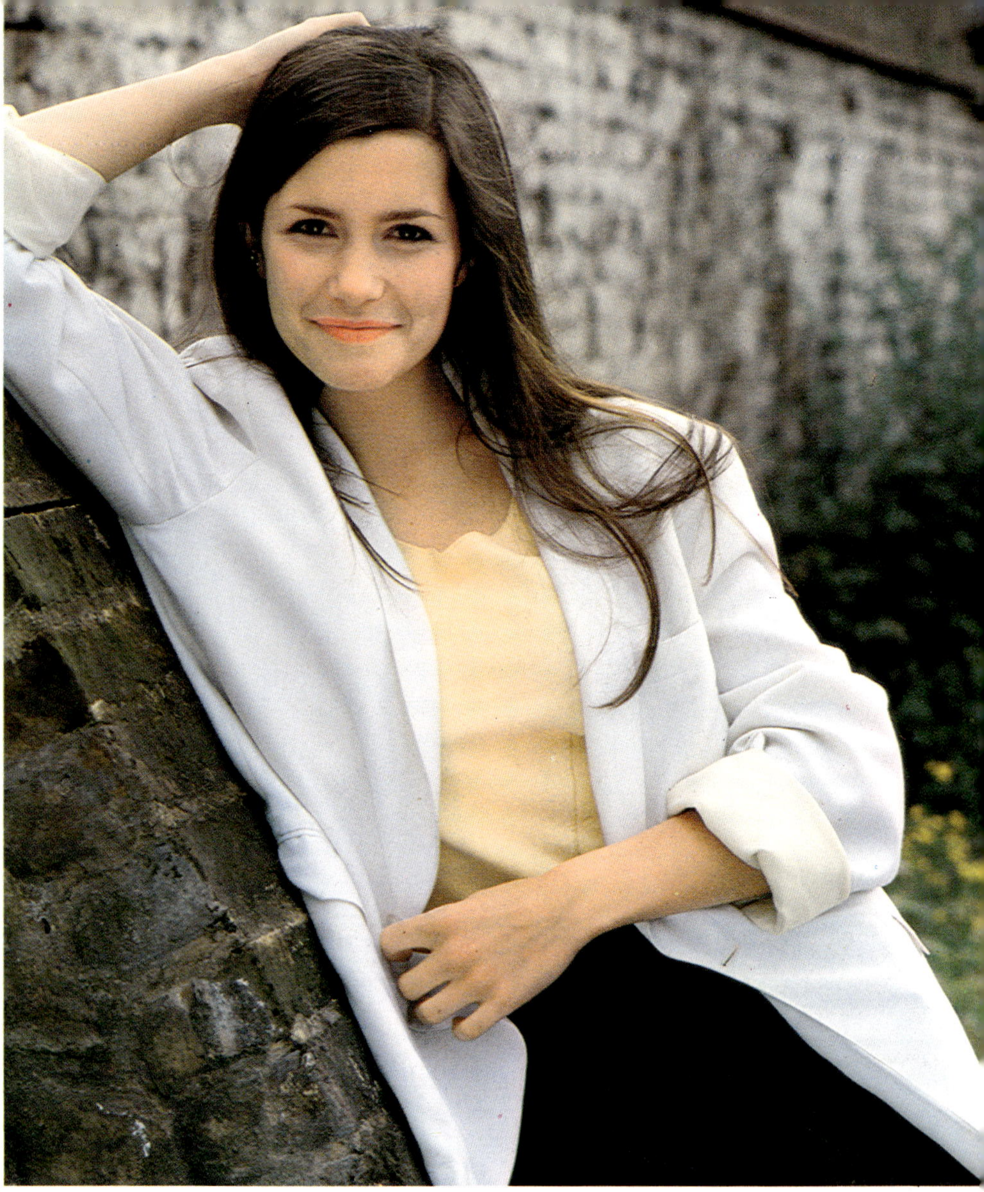

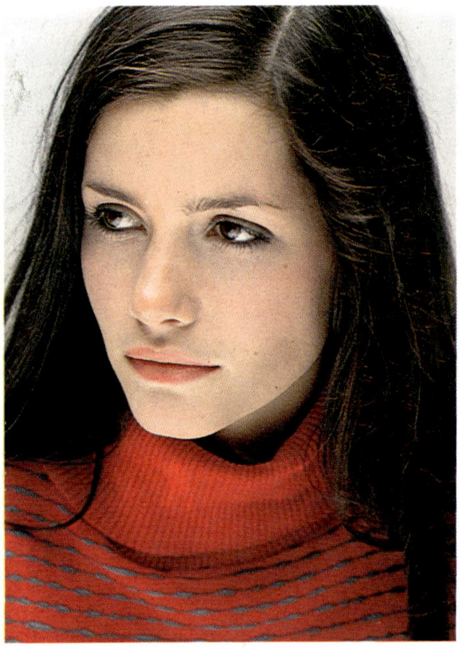

Shiny skin *Watch out for shiny skin highlights, on men as well as women. A touch of powder is all that is needed to eliminate a shiny nose*

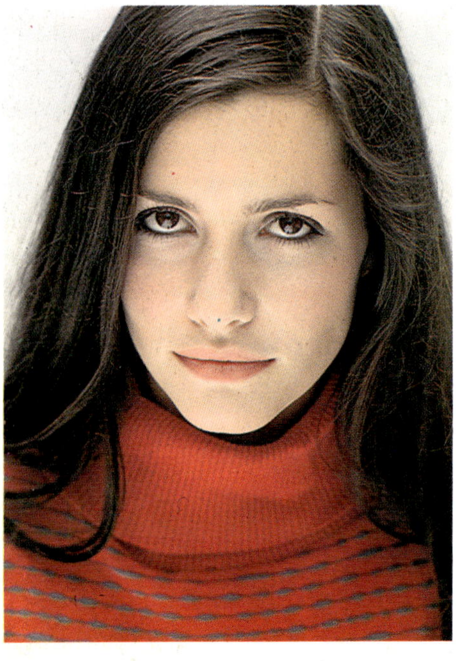

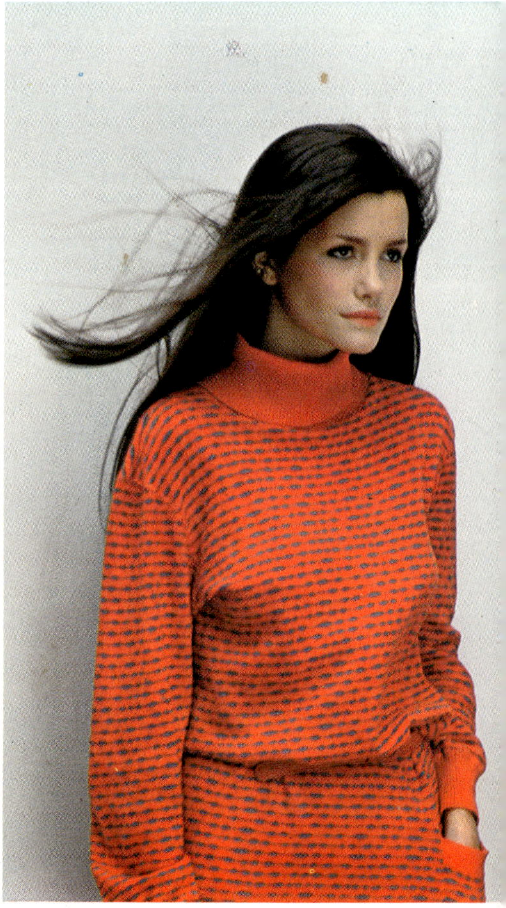

Out of doors *Avoid static poses, such as standing the model on a patch of grass with nothing to do. Look for props, such as trees and walls*

Directing the model

Models who can provide an endless and varied stream of natural poses are rare, and even an experienced model needs to have some sort of direction from the photographer. If you have difficulty in knowing where to start, look out for examples of the type of pictures you are aiming for, and cut them out of magazines and newspapers. A scrapbook made up like this should not be slavishly followed, but makes a good starting point. You may be able to use your scrapbook to show the model the type of pictures you want to take on the session.

Do not forget that some poses are easier for a model to deal with than others. Standing up in an open space without anything to do can be demanding from a model's point of view, and seated or prone poses are much easier—on a chair or bench, the model generally produces far more lively poses and often has somewhere to put hands. Out of doors, look for anything that the model can lean over, lean against or sit on. Benches, trees, walls and balustrades are all useful props. Inside, any piece of furniture can assist a model in finding an original pose.

Even if you start the session with well formed ideas about the poses you want your model to adopt, be pragmatic and try out any ideas that may emerge spontaneously in the course of the session. If any pose seems to be particularly successful, do not be impatient to move on, but stay with it, and work on small changes of position and expression, while retaining the same basic picture.

On the other hand, do not go to the other extreme, and keep the model locked into one position for hours on end. Keep some life and action in the pictures, even literally—if there is enough space, get the model to move around a bit. This is easily done if you are out of doors, because you can prefocus on a fixed point, and have the model walk towards you, or in circles around the camera. Avoid obvious cliches, though—subjects like 'jump for joy' have been done to death.

Indoors, avoiding static poses is more difficult, but you can get the model's hair or clothes moving with a fan or hair dryer or by waving a sheet of cardboard. If the model has long hair, a shake of the head does the job just as well. All these ploys put a bit of movement into an otherwise static picture.

Head and shoulders portraits can be more intimidating for a model than full length pictures, because the camera is so much nearer. Use a long lens if there is enough room to move back—even a 200 mm lens is not too long, but anything with a focal length over 100 mm is good enough. For headshots like this, a mirror placed alongside the model is useful, for a quick check on expression, hair and make up. Prop the mirror up so that the model can see the reflection without a turn of the head. A few fashion photographers use a posing mirror like this out of doors. Fixed to the top of a lighting stand, it is placed next to the model, just out of shot.

If any pose feels unnatural for the model, it is unlikely that it will look good on film, so, in general, use more relaxed postures in which the model feels comfortable and confident. If someone says 'Don't shoot from that side, my other side is better' or 'I never sit like this, I'll look silly', they are probably right, and you should try something else.

Stepping out
Action gives life to pictures—ask the model to walk towards you, preset the focus and release the shutter as soon as the model is sharp

Simulated breeze
Wind-blown hair looks attractive in studio shots. Set the model's hair in motion with a piece of card, electric fan or hair dryer

After the session

It is a matter of common politeness to show the pictures you shoot to the model, unless you are paying the full professional rate—which is considerable. If the model was unpaid, then a set of prints would probably be very welcome. If your pictures are good enough, you may be able to get a steady flow of willing sitters this way, because professional photographers charge high fees for producing a folio of prints for an aspiring model—this should be a fair reward for your model's time and effort.

There is no real secret to working successfully with a model, more than anything it is a question of experience. As you begin to photograph models more and more, your confidence will grow—the results should show in your gradually improving photographs.

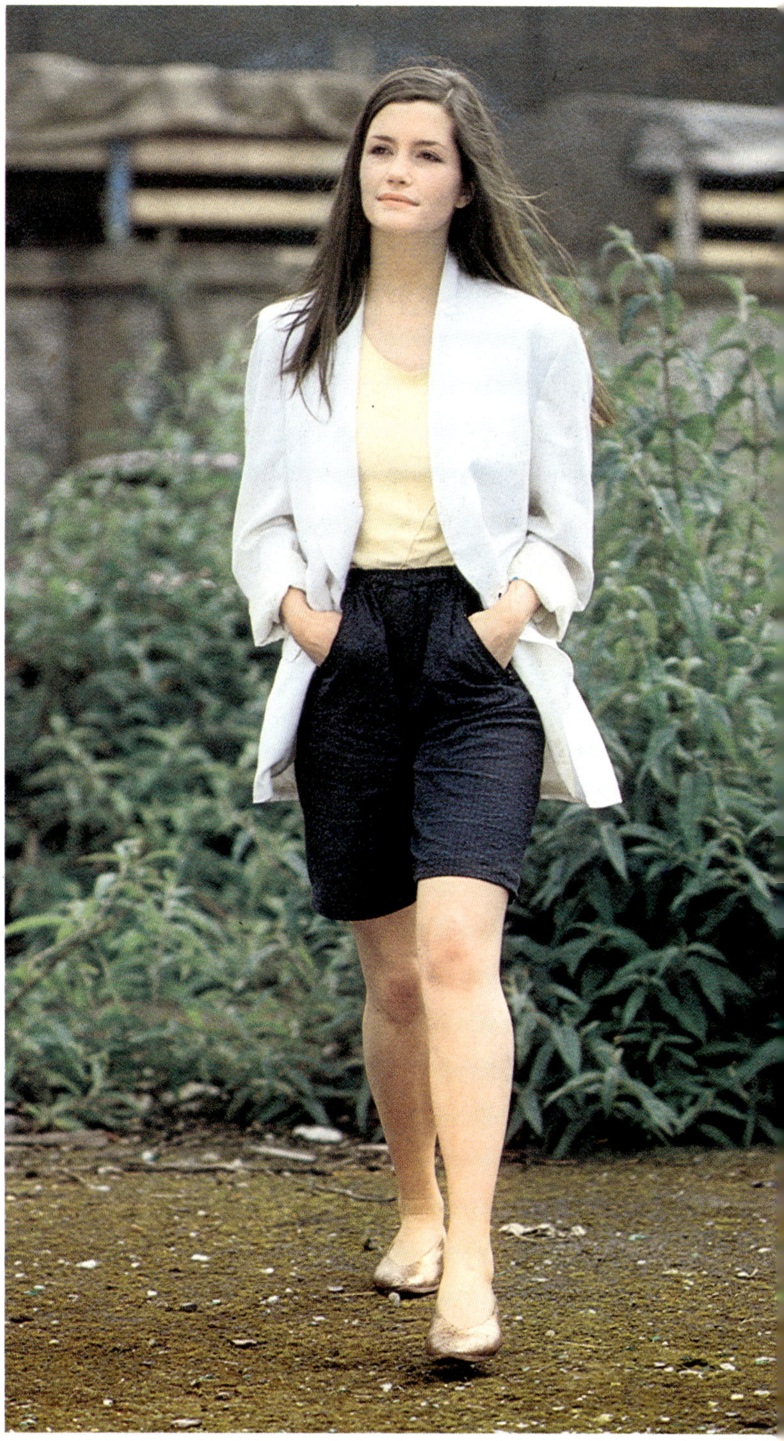

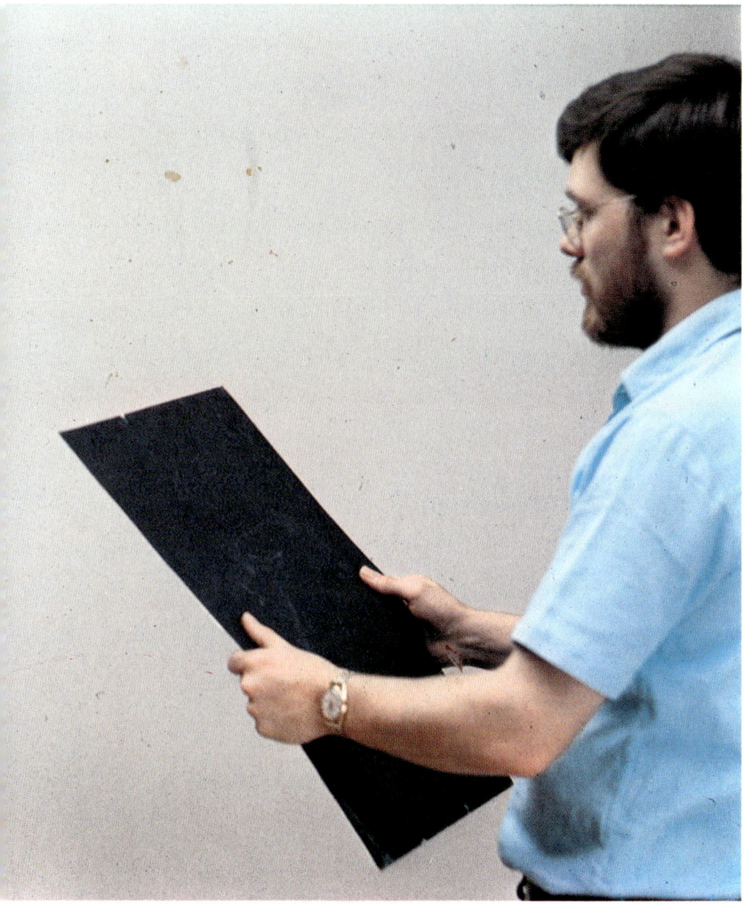

Posing a model

Pictures of people are often described as being 'casual' or 'posed'—usually meaning that subjects look as if they have been caught either quite by chance and therefore look natural, or they appear to be unnaturally stiff and formal. But while casual shots frequently make good pictures, most posed amateur shots do not. This, though, need not be the case—as has often been shown by the great portrait photographers past and present. Few people would say that Snowdon's portraits look posed, despite this being the case. Put simply, such pictures are the result of skilful direction in front of the camera as well as behind it.

Indeed, being able to pose a subject well is an invaluable technique that can give you much greater control over your portrait shots generally and lift your pictures out of the ordinary.

Head and shoulders

In a portrait session, the pose must depend upon what you are trying to achieve. Ask yourself, 'What aspect of this person's character or appearance am I trying to emphasize?'. If your aim is to flatter, then your approach, and your model's pose, must be quite different from a session where your aim is to produce a 'character' picture.

These considerations are especially important with head and shoulders portraits, where attention is principally drawn to the face. A person with a prominent nose might not be pleased with a profile shot—though for a character portrait, the profile might be most appropriate.

Generally, three-quarter face view is the most pleasing for portraits, and this provides, at least, a starting point. Pose the model so that the head can be comfortably turned towards the camera, and the eyes can look directly and easily into the lens. This usually means that the model's shoulders should be angled slightly away from the camera.

For most head and shoulders portraits, it is best to sit models down. This not only helps to make them more comfortable and relaxed—and so less self-conscious—but it also allows you to shoot easily from a variety of angles. In particular, you can shoot from slightly above the subjects' eye level—a viewpoint that is normally very flattering. Use a chair which enables the model to move easily into a variety of poses, but which does not dominate the picture.

A very effective way of using a chair is to get the model to lean into the picture, perhaps sitting sideways on a low-backed chair, and leaning forward, using their arms and hands as a support on the chair back. This has the added advantage that the hands and forearms can be used as elements to strengthen the composition.

A danger of this pose, however, is that the model can easily take on a round shouldered appearance—this can be avoided by making sure that your model's back is kept straight, and that he or she does not lean too far forward over the back of the chair.

It is important not to forget hands and arms in your pose. If you decide to include them in the picture, they must be arranged to contribute positively to the composition. Otherwise, they may simply look ugly. The backs of the hands, in particular, are rather featureless and with the palms away from the camera fingers often seem to hang like bunches of bananas. Use the hands to help create mood, or emphasize the subject's expression and character—look out for natural gestures while shooting and talking to your subject, and try to incorporate these into the pose.

You can sometimes add life to a head and shoulders portrait by seating your model so that their shoulders are turned away from the camera, even with

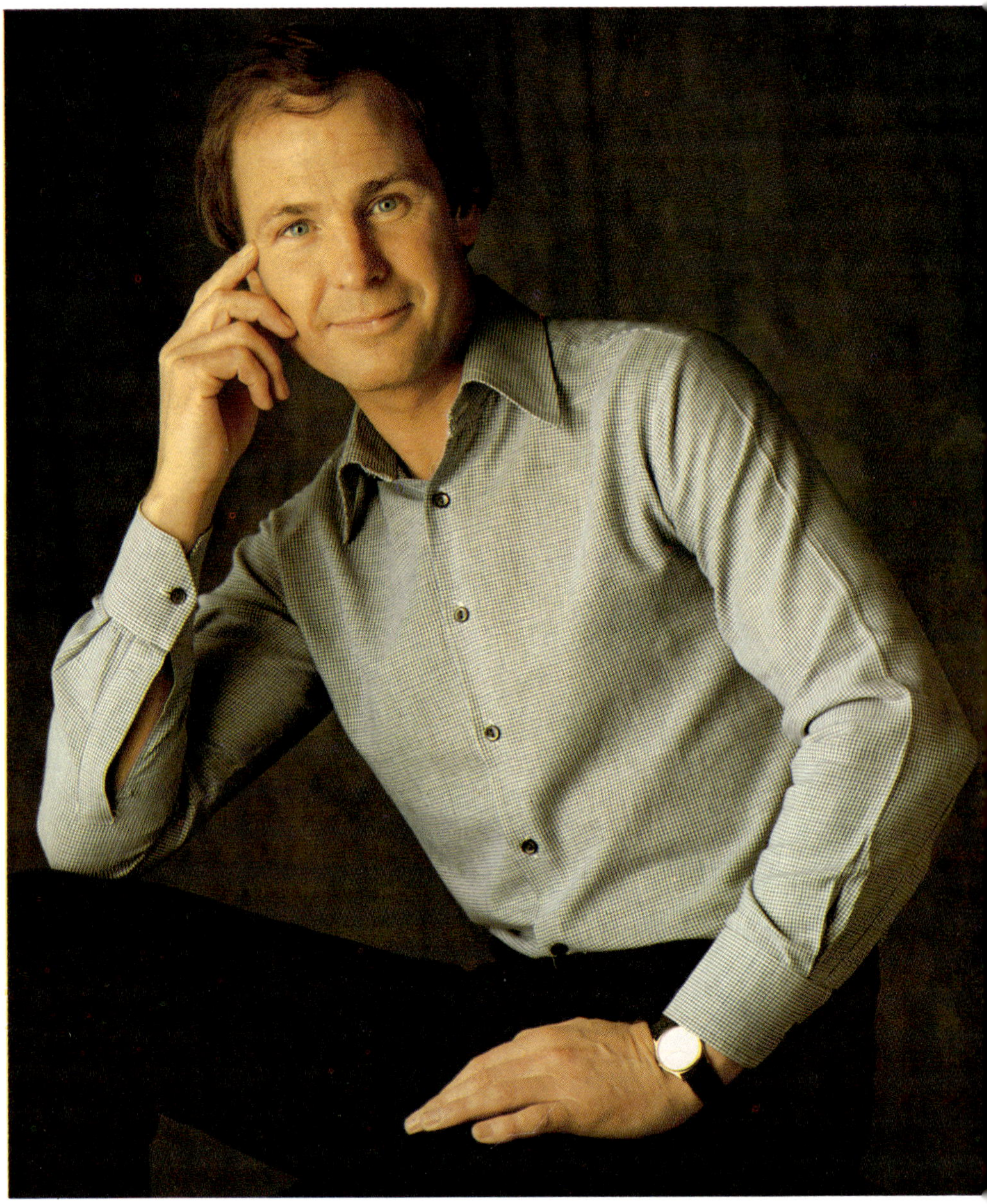

Careful composition *The key to a good portrait is a pose that looks relaxed and natural—a chair often helps*

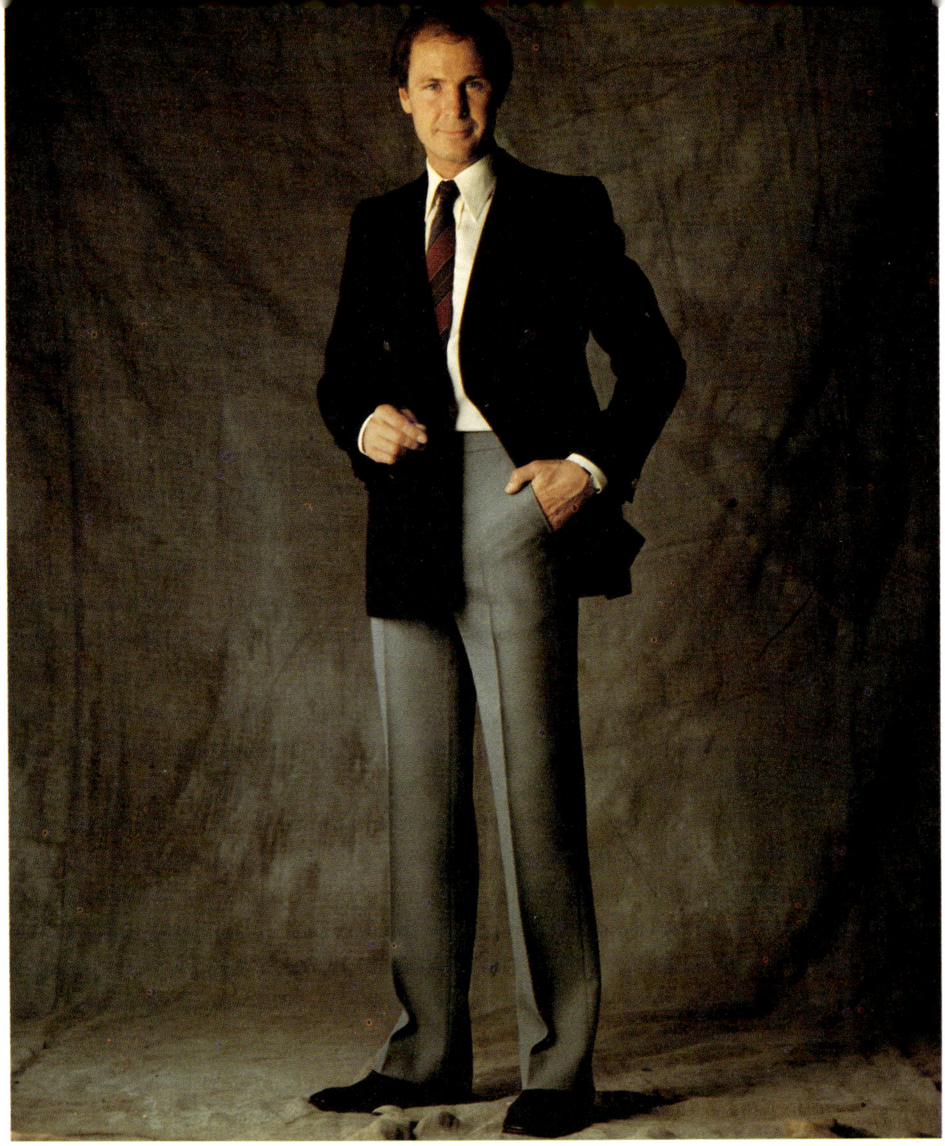

the back slightly towards the lens. Ask them to turn their head back round towards the camera just as the picture is taken, but first make sure that the pose does not create unsightly neck creases.

Half-length portraits

For half- and three-quarter length portraits, a slightly different approach is called for. It is inevitable, for instance, that the model's hands and arms will play an even greater role in shaping the appearance of the final image. A chair again makes a useful prop but may, without care, intrude—if the model leans forward across the chair back, the chair may dominate the picture. Nevertheless a chair can be used in many other ways.

For example, sitting on a chair or stool with the knees drawn up and arms resting on the knees can be a very effective pose for an informal shot. It sometimes helps to provide a box or a stack of books slightly lower for the models to rest their feet on. Arms clasped around a raised knee can also look very natural and informal.

The key to informal poses like this is to give the model something plausible and believable to do in front of the camera. Nothing looks worse than a rigid unnatural pose where the photographer has obviously just said to the model 'do this'. There are many ways of avoiding such a problem—for example, by making sure that the model's hands are fully occupied with maintaining a particular pose. Anybody sitting on a swing, a five-bar gate, or on the edge of a table naturally reaches out to grasp something which will keep them steady, and this produces a strong, energetic composition that can hold a picture together.

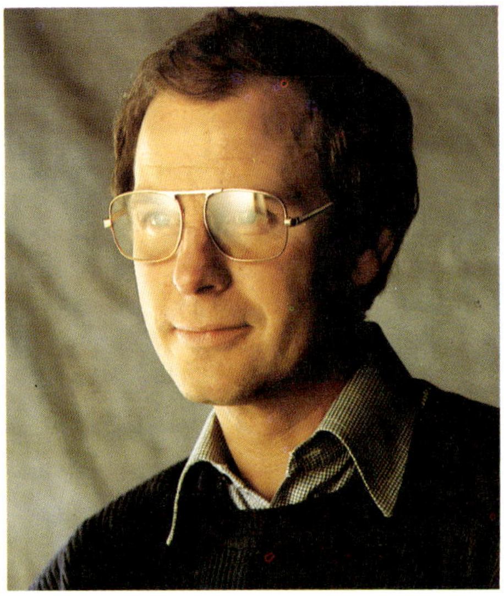

Avoiding reflections *If your sitter wears glasses, you must take special care to avoid reflections of the lights or the sky. This is made much easier if there is a dark surface towards which the sitter can turn his or her head*

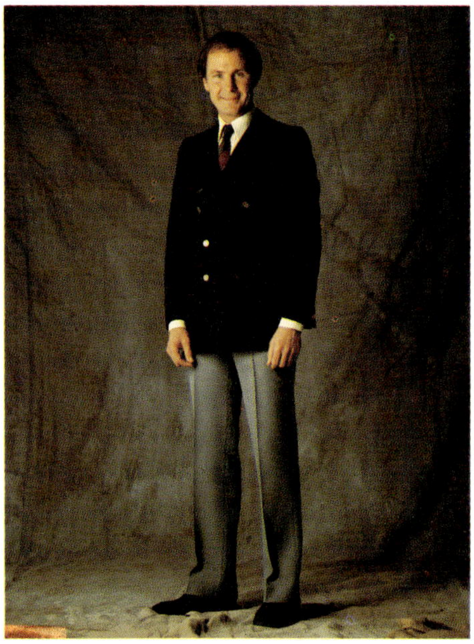

Standing still *Even if your model is perfectly at ease, a standing pose can still present problems. Try to avoid poses where the hands hang limply at the model's sides, as this usually results in stiff, awkward pictures*

Standing poses

Perhaps the most difficult pose, particularly for an inexperienced or self-conscious model, is a freestanding one. Most people feel awkward when asked to stand still for the camera, and the problem is even greater when there are no supports or props to take hold of. Much of the skill of the wedding photographer, for example, is in helping the guests to overcome this problem, although the task is much easier when two or more people are being photographed together.

A good basic technique for a full length standing pose is to ask your model to take a small pace at an angle of

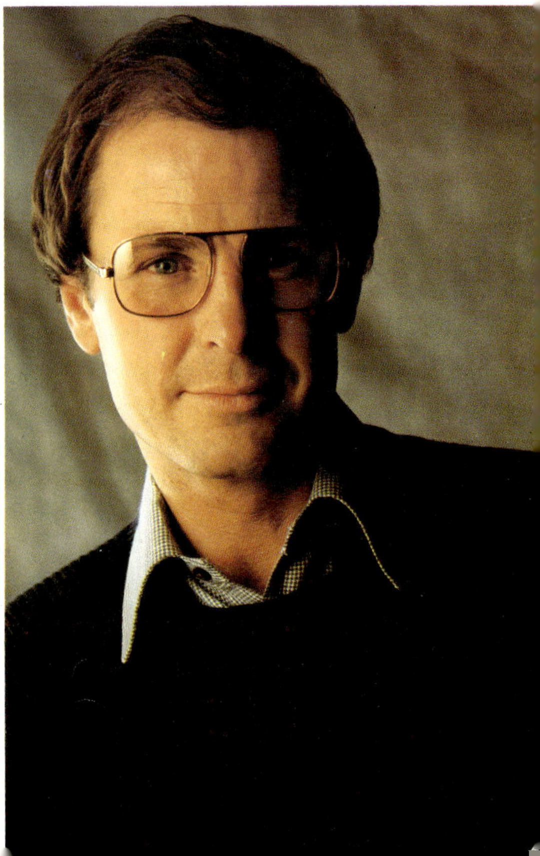

45° to the camera, with his or her weight predominantly on the forward foot. It also helps if the model twists the torso slightly towards the camera, adding movement and life to the picture.

Try to avoid arms hanging loosely—find some pretext for bending one or both arms, with the elbow away from the body, A man, for example, can simply put his hands in his trouser pockets, and a woman can place a hand on her hip or thigh or clasp her hands together at waist level.

If possible, try and get your model to adopt the pose you want by subtle suggestion, rather than by precise direction. If your model cannot readily adopt a certain pose, the pictures are almost certain to look self-conscious and awkward. Good fashion photographs are worth studying for ideas of how a model can look graceful and relaxed when just standing still. In most cases you will find that, although quite static, the model and photographer have managed to introduce a feeling of movement into the picture.

The range of possibilities with a standing pose can be far more varied with nude and glamour pictures—the position and angles of the limbs can be exaggerated, to make an even more dynamic pose. The model's back can be arched and stretched, or the arms raised above the head and clasped behind it, or perhaps entwined in the hair. All these poses help to emphasize the shape and curves of the body, and if done with skill and panache, they can produce very attractive pictures. If the same poses are adopted for conventional photographs, however, they can often look ridiculous.

The freestanding pose is probably more effective with glamour pictures than with any other type, but even so, the addition of props and supports greatly increases the number of possibilities. Most professional photographers who specialize in studio shots of girls have an assosrtment of useful items on hand for

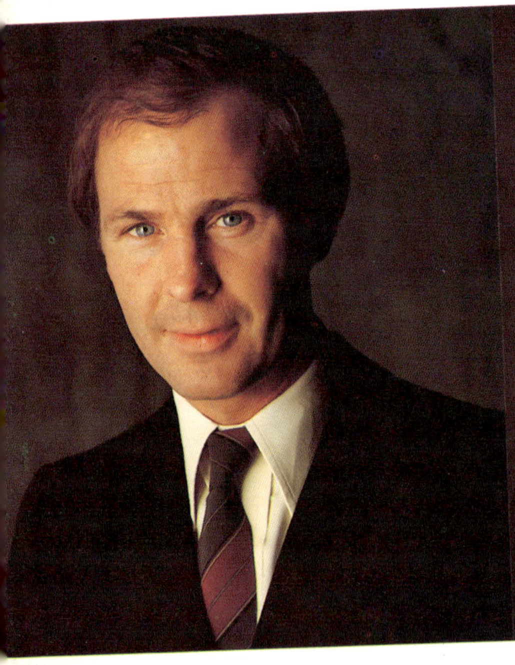

Awkward pose *If your sitter feels uncomfortable, this will inevitably come across in your photographs*

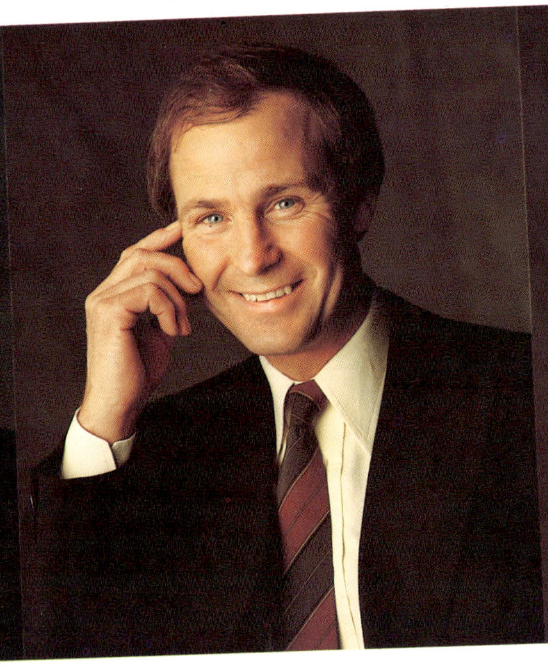

Hands for expression *Take advantage of natural gestures, and try to incorporate them into your pictures*

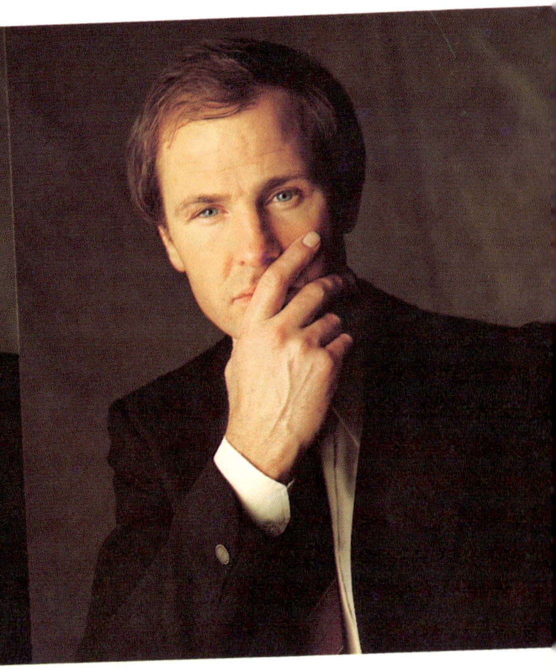

Clumsy fingers *Do not overdo it—hands can sometimes be a distraction, and often come out blank and featureless*

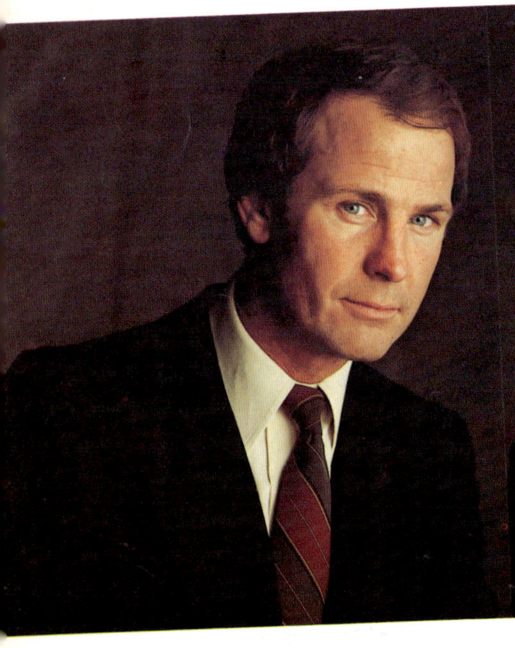

Shifty look *A sidelong glance can occasionally be effective, but here it merely makes the model look shifty*

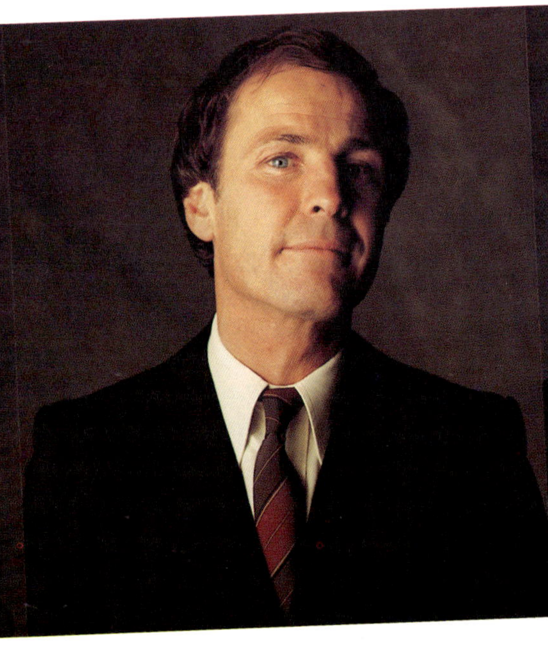

Long neck *Unless you are aiming for a very dramatic picture, try to conceal a model's physical peculiarities*

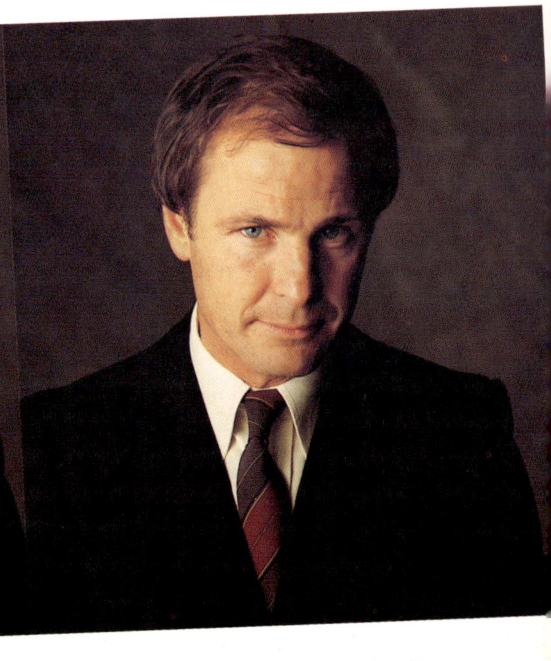

Prominent forehead *If a male sitter has receding or thinning hair, this is emphasized when he looks downwards*

this purpose: a wicker chair to lean against, or a parasol to occupy a model's hands. These and other props are frequently used to aid both the model's pose and the composition of a full length picture.

Besides the more agile standing poses, there are others which would look absurd for conventional portraits, but which are quite acceptable if the model is naked. Poses on the floor are a good example—they are not usually practical for ordinary pictures, unless a very high viewpoint is required, but for glamour photographs or abstract nudes, the floor offers the model greater freedom of movement. The variety of angles and positions for the limbs can be much greater than when sitting or standing, and poses on the floor are particularly suitable where a natural pose is not essential—the model can tense and stretch the body to emphasize lines, shapes and contours.

In addition to greater freedom of movement, posing on the floor also allows more varied camera and lighting angles, which can be an advantage in this kind of picture—it is a simple matter, for example, to shoot from a bird's eye viewpoint when your model is posed on the floor.

Using the setting

For a studio session a roll of paper provides a simple but effective background. For location shots, you must consider the background carefully. The location itself often suggests a suitable pose. An indoor portrait, for example, can make use of furnishings and decor as aids to the model's pose, and as elements of the composition. A fur rug may suggest a languorous reclining pose for a glamour shot. For a formal portrait, you could use a polished desk, with the subject seated, arms folded, or elbows propped in an angular, resolute manner.

If, however, in posing your model you take your cue from the surroundings, always remember that these must not intrude or dominate in the final image.

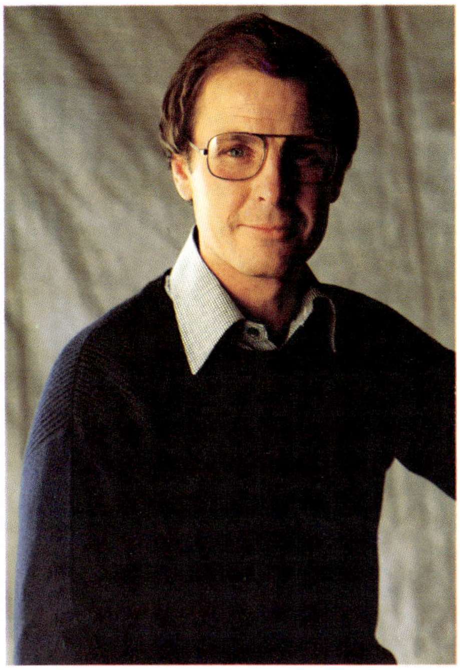

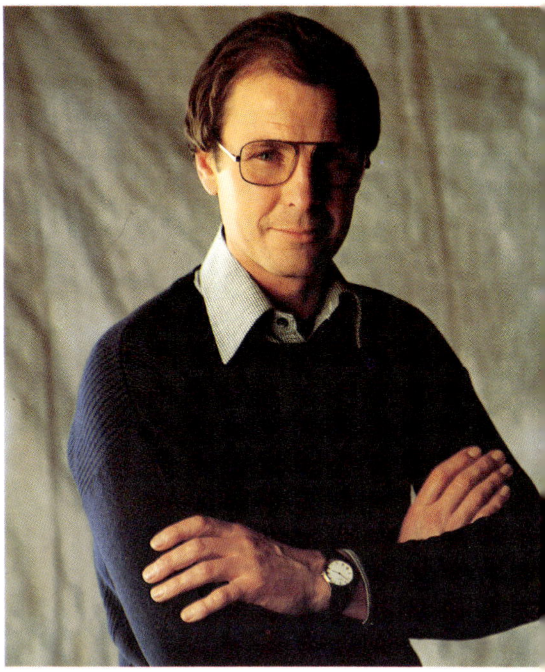

Using the frame *A pose should always be related to the edges of the picture. If you are conscious of the frame edges, you can use them to improve the composition, but carelessness can lead to arms and legs being chopped off*

The human subjects should remain the centre of interest, and all other elements of the picture must play a supporting role—so make sure that the scenery does not upstage the model, perhaps by throwing it out of focus.

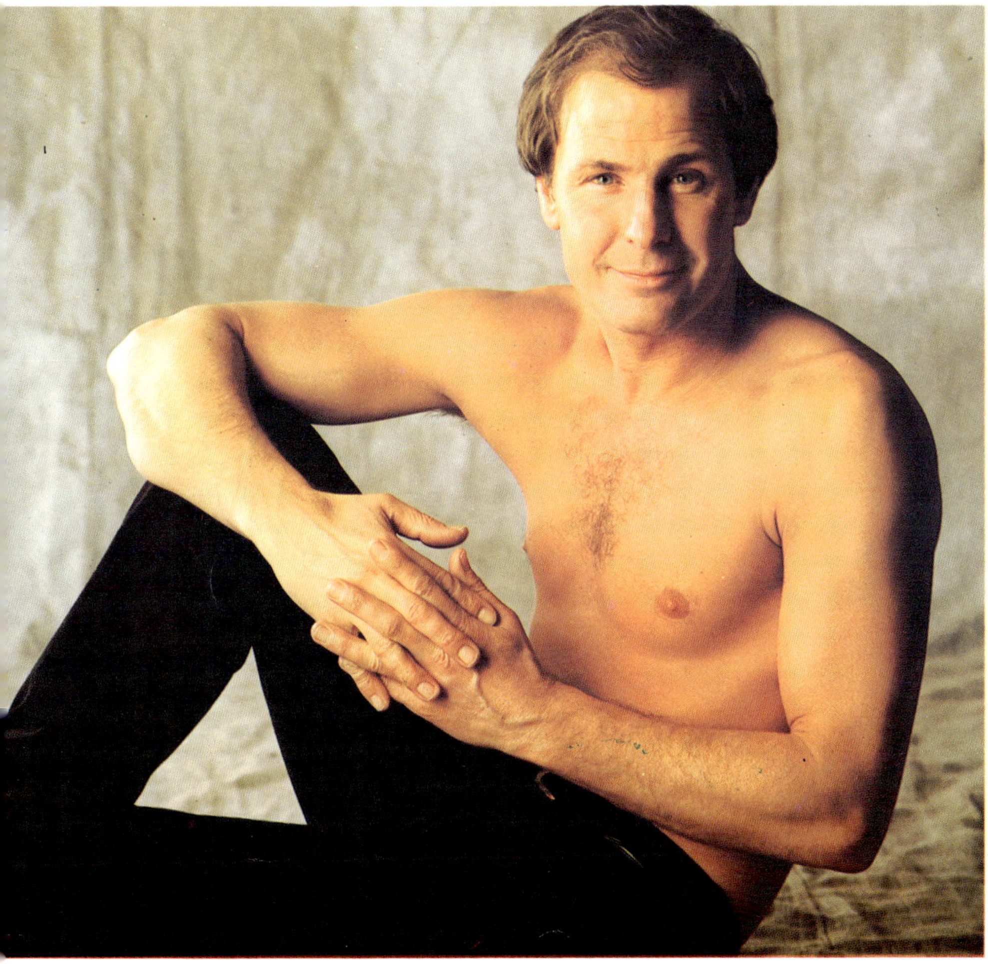

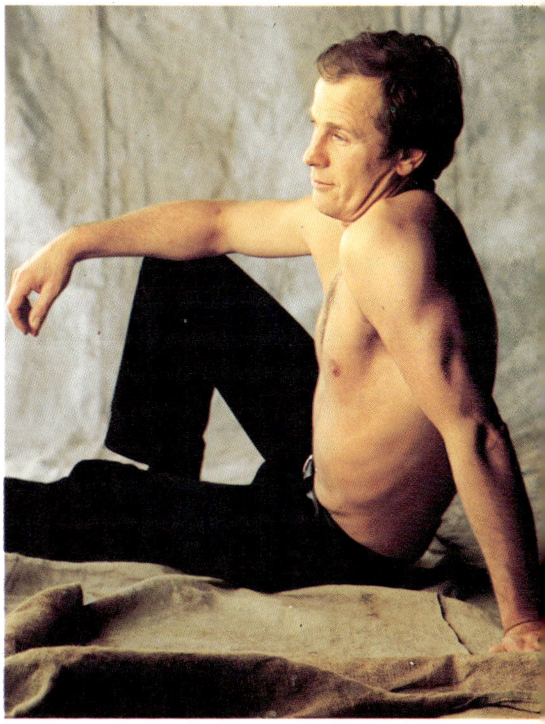

Macho model *Poses on the floor work best with glamour shots—male or female! The pattern of triangles in this graphic composition (left) give the image strength and holds it together.*

Neck creases *If the model's head is turned at an angle, creases in the neck can mar an otherwise good pose*

CHAPTER 19
STUDIO TECHNIQUES
Front and back projection

You do not need to go to the Caribbean to shoot a friend on a tropical beach or to France to picture a bottle of Bordeaux in an 'authentic' setting. You can put all kinds of backgrounds, exotic and mundane, in your pictures without moving from your studio simply by projecting a slide of the scene on to a screen behind the subject.

Slides can be projected either from behind the screen (back projection) or from in front, with the projector close to the camera (front projection). Although you can buy sophisticated—and expensive—equipment designed especially for background projection, you can achieve quite acceptable results using just a normal slide projector.

Most projection techniques are straightforward and the problems occur more in the choice of suitable slides, equipment and the lighting arrangement rather than in taking the shot. Although there are a number of different approaches, certain principles of projection apply to all the methods.

Projection principles

When using either back projection or front projection, it is important to prevent light from the studio lamps falling on to the screen or projection surface. Light spillage of this kind reduces the contrast and colour saturation of the background image. Barn doors, snoots and other masks should be used on the lights to direct the light on to the subject while shielding the screen.

Unless you are using an abstract or obviously non-realistic background it is also important to match the direction and quality of the lighting on the subject with that of the background slide. This may mean using colour balancing filters on the projector to match the colour of the studio lighting.

Matching the lighting in the studio with the lighting in the slide can often be very difficult, particularly if the lighting in the slide is strongly directional. If the scene in the slide is lit by strong sunlight, you may find it impossible to match the angle and intensity in the studio without spilling light onto the projection screen. For this reason, it is usually better to choose a slide in which the lighting is fairly diffuse. With soft lighting, the direction of the light source is much less obvious, and it is much easier to disguise any differences.

For the same reason, it is usually easier to work with slides in which the colours are fairly muted. People expect background colours to be less bright anyway, and it is far easier achieving a match with soft colours than with strong.

Moonlit sky *Front and back projection are most useful for producing surreal or slightly abstract pictures*

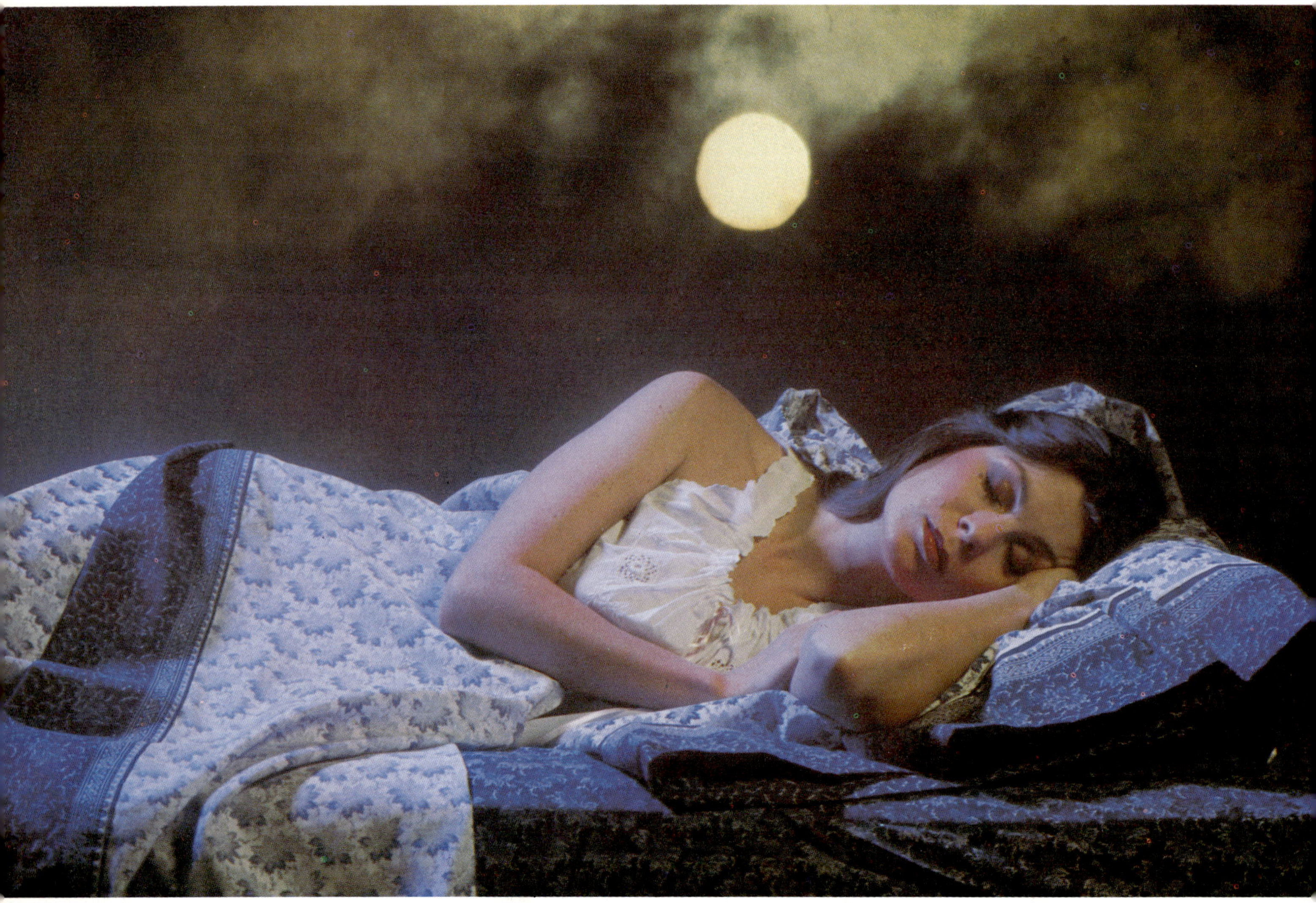

Perspectives in both the subject and screen image must also match. This is especially important if perspective lines are continued or repeated in the background. A shot looking down on a model posed in front of a picture of a street scene shot from ground level would not look right.

Scale also plays an important part here, and you must adjust the image until it is precisely the right size for the subject. If your projector has a zoom lens, you can simply zoom in or out to achieve the right scale. Otherwise, you must move either the projector, the screen or the subject.

Background shots taken on wide angle lenses show an exaggerated distortion toward the sides, especially of strong vertical lines like the edges of buildings. This can be used creatively, but for most applications the background should be distortion free. Ideally, the camera lens should have an angle of view as close to that of the background slide as possible. In fact, the foreshortening effect of a longer than normal lens is often preferred, not only for a tighter image but also because the depth of field is shallower and the inevitable separation of foreground and background looks more natural and not so contrived.

If the background is intended to be far distant, too much depth of field in the slide may ruin the effect—it is sometimes a good idea to have the background out of focus. Do not use a slide with the foreground out of focus or the composite will have two points of focus. The slides used should also be in glass mounts to prevent them from buckling. It is also a good idea to use the largest format possible so that the effect is not ruined by grain—6 × 6 cm slides are ideal.

Projection techniques can be used to recreate the view through a window or door in an interior shot. In this case, the perfect match between the projected image and the main subject is not so important. The studio lighting on the subject does not have to match with the daylight in the slide, for instance, and you can use a wider angle lens. But, depending on the brightness of the exterior and the direction of the sunlight, it may be necessary to backlight the subject to simulate the light coming through the window.

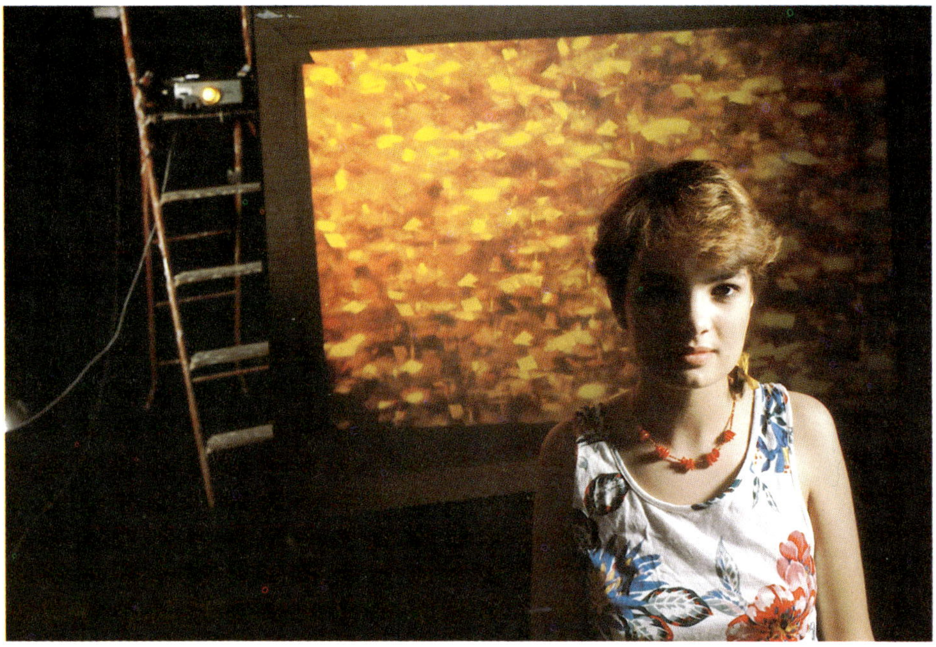

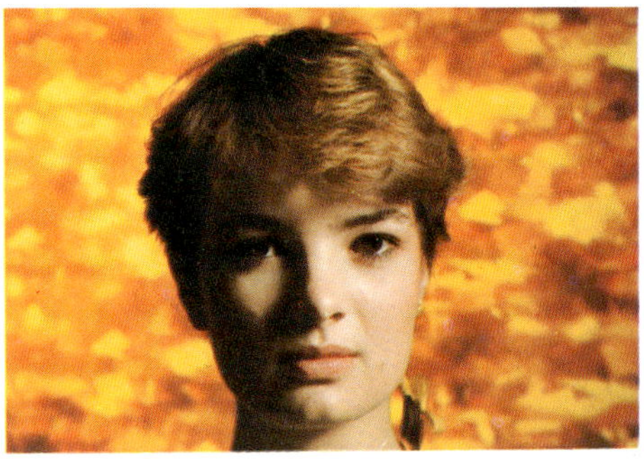

Back projection *The shots above show a basic set-up—using a standard projector and a translucent screen—and the type of result you can easily obtain*

Combined images *The small shots below show the components which are combined to form the main picture. Note how grey the screen is without an image on it*

Front projection

The simplest and cheapest technique is front projection using a standard slide projector to throw an image on to a white surface, such as background paper. The subject is placed in front of this image and lit separately using tungsten or quartz lights, to match the light source of

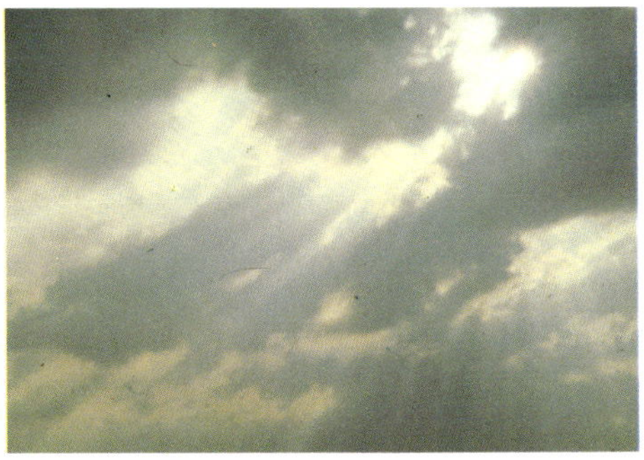

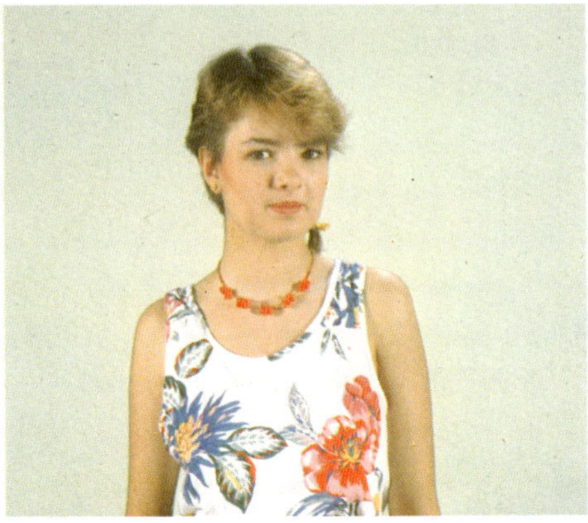

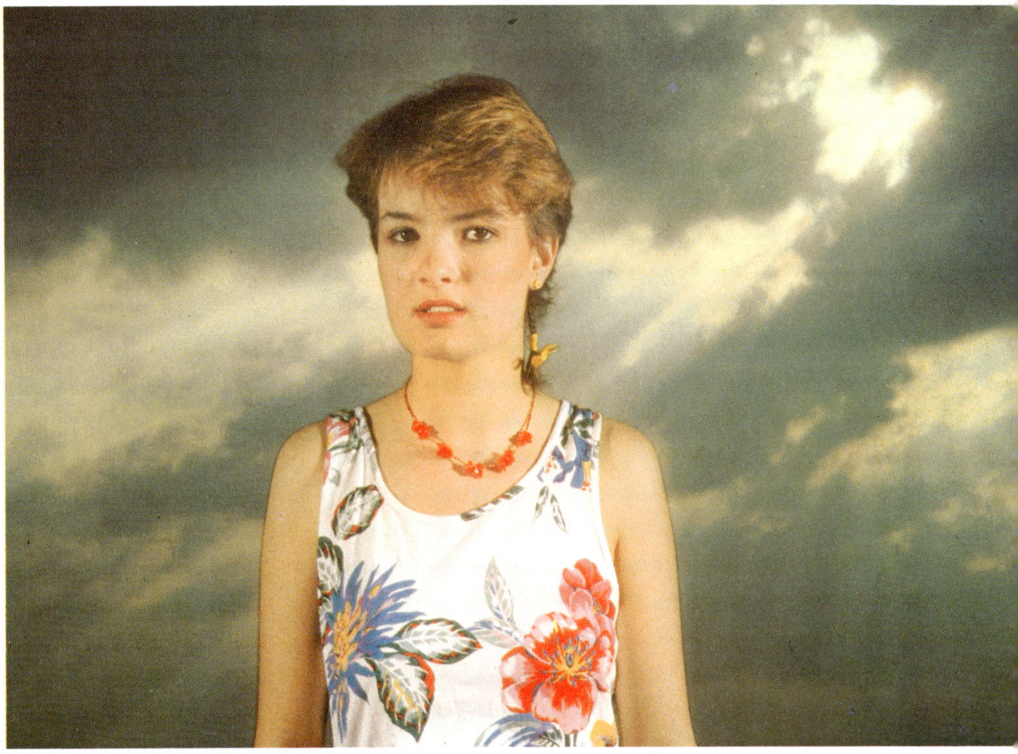

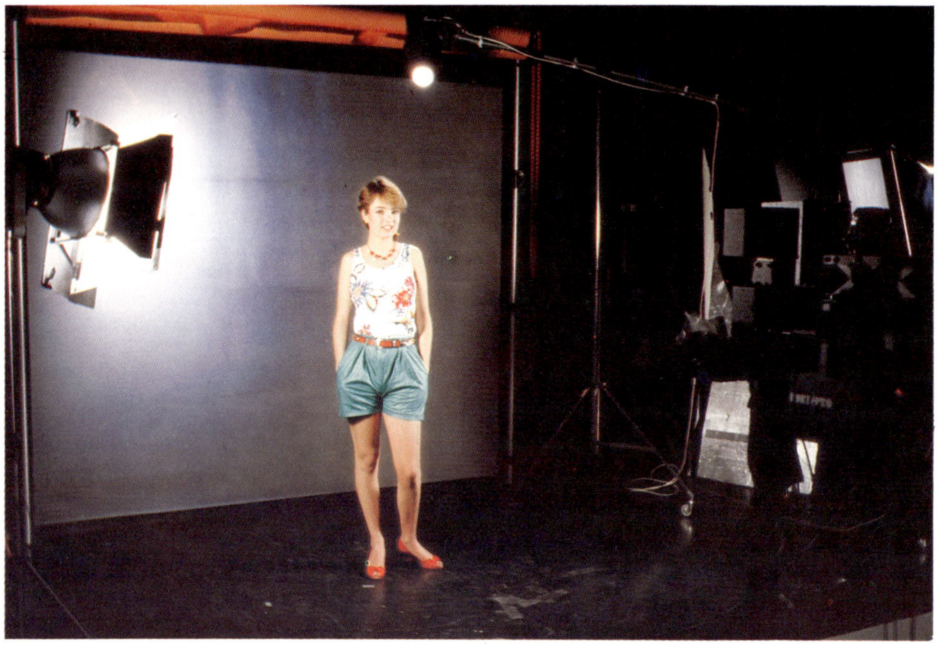

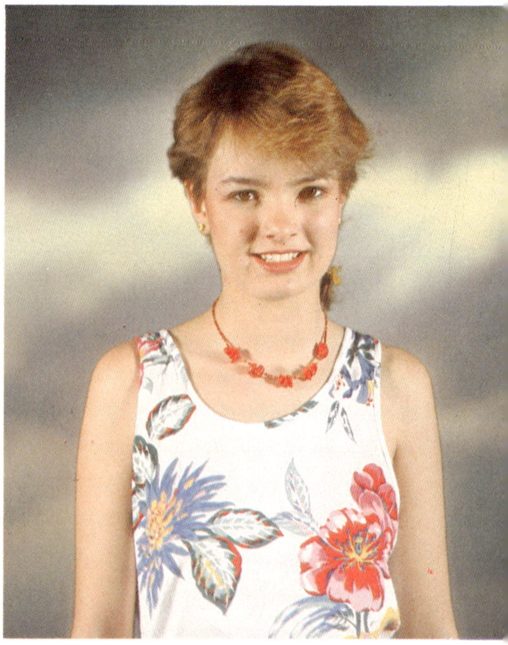

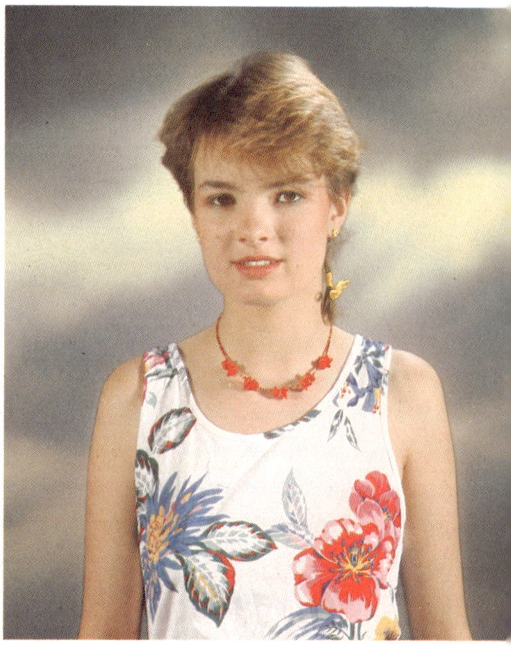

Lighting set-up *Note how the lights in the front projection set-up above are positioned and shielded to avoid light reaching the screen. Backlighting is used (bottom) to remove a black line on the shoulder (top) caused by fringing*

the projector. You should use artificial light film or daylight film with suitable filtration.

The projector must be set up slightly to one side so that it projects *behind* the subject, otherwise the image will show up on the subject as well. This causes some distortion of the image, and so the original picture must be chosen with this in mind. Either use a picture which does not suffer when distorted slightly, such as a landscape, or use the distortion to create interesting effects. Unless you want abstract effects, make the angle between the camera and the projector as small as possible, not only to minimize distortions, but to avoid problems with focusing the projector lens.

If you take background shots specifically for this type of projection, you can try shooting scenes with at least one dark area. With the projector near the camera, you can project the slide directly on to the screen and the subject, with the latter placed so that it is in the dark area of the image. However, although simple, this approach does tend to be rather limiting.

A much more sophisticated and versatile system uses a special projector and screen. This is the type of front projection used by professionals. The projector, which is usually set pointing vertically upwards, throws the image on to a semi-silvered mirror set at 45° in front of the camera lens. This reflects it on to the screen and subject. The camera 'sees' through the mirror, so that the projector beam and camera view are on exactly the same axis and the shadows cast by the subject are directly behind it and out of view.

The screen used with this set-up is a beaded, high gain type which has a very high reflectance and a narrow reflectance angle. This means that the image on the screen is very bright—much brighter than the image falling on the subject. When the film is exposed for the screen, the image on the subject is very underexposed so that very little of it can be seen. Furthermore, when the subject is lit separately, all remaining traces of the projected image are washed out.

Professional units such as the Bowens Front/Pro, use a flash head in the projector to make the exposure, though a modelling light is included for viewing. This means that you can use studio flash units to light the subject. These lights must be kept out of the reflective area of the screen which is roughly 20° to 30° each side of the camera/projector axis, depending on the particular screen.

Although these units are very expensive (the screens alone can cost as much as a roll film SLR), it is possible to hire them, and some studios offer them as additional facilities. The better models have the projector, mirror (or beam-splitter) and camera mount contained in the same unit. This is important as the camera lens and projector beam must be accurately aligned. If they are not the result is a black line, known as *fringing,* round the subject caused by shadows, and producing a 'cardboard cut-out' effect. Front projection systems which have the various components separate can take some time to set up, and accurate alignment is often difficult.

Once the units are set up, they are very easy to use. But to get the best out of them there are a few techniques you can use. For example, it is a good idea to have your subject between one and two metres from the screen. This gives enough separation to allow you to light the subject without spillage on to the screen, but without causing depth of field problems.

Even with properly aligned units, some fringing may occur. To overcome this you should use some backlighting, and possibly some toplighting too. This lightens the edges of the subject, and with some surfaces, such as pale materials or skin, slight flaring often occurs, which improves the image.

Beware of using a camera angle and composition which includes the feet of a standing person. As there is no shadow coming from the feet, the effect is to make the person look as though he or she is floating.

Back projection

Similar problems can occur with back projection. This is the technique which was widely employed in movie work, and is still sometimes used. The advantage of back projection is that it produces results almost as good as those of sophisticated front projection systems, but using much cheaper equipment. The disadvantage is that you need considerable space behind the screen to give a large enough image. It is sometimes necessary to reflect the projector beam off a 45° mirror, or zig-zag it between several mirrors, to cut down on the required space.

With back projection there is no danger of your subject casting shadows or producing fringing. But it is necessary to choose your screen material very carefully if you are not to create other problems.

A wide variety of screens and other materials can be used, to varying degrees of success. Professional back projection screens, as used for movie work and audio–visual displays, are made of acrylic substrates (or glass) which diffuse light evenly (so preventing 'hot spots') and absorb ambient front light. They are supplied in neutral grey and white, as well as a range of tints, and are designed for daylight use. However, the areas behind the screen must be dark if you are to get a bright, detailed and reasonably contrasty image.

As with all non-rigid screens, the material should be stretched tight so that there are no wrinkles, which would otherwise show in the final picture. For this reason, the larger screens are laced on to a frame like a trampoline. If a full-length studio shot is set up, the floor in front of the screen may have to be built up to hide the frame.

Screens of this type can be expensive, but there are cheaper alternatives. 3M make a portable *Polacoat* twin screen unit which carries both front and rear projection screens snapped into a light-weight frame. Table top screens designed for audio–visual displays can be used effectively as backgrounds for small scale still-lifes.

Alternatively, you can make your own screen. Various types of material are available, including a special back projection type, which comes in rolls 1.6 m wide. If a proper screen is not available, sheets of Kodatrace or matt celluloid can be used, as long as they are wrinkle free.

Unfortunately, many materials which might seem suitable for back projection have either a texture or a grain structure. This can show up clearly if the screen is sharply in focus in the final picture. Although it might not matter with abstract backgrounds it makes a realistic effect impossible.

A more difficult problem to overcome is that of hot spots. Proper back projection materials diffuse the light to give even brightness across the whole screen area. Hot spots are reduced by having a thicker screen, but this also cuts down the light level. It is a good idea to experiment with different materials to find the best one for your purposes.

As with the simpler type of front projection, tungsten or quartz lights should be used to light the subject. A few, special back projection systems are available which feature electronic flash sources in the projector. But these are prohibitively expensive for the amateur. Unless you are using a special daylight screen, be careful to shield the screen from the studio lights to prevent a washed-out look. Transparencies taken for back projection should also be of fairly high contrast to compensate for any wash-out remaining. Any type of projector can be used, but space usually dictates a shortish focal length lens, or a mirror system.

Once the equipment is set up, the photography is quite straightforward. Normal metering methods can be used, but for complete control, especially with systems using flash, it is an advantage to have a camera to which a Polaroid back can be fitted. This allows you to check the effect, especially the relative light levels of subject and screen image, before shooting conventional film.

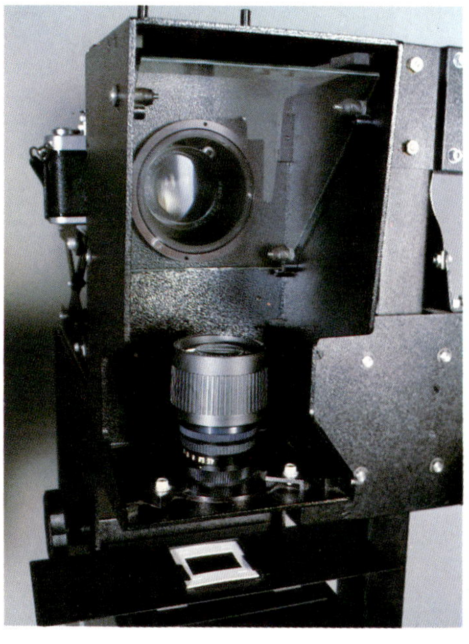

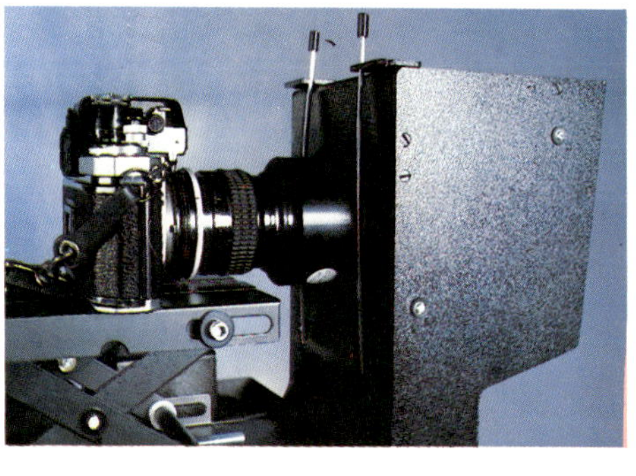

Projection gear
Front projection units (left) use semi-silvered mirrors to throw the image on to the subject. To ensure correct alignment, the camera lens is clamped in place. You can also get good results with simple equipment (right and below). In this case, the image was thrown on to black paper

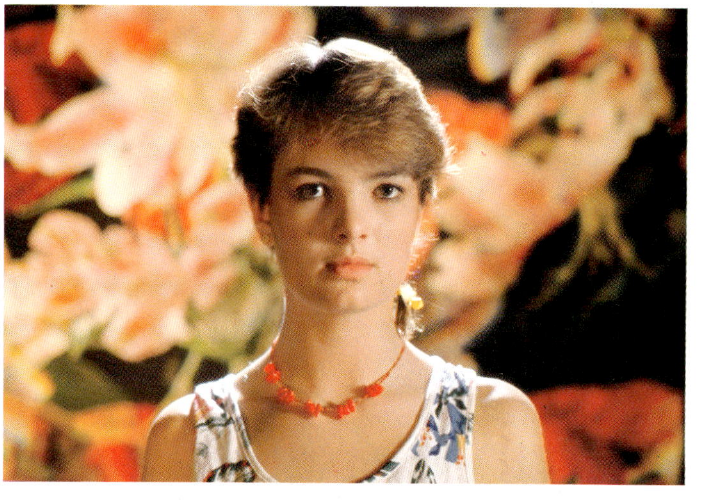

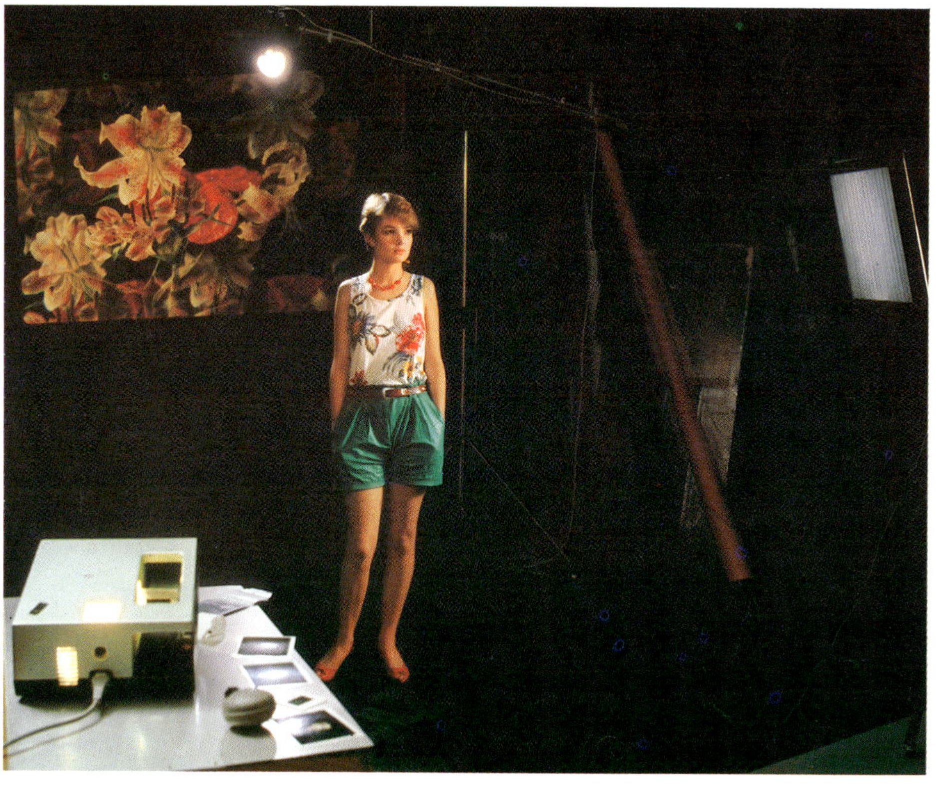

Location studio

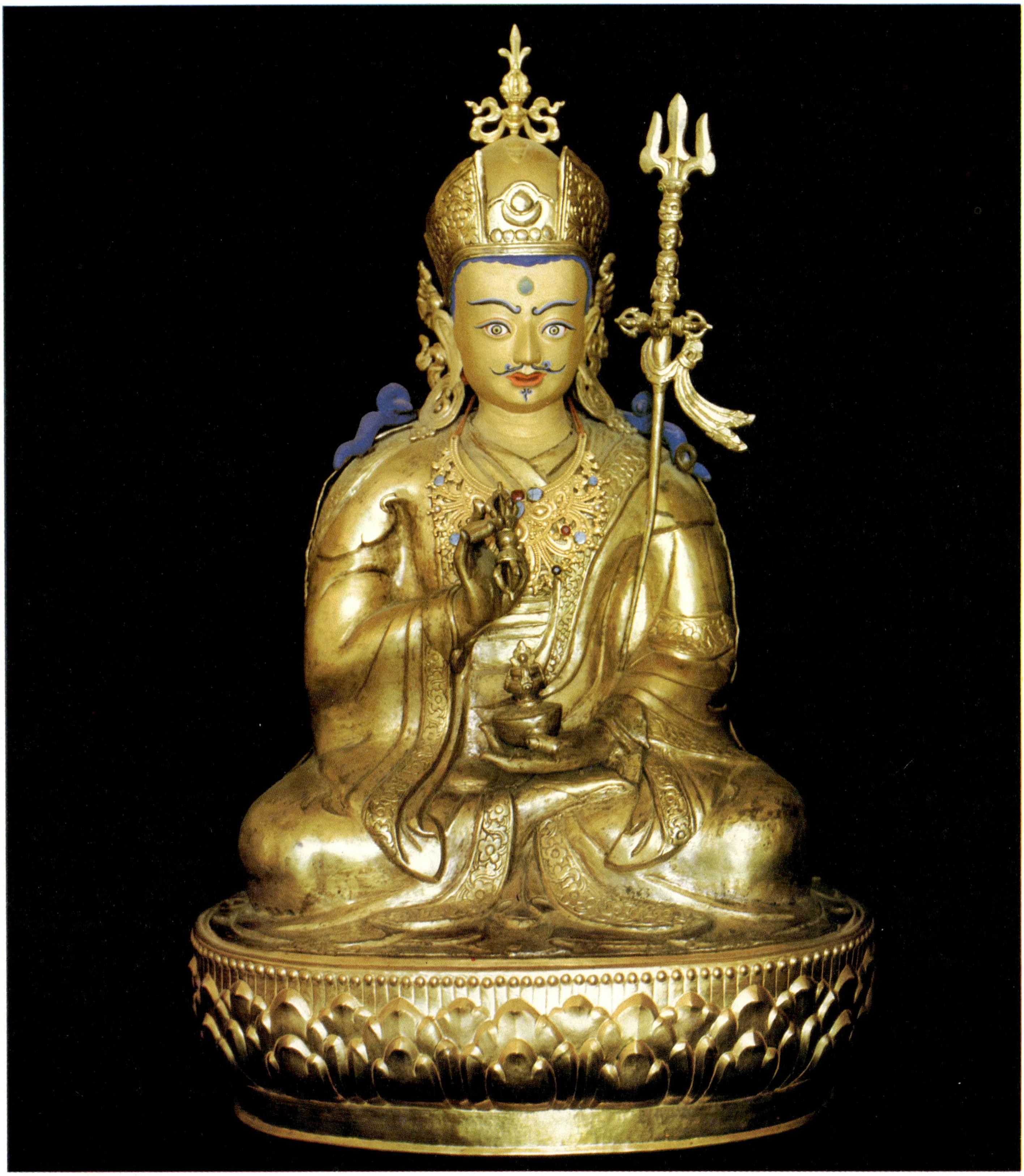

There is usually a distinct difference between a photograph taken in a studio and one taken on location. Both amateurs and professionals regard studio quality as the utmost of which their equipment is capable, but often expect quality to suffer once they are in unfamiliar territory. Yet there are ways of creating studio conditions in even the least promising surroundings.

You might, for example, wish to photograph some interesting object which you discover while on holiday, far from home—a fossil embedded in rocks,

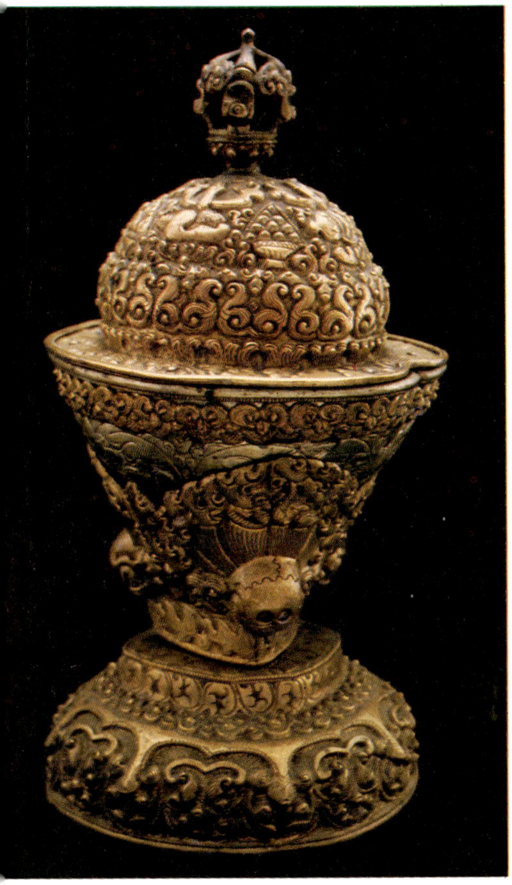

Intense shots *These shots were taken on location in Tibet using tent lighting. The Guru (left) was lit with available window light plus reflectors. The skull bowl (above) suffers from lack of depth of field as small flashguns were used*

a work of art or even an example of local cratsmanship, perhaps. You may be interested in taking photographs of particular objects as part of your hobby, from car badges to antiquities. In each case, the simple snapshot probably will not be adequate, and you will wish that you had better facilities at your disposal.

But if you are prepared to take care over your photography when you are away from home, there is a great deal you can do to improve matters, and even to produce results of studio quality. The main restriction is that you simply cannot carry all the lights and backgrounds that you normally associate with studio work. Even so you can get by with surprisingly little additional load.

The camera and accessories

Although most amateurs automatically expect to use their regular camera, it is worth considering how a professional would approach the problem of taking studio quality pictures on location, maybe in a remote part of the world where service facilities and even simple items are hard or impossible to obtain. The ideal would be a roll film camera with a wide range of facilities, such as camera movements and interchangeable lenses. Some cameras, such as the Linhof Technica 70, offer this. Alternatively, a reliable roll film camera with more restricted facilities, such as a Hasselblad, could be used. If both these were out of the question, a professional might use a top quality 35 mm camera with a range of lenses, including shift and macro lenses.

But whatever the camera, it is important that the shutter should be completely mechanical, using no batteries, or offer manual speeds if the batteries fail. Though batteries are widely available, and you can take spares, they can sometimes let you down at the worst possible moment, and your spares may also turn out to be faulty. Few professionals would feel happy at relying solely on an electronically controlled shutter when at a remote location. Other essentials would be a light meter—again, one using no batteries such as the Weston Master, a full set of filters (see page 246-7) and perhaps a colour temperature meter.

A tripod and cable release are essential. The tripod should be as sturdy as you can bear to carry—a flimsy one is worse than useless.

It is always worth using a viewfinder magnifier when working with 35 mm. This makes focusing much more precise, which is important if you want high quality results.

Backgrounds and lighting

While the equipment you carry must largely depend on what you regularly use and have available, the main problems with attempting studio work on location involve the backgrounds and the lighting.

Large quantities of background paper are obviously not practical, and even small quantities will soon become creased, dirty and useless. Whenever possible, you should use 'natural' backgrounds, and improvise where necessary. This applies particularly to portraits, where it is thoroughly impractical to carry a sufficient area of paper to make any difference. There are, however, two other possibilities.

The first is black velvet. A piece a metre or a metre and a half square will fold down to a very compact bundle, and may be shaken out adequately flat to be used as a backdrop to any local artefacts—pots, knives, small statues, works of art and so on. Because it is such an efficient absorber of light, black velvet simply will not show up in a colour transparency where the subject is correctly exposed. This makes the subject appear to float in space, which can be very effective. The only drawback is that it can become monotonous.

The second possibility is locally obtained fabrics. This is especially true in India, where light cottons in a wide variety of colours are obtainable very cheaply. 'Double width' (two metre) fabric can be used either reasonably smooth, or gathered to give the effect of drapes. Heavier fabrics can be used in the same way as the black velvet to give a little variety.

Unless the background is important, or

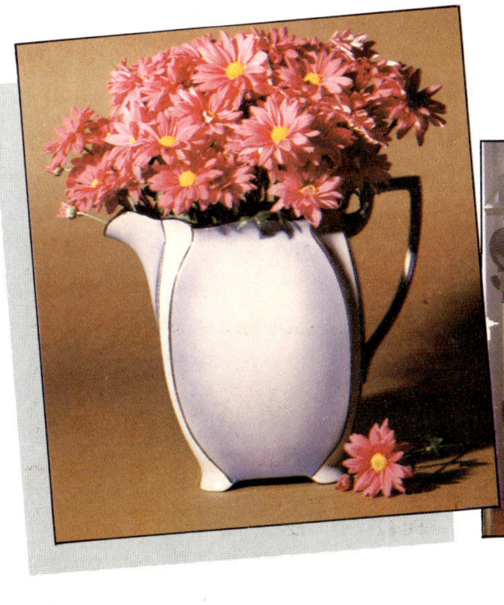

Softer light *Quartz lighting is useful but can give hard shadows (left). Putting a diffuser in front of the lamp (below) gives softer lighting (right)*

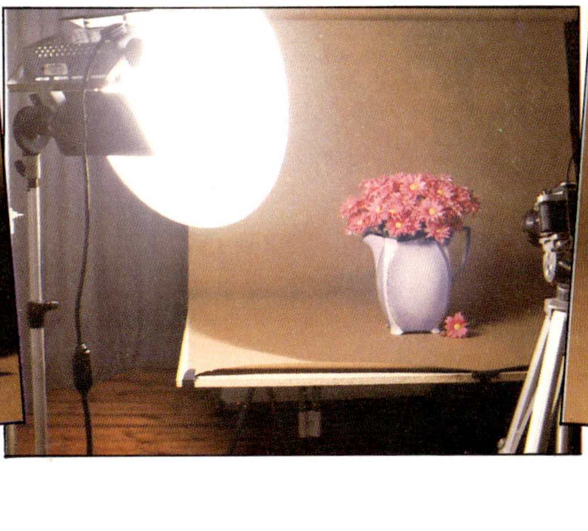

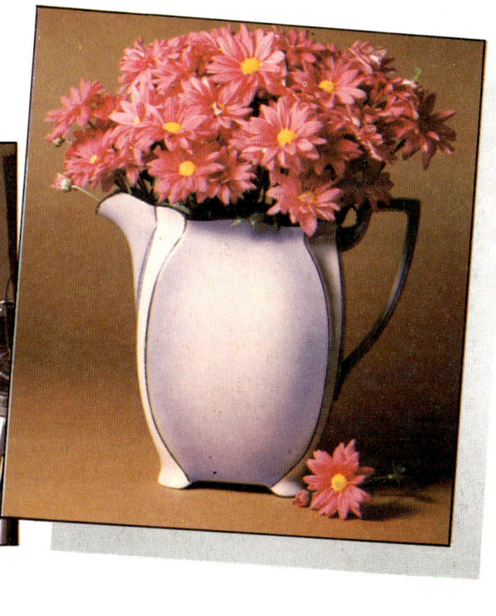

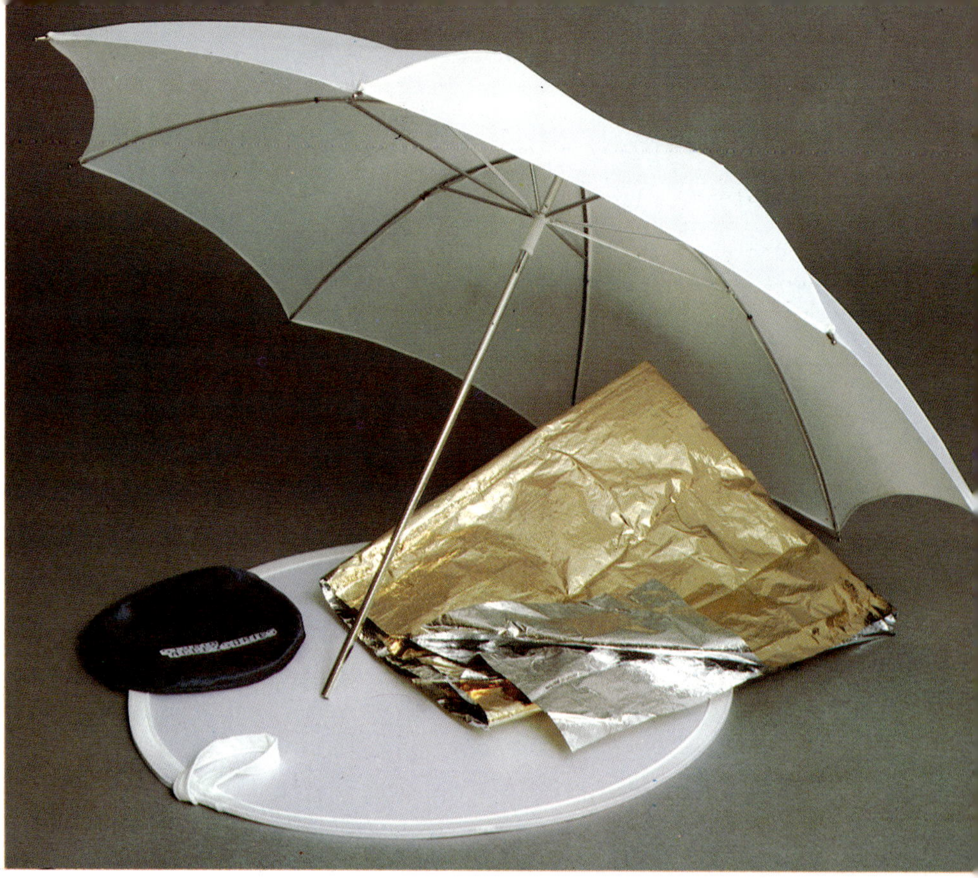

Useful accessories *Above are the best types of reflector—foil, umbrella and Lastolite (which folds to the size of the small blue bag). The bracket (right) allows you to fit a flashgun to a tripod, for easier and more versatile lighting*

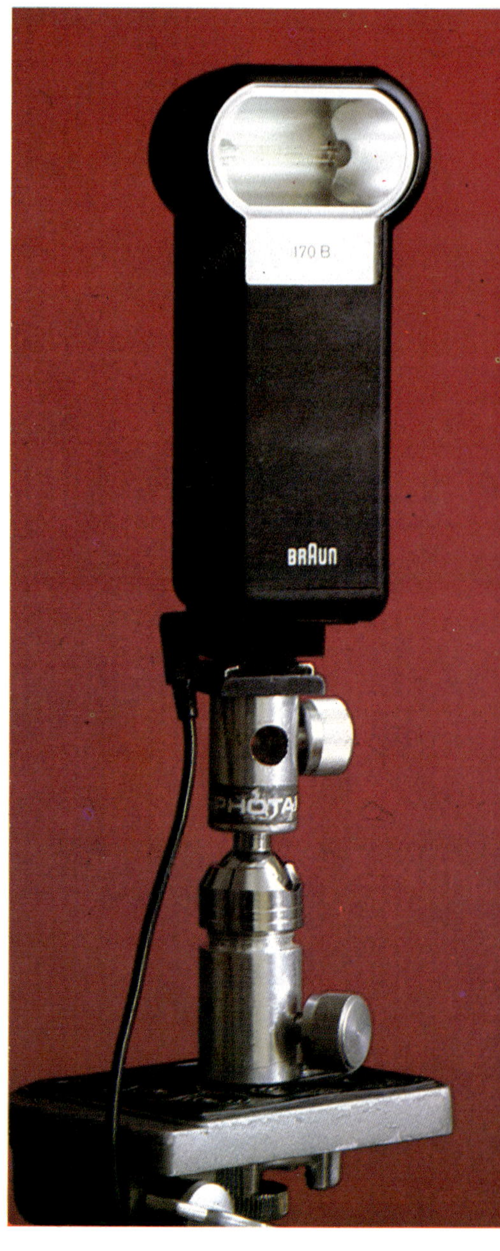

unless the subject is actually resting on it, the best approach is often to use a wide aperture and selective focus so that it is not very clear. Provided there are no violently contrasting patches of colour or brightness, this should not be obvious.

Lighting is even more of a problem. Ideally, you should work with available light whenever possible. This makes no demands on erratic power supplies or heavy, expensive and irreplaceable batteries, but it is also unpredictable in colour, quantity, and harshness.

Each of these variables is, however, controllable. The first, colour, is only important if you are using transparency film, and can usually be corrected with filtration: this is where the colour temperature meter comes in. It cannot easily be corrected, however, if it is changing quickly (for example, at sunset) or if it derives from fluorescent tubes, as in a museum or other building. Evening light can add character to a shot as it becomes redder, but fluorescent lighting (or worse still mixed lighting) is disastrous: a CC20M filter, an FL-D or FL-W (see page 119) may improve fluorescent lighting, but the results will still be unpredictable and possibly unusable. The only real possibilities are moving the subject, turning off the fluorescents and working by daylight, or adding artificial light, such as flash.

Indoors, it may be possible to increase the amount of light simply by opening curtains and doors. You may increase the lighting by several stops in this way. It may also be possible to shoot at another time, when the sun is shining from a different direction. But if the light is simply coming from the wrong direction then reflectors are needed.

Reflectors can be as simple as a sheet of newspaper or a piece of white cloth—even a T-shirt will often make a significant difference—or they may be purpose-made. Three of the most useful possibilities for studio photography on location are: aluminium foil, crumpled and then smoothed out before being stuck on a piece of cardboard or packing case (the crumbling helps prevent 'hot spots' in the reflected light); white fabric stretched over light wooden frameworks (use bought laths or bamboos, or even wood cut from trees); and purpose-made reflectors, such as the Lastolite.

Plain white or textured silver reflectors do not alter the colour of the light—the main difference is that textured silver reflectors are more efficient. Some people use gold coloured reflectors for flattering skin tones.

The plain white reflectors can also be used as diffusers to modify harsh, directional light: a typical diffuser might reflect 50 per cent of the light falling on it and diffuse the other 50 per cent through it. Once again alternatives include large pieces of white cloth. These can be pinned in a window, like curtains. There is also the possibility of using a black Lastolite, or something similar, to shade the subject or to prevent reflections from nearby surfaces.

There comes a point, however, where there is simply not enough light, and reflectors and diffusers are of no use. Very long exposure times should be avoided because of *reciprocity failure* (see page 236). At this juncture, you are forced back on additional lighting. Simple on-camera flash is extremely unlikely to be able to deliver the effects you want, so multiple flash will be needed. An alternative, if the power is reliable and if you can totally exclude other light, is tungsten lighting—preferably tungsten halogen—with plenty of spare bulbs. But this involves carrying a considerable extra load.

The best form of additional lighting is therefore flash. A good set-up will include a large powerful gun, preferably with switchable power, and anything up to half a dozen small guns with slave units. These can be quite inexpensive, costing less than a couple of rolls of transparency film each. With just one extension lead for the big gun, you have a main light source with plenty of fill-in; you can also group the small guns together for greater intensity.

You should make sure if possible that all the guns run on the same size of batteries—the AA pencil-cell size is fairly universal and is easy to carry. An excellent idea is to carry rechargeable (NiCd) batteries, if there is any chance of being able to recharge them. A well-planned expedition will use AA batteries for everything.

To hold small flashguns in place, use

tape or putty-type adhesive. Lightweight tripods can also come in handy, offering you good control over positioning. If you use a tripod, buy the adapters sold for attaching flashguns to lighting stands, which have a tripod screw fitting insert.

A flash meter is also essential, though it is a bad idea to rely on it totally, particularly because you will need a battery to run it. In practice, a Polaroid test is almost the only way to be sure of high quality results (see page 614), but this means you must use a roll film camera with a Polaroid back.

A Polaroid test allows you to check both the effect of the flashguns and the exposure, which you scale up or down according to the speed of the film you are using. It is also true that errors, things left in shot and so on, show up more clearly in a Polaroid than in real life. Even with a Polaroid test, bracketing of exposures is advisable; without a Polaroid, it is essential.

Unduly harsh flash lighting can be softened with reflectors and diffusers, as already described, but for shadowless lighting of small objects (up to, say, 60 cm high), a *tent* is useful. This is no more than a lightweight framework covered in thin white cloth, inside which the subject is placed. Black velvet provides a background, while the top, sides, and front (with a hole cut for the camera lens) diffuse and reflect the light. If you are staying in one place for some time, you can have one made up by the local carpenter, or you can lash one together yourself from sticks and gaffer tape. Some people even take collapsible frames of aluminium. The easiest shape to make, and to work with, is a cube—but if you have two, or better still, three light tripods you can make an excellent tent with these.

The easiest approach is to set up one tripod with a transverse pole which holds the velvet as a backdrop. The second tripod forms an 'A' at the other end, with its third leg extended and gaffer-taped to the tip of the first. With white cloth draped over the whole assembly, and held in place with clips or clamps, the result is a very useful tent.

The result is ideal for photographing small objects under diffuse lighting—you can either use daylight or flash. Even if you shine the flash from one side only the effect of the tent will be to make it quite non-directional. If you are photographing a shiny object it might be neccessary to make sure that the inner framework is completely covered by the white cloth.

Even white cloth can have a slight coloration, so if you are using transparency film you should do a trial run if possible. You may find that an 82 series blue filter will be needed to correct for a yellowish cast, though the bluish colour of flash or even a cloudy day might overcome the colour of the cloth.

But the most important factor in this kind of work is meticulous attention to detail—and for this you need patience.

Setting up a tent

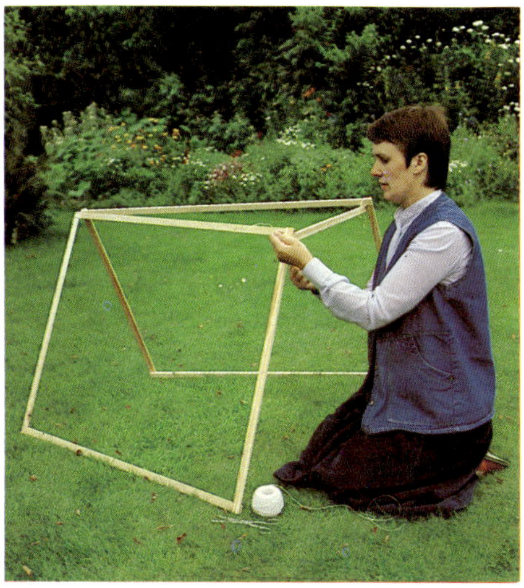

The best material for the frame is thin wood or bamboo which can be either taped or nailed together

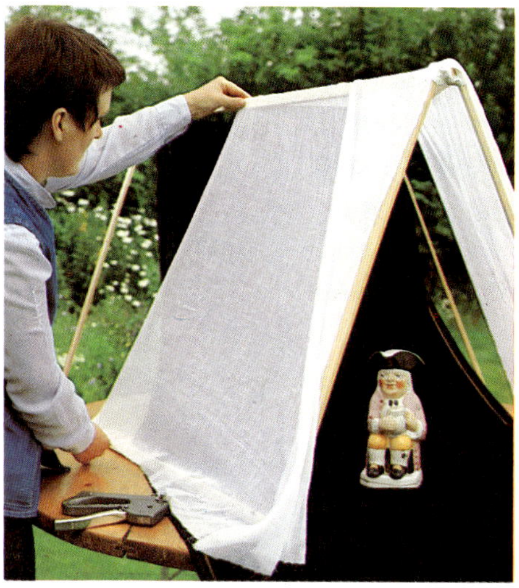

Place the object you want to photograph on a suitable background, and then cover the frame with white cloth

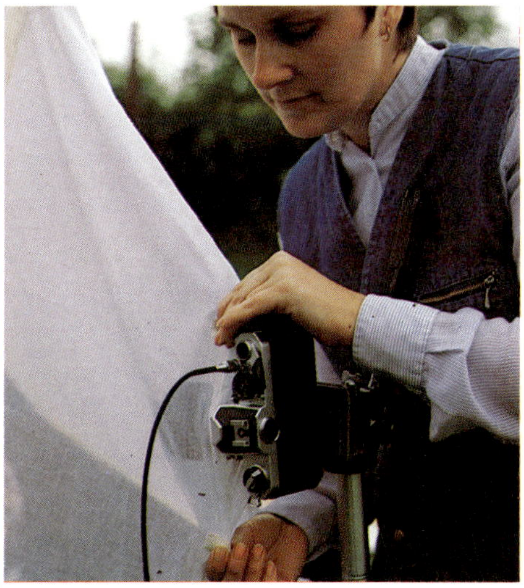

After setting up the camera, preferably on a tripod, cover the front of the tent with cloth, making a hole for the lens

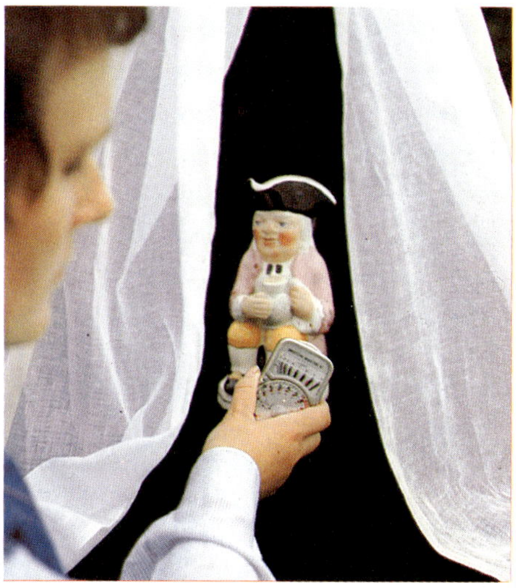

Use a hand-held meter, rather than the camera's built-in one. The best way of metering is the incident light method

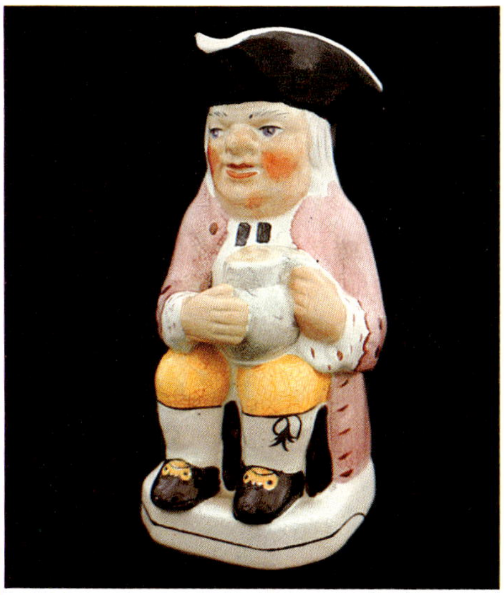

With some types of cloth, especially if it is fairly thick, you will find that the shot has a slight yellow cast

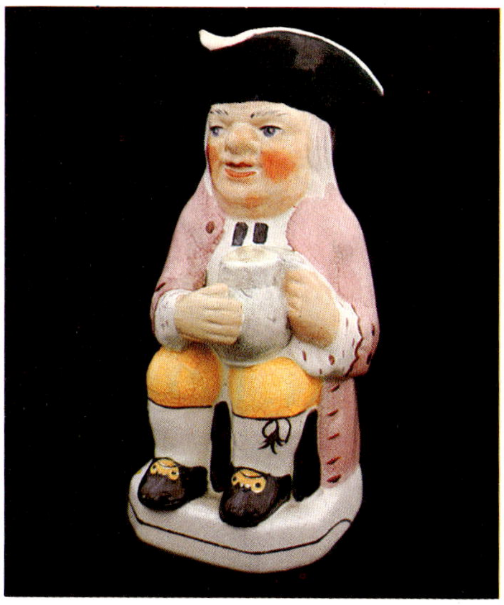

If the light in the tent is too yellow, use an 82 filter to correct. If in doubt, shoot pictures with and without the filter

Still lifes

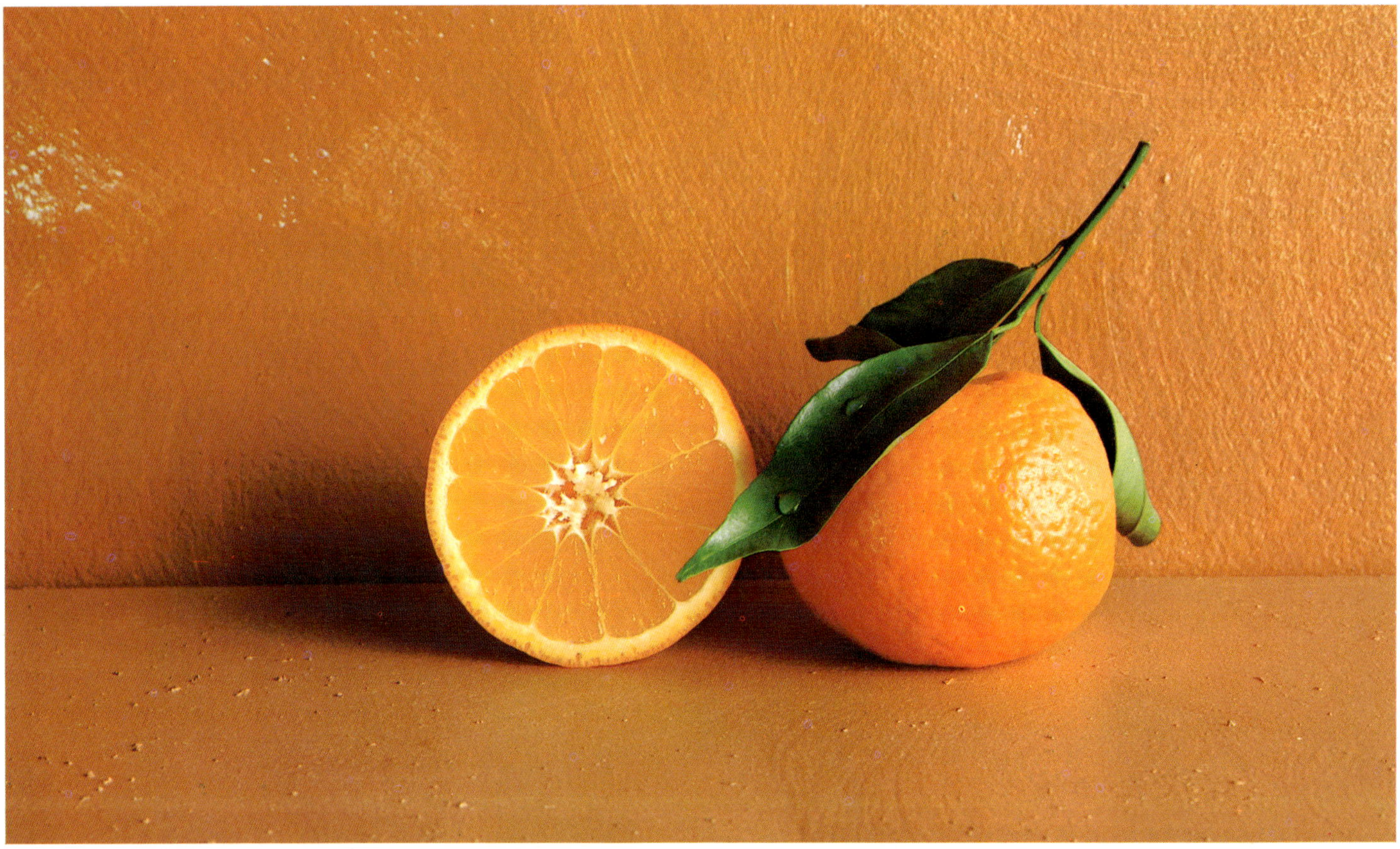

Still life photography is a subject which many people find themselves tackling at some point. The term covers the photography of anything three-dimensional, other than people or animals, which can be brought into the studio or set up as a tableau. The treatment of the subject can range from the purely recording type of shot, such as photographing a valuable vase or necklace for insurance purposes, to the artistic photography of interesting or beautiful objects which you might have collected for the purpose, such as an apple, a stone or a flower. You may become quite involved with this aspect of still life work. Many professionals carry out nothing but still life photography, in the forms of product shots for advertisements or food shots for magazines and books.

The appeal of still life work is that the photographer is in complete control of every aspect—the lighting, the appearance of the subject, the background and the angle of view. An expert can make virtually any subject look good, while on the other hand even a beautiful subject can look dull if the shot is badly set up and poorly lit. So this article covers some basic techniques from which you can develop your own approach.

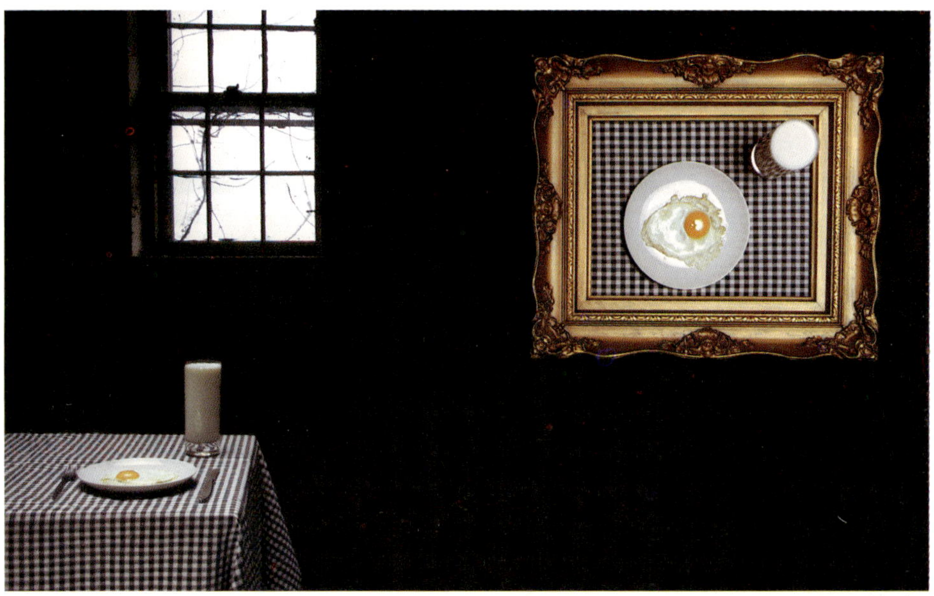

Simple and contrived *The top picture is a classic still life—simple, natural and requiring no special techniques, it relies for its effect on colour and composition. The lower shot shows the other end of the spectrum in that it relies heavily on clever photography and an amusing idea*

Choosing the camera and lens

A standard 35 mm camera is quite suitable for still life work, particularly if you use fine grain film, though larger formats are preferable for the very best results. All modern SLR cameras focus to a reasonably close distance with the standard lens, and a macro lens is only needed for small objects or where it is necessary to stop down to very small apertures to increase the depth of field. A mirror lock-up mechanism and depth of field preview facility are useful, but by no means essential—the mirror lock helps to avoid camera shake and the depth of field preview shows how much of the subject will be in sharp focus.

A medium format SLR, however, will invariably need either an extension tube or a close-up lens, since for many still life subjects the image will be too small at the lens's minimum focusing distance. A Polaroid back can be fitted to some cameras allowing you to check the composition, exposure and lighting before the final picture is taken.

When it comes to choosing a lens, there is much to be said in favour of a focal length somewhat longer than the standard. A longer lens allows you to get farther back from the subject and achieve a good perspective. The more space there is between lens and subject, the more room there is for lighting stands, reflectors and other paraphernalia. It also allows final arrangement of the subject without the risk of knocking things over, which invariably happens when working in a confined area. Furthermore, a lens with a longish focal length is likely to stop down further, which can be useful on those occasions when you need plenty of depth of field.

However, wide angle lenses can prove useful for some types of still life work. Sometimes it can be effective to be right in among the objects being photographed. For instance, a wide angle lens is often used when photographing architectural models, where the idea is to produce a pedestrian's eye view of the project—indeed, drawings are sometimes made from such photographs.

Wide angle lenses used at close distances will produce a strong, dramatic perspective. This can be used creatively, but bear in mind that the 'pulling' effect towards the corners of the image will distort objects if they are situated anywhere except in the middle of the subject matter.

Using a wide angle lens for a still life set could well mean you will need a much larger background than for the same subject photographed with a longer focal length. Sometimes it is possible to move the background and subject closer together, sometimes it is not, in which case a change to a longer focal length is necessary.

Photographers often make use of the strongly converging perspective lines of wide angle images by using lined or patterned backgrounds. The lines appear to meet on the horizon, which may only be a short distance away, making the subject seem somehow larger than life.

One limiting factor of still life work is that one really needs a studio. Photographers go to extraordinary lengths in order to achieve this happy situation at home. A spare room is ideal if it is big enough, but for the larger subjects a considerable amount of space is sometimes needed and you may have to take over another room temporarily. Garages, garden sheds and lofts or attics can also be used, or even just a corner of them, space permitting.

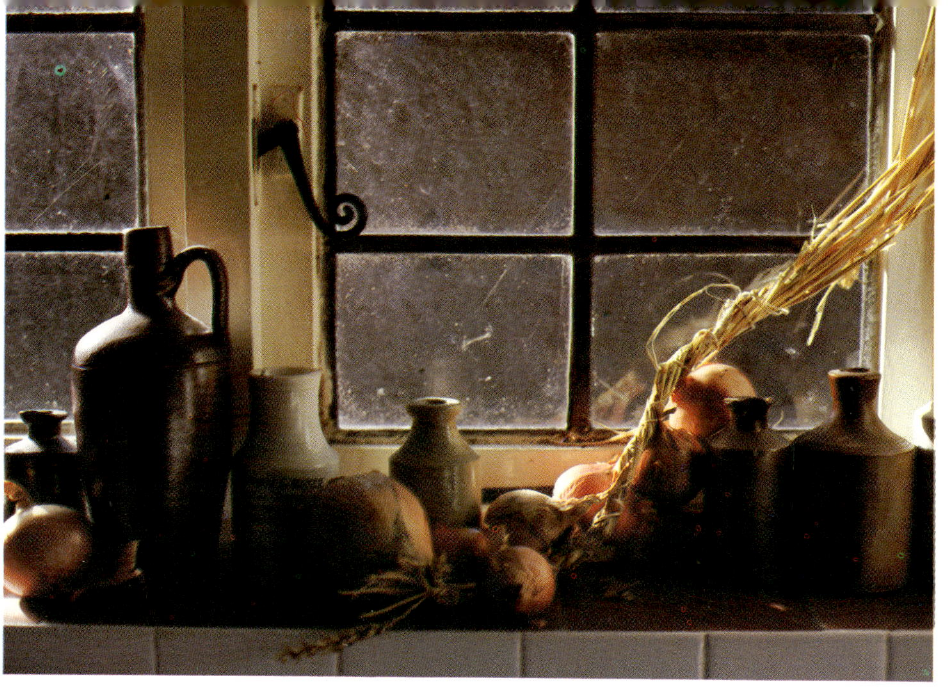

Window light *You do not have to use complex lighting set-ups. With this type of subject the natural light from a window is often more appropriate*

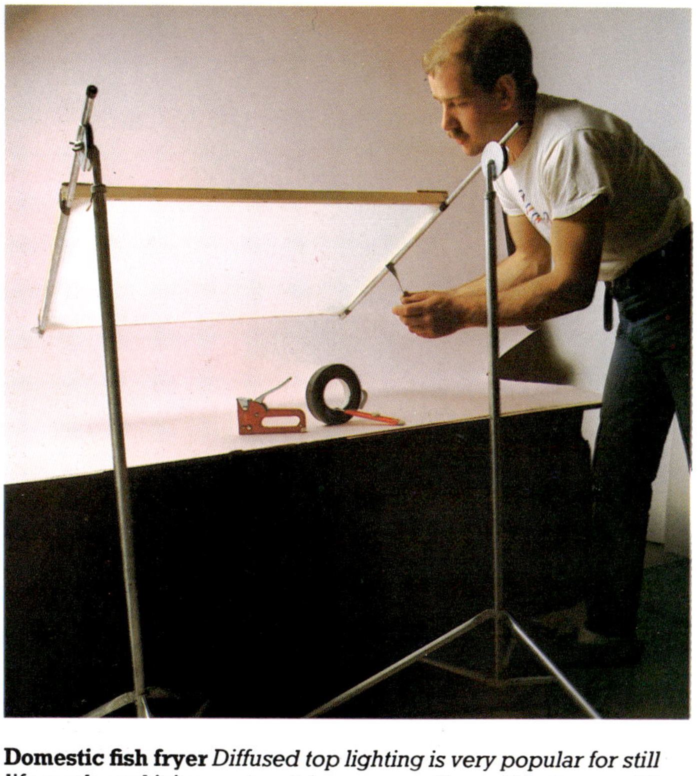

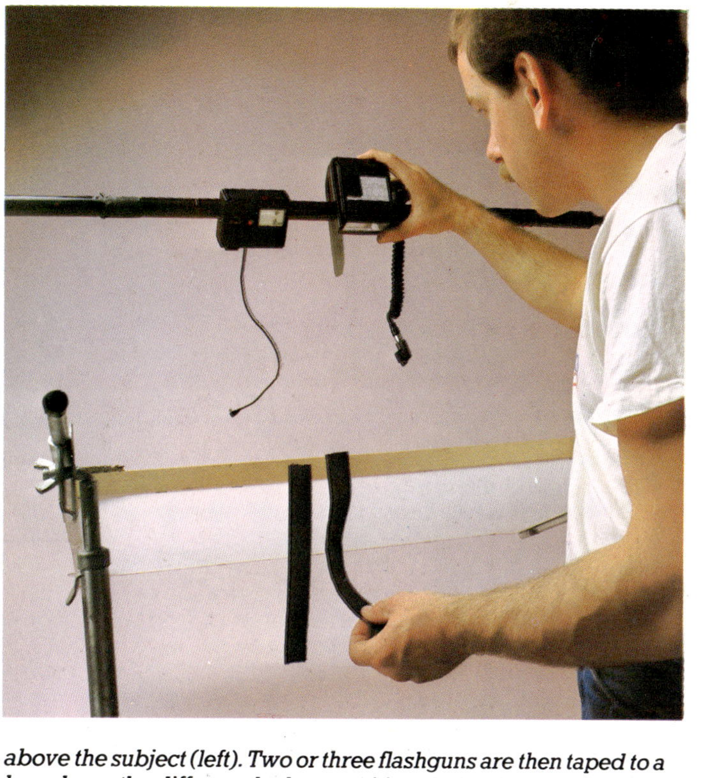

Domestic fish fryer *Diffused top lighting is very popular for still life work, and it is easy to achieve even with small flashguns. All you need is a frame covered with the diffusing material clamped above the subject (left). Two or three flashguns are then taped to a bar above the diffuser, the best positions being found by making experimental test shots*

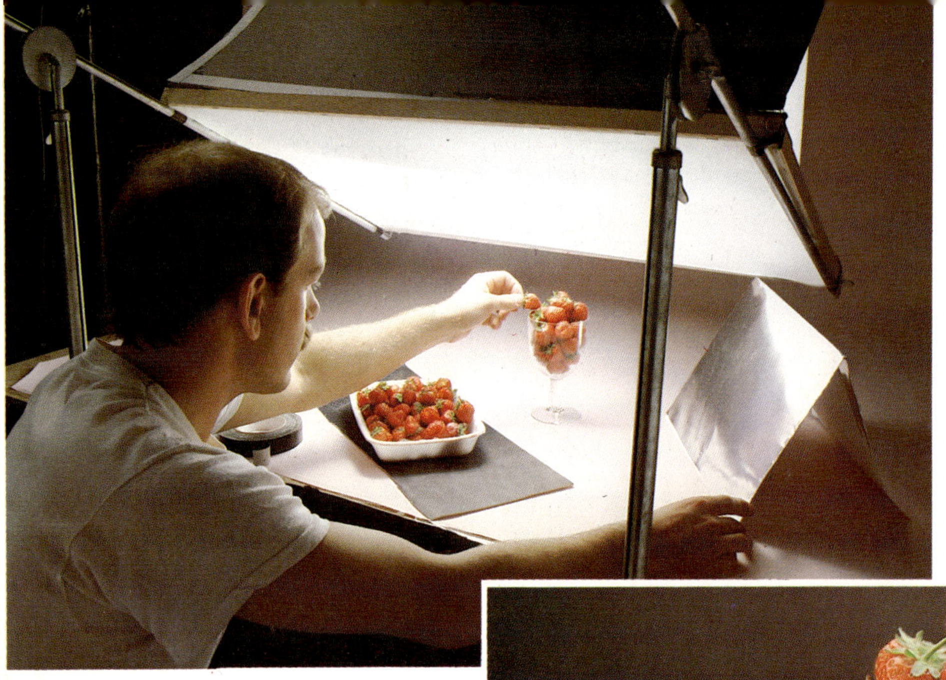

Gradual background *This is the type of lighting used a great deal by professionals. Tilting the diffuser forwards (above) means that only the foreground is lit, the light fading off towards the back (right)*

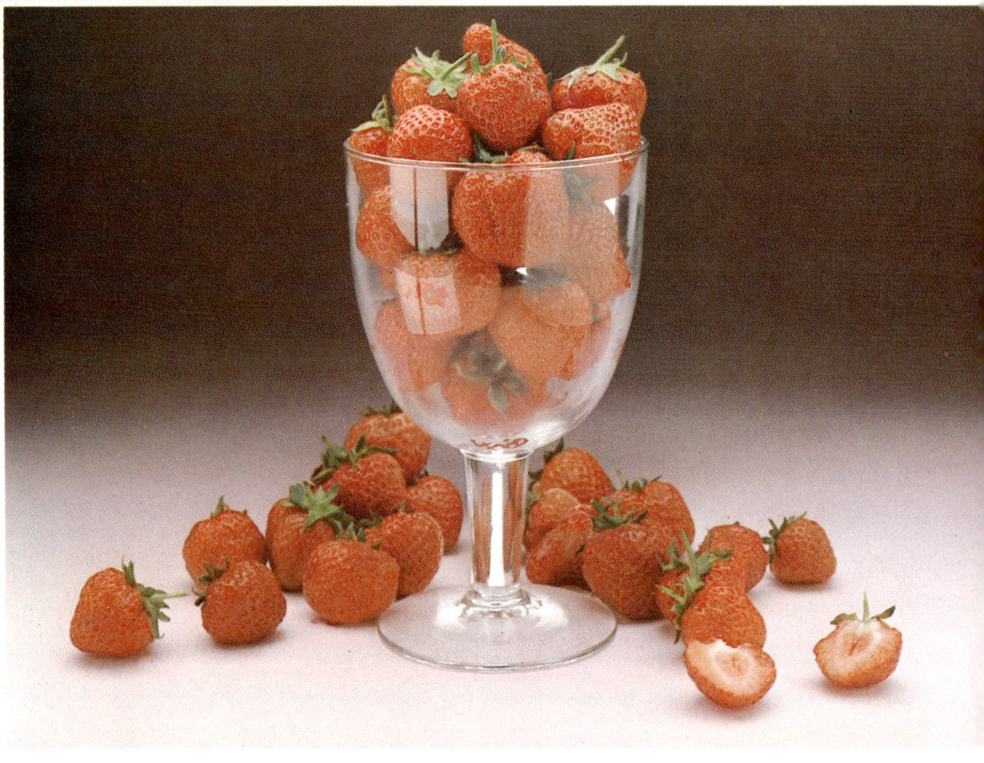

Keep it clean

A good deal of still life work, however, needs only small amounts of space, and it is quite possible to use a tabletop as your studio area. In this case, you may be able to use a corner of a room. But whether you are working in a studio or in the living room, cleanliness is vital.

In photographers' terms, there is nothing more annoying than having spent a lot of time setting up a still life, only to find that the transparency shows fluff, dust or a hair in a most conspicuous place. Apart from the obvious, like not smoking, keeping animals and children away, doors and windows shut, etc, there will still be occasions when dust gets in the wrong place. 'Dust off' aerosols, blower brushes and the like are very useful, but do be careful that you do not just blow dust from one part of the set to another.

Dust and fluff on velvet, flock paper or other fabrics is best removed by winding sticky tape round a finger of the hand to make a sticky brush and then picking the dust off. Some types of plastic, notably perspex, become charged with electrical static quite easily, through routine handling. An anti-static cloth or brush should be used to neutralize the dust-attracting charge. The same brush can also be used for glassware and indeed many other still life objects.

Obstinate fingermarks can be removed with surgical spirit or acetone, but as these are also solvents for some substances, especially plastics, be careful. If you use polish for cleaning, note that some leave waxy deposits which show up on film, so test for this first. Clean clear plastics only with soap and water, and dry then with a clean chamois: or use a special plastic-polish and a clean, soft duster. Some of these polishes are also anti-static, which helps prevent static build-up at source.

Choosing the lighting

The simplest and most readily available form of lighting for still lifes is, of course, daylight. There is a great deal to be said for arranging your subject near a window and using natural light alone for illumination. But the light must be diffuse—direct sunlight will pose impossible problems with contrast. So the window must be north-facing, or the weather must be fairly cloudy. Establish exposure by taking an incident light reading from the subject with a hand-held meter (see pages 41 to 45).

However, there are a number of problems involved in using window light. The first is that the light source often tends to be behind the subject. While backlighting can be attractive, the front of the subject will tend to be deep in shadow. One solution to this problem is to shoot from a high angle, so that the camera view catches the light falling on top of the subject. Unfortunately, this approach will not suit many subjects.

An alternative is to use reflectors to fill in the shadows a little. Many surfaces can be pressed into service as reflectors, from hand mirrors to silver foil. There is no need for the reflector to give a diffuse light, for the window light is already soft, and you will need all the reflection you can get. Even this approach, though, is limited in scope, for the light reflected into the shadows is inevitably much less than the window light behind the subject.

A better solution is to use electronic flash to fill in the shadows. With a small still life, even a tiny portable flashgun should provide more than enough light to balance the light from the window. The problems lie in positioning the gun (it should be off-camera), balancing flash and daylight exposures, and in achieving correct colour balance.

Without a modelling light, it can be difficult to position the flashgun accurately. A bright torch will give you some idea of direction, but no idea of the lighting balance—the flash will be much brighter. The only way to establish the right position, and so the right exposure, is to make an educated guess and a few trials—if you can make a Polaroid test, so much the better.

Start by taking an incident light reading from the subject with a hand-held meter. Remember you will need maximum depth of field for such a close-up subject, set the aperture at *f*/11 or *f*/16. Then set the shutter speed according to the exposure reading. This must be slower than the camera's flash synchronization speed—usually 1/60 or 1/125 second. Now work out how far the flash needs to be from the subject to give correct exposure with the aperture at two stops wider than that set—that is, *f*/5.6 or *f*/8. Set the flash this distance from the subject for your first trials.

Colour balance can be quite a problem, since the daylight will probably have a much higher colour temperature than the flash. The best solution, short of making a double exposure, is to add a warming filter for the sky and ignore the flash, for a slight warmth in the areas lit by flash will probably look quite attractive.

With all these problems, it is clearly worth abandoning daylight altogether and using artificial light alone if you possibly can. If so, however, you will almost certainly need a much more powerful flashgun. Proper studio flash (see pages 178-186) is better still.

A very high proportion of still life work can be lit with a single head and the careful use of additional reflectors and diffusers. The main light should have a large diffusing screen set some way in front of the reflector to soften the shadows. This applies equally to both tungsten and electronic light sources. The diffuser can be a separately mounted unit or a manufacturer's clip-on accessory and its size can vary between about 30 cm and 90 cm square.

A diffuser can be made at home from an offcut of white translucent acrylic sheet or made of any Kodatrace type of sheeting fixed to a frame. It is also possible to use a silvered umbrella as a single soft light source in either reflector or diffuser role.

If you are using tungsten lighting, always remember to keep a reasonable distance between the lamp and the diffuser – the heat thrown out by the lamp is considerable and may constitute a fire risk. Bear the heat of tungsten lamps in mind when you are working with perishable subjects such as food.

Should the subject lend itself to hard lighting, or you require sharp shadows, then use a standard reflector (or spotlight) without a diffuser, and allow a large distance from light and subject.

Setting up the lighting

Since the 1960s, professional photographers have had a strong tendency towards top lighting still life subjects. Bearing esoteric names like Swimming pool, Hazy light and Fish fryer, their top lights are simply large sophisticated equivalents of the diffusing screen already mentioned. Most need an expensive and heavy boom light stand in order to support the weight. Where domestic conditions allow, it is possible to have hooks in the ceiling to support heads and a frame. Otherwise, a length of electric conduit between two stands may be sufficient. These stands can be base weighted for safety with house bricks in a plastic carrier bag.

Still life subjects benefit greatly from a 'falling off' or gradual darkening of the background. The prime requisite is for sufficient space between subject and background in order to effectively throw this area into shadow. Camera viewpoint affects the position of the soft-edged horizon. A fall-off background can be achieved by masking the main light from the background with black card or board. This mask is placed forward of the main light or, in the case of top lighting, on its backedge. A coarse, saw-toothed edge to this mask will soften the line of its shadow.

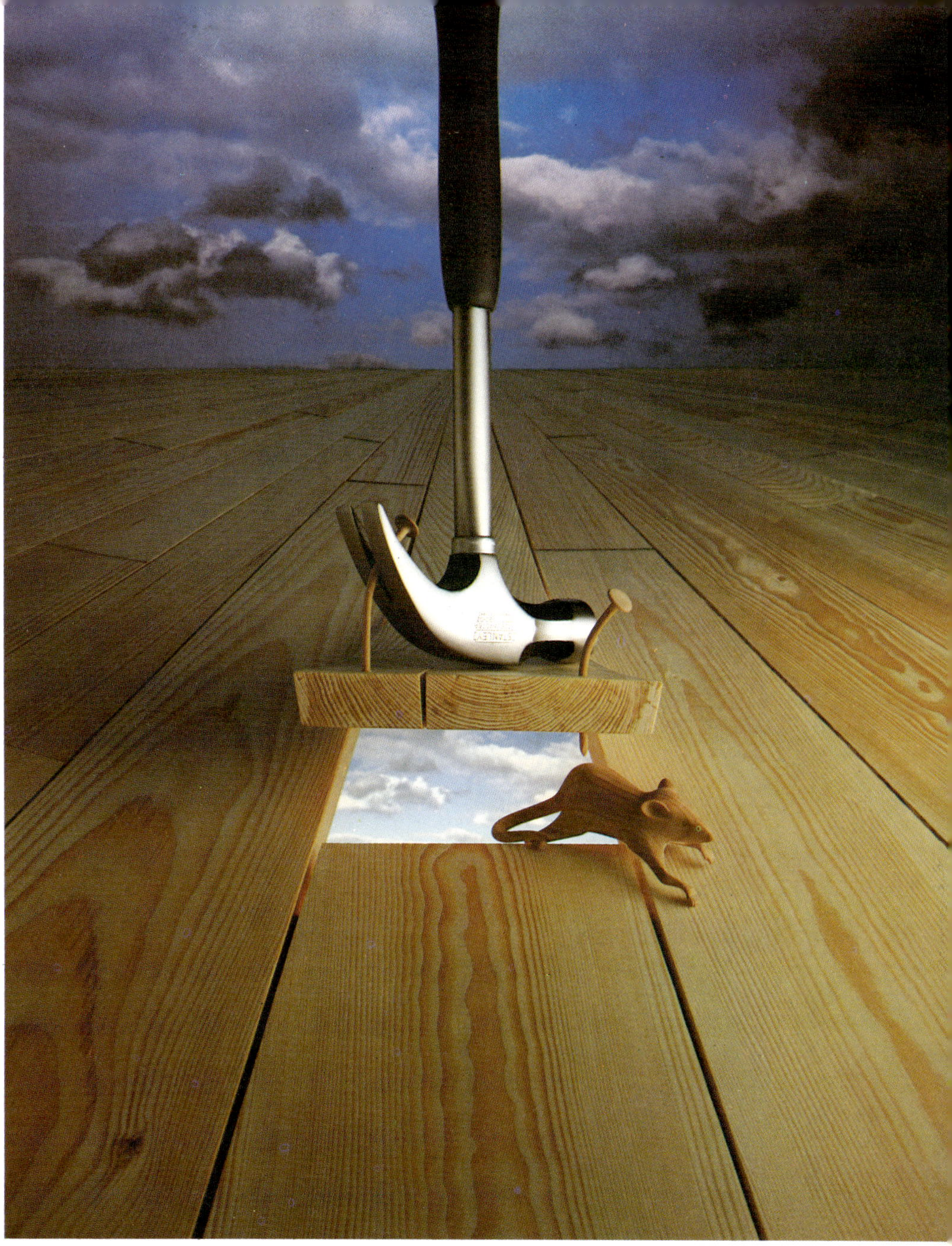

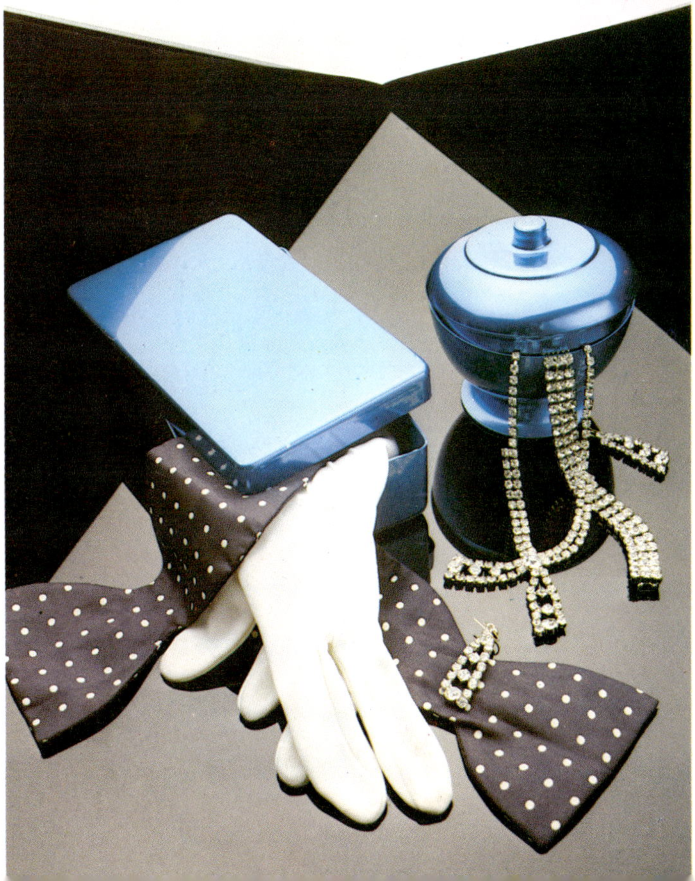

Vanishing trick
To give the effect of a large space in the confines of a studio, the boards used above were made in miniature and tapered, giving a result similar to an ultra-wide angle lens—even though an almost standard focal length lens was actually used

Reflected light
If you use a reflective background the lighting will form an effective part of the background. The bright patch here is a reflection of the fish fryer flash diffuser—part of which can be seen at the top of the picture

Metal and glassware

For those with imagination and patience, photographing still lifes can be an immensely satisfying occupation, giving individually 'crafted' images that are very much your own. Once you have mastered basic lighting techniques, you can usually put all your efforts into choosing and arranging subjects. But certain subjects such as glass and metalware, require a special approach.

Photographing glass

Glass containers make most drinks look instantly more attractive, but glass presents a number of problems for the photographer. Glass must invariably be backlit to some degree. This is the only way in which to do justice to the material and its contents. Glass, because of its transparent (or sometimes translucent) nature only shows up clearly when lit from behind, underneath, or sometimes both together. Those golden glasses of beer in advertisements never seem to look as good on the bar counter, for this very reason.

Sometimes you may see a normally lit photograph shot in an advertisement but the glass container holding beer, wine, perfume, cooking oil, or whatever, within the grouping still glows. This is achieved by the use of an accurately shaped white, silver of gold card reflector placed very carefully in shot behind the subject. Another technique is to have a hole in the background, or base, with a light shining through it, to achieve the same effect.

With glass objects you must use light-

Adding black *When you have a light subject and a light background, the edges of the subject tend to disappear (below). To overcome this, place pieces of black card around the subject (opposite page, bottom left) so that this card is reflected and so makes the edges darker. This gives a better outline and also helps to give a better impression of shape, particularly with rounded subjects such as the glass, here*

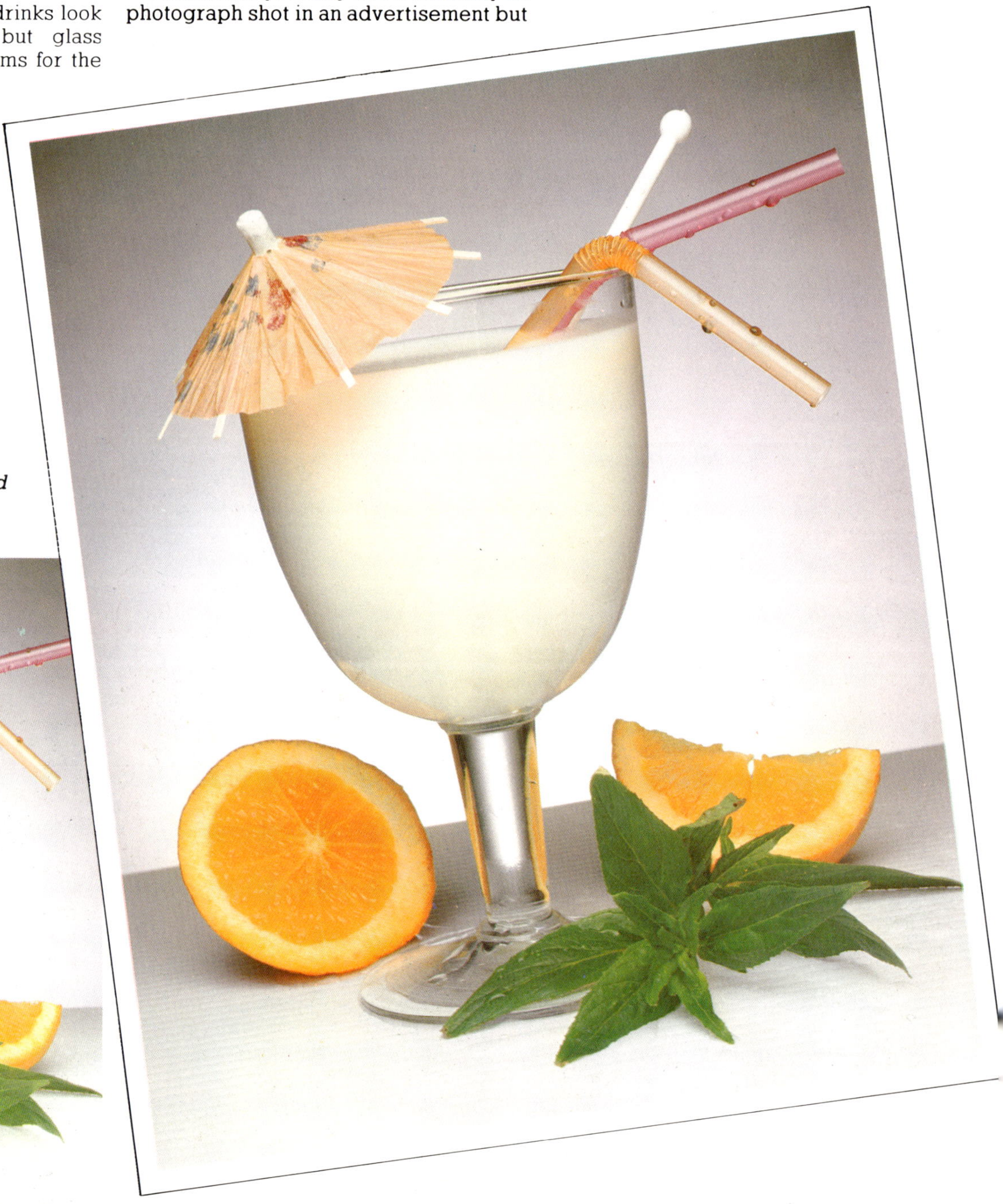

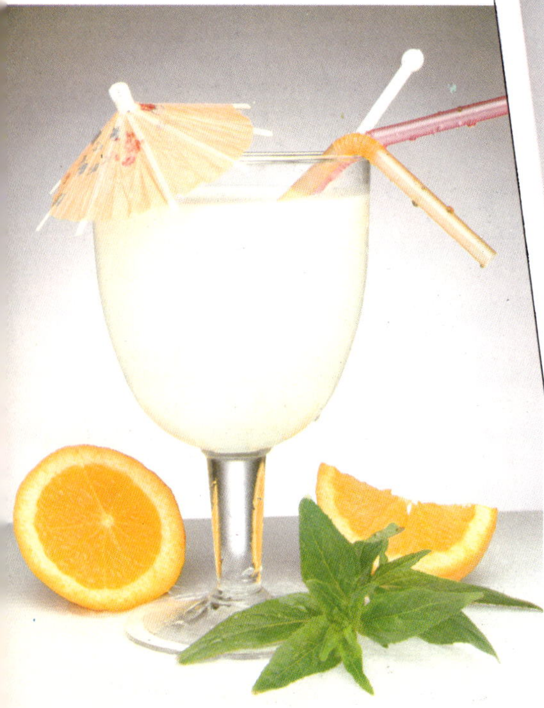

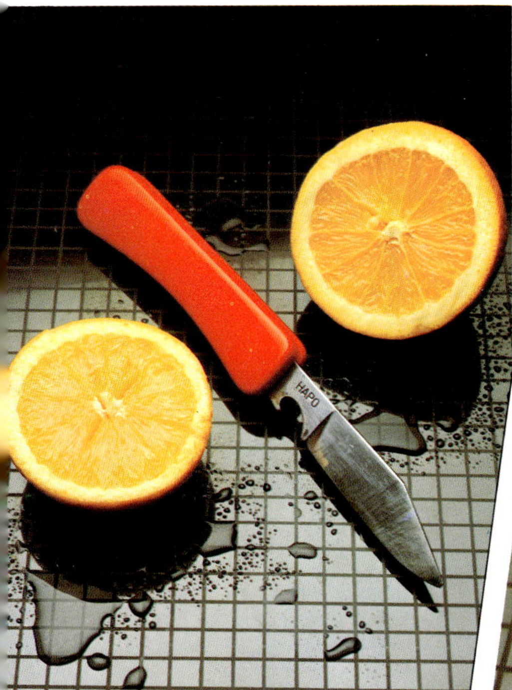

Cleaner cut *Although the lighting in the above shot is adequate for most of the picture, the blade looks rather dull. To give a brighter, cleaner look to the metal, a silver card reflector was positioned out of shot (bottom right) so that it could be seen reflected in the blade. Positioning the reflector is best done while looking through the camera as its effect depends as much on viewpoint as on the position of the card*

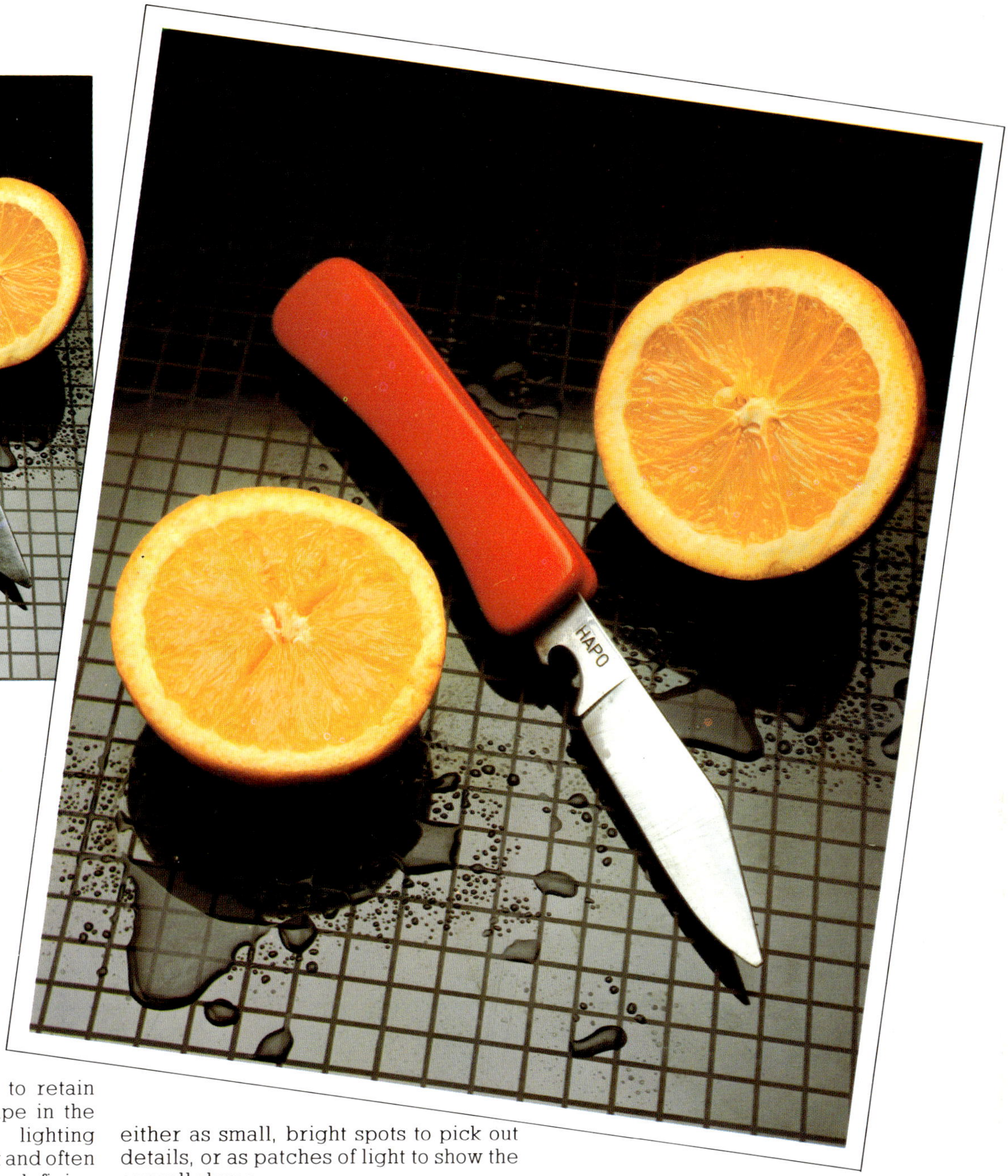

ing very carefully if you are to retain some idea of the object's shape in the photograph. Unsympathetic lighting results in the object looking flat and often confused. Backlighting helps by defining the edges of the object more clearly. But it is also useful to have some highlights on the front surface of your subject—either as small, bright spots to pick out details, or as patches of light to show the overall shape.

To produce small highlights, use a second light with a mask over the front. The mask should have just a small hole in it—maybe three of four millimetres across, though it is advisable to experiment with different sizes. If you are using tungsten lights, make sure there is some space between the mask and lamp reflector for ventilation, and keep checking that the mask is not getting too hot. If you are using flash, a modelling light is essential to determine the position for the light to get the best highlights.

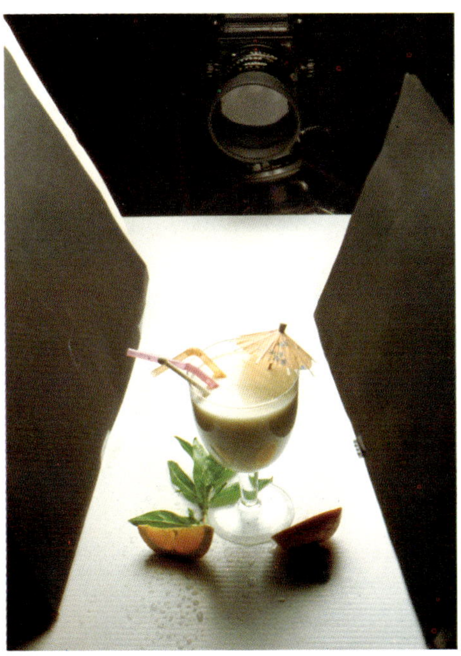

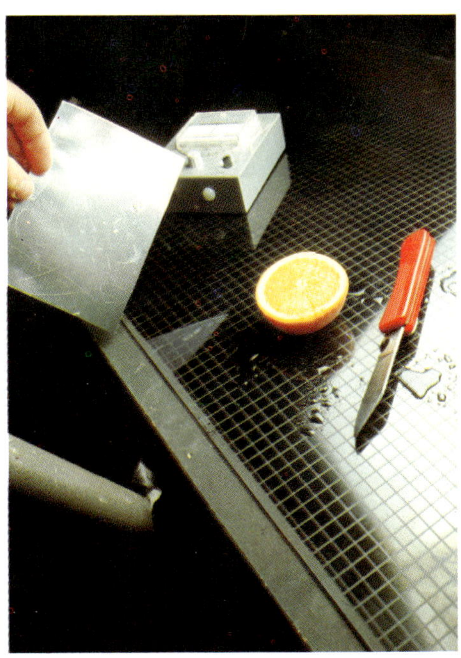

An alternative is to use a torch, similarly masked, and double exposure. The first exposure is the normal one using either flash or tungsten. Then, with the room completely blacked out and the lights off, make a second exposure using the torch. Trial and error is necessary to determine the exposure for the torch, and you may find it necessary to filter this light if you are using flash as your main light. The correct amount of filtration should also be found by experimentation, but precise correction is not usually necessary.

If you are going to do a lot of still life work it may be worth making a special 'chair frame' table like that used by

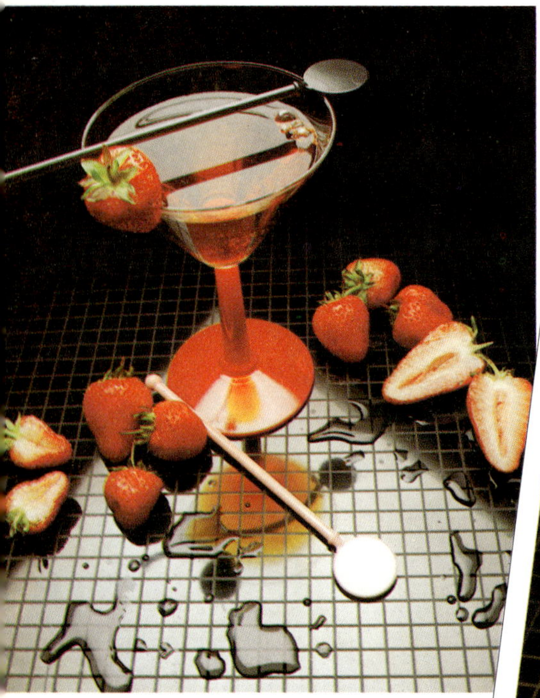

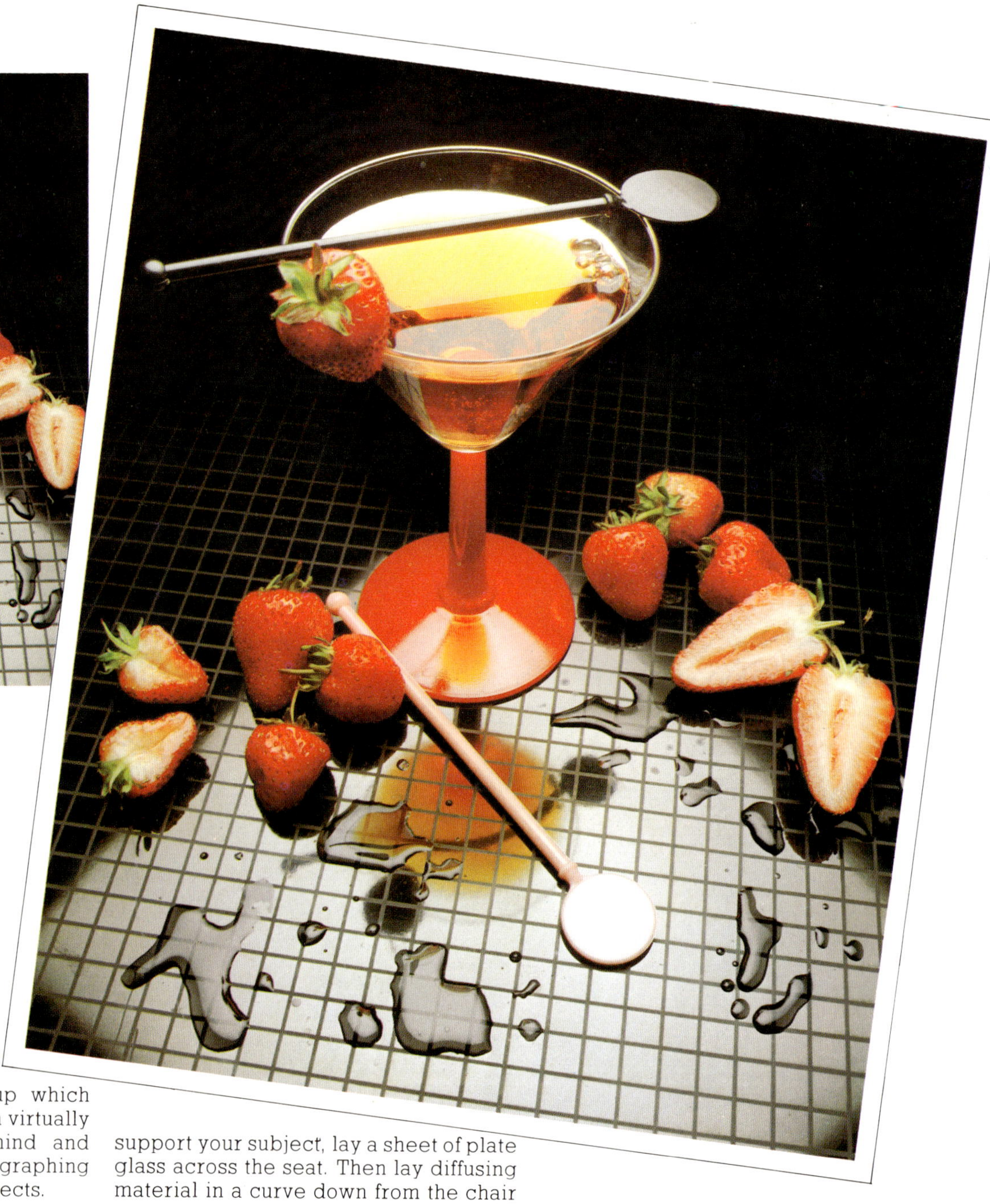

Brighter cocktail *With just the basic lighting set-up (above) the cocktail looks unexciting and dull, with little indication of colour. To liven up the shot a piece of mirrored card was placed in shot but behind the glass (below), so that it reflected light through the drink (right). Apart from making the drink look more attractive, this added highlight also has the effect of making the cocktail the centre of attention in the shot*

professionals. This is a set-up which allows the subject to be lit from virtually any direction, including behind and below, and so is ideal for photographing glassware, as well as other subjects.

The basic structure is similar to an overgrown chair frame with the rear edge of the 'seat' frame missing. To support your subject, lay a sheet of plate glass across the seat. Then lay diffusing material in a curve down from the chair back top to the front of the seat and fix it with tape or staples. The diffusing material can be tracing paper or one of many plastic diffusers available in rolls from professional photographic dealers.

You can make the frame from almost any material, including wood, but make sure that it is strong enough to support fairly heavy objects. Further refinements include using more diffusing materials to add a translucent canopy, sides and front (with a hole cut for the lens) to create a 'tent' (see below).

It is useful to have a fair amount of space around this table to give sufficient room for the lights. If the lights have to be close, the lighting is likely to be uneven, giving 'hot spots'. If space is limited, the only alternative is to use additional layers of diffuser, but this restricts you to soft lighting. Fairly harsh lighting is often very effective with glassware, but has the disadvantage that it leads to strong shadows. This is where the chair frame set-up is useful, because, by adding a second lamp lighting the subject from below, these shadows are either burnt-out or made much paler. This second lamp can also be used for the main lighting source.

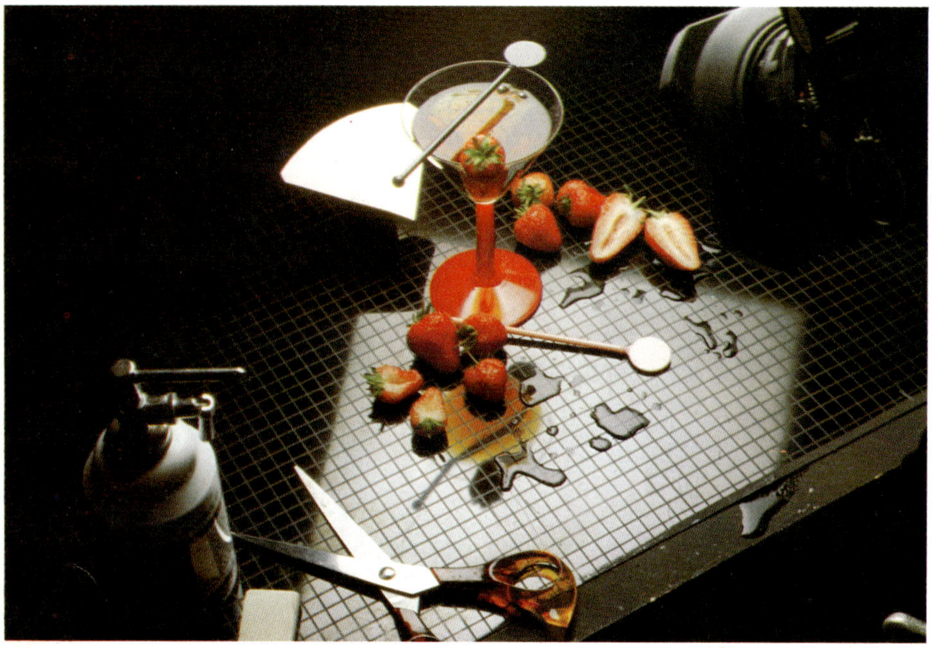

The technique of 'adding black' is most

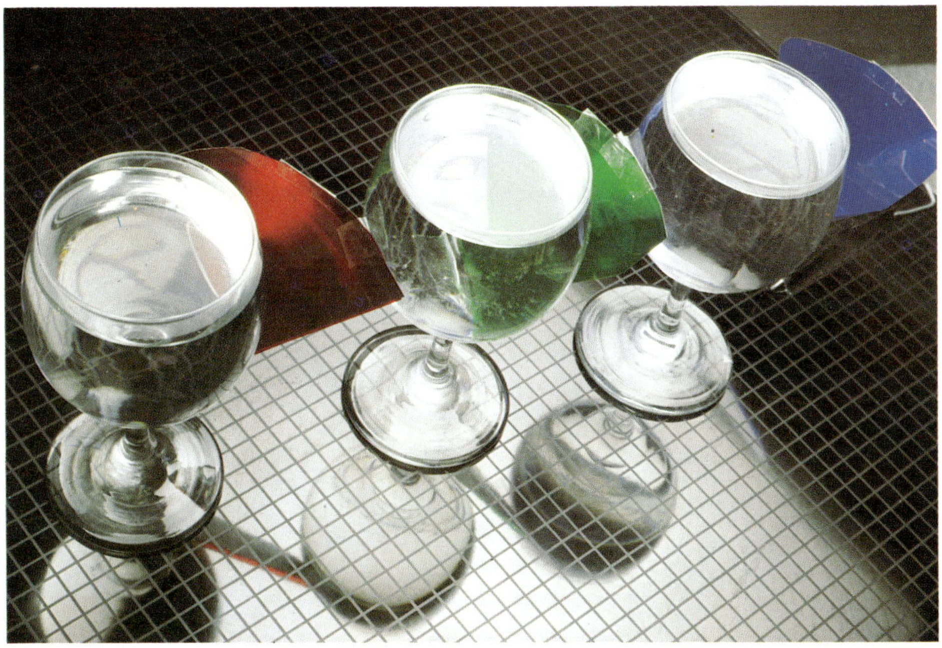

necessary when the edges of a shiny object disappear into a light background. Reflecting black, grey or a colour into the edges can sometimes prevent this happening. The alternative is to use dulling sprays. These are aerosols of paraffin wax in solution and are made in a range of clear matt, semi-matt and black. They are not very expensive and last for years. Do not use them on any mechanical or expensive subjects. Dulling spray can be removed with acetone (nail varnish remover) and a clean soft cloth.

Silverware and metal

The photography of silverware has long been a problem, for no matter where one places a light, or the camera, everything within a 180° radius will be reflected in the subject. Old manuals of photography would recommend spraying the subject with milk, or rolling Plasticine over the surface to dull it. This had the effect of making the subject look washed out and lustreless as if it were made of pewter, or even worse, of clay.

Obviously the problem of reflections also applies to any other polished surface, whether it be brass, copper, chrome, aluminium, or nowadays, metallic finished plastic. The final solution to this situation was the invention of *tent* lighting.

Originally, tent lighting was literally just that—the set was constructed with a metal or wooden frame and covered with butter muslin. A modern tent, at its simplest, is a translucent drum for side views or a cone for top shots. Either of these can be made from tracing paper, or expensively ready-made in translucent acrylic plastic.

Coloured glass *It is very easy to introduce colour into a shot, even when the subject itself is very drab and monochromatic (below). With glass objects, place silver reflectors covered with coloured gels behind them (above) so that the colour is reflected through the glass (right). With other types of subject, the gels can be used as reflectors, similar to that used for the knife (page 215) to add a hint of colour to selected parts of the subject*

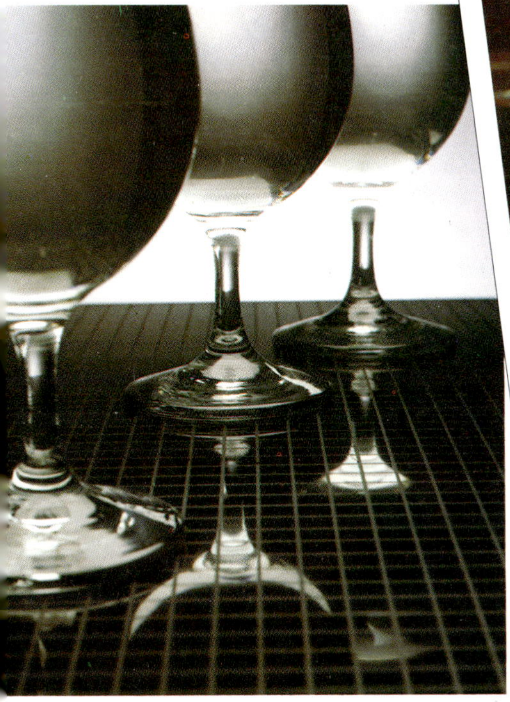

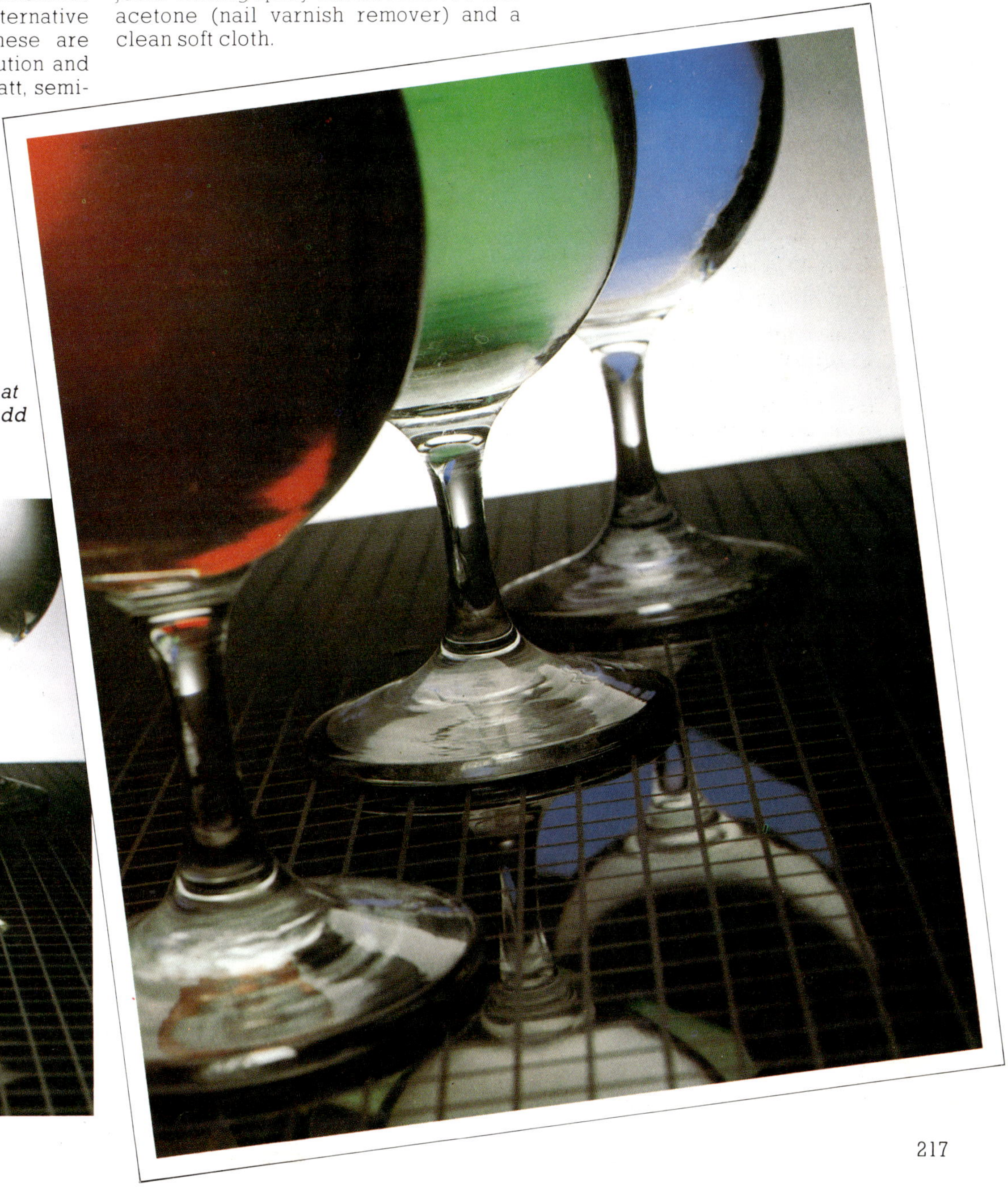

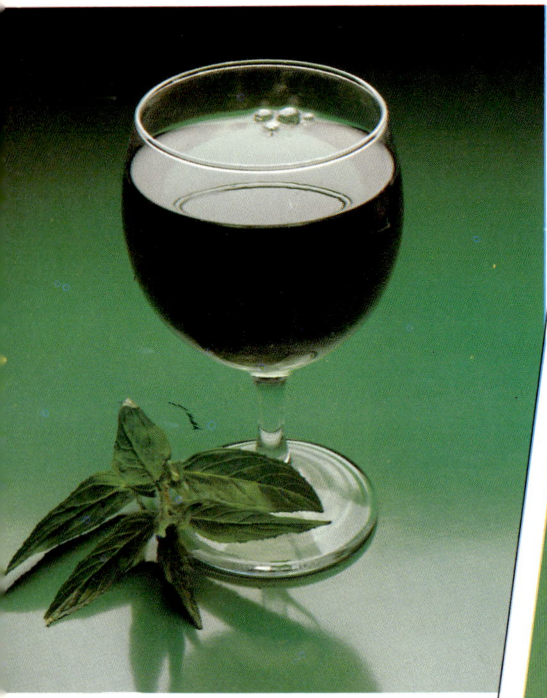

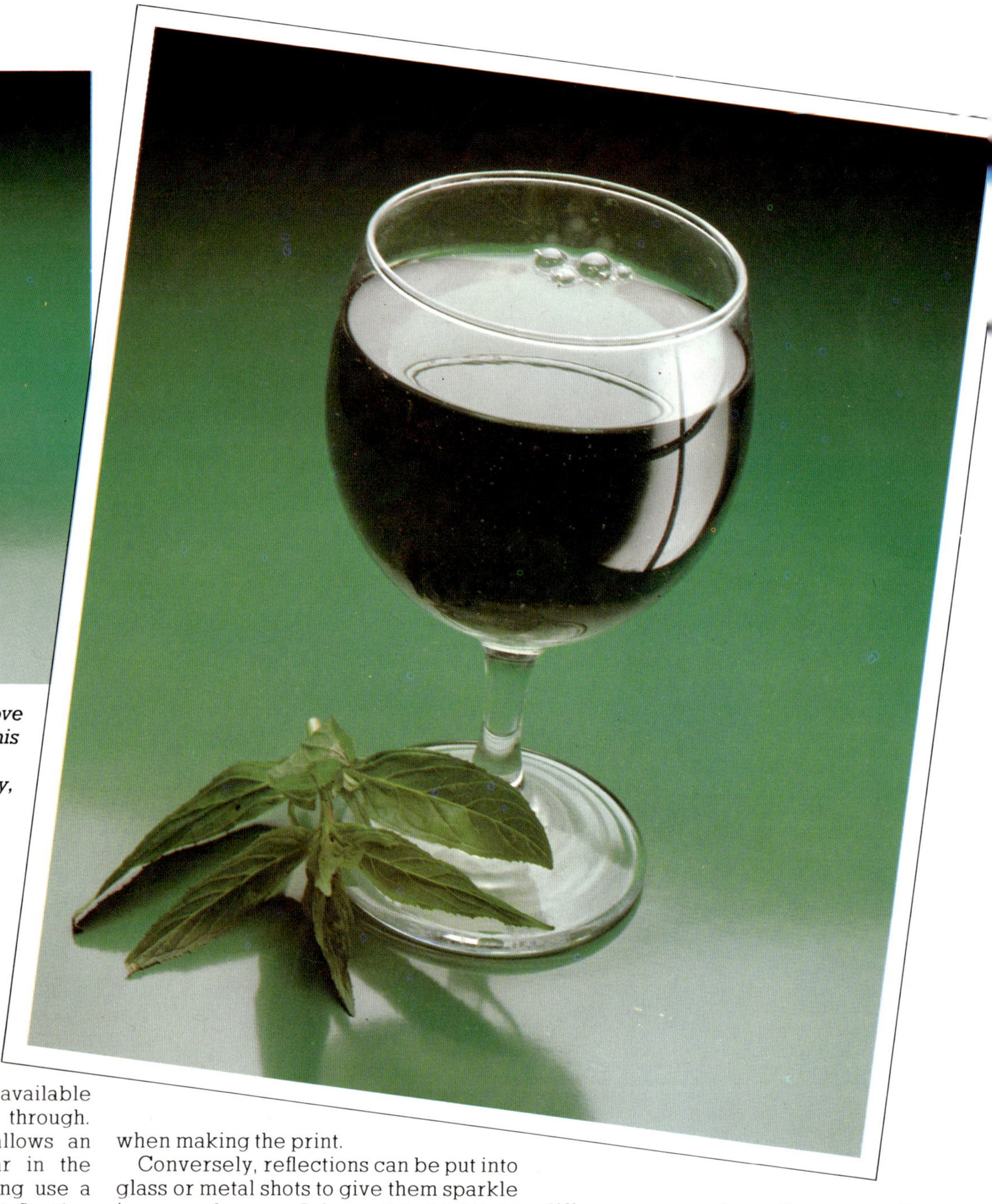

Reflected window *In the shot above the glass looks flat and lifeless. This is mostly due to the lack of highlights in the glass. Fortunately, it is very easy to add highlights using card reflectors. For this shot a reflector was placed to one side (below), the card having been divided into four with tape to simulate a window frame. The size and shape of the highlight are controlled by altering the angle, shape and distance of the reflector*

In either type, a hole must be available for the camera lens to poke through. However, this immediately allows an image of the lens to appear in the subject! To stop this happening use a dulling spray to matt out the reflective area on the subject when using negative film, or, dodge out the unwanted image when making the print.

Conversely, reflections can be put into glass or metal shots to give them sparkle in several ways. A long, thin highlight can be generated by placing a striplight close to the subject. A masked down diffuser can produce the same effect. This is fairly easily done, but bear in mind that the shape of the subject itself may distort the shape of the highlight. This can be overcome by altering the outline of the striplight, of diffuser mask, with black paper and card. It is more than likely, that you will end up with a peculiarly shaped mask over the light source, in order to achieve a regularly shaped highlight in the subject when seen from the camera.

The same technique can be used in reverse, in order to introduce a controlled highlight shape into a dark glossy subject or background surface. Should the latter be of acrylic, or similar, it can be twisted to distort the reflection even more. It is worthwhile experimenting with some specially shaped cardboard cut-outs over a light source, in order to gain some idea of how this can work for you. Smaller highlights, for localized areas, can be induced by the use of handbag mirrors, cooking foil, or with silver, gold or coloured plastic reflective foils mounted on to pieces of cardboard.

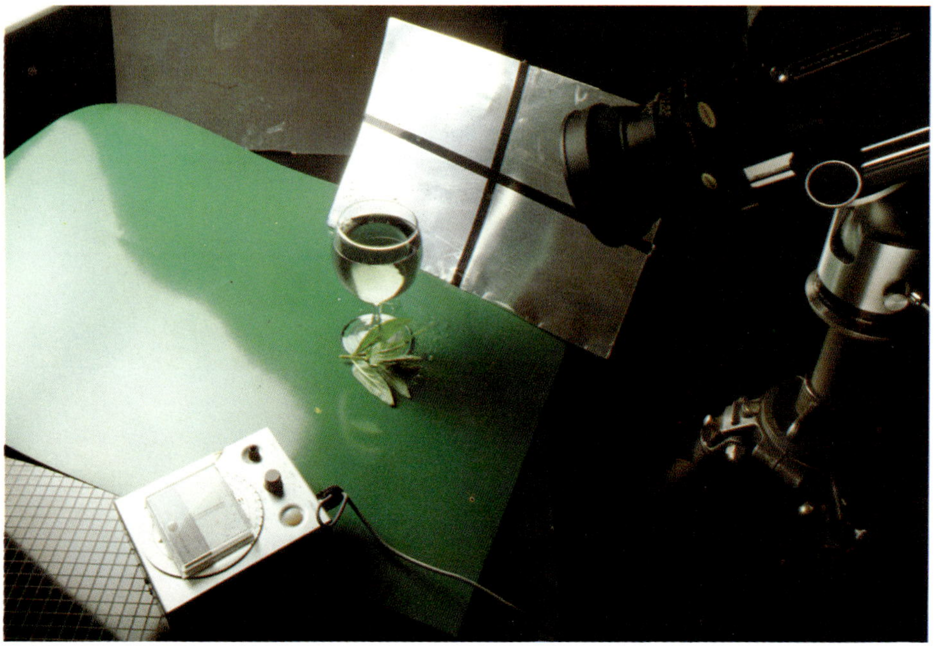

UNDERSTANDING PHOTOGRAPHY

Although modern cameras make photography a simple matter, the technical side of the subject is often baffling, especially to the newcomer. So this section has been compiled to help you understand photography and photographic processes. Among the subjects covered are film speeds, the intricacies of colour temperature, depth of field and how film works. Each subject is clearly explained and accompanied by specially commissioned diagrams and photographs.

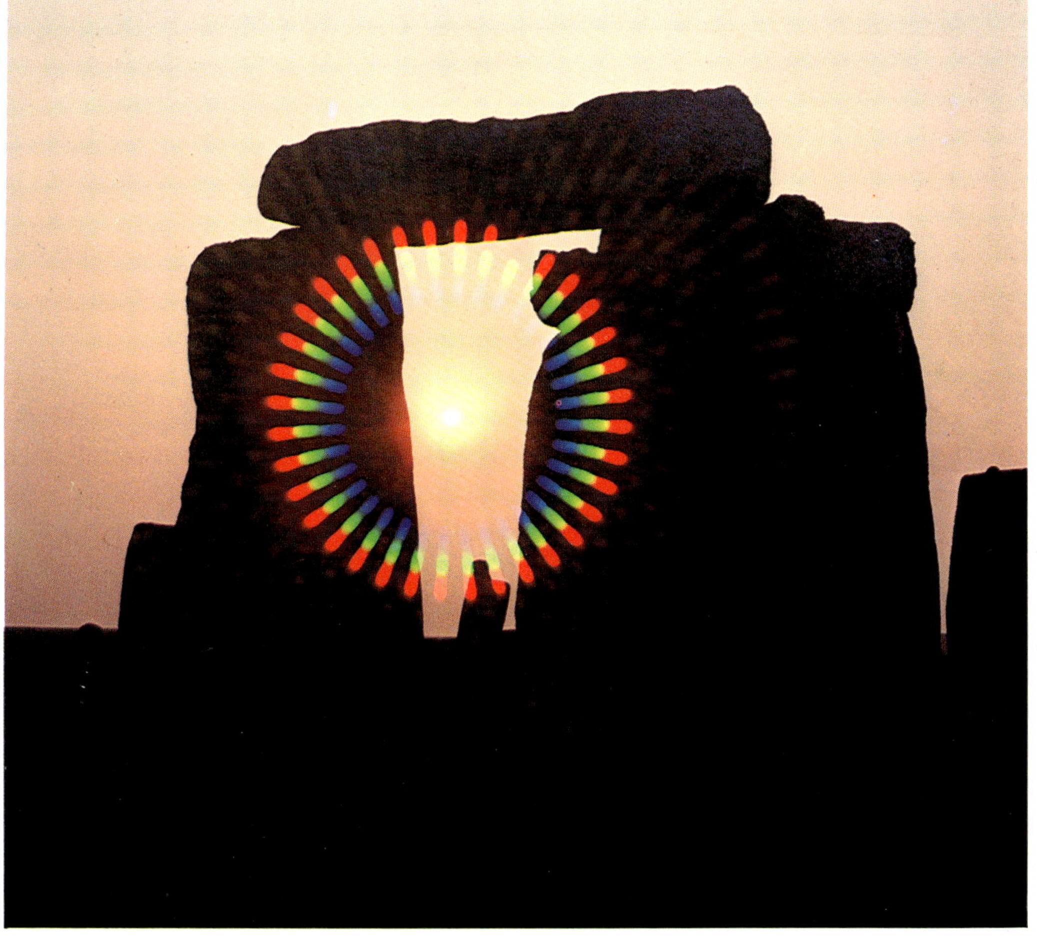

UNDERSTANDING PHOTOGRAPHY
Depth of field

Put simply, depth of field means 'range of sharp focus'. The beginner generally wants to get everything in the picture in focus, but this is not always possible. There are numerous creative uses of focus, but this section is concerned solely with the technical aspects of controlling the depth of field.

The most common way to improve the depth of field is to 'stop down' the lens aperture—that is, reduce the diameter of the lens. The smaller the aperture, the better its depth of field. Remember that small apertures mean large *f*-numbers.

From this, it follows that if you want to get as much of the picture as sharp as possible, you must always close the lens right down—to *f*/16 or *f*/22 if the lens allows it. To keep the same exposure, this means that you have to give a longer shutter speed.

Once the aperture gets smaller than a few millimetres, the picture quality worsens because of the effects of *diffraction*—the result of light travelling past obstacles. The same effect is used in another way to create spikes on highlights in pictures. Many lenses can't be stopped down smaller than *f*/16, since the gain in depth of field would be offset by an overall loss in sharpness.

Another way of controlling depth of field is to use a lens of a different focal length. A telephoto lens has a more restricted depth of field than a standard one, when focused on any particular distance, while a wide angle lens has a greater depth of field. Choice of focal length has as much effect on depth of field as choice of aperture.

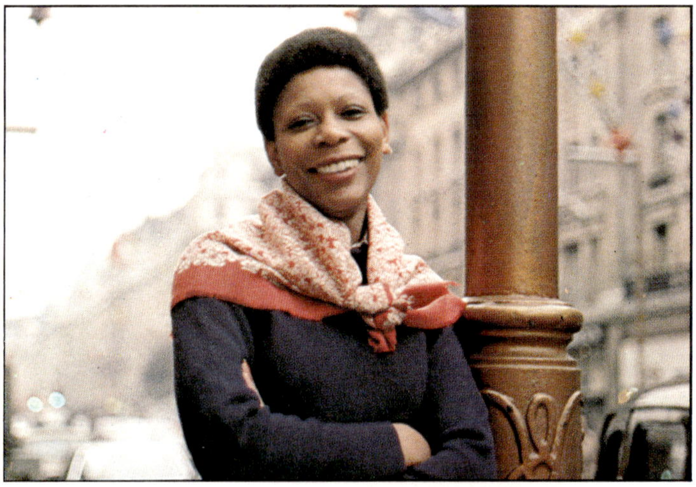

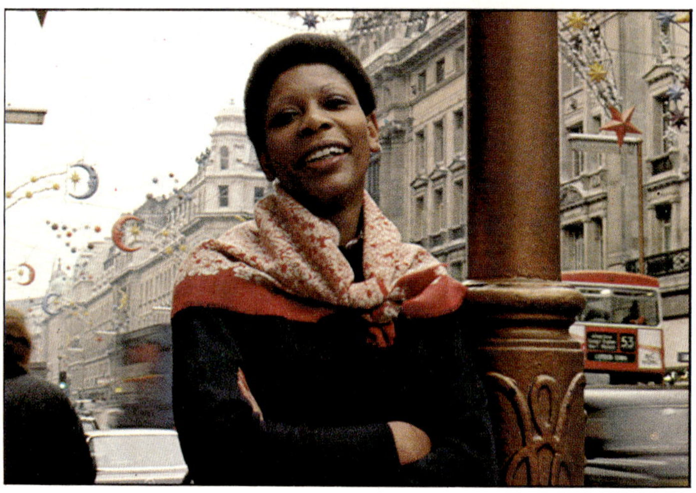

Blurred backgrounds *Using a wide aperture cuts out the background. Stopping down the lens brings it into focus*

How depth of field works

The only reason that a lens has any depth of field at all is that we can tolerate slightly out-of-focus images. Imagine a simple lens focused on an object, as in fig. 1 below.

Rays of light from an object slightly closer will not be focused exactly on the film, but will focus a little way behind it (Fig.2 below) so the slightly closer object will be out of focus on the film.

But unless you enlarge the film a great deal, and look at it closely, you won't notice that the slightly closer object is blurred. The film itself has a grainy nature, which can make it impossible to tell whether or not objects are sharply focused.

These two factors combine to allow a fair tolerance in focus, and the range of sharp focus appears quite wide.

Circles of confusion

The simplest sort of object to deal with is a point of light. A slightly defocused image of a point of light is a small circle, technically known as the *circle of confusion*, rather than a point. The more defocused the image, on either side of the true focus point, the bigger the circle.

Any real object can be thought of as being made up of a large number of points of light, of different colours and brightnesses. Each point produces its own image, and when the image is out of focus all the circles of confusion start to overlap, and the result is a blur.

Stopping down the lens helps to improve the depth of field because if you reduce the lens's aperture, you reduce the size of the circles

1. *Light from the centre of the subject is brought to a focus at the film plane*

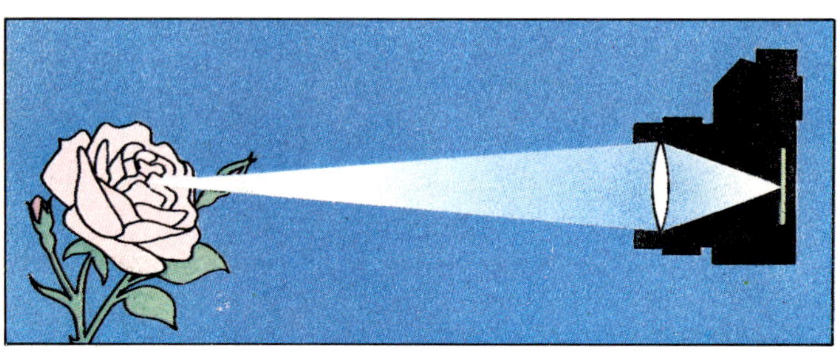

2. *Light from parts of the subject closer to the camera focuses behind the film*

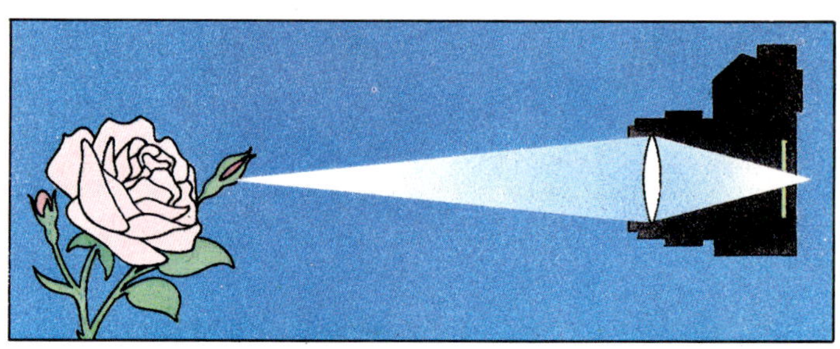

of confusion. So there is a greater chance that slightly out-of-focus images will be acceptably sharp, and depth of field is increased.

Depth of field scales

Many lenses have depth of field scales on their barrels, usually on either side of the focusing mark. These show how much is in focus at any particular *f*-number, read from the focusing scale.

The scale shows another characteristic of depth of field—it is greater on the far side of the focus point. This is worth bearing in mind when you are planning your exact focus point.

Never rely on the scale to give sharp results. Since depth of field depends on tolerance to unsharp images and on the graininess of film, the camera manufacturer has had to make an estimate of what people will put up with. If you are being very critical and are using fine grain film, do not be surprised if you get poorer depth of field than the scale suggests. It is only a guide—remember that only one distance can be truly sharp unless you are using special equipment.

On an SLR, it is possible to see the range of focus on the viewing screen. But many cameras these days view the scene at full aperture all the time, to give a bright view and make focusing easier. On such cameras it is an advantage to have a 'depth of field preview button' which stops the lens down instantly to the taking aperture, giving you a picture of the final depth of field. Though this helps a lot, it has the drawback that the screen goes quite dark making it hard to view. Even so, it is the only sure way to check.

No depth *A bad choice of focus and depth of field means most flowers are blurred*

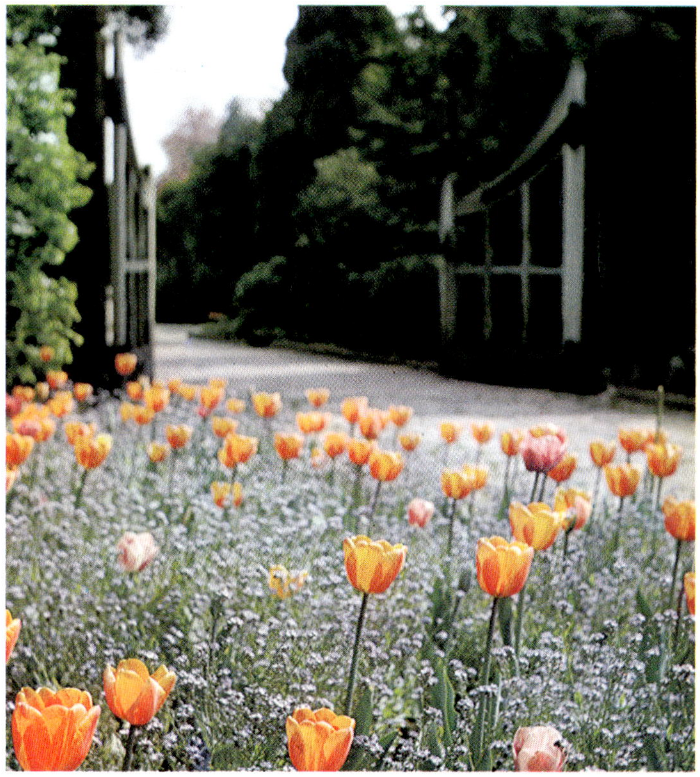

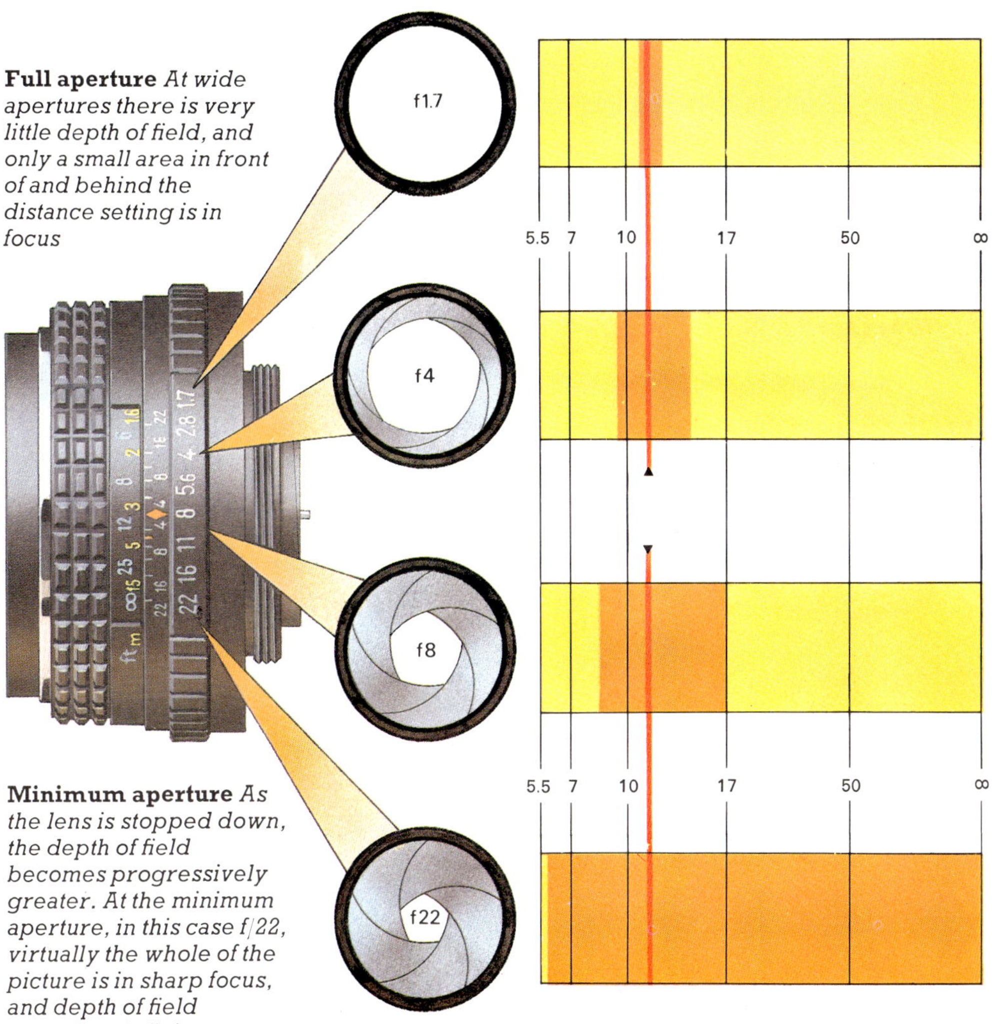

Full aperture *At wide apertures there is very little depth of field, and only a small area in front of and behind the distance setting is in focus*

Minimum aperture *As the lens is stopped down, the depth of field becomes progressively greater. At the minimum aperture, in this case f/22, virtually the whole of the picture is in sharp focus, and depth of field extends to infinity*

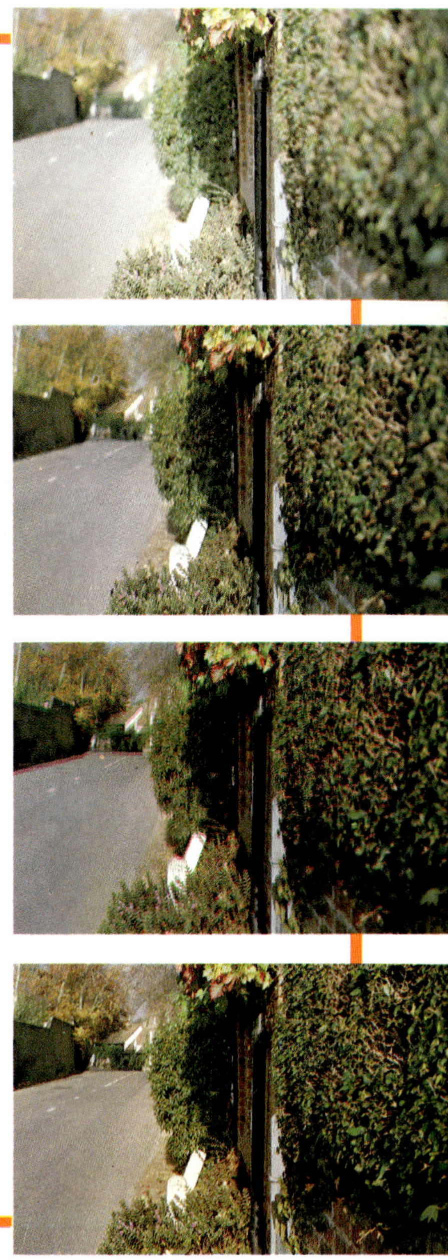

Lenses and apertures

To the newcomer, photography seems to be a world of numbers. There are focal lengths, *f*-numbers, focusing distances, film speeds, shutter speeds . . . not to mention the often intricate designations for camera models.

The *f*-numbers seem the most arbitrary set of all: they run 2, 2.8, 4, 5.6, 8, 11, 16 . . . around the barrel of a lens. There seems no logic to them at first—they are not an obvious series, since they contain such oddities as 2.8 and 5.6. There is a good reason for their choice, but the most important thing is that they are a distinctive set of numbers. Any photographer picking up a new camera or lens can recognize them for what they are, so there is little risk that they will be confused with, for example, the focusing scale.

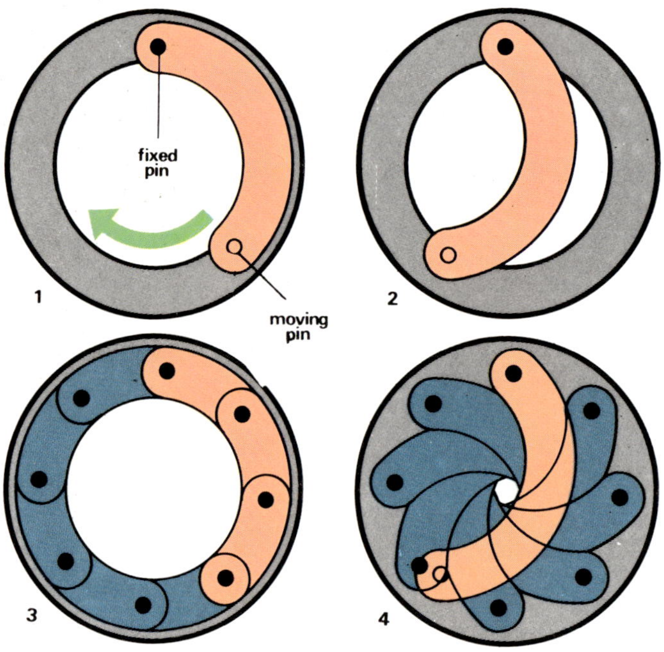

What the numbers mean
The *f*-numbers describe the aperture of the lens—that is, the diameter of the lens opening. Most lenses used in photography have a variable aperture, controlled by means of the iris diaphragm, which has become a symbol for photography. The numbers refer to the aperture at various iris settings.

It is easy to appreciate that the larger the aperture, the more light is let on to the film. So why not simply describe apertures in, say, millimetres? Then a small aperture would be 2 mm and

Diaphragm blades *An iris diaphragm has many blades, each of which moves across the lens opening. One end of each is fixed, the other is attached to a short slot in a ring. Turning this ring moves the blades*

Using aperture to control exposure

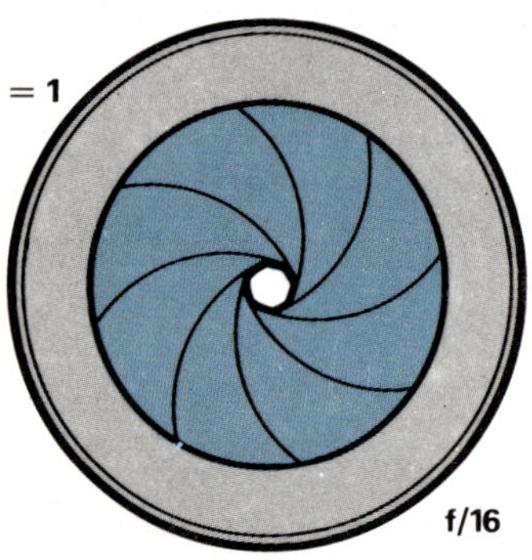

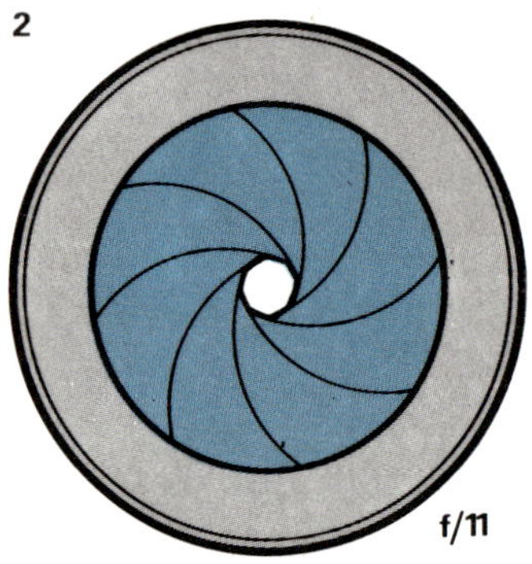

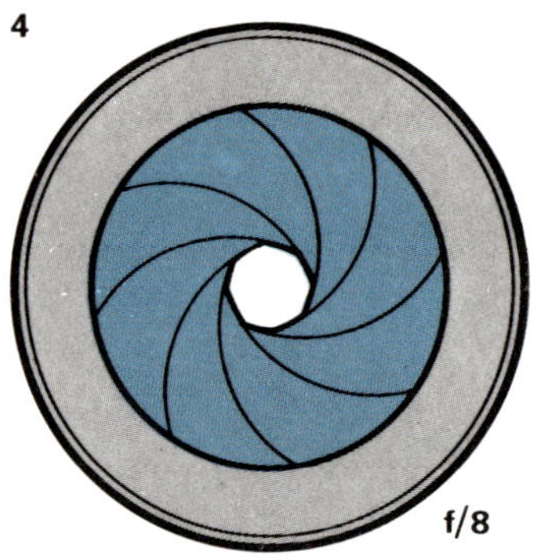

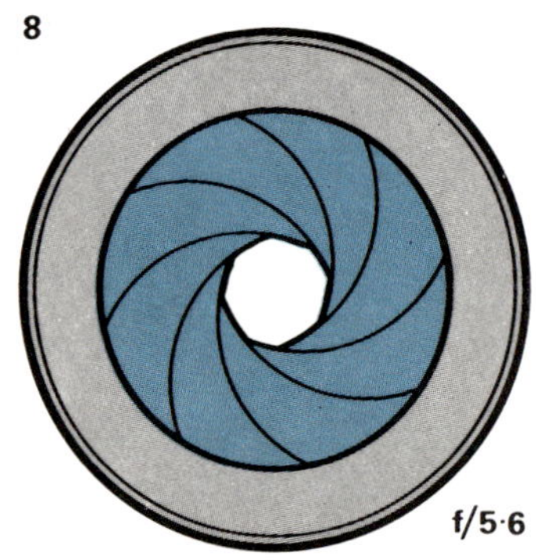

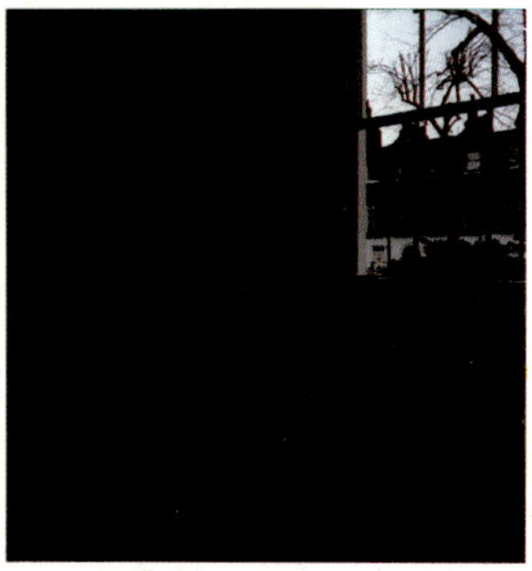

At f/16, the whole image is much too dark

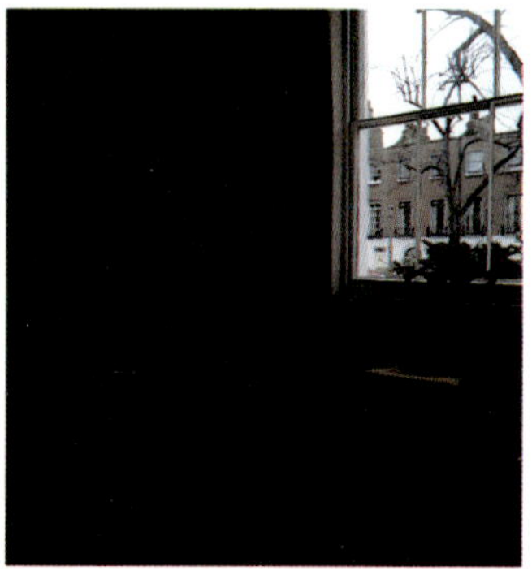

The view outside is correctly exposed at f/11

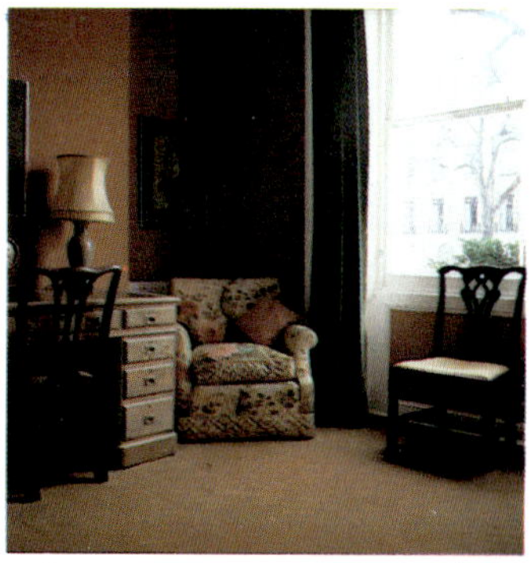

There is a little detail visible indoors by f/8

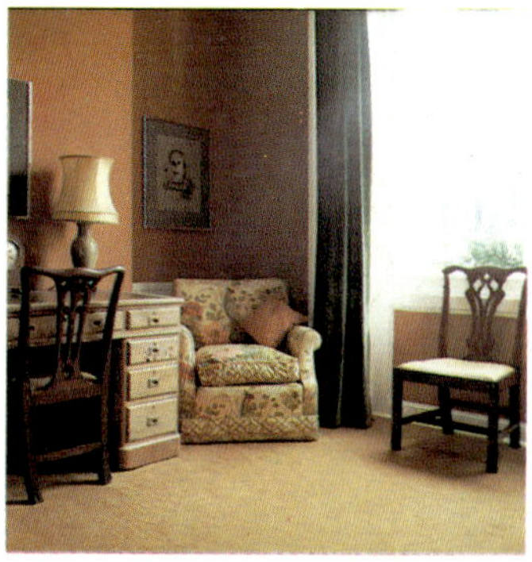

The best picture is produced by using an aperture of f/5.6

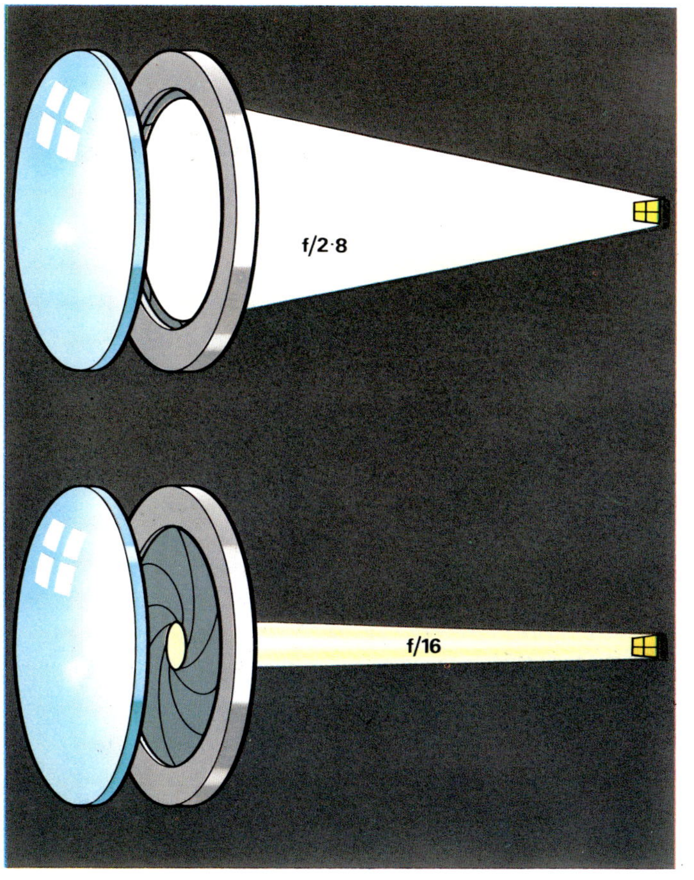

Stopping down *The job of the iris diaphragm is to reduce the effective aperture of a lens. The upper diagram shows the lens at a wide aperture, about f/2.8. Reducing the aperture narrows the 'cone' of light, and when the lens is at f/16 it forms a very dim image*

a large one perhaps 25 mm—a scale which gets larger as the aperture does, compared with the *f*-number scale which, confusingly, runs the opposite way.

The problem is that we are not so much concerned with the amount of light passing through the lens as the actual brightness of the image. This depends not only on the size of the aperture through which the light passes, but also on the *focal length* of the lens you are using.

The focal length of a lens—broadly speaking, the distance from the lens to the film—gives an indication to the photographer of the size that the image of the subject is going to appear on the film. A lens with a long focal length—often called a telephoto lens—produces an image which is bigger than that formed by a standard lens. Conversely, a short focal length lens, that is to say, a wide angle lens, gives an image that is actually reduced in size.

The focal length of the lens, measured in millimetres, is engraved on the front of the barrel. It tells you how far the glass elements of the lens must be placed from the film in order to form an image of distant objects. This is why telephoto lenses are physically longer than standard lenses: the lens elements have to be moved farther from the film.

Since the image formed by a long focus lens is larger than that formed by a standard lens, light from one part of the subject is spread over a larger area when the long focus lens is in use, and is therefore much dimmer. This means that if both lenses have an aperture that is equally wide, the long focus lens will form an image that is larger but less bright.

Calculating the numbers

This is why photographers use the scale of *f*-numbers. These take the focal length into account so that the image brightness for a given subject is always the same at any particular *f*-number—at least in theory.

An *f*-number of a lens is simply its focal length divided by its aperture. For instance, a lens of 50 mm focal length with an aperture of 25 mm has an *f*-number of 2, written *f*/2. Move the iris so as to reduce the aperture to 12.5 mm and it is working at *f*/4. Stop it down still further to 3 mm and it is approximately *f*/16.

When using a lens, the most helpful scale is one that shows changes by a factor of two—that is, with the image brightness doubling or halving. This means that the clear area of the lens doubles or halves. Since area changes with the square of the diameter of the lens, the *f*-numbers are actually the square roots of the numbers in the two-times table. Take the numbers 1, 2, 4, 8, 16, 32, 64 . . . and work out their square roots. You get 1.000, 1.414, 2, 2.828, 4, 5.657, 8, 11.314, 16 . . . These numbers are rounded off to give the familiar series, except that strictly speaking 5.657 is closer to 5.7 than 5.6. So there is logic in the series—each setting is a halving in area of the previous one. It is unfortunate that the series runs the 'wrong' way, and that the numbers seem a little arbitrary. But they are universal and distinctive, and mean a lot.

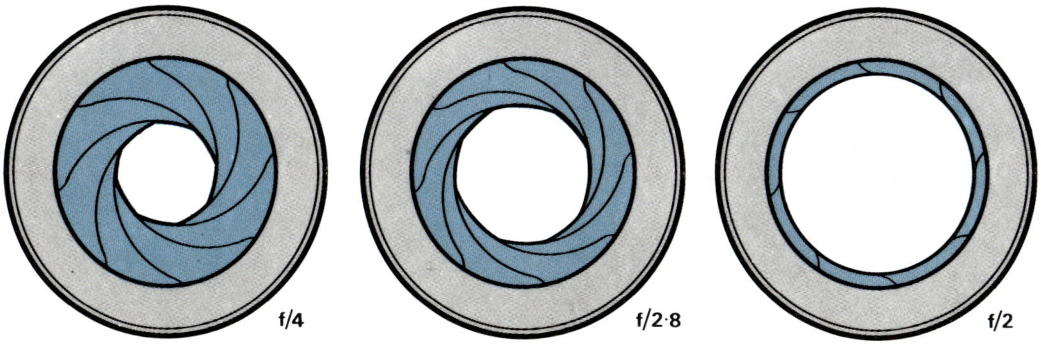

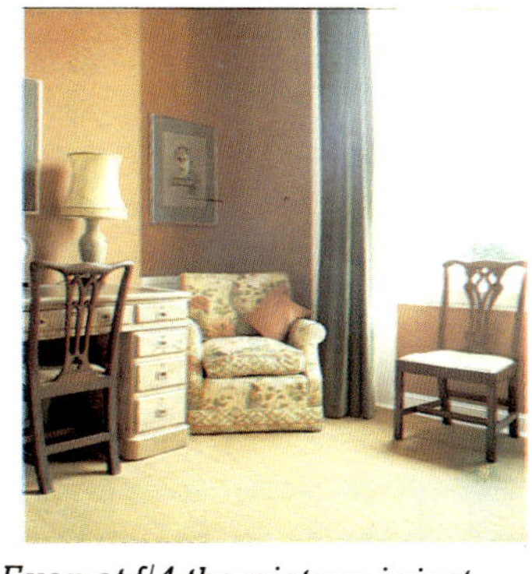

Even at f/4 the picture is just about acceptable

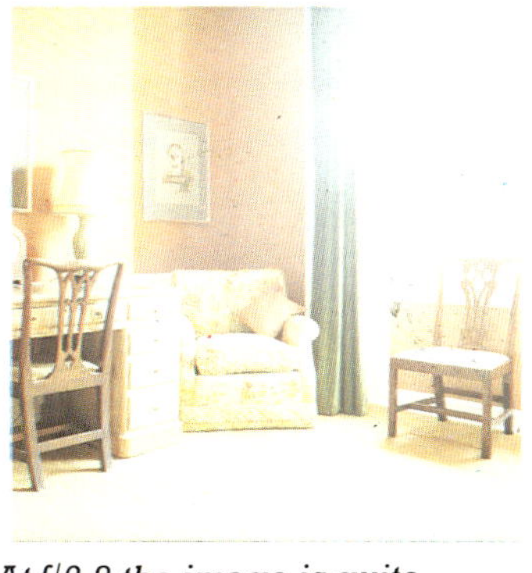

At f/2.8 the image is quite clearly overexposed

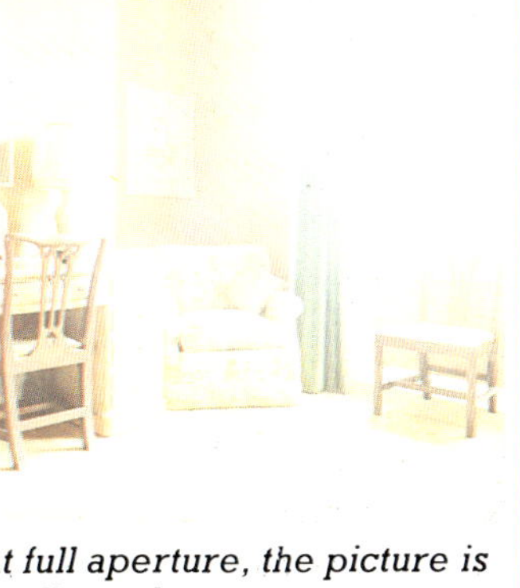

At full aperture, the picture is totally useless

Exposure control *Opening the diaphragm by one stop doubles the area of the aperture, and lets twice as much light reach the film. These pictures show the effect this has on exposure*

Focal length

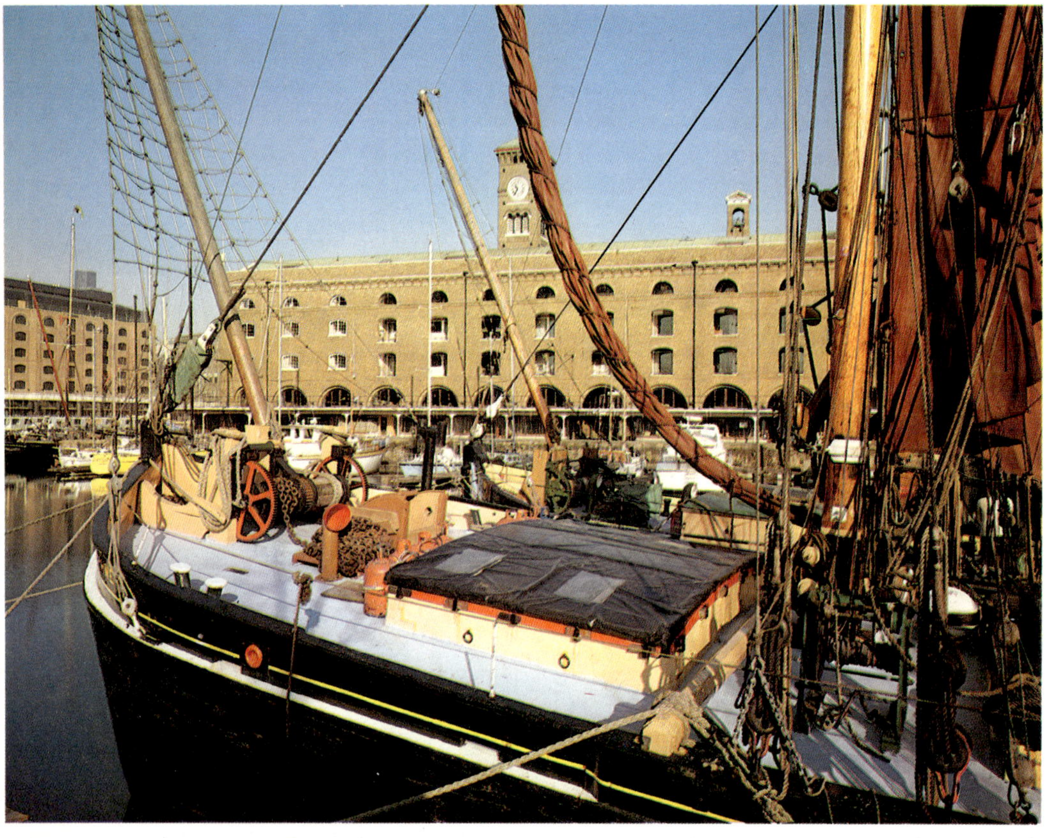

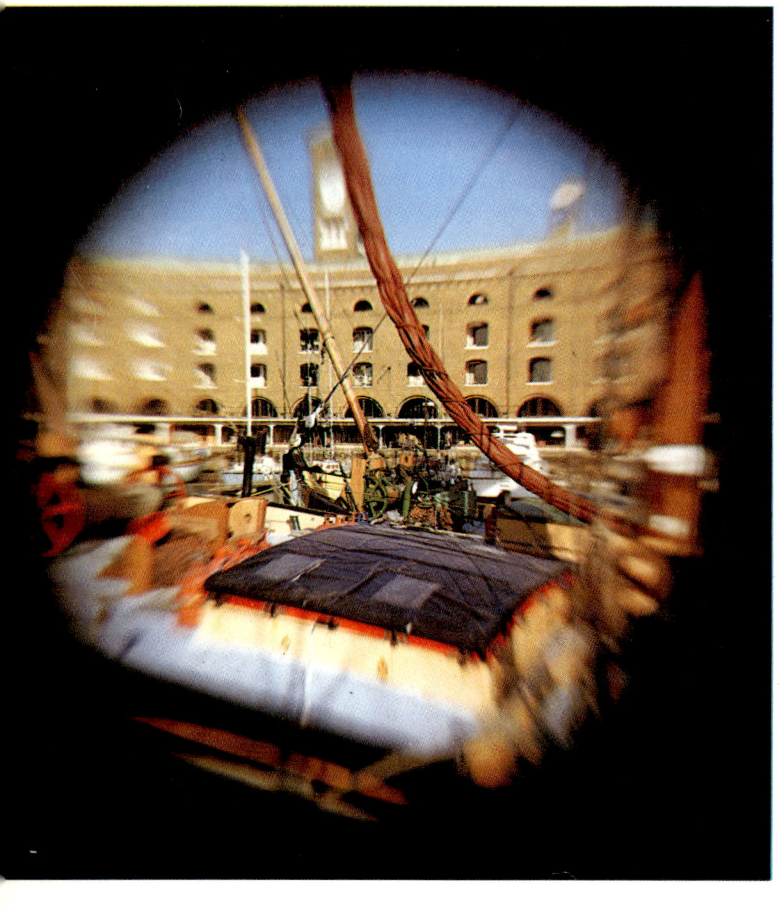

Dock scene *A 90 mm lens designed for use with the large format camera which took this picture has enough covering power. The 90 mm lens for the lower shot was made for use with 35 mm film. The image is the same size, but only the middle is sharp and bright enough to use*

The focal length of a lens is of vital importance because it influences the subject–image relationship in two principal ways. First, focal length governs the size of the image that an object forms on the film in the camera. Secondly, it governs the proportion of the subject that the camera 'sees'—that is, the angle of view.

Image size

If a series of 35 mm cameras with lenses of different focal lengths are lined up side by side, all pointing at the same distant subject, the size of the images on the screens will be different on each camera in the row.

For a distant object the dimensions of the image are proportional to focal length. A lens with long focal length gives a bigger image than a lens with short focal length.

A 500 mm lens gives an image of a distant church spire which is ten times higher than that produced by the standard 50 mm lens. Since the width of the image is also increased tenfold, then the total area of the image projected by the 500 mm lens is 100 times that produced by the 50 mm.

Angle of view

As focal length increases and the image grows bigger, less and less of the subject is included in the picture and the angle of view becomes smaller also.

If it is impossible to move a camera far enough away from a subject to include all of it with the standard 50 or 55 mm lens. Replacing the standard lens by a *wide angle* lens reduces the size of image and includes more of the subject on the film. A wide angle lens is really just a short focal length lens, because as focal length decreases the angle of view gets wider.

A point to bear in mind, since it often causes confusion, is that the effect of focal length on angle of view varies with the film format. So while a 90 mm lens is long with 35 mm cameras, it is standard with medium format cameras. Some typical angles of view for lenses for 35 mm cameras are shown opposite.

Lenses and perspective

If a camera is set up and pointed at a subject such as a building with a figure in the foreground, exposures made from the same point with lenses of different focal lengths will show different angles of view, and different amounts of the subject will be included in the pictures. There will be no differences in perspective as long as the camera is not moved.

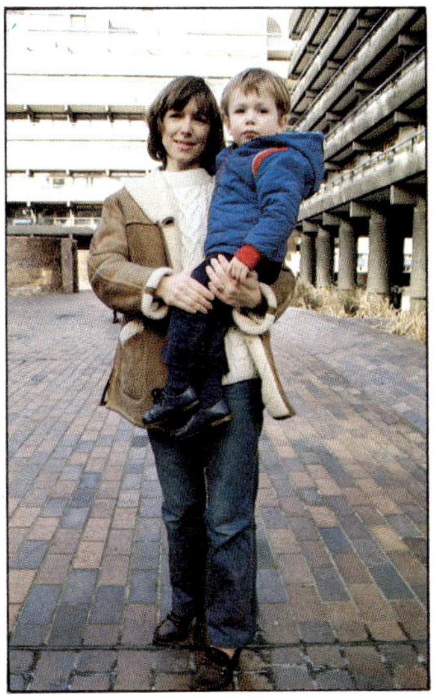

Close viewpoint *Standing near to the subject and using a 28 mm lens results in pictures which seem to be distorted*

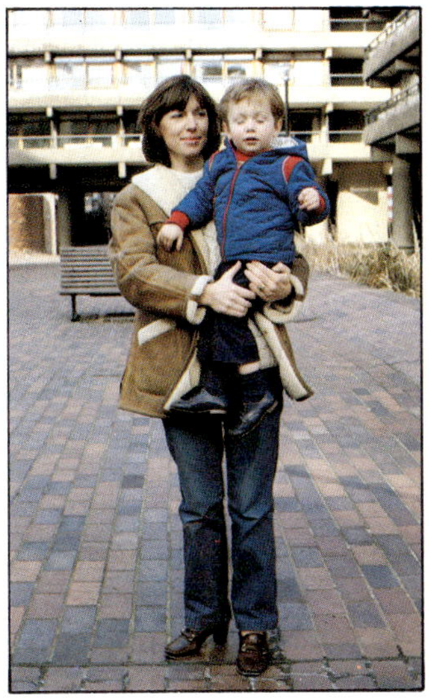

Stepping back *Moving away from the mother and child resulted in normal perspective. A standard lens was used to fill the frame*

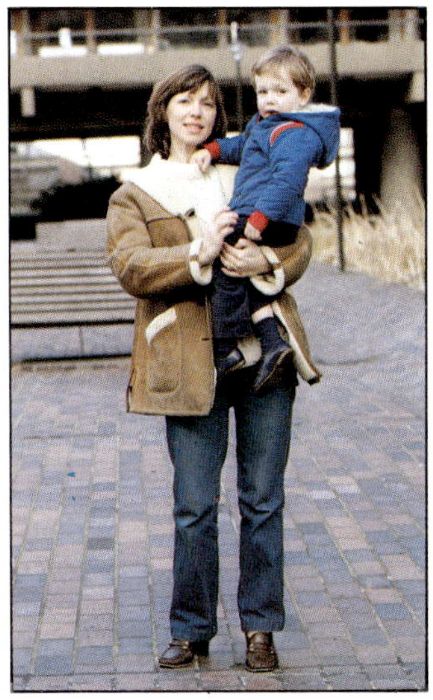

Long shot *From a distance perspective seems flatter, but this was caused by the camera position not by the 105 mm lens used here*

Standard lenses

The normal or standard lens for a 35 mm camera is one with a focal length of around 50 mm. This focal length gives a field of view roughly the same as that over which the eyes give satisfactory sharpness. You cannot, however, really compare a camera with the eyes because the angle through which the eyes give excellent sharpness is only a small proportion of the area we can actually see. Second, we can move eyes to scan a subject and also turn our heads. There is no magic in having a standard lens of 50 mm or so on a 35 mm camera. Many photographers claim that the wider angle of view of a 35 mm lens is preferable, while others maintain that a focal length of about 75 mm is better for general use because it enables the picture space to be filled more easily with the subject.

Telephoto lenses

A telephoto lens is essentially a lens with a long focal length, but it has a special construction that keeps the lens-to-film distance to a minimum. A basic long focal length lens must be placed one focal length away from the film if it is to form an image of a subject at infinity. In the case of a telephoto lens, the lens-to-film distance is considerably reduced so the lens can be made more compact.

With a 200 mm telephoto lens the rear surface may be only 100 mm from the film when the lens is set at infinity. A long focal length lens designed for use on a large format technical or view camera is normally of conventional construction, but small format cameras normally use telephotos.

Retrofocus lenses

A short focus wide angle lens presents problems when used on a single lens reflex camera—as before, to focus on infinity, any lens must be one focal length from the film. If the lens has a focal length of 24 mm, it must be exactly this distance from the film when photographing a distance object. For a single lens reflex camera to operate normally, however, there must be sufficient space for a mirror to be fitted in between the rear of the lens, and the film. 24 mm is not enough of a gap.

This difficulty is overcome by using an inverted telephoto or *retrofocus* construction which makes the lens-to-film distance much longer than the focal length, even when the camera is focused at infinity. In the case of a typical 24 mm wide angle lens the lens-to-film distance may be as much as 35 mm measured from the rear surface of the lens. Some standard 50 and 55 mm lenses are of retrofocus type, as are many of the lenses in the Nikon range.

Covering power

If any lens designed for use on a 35 mm camera is mounted on a 4 × 5 inch technical camera and focused on a distant scene, the focusing screen of the camera will show a circular image, about 50 mm in diameter, the edge of which fades off into darkness. This circular image will just cover the 24 × 36 mm frame with an image which is evenly illuminated and sharp overall. Such a lens has a *covering power* adequate for a 35 mm camera but for nothing bigger than this format.

A lens with a focal length of 90 mm would be a telephoto lens on a 35 mm Leica, a standard lens on a 6 × 6 cm Mamiyaflex and a wide angle lens on a 4 × 5 inch Sinar technical camera. A 90 mm lens for a Leica needs only modest covering power relative to its focal length. The same focal length for a 6 × 6 cm camera would need normal covering power, but a 90 mm lens as a wide angle lens for the 4 × 5 inch format would have to be designed to give a much bigger image. The same 90 mm lens would not serve all three purposes equally well, so each camera format needs a separate lens to give best results.

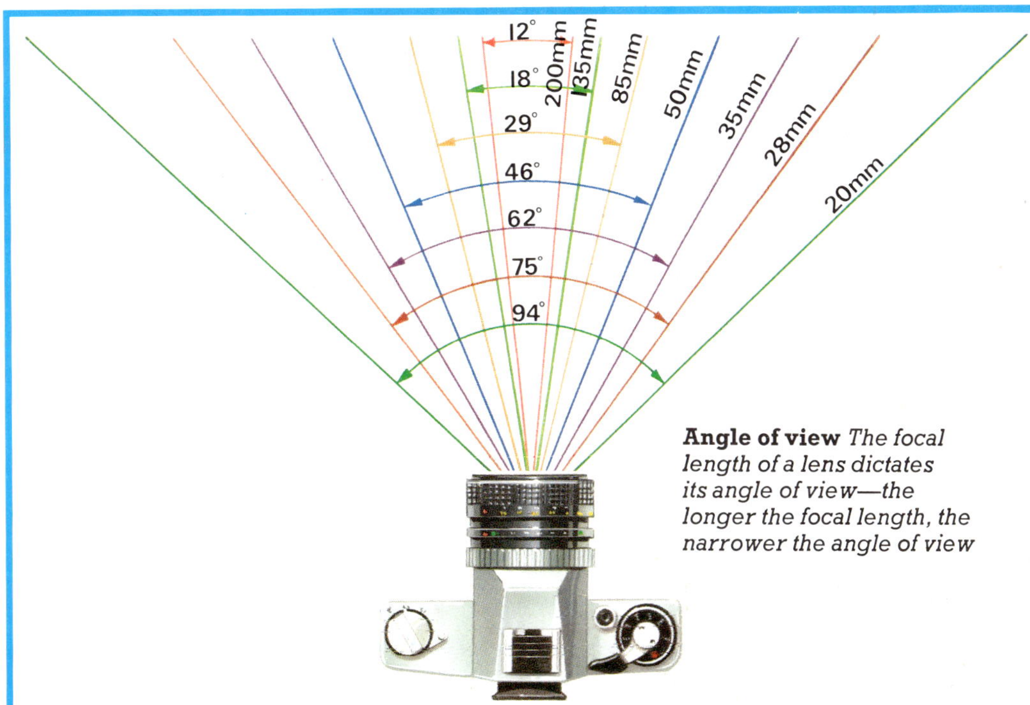

Angle of view *The focal length of a lens dictates its angle of view—the longer the focal length, the narrower the angle of view*

How film works

When you look at a black and white negative or print, all you are seeing is millions of tiny particles of metallic silver embedded in a thin layer of tough jelly. This emulsion is coated onto a thin sheet of plastic material or paper.

Although this may not sound very exciting, it is the basis of all photographs, even colour films and prints. From such mundane beginnings, superb photographs can be produced, and though the process of image formation is often taken for granted, it makes a fascinating story in itself.

Film technology is advancing all the time. Every year the emulsion is refined by the addition of new crystal structures and by improving sensitivity. Here, then, we are going to discuss the basic structure over which these refinements are made.

What is an emulsion ?

The simplest type of emulsion is that used for black and white photography. *Emulsion* is really the wrong word, because the light sensitive layer of film or paper consists of minute crystals of silver compounds *suspended* in gelatin. For historical reasons it is called an emulsion, not a suspension.

It is possible to make a simple emulsion in the kitchen sink. All that is needed is some common salt dissolved in a weak glue of warm cooking jelly.

If a solution of silver nitrate is stirred into this mixture, myriad tiny crystals of silver chloride are formed, turning the gelatin white like milk. The crystals are insoluble in water, so they separate or *precipitate* out. If the emulsion was made in a darkroom under a safelight, instead of in daylight, it could be coated on to paper, dried and used for printing.

The light sensitive compounds used in photographic materials are made by combining silver with chlorine, bromine and iodine. These three chemicals are called *halogens*, and the compounds they form when combined with silver are called *silver halides*. There is a fourth silver halide, silver fluoride, but it is of no interest to photographers because it is soluble in water and would wash out of the gelatin layer. Of the three useful halides, silver bromide is the most sensitive to light and the most important constituent of any emulsion.

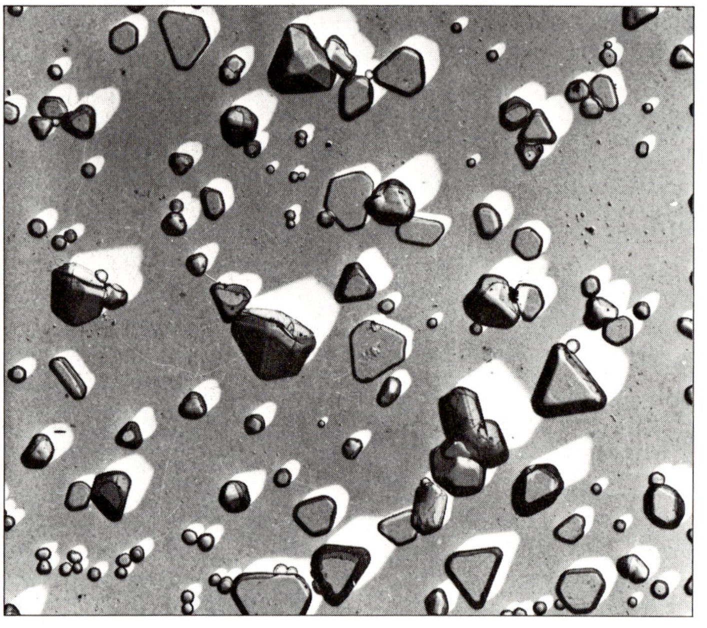

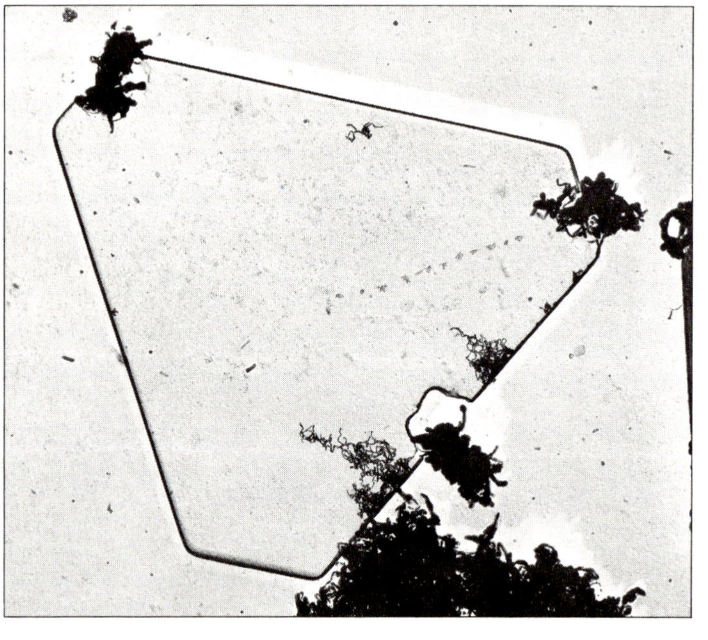

Silver grains *The top picture shows the different sized crystals of silver halide contained in an emulsion. The lower picture shows silver around a part-developed grain*

Development

If a piece of undeveloped film is left in a sunny window for a few minutes it will turn a slate grey. Light converts the silver bromide to very finely divided metallic silver. Bromine gas is liberated and this can be detected by its acrid smell.

In a camera, the exposures given to a film are not enough to produce instant visible silver. Instead, on each crystal that receives more than a certain amount of light, a few atoms of silver are freed. These collect at points on the crystal surface where there are impurities—such as silver sulphide—which have been formed during manufacture.

The images formed in a camera are invisible or *latent* images, and can be revealed only by treating the exposed film in a developer which continues the action of the light. Every crystal with one or more groups of silver atoms on its surface is quickly changed entirely to silver by the reducing agent in the developer.

If a developer is allowed to act for long enough it will reduce all the halide crystals to silver whether they have been exposed or not, but its action on exposed crystals is from 10 to 100 times as fast. In the normally brief development times of a few minutes the exposed areas of a film are blackened and most of the halide crystals are changed completely to silver. In the areas that have received little exposure only a few particles of silver are formed. There is thus a 'negative' image in which the lightest parts of the subject are recorded by the densest parts of the film and the dark parts appear almost transparent or clear.

Gelatin

The gelatin, in which the light sensitive crystals are embedded, has several things to do. It holds the silver halide crystals in place and keeps them evenly distributed on the paper or film backing. It swells in the developer by absorbing water and allows the chemicals to have free access to the halide grains. It also helps development by increasing the rate at which exposed grains develop, while slowing down the unexposed ones.

Development must be stopped before the unexposed grains start to develop by rinsing the film or paper vigorously in water. It can be stopped even more quickly by using a very dilute solution of acetic acid—spirit vinegar—as a stop bath instead of water. This has the effect of neutralizing the alkali contained in every developer and the action stops almost at once. Developing agents, almost without exception, have to be in alkaline solution to work properly.

A stop bath has another important function—it prevents developer contaminating clean solutions.

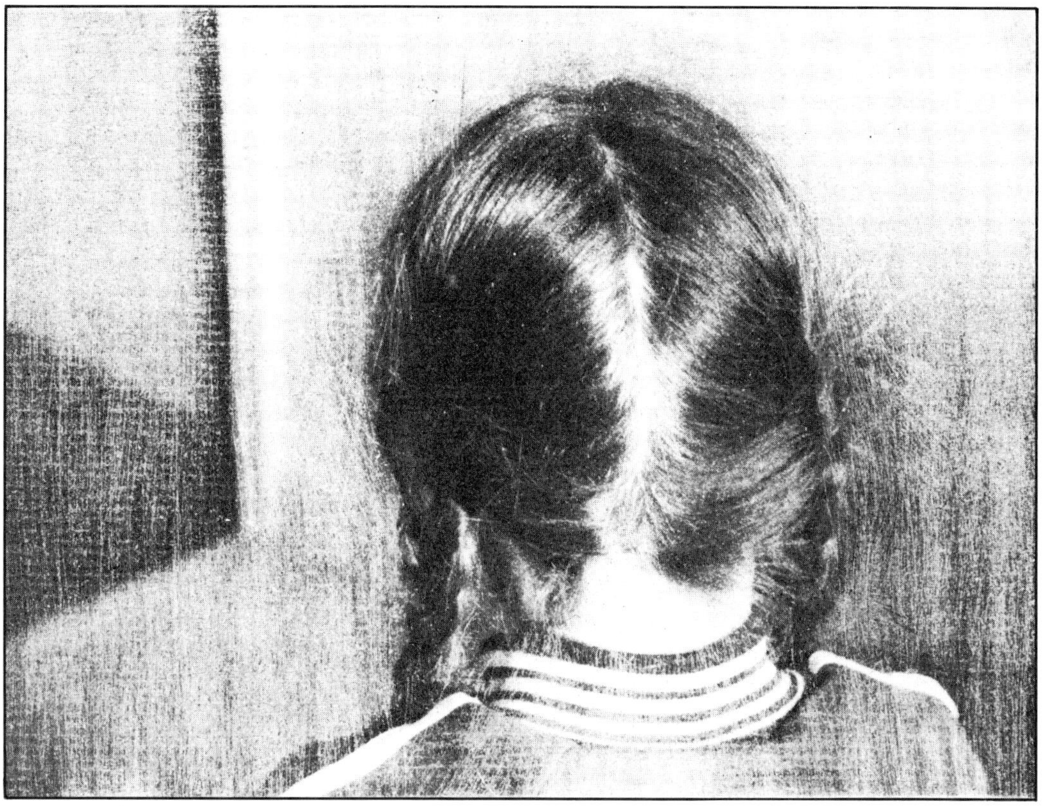

Mari Mahr

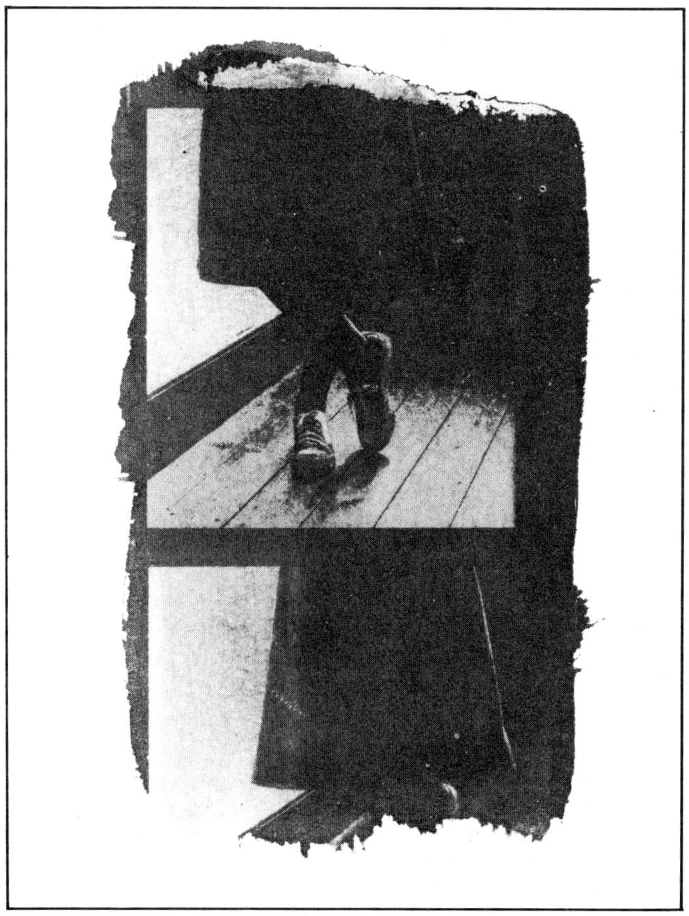

Emulsion paint *These two pictures were printed on to ordinary paper. The photographer first made it light sensitive by painting on a home-made emulsion*

Film development *After exposure, silver bromide crystals in the emulsion are left covered with minute specks of silver (top). During development, each exposed grain is converted entirely to silver (middle). Fixation removes unexposed grains of silver bromide*

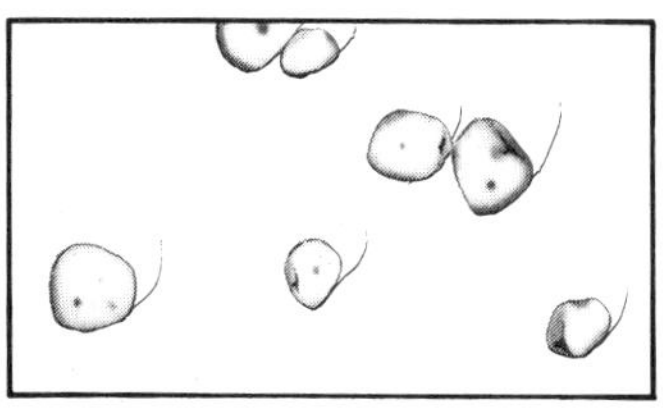

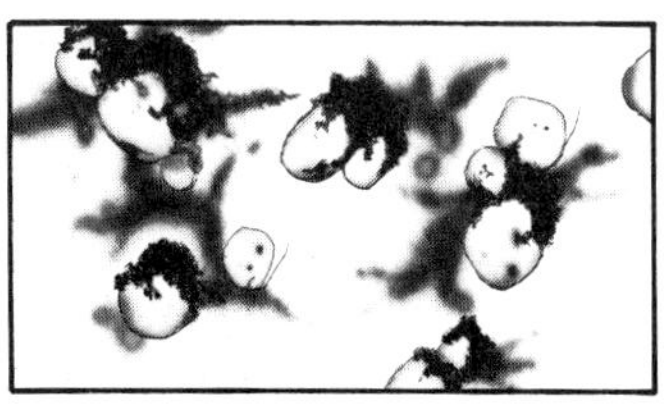

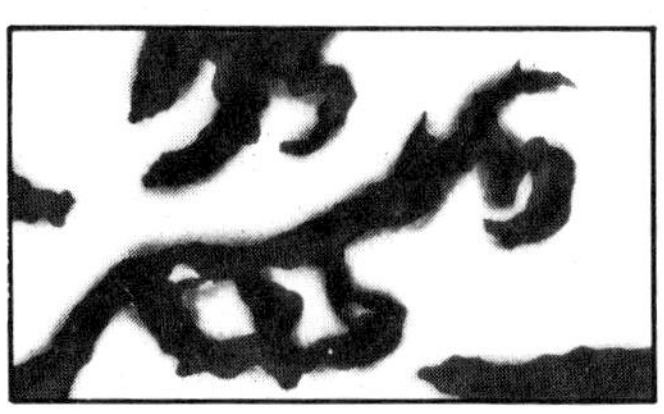

Fixation

After development there is a considerable quantity of silver halide left mixed with the silver image. If this was left on the film or print, it would slowly darken and eventually almost obliterate the image. The silver halides are not soluble in water so a fixing bath is used to convert them to freely soluble compounds. Some of these compounds diffuse out into the fixing bath, and it is the accumulation of silver salts in a fixer that limits its useful life, rather than exhaustion of the solution.

A final wash in running water must be given to all films and papers to remove soluble silver salts and also the fixing chemicals. Any silver salts left in an emulsion slowly darken in light if not removed and fixer eventually decomposes and attacks the silver image, turning it brown in patches.

Commercial emulsions

Emulsions on films and papers are very different from the simple homemade silver chloride type described here.

For a film, the light sensitive compound is mainly silver bromide with traces of silver iodine. The method of precipitation of the halides and their subsequent heat treatment controls the speed and other properties of the material. A slow emulsion has very small halide crystals of fairly uniform size, and a fast one has bigger crystals of much more varied sizes. In a single emulsion the larger crystals or grains are the most sensitive to light.

Colour emulsions are silver halide emulsions just like those of monochrome materials. Additionally, most colour emulsions contain *colour couplers* which eventually form the coloured images making up the final picture. In this process, silver is produced, but it is not required in the final image and so it is removed by converting it back to silver bromide and then fixing it in the normal way. A bleach-fix bath performs both operations in a single process. The final images consist only of minute dye particles suspended in gelatin.

How colour negative film works

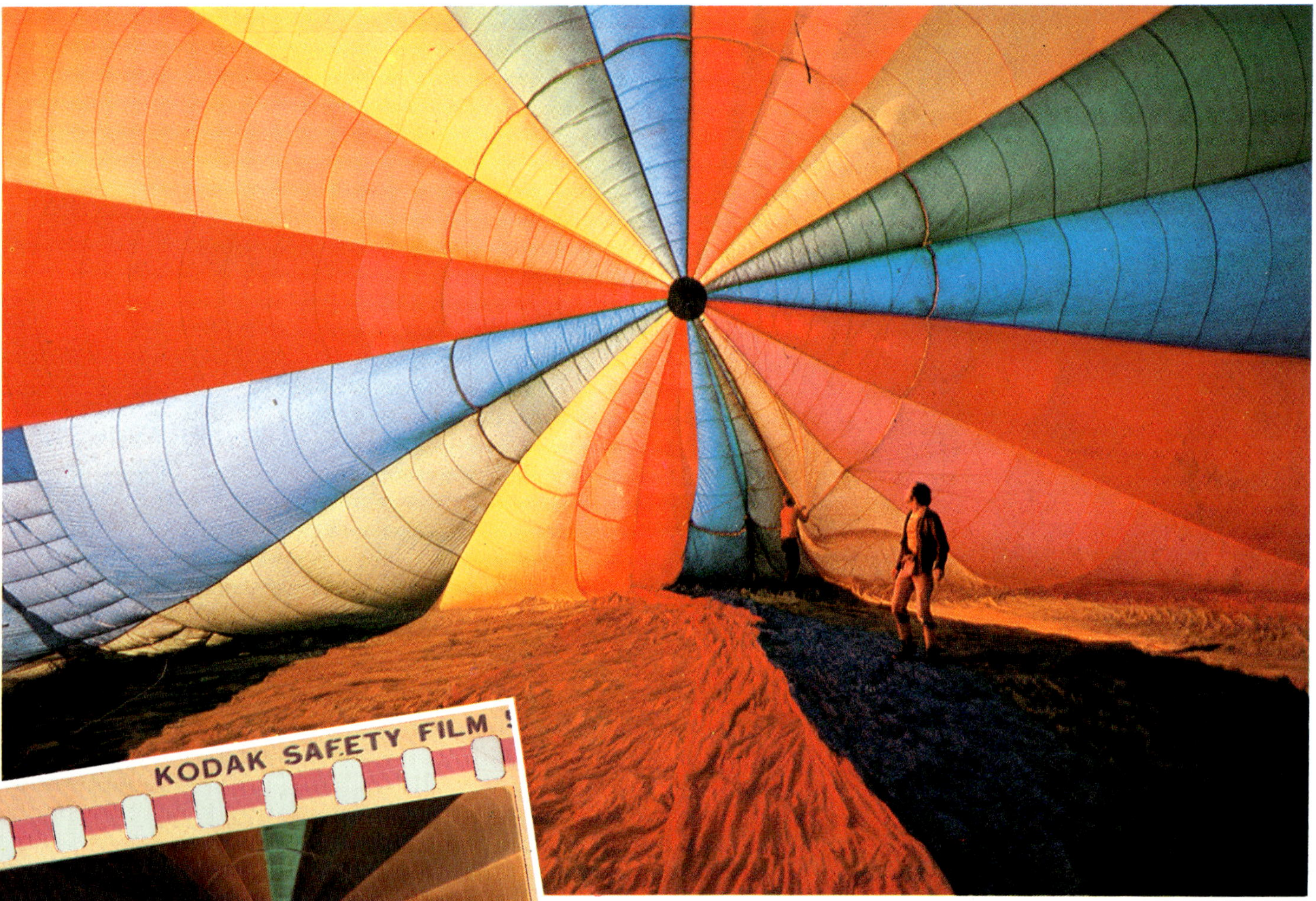

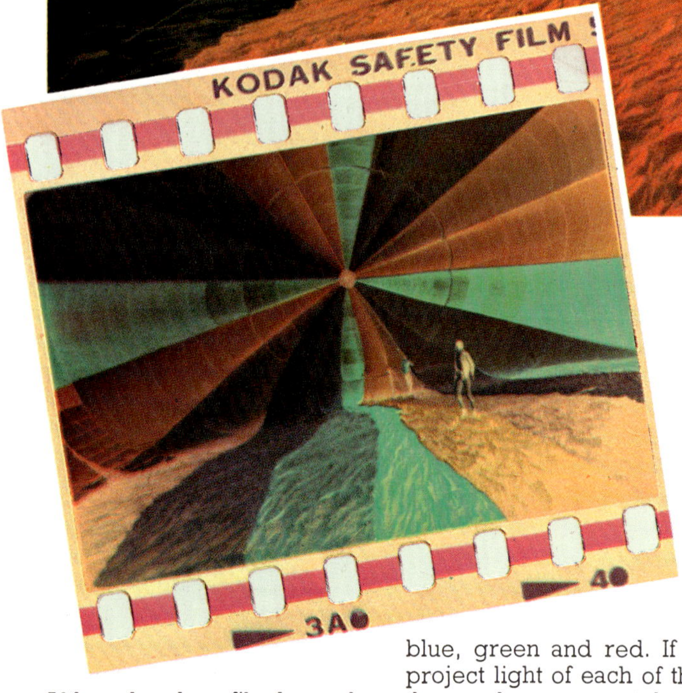

Negative and positive *The tones on a colour negative are reversed, as they are in black and white, but colours, too, appear as their opposites*

Although colour film has only become widely popular in the last 20 or so years, the basic principles are almost as old as photography itself.

Colour negative film, and indeed all colour film, depends upon the discovery in the mid-19th century that coloured light can be split into three *primary colours*: blue, green and red. If you project light of each of these three colours separately onto a screen, you can make white and almost any other colour in the spectrum by overlapping them in different proportions.

Photographic scientists realized that this discovery might provide a basis for colour photography. Just as you can create any colour by mixing blue, green and red, any colour can be divided into its blue, green and red components. By recording the amount of blue light, the amount of green light and the amount of red light reflected from a subject, you have, in effect, recorded the original colour of the subject.

So colour negative film is essentially based on three separate emulsions, one sensitive to blue light, one to green and the other to red. Because there are three layers, all coated together onto a base, such films are called *integral tripacks*.

The top layer is sensitive to blue light and ultraviolet light, and contains silver bromide crystals, without any colour sensitization dyes. Because it is sensitive to ultraviolet light—to which our eyes are blind—this layer of the film receives too much exposure when the light is rich in ultraviolet. As a result pictures at the seaside and at high altitudes, where there is often more ultraviolet, may have a light blue cast and may look overexposed.

The second layer of emulsion is sensitive to both blue and green light. It is a silver bromide emulsion with certain dyes added to make the film react to green light. This layer of the film must only record the green component of the subject, so blue light is filtered out by a yellow barrier layer between the first and second layers.

The yellow barrier layer is not made from dyes or pigments, but is coloured with finely divided silver particles—*colloidal silver*. Colloidal silver is used because it can be removed in processing by a bleach bath.

The final layer of the film, next to the film base, is sensitive to both blue light and to red light. Since the blue light has already been filtered out by the yellow barrier before it reaches this layer, it records only the red component of the subject.

The three emulsion layers, then, each form an image of one of the three primary colours, blue, green and red. Before processing, however, the film is not actually coloured. Colour must be provided by the formation of appropriately coloured dyes in each of the three emulsion layers during processing. The formation of the dyes is controlled by complex organic chemicals known as *colour couplers*. Each of the three emulsion layers contains a different *colour coupler*.

When the film is processed, the developer reacts with the grains of silver in the emulsions to form a silver image just like a black and white negative, and also some by-products. It is the by-products that react with the colour couplers to form the dyes that make the colour image.

Round each grain of silver in the blue sensitive layer, for example, *yellow* dye is formed, and a yellow image appears. The same process happens in the other layers. Where green light has struck the green sensitive layer, a *magenta* image is formed, and where red light has struck the red sensitive later, a *cyan* (blue-green) image is formed.

After colour development, then, there is both a dye image, and a silver image in each emulsion layer. It is difficult to see the colours of the dyes because the black and grey tones of the silver hide them. To convert the negative into the right form the silver image must be bleached away. The bleach used is not ordinary household bleach, but a chemical which converts silver back into silver bromide, without affecting the dye images in each layer. It also bleaches out the yellow filter layer.

After bleaching, the film is immersed in a fixing bath, which makes all the silver bromide soluble in water. This process is similar to the fixing of a black and white film, but the fixer is formulated so as not to affect the dye image.

Finally the film is washed to remove all the soluble compounds, and hung up to dry. The bleach and fixing stages are often combined into one—a '*blix*' *bath*—and the processing routine is no more difficult and only a little longer than developing a black and white film.

A negative image

A colour negative is negative in two senses. Not only are light tones in the subject reproduced as dark in the negative, but all colours in the subject are reproduced as their complementaries in the negative. All these primary colours, which are mixed to form other colours, are rendered as their three *complementary* colours: blue becomes yellow, green is changed to magenta, and red becomes cyan. Just as the printing of a black and white negative gives the image its original values, so too does the printing of a colour negative. Colour printing paper works in a similar way to film and the print is simply a negative image of the negative—a 'positive'.

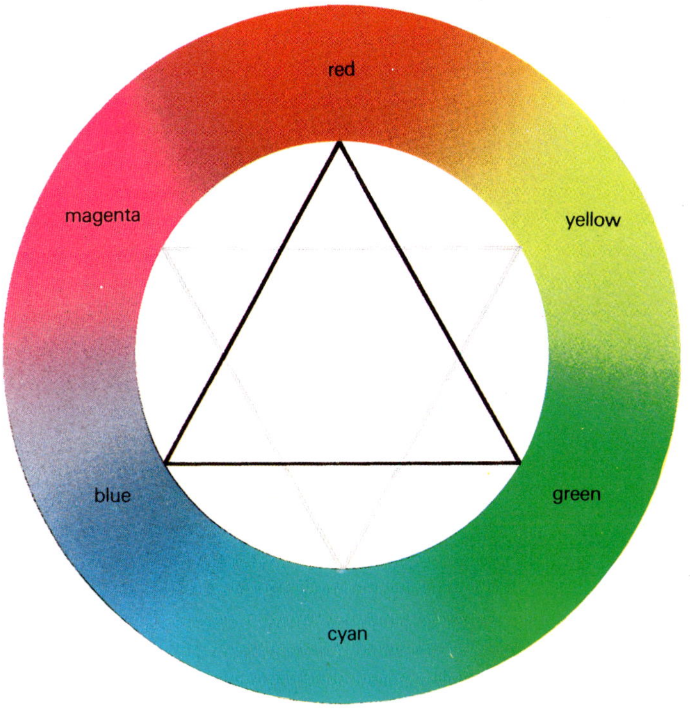

Colour circle *Colour negative film works by recording each of the primary colours as their complementaries. Printing the film reverses the process*

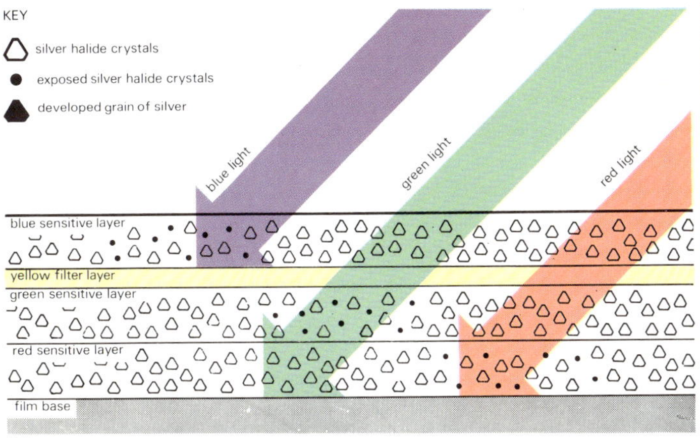

Exposure *Exposure to blue, green and red light forms a latent image in the three emulsion layers, each of which is sensitive to one of the primary colours*

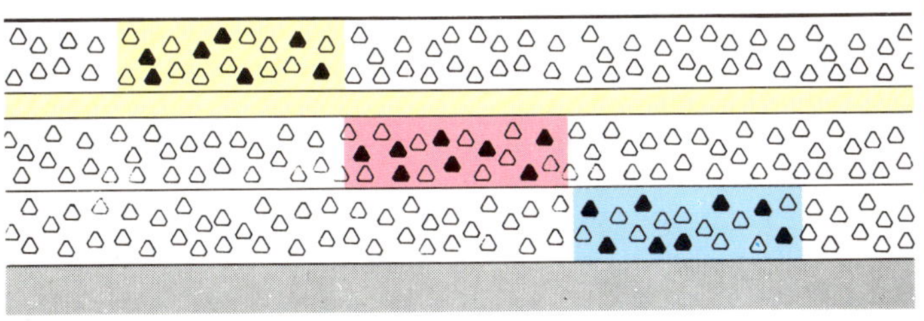

Development *A silver image is produced in the layers of the film where light of the appropriate colours fell. Colour couplers react to form coloured dyes*

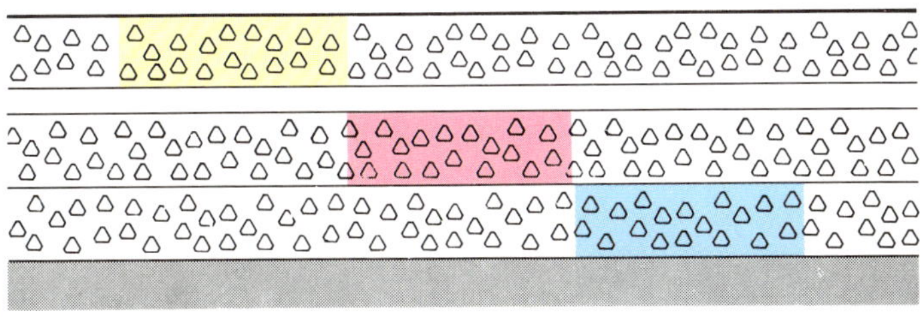

Bleaching *A bleach bath converts the metallic silver back into silver halides, and removes the yellow filter layer*

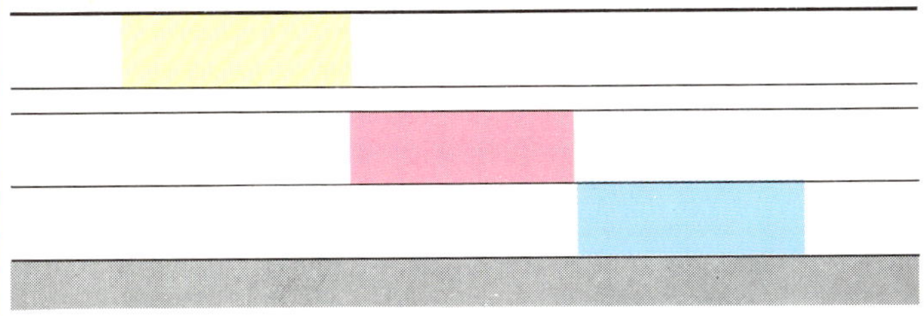

Fixation *The silver halides are removed from the film in the fixing bath, leaving only dye images in each layer, in complementary colours of the light that struck the film*

How colour slide film works

Although neglected for black and white work, slide or reversal film is now immensely popular for colour. Indeed, many professionals use slide film almost exclusively. Like colour negative film, slide film is based on the principle of subtractive synthesis of colour (see page 550), but it differs in a number of significant ways.

The emulsion for colour slide film is basically similar to that of colour negative film—it is an integral tripack, as described on page 551. It consists of three layers, sensitive to blue, green and red light, with a yellow filter 'layer' beneath the blue sensitive layer that prevents blue light from reaching the other two layers. Slide film also resembles colour negative film in that the three layers each contain colour couplers which produce yellow, magenta and cyan dyes.

Exposure of colour slide film is also the same as exposure of colour negatives, and different colours of light form an image in different parts of the emulsion. Blue light forms a latent image in the top, blue sensitive layer. The next layer, which is green sensitive, records a latent image of the green in the subject, and the bottom layer of the film records red light.

The real difference between transparencies and negatives lies in the processing. Since slide and negative emulsions are similar, and the latent image is recorded on the film in a similar manner, processing slide film in the same way as negative film would result in a negative image. So, to give its positive image, slide film must be processed by a particular method, known as *reversal processing*. This is why slide film is also referred to as 'reversal' film. Essentially, reversal processing involves developing the latent negative image on the film and then chemically reversing it to give the final positive.

The first stage in processing is to develop the film in a solution which is very similar to black and white developer. This simply produces a silver image in those parts of the film that have been exposed to light. In the blue sensitive layer, for example, a negative silver image of the blue parts of the subject will appear. The process of development has to be very accurately controlled—the temperature must be accurate to within 0.33°C. This precision is necessary to ensure equal density and contrast in all three emulsion layers.

The second processing step is to 'fog' the film

Three layers *The image on a slide is made up from three separate dye images in yellow magenta and cyan*

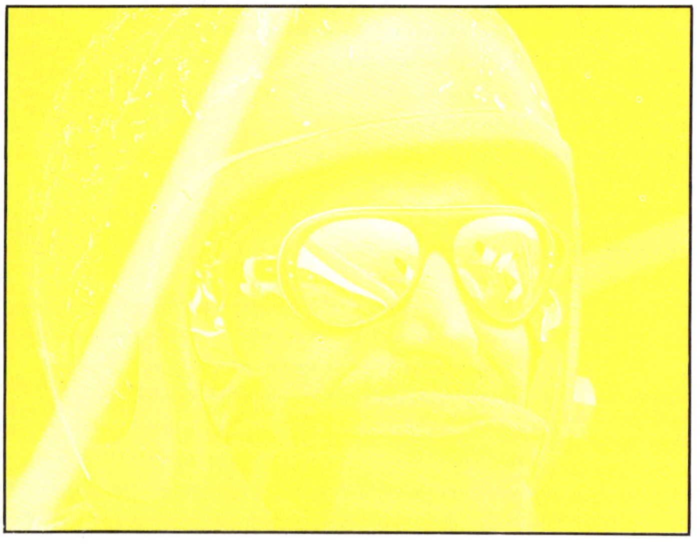

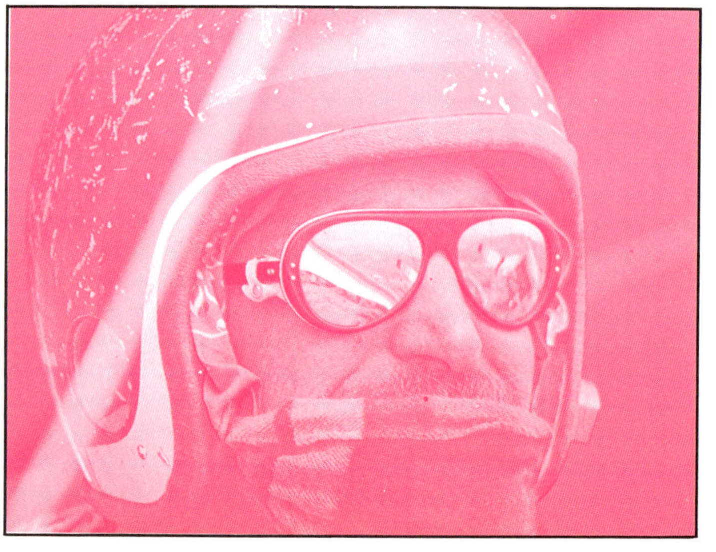

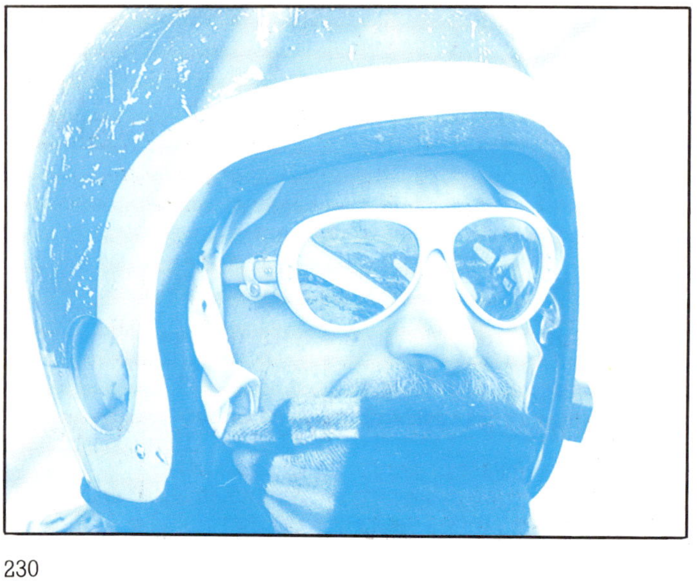

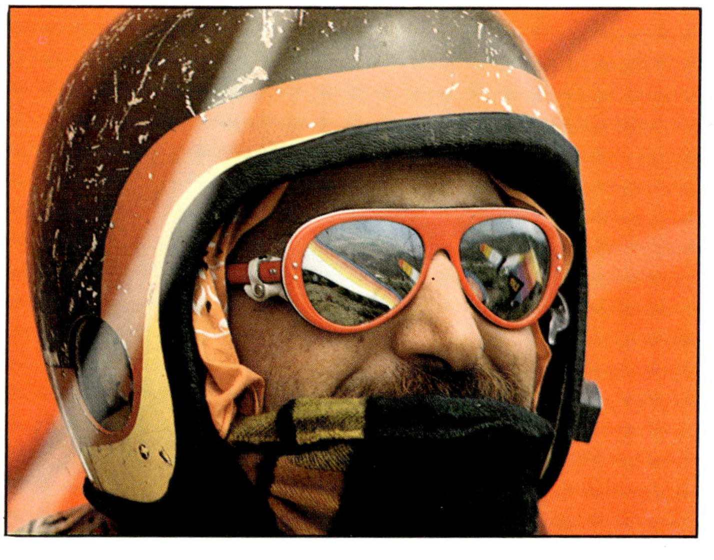

deliberately—either by exposing it to bright white light, or, more commonly, by a chemical fogging agent. The effect of fogging is to make it possible to develop all the silver grains which were not exposed when the picture was taken. The fogging has no effect on the grains that were exposed in the camera, because these were already developed to metallic silver in the first of the processing solutions.

The next stage is to immerse the film in colour developer. This acts in the same way as the developer for colour negative film—it develops the fogged grains of silver, and simultaneously produces development by-products. These combine with the colour couplers in the three emulsion layers, producing coloured images in each layer where the fogged silver is being developed.

At this point in processing, the film is opaque because there is developed silver over the entire frame in addition to the coloured dye images. With the image already recorded in colour, the silver is no longer required and must be removed so that the colour can be seen. To remove it, the film is dipped into a silver bleach bath, which converts the metallic silver back into silver halide. The silver halide is in turn removed by immersing the film in fixing solution, which converts it to soluble compounds. These can then be washed off, to reveal the final positive colour image.

The process works because the coloured dyes form only in the fogged silver areas, not those areas that were exposed in the camera. The colour of the dye in each layer is complementary to the original sensitivity of the layer: the dye is yellow in the blue layer, magenta in the green layer and cyan in the red layer. In the blue sensitive layer, for example, a yellow dye is formed in the fogged silver areas during processing. Since the fogged silver areas in the blue sensitive layer are all the areas that did *not* react during the original exposure—that is, they are the areas with *no* blue in the original scene—the yellow dye corresponds to 'no blue' areas.

Because yellow is complementary to blue, a yellow filter transmits red and green but absorbs blue. When you look at the final slide against normal white light, the yellow dye formed in the 'no blue' areas acts as a filter, allowing green and red light to pass but blocking blue. Blue is therefore seen only in the areas where there is no yellow dye—the areas that were blue in the original scene. The magenta dye similarly reveals the green areas and the cyan dye shows up the red to give a complete positive image.

Kodachrome film

Not all colour slide films have the colour couplers incorporated into the emulsion. One film, Kodachrome, uses colour couplers in the processing solutions instead. These diffuse into the emulsion of the film at a controlled rate during processing. The fogging stage takes place layer by layer, instead of all at once.

Processing Kodachrome is a very complicated procedure and involves up to 24 separate steps. Because of the complexity, home processing the film is impractical and only a few laboratories can handle it. In most countries, the film must be returned to Kodak for processing. Although the Kodachrome process may seem unnecessarily elaborate, it has two important advantages. One is that the permanence of Kodachrome slides is unrivalled—some of the earliest pictures taken on the film show no signs of fading, despite the fact that they were taken in 1935. The second advantage is that the emulsion layers of the film can be made very thin because they do not need to contain bulky colour couplers. This results in a film which gives remarkably sharp results, and an almost grain free image.

Fast colour slides

The emulsion structure of colour slides is not always as simple as the one described here. In fact, many films, particularly fast ones, use several layers, fast medium and slow, for each colour sensitive section of the emulsion. There are also inert gelatin layers between the light sensitive sections, and a protective topcoat.

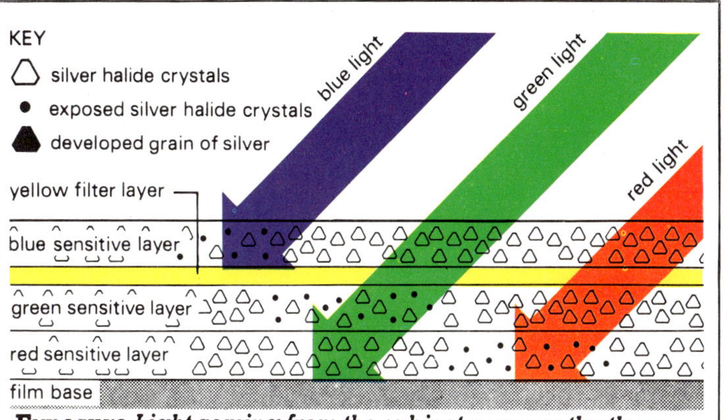

Exposure *Light coming from the subject exposes the three layers of the film. Blue is recorded by the top layer, green by the middle layer, and red by the bottom one*

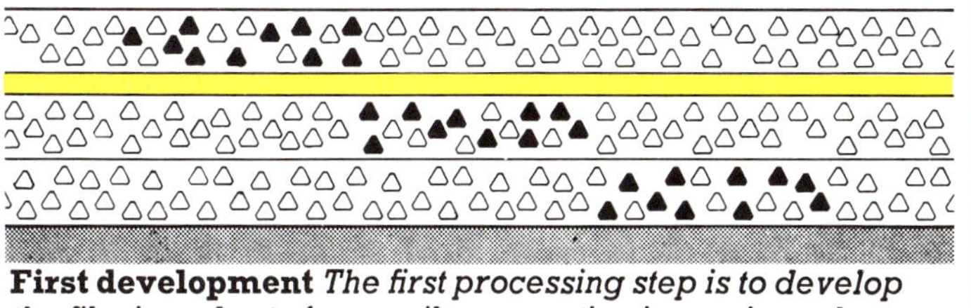

First development *The first processing step is to develop the film in order to form a silver negative image in each of the three layers, corresponding to the exposed areas*

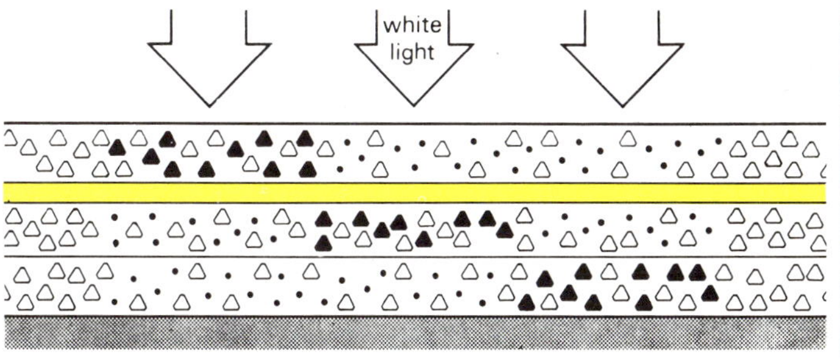

Fogging *The film is fogged, either chemically, or by white light. This forms a latent image in the areas that were not exposed by light coming from the subject*

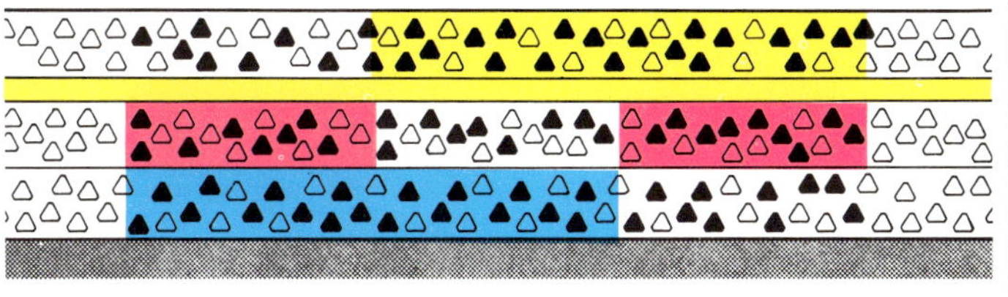

Colour development *This stage forms a positive silver image in each layer, and matching dye images in colours complementary to those that originally exposed the film*

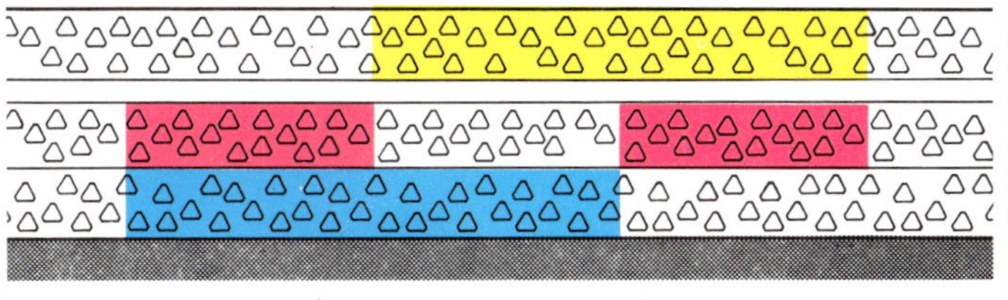

Bleaching *The next process is to bleach out all the silver from the film. This leaves only silver halides, and a coloured dye positive image in each layer*

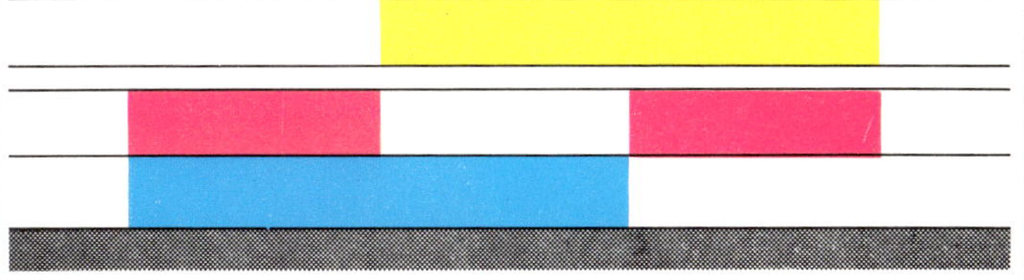

Fixing *Finally, the film is fixed to remove the silver halides and leave the colour image. Where each colour of light fell, a corresponding colour appears*

Film contrast

As a camera user you know something about *contrast*—that is, the contrast between tones in a scene. An outdoor scene in high summer has tones ranging from very bright to black. On a misty day in winter, however, the same objects may be barely distinguishable shades of grey.

You can also see when one of your pictures is hopelessly dull and grey because of lack of contrast. You may also get the occasional picture which is so contrasty that it can be labelled 'soot and whitewash'. A photograph on a misty day can easily become an overall grey with all the subtle tones of the subject lost. A contrasty scene can also come out with inky black shadows and bald white highlights. By understanding how contrast works, you can avoid these extremes.

If you send your colour films away for processing and printing you have to accept the image contrasts that the laboratory thinks are right. With black and white film which you develop and print yourself contrast is very much more under your control, if you know how to handle it.

Eyes work differently from film: they can see a very big range of brightnesses, picking out details in the brightest highlights and the deepest shadows. We expect to see such details in photographs, but there are difficulties. Film is more restricted than the eyes as to the range of tones it can deal with, and some tones are always lost. And even if it were possible to make a perfect negative of the most contrasty subjects a paper print can only show a limited range of brightnesses—about 100 to 1 at most.

A colour slide film is a little better in some respects. It can show a much higher range of brightnesses than a print—up to about 1000 to 1—but it still has its limitations. A subject such as a brightly lit beach, with sunlight reflected off wet sand and a dark foreground, has a brightness range of up to 8000 to 1 between the highlights and the shadows. A photograph can record only part of this range, but one normally ignores detail in the highlights and shadows in favour of the middle range.

Oddly enough, a colour slide that exactly matched the contrast of the scene would look dull and lifeless. We prefer to see the contrast between objects made more apparent than it is in reality. This worsens the problem of maintaining good shadow and highlight detail. A good slide always has greater contrast than the subject it shows, but in the process shadows and highlights lose contrast as the middle tones gain contrast. The increase in contrast is deliberate: it helps to keep the brilliance of the colours of the subject. Loss of detail in the lightest and darkest tones passes unnoticed as long as it is not excessive and provided the middle tones look right.

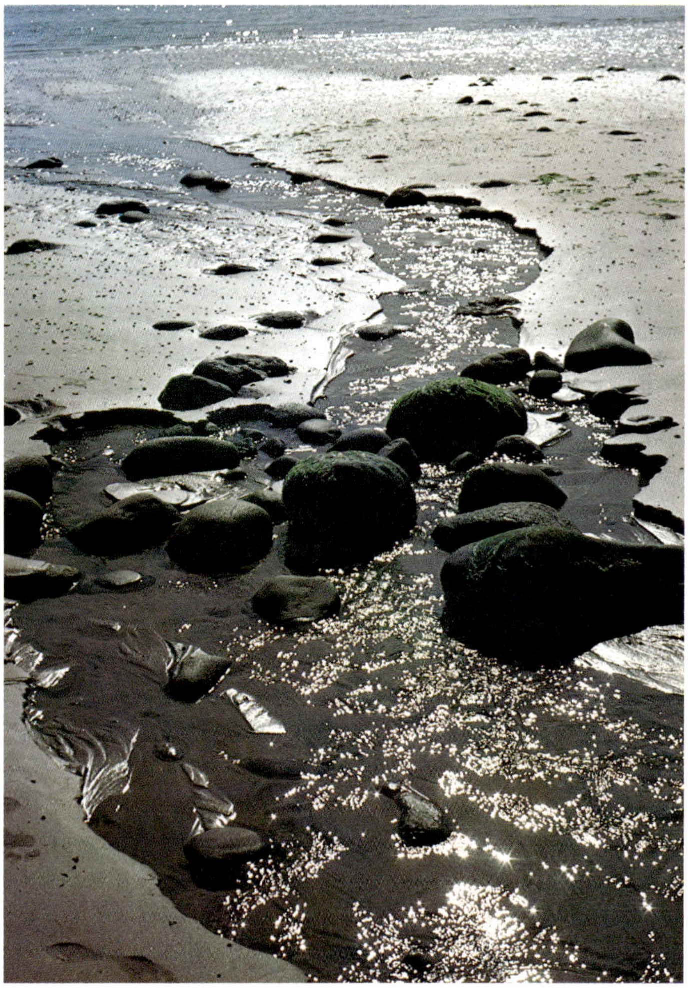

Harsh highlighting *A subject with very high contrast, very difficult to photograph successfully without losing shadow detail*

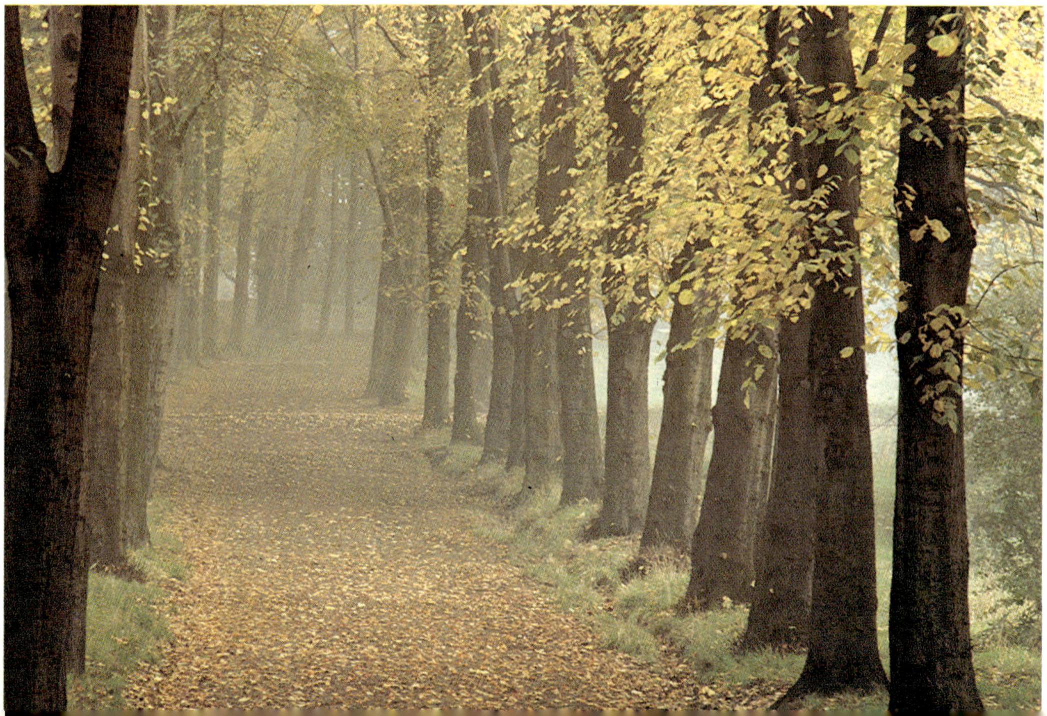

Soft and mellow *This is a scene with little contrast of its own, which often happens in autumn and winter shots especially on a cloudy day*

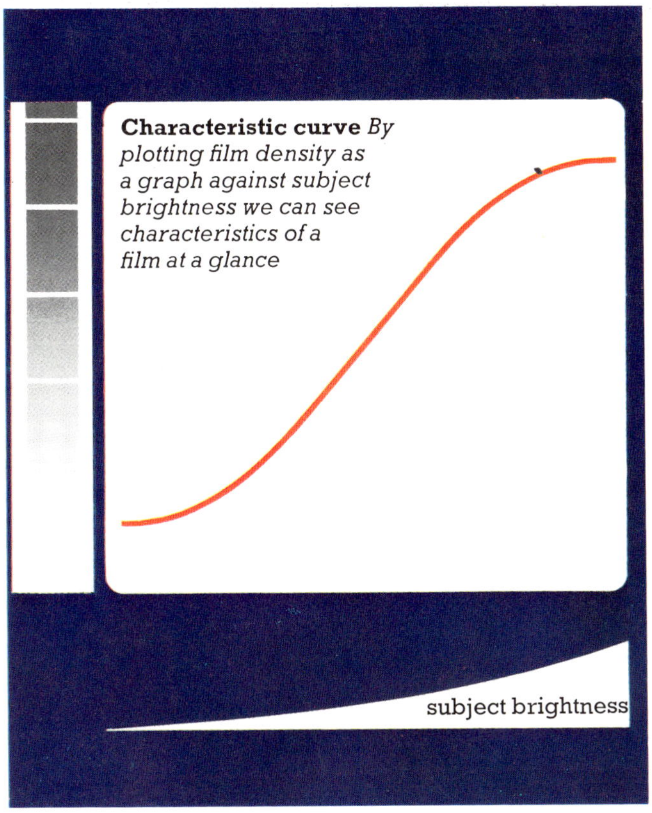

Characteristic curve *By plotting film density as a graph against subject brightness we can see characteristics of a film at a glance*

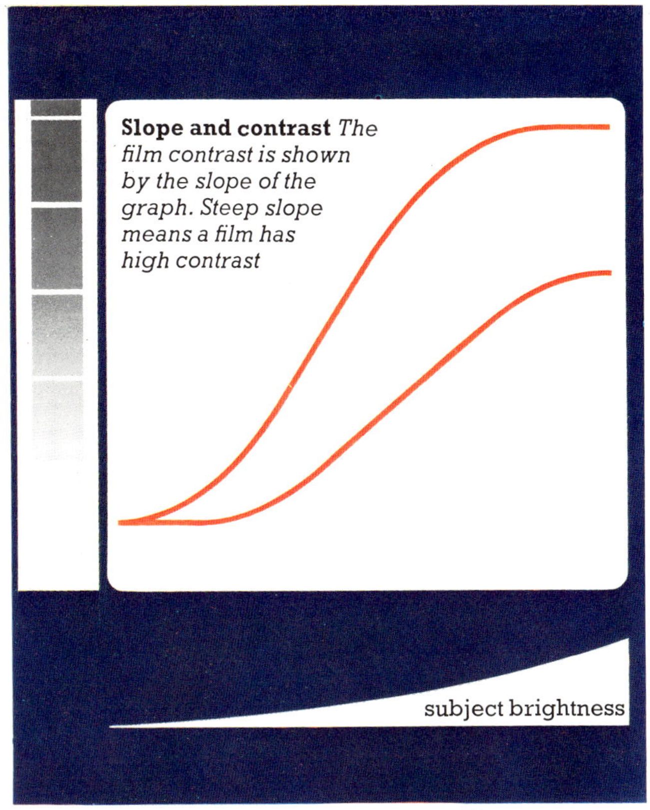

Slope and contrast *The film contrast is shown by the slope of the graph. Steep slope means a film has high contrast*

How to measure contrast

To understand and control the contrast of film and paper photographers use a simple graph. Since it shows the characteristics of the film for which it is drawn, it is called a *characteristic curve*. For all materials, films and papers, it has the same basic shape—a sloping straight line that flattens off at both ends. The steeper the slope, the higher the contrast. It is the straight part of the graph that is of most interest when talking about contrast.

The straight line shows that the greater the exposure, the more effect there is on the film. By plotting a characteristic curve of two different films, one of high and one of low contrast, it is easy to see the difference (fig. 2). The slope of the graph drawn for the high contrast film is much steeper than that of the film of lower contrast. Both curves start at the same point, but film A gets much denser than film B for the same increase in exposure.

Film speed and contrast

The contrast of a film is directly related to the film speed. Fast films have a low contrast. Very slow black and white film, for example, is suitable only for special applications, such as document copying, where extreme contrast is demanded. In the middle of the film speed range—from 50 to 400 ASA (ISO)—film manufacturers aim to produce a range of different films which give a choice of speeds while maintaining approximately the same level of contrast.

Film contrast is affected not only by the film speed, but also by development. As development increases, so does contrast. This can be used to tailor the film contrast to the tonal range of the subject. In the case of colour negative film, any attempts to alter the development run into trouble, as the whole development and printing procedure is arranged to give average contrast. If the range of tones falls outside the recording ability of the film, the resulting print will have bald white highlights and inky black shadows, with the colours probably distorted as well.

Contrast as a number

Because contrast is such an important characteristic of film, and it is inconvenient to have to draw graphs all the time, it is often described by referring to the slope of the characteristic curve. When twice as much exposure produces exactly twice as much effect on the film, the film has a contrast of 1, and with the correct choice of scales the characteristic curve has a slope of 45°. If the exposure has a greater effect, the result is more contrast, and the numerical value of the contrast will be higher too. The numerical value of contrast is sometimes referred to by the Greek letter gamma. Most b & w films have a gamma of 0.5 to 0.8.

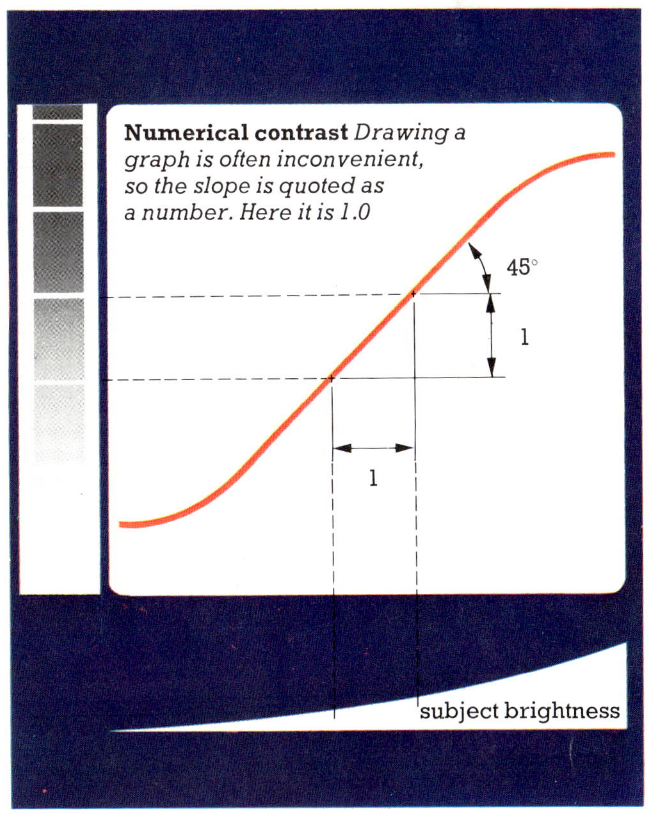

Numerical contrast *Drawing a graph is often inconvenient, so the slope is quoted as a number. Here it is 1.0*

If a film has a contrast of 1, the tones of the subject will be recorded on the film with no increase in contrast. This is sometimes very important. When slides are being copied, for example, the copy should ideally be identical to the original. In practice this is rarely the case, and contrast is usually increased each time a picture is copied.

Lith film has the highest contrast of any photographic material. It is made especially for copying diagrams and other images where the only subject tones are pure black and white and it cannot be used for normal photography.

Film speed and grain size

Modern emulsions are remarkably versatile and perform well over a wide variety of conditions. But to produce high quality negatives, they need precisely controlled exposure and development. Without accurate exposure, the negatives tend to become too thin or too dense; without correct development, contrast is poor.

Density and contrast

Now that the majority of photographers have access to accurate light meters, incorrect exposure is far less common than it used to be. Yet there are still many circumstances in which it is relatively easy to make errors in exposure.

Overexposure combined with too short development produces negatives with insufficient contrast, and though you can sometimes compensate for this by printing on a very hard grade of paper, generally the results are unacceptable.

On the other hand, if a slightly overexposed film is developed for too long, contrast can be so severe that sometimes even a very soft grade of paper cannot yield good prints from negatives. This is essentially because a developer works most actively on the areas of emulsion that have received the most light. Highlights gain in blackness quickly, while shadows blacken only slowly. So as development progresses, the difference in blackness between the highlights and shadows becomes more and more pronounced.

However, the gain in contrast cannot go on indefinitely. Every film has a contrast limit beyond which an increase in development time no longer results in a comparable increase in contrast.

Although, essentially, exposure governs density and development controls contrast, there are occasions when the contrast range can be increased by varying exposure. Controlled overexposure, for instance, is a useful technique for increasing contrast in scenes where the contrast range is small, on a misty day for instance.

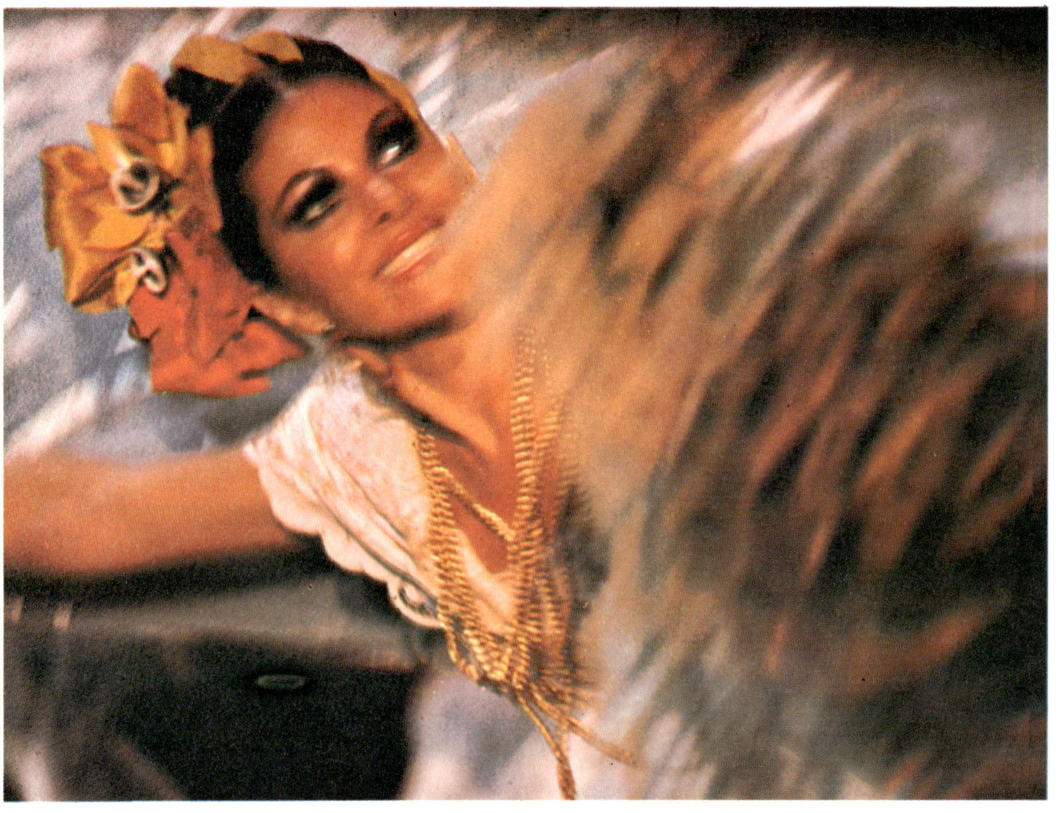

Flamenco dancer *Sometimes photographers overdevelop to gain film speed. Unfortunately, this increases grain and can change the colour balance*

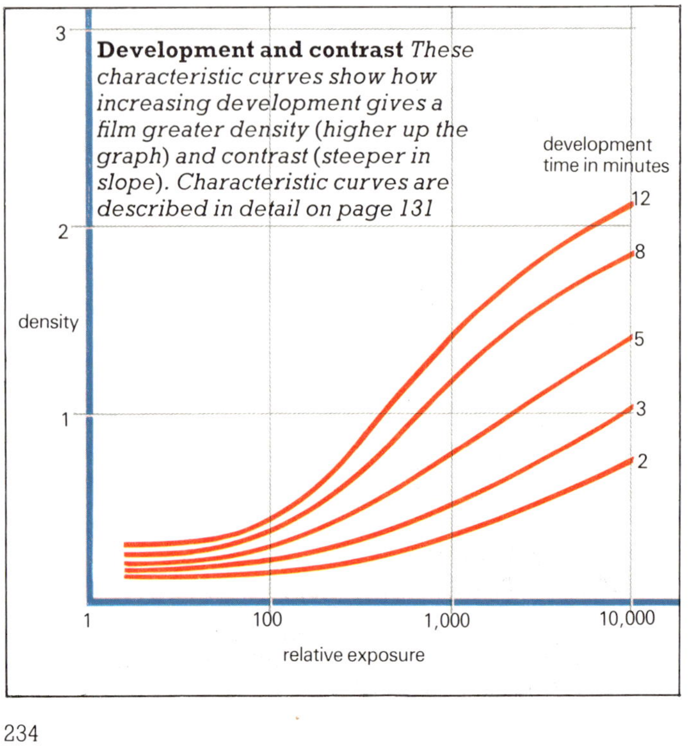

Development and contrast *These characteristic curves show how increasing development gives a film greater density (higher up the graph) and contrast (steeper in slope). Characteristic curves are described in detail on page 131*

Film speed and development

The speed of a black and white film can be increased by developing it for longer than usual, especially if a very active developer is being used. This can be useful in situations where there is not enough light to give full exposure. For example, a 400 ASA (ISO) film can be rated up to 800 ASA, provided it is given the necessary extra development. Manufacturers often suggest development times for increasing speed in the instructions packed with the film or developer.

However, you cannot increase the speed of the film in this way by more than double without severe loss of quality. Pictures can be obtained by rating a film at four or even eight times its official ASA speed and greatly increasing development, but the results are at best only just acceptable as this only increases the blackness of highlights and middle tones in negatives. There is no way of obtaining shadow detail that was not put in the film by exposure. Pictures obtained with a very much uprated film have empty shadows, and contrast in the final print is certain to be too high. A developer goes on developing the higher densities in a film long after the lower densities have reached their limit.

However, extending development beyond a certain point actually decreases contrast, as the film becomes very dense. Since this occurs evenly over the whole negative, it appears as fogging, and the effect is called *chemical fog*. Once the negative has started to fog, the image deteriorates and shadow detail disappears. Some people claim phenomenal increases in speed by push processing, but the loss of shadow detail means that this increase is largely valueless. Nevertheless push processing can provide useful moderate increases in film speed.

Like black and white films, colour slide films can be push processed to increase their speed. Ektachrome 400, for example, can be exposed at up to 1600 ASA provided the time in the first developer of the E-6 process is increased from the normal 6 minutes to 11½ minutes. Tonal and colour quality suffer, but with the extra speed you may be able to shoot in conditions that are otherwise impossible.

Grain size

Graininess is nearly always undesirable in a negative because it reduces definition and can become obtrusive, especially with 35 mm or smaller formats. Grain size generally depends on the film used, but there are ways in which it can be increased or decreased.

If, for instance, a black and white film is slightly overexposed to increase contrast, graininess is also increased. This is because as you give more and more exposure to a monochrome film the light penetrates further and further into the emulsion layer and the silver image becomes thicker and thicker. At the same time, the smaller crystals of silver halide, which are less sensitive to light, become developable. The result is that there is so much silver closely packed in the gelatine that particles clump together to form large grains.

Even if particles do not actually clump together, they may appear to because in the thick emulsion you see many particles on top of each other—an effect known as *optical clumping*.

Just as overexposure increases graininess, so does overdevelopment. With moderate development many of the exposed silver halide crystals are not completely reduced to metallic silver, and the metallic particles remain small. With longer development, however, every exposed crystal is fully reduced and the grains of silver are much larger.

Optical clumping shows up very obviously as graininess on a negative and it is even more of a problem than real clumping—the effects of which are far less noticeable.

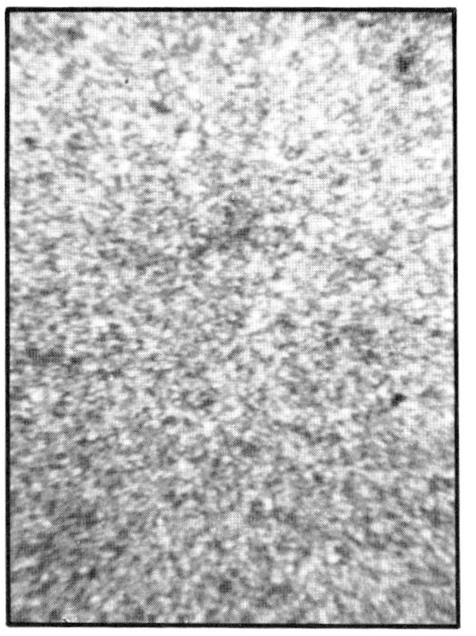

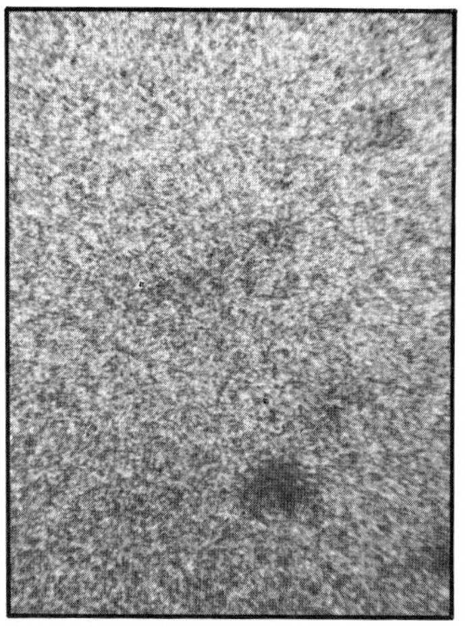

Modern film *Compared to the fast film that was available in 1945 (left), modern film offers remarkable quality. These enlargements show grain from 400 ASA film, old and new*

Speed and grain

Emulsion chemists have succeeded in making increasingly fast film in recent years with remarkably fine grain characteristics. Even a 400 ASA film now has fine enough grain for most purposes provided it is exposed minimally and not overdeveloped. Nevertheless a fast emulsion has larger silver halide crystals than a slow one and it is consequently more grainy. Moreover, graininess is increased by overexposure and overdevelopment far more with fast films than with slow films. A degree of overexposure or overdevelopment that has little effect on the grain of a slow film will have a marked effect on a fast one, so extra care is needed when developing fast film.

The new chromogenic black and white films, such as Ilford XP1 and Agfa-Gevaert Vario-XL, give a grain size normally associated with medium speed films even though they are both rated at 400 ASA. Because of the importance of fine grain with small format cameras this type of film is likely to become very popular.

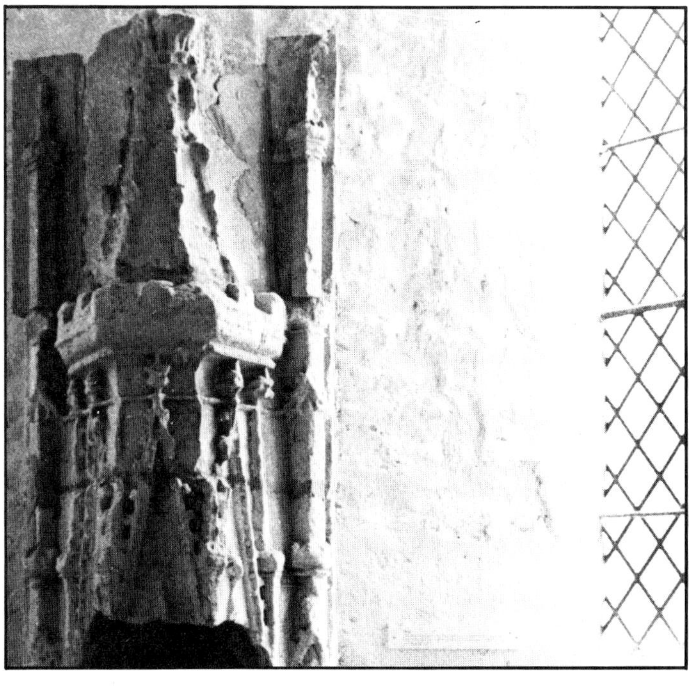

Correct exposure and development *Even when considerably enlarged, film that has had minimum exposure and development does not show an excessive amount of grain*

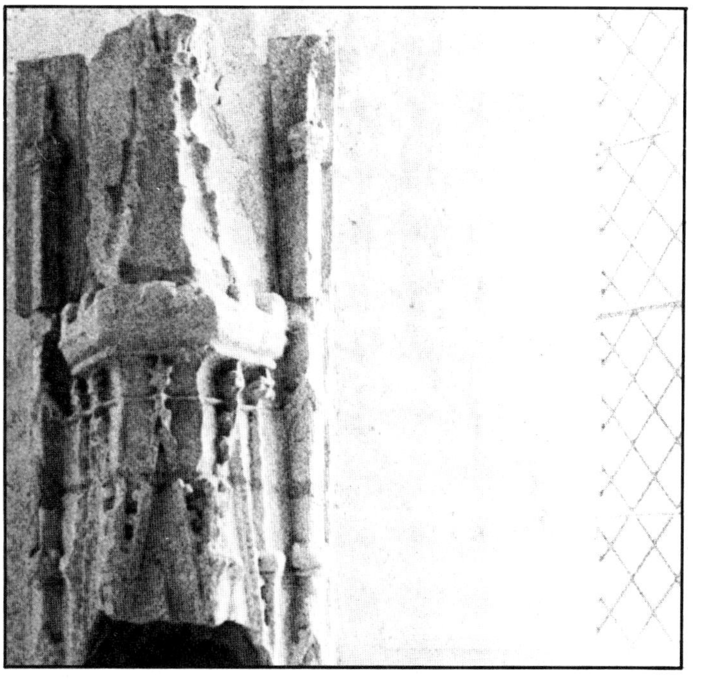

Too much exposure and development *The quality of a negative gets much worse if exposure and development are excessive. The picture is less sharp, and grain is coarser*

Reciprocity failure

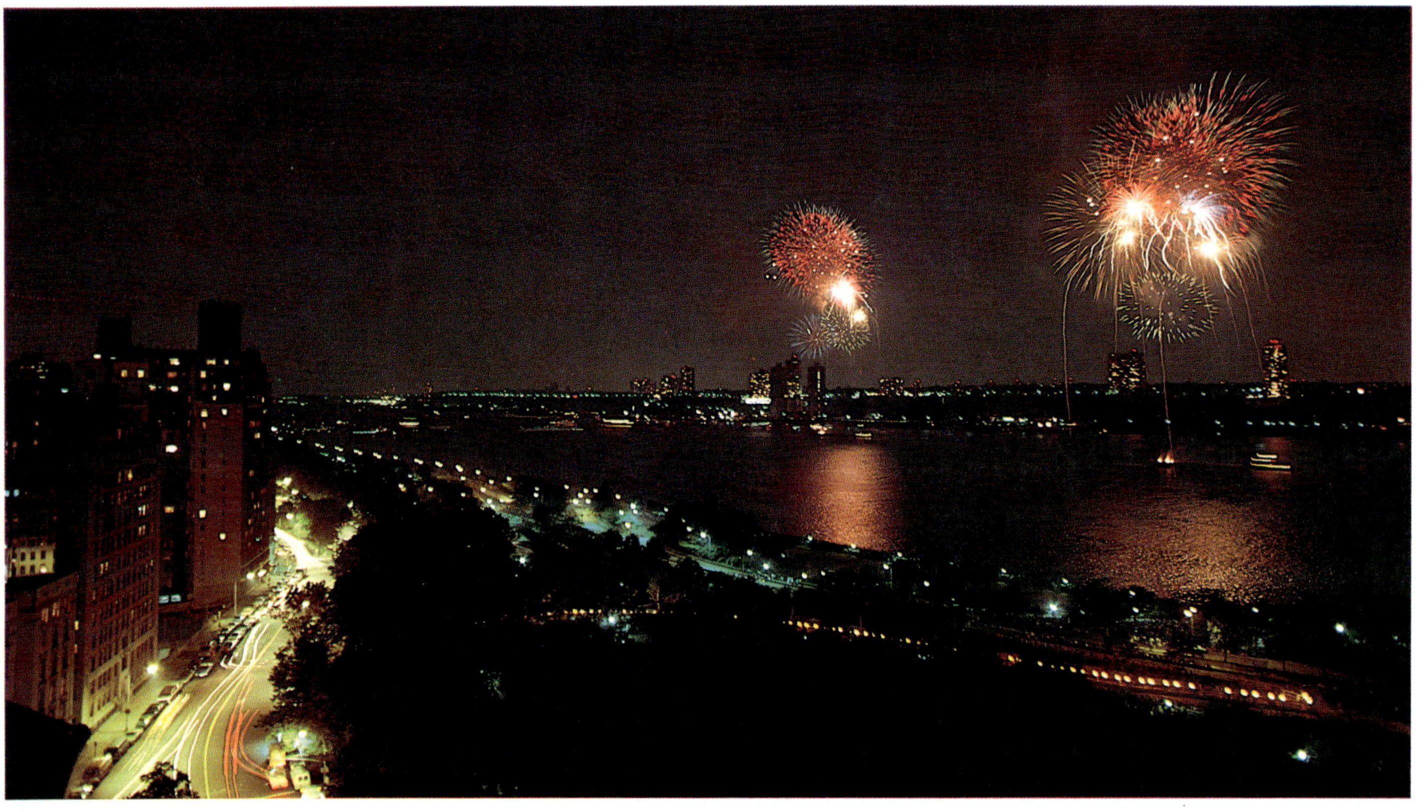

City at night *For long exposure shots like this, the shutter must be held open for longer than the meter indicates, and with colour film, for top results filters must be used*

For every lighting condition, there is a particular range of aperture and shutter speed combinations that gives the correct exposure. The relationship between each of the combinations in the range is normally a simple reciprocal relationship—that is, an increase in the shutter speed must be balanced by a similar decrease in the *f*-number to maintain the correct exposure. So, if you want to double the shutter speed to freeze movement—halving the exposure time—you must double the aperture. A one stop increase in shutter speed thus calls for a one stop decrease on the *f*-scale, two stops extra on the shutter speed dial calls for two stops less on the *f*-scale, and so on.

In normal bright conditions, this relationship, known as the *reciprocity law,* holds true and exposure adjustments are simple. As soon as the light begins to get dim, however, the reciprocity law no longer holds true, and doubling the exposure time does not compensate for halving the aperture.

The practical consequences of the failure of the reciprocity law, known as *reciprocity failure*, are really only significant with very long exposures. When you use exposures longer than about half a second, for example, you must give more exposure than the light meter indicates.

The extra exposure needed varies from one type of film to another, but a typical black and white film needs a two second exposure when the meter indicates one second. This is equivalent to the speed of the film falling to half its rated value.

At longer exposure times, the fall in film speed is even more dramatic. If the indicated exposure for a night shot, for example, is 100 seconds at *f*/2, the photographer needs to hold the shutter open for 1200 seconds at *f*/2 to obtain a correctly exposed picture. This is equivalent to an extra $3\frac{1}{2}$ stops or to exposing a 25 ASA film as if it were only rated at 2 ASA.

Many modern electronic cameras are sold on the claim that they have light meters which 'give exposures as long as five minutes'. Such claims take no account of reciprocity failure, and photographers who try to take advantage of the low light capability of these cameras are liable to be disappointed—all the pictures would be underexposed unless special exposure compensation is given.

Long exposures colour

Black and white films are not the only films to suffer from reciprocity failure. When using colour film, the situation is even more complicated. Colour film has three separate layers of light sensitive emulsion, each recording a different colour of light and each with different characteristics. In particular, each emulsion layer responds differently to low light. The red sensitive layer of the film may obey the reciprocity law down to one second, whereas the blue sensitive layer might fail after five seconds.

The result of reciprocity failure in colour films is that, as well as giving extra exposure, the photographer must use colour filters over the lens. Failure to do this will result in an overall colour cast to the pictures. The strength of this cast depends on the length of the exposure.

Exposure compensation

Each film responds differently to low light intensities, so it is not possible to make hard and fast rules about how much extra exposure to give. The accompanying chart gives general guidelines to the extra exposure needed for black and white film, but it is only approximate. It is impossible to draw such a chart for colour films, and it is necessary to refer to the information published by film manufacturers giving precise details of the extra time and filtration that is required for individual colour film types.

The extra exposure is indicated in three different ways. The first is a factor by which the indicated time should be multiplied. A factor of 3, for example, indicates that when a 5 second exposure is suggested by a meter, the true time is 15 seconds.

The second method is to show the exposure increase needed in *f*-stops. The 3 × exposure increase would be shown as $1\frac{1}{2}$ stops extra exposure.

The third method, given by some film manufacturers, provides different film speed rating for slow shutter speeds. Using this system, a 125 ASA film is rated at 45 ASA for the same five second exposure.

Colour filtration is given in colour correction filter values or *CCs*. CC 50 Y, for example, indicates that at a particular exposure, 50 units of yellow

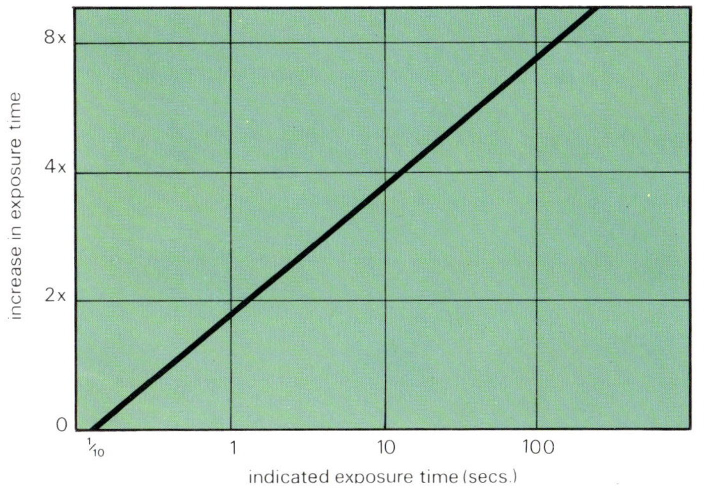

Reciprocity correction *This chart shows the extra exposure needed by black and white films at slow shutter speeds. For colour films, refer to manufacturers' information*

filtration are needed to correct for reciprocity failure. Filter values are standardized regardless of manufacturer origin.

Professional colour films, particularly negative films, are often available in two versions: type S for short exposures and type L for 1/50 second or longer. The colour balance of type L film remains constant for all times from 1/50 second to one minute, although exposure times still need adjustment.

Why does it happen?

The reason for reciprocity failure is tied up closely with the way that individual silver grains are exposed. Light is composed of millions of tiny particles, called photons, and when the camera shutter is open, the film is bombarded with photons. If a grain of silver is to be made developable, it must be struck by at least four photons simultaneously. If photons of light arrive at the silver grains rather sporadically, as they do in dim light, there is less chance that enough photons will strike the silver grains together to form a latent image. In bright light, the number of photons arriving is much higher, and easily exceeds the threshold level.

Very brief exposures

Reciprocity failure also occurs at the other end of the scale, when light is very bright and the exposure time is extremely short. The result is the same, and extra exposure must be given if the pictures are not to be underexposed.

In practice, the only time that such high intensity reciprocity failure is likely to prove a problem is with computer flashguns at very short distances. The circuit that regulates the light output of automatic flashguns according to the subject distance does so by changing the duration of the flash. When the subject is very close to the gun, the duration of the flash is sometimes as short as 1/30,000 second. Exposures as short as this can lead to underexposure and undesirable colour casts. The solution to the problem is to move the flashgun back from the subject.

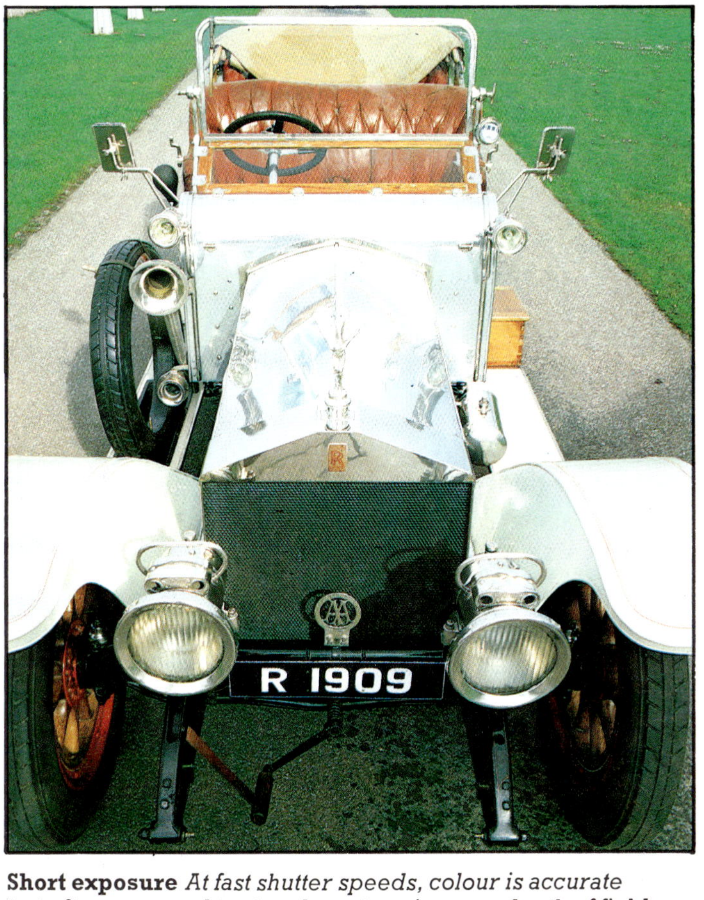

Short exposure *At fast shutter speeds, colour is accurate but often you need to stop down to gain more depth of field, and long time exposures are required*

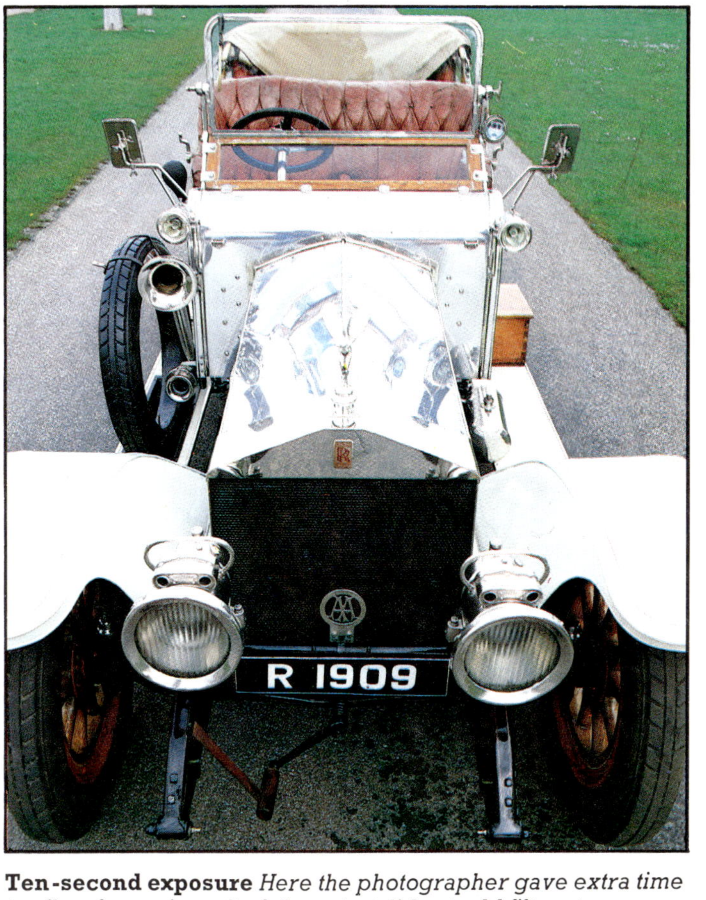

Ten-second exposure *Here the photographer gave extra time to allow for reciprocity failure, but did not add filters to correct the colour shift that occurs at long exposures*

Colour temperature

The most noticeable difference between the light from the sun, and the light from a 40 watt light bulb is that of quantity—the sunlight is obviously much brighter. There is, however, another difference which is of great importance to almost all photographers: light from the sun is of quite a different colour from that of the light bulb.

This difference in colour passes unnoticed most of the time, because the human eye is very accommodating. But if you see someone sitting by a window with their face lit by daylight on one side, and by a light bulb on the other, it is easy to see the difference. The daylight is much bluer than the light from indoors, which is tinged with yellow or orange.

Although our eyes can overlook minor colour shifts like this, colour film cannot. It is manufactured to very rigid specifications as to the colour of light under which it should be used. Most colour transparency film is balanced so that it will give correct results under noon daylight—that is, on a sunny day with blue sky. If photographs are to be taken in light which is not the same colour as daylight, then a filter must be used, either over the source of light, or over the camera lens. If this precaution is not taken, the pictures that result will have an overall colour cast—they will be tinged throughout with a particular colour. If you have ever taken colour pictures indoors by available light, you will be familiar with this problem, because the pictures will all have a yellow or orange colour cast.

In order to be able to correct for the colour cast a guidance system known as *colour temperature* has been developed (see box). Every film is balanced to reproduce colours accurately in certain lighting conditions. The colour temperature system allows the photographer to

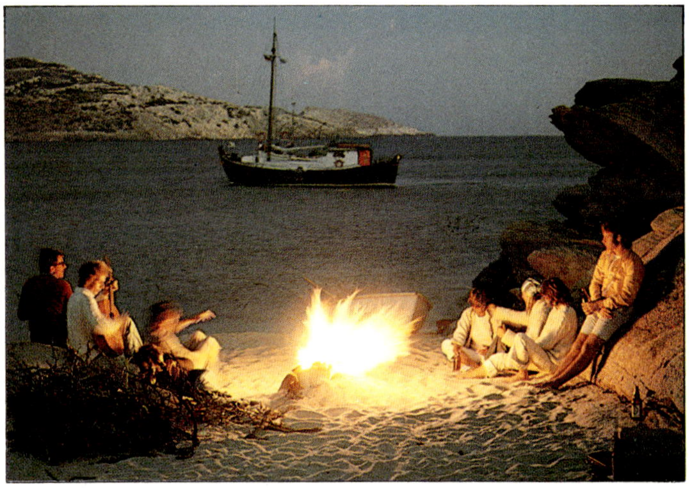

Mixed light *The firelight is too yellow for daylight film and the people's faces have a yellow colour cast*

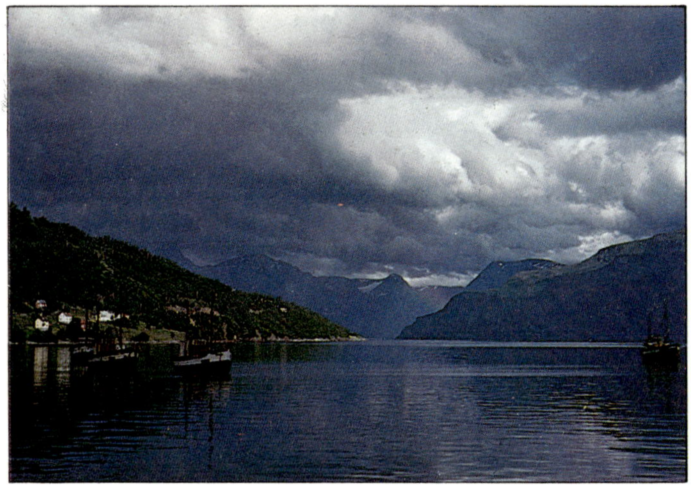

Blue landscape *In overcast weather, pictures will be too blue in colour unless correct filtration is used*

Colour and kelvins

Candles and sunlight *This chart shows, in kelvins, the colour of the most common sources of light for photography*

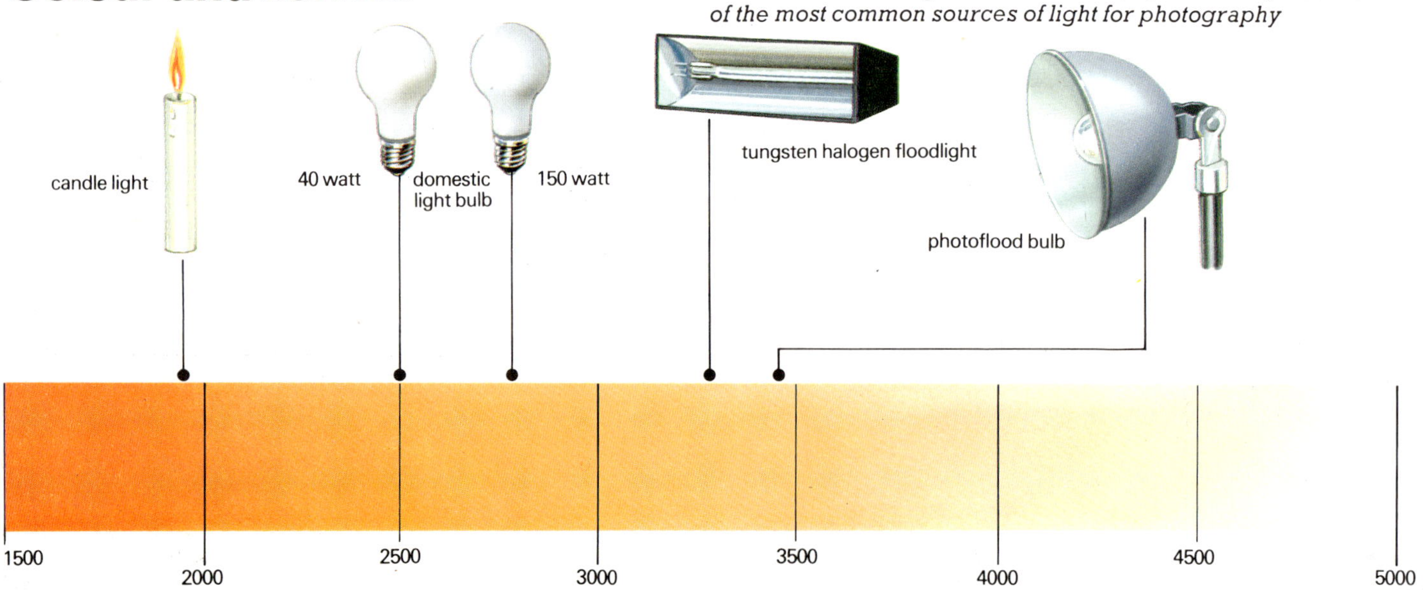

correct the colour cast produced by any lighting system.

Ordinary 'daylight type' colour transparency film is balanced for light with a colour temperature of around 6500K, and if it is to be used indoors under ordinary light bulbs, a blue filter must be used over the lens of the camera. Conversely, if the subject of the pictures is lit only by light from a blue sky—in the shade under a tree, for example—a yellow filter would have to be used.

Which filter ?

The colour temperature system seems complicated at first glance, because there are so many possible colours of light. Fortunately, though, the number of different light sources that are used for photography is small, and manufacturers produce glass and gelatine filters which compensate for most types of lighting.

To take a practical example on an overcast day, the colour of light from the sky lies between 6500K and 7500K, and unless corrected, will produce a blue cast on colour transparency film. This can be compensated for by using a series 81 filter—an 81A, 81B or 81C. The 81A is the palest of the three, and is used in slightly overcast weather, whereas the deepest, the 81C, would be used only on a very dull day. The 81B is the best compromise, and can be used for correction on most overcast days.

Light from the sun is much redder in colour in the morning and evening, and here the correction that is needed lies towards the blue end of the spectrum. An 82A filter produces the correct colour balance within two hours of dawn and dusk.

Tungsten balanced film

Since it is sometimes necessary to take pictures in tungsten lighting in the studio, a few film manufacturers make a slide film that is balanced for use in this light. This is called 'type B' film, or just 'tungsten film'. Most professional lighting gives off a light which has a colour temperature of 3200K, so this is the colour temperature for which tungsten film is balanced.

If you have daylight film in your camera, and you want to take a few pictures under tungsten light, there is a deep blue filter available which can compensate for this—an 80B —but the results may not be perfect. This solution should only really be used as a stop gap measure.

Colour negative film users have fewer problems than photographers who take colour slides, because much of the colour cast which results from incorrect matching of light and film can be compensated for in printing.

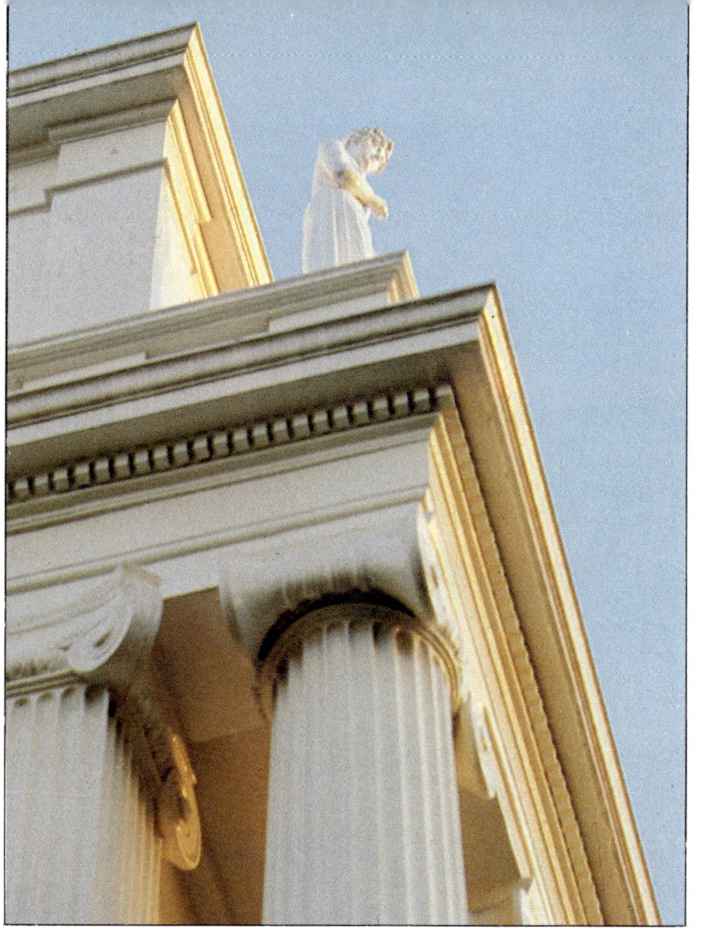

Evening light *Around dawn and dusk the colour temperature drops, and sunlight looks much redder in colour*

Light sources and colour

Photographers use a system called 'colour temperature' to specify the colour of any particular source of light. This system is based on the idea that hot objects glow and give off a particular colour of light at a particular temperature. A hot iron bar, for example, will glow red at fairly low temperatures, and as it is heated further will change colour to orange, through yellow, to white.

By specifying the temperature at which the heated object—actually a theoretical object called a 'perfect black bodied radiator'—gives off light of a certain colour, it is possible to refer to the colour of any light source.

Since this system was devised for scientific use, colour temperature is measured in the units most commonly used in science, which are called kelvins or K. These are the same heat intervals as degrees centigrade, but start at absolute zero—minus 273 degrees centigrade. Consequently, water boils at 373K and freezes at 273K.

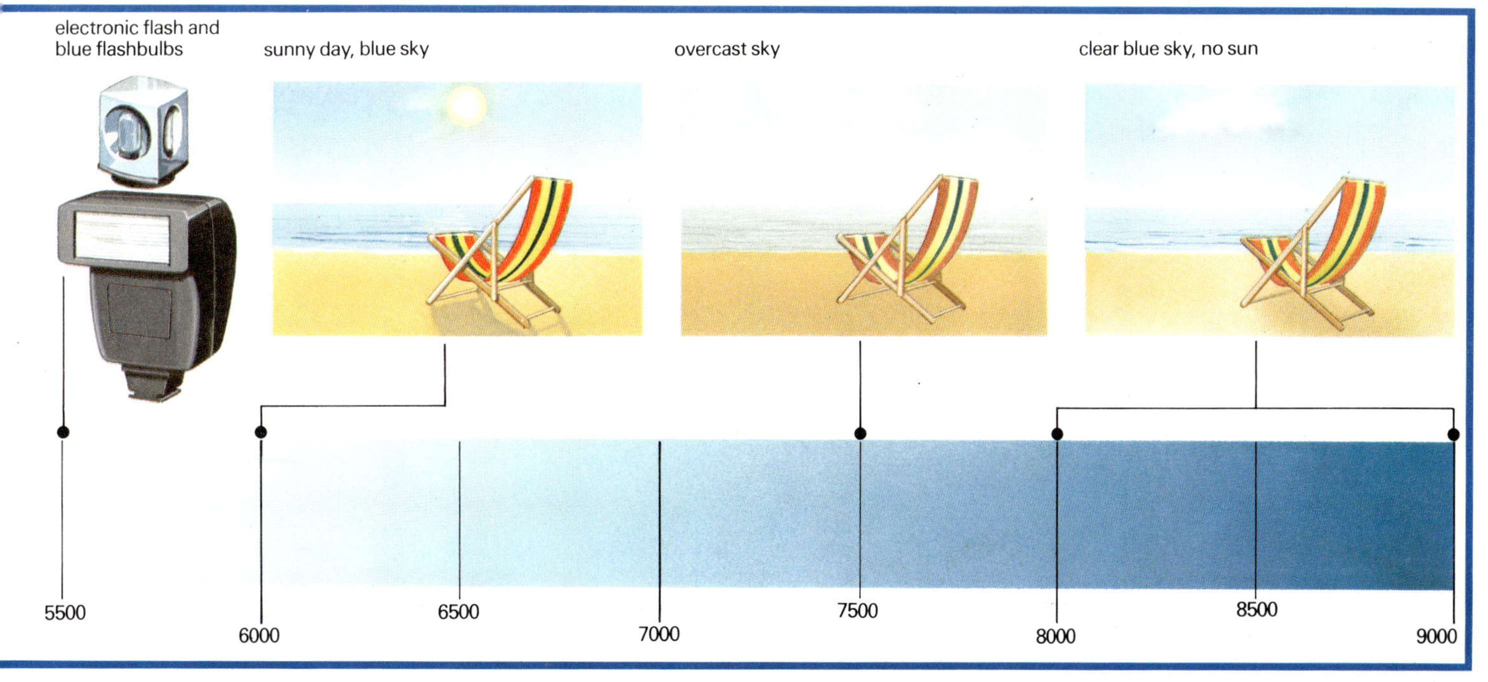

FILTERS AND DATA
Special effects filters

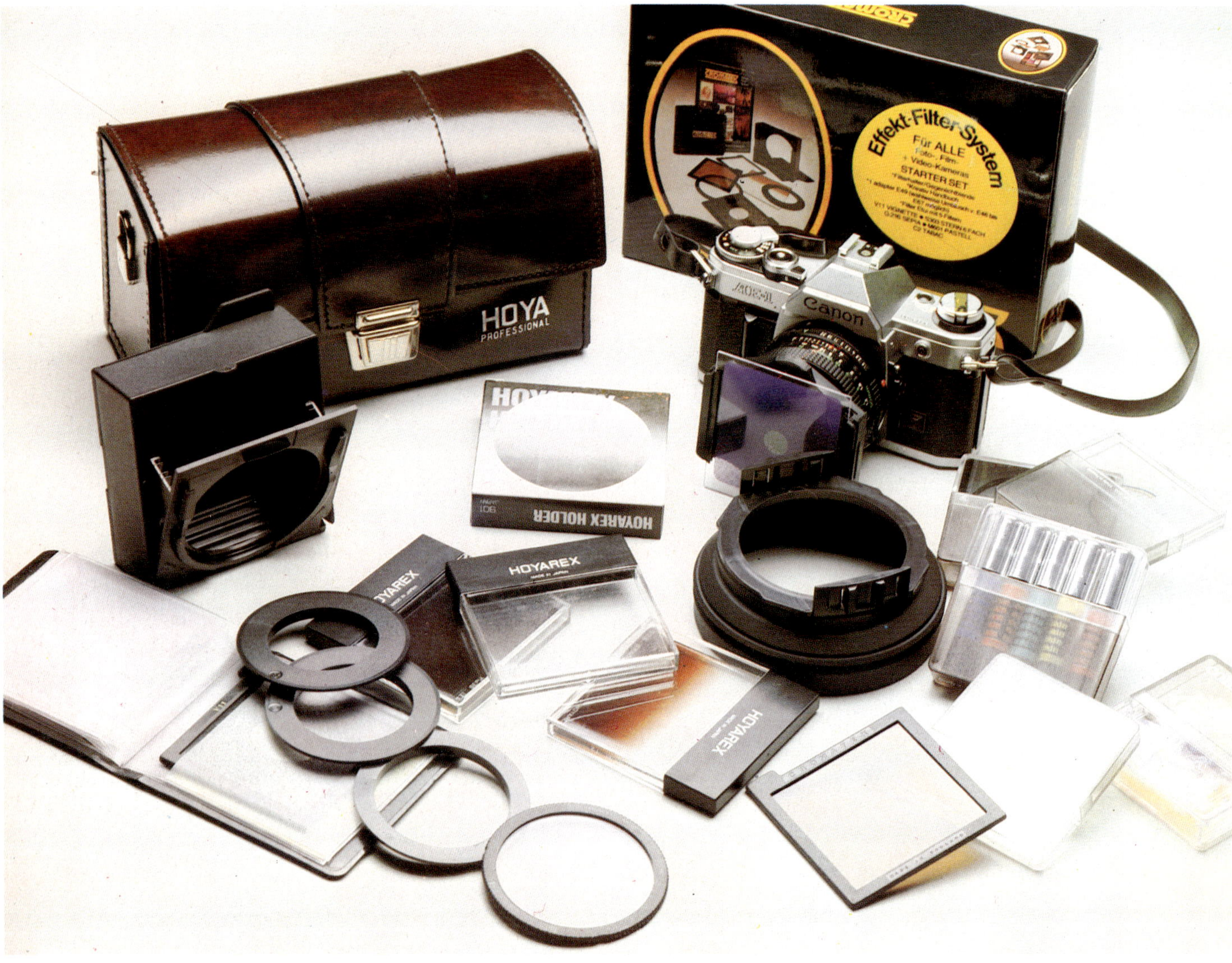

Filter kits *include a range of basic filters and accessories—some of which are not strictly necessary*

Most amateurs are familiar with the use of filters to modify a light source or to achieve faithful rendition of colours. Also intended for the amateur market are filters for special effects, ranging in complexity from simple coloration, through selective magnification to distortion of the image. Before you attempt to use these, it is best to know what effect they give and how easily it is achieved.

Special effects filters are available separately or in kits, and vary in price according to the construction. In the Cokin range, for example, a coloured diffuser costs less than a plastic lens cap, and a 'diffraction universe' costs about the same as a 36 exposure roll of Kodachrome. For about four times as much you can buy a Hoyarex starter kit, complete with Hoya filters and accessories for attaching them to the front of the camera lens.

The basis of the various special effects filter systems is a filter holder, which is attached to the camera lens by an adapter ring that screws into the filter thread. A range of adapters is supplied with some filter systems, but with others you must ensure you buy the correct adapter for your lens.

Filters are slotted into the holder in grooves, which vary in distance from the front of the lens. Filters from one system will not fit into a holder from another system, so it is a good idea to decide on one make only.

Some filters are no more than a shape cut out of black cardboard to form a mask. You can make these simply, to your own design, but the effect is probably not worth the effort. Most special effect filters are outside the scope of the do-it-yourself enthusiast, but you can appreciate the effects better by studying how the filters work.

Probably the most sophisticated filters work by diffraction. These are gratings made from high quality optical glass ruled with parallel lines in one or more directions—they give a star of coloured spot effect. Easily the most creative filters are the Coloured Vaseline and Coloured Varnishes, with which a wide range of coloured effects can be achieved. But they can be a little difficult to handle.

The important thing to remember about special effects filters is that they are for 'special' effects—in other words, they should be used sparingly, when the occasion demands, and not as a substitute for creative composition.

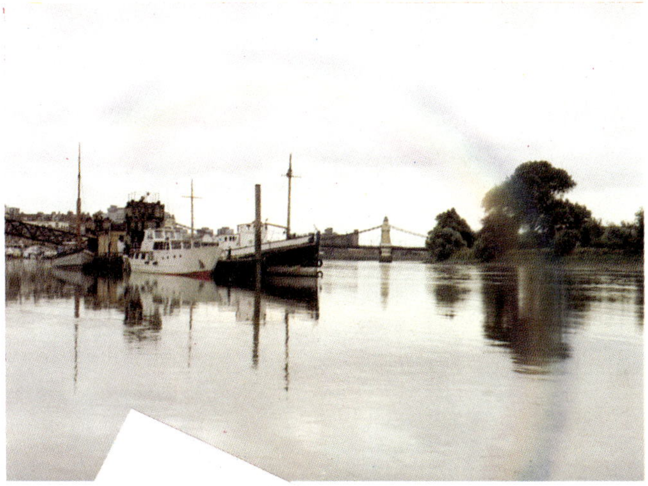

The rainbow effect *is most prominent when this type of subject (a bright sky and reflective water surface) is underexposed. At the correct exposure, the rainbow is 'washed out'. In a real rainbow, the colours occur in the reverse order*

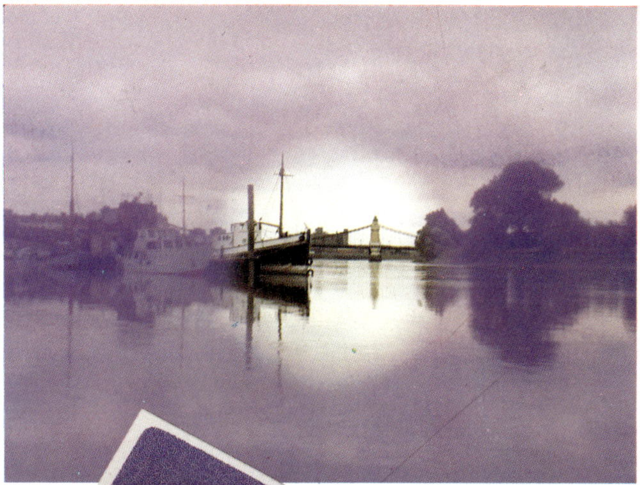

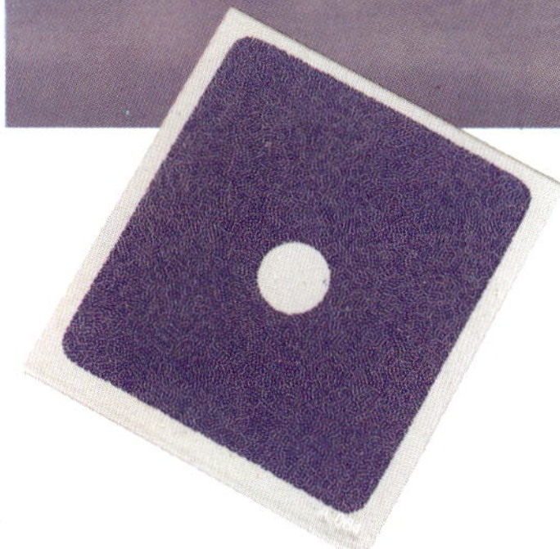

Spot in violet *Essentially this is a diffuser with a clear central spot. There is a choice of several different colours, and the filter can be combined with others, such as a starburst. Focusing through the filter can be a problem*

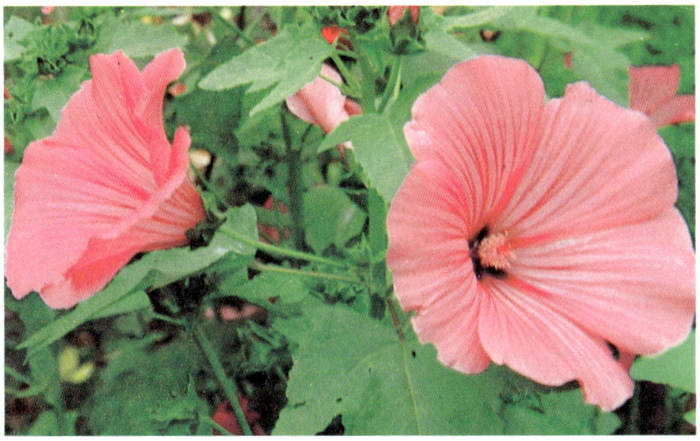

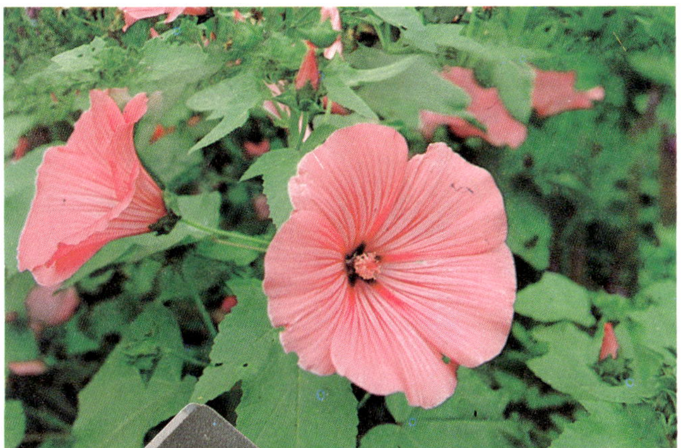

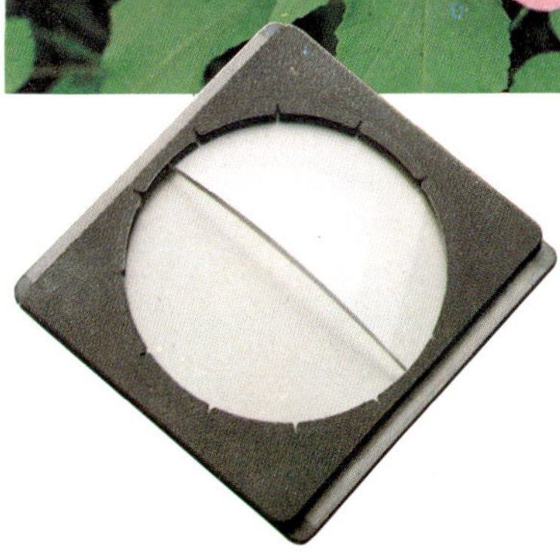

A split field filter *is merely half a lens in a mount, used as a close-up lens for half the field of view. The edge of the lens causes blurring, and the non-uniform magnification causes distortion, as can be seen in the upper shot*

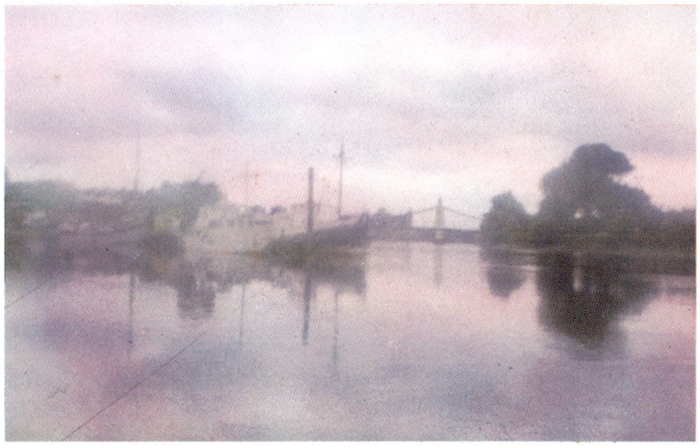

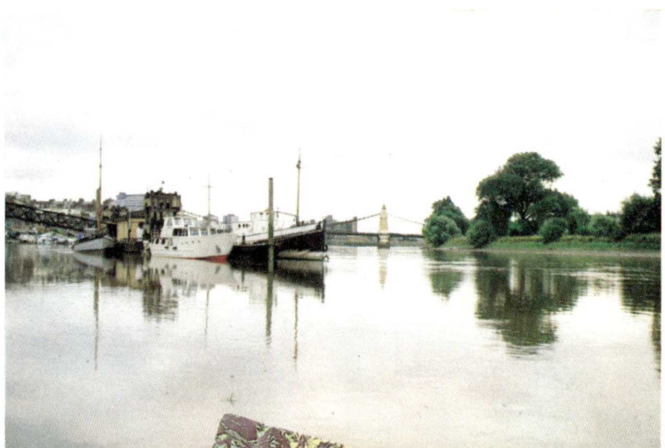

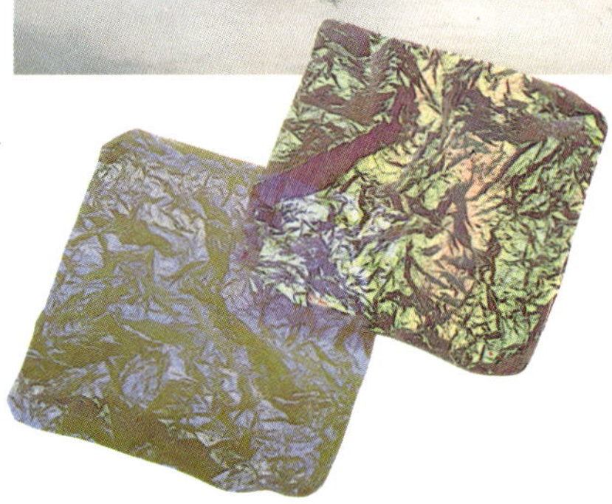

Coloured diffuser *This is supplied as two squares of crumpled plastic, which vary in colour according to the angle of view you use. Shown above are shots with and without the filter*

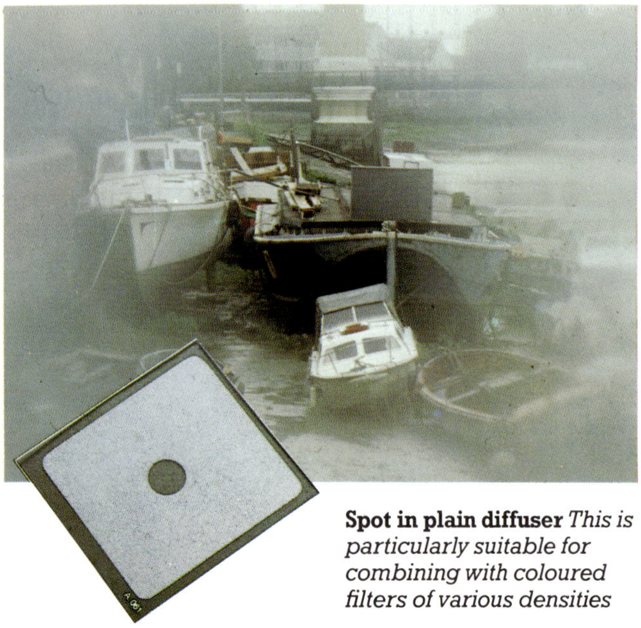

Spot in plain diffuser *This is particularly suitable for combining with coloured filters of various densities*

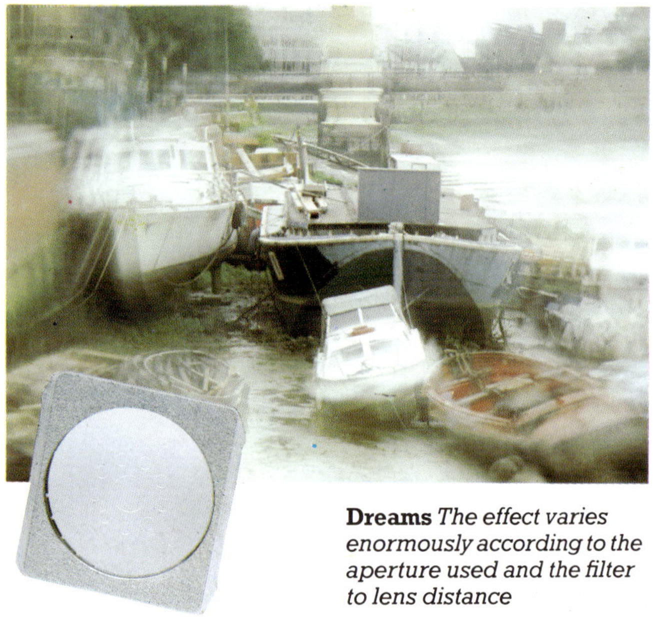

Dreams *The effect varies enormously according to the aperture used and the filter to lens distance*

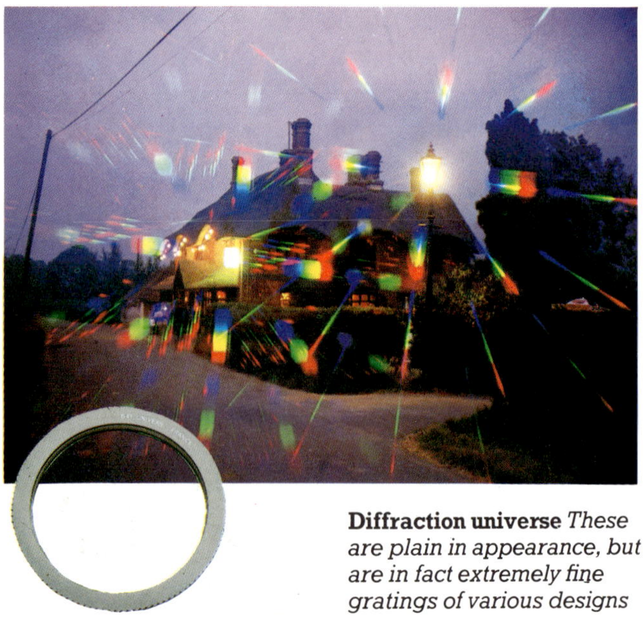

Diffraction universe *These are plain in appearance, but are in fact extremely fine gratings of various designs*

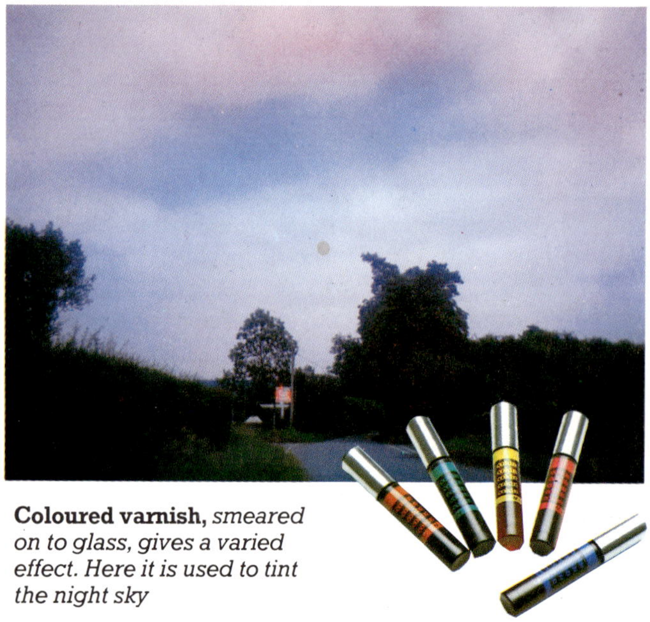

Coloured varnish, *smeared on to glass, gives a varied effect. Here it is used to tint the night sky*

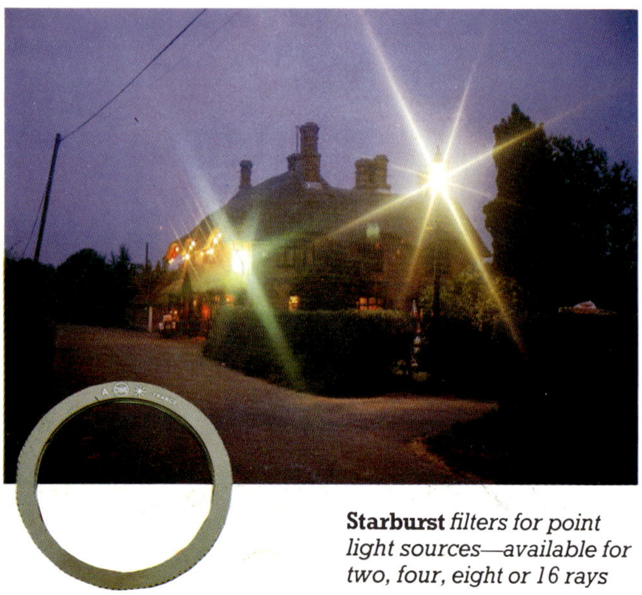

Starburst *filters for point light sources—available for two, four, eight or 16 rays*

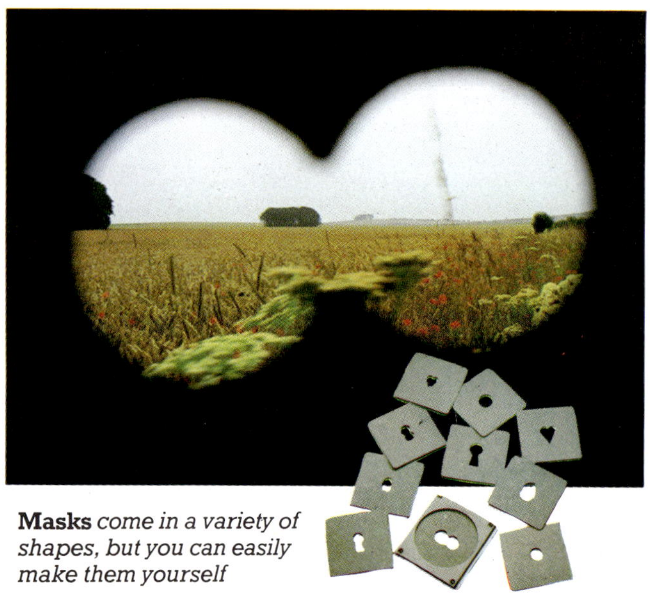

Masks *come in a variety of shapes, but you can easily make them yourself*

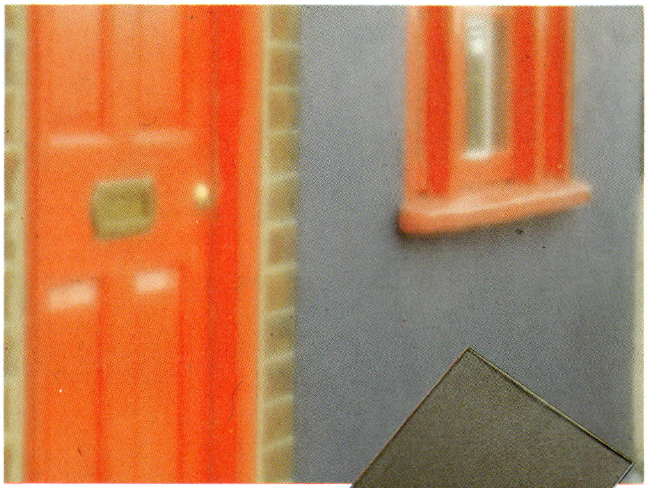

Diffuser *This gives a soft focus effect, the degree of which depends on the grade of the filter*

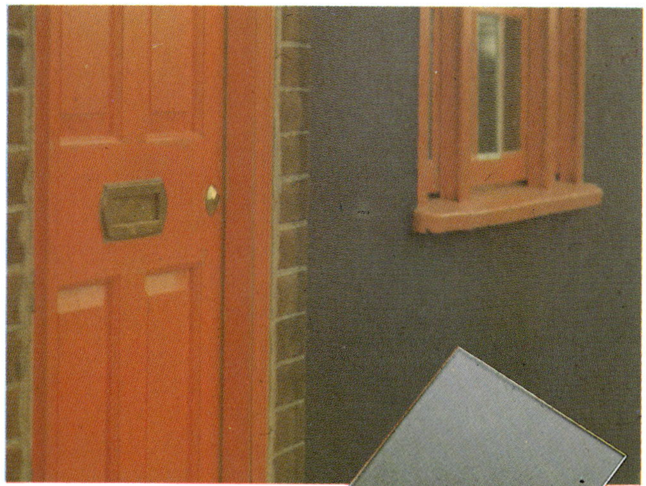

A graduated diffuser *leaves part of the image sharp, so it is easily combined with other coloured filters*

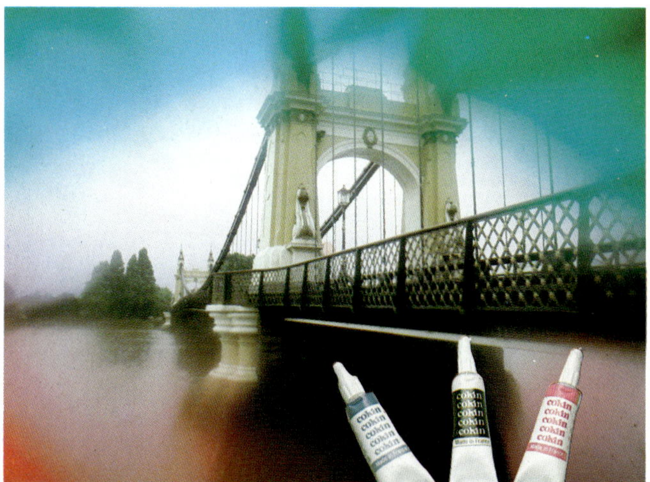

Coloured vaseline, *smeared on to glass, allows you to filter areas of the picture just as you wish*

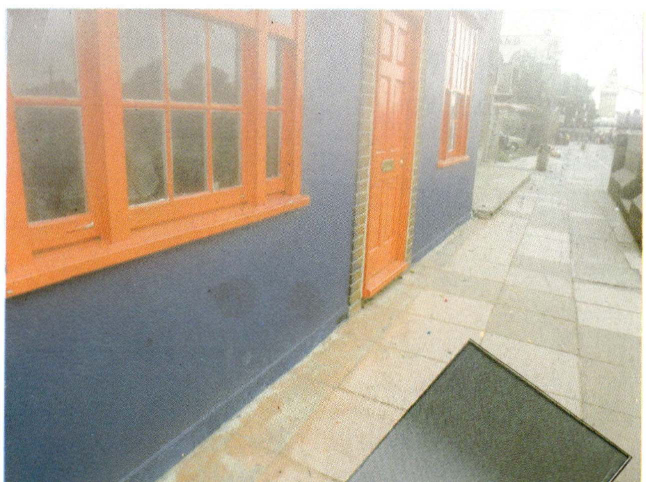

Fog filters *are similar to diffusers. Their effect varies according to the density of the coating on each filter*

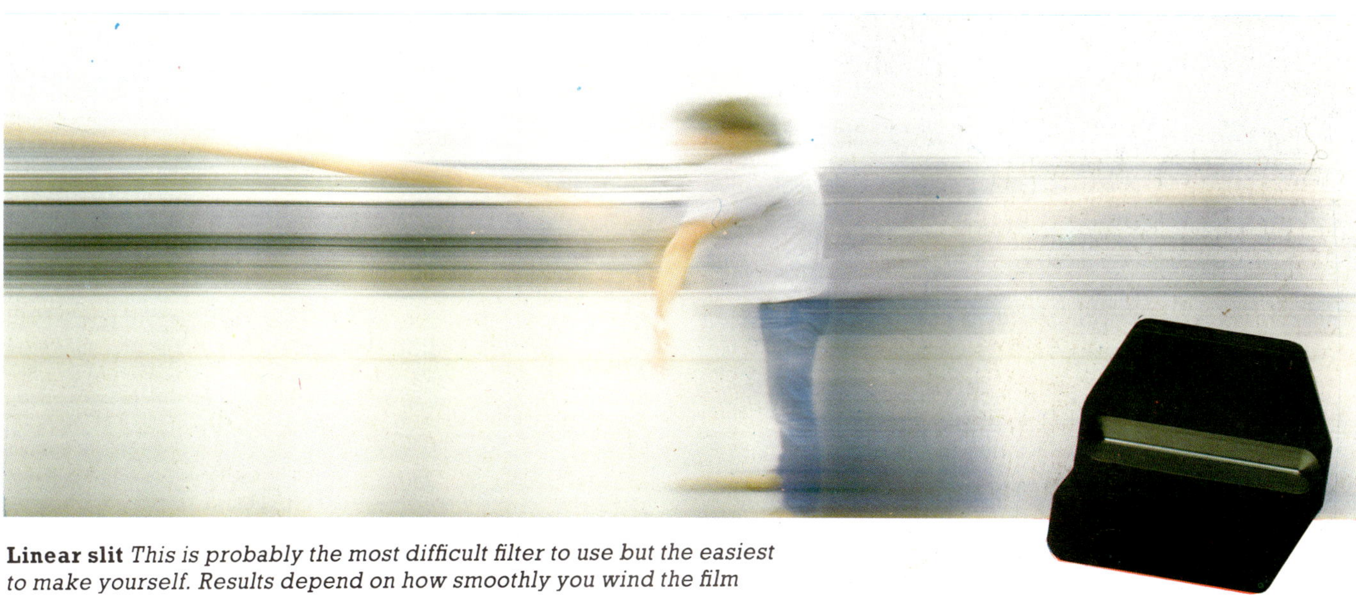

Linear slit *This is probably the most difficult filter to use but the easiest to make yourself. Results depend on how smoothly you wind the film*

Filter data

Many problems in photography can be overcome by the use of suitable coloured filters. And even simple filters can be used creatively to turn an ordinary shot into something worthwhile. As well as special effects filters, there are the straightforward gelatin filters, which are less often mentioned in catalogues. It is useful to know what types there are.

These pages provide a list of most of the filters available in gelatin form, which is the most versatile and wide ranging type. The numbers in the main list refer to the Kodak Wratten number, though the same numbers are used by most other manufacturers too. The filters in each section are listed in order of their density. The additional tables suggest ways of using some of these filters to correct for artificial lighting, and the final one shows exposure increases for a range of colour compensating filters, which are used to 'fine tune' colour temperature.

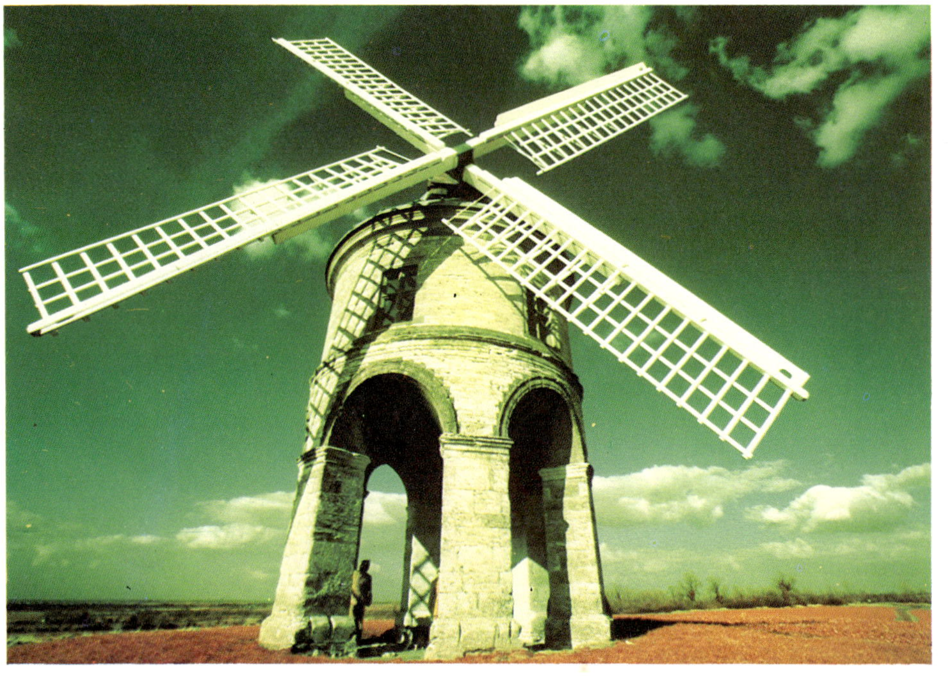

Pink

1A Pale pink These filters, often called *skylight* filters, are used to absorb excess UV radiation. For general photography they are of comparatively little use. However, they do have some effect in reducing the blueness caused by haze at high altitudes. They are also occasionally useful when there is a great deal of UV, such as a snow covered landscape under a blue sky, though an 81A is often better. The glass in modern lens elements usually filters out a sufficient amount of UV, though some photographers use glass versions of this filter as protection for their lenses, in place of the more usual UV types.

Yellows

Yellow filters also absorb ultraviolet radiation. They are sometimes used to filter for haze, particularly in black and white work, and are popular for aerial photography. They are also used to darken blue skies, and increase contrast with black and white film. The darker yellow filters are used with colour infrared (false colour) film to prevent the result being too blue.

2A Pale yellow Absorbs UV below 405 nm. Used to reduce haze at high altitudes
2B Pale yellow Absorbs UV below 390 nm. Better than 2A at reducing haze
2E Pale yellow Absorbs UV below 415 nm. Like the 2B but has more effect on UV
3 Light yellow Often used in aerial photography to correct for excess blue
8 Yellow Gives correct rendition of sky and foliage on black and white film
9 Deep yellow Similar to No. 8, but gives a stronger, more dramatic effect
11 Yellow-green Gives correct rendering in tungsten light on monochrome film
12 Deep yellow Used for haze penetration in aerial photography and for monochrome infrared materials
15 Deep yellow This produces even more dramatic effects than No. 8 or No. 9. It is used for black and white copying of documents on yellowed paper. It is also used for infrared and fluorescence photography

Oranges and reds

These filters are designed to absorb ultraviolet and blue, and also varying amounts of green. With black and white film they are used to increase contrast—for example, to darken blue skies, bring out the grain in wood, or pick out the detail in brick. Red filters are also used for technical work, such as colour separation, colour printing and two-colour photography. The last is a method of producing colour pictures by breaking down the image into two colour components.

16 Yellow-orange filters are mostly used for emphasizing detail in wood and brick, and also widely used for darkening blue skies, in both cases using black and white materials
21 Orange is the most popular orange filter, used to give greater contrast on black and white film
22 Deep orange Commonly used in photomicrography with blue preparations, this filter has greater green absorption than the other orange types
23A Light red Used in colour separation work and also for increased contrast with black and white film
24 Red is used mostly for two-colour photography in conjunction with a 57 (green) filter
25 Red One of the most useful red filters, the 25 reduces haze in black and white aerial shots and filters out excess blue light for monochrome infrared work. It is also used for colour separation and tricolour printing
29 Deep red Principally used for colour separation and tricolour printing

Magentas and violets

These filters principally absorb green, and are mostly used for technical applications, such as reproduction processes and photomicrography. Other magenta filters (CC filters) are used to correct for fluorescent light.

30 Light magenta Used in photomicrography to give increased contrast particularly with green subjects
32 Magenta Used to subtract green
33 Magenta absorbs green strongly and is used in colour reproduction processes to produce masks
34 Deep violet Contrast filter
35 Purple The main use for this filter is to provide contrast in photomicrography. It provides total green absorption and also absorbs some blue and red

Greens

These are mostly used for black and white photography as contrast filters (to lighten foliage for example) and in technical processes such as colour reproduction and colour printing.

54 Deep green This contrast filter absorbs nearly all red and blue light, and a little green light
57 Green Used for two-colour photography with a red (24) filter
58 Green Used as a contrast filter in photomicrography and also for colour separation and tricolour printing
61 Deep green Used for colour separation and tricolour printing work with red (29) and blue (47) filters

Blues and blue–greens

These filters are designed mainly for colour separation work, tricolour printing, contrast effects in photomicrography, and to heighten contrast in black and white work. Blue conversion and light balancing filters are dealt with in a separate section. On black and white film blue filters darken reds. By emphasizing blue tones they can be used to exaggerate mist or fog.

38 Light blue is useful in tungsten lighting with black and white film to prevent red tones from reproducing too light
38A Blue absorbs a large amount of red light, plus a certain amount of ultraviolet and green
44 Light blue–green filters out red and ultraviolet
44A Light blue–green substracts red
45 Blue–green Mostly used in photomicrography, this contrast filter is designed to absorb ultraviolet and red
47 Blue is the filter used to give contrast effects with monochrome film. Also used for colour separation
47B Deep blue This filter is intended mainly for use in colour separation and tricolour printing
50 Deep blue is a monochromat filter (see *narrow band* filters) which transmits the mercury line at 436 nm, and lines at 398, 405 and 408 nm

Narrow band

These are *monochromat* filters which transmit very small parts of the spectrum just one or two hues. As a result, they are very dense and are only used for technical purposes. The most common use for narrow-band, or *narrow cut* filters is in colour separation work, particularly when the separation negatives are being made from transparencies or negatives.

70 Dark red This is used in colour separation work to produce separation positives from colour negatives. It is also used when making colour prints with the tricolour printing method
72B Dark orange–yellow
74 Dark green This transmits only 10 per cent of green light and filters out practically all yellow light from mercury-vapour lamps. This gives monochromatic green light which is useful in experimental optical work as the principal focus, in lenses corrected for one colour, is computed for green light
75 Dark blue–green

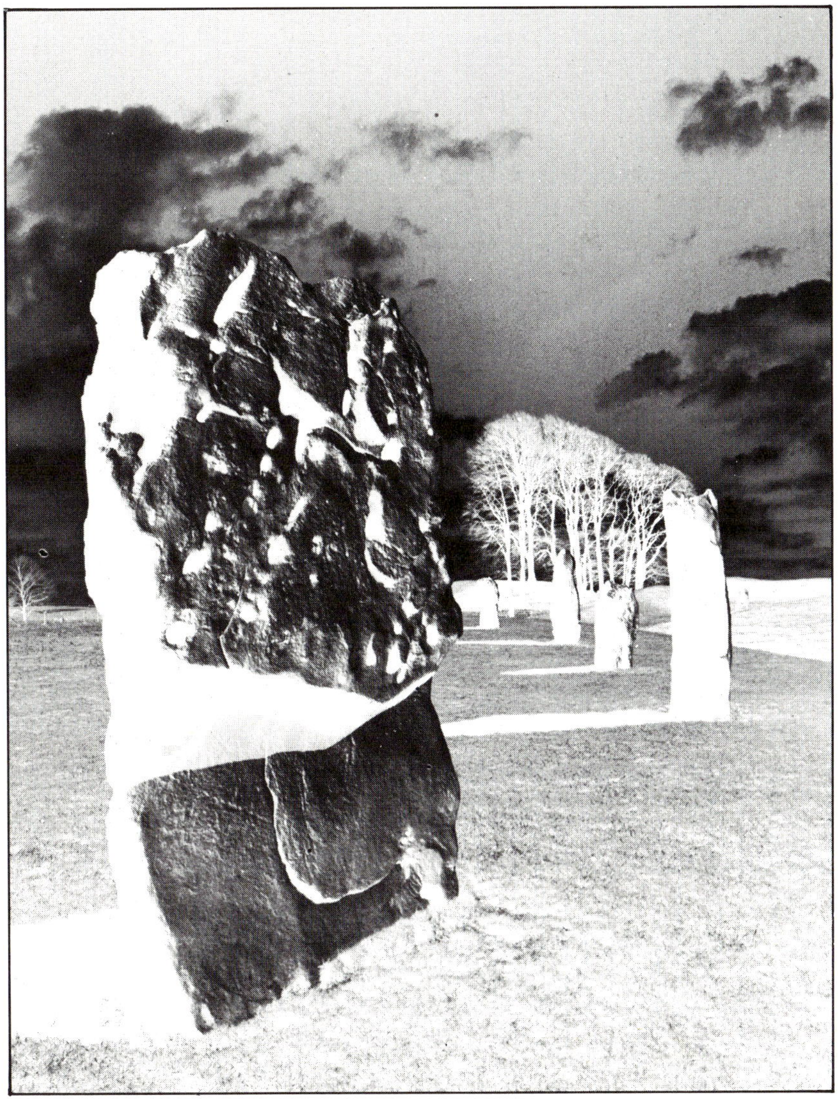

Filtering for effect *The windmill shot was taken on colour infrared film. If no filtration is used this film tends to give results which are very blue. You can use a variety of filters to cut down the amount of blue light, including yellow, orange, red and opaque types. In this case an orange filter was used. The black and white shot was taken on normal film, but a red filter was used to darken the sky and generally increase contrast, producing this dramatic effect*

Conversion

These filters are used to convert daylight to tungsten, or vice versa. They are most commonly used on the camera lens, but they can be used over lights. For example, some photographers use the blue (80) filter over tungsten lights so that they can use them with daylight and daylight film (see picture on page 2598). Use of these filters is dealt with separately.

80 series, blue These are used with daylight film in tungsten lighting. The complete range is: 80A, 80B, 80C
85 series, amber These are used with tungsten film in daylight. The complete range is: 85, 85B, 85BN6, 85C, 85N3, 85N6, 85N9 (includes 0.9 neutral density)

Light balancing

These are paler versions of the conversion filters, and are designed to modify colour temperature for minor corrections. They are nearly always placed over the camera lens. You can use them with conversion filters to give full correction for light sources such as domestic bulbs (see separate table) or to give slight overcorrection for creative effect.

81 series, pale amber These slightly lower the colour temperature. The range is: 81, 81A, 81B, 81C, 81D, 81EF
82 series, pale blue These slightly raise the effective colour temperature. The range is: 82, 82A, 82B, 82C

Balancing colour

If the colour temperature of a light source is 3200K or 3400K then you can use an 80 series filter with daylight film or, in the case of the latter figure, tungsten film. But it is rare that the light is exactly the right colour, so the table below shows you what extra filtration is needed to bring the colour to the above figures.

3200K from	3400K from	Filter	Exposure increase in stops
2490K	2610K	82C + 82C	1⅓
2570K	2700K	82C + 82B	1⅓
2650K	2780K	82C + 82A	1
2720K	2870K	82C + 82	1
2800K	2950K	82C	⅔
2900K	3060K	82B	⅔
3000K	3180K	82A	⅓
3100K	3290K	82	⅓
3300K	3510K	81	⅓
3400K	3630K	81A	⅓
3500K	3740K	81B	⅓
3600K	3850K	81C	⅔
3850K	4140K	81EF	⅔

Miscellaneous

These are filters which do not fit into any of the other categories. They are all intended for various technical applications but are worth knowing about in case you ever come across them.

87 Visually opaque There are two versions of this filter—87 and 87C. Their main use is for infrared work as they absorb all visible light but transmit infrared radiation. This means that the exposure is achieved solely with infrared which is useful for analytical work. And for creative photography it means that the strange effects casued by infrared are even more dramatic
88A Visually opaque Similar to the 87
89B Visually opaque This is also used for infrared photography, particularly aerial work. It transmits radiation of wavelengths between 700 and 800 nm
90 Dark greyish amber This filter is meant for visual use, not for taking pictures with. Looking through the filter, the view is monochromatic and this gives you an idea of how the tones and colours will reproduce on black and white film
92 Red This is used, with 93 and 94, to take densitometer readings of colour films and papers
93 Green Used, with 92 and 94, to take densitometer readings of colour films and papers
94 Blue Used, with 92 and 93, to take densitometer readings from colour films and papers
96 Neutral density See separate table
98 Blue Equivalent to a 47B plus a 2B. Used in colour separation work and tricolour printing
99 Green Equivalent to a 61 plus a 16. Used in colour separation work and tricolour printing

Warm tones *When using flash, the skin tones tend to reproduce slightly too cold. You can produce a much warmer and healthier effect by using an 81A (below)*

Light balance *If you want to have the controllability of tungsten lights but prefer to use daylight film you will have to use an 80 series filter (right)*

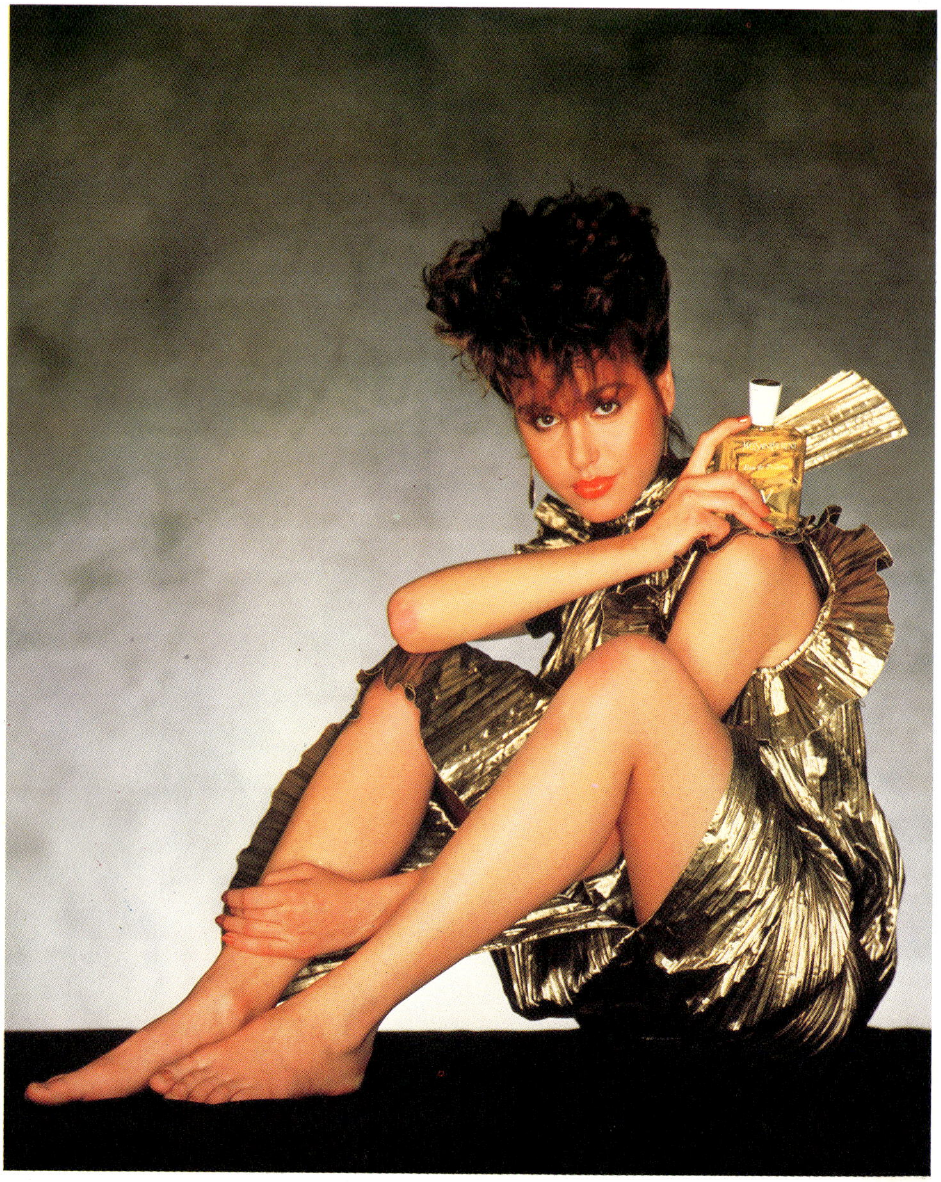

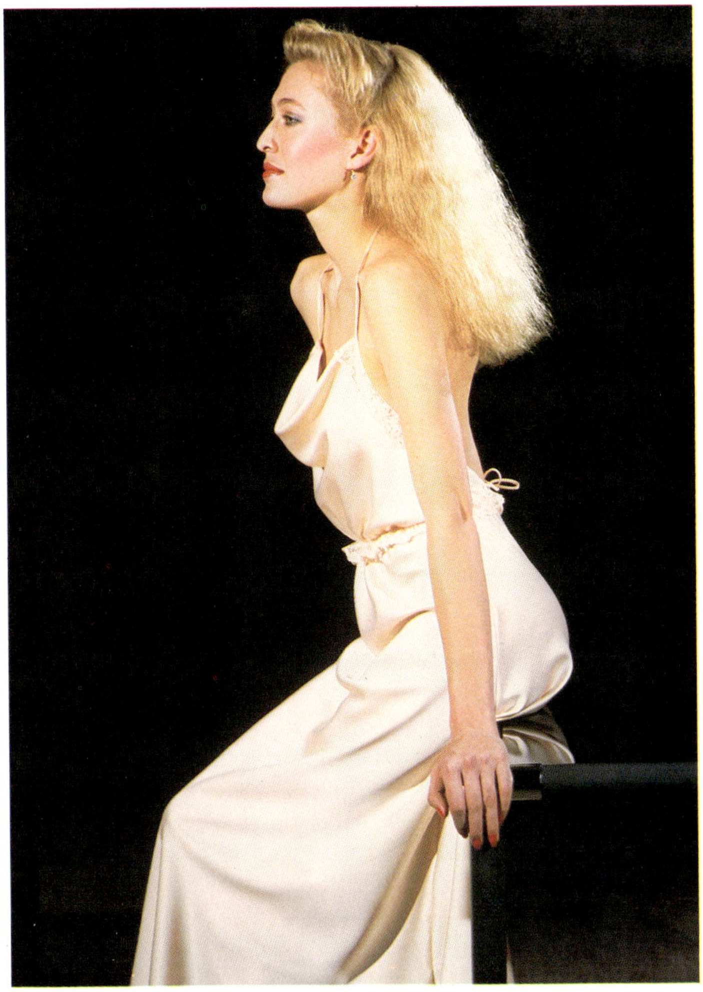

Fluorescent conversion

This table shows the filtration and exposure increase necessary to get acceptable results with different types of fluorescent tube. It is based on Kodak films, but with a little experimentation you can adapt it for other makes. In any case, the figures are only intended as a guide, and for critical results you should always make tests.

Type of tube	Daylight films Neg. films, Ektachrome 200 and Kodachrome 25	Ektachrome 64 and 400, Kodachrome 64	Tungsten films
Daylight	40M + 40Y + 1 stop	50M + 50Y + 1⅓ stops	85B + 40M + 30Y + 1⅔ stops
White	20C + 30M + 1 stop	40M + ⅔ stop	60M + 40Y + 1⅔ stops
Warm white	40C + 40M + 1⅓ stops	20C + 40M + 1 stop	50M + 40Y + 1 stop
Warm white deluxe	60C + 30M + 2 stops	60C + 30M + 2 stops	10M + 10Y + ⅔ stop
Cool white	30M + ⅔ stop	40M + 10Y + 1 stop	10R + 50M + 50Y + 1⅔ stops
Cool white deluxe	20C + 10M + ⅔ stop	20C + 10M + ⅔ stop	20M + 40Y ⅔ stop
Unknown	10B + 10M + ⅔ stop	30M + ⅔ stop	50R 1 stop

Neutral density

Neutral density (ND) filters have no effect on colour, but simply cut down the amount of light entering the lens, allowing you to use a larger stop, longer exposures or to take pictures of objects which are otherwise far too bright (such as the sun). The values listed are the strengths available using single filters, though other strengths can be obtained using combinations. The precise effects of these filters will vary depending on the conditions of use, as there will be reciprocity effects with long exposure times, so you should experiment.

Filter	Filter factor	Transmission (%)	Exposure increase in stops
0.1	1¼	80	⅓
0.2	1½	63	⅔
0.3	2	50	1
0.4	2½	40	1⅓
0.5	3	32	1⅔
0.6	4	25	2
0.7	5	20	2⅓
0.8	6	16	2⅔
0.9	8	13	3
1.0	10	10	3⅓
2.0	100	1	6⅔
3.0	1000	0.1	10
4.0	10,000	0.01	13⅓

Colour compensating (CC)

These filters are very useful for making slight modifications to colour temperature so that you can get the exact colour that you want. They can also be used to give slight colour casts for creative effect. And used in filter packs they can correct for unusual lighting, such as fluorescent (see separate table). When mentioned in tables or articles they are often written without the CC prefix. But in technical information and on the packets they come in, they carry the prefix shown in the table.

Cyan	CC05C	CC10C	CC20C	CC30C	CC40C	CC50C
exposure increase	⅓ stop	⅓ stop	⅓ stop	⅔ stop	⅔ stop	1 stop
Magenta	CC05M	CC10M	CC20M	CC30M	CC40M	CC50M
exposure increase	⅓ stop	⅓ stop	⅓ stop	⅔ stop	⅔ stop	⅔ stop
Yellow	CC05Y	CC10Y	CC20Y	CC30Y	CC40Y	CC50Y
exposure increase		⅓ stop	⅓ stop	⅓ stop	⅓ stop	⅔ stop
Red	CC05R	CC10R	CC20R	CC30R	CC40R	CC50R
exposure increase	⅓ stop	⅓ stop	⅓ stop	⅔ stop	⅔ stop	1 stop
Green	CC05G	CC10G	CC20G	CC30G	CC40G	CC50G
exposure increase	⅓ stop	⅓ stop	⅓ stop	⅔ stop	⅔ stop	1 stop
Blue	CC05B	CC10B	CC20B	CC30B	CC40B	CC50B
exposure increase	⅓ stop	⅓ stop	⅔ stop	⅔ stop	1 stop	1⅓ stop

Photo data

Hyperfocal distance

Any focal length lens has a range of hyperfocal distances—one for each aperture. The hyperfocal distance is that focus setting at which the lens will give the maximum depth of field at that aperture. This depth of field extends from half the hyperfocal distance to infinity and increases as the aperture becomes smaller.

The tables given below indicate the hyperfocal distances for various focal length lenses at different apertures. One of the tables is based on the standard circle of confusion of 0.033 mm, the other is based on a more critical 0.025 mm (see pages 220 to 221). To use the tables, look at the figure indicated for the focal length lens you are using, at the working aperture, and set this distance on the lens. For example, if you are using a 35 mm lens at an aperture of *f*/5.6 you can, by setting the focus to 6.62 m, achieve acceptable sharpness from 3.31 m to infinity.

c × 0·033 mm

Focal length / Aperture	17	21	24	28	35	50	85	100	135	200	300
1·4	6·25	9·54	12·40	16·90	26·50	54·10	156	216	394	856	1948
2	4·37	6·68	8·72	11·80	18·50	37·80	109	151	276	606	1363
2·8	3·12	4·77	6·23	8·48	13·20	27·00	78·1	108	197	432	974
4	2·18	3·34	4·36	5·93	9·28	18·90	54·7	75·7	138	303	681
5·6	1·56	2·38	3·11	4·24	6·62	13·50	39·0	54·1	98·6	206	487
8	1·09	1·67	2·18	2·96	4·64	9·46	27·3	37·8	69·0	151	340
11	0·79	1·21	1·58	2·15	3·37	6·88	19·9	27·5	50·2	110	247
16	0·54	0·83	1·09	1·48	2·32	4·73	13·6	18·9	34·5	75·7	170
22	0·39	0·60	0·79	1·07	1·68	3·44	9·95	13·6	25·1	55·0	123
32	0·27	0·41	0·54	0·74	1·16	2·36	6·84	9·95	17·2	37·8	85·2

c × 0·025 mm

Focal length / Aperture	17	21	24	28	35	50	85	100	135	200	300
1·4	8·25	12·6	16·4	22·4	35	71·4	206	285	520	1142	2571
2	5·78	8·82	11·5	15·6	24·5	50	144	200	364	800	1800
2·8	4·12	6·3	8·22	11·2	17·5	35·7	103	142	260	571	1285
4	2·89	4·41	5·76	7·84	12·2	25	72·2	100	182	400	900
5·6	2·06	3·15	4·11	5·6	8·75	17·8	51·6	71·4	130	285	642
8	1·44	2·20	2·88	3·92	6·12	12·5	36·1	50	91·1	200	450
11	1·05	1·60	2·09	2·85	4·45	9·09	26·2	36·3	66·2	145	327
16	0·72	1·10	1·44	1·96	3·06	6·25	18·0	25	45·5	100	225
22	0·52	0·80	1·04	1·42	2·22	4·54	13·1	18·1	33·1	72·7	163
32	0·36	0·55	0·72	0·98	1·53	3·12	9·03	12·5	22·7	50	112

Close-up exposure increase

When a camera is used for close-up work with the lens mounted on extension tubes or bellows, the *f*-stop markings no longer give an accurate indication of the amount of light reaching the film. Cameras with TTL metering will automatically compensate for this but for manual cameras it is necessary to refer to formulae or tables to calculate the additional exposure requred. Given below are two formulae and a reference table covering most common set-ups.

Estimating magnification can also be difficult. On a 5 × 4 camera, it is possible to measure both the size of the subject and the size of the image on the ground glass screen and so work out the magnification. With 35 mm cameras, the full frame dimensions of 24 × 36 mm give you a basis for calculation. With reproductions of life size or larger, working from the formulae will give optimum accuracy.

$$\text{Required exposure time} = \text{indicated meter exposure} \times \frac{(\text{length of bellows})^2}{(\text{lens focal length})^2}$$

$$\text{Required exposure time} = \text{indicated meter exposure} \times (m + 1)^2$$

Magnification	0·25	0·5	0·75	1	1·25	1·5	1·75	2	3
exposure factor	1·5	2·2	3	4	5	6·5	7·5	9	16

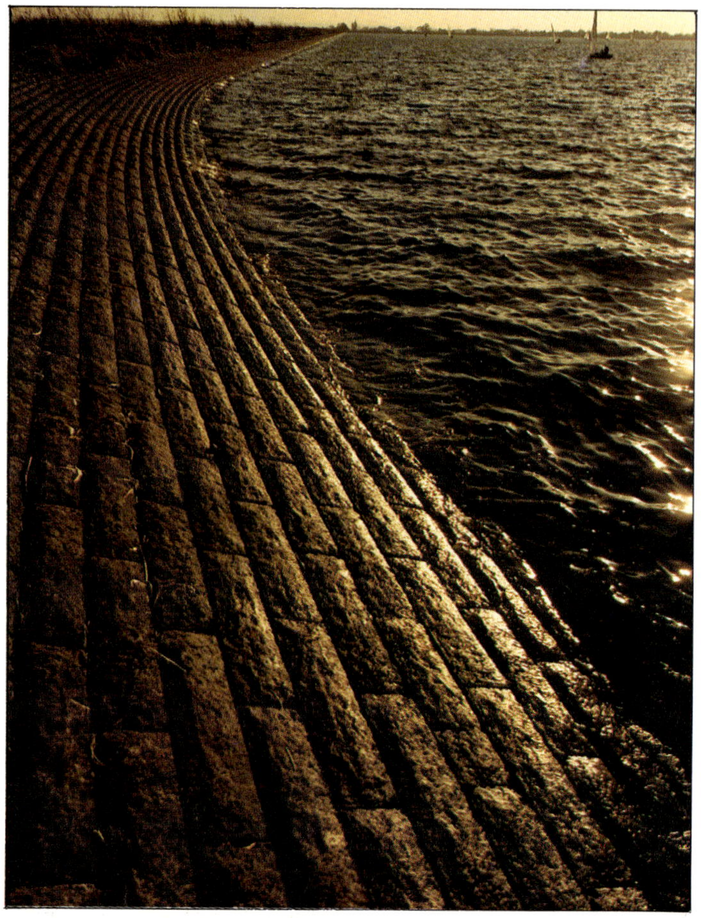

Sharpness control *The lens used for the seascape shot was focused at its hyperfocal distance in order to gain the maximum possible depth of field, extending all the way to infinity. Depth of field in close-up work is much more limited, as shown in the picture of a printed circuit board (far right), so it is essential to use the shallow sharpness creatively, to emphasize part of the subject*

Reciprocity failure compensation

In normal use the speed and colour balance of a film remains unchanged. For example, two shots taken at 1/125 second at f/4 and 1/250 second at f/5.6 of the same subject under the same conditions will have the same density and colour balance. When exposures get very short (1/10,000 second or less) or long (more than one second) the film reacts differently and adjustments have to be made by means of filters and extra exposure. The following table gives some recommended adjustments for the most popular Kodak films. For other films you should experiment, basing your tests on the nearest type of film given below. Alternatively obtain information from the film's manufacturer.

Film	Exposure time (seconds) 1/1000	1/100	1/10	1	10	100
EKTACHROME 64 and 64 Professional (Daylight)	None No filter	None No filter	None No filter	+ 1 stop CC 15B	+ 1½ stops CC 20B	Not recommended
EKTACHROME 160 and 160 Professional (Tungsten)	None No filter	None No filter	None No filter	+ ½ stop CC 10R	Not recommended	Not recommended
EKTACHROME 400 (Daylight)	None No filter	None No filter	None No filter	+ ½ stop No filter	+ 1½ stops CC 10C	+ 2½ stops CC 10C
EKTACHROME 50 Professional (Tungsten)	+ ½ stop CC 10G	None No filter	None No filter	None No filter	+ 1 stop CC 20B	Not recommended
EKTACHROME 200 and 200 Professional (Daylight)	None No filter	None No filter	None No filter	+ ½ stop CC 10R	+ 1 stop CC 15R	Not recommended
KODACOLOR 400	None No filter	None No filter	None No filter	+ ½ stop No filter	+ 1 stop No filter	+ 2 stops No filter
KODACHROME 25 (Daylight)	None No filter	None No filter	None No filter	+ 1 stop CC 10M	+ 1½ stops CC 10M	+ 2½ stops CC 10M
KODACHROME 64 (Daylight)	None No filter	None No filter	None No filter	+ 1 stop CC 10R	Not recommended	Not recommended

Close-up depth of field

Calculating depth of field is often important but never more so than in close-up work where the depth of field available at the working aperture is likely to be both small and very important. It is possible to make rough visual checks on depth of field at different apertures with most SLR and large format cameras but the darkened screen makes such estimates both difficult and crude. For crucial work it is best to refer to a table. The tables printed here show the depth of field available at different apertures and magnifications/reproduction ratios. One of the tables is based on a standard circle of confusion of 0.033 mm—the other uses a figure of 0.025 mm and is recommended for more critical work. In both cases the figures give the depth each side of the main focus—for total depth of field in mm double the figures.

c = 0·033 mm

Mag.	0·1	0·13	0·17	0·2	0·25	0·33	0·5	0·67	1	1·5	2	2·5	3
ratio	1·10	1·8	1·6	1·5	1·4	1·3	1·2	2·3	1·1	3·2	2·1	5·2	3·1
1·4	5·08	3·08	1·87	1·38	0·92	0·56	0·27	0·17	0·092	0·051	0·034	0·025	0·02
2	7·26	4·41	2·67	1·98	1·32	0·08	0·39	0·24	0·13	0·073	0·049	0·036	0·029
2·8	10·1	6·17	3·74	2·77	1·84	1·12	0·55	0·34	0·18	0·10	0·069	0·051	0·041
4	14·5	8·82	5·34	3·96	2·64	1·61	0·79	0·49	0·26	0·14	0·099	0·073	0·058
5·6	20·3	12·3	7·48	5·54	3·69	2·25	1·10	0·68	0·36	0·2	0·13	0·1	0·082
8	29	17·6	10·46	7·92	5·28	3·22	1·58	0·98	0·52	0·29	0·14	0·14	0·11
11	39·9	24·2	14·6	10·8	7·26	4·43	2·17	1·35	0·72	0·4	0·2	0·2	0·16
16	58	35·3	21·3	15·8	10·5	6·44	3·16	1·96	1·05	0·58	0·29	0·29	0·23
22	79·8	48·5	29·3	21·7	14·5	8·26	4·35	2·7	1·45	0·08	0·4	0·4	0·32
32	116	70·6	42·7	31·6	21·1	12·8	6·33	3·92	2·11	1·17	0·59	0·59	0·46
45	163	99·2	60·1	44·5	29·7	18·1	8·91	5·52	2·97	1·65	0·83	0·83	0·66
64	232	141	85·5	63·3	42·2	25·7	12·6	7·85	4·22	2·34	1·18	1·18	0·93

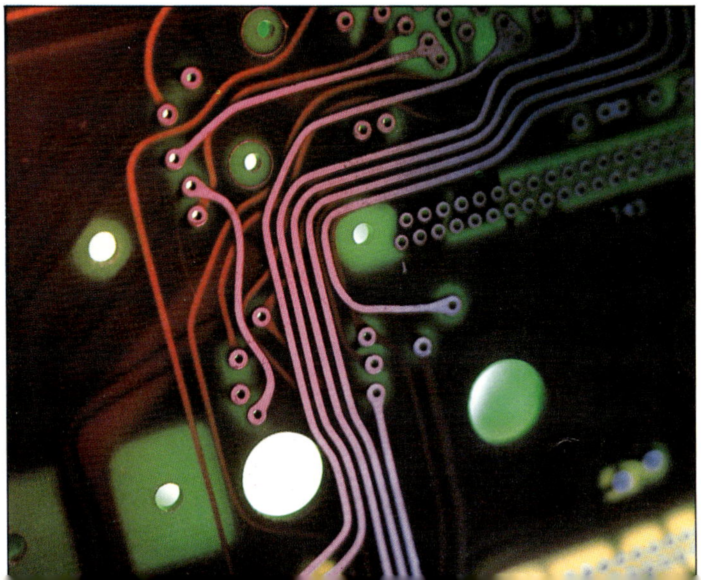

c = 0·025 mm

Mag.	0·1	0·13	0·17	0·2	0·25	0·33	0·5	0·67	1	1·5	2	2·5	3
ratio	1·10	1·8	1·6	1·5	1·4	1·3	1·2	2·3	1·1	3·2	2·1	5·2	3·1
1·4	3·85	2·34	1·41	1·05	0·7	0·42	0·21	0·13	0·07	0·038	0·026	0·019	0·015
2	5·5	3·34	2·02	1·5	1	0·61	0·3	0·18	0·1	0·055	0·037	0·028	0·022
2·8	7·7	4·68	2·83	2·1	1·4	0·85	0·42	0·26	0·14	0·077	0·052	0·039	0·031
4	11	6·68	4·04	3	2	1·22	0·6	0·37	0·2	0·11	0·075	0·056	0·044
5·6	15·4	9·36	5·66	4·2	2·8	1·7	0·84	0·52	0·28	0·15	0·1	0·078	0·062
8	22	13·3	8·09	6	4	2·44	1·2	0·74	0·4	0·22	0·15	0·11	0·088
11	30·2	18·3	11·1	8·25	5·5	3·35	1·65	1·02	0·55	0·3	0·2	0·15	0·12
16	44	26·7	16·1	12	8	4·88	2·4	0·48	0·8	0·44	0·3	0·22	0·17
22	60·5	36·7	22·2	16·5	11	6·71	3·3	2·04	1·1	0·61	0·41	0·3	0·24
32	88	53·4	32·3	24	16	9·77	4·8	2·97	1·6	0·88	0·6	0·44	0·35
45	123	75·2	45·5	33·7	22·5	13·7	6·75	4·18	2·25	1·25	0·84	0·71	0·63
64	176	100	64·7	48	32	19·5	9·6	5·95	3·2	1·77	1·2	0·89	0·71

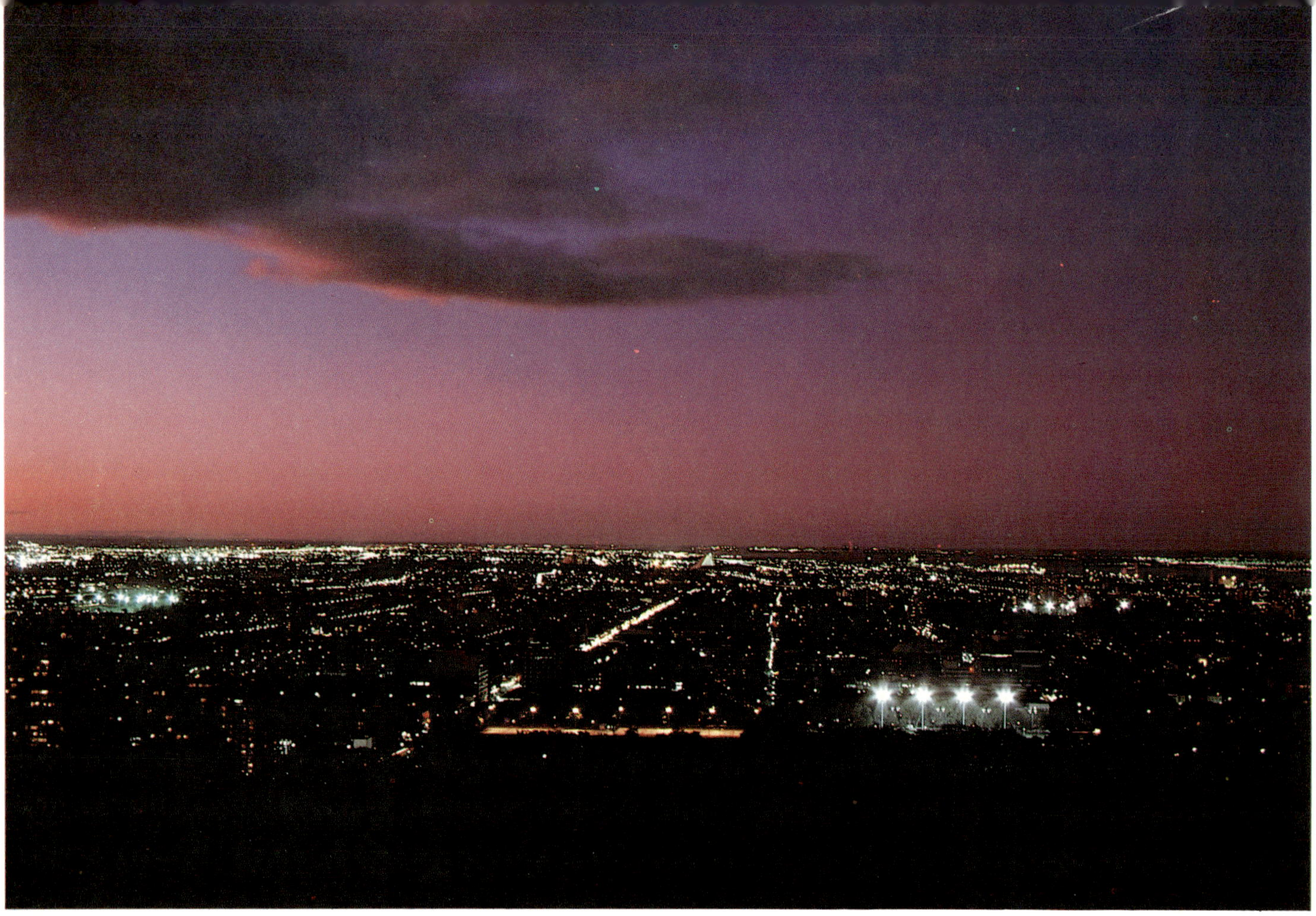

Movie film running times and lengths

Most movie cameras have counters which tell you how much film is left. But it is not always easy to work out what this means in terms of time. Using the table below you can work out how much time you have available or how long a sequence will last.

Film format		Super 8 (72 frames per foot)		16mm (40 frames per foot)	
Projection speed in frames per second		18	24	18	24
Running time and film length		Feet + frames	Feet + frames	Feet + frames	Feet + frames
Seconds	1	0+18	0+24	0+18	0+24
	2	0+36	0+48	0+36	0+48
	3	0+54	1+ 0	1+14	1+32
	4	1+ 0	1+24	1+32	2+16
	5	1+18	1+48	2+10	3+ 0
	6	1+36	2+ 0	2+28	3+24
	7	1+54	2+24	3+ 6	4+ 8
	8	2+ 0	2+48	3+24	4+32
	9	2+18	3+ 0	4+ 2	5+16
	10	2+36	3+24	4+20	6+ 0
	20	5+ 0	6+48	9+ 0	12+ 0
	30	7+36	10+ 0	13+20	18+ 0
	40	10+ 0	13+24	18+ 0	24+ 0
Minutes	1	15+ 0	20+ 0	27+ 0	36+ 0
	2	30+ 0	40+ 0	54+ 0	72+ 0
	3	45+ 0	60+ 0	81+ 0	108+ 0
	4	60+ 0	80+ 0	108+ 0	144+ 0
	5	75+ 0	100+ 0	135+ 0	180+ 0
	6	90+ 0	120+ 0	162+ 0	216+ 0
	7	105+ 0	140+ 0	189+ 0	252+ 0
	8	120+ 0	160+ 0	216+ 0	288+ 0
	9	135+ 0	180+ 0	243+ 0	324+ 0
	10	150+ 0	200+ 0	270+ 0	360+ 0

Coloured sky *The colour of the sky in this shot is due to reciprocity failure. This is one of the occasions when a cast is actually attractive, and so no filtration is needed*

Evening light *The colour temperature of the light source rarely matches the photographic standard of 5500K. But in some cases, such as at sunset, this is not a problem*

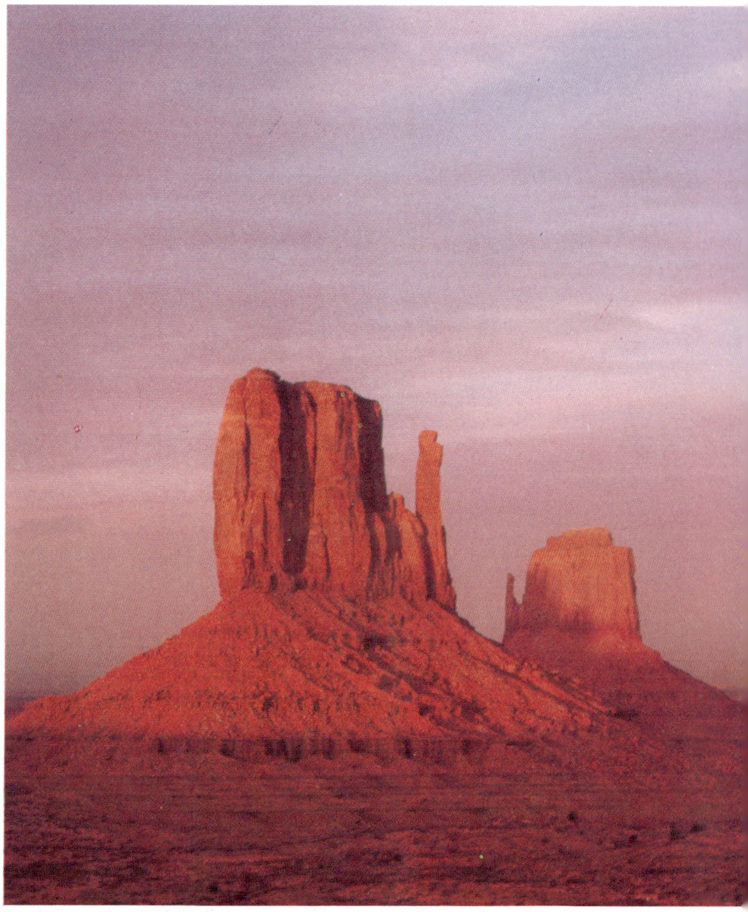

Flash guide numbers

It is essential to know the guide number of your flashgun but manufacturers do not always quote a full set of numbers. By using this table you can work out the guide number of a flashgun at any of the given film speeds, provided that you know one number. For example, if your unit has a guide number of 22 with 64 ASA (ISO) film, simply look down the 64 ASA column until you come to 22. Then, by reading along that row, you can find the number for the other speeds. In this example the unit has a guide number of 40 with 200 ASA film.

The BCPS (beam candle power seconds) rating is a standard measure of light power and is useful for technical applications, such as infrared photography. The joules rating is a more common system of giving the power of a unit, and the power of most studio flash heads is quoted in joules

25	50	64	80	100	160	200	400	BCPS	Joules (watt/seconds)
6	9	10	11	12	16	18	25	300	8
7	10	11	12	14	18	20	28	375	10
8	11	12	14	16	20	22	32	450	12
9	12	14	16	18	22	25	35	600	16
10	14	16	18	20	25	28	40	750	20
11	16	18	20	22	28	32	45	900	25
12	18	20	22	25	32	35	50	1200	32
14	20	22	25	28	35	40	56	1500	40
16	22	25	28	32	40	45	64	1800	50
18	25	28	32	35	45	50	70	2400	64
20	28	32	35	40	50	56	80	3000	80
22	32	35	40	45	56	63	90	3600	100
25	35	40	45	50	63	70	100	4800	125
28	40	45	50	56	70	80	113	6000	160
32	45	50	56	63	80	90	128	7200	200

Sources

Much of the information used in this section was supplied by Kodak. Many of the terms used, such as Wratten, Ektachrome and Kodachrome are Kodak trade names. The hyperfocal distance and depth of field tables were calculated using a Sinclair ZX Spectrum computer.

Colour temperature and mireds

If you want to get accurate colours in your transparencies it is essential to filter for different light sources. Working out the required filtration is easy if you have a colour temperature meter. Otherwise it is difficult to know what colour temperature a particular light source is. The table here gives a guide to the most common or important sources, measured in kelvins. However, the exact colour of any lighting can be affected by the age of bulbs or tubes, the colour of reflectors or surrounding surfaces, and so on. Nevertheless, for all but the most critical conditions, this guide should be sufficiently accurate.

To find the necessary filtration you can use the kelvin/mired scale. Mireds (micro reciprocal degrees) are used because a filter can then be given a set value which applies to any region of the colour temperature range. For example, a filter with a mired shift value of −100 can change the colour temperature from 2000 to 2500 K—a shift of 500 K. But it can also change it from 5000 to 10,000 K—a shift of 5000 K. So filters cannot simply be allotted a colour temperature. The mired scale is derived by dividing the colour temperature into 1,000,000. Blue filters have negative mired values, and red, yellow and amber filters have positive values. Some colour temperature meters, such as the Minolta digital model, give readouts directly in mired values, which are then read off a table to find the correct filters to use. Some approximate mired values are given here for the most common filters, but you should check with the filter's instructions. The point to remember about mireds is that a filter alters the mired value by the same amount whatever the light source, but the change in degrees kelvin varies with the colour temperature of the light.

Candle	1930
Sunrise/sunset	c.2000
40 watt domestic bulb	2650
75 watt domestic bulb	2820
100 watt domestic bulb	2900
200 watt domestic bulb	2980
500 watt photographic lamp	3200
Projector lamps	3100
500 watt photoflood	3400
'Daylight' fluorescent light	4500
Mean noon sunlight	5400
Photographic daylight	5500
Flashcube	5500
Blue flashbulb	6000
Electronic flash tube	6000
Average daylight (sun and sky)	6500
Colour matching fluorescent tube	6500
Overcast daylight	7500
Blue sky	10,000 to 18,000

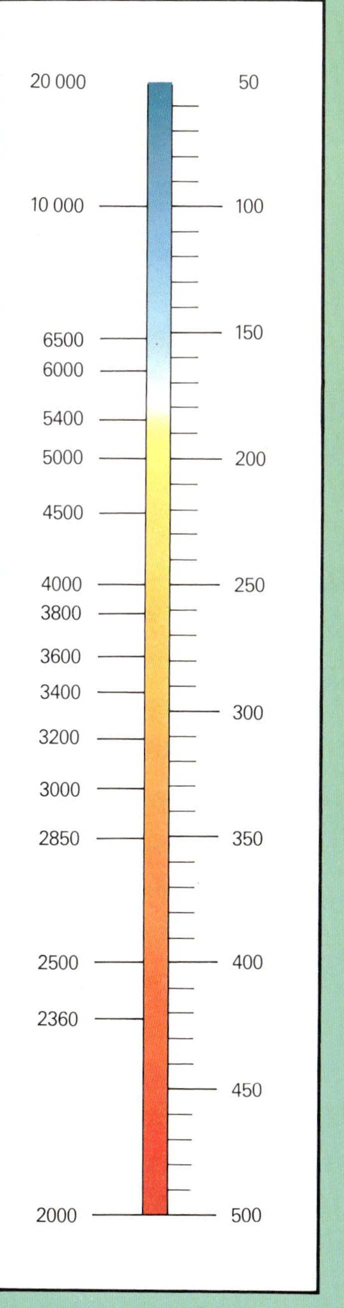

Mired values for common filters

81	+ 10	82	− 10
81A	+ 15	82A	− 20
81B	+ 25	82B	− 30
81C	+ 30	80A	− 130
85B	+ 130	80B	− 110
85C	+ 80	80C	− 80

INDEX

Numbers in italics refer to captions

Picture credits

Table of contents David Hume Kennerly/Contact/Colorific Page 6 Jon Bouchier; 7 Colin Molyneux (top), John Danzig (centre), Sefton Samuels/Sefton Photo Library (bottom left), Jon Bouchier (bottom right); 8 Jon Bouchier, Peter O'Rouke (c); 9 Jon Bouchier, Hans Feurer/Image Bank (cl), Edwourd Berne/fotogram (cr); 10-12 Jon Bouchier; 12 Peter Dazeley (b); 13 Paul Webb (tlr), Peter Dazeley; 14 Peter Dazeley, Colorspirt (br); 15 Coloursport, Peter Dazeley (tr); Ed Buziak (t); 16-19 George Wright; 20-23 Roger Payling; 24 Jon Bouchier (t); 24-25 Homer Sykes; 25 D A Morley (t), Angela Murphy (b); 26 A Petit (t), T Aoptani (b); 27 Paolo Koch/Vision International (1), Richard Winslde (r); 28 Paolo Koch (t), John Coles/Sefton (b); Jean Paul Ferrero/Ardea (t), Frank Hermann (b); 30 John Sims (t), John Heseltine (b); 31 Eve Arnold/Magnum; 32 Kim Sayer; 33 Michael Newton; 34-35 Michael Newton; 36 Malcolm Robertson; 37 Olivier Garros (tl), Chusak Voraphitak (tr), Daniel Barbier (c); M. Edwards (b); 38 Daniel Barbier (t); A Fatras (c), Paolo Kock (cr), Jeremy Coulter (b); 39 Daniel Barbier; 40 Gerard del Vecchio (t), Edouard Berne (c), Peter Keen (b); 41 Tapdance; 42-45 Clay Perry; 46 Ansel Adams 47 Tessa Musgrave; 48; 49 Mimi Jacobs; 50 Robin Laurance; 50-51 Simon Holledge; 51 Eric Schwab (1), Jon Bouchier (r); 52 Northern Piucture Library (t), Peter Keen (bl), Shain Kelly (br); 53 Jon Bouchier; 58 John Heseltine; 59 Clive Sawyer; 60 H Gloaquin; 60-61 John Markham; 61 Jerry Young; 52-64 Kim Sayer; 63 John Garrett (t); 66-69 Jon Bouchier; 67 Richard Massey (br); 68-69 John Sims (t); 70 Ed Buziak; 71 Simon de Courcy Wheeler (b), Leo Mason (t); 72-73 Sergio Dorantes, Ed Buziak (t); 74 John Gardey (t), Sergio Dorantes (b); 75-79 Victor Watts; 76 M P Kahl (br); 77 F L R Jiminez (t); 78 Stewart Fraser (b), Sergio Dorantes (t); 80 Roger Payling (t), Paolo Koch (b); 81 David Burnett (t), Roger Payling (b); 82 Paolo Koch (b); 82-83 George Wright; 84-85 Robin Bath; 85 David Robinson; 86 John de Visser; 86-87 Michael Freeman; 87 Jerry Young; 88 Homer Sykes; 89 Paolo Koch (t), Francois Jalain (b); 90-91 Richard Massey; 91 Duncan Brown (t), Homer Sykes (b); 92 George Wright (t), Jerry Young (b); 93 Ian McKinnell; 94 R Ian Lloyd; 94-95 Dimitri Ilic; 95 Tapdance; 96 Laurie Lewis (b); 96-97 Tapdance (t), Jean-Paul Nacivet (c); 97 Sergio Dorantes; 98 Bill Holden (t), John Heseltine (b); 98 James Walker (t), Arthur Milligan (b); 100-101 Kim Sayer; 100 Irene Windridge (b); 102 Fox Photos; 103-105 Kim Sayer; 106-109 Victor Watts; 110 David Parker; 110-113 Richard & Sally Greenhill; 114 Clay Perry; 115 John Sims (t), Martyn Adelman (b); 116 George Wright (t), Clay Perry (b); 117 Timothy Beddow (t), John Sims (b); 119 Barrie Smith; 120 Sarah King; 121 Michael Freeman; 122 Chris Barker; 122-123 Magda Segal; 123 Penny Tweedie (tl), Clay Perry (tr); 124 Gianfranco Gordoni; 124-125 Brian Griffin; 125 Chuck Fishman (t), Clay Perry (b); 126 Bill Brandt (t); Jenny Baker collection (b); 127 Chris Barker; 128 J P Hautacouer; 129 Homer Sykes (t), LLT Rhodes (b); 130 Homer Sykes (t), Richard and Sally Greenhill; 131 Henri Cartier-Bresson (tr), LLT Rhodes (tr); 132-133 Leo Mason; 133 Stewart Fraser (b); 134 Leo Mason; 135 Colorsport (tl), Fred Mayer/Magnum (tr); 136 Leo Mason; 137 Michael Freeman (tl), Guido Alberto Rossi (tr); 138 Stewart Fraser; 139 Stewart Fraser (t), Colin Elsey (b); 140 MD England; 141 Adrian davies (t), JP Ferrero (b); 142 MP Kahl (b), Gordon Langsden (t); 143 Bernard Rebouleau (t), David & Katie Urry (b); 144 Varin-Visage (t), Jeff Foott (b); 145 Jane Burton; 146 Douglas Armand (t); 147 John F Preedy (tl), David Hosking (tr); Andre Fatras (b); 148 Adrian Davies (t), Francois Merlet (b); 149 Hans Reinhard (t), Frank W Lane (b); 150-151 Roger Payling; 152 Michael Siebert, Patrick Thurston, Michael Siebert, Stephen Dalton/Oxford Scientific Films; 154-157 David Parker; 158-161 Flip Schulke/Seaphot; 162 Jerry Young (t); 162-164 Roger Payling; 164 Michael Maunder (t); 165 Steve Powell (t); 165-169 Jerry Young; 168 Steve Powell (c); 169 David Hoskins (b); 170-173 Kim Sayer; 174 Martyn Adelman; 175-177 Peter Dazeley; 176 Jon Wyand (b); 278 John Cocking; 179 Dave King (c); 179-181 Kim Sayer; 180-181 George Wright (t); 182-185 Victor Watts; 185 Link house Studios (b); 186-193 Julian Calder; 187, 189 Victor Watts (t); 194-197 Jake Wynter; 198-201 Naru; 202-205 Malcolm Hoare; 206 Roger Hicks; 207-209 Michael Newton; 210 Simon de Courcy Wheeler (t), Tony Stone Photo Library (b); 211 Anne Conway (t), Dave King (b); 212-213 Dave King; 213 Ed White (t); 214-218 Dave King; 219 Richard Passmore/Colorific; 220-221 Paul Webb; 222-225 Jon Bouchier; 226 Ilford (t), Kodak (b); 227 Mari Mahr; 228 Arthur Bertrand; 230 Jerry Young; 232 Stephen Madden (t), John Sims (b); 234 Sergio Dorantes; 235 Victor Watts; 236 Michael Evans; 237 Victor Watts; 238 Friedel (t), Francois Roiseaux (b); 239 Paul Webb; 240 Roger Payling; 241-243 John Sims; 244-245 Ed Buziak; 246-247 Wayne Gunther; 248 Jerry Young; 249 Paul Brierley; 250 Steve Mansfield (t) Harold Sund (b);